CULTURAL LAW: INTERNATIONAL, COMPARATIVE, AND INDIGENOUS

Cultural law is a new and exciting field of study and practice. The core themes of linguistic and other cultural rights, cultural identity and differentiation, cultural heritage, traditional knowledge, sports, and religion are of fundamental importance to people around the world, engaging them at the grassroots level and often commanding their daily attention. The related legal processes are both significant and complex.

This unique collection of materials and commentary on cultural law covers a broad range of themes. Opening chapters explore critical issues involving cultural activities, artifacts, and status, as well as the fundamental concepts of culture and law. Subsequent chapters examine the dynamic interplay of law and culture with respect to each of the core themes.

The materials demonstrate the reality and efficacy of international, comparative, and indigenous law and legal practices in the dynamic context of culture-related issues. Throughout the book, the issues are presented at international, national, subnational, tribal, and strictly cultural levels of authority.

James A. R. Nafziger is Thomas B. Stoel Professor of Law and Director of International Programs at the Willamette University College of Law. A former administrative director of the American Society of International Law and President of the American Branch of the International Law Association (ILA), he serves as Chair of the ILA's Cultural Heritage Law Committee. Professor Nafziger is the author of *International Sports Law* and coeditor of *The Cultural Heritage of Mankind* and *Cultural Heritage Issues: The Legacy of Conquest, Colonization and Commerce.*

Robert Kirkwood Paterson is a Professor of Law in the Faculty of Law at the University of British Columbia. He is an editor of the *International Journal of Cultural Property* and rapporteur of the Cultural Heritage Law Committee of the International Law Association, of which he is a Canadian board member. He has written widely on cultural property and international trade law, most recently as coeditor of *Protection of First Nations Cultural Heritage: Laws, Policy, and Reform.*

Alison Dundes Renteln is a Professor of Political Science and Anthropology at the University of Southern California. She is an expert on cultural rights, having authored *The Cultural Defense* and co-edited *Folk Law: Essays on the Theory and Practice of Lex Non Scripta.* She has also served on the California State Bar Commission on Access to Justice and the California Judicial Council Access and Fairness Advisory Committee.

Cultural Law

INTERNATIONAL, COMPARATIVE, AND INDIGENOUS

James A. R. Nafziger
Thomas B. Stoel Professor of Law
Willamette University

Robert Kirkwood Paterson
Professor of Law
University of British Columbia

Alison Dundes Renteln
Professor of Political Science and Anthropology
University of Southern California

CAMBRIDGE
UNIVERSITY PRESS

CAMBRIDGE UNIVERSITY PRESS
Cambridge, New York, Melbourne, Madrid, Cape Town, Singapore,
São Paulo, Delhi, Dubai, Tokyo, Mexico City

Cambridge University Press
32 Avenue of the Americas, New York, NY 10013-2473, USA

www.cambridge.org
Information on this title: www.cambridge.org/9780521865500

First published 2010

Printed in the United States of America

A catalog record for this publication is available from the British Library.

Library of Congress Cataloging in Publication data

Nafziger, James A. R.
Cultural law : international, comparative, and indigenous / James A.R.
Nafziger, Robert K. Paterson, Alison Dundes Renteln.
p. cm.
Includes bibliographical references and index.
ISBN 978-0-521-86550-0 (hardback)
1. Culture and law. 2. Cultural property – Protection – Law and legislation.
3. Multiculturalism – Law and legislation. I. Paterson, Robert K., 1946–
II. Renteln, Alison Dundes. III. Title.
K487.C8N34 2010
344′.09 – dc22 2009047137

ISBN 978-0-521-86550-0 Hardback

Contents

Preface

The inspiration for this book has several sources. The core themes of linguistic and other cultural rights, cultural identity and differentiation, cultural heritage, traditional knowledge, sports, and religion are of fundamental importance to humankind. They are matters that truly engage people at the grass roots, often commanding their daily attention. The related legal processes are both significant and complex. It is therefore not surprising that a vast legal literature has blossomed concerning themes of cultural activity and artifacts. And yet this intellectual development remains on the fringe of legal and social science education. Courses on issues of cultural law or culture and law are few and far between. To the best of our knowledge, this is the first comprehensive coursebook covering a broad range of these issues.

A first source of inspiration for this book, then, is the need we have perceived to bring cultural law more into the mainstream of legal and social science education. A second, related source of inspiration is the opportunity to offer a more integrated, coherent framework for studying the diverse themes of cultural law. Clearly, there are common threads running through these themes and the related legal processes. Certain rules of tort, contract, constitutional, and administrative law, as well as methods and procedures of dispute resolution, recur throughout the book, regardless of the specific cultural theme. Likewise, we consider the role of international law – both customary and conventional – throughout the book. Although the specific topics of "art law," "sports law," "law and religion," "cultural rights," "traditional knowledge," and so on, serve important organizational and analytical purposes, they also minimize the reality of a common framework of cultural law. These discrete rubrics are also misleading insofar as students and practitioners alike may fail to appreciate the possibilities of broader professional specialization in cultural law.

Our effort to develop a suitable framework of cultural law is still a work in progress, but, as a first step, Chapter 1 offers a working definition of cultural law in terms of a set of six relationships between culture and law within which the issues considered in this book could be categorized, although we have not done so. Each of these relationships may be fairly criticized for its breadth, but we believe that, taken together to define cultural law, they offer a constructive and coherent substitute for the vague conjunction, "culture and law." We also think that this set of six relationships highlights a particularly exciting feature of cultural law, namely the dynamic, evolving development of both culture and law under their mutual influence.

Of course, the very concepts of culture and law have been notoriously ambiguous and unstable over time. We are well aware of the definitional dilemmas. We nevertheless are convinced of the importance and efficacy of acquainting law students and lawyers, on the one hand, and cultural specialists, on the other hand, with the definitional issues and characteristics of each other's discipline. Lawyers and cultural specialists must work together. A third source of inspiration for this book, therefore, is the challenge of enhancing interdisciplinary understanding and collaboration, for example, by devoting all of Chapter 2 to the contours of meaning associated with the terms "culture" and "law." To the extent that students and other readers are already familiar with this material, they may wish to skip either Chapter 2 as a whole or parts of it.

A fourth source of inspiration for this book is the importance of demonstrating to students the reality and efficacy of comparative, international, and indigenous law and practices in the real-life context of cultural activity and artifacts. Too often these disciplines otherwise appear arcane or far removed from the immediacy of everyday experience.

A fifth and final source of inspiration for this book is its potential to serve as both a university coursebook and a reference work. We do not claim that the cases, authors' commentary, and other materials in this book are in any way definitive. We have selected the contents, however, with both classroom instruction and ongoing reference needs in mind. Many of the cases and readings are classics, but some are deliberately outside the box, so to speak, to stimulate further inquiry. We also believe that the index at the end of this book will be useful in the classroom, the professional office, and the library.

We have sought to cover as many cultural themes of legal significance to people around the world as possible without running the risk of superficiality. Inevitably, however, space limitations have required us to limit the scope of a few themes (e.g., music and pop culture) and largely to bypass other possible themes (e.g., theater, dance, and cinema) that are already addressed by regimes of general application, such as those that govern intellectual property and constitutional issues – although specific cultural law is beginning to address those themes as well. We have also relied heavily on English-language materials and comparative and indigenous examples from the English-speaking world.

As in any coauthored work, readers may detect variations of style, but we have done our best to establish a uniform structure and style. In doing so, we have generally adhered to conventional legal formatting, such as by the use of footnotes rather than in-text citations or endnotes, and *The Bluebook* system of citation. In keeping with the normal publishing practice, we have eliminated most footnotes within the excerpted materials. Those that we have retained, as well as the authors' own clarifications and explanations, are numbered consecutively within each chapter. Footnote numbers therefore do not necessarily correspond to those in the excerpted sources. Also in keeping with normal publishing practice, we have provided citations to cases, legislation, treaties, and other primary materials only as they become the objects of specific commentary or analysis in this book rather than as they may appear summarily or in lists of examples.

We hope that this volume will inspire others to consider the importance of cultural activities and artifacts in legal processes. We also want to encourage interdisciplinary approaches to the study of law and legal phenomena. Last but not least, we have tried to highlight the significance of analyzing legal processes at all levels: international, national, subnational, tribal, and strictly cultural. Cultural issues are ubiquitous, and the related law is of growing significance. As time goes on, we trust that students and practitioners alike will help expand the range of issues and our understanding of the alternatives for resolving them.

James A. R. Nafziger
Salem, Oregon

Robert Kirkwood Paterson
Vancouver, British Columbia

Alison Dundes Renteln
Los Angeles, California

Acknowledgments

The authors are especially grateful to Andrea Whalen for carrying the burden of processing and formatting the manuscript for this book and for bringing typographical errors and other glitches to the attention of the authors. We also thank Marlowe Caldwell and Kathy Marbut for their skillful computer processing, as well as Roger Clark, Miriam Clavir, Mark Janis, Dennis Karjala, Roberta Kremer, and Jorge A. Sánchez Cordero for their substantive assistance and other support of this project. Students in consecutive yearly seminars at the Willamette University College of Law provided many helpful suggestions as well.

The Hague Academy of International Law and its Centre for Studies and Research graciously granted permission to reprint excerpts appearing in Chapters 3, 4, and 5 that were drawn from pages 145–247 of *The Cultural Heritage of Mankind* (Tullio Scovazzi & James A.R. Nafziger eds. 2008). More broadly, having taken care to obtain permission to reproduce all previously published material, we appreciate the cooperation of publishers and authors who have enabled us to include excerpts of their work in this book. We trust that no previously published material has escaped our attention. Finally, we thank John Berger of Cambridge University Press and Larry Fox and Brigitte Coulton of Aptara for helping steer this book through the production process.

1. Cultural Law: An Introduction

A. The Cultural Dimension of the Legal Process

Legal issues may lead multiple lives. They can be political, economic, social, historical, or cultural. Normally, the particular classification of an issue, in the abstract, is not so important. What is important, however, is to understand how a particular nonlegal dimension may condition the analysis of an issue and the appropriate response to it. Gaining this understanding is a matter not only of viewpoint or specialized information but also of professional skill. It is a skill that is best acquired by gaining a comprehensive understanding of the manifold ways in which a particular dimension of human experience – for our purposes, the cultural dimension – affects the legal process.

The first two chapters in this book address the problem of cultural conflict, the interaction of culture and law, a working definition of cultural law, and the characteristics of both culture and law. The remaining chapters examine the interaction of culture and law in specific contexts of cultural expressions, practices, and activities such as art, traditional knowledge, sports, and religion.

We begin this chapter by considering how the cultural dimension of legal issues in both private sectors and public sectors, including the principle of cultural diversity, may be significant in dispute resolution and ordinary legal discourse. The examples are neither definitive nor comprehensive, but only suggestive. The chapter concludes by broadly defining the discipline of cultural law as a set of relationships.

1. Dispute Resolution amid Cultural Diversity

Yahoo!, Inc. v. La Ligue Contre Le Racisme et L'Antisemitisme
169 F. Supp. 2d 1181 (N.D. Cal. 2001),
rev'd on other grounds and remanded, 433 F.3d 1199 (9th Cir. 2006)

Defendants La Ligue Contre Le Racisme Et L'Antisemitisme ("LICRA") and L'Union Des Etudiants Juifs De France, citizens of France, are non-profit organizations dedicated to eliminating anti-Semitism. Plaintiff Yahoo!, Inc. ("Yahoo!") is a corporation organized under the laws of Delaware with its principal place of business in Santa Clara, California. Yahoo! is an Internet[1] service provider that operates various Internet

[1] The Internet and World Wide Web are distinct entities, but for the sake of simplicity, the Court will refer to them collectively as the Internet. In general, the Internet is a decentralized networking system that

websites and services that any computer user can access at the Uniform Resource Locator ("URL") http://www.yahoo.com. Yahoo! services ending in the suffix, ".com," without an associated country code as a prefix or extension (collectively, "Yahoo!'s U.S. Services") use the English language and target users who are residents of, utilize servers based in, and operate under the laws of the United States. Yahoo! subsidiary corporations operate regional Yahoo! sites and services in twenty other nations, including, for example, Yahoo! France, Yahoo! India, and Yahoo! Spain. Each of these regional web sites contains the host nation's unique two-letter code as either a prefix or a suffix in its URL (e.g., Yahoo! France is found at http://www.yahoo.fr and Yahoo! Korea at http://www.yahoo.kr). Yahoo!'s regional sites use the local region's primary language, target the local citizenry, and operate under local laws.

Yahoo! provides a variety of means by which people from all over the world can communicate and interact with one another over the Internet. Examples include an Internet search engine, e-mail, an automated auction site, personal web page hostings, shopping services, chat rooms, and a listing of clubs that individuals can create or join. Any computer user with Internet access is able to post materials on many of these Yahoo! sites, which in turn are instantly accessible by anyone who logs on to Yahoo!'s Internet sites. As relevant here, Yahoo!'s auction site allows anyone to post an item for sale and solicit bids from any computer user from around the globe. Yahoo! records when a posting is made and after the requisite time period lapses sends an e-mail notification to the highest bidder and seller with their respective contact information. Yahoo! is never a party to a transaction, and the buyer and seller are responsible for arranging privately for payment and shipment of goods. Yahoo! monitors the transaction through limited regulation by prohibiting particular items from being sold (such as stolen goods, body parts, prescription and illegal drugs, weapons, and goods violating U.S. copyright laws or the Iranian and Cuban embargos) and by providing a rating system through which buyers and sellers have their transactional behavior evaluated for the benefit of future consumers. Yahoo! informs auction sellers that they must comply with Yahoo!'s policies and may not offer items to buyers in jurisdictions in which the sale of such item violates the jurisdiction's applicable laws. Yahoo! does not actively regulate the content of each posting, and individuals are able to post, and have in fact posted, highly offensive matter, including Nazi-related propaganda and Third Reich memorabilia, on Yahoo!'s auction sites.

On or about April 5, 2000, LICRA sent a "cease and desist" letter to Yahoo!'s Santa Clara headquarters informing Yahoo! that the sale of Nazi[-] and Third Reich[–]related goods through its auction services violates French law. LICRA threatened to take legal action unless Yahoo! took steps to prevent such sales within eight days. Defendants subsequently utilized the United States Marshal's Office to serve Yahoo! with process

links computers and computer networks around the world. The World Wide Web is a publishing forum consisting of millions of individual Web sites that contain a wide variety of content.

in California and filed a civil complaint against Yahoo! in the Tribunal de Grande Instance de Paris (the "French Court").

The French Court found that approximately 1,000 Nazi[-] and Third Reich[–]related objects, including Adolf Hitler's *Mein Kampf*, *The Protocol of the Elders of Zion* (an infamous anti-Semitic report produced by the Czarist secret police in the early 1900s), and purported "evidence" that the gas chambers of the Holocaust did not exist were being offered for sale on Yahoo.com's auction site. Because any French citizen is able to access these materials on Yahoo.com directly or through a link on Yahoo.fr, the French Court concluded that the Yahoo.com auction site violates Section R645–1 of the French Criminal Code, which prohibits exhibition of Nazi propaganda and artifacts for sale.[2]

On May 20, 2000, the French Court entered an order requiring Yahoo! to (1) eliminate French citizens' access to any material on the Yahoo.com auction site that offers for sale any Nazi objects, relics, insignia, emblems, and flags; (2) eliminate French citizens' access to web pages on Yahoo.com displaying text, extracts, or quotations from *Mein Kampf* and *Protocol of the Elders of Zion*; (3) post a warning to French citizens on Yahoo.fr that any search through Yahoo.com may lead to sites containing material prohibited by Section R645–1 of the French Criminal Code, and that such viewing of the prohibited material may result in legal action against the Internet user; (4) remove from all browser directories accessible in the French Republic index headings entitled "negationists" and from all hypertext links the equation of "negationists" under the heading "Holocaust." The order subjects Yahoo! to a penalty of 100,000 Euros for each day that it fails to comply with the order. The order concludes:

> We order the Company YAHOO! Inc. to take all necessary measures to dissuade and render impossible any access via Yahoo.com to the Nazi artifact auction service and to any other site or service that may be construed as constituting an apology for Nazism or a contesting of Nazi crimes.

Yahoo! asked the French Court to reconsider the terms of the order, claiming that although it easily could post the required warning on Yahoo.fr, compliance with the order's requirements with respect to Yahoo.com was technologically impossible. The French Court sought expert opinion on the matter and on November 20, 2000, "reaffirmed" its order of May 22. The French Court ordered Yahoo! to comply with the May 22 order within three (3) months or face a penalty of 100,000 Francs (approximately US$13,300) for each day of non-compliance. [The confusion of francs and euros in this opinion reflects a transition from the national to the regional currency during the course of the litigation. – *Eds.*] The French Court also provided that penalties assessed against Yahoo! Inc. may not be collected from Yahoo! France. Defendants again utilized the United States Marshal's Office to serve Yahoo! in California with the French Order.

[2] French law also prohibits purchase or possession of such matter within France.

Yahoo! subsequently posted the required warning and prohibited postings in violation of Section R645–1 of the French Criminal Code from appearing on Yahoo.fr. Yahoo! also amended the auction policy of Yahoo.com to prohibit individuals from auctioning:

> Any item that promotes, glorifies, or is directly associated with groups or individuals known principally for hateful or violent positions or acts, such as Nazis or the Ku Klux Klan. Official government-issue stamps and coins are not prohibited under this policy. Expressive media, such as books and films, may be subject to more permissive standards as determined by Yahoo! in its sole discretion.

Yahoo Auction Guidelines (visited Oct. 23, 2001) <http://user.auctions.Yahoo.com/html/guidelines.html>. Notwithstanding these actions, the Yahoo.com auction site still offers certain items for sale (such as stamps, coins, and a copy of *Mein Kampf*) which appear to violate the French Order. While Yahoo! has removed the *Protocol of the Elders of Zion* from its auction site, it has not prevented access to numerous other sites which reasonably "may be construed as constituting an apology for Nazism or a contesting of Nazi crimes."[3]

Yahoo! claims that because it lacks the technology to block French citizens from accessing the Yahoo.com auction site to view materials which violate the French Order or from accessing other Nazi-based content of websites on Yahoo.com, it cannot comply with the French order without banning Nazi-related material from Yahoo.com altogether. Yahoo! contends that such a ban would infringe impermissibly upon its rights under the First Amendment to the United States Constitution. Accordingly, Yahoo! filed a complaint in this Court seeking a declaratory judgment that the French Court's orders are neither cognizable nor enforceable under the laws of the United States.

Defendants immediately moved to dismiss on the basis that this Court lacks personal jurisdiction over them. That motion was denied.[4] . . .

As this Court and others have observed, the instant case presents novel and important issues arising from the global reach of the Internet. Indeed, the specific facts of this case implicate issues of policy, politics, and culture that are beyond the purview of one nation's judiciary. Thus it is critical that the Court define at the outset what is and is not at stake in the present proceeding.

This case is *not* about the moral acceptability of promoting the symbols or propaganda of Nazism. Most would agree that such acts are profoundly offensive. By any reasonable standard of morality, the Nazis were responsible for one of the worst displays of inhumanity in recorded history. This Court is acutely mindful of the emotional pain reminders of the Nazi era

[3] The Court also takes judicial notice that on October 24, 2001, a search on Yahoo.com of "Jewish conspiracy" produced 3,070 sites, the search "Protocols/10 Zion" produced 3,560 sites, and the search "Holocaust /5 'did not happen,'" produced 821 sites. The search "National Socialist Party" led to a Web site of an organization promoting modern-day Nazism.

[4] *See* Yahoo!, Inc. v. La Ligue Contra Le Racisme et L'Antisemitisme, 145 F. Supp. 2d 1168 (N.D. Cal. 2001).

cause to Holocaust survivors and deeply respectful of the motivations of the French Republic in enacting the underlying statutes and of the defendant organizations in seeking relief under those statutes. Vigilance is the key to preventing atrocities such as the Holocaust from occurring again.

Nor is this case about the right of France or any other nation to determine its own law and social policies. A basic function of a sovereign state is to determine by law what forms of speech and conduct are acceptable within its borders. In this instance, as a nation whose citizens suffered the effects of Nazism in ways that are incomprehensible to most Americans, France clearly has the right to enact and enforce laws such as those relied upon by the French Court here.[5]

What *is* at issue here is whether it is consistent with the Constitution and laws of the United States for another nation to regulate speech by a United States resident within the United States on the basis that such speech can be accessed by Internet users in that nation. In a world in which ideas and information transcend borders and the Internet in particular renders the physical distance between speaker and audience virtually meaningless, the implications of this question go far beyond the facts of this case. The modern world is home to widely varied cultures with radically divergent value systems. There is little doubt that Internet users in the United States routinely engage in speech that violates, for example, China's laws against religious expression, the laws of various nations against advocacy of gender equality or homosexuality, or even the United Kingdom's restrictions on freedom of the press. If the government or another party in one of these sovereign nations were to seek enforcement of such laws against Yahoo! or another U.S.-based Internet service provider, what principles should guide the court's analysis?

The Court has stated that it must and will decide this case in accordance with the Constitution and laws of the United States. It recognizes that in so doing, it necessarily adopts certain value judgments embedded in those enactments, including the fundamental judgment expressed in the First Amendment that it is preferable to permit the non-violent expression of offensive viewpoints rather than to impose viewpoint-based governmental regulation upon speech. The government and people of France have made a different judgment based upon their own experience. In undertaking its inquiry as to the proper application of the laws of the United States, the Court intends no disrespect for that judgment or for the experience that has informed it.

...

No legal judgment has any effect, of its own force, beyond the limits of the sovereignty from which its authority is derived. 28 U.S.C. § 1738. However, the United States Constitution and implementing legislation require that full faith and credit be given to judgments of sister states, territories, and

[5] In particular, there is no doubt that France may and will continue to ban the purchase and possession within its borders of Nazi[-] and Third Reich[–]related matter and to seek criminal sanctions against those who violate the law.

possessions of the United States. U.S. CONST. art. IV, §§ 1, cl. 1; 28 U.S.C. § 1738. The extent to which the United States, or any state, honors the judicial decrees of foreign nations is a matter of choice, governed by "the comity of nations." *Hilton v. Guyot*, 159 U.S. 113, 163, 16 S. Ct. 139, 40 L. Ed. 95 (1895). Comity "is neither a matter of absolute obligation, on the one hand, nor of mere courtesy and good will, upon the other." *Hilton*, 159 U.S. at 163–64, 16 S. Ct. 139 (1895). United States courts generally recognize foreign judgments and decrees unless enforcement would be prejudicial or contrary to the country's interests. *Somportex Ltd. v. Philadelphia Chewing Gum Corp.*, 453 F.2d 435, 440 (3d Cir. 1971), *cert. denied*, 405 U.S. 1017, 92 S. Ct. 1294, 31 L. Ed. 2d 479 (1972); *Laker Airways v. Sabena Belgian World Airlines*, 731 F.2d 909, 931 (D.C. Cir. 1984) ("[T]he court is not required to give effect to foreign judicial proceedings grounded on policies which do violence to its own fundamental interests."); *Tahan v. Hodgson*, 662 F.2d 862, 864 (D.C. Cir. 1981) ("[R]equirements for enforcement of a foreign judgment expressed in *Hilton* are that . . . the original claim not violate American public policy . . . that it not be repugnant to fundamental notions of what is decent and just in the State where enforcement is sought").

As discussed previously, the French order's content and viewpoint-based regulation of the web pages and auction site on Yahoo.com, while entitled to great deference as an articulation of French law, clearly would be inconsistent with the First Amendment if mandated by a court in the United States. What makes this case uniquely challenging is that the Internet in effect allows one to speak in more than one place at the same time. Although France has the sovereign right to regulate what speech is permissible in France, this Court may not enforce a foreign order that violates the protections of the United States Constitution by chilling protected speech that occurs simultaneously within our borders. *See, e.g., Matusevitch v. Telnikoff*, 877 F. Supp. 1, 4 (D.D.C. 1995) (declining to enforce a British libel judgment because British libel standards "deprive the plaintiff of his constitutional rights"); *Bachchan v. India Abroad Publications, Inc.*, 154 Misc. 2d 228, 585 N.Y.S.2d 661 (Sup. Ct. 1992) (declining to enforce a British libel judgment because of its "chilling effect" on the First Amendment); *see also Abdullah v. Sheridan Square Press, Inc.*, No. 93 Civ. 2515, 1994 WL 419847 (S.D.N.Y. May 4, 1994) (dismissing a libel claim brought under English law because "establishment of a claim for libel under the British law of defamation would be antithetical to the First Amendment protection accorded to the defendants"). The reason for limiting comity in this area is sound. "The protection to free speech and the press embodied in [the First] amendment would be seriously jeopardized by the entry of foreign [] judgments granted pursuant to standards deemed appropriate in [another country] but considered antithetical to the protections afforded the press by the U.S. Constitution." *Bachchan*, 585 N.Y.S.2d at 665. Absent a body of law that establishes international standards with respect to speech on the Internet and an appropriate treaty or legislation addressing enforcement of such standards to speech originating within the United States, the principle of comity is outweighed by the Court's obligation to uphold the First Amendment.

. . .

In light of the Court's conclusion that enforcement of the French order by a United States court would be inconsistent with the First Amendment, the factual question of whether Yahoo! possesses the technology to comply with the order is immaterial. Even assuming for purposes of the present motion that Yahoo! does not possess such technology, compliance still would involve an impermissible restriction on speech.

Yahoo! seeks a declaration from this Court that the First Amendment precludes enforcement within the United States of a French order intended to regulate the content of its speech over the Internet. Yahoo! has shown that the French order is valid under the laws of France, that it may be enforced with retroactive penalties, and that the ongoing possibility of its enforcement in the United States chills Yahoo!'s First Amendment rights. Yahoo! also has shown that an actual controversy exists and that the threat to its constitutional rights is real and immediate. Defendants have failed to show the existence of a genuine issue of material fact or to identify any such issue the existence of which could be shown through further discovery. Accordingly, the motion for summary judgment will be granted. The Clerk shall enter judgment and close the file.

NOTES AND QUESTIONS

1. By a bare majority (6–5), the Ninth Circuit Court of Appeals reversed on procedural grounds the decision you have just read and remanded the case to the federal court for dismissal without prejudice. In a complicated set of opinions, three of the eleven judges sitting en banc in the case voted to reverse the lower court for a lack of personal jurisdiction and the three others for a lack of ripeness to adjudicate the case. 433 F.3d 1199 (9th Cir. 2006).
2. The case highlights the divergent views on freedom of speech (namely, Internet communications) between France, conditioned by its experience in the 1930s and 1940s, and the United States, under the First Amendment of its U.S. Constitution. As the court observed, "What makes this case uniquely challenging is that the Internet in effect allows one to speak in more than one place at the same time." The carefully written opinion in *Yahoo!, Inc.* confirms the essence of a cultural dimension in what otherwise might be a toss-up on the question of whether one legal system should enforce a judgment of another system that runs contrary to the enforcing system's public policy. Note in particular the court's acknowledgment that "[t]he modern world is home to widely varied cultures with radically divergent value systems. There is little doubt that Internet users in the United States routinely engage in speech that violates, for example, China's laws against religious expression, the laws of various nations against advocacy of gender equality or homosexuality, or even the United Kingdom's restrictions on freedom of the press." Note also the court's sensitivity to "the emotional pain reminders of the Nazi era cause to Holocaust survivors" and its deep respect of the motivations

that underlay the French statutes and the pursuit of relief under them that the defendants sought.

3. The court's discussion of the general principle of comity in international law is instructive, given the lack of international standards to resolve cultural tensions. But in the end, did comity play any role at all, or was it just nice-sounding rhetoric? Ultimately, the court held that "the principle of comity is outweighed by the court's obligation to uphold the First Amendment." Why?
4. During the same period as this litigation, France was vigorously promoting the drafting of what became the UNESCO Convention on the Protection and Promotion of the Diversity of Cultural Expression (2005) (Convention on Cultural Diversity), which we shall examine briefly in the discussion of culture as a human right later in this chapter and again in Chapter 4. Does the French court's decision to apply the statute at issue in *Yahoo!* seem to be an expression of cultural diversity? Indeed, does the statute itself bespeak a tolerance for cultural diversity? Should intolerance of certain behaviors (especially genocide and ethnic cleansing) and symbols (such as Nazi artifacts) be an exception to acceptance of cultural pluralism? To answer that question, the following commentary may be helpful:

> Cultural diversity proves to be an even more elusive concept [than culture], because every culture and interest group has its own unique definition. Constructive ambiguity in this area is at its apex. We must briefly delve into the definitional depths to structure meaning around the concept.
>
> France, original proponent of the *exception culturelle* (cultural exception) to the traditional rules of free trade, interprets diversity as differences between national cultures. . . . The polar opposite view is espoused by the United States, in which diversity refers to the free flow of ideas and expressions – a distinctly nation-neutral (and audiovisual sector liberalizing) approach. Both approaches have intrinsic problems.
>
> UNESCO (United Nations Educational, Scientific, and Cultural Organization) has struggled to reach consensus among its members on this issue and defines cultural diversity as "the manifold ways in which the cultures of groups and societies find expression." This approach creates its own set of problems. Chief among these is its emphasis on the various different means of expressions (a commoditized approach) rather than the differences between cultures (an anthropological/sociological approach).

Johnlee Scelba Curtis, *Culture and the Digital Copyright Chimera: Assessing the International Regulatory System of the Music Industry in Relation to Cultural Diversity*, 13 INT'L J. CULTURAL PROP. 59, 61 (2006).

Do you understand the diametrically opposed interpretations of cultural diversity between those of France and the United States, that framed the core issue in *Yahoo!, Inc.*? It is the French interpretation that motivates and defines the Convention on Cultural Diversity, thereby ensuring the convention's unacceptability within the cultural tradition of the United States.

5. Cultural differences abound in implementing intellectual property and privacy rights. Again, we find tension between French and American expectations:

> North American copyright law has a clause called "fair use," which allows writers to quote phrases here and there without permission from the copyright

> holder. It's minimal, but it's something. American copyright law also allows paraphrasing. . . .
>
> The French do not have fair use for unpublished material. Paraphrase has to be extremely loose. (There must be no echo of the original voice; the imagery and even the tone must be changed.) The French also have a law protecting "private life" – "a loi sur la vie privée" – which means that if you do not like what someone says about you, you can sue.

Hazel Rowley, *Point of Departure: Censorship in France*, 78 AM. SCHOLAR, Winter 2009, at 144. Cultural predilections about privacy are profound. Consider, on the one hand, the relaxed attitude of Europeans toward surveillance cameras and national identification cards and, on the other hand, the relaxed, anything-goes attitude of Americans toward Internet and broadcast communications. Are those attitudes shared across the Atlantic Ocean?

6. Taking account of the cultural diversity dilemma, as highlighted by the examples here, is there any point in trying to develop cross-cultural or international standards to promote, let alone govern, anything as ambiguous as cultural diversity?

David J. Przeracki, *"Working It Out": A Japanese Alternative to Fighting It Out*, 37 CLEV. ST. L. REV. 149 (1989)

In stark contrast to America's legal and cultural heritage, and essential to an understanding of contemporary Japan, is the recognition of the pervasive influence of Confucian philosophy on Japanese society from the earliest times. Best known for its moral philosophy, Confucianism "gives primary emphasis to the ethical meaning of *human relationships*, finding and grounding the moral in the divine transcendence." The relationships one has with others, if harmonious, lead to achievement of the basic Confucian virtue of *jen* (translated as compassion, human-heartedness, or "man-to-manness"). For the Japanese,

> [t]he spirit of harmony and concord [is] expressed in the virtue of *wa*. If people abided by *wa*, disputes would not arise. It is one's duty to avoid discord. *En* is the principle of social tie. The net effect of these two principles [constitutes the foundation of] . . . the Japanese [perspective]. Maintaining the relationship bound together by these two forces is the paramount concern.
>
> [Watts, *Briefing the American Negotiator in Japan*, 16 INT'L LAW. 597, 600 (1982).]

Wa is the principle of harmony which the Japanese feel is a condition of one's being in any relationship, including contractual. Accordingly, *wa* may prevent discord in all activities.

Owing to simple Confucian principles, the Japanese are socialized to avoid interpersonal disputes in every realm, including social and business. The principles of *wa* and *en* are still practiced in contemporary Japan, as evidenced in Japanese contract methodology and Japanese dispute resolution techniques, which are characterized by conciliation, less litigation, and very few lawyers.

It is worthy of reiteration that there exists no concept of right in Japanese society. Historically, the emphasis has been on duty, specifically, a duty to maintain harmonious relationships. As a consequence, the Japanese approach to dispute resolution reverses the order of practice in America; the Japanese strongly prefer extra-judicial, informal means as opposed to litigation. "When a dispute arises, the *relationship* functions as the dispute settling mechanism."

. . .

The procedure by which interpersonal settlements are made has been called "reconcilement." Reconcilement is described as "the process by which parties in the dispute confer with each other and reach a point at which they can come to terms and restore or create harmonious relationships." Japanese confidence in reconcilement is perhaps best exemplified in the "We Can Work It Out" clause which invariably appears at the end of Japanese contracts. The clause will typically take one of two forms:

> If in the future a dispute arises between the parties with regard to the [provisions] . . . stipulated in this contract, the parties will confer in good faith [*Sei-o o motte Kyogi Suru*].
>
> or
>
> . . . will settle [the dispute] harmoniously by consultation [*Kyogi Ni Yori emman Ni Kaiketsu Suru*].
>
> [D. Henderson, Conciliation and Japanese Law 194 (1965).]

The notion of reconcilement recalls the traditional idea that both parties are to blame when a conflict arises (*kenka ryoseibei*) because they both failed to maintain harmonious relations. It is, therefore, in the best interest of each party to settle the dispute privately.

A second level of dispute resolution in Japan is conciliation (*chotei*). Also rooted in Confucian philosophy, and first codified during the Tokugawa Shogunate, conciliation is now provided for in the Civil Conciliation Law of 1951. According to Article 1, "[t]he purpose of this law is to devise, by mutual concessions of the parties, solutions for disputes concerning civil matters, which are consistent with reason and befitting actual circumstances." The negotiations are conducted through a third party (a conciliator or a judge) or a committee. When a compromise is reached, the settlement is enforceable as if determined by a court.

Conciliation is very popular in Japan. Surveys conducted over a three-year period indicate that 80% of Japanese would seek settlement through conciliation. Only 20% would prefer settlement in court (after first attempting reconcilement). The Western practice of arbitration, however, is not very popular in Japan. The Japanese dislike arbitration because it "*imposes* a decision on the parties rather than allowing [them] to mold the outcome under the [influence] of a social superior."

Litigation, consequently, is considered exclusively a last resort. "To bring a case to court emphasizes a failure of society and individuals to resolve suits through traditional means. Any hope of restoring harmony is thus destroyed."

The non-litigious nature of the Japanese is generally attributed to their desire to maintain social harmony. However, several other reasons have been proffered to explain their non-litigious propensities. The first of these is the dearth of effective legal sanctions. In Japanese civil cases, the ultimate sanction is to attach property. While other sanctions include civil fines, the ability to collect them is heavily reliant upon the party's willingness to pay. Another reason is the relative expense to bring suit in Japan. Filing fees, for example, are prorated to the amount in controversy, and can be very costly. A final reason to explain the scarcity of litigation is the modest supply of lawyers in Japan.

NOTES AND QUESTIONS

1. Are the lack of effective legal sanctions in Japan, the relative expense of a lawsuit there, and the modest supply of lawyers more an explanation of nonlitigious propensities of Japanese culture, as the reading suggests, or a reflection of it?
2. A leading authority on Japanese litigation has lamented a lack of explanatory data on the cultural and social dynamics and implications of the historical predisposition against adversarial processes that is attributed to the Japanese. He also offered the following observations, based on several empirical studies:

   > The current consensus, at least tacitly, . . . challenges the view that Japan is exceptional. Despite Japan's relatively lower per capita litigation rates, few if any scholars today assert that Japan is unique. Rather, most seek to discover universally applicable factors that explain Japan's lower rates of litigation. Consequently, the Japanese experience is critically relevant for any general assessment of litigation, arbitration and the role of courts and legal rules.
   >
   > Finally, the Japanese experience teaches us that arbitration – to the extent perceived to produce less predictable outcomes – is a less-preferred means of dispute resolution than litigation. Almost always more costly and often more time consuming as private adjudication, arbitration is not a transparent process. The outcomes produced are not necessarily consistent or certain. They are unpredictable by definition. Arbitration thus inhibits settlement and thereby produces unnecessary serial costs.

   John O. Haley, *Litigation in Japan: A New Look at Old Problems*, 10 Willamette J. Int'l L. & Disp. Resol. 121 (2002).
3. The description of Japanese predispositions to dispute resolution highlights the importance of legal culture. In higher context societies such as Japan, for example, the role of hard law is abbreviated, whereas in lower context societies such as the

United States, it is substantial. The two modern, democratic systems share many economic and political values but differ substantially in the strength of their legal cultures. The significance of the concept has been summarized as follows:

> [T]he term *legal culture* may prove helpful in looking for differences in the degree to which given controversies are subject to law, the role allocated to other expertise, and the part played by "alternatives" to law. It also directs attention to the role of religious or ethnic norms and the ambit of other forms of social control and social ordering. Accompanying and concretizing such differences, explaining and attempting to justify them, there are likely to be contrasting attitudes to the tasks law should be asked to play, to the distinctive approaches to formal and substantive ideas of legality and legitimacy, or concerning the appropriateness of public participation.

David Nelken, *Culture, Legal, in* Encyclopedia of Law & Society 370 (David S. Clark ed., 2007).

According to this observation, why is it important professionally to have an understanding of one's own legal culture as well as foreign legal cultures?

2. Legal Discourse

If law can be viewed as a process of communication, an important responsibility of lawyers, and a demand on the legal profession, is to help avoid disputes and contribute to society by informed, effective communication. The drafting of contracts and of wills are two of the most common professional activities that fulfill this responsibility. In a shrinking world, cross-cultural sensitivities and sensibilities are critical. One is reminded of the disastrous results of linguistic and other cultural lapses such as the attempt to market the Chevrolet Nova by that name in Spanish-speaking countries where the model's name means "doesn't go."

The negotiation process is a routine context in which the cultural dimension of lawyering is common. The following readings highlight issues in both private transactions and diplomacy.

a. International Business Transactions

Daniel C.K. Chow & Thomas J. Schoenbaum, International Business Transactions: Problems, Cases, and Materials 11–13 (2005) (reproduced with the permission of Aspen Publishers)

In an age where people, goods, services, capital, and technology now routinely cross national boundaries, issues of differences and clashes in culture that affect [international transactions] have also become more common. By culture, we refer to the values and norms shared by a group and the group's economic, social, political, and religious institutions. Although consideration of cultural issues may not have been traditionally considered part of the work of an international transactions lawyer, a lawyer who ignores cultural issues in a business transaction does so at his or her own peril in this rapid age of globalization.

[C]ultural and political issues [divide] developing and developed nations as groups and [have] an impact in international policy-making arenas such as the World Trade Organization, the United Nations, and other international organizations. In addition to having an impact in the policy-making arena, cultural differences between countries also have a direct impact on particular [international transactions] in two ways. First, cultural issues should be part of the background "business case" for a private transaction, but unlike economic, legal, and marketing issues, all part of traditional business and legal analysis, cultural issues may be ignored to the detriment of the transaction. For example, when the Walt Disney Company bought a tract of land near Paris to construct Euro Disney, Disney's U.S. management assumed that the promise of jobs and economic development would mean widespread local support for the new theme park. Instead, the local populace valued its traditional agricultural lifestyle over economic development and offered spirited resistance to the Disney project, much to the surprise of Disney's management. In addition, a Disney theme park had been a spectacular success in Japan, but the Japanese were far more receptive to U.S. culture than many of the French, who, if anything, were lukewarm toward American culture. Although these were important considerations, the experienced business and legal officials at Disney never considered the cultural factors. *See* JEANNE M. BRETT, NEGOTIATING GLOBALLY 8 (2002). One possible explanation for the failure of the Disney officials to fully consider the cultural factors is that these factors are not present in the company's transactions in the United States, the business environment to which Disney officials were accustomed, and so were ignored in the company's initial forays into the international market.

A second way that differences in culture can affect international business transactions is in negotiating styles. Lawyers are often called on by their clients to negotiate across cultures: The same lawyer may negotiate a sales contract with a German buyer and a joint venture with a Brazilian partner for the same client. Understanding differences in negotiating styles can be advantageous to the lawyer or business executive. On the other hand, failure to understand cultural differences might result in "value being left on the table" – that is, in a deal where both parties are not as well off as they could be if barriers in culture and negotiating styles could be overcome. Cross-cultural negotiation skills have become highly-sought-after skills in the modern age as we have acquired a better understanding of cultural differences.

According to one view, there are certain prevalent cultural categories that are reflected in negotiation strategies and styles: Individualism versus collectivism, egalitarianism versus hierarchy, and low-context versus high-context communications. *See* BRETT, *supra*, 15–21. Most countries fall into these categories. Individualist cultures place the interests of the individual above those of the collective; hierarchical cultures, unlike egalitarian cultures, emphasize differentiated social status and deference to social superiors and associate social power with social status; negotiators from low-context-communications cultures emphasize direct, explicit communications, whereas those from high-context-communication cultures emphasize indirect communications that must be understood against a complex and often unstated background of social values. *See id.* Negotiators from individualist, egalitarian, and low-context-communications cultures such as China prefer to use indirect negotiation styles that avoid confrontation. Where there is a negotiation between persons with clashing negotiation styles, such as from the United States and China, the difference in styles could lead to poor communication and misunderstanding that result in a less-than-optimal result for both parties. Another, perhaps even greater, concern to lawyers and their clients is that they may be disadvantaged and exploited by the other party's skillful negotiators who are used to working in [a] cross-cultural context. From the viewpoint of the lawyer negotiating on behalf of a client, the goal is to avoid both results that can arise from the pitfalls of culture.

Richard W. Downing, Comment, *The Continuing Power of Cultural Tradition and Socialist Ideology: Cross-Cultural Negotiations Involving Chinese, Korean, and American Negotiators*, 1992 J. Disp. Resol. 105, 125–29

[The author first discusses five Chinese and Korean cultural values that define the stereotypical negotiation behavior of those nationalities: harmony, friendship and affiliation, hierarchy and face, historical experience, and patience. – *Eds.*]

It seems intuitively obvious that negotiations between individuals of different cultures will encounter greater difficulties and take longer to reach agreements. An enormous number of factors may inhibit the settlement of a dispute. For example, parties can never easily communicate their needs to each other, even when they have an extensive background of shared values and experience. In fact, studies show that the greater the similarities of perception and behavior between opposing parties, the more readily they can reach agreement. Therefore, differences in nationality and culture can only add to differences found between individuals within a culture.

A cultural dimension may even exist in the way that parties view the negotiation encounter itself. However, cultural differences *per se* do not interfere with negotiation; instead it is how these differences impact on communication between the parties and on the choice of tactics that causes barriers to settlement. This section tries to ascribe specific difficulties encountered to causes found in the negotiators' cultural heritage and ideology.

A. Harmony

The importance placed on harmony and consensus can create communication difficulties and prevent the development of creative solutions. First, part of the ideal of harmony concerns preventing emotional displays and open conflict between the parties. Generally, suppression of emotion can prove valuable, allowing negotiators to focus on issues instead of being distracted by outbursts and shifts of emotion. However, if foreigners do not follow the courteous and respectful norm (*keqi*) expected of them, their behavior can become quite disruptive. Chinese negotiators tend to react negatively to overtly aggressive behavior and may not consider impoliteness as a mere oversight, but as an insult. The common Western approach of admitting the differences between the parties' positions so as to promote "honest confrontation" might easily backfire. Thus, a lack of understanding of the Chinese desire for harmony during talks can cause frictions that may prevent a mutually beneficial agreement.

A second pitfall caused by this desire for harmony lies in the modes of communication used by negotiators. Chinese or Korean individuals may use subtle gestures or oblique suggestions to convey meaning rather than openly stating information or feelings that might cause disruption. For instance, American negotiators may not recognize that silence or lack of eye contact in their opponents need not indicate disapproval. If they acted on their usual interpretation of these appearances, negotiations might founder needlessly. In a more subtle example, Premier Zhou Enlai quoted a poem written by Mao concerning the evanescence of life. This act has since been understood to express Zhou's recognition of his own failing health, a subject he would be uncomfortable to raise openly. Zhou died several years later of cancer. Chinese officials have made other such subtle references that may have an impact on the progress of negotiation; if their American counterparts fail to recognize them, once again settlement may be jeopardized.

The desire for harmony within a negotiating group may also have a negative impact on bargaining outcomes. Investing creative options proves extremely valuable to settling many disputes. However, the requirement of consensus within many working groups stifles individual initiative. This lack of consensus may well explain some of the difficulties and slowness experienced by negotiations involving Chinese and Korean negotiators, but its exact impact remains very difficult to calculate or even detect.

B. Friendship and Affiliation

Although the building of strong relationships has many positive side-effects, the stress placed upon such bonds by Chinese and Korean negotiators may cause misunderstandings and inhibit the reaching of agreements. In terms of positive effects, perhaps the best way to solve the problem of the lack of similar experience and values of the negotiators, even within one culture, is to build a strong working relationship between the parties. The Chinese emphasis on such relationships can also help to save a contract. Because of the long-term bond created during negotiation, an American business partner might not feel that it needs to respond to its counterpart's failure live up to a contract provision. The foreigner can trust her Chinese "friend" to make up for any minor shortcomings later, and the American has greater inclination to settle disputes so as not to risk the overall relationship. In fact, in 1987 over fifty billion dollars of trade occurred between the PRC and the United States without a single dispute rising to the level of a formal lawsuit. Despite these benefits, differing views of the nature of the relationship itself and of the necessity for written contracts can cause misunderstandings.

First, differing views of the negotiators' relationship may disrupt an otherwise stable agreement. Individuals who value the Confucian model of friendship perceive obligations on the parties that foreigners may not recognize. For example, the American paradigm of a stable relationship seeks strict compliance and predictability after signing a contract. A Chinese partner, however, might regard a relationship as setting up obligations on the part of the American, and would not hesitate to ask small favors. Such requests, in turn, might arouse irritation in the American or even accusations of bad faith. On the other hand, the notion of friendship might create expectations in the Chinese official of deserving such special favors or attention. Ill feelings might arise if the American fails to fulfill these perceived obligations. . . . [T]he concept of friendship can lead to exaggerated expectations of dependency that, if not satisfied, can cause angry reactions and feelings of having been mistreated.

Differing emphasis placed on the relationship and the written expression of it may also create difficulties. Chinese negotiators tend to trust a working relationship more than a contract or treaty that arises from it. This opposite view of the general Western perspective caused misunderstandings when Zhou Enlai entered negotiations with the United States over the 1954 Geneva treaty governing Indochina, a treaty which the U.S. would not sign. Zhou convinced the U.S. government to agree to unilaterally declare that it would not interfere with the treaty's provisions. Although the United States regarded this action as a mere declaration of policy, the PRC then persistently claimed that the U.S. was bound by the 1954 Geneva agreements. The negotiated settlement came to nothing when the United States changed its policy in 1960 and increased its military presence in Vietnam.

Differing views of the importance of contracts and relational bounds also create difficulties in business negotiations. When bargaining over a contract, for example, Chinese negotiators do not like to consider the possibility of the breakup of the relationship, and if they do agree to assigning responsibilities after a breach, they prefer general, uncertain terms. The standard arbitration clause . . . simply states that both parties must try to correct unsatisfactory results and jointly work out the consequences should the contract fail. Obviously, American businesses regard this kind of general statement as completely inadequate. In addition, each side may waste much time trying to educate the other as to the level of specificity and the ultimate form of the contract. American negotiators in particular find this need for explanation frustrating. Thus, different conceptions of the role of contracts, as well as differing ideas on levels of specificity in contracts, can cause barriers to successfully concluding negotiations.

C. Hierarchy and Face

Individuals who hold a concept of hierarchy tend to prefer not to associate with others who have lower status levels, and this preference can prevent the formation of the trusting relationship necessary for successful negotiations. Because lawyers traditionally hold a very low status and were persecuted during the Cultural Revolution along with all intellectuals, perceptions of the status levels of many foreign representatives may hinder negotiation. Although changes since Mao's death made the use of lawyers more legitimate, and the recognition that other cultures may assign status to members in different ways has become more widespread, status consciousness may still limit the ease with which negotiation relationships form.

Ideas of status and face may also affect the ways in which negotiators go about building friendships. Just as important as not injuring another's reputation is the idea of *giving* face: small gestures or comments of respect may fulfill a Chinese negotiator's desire for status recognition. Americans in particular have trouble giving face; although flattery exists between Americans, they often regard it as mere pretense or feel guilty about pumping another's ego. However, failing to show the customary signs of respect will cause offense or inhibit the formation of positive relationships.

NOTES AND QUESTIONS

1. Given the cultural traps identified in the foregoing commentary, why wouldn't it be best for cross-cultural negotiators simply to acknowledge their cultural differences and ask each other to be tolerant? From what you have read, would that overcome the risk of unintended offense?
2. The Chow and Schoenbaum article underscores the significance for lawyers of cultural differences in planning transactions and negotiating agreements. The authors summarize certain prevalent cultural categories: individualism versus collectivism, egalitarianism versus hierarchy, and low-context- versus high-context-communications cultures. They cite the following example of negotiations with the Chinese:

   > A U.S. company had a contract from a German buyer to sell bicycles produced in China. When the first shipment was ready, there was a problem. The bikes rattled. The U.S. buyer did not want to accept the shipment, knowing that they would not be acceptable to the German customer, whose high-end market niche was dominated by bikes that were whisper quiet. What to do? In U.S. culture, the normal approach would be to tell the manufacturer that the rattling bikes were unacceptable and that the problem had to be fixed. In China, such a direct confrontation would be extremely rude and cause much loss of face. Knowing this, the U.S. manager went to the Chinese plant,

> inspected the bicycles, rode a few, and asked about the rattle. "Is this rattle normal? Do all the bikes rattle? Do you think the German buyer will think there is something wrong with the bike if it rattles?" Then he left. The next shipment of bikes had no rattles (citing JEANNE M. BRETT, NEGOTIATING GLOBALLY 8 (2002)).

The authors then ask the following: Under the suggested approach, when does the U.S. manager find out whether the problem has been resolved? Do you see any other issues with this approach? How would you suggest handling this problem without causing loss of face?

3. Professional competence may require not only a grasp of the characteristic cultural values that specifically animate negotiation behavior, as Richard Downing suggests, but also a deeper understanding of foreign culture, as the following observation suggests:

> In order to understand the East Asian negotiating style, Americans who deal with East Asians should explore the history and culture of East Asia. East Asia has a long history that continues to influence the character and style of the inhabitants today. Among East Asian countries, China has the longest continuous history; in fact, the traditional Chinese culture heavily influenced the development of the entire East Asian culture. In modern East Asian business culture, negotiation approaches are rooted in certain Chinese thoughts and studies dating back more than two thousand years. The negotiation styles of the modern East Asians are largely found in *The Art of War*, a book on military strategy and tactics written by Sun Tzu about two thousand five hundred years ago.
>
> As such, before using the typical American negotiation methods when dealing with East Asians, like "problem solving" or "cooperative negotiation," or "adversarial" or "competitive negotiation," Americans should understand the traditional influences behind the East Asian negotiation practices.

John Chu, The Art of War *and East Asian Negotiating Styles*, 10 WILLAMETTE J. INT'L L. & DISP. RESOL. 161, 162–63 (2002).

4. Well-informed generalizations about foreign cultural values and behavior, if skillfully employed, can be helpful, even essential, in negotiations and other professional activities. But overgeneralizations or mindless, unnuanced stereotyping of foreigners and the influence of their culture can be risky, even damaging; skillful employment of cultural information requires much experience and refinement. See James K. Sebenius, *Caveats for Cross-Border Negotiators*, 18 NEGOTIATION J. 121 (2002); Jeffrey L. Rubin & Frank E.A. Sander, *Culture, Negotiation, and the Eye of the Beholder*, 7 NEGOTIATION J. 249 (1991) (cautioning against stereotyping and the self-fulfilling prophesy of expecting differences even when they do not exist or are ineffectual).

b. Diplomacy

In recent years, empirical studies have documented the role of culture in intergovernmental negotiations and diplomacy. These studies focus on the extent to which cultural-based premises can lead to conflicts in negotiation and advocate a more nuanced conceptualization of culture. The scholars not only take care to distinguish culture from national character and stereotypes but also insist that culture is dynamic.

In the thoughtful and practical commentary that follows, Raymond Cohen shows how different assumptions about bargaining affect diplomatic processes. His thesis is that cultural differences not only persist despite the emergence of a global culture but also have an observable effect on diplomatic negotiation. Comparing two styles of negotiation, his emphasis is "not on culture as a single determinant of behavior but on the effect of bilateral negotiation of the cultural gap (often detectable at the linguistic level) between the negotiating parties." The United States is the "baseline culture" against which other cultures are compared and contrasted, though he adds that "this is not meant to imply that American culture is considered superior or normative." The main point is that even subtle cultural differences can affect diplomatic outcomes. As Cohen notes, for example, the concept of saving face is unlikely to cause trouble in Sino-Japanese relations, but it can certainly be problematic in Chinese negotiations with Americans who are unfamiliar with the concept.

Raymond Cohen, Negotiating across Cultures: International Communication in an Interdependent World 215–18, 222–26 (1997) (reproduced with the permission of the United States Institute of Peace)

Culture has been called "the hidden dimension," unseen, yet exerting a pervasive influence on the behavior of individuals, groups, and societies. . . .

Negotiation theorists' dismissal of the effect of culture springs from the assumption that there is a single, universal paradigm of negotiation and that cross-national differences are stylistic and superficial. . . . [T]wo quite different paradigms of negotiation [are, however, apparent]. One is associated with the predominantly verbal and explicit, or *low-context*, communicatory style of the United States. In a nutshell, it is infused with the can-do, problem-solving spirit, assumes a process of give-and-take, and is strongly influenced by Anglo-Saxon legal habits. When theorists posit a universal paradigm of negotiation (usually involving such features as the "joint search for a solution," "isolating the people from the problem," and the "maximization of joint gains"), they are in effect proposing an idealized version of the low-context, problem-solving model. Notice the instrumental assumptions of rationality that underlie the paradigm: people are part of the problem, not the solution; each problem can be solved discretely; goals are defined in terms of material, not psychic, satisfactions.

. . .

There exists another, quite different paradigm of negotiation just as self-consistent and valid in its own terms as that exemplified by [a] low-context, problem-solving approach. This alternative model, associated with a non-verbal, implicit, *high-context* style of communication, predominates in interdependent societies that display a collectivistic, rather than individualistic, ethos. This paradigm was found to mark the negotiating behavior of the non-Western states examined. In contrast to the results-oriented American model, it declines to view the immediate issue in isolation; lays particular stress on long-term and affective aspects of the relationship between the parties; is preoccupied with considerations of symbolism, status, and face; and draws on highly developed communication strategies for evading confrontation.

Putting the two paradigms together in the same room in an intercultural or interparadigmatic encounter produces some interesting reactions. American negotiators tend to be surprised by their interlocutors' preoccupation with history and hierarchy, preference for principle over nitty-gritty detail, personalized and repetitive style of argument, lack of enthusiasm for explicit and formal agreement, and willingness to sacrifice substance to form. They are frustrated by their partners' reluctance to put their cards on the table, intransigent bargaining, evasiveness, dilatoriness, and readiness to walk away from the table without agreement. Non-Western negotiators tend to be surprised by their interlocutors' ignorance of history; preoccupation with individual rights, obsession with the immediate problem while neglecting the overall relationship, excessive bluntness, impatience, disinterest in establishing a philosophical basis for agreement, extraordinary willingness to make soft concessions, constant generation of new proposals, and inability to leave a problem pending. They are frustrated by their American partners' occasional obtuseness and insensitivity; tendency to see things and present alternatives in black-or-white, either-or terms; appetite for crisis; habit of springing unpleasant surprises; intimidating readiness for confrontation; tendency to bypass established channels of authority; inability to take no for an answer; and obsession with tidying up loose ends and putting everything down on paper. Obviously, these are oversimplified depictions, but they do serve to highlight the main points of abrasion in the low-context [and] high-context encounter.

Insistence on the dichotomy may seem overstated in the light of contemporary patterns of interdependence and globalization. But its continuing relevance stems from the existence of an international trend to some cultural *convergence* at the same time as deep-seated *divergence* continues to exist.

. . .

If cross-cultural dissonance can harm a relationship, the converse should be equally true: that cross-cultural synchrony, based on careful attention to the other side's psychological needs, should prove beneficial. This has indeed proved to be so [as in] the example of Senator Mike Mansfield, a superb ambassador to Japan (1977–89). Following a 1981 accident at sea, in which a U.S. nuclear submarine, the *George Washington*, collided with a Japanese freighter, killing two Japanese sailors, passions ran high in Japan. A speedy U.S. naval inquiry, acceptance of liability, and agreement to pay compensation helped defuse the incident. However, the critical step in finally disposing of the affair was taken by Senator Mansfield. Delivering the final report to the Japanese foreign minister, he bowed low according to Japanese custom and apologized in full view of press and television.

"I wanted to let the whole nation know how sorry the U.S. felt by adopting the Japanese manner of apologizing and being sorry," he said. "I deliberately adopted something the Japanese would understand. It was a small price to pay to bring an amicable settlement."

Unless there are shared interests in reaching an accord, however, and a healthy relationship following its conclusion, no amount of cross-cultural sensitivity will help.

. . .

The salience of "personal chemistry" in international affairs may, of course, be overstated. After all, the ongoing conduct of foreign policy is in the hands of a great many agencies and officials. National leaders and high officials are engaged only intermittently. Nevertheless, consultations at the highest level can play a crucial role. Communication between heads of state and foreign ministers brings information authoritatively and promptly to the attention of their respective governments. Commitments are made, directions indicated, agendas set. Where that communication is easy and unencumbered, it may not be possible to brush aside insurmountable differences, but misunderstanding of the other's intentions and gratuitous complications can be avoided. Moreover, without open channels of communication, opportunities to explore common interests may be missed.

A second factor facilitating harmony was the recognition by the United States that there may be certain points of inviolable dogma that are non-negotiable as far as a high-context interlocutor is concerned. However, once such axioms are conceded in principle, it may be possible, in a pragmatic fashion, to arrive at a satisfactory agreement on concrete issues. This approach involves true cross-cultural accommodation, in that it reconciles the deep-seated needs of both sides.

It was this approach that underlay the 1962 Kennedy-Mateos accord paving the way for a resolution of the Chamizal dispute. Once the United States recognized the justice of the Mexican claim (conceded by international arbitration in 1911), Mexico was prepared to be utterly pragmatic in its practical implementation. An identical strategy was followed in 1973, when President Nixon committed the United States to a "just solution" of the Colorado River problem, thereby acknowledging the responsibility of the United States to ensure that usable *water* reached Mexican farmers. Similarly, in the 1969 Okinawa bases negotiations the United States wisely conceded the principle of "home-level reversion" – the return of the Ryukyu and Bonin islands to Japanese administration – thereby guaranteeing both continued U.S. use of the bases and future military cooperation.

The 1972 Shanghai communiqué was yet another example of a generalized framework beneath the philosophical awnings of which pragmatic cooperation could proceed. [The Shanghai communiqué opened up relations and led to formal diplomatic relations between Beijing and Washington, even in the midst of the Chinese Cultural Revolution.] In this case, remarkably, points of difference were not plastered over. But the two countries' opposition to hegemony (that is, Soviet ambitions) was proclaimed and the yawning gap over the Taiwan issue was bridged with the ingenious

U.S. acknowledgment "that all Chinese on either side of the Taiwan Straits maintain there is but one China."

A final ingredient in reaching agreement with high-context negotiators was scrupulous regard for their heightened sensitivity in matters of face. Any whiff of humiliation would doom an agreement to perdition. To obtain the substance of accord it was essential to preserve appearances: to maintain – if necessary, contrive – the impression that the accord was an achievement of the other side, concluded on the basis of mutual respect and equal standing. Striking examples of this pattern were found in the 1971 Japanese devaluation and the 1982 Mexican loan. In the first instance, a 17 percent devaluation of the yen was impossible, but 16.9 percent devaluation was acceptable. In the second case, Mexico was ready to receive a lower effective price for its oil than it could otherwise have obtained, because it rested on a face-saving arrangement. The vital importance of face was also observed in the 1971–72 talks with China, for example, in the terms of the invitation to President Nixon; and in the 1973 negotiations for a cease-fire following the Yom Kippur War, when United Nations checkpoints on the Cairo–Suez road obscured the reality of the blockade of the Egyptian Third Army by Israeli forces. Finally, although it was not always feasible, something unacceptable as an explicit agreement might be palatable as an informal understanding. Over the years, many areas of cooperation, especially with Mexico and Egypt, have been assisted by this expedient. The February 1995 peso rescue package is an example. Political concessions were made by Mexico, but not in the main financial agreement.

. . .

[C]ross-cultural insight is not a panacea or substitute for consonant interests. Furthermore, prior to [a] grasp of the cultural context must come the realization that negotiations do not take place in a vacuum. If negotiators are to succeed they must first have a good feel for the personal abilities, requirements, and freedom of maneuver of opposing delegates, as well as the political strengths and weaknesses, needs, and constraints of the government they represent.

Provided these reservations are borne in mind, there are certain obvious lessons to be drawn from this project. I present them here (for the benefit of the low-context individual faced by a high-context adversary) in the form of ten recommendations for the intercultural negotiator[:]

1. Prepare for a negotiation by studying your opponents' culture and history, and not just the issue at hand. Best of all, learn the language. Immerse yourself in the historical relationship between your two nations. It may explain more than you might expect.

2. Try to establish a warm, personal relationship with your interlocutors. If possible, get to know them even before negotiations get under way. Cultivating contacts and acquaintances is time well spent.

3. Do not assume that what you mean by a message – verbal or nonverbal – is what representatives of the other side will understand by it. They will interpret it in the light of their cultural and linguistic background, not

yours. By the same token, they may be unaware that things look different from your perspective.

4. Be alert to indirect formulations and nonverbal gestures. Traditional societies put a lot of weight on them. You may have to read between the lines to understand what your partners are hinting at. Do not assume that they will come right out with it. Be ultra-careful in your own words and body language. Your partners may read more into them than you intend. Do not express criticism in public. Do not lose your temper. Anything that leads to the loss of face is likely to be counterproductive.

5. Do not overestimate the power of advocacy. Your interlocutors are unlikely to shift their positions simply in response to good arguments. Pressure may bring short-term results, but risks damaging the relationship. Facts and circumstances speak louder than words and are easier to comply with.

6. Adapt your strategy to your opponents' cultural needs. On matters of inviolable principle, attempt to accommodate their instinct for prior agreement with your preference for progress on practical matters. Where haggling is called for, leave yourself plenty of leeway. Start high, bargain doggedly, and hold back a trump card for the final round.

7. Flexibility is not a virtue against intransigent opponents. If they are concerned to discover your real bottom line, repeated concessions will confuse rather than clarify the issue. Nor is there merit in innovation for its own sake. Avoid the temptation to compromise with yourself.

8. Be patient. Haste will almost certainly mean unnecessary concessions. Resist the temptation to labor under artificial time constraints; they will work to your disadvantage. Allow your opponents to decide in their own good time. Their bureaucratic requirements cannot be short-circuited.

9. Be aware of the emphasis placed by your opponents on matters of status and face. Outward forms and appearances may be as important as substance. For face-conscious negotiators, an agreement must be presentable as an honorable outcome. On the other hand, symbolic gains may compensate them for substantive losses.

10. Do not be surprised if negotiation continues beyond the apparent conclusion of an agreement. Implementation is unlikely to be automatic and often requires continuing discussion. To assist compliance, it may help to build a system of graduated, performance-based incentives into the original contract.

NOTES AND QUESTIONS

1. Do American assumptions about negotiation differ markedly from those of diplomats in Asia?
2. In what ways does the concept of saving face affect international diplomacy? How should individuals preparing for meetings ensure that they are aware of sensitivities that exist for the other parties?

3. Does item 7 in Raymond Cohen's list of diplomatic negotiations spell doom for efforts to bridge major policy differences, such as the effort in the first decade of the twenty-first century to negotiate an end to North Korea and Iranian development of nuclear weapons? Or does item 7 make better sense in the wider context of the entire list of recommendations?
4. Carol Gilligan has written that moral reasoning is gendered. In her influential book, In a Different Voice, she contends that women reason more in terms of harm done to relationships than in terms of abstract principles. Assuming her argument is correct, in what specific ways might gender affect diplomatic relations? Do women throughout the world reason in the same way, as Gilligan suggests, or is reasoning itself culturally conditioned?
5. The economist and diplomat John Kenneth Galbraith famously observed that "there are a few iron-clad rules of diplomacy but to one there is no exception: When an official reports that talks were useful, it can safely be concluded that nothing was accomplished." Does the sugar-coated parlance of diplomacy, with its euphemisms, reinforce or overcome cultural misunderstandings?
6. Successful diplomacy normally involves acts as well as communications, of course. Social hospitality and gift-giving have nearly always been instrumental, from the potlatch ceremonies of the Kwakiutls in Canada to the ritualistic swapping of gifts among heads of state today. Scientific evidence suggests, for example, that the Wari empire, which dominated much of Peru between 600 and 1000 A.D., may have relied on a form of diplomatic party-giving featuring a potent mix of corn beer and hallucinogens. See Andrew Curry, *Trophy Skulls and Beer*, Archaeology, Jan.-Feb. 2010, at 38 ("Mountain-top palaces might have functioned like embassies, and could have played a role in a soft-power effort to impress the neighbors with great parties." *Id.* at 39.).

3. Cultural Identity Paradigms

As the following reading makes clear, cross-cultural sensitivity and experience may not be enough in the face of deep-seated, determinative cultural identities. Such identities often perform a positive function in enriching and stabilizing people's lives, but, as we shall see, they also may constrain legal communications, cheapen cultural values, and inhibit options for constructively resolving cultural issues. For example, cultural identities may lead to expansive definitions of a nation's cultural patrimony over archaeological material. It may also limit collaboration in resolving disputes concerning illegally exported material. Entrenched national identities may also encourage unfairness in the sports area, just as religious identities may discourage ecumenical progress in alleviating poverty, social injustice, and environmental degradation. The following reading undertakes the ambitious project of examining the implications of cultural identities for the world order.

Jacinta O'Hagan, *Conflict, Convergence, or Coexistence? The Relevance of Culture in Reframing World Order, in* Reframing the International: Law, Culture, Politics 187–88, 198–210 (Richard Falk, Lester Edwin J. Ruiz & R.B. Walker eds., 2002)

Having now moved into the twenty-first century[,] the calendar turns on a thousand years of human history, a period that has seen technological and social changes that have transformed the social and physical world in which humanity lives. What is the relevance of culture to the world order that is emerging from these processes of transformation? "Culture," it seems, is prevalent in contemporary political commentary and analysis. In many contexts, cultural identity is perceived as defining the parties to conflict. For instance, in the late 1990s, conflict in Indonesia revealed for some the cultural "faultlines" between that state's ethnically and religiously diverse peoples. There were similar concerns with regard to ongoing cultural tension between Muslim and Hindu communities in India and Pakistan. In the Balkans, Kosovo presented a harrowing image of a seemingly ancient and irreconcilable conflict between the region's Albanian Muslim population and the Orthodox Serbs. The disintegration of the former Soviet Empire into ethnic and religiously diverse states produced tension in the Caucasus, in Central Asia, and in Russia itself. In Africa, violence between Hutu and Tutsi people led to the deaths of tens of thousands of people in 1994. Rivalry between Islam and the West appears to pervade the politics of the latter decades of the twentieth and early twenty-first century. There has also been wide debate about "Asian values" as a system that both empowered the dynamic states of the East Asian region and distinguished them from the West. There is, then, a prevalent image of culture as a force that distinguishes and divides ethnic and religious communities, of culture as a source of conflict. This is the pessimistic message underlying Samuel Huntington's "clash of civilizations" image of the post–Cold War world order. But is this the only way to view the influence of culture on contemporary world politics?

... The nature of culture and its relevance to contemporary world order is deeply contested. This is not surprising; culture is a broad and complex term that can be interpreted in many ways.

...

... Perhaps the most prominent and contentious example of the recent revival of interest in culture's role in world order is Samuel Huntington's work on the "clash of civilizations." In this thesis, Huntington suggests that civilizational identity is becoming the organizing principle in the post–Cold War world order. Although Huntington's argument is a controversial one that has been widely contested, it provided something of a centrifugal point around which the arguments relating to culture and civilizations spun in the 1990s. The imagery and language employed in his discussion of "cultural clashes," fault lines, and tectonic plates have powerfully entered into the vocabulary of contemporary academic and political commentary.

Huntington has argued that the end of the Cold War signaled the collapse of ideological identification as a central feature of international relations. However, he also saw modernization and technology as forces that are weakening the role of the nation-state as a political community and enhancing the role of cultural and religious identity in politics. These processes enhance the sense of identity between culturally similar groups and heighten the sense of difference from others. For Huntington, these developments are expressed in economic and political cohesion within civilization groups and increased tension between civilizational groups. In essence, Huntington's thesis is premised on the belief that differences accentuated by proximity accentuates conflict. Culture, as expressed through civilizational communities and alliances, structures relations between the smaller political units or communities. This perspective shifts the focus away from states as the foundation of the international and world order toward broader, culturally based communities. It does not argue that states are no longer significant actors in world politics, but it does suggest that they are becoming the agents of civilizational identity, with their interests increasingly defined along cultural lines.

This perspective projects an image of world order based on the interaction of a number of largely incommensurable civilizations. These are seen as dynamic, in that they rise and fall and are subject to redefinition. However, while Huntington acknowledges that civilizations blend and overlap, he sees the differences between them as real, if not always sharply defined. Most significantly, civilizations are seen as largely incommensurable; their capacity to understand each other is limited. Huntington rejects any suggestion that humanity forms, or is converging toward, a single, universal civilization. Instead, world order comprises a number of coexisting but antagonistic civilizations. . . .

The "clash of civilizations" provides one *reading* of the impact of globalization and modernization of the modern world. However, this perspective suggests that increased interaction raises awareness of the differences between civilizations and invigorates animosities rather than enhancing understanding and cultural convergence. Furthermore, this perspective suggests that modernization does not homogenize societies; modern societies share commonalities but remain culturally distinct. In particular, modernization does not necessarily mean Westernization for Huntington. He firmly rejects the idea that the end of the Cold War will produce the universalization of Western liberal democracy. For Huntington, the norms and values that define the West also distinguish it from other civilizations, making it unique rather than universal. Huntington argues that the spread of Western values and institutions, such as democracy, has been a superficial process, predicated on the strength of the West as a military and economic power, not the innate relevance of these values to all other societies. Huntington's analysis led him to conclude in 1996 that the promotion of Western norms and values as universal is false, immoral, and dangerous. It is false because Western values are not universal. It is immoral because values could only be effectively spread through the projection of force, suggesting some form of imperialism. It is dangerous because it posed the risk of counterreaction. In contrast, the "clash of civilizations" thesis suggests civilizations should pursue policies of consolidation at home and noninterference with other civilizations abroad.

. . . Huntington's analysis of cultural world order has been widely debated and contested. A central criticism is that it overemphasizes conflict between peoples of different civilizations. The thesis allows very little consideration of the constructive and cooperative engagements between civilizations that can be a source of growth and development. In addition, there is little space for exploring the points of commonality and shared experience that link groups and societies across civilizational boundaries and concerns for issues such as management of the global commons or the rights of indigenous peoples.

The "clash of civilizations" image of the cultural world order has also been criticized for its tendency to underplay tensions and conflicts between people from the same civilization. For instance, Huntington's treatment of Islam has been widely criticized as underrating the tension between Muslim societies and exaggerating the influence of radical Islamic elements in these societies. In part, this derives from the tendency of this approach to accentuate the homogeneity of civilizations, portraying them as rather rigid, hermetically sealed entities. This is despite Huntington's definition of civilizations as dynamic. The essentializations of civilizations facilitates viewing tensions in relations between them as primordial and inevitable. This can convey the sense that culture is itself the source of conflict, rather than one factor in the interpretation of a variety of issues in relations between different civilizations.

Cultural World Order as Convergent

. . . The "clash of civilizations," however, presents only one set of assumptions in contemporary political commentary about the nature of cultural world order. This model of world order as a plurality of incommensurable civilizations is particularly contested by liberal critics who convey a much stronger sense of the convergence of societies toward the universal, modern civilization. For them, the increased interaction generated by modernization and globalization is producing powerful forces that encourage the integration of the world along a Western, liberal model. One of the best-known contemporary liberal proponents of this alternative model of world order, one often cited in contrast to Huntington, is Francis Fukuyama. In his "end of History" thesis, Fukuyama projects an image of world order comprising different cultures, but in which humanity as a whole is engaged in a single, civilizing process of development and modernization. Human society is perceived to be on a journey of ideological revelation, the process of History. This journey is toward the most satisfying and efficient political and economic system, a journey that has culminated in the concepts underlying the system of liberal democracy, the "end of History." The West is presented by Fukuyama as at the vanguard of this process, defeating competing models of modernization, such as Marxist-Leninism. Through this victory, the West is perceived as establishing the norm, presenting the standard toward which other societies are moving.

Fukuyama's understanding of this process of human development is premised on a belief that economic modernization and technical change are integrative and homogenizing forces: "all countries undergoing economic modernization must increasingly resemble one another." Over time, these changes tend to "blur the boundaries between civilizations and promote a homogenous set of political and economic institutions among the world's most advanced countries." Furthermore, he argues, economic development encourages "a certain degree of value change in a Western direction."

... Fukuyama then acknowledges the persistence of culture, even recognizing some resistance to homogenization at the level of cultural identity. However, unlike Huntington, he does not assume cultural difference necessarily leads to conflict. Furthermore, his discussion focuses on national rather than broad civilizational cultures. In fact, he attempts to eradicate such notions as a single Asian culture as too simplistic. However, he continues to assume that the institutional models of Western liberal democracy define the parameters within which all societies will evolve. Therefore, he continues to assume a broad process of convergence toward Western institutions and values.

The liberal confidence in modernization as a process that leads to convergence with the Western model was further enhanced by the crisis that befell Asian economies in 1997–1998. The crisis demonstrated for scholars such as Fukuyama that the Asian model of development did not provide a durable and universal model. Cultural differentiation might obstruct but ultimately will not inhibit institutional and, presumably, ideological convergence toward a liberal political and economic system. Consequently, the impression remains of a single civilizing process with "the West" at its forefront.

Cultural World Order as Coexistence

... A more pluralist cultural world order can be found in the "international society" perspective. The vision of world order drawn from the work of authors such as Martin Wight, Hedley Bull, and Adam Watson is pluralist in that it sees the current world order as characterized by a global international society that encompasses a variety of civilizational identities. However, while it is multicivilizational in membership, they conceptualize this modern international society as an outgrowth of Western civilization, and its emergence is interwoven with the political development of the European states system. The West has provided the normative and institutional framework of modern world politics. Through the structures of international society, it has created a single, global political system and the context within which all civilizations function and interact.

These scholars, however, do not argue that international society has created civilizational homogeneity. Within the context of international society, the identity of various civilizations, and particularly the West, remains distinct. The West occupies a privileged position within this society that was constructed around the assumptions, interests, and experiences of Western civilization. The West set the standards, first of race, then [of] religion, and subsequently of governance, which other societies were required to meet to obtain entry into international society. The image of cultural world order that emerges from this analysis is a pluralist but also a hierarchical one, with Western civilization occupying the apex of this hierarchy as the hegemonic or dominant force.

A sense of civilizational hierarchy is even more evident in the perception of cultural world order that we find in the work of Edward Said. In Said, we find a world order that has been structured by the imperialism of the West, used here primarily to represent the imperial powers of Europe and the United States. Said perceives the empires of the nineteenth and early twentieth century [as] establishing a sense of civilizational hierarchy that was constituted, reinforced, and legitimated through the deployment of images of the non-Western societies as less rational, less advanced, and less capable than the West. This hierarchy is perceived as ongoing, perpetuated through a system of cultural hegemony in the postcolonial period in which the projection of law and the maintenance of order and stability provided the basis for a different form of civilizing mission. This continued to legitimate the West's intervention in, and control of, the political and economic affairs of the non-West.

For Said, then, the projection of Western norms and institutions as universal masks the cultural hegemony of the West. However, Said's cultural world order is not one that assumes a convergence with the dominant culture. Instead, it suggests that a gap has been maintained between the dominant and the dominated. Therefore, Said's cultural world order, like Huntington's, is pluralist and critical of Western universalism as a mask of hegemony. However, Said's pluralist world order does not assume that civilizational identities are necessarily segregated and hostile. Difference does not inevitably mean hostility for Said. Rather, he portrays cultures as dynamic, hybrid, heterogeneous, constantly changing in interaction with one another. Said seeks to escape the hegemonic structure of the current world order to achieve one based on mutual respect between cultures, while maintaining an underlying respect for broad human goals.

The Implications of Differing Conceptions of World Order

... Identifying differing conceptions of cultural world order is not just an intellectual exercise. How we view the cultural world order is one of the perspectives that frames the way in which we read political interaction. This is not to argue that the cultural perspective is the only or even necessarily the dominant factor that shapes political perceptions and assumptions. However, assumptions about cultural interaction have significant and differing implications for how the possibilities for political interaction are perceived. This can be illustrated by considering how the three broad models of cultural world order identified in the preceding discussion – the models of conflict, convergence, and coexistence – could provide different readings, analysis, and prescriptions for issues in world politics. We will briefly consider three significant issues in current political debates[:] the issues of ethnic nationalism, globalization, and human rights.

Conceptions of Cultural World Order and Ethnic Nationalism

At the outset, we noted that cultural identity is often associated in contemporary world politics with issues of ethnic nationalism and religious revivalism. In cases such as the emergence of ethnic nationalism during the 1990s in locations such as Kosovo, Bosnia, and in Chechnya and Dagestan, local cultural identities not only became important political identities but [also] were significantly articulated in the context of broader civilizational identities – Islamic and Slavic or Orthodox. . . . This can produce the perception of cultural identity itself being the source of conflict between such communities. This can have serious consequences for the ways in which we might negotiate conflicts in such contexts. Focusing on culture as the essential source of conflict can inhibit dispute resolution and even exacerbate tensions further. It can distract attention from other sources of dispute, based perhaps on issues relating to resources or the distribution of political power that may be interwoven with identity politics. If conflicts over economic or political issues are interpreted as essentially collisions of civilizations based on primordial differences, they are transferred from the realm of the negotiable and the solvable into that of perpetual unsolvable conflict. Furthermore, focusing on the irreconcilability of civilizations, rather than on their techniques for coexistence, can become a self-fulfilling prophecy. The rhetoric of the inability of peoples who see themselves as culturally distinct to peacefully coexist can generate and legitimate policies such as "ethnic cleansing," which can decimate previously heterogeneous communities.

An alternative reading of ethnic nationalism, such as in the Balkans or the Caucasus, can be found in the more liberal convergence perspective. From this perspective, these forces may be treated as temporary and transitional phenomen[a] that do not seriously challenge the broader long-term processes of development. This may inhibit consideration of the importance attached by local communities to local values and beliefs, which can in themselves provide powerful and immediate forces that can shape political interaction, as was the case in Rwanda in 1994. A lack of sensitivity to the cultural context in which policies or institutions have evolved, or to which they will be applied, can produce friction, misunderstanding, resentment, or even the failure of such policies and institutions. Furthermore, the processes of development that the liberal perspective identifies with progress are not universally accepted as positive and desirable. For some, they are associated with the continuing projection of Western control over the non-West. Voices from the developing world have argued that liberal standards are a form of cultural imperialism imposing Western standards under the guise of universal standards.

What of those who conceptualize cultural world order as pluralist and potentially cooperative, how would this perspective view the issue of ethnic nationalism and religious revival? In Edward Said's work there is an effort to find a path between cultural relativism and cultural hegemony. For Said, while nationalism has played a significant role in achieving human emancipation from absolutism and imperialism, there is a danger that these liberating energies could be strangled by narrow, essentialized, or chauvinist forms of nationalism, or "nativism," which continue to reinforce divisions. For Said, while the development of national consciousness is the necessary first stage of anti-imperialism, true liberation requires movement onward from national to "social consciousness." Without such a transformation, national consciousness can produce fundamentalism and despotism rather than liberation. It can produce an essentialized sense of homogeneous and authentic traditions that can be as oppressive as the essentialized images of weakness and inferiority that were projected during imperial control. Said rejects nationalist separatism and triumphalism in favor of seeking a community among cultures and peoples. A key question here is how one attains the conditions of trust and dialogue such a community requires. How can these conditions be achieved in relationships such as between Palestinians and Israelis or ethnic Albanians and Serbs in Kosovo, where the communities have become scarred by fear and insecurity through experiences of violence?

Conceptions of Cultural World Order and Globalization

A second central debate in world politics at this point in time is whether world order is converging or diverging as a result of globalization. How might perceptions of cultural world order frame positions in this debate? An image of world order that assumes the "convergence" of different civilizational identities perceives globalization as enhancing communication and interdependency between different civilizational groups, facilitating institutional and normative homogenization toward the dominant model of modernization. Societies become more similar. While basic cultural differences may remain, these do not impede political, economic, and some measure of normative homogenization. In contrast, an image that perceives the cultural world order as innately conflictual would view the processes of globalization as raising the level of intercivilizational contact, exacerbating tensions between societies from different civilizational identities and enhancing the cohesion within. From the perspective of the pluralist who seeks to encourage coexistence rather than conflict, globalization may be seen as a series of processes that increase contacts and interdependencies but generate a significant resurgence of identity politics, an arena in which civilizational identity becomes increasingly important, but also one in which these identities increasingly intermingle. For Robert Cox, as the material boundaries of civilizations become increasingly mingled in the contemporary world, conceptualizing civilizations as analogous to territorial communities becomes less relevant. Rather than seeking to contain this intermingling through policies that encourage civilizational homogenization and enhanced cohesion, which Cox views as less and less feasible, he accentuates the need for mutual comprehension and dialogue between civilizational identities as paramount for world order. The establishment of a nonhegemonic pluralist world order in this context requires dialogue and mutual respect among different civilizational identities.

Each of these perspectives might provide a slightly different understanding of the processes of regionalism that forms one facet of the globalization debate. For the convergence theorists, the growth of regional arrangements such as the European Union (EU), the North American Free Trade Agreement (NAFTA), [the] Association of South East Asian Nations (ASEAN), and [the] Asia Pacific Economic Cooperation (APEC) is a function of the growing interdependence of societies and their tendency toward integration on an economic and, to some degree in the case of the EU, a political level. Regionalism is a stepping stone for globalization. For Fukuyama, the EU demonstrates the feasibility of moves toward economic integration and the evolution of a pacific union in states prepared to dismantle national boundaries in the pursuit of peace and prosperity. However, for the perspective that emphasizes conflict, regionalism does not signal convergence, but fragmentation. It is a reaction to globalizing trends, with societies resisting universalizing tendencies by strengthening their cultural identity within larger blocks. Huntington, for instance, argues that cooperation is most likely to succeed within, rather than across, civilizational communities. Therefore, the prospects for the EU, based on a homogenous Western civilizational community, are anticipated to be much stronger than those of ASEAN, a regional organization that includes members from a number of different civilizations.

From a more positive pluralist perspective, Richard Falk has reflected on the potential for regionalism to act as a site of resistance to the negative impacts of globalism, which include the relaxation of controls and codes of conduct on multinational corporations and transnational financial institutions, as well as increasing pressure of welfare and labor standards. Regionalism might act as a site for the promotion of positive globalism, in the form of world governance structures that promote sustainability, human rights, development, and demilitarization, while preserving a measure of cultural diversity. Falk acknowledges, however, that to date, regionalism has not necessarily fulfilled this potential, acting in a number of cases to affirm some of the negative dimensions of globalization.

Conceptions of Cultural World Order, Human Rights, and Intervention

A third set of significant issues in contemporary debates on world politics is that of human rights and the efficacy of humanitarian intervention. While there is now widespread commitment among states to the UN conventions on human rights, there is a lack of consensus on how the concepts of human rights should be interpreted and applied. For some, human rights represent the basic, universal principles that protect and respect the dignity and welfare of all humans, regardless of their culture. For others, the human rights regime as it is currently structured reflects the priorities and norms of a dominant culture, the West. It has been argued, particularly, by commentators such as Malaysia's President Mahathir, that the current human rights regime is not sufficiently sensitive to the diversity of social, economic, cultural, and political realities that prevail in different countries. Instead, human rights are often seen to represent Western values, pursued at times to further Western economic and political goals. This is particularly with respect to the emphasis that the West places on the rights of the individual over the rights of the community and on political and civil rights over social and economic. The UN Conference on Human Rights in Vienna in 1993 addressed this issue when the representatives of Asian governments such as Indonesia and China took a strong stand in articulating the need for the human rights regime to respect a variety of cultural perspectives. The position of regional governments in this respect was outlined in the Bangkok Declaration issued just prior to the Vienna Conference.

The human rights debate is a broad and multidimensional one. It was of central importance to politics of 1999, particularly with reference to the crises in Kosovo and in East Timor. In both cases, elements of the international community, led by Western states, justified intervention into Yugoslavia and Indonesia on the grounds of gross violations of human rights. How might different perspectives on the nature of cultural world order influence analysis of these issues? An analysis based on the "clash of civilizations" might argue that intervention in both disputes was premised on a misguided belief in Western "universalism" that projects Western interpretations of norms and values, such as human rights, as universal. Such a perspective would suggest that norms and values are culturally relative. Furthermore, this perspective might suggest that the conflicts in the Balkans and in East Timor were themselves a product of conflictual relations between civilizational identities. In this context, intervention could be read as the interference by the West in the affairs of another civilizational community in an effort to project Western norms and values.

From the perspective of those who see the cultural world order as a convergent one, these interventions could be viewed as marking the progressive emergence of universal norms and values. For instance, the liberal internationalist perspective articulated by British Prime Minister Tony Blair during the early stages of the NATO intervention in Kosovo presented the international community led by the West as having both an interest and a duty in promoting new norms of sovereignty and intervention to promote a more united peaceful and ethical world order. One element of this new norm of sovereignty is that the principles of noninterference must be qualified by considerations of the way in which states treat their citizens regardless of their particular civilizational identity. In this context, it is noteworthy that intervention in both Kosovo and East Timor was undertaken by Western or Western-led forces in order to protect non-Western populations. This could suggest that "civilizational rallying" was not the chief motivation behind the measures taken. Rather, these "human rights" interventions could be perceived as signaling the convergence of different civilizational identities toward the upholding of common norms and values.

However, those who seek to cultivate a more cooperative and egalitarian cultural world order might read these instances of humanitarian intervention with some skepticism. As noted above, while there is a large measure of agreement on the principle of the existence of human rights, there is less consensus on the interpretation and application of these principles. For instance, as noted above, there is a sense that while Western norms and values have an important contribution to make to the universal principles of human rights, the West's interpretations privilege some values over others. Furthermore, the West itself has been selective and inconsistent in its application of these principles, thus undermining the sense of a genuine evaluation of common norms and values. In particular, there is a concern that humanitarian intervention tends to be pursued when it serves the best interests of the most powerful.

In the case of Kosovo, intervention could be interpreted not only as seeking to protect human rights, but also as a means of asserting Western hegemony over a smaller and non-Western state. In East Timor, some disquiet has been voiced in Indonesia and Malaysia with regard to the perceived aggression of the Australian troops, with Australia perceived as acting as an agent for Western hegemony, a "regional deputy sheriff" to the U.S. global policeman. Advocates of a pluralist but nonconflictual cultural world order highlight the necessity for an order that is nondiscriminatory and operates on the basis of equal respect for all participants. This perspective, while valuing the establishment of universal principles to be protected by concerted action from the international community, would advocate that humanitarian interventions be pursued on a consistent, nonselective basis. . . .

Conclusion

Examining assumptions about culture therefore does form an important aspect of the broader project of reframing world order. Important questions surround the issue of how we think about culture. For instance, assumptions about the relevance and role of culture and of cultural identity are ever more prevalent in the politics of states today. However, culture is not something that should or can be examined simply at the level of states. Assumptions about culture and cultural identity can also shape politics within states and at transnational levels. Recognition of a significant relationship between conceptions of civilizational identities and broader assumptions about the nature of the cultural world order is important for studies of world politics as we enter a new millennium. It suggests we need further consideration and investigation of how these assumptions may frame perceptions of the possibilities for global political interaction.

Assumptions of incommensurability in relations between civilizations, as found in Huntington's analysis, could lead to policies of consolidation and homogenization within broad cultural communities, and the pursuit of self-regarding rather than cosmopolitan policies and behavior without. Conversely, assumptions of strong universalist tendencies in civilizational interaction, as found in Fukuyama's work, could lead to policies that accentuate and promote perceived commonalities or potential for these, but perhaps disregard important areas of cultural, social, and political difference.

To assume that it is feasible, and desirable, to establish a cultural world order that is pluralist but not hierarchical challenges policymakers to seek genuine, cross-cultural global dialogue. This in itself is a daunting task. It demands that cultural communities are seen as being distinct but not necessarily immutable, and seen as social constructions rather than essentialized as fixed and given. It encourages policies and strategies that recognize the salient cultural differences, but also strive to identify points of commonality between cultures. Is this an unrealistic approach? It certainly presents a goal that will be challenging and difficult to meet. However, it is perhaps no less a realistic perspective than those that accentuate conflict to the neglect of cooperation and commonality, or convergence to the neglect of significant and meaningful differences. As we move toward a new millennium in which assumptions about culture will continue to powerfully influence our understanding of world order, we might do well to keep in mind Edward Said's observation:

> No one can deny the persisting continuities of long traditions, sustained habitations, national languages and cultural geographies, but there seems no reason except fear and prejudice to keep insisting on their separation and distinctiveness, as if that was all human life was all about. Survival in fact is about the connections between things.

NOTES

1. Samuel Huntington summarized his clash-of-civilizations theory in *The Clash of Civilizations*, 72 Foreign Aff., Summer 1993, at 22 ("It is my hypothesis that the fundamental source of conflict in this new world will not be primarily ideological or primarily economic. The great divisions among humankind and the dominating source of conflict will be cultural. Nation states will remain the most powerful actors in world affairs, but the principal conflicts of global politics will occur between nations and groups of different civilizations. The clash of civilizations will dominate global politics. The fault lines between civilizations will be the battle lines of the future."). But Daniel Chirot, in *A Clash of Civilizations or of Paradigms?* 16 Int'l Soc. 341 (2001), argues that the so-called clash of civilizations is actually the product of uneven modernization. He describes the resistance to modernization as "the hallmark of the most intense cultural clashes in the contemporary world." *Id.* at 356. He concludes on the following sobering note:

> [T]he most bitter clashes of competing cultures will not be mostly between cultures at different evolutionary stages of development, because existing gaps can be closed, as they have been in many cases in the past. Rather, we can predict that both the Huntingtonians and postmodernists are wrong, and that the most severe, irreconcilable cultural clashes will be within societies, between different ideas about how to continue modernization, what to reject and what to accept. We also know that within any society, when the wrong side wins, tragedy will ensue.

Id.

2. When we consider cultural issues, we must be careful to distinguish theory, particularly grand theory, from belief and practice. For example, the global public seems to be skeptical about Samuel Huntington's sweeping clash of civilizations. In an extensive poll of more than twenty-eight thousand people in twenty-seven countries, a BBC poll found that some 56% of all respondents rejected an inevitable conflict between the Islamic world and the West. Perhaps most significantly, 52% attributed ongoing tensions to political powers and interests rather than to religion or culture. On average, three-quarters of the public rejected the clash of civilizations thesis in Canada, Italy, and the United Kingdom. BBC NEWS, BBC WORLD SERVICE POLL (Feb. 19, 2007).

B. Cultural-Legal Interaction

The *Yahoo!* case at the beginning of this chapter introduced the cultural dimension of legal disputes, dramatizing the challenge to legal systems and the transnational principle of comity when cultural values collide. The readings that followed further examined the cultural dimension of dispute resolution, through Japanese cultural predispositions and through legal discourse, with its own risks of conflict between cultural values, in the contexts of diplomatic and business negotiations. Compounding the challenges we face in a world that is both multicultural and globalizing is, as we have seen, the lack of agreement on a definitive interpretation of cultural diversity and on the implications of cultural identity for world order.

This section shifts our focus away from the cultural dimension of both private and public transactions, and away from the overarching process of world ordering, which often involve conflicts between fundamental cultural values. Although we have already observed generally the interaction of law and culture, we will now focus more sharply on the intersection of cultural values and legal prescriptions.

1. Legal Protection of Cultural Values

LYNG v. NORTHWEST INDIAN CEMETERY PROTECTIVE ASS'N, 485 U.S. 439 (1988)

Justice O'Connor delivered the opinion of the Court.

This case requires us to consider whether the First Amendment's Free Exercise Clause prohibits the Government from permitting timber harvesting in, or constructing a road through, a portion of National Forest that has traditionally been used for religious purposes by members of three

American Indian tribes in northwestern California. We conclude that it does not.

I

As part of a project to create a paved 75-mile road linking two California towns, Gasquet and Orleans, the United States Forest Service has upgraded 49 miles of previously unpaved roads on federal land. In order to complete this project (the G-O road), the Forest Service must build a 6-mile paved segment through the Chimney Rock section of the Six Rivers National Forest. That section of the forest is situated between two other portions of the road that are already complete.

In 1977, the Forest Service issued a draft environmental impact statement that discussed proposals for upgrading an existing unpaved road that runs through the Chimney Rock area. In response to comments on the draft statement, the Forest Service commissioned a study of American Indian cultural and religious sites in the area. The Hoopa Valley Indian Reservation adjoins the Six Rivers National Forest, and the Chimney Rock area has historically been used for religious purposes by Yurok, Karok, and Tolowa Indians. The commissioned study, which was completed in 1979, found that the entire area "is significant as an integral and indispensible part of Indian religious conceptualization and practice." Specific sites are used for certain rituals, and "successful use of the [area] is dependent upon and facilitated by certain qualities of the physical environment, the most important of which are privacy, silence, and an undisturbed natural setting." . . . The study concluded that constructing a road along any of the available routes "would cause serious and irreparable damage to the sacred areas which are an integral and necessary part of the belief system and lifeway of Northwest California Indian peoples." Accordingly, the report recommended that the G-O road not be completed.

In 1982, the Forest Service decided not to adopt this recommendation, and it prepared a final environmental impact statement for construction of the road. The Regional Forester selected a route that avoided archeological sites and was removed as far as possible from the sites used by contemporary Indians for specific spiritual activities. Alternative routes that would have avoided the Chimney Rock area altogether were rejected because they would have required the acquisition of private land, had serious soil stability problems, and would in any event have traversed areas having ritualistic value to American Indians. At about the same time, the Forest Service adopted a management plan allowing for the harvesting of significant amounts of timber in this area of the forest. The management plan provided for one-half[-]mile protective zones around all the religious sites identified in the report that had been commissioned in connection with the G-O road.

. . .

After a trial, the District Court issued a permanent injunction prohibiting the Government from constructing the Chimney Rock section of the G-O road or putting the timber-harvesting management plan into effect. The court found that both actions would violate the Free Exercise Clause because they "would seriously damage the salient visual, aural, and environmental qualities of the high country." Finally, the court concluded that both projects would breach the Government's trust responsibilities to protect water and fishing rights reserved to the Hoopa Valley Indians. . . .

[A summary of the litigation in the federal district and appellate courts is omitted. –*Eds.*]

A

The Free Exercise Clause of the First Amendment provides that "Congress shall make no law . . . prohibiting the free exercise [of religion]." It is undisputed that the Indian respondents' beliefs are sincere and that the Government's proposed actions will have severe adverse effects on the practice of their religion. Those respondents contend that the burden on their religious practices is heavy enough to violate the Free Exercise Clause unless the Government can demonstrate a compelling need to complete the G-O road or to engage in timber harvesting in the Chimney Rock area. We disagree.

. . .

The crucial word in the constitutional test is "prohibit." "For the Free Exercise Clause is written in terms of what the government cannot do to the individual, not in terms of what the individual can exact from the government."

Whatever may be the exact line between unconstitutional prohibitions on the free exercise of religion and the legitimate conduct by government of its own affairs, the location of the line cannot depend on measuring the effects of a government action on a religious objector's spiritual development. The Government does not dispute, and we have no reason to doubt, that the logging and road-building projects at issue in this case could have devastating effects on traditional Indian religious practices. Those practices are intimately and inextricably bound up with the unique features of the Chimney Rock area, which is known to the Indians as the "high country." Individual practitioners use this area for personal spiritual development; some of their activities are believed to be critically important in advancing the welfare of the Tribe, and indeed, of mankind itself. The Indians use this area, as they have used it for a very long time, to conduct a wide variety of specific rituals that aim to accomplish their religious goals. According to their beliefs, the rituals would not be efficacious if conducted at other sites than the ones traditionally used, and too much disturbance of the area's natural state would clearly render any meaningful continuation of traditional practices impossible. To be sure, the Indians themselves were far from unanimous in opposing the G-O road, and it seems less than certain that construction of the road will be so disruptive that it will doom their religion. Nevertheless, we can assume that the threat to the efficacy of at least some religious practices is extremely grave.

Even if we assume that we should accept the Ninth Circuit's prediction, according to which the G-O road will "virtually destroy the . . . Indians' ability to practice their religion," the Constitution simply does not provide a principle that could justify upholding respondents' legal claims. However much we might wish that it were otherwise, government simply could not operate if it were required to satisfy every citizen's religious needs and desires. A broad range of government activities – from social welfare programs to foreign aid to conservation projects – will always be considered essential to the spiritual well-being of some citizens, often on the basis of sincerely held religious beliefs. Others will find the very same activities deeply offensive, and perhaps incompatible with their own search for spiritual fulfillment and with the tenets of their religion. The First Amendment must apply to all citizens alike, and it can give to none of them a veto over public programs that do not prohibit the free exercise of religion. The Constitution does not, and courts cannot, offer to reconcile the various competing demands on government, many of them rooted in sincere religious belief, that inevitably arise in so diverse a society as ours. That task, to the extent that it is feasible, is for the legislatures and other institutions.

Respondents attempt to stress the limits of the religious servitude that they are now seeking to impose on the Chimney Rock area of the Six Rivers National Forest. While defending an injunction against logging operations and the construction of a road, they apparently do not *at present* object to the area's being used by recreational visitors, other Indians, or forest rangers. Nothing in the principle for which they contend, however, would distinguish this case from another lawsuit in which they (or similarly situated religious objectors) might seek to exclude all human activity but their own from sacred areas of the public lands. The Indian respondents insist that "*[p]rivacy* during the power quests is required for the practitioners to maintain the purity needed for a successful journey." . . . No disrespect for these practices is implied when one notes that such beliefs could easily require *de facto* beneficial ownership of some rather spacious tracts of public property. Even without anticipating future cases, the diminution of the Government's property rights, and the concomitant subsidy of the Indian religion[] would this case be far from trivial: the District Court's order permanently forbade commercial timber harvesting, or the construction of a two-lane road, anywhere within an area covering a full 27 sections (*i.e.*, more than 17,000 acres) of public land.

The Constitution does not permit government to discriminate against religious that treat particular physical sites as sacred, and a law prohibiting the Indian respondents from visiting the Chimney Rock area would raise a different set of constitutional questions. Whatever rights the Indians may have to the use of the area, however, those rights to not divest the Government of its right to use what is, after all, *its* land.

B

Nothing in our opinion should be read to encourage governmental insensitivity to the religious needs of any citizen. The Government's rights to the use of its own land, for example, need not and should not discourage it from accommodating religious practices like those engaged in by the Indian respondents.

. . .

Perceiving a "stress point on the longstanding conflict between two disparate cultures," the dissent attacks us for declining to "balance[e] these competing and potentially irreconcilable interests, choosing instead to turn this difficult task over to the Federal Legislature." Seeing the Court as the arbiter, the dissent proposes a legal test under which it would decide which public lands are "central" or "indispensable" to which religious, and by implication which are "dispensable" or "peripheral" and would then decide which government programs are "compelling" enough to justify "infringement of those practices." We would accordingly be required to weigh the value of every religious belief and practice that is said to be threatened by any government program. Unless a "showing of 'centrality'" is nothing but an assertion of centrality, the dissent thus offers us the prospect of this Court's holding that some sincerely held religious beliefs and practices are not "central" to certain religions, despite protestations to the contrary from the religious objectors who brought the lawsuit. In other words, the dissent's approach would require us to rule that some religious adherents misunderstand their own religious beliefs. We think such an approach cannot be squared with the Constitution or with our precedents, and that it would cast the Judiciary in a role that we were never intended to play. . . .

IV

The decision of the court below, according to which the First Amendment precludes the Government from completing the G-O road or from permitting timber harvesting in the Chimney Rock area, is reversed. In order that the District Court's injunction may be reconsidered in light of this holding, and in the light of any other relevant events that may have intervened since the injunction issued, the case is remanded for further proceedings consistent with this opinion.

It is so ordered.

Justice Kennedy took no part in the consideration or decision of this case.

Justice Brennan, with whom Justice Marshall and Justice Blackmun join, dissenting.

. . .

I

For at least 200 years and probably much longer, the Yurok, Karok, and Tolowa Indians have held sacred an approximately 25-square-mile area of land situated in what is today the Blue Creek Unit of Six Rivers National Forest in northwest California. As the Government readily concedes, regular visits to this area, known to respondent Indians as the "high country," have played and continue to play a "critical" role in the religious practices and rituals of these Tribes. Those beliefs, only briefly described in the Court's opinion, are crucial to a proper understanding of respondents' claims.

As the Forest Service's commissioned study, the Theodoratus Report, explains, for Native Americans religion is not a discrete sphere of activity separate from all others, and any attempt to isolate the religious aspects of Indian life "is in reality an exercise which forces Indian concepts into non-Indian categories." Thus, for most Native Americans, "[t]he area of worship cannot be delineated from social, political, cultur[al], and other areas o[f] Indian lifestyle." A pervasive feature of this lifestyle is the individual's relationship with the natural world; this relationship, which can accurately though somewhat completely be characterized as one of stewardship, forms the core of what might be called, for want of a better nomenclature, the Indian religious experience. While traditional Western religions view creation as the work of a deity "who institutes natural laws which then govern the operation of physical nature," tribal religions regard creation as an on-going process in which they are morally and religiously obligated to participate. Native Americans fulfill this duty through ceremonies and rituals designed to preserve and stabilize the earth and to protect humankind from disease and other catastrophes. Failure to conduct these ceremonies in the manner and place specified, adherents believe, will result in great harm to the earth and to the people whose welfare depends upon it.

In marked contrast to traditional Western religions, the belief systems of Native Americans do not rely on doctrines, creeds, or dogmas. Established or universal truths – the mainstay of Western religions – play no part in Indian faith. Ceremonies are communal efforts undertaken for specific purposes in accordance with instructions handed from generation to generation. Commentaries on or interpretations of the rituals themselves are deemed absolute violations of the ceremonies, whose value lies not in their ability to explain the natural world or to enlighten individual believers but in their efficacy as protectors and enhancers of tribal existence. Where dogma lies at the heart of Western religions, Native American faith is inextricably bound to the use of land. The site-specific nature of Indian religious practice derives from the Native American perception that land is itself a sacred, living being. Rituals are performed in prescribed locations not merely as a matter of traditional orthodoxy, but because land, like all other living things, is unique, and specific sites possess different spiritual properties and significance. Within this belief system, therefore, land is not fungible; indeed, at the time of the Spanish colonization of the American Southwest, "all . . . Indians held in some form a belief in a sacred and indissoluble bond between themselves and the land in which their settlements were located."

For respondent Indians, the most sacred of lands is the high country where, they believe, prehuman spirits moved with the coming of humans to the Earth. Because these spirits are seen as the source of religious power, "medicine," many of the tribes' ritual and practices require frequent journeys to the area. Thus, for example, religious leaders preparing for the complex of ceremonies that underlie the Tribes' World Renewal efforts must travel to specific sites in the high country in order to attain the medicine necessary for successful renewal. Similarly, individual tribe members may seek curative powers for the healing of the sick, or personal medicine for particular purposes such as good luck in singing, hunting, or love. A period of preparation generally precedes such visits, and individuals must select trails in the sacred area according to the medicine they seek and their abilities, generally moving to increasingly more powerful sites, which are typically located at higher altitudes. Among the most powerful of sites are Chimney Rock, Doctor Rock, and Peak 8, all of which are elevated rock outcroppings.

According to the Theodoratus Report, the qualities "of silence, the aesthetic perspective, and the physical attributes are an extension of the sacredness of [each] particular site." The act of medicine making is akin to meditation: the individual must integrate physical, mental, and vocal actions in order to communicate with the prehuman spirits. As a result, "successful use of the high country is dependent upon and facilitated by certain qualities of the physical environment, the most important of which are privacy, silence, and an undisturbed natural setting. Although few Tribe members actually make medicine at the most powerful sites, the entire Tribe's welfare hinges on the success of the individual practitioners.

...

In the final analysis, the Court's refusal to recognize the constitutional dimension of respondents' injuries stems from its concern that acceptance of respondents' claim could potentially strip the Government of its ability to manage and use vast tracts of federal property. In addition, the nature of respondents' site-specific religious practices raises the specter of future suits in which Native Americans seek to exclude all human activity from such areas. These concededly legitimate concerns lie at the very heart of this case, which represents yet another stress point in the longstanding conflict between two disparate cultures – the dominant Western culture, which views land in terms of ownership and use, and that of Native Americans, in which concepts of private property are not only alien, but contrary to a belief system that holds land sacred. Rather than address this conflict in any meaningful fashion, however, the Court disclaims all responsibility for balancing these competing and potentially irreconcilable interests, choosing instead to turn this difficult task over to the Federal Legislature. Such an abdication is more than merely indefensible as an institutional matter: by defining respondents' injury as "nonconstitutional," the Court has effectively bestowed on one party to this conflict the unilateral authority to resolve all future disputes in its favor, subject only to the Court's toothless exhortation to be "sensitive" to affected religions. In my view, however, Native Americans deserve – and the Constitution demands – more than this.

Prior to today's decision, several Courts of Appeals had attempted to fashion a test that accommodates the competing "demands" placed on federal property by the two cultures. Recognizing that the Government normally enjoys plenary authority over federal lands, the Courts of Appeals required Native Americans to demonstrate that any land-use decisions they challenged involved lands that were "central" or "indispensable" to their religions practice. Although this requirement limits the potential number of free exercise claims that might be brought to federal land management decisions, and thus forestalls the possibility that the Government will find itself ensnared in a host of Lilliputian lawsuits, it has been criticized as inherently ethnocentric, for it incorrectly assumes that Native American belief systems ascribe religions significance to land in a traditionally Western hierarchical manner....

III

Today, the Court holds that a federal land-use decision that promises to destroy an entire religion does not burden the practice of that faith in a manner recognized by the Free Exercise Clause. Having thus stripped respondents and all other Native Americans of any constitutional protection against perhaps the most serious threat to their age-old religious practices, and indeed to their entire way of life, the Court assures us that nothing in its decision "should be read to encourage governmental insensitivity to the religious needs of any citizen." I find it difficult, however, to imagine conduct more insensitive to religious needs than the Government's determination to build a marginally useful road in the face of uncontradicted evidence that the road will render the practice of respondents' religion impossible. Nor do I believe that respondents will derive any solace from the knowledge that although the practice of their religion will become "more difficult" as a result of the Government's actions, they remain free to maintain their religions beliefs. Given today's ruling, that freedom amounts to nothing more than the right to believe that their religion will be destroyed. The safeguarding of such a hollow freedom not only makes a mockery of the "'policy of the United States to protect and preserve for American Indians their inherent right of freedom to believe, express, and exercise the[ir] traditional religions,'" it fails utterly to accord with the dictates of the First Amendment.

I dissent.

Church of the Lukumi Babalu Aye, Inc. v. City of Hialeah, 508 U.S. 520 (1993)

Justice Kennedy delivered the opinion of the Court....

The principle that government may not enact laws that suppress religious belief or practice is so well understood that few violations are recorded in our opinions. Concerned that this fundamental nonpersecution principle of the First Amendment was implicated here, however, we granted certiorari.

Our review confirms that the laws in question were enacted by officials who did not understand, failed to perceive, or chose to ignore the fact that their official actions violated the Nation's essential commitment to religious freedom. The challenged laws had an impermissible object; and in all events the principle of general applicability was violated because the secular ends asserted in defense of the laws were pursued only with respect to conduct motivated by religious beliefs. We invalidate the challenged enactments and reverse the judgment of the Court of Appeals.

I

A

This case involves practices of the Santeria religion, which originated in the 19th century. When hundreds of thousands of members of the Yoruba people were brought as slaves from western Africa to Cuba, their traditional African religion absorbed significant elements of Roman Catholicism. The resulting syncretion, or fusion, is Santeria, "the way of the saints." The Cuban Yoruba express their devotion to spirits, called *orishas*, through the iconography of Catholic saints, Catholic symbols are often present at Santeria rites, and Santeria devotees attend the Catholic sacraments.

The Santeria faith teaches that every individual has a destiny from God, a destiny fulfilled with the aid and energy of the *orishas*. The basis of the Santeria religion is the nurture of a personal relation with the *orishas*, and one of the principal forms of devotion is an animal sacrifice. The sacrifice of animals as part of religious rituals has ancient roots. Animal sacrifice is mentioned throughout the Old Testament, and it played an important role in the practice of Judaism before destruction of the second Temple in Jerusalem. In modern Islam, there is an annual sacrifice commemorating Abraham's sacrifice of a ram in the stead of his son.

According to Santeria teaching, the *orishas* are powerful but not immortal. They depend for survival on the sacrifice. Sacrifices are performed at birth, marriage, and death rites, for the cure of the sick, for the initiation of new members and priests, and during an annual celebration. Animals sacrificed in Santeria rituals include chickens, pigeons, doves, ducks, guinea pigs, goats, sheep, and turtles. The animals are killed by the cutting of the carotid arteries in the neck. The sacrificed animal is cooked and eaten, except after healing and death rituals.

Santeria adherents faced widespread persecution in Cuba, so the religion and its rituals were practiced in secret. The open practice of Santeria and its rites remains infrequent. The religion was brought to this Nation most often by exiles from the Cuban [R]evolution. The District Court estimated that there are at least 50,000 practitioners in South Florida today.

B

Petitioner Church of the Lukumi Babalu Aye, Inc. (Church) is a not-for-profit corporation organized under Florida law in 1973. The Church and its congregants practice the Santeria religion. The president of the Church is petitioner Ernesto Pichardo, who is also the Church's priest and holds the religious title of *Italero*, the second highest in the Santeria faith. In

April 1987, the Church leased land in the City of Hialeah, Florida, and announced plans to establish a house of worship as well as a school, cultural center, and museum. Pichardo indicated that the Church's goal was to bring the practice of the Santeria faith, including its ritual of animal sacrifice, into the open. The Church began the process of obtaining utility service and receiving the necessary licensing, inspection, and zoning approvals. Although the Church's efforts at obtaining the necessary licenses and permits were far from smooth, it appears that it received all needed approvals by early August 1987.

The prospect of a Santeria church in their midst was distressing to many members of the Hialeah community, and the announcement of the plans to open a Santeria church in Hialeah prompted the city council to hold an emergency public session on June 9, 1987.

. . .

In September 1987, the city council adopted three substantive ordinances addressing the issue of religious animal sacrifice. Ordinance 87–52 defined "sacrifice" as "to unnecessarily kill, torment, torture, or mutilate an animal in a public or private ritual or ceremony not for the primary purpose of food consumption," and prohibited owning or possessing an animal "intending to use such animal for food purposes." It restricted application of this prohibition, however, to any individual or group that "kills, slaughters or sacrifices animals for any type of ritual, regardless of whether or not the flesh or blood of the animal is to be consumed." The ordinance contained an exemption for slaughtering by "licensed establishment[s]" of animals "specifically raised for food purposes." Declaring, moreover, that the city council "has determined that the sacrificing of animals within the city limits is contrary to the public health, safety, welfare and morals of the community," the city council adopted Ordinance 87–71. That ordinance defined sacrifice as had Ordinance 87–52, and then provided that "[i]t shall be unlawful for any person, persons, corporations or associations to sacrifice any animal within the corporate limits of the City of Hialeah, Florida." The final Ordinance, 87–72, defined "slaughter" as "the killing of animals for food" and prohibited slaughter outside of areas zoned for slaughterhouse use. The ordinance provided an exemption, however, for the slaughter or processing for sale of "small numbers of hogs and/or cattle per week in accordance with an exemption provided by state law." All ordinances and resolutions passed the city council by unanimous vote. Violations of each of the four ordinances were punishable by fines not exceeding $500 or imprisonment not exceeding 60 days, or both.

Following enactment of these ordinances, the Church and Pichardo filed this action . . . in the United States District Court for the Southern District of Florida. Named as defendants were the city of Hialeah and its mayor and members of its city council in their individual capacities. Alleging violations of petitioners' rights under, *inter alia*, the Free Exercise Clause, the complaint sought a declaratory judgment and injunctive and monetary relief. The District Court granted summary judgment to the individual defendants, finding that they had absolute immunity for their legislative acts and that the ordinances and resolutions adopted by the council did not constitute an official policy of harassment, as alleged by petitioners.

. . .

It is a necessary conclusion that almost the only conduct subject to Ordinances 87–40, 87–52, and 87–71 is the religious exercise of Santeria church members. The texts show that they were drafted in tandem to achieve this result. We begin with Ordinance 87–71. It prohibits the sacrifice of animals, but defines sacrifice as "to unnecessarily kill . . . an animal in a public or private ritual or ceremony not for the primary purpose of food consumption." The definition excludes almost all killings of animals except for religious sacrifice, and the primary purpose requirement narrows the proscribed category even further, in particular by exempting kosher slaughter. We need not discuss whether this differential treatment of two religions is itself an independent constitutional violation. It suffices to recite this feature of the law as support for our conclusion that Santeria alone was the exclusive legislative concern. The net result of the gerrymander is that few if any killings of animals are prohibited other than Santeria sacrifice, which is proscribed because it occurs during a ritual or ceremony and its primary purpose is to make an offering to the *orishas*, not food consumption. Indeed, careful drafting ensured that, although Santeria sacrifice is prohibited, killings that are no more necessary or humane in almost all other circumstances are unpunished.

Operating in similar fashion is Ordinance 87–52, which prohibits the "possess[ion], sacrifice, or slaughter" of an animal with the "inten[t] to use such animal for food purposes." This prohibition, extending to the keeping of an animal as well as the killing itself, applies if the animal is killed in "any type of ritual" and there is an intent to use the animal for food, whether or not it is in fact consumed for food. The ordinance exempts, however, "any licensed [food] establishment" with regard to "any animals which are specifically raised for food purposes," if the activity is permitted by zoning and other laws. This exception, too, seems intended to cover kosher slaughter. Again, the burden of the ordinance, in practical terms, falls on Santeria adherents but almost no others: If the killing is – unlike most Santeria sacrifices – unaccompanied by the intent to use the animal for food, then it is not prohibited by Ordinance 87–52; if the killing is specifically for food but does not occur during the course of "any type of ritual," it again falls outside the prohibition; and if the killing is for food and occurs during the course of a ritual, it is still exempted if it occurs in a properly zoned and licensed establishment and involves animals "specifically raised for food purposes."

. . .

The legitimate governmental interests in protecting the public health and preventing cruelty to animals could be addressed by restrictions stopping far short of a flat prohibition of all Santeria sacrificial practice. If improper disposal, not the sacrifice itself, is the harm to be prevented, the city could have imposed a general regulation on the disposal of organic garbage. It did not do so. Indeed, counsel for the city conceded at oral argument that, under the ordinances, Santeria sacrifices would be illegal even if they occurred in licensed, inspected, and zoned slaughterhouses. Thus, these broad ordinances prohibit Santeria sacrifice even when it does not threaten the city's interest in the public health....

Under similar analysis, narrower regulation would achieve the city's interest in preventing cruelty to animals. With regard to the city's interest in ensuring the adequate care of animals, regulation of conditions and treatment, regardless of why an animal is kept, is the logical response to the city's concern, not a prohibition on possession for the purpose of sacrifice. The same is true for the city's interest in prohibiting cruel methods of killing. Under federal and Florida law and Ordinance 87–40, which incorporates Florida law in this regard, killing an animal by the "simultaneous and instantaneous severance of the carotid arteries with a sharp instrument" – the method used in kosher slaughter – is approved as humane. The District Court found that, though Santeria sacrifice also results in severance of the carotid arteries, the method used during sacrifice is less reliable and therefore not humane. If the city has a real concern that other methods are less humane, however, the subject of the regulation should be the method of slaughter itself, not a religious classification that is said to bear some general relation to it.

...

The city concedes that "neither the State of Florida nor the City has enacted a generally applicable ban on the killing of animals." It asserts, however, that animal sacrifice is "different" from the animal killings that are permitted by law. According to the city, it is "self-evident" that killing animals for food is "important"; the eradication of insects and pests is "obviously justified"; and the euthanasia of excess animals "makes sense." These *ipse dixits* do not explain why religion alone must bear the burden of the ordinances, when many of these secular killings fall within the city's interest in preventing the cruel treatment of animals.

The ordinances are also underinclusive with regard to the city's interest in public health, which is threatened by the disposal of animal carcasses in open public places and the consumption of uninspected meat. Neither interest is pursued by respondent with regard to conduct that is not motivated by religious conviction. The health risks posed by the improper disposal of animal carcasses are the same whether Santeria sacrifice or some nonreligious killing preceded it. The city does not, however, prohibit hunters from bringing their kill to their houses, nor does it regulate disposal after their activity. Despite substantial testimony at trial that the same public health hazards result from improper disposal of garbage by restaurants, restaurants are outside the scope of the ordinances. Improper disposal is a general problem that causes substantial health risks, but which respondent addresses only when it results from religious exercise.

The ordinances are underinclusive as well with regard to the health risk posed by consumption of uninspected meat. Under the city's ordinances, hunters may eat their kill and fishermen may eat their catch without undergoing governmental inspection. Likewise, state law requires inspection of meat that is sold but exempts meat from animals raised for the use of the owner and "members of his household and nonpaying guests and employees." The asserted interest in inspected meat is not pursued in contexts similar to that of religious animal sacrifice.

Ordinance 87–72, which prohibits the slaughter of animals outside of areas zoned for slaughterhouses, is underinclusive on its face. The ordinance includes an exemption for "any person, group, or organization" that "slaughters or processes for sale, small numbers of hogs and/or cattle per week in accordance with an exemption provided by state law." Respondent has not explained why commercial operations that slaughter "small numbers" of hogs and cattle do not implicate its professed desire to prevent cruelty to animals and preserve the public health. Although the city has classified Santeria sacrifice as slaughter, subjecting it to this ordinance, it does not regulate other killings for food in like manner.

We conclude, in sum, that each of Hialeah's ordinances pursues the city's governmental interests only against conduct motivated by religious belief. The ordinances "ha[ve] every appearance of a prohibition that society is prepared to impose upon [Santeria worshippers] but not upon itself." This precise evil is what the requirement of general applicability is designed to prevent.

. . .

The Free Exercise Clause commits government itself to religious tolerance, and upon even slight suspicion that proposals for state intervention stem from animosity to religion or distrust of its practices, all officials must pause to remember their own high duty to the Constitution and to the rights it secures. Those in office must be resolute in resisting importunate demands and must ensure that the sole reasons for imposing the burdens of law and regulation are secular. Legislators may not devise mechanisms, overt or disguised, designed to persecute or oppress a religion or its practices. The laws here in question were enacted contrary to these constitutional principles, and they are void.

Reversed.

NOTES AND QUESTIONS

1. After the Supreme Court's decision in *Lyng*, "the political process responded to interests the judiciary had not protected, and the Bureau of Land Management relocated the road." Christopher L. Eisgruber & Lawrence G. Sager, *The Vulnerability of Conscience: The Constitutional Basis for Protecting Religious Conduct*, 61 U. Chi. L. Rev. 1245 (1994). Does this suggest the efficacy of a separation of powers (legislative and judicial) in ultimately resolving a sensitive cultural issue?
2. How can you reconcile the opposite results on the issue of religious freedom in *Lyng* and *Church of the Lukumi Babalu Aye*? In the absence of the First Amendment – in other words, if neither of the two cases had involved a constitutional

question – can you construct an argument based on the protection of a religious minority's cultural values that would adequately address the respective issues in the two cases, or is the argumentation and the justiciability of the issues dependent on the supremacy of constitutional protection? Does Justice Brennan's strong dissent in *Lyng* offer any arguments for a nonconstitutional resolution of the dispute?

3. In 2009 *Forbes* magazine named Hialeah, Florida, the site of the dispute in *Church of the Lukumi Babalu Aye*, as one of the "ten most boring cities" in the United States. Evidently, Santeria practices have had little effect on the city's equanimity, even after the Supreme Court decision.
4. In Chapter 2, we return to the theme of a tribe's cultural attachment to land as an example of indigenous cultural law.

2. Cultural Relativism and Universalism in the Legal Process

Jacqueline Nolan-Haley, Harold Abramson, & Pat K. Chew, International Conflict Resolution: Consensual ADR Processes 78–82 (2005) (reprinted with the permission of Thomson Reuters)

Dilemma One

A delegation of American feminists attends a United Nations World Conference on Women in China, where delegations from countries all over the world meet. A critical issue arises: Given profound cultural differences among women from different countries, how can feminists maintain a global political movement while avoiding charges of cultural imperialism?

Dilemma Two

You are a judge in a criminal case where the defendant is a recent immigrant to the United States. What if the defense presents cultural evidence as an excuse for her otherwise criminal conduct? Should the immigrant defendant be judged according to her own cultural standards rather than those of the relevant jurisdiction?

Dilemma Three

A company is considering doing business in a foreign country where there are discriminatory employment practices and lax environmental protection laws. Should the company go along with the practices of the host country? Should the company reject the practices even though that decision would put them at a competitive disadvantage? Should the company simply refuse to do business in that country altogether?

Dilemma Four

You are asked to resolve the case of an employee who has worked for your company for sixteen years. Though her work has been excellent for fifteen years, it has been unsatisfactory for the past year. If there is no reason to expect that performance will improve, should the employee be (a) dismissed on the grounds that job performance should remain the grounds for dismissal, regardless of the age of the person and his previous record; or (b) is it wrong to disregard the fifteen years the employee has been working for the company?

Two models, those of cultural relativism and of universalism, offer very useful conceptual tools for trying to reconcile these dilemmas. The *cultural relativist model* essentially advocates a deference to each culture and their cultural practices: "When in Beijing, do as the Chinese do!" The *universalist model*, in contrast, argues that there should be uniform global standards [to which] all countries should adhere.

Each approach presents its own challenges. Under the cultural relativist model, the presumption is that cultural practices are clearly identifiable. . . . [D]efining the "culture" and its attributes is seldom easy. Among other nuances, cultures are always changing, and there are often competing political, religious, or social authorities for defining cultural practices.

The universalist model also has definitional challenges. How and who decide what constitutes the universal norm? To what extent are these standards determined by global consensus versus the decision of a dominating and domineering group of countries, individuals, or interests?

Let's revisit the dilemmas posed above. Consider the varied perspective[s] on how to reconcile these differences and on what roles the cultural relativist and universalist models play.

Dilemma One

Feminist responses to this charge [of cultural imperialism] are complicated and sometimes conflicting. On the one hand, feminists note that culture and religion are often cited as justifications for denying women a range of basic rights, including the right to travel, rights in marriage and divorce, the right to own property, even the right to be protected by the criminal law on an equal basis with men. Women have much to lose, therefore, in any movement away from a universal standard of human rights in favor of deference to culture. On the other hand, feminists acknowledge that feminism itself is grounded in the importance of participation, of listening to and accounting for the particular experiences of women, especially those on the margins of power. Indeed, much feminist criticism of traditional human rights approaches has focused on the tendency of international policymakers to exclude women's experiences and women's voices. Thus, the claim that Western concepts of women's equality are exclusionary or imperialist strikes at the heart of one of feminism's central commitments – respect for difference.

In short, both the move to expand universal human rights to include those rights central to women's condition and the move toward a relativist view of human rights are consistent with and informed by feminist theory. Indeed, the tension between them reflects a tension within feminism itself, between describing women's experience collectively as a basis for political action and respecting differences among women.

(From Tracy E. Higgins, *Anti-Essentialism, Relativism, and Human Rights*, 19 HARV. WOMEN'S L.J. 89–105, 111–15 [1996].)

Dilemma Two

Allowing sensitivity to a defendant's culture to inform the application of laws to that individual is good multiculturalism. It also is good progressive criminal defense philosophy, which has as a central tenet the idea that the defendant should get as much individualized (subjective) justice as possible.

For legal scholars and practitioners who believe in a progressive civil and human rights agenda, these illustrations also raise an important question: What happens to the victims – almost always minority women and children – when multiculturalism and individualized justice are advanced by dispositive cultural evidence? The answer, both in theory and in practice, is stark: They are denied the protection of the criminal laws because their assailants generally go free, either immediately or within a relatively brief period of time. More importantly, victims and potential victims in such circumstances have no hope of relief in the future, either individually or as a group, because when cultural evidence is permitted to excuse otherwise criminal conduct, the system effectively is choosing to adopt a different, discriminatory standard of criminality for immigrant defendants, and hence, a different and discriminatory level of protection for victims who are members of the culture in question. This different standard may defeat the deterrent effect of the law, and it may become precedent, both for future cases with similar facts, and for the broader position that race – or national origin-based applications of the criminal law are appropriate. Thus, the use of cultural defenses is anathema to another fundamental goal of the progressive agenda, namely the expansion of legal protections for some of the least powerful members of American society: women and children.

(From Doriane Lambelet Coleman, *Individualizing Justice through Multiculturalism*, 96 COLUM. L. REV. 1093, 1099, 1156–65 [1996].)

Dilemma Three

There are some hard truths that might guide managers' actions, a set of what I call core human values, which define minimum ethical standards for all companies. The right to good health and the right to economic advancement and an improved standard of living are two core human values. Another is what Westerners call the Golden Rule, which is recognizable in every major religious and ethical tradition around the world. In Book 15 of his *Analects*, for instance, Confucius counsels people to maintain reciprocity, or not to do to others what they do not want done to themselves.

Although no single list would satisfy every scholar, I believe it is possible to articulate three core values that incorporate the work of scores of theologians and philosophers around the world. To be broadly relevant, these values must include elements found in both Western and non-Western cultural and religious traditions. . . .

In the spirit of what philosopher John Rawls calls *overlapping consensus*, one can see that the seemingly divergent values converge at key points. Despite important differences between Western and non-Western cultural and religions traditions, both express shared attitudes about what it means to be human. First, individuals must not treat others simply as tools; in other words, they must recognize a person's value as a human being. Next, individuals and communities must treat people in ways that respect people's basic rights. Finally, members of a community must work together to support and improve the institutions on which the community depends. I call those three values *respect for human dignity*, *respect for basic rights*, and *good citizenship*.

(From Thomas Donaldson, *Values in Tension: Ethics Away from Home*, HARV. BUS. REV. Sept.–Oct. 1996, 3, 12.)

Dilemma Four

There is great potential for conflict when people from cultures having different orientations must deal with one another. This is particularly true when people who value universal rules deal with people who think each particular situation should be examined on its merits and that different rules might be appropriate for different people. Westerners prefer to live by abstract principles and like to believe these principles are applicable to everyone. To set aside universal rules in order to accommodate particular cases seems immoral to the Westerner. To insist on the same rules for every case can seem at best obtuse and rigid to the Easterner and at worst cruel.

[In a study by Hampden-Turner and Trompenaar on this case], more than 75 percent of Americans and Canadians felt the employee should be let go. About 20 percent of Koreans and Singaporeans agreed with that view. . . . As these results show, Westerners' commitment to universally applied rules influences their understanding of the nature of agreements between individuals and between corporations. By extension, in the Western view, once a contract has been agreed to, it is binding – regardless of circumstances that might make the arrangement must less attractive to one of the parties than it had been initially. But to people from interdependent, high-context cultures, changing circumstances dictate alterations of the agreement.

(From RICHARD E. NISBETT, THE GEOGRAPHY OF THOUGHT: HOW ASIANS AND WESTERNERS THINK DIFFERENTLY . . . AND WHY 64–66 [2003].)

NOTES

1. On the debate between cultural relativism and universalism in human rights law, see Ida L. Bostian, *Cultural Relativism in International War Crimes Prosecutions: The International Criminal Tribunal for Rwanda*, 12 ILSA J. INT'L & COMP. L. 1 (2005) (detailing the need to "strike a balance" between cultural relativism and universalism "that will recognize legitimate cultural differences – particularly when those differences may make it more difficult to uncover the truth about what occurred – but without ignoring the danger of using cultural relativism as a shield behind which to hide atrocities. A mild cultural relativism is the best way to accomplish these goals . . . by establishing hybrid tribunals and/or by international tribunals exercising jurisdiction only where the domestic courts are unable or unwilling to do so.").
2. When rules of law and cultural predispositions or expressions collide, as they often do, the resulting upheavals may alter the law, conflicting cultural values, or both. This dynamic process is continuous and important, as the following commentary suggests:

   > [L]aw and culture cannot fully answer the normative law reform question. This is because law and culture operate in a reflexive loop, each influencing the other. Accordingly, a change in law may actually change culture over time. Thus, a legal reform or transplant from another system may be rejected because of a lack of cultural fit, but alternatively it may be adopted and ultimately come to seem natural, thereby effectuating broader cultural shifts.

   [As an example, the author notes the unexpected enthusiasm for alternative dispute resolution in the traditionally adversarial culture of the United States. – *Eds.*].

   > As communication technologies, trade, and migration blur cultural boundaries and even begin to undermine relatively stable ideas about the majority religious, racial, and ethnic groupings that comprise a state, law will face greater pressure to incorporate foreign cultural practices. Yet, at the same time, there are bound to be backlashes, as cultures fight fiercely to retain their dispute resolution mechanisms and legal cosmology just as surely as they resist other perceived encroachments.
   >
   > Negotiating this complex interplay between cultural bricolage and cultural essentialism is bound to be the crucial question for comparative law in this new era. We will need to develop a jurisprudence for an increasingly hybrid world where cultural conceptions remain crucial, but are in flux.

   Paul Schiff Berman, *The Enduring Connections between Law and Culture*, 57 AM. J. COMP. L. 249, 256, 257 (2009) (reviewing LAWRENCE ROSEN, LAW AS CULTURE: AN INVITATION (2006) and OSCAR G. CHASE, LAW, CULTURE, AND RITUAL: DISPUTING SYSTEMS IN CROSS-CULTURAL CONTEXT (2005)).

3. The Cultural Defense

Dilemma 2 in the last reading involves the cultural defense, which litigants invoke to justify a modification of applicable law and due process.[6] When individuals follow their time-honored traditions, usually doing so occurs without any sort of incident or governmental interference. On those occasions, however, when authorities ban customs, individuals may claim that the policy impinges on their right to culture. If they are prosecuted for violating state law, they sometimes use the legal strategy of a cultural defense. Even though no national legal system has officially adopted the cultural defense as an official policy, judges have made reference to cultural considerations in numerous cases. In some of the cases, the defendant may have difficulty persuading the court that the cultural practice is "genuine" or "authentic." As we shall see in Chapter 2.B, the invocation of a recognized body of traditional customary law may strengthen this defense, but in general, it has not led to its successful application. Consider a few examples that illustrate how the law treats cultural arguments regarding different worldviews.

Some cases reflect differing beliefs about the significance of animals. *United States v. Tomono* is an example of judicial treatment of cultural factors in sentencing a defendant convicted of reptile smuggling. Kei Tomono was accused of violating U.S. laws concerning wildlife and smuggling. A twenty-six-year-old, college-educated Japanese national, Tomono ran an import-export business known as Amazon International based in Chiba, Japan.

On one trip to the United States in April 1996, he had 60 pig-nosed, or Fly River, turtles and 113 Irian Jaya snake-necked turtles in his luggage, which he intended to sell. Later, in August 1997, he made another trip from Japan to San Francisco to attend a reptile breeders' conference, this time carrying with him six red mountain racer snakes and two Mandarin rat snakes in his luggage. On both occasions, he filled out the standard customs declaration form denying that he was carrying any "fruits, plants, food, soil, birds, snails, other live animals, wildlife products, farm products." Government agents had searched his luggage in San Francisco, without his knowledge. Although he was permitted to fly on from San Francisco to Orlando, once he reached Florida, a U.S. Fish and Wildlife Service agent asked to search his luggage. He consented, the snakes were found, and he and his traveling companion were taken into custody. The creatures were said to be worth approximately $70,000.[7]

A grand jury indicted him for violations of the federal antismuggling act and the Lacey Act, which forbids the import, export, sale, and possession of fish or wildlife taken in violation of federal, state, or foreign law. The violations dealt not only with the possession and intended sale of the creatures but also with the failure to declare them to customs.

Charged with violations of the Lacey Act and the federal antismuggling act, Tomono decided to plead guilty. Tomono argued for a downward departure under the sentencing guidelines. His position was that, because of cultural differences between Japan and the United States, he "was unaware of the serious consequences of his actions, and that these actions constituted a factor not considered by the Sentencing Commission that should be taken into account in calculating his sentence."[8]

[6] *See generally* Cultural Issues in Criminal Defense (Linda Friedman Ramirez ed., 3d ed. 2010); Alison Dundes Renteln, The Cultural Defense 110–12 (2004), from which the examples in the text are taken.

[7] Jim Leusner & Susan Jacobson, *2 Dealers of Reptiles Go to Jail*, Orlando Sentinel, Aug. 17, 1997.

[8] United States v. Tomono, 143 F.3d 1401 (11th Cir. 1998).

Taking his cultural background into consideration, the district court reduced his sentence.[9] At the sentencing hearing, Judge Ann Conway stated:

> Basically, the court agrees with the defense that the cultural differences in this case give the court a basis to depart downward that is not otherwise available or covered by the Sentencing Guidelines. . . . The court finds that Mr. Tomono's not declaring [the animals] to the U.S. Customs could be well the result of the cultural differences and his misunderstanding of the laws and the forms. The court is departing three levels downward because the cultural difference would be demonstrated by the difference in the market value in Japan versus the difference in the market value in the [United States].

The judge explicitly distinguished between cultural differences and national origin: "Even though culture might be related to a person's origin, not every person who has the same national origin has the same culture and background. Culture extends beyond just national origin and includes factors such as beliefs, religion, laws, morals, and practices."

The court made it clear that it was basing the sentence not on national origin but on cultural differences. In particular, the court noted that the turtles in question were not endangered species in Japan and that Tomono would not have been arrested there. The court also made a special point of the "unique" place of reptiles in Japanese culture, and of the fact that Tomono is widely respected for his work in the field of herpetology. Furthermore, the court was influenced by Tomono's apparent ignorance of American law. Because Tomono had been to the United States on only two or three occasions and ostensibly was unfamiliar with the laws, the court was sympathetic to his argument. On the basis of the specific facts in this case, the court sentenced Tomono to five years' probation (unsupervised, provided he leave the United States), a $5,000 fine, and another "assessment" of $200.

The government appealed the downward departure of his sentence, presenting arguments that provided the basis for the court of appeals' decision. The government argued that downward departures for factors not adequately considered by the sentencing guidelines should be an uncommon occurrence. The offense at the center of this case, namely foreign nationals' smuggling of wildlife into the United States, is routine. Because defendants generally come from different cultures, a downward departure in a case such as this would lead to rampant misuse of the guidelines. Downward departures based on culture would be a common occurrence, something not anticipated by the policy.

Another part of the prosecution's argument was that the motivation for smuggling was economic and not cultural. This motivation applies also to smugglers of drugs, contraband, and so on. The basic point the government wished to make was that the sentencing guidelines are to permit departures only for rare or unique circumstances. The prosecution emphasized what it regarded as a contradiction. Tomono claimed ignorance of the law but admitted knowledge of U.S. policy during the plea negotiation.

[9] United States v. Tomono, 97 CR-127-ORL-22, Dec. 4, 1997. The Court of Appeals for the Eleventh Circuit explained the lower court's behavior as follows: "the district court granted a three-level downward departure for what it termed cultural differences." 143 F.3d at 1403. Before making the downward departure, the court had reduced his level of culpability because of his acceptance of responsibility. In American culture, showing remorse and accepting responsibility are considered extremely desirable.

He also was aware of U.S. regulations on trade in wildlife and federal health regulations prohibiting the importation of turtles of less than four inches in carapace (shell) length.

The government argued that following the logic of the district court's decision would result in two different sets of sentencing guidelines, one for U.S. citizens and one for foreign nationals. The government's brief rejects, in principle, the notion that the norms in other legal systems should influence the disposition of cases in the United States, arguing that such circumstances are so common as to result in routine downward departures not contemplated by the Sentencing Commission.

On appeal, the court rejected all strands of the cultural differences argument. The court found as follows: that the guidelines also took into account the endangered status of turtles,[10] that there was no evidence in the record supporting the unique place reptiles occupy, that counsels' arguments alone were usually not enough to justify departures from the sentencing guidelines, and that Tomono showed familiarity with U.S. policies during the plea negotiation. The government had to show that the defendant knew the wildlife was illegal, not that the defendant was specifically aware of the existence of the Lacey Act.

The court of appeals concluded that there were insufficient grounds for a downward departure. The district court therefore had abused its discretion when it took the case "out of the heartland of the guidelines.... [C]onsidering 'cultural differences' attributable solely to a defendant's country of origin comes uncomfortably close to considering the defendant's national origin itself, in contravention of the guidelines.... We need not decide whether 'cultural differences' may ever be an appropriate ground upon which to depart from the guidelines."[11] The court vacated the sentence and remanded it for resentencing. Tomono was deported to Japan.

Judge Roney, writing in dissent, began with the proposition that the Sentencing Commission had not prohibited the consideration of culture. Because it is permissible to base a downward departure on cultural differences, according to Judge Roney, the crucial question is whether the sentencing court abused its discretion. Emphasizing that the trial court is in a "preferred position" to understand what justice requires in particular circumstances, he eloquently defended the use of discretion by the district court. After explaining that "discretion" means that a decision either way is not wrong, he concluded that the district court judge in *United States v. Tomono* did not abuse her discretion.

In the United States, it remains unclear whether cultural differences can legitimately be referred to in sentencing. The decisions thus far are from the circuit courts and, as a consequence, are binding only on the states within the court's region. The appellate decisions, in any event, have not resolved the question of whether the prohibition against considering national origin encompasses cultural differences.

In another case, *Siripongs v. Calderon*,[12] the issue was whether the failure to consider cultural factors during the death penalty phase was a serious constitutional error. Jaturun ("Jay") Siripongs, a Thai national, participated in a robbery of a convenience store, the

[10] "The fact that the turtles may or may not be endangered is already considered in the applicable guideline, which mandates a four-level enhancement if the wildlife in question is listed in the Endangered Species Act of the Convention on International Trade in Endangered Species. See U.S. Sentencing Guidelines Manual S 2Q2.1(b)(3)(B)."

[11] *Tomono*, 143 F.3d at 1404.

[12] Siripongs v. Calderon, 133 F.3d 732 (9th Cir. 1998).

Pantai market, during which two clerks were killed.[13] Convicted of two murders with special circumstances, he received a death sentence in 1983. Though he admitted to being present at the robbery, he professed that he was innocent of the murders and that his accomplices were responsible for the killings. He was, however, unwilling to name the accomplices.[14] Because he would not furnish information about them, the court did not find his account credible. His lawyer, a public defender, did not present psychological or cultural evidence that might serve as mitigating factors during the finding of guilt or during sentencing phase of the trial.[15]

After the California Supreme Court affirmed the judgment,[16] Siripongs filed a petition for writ of habeas corpus in the federal district court, alleging, among other things, that his lawyer's failure to present mitigating evidence constituted a violation of his Sixth Amendment right to effective assistance of counsel. The district court declined to allow Siripongs to present evidence and ruled on summary judgment for Calderon. The first time the court of appeals heard the case it concluded that Siripongs should have the opportunity to argue that his legal counsel was ineffective, on the basis of a complete factual record. The court therefore remanded the case for an evidentiary hearing on the question of whether Siripongs's attorney had failed to provide adequate legal representation during both the guilt-finding and penalty phases of the trial.[17] After hearing evidence for eight days, the district court ruled against Siripongs. The Ninth Circuit, the second time it heard the case,[18] did not decide whether the lawyer's failure to develop the expert testimony constituted deficient performance but simply concluded that the lawyer made a reasonable choice to forgo the testimony of Siripongs's mother because of a fear her testimony would be impeached.[19]

The cultural argument central to this case was whether the refusal to name the accomplices was culturally motivated. An expert in Thai culture, Herbert Phillips, professor of anthropology at the University of California, Berkeley, explained that the reluctance to snitch was "consistent with deeply embedded Thai cultural values, including cultural concepts of shame and dishonor, and with Thai religious beliefs." Siripongs did not "snitch" because it would interfere with duty to made amends for his wrongdoing in the next life. Ostensibly saving face, Siripongs avoided bringing even greater shame on his family by refusing to implicate others in the wrongdoing.[20] There was also the possibility that his family might experience retaliation had he divulged his accomplices.

[13] Afterward, Siripongs used the victims' credit cards. This may suggest that – subconsciously, at least – he wanted to be caught. Affidavit of Herbert Phillips, professor of anthropology, University of California, Berkeley, Nov. 14, 1991.

[14] One especially puzzling aspect of the case is the accomplice defense. Much of the cultural evidence pertained to the question of whether another person had committed the murders. Even if that were true, Siripongs could still receive the death penalty. Pulling the trigger is not a prerequisite to the imposition of capital punishment.

[15] "Siripongs'[s] counsel put on no witnesses during the guilt phase and called none of Siripongs'[s] personal friends or family members during the penalty phase." *Siripongs*, 133 F.3d 732 at 734.

[16] People v. Siripongs, 754 P.2d 1306 (Cal. 1988), *cert. denied*, 488 U.S. 1019 (1989).

[17] Siripongs v. Calderon, 35 F.3d 1308 (9th Cir. 1994), *cert. denied*, 512 U.S. 1183 (1995).

[18] The Ninth Circuit Court had to evaluate a record consisting of thirty volumes of transcripts!

[19] *Siripongs*, 133 F.3d 732 at 735.

[20] Siripongs never told his family about his arrest; they learned from the local Thai-language paper. Phillips notes that this is consistent with "the cultural expectation that an individual endeavor not to cause his family shame. By so doing, Mr. Siripongs can get on with his own death, begin to compensate for the evil, the 'baap,' with more good, the 'boon,' if not in this life, then in future lives."

In his affidavit, Professor Phillips explained the multifaceted cultural argument, emphasizing particularly the important Thai concept of shame:

> The Thai concept of merit and de-merit arises from a strong belief that if a Thai commits a bad or evil act, he must work extremely hard in doing good things to compensate for what he has done. The Thai notion is not to be punished for the evil act, because it is done and cannot be reversed. Rather, the Thai notion is that you have to make up for the evil act by compensating for it with merit. There is a cash register notion of merit and de-merit known as "boon" and "baap." "Boon" means goodness and "baap" means sin. There is a constant dialectic between boon and baap throughout life for all Thais, as they struggle continually to compensate for the baap they have made with more and more boon. . . .
>
> I understand that Mr. Siripongs has refused to identify his accomplices. Such behavior makes sense from a cultural perspective even if ultimately it leads to Mr. Siripongs' death. From a Thai perspective, it would have been a useless act for Mr. Siripongs to identify the actual murderer. Making known his accomplices' identities would not reverse what had happened. The two people who had been killed would remain dead. From a cultural perspective, therefore, identifying his accomplices would have served no purpose for Mr. Siripongs. Thus, Mr. Siripongs' refusal to identify the accomplices does not necessarily mean that Mr. Siripongs killed either victim or intended death to result. Such behavior in fact is culturally appropriate under these circumstances.
>
> The cultural notion at work here is that assignment of blame is not the critical issue. The critical issue, from the perspective of Thai culture, is that the robbery got out of control. In Thai culture, "khwaan" refers to an individual's soul, which is the source of an individual's identity in the most profound sense of the term. In periods of extreme emotional stress, a Thai's "khwaan" leaves his body, causing him to be out of control. In this case, Mr. Siripongs' behavior appears to demonstrate that he believed he had lost his "khwaan" when the robbery got out of control and his accomplice committed the homicides. With the two victims already dead, from Mr. Siripong[s]'s perspective, it made no sense to assign blame for the homicides to the actual murderer. Importantly, even if he had done so he could not have regained his "khwaan." This could only be done by regaining a state of personal and social equilibrium and by compensating for the evil or "baap" that he had committed. . . . [T]his is exactly what he did by creating a trail that resulted in his quick arrest and punishment.

Professor Phillips pointed out another cultural factor, namely the Thai concept of supernatural moral justice. According to the Thai worldview, a Thai person, if not punished in this life, will receive his or her due in future lives. Phillips also speculated that if the accomplices were relatives, Siripongs might have declined to identify them. Because of the Thai notions of deference to authority and of reciprocal obligations, from the Thai perspective, Siripongs's actions made some sense.

Another important cultural difference pointed out by Phillips concerns the display of emotions. In Thai culture, it is considered inappropriate to express emotion. Phillips suggested that those during the trial who observed Siripongs's "stoical demeanor" might have misconstrued this body language: "To be 'ning,' or free of emotional demonstration, in the context of a criminal trial in which a Thai is accused of committing two murders is completely appropriate behavior. In fact, any outward expression of emotion would be culturally highly improper."

The appellate court was skeptical of the cultural arguments because Siripongs seemed too Americanized. The court noted that he had cooperated with law enforcement, that he was no longer a practicing Buddhist, and that he preferred the American value system.

Another basis for the Sixth Amendment challenge was that Siripongs's lawyer had not pursued his client's interests energetically, to say the least. Not only was this his first capital case, but also he was simultaneously running for Congress. Arguably, the political campaign had distracted him from preparing properly for the trial.[21] He never gathered any evidence about Siripongs's background from Thailand; his investigators had planned a trip to Thailand but later canceled it. No explanation for this was ever provided. Some aspects of Siripongs's background might have influenced the jury – for example, he apparently had been raised by an uncle who ran a prostitution business, he may have been sexually abused as a child, and he was an ex–Buddhist priest. His lawyer even allowed the prosecution to present evidence he knew to be false.[22] During the penalty phase of the trial, the jury never heard any mitigating evidence concerning Siripongs's life in Thailand.[23] His lawyer also never called Siripongs's mother to testify on his behalf, even though she sat in the courtroom on a daily basis.

In 1995 Siripongs's new lawyers presented evidence showing that his trial attorney's performance fell below constitutional standards. They argued that the failure to develop "potentially meritorious defenses" constituted deficient representation. Because this was a capital case, the attorney's duty to investigate was particularly crucial. Because death is final and irreversible, it is always imperative that defense counsel search for any potentially mitigating evidence.

Ultimately, however, the appellate court did not find the lawyer's performance deficient. It concluded that the system had operated correctly: "Our decision is made with the confidence that must accompany a decision that upholds a sentence of death."[24] The court concluded not only that Siripongs was responsible for the killing but also that his crime must have been premeditated. Because he knew the store clerks and realized that, if left alive, they would be able to identify him, he must have planned to rob the store and murder the clerks. The defense's response was that, because that the owner of the store was apparently involved in selling stolen jewelry, this would have deterred the owner from reporting the robbery for fear of being arrested.

Siripongs's new lawyers filed a petition for the writ of certiorari, whose main argument was that Siripongs should have had an opportunity to resolve the Sixth Amendment

[21] Although the Ninth Circuit found this matter "troublesome" the first time it heard the case, the second time it concluded that his campaign had not interfered with his trial preparations. *Siripongs*, 133 F.3d 732 at 737.

[22] Evidently a rap sheet from Thailand showed Siripongs had been convicted of one crime, a nonviolent burglary. It was translated improperly in the California court, but despite having a corrected copy, his lawyer did not rectify the error in the court record.

[23] The lawyer failed to notice that the court interpreter was a friend of victim's husband, something that at the very least created the appearance of bias.

[24] *Siripongs*, 133 F.3d 732 at 737.

argument and that the district court had failed to conduct adequate investigation to made this determination. The lawyers also argued that the appellate court had misinterpreted Supreme Court precedent, putting its ruling in conflict with other circuits on the duty that counsel have to investigate mitigation evidence.[25] Despite these arguments, Siripongs was executed in 1998.[26]

It is impossible to know whether the evidence relating to a defendant's cultural background would have influenced the jury's decision about whether to impose the death penalty. There is, of course, a chance that it might have. Even those who support the death penalty will be troubled by the possibility that a defendant could be sentenced to death merely because of his body language. Given that there is nothing in the legal system that formally prohibits the consideration of cultural factors, this information should be presented to prevent any potential miscarriage of justice.

Failure to consider cultural evidence can be challenged on various grounds. Such failure can lead to the imposition of excessive punishment – that is, a disproportionately harsh penalty. Another possible line of argument is that a court's refusal to consider cultural evidence violates a defendant's right to freedom of expression. The defense counsel's failure to present the evidence could be considered malfeasance, a violation of the defendant's right to effective assistance of counsel. The emerging norm seems to be that lawyers should go to some lengths to discover the background of their clients, to the extent that it might mitigate their sentences. Ignorance of other cultures is no longer acceptable.

Some commentators might object to cultural evidence even at sentencing as a matter of principle, because it offends notions of equal justice. Defendants should be treated equally under the law. The problem with this argument is that the motivations and demeanor of the average defendant from the dominant culture will be understood and therefore generally not be subject to misinterpretation. To avoid misunderstandings, justice requires the consideration of the cultural background of defendants at all stages of legal process, most certainly during the sentencing phase of the trial.

In some cases, the question is not one of appropriate sentencing but rather of whether the act itself constitutes a crime. For example, a Nigerian national, Dr. Gregory Ezeonu, was prosecuted in New York for statutory rape of his second, or junior, wife, Chiweta,

[25] Motion for Leave to Proceed in forma pauperis and Petition for Writ of Certiorari. October Term, 1997. If this petition failed, his lawyers planned to advance an argument along the lines of the *Breard* case. Daniel Breard, a national of Paraguay, was convicted of murder in Virginia. While on death row, he filed a lawsuit in which he alleged that the failure of the Virginia authorities to permit him to speak with his embassy was a serious error, a violation of the Vienna Convention on Consular Relations, to which the United States is a party. When a national of another country is accused of a crime, according to public international law, he or she is supposed to have access to his consulate. The U.S. Supreme Court declined to intervene, despite an international outcry including a plea from the World Court. Siripongs, like Breard, was tried for a capital crime without ever having the opportunity to consult his embassy. Robert F. Brooks & William H. Wright Jr., *States Deny Treaty Rights to Foreign Defendants*, NAT'L L.J., Nov. 4, 1996, at B8.

[26] Many pleaded for Siripongs's life, including relatives of victims, two jurors who had recommended the death penalty, Pope John Paul II, and even the warden of San Quentin Prison and a death-row prison guard. Richard Marcosi & Daniel Yi, *Friends and Foes Offer Conflicting Pictures of Killer*, L.A. TIMES, Nov. 15, 1998, at A34. Neither Republican Governor Pete Wilson nor Democratic Governor Gray Davis granted his plea for clemency. Richard Marcosi, *Siripongs Gets New Execution Date; Will Take Appeal to Davis*, L.A. TIMES, DEC. 15, 1998, at A3; Richard Marcosi & Greg Hernandez, *Convicted Killer Siripongs Put to Death*, L.A. TIMES, Feb. 9, 1999, at A1, A18; Richard Marcosi, *Attorney Has Case of a Lifetime*, L.A. TIMES, Dec. 3, 1998, at B1, B6.

who was thirteen years old.[27] (The record does not reveal from which of hundreds of ethnic groups in Nigeria Ezeonu came; polygamy is practiced among only some groups.) Dr. Ezeonu was a psychiatrist affiliated with Harlem Hospital. His children were removed from the household by the Child Welfare Administration. When detectives went to his apartment to discuss his children, he evidently invited them in and volunteered that he was interested in "giving Chiweta sex education." His defense was that he had been married concurrently under both New York and Nigerian law. The court therefore had to evaluate the status of the second marriage and the second wife in New York. Although generally a marriage is recognized if valid where consummated, the court concluded that where recognition would be "repugnant to public policy," the general rule does not apply. The court thought it was obvious that polygamy was against public policy.

In what was apparently a case of first instance for New York, the court held that bigamy was no defense to the charge of statutory rape. Furthermore, the court explicitly expressed disinterest in hearing witnesses from Nigeria who allegedly had observed the marriage ceremony or were prepared to discuss marriage customs. Although Nigerian law and custom may permit a junior wife, New York does not recognize such status. Because at the time of his "marriage" to the complainant, Dr. Ezeonu was already married, his second marriage was void even were it to have been legally consummated in Nigeria. Consequently, Dr. Ezeonu was not married to Chiweta, the thirteen-year-old, for purposes of prosecution for statutory rape.

NOTES AND QUESTIONS

1. In a lower-context legal culture such as that of the United States, is there a greater or lesser need for the cultural defense than in a higher-context legal culture where cultural considerations already are more determinative of outcomes in transactions and dispute resolution?
2. What criticisms might anthropologists likely make of the use of culture in the summarized cases?
3. Does the consideration of culture in the foregoing cases violate equal protection of the law? From the point of view of the victims, is it fair to mitigate the defendants' punishment simply by virtue of having come from another country?
4. What are the arguments for and against allowing cultural factors during the guilt-finding phase or the penalty phase of trials?
5. In your view, should the prohibition against the consideration of national origin preclude the possibility of admitting cultural evidence?
6. In Chapter 2.B, we return to issues related to the cultural defense in the context of a discussion about customary law.

4. Separate Legal Systems

Another way to adjudicate culture issues besides considering a cultural defense to the normal legal process is for the dominant legal system to delegate decision making to special tribunals within the ethnic minority or indigenous community. Although this approach might seem surprising, there is precedent for allowing religious minorities to

[27] People v. Ezeonu, 155 Misc. 2d 344, 588 N.Y.S.2d 116 (1992).

settle their conflicts within religious tribunals. For example, Orthodox Jews settle disputes in the *bet din*. The main argument for doing so is its consistency with the principle of religious freedom that is often if not normally guaranteed by national constitutions. One major objection to such tribunals is that the state, by allowing religious institutions to settle their own disputes, violates the principles of equal protection and the separation of church and state. Another worry is that religious judges may misinterpret secular law. Another serious concern is that the male elites of the minority community may render decisions that do not afford adequate protection to women's rights. We shall return to these issues in the context of religious values in Chapter 9.

NOTE

For an example of issues related to separate legal systems, see, e.g., Mark Landler, *German Judge Cites Koran, Stirring Up Cultural Storm*, N.Y. TIMES, Mar. 23, 2007, at A10. "Under Israeli law, the religious courts have exclusive jurisdiction in matters of divorce between spouses who are both Jewish, Muslim, or Christian belonging to one of the recognized religious communities or who are both Druze." TALIA EINHORN, PRIVATE INTERNATIONAL LAW IN ISRAEL 212 (2009).

5. Globalization of Mass Culture

"Jamaica called. They want their culture back."

The globalization of cultural values, artifacts, and practices – for good or bad – is a characteristic of our times. As in the cartoon, cultural globalization may be viewed as a threat to local, national, or regional identities and control. The improper appropriation of culture may be particularly offensive. Even more threateningly, the McDonaldization of mass culture may result in an unwanted displacement of cherished traditions. On the other hand, the process of globalization helps spread otherwise remote and inaccessible culture for the enjoyment and benefit of all humanity. The process also universalizes fundamental benefits such as standards and expectations of human rights.

The widespread use of computers in a universe of cyberspace has, of course, facilitated globalization. A particularly interesting development at the intersection of culture and law has been the rapid growth of open sourcing of knowledge. This development, with its profoundly participatory and democratic implications, has engaged the entire world in cultural projects such as Wikipedia. If the culture defense and separate legal systems represent centrifugal tendencies in global society, open sourcing in cyberspace is a markedly centripetal tendency.

As the following reading suggests, the rhetoric and very idea of open sourcing bear similarities to the collective process of creativity and innovation in traditional societies. Moreover, open sourcing has profound implications for an important artifact of modern economies: copyright protection. The effect of open sourcing on copyright law is thus a significant example of the effect of mass culture on law.

Siva Vaidhyanathan, *Open Source as Culture – Culture as Open Source*, *in* Open Source Annual 346 (2007)

Copyright is a limited monopoly, granted by the state, meant to foster creativity by generating a system of presumed incentives. The copyright holder must have enough faith in the system to justify her investment. The copyright holder's rights to exclude are limited by some public values such as education and criticism. This is the standard understanding of copyright law's role and scope. But while acknowledging the interests of the public, it omits the voice of the public itself. In other words, the system cannot thrive if the public considers it to be captured, corrupted, irrelevant, or absurd.

The rise and success of Open Source models foster a general understanding that copyright is not a single right bestowed upon one brilliant individual author, but is instead a "bundle" of rights that a copyright holder (individual, corporation, organization, or foundation) may license. Most importantly, these experiments and project[s] show that "all rights reserved" need not be the default state of copyright protection. For many, "some rights reserved" serves the interests of creators better than the absolutist proprietary model.

As the rhetoric of Open Source and the politics of traditional knowledge and culture emerge in starker relief within the topography of copyright and cultural policy debates, their themes tend to converge. As anthropologist Valdimar Hafstein describes the tension between copyright systems as dictated by the industrialized world and modes of communal cultural production that are best (albeit not exclusively) demonstrated in developing nations, he uses terms that could just as easily be applied to technological peer production. "Creativity as a social process is the common denominator of these concepts and approaches," Hafstein writes. "From each of these perspectives, the act of creation is a social act. From the point of view of intertextuality, for example, works of literature are just as much a product of society or of discourse as they are of an individual author or, for that matter, reader." Traditional cultural knowledge, communally composed and lacking distinct marks of individual authorship, is "a node in a network of relations: not an isolated original, but a reproduction, a copy," Hafstein explains. Nothing about Hafstein's descriptions of the politics of traditional knowledge offers a resolution to that particular source of friction in global intellectual property battles. The converging rhetorics, however, reveal the extent to which innovation and creativity often (perhaps most often) lie outside the assumptions of incentives and protectionism upon which high levels of corporate copyright protection rest.

The Open Source model of peer production, sharing, revision, and peer review has distilled and labeled the most successful human creative habits into a political movement. This distillation has had costs and benefits. It has been difficult to court mainstream acceptance for such a tangle of seemingly technical ideas when its chief advocates have been hackers and academics. Neither class has much power or influence in the modern global economy or among centers of policy decision-making. On the other hand, the brilliant success of overtly labeled Open Source experiments, coupled with the horror stories of attempts to protect the proprietary model, have added common sense to the toolbox of these advocates.

C. Cultural Law

1. A Working Definition

What exactly do we mean by "cultural law"? In general, the term embraces a panoramic range of human behavior, expressions, and activities pertaining to family and social norms, rules of etiquette, folklore, folk art, religion, art, architecture, media, sports, recreation, music, language, literature, drama, dance, other performing arts, and significant relations among these phenomena. Cultural law may be best defined in terms of several distinct functions related to this broad range of subject matter. Accordingly, we can establish that the term "cultural law" refers to a set of relationships between law and culture. The two social constructs are inseparable. These relationships can be summarized as follows:

1. Law embodies culture and formalizes its norms.
2. Law promotes, protects, conditions, and limits cultural attributes and expressions.
3. Law harmonizes cross-cultural differences, confirms cultural rights, and establishes international standards.
4. Culture reinforces legal rules.
5. Culture conditions and constrains the adoption, interpretation, and vitality of legal rules.
6. Cultural expressions and symbols promote legal relationships.

2. Culture-Related Terminology

The term "culture" is notoriously ambiguous. In fact, it has been described as one of the two or three most complicated words in the English language. It has at least three different meanings: a set of desirable characteristics and goals of the civilized world; the norms and other characteristics of particular groups or societies; and specific works of art, literature, music, and other expressions. We can speak therefore of "high culture," "a cultural experience," "low culture," "cultural life," "multiculturalism," "corporate culture," "political culture," "military culture," "culture of corruption," "cultural diversity," "culture wars," "cultural bias," "counterculture," the "drug culture," and "debt culture." When the baseball superstar Alex Rodriguez was compelled to admit his use of performance-enhancing drugs, including steroids, during at least three seasons several years earlier, he blamed it on "a different culture" of baseball then.[28]

The range of meanings is mind boggling, and the resulting confusion is rampant. For example, in early reports about pleas for the 2012 Olympic Games in London, the British excitedly urged its readers and audiences not to be carried away by the thoughts of pole-vaulters, swimmers, and gymnasts alone but to carry a torch for "culture" as well as if sports were somehow distinct from culture. The news accounts then trumpeted the usual Olympic plans to feature art exhibits, musical events, and poetry at the games, without ever recognizing that sport itself is culture. Chapter 2.A offers a variety of perspectives on the concept of culture.

Terms derived from "culture" are also important to lawyers, businesspeople, diplomats, and professionals, not to mention national interests. For example, the framework of the antiprotectionist North American Free Trade Agreement (NAFTA),[29] which is thoroughly hostile to national trade barriers, includes an exception for cultural industries. This exception removes from the scope of NAFTA any measure adopted or maintained with respect to cultural industries.[30] Such measures include, for example, "the publication, distribution, or sale of books, magazines, periodicals or newspapers in print or machine readable form but not including the sole activity of printing or typesetting any of the foregoing." The parties included the "cultural industries exception" to the national treatment obligation in NAFTA to ensure that they (mostly Canada) could protect and provide support to industries preserving and producing works significant to national culture that otherwise might be jeopardized by the freer import of alternative goods and services from other parties. The cultural industries exception operationalizes the core value of cultural identity that was discussed earlier in this chapter.

In 2007 a NAFTA arbitration under the rules of the UN Commission on International Trade Law (UNCITRAL), and administered through the International Centre for Settlement of Investment Disputes (ICSID), delivered an award and opinion resolving a long-standing dispute between United Parcel Services of America, Inc. (UPS) and the Government of Canada (Canada).[31] The dispute involved conflicting interpretations of NAFTA, in particular, provisions in chapter 11 (investments), chapter 15 (monopolies

[28] *See generally* SELENA ROBERTS, A-ROD (2009); Selena Roberts & David Epstein, *Confronting A-Rod*, SPORTS ILLUSTRATED, Feb. 16, 2009, at 28.

[29] North American Free Trade Agreement, U.S.-Can.-Mex., Dec. 17, 1992, 32 I.L.M. 289 (1993) [hereinafter NAFTA].

[30] Article 2106 of NAFTA, *id.*, provides as follows:

> Notwithstanding any other provision of this Agreement, as between Canada and the United States, any measure adopted or maintained with respect to cultural industries, except as specifically provided in Article 302 (Market Access – Tariff Elimination), and any measure of equivalent commercial effect taken in response, shall be governed under this Agreement exclusively in accordance with the provisions of the *Canada-United States Free Trade Agreement.* The rights and obligations between Canada and any other Party with respect to such measures shall be identical to those applying between Canada and the United States.

[31] United Parcel Serv. of Am. v. Canada, Merits (NAFTA Ch. 11 ARB. TRIB. June 11, 2007), 46 I.L.M. 922 (2007).

and state enterprises), as well as the relationship between the two chapters. Put simply, UPS claimed that Canada, directly and through its agent Canada Post, a Crown corporation, had harmed UPS and UPS subsidiaries in Canada by breaching its obligations under NAFTA to ensure that UPS and its investments received the requisite treatment to which foreign investors are entitled.

Among the issues in *United Parcel Service v. Canada* was whether Canada could premise its discriminatory treatment by Canada Post against UPS in the cultural industries exception. In a controversial decision, the tribunal, in a 2–1 decision, ruled that the nationwide distribution of mail was a "cultural industry" falling within the exception. (The tribunal also ruled in favor of Canada's other defenses to discriminatory treatment.)

As we shall see in Chapters 3 and 5, another term, "cultural heritage," is normally limited to the tangible or material objects and intangible ideas related to such objects in the sense of the traditional but problematic term "cultural property." Cultural heritage law, like cultural law as a whole, is best defined in terms of its functions. Essentially, cultural heritage law helps protect the physical integrity of cultural material; facilitates cooperation in its protection, transfer, and return; rectifies wrongful activity; imposes penal sanctions in response to criminal activity; and provides formal and informal mechanisms and rules for resolving related disputes.

3. Culture as a Human Right

a. Applicable Law

Culture as an internationally protected human right has two modern sources: the peace movements of the late nineteenth century and the several peace treaties that addressed the territorial renovation of Europe after the First World War. The two Hague Conferences of 1899 and 1907 produced consecutive conventions and regulations that first codified the protection of cultural heritage in humanitarian law. Concurrently, a related concept of cultural internationalism emerged from the same nineteenth-century peace movements, offering an ambitious antidote to mounting political tensions in Europe. Unfortunately the guns of August 1914 tolled the progress of cultural internationalism. After the war, however, such intellectuals as Romain Rolland, Paul Valéry, Marie Curie, Henri Bergson, and Albert Einstein sought to restore the concept to a position of centrality in diplomatic discourse. The postwar peace treaties, informed by Wilsonian self-determinism, established a foundation for modern human rights law in their provisions for protection of cultural minorities within the emerging boundaries of Eastern Europe.

The gathering storm of the Second World War again demolished the fragile structure of cultural internationalism. In the war's aftermath, however, a blend of cultural internationalism and nationalism – not unlike today's cosmopolitanism – inspired an emphasis on cultural diplomacy. The idea was for governments to rely on a form of public diplomacy that emphasized culture in a broad sense. It was to equip governments with what we now call soft power, in Joseph Nye's famous phrase. More recently, the UN Covenants on Civil and Political Rights and on Social, Economic and Cultural Rights and other human rights instruments have provided a new vocabulary and legal framework for culture-based claims. The essay by Jacinta O'Hagan earlier in this chapter introduced the role of human rights in the world order. In this section, we focus on cultural rights specifically.

"Culture" has multiple meanings in international human rights law. International instruments often refer to culture in terms of a right to culture or to the protection of one or another forum of cultural diversity. The most important conceptualization is in article 27 of the International Covenant on Civil and Political Rights (ICCPR):

> In those states in which ethnic, religious, and linguistic minorities, exist, persons belonging to such minorities shall not be denied the right, in community with the other members of their group, to enjoy their own culture, to profess their own religions, or to use their own language.

Although this is generally known as the minority rights provision, it has been broadly construed to afford protection of cultural matters for many different types of groups, including indigenous peoples (who may form a majority in some countries) and immigrants. Not only do many individuals and groups avail themselves of these rights, according to the Human Rights Committee, which monitors compliance with the ICCPR and interprets its provisions in the reporting and review process, but also cultural rights themselves are broad in scope. The Committee's general comment on article 27 offered an interpretation of the scope of cultural rights, as follows:

> [C]ulture manifests itself in many forms, including a particular way of life associated with the use of land resources, specially in the case of indigenous peoples. That right may include such traditional activities as fishing or hunting and the right to live in reserves protected by law. The enjoyment of those rights may require positive legal measures of protection and measures to ensure the effective participation of members of [minority] communities in the decisions that affect them.

According to article 15(1) of the International Covenant on Economic, Social, and Cultural Rights, states parties are obligated to protect the right of everyone to take part in cultural life. Culture, in this context, is associated with creative activities in which individuals cooperate. It is linked to the acquisition of knowledge, rituals associated with a way of life, and forms of communication. The international community has used the definition of culture in this article as a basis for developing provisions in the instruments of the UN Educational, Scientific, and Cultural Organization (UNESCO). The notion of culture was subsequently defined in the Recommendation on Participation by the People at Large in Cultural Life and Their Contribution to It (1976). In the preamble to the Recommendation, the concept was set forth as follows:

> [C]ulture is not merely an accumulation of works and knowledge which an elite produces, collects and conserves in order to place it within reach of all; or that a people rich in its past and its heritage offers to others as a model which their own history has failed to provide for them; and that culture is not limited to works of art and the humanities.

Despite the idea expressed that culture should be broadly construed, the standard view is that this article deals with science and technology, the protection of intellectual property, and general elite forms of culture (i.e., culture with a capital *C*).

UNESCO adopted, first, a Universal Declaration and, subsequently, a Convention on the Protection and Promotion of Diversity of Cultural Expression, as we saw earlier in this chapter. The Convention's preamble mentions language and intellectual property rights as well as the rights of minorities and indigenous peoples:

> "Cultural content" refers to the symbolic meaning, artistic dimensions and cultural values that originate from or express cultural identities.
>
> "Cultural expressions" are those expressions that result from the creativity of individuals, groups and societies and that have cultural content.

In those states with ethnic, religious, or linguistic minorities or persons of indigenous origin, International Labor Organization Convention No. 169 on Indigenous and Tribal Peoples provides a collective right – a so-called third-generational right – to cultural integrity. Also, article 30 of the Convention on the Rights of the Child guarantees a child of such persons the right, in community with other members of his or her group, to enjoy his or her own culture, to profess and practice his or her own religion, and to use his or her own language. This provision is an important formulation, as the integrity of cultural groups depends ultimately on the cultural identities of their children.

The Convention on the Rights of Persons with Disabilities contains by far the most elaborate provision for cultural rights. The Convention was opened for signature in 2007, with the highest number of signatories on its opening day (eighty-two) in the history of the UN Conventions. It is intended to promote a paradigm shift in attitudes and approaches of states parties toward persons with disabilities so that they no longer are viewed as objects of charity, medical treatment, and social protection but rather as subjects of law capable of exercising human rights on their own. Article 30, on participation in cultural life, leisure, and sport, reads as follows:

> 1. States Parties recognize the right of persons with disabilities to take part on an equal basis with others in cultural life, and shall take all appropriate measures to ensure that persons with disabilities:
>   a. Enjoy access to cultural materials in accessible formats;
>   b. Enjoy access to television programmes, films, theatre and other cultural activities, in accessible formats;
>   c. Enjoy access to places for cultural performances or services, such as theatres, museums, cinemas, libraries and tourism services, and, as far as possible, enjoy access to monuments and sites of national cultural importance.
> 2. States Parties shall take appropriate measures to enable persons with disabilities to have the opportunity to develop and utilize their creative, artistic and intellectual potential, not only for their own benefit, but also for the enrichment of society.
> 3. States Parties shall take all appropriate steps, in accordance with international law, to ensure that laws protecting intellectual property rights do not constitute an unreasonable or discriminatory barrier to access by persons with disabilities to cultural materials.
> 4. Persons with disabilities shall be entitled, on an equal basis with others, to recognition and support of their specific cultural and linguistic identity, including sign languages and deaf culture.
> 5. With a view to enabling persons with disabilities to participate on an equal basis with others in recreational, leisure and sporting activities, States Parties shall take appropriate measures:
>   a. To encourage and promote the participation, to the fullest extent possible, of persons with disabilities in mainstream sporting activities at all levels.

b. To ensure that persons with disabilities have an opportunity to organize, develop and participate in disability-specific sporting and recreational activities and, to this end, encourage the provision, on an equal basis with others, of appropriate instruction, training and resources;
c. To ensure that persons with disabilities have access to sporting, recreational and tourism venues;
d. To ensure that children with disabilities have equal access with other children to participation in play, recreation and leisure and sporting activities, including those activities in the school system.

Although these cultural rights are sometimes regarded as the least developed category of human rights, they are unquestionably a part of international human rights law. Cultural rights have been highly controversial because their protection sometimes requires that other human rights be limited. Also, there is substantial debate about the proper interpretation of cultural rights, about which individuals are entitled to invoke them, and about what obligations governments have to enforce these rights.

A crucial question is often how to balance the legal protection of particular cultural rights, such as that of religious expression or family integrity, against other human rights, such as women's rights and children's rights. The interrelationships and tensions among different types of human rights will be especially apparent in Chapter 9, which covers religion.

Many feminist theorists reject the proposition that cultural rights deserve legal protection because of their concern that protecting these rights will undermine gender equality. Although their work is often framed as a critique of multiculturalist relativity, these analysts are essentially denying the validity of cultural rights or are limiting the scope of certain cultural rights. However, such feminist objections do not appear to apply to the numerous traditions that have no connection to gender. Moreover, feminist theorists raise fewer objections to the protection of cultural rights when cultures do not imprison those who seek to exit, particularly women wishing to flee from oppressive customs. Sometimes, too, the respective rights are mutually reinforcing, for example, when women wear the veil in countries that prohibit this type of religious garb.

In practice, the international recognition of cultural rights implies that governments must honor them. Because this obligation is not absolute, however, cultural rights must sometimes yield to countervailing considerations. The challenge, naturally, is to distinguish between valid and invalid reasons for overriding cultural traditions and practices insofar as they may threaten public health, safety, or morals.

b. Claims

(i) Food. The most common examples of cultural relativity in civil society are food taboos, given that foodways are a significant part of a community's way of life. Many cultural conflicts have centered on meat. In India, beef is not eaten because the cow is sacred, and dogs are not eaten in the United States because the dog is a pet, typically regarded as a full-fledged member of the family. In a celebrated case, two Cambodians were arrested in Long Beach, California, after they had butchered a German Shepherd dog for dinner.

David Haldane, *Culture Clash or Animal Cruelty? Two Cambodian Refugees Face Trial after Killing Dog for Food*, L.A. Times, Mar. 13, 1989, at 1 (reprinted with permission)

These are the facts on which everyone agrees: Late last June, Sokheng Chea, 32, and Seng Ou, 33, both Cambodian refugees, decided to eat a 4-month-old German Shepherd puppy that a co-worker had given them as a pet. Holding the dog down on the kitchen floor of Ou's Long Beach apartment, they hit it over the head with a blunt instrument, slashed its throat and began skinning it. That is when the police arrived. Alerted by a neighbor who had heard the dog's yelps, they arrested the two men. And last week, Chea and Ou went on trial at Long Beach Municipal Court for misdemeanor cruelty to animals, an offense that carries a maximum penalty of a year in jail and a $2,000 fine.

The only disagreement is over whether what they did is illegal. The prosecution contends that the killing was a crime because it was carried out in an unnecessarily cruel way. The defense counters that the dog was killed humanely in a manner consistent with contemporary slaughterhouse practices, and that the two recent immigrants were following their own national customs with no idea that they were offending American sensibilities.

Underlying everything, the lawyers agree, is a resounding clash of cultural values and a basic question: Just how much is America willing to bend to accommodate the new wave of immigrants who are daily arriving on its shores? "If the dog had been some other kind of animal – like a chicken or a duck or a pig – these people wouldn't be in court," said Joe Beason, an attorney representing Chea. "While [Americans] consider it completely acceptable to go out and shoot a deer, those same hunters would disapprove of killing a dog for food." Countered Sarah Lazarus, the prosecutor in the case: "We intend to prove that this was cruelty. It's cultural to the extent that each segment of our society has its own cultural customs, but some of [those customs] can be woven into the fabric of our society and others cannot."

The court proceedings have been closely monitored by animal-rights activists. "We do not accept these things in our society, and we would hope that the court will deal with [these men] with the appropriate severity," said Jerye Mooney, coordinator of the Fund for Animals, a national organization based in Torrance that is pushing for legislation to specifically prohibit the killing of dogs and cats for human consumption. Similar legislation, inspired by reports that Southeast Asian refugees had been foraging for stray dogs and other animals in San Francisco's Golden Gate Park, was defeated by [a California] Assembly committee in 1981.

"I would like to see these other cultures contained," said Sabina Hubbard, chairwoman of the Orange County chapter of the Pet Assistance Foundation. "We don't want these [practices] to spread."

. . .

According to local Asian leaders, dogs and cats are considered delicacies in some Southeast Asian countries. Two years ago, officials of the Society for the Prevention of Cruelty to Animals reported an increase in the number of dogs and cats being killed for food in Los Angeles County, a trend they attributed to the influx of Southeast Asian refugees. But Lazarus said that, to her knowledge, this is the first incident in which enough evidence existed to bring the matter to court.

The trial – which has already resulted in at least one death threat against the defendants – has raised the hackles of some local Southeast Asian leaders who fear that the publicity may result in anti-Asian bias. "I am very concerned," said Vora H. Kanthoul, associate executive director of the United Cambodian Community, a social service agency based in Long Beach. While the eating of dogs is not uncommon in such countries as Korea, the Philippines and Vietnam, he said, it was highly unusual in Cambodia until the 1970s, when people there were near starvation during the regime of Pol Pot, a brutal Communist dictator. "During the war, a lot of things happened and they ate anything to survive," Kanthoul said. "It's unfortunate that [these men] were caught because it's blown everything out of proportion."

Responding to a pretrial motion last week, Judge Bradford L. Andrews ruled that killing a dog for food is not in itself a violation of the law. To win its case, therefore, he said, the prosecution must prove that the dog was "maimed, wounded, tortured, mutilated or tormented" in a manner beyond that required to prepare it as food. Lazarus said that as the trial progresses, she intends to produce an eyewitness and a veterinarian who will testify that the dog was killed with unnecessary cruelty. Beason says he has an autopsy report indicating that the killing was done in a manner consistent with livestock slaughter techniques and that there is no direct evidence of inhumane treatment.

As for the cultural issue, both say it will ultimately have to be resolved out of court. "When you bring someone into this country, you take the whole person," Beason said. "You don't just extract them from their culture, you bring the culture with them."

When the prosecutors realized there was no state law prohibiting the consumption of dogs, they decided to prosecute the men under the general animal cruelty law. What is construed as cruelty to animals varies over time and across cultures, however. Eventually, the special legislation was enacted that prohibited the consumption of pets but did not specify which animals constitute pets.

The following federal court opinion involved the related issue of whether the state of Illinois could prohibit the slaughter of horses for import of their meat to France, where horsemeat is considered a delicacy. The case reflects a clash between American and European cultural values that was ultimately resolved on constitutional grounds.

CAVEL INTERNATIONAL, INC. v. MADIGAN, 500 F.3d 551 (7th Cir. 2007) *cert. denied*, 128 S. Ct. 2950 (2008)

POSNER, *Circuit Judge*. Horse meat was until recently an accepted part of the American diet – the Harvard Faculty Club served horse-meat steaks until the 1970s. No longer is horse meat eaten by Americans, though it is eaten by people in a number of other countries, including countries in Europe; in some countries it is a delicacy. Meat from American horses is especially prized because our ample grazing land enables them to eat natural grasses, which enhances the flavor of their meat.

Cavel International, the plaintiff in this case, owns and operates the only facility in the United States for slaughtering horses. Until recently it was one of three such facilities, but the other two, both in Texas, stopped slaughtering horses after the Fifth Circuit upheld a Texas law similar to the Illinois law challenged in this case. *Empacadora de Carnes de Fresnillo, S.A. de C.V. v. Curry*, 476 F.3d 326, 336–37 (5th Cir. 2007).

...

The Act is fully applicable to Cavel, even though, because there is no U.S. domestic market for horse meat as a human food, Cavel's entire output is exported to such countries as Belgium, France, and Japan. Indeed, Cavel is the subsidiary of a Belgian company.

On May 24 of this year, the Illinois Horse Meat Act, 225 ILCS 635, was amended to make it unlawful for any person in the state either "to slaughter a horse if that person knows or should know that any of the horse meat will be used for human consumption," or "to import into or export from this State, or to sell, buy, give away, hold, or accept any horse meat if that person knows or should know that the horse meat will be used for human consumption." (Prior to the amendment, the statute merely required a license to slaughter horses and imposed various inspection, labeling, and other regulatory restrictions on licensees. The prohibition has made these provisions academic). Cavel claims that the amendment violates both the federal Meat Inspection Act and the commerce clause – the provision in Article I, section 8, of the federal Constitution that in terms merely empowers Congress to regulate interstate and foreign commerce but that has been interpreted to limit the power of states to regulate interstate and foreign commerce even in the absence of federal legislation inconsistent with the state regulation.

[A] state is permitted, within reason, to express disgust at what people do with the dead, whether dead human beings or dead animals. There would be an uproar if restaurants in Chicago started serving cat and dog steaks, even though millions of stray cats and dogs are euthanized in animal shelters. A follower of John Stuart Mill would disapprove of a law that restricted the activities of other people (in this case not only Cavel's owners and employees but also its foreign consumers) on the basis merely of distaste, but American governments are not constrained by Mill's doctrine.

The fact that [Governor Rod Blagojevich's] signing statement acknowledges the role of the Hollywood actress Bo Derek, author of the book *Riding Lessons: Everything That Matters in Life I Learned from Horses* (2002), in outlawing the slaughtering of horses could be thought to inject a frivolous note into a law that forces the closing of a business that has very little to do with the people of Illinois. But this is not a basis for invalidating a nondiscriminatory statute that interferes minimally with the nation's foreign commerce and cannot be said to have no rational basis.

NOTES AND QUESTIONS

1. Ultimately there will be cultural clashes over what individuals eat. Perhaps the French adage "chacun à son goût" – "each to his or her own taste" – may best capture the essence of cultural relativity in taste. In a democratic political system, however, what is the state interest in regulating the consumption of particular animals? Why is the consumption of dogs and horses more repugnant than the consumption of cows? Could the state mandate vegetarianism?
2. In these kinds of food fights, public law and policy blocked people's access to nutrition. Another issue involves the protection of ethnic minorities from food that offends their dietary practices. Some of the controversies hinge on the improper preparation of food. In other instances, the plaintiffs claim damages for injury from which majority populations are spared. For example, a Hindu man ordered a bean burrito at Taco Bell but was given a beef burrito instead. When he took a bite of it, he claimed to have been severely traumatized, and he sued for damages.

   In another case, Hindus discovered that McDonald's was surreptitiously seasoning french fries with beef flavoring without disclosing this information, a practice that obviously violated the Hindu dietary prohibition against the consumption of beef. One of the plaintiffs was said to be horrified when he found out: "I feel sick in the morning every day, like I want to vomit. . . . Now it is there in my mind that I have done this sin."[32]

   Although the effect of this practice was especially problematic for Hindus, it was also repulsive to vegetarians whose diet is often simply a matter of nonreligious choice. The question of food preparation is also important to vegetarians, who at times have joined forces with Hindus. When vegetarian law students joined forces with the Hindus, they first filed a lawsuit in Seattle. Following this, additional suits were filed in other states. Eventually, McDonald's, although denying it had ever claimed that the French fries were "vegetarian," settled the lawsuit by paying each of the eleven named plaintiffs $4,000 each, by donating $10 million to Hindu and other groups, by creating a dietary advisory board, and by posting an apology on the McDonald's Web site.[33]
3. Some courts have concluded that laws specifically governing Jewish kosher food are unconstitutional, as they cause excessive entanglement with religion in violation of the First Amendment to the U.S. Constitution.[34] In Quebec in the mid-1990s, there was controversy about whether kosher products could be sold if the labels were in English only.[35] Although Jewish communities have developed certification

[32] Laura Goodstein, *For Hindus and Vegetarians, Surprise in McDonald's Fries*, N.Y. Times, May 20, 2001, at 1, 18.

[33] Herbert G. McGann, *McDonald's Settles Beef over Fries*, CBS News, June 5, 2002.

[34] *See, e.g.*, Commack v. Self-Service Kosher Meats v. Weiss, 294 F.3d 415 (2d Cir. 2002), *cert. denied*, 537 U.S. 1187 (2003); Ran-Dav's County Kosher, Inc. v. New Jersey, 608 A.2d 1353 (N.J. 1992).

[35] *Quebec to Convene Kosher Label Panel*, L.A. Times, Apr. 13, 1996, at A5.

programs, Muslims in the United States have encountered fraud in the sale of halal food despite efforts by the U.S. Department of Agriculture to combat it.

(ii) The Environment. In many disputes, environmental rights and the right to culture are mutually reinforcing. The cultural argument reinforces the demand for environmental protection. Litigation in which indigenous peoples have challenged the desecration of sacred sites has included a claim that harm to the environment also undermines their way of life. In the *Yanomami* case (1985), the Inter-American Commission on Human Rights held that failure of the Brazilian government to prevent development that destroyed the Yanomami way of life constituted "ethnicide." In cases such as these, environmental rights and cultural rights coincide, revealing a confluence of rights claims, whereas in many other contexts, environmental rights claims conflict with cultural rights claims.

At the crux of many cases are cultural differences concerning the use of various types of endangered species. Despite the existence of international conventions such as the Convention on International Trade in Endangered Species of Wild Fauna and Flora (CITES), designed to prevent the killing of animals thought to be near the brink of extinction, in some Asian countries, these animals are considered necessary for cultural or religious practices among some segments of the population. Animal parts may be needed for medicinal purposes, they may be used as aphrodisiacs, or they are regarded as having supernatural powers.

On the one hand, animal rights activists and environmentalists contend that some creatures deserve protection for their own sake and to preserve biodiversity, a human value deemed intrinsically valuable. On the other hand, representatives of some cultures and some indigenous leaders maintain that they are entitled to use animals for legitimate reasons such as medicinal purposes, despite international criticism. In these disputes, they invoke the right to culture and the right to religious freedom to justify their policy position. (As we saw earlier, these rights are also invoked to support a cultural defense in courts of law.)

For the most part, the international community has not recognized cultural rights arguments when they have clashed with environmental rights in the context of endangered species policy. For example, when the international community concluded that Taiwan had failed to enforce CITES adequately because it allowed the sale of tiger and rhinoceros parts, the Clinton administration in 1994 imposed economic sanctions that prohibited the American import of Taiwanese products made from wild species. This represented more than $20 million in trade.

Within the United States, there have also been domestic prosecutions of individuals engaged in the sale of endangered species parts contrary to endangered species law and the Lacey Act. The federal government has sponsored raids of Asian medicine shops in Chinatown in San Francisco and elsewhere and has conducted sting operations such as Operation Chameleon, in which the Justice Department and U.S. Fish and Wildlife Service in 1998 arrested "Anson" Keng Liang Wong, allegedly the largest illegal reptile dealer in the world.

In one U.S. case, *Kei Tomono v. United States*, a Japanese man who ran an import-export business was caught with turtles and snakes in his suitcase as he was entering the United States. Although he agreed to plead guilty, he argued that the court should take his cultural background into account to mitigate his sentence. His contention was that reptiles occupy a unique place in Japanese culture, that the creatures are not regarded as endangered in Japan, and that he was unaware that exporting the animals was illegal. The appellate court ultimately rejected the request for a downward departure from the sentence specified in the federal sentencing guidelines, thus declining to mitigate his sentence. To be sure, the validity of Tomono's arguments may not be convincing, as he was college educated and had been involved in the reptile business for several years, but it is conceivable that such claims have merit in other cases. For the most part, however, cultural defenses of this sort have generally not succeeded.

In some circumstances, both national governments and international organizations have tried to accommodate communities by issuing permits to allow hunting. The question is, What sorts of policies are most likely to achieve the goal of protecting cultural rights as well as environmental rights, such as the right to biodiversity? One noteworthy attempt to balance both concerns was a memorandum from President Clinton.

Memorandum on Distribution of Eagle Feathers for Native American Religious Purposes, Weekly Comp. Pres. Doc. 30 (17) (Apr. 29, 1994), at 935–37

Policy Concerning Distribution of Eagle Feathers for Native American Religious Purposes

Memorandum for the Heads of Executive Departments and Agencies

Eagle feathers hold a sacred place in Native American culture and religious practices. Because of the feathers' significance to Native American heritage and consistent with due respect for the government-to-government relationship between the Federal and Native American tribal governments, this Administration has undertaken policy and procedural changes to facilitate the collection and distribution of scarce eagle bodies and parts for this purpose. This memorandum affirms and formalizes executive branch policy to ensure that progress begun on this important matter continues across the executive branch.

Today, as part of an historic meeting with all federally recognized tribal governments, I am directing executive departments and agencies (hereafter collectively "agency" or "agencies") to work cooperatively with tribal governments and to reexamine broadly their practices and procedures to seek opportunities to accommodate Native American religious practices to the fullest extent under the law.

As part of these efforts, agencies shall take steps to improve their collection and transfer of eagle carcasses and eagle body parts ("eagles") for Native American religious purposes. The success of this initiative requires the participation, and is therefore the responsibility, of all Federal land managing agencies, not just those within the Department of the Interior. I therefore direct each agency responsible for managing Federal lands to diligently and expeditiously recover salvageable eagles found on lands under their jurisdiction and ensure that the eagles are promptly shipped to the National Eagle Repository ("Repository"). To assist agencies in this expanded effort, the Secretary of the Interior shall issue guidelines to all relevant agencies for the proper shipment of eagles to the Repository.

After receiving these guidelines, agencies shall immediately adopt policies, practices, and procedures necessary in accordance with these guidelines to recover and transfer eagles to the Repository promptly.

I support and encourage the initial steps taken by the Department of the Interior to improve the distribution of eagles for Native American religious purposes. In particular, the Department of the Interior shall continue to adopt policies and procedures and take those actions necessary to:

(a) ensure the priority of distribution of eagles, upon permit application, first for traditional Native American religious purposes, to the extent permitted by law, and then to other uses;
(b) simplify the eagle permit application process quickly and to the greatest extent possible to help achieve the objectives of this memorandum;
(c) minimize the delay and ensure respect and dignity in the process of distributing eagles for Native American religious purposes to the greatest extent possible;
(d) expand efforts to involve Native American tribes, organizations, and individuals in the distribution process, both at the Repository and on tribal lands, consistent with applicable laws;
(e) review means to ensure that adequate refrigerated storage space is available to process the eagles; and
(f) continue efforts to improve the Repository's ability to facilitate the objectives of this memorandum.

The Department of the Interior shall be responsible for coordinating any interagency efforts to address continuing executive branch actions necessary to achieve the objectives of this memorandum.

We must continue to be committed to greater intergovernmental communication and cooperation. In addition to working more closely with tribal governments, we must enlist the assistance of, and cooperate with, State and local governments to achieve the objectives of this memorandum. I therefore request that the Department of the Interior work with State fish and game agencies and other relevant State and local authorities to facilitate the objectives of this memorandum.

With commitment and cooperation by all of the agencies in the executive branch and with tribal governments, I am confident that we will be able to accomplish meaningful progress in the distribution of eagles for Native American religious purposes.

The Director of the Office of Management and Budget is authorized and directed to publish this memorandum in the Federal Register.

There were, unfortunately, several difficulties associated with the implementation of this effort. First, there was an insufficient number of eagle feathers. Second, the National Eagle Repository was unable to respond quickly enough to requests. Requiring Native Americans to submit a request by FedEx and then wait for it to come in the mail was compared to waiting in line to enter a church days after a death occurred. Third, it was ethnocentric to assume that the use of feathers was by itself important. Instead, it was just as important – culturally – to hunt the eagles for their feathers. In other words, the hunt was itself a crucial aspect of the ritual.

The International Whaling Commission has granted exemptions from the policy against the killing of bowhead and other whales by indigenous communities. This cultural accommodation represents a compromise that accommodates both environmental rights and cultural rights. If indigenous groups agree to take only a few creatures, the resulting depletion of whale stocks will not risk endangering the species.

One major difficulty has been that other groups have objected to the exemption, asserting that it violates equal protection to make an exception for indigenous peoples but not for them. Japanese and Norwegian whaling communities, whose way of life also depends on the taking of whales, have advanced this argument. They hold that policies intended to stop whaling are a form of cultural imperialism. Some members of indigenous groups also criticize the policy as ethnocentric, in part because the need to request exemptions is seen as paternalistic. The "authenticity" of the cultural traditions of hunting is also controversial. As culture is not static, this objection seems to lack force, as groups may prefer to use electric harpoon guns rather than spears. Cultural rights arguments ought not to depend on the method of killing, however.

The real question is how to reconcile competing rights claims. Which should take precedence, environmental rights or cultural rights? In this context, cultural communities find insulting the assumption that they would hunt or fish any species to the point of extinction. They claim that it was, after all, colonial powers that depleted natural resources to such an extent. In the final analysis, minority groups and indigenous peoples will have only the benefit of diverse species for whatever purpose, if they are not extinct. This logic would seem to suggest that environmental rights, despite being recognized later in time, trump cultural rights claims. Whether or not one agrees with this argument, it is clear that greater attention to the hierarchy of human rights claims is needed.

(iii) Disabilities. As we have seen, the first human rights treaty of the twenty-first century, the Convention on the Rights of Persons with Disabilities, provides comprehensive legal protection for individuals with disabilities. Protected persons find that their representations in folklore, popular culture, and other media perpetuate negative stereotypes. It has been a standard plot device to have villains portrayed as persons with disabilities, as in comic strips. Actors with disabilities often face dilemmas when their chance to be in television programs and films requires playing a role that reinforces stereotypes about persons with disabilities.

Another difficulty is that sometimes persons with disabilities may defend a custom that perpetuates stereotypes that are detrimental to the image of the group as a whole. This occurred in a controversy that involved the so-called sport of dwarf throwing that the UN Human Rights Committee ultimately addressed.[36] France claimed that the ban on the sport was consistent with public order, but a man whose livelihood depended on this activity challenged the ban saying that it violated his human rights under the ICCPR.

[36] Manuel Wackenheim v. France, Comm. No. 854/1999: France 20/07/2002, CCPR/C/75/D/854 1999 (Jurisprudence).

One might wonder whether dwarfs constitute a cultural group for legal purposes. To the extent that a disabled community has a strong sense of social solidarity, speaks a distinct language, and experiences differential treatment from members of the majority, that group is arguably a cultural minority. Although there is little question that the Deaf represent a cultural group, it is less clear whether other disability communities do. There is also a debate about whether there is such a thing as disability culture.

QUESTIONS

> The Convention on the Rights of Person with Disabilities obligates states parties to equalize opportunities for persons with disabilities. If you were an attorney representing an individual whose employment was terminated because of deafness, how would you invoke the new treaty? A deaf woman who worked as a lifeguard with the YMCA was dismissed after a year because of her condition. When she was informed that her disability made her ineligible, she sued. Leaving aside the specific requirements of such legislation as the Americans with Disabilities Act, should hearing facility be a bona fide occupational qualification to be a lifeguard?

(iv) Family Life and Marriage. An important part of life is the opportunity to marry and have a family. As there are vastly different systems of marriage around the world, conflicts may arise over the proper age of marriage, whether individuals should have the right to choose their spouses, whether the spouse must be of the opposite sex, whether a husband may take more than one wife, and so on. Fascinating jurisprudential issues arise when state legal systems are faced with marriages that are considered valid in the countries where they were celebrated but are not in accordance with the law where a husband and wife may have relocated. The following case received considerable attention. It involved Bangladeshi parents who decided that their son, a man aged twenty-six with intellectual disabilities including autism who had the skills expected of an average three-year-old, would marry an older woman. According to English law, the son lacked capacity to consent to marriage. According to Bangladeshi law, however, it was a valid marriage. The matter was further complicated insofar as the marriage ceremony took place over the phone, thereby raising a question about the appropriate *lex loci celebrationis* (the law of the place of the marriage).

City of Westminster Social & Community Services Department v. IC, [2008] EWCA Civ. 198

Expert evidence was given by Professor Menski, professor of South Asian laws at the School of Oriental and African Studies at the University of London. His evidence and conclusions were unchallenged. As to the marriage this was his evidence:

> The "marriage" needs to be contracted in an "Islamically accepted form," which in this case he finds it to have been, even though the bride, the Khazi officiating, many of her relatives as well as IC's relatives, in particular the father, were in Bangladesh, and IC was with his siblings and an Imam from a local mosque in London, there being

> speaker-phone communication between the two parties. This form of celebration of marriage (at the telephone) is increasingly common and accepted as entirely valid.

As to the communication between those in this jurisdiction and those in Bangladesh, these were the judge's findings:

> Irrespective of IC's ability or inability to consent, the father of IC (his marriage guardian) "may legitimately act in the best interests of his Ward to arrange, solemnize and contract a marriage for that individual which binds that individual and the spouse in all respects. . . .
>
> It is said that in the course of the marriage ceremony IC said the word "yes" in ostensible consent to his marriage, although his overall mental capacity should not be ignored, included within which is the possibility of coaching, or, more probably than not, echolalia from which he suffers, leading, depending on the phrasing of the question put to him, to such an answer. Irrespective of the status of that "yes" it is, in this case, the father's agreement to the marriage as the lawful marriage of an incapacitated son which is sufficient under the provisions of traditional Islamic law to constitute an appropriate consent.

Aleem v. Aleem
947 A.2d 489 (Md. 2008)

Cathell, J.

Farah Aleem filed suit for a limited divorce from her husband, Irfan Aleem, in the Circuit Court for Montgomery County. The husband thereafter filed an Answer and Counterclaim. He raised no jurisdictional objections. Without, however, any advance notification to the wife, and while the Montgomery County action was pending (between the filing of the action for a limited divorce and the filing of the amended complaint for an absolute divorce), the husband, a Muslim and a national of Pakistan, went to the Pakistan Embassy in Washington, D.C., and performed *talaq*[37] by executing a written document that stated:

> Now this deed witnesses that I the said Irfan Aleem, do hereby divorce Farah Aleem, daughter of Mahmood Mirza, by pronouncing upon her Divorce/Talaq three times irrevocably and by severing all connections of husband and wife with her forever and for good.
>
> 1. I Divorce thee Farah Aleem
> 2. I Divorce thee Farah Aleem
> 3. I Divorce thee Farah Aleem. . . .

[37] Apparently, under Islamic law, where that Islamic law has been adopted as the secular law of a jurisdiction, such as Pakistan, a husband has a virtual automatic right to *talaq* (i.e., to divorce his wife by acknowledging "I divorce thee" three times), but the wife only has a right to *talaq* if it is in the written marriage agreement or if he otherwise delegates that right to her. In the present case the husband did not grant the wife the right to *talaq*. While the nature of *talaq* is relevant to the issues here presented, the wife does not claim that the husband "granted" her that right and accordingly that is not a factual issue in this case.

Petitioner posits that the performance by him of *talaq* under Islamic religious and secular Pakistan law, and the existence of a "marriage contract," deprived the Circuit Court for Montgomery County of jurisdiction to litigate the division of the parties' marital property situated in this country.[38] The trial court found that the marriage contract entered into on the day of the parties' marriage in Pakistan specifically did not provide for the division of marital property and thus, for that reason alone, the agreement did not prohibit the Circuit Court for Montgomery County from dividing the parties' marital property under Maryland law. The Court of Special Appeals agreed and stated "[t]hus, the Pakistani marriage contract in the instant matter is not to be equated with a premarital or post-marital agreement that validly relinquished, under Maryland law, rights in marital property." *Aleem v. Aleem*, 175 Md.App. 663, 681, 931 A.2d 1123, 1134 (2007). The Court of Special Appeals further stated:

> If the Pakistani marriage contract is silent, Pakistani law does not recognize marital property. If a premarital or post-marital agreement in Maryland is silent with respect to marital property, those rights are recognized by Maryland law.... In other words, the 'default' under Pakistani law is that Wife has no rights to property titled in Husband's name, while the 'default' under Maryland law is that the wife has marital property rights in property titled in the husband's name. We hold that this conflict is so substantial that applying Pakistani law in the instant matter would be contrary to Maryland public policy.
>
> Our holding in this case only relates to instances where Islamic law, or parts thereof such as *talaq*, is also the secular (civil) law of a country whose judgments we are urged to accept under the doctrine of comity. In other words, we address Islamic law only to the extent it is also the civil law of a country. The viability of Islamic law as a religious canon is not intended to be affected.

Petitioner presents two questions for our review:

1. [Did] the Court of Special Appeals disregard[] fundamental principles of international comity and conflicts of laws in refusing to recognize a Pakistani divorce because Pakistan and Maryland employ different 'default rules' for the division of property between spouses[?]
2. [Did] the Court of Special Appeals disregard[] fundamental principles of international comity and conflicts of laws in concluding that Pakistan lacked jurisdiction to dissolve the parties' marriage because the parties resided in Maryland on diplomatic visas[?]

The Relevant Facts

The parties, both citizens of Pakistan, were married in Pakistan in 1980. The marriage was arranged by the families of the parties. In accordance

[38] The "marital property" as it would be defined under Maryland law included the husband's pension from World Bank valued at approximately one million dollars, real property valued at $850,000, personal property valued at approximately $80,000, and two or more vehicles.

with Pakistani custom there was a written agreement presented to the wife on the day of the wedding for her to sign. At that time she was 18 years old and her husband was 29 years old. She had just graduated from high school and he was a doctoral candidate at Oxford University in England. . . .

T[he] agreement provided for a "dower" of 51,000 rupees[39] the payment of which was "deferred." There was no other express or implied waiver of any property rights of either party. During the presentation of the agreement, the wife was advised by her uncle who was acting as a "vakil." There is no evidence in this case, however, that the wife's uncle was a lawyer.[40] Under Pakistani law, unless the agreement provides otherwise, upon divorce all property owned by the husband on the date of the divorce remains his property and "the wife has [no] claim thereto." The opposite is also applicable. The husband has no claim on the property of the wife. In other words, upon the dissolution of the marriage, the property follows the possessor of its title.

Shortly after their marriage, the husband moved to England. The wife joined him later and they resided there for four years while he completed his studies. They then moved to the United States and began to reside in Maryland while the husband worked at the World Bank. They maintained a residence in this State for 20 years and resided here at the time the wife filed for divorce and the husband went to the Pakistan Embassy and performed *talaq*. The parties have two children, both of whom were born in this country, are United States citizens, and reside in this country. The wife is now a resident of Maryland, and holds a green card status.

The central issue in the present case concerns the wife's attempt to have the husband's pension from the World Bank, which relates primarily to his work performed while he was a resident of this country, declared to be "marital property" and to have other property declared marital property and thus be entitled to half of that pension and property under Maryland law.

[39] While the dower was deferred at the time of the contract, it appears that when Irfan Aleem attempted to divorce Farah Aleem, that a sum of $2,500 was mentioned as a "full and final" settlement. Under Islamic law as it is in the civil law of Pakistan, a man, upon marriage, can defer the payment of the "dower" (*mahr* in Urdu) but he cannot divorce the wife by *talaq* unless he then pays the *mahr* to the wife. In a pleading filed in the Circuit Court for Montgomery County by the husband, *mahr*, is explained as follows:

> . . . Dower can be used as a means of controlling the husband's power of divorce, since upon dissolution of the marriage he is requi[r]ed to pay the total amount of the dower at once. . . . [T]he wife's claim for any unpaid portion of her dower is an unsecured debt which is due from her husband. . . . Dower is a major part of the husband' financial commitment to his wife.

In the present case, the sum of $2,500 represents payment of the *mahr* to the wife. It is the husband's position that payment of *mahr* of $2,500 is all that is due the wife, as opposed to the one half of almost two million dollars that she might be entitled to under Maryland law (It is unclear how the *mahr* would affect the position of the Pakistani courts in respect to properties titled in both names. The primary property focus in the present case is the petitioner's pension – which is titled only in the husband's name.). This stark discrepancy highlights the difference in the public policies of this State and the public policies of Islamic law, in the form adopted as the civil, secular law of countries such as Pakistan.

[40] Apparently, under Pakistani law a "vakil" performs the function of a legal advisor and often is a lawyer.

Discussion

More than a hundred years ago, the Supreme Court of the United States, in an extensive discussion relating to the judgments of foreign countries, discussed the comity due judgments of foreign countries and full faith and credit issues. [The Court provides an historical overview from that opinion.] ... "As to judgments of courts of foreign countries, there is no constitutional requirement of recognition. It is a matter of comity." *Telnikoff v. Matusevitch*, 347 Md. 561, 702 A.2d 230 (1997) (a "certified question" case), is perhaps the most modern and seminal of our cases on comity between Maryland and foreign countries. It did not involve issues of marital property or other domestic law issues, but involved primarily the law of defamation and the constitutional guarantees of freedom of speech. *Telnikoff*, however, did restate with clarity the issues that relate to comity and their application generally. As stated above, the case involved the difference between the laws of libel of England and of Maryland. An English citizen had obtained a judgment in the courts of England based upon a libel occurring in England. He sought to have the judgment enforced in this country and Matusevitch brought an action to preclude the enforcement. We stated as follows:

> Telnikoff argues that the English libel judgment is entitled to recognition under principles of "comity." Matusevitch, on the other hand, asserts that the English judgment is repugnant to the public policy of the United States and Maryland and, therefore, should be denied recognition.
>
> The recognition of foreign judgments is governed by principles of comity.... "Although more than mere courtesy and accommodation, comity does not achieve the force of an imperative or obligation. Rather, it is a nation's expression of understanding which demonstrates due regard both to the international duty and convenience and to the rights of persons protected by its own laws").. . .
>
> Although foreign judgments are entitled to a degree of deference and respect under the doctrine of comity, courts will nonetheless deny recognition and enforcement to those foreign judgments which are inconsistent with the public policies of the forum state....

The justification for the public policy exception to the recognition of foreign judgments as articulated by the United States Court of Appeals for the District of Columbia Circuit in *Laker Airways v. Sabena, Belgian World Airlines*, 235 U.S. App. D.C. 207, 731 F.2d 909, 937 (D.C.Cir.1984), is as follows:

> There are limitations to the application of comity. When the foreign act is inherently inconsistent with the policies underlying comity, domestic recognition could tend either to legitimize the aberration or to encourage retaliation, undercutting the realization of the goals served by comity. No nation is under an unremitting obligation to enforce foreign interests which are fundamentally prejudicial to those of the

> domestic forum. Thus, from the earliest times, authorities have recognized that the obligation of comity expires when the strong public policies of the forum are vitiated by the foreign act.' . . .

In determining non-constitutional principles of law, courts often rely upon the policies and requirements reflected in constitutional provisions. . . . ("Although [Article 46 of the Maryland Declaration of Rights] may not directly apply to private employers, it nonetheless establishes a public policy in Maryland that an individual should not be subjected to sex-based discrimination.")

The Court of Special Appeals, in *Wolff v. Wolff*, 40 Md. App. 168, 389 A.2d 413 (1978), noted as follows:

> "The full faith and credit clause . . . does not apply to a divorce obtained in a foreign country. Courts of the United States are not required by federal law to give full force and effect to a judgment granted in a foreign nation. On the other hand, judgments of courts of foreign countries are recognized in the United States because of comity. . . . This principle is frequently applied in divorce cases. . . . The principle of comity, however, has several important exceptions and qualifications. A decree of divorce will not be recognized by comity where it was obtained by a procedure which denies due process of law in the real sense of the term, or was obtained by fraud, or where the divorce offends the public policy of the state in which recognition is sought. . . . " (Citations omitted.)

The Maryland Legislature declared Maryland's public policy in regard to property acquired during a marriage, stating in the preamble to Chapter 794 of the Acts of 1978, that "the property interests of the spouses should be adjusted fairly and equitably." And furthermore, from the record in the present case, it appears that under Islamic law, which, albeit with certain modifications, has been adopted as the law in Pakistan, only the husband has an independent right to *talaq*, i.e., to use *talaq* to divorce his wife.[41] The wife may only utilize *talaq* if the husband has given her that right in the contract of marriage. In the case at bar, the wife was not granted the right of *talaq* by her husband. It appears, also from the record, that the husband may utilize *talaq* with no prior notice to the wife. It is clear as well, as we point out above, that, under Pakistani law, upon a divorce there is no equitable division of marital property, i.e., property acquired by the parties during the marriage, unless the marriage "contract" so provides . . .

[41] Here the Court refers to a synopsis of the Pakistani law of divorce in a House of Lords decision. The rules require the husband who exercises his unilateral right to notify the chairman of the local council immediately. "Although [the chairman] is required to convene an arbitration council to attempt the reconciliation of the parties, their attendance is not obligatory and the divorce will become effective, unless the wife is pregnant, once 90 days have elapsed from the date on which the chairman received notice of the *talaq*."

On November 7, 1972, the people of Maryland ratified the Equal Rights Amendment, now found as Article 46 of the Maryland Declaration of Rights. It provides: "Equality of rights under the law shall not be abridged or denied because of sex." Accordingly, in the first instance, the enforceability of a foreign *talaq* divorce provision, such as that presented here, in the courts of Maryland, where only the male, i.e., husband, has an independent right to utilize *talaq* and the wife may utilize it only with the husband's permission, is contrary to Maryland's constitutional provisions and thus is contrary to the "public policy" of Maryland. Moreover, if we were to recognize the use of *talaq*, controlled as it is by the husband, a wife, a resident of this State, would never be able to consummate a divorce action filed by her in which she seeks a division of marital property, because a husband who is a citizen of any country in which Islamic law, *adopted as the civil law*, prevails could go to the embassy of that country and perform *talaq*, and divorce her (without prior notice to her) long before she would have any opportunity to fully litigate, under Maryland law, the circumstances of the parties' dissolution of their marriage.[42]

Talaq lacks any significant "due process" for the wife, and its use moreover, directly deprives the wife of the "due process" she is entitled to when she initiates divorce litigation in this State. The lack and deprivation of due process is itself contrary to this State's public policy.

Petitioner directs the Court's attention to the practice in Pakistan of having a Council of Arbitration available to the wife. That practice, however, only applies if the parties want to reconcile and it addresses only that possibility. In a situation where both parties seek divorce, as here, it has virtually no application. Its function was explained at the trial level by a letter from Muhammad Najeeb, Chairman of the Arbitration Council in the Clifton Cantonment, Karachi, Pakistan, to the attorney for the wife, as follows:

> Please refer to your letter dated 15th Dec., 2003, on behalf of your client, Mst. Farah Aleem, I may inform you that the marriage was solemnized in Pakistan within the jurisdiction of this Union Council and that both your client and Mr. Aleem are Pakistani citizens and therefore this Union Council has jurisdiction in the matter. We had sent notices to your client as provided under Section 7 of the Muslim Family Laws Ordinance 1961. The purpose of notices is to ascertain whether both parties want to reconcile in which case the divorce shal[l] not become final. In case both parties or any one of them does not want reconciliation, the divorce shall become final after 90 days of such notice. . . . Mr. Aleem had responded in writing that he does not want to reconcile but there is no intimation from your client [in] []spite of

[42] In a letter from respondent's counsel to the Arbitration Council, respondent points out that the husband's performance of *talaq* was designed to circumvent Maryland law. She stated in relevant part as follows:

> Mr. Aleem is obligated to provide Ms. Aleem with both child support and alimony pursuant to Order of Court. Mr. Aleem, by seeking a divorce in Pakistan, is attempting to circumvent the laws of the state of Maryland, and the Order of our Court, notwithstanding that he has submitted to the Court's jurisdiction, to this day has counsel here in Maryland, and has regularly sought our Court's relief.

> the fact that your client has received the notice which will be presumed that she does not want any reconciliation. *It may also be mentioned that [the] function of the Arbitration Council is **only** to see whether both husband and wife want to reconcile and live again as husband and wife.* (Emphasis added.)

Additionally, as indicated above, Maryland has enacted a comprehensive statutory scheme designed to effectuate a fair division of property acquired by the parties during the time of their marriage, just as the pension at issue in this case was acquired.[43] To accept *talaq* and to accept the silence of the "contract" signed by the wife on the day of her marriage in Pakistan, as a waiver of her rights to marital property acquired during the marriage, is, in direct conflict with our public policy. Additionally, the Pakistani statutes proffered by petitioner as establishing that all of the property titled in his name, however and whenever acquired, is his property free of any claim by the wife arising out of the marriage, are also in direct conflict with the Maryland statute governing those same issues.

. . .

The *talaq* divorce of countries applying Islamic law, unless substantially modified, is contrary to the public policy of this state and we decline to give *talaq*, as it is presented in this case, any comity. The Pakistani statutes providing that property owned by the parties to a marriage, follows title upon the dissolution of the marriage unless there are agreements otherwise, conflicts with the laws of this State where, in the absence of valid agreements otherwise or in the absence of waiver, marital property is subject to fair and equitable division. Thus the Pakistani statutes are wholly in conflict with the public policy of this State as expressed in our statutes and we shall afford no comity to those Pakistani statutes.

Additionally, a procedure that permits a man (and him only unless he agrees otherwise) to evade a divorce action begun in this State by rushing to the embassy of a country recognizing *talaq* and, without prior notice to the wife, perform "I divorce thee . . . " three times and thus summarily terminate the marriage and deprive his wife of marital property, confers insufficient due process to his wife. Accordingly, for this additional reason the courts of Maryland shall not recognize the *talaq* divorce performed here.

We answer no to each of petitioner's questions.

Judgment affirmed; costs to be paid by Petitioner.

NOTES AND QUESTIONS

1. How would the Convention on the Rights of Persons with Disabilities have applied in *City of Westminster*? Explain how the judge might have ruled, had the treaty been incorporated into the reasoning.

[43] The *mahr*, deferred in the marriage certificate, would not normally be classified under Maryland law as marital property in any event, as it may not have been "acquired" during the marriage.

2. As a matter of public policy concerning individuals with intellectual disabilities, should the presumption be in favor or against authorizing marriage?
3. Tacit assumptions underlie marriage law judgments. In North America and Western Europe child marriage not only is presumptively invalid but also may constitute statutory rape. It is also noteworthy that at the same time that same-sex marriage is becoming increasingly accepted worldwide, polygamy is increasingly condemned. Plural marriage may result in both criminal prosecution and exclusion of immigration applicants. In 2008 the Spanish Supreme Court upheld a lower court ruling that had denied a Senegalese man's naturalization because he had two wives. The court concluded that polygamy, unlike same-sex marriage, was not merely illegal in Spain but contrary to the Spanish public order. Sentencia de la Audiencia Nacional, sec. 3, March 11, 2008 (JUR 2008\164675).
4. As *Aleem v. Aleem* demonstrates, divorce practices also reveal important cultural differences such as whether a religious form of divorce – for example, by unilateral repudiation (as by *talaq*) – can be legally recognized. The *Aleem* opinion raises broader legal questions of recognition and enforcement of foreign law that are very common and important in the international legal system. First, what is comity? Does it have limits? How does comity compare with full faith and credit in U.S. constitutional law? Second (and related to the first question), how far should public policy extend to bar the normal recognition and enforcement of foreign law? How, specifically, were comity and public policy applied or not in *Aleem*?
5. Do you agree with the court's analysis of *talaq* in *Aleem*? For an argument that the dispute could have been resolved by focusing on jurisdiction rather than comity, see Rajni K. Sekhri, Aleem v. Aleem: *A Divorce from the Proper Comity Standard – Lowering the Bar that Courts Must Reach to Deny Recognizing Foreign Judgments*, 68 U. Md. L. Rev. 662 (2009). If men and women both had the right to divorce via *talaq*, would this method be more acceptable and not against public policy? Should legal systems facilitate the dissolution of unhappy unions in a more cost-effective manner? Other courts take the view that they should not recognize the *talaq* or "triple divorce" because it is inconsistent with due process and violates public policy. See the per curiam decision *Tarjkonda v. Pinjari*, 2009 LEXIS 733 (Mich. App.) (unpublished).
6. To what extent does it or should it matter where the *talaq* is pronounced and whether it is in the context of a polygamous marriage? Consider, for example, the case of *Radwan v. Radwan*, 3 All E. R. 967 (1972), (Fam. Div. London). An Egyptian husband married an English woman in the Egyptian consulate in Paris; she was his second wife. After living together for several years, the husband pronounced the *talaq* in the Egyptian embassy in London, a procedure that was considered valid in Egypt but not in England. The wife filed for divorce in court, claiming that English law did not recognize this unilateral form of divorce performed in a consulate. The husband argued that he had already secured a valid *talaq* divorce. The judge identified the central issue:

> The question for my decision is whether by English law the Consulate General of the United Arab Republic is part of a country outside the British Isles within the meaning of the Recognition of Divorces and Legal Separations Act of 1971. By that Act the relevant sections providing for recognition will have effect in

> respect of overseas divorces if they have been obtained by means of judicial or other proceedings in any country outside the British Isles, and it is necessary for the efficacy of the *talaq* divorce that it should have been obtained outside the British Isles by reason of the fact that at the material time the husband had acquired English domicile.
>
> Curiously, the question has not arisen for decision in England before, that is, the question whether the premises of an embassy or consulate are part of the territory of the sending state as compared to the territory of the receiving state.

The judge considered case law on whether diplomatic premises should be considered the territory of the sending or receiving state and found that relevant treaties were silent on the question of extraterritoriality. He concluded that the husband had not divorced his English wife "outside of England" when he performed the *talaq* in the Egyptian consulate because the embassy could not be considered to be on Egyptian territory outside of England. The law (the Recognition of Divorces and Legal Separations Act of 1972) required that the *talaq* be performed outside of England because the husband had acquired English domicile. Subsequently, in his consideration of the wife's claim, the same judge ruled against her. Because the marriage was performed in France (albeit in the Egyptian consulate), it was controlled by French law, and France, like England, did not accept the extraterritorial fiction that the consulate was Egyptian territory: Under French law, the marriage was not valid in the first place. *Radwan v. Radwan* II, 3 All E. R. 1026 (1972). Do you agree with the court's reasoning in the two *Radwan* decisions? Or should marriages and divorces in consulates and embassies be treated as though they occurred in the homeland?

7. When Muslim couples travel abroad, courts sometimes grapple with the question of how best to evaluate the custom of *mahr*. For insightful commentary on this challenge, see Ann Lazueuer Estin, *Toward a Multicultural Family Law*, 38 Fam. L. Q. 501–27 (2004); Bharathi Anandhi Venkatraman, *Islamic States and the United Nations Convention on the Elimination of All Forms of Discrimination Against Women: Are the Shari'a and the Convention Compatible?*, 44 Am. U. L. Rev. 949 (1995). For an argument in favor of recognition, see M. Jindani, *The Concept of Mahr in Islamic Law: The Need of Statutory Recognition by English Law*, Y.B. Islamic & Middle Eastern L. 219–27 (2004–5). See also Azizah Al-Ilibri, *Islam, Culture, and Religion*, 12 Am. U. J. Int'l & Pol. 1 (1997).
8. In Israel:

> Jewish divorce is effected by the civil law husband delivering to his wife a *get* (bill of divorce). Personal attendance is not required. The spouses may appoint agents to give and accept the *get*. The rabbinical court only ensures that Jewish law is observed. The spouses do not [profess] any faith. No reference is made to God, either in the *get* or during its delivery. For Reform Jews, a civil divorce is sufficient. However, if the divorced spouse would later on wish to marry an Orthodox or Conservative Jew, he or she would still need a religious divorce. The husband may not divorce his wife against her will. Consent has always been a proper ground for divorce. Each spouse may also demand divorce upon justified grounds. Yet, even when justified grounds exist for

> demanding divorce, the rabbinical court's judgment does not by itself dissolve the marriage. The court's role is to help enforce rights that already exist. The spouses remain married until a *get* is delivered, an act to which they must both agree.

Talia Einhorn, Private International Law in Israel 213 (2009).

If the husband refuses to deliver the *get*, his wife is trapped indefinitely in a limbo state, unable to move on and establish a new life. The question of whether civil courts can intervene to order the husband to grant the *get* is problematic. From the religious point of view, the *get* must be of the husband's own free will in order to be valid. From the secular perspective, it violates the principle of the separation of church and state for civil courts to interfere in religious affairs. Interestingly, this has been a worldwide concern. For a comprehensive overview, see Esther Tager, *The Chained Wife*, Neth. Q. Human Rights 4, 425–57 (1999).

In *Bruker v. Marcovitz*, [2007] 3 S.C.R. 607, 2007 SCC 54, the Supreme Court of Canada ruled that a secular court could address and then reject a husband's refusal to grant a *get* to his wife, as they had formally agreed, even though the question was rooted in religious practice. In other words, the husband was not shielded from the wife's legal claim for a divorce despite a Canadian constitutional guarantee of freedom of religion. For commentary on this case, see Kevin L. Boonstra, *How to Get a Get*, Liberty, May/June 2009, at 17.

4. Coda: Examples of Cultural Law from the World of Music

Throughout this chapter we have seen examples of the diverse relationships between culture and law that form the framework of cultural law. Subsection 1 defined cultural law in terms of six functional relationships between culture and law. Examples of each of these relationships, as follows, are all drawn from a neglected aspect of cultural law: music.

a. Law Embodies Culture and Formalizes Its Norms

It has been said that "[c]ulture is like a map,"[44] providing "an abstract description of trends toward uniformity in the words, deeds, and artifacts of a human group."[45] If so, it follows that a primary function of law, whether formal or informal, state-centered or not, is to embody culture and formalize its norms in a society.

Music, often accompanied by dance, sometimes establishes "trends toward uniformity" that symbolize or even constitute a kind of legal order, particularly in traditional, often tribal societies. In such highly contextual societies, where legal texts are apt to be only incidental, music-driven ritual may itself serve to define important social expectations. One example involves ritual singing and the use of sacred flutes among the Mehinaku people of Brazil to confirm gender roles, related taboos, and authorization of otherwise prohibited violence.[46] Although modern, more textual societies seldom rely on music itself to define legal rules, their laws do express normative support of music.

[44] Clyde Kluckhohn, Mirror for Man 26 (1949).
[45] *Id.*
[46] Thomas Gregor, Anxious Pleasures 98 (1985).

Tax deductions for contributions to music (and other cultural) organizations are one example. In the following chapters we shall observe how other cultural artifacts shape the law as well.

b. Law Promotes, Protects, Conditions, and Limits Cultural Attributes and Expressions

Johnlee Scelba Curtis, *Culture and the Digital Copyright Chimera: Assessing the International Regulatory System of the Music Industry in Relation to Cultural Diversity*, 13 Int'l J. Cultural Prop. 59–60, 63–64, 66–69, 77, 80, 81, 84–85 (2006)

As the digital revolution sweeps the globe, the world's cultural property is rapidly being translated into ones and zeros. Simultaneously, the technologies of the Internet, advanced electronics, telephony, and personal computers are constantly converging – often in completely unexpected ways. Technological growth is first spawned, it seems, through the venue of entertainment (where commercially profitable applications have been most readily discovered). Historically, the initial form of entertainment to be widely digitalized was music – through the delivery technology of the compact dis[c]. As both a form of cultural property and a form of entertainment, music has played a central role in the ongoing debate over digital rights in the new era of digital networked environments. Almost constantly, the news has showcased the series of recent law suits that the Recording Industry Association of America (RIAA) has brought before judges, hoping to gain substantial protection against the increased piracy threats the digital revolution has incurred as well as test the limits of the current content regulation regimes.

Views of the present regulatory means of reducing online music piracy and copyright infringement seem polarized. On one side of the ideological spectrum, the "cultural conglomerates" posit that their copyrights are property rights that must be afforded the same protection, as are owners of other types of property. This means supporting extended copyright terms, expanded content usage controls, and fighting Internet downloads or *thefts* of their contents. On the other side, *free culturists* believe that cultural property belongs to the *commons* (to everyone in society). This means that they see copyrights as protectionist instruments that distribute monopoly rights to a handful of cultural enterprises; and they believe that this only serves to afford those corporations monopoly rents, thereby causing market failures within the sector of cultural commodities.

An objective view presents a more subtle explanation. Borrowing the parlance of Lawrence Lessig, this debate is a chimera, because both sides are, at the same time, right *and* wrong. One side wants *all rights reserved* to be the copyright norm in the digital networked environment, which would stifle creativity, innovation, and diversity of production. The other side wants *no rights reserved* to remain the norm within the digital[,] which would undermine the investments of the cultural industries and, ironically, the existing cultural habitat of the media market. Between the reactive responses of cultural industries to the digital revolution and the outraged responses by content-hungry consumers, perhaps it is possible [to] divine the impact of the copyright system on cultural diversity.

. . .

The definition of *cultural products* has also been subject to considerable debate (especially as the digital environment blurs definitional boundaries) largely because specific linguistic subtleties can drastically alter legal meaning. Industry leaders interpret their goods and services as mere *entertainment.* This language enables cultural goods and services to be subject to the international trade liberalization rules of the World Trade Organization (WTO). Others have interpreted cultural goods and services as *societal achievements.* This language would justify special treatment for cultural goods and services. The absence of a consensual definition of cultural goods and services has enabled the current *status quo* of stagnant international legal protections of cultural diversity.

. . .

Cultural content of the musical form has existed before recorded history. The concept, however, that such content is property in a proprietary sense is relatively modern. Current copyright law protects a composer's proprietary claims over a wide variety of uses of music, including: written representations in notation form, as part of a dramatic or audiovisual work, and when embodied in a recording. This section adopts a historical approach. Examining several historical periods can help identify how, when, and why music evolved into property.

. . .

In ancient Greece and Rome, the concept of proprietary claims to music did not yet exist. Although little notated Greek music has survived ([as a result of] the papyrus medium), scholars have written enough for us to ascertain the philosophies and practices of music in ancient Greece. Musical notation on various primitive surfaces was developed after the fourth century BC, but music consisted of intangible and communal expressions. The Greeks believe music was different [from] spoken language – one was to be written down (Greek) and the other was not (music). Music was considered an art form bestowed to man by the gods through the intercession of the Muses – specifically, Euterpe, the musical muse. As part of the *quadrivium* of mathematical liberal arts, music was a force of nature to be studied but incapable of being owned by a mortal. In our modern world, we use music's ability to stimulate emotional responses and sell it as a commodity.

The ancient Greeks viewed music as a reflection of balance and harmony, as well as a power that could be disruptive to the social order if not controlled. Both Plato and Aristotle believed that compulsory music education was necessary to enable free citizens to control their own emotions. Plato felt that music was so powerful a force that all aspects of music should be under strict government control. Aristotle agreed that musical education was vital [to] society but disagreed with Plato's idea of state-paid and chosen musicians (because that would prevent musicians from being *free men*). The idea that a composer would have proprietary rights to a melody was a concept foreign to the Greeks, because their perception of music was linked to a divine system – one that ordered their world. Although authors (poets, playwrights, philosophers, etc.) were attributed their works, the melodies they often wrote to accompany their texts remained unattributed. When political power shifted from Greece to Rome, the Romans looked to the Greeks for ideological inspiration. Despite the impressive innovations of Roman law, however, there is no evidence that Roman law supported proprietary claims of musical expression and composition, even though some have posited that their tenets of contract and intangible property are the *philosophical roots* of those contemporary laws.

In medieval Europe several elements fused to form the foundations of property rights in music. First, the notation of music in physical form was again attempted – now on less-ephemeral media. This made music a physical embodiment of an intellectual endeavor (instead of a momentary, *otherworldly* phenomenon). Second, the profession of music composition emerged, and the demand for musical compositions grew. Third, urbanization and increased trade made music more of a commodity. Because the Catholic Church was the most influential political and social institution in medieval European life, music was dominated by liturgy and the chant style of composition. The Church directly regulated chants. Secular music, however, was controlled by the feudal system. Only fragments of the secular tradition were embodied in written form. During that period, the concept of property did not attach to the discipline of either music performance or composition. Although, as the job of musical production evolved from slave labor to the labor of the Church, the evolution of music from the property of nature to the property of individuals took root. When the Church developed a system of written notation to preserve the *divinely inspired* chants, the necessity for musical literacy and technical proficiency soon followed. The tool of notation sparked new innovation and forms of expression. Secular music began the tradition of love songs (sung by troubadours). Musical guilds were then established to make the first proprietary claims to music.

The legal protection of guilds greatly evolved the notion of musical performance but had no effect on written music itself, because guilds were granted official monopolies on public performance by towns. Further, membership in a guild became a professional requisite for a musician in the era. The fourteenth century produced even higher levels of achievement in the musical arts. Books of compositions were printed, notation had become ubiquitous, and the commoditization of music had started, but that commodity was not consistently attributed to the composer/artist. Clearly, however, the foundations of property rights were laid during the Middle Ages largely because of innovation-based commoditization.

During the Renaissance, the philosophy of humanism, the further development of composition, and the rise in the number of famous composers caused music to emerge as a form of property. This had legal ramifications.

For the first time, proprietary claims were made by publishers of music they sold. The increasing status of the composer culminated in Flemish composer Orlando Lassus'[s] attempt to control the printing of his music. Control at this time was different from today's copyright protections. In the Renaissance control meant the publisher's right to publish and vend copies of musical scores. In 1440 Johan Gutenberg's revolutionary invention, the printing press, helped spur this conceptual evolution. The conceptual evolution sparked a legal revolution, but one that took 200 years to occur. When it did, the commoditization of music was complete, and property rights in compositions were first recognized. The Renaissance laws regulating printed books also applied to publications of music notation. The main musical customers during the period were wealthy aristocrats and the Church (but with advances in printing techniques, publications were increasingly available to the public at large). The law granted limited monopolies in expressive and technological innovation and included controls on the content itself through licensing and guild rules of publishing. Legal protection over musical works was granted to encourage increased expressive productivity, as well as increased technological innovation in the printing of music. Exclusive rights were granted to publish and sell copies of music for limited times in limited geographical areas.

Thus, in ancient Greece and Rome, music was viewed as separate from words, and treated very differently. Music was given no property rights, and composers were not acknowledged as the source of inspiration. In the Middle Ages, notation was redeveloped; musical composition was considered a viable activity; and music guilds were formed to give exclusive performance rights legal force. The Renaissance brought the innovation of efficient publishing to musical composition. This caused the evolution of the concept of property rights to include published music. The rights granted to publishers helped them compete against other publishers and other geographical market entrants. The common logical theme that runs through the history is that material conditions determining the commoditization of music directly impacted the concept of private property in each era. The legal concept of property was malleable to changes in the material conditions existing at the particular time. This brief historical journey has hardly been without purpose. We should observe a pattern: conceptual changes in the law brought about by the conversion of technological and philosophical stimuli. In the current battle over the future of music in the digital networked environment, it is wise to refer to the battles of the past and recognize that changes in material conditions and circumstances often can make existing legislation and market strategies obsolete.

...

Permission is increasingly required for the most mundane and innocent of endeavors. Campers have, for generations, been able to tell stories and sing tunes like "Row, Row, Row Your Boat" around a campfire without asking for permission. [The] American Society of Composers, Authors and Publishers (ASCAP), the performance rights body that licenses copyrighted works for nondramatic public performances, believes it is entitled to determine the terms for such *performances.* ASCAP reasoned that because hotels, restaurants, and resorts must pay for the right to perform recorded music, summer camps should be required to pay for licenses, too. Under copyright law a public performance occurs "where a substantial number of persons outside of a normal circle of a family and its social acquaintances is gathered." Thus ASCAP was technically correct. ASCAP initially demanded that the American Camping Association purchase a license fee of $1,200 per season per camp.

. . .

The current copyright regime has enumerated benefits that should be retained, but it exhibits more banes than blessings in the context of promoting and sustaining cultural diversity in musical commodities.

While *discovering* rural musicians may help small numbers of them become recognized internationally, musical diversity is destroyed when the world's cornucopia of music is *mixed* and *edited* by a handful of media interests. Although it may be beneficial for the world to have access to American cultural goods, it is not beneficial, in cultural diversity terms, for the world to be awash in the culture of only one nation. Further, although a harmonization of national intellectual property laws into negotiated instruments-in-progress like TRIPS [part of the international trade regime related to cultural law, to be discussed in Chapter 6 – *Eds.*] may eventually serve the public good, such a system is ineffective without strict international enforcement. The current legal regime of copyright (both regionally in the United States and as implemented internationally in negotiated agreements) is unable to provide a predictable, enforceable, harmonized, and balanced international market for cultural commodities amid the wide proliferation of digital and network technologies. The historical analysis we have explored has shown that, in new eras, new legal philosophies are born. [The authors refer to an analysis of current issues such as the copyright on all group singing of "Row, Row, Row Your Boat" – *Eds.*] [That] shows how the current copyright regime can hurt innovation, creativity, and diversity – the very fundamentals that it was ostensibly created to service.

Clearly we have entered a new era – the era of the *digital music revolution.* There are new material circumstances that simply were not present in former eras. Digital reproduction has rendered copies of music distortion free; the World Wide Web has connected music fans (and their collections); physical music media [have] been relegated to secondary importance in light of customizable playlists and digital music players with ever-doubling storage capacities; and affordable digital music studios have democratized musical production. Just as past technological breakthroughs have spawned new regulatory policies, the international regulatory schemes governing digital music must reflect this paradigm shift.

. . .

It is clear that not only do copyright rules need to adjust to balance both consumer and artist interests with the interests of the producers, but copyright also must broadly reform its communication policy and reflect the needs of both digital and cultural ecosystems.

. . .

The chimerical debate over copyright in the digital networked environment yields many rationales and challenges for adjusting the current system. In the adjustment process, only if the goal of promoting cultural diversity takes a heightened role can a true balancing of interests be reached. The debate over the preferable legislative tools for that balancing continues. With rapid convergence and technological growth as the two-dimensional reality of the digital age, smart legislators will seek measures that not only meet the needs of corporate interests (necessary for ongoing technological innovation and cultural development), but also strive to promote cultural diversity among cultural industry goods (necessary for long-term sustainability of cultural markets and human rights). What a sweet sound that would be for citizens and consumers of all cultures!

---

c. Law Harmonizes Cross-Cultural Differences, Establishes International Standards, and Confirms Cultural Rights

Jerry L. Weinstein, *Musical Pitch and International Agreement*, 46 Am. J. Int'l L. 341 (1952)

To what extent may it be said that a standard musical pitch has been established by international agreement? This question was recently raised before UNESCO by the Austrian Delegation. The matter has an interesting history of international agreement and practice and is one of much importance to the international musical world. Specifically, the question is one of the establishment of a standard pitch for the note A above middle C; or how many times, measured in cycles per second, should the note A vibrate?

The musical performer, especially the singer, whose voice and ear are trained to a given pitch and cannot readily be altered, is faced with substantive technical difficulties owing to the contemporary international musical cleavage. In certain European countries and in the United States the standard pitch is A = 440 cps (cycles per second), whereas in the other European countries the standard pitch is A = 435 cps.

In the eighteenth century and onwards, the standard pitch in use was the so-called "classical" pitch of A = 422 cps, to which Bach, Mozart, and Beethoven wrote, but by the middle of the nineteenth century the number of vibrations had increased in practice to 435. In an early effort to obtain wide recognition of this pitch, the French Government in 1859 deposited at the Paris Conservatory of Music a standard tuning fork which was to be the standard pitch or "diapason." The frequencies generated by vibrations of this fork were stated to be 435 cps for A above middle C. It was no doubt in view of the establishment of this standard pitch that on January 12, 1885, it was officially announced in London that Queen Victoria had sanctioned the adoption of this "*diapason normal*," as the French standard was called, for her private band, and that it would in [the] future be used at state concerts.

In the same year 1885, at the instigation of the Austrian Minister of Culture and Instruction, a conference was held in Vienna for the purpose of establishing a "standard diapason." The governments of Italy, Austria, Hungary, Prussia, Russia, Saxony, Sweden, and Württemberg were represented. The conference was held from November 16 to 19, and the principal resolution unanimously adopted called for the establishment of "one international '*diapason normal*' to be set at A = 435 cps." The conference recommended governments to take steps for the adoption of this standard pitch for all musical purposes, and in all musical institutions, public and private.

It would seem[,] therefore[,] that A = 435 cps as the standard pitch was widely accepted at the end of the last century, for Great Britain had followed the standard pitch set up by France, the Vienna Conference did likewise, while musical groups and instrument makers in the United States also conformed to this pitch.

In accordance with this internationally accepted practice of using A = 435 cps as the standard musical pitch, the resolutions of the 1885 Vienna Conference, though mistakenly termed "Convention," and with a minor error as regards dates, were incorporated into the Treaty of Versailles in 1919. By Article 282 of that treaty, certain multilateral treaties, conventions and agreements of an economic or technological character, subsequently enumerated, were to be regarded as being in effect as between Germany and those Allied and Associated Powers who were parties to them. No. 22 of the conventions listed was: "Convention of November 16 and 19, 1885, regarding the establishment of a concert pitch." Similar provisions were included in Article 234 of the Treaty of Peace of St. Germain with Austria in 1919, and in Article 217 of the Treaty of Peace of Trianon with Hungary in 1920.

After the Peace Treaties, however, due to the progressive development in laboratory technique and the manufacture of musical instruments, a move was made to further increase the number of vibrations from 435 to 440 cps. This change gained wide recognition in the United States and was adopted as the standard pitch by the Musical Industries Chamber of Commerce in 1925, and by the American Standards Association in 1936, thus acquiring the status of an industrial standard.

The change also took effect in Europe, and under the auspices of the International Standards Association, an international conference was held in London in May 1939, in order to accord international recognition to A = 440 cps as the new pitch. The governments of France, Germany, Great Britain, Holland and Italy were represented, while the governments of the United States and Switzerland sent official messages. Six of the seven countries represented independently proposed the adoption of A = 440 cps as the standard musical pitch, and this was unanimously accepted by the conference.

The advent of the [S]econd World War temporarily jeopardized the chance of a wider international acceptance of this standard pitch by use, and today many European countries still adhere to the older standard pitch of A = 435 cps. A further minor complexity is that in the United States the standard pitch A = 440 cps is the minimum in use, since, for example, the Boston Symphony Orchestra, probably the highest-pitched orchestra in the world, is tuned to a pitch of A = 444 cps.

This, then, is the nature of the present international musical divergence: Should A vibrate 435 or 440 cycles per second? There is much hope inspired by the experience of past international agreement and practice on the matter that the time is not far distant when UNESCO or a third international conference will settle what is, at least culturally, a vexed question.

NOTES AND QUESTIONS

1. In 1995 the International Organization for Standardization settled the "vexed question" by confirming 440 cps (or "Hz" for hertz), a decision that it later reiterated. Today A = 440 Hz is the most common, though not universal, standard. For example, baroque music ensembles have generally agreed on a standard of A = 415 Hz.
2. Much ado about nothing? Although the debate about a universal proper pitch standard may seem rather distant from the mainstream of lawyering, if not trivial, the role of both intergovernmental and nongovernmental standardization of weights, measures, practices, and so on, is of growing significance in practice. In some contexts, such as trade usage, cultural differences would seem to be tangential. In reality, however, cultural differences readily explain the need for international standardization and engage the work of lawyers who have to deal with divergent usages.

d. Culture Reinforces Legal Rules

Culture is not value-free. It may even reinforce grossly unjust legal rules, practices, and regimes. For example, Nazi Germany's aggressive employment of "high culture" (as opposed to "degenerate art") to enhance the regime's image led to massive plundering of cultural resources, principally fine art, throughout Europe. Herbert Gerigk, a music expert, led a relentless search in occupied France for rare instruments, manuscripts, and other musical treasures. His zeal in doing so earned him steady employment by Alfred Rosenberg as well as Joseph Goebbels' approval and extension of funds to him.[47] Gerigk's musical treasure hunt reinforced the authority of the administrative orders and rules in an otherwise dicey, bureaucratically complicated system of plunder and the Nazi regime as a whole.

e. Culture Conditions and Constrains the Adoption, Interpretation, and Vitality of Legal Rules

Steve Jones, *Music That Moves: Popular Music, Distribution and Network Technologies*, 16 Cultural Stud., no. 2, at 213, 221–22 (2002) (reprinted with permission of Taylor and Francis Group)

[47] *See* Jonathan Petropoulos, Art as Politics in the Third Reich 152–53 (1996).

Processes employed in the past by the music industry to exert control over the flow of music (and, in the case of immigration laws, of musicians themselves) are rendered useless when the medium of distribution undergoes a paradigmatic change from analogue to entirely digital, from physical good to digital code. The legal controls the music industry could exert relied on an infrastructure of transportation that provided gate-keeping opportunities. Customs checkpoints, warehouses, retail outlets and even radio stations were subject to legal authority due to their [situatedness] in space (they could be found, discovered) and in time (they would stay put in space sufficiently long to be found). The lesson of movement has not escaped pirate radio operators who would frequently change locations and frequencies to avoid arrest.

It is likely that in the future the locus of control of online music will reside in the Internet's infrastructure, in the routers, or perhaps the Internet protocol itself. Such points are the ones most clearly available for gate-keeping, and are the ones at which movement is controlled. They form the only locus at which one might monitor and act upon exchange at Internet speed and at great volume. They also, however, create serious issues of loss of privacy and surveillance. It is noteworthy that those loci of exchange are prone to greatest corporate control after industrial consolidations like that of America Online and Time-Warner.

The focus on copyright has also overshadowed the wider implications of digital distribution. The disruption of the loci of exchange also disrupts a connection between the social and financial. High-speed distribution makes it impossible, for all practical purposes, for humans to negotiate an exchange, unless the exchange is forced to a slower rate by artificially interrupting the process. Downloading music using [MP3] software like Napster, Gnutella, and so on, is on the one hand a human-machine interaction that obliterates traditional place – and point-of-purchase interaction. However, on the other hand, such software incorporates opportunities for messaging and chat that allow reconfiguration to new forms of connection between consumers (and purveyors) of music.

---

f. Cultural Expressions and Symbols Promote Legal Relationships

Daniel J. Wakin, *North Koreans Welcome Symphonic Diplomacy*, N.Y. Times, Feb. 27, 2008, at A10 (reprinted with the permission of the *New York Times.* All rights reserved)

PYONGYANG, North Korea – As the New York Philharmonic played the opening notes of "Arirang," a beloved Korean folk song, a murmur rippled through the audience. Many in the audience perched forward in their seats.

. . .

It was the first time an American cultural organization had appeared here, and the largest contingent of United States citizens to appear since the Korean War. The trip had been suffused with political importance since North Korea's invitation came to light last year. It was seen by some as an opening for warmer relations with the United States, which North Korea has long reviled.

. . .

The concert evoked other orchestra missions to repressive states, like the Boston Symphony Orchestra's visit to the Soviet Union in 1956, followed soon after by a Philharmonic visit, and the Philadelphia Orchestra's trip to China in 1973.

Elisabetta Povoledo, *China Orchestra Plays for Pope for First Time, Hinting at Thaw*, N.Y. Times, May 8, 2008, at A6 (reprinted with the permission of the *New York Times*. All rights reserved)

The China Philharmonic Orchestra performed Mozart's Requiem with the Shanghai Opera House Chorus for Pope Benedict XVI on Wednesday, an unprecedented concert that could signal a thaw in the historically chilly relations between the Vatican and the Chinese government.

The event evoked memories of Ping-Pong diplomacy, which helped lead to the restoration of relations between the United States and China in the 1970s, with music instead of sports as the bonding agent.

"Music, and art in general, can serve as a privileged instrument for encounter and reciprocal knowledge and esteem between different populations and cultures," Benedict said after the concert, which was held in the Paul VI Audience Hall at the Vatican. "A means attainable by all for valuing the universal language of art."

China and the Vatican have not had diplomatic relations since the 1950s, though each side has made conciliatory signs in recent years.

NOTES

1. Perhaps the best-known examples of the use of cultural expressions and symbols to promote legal relationships has been in the sports arena. The "ping-pong diplomacy" between the United States and China in the 1970s and "tennis diplomacy" between South Korea and China in the 1980s are prime examples. In 2008 and 2009 Armenia and Turkey engaged in several phases of "soccer diplomacy" involving attendance of the presidents of the two countries at World Cup qualifying football/soccer games between their respective national teams. The diplomacy served as the principal symbol of a rapprochement between the two countries that may lead eventually to the first diplomatic relations between the traditionally hostile neighbors and the opening of their border for the first time since 1993. See Mark Landler & Sebnem Arsu, *Long-Bitter Turkey and Armenia Struggle to Normalize Ties*, N.Y. Times, Oct. 11, 2009, at A5; Sebnem Arsu, *Armenians and Turks Agree on Ties*, N.Y. Times, Sept. 1, 2009, at A4.
2. In addition to "ping pong" and other sports-related diplomacy, joint archaeological and historic preservations projects have also helped foster better relationships between divided countries. See, e.g., Michael Theodoulou, *Ancient Walls Unite Divided Cypriots*, Christian Sci. Monitor, Apr. 3, 2008 (The restoration

of a medieval and Renaissance quarter of Famugusta, within the internationally unrecognized northern half of Cyprus, has united estranged Greek and Turkish communities.). See also James Brooke, *Rebuilding Temple, Narrowing a Gap*, N.Y. Times, Oct. 2, 2005, at 6 (describing a joint North Korean-South Korean project to rebuild the Holy Valley Temple in Singye, North Korea, and concluding with the following observation:

> Culture is the way to find common ground for both Koreas, [the head monk said,] after walking barefoot over the polished pine floor boards of the new temple. "As for culture and sentiment, we have a lot in common. But when it comes to politics, economy, and defense, it is a long process."
>
> The central link between music and law is interpretation. Both fields depend on textual interpretation. In music, scores provide the texts. In law, the texts are constitutions, statutes, ordinances, regulations, and cases. In each field, interpretation of texts is of immense importance.
>
> . . .
>
> The similarities between music and law are suggestive. They say something significant about the process of interpretation, something that goes beyond the boundaries of any particular discipline. There is, of course, no single orthodox interpretation of Mozart's Symphony in G Minor, any more than there is one authoritative reading of the Due Process Clause of the Fourteenth Amendment. Everything turns on the outlook of the interpreter, his background, his intellect, his hopes and his aspirations.
>
> Music and law are both functions of their creators, and reflections of their minds and their reactions to the world in which they live. Just as we experience the world through the ears and mind of a Beethoven, Brahms, or Stravinsky when we hear their music, so we understand the world through the minds of the Framers, a particular legislature, or a judge, when we read their work product. We are in contact with minds and we must attempt identification with those minds. The closer the identification, the closer it is possible to come to an understanding of the creator's work.

Daniel Kornstein, The Music of the Laws 107, 110 (1982).

2. Culture and Law: The Basics

A. Culture

1. The Issues

In the following conversation, the participants, who come from several professional fields, discuss their respective understandings of culture. In the course of their remarkable discussion, they cover most of the basic issues about the concept of culture. We will have occasion throughout the book to draw on their insights.

Clyde Kluckhohn & William H. Kelly, *The Concept of Culture, in* The Science of Man in the World Crisis 78–106 (Ralph Linton ed., 1980)

THE LAWYER: At the last meeting of this little discussion group of ours, we got into quite an argument about "culture" as a technical term in anthropology – exactly what anthropologists mean by it and whether it is any use or not. The big dictionaries and even the anthropological books here in the club library didn't help us out very much. We did gather that the anthropological conception, like all the other scientific and popular usages, carries with it an implication of human interference, of something being added to, or altered from, a state of nature. But we found ourselves wishing that we could ask questions which might clear up points which were sidestepped or simply not discussed by these formal statements. We therefore prevailed upon you gentlemen to come here and let us put you on the spot.

THE HISTORIAN: Was I right in insisting last time that the anthropologist's conception of culture is much more inclusive than the historian's?

FIRST ANTHROPOLOGIST: Yes, to anthropologists a humble cooking pot is as much a cultural product as is a Beethoven sonata.

THE BUSINESSMAN: I am relieved to hear that. For my wife a person who has culture is a person who can talk about Debussy, T. S. Eliot, Picasso, and those people.

THE LAWYER: Do anthropologists apply the term "culture" to our civilization? Isn't there a difference between "culture" and "civilization"?

SECOND ANTHROPOLOGIST: To most anthropologists, a civilization is simply a special type of a culture, namely, a complex or "high" culture. More specifically, a civilization is – as the derivation of the word itself suggests – the culture of a people who live in cities. People who have lived in cities have invariably possessed a somewhat complex way of life, and have almost always had a written language.

THIRD ANTHROPOLOGIST: Perhaps it would also be well to state for the record that anthropologists have never followed another distinction which certain sociologists have made between culture and civilization. This usage discriminates between "civilization" as comprising the sum total of human "means" and "culture" as constituting the collectivity of human "ends."

FIRST ANTHROPOLOGIST: Many educated people seem to have the notion that "culture" applies only to exotic ways of life or to societies where relative simplicity and relative homogeneity prevail. Some sophisticated missionaries, for example, will use the anthropological conception in discussing the special modes of living of South Sea Islanders, but seem amazed at the idea that it could be applied equally to the inhabitants of New York City. And social workers in New York City will talk about the "culture" of a colorful and well-knit immigrant group, but boggle at utilizing the concept toward understanding the behavior of staff members in the social service agency itself.

THE ECONOMIST: A moment ago you used the term "society." This brings me to a point which I have found confusing in certain recent more or less popular writings of anthropologists. Sometimes the terms "culture" and "society" seem to have been used almost as synonyms.

FIRST ANTHROPOLOGIST: There would be fairly general agreement in our profession that this is undesirable. The usage which has attained almost complete acceptance among us can be put simply, though not altogether precisely, as follows: A "society" refers to a group of people who have learned to work together; a "culture" refers to the distinctive ways of life of such a group of people.

THE PHILOSOPHER: In my language, then, "a culture" is an abstraction, whereas "a society" is not?

THIRD ANTHROPOLOGIST: That is certainly correct in the sense that you can see the individuals who make up a society, while you never see "culture." However, the statement must not be made to imply that the processes of inference and abstraction are not involved in many of the specific problems of deciding where one society leaves off and another begins. Some anthropologists assert that such problems can always be resolved by sufficiently detailed observation of the frequencies with which human beings in a defined territory interact. This is doubtless a valid operation by which to decide what individuals constitute "a society," but we should be deluding ourselves if we pretended that reasoning were not as necessary as observation to the delimitation of a society.

SECOND ANTHROPOLOGIST: I can't agree with your first statement that culture is never observed directly. What does an anthropologist actually do when he is working in the field? Yes, he sees the human organisms who make up a society. He sees not only them, but also their behavior. He likewise sees the objects they have made and all of the alterations which they produced in their natural environment. What the anthropologist does is to record the distinctive ways of behaving which he sees and those results of behavior which are also characteristic. These constitute the culture of the group.

THIRD ANTHROPOLOGIST: There is no doubt that you have rightly described what anthropologists actually do in the field. But those recordings which you have mentioned I would prefer to consider as the anthropologist's raw data. Both "society" and "culture" are conceptual constructs. In each case, although in importantly different ways, the anthropologist has added to or subtracted from what he actually saw. Both the society and the culture which he portrays are conceptual models – not firsthand recordings of all he observed.

THE PSYCHOLOGIST: Let me see if I can translate into my own lingo. Culture means the totality of social habits.

FIRST ANTHROPOLOGIST: "Habit" is too neutral a term. It would be more exact to say "socially valued habits," for a group is never affectively indifferent to its culture.

THE PSYCHOLOGIST: I suppose that branch of psychology which is most intimately related to "culture" is what we today call "learning theory." Wouldn't you agree that the transmission of culture can be understood only in so far as learning and teaching are understood?

FIRST ANTHROPOLOGIST: Yes, inasmuch as all human beings of whatever "races" seem to have about the same nervous systems and biological equipment generally, we would anticipate that the basic processes of learning are very similar if not identical among all groups. We therefore look to the psychologist to inform us about the laws of learning. On the other hand, we can show that *what* is learned, from whom learning takes place, and when the learning of certain skills usually occurs, [vary] according to culture. Also, I should like to point out that there is one danger in speaking of culture as being "taught." "Teaching" is not limited, as in the popular sense, to conscious instruction. Individuals learn – "absorb" more nearly suggests, in nontechnical language, the process – much of their culture through imitation of both the "matched-dependent" and "copying" types. Take, for example, those gestures and expressive movements ("motor habits") which are observed as characteristic of certain groups. Every anthropologist regards these as cultural phenomena, and yet only in dancing schools, armies, and the like is explicit instruction as to posture, and so forth, given.

THE PSYCHOLOGIST: If I am not mistaken, C. S. Ford has defined culture as consisting of "traditional ways of solving problems" or "learned problem solutions."

THIRD ANTHROPOLOGIST: It is true that any culture is, among other things, a set of techniques for adjusting both to the external environment and to other men. In so far as Ford's statement points to this fact, it is helpful, but it will not do as a synoptic definition. For cultures create problems as well as solving them. If the lore of a people states that frogs are dangerous creatures, or that it is not safe to go about at night because of were-animals or ghosts, threats are posed which do not arise out of the inexorable facts of the external world. This is why all "functional" definitions of culture tend to be unsatisfactory: they disregard the fact that cultures create needs as well as provide a means of fulfilling them.

THE PSYCHIATRIST: In fact, my profession has always tended to think of culture as something which was repressive to the "natural" nature of man, as something which produced needless neuroses by demands and thwartings during the process of molding individuals into shapes uncongenial to their native temperament.

THIRD ANTHROPOLOGIST: This seems to us to be another half-truth. Culture is *both* fulfilling and frustrating.

FOURTH ANTHROPOLOGIST: I have held my peace, but at this point I really must protest. Where is this "culture" which you talk about as doing this and that? If anthropology is to become a natural science, it must deal only in empirical and observable entities. In spite of the fact that most archeologists, ethnologists, and social anthropologists still feel that "culture" is their master concept, I maintain we would get further if we stuck to human interaction with other humans and with the natural environment. You can see those things, but has any of you ever seen "culture"?

FIRST ANTHROPOLOGIST: I freely admit that to say "culture" does something is an inexact or metaphorical way of speaking. But this is merely a convenient shorthand expression in place of the long-winded though admittedly more precise "the human representatives of the group which share this culture do thus and so." As for "seeing": your admired natural scientists have never seen "gravity" or "evolution." And yet they find the introduction of these concepts indispensable for making the facts intelligible and for predicting them. "Culture" is an abstract generalizing concept, as essential to the understanding and prediction of events in the human world as is gravity to the understanding and prediction of events in the physical world.

SECOND ANTHROPOLOGIST: I accept and use the concept "culture," but I shy away from these high abstractions. I think it is better to stick to a more traditional definition, such as: "Culture is that complex whole which includes artifacts, beliefs, art, all the other habits acquired by man as a member of society, and all products of human activity as determined by these habits."

FIRST ANTHROPOLOGIST: That is all right as a descriptive statement of what students of culture investigate. But as a definition I find it awkward. The enumeration is incomplete, and experience shows that in definitions by enumeration those elements which are not explicitly stated tend to be forgotten even though they be implied. You, for example, have not even mentioned language.

THIRD ANTHROPOLOGIST: I would file two other objections. First, the definition is too intellectualistic. One gets no hint that people are other than affectively neutral toward their culture. This is just a list of culture content. Except, possibly, for the single word "whole," there is no indication that culture has organization as well as content.

THE ECONOMIST: How about "social heredity" as a brief abstract definition of culture?

THIRD ANTHROPOLOGIST: This definition has been widely current and has been of much utility in drawing attention to the fact that human beings have a social as well as a biological heritage. The principal drawbacks to this conception of culture are that it implies too great stability of culture and too passive a role on the part of man. It suggests that man gets his culture as he gets his genes – without effort and without resistance. It tends too much to make us think of the human being as what Dollard has called "the passive porter of a cultural tradition." Men are, as Simmons has recently reminded us, not only the carriers and the creatures of culture – they are also creators and manipulators of culture. "Social heredity" suggests too much of the dead weight of tradition.

THE PSYCHIATRIST: Yes, culture is not merely a "given." Really, in a strictly literal sense, it is not a "given" at all – it is only available. Indeed, [José] Ortega y Gasset has defined culture as "that which is sought." The phrase "social legacy" perhaps avoids some of these difficulties, but even this is hardly satisfactory. One wants a definition which points to the fact that the irreducible datum of the social scientist is the individual and his behavior. From the angle of individual psychology, no definition of culture is adequate which does not make us aware of the active role of the individual as regards his culture and of the fact that he has an impulse to enjoy life.

THE BUSINESSMAN: Much of what has been said was mildly diverting as an exhibition in logical adroitness, but frankly I still don't altogether see why anybody bothers about "culture" at all.

FIRST ANTHROPOLOGIST: Well, one of the interesting things about human beings is that they try to understand themselves and their own behavior. While this has been particularly true of Europeans in recent times, there is no group which has not developed a scheme or schemes to explain man's actions. I would claim that the concept of culture is essential to such understanding.

SECOND ANTHROPOLOGIST: I would phrase the case a little differently. Science is concerned with all observable phenomena, including man himself and his behavior. "Culture" is a convenient descriptive category for organizing our objective reports on human behavior.

THE PHILOSOPHER: It strikes me that the last two statements contain the key to much of our apparent disagreement. For some anthropologists "culture" is primarily a descriptive concept; for others it is primarily an explanatory concept. So-called "definitions" are always constructed from a point of view – which is all too often left unstated. Not all definitions are substantive (that is, "descriptive"). Nor is "explanatory" the only other alternative. Some of the definitions which have been partially stated or implied have been "functional"; others may be characterized as epistemological – that is, they have been intended to point toward the type of phenomena from which we gain our knowledge of "culture." There is also the point that some definitions look toward the actions of the individual as the starting point of all assertions, whereas others, while perhaps admitting these as ultimate referents, depart from abstractions attributable to groups. However, the distinction between "explanatory" and "descriptive" seems to be most central.

"Culture" as an Explanatory Concept

THIRD ANTHROPOLOGIST: By "culture" we mean those historically created selective processes which channel men's reactions both to internal and to external stimuli.

SECOND ANTHROPOLOGIST: That is certainly an "analytical abstraction" all right.

THIRD ANTHROPOLOGIST: That is precisely the idea: that with this concept certain aspects of the concrete phenomena may be analyzed out, and thus whole events may be better "explained" and predicted.

FIRST ANTHROPOLOGIST: Very neat. And it seems to me to cover the ground. It avoids the difficulty lurking in those many definitions of culture which employ the phrase "acquired by man as a member of society." That phrase seems to suggest that "culture" as an explanatory concept refers *only* to dimensions of the behavior of individuals resultant upon their membership in a particular society (either through birth or through later affiliation). But "culture" also helps us to understand such processes as "diffusion," "culture contact," "acculturation."

THIRD ANTHROPOLOGIST: Yes, culture as an explanatory concept is useful alike in analyzing actions of individuals (whether treated as individuals or as groups) and in elucidating geographical distributions of artifacts or forms of behavior and historical sequences.

FIRST ANTHROPOLOGIST: One could perhaps rephrase your definition along substantive lines by saying that by culture we mean those historically created definitions of the situation which individuals tend to acquire by virtue of participation in or contact with groups which tend to share ways of life which are in some respects distinctive.

FOURTH ANTHROPOLOGIST: Even I find some merit in the explanatory definition proposed. You at least make some concession to a behavioristic approach when you speak of "reactions" and "stimuli."

THIRD ANTHROPOLOGIST: Naturally I would agree that any concept or proposition in social science must be ultimately referable back to human behavior. Even when we deal with distribution of "culture traits," we must not forget that we are dealing with products of human hands, with traces left by human activity.

FOURTH ANTHROPOLOGIST: But why did you find it necessary to include "*internal* stimuli"?

THIRD ANTHROPOLOGIST: When a man eats, he is reacting to an internal "drive," namely, hunger contractions consequent upon the lowering of blood sugar and so forth, but his precise reaction to these internal stimuli cannot be predicted by physiological knowledge alone. Whether a healthy adult tends to "feel hungry" twice, three times, or four times a day and the hours at which these "feelings" tend to recur is a question of culture. *What* he eats is of course limited by sheer objective availability, but is also partly regulated by culture. It is a biological fact that some types of berries are poisonous, but it is a cultural fact that, a few generations ago, most Americans considered tomatoes to be poisonous and refused to eat them. On the other hand, milk, which we regard as a healthful and pleasing food, is regarded by certain peoples of the earth as either dangerous or disgusting. Such selective, discriminative use of the environment is characteristically cultural. In a still more general sense, too, the process of eating is channeled by culture. Whether a man eats to live, lives to eat, or eats and lives is partly individual idiosyncrasy, but there are also marked correlations of individual tendencies along these lines with cultural groups.

SECOND ANTHROPOLOGIST: Why do you use the word "reaction" instead of more straightforward "action"?

THIRD ANTHROPOLOGIST: Because "reaction" comes nearer to conveying the feeling tone which is associated with all selective designs for living.

FOURTH ANTHROPOLOGIST: I am partially convinced, but I must once more come back to my question: Why did you introduce this unseen "culture"?

THIRD ANTHROPOLOGIST: There is no human being, if he be even a few weeks old, who reacts completely freshly to any stimulus situation. Very few human responses indeed can be explained entirely through even the most complete knowledge of the individual biological equipment, private experience up to that point, and the objective facts of the given situation.

FOURTH ANTHROPOLOGIST: But where does "culture" come from? You seem to invoke it as a kind of *deus ex machina.*

THIRD ANTHROPOLOGIST: Culture is, as it were, the precipitate of history. It includes those aspects of the past which, usually in altered form, live on in the present. In more than one sense "history is a sieve."

THE BIOLOGIST: Do you mean that culture consists of those ways of meeting situations which prove to have survival value?

THIRD ANTHROPOLOGIST: This is a large and important part of the truth. The process of culture may well be regarded as something added to man's innate biological capacities; it provides instruments which enlarge or may even substitute for biological functions and which to a limited degree compensate for biological limitations – as in insuring that the biological fact of death does not always mean that what the dead individual has learned is lost to humanity. Nevertheless, I believe this to be a dangerously misleading formulation unless it is properly explained and qualified. In the first place, as [Ralph] Linton and others have documented, it is an observed fact that most groups elaborate certain aspects of their culture far beyond maximal relative utility or survival value. In other words, not all culture is adaptive – in the sense of promoting sheer physical survival. At times indeed it does exactly the opposite. We must bring in the concept of adjustment (that is, lowering of tension) as well as that of adaptation. In the second place, aspects of culture which once directly promoted survival may persist even after they have ceased to have survival value. An analysis of contemporary Navaho culture will disclose many features which cannot possibly be construed as adaptations to the total environment in which Navahos now find themselves. However, it is altogether likely that these represent survivals, with modifications which have occurred during the centuries, of cultural forms which were adaptive in one or another environment in which certain ancestors of the contemporary Navaho lived prior to entering the Southwest.

FIRST ANTHROPOLOGIST: In other words, you are saying that no way of reacting is taken over by the group unless it has direct adaptive or adjustive value for individuals as such (or as constituting a group) at the time the design for living becomes cultural.

THIRD ANTHROPOLOGIST: Right. The main point is that, as [Franz] Boas so often insisted, we cannot account for complex historical changes by any simple formula. While many patterned ways of reacting unquestionably represent almost inevitable responses to an external environment in which the group lives or once lived, there are certainly also many cases where the inexorable conditions of action merely limit the possibility of response rather than eventually compelling one and only one mode of adaptation. These "choices" are probably themselves determined – if we make our theoretical system wide enough to encompass all possible types of factors. But, within the more usual frame of reference, they are the "accidents of history." Let me give an example or two. In a society where the chief really has great power, one particular chief happens to be born with an endocrine imbalance which brings about certain (to that group) unusual idiosyncrasies in personality. By virtue of his position, he is able to bring about certain modifications in the way of life of his group (say, in religion) which are congenial to his "temperament." It may be argued, and it may be true, that no amount of authority could insure the persistence of such alterations unless they somehow had adjustive or adaptive value for more than a single individual.

I do not believe that the empirical evidence bearing on this problem has been sufficiently analyzed to permit a definite answer to the question. But what is certain is that such a circumstance has been known to be followed by relatively temporary or relatively enduring changes in group designs for living – sometimes primarily in the form of strong "reaction formations." The fact of the chief's position and all that was consequent upon it is not an accident from the point of view of the theoretical systems usually employed in analyzing such steps. The unusual temperament is, however, due to an "accident of the genetic process."

Or, suppose that in the same group a chief dies as a relatively young man, leaving an infant as his heir. This has been observed to result in a marked crystallization of two factions around two rival older relatives, each of whom has about an equally valid claim to act as "regent." Through these circumstances a complete and lasting splitting off of two groups has been observed to take place. Each group thereafter has pursued its own separate destiny, and the end result is the formation of two distinguishable variants of what was at one time a more or less homogeneous culture. Now, to be sure, it is likely that the original factional lines had their bases in "economic," demographic, or other "external" conditions. Yet, had it not been for the "accidental" death of the one chief in his early maturity, the society might have indefinitely continued intact as an equilibrium of opposed tendencies. In short, the form and the mesh of the "sieve which is history" must be seen and shaped not only by the total "environment" at any given point in time but also by individual "psychological" and "accidental" factors.

FIRST ANTHROPOLOGIST: Could we then say that culture includes all those ways of feeling, thinking, and acting which are not inevitable as a result of human biological equipment and process and (or) objective external situations?

THIRD ANTHROPOLOGIST: My objection to that definition would be: first, that this defines culture as a "residual category" – which is logically undesirable; second, I believe it is better to mention explicitly the time dimension as indicated by the phrase "historically created."

FIRST ANTHROPOLOGIST: This suggests also the cumulative nature of culture.

THIRD ANTHROPOLOGIST: Yes, provided we remember that in another sense culture is not exactly "cumulative." Culture at any given time-point has likewise the property of uniqueness. That is why it is absolutely essential to include the word "selective" in any definition.

THE LAWYER: I can see that there has been a selection of possible modes of behavior and that these selections then may become established in a group, but aren't you overemphasizing this aspect? It seems to me that in common sense terms if we understand human nature, and if we then make our interpretation in the light of the concrete situation at hand, we get along very well.

FIRST ANTHROPOLOGIST: No, if you will look beyond the records of our own time and place you will find that the matter is not so simple. There are certain recurrent and inevitable human problems, and the ways in which man can meet them are limited by his biological equipment and by certain facts of the external world. Anthropologists have perhaps in recent years been too much preoccupied with the diversity found upon the earth and have neglected the basic similarities. But apart from these important but very general resemblances, the conception of one single, unchanging "human nature" is a reassuring fiction of folklore. When it comes to details, there are "human natures."

For example, old age is a situation to which all human beings who live long enough must adjust. But we find that in some human societies the old, regardless of their particular achievements, are entitled to respect and even to authority. In other societies, we find that the old, again regardless of individual differences, are ordinarily treated with relative indifference or active contempt. In still other societies, whether or not an aged person is treated with deference or with neglect seems to depend on his own past history rather than upon his period of life. Thus we see that though age is a biological fact it is always culturally defined. This fact of the plasticity of "human nature" is the widest and the most certain induction which anthropologists can derive from the cross-cultural record. The precise *forms* which biological and social processes take are myriad, and these *forms* are cultural.

Let us take an instance where, as so often, biological and social facts are intertwined. In many human groups which have been described, the physically weak have been, almost without qualification, at a disadvantage. In some groups, however, it has been observed that there have been effective deterrents against the strong taking advantage of the weak. Bullying has been punished by social disapproval and hence has actually been relatively rare. In a few societies, there is a tendency to give privileged positions to the physically weak or to certain types of the physically weak. Just as sociobiological situations or purely social situations can be stylized, so also some purely biological situations may be stylized.

Take vomiting, for example. Vomiting is a biological event and it can be produced by causes which are solely biological. But in other cases, although individual differences in neurological equipment and in previous experience play their part, the event sequence which would lead up to vomiting could never be predicted purely on the basis of biological knowledge. For instance, Americans who have eaten rattlesnake have been known to vomit upon being told what they had been fed. Since rattlesnake meat is perfectly nutritious, the vomiting is produced by some extrabiological factor. Similar illustrations could be given for other biological processes, such as weeping and fainting. These biological processes are also caught in a cultural web, as it were.

Here is a particularly telling example. The newborn infant excretes whenever tensions in bladder and colon reach a certain level of intensity. Before long, however, biological rhythms have surrendered to superimposed designs which are not directly derived from the facts of biology. Most adult human beings in normal health defecate only once or at most twice during a day. This tends to occur within rather fixed hours and, in many human groups, only at certain designated places and under defined conditions as to who else may (should) or may (should) not be present. So interesting and so vital is the interrelation of the biological and the cultural dimensions of human behavior that some anthropologists feel the study of these connections to be the differential feature of anthropology.

THE PSYCHOLOGIST: Isn't this just a kind of "conditioning"?

THE BIOLOGIST: Yes, couldn't we call it simply "environmental conditioning"?

FIRST ANTHROPOLOGIST: A very special sort of conditioning. No group deliberately sets out to train its children to vomit under certain circumstances. This result, rather, is a kind of incidental by-product of a style of life or of some aspect of such a style of life.

THIRD ANTHROPOLOGIST: The naïve – and very powerful – view is that we have individual organisms (they can be seen) and that they exist in an external world (which can also be seen and described). This is the view which "common sense" takes, and it is very hard to shake oneself out of this apparently sensible formula. But it simply won't cover the facts; the awareness of the external environment is too highly selective for that. Put down various groups of adults who have been trained in different social traditions in the same desert island. What they see in their surroundings will not be identical at all. Nor will, of course, the techniques by which they endeavor to adjust themselves to the surroundings. Between culturalized men and their environment there exists, as it were, a screen which is intangible and invisible but none the less real. This screen is "culture."

THE PSYCHOLOGIST: In trying to understand a single concrete act on the part of an individual I have found it helpful to ask these questions:

1. What are the innate endowments and limitations of the individual?
2. What has his total experience been prior to the act we are studying?
3. What is his immediate situation?

FIRST ANTHROPOLOGIST: No one of these variables can be elucidated in a completely satisfactory manner without introducing the concept "culture."

1. Except in the case of newborn babies and of individuals born with clear-cut structural or functional abnormalities we can observe "innate endowments" only as modified by cultural training. In a hospital in New Mexico where Zuni Indian, Navaho Indian, and white American babies are born it is possible to classify the newly arrived infants as hyperactive, average, and hypoactive. Some babies from each "racial" group will fall into each category, though a higher proportion of the white babies will fall into the hyperactive class. But if a Navaho baby, a Zuni baby, and a white baby – all classified as about equally hyperactive at birth – are again observed at the age of two years, the Zuni baby – as *compared with the white child* – will no longer seem given to quick and restless activity, though he may seem so as compared with other Zunis of the same age. The Navaho child is likely to fall in between as contrasted with the Zuni and the white though he will probably still seem hyperactive if seen against the standard of a series of Navaho youngsters.
2. The sheer factual description of the individual's experience doesn't get us very far. His interpretation of these events is indispensable, and this will be made, at least in part, in terms of norms current in his group. Losing a mother tends to mean one thing in one society, quite a different thing in another society.
3. Naturally, the immediate situation as well as past experience is reacted to, not in purely rational or objective fashion but in terms of the situation as meaningfully defined by the participant. Almost no human situations are viewed in ways which are altogether a consequence of the individual's experience. Culture is – among other things – a set of ready-made definitions of the situation which each participant only slightly retailors in his own idiomatic way.

THE BIOLOGIST: May we get back to some examples?

THIRD ANTHROPOLOGIST: If we are to begin at the beginning we start off, I suppose, with the basic observation of the diversity of human behavior. A few years ago a young man of American parentage[,] but who had been reared in a Chinese family from infancy on, paid his first visit to America. Reporters commented not only upon his apparently complete bewilderment in the American way of life, but also upon the fact that his walk, arm and hand movements, and facial expression were "Chinese – not American." They insisted that one had to fix one's attention upon his blond hair and blue eyes to convince oneself that he was of white stock at all. Here the point is that an individual's acts and attitudes not only failed to resemble those of his own close relatives in this country but that they resembled those of all members of an alien physical group and contrasted with those of all members of his own physical group.

To take a less dramatic but better-known illustration, a third generation Italian, unless he has been reared in the Italian colony of a large American city, shows "social habits" which resemble those of "Old Americans" much more closely than they do those of residents of Italy. The influence of the various domestic and geographical environments in which these Italian-Americans grew up was not so powerful but that we can recognize common tendencies in all of them which ally them to other "Americans." The variations and similarities which obtain between groups of human beings must also both be clarified. Groups of the same strain of physical heredity show great differences in behavioral norms and groups of unquestionably different strains show great similarities.

It has been remarked by many observers in the Japanese relocation centers that Japanese who have been born and brought up in this country, especially those who were reared apart from any large colony of Japanese, resemble their white neighbors in all behavioral characteristics much more closely than they do their own Japanese relatives who had been educated in Japan and then immigrated to this country.

THE PSYCHOLOGIST: This proves that human beings can learn from each other – and we knew that already. What proof is there that if all white Americans were wiped out the Japanese-American wouldn't eventually revert to designs for living highly similar to those characteristic of the Japanese of Japan?

THIRD ANTHROPOLOGIST: Obviously, there can be no certain answer to such a hypothetical question. But note carefully that the concept of culture as I have phrased it in no way denies the possible importance of innate factors. It does not assert the patent absurdity that the behavior of all Japanese (of Japan) or the behavior of all white Americans is minutely identical. It says merely that the behavior of each group though showing much individual variation still shows certain common tendencies within the one group which contrast sharply with those within the other group. Since the common tendencies of the American group are also to a perceptible degree exhibited by large numbers of individuals of Japanese racial stock – although it is not claimed that their behavior shows precisely the same modalities as the white Americans – it is argued that these shared trends may be attributed to the presence and influence of communicable designs for living.

THE ECONOMIST: Perhaps if Japan were depopulated and colonized by white Americans these would, within a certain number of generations, develop social definitions of the situation which would hardly be distinguishable from those characteristic of the Japanese today.

THIRD ANTHROPOLOGIST: The natural environments of the United States are very various, and yet the Americans of the arid Southwest and of rainy Oregon still behave in ways which are easily distinguishable from inhabitants of the Australian desert on the one hand and from those of verdant England on the other. Tribes like the Pueblo and Navaho, living in substantially identical natural and biological environments, still manifest very different ways of life. The English who live in the Hudson Bay region and those who live in British Somaliland still share common designs for living. It is true, of course, that the different natural environments are responsible for observable alterations. But the striking fact is that, in spite of the tremendous environmental differences, shared designs for living still persist.

The inhabitants of two not widely separated villages in New Mexico, Ramah and Fence Lake, are both of the so-called "Old American" physical stock. Almost certainly a physical anthropologist would say they represented random samples from the same physical population. The rocky tablelands, the annual rainfall and its distribution, the flora and fauna surrounding the two villages hardly show perceptible variations. The density of population and the distance from a main highway [are] almost exactly the same in the two cases. Nevertheless, even the casual visitor immediately notices distinctions. There are characteristic differences in dress; the style of the houses is different; there is a saloon in one town and not in the other. A completion of this catalog would conclusively demonstrate that very different patterns of life prevail in the two settlements. Why? Primarily because the two villages represent variants of the general Anglo-American social traditions. They have slightly different cultures.

THE PHILOSOPHER: There are two questions upon which I must pin you down. The first is: where is the locus of culture – in society or in the individual?

THIRD ANTHROPOLOGIST: Asking the question that way poses a false dilemma. Remember that "culture" is an abstraction. Hence culture as a concrete, observable entity does not exist anywhere – unless you wish to say that it exists in the "minds" of the men who make the abstractions. The objects and events from which we make our abstractions do have an observable existence. But culture is like a map. Just as a map isn't the territory but an abstract representation of the territory so also a culture is an abstract description of trends toward uniformity in the words, acts, and artifacts of human groups. The data, then, from which we come to know culture are not derived from an abstraction such as "society" but from direct observable behavior and behavioral products. Note, however, that "culture" may be said to be "supraindividual" in at least two nonmystical, perfectly empirical senses:

1. Objects as well as individuals manifest culture.
2. The continuity of culture never depends upon the continued existence of any particular individuals.

THE PHILOSOPHER: Very good. Now my second question: Can "culture" ever be said to be the cause of anything?

THIRD ANTHROPOLOGIST: Not in any very strict or exact way of speaking. In the first place, I would always question the advisability of using the term "cause" in any social science theory. Too much of a unidirectional force is implied. Rather I should use "determinant" with its connotation of interdependence of the relevant forces. But even to say "culture determines" is a very inexact and elliptical way of speaking, justified perhaps in certain circumstances by the convenience of brevity. Inexact, however, it is, because no concrete phenomenon is ever completely and solely determined by culture.

Sometimes, to be sure, culture may be the "strategic factor" – that is, the crucial element that determines that a given act tends to be differently carried out in one group than in another or that the act is somehow not what we would anticipate from a knowledge of the physical and biological forces operative. But "cultural determinism" in any simple or literal sense is as objectionable as any other class of unilateral determinism such as "geographical determinism" or "economic determinism." Although, in the concrete, the influence of culture is always mediated by men or artifacts, one is nevertheless justified in speaking of culture as a determinant of events when a discussion is being carried on at a high level of abstraction – provided the degree of abstraction is not lost sight of. The point may become clearer from an analogy – though all analogies (including this one!) are dangerous.

Suppose a man who has a plague which is thought to be due to a postulated but unseen virus enters a city and infects the population. What "causes" the epidemic – the man or the virus? Clearly, either answer is equally correct depending upon the conceptual system within which one is working. We should be too close to reifying an abstraction if we said that, in similar fashion, either men or things can become "hosts" to culture. Also, this metaphor, like the definition of culture as "social heredity" implies too passive a relationship between men and culture – as if culture were a bacteria acquired entirely casually and unknowingly by contact. And yet the simile remains tantalizing. One may even point out that it is less misleading than "social heredity," for genes are acquired in fixed and immutable form – once and for all – at birth, whereas bacteria change with the host and in time, though a given species remains recognizable in spite of this variation according to different hosts.

THE PHILOSOPHER: Could you relate what you have just said to the arguments over the proposition of [Oswald] Spengler, [Pitirim] Sorokin, and others that cultures have their own independent laws of growth and decay?

THIRD ANTHROPOLOGIST: If what I have said is correct, anthropologists have probably been too hasty in their rejections of these theories. The theories you mention have, to greater or lesser degree, been phrased unfortunately so that condemnations of them as "mystical" or "metaphysical" can be given superficial plausibility. But an anthropologist who really wishes to understand these interpretations can "translate" them into his own conceptual scheme so that, if the levels of abstraction [can] be kept straight, they seem to merit partial acceptance or at least careful reexamination. For, while no culture is "superorganic" in the sense that it would continue to "exist" after all the human beings who shared it had died and all the nonhuman manifestations of that culture had been destroyed, still a culture that is a going concern has properties which exhibit some independence from the other forces with which the culture is in interaction. One of the diagnostic features of a culture is its selectivity. Most specific needs can be satisfied in a wide variety of ways but "the culture selects" only one or a very few of the organically and physically possible modes. "The culture selects" is, to be sure, a metaphorical way of speaking. The *original* choice was necessarily made by an individual and then followed by other individuals (or it wouldn't have become culture). But from the angle of those individuals who later learn this bit of culture the existence of this element in a design for living has the *effect* of a selection which was not made by these human beings as a reaction to their own particular situation but was rather a choice made by individuals long gone but which still tends to bind our contemporary actors. Such a selective awareness of the natural environment, such a stereotyped interpretation of man's place in the world is not merely inclusive; by implication it also excludes other possible alternatives. Because of the "strain toward consistency" in cultures such inclusions and exclusions are meaningful far beyond the specific activity which is overtly involved.

Just as the "choice" of an individual at a crucial epoch commits him in certain directions for the rest of his life, so the original bents, trends, "interests" which become established in the designs for living of a newly formed society tend to channel a culture in some directions as opposed to others. Subsequent variations in the culture – both those which arise internally and those which are a response to contact with other cultures or to changes in the natural environment – are not random. In some sense, at least, there is probably "cultural orthogenesis" as well as biological orthogenesis.

THE LAWYER: Now I only wonder how you are going to make the transition from "culture" to "a culture." No physicist speaks of "a gravity."

FIRST ANTHROPOLOGIST: Surely when the physicist "explains" the falling of certain concrete bodies at a given time and place he must – if he is to be precise as to details – get beyond the general principle of "gravity." He must describe the particular field of gravity which affected those bodies at just that time. Similarly "a culture" is just a convenient short expression for "a special field of that force known as culture."

"CULTURE" AS A DESCRIPTIVE CONCEPT

THE PHYSICIAN: Can we say that culture in general as a descriptive concept means the accumulated treasury of human creation: books, paintings, buildings, and the like; the knowledge of ways of adjusting to our surroundings, both human and physical; language, customs, and systems of etiquette, ethics, religion, and morals that have been built up through the ages?

FIRST ANTHROPOLOGIST: In referring to culture as "a storehouse of adjustive responses" and as a human creation you strike notes upon which we would all now agree. But the objections to an enumerative definition and to a definition which lists, in part, concrete phenomena are serious.

SECOND ANTHROPOLOGIST: Yes, I also now fully share the view that, even at a descriptive level, culture must be considered as an abstraction. Even a "culture trait" is, in a sense, an "ideal type." Take, for instance, the alarm clock. No two are ever exactly alike: some are large, some are small; some work perfectly and others don't; some are shiny and some are painted in soft colors. If we examine minutely enough several which have just been produced by the same factory, we should find that even these show small differences.

THE BUSINESSMAN: Let me take this idea a little further. A bank is a general term applying to all the specific institutions that conduct certain types of financial transactions. Doesn't culture, then, as a descriptive concept mean the sum of all such generalizations?

FIRST ANTHROPOLOGIST: I would prefer to say "a summation of all the ideas for standardized types of behavior."

THIRD ANTHROPOLOGIST: The notion of defining culture, in a descriptive sense, as a set of blueprints for action in the widest sense (including feeling, of course) is very attractive. And it is probably perfectly sound, provided that it is clearly realized that such a statement is made from the standpoint of the observer, the student of culture, rather than from that of the participant in culture. For the participant much of culture is unverbalized and probably in a still wider sense implicit.

THE PSYCHIATRIST: I agree. I have always protested against such statements as "culture consists of ideas" because we know well from comparative psychiatry that there is also such a thing as "culturally standardized unreason."

FIRST ANTHROPOLOGIST: Yes, while a great deal of culture is cognitive and is cognitively transmitted, the place of feeling bulks enormously.

THE ECONOMIST: Perhaps we need three categories: rational, irrational, and nonrational.

THIRD ANTHROPOLOGIST: Quite. In [Vilfredo] Pareto's jargon, some of culture is "logical," some is "illogical," but probably the highest proportion is "nonlogical."

FOURTH ANTHROPOLOGIST: May we then give the following substantive definition: *By culture we mean all those historically created designs for living, explicit and implicit, rational, irrational, and nonrational, which exist at any given time as potential guides for the behavior of men.*

THE LAWYER: I have only one question: Why is it necessary to say "at any given time"?

FOURTH ANTHROPOLOGIST: Because culture is constantly being created and lost. No definition must suggest that culture is static or completely stable.

SECOND ANTHROPOLOGIST: Does "designs for living" mean that you intend the concept to include only "theory" – that is, the ways in which things ought to be done or felt?

FOURTH ANTHROPOLOGIST: No, "design" denotes both "theory" and "practice." In our own professional jargon[,] "design" is meant to designate both "behavioral patterns" and "ideal patterns." Remember that culture is always a conceptual construct. The anthropologist not only observes that people say (or otherwise indicate) that they have certain standards for behavior, violations of which are punished by great or small sanctions; he equally notes that even disapproved behavior systems tend to fall into certain modalities. From the observer's standpoint it is as if people were unconsciously adhering to certain "blueprints" or "designs" also for conduct which is prohibited or indifferent from the standpoint of shared "moral" norms.

THE LAWYER: May we have a definition of "a culture," in the descriptive sense?

FIRST ANTHROPOLOGIST: *A culture is a historically derived system of explicit and implicit designs for living, which tends to be shared by all or specially designated members of a group.*

THIRD ANTHROPOLOGIST: That satisfies me. The word "system" does a lot of work in that definition. It suggests abstraction. It directly implies that a culture is organized, that it is selective.

THE PSYCHOLOGIST: I like the word "tends." Some of us have in the past felt cheated because we have been assured that studying a culture would give us the common ground against which various personality figures emerged. Our own investigations along this line seem to indicate that it was misleading to depict any single background as being in any literal sense "common" to all members of any group.

FIRST ANTHROPOLOGIST: Yes, just as "tends" reminds us that no individual thinks, feels, or acts precisely as the "design" indicates that he will or should, so also "specially designated" is a reminder that not all of the "blueprints" which constitute a culture are meant to apply to each and every individual. There are sex differentials, age differentials, class differentials, prestige differentials, and so on.

THIRD ANTHROPOLOGIST: It seems to me that you have enunciated two related but separate propositions. It is important that we should not mix them. First, there is the proposition that the sharing is tendency rather than fact. As L. K. Frank puts it, what we can actually observe is the "idiomatic version of each personality's utilization of cultural patterns." And he goes on to make a useful analogy something along these lines: We can abstract the regularities and uniformities and likewise observe the personality distortions and skewings, as we have learned to observe the statistical regularities of a gas but also recognize and acknowledge the irregular and non-conforming behavior of individual molecules of that gas. Second, there is the proposition of the compartmentalization and segmentation of a culture. While each individual's utilization of pattern is idiomatic, some sets of patterns are always felt as appropriate for certain categories of individuals. A background of culture is to be regarded as approximately constant – not for every individual in all groups which have some continuity and functional wholeness, but rather for those who occupy the same set of statuses or perform about the same roles within the total group.

FIRST ANTHROPOLOGIST: Correct. But this important fact must not obscure another fact of equal or greater significance. At least in those groups which have some historical continuity and which are generally designated as "societies," all individuals tend to share common interpretations of the external world and man's place in it. To some degree every individual is affected by this common "view of life." A culture is made up of overt patterned ways of behaving, feeling, and reacting. But it also includes a characteristic set of unstated premises or hypotheses which vary greatly in different societies. Thus one group unconsciously assumes that every chain of actions has a goal and that when this goal is reached tension will be reduced or disappear. To another group, thinking based upon this assumption is meaningless: they see life not as a series of purposive sequences but as made up of experiences which are satisfying in and of themselves, rather than as means to ends.

THE PHILOSOPHER: Are you saying that each culture is integrated about certain dominant interests and in accord with certain postulates and assumptions?

THIRD ANTHROPOLOGIST: Probably very few cultures indeed can be regarded as completely integrated systems. Most cultures, like most personalities, can be regarded as equilibria of opposed tendencies. But even in cultures which do not approach complete integration one may detect certain recurrent themes in a variety of specific contexts.

THE PSYCHOLOGIST: Are you talking about what some anthropologists have called the "absolute logics," of a people or about what others refer to as "the logic of the sentiments?"

THIRD ANTHROPOLOGIST: Both. Every people not only has a sentiment structure which is to some degree unique but also a more or less coherent body of distinctive presuppositions about the world. This last is really a borderland between reason and feeling. Perhaps in a certain ultimate sense the "logic" of all peoples is the same. But their premises are certainly different.

THE PHILOSOPHER: Do you mean the conscious, the stated premises – what a logician would call the "postulates" – or the unstated premises or "assumptions"?

THIRD ANTHROPOLOGIST: Both. Certainly some of the most critical premises of any culture are often unstated, even by the intellectuals of the group. Likewise the basic categories of "thinking" are implicit, save, perhaps, to a tiny minority in rationally sophisticated societies like our own.

FOURTH ANTHROPOLOGIST: If the premises and the system of categories are unconscious, how are they transmitted?

FIRST ANTHROPOLOGIST: Mainly, probably, through the language. Especially the morphology of a language preserves the unformulated philosophy of the group. For example, Dorothy Lee has shown that among the Trobriand Islanders "the sequence of events does not automatically fall into the mold of causal or telic relationship." Because of the mold which grammar imposes upon their "thinking" these people find certain types of communication with Europeans difficult since Europeans almost inevitably talk in causal terms. The very morphology of any language inevitably begs far-reaching questions of metaphysics and of values.

A language is not merely an instrument for communication and for rousing the emotions. Every language is also a device for categorizing experience. The continuum of experience can be sliced very differently. We tend all too easily to assume that the distinctions which Indo-European languages (or our own particular language) force us to make are given by the world of nature. As a matter of fact, comparative linguistics shows very plainly that any speech demands unconscious conceptual selection on the part of its speaker. No human organism can respond to all the kaleidoscopic stimuli which impinge upon it from the external world. What we notice, what we talk about, what we feel as important [are] in some part a function of our linguistic patterns. Because these linguistic habits tend to remain as unquestioned "background phenomena," each people tends to take its fundamental categories, its unstated basic premises for granted. It is assumed that others will "think the same way," for "it's only human nature." When others face the same body of data but come to different conclusions, it is seldom thought that they might be proceeding from different premises. Rather, it is inferred that they are "stupid" or "illogical" or "obstinate."

FOURTH ANTHROPOLOGIST: How does it happen that different people have different systems of categories?

FIRST ANTHROPOLOGIST: A language is one aspect of a culture. Therefore, we must refer to the "accidents of history" and to all the other forces which we mentioned as producing the forms of culture. Each individual tends to classify his experiences along the lines laid down by the grammar to which he is habituated, but the grammar itself is a cultural product. Dorothy Lee has made this point very well:

> True enough, the thought of the individual must run along its grooves; but these grooves, themselves, are a heritage from individuals who laid them down in an unconscious effort to express their attitudes toward the world. Grammar contains in crystal[l]ized form the accumulated and accumulating experience, the Weltanschauung of a people.

THIRD ANTHROPOLOGIST: There is perhaps also another angle to the perpetuation of cultural organization, particularly at the implicit level. This is the culturally prescribed system of child training. If all adults have been subjected to about the same deprivations and frustrations during socialization, they tend to see life in somewhat the same terms. Roheim says, "The dominant idea of a culture may be an addiction but it is always a system formation that can be explained on the basis of the infantile situation." Margaret Mead deals with the relation of "infantile traumas" to the one or more focal points in each culture under the conception of "plot in culture."

FOURTH ANTHROPOLOGIST: Although partially won over, I am still happy about this term "implicit culture."

THIRD ANTHROPOLOGIST: A conception of this order is made necessary by certain eminently practical considerations. It is well documented that programs of the British Colonial services or of our own Indian service which have been carefully thought through for their continuity with the cultural inventory and with the overt cultural patterns, nevertheless fail to work out. Intensive investigation also does not reveal any flaws in the set-up at the technological level. The program is sabotaged by resistance which must be imputed to the manner in which the members of the group have been conditioned by *implicit* designs for living to think and feel in ways which were unexpected to the administrator.

FIRST ANTHROPOLOGIST: Students of culture change are also agreed that the way in which a group accepts, rejects, or readapts borrowed elements cannot be fully understood in terms of direct and explicit functions. The process is also related to the cultural structure, including those portions of it which are implicit. Even after the content of the culture of a group of American Indians has become completely European, its way of life still somehow retains a distinctive flavor, as if the "container" remained "aboriginal."

THIRD ANTHROPOLOGIST: We would freely admit that conceptual instruments which are objective enough and precise enough to deal with the patterning of implicit culture are only beginning to be evolved. The importance of tacit cultural premises and categories is probably obvious enough. But the sheer statement of the presence and absence of these (and of all other features of culture, whether implicit or explicit) is not enough. The full significance of any single element in a cultural design will be seen only when that element is viewed in the total matrix of its relationship to other elements and indeed to other designs. Naturally, this includes accent or emphasis, as well as position. Accent is manifested sometimes through frequency, sometimes through intensity. The indispensable importance of these questions of arrangement and emphasis may be driven home by an analogy.

Take a musical chord made up of three notes. If we are told that the three notes in question are A, B, and G, we receive information which is fundamental. But it alone will not enable us to predict the type of sensation which the playing of this chord is likely to evoke in us or in other specified visitors. We need many different sorts of relationship data. Are the notes to be played in that or some other order? What duration will each receive? How will the emphasis, if any, be distributed? We also need, of course, to know whether the chord will be played in the key of C or in the key of B-flat minor, and whether the instrument is to be a piano or an accordion.

The Utility of the Concept "Culture" in its Various Senses

THE BUSINESSMAN: I'd like to interject a practical question: What good is this concept so far as the contemporary world is concerned? What can you do with it?

FIRST ANTHROPOLOGIST: First and foremost I would insist that its use lies in the aid the concept gives to man's endless quest to understand himself and his own behavior. For example, this relatively new idea makes some of the questions which trouble one of the most learned and acute thinkers of our age, Reinhold Niebuhr, seem pseudo-problems. In his recent book *The Nature and Destiny of Man*[,] he argues that the universally human sense of guilt or shame and man's capacity for self-judgment [necessitate] the assumption of supernatural forces. But these facts are susceptible of self-consistent and relatively simple "explanation" in purely naturalistic terms through the concept of culture. Social life among humans never occurs without a system of "conventional understandings" which are transmitted more or less intact from generation to generation. Any individual is familiar with some of these and they constitute a set of standards against which he judges himself. To the extent that he fails to conform he experiences discomfort, because the intimate conditioning of infancy and childhood puts great pressure on him to internalize these norms, and his unconscious tendency is to associate withdrawal of love and protection or active punishment with deviation.

This and other issues which have puzzled philosophers and scientists for countless generations become fully or partially understandable by means of this fresh conceptual instrument. But if your interest is in action rather than thought, the principal claim which can be made for culture is that it helps us enormously toward predicting human behavior. One of the reasons that such prediction has not been very successful thus far has been that it has been carried out, for the most part, on the naïve assumption of a minutely homogeneous "human nature." In the framework of this assumption all human thinking proceeds from the same premises; all human beings are motivated by the same needs and goals. But in the cultural framework we see that, while the ultimate logic of all peoples may be the same (and thus communication and understanding are possible), the thought processes depart from radically different premises – especially unconscious or unstated premises. But those who have the cultural outlook are more likely to look beneath the surface and bring the culturally determined premises to the light of day. This may well not bring about immediate agreement and harmony, but it will at least facilitate a more rational approach to the problem of "international understanding" and to diminishing friction between groups within a nation.

The conception of culture also encourages paying attention to the more concrete aspects of ways of life other than our own. It suggests, for example, the usefulness of knowledge of alien "customs" if we wish to predict how a foreign people will behave in a certain situation and of respect for these same customs if we wish to get along with that foreign people.

A culture is not only a reticulum of patterned means for satisfying needs but equally a network of stylized goals for individual and group achievement. If we need to predict human action we must not assume that the effective motivations in all human groups are the same. Even the primary drives, like hunger and sex, though biological "givens," are subtly modified and channeled by culture. What kind of food, what type of sexual experience will be most striven after cannot be predicted through biological knowledge alone. There exists for every human group "secondary drives." Among us, for example, the "need" for cars or radios often goads individuals even harder than that for sexual satisfaction. Every culture is also a structure of expectancies. If we know a culture, we know what various classes of individuals within it expect from each other – and from outsiders of various categories. We know what types of activity are held to be inherently gratifying.

SECOND ANTHROPOLOGIST: One great contribution is that of providing some persons with some detachment from the conscious and unconscious emotional values of their own culture. The phrase "some detachment" must be emphasized. An individual who viewed the designs for living of his group with complete detachment would almost certainly be disoriented and unhappy. But I can prefer (that is, feel affectively attached to) American manners while at the same time perceiving certain graces in English manners which are lacking or more grossly expressed in ours. Thus while unwilling to forget that I am an American and hence with no desire to ape English drawing room behaviors, I can still derive a lively pleasure from association with English people on "social" occasions. Whereas if I have no detachment, if I am utterly provincial, I am likely to regard English manners as utterly ridiculous, uncouth, perhaps even immoral. With that attitude I shall certainly not get on well with the English and I am likely to resent bitterly any modification of our manners in the English or any other direction. Such attitudes clearly do not make for international understanding, friendship, and cooperation. They equally make for a too rigid social structure.

Anthropological documents and anthropological teachings are valuable, therefore, in that they tend to emancipate individuals from a too perfervid allegiance to every item in the cultural inventory. The person who has been exposed to the anthropological perspective by incongruity is more likely, on the one hand, to "live and let live" both within his own society and in his dealings with members of other societies; on the other hand, he will probably be more flexible in regard to needful changes in social organization to meet changed technological structure and changed economies.

THIRD ANTHROPOLOGIST: In a way, I would say that the most important implication of "culture" for action is the profound truth (so frequently overlooked by every sort of "social planners") that you can never start with a clean slate so far as human beings are concerned. No human being or group of human beings can ever freshly see the world in which they move. Every human is born into a world defined by already existing cultural patterns. Just as an individual who has lost his memory is no longer "normal," so the idea that at any point in its history a society can become completely emancipated from its past culture is inconceivable. This is the source of the tragic failure of the Weimar constitution in Germany. Seen in detached context, it was an admirable document. But it failed miserably in actual life, partly because it provided for no continuity with existent designs for acting, feeling, and thinking. Finally, as the word "design" in our definitions implies, every culture has organization as well as content. This fact carries with it the highly practical warning to administrators and lawmakers that a "custom" which it is desired to abolish or modify cannot be isolated. Any change may have repercussions in areas of behavior where they are least expected. While serious anthropologists disavow all messianic pretensions and make no claim that "culture" is any "philosopher's stone" which will end all problems, nevertheless the explanatory concept does carry an overtone of legitimate hope to troubled men.

---

2. Relativism and Incommensurability

One of the main challenges in the study of cultural systems is epistemological in nature. The question is whether it is possible for an observer in one society to accurately and fully comprehend the meaning of rituals, symbols, and artifacts in another society. Some take the view that it may not be possible because certain phenomena are incommensurable; that is, that there are no corresponding analogues in the observer's culture.

Peter Winch, *Understanding a Primitive Society*, 1 Am. Phil. Q. 1, 307, 315 (1964)

[In this famous essay, the author inquires whether a person who has grown up accepting science can fully comprehend the worldview of those who embrace supernatural explanations for events. The question is whether the contrasting systems of belief – magic versus science – are so incompatible with each other as to inhibit someone socialized in one system of belief from grasping the logic in the other. In his treatment of the beliefs of the African Zande people, the author observes the following. – *Eds.*]

[The Zande] believe that certain of their members are witches, exercising a malignant occult influence on the lives of their fellows. They engage in rites to counteract witchcraft; they consult oracles, and use magic medicines to protect themselves from harm.

An anthropologist studying such a people wishes to make those beliefs and practices intelligible to himself and his readers. This means presenting an account of them that will somehow satisfy the criteria of rationality demanded by the culture to which he and his readers belong: a culture whose conception of rationality is deeply affected by the achievements and the methods of the sciences, and one which treats such things as a belief in magic or the practice of consulting the oracles as almost a paradigm of the irrational. The strains inherent in this situation are very likely to lead the anthropologist to adopt the following posture: We know that Zande beliefs in the influence of witchcraft, the efficacy of magic medicines, the role of oracles in revealing what is going on and what is going to happen, are mistaken, illusory. Scientific methods of investigation have shown conclusively that there are no relations of cause and effect such as are implied by these beliefs and practices. All we can do then is to show how such a system of mistaken beliefs and inefficacious practices can maintain itself in the face of objections that seem to us so obvious. . . .

Something else is also suggested by this discussion: the forms in which rationality expresses itself in the culture of a human society cannot be elucidated simply in terms of the logical coherence of the rules according to which activities are carried out in that society. For, as we have seen, there comes a point where we are not even in a position to determine what is and what is not coherent in such a context of rules, without raising questions about the point which following those rules has in the society. . . . The conception of reality is indeed indispensable to any understanding of the point of a way of life.

Clearly, interpretations of other cultures are both influenced and constrained by our own worldviews. We must be aware of our cultural biases. Even then, some degree of misinterpretation is probably inevitable.

3. Anthropological Definitions and Concepts

As we shall see, there are many different definitions of culture, which often vary according to one's professional discipline. Writers may define culture as though it consisted entirely of written texts or high culture, by which they mean novels, poetry, and plays, whereas scientists may think of mold when they hear the term. Social scientists are inclined to interpret culture as mass or popular culture. They refer to the media such as television, radio, and the so-called new media, whose emergence has been facilitated by the Internet.

For those who study high culture and popular culture, one can identify the individuals who created a particular cultural form. By contrast, the term "culture" in the fields of anthropology and folklore has historically referred to traditional culture or what we might call a way of life. Cultural artifacts and patterns of expression usually belong to an entire community so as to make it all but impossible to determine the identity of the person or perhaps the small group who created them. Also, traditional cultural expressions are more likely to vary over time and exist in multiple forms. Shakespeare's *King Lear* may always be essentially the same, no matter when one reads it or whatever the particular staging of it, and *Star Wars* may be the same no matter how many times one watches it, but there are many substantial versions of the Cinderella theme in folklore that ensure that its telling will continue to evolve throughout the ages.

a. Early Definitions

Over the years there has been substantial debate about the definition of culture.[1] Several early formulations presumed that some cultures were superior to others, thereby giving rise to a theory of cultural evolutionism. In the late nineteenth century, however, the English anthropologist E. B. Tylor rejected that presumption, offering instead an early but enduring definition of culture: "Culture or civilisation, taken in its wide ethnographic sense, is that complex whole that includes knowledge, belief, art, morals, law, custom, and any other capabilities and habits acquired by man as member of society."[2] Tylor, who was said to have been influenced by German historians, referred to anthropology as the science of culture. Another famous explanation of culture, as follows, distinguished it from civilization.

Bronislaw Malinowski, *Culture*, *in* Encyclopaedia of the Social Sciences 621, 645 (Edwin R.A. Seligman ed., 1937)

Man varies in two respects: in physical form and in social heritage, or culture. . . . This social heritage is the key concept of cultural anthropology, the other branch of the comparative study of man. It is usually called culture in modern anthropology and social science. The word ["]culture["] is at times used synonymously with civilization, but it is better to use the two terms distinctively, reserving civilization for a special aspect of more advanced cultures. Culture comprises inherited artifacts, goods, technical

[1] For incisive analyses, see David Bidney, *The Concept of Culture and Some Cultural Fallacies*, 46 Am. Anthropologist 30 (1944); Paul Bohannan, *Rethinking Culture: A Project for Current Anthropologists*, 14 Current Anthrop. 357 (1973).

[2] E.B. Tylor, 1 Primitive Culture 1 (1871).

processes, ideas, habits and values. Social organization cannot be really understood except as a part of culture; and all special lines of inquiry referring to human activities, human groupings, and human ideas and beliefs can meet and become cross[-]fertilized in the comparative study of cultures. . . . Culture is then essentially an instrumental reality which has come into existence to satisfy the needs of man in a manner far surpassing any direct adaptation to the environment. Culture endows man with an additional extension of his anatomical apparatus, with a protective armor of defenses and safeguards, with mobility and speed through media where his direct bodily equipment would have entirely failed him. Culture, the cumulative creation of man, extends the range of individual efficiency and of power of action; and it gives a depth of thought and breadth of vision undreamed of in any animal species. The sources of all this [consist] in the cumulative character of individual achievements and in the power to share in common work. Culture thus transforms individuals into organized groups and gives these an almost indefinite continuity.

---

b. Later Definitions: The Influence of Relativism

At the beginning of the twentieth century, Franz Boas challenged cultural evolutionism, introducing relativism to the discipline of anthropology. Between 1900 and 1950, Boas's approach was the dominant view of culture. According to Boas, "Culture embraces all the manifestations of social habits of a community, the reactions of the individual as affected by the habits of the group in which he lives, and the products of human activity as determined by these habits."[3]

Boas's conceptualization was thoroughly egalitarian in its implications. It was therefore used in a highly beneficial way to challenge racist ideology. One of Boas's students, Ruth Benedict, however, formulated cultural relativism in a controversial way. In *Patterns of Culture*, she described the status of cultural systems as having "equally valid patterns of life."[4] The difficulty with this formulation is that a relativist has no absolute standard by which to evaluate the relative status of different cultural systems and thereby conclude that they have equal validity. That is to say, a relativist who contends that norms of validity are determined within a particular social context, from an internal point of view, cannot then appeal to a norm that is external to cultures by means of which to judge the validity of those cultures. Benedict's unfortunate conceptualization led to the criticism that cultural relativism is self-refuting.

Other ways to theorize about cultural relativism avoid this fallacy. Melville Herskovits, another student of Boas's, maintained that "[e]valuations are relative to the social context in which they are made." If we modify his statement so that it reads instead "some evaluations are relative to the social context in which they are made," the theory is no longer self-contradictory. This means that some transcultural assessments may legitimately be

[3] Franz Boas, *Anthropology*, *in* 2 Encyclopedia of the Social Sciences, (1937).

[4] Ruth Benedict, Patterns of Culture 278 (1934).

made that are not relative to the social context; hence, relativism does not undercut its own validity.

Another challenge to relativists is the implication that their theory requires tolerance, thereby undermining their ability to criticize moral practices in other cultures. There was no reason, however, why the theory had to be construed in this way. The mere fact that one acknowledges the existence of multiple ethical systems in different cultures does not require that one accept them. As Robert Redfield put it:

> The two parts of the doctrine are not logically or necessarily interdependent. The first part says that people are brought up to see the value in things that their local experience has suggested. The second part says that we should respect all cultures. But there is no true "therefore" between these two parts. It cannot be proved from the proposition that values are relative, that we ought to respect all systems of values. We might just as well hate them all.[5]

The theory of cultural relativism is more properly understood as a descriptive theory that simply acknowledges the existence of differing systems without requiring that one take a position on their validity, let alone a hierarchy.

The early history of anthropology as a discipline witnessed a schism between British social anthropologists, who primarily studied social structure, and American anthropologists, who mainly focused on culture. Consequently, the search for a definition of culture seems to have taken place primarily in the United States, and within American anthropology there were numerous definitions. A. L. Kroeber and Clyde Kluckhohn compiled several hundred of these definitions in their book *Culture: A Crucial Review of Concepts and Definitions* (1952), which was part of an effort to come up with a working definition for the social sciences. In the end, they proposed the following formulation:

> Culture consists of patterns, explicit and implicit, of and for behavior acquired and transmitted by symbols, constituting the distinctive achievement of human groups, including their embodiments in artifacts; the essential core of culture consists of traditional (i.e., historically derived and selected) ideas and especially their attached values; cultural systems may, on the one hand, be considered, as products of action, on the other as conditioning elements of further action.[6]

This influential approach is known as the pattern theory of culture.

c. Postmodern Theory and Cultural Studies

With the rise of postmodern theory, culture became a contested concept in the social sciences and humanities. This was accompanied by a reconsideration of anthropological fieldwork as an objective method. Clifford Geertz, in *The Interpretation of Culture,*

[5] Robert Redfield, The Primitive World and Its Transformations 146–47 (1962); *see also* Alison Dundes Renteln, *Relativism and the Search for Human Rights*, 90 Am. Anthropologist 56 (1988).

[6] A.L. Kroeber & Clyde Kluckhohn, Culture: A Crucial Review of Concepts and Definitions 181 (1952).

emphasized the subjective nature of ethnography, which he called "thick description."[7] Despite the leading role anthropologists had played in championing the study of culture, some of them questioned its continuing validity, claiming that any attempt to characterize a culture risks essentializing the group. The gist of the argument is that describing cultures *in toto* leads to oversimplifying them insofar as there are many subgroups within a culture, among which there can be internal disagreement over cultural practices.

Culture was contested not only within the field of anthropology. Among those challenging the notion were sociologists and historians who thought the standard view of culture treated it as a static concept. They also stressed that customs can be easily modified and manipulated. For many, the key idea was that cultural traditions are socially constructed to achieve political objectives, usually of those wielding power.

Eric Hobsbawm, in his study of British monarchical tradition, coined the term "invented tradition," a concept that stresses the production and malleability of culture by elites for political purposes. He questioned the assertion that particular cultural traditions were actually as well established as many believed. In his influential book *The Invention of Tradition*, he argues, "'Traditions' which appear or claim to be old are often quite recent in origin and sometimes invented."[8] For instance, although the Scottish kilt seems ancient, it is really a recently invented tradition. In contrast, he argues that genuinely ancient material has also been used to invent traditions. Thus, folk songs were revised for nationalist purposes. Hobsbawm draws a distinction between tradition and custom, arguing that custom varies but that tradition is apt to be more static:

> Custom is what judges do; "tradition" (in this instance invented tradition) is the wig, robe and other formal paraphernalia and ritualized practices surrounding their substantial action. The decline of "custom" inevitably changes the "tradition" with which it is habitually intertwined.[9]

The traditions consciously invented in the period after the Industrial Revolution fit a typology.[10]

One important branch of postmodern theory is what came to be known as cultural studies, an intellectual movement that has been described as a "tendency across

[7] Clifford Geertz, *Thick Description: Toward an Interpretive Theory of Culture*, *in* The Interpretation of Cultures 307 (1971).

[8] Eric Hobsbawm, *Introduction: Inventing Traditions*, *in* The Invention of Tradition 1 (Eric Hobsbawm & Terence Ranger eds., 1984).

[9] *Id.* at 2–3.

[10] They seem to belong to three overlapping types: (1) those establishing or symbolizing social cohesion or the membership of groups, real or artificial communities; (2) those establishing or legitimizing institutions, status, or relations of authority; and (3) those whose main purpose was socialization, the inculcation of beliefs, value systems, and conventions of behavior. Although traditions of the first two types were certainly devised (as those symbolizing submission to authority in British India), it may be tentatively suggested that the first type was prevalent, and the other functions regarded as implicit in or flowing from a sense of identification with a community and/or the institutions representing, expressing, or symbolizing it such as a nation.

Id. at 9.

various disciplines, rather than a discipline itself."[11] In contrast to mainstream anthropology's emphasis on careful ethnography in the field, the cultural studies approach uses the technique of deconstruction. It seeks to identify the power relations implicit in social systems to reveal how culture serves power elites and enhances their hegemony.[12]

Cultural studies can be traced to French structuralists (Ferdinand de Saussure, Claude Lévi-Strauss, and Roland Barthes) and poststructuralists (Michel Foucault, Pierre Bourdieu). A leading institution in this movement was the University of Birmingham Center for Contemporary Cultural Studies (CCCS) during the 1960s.[13]

Postcolonial theory also relied on these techniques. Cultural studies influenced the study of imperialism and colonialism and inspired Edward Said to call attention to Eurocentric views in colonial scholarship, noting the tendency to view the "other" in binary categories, a framework that came to be known as Orientalism.[14] Another strand of postmodern thought maintains that globalization has led to a universal culture of McDonald's, the Gap, and other shared commodities. Although there is some truth to the claim that the Internet, air travel, and other technological innovations have blurred cultural differences, individuals have not, however, discarded their cherished cultural heritages.

d. The Contemporary Defense of the Concept of Culture

Despite the popularity of the postmodern critiques of culture, the concept of culture is alive and well, as the following reading confirms.

[11] A Companion to Cultural Studies 1 (Toby Miller ed., 2001).

[12] What is distinctive about cultural studies is an analytic focus on the form and content of culture that draws heavily on French structuralism and its legacy. This approach looks on culture as being like a linguistic system or text that can be decoded in terms of its constituent signs, symbols, myths, narratives, language games, discourses, and codes. Such an understanding calls for cultural analysis as a form of hermeneutic activity, in which the analyst uncovers and redescribes core features of overarching systems of meaning. Central to this endeavor is a desire to assert the relative autonomy of culture, that is, to treat culture as an independent variable that should be understood neither as a simple reflection of hidden interests nor as a set of functionally determined values and norms. The process of analysis therefore involves decoding, interpreting, and recoding the cultural system before going on to trace the contingent ways that culture is articulated with concrete social practices and structures.

Philip Smith, *Cultural Studies, Overview*, *in* 1 Encyclopedia of Violence, Peace, and Conflict 525–38 (1999).

[13] Spearheaded by Stuart Hall, the Birmingham school drew heavily on the work of Antonio Gramsci. Gramsci's key concept of hegemony emphasizes the role of consciousness in maintaining class domination by short-circuiting critical thinking and by defining reality in particular ways. Drawing on Gramsci's idea of a war of position, Hall argued that it is vacuous to speak of a single dominant ideology (e.g., capitalism), but rather we must look at the contingent discourses and struggles though which a plurality of hegemonic discourses are reproduced and challenged. With this credo in mind, the members of the CCCS undertook a variety of empirical studies, many of them ethnographic, charting hegemonic and counterhegemonic discourses in areas such as racism and immigration, strikes and industrial conflict, law-and-order politics, and youth subcultures. Typically these empirical investigations combined Gramsci with other French Marxist influences such as Althusser, Barthes, and De Certeau. The common substantive theme, however, was the way a politics of repression could be legitimized.

Id. at 532–33.

[14] Edward Said, Culture and Imperialism (1994).

Richard A. Shweder, *Culture: Contemporary Views, in* 5 International Encyclopedia of the Social & Behavioral Sciences 3151, 3157 (Neil Smelser & Paul Baltes eds., 2001) (reprinted with permission of Elsevier Ltd.)

It is important to recognize that valid social criticism and questions of moral justification are not ruled out by the "standard view" of "culture." Nothing in the Kroeber and Kluckholn formulation[15] suggests that the things that other peoples desire are in fact truly desirable or that the things that other peoples think are of value are actually of value. Consensus does not add up to moral truth. In other words, a definition of culture *per se* is not a theory of the "good." From a moral point of view, one need not throw out the idea of culture just because some tyrant puts the word "culture" to some misuse, or because at times some ethnic groups enter into geopolitical conflict.

The idea of culture also does not imply passive acceptance of received practice. . . . Even fully rational, fully empowered . . . human beings discover that membership in some particular tradition of meanings and values is an essential condition for personal identity and individual happiness. . . .

The idea of culture also does not imply the absence of debate, contestation, or dispute among members of a group. Nor does it necessarily imply the existence of within group homogeneity in knowledge, belief, or practice. Every cultural system has experts and novices; one does not stop being a member of a common culture just because cultural knowledge is distributed and someone knows much more than you do about (e.g.) how to conduct a funeral or apply for a mortgage. One does not stop being a member of a common culture just because there are factions in the community. The claim that there are between group cultural differences has never implied the absence of within group differentiation or that there is no variation around the mean.

The idea of "culture" does not imply that every item of culture is in the possession or consciousness of every member of that culture. The idea of culture merely directs our attention to those ideas about what is true, good, beautiful, and efficient that are acquired by virtue of membership in some group. Not everything has to be shared for a "culture" to exist. Members of a cultural community do not always agree about this or that, but they do take an interest in each other's ideas about what is true, good, beautiful, and efficient because those ideas (and related practices) have a bearing on the perpetuation of their way of life, and what they share is that collective inheritance. Since the standard view does not assume that a culture is a well-bounded, fixed, and homogenous block, the critique of the concept of "culture" that starts with the observation of internal variation and ends "therefore there is no cultural system" should have been a nonstarter.

The idea of culture also does not imply that other kinds of peoples are "other," in the sense of being less than human or possessing qualities that entitle us to intervene in their way of life. We live in a multicultural

[15] This formulation – the pattern theory of culture – is set forth in the text at note 6, *supra*.

world consisting (as Joseph Raz has put it) "of groups and communities with diverse practices and beliefs, including groups whose beliefs are inconsistent with one another." The aspirations (a) not to lose your cultural identity, (b) not to assimilate to mainstream pressures, (c) not to be scattered throughout the city, country or world, (d) not to glorify the Diaspora, and (e) not to join the highly individualistic and migratory multinational, multiracial but (in many ways) monocultural cosmopolitan elite are real and legitimate aspirations, and those aspirations cannot be properly understood by treating them as illusions. They are certainly not the only legitimate aspirations in a multicultural world; there is much that can be said in favor of a liberal cosmopolitan life. But they are legitimate aspirations. Even in a "global" world, cultural communities and ethnic groups are not going to disappear. We cannot avoid the question, what form does and should multiculturalism take in our emerging postmodern society? Perhaps that is one reason that so many social scientists and public policy analysts look to anthropology for a useful concept of "culture," not for no concept of culture at all.

NOTES AND QUESTIONS

1. What are the main differences in the way that culture was conceptualized in early-twentieth-century anthropology as compared with cultural studies at the end of the twentieth century?
2. How do the contemporary debates about the concept of culture affect the ability of scholars to do fieldwork? To what extent should ethnography remain a viable methodology?
3. Are there any common concerns in the various formulations of culture? Virtually all theories of culture emphasize that it must be viewed as dynamic. Communities may consciously choose to discard anachronistic or objectionable traditions. When they do not, individuals may decide that they wish to opt out of their societies, which admittedly may be difficult to accomplish in some places. As a theoretical matter, however, this means that, despite the tremendous power of culture in shaping perception and influencing behavior, human agency remains important and should not be discounted. In short, although cultural forces certainly affect individuals, they do not determine their actions.
4. How useful is the concept of culture? See Lila Abu-Lughod, *Writing against Culture, in* Recapturing Anthropology: Working in the Present 137–62 (Richard G. Fox ed., 1991), and Christoph Bruman's eloquent response, *Writing for Culture: Why a Successful Concept Should Not Be Discarded*, 50 Current Anthrop. S1–S13 (1999) and comments in response at S13–S27.

4. Enculturation: How Culture Affects Perception and Behavior

Every person is born into a culture and acquires the values of that society by enculturation. Culture influences both perception and behavior in myriad ways. Remarkably, individuals are, for the most part, unconscious of the processes by which this occurs.

The symbolic meaning of numbers provides a classic example of how culture affects social understandings of normalcy. For example, although turning forty is considered a major life transition in some societies, it is not universally regarded in this way because the number forty means different things in different societies. Similarly, in the United States, but not elsewhere, the number thirteen is an unlucky number. In China, four is an unlucky number because the word for it is a homonym for the word for death. But the number eight is considered lucky in China, thereby explaining why the Beijing Olympic Organizing Committee decided to begin the 2008 Summer Games there on August 8, 2008, at 8:08 p.m. The number three is also a cultural artifact: "trichotomy exists but it is not part of the nature of nature. It is part of the nature of culture."[16]

Color symbolism also often serves as an illustration of cultural differences in perception. At funerals, for example, black is the color customarily worn in North America and Europe, but in China it is white. In the West, a bride usually wears a white gown, whereas a bride wears red at a traditional wedding ceremony in China.

There is also enormous cultural variation in the meaning of particular gestures. What is useful at home can be embarrassing, if not lethal, abroad.

What's A-O.K. in the U.S.A. Is Lewd and Worthless Beyond, N.Y. Times, Aug. 18, 1996, at E7

(Reuters) – The opening session of Bangladesh's new Parliament turned into chaos Sunday after opposition legislators reacted with fury to an alleged offensive thumb gesture by Shipping Minister A.S.M. Abdur Rab. The gesture is considered a grave insult in Bangladesh. "This is a dishonor not only to Parliament but to the nation," said the deputy leader of the opposition Bangladesh Nationalist Party, Badruddoza Chowdhury. "The minister must apologize for his showing of the thumb. And the speaker must ask the minister to do so," he said amid shouting from his party colleagues.

What had the shipping minister done to provoke such wrath? He gave the old thumbs-up. While in the United States, that's just a friendly sign for "All right!" or "Good going!"; in Bangladesh, Australia and other parts of the world, particularly in Islamic countries, that jaunty gesture is the exact equivalent of an upraised middle finger. Yes, it is what is known to generations of high school students as "flipping the bird." That may explain why one American newspaper correspondent's interviews with the random Islamic men on the street inevitably ended with the men furious. The correspondent wound up all of his interviews with a clap on the back, a big grin, and a hearty thumbs-up.

The thumbs-up is not the only gesture whose meaning an American innocent abroad could mistake. There is a huge array of cross-cultural gaffes to be made. Here are some examples, excerpted from "Gestures: The Do's and Taboos of Body Language Around the World," by Roger E. Axtell (1991, reprinted by permission of the publisher, John Wiley & Sons, Inc.).

[16] Alan Dundes, *The Number Three, in* Interpreting Folklore 134 (Alan Dundes ed., 1980).

The A-O.K.

The "A-O.K." sign, with the thumb and index finger joined in a circle, has insulting and scatological connotations in many Latin American countries. So, when then Vice President Richard M. Nixon, who always had a certain grace problem, landed on one of his trips south of the border in the 1950's and emerged to greet a crowd with both hands up in a double "A-O.K.," he was, in effect, telling the welcomers to – well, you get the picture.

The A-O.K. does no better elsewhere: A Frenchman, particularly in the South of France, would read that very same gesture as meaning "zero" or "worthless." I once took a hotel room in France and when the concierge asked "Is your room satisfactory?" I replied with the "O.K." sign. With a shrug of irritation, the concierge said, "If you don't like it, we'll just have to find you another room."

In Japan, the thumb and forefinger making a circle is used as [a] symbol for money.... Because of this use, the gesture could have serious consequences when incorrectly used. Imagine a Western businessperson who has negotiated a contract with a Japanese and, at the conclusion, casually makes the O.K. sign.... The Japanese might say to himself "[O]h! he's giving me the sign for 'money.'... Is he asking for a bribe?"

Patting a Child's Head

In India, Sri Lanka and Thailand, patting a child on the head would be shocking and offensive because the head is believed to be the seat of the soul.

"V" for Victory

You think it means "victory" or "peace." But that isn't all it means in England: There, if the palm and fingers face inward, it means 'Up yours!' especially if executed with an upward jerk of the fingers. There may be a connection between the two meanings that dates back 500 years, when the French used to cut off the middle finger and forefinger of the English archers they captured in battle: After the battles of Agincourt and Crecy, so the story goes, where the French were heavily defeated by the expert English archers, the surviving French were marched off the battlefield to the taunts of the victorious English. The English added further insult to the French by holding up their hands, forefinger and middle finger stiffly upright, palms inward, to show both fingers fully intact.

The "Hook 'Em Horns" Sign

The "hook 'em horns" sign, two outside fingers with the pinky and index finger raised up and the middle two fingers folded down, may be beloved of fans of the University of Texas football team, the Longhorns, and it is a good luck gesture in Brazil and Venezuela. Upside down, it is used in American baseball to signify "two outs." But in parts of Africa it is a curse. It is not much appreciated in Italy either: For millions of Italians it is the cornuto, and it signifies an entirely different meaning. It says, "You are being cuckolded." In more kindly terms, one person is signaling to the other that "Your spouse is being unfaithful."

Oh, Waiter!

Here the gesture for hailing a waiter is one arm halfway up in the air, sometimes with the index finger slightly raised. But in Japan that is rude. And in Germany it may bring more than you bargained for: In places like Germany, the signal . . . means "two," because two fingers (one finger and a thumb) are being held upright. So an American might be signaling in this fashion and then saying "Waiter – some water, please," and a German waiter would bring two glasses of water. To order one glass, try the thumbs-up.

Finger Beckoning

In certain places, scratching the air, hissing and even making kissing noises may be preferable to using another common American gesture, curling the index finger in and out, to beckon a waiter. In countries as widespread as Yugoslavia and Malaysia, that gesture is used only for calling animals. Therefore, using it to beckon a human would be terribly impolite. In Indonesia and Australia, it is also used for beckoning "ladies of the night."

Tapping Head with Forefinger

It means "smart" here. In Holland, if the finger is tapped to the center of the forehead, it means "he's crazy."

He's Crazy

Rotating the forefinger around in front of the ear has two entirely different meanings. In the United States it usually connotes that someone or something is "crazy." In Argentina, it can be a signal to indicate "you have a telephone call."

Stop

Here we know it as the signal for "Stop!" or "That's enough." In Greece, it is called the Moutza, or hand push, and it has filthy roots: The [M]outza reaches back into ancient Greek history when fecal matter and dirt were hurled or pushed into the face of war prisoners. . . . And in West Africa this gesture means "You could have any one of five fathers!" which is another way of calling a person a bastard.

B. Law

1. Jurisprudential Foundations

Political and legal systems vary enormously in their commitment to the promotion, protection, and regulation of cultural activity and expression. If we take account of unwritten law, the *lex non scripta*, among some groups and peoples, all culture forms a kind of customary law. Even if we consider only state legal systems, we find great variation. Bhutan's four pillars of gross national happiness, which support all national policy, include cultural preservation along with sustainable development, environmental protection, and good governance. Short of that level of commitment, some legal systems have constitutional provisions for the promotion, protection, and regulation of culture; some have ministries of culture; some have only a cultural advisory council or commission; and some have no institutional mechanism at all that is focused on culture.

This section provides an overview of jurisprudential foundations that are important to cultural law, as well as an introduction to international, comparative, and indigenous law. Some of the commentary that follows may already be familiar to those who have studied these subjects or related subjects such as legal anthropology and jurisprudence. We first explore some issues regarding the concept of law as a whole.

a. Natural Law and Legal Positivism

In the sphere of cultural law, we are inevitably confronted with a fundamental question about authority and legitimacy: must a proposition of law, as a tool of justice, be inherently moral to be valid? The vast literature on the nature of law reveals an endless debate about the relationship between law and morality. The bookends of this literature, so to speak, are the contending approaches of natural law and legal positivism.

The natural law approach posits the existence of a natural order of things or a higher law in which law and morality largely coincide. An immoral rule or other proposition therefore cannot be called law. Twentieth-century refinements of natural law theory argue that a legal system must have an inner core of moral justification associated with the elusive concepts of fairness and justice and characteristically is more a matter of fair and just procedures than of particular substance.

Michael H. Hoeflich, *Natural Law Theory*, *in* The Oxford Companion to American Law 587 (Kermit L. Hall ed., 2002) (reprinted with the permission of Oxford University Press)

Theories of natural law have played an important role in the development of Western jurisprudence for more than two millennia. Both Plato and Aristotle developed their legal and political theories in part on the assumption that there were laws of universal applicability, found in nature, that were both unchangeable and a standard against which all human, positivist laws could be measured. These theories of natural law were adopted and adapted by the Roman lawyers, and played some role in Roman legal theory. They are found both in the writings of the Roman jurists contained in the *Digest*, one of the constituent parts of the *Corpus Juris Civilis*, and especially in the legal and political writings of Cicero.

During the Middle Ages, natural law theories were further adopted into the laws of the Catholic Church, and became the basis for the theoretical elaboration of law in the writings of Thomas Aquinas. In the early modern period, natural law continued to be a vital force in legal theory on the European continent. Jurists such as [Hugo] Grotius, [Samuel von Pufendorf], and [Francisco Suárez] used natural law as a platform on which to develop their theories of international law. [Niccolò Machiavelli] and [Richard] Hooker used natural law for their theoretical elaborations of notions of sovereignty. Indeed, no European jurist prior to the beginning of the nineteenth century was able to ignore natural law theory. One could argue whether there was such a thing as natural law, but the strength of the natural law tradition was so great that no writer on legal or political subjects for more than two thousand years could fail to deal with it.

In England and the United States, interest in natural law theory was also strong. Many of the crucial debates between Edward Coke and Francis Bacon on the nature of sovereignty and the authority of the common law centered on their differing conceptions of the relationship between natural law and common law. Especially important in these debates and the development of natural law theories in the common law world was the tradition, dating back to Roman law, of seeing natural law as an embodiment of "pure reason" [*recta ratio*]. This notion of natural law as pure reason, combined with the concept that common law, too, was the embodiment of reason, permitted common law jurists to develop a working theory of the congruence between natural law and common law.

In the sphere of public law, natural law theories were of particular importance. The use of natural law theories as a basis for developing concepts of sovereignty in the sixteenth and seventeenth centuries led to the later transformation of these theories into a basis for the development of theories of inherent "natural rights." The works of political theorists such as Montesquieu, [Thomas] Hobbes, and above all, John Locke, wrestled with the crucial issues of whether natural law bestowed certain inalienable natural rights upon individuals, rights that could not be abrogated by positivist laws created either by monarchs or legislatures. Thus, natural law theory in the hands of men such as [John] Locke could be used to create a consistent theory of the right of individuals and groups in order to resist the imposition of positive laws that were in derogation of inalienable rights. Natural law was thus able to be used by jurists and political theorists as a basis for justifying the revolutionary movements of the late eighteenth century. Natural law was, in the words of Edward S. Corwin [a leading American legal scholar], a principal source of the "higher law" theories that helped formulate a distinctively American constitutional jurisprudence and the ideas of "inalienable" rights, particularly to liberty and property and the correlative right of due process, which [underlie] so much of American constitutional law.

. . .

Much of the abolitionist writing in both England and the United States during the eighteenth and early nineteenth century began from the position that slavery as an institution contravened natural law and the inherent rights of human beings and therefore was illicit and invalid.

. . .

Natural law theories met with strong opposition in the latter part of the nineteenth century and the beginning of the twentieth with the rise of new jurisprudential movements such as pragmatism and the historical school. Some of the most prominent American jurists, particularly Oliver Wendell Holmes Jr., vehemently argued against the legitimacy of natural law. While natural theories did not disappear from the legal horizon, they were certainly in eclipse. In the twentieth century, however, they enjoyed something of a limited renaissance.

. . .

The so-called rights revolution of the second half of the twentieth century owes much to the later-eighteenth-century theories of natural law, and the influence of Locke and other theorists is clear in the development of the law in several areas, including, for instance, the development of the idea of a constitutional right to privacy.

Legal positivists, on the other hand, challenge the basic premise of natural law, arguing that law and morality are distinct. For them the morality of a legal system is independent of whether it "counts" as a legal system. In their view, the law is tied to the apparatus of the state, making authority paramount.

John Austin, a nineteenth-century English philosopher, defined what has become the classic definition of legal positivism. "A law," he wrote, is simply "a command which obliges a person or persons to a course of conduct." This conceptualization did not provide for changes in the political or legal order, in particular for the often problematic transition of authority from one sovereign to another. Moreover, a literal application of legal positivism can be troublesome. For example, a robber who orders someone at gunpoint to hand over his wallet would fit the definition of legal authority, a clearly preposterous result.

H. L. A. Hart, a twentieth-century English legal philosopher, suggested that this conclusion demonstrated the inadequacy of Austin's version of legal positivism. In its place he offered a refined theory, proposing that we conceptualize the law to be comprised of primary rules and secondary rules. Whereas primary rules are the ordinary ones by which society operates – for example, do not murder your parents, do not walk on the grass, and do not exceed the speed limit – secondary rules are those that tell us how to change rules, how to settle conflicts among rules, and how to identify valid rules. The most famous of the secondary rules is known as "the rule of recognition." Although this is intended to steer people toward those primary rules that are valid, thereby resolving doubts about their legitimacy, Hart does not provide any means for us to know which secondary rules are valid.

Legal positivism has contributed to a strong bias toward the view that state law is the true, if not only, law, an assumption that leads to a narrow and erroneous concept of legal systems. For example, a blinkered concept of law as no more or less than the command of a sovereign would seem to effectively exclude international law, customary or indigenous law, and ecclesiastical law. Not surprisingly, H. L. A Hart, although a more sophisticated positivist than John Austin, explicitly questioned whether such normative systems meet the minimal requirements for "law."

The divergent views of natural lawyers and legal positivists are most apparent when one examines specific issues. In a famous debate in the *Harvard Law Review*, Lon Fuller, a natural lawyer, and H. L. A. Hart took up the question of whether the authoritative practices of the Nazis, enshrined in statutes that authorized mass killing, amounted to "law." They analyzed the case of a Nazi wife who informed the authorities that her husband had criticized the Third Reich while he was home on leave from the war, although she was under no legal obligation to do so. The husband was subsequently arrested and sentenced to death but instead was subsequently sent to the front. After Germany's defeat, the Nazi wife was prosecuted under a statute that made it a crime to deprive a person of his freedom. Her defense was that because she had acted in accordance with a Nazi law that was valid at the time, she had not committed any crime. Hart argued as follows:

> Many of us might applaud the objective – that of punishing a woman for an outrageously immoral act – but this was secured only by declaring a statute established since 1934 not to have the force of law, and at least the wisdom of this course must be doubted. There were, of course, two other choices. One was to let the woman go unpunished; one can sympathize with and endorse the view that this might have been a bad thing to do. The other was to face the fact that if the woman were to be punished it must be pursuant to the introduction of a frankly retrospective law and with a full consciousness of what was sacrificed in securing her punishment in this way. Odious as retrospective criminal legislation and punishment may be, to have it pursued openly in this case would at least have had the merits of candour. It would have made plain that in punishing the woman a choice had to be made between two evils, that of leaving her unpunished and that of sacrificing a very precious principle of morality endorsed by most legal systems. H. L. A. Hart, *Positivism and the Separation of Law and Morals*, 71 HARV. L. REV. 619 (1958).

Fuller, whose modern version of natural law was informed by the recognition of an "inner morality" of laws identified with fairness and due process, concurred on the retroactive applicability of the post-Nazi law in this case. Interestingly, he took this position despite its incompatibility with a core idea of legality that rules must be announced in advance in order to give individuals the opportunity to conform their behavior to them.

The same issue of retroactive imposition of penal law arose in the 1990s when East German border guards, having shot and often killed persons fleeing across the Berlin wall to West Germany, were prosecuted for doing so after the fall of the Berlin wall. Their defense was that they were simply following the existing law and superior order that were in effect at that time.

Streletz, Kessler and Krenz v. Germany; K.-H. W. v. Germany, as summarized by Beate Rudolf, *in* 95 AM. J. INT'L L. 904 (2001)

In a landmark judgment, *Streletz, Keller and Krenz v. Germany*, the European Court of Human Rights (ECHR) unanimously held that criminal prosecution of the leaders of the German Democratic Republic (GDR) for ordering to kill individuals attempting to flee the GDR is compatible with the principle *nullum crimen sine lege* and consequently with the prohibition on retroactive criminal laws under the European Convention on Human Rights. In a second judgment, *K.-H. W. v. Germany*, with three of the seventeen judges dissenting, the Court affirmed this holding as applied to the criminal responsibility of a low-ranking soldier.

The three applicants in *Streletz* occupied senior positions in the GDR government and in the leadership of the ruling Socialist Unity Party. They were members of the National Defense Council beginning in 1971, 1967, and 1983, respectively, and continuing through the time that the borders opened in 1989. After the unification of Germany, the applicants were prosecuted in the Berlin Regional Court and, in connection with the deaths of seven young men who had attempted to flee the GDR between 1971 and 1989 and were killed by East German border guards or antipersonnel mines, sentenced to prison terms ranging from five to seven years for incitement to commit intentional homicide. The sole applicant in *K.-H. W.* was a member of the East German border guards from 1971 until 1989. In 1972, he and another border guard shot an individual who tried to swim from East Berlin to West Berlin. The Berlin Regional Court found the guard guilty of intentional homicide and sentenced him to juvenile detention for one year and ten months, suspended on probation.

In 1961, the GDR fortified its borders with West Berlin and the Federal Republic of Germany (FRG). This fortification was later reinforced by automatic-fire systems and antipersonnel mines, and came to be known as the "Wall." According to FRG prosecutors, 264 persons lost their lives attempting to flee the GDR between 1961 and 1989; organizations representing the victims' families speak of almost 1,000 dead. The important decisions regarding the establishment and consolidation of the border-policing regime, as well as regarding orders to shoot to kill . . . were made by the GDR's National Defense Council. In particular, the council ordered the installation of the automatic-fire system and the laying of the antipersonnel mines in the "death strip" along the border. From 1961 onwards, pursuant to instructions from the council, the defense minister regularly issued orders – using the same language as the council – that "border violators," or what the ECHR referred to as "fugitives," were to be either arrested or "annihilated." Consequently, rather than punishing soldiers for the killings at the border, the GDR decorated and rewarded them for having killed individuals attempting to flee. The soldiers were also ordered, however, to keep silent about the incidents.

Articles 112 and 22 of the GDR's Criminal Code prohibited homicide and incitement to commit homicide, respectively. Section 17(2)(a) of the People's Police Act 1968, which was replaced in 1982 by the similarly worded Article 27(2) of the State Borders Act, permitted the use of firearms when needed to prevent the commission or continuation of a "serious crime." And Article 213 of the Criminal Code declared that illegally crossing the border constituted a serious crime if committed "by dangerous means or methods." Courts of the GDR ensured the border guards' impunity by regarding the mere use of instruments – such as a ladder or rope – for crossing the border as satisfying the condition of dangerousness. This interpretation was confirmed in a formal statement issued jointly by the GDR's Supreme Court and the supreme prosecutor.

The Unification Treaty between the FRG and the GDR provides, in principle, that for all criminal acts committed before unification, the applicable law is that of the place where the offense was committed. Courts are required, however, to apply the FRG's criminal law in place at the time if it was more lenient than the applicable GDR statutes. Subject to this qualification, FRG courts have thus been obligated to apply the criminal law of another state, the GDR. This compromise approach reflects both the unwillingness of the FRG to incorporate the criminal law of an undemocratic regime into its own legal order, and the intention of the GDR to ensure that its citizens would continue to be judged according to the law in force at the time when the criminal acts took place.

The Berlin Regional Court – the trial court – found that the GDR's border[-]policing regime "flagrantly and intolerably infringed elementary precepts of justice and human rights protected under international law." Thus, the court applied what has come to be known as Radbruch's formula of "statutory injustice": statutory law that is in intolerable contradiction with the requirements of justice is void and should not be applied. For this reason – and citing two leading decisions of the German Federal Court of Justice – the regional court concluded that GDR state practice with regard to these provisions could not be used by applicants as a defense. Consequently, it sentenced them under the Criminal Code of the FRG, which was more lenient than the relevant provisions of the GDR's criminal law.

On appeal, the Federal Court of Justice, in separate opinions, affirmed the convictions of Streletz and Kessler, of K.-H. W., and of Krenz. Referring to earlier judgments of its own, the court pointed out that the border regime and the order to "annihilate" fugitives served the purpose of deterring the population from exercising their internationally recognized human right to leave their own country. Likewise, killing the fugitives at the border constituted an arbitrary deprivation of life in violation of established international law. The GDR's border policy was one that "put the prohibition of crossing the border above the right to life" and that, as such, violated internationally protected precepts of justice and human rights. Cited as authorities in this context were both the International Covenant on Civil and Political Rights and the Universal Declaration of Human Rights. The court thus concluded the border-policing regime violated known requirements of international law. The court also emphasized that the GDR Constitution and the State Borders Act themselves contained provisions that reflected the principle of proportionality; the use of lethal force was justified under those provisions only when a fugitive endangered the life or limb of another person. Except for such situations (which were not at issue in any of the present applications), the State Borders Act could not be used by the applicants either to justify the use of lethal force or to defend against their criminal convictions.

Germany's Federal Constitutional Court upheld the convictions of all four applicants. The court acknowledged that Article 103(2) of the FRG's constitution, or Basic Law, dictates that an "act can be punished only if it was a punishable offense by law before the act was committed." This article is an expression of the rule of law and is fundamental to preserving the trust of citizens. A citizen thereby knows how to "regulate his conduct, on his own responsibility, in such a way as to avoid committing a punishable offence." This assurance and the trust that it creates do not deserve protection, however, in the case of enforcing the criminal laws of a "State that neither practiced democracy and the separation of powers nor respected fundamental rights," and that, in particular, "statutorily defined certain acts as serious criminal offences" while providing border guards with a legal justification for committing those same acts, notwithstanding written law and human rights. In the opinion of the Federal Constitutional Court, to accept a justification for such "grave breach[es]" of internationally recognized human rights – and to reverse the judgments of the Federal Court of Justice – would be contrary to "objective justice," which "embraces the need to respect [these] rights."

The ECHR examined the applicants' complaints under Article 7(1) of the European Convention on Human Rights whose articulation of the principle *nullum crimen sine lege* requires that the "written as well as unwritten law" be analyzed in relation to the question of whether the applicants' actions were criminal under GDR law. Pointing to the "principle of proportionality and the principle that human life must be preserved" as expressed in Article 17(2)(a) and (4) of GDR's People's Police Act, in Article 27(1), (4), and (5) of its State Borders Act, and in Article 30(1) and (2) of its Constitution, the ECHR held that the applicants' convictions complied with what was required under the written law of the GDR.

The ECHR then turned to the problem of whether the unwritten law of the GDR – in particular, the practice of the GDR state organs – could serve as a ground for justifying the border guards' killing of fugitives. The Court found that the objective pursued by that practice was the preservation of the GDR's existence, but that this objective was limited by the GDR Constitution and legislation, according to which human life was the supreme value. The Court concluded that the indiscriminate effects of antipersonnel mines and automatic-fire systems, as well as the categorical nature of the orders given to the border guards, flagrantly violated both the GDR Constitution and the ICCPR [International Covenant on Civil and Political Rights], which was ratified by the GDR in 1974. For these reasons, GDR state practice could not serve as a justification for the applicants' conduct. With respect to the first three applicants, in particular, the Court also stressed that they could not justify their conduct based on state practice, as they themselves were responsible for implementing or maintaining it. Moreover, the Court noted in passing that the mere reference to a practice could not suffice as a justification, thus alluding to the fact that the state practice was kept secret, reflecting the applicants' own conviction that their deeds were unjust.

In rejecting the argument of the applicants in *Streletz* that they could not have foreseen that their actions constituted criminal offenses, as required by Article 7(1) of the European Convention, the Court stated:

> The broad divide between the GDR's legislation and its practice was to a great extent the work of the applicants themselves. Because of the very senior positions they occupied in the State apparatus, they

> evidently could not have been ignorant of the GDR's Constitution and legislation, or of its international obligations and the criticisms of its border-policing regime that had been made internationally.

The Court also noted that the applicants had self-consciously superimposed "secret orders and service provisions" on existing GDR statutes – which were required in an effort to ensure that the border regime did not violate those very statutes. This effort, however, ultimately failed. As the Court concluded – in both the *Streletz* and *W.* judgments – the resulting "[state] practice, which emptied of its substance the legislation on which it was supposed to be based, and which was imposed on all organs of the GDR, including its judicial bodies, cannot be described as 'law' within the meaning of Article 7."

With respect to the fourth applicant (K.-H. W.) and the question of foreseeability, the ECHR observed that "even a private soldier could not show total, blind obedience to orders which flagrantly violated not only the GDR's own legal principles but also internationally recognized human rights." The Court emphasized that the relevant legal norms were accessible, that the applicant had voluntarily enlisted with the border guards, and that he could not have been ignorant of the restrictive policy on the freedom of movement. Consequently, he had been aware of the possibility of having to shoot unarmed persons who were merely trying to leave the country. On this point, three judges dissented. For them, the decisive question was whether, in view of the GDR's failure to prosecute, the fourth applicant's criminal responsibility could be deduced from international law at the material time. Although the border regime itself could be regarded as a crime against humanity in the 1970s, these three judges were not convinced that an individual's participation in that same regime would have resulted in international criminal responsibility at the time that the relevant acts were committed.

In reflecting upon the issues presented in the *Streletz* and *W.* cases, the ECHR remarked that "the problem Germany had to deal with after reunification as regards the attitude to adopt vis-à-vis persons who had committed crimes under a former regime has also arisen for a number of other States which have gone through a transition to a democratic regime." The Court held that "it is legitimate for a State governed by the rule of law to bring criminal proceedings against persons who have committed crimes under a former regime." Likewise, it was entitled to interpret and apply the former regime's legal provisions applicable at the material time in light of the principles of the rule of law; "contrary reasoning would run counter [to] the very principles on which the system of protection put in place by the [European] Convention is built."

In addition to considering the applicants' convictions under German law in relation to Article 7 of the European Convention, the ECHR also considered those convictions under international law in relation to that article. Were the German courts correct in holding that "at the time that they were committed, the applicants' acts constituted offences defined with sufficient accessibility and foreseeability under international law, particularly the rules of international law on the protection of human rights?" In arriving at an affirmative answer, the ECHR stressed that all of the applicants knew or should have known that the border-policing regime "disregarded the need to preserve human life" and "infringed the right to . . . freedom of movement," both of which are internationally protected rights. Moreover, as early as 1968, the GDR's Criminal Code (Article 95) provided that "individual criminal responsibility was to be borne by those who violated the GDR's international obligations or human rights and fundamental freedoms."

Criminal prosecution of acts perpetrated by a repressive regime poses a fundamental dilemma for a democratic state committed to the rule of law. If it respects the practice of impunity prevalent in the previous regime, it may ratify the injustices and human rights violations committed by it. But if it prosecutes, it may violate the principle *nullum crimen sine lege* and thus the very foundations of its own legal order and legitimacy. Faced with this dilemma, the ECHR opted for a restrictive understanding of the principle *nullum crimen sine lege*, limiting its full protective function to norms enacted by a state under the rule of law. The Court's reasoning raises two questions, however. First, in an effort to determine whether applicants' actions violated the law in force at the relevant time, was it sufficient to focus exclusively on the wording of GDR statutes? Second, under what circumstances can one justify exceptions to the principle of nonretroactivity?

In interpreting the GDR's Constitution, statutes, and treaties, the ECHR took them seriously, at face value, and without regard to the practice of the GDR's political and judicial organs. Like the Federal Court of Justice, the Court may be criticized for disregarding the fact that it was not merely the application of the law that was perverted in the GDR, but the legal system as such. In substituting for the actual, perverted language of statutes a new and different understanding that respects the rule of law, the Court misrepresented the character of the prior unjust regime, in which statutes were used to provide every state action with the cover of legality. The Court's approach involved not just a simple change in the interpretation of GDR law, but rather the creation of new law.

Despite the above problem with the ECHR's approach to GDR law, exposing the conflict between the actual practice of the GDR, on the one hand, and its Constitution, statutes, and international obligations, on the other, is not merely a matter of politics or Cold War propaganda. From the point of view of international human rights law, based on the rule of law, if a state articulates a set of written rules and calls it "law," it creates the justified expectation that these rules will be applied in accordance with the ordinary understanding that would emerge under a system that respects the rule of law. This conclusion is particularly warranted if that system expressly presents itself as satisfying the rule of law and the requirements of human rights. Moreover, if arbitrary and largely secretive state practice is considered to have the capacity to alter the meaning of a statutory rule on a matter as fundamental as the prohibition of killing another human being, the idea of law – as the antithesis of arbitrariness – may itself disappear. It is at this point, and for this reason, that a court bound by the rule of law must not show the usual deference to the practice of another state's legal and political institutions with respect to statutory and constitutional interpretation. Any other approach would result in accepting "unlimited interpretation," by which law becomes a mere cloak for arbitrariness. The rejection of the foreign "law" in this case is functionally comparable to a court's application of the public policy ("ordre public") exception in a private law case involving choice of law.

By holding that such arbitrary practice does not constitute "law" in the sense required by Article 7 of the European Convention, the ECHR Court rejected an understanding of law as being a mere system of de facto rules. In that type of system, individuals bound by a legal norm could always hide behind the acts of others under the guise of state practice, and would not be required to assess by themselves the legality of their own acts. In rejecting such a position, the Court emphasized individual responsibility for one's own deeds.

With respect to the second question – that of the exceptions to the principle of nonretroactivity – the ECHR found no fault with the German courts' application of Radbruch's formula in the light of international human rights. This approach has been criticized as being "natural law jurisprudence disguised as enlightened positivism," but the fact remains that the refusal to accept the GDR practice as a defense serves to uphold basic human rights, especially the right to life, under an applicable international treaty – a treaty that is itself positive law. That said, the judgments do not satisfactorily answer the question of which violations of international law warrant an exception to the principle of nonretroactivity. Some jurists have suggested that only crimes under international law should be capable of justifying such exceptions. The decisions of the Federal Court of Justice, the Federal Constitutional Court, and ECHR, however, could be understood as giving a different answer. They are all based on the position that no state has the right to use deadly force to imprison its own population within its borders. This position, broadly conceived, may reflect what some commentators see as the emerging human right to democracy: as applied to this situation, state interests cannot justify restrictions on fundamental human rights if the purpose of those restrictions is the preservation of an undemocratic order that does not respect the rule of law. By the same token, the principle of nonretroactivity cannot be invoked in such circumstances to avoid prosecution for unjustified killing.

Although the *Streletz* and *W.* judgments concerned the unique case of the FRG's having to judge the crimes committed by officials of another state – the GDR – under the laws of that very state, the fundamental tension between positive law and the demands of justice was the same as that for any state facing its own repressive past. Since the courts of such a state have the authority to reinterpret statutes, the question is whether defendants can plead that they could not foresee the change in interpretation and that their acts, therefore, were excused. The ECHR's reasoning in *Streletz* would preclude such a plea, however. All state officials would be required to assess whether their actions would infringe upon fundamental human rights and have the effect of maintaining a regime that disregards the people's rights to democracy and to live in a society governed by the rule of law.

NOTES AND QUESTIONS

1. What are two major differences between the legal positivist and natural law schools of jurisprudence? Are natural law and legal positivism ever compatible or coexistent? How would thinkers in each school view the death penalty as a matter of public policy?
2. How would a legal positivist and a natural law thinker, respectively, analyze the legality of marriage contracts between same-sex couples in a jurisdiction whose family law code limits marriage to that between one man and one woman?
3. Do you agree with Radbruch's formula of statutory injustice – that a statutory law contradicting the requirements of justice is void and should not be applied? Is the formula, as applied in the two GDR cases, an application of natural law theory or "natural law jurisprudence disguised as enlightened positivism"? How did the ECHR reconcile its decision with the principle of nonretroactivity? Of what importance to the decision was "the emerging right of democracy"? Are human rights a product of natural law, legal positivism, or both? Would H. L. A. Hart's rule of recognition support the decision?
4. Did the ECHR faithfully apply the law of the GDR, as the German unification agreement required? Should the court have recognized GDR practice as well as the letter of the law?
5. The Nuremberg and Tokyo war crimes tribunals after the Second World War, which prosecuted and sentenced (even to death) German and Japanese officials, refused to accept the defense that some of those officials were simply acting under the orders of their superiors. Analyze the Court's treatment of this principle as applied to the senior officials and the border guard. To what extent is the reasoning compatible with international human rights norms ensuring the right to a fair trial?
6. What are the implications of the reasoning for the use of force to protect borders?
7. Do the two GDR cases suggest that they mean symbiotic – that is, more or less dependent on each other in their application to real cases? Under what circumstances, if any, is the defense of superior orders nevertheless acceptable?

b. Other Schools of Jurisprudence

Besides natural law and legal positivism, a third jurisprudential approach, the historical school of jurisprudence, rejects the abstract theorizing of positivists and adopts instead a view of law that puts it squarely in its historical context. The Baron Montesquieu may have been the first proponent of that view. In his classic work *The Spirit of the Laws*, he explains how legal systems reflect the social mores of the communities and times in which they exist. The key idea was that law reflects the value system of a given society during a given period of history. The German legal thinker Karl von Savigny coined the word *Volksgeist* ("spirit of the people") to convey that idea. Law is a mirror of societal values. Some nineteenth-century disciples of the historical school – for example, Sir Henry Maine – offered a theory of legal evolution according to which societies adopt new legal systems as they advance from one level of civilization to the next.

In the twentieth century, a law-and-society movement in North America argued that law must always be examined in its social context. Scholars who joined this movement came from a variety of disciplines, such as anthropology, economics, politics, psychology, and sociology. What they had in common was a belief in the necessity of conducting empirical investigation to ascertain the nature of institutions that constitute a legal system. One branch of this movement, influenced by the political scientist Harold Lasswell, developed a policy-oriented jurisprudence based on a functional system of decision making that took into account a set of base values and options for the exercise of power.

Sociological jurisprudence, as developed by the great American legal thinker Roscoe Pound, focused attention on analyzing the various interests of parties in disputes. An offshoot of this, legal realism, concentrated on the institutional apparatus of the legal systems. Rooted in behaviorism, legal realists maintain that if one wishes to know how the law works, it is crucial to study the actors – especially judges, lawyers, police officers, juries, and other players who make the decisions. Carried out to its fullest extent, legal realism would teach that if one really wants to understand how the legal system functions on a particular day, it may be helpful to know what the judge had for breakfast that morning. Consequently, this approach has sometimes been referred to, in jest, as the gastronomic theory of jurisprudence.

The latter quarter of the twentieth century witnessed the rise of critical legal studies (CLS), a more or less postmodern approach that drew on Marxist theory and sociological jurisprudence to deconstruct the law, revealing the arbitrary nature of legal doctrines, as indeterminate. For the most part, CLS scholars focused on the relative bargaining power of those involved in litigation, highlighting the hegemonic power of legal elites. This movement shifted the focus back to formal doctrines and away from institutional analysis. Critical legal studies itself came under attack for its cultural bias, splintering into such one-issue theories as feminist jurisprudence, critical race theory, critical Latino theory, and queer theory. Another school of jurisprudence, law and economics, also emerged during the last quarter of the twentieth century, and is based on the view that legal issues are best understood and resolved by economic analysis.

NOTE

1. The legal realism movement was rooted in the objective jurisprudence of Justice Oliver Wendell Holmes Jr., who defined law as the prediction of court outcome. The movement profoundly affected American legal thinking, not only in the formal sense of professional counseling, advocacy, and judging but also in a broader sense of understanding that law reflects culture. The pioneering collaboration between the legal scholar Karl Llewellyn and the anthropologist E. Adamson Hoebel produced a pathfinding study:

   > In *The Cheyenne Way* (1941), Hoebel and Llewellyn utilized the legal realist case method – which had entered American jurisprudence and legal education via the German historical jurisprudence of von Savigny – to distill the essence

> of the Cheyenne way of life, as expressed in Cheyenne law. To do this, the scholars focused on what they called *trouble cases*, meaning conflicts resolved in public forums. Their assumption that trouble cases were a better window into the core of local legal principles than were other possible types of law (such as administrative or regulatory) was to become methodologically conventional for many legal anthropologists even as theoretical frameworks shifted. The general idea that law reflects culture was to continue as a major theme in legal anthropology, eloquently crystallized later in the work of Clifford Geertz and his followers. Fieldwork conducted in the 1950s by noted legal anthropologists such as Elizabeth Colson and Leopold Pospíšil expanded the scope of research into disputed cases, asking wider questions about how resolution of these cases was tied to the overall structure of societies.

Mark Goodale & Elizabeth Mertz, *Anthropology of Law*, *in* ENCYCLOPEDIA OF LAW & SOCIETY 68, 70 (David S. Clark ed., 2007).

2. International Law

a. Introduction

The origins of modern international law lie in the writings of the sixteenth-century Spanish natural lawyers Francisco Suárez and Francisco de Vittoria, and the seventeenth-century Dutch natural lawyer Hugo Grotius, in his seminal writings on the use of force and law of the sea. "International law" is a term coined by the eighteenth- and early-nineteenth-century English positivist Jeremy Bentham that has replaced the earlier term, "law of nations." Bentham was a utilitarian, whose global vision of seeking the greatest happiness for the greater number relied on governance by a system of nation-states. This system would need to address such fundamental issues as the use of force, trade, environment, law of the sea, and many other matters.

From its earliest days, the law of nations accorded a limited legal status to nonstate actors as well as legal actors. For example, eighteenth-century rules of international law condemned pirates as *hostis humani generis* (enemies of humanity). During the second half of the twentieth century, jurists realized that international organizations, nongovernmental entities, and individuals are all international legal actors or, in the vocabulary of international law, enjoy international personality. In the twenty-first century, substantial attention has been focused on such legal actors as the United Nations and its specialized agencies as well as nongovernmental organizations, such as the International Committee of the Red Cross; the Olympic Movement; and multinational corporations. Moreover, with the rise of international human rights law in the last half of the twentieth century, individuals are unquestionably major actors as both objects and subjects of international law.

An important effect of the recasting of the law of nations as international law was to divide the field between public and private international law. Consequently, until the latter half of the twentieth century, the scope of public international law was limited to legal relationships among nation-states. They alone had international legal personality or, in other words, were subjects and objects of international law.

In the past few decades, however, public international law has, in effect, returned to the earlier vision of the law of nations, embracing today not only nation-states but also international organizations, nongovernmental organizations, and individuals. Of course, the extent to which each of those enjoys international legal personality depends on the context. For example, unlike states, individuals cannot use force but are subjects and objects of internationally protected human rights.

Meanwhile, private international law, rooted in medieval and early modern doctrine, blossomed. Private international law generally refers to three sets of procedural issues in dispute resolution: jurisdiction, choice of law, and enforcement of judgments. To a great extent, the applicable rules are national (or subnational in the case of some federal systems such as the United States). Although regional rules of private international law, particularly in Europe, and several private international law treaties are important, public international law may also govern more or less private legal relationships.

The international law that applies to cultural issues is largely public international law. The term "international law" therefore generally refers to public international law. In Chapter 5, however, we have occasion to consider private international law in the context of disputes concerning claims for the return, restitution, and repatriation of cultural material to countries of origin.

A postcolonial issue, primarily since the Second World War, has been the extent to which states in the so-called third world are bound by public international law when they played little role in the development of standards. This issue is sometimes framed as a question of whether there is a Western or Eurocentric bias reflected in international instruments. Although a comprehensive treatment of this matter is beyond the scope of this chapter, it is worth bearing in mind the possibility that legal standards, not only global ones, may be culturally biased. It is also noteworthy that jurists in other parts of the world may call into question well-established standards whose validity Western jurists take for granted.

b. Sources

Article 38 of the governing Statute of the International Court of Justice (ICJ) provides the most widely accepted checklist of the sources of public international law. It is written in terms of proceedings before the ICJ, whose decisions under Article 59 of the Statute, have "no binding force except between the parties and in respect of that particular case." Nevertheless, in practice among international lawyers, Article 38's applicability is not limited in that way:

Article 38

1. The Court, whose function is to decide in accordance with international law such disputes as are submitted to it, shall apply:
   a. international conventions, whether general or particular, establishing rules expressly recognized by the contesting states;
   b. international custom, as evidence of a general practice accepted as law;
   c. the general principles of law recognized by civilized nations;
   d. subject to the provisions of Article 59, judicial decisions and the teachings of the most highly qualified publicists of the various nations, as subsidiary means for the determination of rules of law.
2. This provision shall not prejudice the power of the Court to decide a case *ex aequo et bono*, if the parties agree thereto.

International conventions are also known by a variety of other names, such as "international agreements," "treaties," "exchanges of notes," "agreed minutes," "memoranda of agreement," "memoranda of understanding," "*modi vivendi*" – and, in specific contexts, "charters," "pacts," "concordats," and "protocols." Whatever the name, the legal status of these arrangements is the same unless otherwise stipulated. They are written instruments, a little like ordinary contracts, which specify rights and duties to govern the behavior of states and other entities with international legal personality.

An axiom of international law is *pacta sunt servanda*: treaties are binding. They enter into force after the requisite number of states parties have ratified them according to the convention, and treaties are binding only on those states that have willingly undertaken the stipulated obligations by giving explicit consent to be bound by ratification or other specified accession. Although states may submit reservations (freeing themselves from a particular obligation or obligations), understandings, and declarations at the time of ratification, their qualifications of particular obligations may not be inconsistent with fundamental objects and purposes of a treaty. The international community has discouraged reservations to human rights treaties, which have tended to be excessive. On occasion a state has tried to enter a reservation to a human rights treaty that other states regard as incompatible with the regime; this leaves open the question of whether the state is bound by the treaty *in toto*, by the treaty minus the provision to which it entered the reservation (which would be severed from it), or not at all. The rules regarding treaty interpretation are codified in the Vienna Convention on the Law of Treaties, which is known as the treaty on treaties.

Another major source of law is custom. In Roman law, the term for the body of customary norms is *ius gentium*. Two requirements determine whether a particular norm expresses "international custom, as evidence of a general practice accepted as law." There is, first, an objective factor: sufficiently widespread and repeated practice by states and other international legal actors. Second, there is a subjective factor, known as *opinio juris sive necessitatis*, by which the established practice must be followed out of a sense of legal obligation. The second element is necessary because states and other international legal actors might behave in a particular way out of habit or as a matter of convenience but not feel compelled by any sense of a legal obligation to act in that manner. For example, merely because states communicate with each other on white paper or by e-mail does not mean that such practices are legally compelling on them as custom. Once jurists concur that a norm is part of customary international law, it is by definition binding on all states. In this regard, customary law is more powerful than treaty law because treaties are binding on only those states that have ratified them.

Although customary international law is ordinarily universal, it is often limited to particular subject matter – for example, cultural heritage, sports, or the use of force – and to particular groups of persons. Indeed, one of the oldest examples of custom, dating back to the Rhodian Code of ancient Greece and medieval practices – is the *lex mercatoria*, the customary norms of the transnational commercial community. States recognize this important body of custom at least to the extent that it facilitates the interpretation of commercial contracts on the presumption that parties intended to be bound by the *lex mercatoria*. As we shall see, a similar notion of *lex sportiva* is emerging from arbitration of international sports-related disputes.

Customary international law may also be regional. For instance, in South America, the right of asylum was asserted as a customary right, even though international law does not otherwise recognize it. In *Colombia v. Peru*, a case decided by the ICJ in 1950, the court rejected the claim that asylum was a matter of regional customary law but recognized the legitimacy of regional custom.

One issue related to customary law is whether it is binding on a persistent objector, that is, usually a state that repeatedly refuses to be bound by a particular rule of custom. Another issue is that of the existence of a customary rule that appears to depend on an intertemporal paradox. As one scholar aptly put it, "How can something be accepted as law before it has actually developed into law?" Herein lies the difficulty. If a norm can become customary law only when states act in accordance with it and believe that they are obligated to adhere to it, then how can they be bound before the moment when the norm has been recognized as binding? Each state must believe, mistakenly perhaps, that it is bound with other states in the process of establishing the norm in the corpus of customary international law.

Of course, many states violate international law in practice even if they acknowledge that its customary standards are legally binding. Thus, they fail to comply with the general practice of states. Some have argued, therefore, that international custom should be based simply on the standards that state representatives publicly declare are binding on their governments. Although this approach avoids the problem of having to show that state behavior reflects respect for a given norm, it conflates *opinio juris* and state practice. On this view, all that must be shown is what states say that they believe they are obligated to respect, rather than *opinio juris* and what they actually feel compelled by law to observe in practice.

Customary norms are often codified in international agreements, in which case they may be considered both customary and conventional, such as the prohibition against torture by states. It is important, nevertheless, to know when norms are customary, because a state that has not ratified a particular convention may claim not to be bound by a standard. If the norm is part of customary law, however, the state is bound by the norm irrespective of whether it is a party to the pertinent convention.

Treaties, unlike customary international law, normally provide for any or all of the following procedures – enforcement mechanisms, review conferences, and dispute resolution – thereby making it easier to hold states accountable for violations of international standards. Many treaties establish a committee of experts to monitor compliance with the provisions of the treaty. Accordingly, states are expected to submit periodic reports that document the extent to which their domestic legal systems adhere to the stipulated standards.

In general, treaty and custom are considered to have equal authority. Questions about which supersedes the other are resolved by the last-in-time rule. This is based on the maxim *lex posterior derogate priori*, or "a later law repeals an earlier law."

This brings us, finally, to several ancillary sources of international law, as identified in article 38 of the Statute of the ICJ. "The general principles of law" refer, first, to principles that can be distilled from those employed widely in domestic legal systems, such as good faith, equitable canons (e.g., the clean-hands doctrine), and collateral estoppel. The term also refers to universally accepted principles of international law itself, such as *pacta sunt servanda* and comity. In the largely abandoned socialist world, Soviet jurists argued that general principles were only those drawn from positive international law (conventions and firmly established customary practices) to which the socialist countries, after the Bolshevik Revolution, had consented, but that view was never broadly adopted.

The two "subsidiary means for the determination of rules of law" represent a compromise between the civil law (particularly German) penchant for consulting "the teachings of the most highly qualified publicists" and the common law reliance on "judicial decisions." Both of these secondary sources, however, are regarded primarily as techniques for properly interpreting the three main sources: international conventions, custom, and general principles.

Finally, the parties to a dispute may agree to have it resolved *ex aequo et bono* ("according to what is right and good"). Accordingly, the ensuing resolution of their dispute will ignore hard law and rely instead on principles of fairness and justice and generally on the basis of a friendly settlement of the dispute or reasonable adjustment of the relations between the parties. This source is not to be confused with general principles of equity, based on more or less established legal principles and doctrine.

3. Comparative Law

a. Introduction

One way to identify or confirm new norms of international law is by means of the comparative method. By examining the codes or constitutions of national legal systems, one can find shared principles of law that may be codified in new international agreements. The existence of a global consensus on either international custom or general principles of law paves the way to the confirmation of international rules.

Although comparative law is a useful tool for ascertaining the content of international legal custom, it has much broader application as a discipline for the use and adoption of foreign law. The emergence of comparative law coincided with the rise of nationalism in Europe, prompting scholars to view law as an essential device for promoting social cohesion. There is no question that the law was used strategically to create a sense of national solidarity and as a means of inculcating important cultural values. Although there is considerable variation around the world in the way courts and other legal institutions function, there are also commonalities in legal systems, which have been delineated in the form of ideal types that collectively came to be known as families of law.

As a rough analytic construct rather than a precise description, the traditional framework includes three families: primarily common law, civil law, and socialist law, even though some regard socialist law as a category of civil law. It is particularly useful to be familiar with the key distinctions between common law and civil law traditions because, despite their British and continental European origins, respectively, they served as a basis for legal systems around the globe. Thus, Japanese and Chinese law are based on the German code; Latin American codes are based on the French and Spanish codes; and, not surprisingly, the laws of former colonies are based on those of their European mother countries. Because national legal systems vary widely within this general framework – witness the complicated federal systems in the United States and Canada or the hybrid civil law and socialist system of China – we speak generally of the "traditions" of common law and civil law.

The families-of-law approach has been subject to a number of criticisms. The most serious is that the ideal types rely on oversimplification. Considering the wide range of legal systems that exist and fall under each family, it is misleading to treat them as similar. Another challenge is that many legal systems are "mixed," such as Louisiana law in the

United States and that of Quebec in Canada. Indeed, all states have codes of law in the civil law tradition on such topics as family law and criminal law, and all states turn to judicial decisions for guidance, as in the common law tradition. Important codes include the Uniform Commercial Code, which has been adopted by all states in the United States, the Internal Revenue Code of the United States, and so on.

Another criticism of the families-of-law approach in comparative law is that the unit of analysis is too restrictive. Why should the focus be only on state law? This apparently reflects the legal positivist conception of law that we introduced at the beginning of this chapter. Instead, decisions are made not only by state courts but also by subnational tribunals, for example, trial courts, dispute settlement mechanisms such as the Roma *kris*, and international courts. Furthermore, we need not study systems *in toto*. Instead, we can compare juries in various countries, the role of cameras in the courtroom, specific doctrines like the hearsay rule in evidence codes, the duty to rescue, and so on. Fortunately, in the past few decades, comparative law research has been moving beyond the traditional families-of-law approach. Although the families-of-law approach is of historical interest, it is increasingly less relevant as systems continue to borrow from one another or experience the imposition of foreign law following armed conflict.

b. The Common Law Tradition

John V. Orth, *Common Law*, *in* The Oxford Companion to American Law 125 (Kermit L. Hall ed., 2002) (reprinted with the permission of Oxford University Press)

Originating in the decisions of English judges of the early Middle Ages and systematically developed since the twelfth century, the common law eventually spread with English settlements throughout much of the world. Once referred to as "unwritten law" (*lex non scripta*), the common law was, in fact, gathered from the written reports of judicial decisions and in consequence was also called case law as opposed to law found in legislative enactments or statute law. Common law is sometimes contrasted with equity, the distinctive rights and remedies historically administered by the English Court of Chancery; today the administration of law and equity are merged in England and most American states.

Historical Roots. In medieval England royal courts dispensed justice in cases in which important national interests were at stake, such as the ownership of landed estates or violations of the King's peace. Lesser or local disputes were resolved by other courts, often applying their own special rules. Common to the whole country, the decisions of the royal courts laid the foundations of the English legal system prior to the adoption of any statutes. King Henry II in the twelfth century provided the institutional framework for regular development by organizing an integrated judicial system. Eventually three common law courts emerged: the Court of Common Pleas, the Court of King's Bench, and the Court of Exchequer – an arrangement that endured until the nineteenth century when the Judicature Acts (1873–75) put the English court system on its modern basis.

The oldest book on the common law, a brief treatise *On the Laws and Customs of England*, written in Latin, dates to the twelfth century and is attributed to Ranulf de Glanvill, an important figure in King Henry's government. In keeping with the common law's origin in judicial decisions, the book is organized around writs, the forms used to initiate legal proceedings and define remedies for specific wrongs. Glanvill includes much information about medieval litigation and is an early example of the common law's characteristic method of reasoning, posing hypothetical cases and seeking guidance from prior decisions. The impressive progress of the common law over the next hundred years is evident from another monumental work, also in Latin and also entitled *On the Laws and Customs of England*, composed in the mid-thirteenth century and attributed to Henry de Bracton, a royal judge. Although obviously acquainted with ancient Roman law and the latest developments in canon law, Bracton largely reflects the indigenous development of English law in the work of the courts. Singling out for special study the decisions of one or two judges, Bracton illustrates the heroic role assigned to the judge in the literature of the common law. Five hundred years were to pass before another systematic exposition of the common law appeared, this time in English: Sir William Blackstone's four-volume *Commentaries on the Laws of England* (1765–69).

During the centuries between Bracton and Blackstone, the makers of the common law concentrated on filling in the details, especially the almost incredible complexities of the law of real property. Typical of the new emphasis was Sir Thomas Littleton's short treatise *On Tenures*, published in 1481. Not in English or even in Latin but in Law French, the argot of English lawyers for centuries after the Norman Conquest, Littleton offered a scientific account of English land law, long the heart of the common law. Practical in organization and emphasis, Littleton's treatise was inward looking, wholly unaffected by non-English influences – the perfect example of the common law's hermetic tendencies. After a century and a half, Littleton's *On Tenure* was updated in a voluminous commentary by Sir Edward Coke; *Coke on Littleton* quickly became a classic of the common law. Displaying an astounding mastery of ancient precedent and an uncanny ability to restate it in a manner relevant to current conditions, Coke's work ensured that modern Anglo-American property law would be erected on firm medieval foundations. In commentaries on the statutes, criminal law, and the courts, Coke also developed the concept of due process and emphasized the political implications of the rule of law as a restraint on arbitrary power.

Centered on judicial decisions, the common law early developed a tradition of case reports, beginning with the medieval Year Books in Law French. Modern law reporting began in the sixteenth century with the immensely influential reports in English prepared by Sir Edward Coke, the source for such arcana of the common law as the Rule in Shelley's Case and the Rule in Wild's Case. Access to the reports was facilitated by a series of books known as "abridgements," which catalogued cases under topics arranged alphabetically, the ancestors of modern legal encyclopedias such as *Halsbury's Laws of England* and *American Jurisprudence.*

Born in the decisions of individual cases, the common law continued into the modern period to be developed more by judicial decision than by legislation. Property law, the primary legal interest of the landed aristocracy, evolved slowly as entails gave way to strict settlements, and mortgages facilitated the economic exploitation of land. With the growth of the British Empire and the spread of international trade, novel questions of commercial law required the renovation of the common law of contracts and the development of new legal arrangements such as insurance and joint ventures. Lord Mansfield, chief justice of the Court of King's Bench in the late eighteenth century, exploited the common law's flexibility to the fullest and laid down new law to deal with the unprecedented new realities.

From the beginning, the English legal profession was divided into barristers and solicitors. Barristers had a monopoly on practice before the common law courts, and from their ranks the judges were recruited, forging the link between practice and judging that distinguishes the common law to this day. Legal advice on family settlements, property transactions, and business in general was the preserve of solicitors, earlier referred to as attorneys. Legal education necessarily followed this functional division. Barristers were trained in the Inns of Court, medieval hostelries that developed into a combination law school and professional club. Solicitors had comparable but less prestigious accommodations. After the medieval period the educational functions of the Inns atrophied, although students, including numerous framers of the United States Constitution, continued to visit frequently. Realistically, a form of professional apprenticeship was the only means of legal education until organized curricula in law appeared at English universities in the nineteenth century. Although the professional division into barristers and solicitors was briefly attempted in some of the older American colonies like Virginia, it proved too costly and too deeply rooted in English institutions to survive transplantation to America where a unified bar became the norm.

...

Throughout its long history the common law was shaped by great judges; their rulings provided the substance of the law, their written opinions formed its basic texts, their sayings and idiosyncrasies became its lore. Promotion to the bench was the crown of many careers in law; recruitment from the ranks of practicing lawyers and successful politicians – often one and the same – linked the judiciary and the world of practical affairs. Coming from such backgrounds, common law judges were often impatient with purely abstract concepts and naturally inclined to consider practical results. Custodianship of the Constitution endowed them not only with awesome power but also with a sense of high purpose. Ordering an end to racial segregation in public schools, Supreme Court Chief Justice Earl Warren discarded the legal fiction of "separate but equal" and declared that "separate educational facilities are inherently unequal," setting off a social revolution that spread far beyond the classrooms. (*Brown v. Board of Education* (1954)).

. . .

More than a set of ancient rules, the common law also became a set of procedures guaranteeing fairness in the resolution of disputes. Although procedural regularity is most important in criminal law, where the individual faces the might of the state, it is important in civil litigation as well. The ability of the common law over the centuries to command the respect of the public was largely dependent on the widespread perception of its fundamental fairness. The popularity of the common law at the time of American Independence derived from its historic association with due process, the legal code word for fair play. Rules may often be settled one way or another; the common law and the civil law, for example, reach opposing results in numerous cases. In the abstract it is usually difficult to develop enthusiasm for one rule over another, but a reputation for impartial decision making after an opportunity to be heard is what grounds a legal system in popular esteem. The common law in the Anglo-American world is synonymous for the most part with the rule of law.

Beyond specific rules and procedures, the common law also embodies a certain way of handling legal problems. Born in the courts, the common law was always primarily focused on resolving individual disputes. Judge-centered in the sense that it was historically expressed in the decisions of the judges, the common law is in another sense centered on the litigants. The parties generally control the presentation of their own cases, and the judge plays a relatively passive role, limited by and large to deciding which side has the better argument. In consequence, the common law developed a deep-seated attachment to the adversarial process, which in turn fostered a frame of mind that assumes two sides to every case.

. . .

Relation to Civil Law. Although common law is often divided into criminal and civil law, the former concerned with public order and the latter with private rights such as property and contracts, civil law has also another and different meaning: the entire legal system derived from Roman law as expressed in the *Corpus juris civilis*, the definitive summation promulgated by the Emperor Justinian in the sixth century. Roman law was never entirely forgotten in Europe, and the Church through its own canon law and general Latin culture kept alive some knowledge of the Roman past. Clerically trained English jurists like Bracton were obviously familiar with Roman law, and in Britain the Scottish legal system was (and remains) a civil law system with its own distinct forms and terminology. But the common law generally developed in isolation from these influences and was already fully formed within the fifteenth century, during the Renaissance, classical sources were rediscovered. The logical arrangement and cultural prestige of the rediscovered *Corpus juris civilis* attracted academic English attention but was far less significant an influence on English law than on European legal systems. In America, Louisiana alone among the states retains an integrated civil law system, one based in Spanish and French colonial traditions, but many Western states preserve some civil law contributions, such as the community property system whereby husbands and wives are presumed to share equally in property acquired during marriage.

Revived interest in the *Corpus juris civilis* resulted eventually in the adoption by various European countries of legal codes, rigorously logical statements of basic rules and practices, such as the French Code Civil adopted after the French Revolution and often referred to as the Code Napoleon.

In the courtroom, as noted in the above reading, the common law tradition is essentially adversarial, dependent on the parties for the general framing of issues in the form of pleadings as well as the production of (generally oral) evidence. Juries of laypersons decide the facts in criminal cases throughout common law systems and, principally in the United States, also in civil (noncriminal) cases as well. The judge plays a fairly passive role, ruling on motions presented by the parties; keeping the trial efficient; and framing factual issues for consideration by a jury, if there is one in a particular trial. The judge's decision, however, not only is binding on the immediate parties in a case but also serves as precedent in future cases within the same jurisdiction. Thus, in making decisions, judges generally derive legal principles inductively by reviewing past cases relevant to the issue at hand. Once they identify the binding principle or *ratio decidendi*, the decision becomes established as precedent, which judges in future cases within the same court system (jurisdiction) are obligated to follow. *Stare decisis*, or the practice of following principles established in past precedent, is one of the most significant features of common law.

Because common law judges are bound by precedent, they are required to look to the past for guidance. This makes the common legal tradition inherently conservative, something that makes it difficult to render decisions designed to effect social change. As a consequence, judges have devised techniques for avoiding the full import of past decisions, such as by distinguishing the present case from the precedent on the facts, by reinterpreting the doctrine, or by sometimes simply ignoring the precedent on the basis of policy or opposing principles. Thus, even though the common law may be conservative in theory because of the weight of precedent as *stare decisis*, judges find ways to circumvent inconvenient precedents. Social change is thereby achieved through a gradual, incremental process.

There is no single way to select judges in the common law. In some jurisdictions they are appointed, and in others they are elected. Regardless of the manner of selection, judges are not required to complete any specialized educational training before going on the bench, which is a marked difference from the civil law.

c. The Civil Law Tradition

The most distinctive characteristic of the civil law tradition is the use of all-encompassing legal codes that are designed to cover all eventualities. Thus, in contrast to the common law system, in which judges play a particularly crucial role in fashioning the law itself, courts are more inquisitorial than adversarial. They rely on written more than oral evidence that is presented in stages determined by judges rather than at one big, mostly oral trial, as in the common law tradition. Judges in the civil law play a much more active role in seeking evidence and organizing a case before them, but their decision is binding only on the parties to a particular case. They are regarded as bureaucrats or government functionaries who must attend special schools to be trained after they complete their legal education. Generally they enjoy a somewhat lower professional status vis-à-vis legislators than in common law systems.

Just as the selection of judges differs considerably, likewise the treatment of criminal defendants is significantly different. Unlike common law systems, civil law systems do not generally have juries to decide the facts, although laypersons are sometimes included in the adjudicative process. Because there is no presumption of innocence, some common law commentators erroneously refer to civil law as having the presumption of guilt. Instead, the safeguards existed prior to the trial. A magistrate (*juge d'instruction*) reviews the dossier to determine whether the state has gathered sufficient incriminating evidence to warrant a trial. If the evidence is scanty, the accused is released, but if the file contains a great deal of information implicating the defendant in the alleged crime, the judge refers the case to trial. As most of those who proceed to trial are eventually convicted, this gives rise to the mistaken impression that the criminal justice process in civil law systems operates on the basis of a presumption of guilt. As we have seen, however, procedural safeguards exist but are applied at an earlier, pretrial stage of a criminal process.

Socialist law is usually presented as a separate and discrete family of law, though it was based on the established civil law tradition in each of the socialist countries. Scholars often characterize it as highly politicized, arguing that the socialist codes of law, albeit based on Western European models, were designed to inculcate communist values. Although this characterization was widely accepted, it is of course spurious to think that only socialist legal systems have promoted ideological values. Historically, common law systems promoted individual property rights, the French Napoleonic code featured administrative procedures, and the German code emphasized social legislation and the performance of duties. All legal systems reflect the value systems of the societies in which they operate to varying degrees.

d. Beyond the Common Law and Civil Law Traditions

What attitude did the families of law take toward cultural traditions? Historically, to the extent that all legal systems have been used to promote national identity, judges declined to recognize the customary law of ethnic minority groups because this might jeopardize national unity. The Soviet Union prohibited all religions and the survival of local custom. Some civil law countries such as France were also inclined to deny cultural rights to minorities. This reflected the notion that there were no minorities in France. Common law countries such as the United Kingdom and the United States interpreted constitutional rights in such a way as to promote national unity, sometimes to the detriment of ethnic and religious minorities and indigenous peoples.

An important issue concerns the transplantation of legal rules and procedures from one system to another. Transplantation refers to the legal borrowing or reception of a legal norm or rule from another legal system. The cultural dynamics are profound. One view of transplantation of norms and rules is that they can take root only in a legal culture similar to that of the country of origin. An opposing view, however, is that transplantations occur and have always occurred successfully, since the famous Mesopotamian Code of Hammurabi (around 1760 BCE), purely on the basis of expediency and practicality, regardless of cultural conditions.

This debate was at the heart of two law and development movements of the last half of the twentieth century, by which transplantation became a very common technique for quickly installing legal systems: first, in newly independent countries after colonizations and, later, in former socialist countries after the end of the Cold War. In the end, can such wholesale legal borrowing be successful if it is not rooted in the culture that produced the law or procedure? As it turns out, despite speculation that globalization would result in the adoption of similar legal systems around the world, there continues to be remarkable and significant variation in legal content and practices across the globe. The literature on this question of legal transplants continues to be an exciting subject in the field of legal studies.

e. The Judicial Use of Foreign Law

One contentious issue related to comparative law is the practical question of whether rulings of a foreign legal system should be consulted for the nonbinding guidance they can provide in resolving a dispute. In landmark decisions centering on crucial human rights issues, judges have increasingly invoked the legal reasoning of their colleagues in foreign legal systems. Should they do so? In *Roper v. Simmons*, the U.S. Supreme Court said yes, thereby ruling that juvenile executions violate the U.S. Constitution's prohibition under the Eighth Amendment against cruel and unusual punishment. Although the Court's use of foreign and international legal authority concerning capital punishment for minors was not dispositive, it nevertheless influenced the outcome of the case. Both Justice Kennedy's opinion for the majority and the debate between dissenting Justices O'Connor and Scalia, as follows, are already classics concerning the judicial use of foreign law.

Roper v. Simmons,
543 U.S. 551 (2005)

Kennedy, J.:

This case requires us to address, for the second time in a decade and a half, whether it is permissible under the Eighth and Fourteenth Amendments to the Constitution of the United States to execute a juvenile offender who was older than 15 but younger than 18 when he committed a capital crime. In *Stanford v. Kentucky* (1989), a divided Court rejected the proposition that the Constitution bars capital punishment for juvenile offenders in this age group. We reconsider the question.

. . .

Our determination that the death penalty is disproportionate punishment for offenders under 18 finds confirmation in the stark reality that the United States is the only country in the world that continues to give official sanction to the juvenile death penalty. This reality does not become controlling, for the task of interpreting the Eighth Amendment remains our responsibility. Yet at least from the time of the Court's decision in *Trop*, the Court has referred to the laws of other countries and to international authorities as instructive for its interpretation of the Eighth Amendment's prohibition of "cruel and unusual punishments."

As respondent and a number of amici emphasize, Article 37 of the United Nations Convention on the Rights of the Child, which every country in the world has ratified save for the United States and Somalia, contains an express prohibition on capital punishment for crimes committed by juveniles under 18. United Nations Convention on the Rights of the Child, Art. 37. No ratifying country has entered a reservation to the provision prohibiting the execution of juvenile offenders. Parallel prohibitions are contained in other significant international covenants. See ICCPR, Art. 6(5), 999 U.N.T.S., at 175 (prohibiting capital punishment for anyone under 18 at the time of offense) (signed and ratified by the United States subject to a reservation regarding Article 6(5), as noted, supra, at 567, 161 L. Ed. 2d, at 20); American Convention on Human Rights: Pact of San Jose, Costa Rica, Art. 4(5), Nov. 22, 1969, 1144 U.N.T.S. 146 (entered into force July 19, 1978) (same); African Charter on the Rights and Welfare of the Child, Art. 5(3), OAU Doc. CAB/LEG/24.9/49 (1990) (entered into force Nov. 29, 1999) (same).

Respondent and his amici have submitted, and petitioner does not contest, that only seven countries other than the United States have executed juvenile offenders since 1990: Iran, Pakistan, Saudi Arabia, Yemen, Nigeria, the Democratic Republic of Congo, and China. Since then each of these countries has either abolished capital punishment for juveniles or made public disavowal of the practice. In sum, it is fair to say that the United States now stands alone in a world that has turned its face against the juvenile death penalty.

Though the international covenants prohibiting the juvenile death penalty are of more recent date, it is instructive to note that the United Kingdom abolished the juvenile death penalty before these covenants came into being. The United Kingdom's experience bears particular relevance here in light of the historic ties between our countries and in light of the Eighth Amendment's own origins. The Amendment was modeled on a parallel provision in the English Declaration of Rights of 1689, which provided: "[E]xcessive Bail ought not to be required nor excessive Fines imposed; nor cruel and unusual Punishments inflicted." As of now, the United Kingdom has abolished the death penalty in its entirety; but, decades before it took this step, it recognized the disproportionate nature of the juvenile death penalty; and it abolished that penalty as a separate matter. In 1930 an official committee recommended that the minimum age for execution be raised to 21. Parliament then enacted the Children and Young Person's Act of 1933, which prevented execution of those aged 18 at the date of the sentence. And in 1948, Parliament enacted the Criminal Justice Act, prohibiting the execution of any person under 18 at the time of the offense. In the 56 years that have passed since the United Kingdom abolished the juvenile death penalty, the weight of authority against it there, and in the international community, has become well established.

It is proper that we acknowledge the overwhelming weight of international opinion against the juvenile death penalty, resting in large part on the understanding that the instability and emotional imbalance of young people may often be a factor in the crime. The opinion of the world community, while not controlling our outcome, does provide respected and significant confirmation for our own conclusions. . . . It does not lessen our fidelity to the Constitution or our pride in its origins to acknowledge that the express affirmation of certain fundamental rights by other nations and peoples simply underscores the centrality of those same rights within our own heritage of freedom.

The Eighth and Fourteenth Amendments forbid imposition of the death penalty on offenders who were under the age of 18 when their crimes were committed. The judgment of the Missouri Supreme Court setting aside the sentence of death imposed upon Christopher Simmons is affirmed.

It is so ordered.

Justice O'Connor, dissenting:

I turn, finally, to the Court's discussion of foreign and international law. Without question, there has been a global trend in recent years towards abolishing capital punishment for under-18 offenders. Very few, if any, countries other than the United States now permit this practice in law or in fact. While acknowledging that the actions and views of other countries do not dictate the outcome of our Eighth Amendment inquiry, the Court asserts that "the overwhelming weight of international opinion against the juvenile death penalty . . . does provide respected and significant confirmation for [its] own conclusions." Because I do not believe that a genuine national consensus against the juvenile death penalty has yet developed, and because I do not believe the Court's moral proportionality argument justifies a categorical, age-based constitutional rule, I can assign no such confirmatory role to the international consensus described by the Court. In short, the evidence of an international consensus does not alter my determination that the Eighth Amendment does not, at this time, forbid capital punishment of 17-year-old murderers in all cases.

Nevertheless, I disagree with Justice Scalia's contention, that foreign and international law have no place in our Eighth Amendment jurisprudence. Over the course of nearly half a century, the Court has consistently referred to foreign and international law as relevant to its assessment of evolving standards of decency. This inquiry reflects the special character of the Eighth Amendment, which, as the Court has long held, draws its meaning directly from the maturing values of civilized society. Obviously, American law is distinctive in many respects, not least where the specific provisions of our Constitution and the history of its exposition so dictate. But this Nation's evolving understanding of human dignity certainly is neither wholly isolated from, nor inherently at odds with, the values prevailing in other countries. On the contrary, we should not be surprised to find congruence between domestic and international values, especially where the international community has reached clear agreement – expressed in international law or in the domestic laws of individual countries – that a particular form of punishment is inconsistent with fundamental human rights. At least, the existence of an international consensus of this nature can serve to confirm the reasonableness of a consonant and genuine American consensus. The instant case presents no such domestic consensus, however, and the recent emergence of an otherwise global consensus does not alter that basic fact.

. . .

Justice Scalia, dissenting:

Though the views of our own citizens are essentially irrelevant to the Court's decision today, the views of other countries and the so-called international community take center stage.

The Court begins by noting that "Article 37 of the United Nations Convention on the Rights of the Child, which every country in the world has ratified save for the United States and Somalia, contains an express prohibition on capital punishment for crimes committed by juveniles under 18." The Court also discusses the International Covenant on Civil and Political Rights (ICCPR), which the Senate ratified only subject to a reservation that reads:

> The United States reserves the right, subject to its Constitutional constraints, to impose capital punishment on any person (other than a pregnant woman) duly convicted under existing or future laws permitting the imposition of capital punishment, including such punishment for crimes committed by persons below eighteen years of age.

Unless the Court has added to its arsenal the power to join and ratify treaties on behalf of the United States, I cannot see how this evidence favors, rather than refutes, its position. That the Senate and the President – those actors our Constitution empowers to enter into treaties, see Art. II, § 2 – have declined to join and ratify treaties prohibiting execution of under-18 offenders can only suggest that our country has either not reached a national consensus on the question, or has reached a consensus contrary to what the Court announces. That the reservation to the ICCPR was made in 1992 does not suggest otherwise, since the reservation still remains in place today. It is also worth noting that, in addition to barring the execution of under-18 offenders, the United Nations Convention on the Rights of the Child prohibits punishing them with life in prison without the possibility of release. If we are truly going to get in line with the international community, then the Court's reassurance that the death penalty is really not needed, since "the punishment of life imprisonment without the possibility of parole is itself a severe sanction," gives little comfort.

It is interesting that whereas the Court is not content to accept what the States of our Federal Union say, but insists on inquiring into what they do (specifically, whether they in fact apply the juvenile death penalty that their laws allow), the Court is quite willing to believe that every foreign nation – of whatever tyrannical political makeup and with however subservient or incompetent a court system – in fact adheres to a rule of no death penalty for offenders under 18. Nor does the Court inquire into how many of the countries that have the death penalty, but have forsworn (on paper at least) imposing that penalty on offenders under 18, have what no State of this country can constitutionally have: a mandatory death penalty for certain crimes, with no possibility of mitigation by the sentencing authority, for youth or any other reason. I suspect it is most of them. To forbid the death penalty for juveniles under such a system may be a good idea, but it says nothing about our system, in which the sentencing authority, typically a jury, always can, and almost always does, withhold the death penalty from an under-18 offender except, after considering all the circumstances, in the rare cases where it is warranted. The foreign authorities, in other words, do not even speak to the issue before us here.

More fundamentally, however, the basic premise of the Court's argument – that American law should conform to the laws of the rest of the world – ought to be rejected out of hand. In fact the Court itself does not believe it. In many significant respects the laws of most other countries differ from our law – including not only such explicit provisions of our Constitution as the right to jury trial and grand jury indictment, but even many interpretations of the Constitution prescribed by this Court itself. The Court-pronounced exclusionary rule, for example, is distinctively American. When we adopted that rule in *Mapp v. Ohio* (1961), it was "unique to American jurisprudence." Since then a categorical exclusionary rule has been "universally rejected" by other countries, including those with rules prohibiting illegal searches and police misconduct, despite the fact that none of these countries "appears to have any alternative form of discipline for police that is effective in preventing search violations." England, for example, rarely excludes evidence found during an illegal search or seizure and has only recently begun excluding evidence from illegally obtained confessions. Canada rarely excludes evidence and will only do so if admission will "bring the administration of justice into disrepute." The European Court of Human Rights has held that introduction of illegally seized evidence does not violate the "fair trial" requirement in Article 6, § 1, of the European Convention on Human Rights.

The Court has been oblivious to the views of other countries when deciding how to interpret our Constitution's requirement that "Congress shall make no law respecting an establishment of religion. . . . " Most other countries – including those committed to religious neutrality – do not insist on the degree of separation between church and state that this Court requires. For example, whereas "we have recognized special Establishment Clause dangers where the government makes direct money payments to sectarian institutions," countries such as the Netherlands, Germany, and Australia allow direct government funding of religious schools on the ground that "the state can only be truly neutral between secular and religious perspectives if it does not dominate the provision of so key a service as education, and makes it possible for people to exercise their right of religious expression within the context of public funding." England permits the teaching of religion in state schools. Even in France, which is considered "America's only rival in strictness of church-state separation," "[t]he practice of contracting for educational services provided by Catholic schools is very widespread."

And let us not forget the Court's abortion jurisprudence, which makes us one of only six countries that allow abortion on demand until the point of viability. Though the Government and amici in cases following *Roe v. Wade* (1973) urged the Court to follow the international community's lead, these arguments fell on deaf ears. The Court's special reliance on the laws of the United Kingdom is perhaps the most indefensible part of its opinion. It is of course true that we share a common history with the United Kingdom, and that we often consult English sources when asked to discern the meaning of a constitutional text written against the backdrop of 18th-century English law and legal thought. If we applied that approach today, our task would be an easy one. As we explained in *Harmelin v. Michigan*, 501 U.S. 957, 973–974, 115 L. Ed. 2d 836, 111 S. Ct. 2680 (1991), the "Cruell and Unusuall Punishments" provision of the English Declaration of Rights was originally meant to describe those punishments "'out of [the Judges'] Power'" – that is, those punishments that were not authorized by common law or statute, but that were nonetheless administered by the Crown or the Crown's judges. Under that reasoning, the death penalty for under-18 offenders would easily survive this challenge. The Court has, however – I think wrongly – long rejected a purely originalist approach to our Eighth Amendment, and that is certainly not the approach the Court takes today. Instead, the Court undertakes the majestic task of determining (and thereby prescribing) our Nation's current standards of decency. It is beyond comprehension why we should look, for that purpose, to a country that has developed, in the centuries since the Revolutionary War – and with increasing speed since the United Kingdom's recent submission to the jurisprudence of European courts dominated by continental jurists – a legal, political, and social culture quite different from our own. If we took the Court's directive seriously, we would also consider relaxing our double jeopardy prohibition, since the British Law Commission recently published a report that would significantly extend the rights of the prosecution to appeal cases where an acquittal was the result of a judge's ruling that was legally incorrect. We would also curtail our right to jury trial in criminal cases since, despite the jury system's deep roots in our shared common law, England now permits all but the most serious offenders to be tried by magistrates without a jury.

The Court should either profess its willingness to reconsider all these matters in light of the views of foreigners, or else it should cease putting forth foreigners' views as part of the reasoned basis of its decisions. To invoke alien law when it agrees with one's own thinking, and ignore it otherwise, is not reasoned decisionmaking, but sophistry.

The Court responds that "[i]t does not lessen our fidelity to the Constitution or our pride in its origins to acknowledge that the express affirmation of certain fundamental rights by other nations and peoples simply underscores the centrality of those same rights within our own heritage of freedom." To begin with, I do not believe that approval by "other nations and peoples" should buttress our commitment to American principles any more than (what should logically follow) disapproval by "other nations and peoples" should weaken that commitment. More importantly, however, the Court's statement flatly misdescribes what is going on here. Foreign sources are cited today, not to underscore our "fidelity" to the Constitution, our "pride in its origins," and "our own [American] heritage." To the contrary, they are cited to set aside the centuries-old American practice – a practice still engaged in by a large majority of the relevant States – of letting a jury of 12 citizens decide whether, in the particular case, youth should be the basis for withholding the death penalty. What these foreign sources "affirm," rather than repudiate, is the Justices' own notion of how the world ought to be, and their diktat that it shall be so henceforth in America. The Court's parting attempt to downplay the significance of its extensive discussion of foreign law is unconvincing. "Acknowledgment" of foreign approval has no place in the legal opinion of this Court unless it is part of the basis for the Court's judgment – which is surely what it parades as today.

David G. Savage, *Scalia to Congress: Butt Out of Court's Use of Foreign Law*, L.A. Times, May 19, 2006, at 1 (reprinted with permission)

Justice Antonin Scalia said Thursday he was strongly opposed to using foreign law to decide constitutional cases in the Supreme Court but also was opposed to having Congress outlaw the practice.... His oft-stated skepticism about the role of foreign laws has been taken up by a group of House Republicans, who introduced a measure saying legal decisions interpreting the Constitution "should not be based on judgments, law or pronouncements of foreign institutions." Scalia said Thursday he did not welcome the intervention. He told the lawmakers that he did not think the justices should second-guess how Congress makes its decisions. The same applies in reverse, he added. "No one is more opposed to using foreign law than I am, but I'm darned if I think it's up to Congress to direct the Supreme Court how to make its decisions," he said....

In February, he said only "idiots" would believe the Constitution must change with society. Several of his colleagues are on record as saying the Constitution should indeed change with society. In March, he said it was "crazy" to believe foreigners captured in a war are entitled to a full jury trial. That was a couple of weeks before the Supreme Court took up such a case.

On Thursday, Scalia stuck to a familiar legal topic, albeit one that has divided the high court and much of the nation's legal community. The issue is whether the justices should consider the opinions of foreign courts in deciding cases under the U.S. Constitution. The question has been caught up in the culture wars over gays, abortion, religion and the death penalty.

In recent years, four of Scalia's colleagues – Justices Ruth Bader Ginsberg, John Paul Stevens, Stephen G. Breyer and Anthony M. Kennedy – have given speeches saying the opinions of foreign courts should influence U.S. legal thinking though outside views are not decisive. Three years ago, when the Supreme Court struck down as unconstitutional a Texas law that made private sex between gay adults a crime, the majority noted in passing that the European Court of Human Rights had come to a similar conclusion two decades earlier. Two years ago, the court struck down state laws that permitted the death penalty for murderers younger than 18. Kennedy noted that the United States stood nearly alone in condemning juvenile killers to death. Scalia dissented sharply in both cases, faulting the majority for following the view of "like-minded foreigners" and repeating his view that the Constitution "means just what it meant when it was adopted."

NOTES AND QUESTIONS

1. The debate about the juridical status of foreign law in U.S. constitutional practice reflects the hostility of some judges such as Justice Scalia to consult, let alone apply, legal reasoning from other jurisdictions, however helpful it might be in deciding the issues before the Court. Other judges note a long history of making use of foreign authority in nonconstitutional cases as a source of new ideas and a technique for determining important trends in addressing issues. These judges argue that foreign authority can be very useful in constitutional cases as well, stopping short of actually applying the authority as common law.
2. Do you agree with Justice Scalia that only "idiots" believe that the U.S. Constitution is a dynamic instrument whose interpretation must change with society? In other words, do you agree with him that the Constitution should always be interpreted in terms of the original intent of the Constitution's framers?
3. In your view, what are the advantages and disadvantages of incorporating judicial reasoning from abroad to interpret the Constitution and, more generally, in non-constitutional cases? Would your arguments apply with equal force in common law and civil law systems?
4. As the newspaper item notes, in interpreting the Constitution, the U.S. Supreme Court has increasingly consulted foreign law not as authority but as a source of ideas and an indication of global practices. Note, for example, the following opinions of the Court: *Lawrence v. Texas*, 539 U.S. 558, 573 (2003) (citing a decision of the European Court of Human Rights to strike down as unconstitutional a state law that had criminalized consensual homosexual conduct); *Grutter v. Bollinger*, 539 U.S. 306, 344 (2003) (Ginsburg, J., concurring; citing the International Convention on the Elimination of All Forms of Racial Discrimination and the Convention on the Elimination of All Forms of Discrimination against Women as support for the constitutionality of a law school's affirmative action policies); and *Atkins*

v. Virginia, 536 U.S. 304, 316 (2002) (prohibiting state executions of the mentally retarded by taking into account a strong global consensus against such a practice).

5. The U.S. Supreme Court has also applied general international law in hundreds of cases, besides treaties to which the Senate has given its advice and consent as the law of the land under the Constitution's supremacy clause. The Court also applies a principle that Chief Justice Marshall first articulated more than two hundred years ago: "an act of Congress ought never be construed to violate the law of nations if any other possible construction remains." *Murray v. The Schooner Charming Betsy*, 6 U.S. (2 Cranch) 64 (1804). This principle is therefore known as the *Charming Betsy* principle. Even Justice Scalia agrees with it, as he made clear in a dissenting opinion in *Hartford Fire Insurance Co. v. California*, 509 U.S. 764 (1993).
6. To what extent do international law principles dictate whether it is proper to refer to decisions in other jurisdictions?
7. Should international criminal tribunals cite cases from national legal systems? Why? Why not?

f. Customary Law

Gordon R. Woodman, *Customary Legal Norms*, *in* Encyclopedia of Law & Society 379, 380, 381 (David S. Clark ed., 2007)

Custom is a source of law in many nation-states as well as in international law. Although it is of inferior authority to legislation and scholars often give it less attention than statutory law and judicial decision making, in many states it is the source of legal norms of great importance in the lives of many subjects. Customary legal norms have legal authority prior to their recognition. Organs of state law enforce them on the ground that they already have the quality of law. Such norms are sometimes required to have received long observance, and to be regarded as obligatory, before they can be recognized in the communities in which they are observed. State organs also usually assert a discretionary authority to override custom when they consider it would be wrong to recognize it.

There are many examples of such customary laws, including the following:

1. Customs that people observe in particular localities
2. Some elements of English common law, which judges have historically stated to be "the common custom of the realm"
3. Customary laws of indigenous minority peoples, the best publicized instances being in North and South America, Australia, and New Zealand
4. Customary laws of the various ethnic groups that constitute the populations of states in sub-Saharan Africa
5. Observed religious laws, significant in many parts of the world

6. Customary norms of international law as well as *lex mercatoria*, the customary norms of the worldwide commercial community

. . .

In many jurisdictions, customary norms observed in particular localities are recognized as effecting valid variations in generally applicable norms of state law. Certain communities, for example, may observe different rules of inheritance law from those of the general population. It is normally required, as a condition of recognition, that the customs be proven "ancient" in origin, sometimes with periods such as forty or sixty years. Moreover, state institutions exercise the power to refuse recognition to such customs on the ground that they are (in the eyes of state law) unreasonable or contrary to public order. Local custom as a source of state law tends to decline in importance as a state modernizes; the proportion of the law consisting of legislation increases; and the population becomes more homogeneous in some sense.

. . .

It might appear that religious laws are not within the scope of custom, since they derive their authority and content from religious inspiration rather than popular observance. However, in state practice, jurists often treat religious laws as indigenous customary laws, and these laws have been accorded recognition in the same terms as other customary laws. This has been most notably the case in South and Southeast Asia, where Islamic law and Hindu law have received widespread normative and institutional recognition. In India, both Hindu and Islamic laws, but also the traditional customary laws of the "scheduled tribes," receive state recognition.

T.W. Bennett, *Comparative Law and African Customary Law*, *in* The Oxford Handbook of Comparative Law 641 (Mathias Reimann & Reinhard Zimmermann eds., 2006) (reprinted with permission of Oxford University Press)

Customary law grows out of the social practices which a given jural community has come to accept as obligatory. It is a pervasive normative order, providing the regulatory framework for spheres of human activity as diverse as the family, the neighbourhood, the business of merchant banking, or international diplomacy. Because custom is so diverse and so wide-ranging, it is clearly impossible to consider all possible systems. . . .

In certain legal systems, custom has been elevated to a position of honour, respected by courts and law-makers as a national tradition; the laws of Maoris in New Zealand and Aboriginals in Australia are recent examples. For the most part, however, lawyers pay custom little attention. It will be no surprise, then, to discover that customary law is a latecomer to the discipline of comparative law.

The main reason for this neglect would seem to lie in the fact that lawyers take as their model for law the system that evolved in Europe. On this understanding, they believe that the primary sources of law are those endorsed by the state – legislation and precedent – and not the potentially anarchic social practices of local communities. Hence, legal scholars everywhere tend to regard custom as a somewhat primitive regime, one less worthy of study than "law."

The history of comparative law has, in fact, been markedly Eurocentric. It was only in the fifteenth and sixteenth centuries that lawyers in Europe started looking to the wider world. Initially, their interest was sparked by the conquest of the Americas and the opening of trade routes to the East, events which aroused a taste for the exotic and a self-conscious reflection on European culture. Attention was drawn to the indigenous laws of sub-Saharan Africa only very much later, once the scramble for colonies was over, and the colonial powers were confronting the problem of governing their possessions.

Eventually, all the European administrations had to recognize the unwritten laws of their subject peoples for the simple reason that they suffered chronic shortages of personnel and finance. Because lawyers lacked the skills necessary to determine the content of these laws, however, the job was relegated to anthropologists. Thus, as will be apparent below, the study of custom has been dominated by social anthropology.

In so far as comparative lawyers were prepared to consider customary law, they dwelt on the substance of the rules. . . . [B]ecause customary laws are confined to small, more or less self-contained, communities, they are not immediately accessible to outsiders. Hence the great problem with customary law: ascertaining the rules.

Customary law is often unwritten. It is then a matter of oral history and ritualized activity. As such, it is often known as folk law: "a socially defined group's orally transmitted traditional body of obligations and prohibitions, sanctioned or required by that group, binding upon individuals or subsets of individuals (for example, clans) under pain of punishment or forfeiture."[17] Thus, folkloristic forms include, for example, games, proverbs, and songs. Of course, when folk law norms are codified in written form, documented in scholarly works, or interpreted in formal court proceedings, the standard definition of folk law as unwritten law or *lex non scripta* may be insufficient.

A folk is properly defined as any group that shares a common linking factor such as nationality, religion, ethnicity, occupation, locality, or family. Every folk has a legal system. Because there are innumerable folks systems throughout the world, it is obviously futile to characterize them in any universal sense. They do share certain common characteristics, the most prominent of which is that it consists of unwritten law or "*lex non scripta.*" As it is generally unwritten, folk law is subject to multiple interpretations, it is dynamic, and it reflects the values of the people to whom it applies. Of course, when folk law norms are codified in written form, documented in scholarly works, or interpreted in court decisions, the standard definition of folk law may be insufficient.

It can be challenging to study folk law because it is unwritten. Major works have been written on techniques for ascertaining the law that addresses questions such as whether

[17] Folk Law: Essays on the Theory and Practice of Lex Non Scripta xiii (Alison Dundes Renteln & Alan Dundes eds., 1994).

researchers can rely on informants or should themselves observe proceedings to learn about particular norms. The methodology of proving the existence of folk law has been important not only to anthropologists but in law practice and adjudication. Much of the seminal work in this field focused on colonial Africa. Restatements or attempts to codify folk law were criticized as being a form of colonial social control, while others viewed such efforts as reflecting a conservative "retribalization" or "internal pacification," clearly not for the benefit of the groups whose laws were codified.

The study of folk law has focused on both specific rules and cases. Studies concentrating on rules have the disadvantage of missing the importance of legal processes through which customary law is interpreted and enforced. On the other hand, works that focus on cases may give the impression that a problem case is representative of the nature of a particular legal system. In court cases it was sometimes necessary to ascertain particular customary laws, which usually had to be specially pleaded as a question of fact. In colonial courts this meant that colonial peoples had to prove the validity of their own law to judges who were typically foreigners. Because of the difficulty of proving the existence of unwritten norms, judges in the dominant culture have often been unwilling to recognize folk law. On those occasions when they have been prepared to recognize folk law, they may have nevertheless refused to give it much weight if they viewed the customs as "repugnant" or contrary to "public policy." To make that clear, colonial legislation often contained "repugnancy clauses," which expressly prohibited traditions repugnant to "natural justice" such as infanticide, sati, and polygamy. One of the classic examples of colonial legal systems having to grapple with indigenous beliefs involved the use of a witchcraft defense.

To make matters more complicated, ascertaining the applicable rule or rules may offend the folk law of some groups if disclosing rules is unacceptable. For example, when Native Americans file lawsuits to protect their sacred sites, courts may require that they reveal precisely what landscapes are sacred. Divulging this information, however, may violate the folk law of the group in question.

Some aspects of folk law concern not the substantive content of the rules by which societies operate but instead legal processes and legal symbolism. Folk law includes the consideration of furniture arrangements in courtrooms, procedures for concluding a deal, such as by shaking hands, particular judicial attire, and the weapons allowed for law enforcement. There are also studies of the legal symbolism of the mace, instruments of punishment, and execution. The custom of having a child divide a piece of pie into two and then allowing the other child to select his "half" first is an example of children's folk legal custom. Another rich area of folk law is legal proverbs. For example, Americans are familiar with the castle doctrine ("A man's home is his castle") as well as "possession is nine-tenths of the law."

Classic ethnographic studies in anthropological jurisprudence have examined the rules governing retaliation for homicide such as the Albanian blood feud, the vendetta in Morocco, and feuding in Montenegro. Legal customs specify precisely which relative is to avenge a death, how many hours after the murder revenge should be taken, under what circumstance blood money may be paid to prevent a retaliatory killing, and so forth. These studies demonstrate how rule-governed these societies are.

One of the empirical questions in legal anthropology has been to characterize the standards employed in legal systems. Max Gluckman's famous book[] *The Judicial Process among the Barotse of Northern Rhodesia*[] contains numerous cases that he recorded when he did fieldwork among the Barotse, a Bantu people in what is now Zambia. His interpretation of the data is that the Barotse used the "reasonable person" standard in adjudication.

Max Gluckman, The Judicial Process among the Barotse of Northern Rhodesia 134–41 (1955)

CASE 28: THE CASE OF CROSS-COUSIN ADULTERY

Thus at Namalya Kuta under Nawala (R42) an Mbunda accused another Mbunda, one of my servants, of committing adultery with his wife. His case was that the defendant had given his wife a mat and a basket of meal. The defendant proved that the woman was his mother's brother's daughter, therefore his "sister" by Lozi custom, and he was entitled to make gifts to her. NAWALA and the other Lozi held that had he been a Lozi, he would have been acquitted. "For were you a Lozi, she would be your sister indeed, though even a Lozi makes gifts to his sister in public. But we know you Mbunda do not call the daughter of your mother's brother 'my sister,' and you can marry her. If you can marry her, you can commit adultery with her. If you were making presents to her because she is your relative, you should have given the things through her husband. Then he would have thanked you, for you would have been giving them to him. But you gave them on the side: you gave to her as your mistress. You will pay him [money], and she will give us [money] to send to the kuta." [Four years later the defendant admitted his guilt to me.]

Other presumptions held by the male judges about women influence their decisions, for men have certain ideas about the customary ways of women. In "The Case of the Schoolboy Adulterer," for one judge it was reasonable for a woman to accuse an innocent man of being her lover in order to protect her true lover, and this is what he, with many other men, believes girls are taught during the puberty seclusion. Another judge, who has been caught himself in an analogous situation, has learnt that adulteresses reveal the names of their true lovers; this then is reasonable behaviour for an adulteress. His personal experience rebuts the above presumption. Men also believe that it is customary for women, especially for a woman and her husband's sister, to tell each other of their affairs. The judges are thus working with a series of presumptions based on social and personal belief, and also personal experience. Here men are arguing in terms of what they believe women do and what women's customs are, and I cannot say whether their presumptions are sound or not.

These last presumptions, like others cited earlier, illustrate that for the kuta there are acts of behaviour which can only be reasonably explained on the assumption that the doer is an adulterer or adulteress. It is a false paradox, abut perhaps illuminating, to say that the kuta has a view of the "reasonable and customary" adulterer and adulteress. For lovers and their mistresses behave in certain standardized ways, which are not those of the innocent. These ways are well known, and assemble into social stereotypes.

ING'UNDE began his judgement: "I follow . . . because of the tempting seductiveness of women. We know them, because we have our sweethearts."

When the defendant said under cross-examination that he just took the orange because he was offered it, one judge countered: "Come on, you cannot deceive us; we all have our mistresses and know how a woman behaves with her lover."

. . .

The preceding case [illustrates] that a Barotse kuta cross-examines and assesses evidence by the standard of how a reasonable man or woman would have behaved, meticulously according to custom: refusing oranges from another man's wife and making a point of showing him her letters tempting to adultery. . . . But the legal significance of reasonable and customary behaviour extends far beyond its use in cross-examination and in assessing evidence to provide for judgment. The issue before the kuta may turn from a narrow, legally enforceable claim into an examination of whether the parties observed the obligations due to each other. . . . The problem of whether a person has fulfilled his obligations to another may be simple, if there is no clear breach of custom; or it may be complex in that a norm such as "A husband must care for his wife," has to be applied to varying circumstances. Thus, a wife may claim divorce from her husband on the grounds that he has committed an absolute breach of custom which cannot be remedied by damages or apology.

CASE 29: THE CASE OF A URINATING HUSBAND

A drunken husband, sleeping with one wife, when going out to urinate, turned at the wrong door, entered his other wife's room, and urinated on her. Induna Ishewambuta (Namakau Kuta) granted both wives immediate divorce: a husband must not mix his sexual actions with two wives.

CASE 30: THE CASE OF THE WIFE'S GRANARY

A wife was away visiting her parental home. Some of her kin came to her husband's home and he took food from her granary for them. Later people came prepared to pay a good price for grain for a feast: her husband took some of her grain and sold it, and on her return gave her the money. She claimed divorce and was granted it by the Lialui Kuta despite his protests that he was dispensing hospitality to her kin and selling the grain to her advantage, because it is prohibited for a husband to go to his wife's granary.

But a wife usually seeks a divorce by asking the kuta to declare that her husband has behaved so unreasonably that he no longer regards or treats her as a wife. This, in Lozi thinking, is why they have passed statutes to divorce women from men who have gone to White country for more than a certain number of years, a number which has steadily been reduced. It is unreasonable for a man to expect his wife to live alone for too long a period.

NOTES AND QUESTIONS

1. Although most societies make reference to notions of reasonableness in legal contexts, it is unclear whether the Barotse invoked the same standard used in the common law. What insights about the nature of reasonableness does Gluckman's study of Barotse jurisprudence afford us? His scholarship has been influential not only for demonstrating what techniques should be used in ethnographic studies of law but also for showing the dangers of projecting one's own legal categories onto one's data. This raises the question as to what linguistic terms researchers should use when they describe indigenous legal systems. A well-known debate between Max Gluckman and Paul Bohannan centered on this methodological challenge. Whereas Gluckman favored an approach that used the terms of the researcher's legal systems, Bohannan argued that the researcher should use the native terms linked to folk categories. Although Bohannan's approach avoids the risk of distortion, using only native terms for legal concepts complicates any serious effort to engage in comparative analysis.
2. The study of customary law is based on ethnographic fieldwork. Bronislaw Malinowski, whose observations we read earlier in this chapter, was a pioneering figure in developing this set of research techniques to gather empirical data about legal institutions. His study of penal law, *Crime and Custom in Savage Society* (1926), is a classic ethnography of law, as it offers insight into the relationship between social structure and legal processes. According to Malinowski, reciprocal obligation is the basis for social life, but his analysis was thought to be overinclusive with respect to the legal phenomena it encompassed.
3. Many types of dispute settlement mechanisms are used in indigenous legal systems. There are song duels, joking relationships, ordeals, shunning and banishment, and others. These serve to diffuse conflict and settle disputes that might be handled through adjudication in the modern state systems.
4. As a result of the impact of colonialism, it is nearly impossible to characterize legal systems built on custom as they existed before culture contact. Laura Nader's landmark study *Harmony Ideology: Justice and Control in a Zapotec Mountain Village* (1990) demonstrates the importance of recognizing the interaction among legal systems to see what larger social forces influenced the formation of particular indigenous legal rules and systems. In the United States, for example, forcing Native Americans onto reservations and sending their children to off-reservation boarding schools so they would become assimilated helped forge a pan-Indian social solidarity that gave rise to social movements such as American Indian movement. The emergence of the Native American Church was also partly a consequence of the colonial pressures exerted on Native Americans. State interference with the indigenous way of law affected the operation of indigenous law systems so as to complicate efforts to study them. Despite the reality that indigenous law has changed, scholars remain fascinated by some of the traditional techniques. For example, the flourishing restorative justice movement was inspired by indigenous folkways.
5. In some extraordinary cases, judges apply customary law in modern legal systems. For example, a trial judge in the state of Washington postponed final sentencing for Tlingit teenagers who had beaten a pizza-delivery man in order to allow their tribe to apply a customary sanction of banishment for a period of eighteen months.

Accordingly, the judge turned the convicted teenagers over to their tribal elders for banishment to remote islands off the coast of Alaska. The state of Washington appealed the sentence. If you were an appellate judge, how would you rule? For an argument that the judge's decision was inconsistent with the Eighth Amendment, see Stephanie Kim, Note, *Sentencing and Cultural Differences: Banishment of the American Indian Robbers*, 29 JOHN MARSHALL L. REV. 239 (1995). For the appellate court reversal of the judge's decision, see *State of Washington v. Simon P. Roberts et al.*, 894 P.2d 1340 (Wash. 1995). For defenses of incorporating tribal jurisprudence, see Clare E. Lyon, Note, *Alternative Methods for Sentencing Youthful Offenders: Using Traditional Tribal Methods as a Model*, 4 AVE MARIA L. REV. 211 (2006); Stacie S. Polaschuk, Note, *Following the Lead of the Indian Child Welfare Act: Expanding Tribal Court Jurisdiction over Native American Juvenile Delinquents*, 69 S. CAL. L. REV. 1191 (1996).

6. In 1996 Canada amended its criminal code so as to incorporate many of the recommendations of a report of the Canadian Sentencing Commission concerning the overrepresentation of native people in Canadian prisons and other correctional facilities. Among the new provisions was section 718.2(e), which states that "all available sanctions other than imprisonment that are reasonable in the circumstances should be considered for all offenders, with particular attention paid to the circumstances of aboriginal offenders." See Susan Haslip, *Conditional Sentencing and the Over-representation of Aboriginal Offenders in Penal Institutions*, 5 GONZ. J. INT'L L. (2001–02). In *R. v. Gladue*, [1999] 1 S.C.R. 688, the Supreme Court of Canada ruled that section 718.2(e) was inapplicable in a case involving a three-year sentence for manslaughter because, although both the offender and her victim were aboriginal persons, they lived in urban areas off-reserve.

   Another Canadian case, *Thomas v. Norris*, [1992] 2 C.N.L.R. 139 (B.C.S.C.), involved a civil claim for damages for assault and battery and false imprisonment. The defendants claimed that they had a constitutionally protected right to initiate the plaintiff, according to their own practices, into the Coast Salish Big House Tradition. The court dismissed this argument as follows:

   > Placing the aboriginal right at its highest level, it does not include civil immunity from coercion, force, assault, unlawful confinement, or any other unlawful tortuous conduct on the part of the defendants. While the plaintiff may have special rights and status in Canada as an Indian, the "original" rights and freedoms he enjoys can be no less than those enjoyed by fellow citizens, Indian and non-Indian alike.

4. Indigenous Law

Much of the earlier discussion about customary law and folk law pertains to the law of indigenous peoples. Although there is no agreed-on definition, the term "indigenous" generally refers to identifiable groups or peoples who are "native" in a territory, generally having been the first to settle there.

At the international level, a body of soft law focuses on indigenous peoples. The United Nations has taken a number of initiatives, beginning in 1982 with the establishment by the then Commission on Human Rights (now Human Rights Council) of the Working Group on Indigenous Populations and culminating in 2008 with the UN General Assembly's adoption of the UN Declaration on the Rights of Indigenous Peoples. An international agreement drafted and monitored by the International Labor Organization, a specialized agency of the United Nations, is also noteworthy. That agreement is the Convention Concerning Indigenous and Tribal Peoples (No. 69).

The commentary that follows highlights the value of indigenous law study, the mutual relationship between law and culture, and the protection of indigenous cultural artifacts as a prelude to the chapters that follow.

Daniel P. Strouthes, *Legal Systems of Aboriginal and Indigenous Peoples, in* 1 Encyclopedia of Law & Society 1, 2 (David S. Clark ed., 2007)

To understand law in depth, one must understand as many human legal systems as possible. The study of indigenous law has provided much helpful data, especially pertaining to making and testing useful generalizations. Using non-Western data, for example, we may conclude that non-Western nonstate legal systems make more use of the personality principle of law (law applied by status rather than by territory) than Western state systems do.

On the other hand, Western legal scholars have claimed, for instance, that the concept of *res judicata*, the idea that at some point in litigation a judicial system will make a final decision that cannot be altered, is to be found in *all* legal systems. *Res judicata's* advantage is that even an erroneous final judgment settles the dispute so that the parties may resume their lives rather than pursue litigation forever. However, Tibetan civil law allows a party to reopen a case at any time, a feature that Tibetans point to with pride. Why do Tibetans see no advantage to *res judicata* in civil cases (they use it in criminal cases)? Tibetan society has traditionally been one of small, very poor agricultural villages. Tibetans realize that if courts make final decisions in civil cases, the parties to the dispute, mainly neighbors, may not reconcile to the point that they could work together – in fact, long-standing hatred might result from the judicial decision. Absence of res judicata forces the parties to come to a mutually agreeable conclusion.

. . .

The student of indigenous legal systems quickly realizes the tremendous breadth of behaviors dealt with, the means of controlling those behaviors, and especially ideas of justice.

. . .

The study of non-Western legal systems usually reveals features central to the culture and society. Because law represents a powerful adaptive tool, a study of the society's laws provides a vivid look at the exigencies of life in that society. In addition, since most non-Western societies have few resources to utilize on law, making a law suggests that its members are saying that they consider this behavior very important to the group.

In some Shoshone groups, for instance, life before European settlement was harsh due to an arid environment, so much so that marriage was essential to survival. In these groups, therefore, the law required both the levirate (in which a widow marries her husband's brother) and the sororate (in which a widower marries his wife's sister).

The Cheyenne of the American Great Plains made it illegal for a man to hunt alone for bison, a herd animal that has the ability to cover large distances quickly. The Cheyenne depended on bison, and so if one lone hunter frightened the herd away before a large group of hunters made enough kills to feed the entire group, the Cheyenne would face hardship and even starvation.

In Uganda, raising cattle is an exceedingly risky business, yet vital to survival, so the Sebei developed a type of legally enforceable contract to spread this risk among multiple people, called *namanya*. In *namanya*, one party exchanges a bullock for a productive cow, which remains the property of the second party. The first party cares for the cow, enjoying whatever milk it produces, until it produces a heifer, which he keeps and then returns the original cow to the second party. All bullocks produced go to the second party. If the cow dies, is infertile, or produces only bullocks, the second party furnishes the first party with a replacement. An individual normally has several *namanya* contracts in force at any one time, both as cow-giver and as recipient.

NOTES

1. Two leading folklorists have identified the characteristic social outcomes of the most prominent ideologies, as cultural artifacts, of the twentieth century: their characterizations provide amusing variations on the Ugandan practice of *namanya* in the reading above.

   > Socialism . . . If you have two cows, you give your neighbor one.
   >
   > Communism . . . If you have two cows, you give them to the government and the government gives you some milk.
   >
   > Fascism . . . If you have two cows, you keep the cows and give the milk to the government and the government then sells you some of the milk.
   >
   > New-Dealism . . . If you have two cows, you shoot one and milk the other and then pour the milk down the drain.
   >
   > Nazism . . . If you have two cows, the government shoots you and keeps the cows.
   >
   > Capitalism . . . If you have two cows, you sell one and buy a bull.

   ALAN DUNDES & CARL R. PAGTER, URBAN FOLKLORE FROM THE PAPERWORK EMPIRE 59 (1978).
2. David Strouthes concludes his commentary on the legal systems of aboriginal and indigenous peoples, herein, with the following observation (from p. 5):

   > Some indigenous peoples are increasingly asking the dominant state to use its own legal systems to protect the rights that indigenous systems recognize but cannot control. For example, each Australian aborigine group has a different origin story, a "dreaming," a reference to the "dreamtime," or time of human

creation. Thus, each group has a separate set of symbols that pertain to its own origin story, and thereby the right to use those symbols. Now that Australian aboriginal art has become big business, many aborigines, whose use these symbols in their art, have pressed the Australian government to prevent all but members of each group from making use of that group's dreamtime symbols, thus preserving their monopolies.

Case of the Saramaka People v. Suriname, 2007 Inter-Am. Ct. H.R. (ser. C) No. 172 (Nov. 28, 2007)

I. Introduction of the Case and Subject of the Dispute

1. On June 23, 2006, in accordance with the provisions of Articles 50 and 61 of the American Convention [on Human Rights], the Inter-American Commission on Human Rights (hereinafter "the Commission" or "the Inter-American Commission") submitted an application to the Court against the State of Suriname (hereinafter "the State" or "Suriname").... On June 19, 2006, the Commission concluded that "the matter had not been settled" and, consequently, submitted this case to the jurisdiction of the Court.

2. The application submits to the Court's jurisdiction alleged violations committed by the State against the members of the Saramaka people, an allegedly tribal community living in the Upper Suriname River region. The Commission alleged that the State has not adopted effective measures to recognize their right to the use and enjoyment of the territory they have traditionally occupied and used, that the State has allegedly violated the right to judicial protection to the detriment of such people by not providing them effective access to justice for the protection of their fundamental rights, particularly the right to own property in accordance with their communal traditions, and that the State has allegedly failed to adopt domestic legal provisions in order to ensure and guarantee such rights to the Saramakas.

3. The Commission asked the Court to determine the international responsibility of the State for the violation of Articles 21 (Right to Property) and 25 (Right to Judicial Protection), in conjunction with Articles 1(1) and 2 of the American Convention [on Human Rights]. Furthermore, the Commission requested that the Court order the State to adopt several monetary and non-monetary reparation measures.

...

11. In its application before the Court, the Commission defined the factual basis for the present case under the heading "Statement of Facts." Here, the Commission included the following statement: "[d]uring the 1960s, the flooding derived from the construction of a hydroelectric dam displaced Saramakas and created the so-called 'transmigration' villages." This one line is the only reference in the Commission's application regarding the alleged displacement of members of the Saramaka people due to the construction of a dam, which the representatives referred to as the Afobaka

dam that in the 1960s flooded alleged traditional Saramaka territory. The Court observes that the Commission did not develop in the application any legal arguments regarding the alleged international responsibility of the State for these acts.

12. The representatives submitted an additional and rather detailed, three-and-a-half[-]page account of certain facts not contained in the application, regarding the alleged "ongoing and continuous effects" associated with the construction of the Afobaka dam. Accordingly, under the heading of "Facts" in their brief containing pleadings, motions, and evidence, the representatives described, *inter alia*, the following alleged facts: the lack of consent by the Saramaka people for said construction; the names of the companies involved in the construction of the dam; various figures regarding the amount of area flooded and the number of displaced Saramakas from the area; the compensation that was awarded to those displaced persons; the lack of access to electricity of the so-called "transmigration" villages; the painful effect the construction had on the community; the reduction of the Saramaka people's subsistence resources; the destruction of Saramaka sacred sites; the lack of respect for the interred remains of deceased Saramakas; the environmental degradation caused by foreign companies that have received mining concessions in the area, and the State's plan to increase the level of the dam to increase power supplies, which will presumably cause the forcible displacement of more Saramakas and which has been the object of a complaint filed by the Saramakas before domestic authorities in the year 2003.

...

Non-Compliance with Article 2[18] (Domestic Legal Effects), and Violation of Articles 3[19] (Right to Juridical Personality), 21[20] (Right to Property) and 25[21] (Right to Judicial Protection) of the American Convention, in relation to Article 1(1)[22] (Obligation to Respect Rights) thereof

[18] Article 2 establishes that, "[w]here the exercise of any of the rights or freedoms referred to in Article 1 is not already ensured by legislative or other provisions, the States Parties undertake to adopt, in accordance with their constitutional processes and the provisions of this Convention, such legislative or other measures as may be necessary to give effect to those rights or freedoms."

[19] Article 3 establishes that "[e]very person has the right to recognition as a person before the law."

[20] Article 21 establishes, *inter alia*, that "1. Everyone has the right to the use and enjoyment of his property. The law may subordinate such use and enjoyment to the interest of society. 2. No one shall be deprived of his property except upon payment of just compensation, for reasons of public utility or social interest, and in the cases and according to the forms established by law."

[21] Article 25 establishes that "1. Everyone has the right to simple and prompt recourse, or any other effective recourse, to a competent court or tribunal for protection against acts that violate his fundamental rights recognized by the constitution or laws of the state concerned or by this Convention, even though such violation may have been committed by persons acting in the course of their official duties. 2. The States Parties undertake:

a. to ensure that any person claiming such remedy shall have his rights determined by the competent authority provided for by the legal system of the state;
b. to develop the possibilities of judicial remedy; and
c. to ensure that the competent authorities shall enforce such remedies when granted."

[22] Article 1(1) establishes that "[t]he States Parties to this Convention undertake to respect the rights and freedoms recognized herein and to ensure to all persons subject to their jurisdiction the free and full

77. In light of the interrelatedness of the arguments submitted to the Court in the present case, the Tribunal will address in a single chapter the alleged non-compliance with Article 2, and violations of Articles 3, 21, and 25 of the Convention. Accordingly, the Court will address the following eight issues: first, whether the members of the Saramaka people make up a tribal community subject to special measures that ensure the full exercise of their rights; second, whether Article 21 of the American Convention protects the right of the members of tribal peoples to the use and enjoyment of communal property; third, whether the State has recognized the right to property of the members of the Saramaka people derived from their system of communal property; fourth, whether and to what extent the members of the Saramaka people have a right to use and enjoy the natural resources that lie on and within their alleged traditionally owned territory; fifth, whether and to what extent the State may grant concessions for the exploration and extraction of natural resources found on and within alleged Saramaka territory; sixth, whether the concessions already issued by the State comply with the safeguards established under international law; seventh, whether the lack of recognition of the Saramaka people as a juridical personality makes them ineligible under domestic law to receive communal title to property as a tribal community and to have equal access to judicial protection of their property rights; and finally, whether there are adequate and effective legal remedies available in Suriname to protect the members of the Saramaka people against acts that violate their alleged right to the use and enjoyment of communal property.

A. The Members of the Saramaka People as a Tribal Community Subject to Special Measures That Ensure the Full Exercise of Their Rights

78. The Commission and the representatives alleged that the Saramaka people make up a tribal community and that international human rights law imposes an obligation on the State to adopt special measures to guarantee the recognition of tribal peoples' rights, including the right to collectively own property. The State disputed whether the Saramaka people could be defined as a tribal community subject to the protection of international human rights law regarding their alleged right to collectively own property. The Court must therefore analyze whether the members of the Saramaka people make up a tribal community, and if so, whether it is subject to special measures that guarantee the full exercise of their rights.

79. First of all, the Court observes that the Saramaka people are not indigenous to the region they inhabit; they were instead brought to what is now known as Suriname during the colonization period. Therefore, they are asserting their rights as alleged tribal peoples, that is, not indigenous to the region, but that share similar characteristics with indigenous peoples, such as having social, cultural and economic traditions different from

exercise of those rights and freedoms, without any discrimination for reasons of race, color, sex, language, religion, political or other opinion, national or social origin, economic status, birth, or any other social condition."

other sections of the national community, identifying themselves with their ancestral territories, and regulating themselves, at least partially, by their own norms, customs, and traditions.

A.1) The Members of the Saramaka People as a Distinct Social, Cultural and Economic Group with a Special Relationship with its Ancestral Territory

80. According to the evidence submitted by the parties, the Saramaka people are one of the six distinct Maroon groups in Suriname whose ancestors were African slaves forcibly taken to Suriname during the European colonization in the 17th century. Their ancestors escaped to the interior regions of the country where they established autonomous communities. The Saramaka people are organized in twelve matrilineal clans (*lös*), and it is estimated that the contemporary size of the Saramaka population ranges from 25,000 to 34,000, which is spread over 63 communities on the Upper Suriname River and in a number of displaced communities located to the north and west of said area.

81. Their social structure is different from other sectors of society inasmuch as the Saramaka people are organized in matrilineal clans (*lös*), and they regulate themselves, at least partially, by their own customs and traditions. Each clan (*lö*) recognizes the political authority of various local leaders, including what they call Captains and Head Captains, as well as a *Gaa'man*, who is the community's highest official.

82. Their culture is also similar to that of tribal peoples insofar as the members of the Saramaka people maintain a strong spiritual relationship with the ancestral territory they have traditionally used and occupied. Land is more than merely a source of subsistence for them; it is also a necessary source for the continuation of the life and cultural identity of the Saramaka people. The lands and resources of the Saramaka people are part of their social, ancestral, and spiritual essence. In this territory, the Saramaka people hunt, fish, and farm, and they gather water, plants for medicinal purposes, oils, minerals, and wood. Their sacred sites are scattered throughout the territory, while at the same time the territory itself has a sacred value to them. In particular, the identity of the members of the Saramaka people with the land is inextricably linked to their historical fight for freedom from slavery, called the sacred "first time." During the public hearing in this case, Head Captain Wazen Eduards described their special relationship with the land as follows:

> The forest is like our market place; it is where we get our medicines, our medicinal plants. It is where we hunt to have meat to eat. The forest is truly our entire life. When our ancestors fled into the forest they did not carry anything with them. They learned how to live, what plants to eat, how to deal with subsistence needs once they got to the forest. It is our whole life.

83. Furthermore, their economy can also be characterized as tribal. According to the expert testimony of Dr. Richard Price, for example, "the very great bulk of food that Saramaka eat comes from . . . farms [and] gardens" traditionally cultivated by Saramaka women. The men, according to Dr. Price, fish and "hunt wild pig, deer, tapir, all sorts of monkeys, different kinds of birds, everything that Saramakas eat." Furthermore, the women gather various fruits, plants and minerals, which they use in a variety of ways, including making baskets, cooking oil, and roofs for their dwellings.

84. Thus, in accordance with all of the above, the Court considers that the members of the Saramaka people make up a tribal community whose social, cultural and economic characteristics are different from other sections of the national community, particularly because of their special relationship with their ancestral territories, and because they regulate themselves, at least partially, by their own norms, customs, and/or traditions. Accordingly, the Court will now address whether and to what extent the members of the tribal peoples require special measures that guarantee the full exercise of their rights.

A.2) Special Measures of Protection Owed to Members of the Tribal Community That Guarantee the Full Exercise of Their Rights

85. This Court has previously held, based on Article 1(1) of the Convention, that members of indigenous and tribal communities require special measures that guarantee the full exercise of their rights, particularly with regards to their enjoyment of property rights, in order to safeguard their physical and cultural survival. Other sources of international law have similarly declared that such special measures are necessary. Particularly, in the *Moiwana* case, this Court determined that another Maroon community living in Suriname was also not indigenous to the region, but rather constituted a tribal community that settled in Suriname in the 17th and 18th century, and that this tribal community had "a profound and all-encompassing relationship to their ancestral lands" that was centered, not "on the individual, but rather on the community as a whole." This special relationship to land, as well as their communal concept of ownership, prompted the Court to apply to the tribal Moiwana community its jurisprudence regarding indigenous peoples and their right to communal property under Article 21 of the Convention.

86. The Court sees no reason to depart from this jurisprudence in the present case. Hence, this Tribunal declares that the members of the Saramaka people are to be considered a tribal community, and that the Court's jurisprudence regarding indigenous peoples' right to property is also applicable to tribal peoples because both share distinct social, cultural, and economic characteristics, including a special relationship with their ancestral territories, that require special measures under international human rights law in order to guarantee their physical and cultural survival.

B. The Right of Members of Tribal Peoples to the Use and Enjoyment of Communal Property in Accordance with Articles 21, 1.1, and 2 of the American Convention

87. The Court will now address whether Article 21 of the American Convention recognizes the rights of members of tribal peoples to the use and enjoyment of communal property.

B.1) Right to Communal Property under Article 21 of the American Convention

88. This Court has previously addressed this issue and has consistently held that:

> the close ties the members of indigenous communities have with their traditional lands and the natural resources associated with their culture thereof, as well as the incorporeal elements deriving there from, must be secured under Article 21 of the American Convention.

89. Likewise, in the *Mayagna* case, the Court considered that "Article 21 of the Convention protects the right to property[,] which includes, among others, the rights of members of . . . indigenous communities within the framework of communal property." Similarly, in the *Sawhoyamaxa* case, the Court considered "that indigenous communities might have a collective understanding of the concepts of property and possession, in the sense that ownership of the land 'is not centered on an individual, but rather on the group and its community.'" Moreover, the Court held in the *Yakye Axa* case that "both the private property of individuals and communal property of the members of . . . indigenous communities are protected by Article 21 of the American Convention."

90. The Court's decisions to this effect have all been based upon the special relationship that members of indigenous and tribal peoples have with their territory, and on the need to protect their right to that territory in order to safeguard the physical and cultural survival of such peoples. In this sense, the Court has declared that:

> the close ties of indigenous people with the land must be recognized and understood as the fundamental basis of their cultures, their spiritual life, their integrity, and their economic survival. For indigenous communities, [their relationship with] the land is not merely a matter of possession and production but a material and spiritual element, which they must fully enjoy . . . to preserve their cultural legacy and transmit it to future generations.

91. In essence, pursuant to Article 21 of the Convention, States must respect the special relationship that members of indigenous and tribal peoples have with their territory in a way that guarantees their social, cultural, and economic survival. Such protection of property under Article 21 of the Convention, read in conjunction with Articles 1(1) and 2 of said instrument, places upon States a positive obligation to adopt special

measures that guarantee members of indigenous and tribal peoples the full and equal exercise of their right to the territories they have traditionally used and occupied.

B.2) Interpretation of Article 21 of the American Convention in the Present Case

92. The Court recognizes that it has arrived at such an interpretation of Article 21 in previous cases in light of Article 29(b) of the Convention, which prohibits an interpretation of any provision of the Convention in a manner that restricts its enjoyment to a lesser degree than what is recognized in the domestic laws of the State in question or in another treaty to which the State is a party. Accordingly, the Court has interpreted Article 21 of the Convention in light of the domestic legislation pertaining to indigenous peoples' rights in Nicaragua and Paraguay, for example, as well as taking into account the International Labor Organization's Convention (No. 169) concerning Indigenous and Tribal Peoples in Independent Countries (hereinafter "ILO Convention 169").

93. As will be discussed *infra*, Suriname's domestic legislation does not recognize a right to communal property of members of its tribal communities, and it has not ratified ILO Convention 169. Nevertheless, Suriname has ratified both the International Covenant on Civil and Political Rights as well as the International Covenant on Economic, Social, and Cultural Rights. The Committee on Economic, Social, and Cultural Rights, which is the body of independent experts that supervises States parties' implementation of the ICESCR, has interpreted common Article 1 of said instruments as being applicable to indigenous peoples. Accordingly, by virtue of the right of indigenous peoples to self-determination recognized under said Article 1, they may "freely pursue their economic, social and cultural development," and may "freely dispose of their natural wealth and resources" so as not to be "deprived of [their] own means of subsistence." Pursuant to Article 29(b) of the American Convention, this Court may not interpret the provisions of Article 21 of the American Convention in a manner that restricts its enjoyment and exercise to a lesser degree than what is recognized in said covenants. This Court considers that the same rationale applies to tribal peoples due to the similar social, cultural, and economic characteristics they share with indigenous peoples.

94. Similarly, the Human Rights Committee has analyzed the obligations of State Parties to the ICCPR under Article 27 of such instrument, including Suriname, and observed that "minorities shall not be denied the right, in community with the other members of their group, to enjoy their own culture[, which] may consist in a way of life which is closely associated with territory and use of its resources. This may particularly be true of members of indigenous communities constituting a minority."

95. The above analysis supports an interpretation of Article 21 of the American Convention to the effect of calling for the right of members of

indigenous and tribal communities to freely determine and enjoy their own social, cultural and economic development, which includes the right to enjoy their particular spiritual relationship with the territory they have traditionally used and occupied. Thus, in the present case, the right to property protected under Article 21 of the American Convention, interpreted in light of the rights recognized under common Article 1 and Article 27 of the ICCPR, which may not be restricted when interpreting the American Convention, grants to the members of the Saramaka community the right to enjoy property in accordance with their communal tradition.

96. Applying the aforementioned criteria to the present case, the Court thus concludes that the members of the Saramaka people make up a tribal community protected by international human rights law that secures the right to the communal territory they have traditionally used and occupied, derived from their longstanding use and occupation of the land and resources necessary for their physical and cultural survival, and that the State has an obligation to adopt special measures to recognize, respect, protect and guarantee the communal property right of the members of the Saramaka community to said territory.

C. The Property Rights of the Members of the Saramaka People Derived from Their System of Communal Property (Article 21 of the Convention in Conjunction with Articles 1(1) and 2 Thereof)

97. Having declared that the American Convention recognizes the right of the members of the Saramaka people to the use and enjoyment of property in accordance with their system of communal property, the Court will now proceed to analyze whether the State has adopted an appropriate framework to give domestic legal effect to this right.

98. This Court, in the *Moiwana* case, already addressed the general issue regarding communal property rights of indigenous and tribal peoples in Suriname. There, the Court held that the State did not recognize [that such peoples had] a collective right to property. The Court observes that such conclusion is further supported by a variety of international bodies and organizations that have also addressed this issue. The United Nations Committee on the Elimination of Racial Discrimination, the United Nations Human Rights Committee, and the United Nations Commission on Human Rights' Special Rapporteur on the situation of human rights and fundamental freedoms of indigenous people have all observed that Suriname does not legally recognize the rights of members of indigenous and tribal peoples to their communal land, territories, and resources.

99. The State also acknowledged that its domestic legal framework does not recognize the right of the members of the Saramaka people to the use and enjoyment of property in accordance with their system of communal property, but rather a privilege to use land. Nevertheless, the State provided four alleged reasons as to why it should not be held accountable for this in the present case. First, the State asserted that the lack of clarity regarding

the land tenure system of the Saramaka people, particularly regarding who owns the land, presents a practical problem for State recognition of their right to communal property. Second, certain "complexities and sensitivities" regarding the issue of collective rights have not permitted the State to legally recognize such rights. The State suggested that legislation providing for "special treatment" for indigenous and tribal groups raises questions of State sovereignty and discrimination with regard to the rest of the population. Thirdly, the State argued that judge-made law could recognize rights to communal property, but the members of the Saramaka people have refused to apply to domestic courts for said recognition. Finally, the State argued that its domestic legislation recognizes an "interest," rather than a right, to property of members of the Saramaka people. The Court will address each issue in said order.

C.1) Land Tenure System of the Members of the Saramaka People

100. First, the issue regarding the alleged lack of clarity of the members of the Saramaka people's traditional land ownership regime was thoroughly addressed by the parties, witnesses, and expert witnesses in the present case. From the evidence and testimonies submitted before the Court, it is clear that the *lös*, or clans, are the primary land-owning entities within Saramaka society. Each *lö* is highly autonomous and allocates land and resource rights among their constituent *bëë* (extended family groups) and their individual members in accordance with Saramaka customary law. Pursuant to this customary law, the Captains or members of a *lö* may not alienate or otherwise encumber the communal property of their *lö*, and a *lö* may not encumber or alienate their lands from the collectively held corpus of Saramaka territory. On this last point, Head Captain and *Fiscali* Eddie Fonkie explained that "[i]f a *lö* tried to sell its land, the other *lö* would have the right to object and to stop [such transaction] because it would affect the rights and life of all Saramaka people. The *lö* are very autonomous and . . . do not interfere in each other's affairs unless it affects the interests of all Saramaka people." This is because the territory "belongs to the Saramakas, ultimately. [That is,] it belongs to the Saramakas as a people."

101. In any case, the alleged lack of clarity as to the land tenure system of the Saramakas does not present an insurmountable obstacle for the State, which has the duty to consult with the members of the Saramaka people and seek clarification of this issue, in order to comply with its obligations under Article 21 of the Convention, in conjunction with Article 2 of such instrument.

C.2) Complexity of Issues Involved and the State's Concern Regarding Discrimination against Non-Indigenous or Non-Tribal Members

102. Two additional related arguments submitted by the State as to why it has failed to legally recognize and protect the land-tenure systems of indigenous and tribal communities' are the alleged "complexities and

sensitivities" of the issues involved, and the concern that legislation in favor of indigenous and tribal peoples may be perceived as being discriminatory towards the rest of the population. Regarding the first issue, the Court observes that the State may not abstain from complying with its international obligations under the American Convention merely because of the alleged difficulty to do so. The Court shares the State's concern over the complexity of the issues involved; nevertheless, the State still has a duty to recognize the right to property of members of the Saramaka people, within the framework of a communal property system, and establish the mechanisms necessary to give domestic legal effect to such right recognized in the Convention, as interpreted by this Tribunal in its jurisprudence.

103. Furthermore, the State's argument that it would be discriminatory to pass legislation that recognizes communal forms of land ownership is also without merit. It is a well-established principle of international law that unequal treatment towards persons in unequal situations does not necessarily amount to impermissible discrimination. Legislation that recognizes said differences is therefore not necessarily discriminatory. In the context of members of indigenous and tribal peoples, this Court has already stated that special measures are necessary in order to ensure their survival in accordance with their traditions and customs. Thus, the State's arguments regarding its inability to create legislation in this area due to the alleged complexity of the issue or the possible discriminatory nature of such legislation are without merit.

C.3) Judge-Made Law

104. Additionally, the State argued that judge-made law could recognize collective property rights, but that the members of the Saramaka people have refused to apply to domestic courts for said recognition. First and foremost, a distinction should be made between the State's duty under Article 2 of the Convention to give domestic legal effect to the rights recognized therein, and the duty under Article 25 to provide adequate and effective recourses to remedy alleged violations of those rights. The Court will address *infra*, in its analysis of the alleged violation of Article 25 of the Convention, the effectiveness of the recourses mentioned by the State, including those available under article 1386 of Suriname's Civil Code, to remedy alleged violations of the right to property of members of the Saramaka people in conformity with their system of communal property.

105. The Court observes that although so-called judge-made law may certainly be a means for the recognition of the rights of individuals, particularly under common-law legal systems, the availability of such a procedure does not, in and of itself, comply with the State's obligation to give legal effect to the rights recognized in the American Convention. That is, the mere possibility of recognition of rights through a certain judicial process is no substitute for the actual recognition of such rights. The judicial

process mentioned by the State is thus to be understood as a means by which said rights might be given domestic legal effect at some point in the future, but that has not yet effectively recognized the rights in question. In any case, the right of the members of the Saramaka people in particular, or members of indigenous and tribal communities in general, to collectively own their territory has not, as of yet, been recognized by any domestic court in Suriname.

. . .

115. In sum, the State's legal framework merely grants the members of the Saramaka people a privilege to use land, which does not guarantee the right to effectively control their territory without outside interference. The Court has previously held that, rather than a privilege to use the land, which can be taken away by the State or trumped by real property rights of third parties, members of indigenous and tribal peoples must obtain title to their territory in order to guarantee its permanent use and enjoyment. This title must be recognized and respected, not only in practice, but also in law, in order to ensure its legal certainty. In order to obtain such title, the territory traditionally used and occupied by the members of the Saramaka people must first be delimited and demarcated, in consultation with such people and other neighboring peoples. In this regard, the Court has previously declared that "a strictly juridical or abstract recognition of indigenous lands, territories or resources lacks true meaning where the property has not been physically established and delimited."

. . .

D. The Right of the Members of the Saramaka People to Use and Enjoy the Natural Resources That Lie on and within Their Traditionally Owned Territory

118. An issue that necessarily flows from the assertion that the members of the Saramaka people have a right to use and enjoy their territory in accordance with their traditions and customs is the issue of the right to the use and enjoyment of the natural resources that lie on and within the land, including subsoil natural resources. In the present case, both the State and the members of the Saramaka people claim a right to these natural resources. The Saramakas claim that their right to use and enjoy all such natural resources is a necessary condition for the enjoyment of their right to property under Article 21 of the Convention. The State argued that all rights to land, particularly its subsoil natural resources, are vested in the State, which can freely dispose of these resources through concessions to third parties. The Court will address this complex issue in the following order: first, the right of the members of the Saramaka people to use and enjoy the natural resources that lie on and within their traditionally owned territory; second, the State's grant of concessions for the exploration and extraction of natural resources, including subsoil resources found within Saramaka territory; and finally, the fulfillment of international law guarantees regarding the exploration and extraction concessions already issued by the State.

119. First, the Court must analyze whether and to what extent the members of the Saramaka people have a right to use and enjoy the natural resources that lie on and within their traditionally owned territory. The State does not contest that the Saramakas have traditionally used and occupied certain lands for centuries, or that the Saramakas have an "interest" in the territory they have traditionally used in accordance with their customs. The controversy lies regarding the nature and scope of said interest. In accordance with Suriname's legal and constitutional framework, the Saramakas do not have property rights *per se*, but rather merely a privilege or permission to use and occupy the lands in question. According to Article 41 of the Constitution of Suriname and Article 2 of its 1986 Mining Decree, ownership rights of all natural resources vest in the State. For this reason, the State claims to have an inalienable right to the exploration and exploitation of those resources. On the other hand, the customary laws of the Saramaka people allegedly vest in its community a right over all natural resources within and subjacent to or otherwise pertaining to its traditional territory. In support of this assertion, the Court heard testimony from a Saramaka Captain to the effect that the Saramaka people have a general right to "own everything, from the very top of the trees to the very deepest place that you could go under the ground."

120. In this regard, this Court has previously held that the cultural and economic survival of indigenous and tribal peoples, and their members, depend on their access and use of the natural resources in their territory "that are related to their culture and are found therein," and that Article 21 protects their right to such natural resources. Nevertheless, the scope of this right needs further elaboration, particularly regarding the inextricable relationship between both land and the natural resources that lie therein, as well as between the territory (understood as encompassing both land and natural resources) and the economic, social, and cultural survival of indigenous and tribal peoples, and thus, of their members.

121. In accordance with this Court's jurisprudence as stated in the *Yakye Axa* and *Sawhoyamaxa* cases, members of tribal and indigenous communities have the right to own the natural resources they have traditionally used within their territory for the same reasons that they have a right to own the land they have traditionally used and occupied for centuries. Without them, the very physical and cultural survival of such peoples is at stake. Hence the need to protect the lands and resources they have traditionally used to prevent their extinction as a people. That is, the aim and purpose of the special measures required on behalf of the members of indigenous and tribal communities is to guarantee that they may continue living their traditional way of life, and that their distinct cultural identity, social structure, economic system, customs, beliefs and traditions are respected, guaranteed and protected by States.

122. As mentioned above, due to the inextricable connection members of indigenous and tribal peoples have with their territory, the protection of their right to property over such territory, in accordance with Article 21

of the Convention, is necessary to guarantee their very survival. Accordingly, the right to use and enjoy their territory would be meaningless in the context of indigenous and tribal communities if said right were not connected to the natural resources that lie on and within the land. That is, the demand for collective land ownership by members of indigenous and tribal peoples derives from the need to ensure the security and permanence of their control and use of the natural resources, which in turn maintains their very way of life. This connectedness between the territory and the natural resources necessary for their physical and cultural survival is precisely what needs to be protected under Article 21 of the Convention in order to guarantee the members of indigenous and tribal communities' right to the use and enjoyment of their property. From this analysis, it follows that the natural resources found on and within indigenous and tribal people's territories that are protected under Article 21 are those natural resources traditionally used and necessary for the very survival, development and continuation of such people's way of life.

123. Thus, in the present case, the Court must determine which natural resources found on and within the Saramaka people's territory are essential for the survival of their way of life, and are thus protected under Article 21 of the Convention. Consequently, the Court must also address whether and to what extent the State may grant concessions for the exploration and extraction of those and other natural resources found within Saramaka territory.

E. The State's Grant of Concessions for the Exploration and Extraction of Natural Resources Found on and Within Saramaka Territory

124. The Commission and the representatives alleged that land concessions for forestry and mining awarded by the State to third parties on territory possessed by the Saramaka people, without their full and effective consultation, violate their right to the natural resources that lie on and within the land. The State asserted that all land ownership, including all natural resources, vests in the State, and that, as such, the State may grant logging and mining concessions within alleged Saramaka territory, while respecting as much as possible Saramaka customs and traditions.

E.1) Restrictions on the Right to Property

125. This brings the Court to the issue of whether and to what extent the State may grant concessions for the exploration and extraction of natural resources found within Saramaka territory. In this regard, the State argued that, should the Court recognize a right of the members of the Saramaka people to the natural resources found within traditionally owned lands, this right must be limited to those resources traditionally used for their subsistence, cultural and religious activities. According to the State, the alleged land rights of the Saramakas "would not include any interests on forests or minerals beyond what the Tribe traditionally possesses and uses

for subsistence (agriculture, hunting, fishing etc.), and the religious and cultural needs of its people."

126. The State seems to recognize that resources related to the subsistence of the Saramaka people include those related to agricultural, hunting and fishing activities. This is consistent with the Court's previous analysis on how Article 21 of the Convention protects the members of the Saramaka people's right over those natural resources necessary for their physical survival. Nevertheless, while it is true that all exploration and extraction activity in the Saramaka territory could affect, to a greater or lesser degree, the use and enjoyment of some natural resource traditionally used for the subsistence of the Saramakas, it is also true that Article 21 of the Convention should not be interpreted in a way that prevents the State from granting any type of concession for the exploration and extraction of natural resources within Saramaka territory. Clean natural water, for example, is a natural resource essential for the Saramakas to be able to carry out some of their subsistence economic activities, like fishing. The Court observes that this natural resource is likely to be affected by extraction activities related to other natural resources that are not traditionally used by or essential for the survival of the Saramaka people and, consequently, its members. Similarly, the forests within Saramaka territory provide a home for the various animals they hunt for subsistence, and it is where they gather fruits and other resources essential for their survival. In this sense, wood-logging activities in the forest would also likely affect such subsistence resources. That is, the extraction of one natural resource is most likely to affect the use and enjoyment of other natural resources that are necessary for the survival of the Saramakas.

127. Nevertheless, the protection of the right to property under Article 21 of the Convention is not absolute and therefore does not allow for such a strict interpretation. Although the Court recognizes the interconnectedness between the right of members of indigenous and tribal peoples to the use and enjoyment of their lands and their right to those resources necessary for their survival, said property rights, like many other rights recognized in the Convention, are subject to certain limitations and restrictions. In this sense, Article 21 of the Convention states that the "law may subordinate [the] use and enjoyment [of property] to the interest of society." Thus, the Court has previously held that, in accordance with Article 21 of the Convention, a State may restrict the use and enjoyment of the right to property where the restrictions are: a) previously established by law; b) necessary; c) proportional, and d) with the aim of achieving a legitimate objective in a democratic society. In accordance with this Article, and the Court's jurisprudence, the State will be able to restrict, under certain circumstances, the Saramakas' property rights, including their rights to natural resources found on and within the territory.

128. Furthermore, in analyzing whether restrictions on the property right of members of indigenous and tribal peoples are permissible, especially

regarding the use and enjoyment of their traditionally owned lands and natural resources, another crucial factor to be considered is whether the restriction amounts to a denial of their traditions and customs in a way that endangers the very survival of the group and of its members. That is, under Article 21 of the Convention, the State may restrict the Saramakas' right to use and enjoy their traditionally owned lands and natural resources only when such restriction complies with the aforementioned requirements and, additionally, when it does not deny their survival as a tribal people.

E.2) Safeguards against Restrictions on the Right to Property That Deny the Survival of the Saramaka People

129. In this particular case, the restrictions in question pertain to the issuance of logging and mining concessions for the exploration and extraction of certain natural resources found within Saramaka territory. Thus, in accordance with Article 1(1) of the Convention, in order to guarantee that restrictions to the property rights of the members of the Saramaka people by the issuance of concessions within their territory do not amount to a denial of their survival as a tribal people, the State must abide by the following three safeguards: First, the State must ensure the effective participation of the members of the Saramaka people, in conformity with their customs and traditions, regarding any development, investment, exploration or extraction plan (hereinafter "development or investment plan") within Saramaka territory. Second, the State must guarantee that the Saramakas will receive a reasonable benefit from any such plan within their territory. Thirdly, the State must ensure that no concession will be issued within Saramaka territory unless and until independent and technically capable entities, with the State's supervision, perform a prior environmental and social impact assessment. These safeguards are intended to preserve, protect and guarantee the special relationship that the members of the Saramaka community have with their territory, which in turn ensures their survival as a tribal people.

130. These safeguards, particularly those of effective participation and sharing of benefits regarding development or investment projects within traditional indigenous and tribal territories, are consistent with the observations of the Human Rights Committee, the text of several international instruments, and the practice in several States Parties to the Convention. In *Apirana Mahuika et al. v. New Zealand*, for example, the Human Rights Committee decided that the right to culture of an indigenous population under Article 27 of the ICCPR could be restricted where the community itself participated in the decision to restrict such right. The Committee found that "the acceptability of measures that affect or interfere with the culturally significant economic activities of a minority depends on whether the members of the minority in question have had the opportunity to participate in the decision-making process in relation to these measures and whether they will continue to benefit from their traditional economy."

131. Similarly, Article 32 of the United Nations Declaration on the Rights of Indigenous Peoples, which was recently approved by the UN General Assembly with the support of the State of Suriname, states the following:

1. Indigenous peoples have the right to determine and develop priorities and strategies for the development or use of their lands or territories and other resources.
2. States shall consult and cooperate in good faith with the indigenous peoples concerned through their own representative institutions in order to obtain their free and informed consent prior to the approval of any project affecting their lands or territories and other resources, particularly in connection with the development, utilization or exploitation of mineral, water or other resources.
3. States shall provide effective mechanisms for just and fair redress for any such activities, and appropriate measures shall be taken to mitigate adverse environmental, economic, social, cultural or spiritual impact.

132. More importantly, the District Commissioner of Sipaliwini in Suriname, who testified before the Court on behalf of the State, recognized the importance of consulting with the traditional authorities of the Saramaka people prior to authorizing concessions that may affect "communities in the direct vicinities." Nonetheless, the Court considers that the actual scope of the guarantees concerning consultation and sharing of the benefits of development or investment projects requires further clarification.

E.2.a) Right to Consultation and, Where Applicable, a Duty to Obtain Consent

133. First, the Court has stated that in ensuring the effective participation of members of the Saramaka people in development or investment plans within their territory, the State has a duty to actively consult with said community according to their customs and traditions. This duty requires the State to both accept and disseminate information, and entails constant communication between the parties. These consultations must be in good faith, through culturally appropriate procedures and with the objective of reaching an agreement. Furthermore, the Saramakas must be consulted, in accordance with their own traditions, at the early stages of a development or investment plan, not only when the need arises to obtain approval from the community, if such is the case. Early notice provides time for internal discussion within communities and for proper feedback to the State. The State must also ensure that members of the Saramaka people are aware of possible risks, including environmental and health risks, in order that the proposed development or investment plan is accepted knowingly and voluntarily. Finally, consultation should take account of the Saramaka people's traditional methods of decision-making.

134. Additionally, the Court considers that, regarding large-scale development or investment projects that would have a major impact within

Saramaka territory, the State has a duty, not only to consult with the Saramakas, but also to obtain their free, prior, and informed consent, according to their customs and traditions. The Court considers that the difference between "consultation" and "consent" in this context requires further analysis.

135. In this sense, the U.N. Special Rapporteur on the situation of human rights and fundamental freedoms of indigenous people has similarly observed that:

> [w]herever [large-scale projects] occur in areas occupied by indigenous peoples it is likely that their communities will undergo profound social and economic changes that are frequently not well understood, much less foreseen, by the authorities in charge of promoting them. . . . The principal human rights effects of these projects for indigenous peoples relate to loss of traditional territories and land, eviction, migration and eventual resettlement, depletion of resources necessary for physical and cultural survival, destruction and pollution of the traditional environment, social and community disorganization, long-term negative health and nutritional impacts as well as, in some cases, harassment and violence.

Consequently, the U.N. Special Rapporteur determined that "[f]ree, prior and informed consent is essential for the [protection of] human rights of indigenous peoples in relation to major development projects."

136. Other international bodies and organizations have similarly considered that, in certain circumstances, and in addition to other consultation mechanisms, States must obtain the consent of indigenous and tribal peoples to carry out large-scale development or investment projects that have a significant impact on the right of use and enjoyment of their ancestral territories.

137. Most importantly, the State has also recognized that the "level of consultation that is required is obviously a function of the nature and content of the rights of the Tribe in question." The Court agrees with the State and, furthermore, considers that, in addition to the consultation that is always required when planning development or investment projects within traditional Saramaka territory, the safeguard of effective participation that is necessary when dealing with major development or investment plans that may have a profound impact on the property rights of the members of the Saramaka people to a large part of their territory must be understood to additionally require the free, prior, and informed consent of the Saramakas, in accordance with their traditions and customs.

E.2.b) Benefit-Sharing

138. The second safeguard the State must ensure when considering development or investment plans within Saramaka territory is that of reasonably

sharing the benefits of the project with the Saramaka people. The concept of benefit-sharing, which can be found in various international instruments regarding indigenous and tribal peoples' rights, can be said to be inherent to the right of compensation recognized under Article 21(2) of the Convention, which states that

> [n]o one shall be deprived of his property except upon payment of just compensation, for reasons of pubic utility or social interest, and in the cases and according to the forms established by law.

139. The Court considers that the right to obtain compensation under Article 21(2) of the Convention extends not only to the total deprivation of property title by way of expropriation by the State, for example, but also to the deprivation of the regular use and enjoyment of such property. In the present context, the right to obtain "just compensation" pursuant to Article 21(2) of the Convention translates into a right of the members of the Saramaka people to reasonably share in the benefits made as a result of a restriction or deprivation of their right to the use and enjoyment of their traditional lands and of those natural resources necessary for their survival.

140. In this sense, the Committee on the Elimination of Racial Discrimination has recommended not only that the prior informed consent of communities must be sought when major exploitation activities are planned in indigenous territories, but also "that the equitable sharing of benefits to be derived from such exploitation be ensured." Similarly, the Special Rapporteur on the situation of human rights and fundamental freedoms of indigenous peoples has suggested that, in order to guarantee "the human rights of indigenous peoples in relation to major development projects, [States should ensure] mutually acceptable benefit sharing. . . . " In this context, pursuant to Article 21(2) of the Convention, benefit sharing may be understood as a form of reasonable equitable compensation resulting from the exploitation of traditionally owned lands and of those natural resources necessary for the survival of the Saramaka people.

F. The Fulfillment of the Guarantees Established under International Law in Relation to the Concessions Already Granted by the State

141. Having declared that the Saramakas' right to use and enjoy their traditionally owned lands necessarily implies a similar right with regards to the natural resources that are necessary for their survival, and having set safeguards and limitations regarding the State's right to issue concessions that restrict the use and enjoyment of such natural resources, the Court will now proceed to analyze whether the concessions already issued by the State within Saramaka territory complied with the safeguards mentioned above.

. . .

153. Not only have the members of the Saramaka people been left with a legacy of environmental destruction, despoiled subsistence resources, and

spiritual and social problems, but they received no benefit from the logging in their territory. Government statistics submitted into evidence before the Court prove that a considerable quantity of valuable timber was extracted from the territory of the Saramaka people without any compensation.

154. In conclusion, the Court considers that the logging concessions issued by the State in the Upper Suriname River lands have damaged the environment and the deterioration has had a negative impact on lands and natural resources traditionally used by members of the Saramaka people that are, in whole or in part, within the limits of the territory to which they have a communal property right. The State failed to carry out or supervise environmental and social impact assessments and failed to put in place adequate safeguards and mechanisms in order to ensure that these logging concessions would not cause major damage to Saramaka territory and communities. Furthermore, the State did not allow for the effective participation of the Saramakas in the decision-making process regarding these logging concessions, in conformity with their traditions and customs, nor did the members of the Saramaka people receive any benefit from the logging in their territory. All of the above constitutes a violation of the property rights of the members of the Saramaka people recognized under Article 21 of the Convention, in connection with Article 1.1 of said instrument.

. . .

157. With regard to the concessions within Saramaka territory that have already been granted to private parties, including Saramaka members, the Court has already declared that "when indigenous communal property and individual private property are in real or apparent contradiction, the American Convention itself and the jurisprudence of the Court provide guidelines to establish admissible restrictions to the enjoyment and exercise of those rights." Thus, the State has a duty to evaluate, in light of the present Judgment and the Court's jurisprudence, whether a restriction of these private property rights is necessary to preserve the survival of the Saramaka people.

158. From all of the above considerations, the Court concludes the following: first, that the members of the Saramaka people have a right to use and enjoy the natural resources that lie on and within their traditionally owned territory that are necessary for their survival; second, that the State may restrict said right by granting concessions for the exploration and extraction of natural resources found on and within Saramaka territory only if the State ensures the effective participation and benefit of the Saramaka people, performs or supervises prior environmental and social impact assessments, and implements adequate safeguards and mechanisms in order to ensure that these activities do not significantly affect the traditional Saramaka lands and natural resources; and finally, that the concessions already issued by the State did not comply with these safeguards. Thus, the Court considers that the State has violated Article 21 of the Convention, in conjunction with Article 1 of such instrument, to the detriment of the members of the Saramaka people.

G. The Lack of Recognition of the Saramaka People as a Juridical Personality Makes Them Ineligible under Domestic Law to Receive Communal Title to Property as a Tribal Community and to Have Equal Access to Judicial Protection of Their Property Rights

159. The [Saramaka] representatives alleged that the State has violated its obligations under Article 3 of the Convention by denying the Saramaka people of their right to recognition of their legal personality. According to the representatives, the lack of recognition of the Saramaka people as a juridical personality makes them ineligible under domestic law to receive communal title to land as a tribal community. Only individual members of the Saramaka community, acting as individuals, may receive a leasehold on State land. The representatives request, therefore, that the State recognize the juridical personality of the Saramaka people as a distinct people, in accordance also with their right to self-determination.

...

162. Substantially, the State first questioned the cohesion of the Saramaka people as "an independent bearer of rights and obligations governed by its own laws, regulations and customs, as the concept of judicial [*sic*] personality provided for in [A]rticle 3 of the Convention presumes." Secondly, the State argued that the American Convention guarantees that every "person" has the right to be recognized as such before the law and not as a "distinct people," as argued by the representatives. Finally, the State argued that it is possible for the Saramaka people to "approach the civil courts requesting a declaratory decision recognizing the tribe as a legal entity."

...

164. The State's first argument is that the voluntary inclusion of some of the members of the Saramaka people in "modern society" has affected their cultural distinctiveness, such that it would be difficult to define them as a distinct legal personality. That is, the State questions whether the Saramaka can be legally defined in a way that takes into account the different degrees to which various self-identified members of the Saramaka people adhere to traditional laws, customs, and economy, particularly those living in Paramaribo or outside of the territory claimed by the Saramaka. In this regard, the Court has already declared that the Saramaka people can be defined as a distinct tribal group, whose members enjoy and exercise certain rights, such as the right to property, in a distinctly collective manner. The fact that some individual members of the Saramaka people may live outside of the traditional Saramaka territory and in a way that may differ from other Saramakas who live within the traditional territory and in accordance with Saramaka customs does not affect the distinctiveness of this tribal group nor its communal use and enjoyment of their property. Moreover, the question of whether certain self-identified members of the Saramaka people may assert certain communal rights on behalf of the juridical personality of such people is a question that must be resolved by the Saramaka people in accordance with their own traditional customs and norms, not by the State or this Court in this particular case. Accordingly, the lack of individual identification with the traditions and laws of the

Saramaka by some alleged members of the community may not be used as a pretext to deny the Saramaka people their right to juridical personality.

165. Having emphasized that the Saramaka people are a distinct tribal group, whose members enjoy and exercise certain rights collectively, the Court will address the State's second argument regarding the possibility of recognizing the legal personality of a distinct group rather than that of its individual members.

. . .

168. The Court observes that the recognition of the juridical personality of individual members of a community is evidently necessary for their enjoyment of other rights, such as the right to life and personal integrity. Yet, such individual recognition fails to take into account the manner in which members of indigenous and tribal peoples in general, and the Saramaka in particular, enjoy and exercise a particular right; that is, the right to use and enjoy property collectively in accordance with their ancestral traditions.

169. The Court observes that any individual member of the Saramaka people may seek judicial protection against violations of his or her individual property rights, and that a judgment in his or her favor may also have a favorable effect on the community as a whole. In a juridical sense, such individual members do not represent the community as a whole. The decisions pertaining to the use of such individual property are up to the individual and not to the Saramaka people in accordance with their traditions. Consequently, a recognition of the right to juridical personality of the Saramaka people as a whole would help prevent such situations, as the true representatives of the juridical personality would be chosen in accordance with their own traditions, and the decisions affecting the Saramaka territory will be the responsibility of those representatives, not of the individual members.

170. A similar situation has occurred in the present case, whereby the State has constantly objected to whether the twelve captains of the twelve Saramaka clans (*lös*) truly represent the will of the community as a whole. The State additionally asserted that the true representative of the community should be the *Gaa'man*, and not others. This controversy over who actually represents the Saramaka people is precisely a natural consequence of the lack of recognition of their juridical personality.

171. The recognition of their juridical personality is a way, albeit not the only one, to ensure that the community, as a whole, will be able to fully enjoy and exercise their right to property, in accordance with their communal property system, and the right to equal access to judicial protection against violations of such right.

172. The Court considers that the right to have their juridical personality recognized by the State is one of the special measures owed to indigenous and tribal groups in order to ensure that they are able to use and enjoy

their territory in accordance with their own traditions. This is a natural consequence of the recognition of the right of members of indigenous and tribal groups to enjoy certain rights in a communal manner.

173. In this case, the State does not recognize that the Saramaka people can enjoy and exercise property rights as a community. Furthermore, the Court observes that other communities in Suriname have been denied the right to seek judicial protection against alleged violations of their collective property rights precisely because a judge considered they did not have the legal capacity necessary to request such protection. This places the Saramaka people in a vulnerable situation where individual property rights may trump their rights over communal property, and where the Saramaka people may not seek, as a juridical personality, judicial protection against violations of their property rights recognized under Article 21 of the Convention.

174. In conclusion, the members of the Saramaka people form a distinct tribal community in a situation of vulnerability, both as regards the State as well as private third parties, insofar as they lack the juridical capacity to collectively enjoy the right to property and to challenge before domestic courts alleged violations of such right. The Court considers that the State must recognize the juridical capacity of the members of the Saramaka people to fully exercise these rights in a collective manner. This may be achieved by implementing legislative or other measures that recognize and take into account the particular way in which the Saramaka people view themselves as a collectivity capable of exercising and enjoying the right to property. Thus, the State must establish, in consultation with the Saramaka people and fully respecting their traditions and customs, the judicial and administrative conditions necessary to ensure the recognition of their juridical personality, with the aim of guaranteeing them the use and enjoyment of their territory in accordance with their communal property system, as well as the rights to access to justice and equality before the law.

175. The State's failure to do so has resulted in a violation, to the detriment of the members of the Saramaka people, of the right to the recognition of their juridical personality pursuant to Article 3 of the Convention in relation to their right to property under Article 21 of such instrument and their right to judicial protection under Article 25 thereof, as well as in relation to the general obligation of States to adopt such legislative or other measures as may be necessary to give effect to those rights and to respect and ensure their free and full exercise without discrimination, pursuant to Articles 2 and 1(1) of the Convention.

H. The Availability of Adequate and Effective Legal Remedies in Suriname to Protect the Saramaka People against Acts That Violate Their Right to Property

[See Notes and Questions, which follow.]

NOTES AND QUESTIONS

1. What follows is a summary of the legal remedies that the Inter-American Court of Human Rights ordered the Suriname government to pay to the Saramaka people:

   > In the ambit of reparations, the Court considered the members of the Saramaka people as the injured party, without having to name them individually. The Court determined several measures to guarantee nonrepetition, including: demarcating territories; recognizing collective juridical capacity; and perfecting internal laws on consultations, EIAs, and judicial protection. As measures of satisfaction, the Court ordered the state to translate its judgment into Dutch and to finance two radio broadcasts, in the Saramaka language, of the decision's key paragraphs. Then, in relation to compensation, the Court considered that the Saramaka people had obtained no benefit from the timber extracted from their territory and that the logging concessions had resulted in environmental damage; Suriname was therefore ordered to pay US$75,000 in compensation for such material damage. The Court also considered that the immaterial damage caused to the Saramaka people by "alterations to the very fabric of their society" – including the impact of the environmental damage on their spiritual connection with their territory, as well as the suffering and distress endured as a result of the long struggle for legal recognition – entitled them to a just compensation. Finally, on equitable grounds, the Court ordered the state to allocate US$600,000 to a community development fund to finance, among other things, educational, housing, agricultural, and health projects.

   Marcos A. Orellana, *Saramaka People v. Suriname*, 102 Am. J. Int'l L. 841, 845–46 (2008).

2. A serious issue is often whether remedies ordered by the court will ever be fully satisfied. Note the following commentary:

   > In Paraguay, two cases in the past few years, *Yakye Axa Indigenous Community v. Paraguay* and *Sawhoyamaxa Indigenous Community v. Paraguay*, have brought before the Court the issue of indigenous communities' right to their traditional lands. In these cases, the displacement of indigenous communities from their lands caused their members to live in deplorable conditions and sometimes to die as a result of the state's subsequent failure to provide necessary medical services. Yet the state has not complied with the most important element of the Court's determinations on reparations: giving possession of the lands to the communities. The Court noted in February 2007 that since the publication of the judgment in *Sawhoyamaxa*, the state's failure to implement its orders on providing basic services to the community had led to the deaths of four additional individuals and the hospitalization of five more.

   James L. Cavallaro & Stephanie Erin Brewer, *Reevaluating Regional Human Rights Litigation in the Twenty-First Century: The Case of the Inter-American Court*, 102 Am. J. Int'lL. 768, 786–87 (2008).

   What enforcement measures should the Saramaka people pursue if the required remedies are not forthcoming?

3. *Saramaka People* is the first decision of an international tribunal to assimilate the status of a nonindigenous minority group to that of an indigenous group for purposes of protecting their right to govern the use and enjoyment of natural resources within their traditional lands. Earlier decisions of the court had established the ownership rights of individuals and peoples in their traditional lands. The seminal case was *Mayagna (Sumo) Awas Tingni Community v. Nicaragua*, 2001 Inter-Am. Ct. H.R. (ser. C) No. 79 (Aug. 31, 2001). Subsequent cases include *Moiwana Village v. Suriname*, 2005 Inter-Am. Ct. H.R. (ser. C) No. 124 (June 15, 2006); *Yakye Axa Indigenous Community v. Paraguay*, 2005 Inter-Am. Ct. H.R. (ser. C) No. 125 (June 17, 2005); and *Sawhoyamaxa Indigenous Community v. Paraguay*, 2006 Inter-Am. Ct. H.R. (ser. C) No. 146 (Mar. 29, 2006).

   At least one national court concurs. *Cal v. Attorney General* (S. Ct. Belize, Oct. 18, 2007), 46 I.L.M. 1022.
4. How does the court establish that the Saramaka people merit special protection of their natural resources even though they are "not indigenous to the region they inhabit"? Is it easy to distinguish indigenous from nonindigenous status? Would all settlers in the same region merit special protection? If not, why should the Saramaka people be treated differently (i.e., better) than other people under Suriname law? Why, even as a matter of cultural survival, does the court establish that Suriname owes obligations to the Saramaka people to enable them to relatively untrammeled use and enjoyment of traditionally owned land and its natural resources if they were not the original settlers there?
5. What is the role of customary law in the court's determination of the special rights of the Saramaka peoples? Does the *Saramaka* opinion itself establish an extension of the customary law to collective rights in natural resources or will that right need to be repeatedly confirmed over time to acquire the status of international custom? Besides customary law, what is the precise role of international and regional law in establishing the government of Suriname's obligations? On what specific basis did the Court determine that the Suriname government had failed to comply with its obligations under article 21, in connection with article 1.1, of the American Convention on Human Rights?
6. If cultural survival is the issue, is it clear what natural resources are necessary to the Saramaka people's survival and whether they are entitled to legal control over all of the natural resources within their lands or just those necessary to their cultural survival?
7. Why did it matter whether Suriname law recognized the Saramaka people collectively as opposed to the individual status of tribal members? Doesn't the gradual assimilation of Saramaka individuals into the larger society undermine the contention that the people as a whole should enjoy legal personality?
8. Under article 21 of the American Convention, what specific principles govern the extent to which a state may restrict a tribe's use and enjoyment of their natural resources? What safeguards apply to state restrictions? When is consultation required? When is actual consent required? When does a project have a major impact on the use and enjoyment of natural resources? Suppose that application of the safeguards interferes with an investment project under a concession agreement entered into by the Suriname government. Should such an agreement nullify the

protective effect of the safeguards or at least complicate the resolution of a dispute by arbitration as may be provided under such an agreement?

9. See generally Siegfried Wiessner, *Rights and Status of Indigenous Peoples: A Global Comparative and International Legal Perspective*, 12 Harv. Hum. Rts. J. 57, 127 (1999); S. James Anaya & Robert Williams Jr., *The Protection of Indigenous Peoples' Rights over Lands and Natural Resources under the Inter-American Human Rights System*, 14 Harv. Hum. Rts. J. 33 (2001); S. James Anaya, Indigenous Peoples in International Law 61–72 (2d ed. 2004).

5. Legal Pluralism

Legal pluralism refers to the existence of multiple legal orders within the same territory. For example, in Morocco, we find customary law courts of the Berber people, Sharia courts that enforce Islamic law, and the courts of the state. Similarly, in the United States, we find state courts, federal courts, tribal courts, religious tribunals, and the dispute settlement mechanisms of ethnic groups such as the *kris* of the Roma people.

Of course, legal pluralism does not attribute coequality to all legal systems. Normally, the state system is dominant. Also, it is not always clear whether customary practices necessarily qualify as a legal system. Another question is how to weigh and evaluate the component legal systems. A failure to coordinate the decisions of multiple tribunals, for example, may run the risk of double jeopardy, whereby a person who is subject to both customary and state law is exposed to prosecution and punishment twice for the same offense. The counterargument is that each system classifies the offense differently so that, even though the two courts are analyzing the same set of facts, technically speaking, the offense is different.

Werner Menski, Comparative Law in a Global Perspective: The Legal Systems of Asia and Africa 173–74, 183–84 (2d ed. 2006)

The usefulness of trying to define "law" has been questioned by many writers, and the concept itself has created hostility in many parts of the world. Positivist analysis has been criticized for being too narrowly focused on rules, natural law theories are viewed with suspicion for ending up as religious positivism, and socio-legal approaches face fears about fuzziness. Earlier, [Karl] Olivecrona found that a definition of the supposed concept of law cannot be given. The simple model of law as a system of rules is perhaps nothing more than a tool of description. It is superficial and false to treat law as only composed of the totality of rules: Each law in fact constitutes a *system*. Such a system may be changed by law-makers, yet there is something, supposedly universal, beyond these rules which one can also study as "law."

A postmodern approach would question attempts to universalize one particular concept of law and emphasise instead its inherent plurality. . . . [A] general definition of law within the conceptual context of legal pluralism may be misleading, because the indicia of "the legal" are more like a continuum or more complex mix of attributes, which it is not necessary to set off artificially from closely related phenomena except for pragmatic reasons in quite specific contexts.... "[G]eneric statements of the functions of law are of limited value. A comparatist has to examine not only rules and functions, but also the context in which legal problems arise. Only by understanding this context or institutional setting can we make effective comparison." This leads to the argument that looking for law as an ordered system is itself highly problematic.

...

While the dominant model of law appears to be that "law" is first and foremost what the state, in whatever form, has laid down as a body of rules applying to its citizens (and, in many cases, to everyone within the jurisdiction of that state), a wider definition of law would also need to take account of the presence of bodies of rules made by groups of people for themselves, and of religious or ethical/moral laws and concepts. Where a particular community, perhaps within a state, or perhaps in the absence of a state (though that is rare, nowadays) makes bodies of rules for itself, we may speak of customs, social norms or different types of [a] semi-autonomous legal field. The critical question, again, remains whether we are prepared to accept that such customs and norms are a form of law. Following [Masaji] Chiba, we may assume without difficulty that certain customs may be co-opted by a state as law, in which case they might no longer be seen as customs, but as "official law" while other customs will be treated merely as local norms without binding legal value. But does this make them less effective in social reality? And, what if the effect of legislation is the emergence of new customs, a new "living law"? These are complex issues to which no easy answers are found unless we open our eyes to plurality-consciousness and recognize that no accepting plurality creates barriers to holistic legal analysis.

Similarly, by considering religion as a source of law, we may find that certain state laws have silently incorporated religious norms and rules into their official legal system. The more critical question is what happens if a state refuses to do so, as is today the case in Northern states with large Southern ethnic minority and migrant populations. Again, such arguments are dependent on worldviews and personal opinions, and are therefore intractable. From the perspective of certain religions, God's law may be treated as superior to any form of state law. But controversies will start with the basic question whether there is God, of whatever name or description. At the end, a plurality-conscious, global definition of law that includes every possible stakeholder turns out so general that it seems meaningless. Law then becomes, in a form of English that remains open to all possible kinds of interpretation, simply:

- A body of rules established by an entity.

A legal system, in the same vein, would then be something like a body of rules applied by an entity, which may be a collection of entities, in specific contexts. The notion of "system" increases the perception of dynamism, but law itself is internally dynamic from the very start. This discussion was not designed to show the absurdity of efforts to define law, but to illustrate that a universal definition of law is only feasible if it accounts for the immensely plural phenomenon of law itself. As a working hypothesis for a globally conscious understanding of law, the following propositions and consequences arise from the above discussion:

- law is a phenomenon that is universal but manifests itself in many different ways;
- law constantly needs to be worked out or negotiated in a culture-specific social context, and is thus inherently dynamic and flexible; [and]
- law not only takes different forms but also has different sources;
- these sources, in essence different manifestations of the state, society, and religion/ ethics, compete and interact in various ways;
- any given body of such rules will also contain components of the other two elements, which adds another (generally invisible) layer of plurality;
- lawyers as professionals and theorists have tended to emphasise the centrality of state law and have thereby underplayed the role of non-state sources of the law including ethics, and particularly society and the element of culture, seriously underestimating the potential for the co-existence of various rule systems;
- whether something is legal or not may well ultimately be determined by lawyers, but they have used the alleged centrality of law to promote a worldview in which "law" is dominant. One might call this "legal determinism," a form of positivism, which turns out as legal centralism;
- this may not be a view consistent with people's experiences anywhere in the world;
- such legal centralism therefore needs to be challenged and a wider, global perspective on law needs to be taken.

Within such a global framework for the comparative study of law and legal systems, it is evident that a narrow approach to law as state law leads neither to appropriate understanding of non-European societies and cultures nor to satisfactory analysis of the phenomenon of law even in its European manifestations. If we do not want to be mere technicians of a particular national law or end up in Eurocentric dark alleys or circular parts of the legal maze, arguing that law is simply law because someone said so, taking a pluralist legal perspective is an inevitable requirement. To state this is easy; to perform the necessary tasks is an enormous challenge.

QUESTION

According to Werner Menski, what has been the role of lawyers in defining law? Could it be otherwise? In Chapter 2, we focus on definitions of law.

Leopold J. Pospisil, The Ethnology of Law 30–31, 43–44, 46, 48, 109–11 (2d ed. 1978) (reprinted with the permission of Pearson Education, Inc.)

Having decided on principles abstracted from decisions as the form of law, we must identify the basic characteristics of those decisions that merit being called legal. My studies of European legal systems and of ethnographic literature, as well as my research among three tribal peoples and civilized Tirolean peasants of Western Austria, have led me to the conclusion that legal decisions, and therefore the law contained in them, have four major attributes whose existence defines social phenomena as law. The four attributes in their logical sequence are authority, intention of universal application, *obligatio* (not to be confused with obligation), and sanction.

. . .

AUTHORITY

Any decision that can be called legal – in other words, that exercises social control – has to be accepted by the parties to a dispute, or its provisions have to be forced on them if they protest and resist. Such a decision obviously cannot be handed down by everyone in a society. It requires an individual who possesses enough power to enforce the verdict – by persuasion or by psychological or physical compulsion. A person or group possessing such power I shall call legal authority. In our society such an authority is often specialized and represented by a judge; in an overwhelming number of tribal and non-Western civilized societies, a legal authority combines in her person additional and nonlegal functions, such as political, economic, or religious leadership. Headman, chief, father, paterfamilias of an extended family, council of elders, high priest, and magistrate are some forms the non-Western legal authority may assume. As a consequence, the identity of the legal authority in a particular group will be most likely to coincide with that group's political leadership.

. . .

INTENTION OF UNIVERSAL APPLICATION

The fact that a decision is passed by an authority does not make it "legal." A tribal authority, a chief, a headman, or a council of elders or important men usually hands down not only legal judgments but also political decisions. Consequently, it is necessary to distinguish the two sets of phenomena by an additional criterion which constitutes a second attribute of law. This attribute, which I have found in all the societies I have investigated and to which explicit or implicit references exist in the ethnographic literature, I call "intention of universal application." It requires that the legal authority making the legal decision *intend* it to be applied to all similar or "identical" cases in the future. It should be noted that what is required here is only that there be an intent on the part of the authority to utilize in the future the principle contained in his decision – not that the principle already be a part of a "going order" manifested in an established custom, rule, or series of precedents. Although precedents are usually relied on, a decision may be unprecedented and introduce a new principle that becomes part of the legal inventory. We can regard it as new "legislation." As a consequence, I recognize as law a principle contained in an unprecedented decision when it incorporates, implicitly or explicitly, the intention of the authority that it apply to all similar cases in the future. That such legislative acts are not the monopoly of the civilized societies is well documented by instances reported in the ethnographic literature.

...

OBLIGATIO

Comparative research into legal decisions reveals another attribute of law, which I have called *obligatio*. The term is derived from Roman law, where it originally applied to contracts or relationships of litigants and was often defined as *iuris vinculum* – a legal tie between the two parties. Employed as a label for my third criterion of law, *obligatio* refers to that part of the legal decision which defines the rights of the entitled and the duties of the obligated parties. It describes the social-legal relationship of the two litigants as it supposedly existed at the time of the violation of the law, together with the delict which unbalanced that relation. Lawyers often refer to this part of the decision as the "factual basis for the verdict." *Obligatio*, then, is not one-sided obligation; it is two-directional, combining the statement of the rights of the person who suffered a loss because of the illegal act of the defendant, and the identification of the duties (an action or a sufferance) of the defendant, who by his action violated a legally approved relationship. If one of these components of *obligatio* is missing, a decision cannot be regarded as legal. Specifying a right of one party but not at the same time imposing a duty on another falls short of the basic prerequisites of law. A Kapauku Papuan trouble case, for example, in which the authority recognized the liability of a negligent individual who caused the death of a pig entrusted to him but failed to affirm the right of the plaintiff for compensation cannot be regarded as legal.

...

SANCTION

Sanction has often been regarded as the essential ingredient of all law. A few authors have gone so far as to equate sanction with law, and have elevated it to serve as the single and exclusive criterion of law. In spite of the importance of legal sanction, such an extreme position must be erroneous. Sanctions alone are incapable of defining phenomena as laws for the simple reason that many nonlegal (e.g., political) decisions, which are made *ad hoc*, do carry sanctions. As explained above, political decisions are not legal, because they lack the important attribute of the intention of universal application – the ideal component of law.

...

Law does not just float around in an unstructured way, as it often seems to be portrayed in ethnographies to do. On the contrary, it *always* pertains to specific groups and subgroups of a society. These groups have to be functioning and politically united. Consequently, there is no law on the politically ununited tribal level of the Kapauku or Nuer tribes, or on the level of the German-speaking society. However, this does not mean, as is often erroneously assumed, that the Kapauku and Nuer – or, God, forbid, the Germans – have no law! It simply means that law pertains to politically united subdivisions of these societies – political confederacies of lineages, or states. As a logical consequence, I recognize a multiplicity of legal systems within a "tribe" or a "state society": there are as many legal systems within a given society as there are functioning subgroups. These form an overall configuration that reflects precisely the pattern of the society's subgroups, or, as I prefer to call it, societal structure. Since these legal systems differ in their content from subgroup to subgroup, and from one level of inclusiveness (legal level) to another, to the point of contradiction, the question of whether an observance is law or not must always be decided on the basis of its relation to a specific group. What appears as mere custom on one societal level (let us say tribal) may well be a law on another level (for example, a lineage). Thus a law is a relative phenomenon – relative to the point of reference in the societal structure with which it is inseparably bound, of which it is a normative expression.

. . .

[L]aw as an integral part of the rest of the culture has been conceived of as an ever-changing, dynamic phenomenon. As such it exhibits an additional type of relativity. The same law that is customary (that is, internalized by the majority of the members of the group) on the society level, for example, appears as authorization from the perspective of those subgroups that have not had enough time or the desire to internalize it, in spite of the fact that their subgroup authorities enforce the measure.

. . .

Law cannot escape the recognition of its relativity to the group in which it exists and to the members of that group, whose lives it shapes and often protects. Paradoxically, replacing orthodox thinking in terms of absolutes by recognizing the relativity of law makes this concept relevant to the societal structure – it makes it an integral part of the sociocultural matrix in which legal phenomena exist.

3. Cultural Heritage Law: Introduction

A. The Definitional Framework

Broadly speaking, the term "cultural heritage" refers to all of the myriad manifestations of culture that human beings have inherited from their forebears. These manifestations include, for example, art, architecture, rural and urban landscapes, crafts, music, language, literature, film, documentary and digital records, folklore and oral history, culinary traditions, traditional medicine, ceremonies and rituals, religion, sports and games, recreational practices such as hunting and fishing, and dance and other performing arts. In a narrower sense, however, the term "cultural heritage" is often limited to tangible or material objects – essentially, cultural material or objects – and intangible ideas related to such objects. We commonly associate this narrower definition with the legal concept of property whether we are referring to physical or intellectual property. Accordingly, the terms "cultural property" and "cultural heritage" sometimes are used interchangeably. Strictly speaking, however, the term "property" connotes ownership and imputes rights to owners and possessors of objects.

The multiple meanings of the term "cultural heritage" may lead to confusion, as is apparent in diverse efforts not only to protect culture itself but also to enhance its meaning in people's lives. Difficult questions arise that may challenge presumed values. Take three examples.

First, when in 2001 the Taliban, claiming Islamic authority, destroyed two colossal statutes of Buddha at Bamiyan in Afghanistan, was that a total loss of the cultural heritage (in the narrower sense of the term) or a mitigated loss of heritage (in the broader sense of the term, taking into account sectarian religious values, however controversial they are)?

Second, the governments of Australia and Western Australia have declined to fully protect extraordinary petroglyphs, many of which are between twenty thousand and thirty thousand years old, on the Burrup Peninsula. Some five hundred thousand to 1 million of them – standing stones, stone circles, and grinding stones, including what may be the earliest known depictions of human faces – are scattered all over the peninsula, constituting perhaps the largest concentration of rock art in the world. Known as the Dampier rock art, the petroglyphs have been seriously threatened by iron-mining and industrial developments, including potentially explosive fertilizer plants and a multibillion-dollar gas-processing plant in the area – the largest ever resource project in Australia.

In 2007 most but not all of the area was added to Australia's Natural Heritage List, thereby precluding further development of the protected portion, but the administrative measure excluded the site of the gas-processing plant and surrounding property. Given the profusion of the art, should the entire area be declared entirely off-limits to economic development? In other words, to what extent should the preservation of cultural heritage trump further economic development, whether public or private, that may accrue directly to the benefit of people? Should normal property law govern decision making in such situations?

Third, the Chinese government, also in the interest of economic development as well as control of destructive flooding, protected only part of a vast cultural heritage that was itself threatened by inundation resulting from construction of the massive Three Gorges Dam project on the Yangtze River. The lost heritage included prehistoric human remains and artifacts, shrines, ancestral temples, and buried artifacts.

More broadly, what should be the scope of cultural heritage management? How should scarce financial resources to protect indigenous heritage be allocated between, on the one hand, the preservation, display, and repatriation of physical objects and, on the other hand, efforts to protect indigenous peoples from assimilation and globalization? These are not just semantic questions; rather, they bespeak larger issues of cultural survival, elitism, and commodification of culture by which heritage becomes simply a historical product subject to commercial exploitation. To borrow a term from environmental law, "sustainability" may be a key to exercising stewardship over global heritage.

Lyndel V. Prott & Patrick J. O'Keefe, *"Cultural Heritage" or "Cultural Property"?*, 1 Int'l J. Cultural Prop. 307, 309, 310–11 (1992)

Is it time for law and lawyers to recognize that the term "cultural heritage" is rightfully superseding that of "cultural property"? To our minds the answer can only be "Yes." Our argument in brief is first, that the existing legal concept of "property" does not, and should not try to, cover all that evidence of human life that we are trying to preserve: those things and traditions which express the way of life and thought of a particular society; which are evidence of its intellectual and spiritual achievements. On the other hand, they can be encompassed by the term "heritage" which also embodies the notion of inheritance and handing on. This is central to our second objection to the existing legal concept of property; that "property" does not incorporate concepts of duty to preserve and protect....

The fundamental policy behind property law has been seen as the protection of the rights of the possessor. If this policy is carried to its logical conclusion then the owner can be buried with a painting that he purchased for millions of dollars but which represents a peak achievement of human culture. The fundamental policy behind cultural heritage law is protection of the heritage for the enjoyment of present and later generations.... Property connotes ownership.... Heritage creates a perception of something handed down; something to be cared for and cherished.[1]

Another problem that inheres in the definition of cultural heritage is its geographic compass. Is the term to be closely associated with particular national patrimonies or is it more eclectic? If the latter, to what extent can legitimate claims be based on an expansive

[1] *See also* Lucille A. Roussin, *Cultural Heritage and Identity*, 11 Cardozo J. Int'l & Comp. L. 707 (2003).

theory of a universal patrimony or heritage? Perhaps the most intractable problem, however, is, as we observed in Chapters 1 and 2, how to define "culture" itself. The term's varied meanings ("high culture," "popular culture," "cultural diversity," "drug culture," and so on) bespeak the need for clear definitions in legislation and specific treaties. The context in which the term appears may also be determinative. Despite the definitional problems, however, the scope of cultural heritage law will become clearer after we identify the leading actors in the following section.

NOTE

For further discussion of these issues, see Tolina Loulanski, *Revising the Concept for Cultural Heritage*, 13 Int'l J. Cultural Prop. 207 (2006).

B. Individual and Nongovernmental Organization Actors

Cultural heritage law relies, of course, on the legislative, judicial, and executive-administrative authority of governments and intergovernmental organizations. Most of this study focuses on this authority. Individuals and nongovernmental organizations (NGOs) primarily associated with cultural heritage, however, also play an essential role in the drama of cultural heritage law and merit special attention in this introduction. These actors can be divided into seven categories, as follows:

1. Private dealers, auction houses, and collectors
2. Museums and art galleries
3. Anthropologists and archaeologists
4. Indigenous and minority ethnic groups
5. Artists
6. Historic preservationists, archivists, and art historians
7. Criminals and criminal organizations

Maritime salvors and military personnel, to be discussed later in this study, also have a role. Also, related organizations such as those representing architects, charitable foundations, and scientific or cultural advocacy groups play supporting roles.

1. Private Dealers, Auction Houses, and Collectors

Private dealers, auction houses, and collectors are the only principal actors in cultural heritage whose activities are primarily commercial, involving the buying and selling of cultural objects. In some instances, the activities of private collectors and other actors are entwined, such as when they donate objects and collections to museums. It is obvious that private dealers, auction houses, and collectors generally do not favor restrictions on the ownership or movement of art and other cultural objects. Instead, they usually support an open and legitimate world market in the objects they collect. As we shall see, cultural law can help blend purely cultural and economic identities, values, and functions of both material and immaterial heritage. Dealers, auction houses, and collectors tend to emphasize the importance of private ownership of cultural material and to focus on the object itself. Archaeologists and other cultural scientists, however, tend to emphasize the importance of the public interest in cultural material and focus more on the context of the object.

International and regional associations of dealers and collectors include the Confédération Internationale des Négociants en Oeuvres d'Art (CINOA), the International League of Antiquarian Booksellers (ILAB), and the International Association of Dealers in Ancient Art (IADAA). Although the first two of these associations are concerned primarily with the routine legal and business problems affecting their membership, the latter responds to shared concerns about the illegal excavation and sale of archaeological material. To this end, the IADAA, formed in 1993, has strict requirements of membership and a code of ethics and practice. A skeptic might conclude that, like other self-regulatory bodies, the IADAA exists to stave off outside regulation of the trade conducted by its members. Nevertheless, its self-regulation encourages at least a minimum uniform level of professional responsibility. The only material sanction the organization has, that of withdrawing the status of membership, is generally effective in enforcing the standards set by the IADAA Code.

The IADAA has taken steps to establish a database in London of stolen antiquities. Other such databases include those of the Art Loss Register (ALR) (United Kingdom), the International Foundation for Art Research (IFAR) (United States), Interpol (France), and national agencies such as the Federal Bureau of Investigation (United States) and the Royal Canadian Mounted Police (Canada). National NGOs include the Art Dealers Association of America and the Antique Tribal Art Dealers Association (United States), and the British Antique Dealers Association (BADA) and the Society of Fine Art Auctioneers and Valuers (United Kingdom). Clubs of collectors, whose memberships are usually but not always local or national, include, for example, the American Ceramic Society and the Oceanic Art Society (Australia). A recent addition to the NGOs with a collectors' perspective is the nonprofit American Council for Cultural Policy (ACCP). Founded in 2002, this association of collectors, academics, and former museum officials seeks to advance the interests of collectors and museums, which it sees as compromised by the archeologists, academics, and governments that seek to restrict open trade in artifacts and antiquities.

The role of collectors themselves in encouraging questionable and illegal practices merits attention. As consumers, so to speak, of cultural heritage, they are at the end of the treasure chain. Arguably, they fuel the market for artifacts.[2] Often, NGOs do not play a significant role in restraining questionable and excessive activities of constituent dealers, collectors, and auction houses. That role is best assigned to governments and intergovernmental organizations. However, NGOs are significant in preserving healthy art markets and developing shared codes of practice.

The following case, which reads like a Hollywood script, describes in rich detail the actors in a murky underworld of looting, smuggling, and illegal transfer of art. The case highlights the role of private dealers, collectors, and financial institutions and museums in art-related transactions.

Autocephalous Greek-Orthodox Church of Cyprus v. Goldberg, 917 F.2d 278 (7th Cir. 1990)

In the early sixth century, A.D., a large mosaic was affixed to the apse of the Church of the Panagia Kanakaria ("Kanakaria Church") in the village

[2] Ricardo J. Elia, *Looting, Collecting, and the Destruction of Archaeological Resources*, 6 Nonrenewable Resources, no. 2, at 85, 86–88, 97 (1997).

of Lythrankomi, Cyprus. The mosaic, made of small bits of colored glass, depicted Jesus Christ as a young boy in the lap of his mother, the Virgin Mary, who was seated on a throne. Jesus and Mary were attended by two archangels and surrounded by a frieze depicting the twelve apostles. The mosaic was displayed in the Kanakaria Church for centuries, where it became, under the practices of Eastern Orthodox Christianity, sanctified as a holy relic. It survived both the vicissitudes of history, *see Autocephalous*, 717 F. Supp. at 1377 (discussing the period of Iconoclasm during which many religious artifacts were destroyed), and, thanks to restoration efforts, the ravages of time.[3]

Testimony . . . established that the Kanakaria mosaic was one of only a handful of such holy Byzantine relics to survive into the twentieth century. Sadly, however, war came to Cyprus in the 1970s, from which the mosaic could not be spared.

The Cypriot people have long been a divided people, approximately three-fourths being of Greek descent and Greek-Orthodox faith, the other quarter of Turkish descent and [Muslim] faith.[4] No sooner had Cyprus gained independence from British rule in 1960 than this bitter division surfaced. Civil disturbances erupted between Greek and Turkish Cypriots, necessitating the introduction of United Nations peacekeeping forces in 1964. (U.N. forces still remain in Cyprus.) Through the 1960s, the Greek Cypriots, concentrated in the southern part of the island, became increasingly estranged from the Turkish Cypriots, concentrated in the north.[5]

The tensions erupted again in 1974, this time with more violent results. In July 1974, the civil government of the Republic of Cyprus was replaced by a government controlled by the Greek Cypriot military. In apparent response, on July 20, 1974, Turkey invaded Cyprus from the north. By late August, the Turkish military forces had advanced to occupy approximately the northern third of the island. The point at which the invading forces stopped is called the "Green Line." To this day, the heavily-guarded Green Line bisects Nicosia, the capital of the Republic, and splits the island from east to west.

The Turkish forces quickly established their own "government" north of the Green Line. In 1975, they formed what they called the "Turkish Federated State of Cyprus" ("TFSC"). In 1983, that administration was dissolved, and the "Turkish Republic of Northern Cyprus" ("TRNC") was formed. These "governments" were recognized immediately by Turkey, but all other nations in the world – including the United States – have never recognized them, and continue to recognize the Republic of Cyprus ("Republic"),

[3] For more on the history, significance and restoration of the Kanakaria mosaic, *see* A. Megaw & E. Hawkins, The Church of the Panagia Kanakaria at Lythrankomi in Cyprus: Its Mosaics and Frescoes (1977).

[4] For a full treatment of the preindependence history of Cyprus, *see* Hill, A History of Cyprus (4 vols. 1949).

[5] This anxious period of Cypriot history is examined in T. Ehrlich, *Cyprus, The "Warlike Isle": Origins and Elements of the Current Crisis*, 18 Stan. L. Rev. 1021 (1966).

plaintiff-appellee in this action, as the only legitimate government for all Cypriot people.

The Turkish invasion led to the forced southern exodus of over one-hundred thousand Greek Cypriots who lived in northern Cyprus. Turkish Cypriots living in southern Cyprus (and tens of thousands of settlers from mainland Turkey) likewise flooded into northern Cyprus, resulting in a massive exchange of populations.

Lythrankomi is in the northern portion of Cyprus that came under Turkish rule. Although the village and the Kanakaria Church were untouched by the invading forces in 1974, the villagers of Greek ancestry were soon thereafter "enclaved" by the Turkish military. Despite the hostile environment, the pastor and priests of the Kanakaria Church continued for two years to conduct religious services for the Greek Cypriots who remained in Lythrankomi. Hardy as they must have been, these clerics, and virtually all remaining Greek Cypriots, were forced to flee to southern Cyprus in the summer of 1976. Church of Cyprus officials testified that they intend to re-establish the congregation at the Kanakaria Church as soon as Greek Cypriots are permitted to return safely to Lythrankomi. (Thirty-five thousand Turkish troops remain in northern Cyprus.)[6]

When the priests evacuated the Kanakaria Church in 1976, the mosaic was still intact. In the late 1970s, however, Church of Cyprus officials received increasing reports that Greek Cypriot churches and monuments in northern Cyprus were being attacked and vandalized, their contents stolen or destroyed. (Such reports were necessarily sketchy and unverifiable as officials from the Republic and Church of Cyprus have been denied access to northern Cyprus.) In November 1979, a resident of northern Cyprus brought word to the Republic's Department of Antiquities that this fate had also befallen the Kanakaria Church and its mosaic. Vandals had plundered the church, removing anything of value from its interior. The mosaic, or at least its most recognizable and valuable parts, had been forcibly ripped from the apse of the church. Once a place of worship, the Kanakaria Church had been reduced to a stable for farm animals.

Upon learning of the looting of the Kanakaria Church and the loss of its mosaics (made plural by the vandals' axes), the Republic of Cyprus took immediate steps to recover them.... [T]hese efforts took the form of contacting and seeking assistance from many organizations and individuals, including the United Nations Educational, Scientific and Cultural Organization ("UNESCO"); the International Council of Museums; the International Council of [Monuments] and Sites; Europa Nostra (an organization devoted to the conservation of the architectural heritage of Europe); the Council of Europe; international auction houses such as Christie's and Sotheby's; Harvard University's Dumbarton Oaks Institute for Byzantine Studies; and the foremost museums, curators and Byzantine scholars throughout the world. The Republic's United States Embassy

[6] A fascinating, firsthand account of current conditions in Cyprus appears in M. A. Weaver, *Report from Cyprus*, New Yorker, Aug. 6, 1990, at 65–81.

also routinely disseminated information about lost cultural properties to journalists, U.S. officials and scores of scholars, architects and collectors in this country, asking for assistance in recovering the mosaics. The overall strategy behind these efforts was to get word to the experts and scholars who would probably be involved in any ultimate sale of the mosaics. These individuals, it was hoped, would be the most likely (only?) actors in the chain of custody of stolen cultural properties who would be interested in helping the Republic and Church of Cyprus recover them.

The Republic's efforts have paid off. In recent years, the Republic has recovered and returned to the Church of Cyprus several stolen relics and antiquities. The Republic has even located frescoes and other works taken from the Kanakaria Church, including the four mosaics at issue here. These four mosaics, each measuring about two feet square, depict the figure of Jesus, the busts of one of the attending archangels, the apostle Matthew and the apostle James.

To understand how these pieces of the Kanakaria mosaic resurfaced, we must trace the actions of appellant Peg Goldberg and the other principals through whose hands they passed in 1988.

Peg Goldberg is an art dealer and gallery operator. Goldberg and Feldman Fine Arts, Inc., is the Indiana corporation that owns her gallery in Carmel, Indiana. In the summer of 1988, Peg Goldberg went to Europe to shop for works for her gallery. Although her main interest is 20th century paintings, etchings and sculptures, Goldberg was enticed while in The Netherlands by Robert Fitzgerald, another Indiana art dealer and "casual friend" of hers, to consider the purchase of "four early Christian mosaics." In that connection, Fitzgerald arranged a meeting in Amsterdam for July 1st. At that meeting, Fitzgerald introduced Goldberg to Michel van Rijn, a Dutch art dealer, and Ronald Faulk, a California attorney. Van Rijn and Faulk were strangers to Goldberg. All she knew about them was what she learned in their few meetings, which included the fact that van Rijn, a published expert on Christian icons (she was given a copy of the book), had been convicted by a French court for art forgery; that he claimed to be a descendant of both Rembrandt and Rubens; and that Faulk was in Europe to represent Fitzgerald and van Rijn.

At that first meeting in Amsterdam on July 1, 1988, van Rijn showed Goldberg photographs of the four mosaics at issue in this case and told her that the seller wanted $3 million for them. Goldberg testified that she immediately "fell in love" with the mosaics. Van Rijn told her that the seller was a Turkish antiquities dealer who had "found" the mosaics in the rubble of an "extinct" church in northern Cyprus while working as an archaeologist "assigned (by Turkey) to northern Cyprus." (Goldberg knew of the Turkish invasion of Cyprus and of the subsequent division of the island.) As to the seller, Goldberg was also told that he had exported the mosaics to his home in Munich, Germany[,] with the permission of the Turkish Cypriot government, and that he was now interested in selling the mosaics quickly because he had a "cash problem." Goldberg was not initially given the seller's identity. Goldberg also learned that

Faulk, on behalf of Fitzgerald and van Rijn, had already met with this as-yet-unidentified seller to discuss the sale of these mosaics. Her interest quite piqued, Goldberg asked Faulk to return to Munich and tell the seller – whose identity, she would eventually learn, was Aydin Dikman – that she was interested.

Faulk dutifully took this message to Dikman in Munich, and returned to Amsterdam the following day. Faulk returned from that meeting with a contract he signed as agent for van Rijn to purchase the mosaics from Dikman for $350,000. When Goldberg met with Faulk on July 2, she was not told of this contract, however. Faulk merely informed her that Dikman still had the mosaics (though he was "actively negotiating with another buyer"), and that, in Faulk's opinion the export documents he had been shown by Dikman were in order. Faulk apparently showed Goldberg copies of a few of these documents, none of which, of course, were genuine, and at least one of which was obviously unrelated to these mosaics. . . .

The next day (all of this happening rather fast), the principals gathered again in Amsterdam. Goldberg, van Rijn, Fitzgerald and Faulk agreed to "acquire the mosaics for their purchase price of $1,080,000 (U.S.)." The parties agreed to split the profits from any resale of the mosaics as follows: Goldberg 50%; Fitzgerald 22.5%; van Rijn 22.5%; and Faulk 5%. A document to this effect was executed on July 4, 1988, which document included a provision reading, "This agreement shall be governed by and any action commenced will be pursuant to the laws of the state of Indiana."

In those hectic early days of July, Goldberg contacted Otto N. Frenzel III, a friend and high-ranking officer at the Merchants National Bank of Indianapolis ("Merchants"), and requested a loan from Merchants of $1.2 million for the purchase of the mosaics. She told Frenzel that she needed $1,080,000 to pay van Rijn and the others, and she required the additional $120,000 to pay for expenses, insurance, restoration and the like. Merchants assured her that financing could be arranged, if she could provide appraisals and other documents substantiating the transaction. With Fitzgerald's and van Rijn's help, Goldberg obtained the appraisals (all three of which valued the mosaics at between $3 and $6 million), and sent them to Merchants. That done, she and Fitzgerald hurried to Geneva, Switzerland, for the transfer of the mosaics, which was to take place on July 5. After arriving in Switzerland, Goldberg learned that her requested loan had been approved by Merchants and the money would be forthcoming, though a few days behind schedule. Her financing secured, Goldberg proceeded to the July 5 meeting as scheduled. She could not yet turn over the money, but she wanted to get a look at what she was buying.

The July 5 meeting was held in the "free port" area of the Geneva airport, an area reserved for items that have not passed through Swiss customs. Faulk and Dikman arrived from Munich with the mosaics, which were stored in crates. Dikman introduced himself to Goldberg and then left; this brief exchange was the only time the two would meet. Goldberg then inspected the four mosaics. She testified that she "was in awe," and that, despite some concern about the mosaics' deteriorating condition, she wanted them "more than ever."

During the few days that Goldberg waited in Switzerland for the money to arrive from Merchants, she placed several telephone calls concerning the mosaics. She testified that she wanted to make sure the mosaics had not been reported stolen, and that no treaties would prevent her from bringing the mosaics into the United States. She called UNESCO's office in Geneva and inquired as to whether any treaties prevented "the removal of items from northern Cyprus in the mid- to late-1970s to Germany," but did not mention the mosaics. She claims also to have called, on advice from an art dealer friend of hers in New York, the International Foundation for Art Research ("IFAR"), an organization that collects information concerning stolen art. She testified that she asked IFAR whether it had any record of a claim to the mosaics, and that, when she called back later as instructed, IFAR told her it did not. [At trial, however, it became apparent that neither Goldberg nor IFAR had any record of any such search such as a bill for services. The district court judge also questioned Goldberg's testimony that she had telephoned customs officials in the United States, Switzerland, Germany, and Turkey.] The only things of which [the district court] was sure was that Goldberg did *not* contact the Republic of Cyprus or the TRNC (from one of whose lands she knew the mosaics had come); the Church of Cyprus; "Interpol," a European information-sharing network for police forces; nor "a single disinterested expert on Byzantine art." . . .

However Goldberg occupied her time from July 5 to July 7, on the latter date the money arrived. Goldberg took the $1.2 million, reduced to $100 bills and stuffed into two satchels, and met with Faulk and Fitzgerald at the Geneva airport. As arranged, Goldberg kept $120,000 in cash and gave the remaining $1,080,000 to Faulk and Fitzgerald in return for the mosaics. Faulk and Fitzgerald in turn split the money with van Rijn, Dikman and their other cohorts as follows: $350,000 to Dikman (as per Faulk and van Rijn's prior agreement with him); $282,500 to van Rijn; $297,500 to Fitzgerald; $80,000 to Faulk; and $70,000 to another attorney in London. Along with the mosaics, Goldberg received a "General bill of sale" issued by Dikman to Goldberg and Feldman Fine Arts, Inc. The following day, July 8, 1988, Goldberg returned to the United States with her prize.

Back home in Indiana, Goldberg took what she had left of her $120,000 cut and deposited it into several of her business and personal bank accounts. After paying for the insurance and shipment of the mosaics, as well as a few unrelated art purchases, that sum amounted to approximately $70,000. Her friends and business associates in Indiana soon took quite an interest in her purchase; literally. For large sums of money, Frenzel, Goldberg's well-placed friend at Merchants, and another Indiana resident named Dr. Stewart Bick acquired from van Rijn and Fitzgerald substantial interests in the profits from any resale of the mosaics.

Peg Goldberg's efforts soon turned to just that: the resale of these valuable mosaics. She worked up sales brochures about them, and contacted several other dealers to help her find a buyer. Two of these dealers' searches led them both to Dr. Marion True of the Getty Museum in California. When told of these mosaics and their likely origin, the aptly-named Dr. True explained to the dealers that she had a working relationship with the Republic of Cyprus and that she was duty-bound to contact Cypriot officials about them. Dr. True called Dr. Vassos Karageorghis, the Director of the Republic's Department of Antiquities and one of the primary Cypriot officials involved in the worldwide search for the mosaics. Dr. Karageorghis verified that the Republic was in fact hunting for the mosaics that had been described to Dr. True, and he set in motion the investigative and legal machinery that ultimately resulted in the Republic learning that they were in Goldberg's possession in Indianapolis.

After their request for the return of the mosaics was refused by Goldberg, the Republic of Cyprus and the Church of Cyprus (collectively "Cyprus") brought this suit in the Southern District of Indiana for the recovery of the mosaics. [The district court awarded possession of the mosaics to the Church of Cyprus. Goldberg then appealed.]

The Court of Appeals addressed five issues: (1) jurisdiction; (2) choice of law; (3) timeliness of the action; (4) the requirements of a replevin action; and (5) the effect of Turkish occupation of Northern Cyprus, from which the mosaics were taken, on the rights of the plaintiff. These issues will be revisited in Chapter 5. To summarize, the appellate court held that the requirements for federal jurisdiction were satisfied; that the law of Indiana, the defendant's domicile and place of final performance, applied, as did the law of Switzerland, the country in whose airport "free port" the mosaics were transferred to the defendant; that the action was timely; that the plaintiff was entitled to possession of the mosaics; and that the confiscatory decrees of occupying Turkish forces did not divest the plaintiff of claim of title.

NOTES AND QUESTIONS

1. A superb account of the *Goldberg* saga appears in Dan Hofstedter, *Annals of the Antiquities Trade, The Angel on Her Shoulder I, II*, New Yorker, July 13, 1992, at 36; July 20, 1992, at 38.
2. Chief Judge Bauer began his opinion by quoting from *The Siege of Corinth*, in which Lord Byron lamented war's capacity to "reduce our grandest and most sacred temples to mere 'fragments of stone.'" *Goldberg*, 917 F.2d at 293. Judge Bauer concluded his opinion by observing that

   > [o]nly the lowest of scoundrels attempt to reap personal gain from this collective loss. Those who plundered the churches and monuments of war-torn Cyprus, hoarded their relics away, and are now smuggling and selling them for large sums, are just such blackguards. The Republic of Cyprus, with diligent effort and the help of friends . . . has been able to locate several of these stolen antiquities; items of vast cultural, religious (and, as this case demonstrates, monetary) value. Among such finds are the pieces of the Kanakaria mosaic at issue in this case.

The court clearly viewed its role not only in rectifying wrongful activity but in deterring "the lowest of scoundrels" and "blackguards" from any further looting, thereby protecting cultural heritage. Judge Bauer's observation thereby reflects two functions of the court's decision: rectification and protection.

3. The court acknowledged that its decision primarily affected a naive (though not completely innocent) art gallery owner rather than the thieves and shadowy intermediaries who drive the illegal market in antiquities and art. Is that fair? Shouldn't a naive defendant have received a measure of judicial protection, too? Concerned that its decision might "seem too harsh," the court concluded that

> those who wish to purchase art work on the international market, undoubtedly a ticklish business, are not without means by which to protect themselves. Especially when circumstances are as suspicious as those that faced Peg Goldberg, prospective purchasers would do best to do more than make a few last-minute phone calls. As testified to at trial, in a transaction like this, "All the red flags are up, all the red lights are on, all the sirens are blaring." . . . In such cases, dealers can (and probably should) take steps such as a formal IFAR search; a documented authenticity check by disinterested experts; a full background search of the seller and his claim of title; insurance protection and a contingency sales contract; and the like. If Goldberg would have pursued such methods, perhaps she would have discovered in time what she has now discovered too late: the Church has a valid, superior and enforceable claim to these Byzantine treasures, which therefore must be returned to it.

Id. at 294.

If prospective buyers of cultural material have a duty of diligence in entering into a transaction, what should be the minimum standard for that duty? Should the characteristic confidentiality of the art market be taken into account in establishing that standard?

4. Italian authorities charged that Marion True, a former antiquities curator at the J. Paul Getty Museum in Los Angeles, and Robert Hecht, an American dealer in classical artifacts, acquired objects that were illegally excavated in Italy. In a rather sensational trial, the prosecution called on expert witnesses who claimed that wealthy collectors, including individuals and museums, are at the heart of the problem of illegal trafficking. In particular, these witnesses testified that the tax and other incentives for private donations of material to museums represented a sophisticated method of laundering artifacts. (A report in 2007 by the Association of Art Museum Directors indicated that private individuals had donated more than 90% of all art collections held in public trust by constituent museums.) Should such general testimony be admissible against individual defendants? Are criminal prosecutions justifiable in part to deter others from illegal trafficking and to encourage the art market, especially auction houses, to require detailed provenance in all commercial transactions?

5. Ricardo Elia questions the distinction between legitimate and illicit markets. Instead, he argues, as follows, that looting is an economic system for which collectors and the general public are ultimately responsible:

> The illicit removal of objects from archaeological sites is one element of a single economic system that may be termed the antiquities market. The system has

three main components: the creation of an inventory or supply of antiquities, acquired either by looting objects from archaeological sites or by producing fakes; their distribution to dealers, often by smuggling the objects out of the country of origin; and ultimately their purchase by collectors, assisted by a variety of specialists, including art historians, conservators, materials analysts, and curators.

The system operates according to the economic laws of supply and demand. The primary cause of looting is collecting. Collectors, both private and institutional (i.e., museums), acquire archaeological objects for their artistic, aesthetic, and investment values. These values may be appreciated without regard for the contextual information required by archaeologists, who are concerned primarily with the scientific and historical information potential of the objects. The collectors, especially at the high end of the market, are often wealthy individuals and prominent figures in society; it is they who create the initial demand for antiquities. Collectors purchase antiquities from dealers, who finance and operate a network of runners, couriers, and smugglers; these agents of the dealers, in turn, pay the looters who furnish the supply of antiquities through their clandestine digging at archaeological sites.

The antiquities market operates as a black market, or, more accurately, as a "double market" – a single market combining elements of both black market and legal market. Many aspects of the system are illegal or carried out in secret, especially in the countries of origin, where objects are illegally looted from sites and often smuggled across national borders. Once material enters the market, business transactions between looters and dealers' agents, dealers and collectors, and collectors and museums are protected by a tradition of secrecy and nondisclosure. Generally, however, once a looted object enters the commerce of art-acquiring countries – especially nations like the United States, the United Kingdom, Germany and Japan – the antiquities market is not only legal and protected by national laws and policies that favor purchasers and possessors, but also a status-producing arena for collectors who can afford to purchase, display, and donate valuable antiquities.

Because the antiquities market system operates for much of the time as a black market, the causal link between collecting and looting is frequently blurred. At any given moment, only individual elements of the system are visible, and they tend to be treated as if they were independent activities. Only rarely are we afforded a glimpse of how the individual components operate as integral parts of a single system, especially in the occasional circumstance when a looting case is cracked and one can follow the flow of looted material from the archaeological site through the market to its final destination.

The plundering of tombs of the Moche culture in Sipán, Peru[,] provides a glimpse of how the system operates. Local villagers looted an undisturbed elite tomb at the Sipán site in 1987. Squabbling among the looters over the division of the artifacts brought the case to the attention of the police; arrests were made, and investigations eventually allowed the details of the case to be reconstructed. Many of the Sipán artifacts had been acquired in Lima by an American expatriate who regularly arranged to smuggle Precolumbian

> artifacts out of Peru; another sizable collection of Sipán material was acquired by a well known Peruvian collector. The expatriate sold a quantity of Sipán artifacts to an American entrepreneur, who had the artifacts smuggled into London. From there they were shipped into the United States, listed as personal items and accompanied by phony papers stating that the artifacts had been acquired prior to Peru's 1929 cultural patrimony law. The American dealer sold the artifacts to numerous collectors, including corporate executives, museum board members, and even a Nobel laureate. (The Sipán case eventually led to lawsuits; the American entrepreneur pleaded guilty to smuggling and served a prison sentence, and some of the looted objects were returned to Peru. Peruvian archaeologists excavated three additional unplundered elite tombs at Sipán, so rich that they earned the nickname "King Tut's tomb of the New World." Finally, in 1990, the United States signed an emergency measure banning the import of Sipán artifacts from Peru.)
>
> While efforts have largely focused on the supply side of the antiquities market, little attention has been paid to the demand side – the collectors who cause the illicit market to flourish in the first place. Since collecting creates the demand that leads to looting, any reduction in demand should lead to a reduction in looting. Unfortunately, changing the behavior of collectors will require a major shift in public attitudes. Collectors have traditionally held an honored place in our society. The "great collectors" frequently occupy positions of power and authority; they are revered as connoisseurs and pursued by solicitous dealers and curators. If they donate their collections to museums, they are immortalized by having museum wings named after them and receive public subventions, in the form of tax breaks, for their beneficence. Changing the culture of collecting will require educating not so much the collectors but the general public, which supports collecting in a vague way as a form of socially sanctioned behavior. The destruction of archaeological resources from looting is only likely to be diminished when the collecting of unprovenienced antiquities becomes regarded as antisocial behavior – like the poaching of endangered animals; the burning of the rainforests; smoking in public; or the wearing of animal furs.

Ricardo J. Elia, *Looting, Collecting, and the Destruction of Archaeological Resources*, 6 Nonrenewable Resources, no. 2, at 85, 86–88, 97 (1997).

Do you agree? If not, how do you reconcile the innocence of collectors with laws of supply and demand that drive most markets, including those in antiquities and art? If you do agree with Professor Elia's argument, what should lawmakers, lawyers, and diplomats do about a problem initiated by diverse collectors around the world?

6. A leading museum director and skeptic about both measures to regulate acquisitions and cooperation in the repatriation of art to countries of origin has written flatly, "At base, works of art are chattels: the stuff of economic exchange." James Cuno, *Art as Chattel: Collectors and the Making of the Great Modern Museums*, Harv. Mag., Nov.–Dec. 2008, at 31. Do you agree? Should art be simply commodified? Are there other values that compete with the economic significance of

art? In Chapter 7, we return to the role of collectors and the practice of collecting in the museum industry.

7. A somewhat more nuanced but also positive view of collectors is the following:

> The looting of sites is deplorable, but it is an ironic twist of circumstance that plundered pots of unknown provenience have opened up for us a rich world of iconography and glyphs that we could not have conceived of a decade ago. It is tragic to lose the specific archaeological context of a tomb freshly unearthed; yet archaeologists have sometimes been simply unable to read what they have uncovered. They have often ignored or discarded materials that might prove invaluable to epigraphers or art historians. In their quest for scientific absolutes they have ignored the ephemeral carriers of cultural information. In their search for the prosaic they have overlooked clues to history, religion, and myth. It has been pointed out that the Rosetta stone was not found in context by archaeologists, but nonetheless it served to open Egyptian hieroglyphs for all scholars.
>
> A true collector collects to share. I repeat: Collectors and scholars must work together to reassemble scattered information. We in this country were long apathetic to the looting of our own ancient sites. Looting must be stopped by solid laws and the enforcement of those laws in the countries where it happens. Once artworks have been cast into the world, they must be conserved and used. It has historically been the role of the collector, the museum, and the teacher to do this.

Gillett G. Griffin, *In Defense of Collectors*, NAT'L GEOGRAPHIC, April 1986, at 462, 465. The problem, of course, is to develop the desired working relationship among collectors, scholars, and museums. As we shall see in the chapters that follow, this is an emerging theme of cultural heritage law.

8. Artifact collectors sometimes assist professional archaeologists. The relationship can even be symbiotic. In the words of one archaeologist, collectors are "'our eyes and ears.... They collect artifacts along the eroding riverbanks year-round. Their findings enhance our knowledge.' In return the archaeologists help the collectors identify and record what they find." Cynthia Barnes, *Saving a Stone Age Site*, NAT'L GEOGRAPHIC, Oct. 2005, at 92–96.
9. Collecting may also inspire cultural developments. For example, Frank Lloyd Wright, the renowned architect, was an avid collector of *ukiyo-e* ("floating world") prints from nineteenth-century Japan. He acknowledged that collecting the prints, which numbered around five thousand in his collection, might have been an obsession. They unquestionably inspired his architecture, and his occasional sale of some prints helped subsidize his architectural work, although he had to reclaim several of them and repay purchasers when it became apparent that the prints had been retouched (prior to his sale of them). Eventually, he forfeited the bulk of his collection to the Bank of Wisconsin for failure to repay collateral on a loan.

Diego Rivera, Mexico's great muralist, drew inspiration for his depictions of ancient Indian life and artistic style from a massive personal collection of nearly sixty thousand pre-Columbian objects. He deposited his collection in the Anahuacalli Museum in Mexico City that is open to the public. The objects had a direct and profound effect not only on Rivera's art but also on Mexican society in general because of his extraordinary influence in using mural art to inspire Mexican national identity and solidarity. Although his agenda was unquestionably romantic and ideological, his art collection helped reshape the national character after the Mexican Revolution. Rivera's murals, especially a famous work on industry and its role in society, also strongly influenced the work of Thomas Hart Benton, Ben Shahn, and other artists in the United States during the period between the two world wars. *See* Linda Downs, Diego Rivera: The Detroit Industry Murals (Detroit Institute of Arts 1999); Betty Ann Brown, *The Past Idealized: Diego Rivera's Use of Pre-Columbian Imagery*, in Diego Rivera: A Retrospective (Founders Society, Detroit Institute of Arts ed., 1986). Might such a social purpose and achievement justify substantial collecting despite its potential for encouraging the looting and commodification of cultural material? See also a proposal to adopt "a new value" of protecting the stream of creative expression by maximizing the access of artists to the work of their predecessors, thereby encouraging a freer international movement of cultural material. Stephen K. Urice, *The Beautiful One Has Come – To Stay*, *in* Imperialism, Art, and Restitution 135, 156 (John Henry Merryman ed., 2006).

2. Museums and Art Galleries

Museums and art galleries, whether private or public, have been undergoing profound changes in recent years. These changes have been driven by two main forces: a scarcity of financial resources and widespread changes in the perceived mandate of publicly funded institutions in light of changing public tastes and values. The extent of these changes varies with the characteristics of a particular institution and the country in which it is located. Evidence of these changes is the number of blockbuster exhibitions staged by major museums and the trend in the character of trustees and senior staff members toward greater ethnic and other cultural diversity.

The leading organization of museums at the international level is the International Council of Museums (ICOM), a Paris-based organization founded in 1946. Enjoying consultative status with the UN Educational, Scientific and Cultural Organization (UNESCO), ICOM has issued guidelines and codes on such matters as ethical acquisition practices and professional ethics. It also collaborates closely with UNESCO on matters of mutual concern, such as documentation, the development of international legislation, and codification of norms to protect cultural heritage.

In addition, ICOM has played a major role in raising the professional standards of museums worldwide. Its efforts in this regard have dealt with museum concerns ranging from security to illegal trafficking in antiquities and archaeological material. Although ICOM standards lack legal compulsion, they operate as a kind of soft law whose persuasive qualities are enhanced by the status of ICOM itself. Of special interest are the Museums Exchange Program, initiated by ICOM in 1978, and the 1979 study of ICOM's Executive Committee, titled "Study of the Principles, Conditions, and Means for the Restitution or Return of Cultural Property in View of Reconstituting Dispersed Heritage." Besides ICOM, another important NGO at the international level is the International Congress of Maritime Museums.

National or regional associations of museums are also significant in, for example, promulgating codes of ethics and conduct binding on their members. Such associations include the Canadian Museums Association, the American Association of Museums, and the Commonwealth Association of Museums. Individual institutions also promulgate their own rules to govern acquisitions, deaccessions, and the repatriation of cultural objects.

3. Anthropologists and Archaeologists

The professions of anthropology and archaeology, to the extent that they may be differentiated, are both concerned with culture in context. They therefore oppose dealing with cultural material in any way that disturbs context or otherwise creates risks to knowledge about its place of origin and other information concerning its content and character. In negotiating with national authorities to carry out exploration and excavation, archaeologists often confirm their support of efforts by host governments to prohibit or restrict trade in excavated material.

The oldest international association of archaeologists is the International Union of Prehistoric and Protohistoric Sciences (IUPPS), based at the University of Ghent (Belgium). Founded in 1931, the IUPPS's membership consists of professional archaeologists in more than 140 countries. The organization sponsors large-scale excavations and promotes research in prehistoric and protohistorical archaeology. Other noteworthy NGOs include the American Anthropological Association, the Archaeological Institute of America, the Society for American Archaeology (United States), and the Institute for Archaeologists (United Kingdom). The World Archaeological Congress recently asserted itself as an international NGO with a special commitment to social justice for indigenous peoples in relation to the practice of archaeology.

Many archaeological associations oppose all trade – legitimate and illegitimate – in excavated material. Their prophylactic approach is designed to maximize the preservation of information about objects and sites. The difficulties in doing so are the twin realities of the widespread pillage of sites and the appetite of museums, other institutions, and individual collectors for high-quality objects.

A leading anthropology NGO is the International Union of Anthropological and Ethnological Sciences (IUAES), which was established in 1948 and is based at Leiden University in the Netherlands. The IUAES seeks to further anthropological and ethnological studies in related fields, such as folklore, paleontology, and human genetics. The organization includes the Commission on Folk Law and Legal Pluralism.

4. Indigenous and Minority Ethnic Groups

One of the most significant changes to the cultural heritage landscape in recent years has been the expanded role of indigenous peoples and minority ethnic groups in gaining greater access to or return of cultural objects associated with their people; in sharing information and discussing mutual problems with one another across national boundaries; and in questioning standing professional assumptions and activities of museums, anthropologists, and archaeologists.[7]

[7] This book uses the common expression "indigenous peoples" even though its meaning is ambiguous. A confusing array of related terms, often used synonymously, includes "indigenous ethnic minorities," "aboriginals," "minority nationalities," and "tribal groups." *See generally* Lejo Sibbel, Good Governance and Indigenous Peoples in Asia 12–18 (2005) (summarizing the lack of agreement on the term "indigenous peoples" even though governments, in effect, recognize their existence). One commentator has referred

The World Council of Indigenous Peoples and the International Indian Treaty Council were the first groups of indigenous peoples to obtain NGO status with the Economic and Social Council of the United Nations. There are now more than a dozen such organizations. Some of them are national, such as the Grand Council of the Cree (Canada). Others are international, such as the International Work Group for Indigenous Affairs, based at the University of Copenhagen; Survival, based in London; and Cultural Survival, based in Cambridge, Massachusetts. Some of the organizations have helped shape the cultural heritage agenda by providing substantial support for indigenous groups. For example, in 1994 the initiative of a Mayan elder at a Cultural Survival meeting in Guatemala led to the UN General Assembly's adoption of the Declaration of the International Decade of the World's Indigenous People. All of these support organizations endorse demands for repatriation of cultural objects to indigenous groups, for example, when a national museum is asked to repatriate objects or when indigenous representatives ask a foreign museum for access to material.

Two intergovernmental initiatives, in particular, have shaped the work of NGOs. The Declaration on the Rights of Indigenous People, adopted by the United Nations, addresses cultural heritage law issues. Also, the UN Sub-Commission Work Group on Indigenous Peoples has been a major forum for indigenous groups to express their rights.

5. Artists

As a whole, the living creators of artworks are apt to be open minded about cultural heritage issues such as those involving the return or restitution of material because their stake is only partly commercial. Most organizations of artists represent the various media in which these creative people work.

Organizations representing working artists include, for example, the Society of Wildlife Artists (United Kingdom), the International Academy of Ceramics (Switzerland), Art Workers Guild (United Kingdom), the Pacific Arts Association (United States), the American Society of Contemporary Artists, the National Association of Women Artists (United States), and International Black Writers and Artists (United States). A leading organization of professional teachers and scholars in the field is the College Art Association (United States), which has assumed leadership in managing and regulating cultural heritage through its educational programs, meetings, codes of conduct, and publications.

6. Historic Preservationists, Archivists, and Art Historians

The leading international NGO dedicated to preserving monuments and sites is the International Council on Monuments and Sites, based in Paris. Founded in 1965, its membership embraces persons and institutions concerned with the conservation, restoration, and protection of historic buildings, monuments and sites. Like-minded organizations include the National Trust for Historic Preservation (United States), the American Association for State and Local History, the Association for Preservation of Technology International (United States), the Ancient Monuments Society (United Kingdom), and the Institute of Historic Building Conservation (United Kingdom).

to the term as a dynamic abstraction that draws from the culture of diverse societies and institutions. *See* Benedict Kingsbury, *Indigenous Peoples in International Law: A Constructivist Approach to the Asian Controversy*, 92 Am. J. Int'l L. 414 (1998).

The National Trust for Historic Preservation, a private nonprofit advocacy group, helps promote the governmental National Register of Historic Places. A site listed on the National Register must be more than fifty years old. It must also be associated with a significant historical trend or event, serve as an outstanding or distinctive example of period architecture, or possibly yield archaeological information. Listings may offer owners of registered properties tax breaks, protection from demolition, a cachet of renown, and perhaps a boost in property value.

Archivists are represented by the International Council on Archives, formed in Paris under the auspices of UNESCO. It consists of national and international archival associations in more than 180 countries and supports the reconstruction of the archival heritage in developing countries. One such professional organization of archivists is the Academy of Certified Archivists (United States), founded in 1989, which offers certification and referral programs.

7. Criminals and Criminal Organizations

Many aspects of cultural heritage have given rise to criminal responsibility. Most of the pertinent criminal laws are national, federal, state, or provincial. Historically, international law regulating criminal activities associated with cultural heritage has been limited and difficult to enforce. The Nuremberg war tribunals after the Second World War, however, initiated prosecutions against alleged perpetrators of deliberate destruction and looting of cultural material in the time of armed conflict. Contemporary international war crimes tribunals have continued the practice.

A major incentive for criminal activity involving cultural heritage is pecuniary. Another incentive is sheer acquisitiveness or greediness. Sometimes more subtle motivations can be discerned, such as the humiliation of or retribution against owners or creators as well as the suppression or hiding of works of art perceived as indecent. Five major categories of criminals are directly connected with cultural material: forgers, fakers, and defrauders; thieves; grave robbers and other illegal excavators; smugglers; and war criminals.

a. Forgers, Fakers, and Defrauders

Trial of the Century, Archaeology, Mar.–Apr. 2005, at 14

Eighteen months after the Israel Antiquities Authority (IAA) first announced that the James Ossuary, a first century A.D. limestone bone box engraved with the words "James, son of Joseph, brother of Jesus," and the Jehoash Inscription, a tablet purporting to be a 2,800-year-old account of repairs to the Temple in Jerusalem, were forgeries, the country's Justice Ministry handed down indictments against five men. The group includes four antiquities dealers, among them ossuary owner Oden Golan, and the former head of the antiquities laboratory at the Israel Museum. According to the indictments, the five were allegedly members of a ring that skillfully faked biblical artifacts by adding inscriptions to real ones or by faking them altogether. Setting the stage for the indictments was the formal admission by the Israel Museum a few weeks earlier that their treasured ivory pomegranate, an artifact that supposedly carried an inscription associating it with Solomon's Temple, was a forgery – one crafted by the ring under indictment... [As of January 2010 the criminal trial was still pending].

Yuval Goren, who analyzed many of the forgeries, predicts that in the long term, the result will be "a disaster for Hebrew epigraphy." Technology has made text replication so accurate, he believes, that the style and language of the ancient writing used may no longer be sufficient criteria by which to judge the authenticity of an artifact....

[T]he biggest impact the trial and resultant revelations may have... is on the attitude the public will have toward biblical archaeology. People may think, "Everything is a fake, so what are we left with? What can we believe, what can't we believe?" It won't be good for archaeology.

College Art Association, A Code of Ethics for Art Historians and Guidelines for the Professional Practice of Art History (1995)

At present there are no laws that provide for the confiscation or destruction of fakes and forgeries that have not entered the country illegally. The harm that is done by the continued circulation of fakes and forgeries is to truth, to the reputation of the artist, or to an older culture by misrepresentation of the nature and quality of its art in the eyes of art historians and the public. Fakes impair the value of authentic works of art in public as well as private collections and distort the art market. An art historian who made his or her reputation through knowledge and connoisseurship of the work of a given artist or culture has a moral obligation to these sources to expose fakes and forgeries when to do so comes within his or her competence and can be established beyond a reasonable doubt. It is recognized that the detection and exposure of fakes can be time-consuming. For an art historian to turn away from this activity on the grounds that he or she does not have the time is to pass this obligation on to others who may or may not be competent to expose the crimes involved and the effect could be a diminution of the quality of the profession. It is further recognized that art historians are concerned about legal actions taken as a result of their judgment. The most probable theories are the torts of disparagement and defamation. It is unlikely that an art historian exercising due care by providing a well reasoned, scholarly opinion will lose in the defense of such a suit. Art historians are least at risk from law suits based on their reasonable opinions, when such opinions are provided to the owner of the work at the request of such owner. In the absence of other types of error and omissions insurance, art historians may be able to obtain insurance against defamation suits available under certain home insurance policies.

Fakes and forgeries of cultural material provoke the same high level of revulsion as any acts of dishonesty. Even experienced experts are vulnerable to sophisticated fakes, and many indigenous peoples see themselves as defamed by what they regard as a form of fakery, namely, the commercial or professional exploitation of various aspects of their cultures. The only exception to the general revulsion against forgers and fakers may occur when their work is a deliberate part of the artistic agenda such as that of the surrealist Salvador Dalí, who encouraged commercial knock-offs of some of his art.

Fakes are, quite simply, objects that are not genuine examples of what they purport to be but do not necessarily purport to be anything more than copies. A forgery is an object that has been made with the intention of deceiving others into thinking that it is something other than it actually is. Both are attempts to enhance the importance of a particular object in the eyes of others, usually for financial reasons. With the growth in the size of the art market and the huge increase in market value of many works of art, the incentive to forge copies of objects and pass them off as originals has increased enormously.

The issues of art fakery and forgery are highly complex. Some fakes may themselves become valuable collectibles, as with some of Dalí's work and that of notorious master forgers. Sometimes the purported worthlessness of fakes is disputed on the basis that if they have been credible enough to fool even experts, then there is no reason to dismiss them because of their identity. The market, however, tends to devalue this perspective by assigning far less value to fakes or alleged fakes than it does to originals.

Fraudulent practices relating to works of art are not limited to the production of near-perfect replicas of original works. For example, an English resident donated large sums to the Tate Gallery in order to be given privileged access to its library. Once inside, he inserted fake provenances of "works of art" by artists represented in the Gallery's collection. These artificial "provenances" itemized contemporary fakes and thereby attempted to legitimate their status. Another instance of art fraud is the invention of a provenance to enhance the value of an original work of art. Especially when there is a prevalence of fakes of particular objects, such as certain antiquities or tribal objects, a connection with a prestigious prior owner will enhance the likelihood of an object commanding a good price in the art market.

The distinction between skilled restoration and outright deception is also problematic. The seller may not even be aware of the extent of such modification of original material. On the other hand, the buyer to whom the level of restoration is revealed may feel profoundly cheated.

The producers of fakes and forgeries may be criminally responsible for engaging in fraud, counterfeiting, forgery or false pretenses. Prosecutions have not been successful overall in dealing with the forgery of art works. The high burden of proof is rarely met by the prosecution because of the characteristic complexity and ambiguity of fine art transactions. New York State is unusual in specifying that art forgery is a distinct criminal offense, but the creation of a work of art resembling that of a well-known artist is not necessarily a crime. The suspect may successfully claim that he or she had no idea the work would ever be sold in suspicious circumstances.

Apart from criminal proceedings, the sale and purchase of fake works of art may result in civil liability. In the United States, for example, honest buyers may rely on various provisions of the Uniform Commercial Code such as those relating to misdescription and breaches of warranty. Success in such cases is often elusive, however, since courts may not be prepared to impose liability in transactions between two ostensibly well-informed and sophisticated individuals, galleries, or institutions.

NOTE

Several museums have candidly displayed expert forgeries of artwork. These exhibitions represent a substantial change in the relationship between museums and the public. A new recognition of transparency and a stronger commitment to education have prompted museums to admit their acquisition mistakes and to encourage public awareness of dishonest trading in cultural material. A broader mission of the new openness is to redefine the role of museums, once seen as citadels of cultural authority, as places fundamentally for the exchange of ideas and opinion. See Mattiew Shaer, *Faking It, Artfully*, CHRISTIAN SCI. MONITOR, Sept. 5, 2008, at 13.

b. Thieves

Art heists have become major media events in recent years. Indeed, the media rush to report instances of art theft, from the spectacular and still-unsolved robbery in 1990 of masterpieces at Boston's Isabella Stewart Gardner Museum to the successive heists of works by Edvard Munch in Oslo that were later recovered.

Stolen art and artifacts ranks third on the roster of illegal trafficking, behind only contraband drugs and arms. Although the precise scope and dynamics of art theft vary enormously, there is increasing evidence that drug cartels and other gangs of organized criminals are involved with art theft and illicit trade in cultural material. Valuable art objects are convenient items to purchase with the proceeds of illicit activities. Not surprisingly, therefore, the laundering of money through art transactions, facilitated by the confidentiality and privacy that characterize the private art market, is a growing problem.

The singularity of art objects often makes them desired just for the pleasure of their possession. This is less of a factor with other valuable chattels such as jewels and automobiles because they are normally fungible and can be acquired almost anywhere by anyone with the requisite financial resources. Valuable art, in contrast, is unique. It may be capable of acquisition only by illegal means if it already belongs to a museum or a private collector.

The effectiveness of criminal (penal) law does not depend on specific legislation addressed to theft of cultural heritage. In the United States, for example, the National Stolen Property Act (NSPA) makes it an offense to bring property into the country that has been stolen abroad. As we shall see, this law has given effect to some foreign patrimony laws that deem certain cultural material as belonging to the state and that forbid its export. This may mean that a person possesses material that he or she does not own and that is, therefore, stolen. Some argue that national courts should not enforce foreign patrimony laws that run counter to public policy. Others argue that national laws in countries of importation are needed to provide effective measures against the international trade in stolen art. Despite such concerns, the United Kingdom and other countries have passed similar laws that can be considered analogous to those criminalizing offshore sexual exploitation of foreign minors.

Another way for states to prosecute art criminals is under statutes that allow the seizure of ill-gotten proceeds, such as under the Racketeer Influenced and Corrupt Organizations Act (RICO) of the United States. Of course, theft not only is a crime everywhere but also may lead to civil proceedings, such as the common law actions of replevin or conversion that are brought by the owners or persons otherwise entitled to possess the property. Often, however, the thief is undiscoverable or civil actions fail under either continental European protections of bona fide purchasers, statutes of limitation, or rules of repose. In some cases, the person in possession of stolen goods, the receiver, will also have committed a criminal offense if he or she is aware that the property is stolen.

Law-enforcement systems in the United Kingdom, the United States, and elsewhere have set up special departments to deal with art crimes, including theft. The problem, however, is that crimes involving cultural material often have low priority, and efforts to detect them are disbanded or have funding support reduced whenever more pressing objectives, such as the detection and prevention of terrorist activities, arise. At the international level, national police agencies are linked by Interpol, which was established in 1923 to promote and establish police cooperation among member states. With respect to stolen cultural material, Interpol is mainly a clearing agency that circulates pertinent information.

Nonprofit organizations such as the International Foundation for Art Research (IFAR), based in New York, also collect and share information related to stolen or missing art works. It was IFAR that established the first archive of stolen art and published reports that could be consulted by prospective buyers. Even after closing its registry of stolen material in deference to the Art Loss Registry in London, IFAR has continued to play a pivotal role in ensuring the detection of the whereabouts and the recovery of stolen art objects. There is little likelihood that the theft of cultural material will ever cease, just as legitimate art collecting is unlikely ever to come to an end, but there is growing evidence that current levels of art theft can be significantly reduced through greater information sharing and international cooperation as well as technological advances and augmented resources.

A decision of the English Court of Appeal, *Bumper Development Corp. v. Commissioner of Police for the Metropolis*,[8] is remarkable for its exploration of the global market in looted antiquities. A Canadian corporation purchased a twelfth-century bronze sculpture of the Hindu god Siva from a London art dealer. After London police seized the sculpture on suspicion of being stolen, the Canadian buyer sued in tort, on a theory of detinue and conversion, claiming the return of the object and damages.

NOTE

For a glimpse of the foibles of art thieves, see Randy Kennedy, *Where You Going with That Monet?* N.Y. Times, Feb. 17, 2008, at 1 (Wk. in Rev.) ("The art thief, in general, is not the brightest paint in the box.").

Bumper Dev. Corp. v. Comm'r of Police for the Metropolis, [1991] 1 W.L.R. 1362 (C.A.)

General introduction

In August or September 1976 an Indian, variously described as a "coolie" or "landless labourer," called Ramamoorthi who lived in a hut near the site of a ruined Hindu temple at Pathur in the State of Tamil Nadu was excavating

[8] *Bumper Dev. Corp. v. Comm'r of Police for the Metropolis*, [1991] 1 W.L.R. 1362 (C.A.).

sand or similar material when his spade struck a metal object. There was a suggestion that it might have been a year earlier, but this was not accepted by Ian Kennedy J., whose finding has not been questioned. The place where he was excavating was close to the hut in which he lived and was either immediately adjacent to or formed part of the site of the temple. The name of the temple was the Arul Thiru Viswanatha Swami Temple to which we shall refer as "the temple." The object which Ramamoorthi struck formed part of a series of bronze Hindu idols later identified as members of a "family" and was a major idol known as a Siva Nataraja. We shall refer to the Siva Nataraja as the "Pathur Nataraja" and the assembly of idols as the "Pathur bronzes." The overwhelming probability is that they formed part of the religious objects in the temple which had been endowed in the late 13th century by a Hindu notable called Avui Thiru Viswanatha. It was later accepted by all parties that the temple had lain in ruins and unworshipped for a matter of centuries.

Notwithstanding his lowly status Ramamoorthi realized that he had discovered objects of value. He reburied them temporarily in the same pit and contacted a friend called Dorai. Dorai came to Pathur, inspected the find and departed saying that he would find a buyer. A few days later Dorai returned with two men, Pillai and Meivel, who proposed to take the Nataraja away to sell it. This was not acceptable to Ramamoorthi unless he was paid for it. The three men departed but a few days later they returned again, this time accompanied by a dealer called Chandran for whom Meivel was a "runner." Chandran was not called to give evidence, but two others, who were in the party[,] were called as witnesses. These were Hussain, who was a part-time dealer in stolen idols and a local government official, and Balraj Nadur, who was a major dealer in stolen idols. Of the objects discovered by Ramamoorthi, the Nataraja attracted particular attention from the dealers and was quickly sold, first to Chandran who sold it on down the line via Hussain and Balraj Nadar. The last identified buyer was a man called Valar Prakash, who has not been traced but was last known to be in Madras.

Of the religious objects discovered by Ramamoorthi which were recognized as being of the Chola period it is necessary only to describe the Nataraja in detail. The Siva Natarajas are representations of the Hindu God Siva who is found in various forms. The Siva Nataraja can be described in a thumbnail sketch as the god standing with his right foot upon a dwarf and surrounded by a "halo" which represents the flames issuing from the mouths of two crocodiles situated to the left and right of the dwarf. At the top of the halo in some Natarajas there is to be found a design either in the form of a mask or a rosette or similar adornment known as a "Kurti Muka." Round the halo there are a number of "flames" issuing radially from the halo. Depending upon the period when and the area in which they were made the Siva Natarajas vary in many respects. The one with which this appeal is concerned is circular; but many others are oval in shape. The Nataraja with which this appeal is concerned had a lotus base mounted on a square-shaped peedam or pedestal.

Returning to Siva, the design again varies according to date and place. The Chola Natarajas have a number of identifying features, some of which are relevant and to which it would be convenient to refer in outline. The god has two right and two left arms and hands but only two legs, right and left. He has on each side of his head horizontally flowing hair described as jettas. Various objects and representations are imposed upon or incorporated in the jettas including a particular one called a "ganga." In one of his right hands and around the wrist there is coiled a snake – a cobra. In one of his left hands he holds another flame. This very brief description will suffice for the moment.

Between 1974 and 1977 there were circulating in London at least two and almost certainly more Siva Natarajas. It was common ground that throughout the world there are many hundreds if not thousands of Siva Natarajas; most of which were, of course, associated with the many Hindu temples and which over the centuries have been objects of worship both in India and in other places where the inhabitants embraced the Hindu religion. There were and are Siva Natarajas in many leading museums and in the present century at least they have been recognized as valuable artefacts dealt in by those who specialize in Eastern religious items. However, it may fairly be assumed that there were not very many Siva Natarajas circulating in the London market in the 1970s and fewer which showed signs of having been buried for centuries. There were certainly two which had been traced as having been stolen from temples in India in current worship and which were impounded by the Metropolitan Police and returned to their appropriate owners. The Siva Nataraja or Natarajas with which this appeal is concerned were, however, objects which had long been buried and had accordingly deteriorated as a result.

Returning to the position in London in the years 1974–1977 an "antique Nataraja," that is to say[,] one which had been buried and had suffered accordingly, was, according to the evidence of Dr. Presencer, shown to him in May 1976 in London. We will refer to this as "the London Nataraja" since there seems to be little dispute that this was the same Nataraja that was bought by the Bumper Development Corporation ("Bumper"). If this was true then it would establish that the London Nataraja could not have been the one excavated by Ramamoorthi. There is now, as a result of additional evidence which was admitted during the appeal, further evidence of an antique Nataraja being offered on the London market as early as Easter 1974. This evidence came from an American dealer who specialized in these objects named Robert Ellsworth.

Information came to the state officials in Tamil Nadu as a result of which criminal investigations were put in hand. Statements were taken from Ramamoorthi and the others about the discovery and subsequent history both of the Pathur Nataraja and of the Pathur bronzes. The statements taken in India from Ramamoorthi, Hussain and others have formed part of the evidence at the trial from which this appeal results.

On 10 June 1982 Bumper purchased in good faith the London Nataraja from a dealer called Sherrier. It is common ground that Sherrier produced a false provenance of the Nataraja for the purpose of the sale. It was whilst it had been sent to the British Museum for appraisal and conservation that the London Nataraja was seized by the Metropolitan Police as part of a policy of returning religious artefacts, which it was thought had been stolen, to their owners in India. Bumper brought the action against the Commissioner of Police of the Metropolis and two of his officers in detinue and conversion claiming the return of the Nataraja and damages. The present proceedings result from the position taken by the defendants as interpleaders and the addition of others as "claimants" to the London Nataraja. Returning to the temple site at Pathur, amongst the surviving ruins and materials there was a stone object of religious worship known as a Sivalingam. In the normal Hindu temple of this period this stone would have been positioned in the sanctum and would be the focus of religious worship. It is a carefully fashioned stone object representing a phallus. It has survived and was discovered amongst the ruined remains of the temple. Since the inception of these proceedings it has been reinstated as an object of religious worship at the site of the temple.

Current proceedings

The court has before it an appeal by Bumper from an order of Ian Kennedy J. made on 17 April 1989 as a result of a judgment delivered by him on the trial of a preliminary issue. The claimants are the Union of India as first claimant, the State of Tamil Nadu as second claimant. Thiru Sadagopan who claims as the "fit person" of the temple on his own behalf as third claimant, and on behalf of the temple itself as fourth claimant. The Sivalingam was added as fifth claimant at a late stage of the trial of the issue. The nature and locus standi of the fifth claimant will be described subsequently in this judgment. Although the Union of India now makes no claim to the London Nataraja, it underwrites any liability in costs which may be incurred by the other claimants in the present proceedings.

The issue which was tried by the judge related to the title possessed by the various parties to the London Nataraja. The matter fell for consideration into two separate stages. namely (1) were the London Nataraja and the Pathur Nataraja one and the same object and (2) if, and only if, it was established that they were, did any of the claimants have a title to the Nataraja superior to Bumper's? The judge delivered his judgment in two parts accordingly and in this court the argument has been dealt with in the same way.

The claimants' case was based upon the evidence of Ramamoorthi and others who were involved with the Pathur Nataraja in India in 1976 and who purported to identify the London Nataraja as being the same as the Pathur Nataraja. The claimants' case was supported by expert evidence relying upon a stylistic similarity between the London Nataraja and the Pathur bronzes and by expert metallurgical and geological and entomological evidence intended to support a connection between the Pathur bronzes and the London Nataraja. Bumper's case depended upon the direct evidence of Dr. Presencer who identified the London Nataraja as an object which he saw in London on 13 May 1976. This date was some four or five months prior to the excavation of the Pathur Natarajas, and if established effectively disposed of the claimants' case. This evidence was supported by a soil analysis which demonstrated that material attached to or inside the base of the London Nataraja was geomorphologically incompatible with the geology of the excavation site. Bumper in its turn relied upon metallurgical evidence to show not similarity but dissimilarity between the London Nataraja and the other Pathur bronzes.

After a trial lasting some 34 days between 17 November 1986 and 26 April 1987, Ian Kennedy J. reserved judgment which he delivered on 17 February 1988. On the question of identity the judge preferred the evidence of the claimants and rejected the evidence of Dr. Presencer. On the second stage the judge held that the fourth claimant, namely the temple, suing by its fit person, custodian or next friend, the third claimant, had proved a title to the Nataraja superior to that of the title of Bumper. Alternatively the judge held that the pious intention of the 12th-century notable who gave the land and built the Pathur Temple remained herein and was personified by the Sivalingam of the temple which itself had a title superior to that of Bumper. Finally he held that the second claimant had a superior title to that of Bumper. This was based upon the state's right under local legislation.

With the consent of the parties, Ian Kennedy J. further assessed damages flowing from the alleged conversion and detinue of the Nataraja by Bumper and ordered damages in the sum of £5 to be paid to the fourth plaintiff. Bumper appeals against the finding that the London Nataraja was the same as the Pathur Nataraja. They further appeal against the findings that they did not base a title to the London Nataraja superior to the claimants and claim a declaration that each of the plaintiffs in the issue (the claimants) had failed to prove that it had any title which would be recognized by the English court; alternatively Bumper seeks an order for a retrial of the issue; in the further alternative Bumper seeks a retrial of that part of the trial of the issue relating to the legal capacity in India of the temple and/or the Sivalingam to hold title to property and pursue an action in England either directly or through the third claimant in respect thereof. In addition. Bumper applied for leave to adduce further evidence in support of their appeals against the judge's order.

On their part the claimants cross-appeal, firstly asserting that the judgment ought to [be] upheld on metallurgical evidence which was not relied upon by the judge. They further appeal against the judge's order in damages, seeking an award in the sum of £236,250. It is now convenient to deal with the two stages independently.

[His Lordship considered the evidence regarding the identity of the Natarajas and said that the court was of the opinion that Ian Kennedy J. had reached the right conclusion on that issue (namely, that the London Nataraja and the Pathur Nataraja were one and the same object). Accordingly, the court dismissed Bumper's appeal on that issue. His Lordship then considered whether, if it was established that the London and the Pathur Nataraja were the same object, any of the second to fifth claimants had established a better title to it than Bumper. His Lordship referred to the grounds of appeal, to the events at Pathur and in Tamil Nadu consequent on the discovery of the Nataraja and the Pathur bronzes, and to the relevant Hindu legislation and continued:]

Proof of foreign law

It is clear that the true status in Hindu law of the third, fourth and fifth claimants in the sense that they can enjoy a title to the Nataraja is central to the issues raised. We propose to use the expression "juristic entity" as being a person, body of persons or object who or which is recognized by the law concerned as being capable of enjoying legal possession of or title to an object and of suing or being sued in respect thereof.

Ian Kennedy J. reviewed at length the evidence of Hindu law not only as set out by textbook writers and in judgments delivered in the Indian courts, but also the oral evidence given before him by the expert witnesses before reaching his conclusions as to which claimants would be acceptable as juristic entities in the courts of Tamil Nadu, and whether and if so, what circumstances such a party could claim a title to the Nataraja. However, before coming to consider the evidence on this aspect of the case, it is convenient to consider the position in English courts. It is trite law that foreign law in our courts is treated as a question of fact which must be proved in evidence. In the absence of any evidence to the contrary, it is to be assumed to be the same as English law. It is however the duty of the judge when faced with conflicting evidence from witnesses about a foreign law to resolve those differences in the same way as he must in the case of other conflicting evidence as to facts.

. . . [W]e have come to the conclusion that the judge was not entitled to reject the evidence of the experts to the effect that Sadogopan did not have a sufficient continuity of association with the temple to qualify as a "de facto" trustee. Furthermore, we have also come to the conclusion that Mr. Calcutta [counsel for the plaintiffs] was correct in submitting that Ian Kennedy J. was not entitled to rely upon his own researches based on passages from *B.K. Mukherjea on The Hindu Law of Religious and Charitable Trust*, 5th ed. (1983) without having the assistance of the expert witnesses and the submissions of counsel. However, when the transcript of [expert witness] Mr. Vadivelu's evidence is considered, it is clear that the paragraphs to which the judge referred had already been referred to by Mr. Vadivelu in his reports and were adopted by him in evidence. There is therefore admissible evidence in support of the paragraphs in the textbook upon which the judge's research was based. Mr. Calcutta's submission therefore becomes largely academic.

[His Lordship then proceeded to consider the evidence relating to the third claimant and to the claim of the temple and stated that in the court's judgment there was sufficient evidence before Judge Kennedy to justify his findings that, under Hindu law, the temple (the fourth claimant) was a juristic entity and the third claimant, Thiru Sadagopan, had the right to sue and be sued on behalf of the temple.]

The English courts

Having held that the temple is a legal person under the law of Tamil Nadu acceptable in the courts of that state as a party which, with the third claimant acting as representative, could have sued for the recovery of the Nataraja, we must now decide whether, as the judge held, it is likewise acceptable in the courts of this country.

The question whether a foreigner can be a party to proceedings in the English courts is one to be determined by English law as the lex fori. In the case of an individual no difficulty usually arises. And the same can be said of foreign legal persons which would be recognized as such by our own law, the most obvious example being a foreign trading company. It could not be seriously suggested that such a company could not sue in the English courts to recover property of which it was the owner by the law of the country of its incorporation.

The novel question which arises is whether a foreign legal person which would not be recognized as a legal person by our own law can sue in the English courts. The particular difficulty arises out of English law's restriction of legal personality to corporations or the like, that is to say[,] the personified groups or series of individuals. This insistence on an essentially animate content in a legal person leads to a formidable conceptual difficulty in recognizing as a party entitled to sue in our courts something which on one view is little more than a pile of stones.

There is an illuminating treatment of legal personality in *Salmond on Jurisprudence*, 12th ed. (1966), at pp. 306–308:

> "Legal persons, being the arbitrary creations of the law, may be of as many kinds as the law pleases. Those which are actually recognized by our own system, however, are of comparatively few types. Corporations are undoubtedly legal persons, and the better view is that registered trade unions and friendly societies are also legal persons though not verbally regarded as corporations. . . . No other legal persons are at present recognized by English law. If, however, we take account of other systems than our own, we find that the conception of legal personality is not so limited in its application, and that there are several distinct varieties, of which three may be selected for special mention. They are distinguished by reference to the different kinds of things which the law selects for personification. The first class of legal persons consists of corporations, as already defined, namely, those which are constituted by the personification of groups or series of individuals. The individuals who thus form the corpus of the legal person are termed its members. The second class is that in which the corpus, or object selected for personification, is not a group or series of persons, but an institution. The law may, if it pleases, regard a church or a hospital, or a university, or a library, as a person. That is to say, it may attribute personality, not to any group of persons connected with the institution, but to the institution itself. Our own law does not, indeed, so deal with the matter. The person known

> to the law of England as the University of London is not the institution that goes by that name, but a personified and incorporated aggregate of human beings, namely, the chancellor, vice-chancellor, fellows, and graduates. It is well to remember, however, that notwithstanding this tradition and practice of English law, legal personality is not limited by any logical necessity, or, indeed, by any obvious requirement of expediency, to the incorporation of bodies of individual persons."

Thus *Salmond on Jurisprudence* recognizes the possibilities which may not be far-fetched, of (say) a foreign Roman Catholic cathedral having legal personality under the law of the country where it is situated; and, in order to make the concept more comprehensible, let it be assumed that it is given that personality by legislation specifically empowering it to sue by its proper officer for the protection and recovery of its contents. It would, we think, be a strong thing for the English court to refuse the cathedral access simply on the ground that our own law would not recognize a similarly constituted entity as a legal person. The touchstone for determining whether access should be given or refused is the comity of nations, defined by the *Shorter Oxford English Dictionary*, 3rd ed. (1933) as:

> "The courteous and friendly understanding by which each nation respects the laws and usages of every other, so far as may be without prejudice to its own rights and interests."

Arguing from the example of a Roman Catholic cathedral and in the belief that no distinction between institutions of the Christian church and those of other major religions would now be generally acceptable, we cannot see that in the circumstances of this case there is any offence to English public policy in allowing a Hindu religious institution to sue in our courts for the recovery of property which it is entitled to recover by the law of its own country. Indeed we think that public policy would be advantaged. As Cardozo J. said in *Loucks v. Standard Oil Co. of New York* (1918) 224 N.Y. 99, 111:

> "The courts are not free to refuse to enforce a foreign right at the pleasure of the judges, to suit the individual notion of expediency or fairness. They do not close their doors unless help would violate some fundamental principle of justice, some prevalent conception of good morals, some deep-rooted tradition of the common weal."

As Viscount Simonds said in *National Bank of Greece & Athens S.A. v. Metliss*, A.C. 509, 525 (1958), in reference to a comparable question of private international law, "[I]n the end and in the absence of authority binding this House, the question is simply: What does justice demand in such a case as this?"

The form of Lord Simonds'[s] question suggests that it is undesirable for us to go further than is necessary for a decision in this case. We emphasize that it is essential to our decision that the third claimant, although not himself a competent party, is empowered by the constitution of the temple to take all necessary steps in the proceedings on its behalf, very much as they would be taken by the next friend or guardian ad litem of a minor or a patient. Steps for which the third claimant is responsible will therefore include giving security for costs, affording discovery and doing other acts at interlocutory stages and in course of the trial itself. It is, however, no objection to the temple's participation in the proceedings that R.S.C., Ord. 80 makes no provision for such a case. The court will provide for all necessary steps to be taken under its inherent jurisdiction to regulate its own procedure.

We therefore hold that the temple is acceptable as a party to these proceedings and that it is as such entitled to sue for the recovery of the Nataraja.

We are fortified in reaching this conclusion since it accords with what we consider to be the intent and purpose behind the principles of comity. Furthermore it avoids the danger of there being any fetter of an artificial procedural nature imported from the lex fori which might otherwise stand between a right recognized by and enforceable under the lex causae.

[His Lordship considered the claim of the Sivalingam and said that, in view of the court's conclusion that the fourth claimant (the temple) had title to sue, it was unnecessary to decide whether the Sivalingam was a juristic entity for the purpose of English law. His Lordship then considered whether any of the claimants' claims was defeated by the provisions of the Limitation Act, 1980, and upheld Justice Kennedy's conclusion that in taking and keeping the idols he had found that Ramamoorthi acted dishonestly so as to bring his conduct within section 4(5) of the Act of 1980. Finally, His Lordship considered the effect of the Indian Treasure Trove Act, 1878 (No. 6 of 1878), and concluded: "For the reasons set out in this judgment we dismiss the appeal on the ground that Ian Kennedy J. correctly decided that the temple had a title to the Nataraja superior to that enjoyed by Bumper."]

After the court upheld the claim to title by the Indian temple and others, the plaintiff's only recourse was to seek return of the purchase price it had paid the London vendor. This is consistent with the Anglo-American legal principle that a bona fide purchaser of stolen goods cannot obtain good title against their original owner. Aside from the plaintiff's possible recourse against the dealer in another action, the outcome in *Bumper* was that a wealthy but apparently honest Canadian collector lost possession of its recent purchase on the London art market without other forms of redress, whereas the intermediaries in this process – the London dealer and those responsible for taking the sculpture in India – apparently remained unscathed. A source country (India) thereby recovered a stolen antiquity from a market country (England). Further disappointment awaited the Canadian plaintiff, the Bumper Development Corporation, however, when India sought to enforce the award of costs by the English courts in its favor. The Alberta Court of Queen's Bench agreed to do so despite arguments to the contrary that centered on public policy.

The question of whether an inanimate object, such as the temple, may be a legal person entitled to sue for recovery of part of itself is one of standing. The following judicial opinion raised that issue in an inheritance-related case more than sixty-five years before *Bumper*. We consider issues of standing more specifically in Chapter 5(C).

Mullick v. Mullick,
[1925] L.R. 52 Ind. App. 245, 250–52

One of the questions emerging at this point is as to the nature of such an idol, and the services due thereto. A Hindu idol is, according to long established authority, founded upon the religious customs of the Hindus, and the recognition by courts of law, a "juristic entity." It has a juridical status with the power of suing and being sued. Its interests are attended to by the person who has the deity in his charge and who is in law its manager with all the powers which would, in such circumstances, on analogy, be given to the manager of the estate of an infant heir. It is unnecessary to quote the authorities; for this doctrine, thus simply stated, is firmly established.

A useful narrative of the concrete realities of the position is to be found in the judgment of Mukerji J. in *Rambrahma Chatterjee v. Kedar Nath Banerjee*: "We need not describe here in detail the normal type of continued worship of a consecrated image – the sweeping of the temple, the process of smearing, the removal of the previous day's offerings of flowers, the presentation of fresh flowers, the respectful oblation of rice and flowers and water, and other like practices. It is sufficient to state the deity is, in short, conceived as a living being and is treated in the same way as the master of the house would be treated by his humble servant. The daily routine of life is gone through with minute accuracy; the vivified image is regaled with the necessaries and luxuries of life in due succession, even to the changing of clothes, the offering of cooked and uncooked food, and the retirement to rest."

The person founding a deity and becoming responsible for these duties is de facto and in common parlance called shebait. The responsibility is, of course, maintained by a pious Hindu, either by the personal performance of the religious rites or – as is the case of Sudras, to which caste the parties belonged – by the employment of a Brahman priest to do so on his behalf. Of the founder, any time before his death, or his successor likewise, may confer the office of shebait on another.

The testator Mutty Lal Mullick did not adopt the latter course, but he acted as shebait with the Brahmin assistant referred to. After his death his widow officiated similarly as the ministrant of the worship, and she used, as directed, the endowed funds specially destined for the upkeep and worship of the deity. After the adopted son Jadulal reached the age of twenty he then became de facto the person, charged with the same duties, to be performed as fully as his adoptive father and mother had performed them.

It must be remembered in regard to this branch of the law that the duties of piety from the time of the consecration of the idol are duties to something existing which, though symbolizing the Divinity, has in the eye of the law a status as a separate persona. The position and rights of the deity must, in order to work this out both in regard to its preservation, its maintenance and the services to be performed, be in the charge of a human being. Accordingly he is the shebait custodian of the idol and manager of its estate. And so, paying proper respect to the religious proprieties of the case, the father, mother and adopted son were successively and de facto ministrants and custodians of this idol.

NOTES AND QUESTIONS

1. The Canadian proceedings in *Bumper* involved an action by the Indian parties seeking recognition and enforcement of the English judgments against Bumper Development Corp. Bumper resisted enforcement, alleging that the judgment was contrary to the public policy of Canada, as reflected by its having acceded to a UNESCO convention against illegal trafficking in cultural property that is discussed later in this book. Bumper also counterclaimed for compensation from India for the loss of the bronze and pleaded a right to set off such compensation, together with its own English costs, against the Indian claims.

   Bumper did not argue that the English courts lacked jurisdiction or that the English judgment was not final or conclusive under English law. It advanced five defenses, however, to the registration of the English judgment in Alberta:

   (a) That the judgments of the English courts were obtained by fraud on the English courts
   (b) That India, as a cosignatory of the UNESCO convention, on equitable grounds, could not pursue its claim for costs and damages
   (c) That the English judgments were contrary to public policy
   (d) That one of the named Indian plaintiffs (the ruined temple) had no status or standing in Alberta
   (e) That the Indians were not entitled to interest on the English judgment debts, as provided for under English law

   Fraud: On this question, the court examined the law in England, Canada, and Australia. Mr. Justice Fraser found that in three Canadian provinces (Nova Scotia, Ontario, and British Columbia), courts had rejected the English Court of Appeal decision in *Abouloff v. Oppenheimer*, [1882] 10 Q.B.D. 295. That case stood for the position that enforcement of a foreign judgment might be resisted on the basis of fraud, even though that made it necessary for the English court to investigate the very facts that had already been adjudicated in the foreign judgment. According to Justice Fraser, the view in the three Canadian jurisdictions was that, for a foreign judgment to be impeached, the alleged fraud had to constitute something external to the proceedings and not merely amount to allegations of false statements at trial that had eventually been subject to the court's adjudication. The *Abouloff* decision had also been the subject of adverse comment by the House of Lords. In the light of this criticism, Justice Fraser held that *Abouloff* did not apply in Alberta, where for a judgment to be considered as having been obtained by fraud there had to be newly discovered material facts that were not before the foreign court or proof that the defendant had not had an adequate opportunity to present its case.

Looking at the facts, the Alberta court concluded that the English trial decision against Bumper had been premised on the finding that the bronze purchased by Bumper and the example excavated near the temple in India were one and the same. This conclusion arose from a rejection of the evidence of an expert English witness who had testified to seeing the bronze in London before the date of its alleged excavation in India. The Alberta court found no basis for an argument that evidence existed that had not been known during the trial. In its view, there were no newly discovered material facts that had not been presented to the foreign court and from which it could be deduced that the foreign judgment had been obtained by fraud. Bumper had not, in the Alberta court's view, been deprived of an adequate opportunity to present its case, and the fraud exception to enforcement of foreign judgments did not allow for the reargument of the case based on evidence before the foreign court or that could have been put before it had Bumper chosen to do so.

The Alberta court conceded that its findings on the fraud defense might have been different if it had followed English law as set out in *Abouloff.* However, there were convincing reasons for it not to do so, not the least of which was the increasing readiness of Canadian courts to favor the finality following from a strict interpretation of defenses to the enforcement of foreign judgments. This policy is well illustrated by the 1990 decision in *Morguard Investments Ltd. v. de Savoye*, [1990] 76 D.L.R. (4th) 256 (S.C.C.), where the Supreme Court of Canada departed from English legal tradition by adding to the grounds available to enforce foreign judgments proof of a real and substantial connection between the dispute and the foreign jurisdiction. Although this issue did not arise in *Bumper*, the remarks of one Supreme Court justice are supportive of the approach in that case. Justice La Forrest stated in *Morguard*:

> Accommodating the flow of wealth, skills and people across state lines has now become imperative. Under the circumstances, our approach to the recognition and enforcement of foreign judgments would appear ripe for reappraisal. Certainly, other countries, notably the United States and members of the European Economic Community, have adopted more generous rules for the recognition and enforcement of foreign judgments to the general advantage of litigants.

This statement of international comity in connection with international transactions is also reflected in recent changes in Canadian statutory law relating to the enforcement of foreign arbitration awards.

Equity: The Alberta Court also rejected Bumper's argument that the Union of India had been "unjustly enriched" by obtaining the return of the bronze to India, since the English judgment amounted to a "juristic reason for any enrichment" and a complete answer to Bumper's defense. It based this reasoning on the explanation of the concept of unjust enrichment in the well-known decision of the Supreme Court of Canada in *Pettkus v. Becker*, [1980] 2 S.C.R. 834.

Public Policy: The defense to enforcement of the English judgment that has most interest to cultural property lawyers was that based on Canada's status as a signatory to the UNESCO convention. This was also the only argument that raised issues specifically connected to the subject matter of the action – cultural property.

One of the most controversial aspects of the English decision in *Bumper* was that, inasmuch as the United Kingdom was not then a signatory to the UNESCO convention against illegal trafficking in cultural property [to be discussed later in this book], the court justified the return of the Nataraja to India by using common law principles. That was so even though its innocent purchaser, Bumper, was left without any right to claim compensation from the United Kingdom.

As we shall see in greater detail in Chapter 4, Canada is a party to the UNESCO convention and has implemented its provisions into federal law in the form of the Cultural Property Export and Import Act. Pursuant to that law, if the bronze had been illegally imported into Canada, the Union of India could request its return, but any innocent purchaser for value could also claim compensation from the source country (India). Of course, none of these events occurred. The bronze never came to Canada, and Canada never played any role in its return to India. There was no return of foreign cultural property pursuant to the provisions of the Canadian statute, so the condition precedent for an order of compensation under the terms of that act never existed.

Bumper argued, however, by way of counterclaim, that the right to claim compensation under the convention created a principle recognized by Canadian policy that would allow Bumper to claim compensation. Justice Fraser rejected this argument on the basis that conventional international law only becomes part of Canadian law once implemented by legislation. The UNESCO convention, he thought, only gave rise to consequences under domestic law insofar as it took the form of legislation. Although this had in fact occurred, the Canadian legislation was not, on the facts, accessible to either India or Bumper. The only exception suggested to this would be if the bronze had been illegally removed to Canada, in which case Canada itself might be under an international legal obligation (perhaps pursuant to article 13(d) of the convention) to facilitate its return to India. Even then, however, Bumper's private domestic legal claim to compensation would need to be based on the Canadian federal legislation, not on the convention.

It was also argued that by bringing proceedings in England and therefore avoiding liability to pay compensation, the Indian claimants should not be able to enforce their award in Alberta. The court rejected this argument on the basis that there were several reasons – not in least, the location of the bronze – for the claimants to have pursued their remedy in the English courts.

The main difficulty for Bumper was that the provisions of the UNESCO convention and Canadian legislation implementing its provisions simply do not envision a situation in which property is returned by one market state when an innocent purchaser resides in another such state. Although the English courts were able to fashion arguments in favor of comity to ensure the return of the stolen bronze, they were unable to find any common law basis to address the claims of an innocent buyer. The Alberta court was unable to find a violation of any principle of Alberta law in the determination as to title by the English courts. In claiming a right to compensation, Bumper was, in effect, asking the Alberta court to fashion a remedy on the basis that one should exist on grounds of public policy – a tall order under any legal system.

What is unusual about the reasoning of Justice Fraser on the issue of public policy is that it mainly addressed Bumper's claim for compensation and dealt much less clearly with Bumper's argument against enforcement of the English judgment for reasons of public policy. The court clearly rejected public policy as a basis for not enforcing the English judgment, but it did not make clear which public policy arguments related to the claim for compensation and which related purely to the issue of enforcement. The court seemed to reject public policy as a ground for nonenforcement primarily because it perceived the reasoning of the English courts on the issue of title to be in all likelihood the same or similar to what could have been expected from an Alberta court. It is arguable that the public policy rationales concerning the UNESCO convention – which were rejected insofar as the claim to compensation was concerned – were not adequately considered in relation to the enforcement of the English judgment.

Standing: As we have seen, the trial judge, Justice Kennedy, had awarded the temple itself (suing through Thiru Sadagopan, a public official in control of its affairs) damages of £5 (raised on appeal to £1,000). Bumper argued, in the enforcement proceedings, that the temple had no status or standing before the Alberta courts to enforce its claim. Justice Fraser could see no reason not to apply the findings of the English Court of Appeal, which had been prepared to accept the temple's legal personality under the law of Tamil Nadu on the basis of comity of nations. It was likely, he thought, that an Alberta court would have dealt with the issue of the temple's standing in the same way.

Interest: The last argument Bumper made to resist enforcement was that the plaintiffs were not entitled to interest on the English judgment debts. The court dismissed this argument on the basis of authority that, so long as the foreign judgment itself stipulated payment of interest, interest was payable, according to the rate specified under the foreign law, up to the date of the registration of the foreign judgment.

Bumper raised several issues by way of counterclaim. All of these were dismissed by way of summary judgment on the basis that they had no reasonable prospect of success. Most of these claims matched the arguments raised in resistance to enforcement of the English judgment, and their reasons for dismissal matched those reasons as well. Bumper's only success was a claim to set off costs awarded Bumper by the English courts. Assuming English law to be the same as Alberta law (in the absence of evidence to the contrary) the judge granted a right to set off.

2. The English decisions in *Bumper* are based on findings about title. Unlike in some legal systems, India and its coclaimants were able to establish title to the Nataraja and to enforce a right of possession against an innocent purchaser of what was assumed to be stolen property.

   The Alberta judgment in *Bumper* had less to do with cultural heritage law than with the recognition of a high foreign award of costs. In contrast to countries like the United States, Canadian courts award costs as part of a judgment, in the same manner as courts in the United Kingdom. Even U.S. courts, however, enforce foreign judgments for costs in the absence of any contrary public policy justifications. Recognition of the English judgment in *Bumper* accorded with a narrowing of the ability of courts to resist enforcement of foreign judgments. At the end of the day, India had secured the return of stolen cultural property, and the consequences of the English judgment in its favor were perfected by the Canadian courts. The novelty and originality of the English courts' findings on repatriation of cultural property in *Bumper* were insufficient to undermine the strength of the comity on which recognition of the foreign judgment was based. On the *Bumper* case generally, see S. Ghandi & J. James, *The God That Won*, 1 INT'L J. CULTURAL PROP. 369 (1992); J. GREENFIELD, THE RETURN OF CULTURAL TREASURES 177–86 (1989).

3. The enforcement in U.S. courts of foreign judgments for costs against the losing side is discussed in *Ackermann v. Levine*, 788 F.2d 830 (2d Cir. 1986), and *Somportex Ltd. v. Philadelphia Chewing Gum Corp.*, 453 F.2d 435 (3d Cir. 1971). In *Conte v. Flota Mercante Del Estado*, 277 F.2d 664 (2d Cir. 1960), Justice Friendly found the U.S. practice of not awarding costs (except as an element of damages) to be "a deliberate departure from the English practice, stemming initially from the colonies' distrust of lawyers and continued because of a belief that the English system favored the wealthy and unduly penalized the losing party," *id.* at 672 (*citing* A.L. Goodhart, *Costs*, 38 YALE L.J. 849 (1929)).
4. Do you think knowledge of a case such as *Bumper* would deter other would-be purchasers of valuable antiquities in market countries such as the United Kingdom? Do you think the result in *Bumper* could limit the number of similar thefts of cultural material in source countries, such as India?

c. Grave Robbers and Other Illegal Excavators

Perhaps the most compelling example of criminal activity associated with cultural heritage is the illegal excavation and pillage of archeological sites to recover cultural objects for sale, often if not typically on the global market. The rise of affluence in the West has fed a seemingly insatiable appetite for antiquities over a full range of quality and value. As the supply of legitimately acquired objects decreases with its movement into private collections and museums, the demand only increases for similar objects. Because most countries impose considerable restrictions on the recovery of antiquities from sites and the removal of any such material from its country of origin, the only source of new objects is their acquisition from illegitimate sources.

The common pattern is for poor locals or opportunistic visitors to uncover objects and sell them to local dealers, who send them out of the country of origin to other dealers in Western countries for sale to collectors and museums. The *chicleros* of Central America and *tombaroli* of Italy, for example, are eager to facilitate this stream of commerce. The major markets for stolen material are the United States, Western Europe, and Japan. Prospective buyers lurk elsewhere, however, especially in the Middle East, other Asian countries, Latin America, and Russia.

It is clear that the unauthorized and undocumented removal of objects from the ground results in a loss of information about their context and consequent confusion about the culture from which the objects came. Unfortunately, recognition of the problem has not led to adequate responses. Legal systems differ enormously in their ability to afford protection to sites and to reduce illegal access to them. Some systems designate national historic sites. Others vest ownership of any unexcavated historical objects in the state and make their removal an offense. Most states limit any access to archaeological sites to persons with official permission, and many make the export of locally sourced antiquities an offense. Very few states, however, can adequately police their territory to mop up illegal excavation and removal of objects. Also, it is difficult to reach agreement even on what constitutes illegal trafficking in antiquities, given the myriad ways of acquiring and collecting them since antiquity itself.

Some museums and many collectors do not share these concerns. Apart from those who are prepared to take the risk of knowingly being party to illegal excavations, others argue that the movement of the products of such activities into the hands of passionate collectors actually enhances the level of appreciation accorded to individual objects and the likelihood that they will be adequately protected and cared for. This perspective is not a popular one among professional and governmental regulatory circles, in which some have forecast the eventual demise of even the legitimate antiquities market.

Because of the transnational nature of the trade in illegally excavated material and the frequent lack of resources or inclination to enforce laws at the sites themselves, any reduction in the level of that trade must rely on international cooperation among police agencies and governments. The prevention of illegal excavations may be a realistic objective in countries with the economic and educational resources to stem such activities at their source, but in most developing countries, the realities of poverty, police corruption, and political instability make this unlikely. Even in wealthy countries, the association of drug profits with the trade in illicit antiquities can make law enforcement problematic.

International organizations, led by UNESCO, have a long record of rule making and facilitation of enforcement to deter and overcome illicit excavation, as have national legal systems. In 2003, for example, the United Kingdom passed the Dealing in Cultural Objects (Offences) Act, c. 27, which outlaws the handling of items with knowledge that they were illegally removed from a site anywhere in the world after 2003. Despite initial opposition from the London art trade, the new law's applicability is not as broad as many first thought. It does not apply to thefts from museums or to objects illegally excavated prior to the coming into force of the legislation. Early concerns that the law would exclude England from the world art market have subsided, and it now appears that it may represent what could be a pattern of such laws in other market states.

d. Smugglers (Illegal Export and Import)

William H. Honan, *Rare Pre-Columbian Relics, at Any Cost*, N.Y. Times, July 31, 1995, at 1

In a 15-minute videotape that tomb robbers in Guatemala are circulating among art dealers and archeologists, there are several views of a milky-colored limestone slab, about 4 by 5 feet. It is the Cancuen panel, a sort of Maya Rosetta stone covered with hieroglyphic signs carved on it 1,500 years ago. For $75,000, anyone can buy a chunk. Actually, the Cancuen panel is priceless, a historically significant treasure that turned up during the present explosion of discoveries about the lost civilizations of Mesoamerica. It is also indicative of a dramatic increase in the rampant and brazen looting of archeological sites in Central America that dates to the early years of the century.

With pre-Columbian artworks fetching record prices at auctions everywhere, unscrupulous dealers in the United States and Europe ignore legal constraints, while thieves threaten, terrorize or even kill anyone who stands in their way. United States Customs Service officials, concentrating on the drug trade, can do little to stem the flood of illicit antiquities into this country. "We're fighting a battle of incredible proportions," said Richard Hansen, a research scientist at the University of California at Los Angeles, who is the director of a large Guatemalan excavation. "In the last two years, 100 percent of the several hundred ancient structures at an important site in north central Guatemala have been looted. The earth is so pockmarked it looks like No Man's Land in World War I."

This dark outlook was seconded by more than two dozen archeologists, art historians, art dealers and law-enforcement officials interviewed in recent weeks. And one successful smuggler, Val Edwards, who can document his 10-year career on the wrong side of the law, paints an even gloomier picture. Mr. Edwards, who was interviewed in New York during several months, contended that throughout the past decade he covertly brought to the United States approximately 1,000 museum-quality artworks removed from ancient burial sites in Mexico and Guatemala. Customs was no problem, he said. He posed as a businessman buying restaurant equipment and cheap reproductions of ancient artifacts for a Mexican restaurant he said he was planning to open. Mr. Edwards has never been arrested and, in 10 years, his bags have been thoroughly searched only once, and then with an eye out for drugs rather than antiquities. He is negotiating a plea bargain with the authorities to try to reduce the penalty for having made false declarations to Customs officials.

Mr. Edwards said he decided to tell his story because he was cheated by his partners and is now repelled by the life of an outlaw. He was able to demonstrate how the illicit trade in pre-Columbian artwork supplies even the most reputable dealers in New York. He provided numerous photographs that he said he had taken in various hotel rooms showing pre-Columbian artworks he smuggled into the United States and delivered in New York to a Latin American entrepreneur who headed the smuggling ring. One photograph showed an elaborately decorated, bucket-like brazier and several others showed different views of the monumental figure of a priest broken into several pieces. Both objects match pictures of pieces displayed in the sales catalogue published by Sotheby's, the art auction house, for its Nov. 15, 1994, sale of pre-Columbian art. Ian Graham, director of the Maya Corpus Project at Harvard University, which attempts to publish all known Maya hieroglyphs and sculptures, said after comparing the photographs provided by Mr. Edwards with those in the Sotheby's catalogue that the two pieces shown in the photographs were identical to those in the catalogue. "There's no question about it," he said. "Although the figure of a priest has been greatly restored, there are tiny discolorations and nicks which correspond exactly."

While two records were set at the Nov. 15 auction, the bidding was not high enough on the brazier and the figure of a priest to satisfy the sellers, and both objects were returned to their owners. Stacy Goodman, vice president and head of Sotheby's pre-Columbian department, said that while her company's policy prohibited revealing the names of those who consign artworks for auction, she could say that the brazier had been offered for sale by a European collector. When pressed for more information about where the piece had come from, Ms. Goodman said a few days later that the European collector said she had acquired it from Leonardo Patterson, a Costa Rican dealer then living in Munich. Ms. Goodman expressed shock when told that Mr. Patterson had a history of problems with the law. But there is no indication that Sotheby's was a knowing participant in an illegal transaction. In 1984, Mr. Patterson was convicted of fraud for trying to sell a fake pre-Columbian fresco in Boston. A year later, while still on probation for the first felony conviction, he was arrested at the Dallas–Fort Worth airport and later convicted of illegally importing into the United States a pre-Columbian ceramic figure dated between 650 and 850 A.D. He also had with him 36 sea turtle eggs, a violation of the Endangered Species Convention.

In an interview, Mr. Patterson, who was recently named a counselor to the Costa Rican Mission to the United Nations, denied any wrongdoing in connection with the brazier. He also said he had known Mr. Edwards for many years and had traveled widely with him, although never for an illegal purpose. He said Mr. Edwards's photograph of the brazier had been taken years ago in Europe.

Franklin J. Barr, Mr. Patterson's lawyer, said in a letter that the brazier had been "in Mr. Patterson's personal collection for almost 30 years." He also said that Mr. Patterson's conviction in Texas was "a blight on the United States Customs Department and our legal and judicial systems." He said the pre-Columbian artwork Mr. Patterson had with him when arrested consisted of newly made "souvenirs," and that his client had been unfairly sentenced to a year in prison for having possessed turtle eggs that "99.9999 percent of American citizens" would not have recognized as being illegal. Mr. Barr also provided a recording of telephone conversations between Mr. Edwards and Mr. Patterson made by Mr. Patterson last spring. In them, Mr. Edwards's voice can be heard offering to keep Mr. Patterson's name out of [t]he *New York Times* in exchange for a cash payment of "25 big ones," presumably $25,000. Mr. Edwards responded that the tapes had been edited so as "to conceal the fact that Patterson attempted to bribe me." Mr. Patterson's lawyer denied the accusation.

Ms. Goodman, who has been head of Sotheby's pre-Columbian department for 10 years, said she had accepted consignment of the figure of a priest from a reputable New York dealer who had been handling pre-Columbian art for more than 15 years. Ms. Goodman said she had researched the two objects as she always did, and "felt comfortable putting them into auction."

Asked whether she considered her research sufficiently diligent in view of the widespread illicit traffic in her field of specialization, and the apparent ease with which the brazier and figure of a priest moved from the hands of men like Mr. Patterson and Mr. Edwards into her sale, Ms. Goodman said: "We do make mistakes." She added, "We could not stay in business if I interrogated our clients." She said that Sotheby's requires consignees to sign both a guarantee that they have no reason to believe that the property was illegally imported, and an agreement that specifies, among other things, that the property is free from "claims of governments or government agencies." Sotheby's clearly dominates the field in the United States. No other auction house presents regular sales of pre-Columbian artworks, and a number of dealers have recently abandoned the field, citing the risks involved.

Many defend the rights of law-abiding dealers and collectors who value pre-Columbian works more as art than as information. Gillett G. Griffin, a lecturer in art and archeology at Princeton University and curator of pre-Columbian art at the Art Museum of Princeton, said that while he could not condone looting, "it's healthier for many of these objects to be well cared for in a museum than in the ground in some areas where there's no guarantee of their safety." But most archeologists contend that even the lawful trade stimulates the illicit market, and that once an object is removed from its context in a burial mound or tomb it almost always loses its capacity to serve as a messenger from the ancient past.

Mr. Edwards said his smuggling expeditions would usually begin when a back-country villager telephoned a Latin American entrepreneur, the man for whom Mr. Edwards said he worked for 10 years, to report the discovery of a burial mound or tomb containing precious objects. The businessman would then summon Mr. Edwards from New York, frequently paying for his flight to Mexico City by giving him the number and expiration date of his Visa card. Mr. Edwards has receipts for numerous such travel expenses. The entrepreneur, through his lawyer, Carl R. Soller, has denied any involvement in these activities. Mr. Soller said Mr. Edwards had no credibility because he had attempted to extort money from his client. "That gives me a moment of pause," Mr. Soller said. "He's doing what he's doing for monetary gain." Mr. Soller said that the travel receipts with both his client's and Mr. Edwards's name on them "prove only that he's gone to Mexico and back."

Mr. Edwards said that shortly after arriving in Mexico City, he and his associate would set out for the jungle by car. On a few occasions, Mr. Edwards said, they visited archeological sites and observed the illegal digging in progress. Once, Mr. Edwards said, he was frightened off by gunfire, and he learned that killings between rival looters were common in the area. Generally, however, when they arrived at the village from which the call had been made, they would be invited into a thatched-roof hut and shown a collection of artworks, many still caked with mud. Once prices were agreed on, Mr. Edwards said, the Latin American entrepreneur would make a down payment with cash.

On the return journey to Mexico City, Mr. Edwards explained, the two men would never transport the artworks in their car. "There's a lot of marijuana-growing in these remote areas, and there are roadblocks where the police are looking for drugs," Mr. Edwards said. Instead, villagers would take the works or art in bundles on a bus to Mexico City. "The soldados wouldn't stop the buses because if they opened every bundle the villagers were carrying, the bus would never get through," Mr. Edwards said. After arriving at the bus depot in Mexico City, the villagers would deliver the artworks to a local house, where they would be paid the balance due them in cash. "I would bring over my luggage," Mr. Edwards said, "and we would pack the stuff in the suitcases, and usually in two large boxes also."

Mr. Edwards said that most pieces he took through Customs were small to medium in size, but at least two were large. "One figure was so big we had to cut it up," he said. "When I reassembled it on a bed in my hotel room, it looked like a human being lying there." Mr. Edwards said the businessman would generally take the flight to the United States with him, although they would pretend not to know each other. "After all," Mr. Edwards said he was told, "I was being paid $1,500 a pop to assume the risk alone." Mr. Edwards, who has bushy dark hair, flashing eyes and a theatrical manner, contradicts the stereotype of a stealthy, unobtrusive smuggler. He said he prepared himself meticulously for "the moment of truth" when he would have to pass through United States Customs. "I played the role of a businessman," Mr. Edwards said. "I told Customs I was planning to open a Mexican restaurant in New York, and was over there stealing ideas for decor, and buying restaurant equipment like tortilla machines. I had blueprints of restaurants I'd cut out of magazines."

One trick he learned was to avoid having his passport stamped. "You can get into Mexico without a passport," he said. "A driver's license will do, and that way nothing gets stamped. If you get your passport stamped, and they see you've just come in for six hours or a day, they'll ask questions." He also practiced diversion. "You're only allowed to bring in two liters of liquor tax free," he said, "so I'd buy two liters of tequila and two of Kahlua. When I got to Customs, I'd say: 'Look, I've got two extra bottles of liquor. What's the procedure?' Nine times out of 10, they'd say, 'Ah, go on.'" Mr. Edwards said that he never took pleasure in testing wits with Customs officials. "I enjoyed the excitement of flying off to Mexico on a whim," he said. "I liked the jet-set part of it. But getting off the plane after the return flight: that's the longest walk. That's when your mouth would dry up. I loathed it. I started getting sick, having nosebleeds. I was drinking a lot to forget about the risks involved." Mr. Edwards said that once he and his associate had arrived in New York, they would usually take a limousine to the Hotel Edison in Midtown Manhattan, where they unloaded the boxes and suitcases in the businessman's room. Mr. Edwards said he was not permitted to be present when dealers came to the hotel to make purchases.

Michael Coe, a professor emeritus of archeology at Yale University who has made a study of the illicit traffic in pre-Columbian antiquities, said that while it is highly unusual for someone as experienced as Mr. Edwards to tell what he knows, Mr. Coe believes that Mr. Edwards's story and evidence ring true. Throughout southern Mexico and most of Central America can be found hundreds of thousands of ancient burial sites. These contain the remains of the Maya, Olmec, Aztec, Zapotec and nearly a dozen earlier or later civilizations that rose and toppled in the region before the Spaniards arrived at the beginning of the 16th century. Looting these burial sites is often accompanied by violence just as in the past. Arthur Demarest, an archeologist at Vanderbilt University, said that looters recently eviscerated two guards and hung their corpses from trees at the Machaquilla site in the Peten region. But archeologists also deplore the looting itself, fearing that quantities of information about ancient Mesoamerica are slipping away, never to be recovered. R. E. W. Adams, a University of Texas archeologist, spoke for most of his colleagues when he said: "Looting is like tearing pages from a history book."

Apart from cultural patrimony laws that vest title to all unexcavated antiquities in the state, many legal systems prohibit the export of cultural property of local origin. Sometimes these laws are fairly universal in terms of the scope of material to which they apply, for example, to all antiquities more than two or three hundred years old. In other cases, they are more selective and limit the export only of certain classes of objects according to cultural categories or monetary value thresholds. We shall return to this topic in Chapter 4.

Such laws have faced two significant problems in terms of their enforcement. First, export controls are notoriously difficult to enforce, a difficulty that has become only more real as national boundaries have become more porous. Many persons engaged in transactions involving cultural heritage are unaware that such laws even exist. Also, some former colonial states have little early material culture remaining to be subject to export controls, as in several West African and Pacific Island countries. If export controls are so draconian as to bar the export of all archaic material regardless of its value, they are more likely to be ignored, and their very existence may create a black market for controlled objects. Second, many countries refuse to recognize or enforce the export laws of another sovereignty. Such laws are considered public laws akin to tax or penal legislation in which other states have no public policy investment or whose enforcement is regarded as an infringement of the sovereignty of the importing state. The normal rules of private international law therefore have been disappointing. Instead, as has been the case with illegally excavated antiquities, the most potent force for legal change in relation to export controls has arisen from international cooperation and the legal instruments on which it is based.

NOTES

1. For a fascinating account of "one of the biggest antiquities-smuggling rings in history" (in India), see Patrick Radden Keefe, *The Idol Thief*, NEW YORKER, May 7, 2007, at 58. The mastermind, eventually standing trial, confessed that he took advantage of the free-trade zone and lax inspections in Switzerland by shipping items through Geneva,

   > where he maintained three shell corporations. These companies would buy and sell the objects among themselves, to launder the provenance, before forwarding them to auction houses and collectors elsewhere. The auction

> houses could claim to be accepting antiquities not from India but from a Swiss company that had bought them from another Swiss company – even if the companies shared the same business address and the antiques had been on Swiss soil for less than a week. . . . [T]wo companies alone had consigned some ninety-three lots to Sotheby's sales. Sotheby's often paid his commission through a dummy bank account, Ghiya [the mastermind] explained. To get cash back into India, Ghiya used hawala, a paperless money-remittance system that is widely used in India and by diasporic South Asian communities throughout the world and is virtually untraceable.

Id. at 66.

2. A detailed report on illegal trafficking in Egyptian antiquities is particularly instructive as a case study. The report is neatly divided into several categories of actors and institutions with which we have been concerned: the smuggler, the expert, the dealer, the free port, the gallery, the buyer, and the recovery. See Barry Meier & Martin Gottlieb, *An Illicit Journey Out of Egypt, Only a Few Questions Asked*, N.Y. Times, Feb. 23, 2004, at A1.
3. In *Looters Rob Graves and History*, Nat'l Geographic, April 1986, at 452, the renowned Mesoamerican archaeologist and Mayan linguist Ian Graham describes the dynamics of looting and smuggling initiatives at the Río Azul site in Guatemala.

e. War Criminals

War and other physical conflicts have long played a major role in the destruction and pillage of cultural heritage. Most recently, during the armed conflict in Iraq, the world has seen the dangers cultural heritage can face. Though the scale of recent looting and destruction in Iraq eventually turned out to be smaller than many had feared, it was still substantial enough to renew concerns about the adequacy of existing legal and physical protection of cultural heritage during armed conflict. As the international law of war has developed, so, too, have the obligations of states regarding cultural material in the context of armed conflict. The prosecutions of major Nazi war criminals in the Nuremberg and Tokyo trials following the Second World War firmly established confiscation, destruction, and damage to cultural property as war crimes subject to prosecution and punishment. Contemporary war crimes tribunals, such as the International Criminal Tribunal for the Former Yugoslavia and the International Criminal Court, also confirm that pillage of cultural material is a war crime. We shall return to this topic in Chapter 4.

C. The International Legal Framework: A Summary

Despite a long history of efforts to stem illegal activity involving cultural heritage, it is mostly in recent decades that the global community has acted deliberately to construct a specific, comprehensive regime of law for regulating and protecting the heritage. Among the earliest specific multilateral agreements were the Roerich Pact (1935),[9] to

[9] Treaty on the Protection of Artistic and Scientific Institutions and Historic Monuments, *done* Apr. 15, 1935, 167 L.N.T.S. 289.

protect monuments in Western Hemisphere states, and the Hague Convention (1954),[10] to protect cultural material in time of armed conflict. In the late 1960s, however, four developments sparked efforts to develop a more comprehensive regime to protect the heritage. First, concerned archaeologists began to blow the whistle on illegal excavations, trafficking, and acquisitions. Second, Latin American governments, particularly Mexico, brought pressures on import states, particularly the United States, to cooperate in barring the importation of significant cultural material and in returning it to countries of origin. Third, native peoples' movements sparked efforts to regain possession of indigenous material. Fourth, more sophisticated thefts and the growing role of organized crime alerted law enforcement authorities to the need for better legal controls. Illegally traded cultural material was fast assuming third place behind drugs and weapons as international contraband. In response to these developments, intergovernmental and nongovernmental organizations enlisted the cooperation of national governments and private institutions in fashioning the rules and procedures that form the framework of cultural heritage law.

The emerging regime of cultural heritage law performs five interrelated functions: protection, cooperation, rectification, criminal justice, and dispute resolution. Accordingly, the law seeks to protect the physical integrity of cultural material; facilitates cooperation in its protection, transfer, and return; rectifies wrongful activity by means of civil remedies and otherwise; imposes penal sanctions in response to criminal activity; and provides formal and informal mechanisms and rules for resolving related disputes. Before looking at each of these functions in detail, it may be helpful to summarize the principal legal instruments. Treaties by UNESCO are dominant, just as cultural heritage law, broadly defined, has become central to UNESCO since 1954.

Principal instruments that were designed specifically for the protection of cultural heritage include the UNESCO Convention Concerning the Protection of the World Cultural and Natural Heritage (1972),[11] the UNESCO Convention for the Safeguarding of the Intangible Cultural Heritage (2003),[12] the UNESCO Convention on the Protection and Promotion of the Diversity of Cultural Expression (2005),[13] the Hague Convention for the Protection of Cultural Property in the Event of Armed Conflict (1954),[14] and the Council of Europe's Convention on the Protection of the Archaeological Heritage (1992).[15] Other instruments, as we shall see, also help protect the cultural heritage.

The salient instrument for cooperation in avoiding and responding to illegal activity involving cultural heritage is the UNESCO Convention on the Means of Prohibiting and Preventing the Illicit Import, Export and Transfer of Ownership of Cultural Property

[10] Convention for the Protection of Cultural Property in the Event of Armed Conflict, *done* May 14, 1954, 249 U.N.T.S. 240.

[11] Convention Concerning the Protection of the World Cultural and Natural Heritage, *done* Nov. 23, 1972, 1037 U.N.T.S. 151.

[12] *Adopted* Oct. 17, 2003, UNESCO Doc. Misc/2003/CLT/CH14.

[13] *Adopted* Oct. 20, 2005, UNESCO Doc. CLT-2005/CONVENTION DIVERSITE-CULT-REV. On issues of cultural diversity as related to the 2005 Convention, *see* Johnlee Scelba Curtis, *Culture and the Digital Copyright Chimera: Assessing the International Regulatory System of the Music Industry in Relation to Cultural Diversity*, 13 INT'L J. CULTURAL PROP. 59 (2006).

[14] *Signed* May 14, 1954, 249 U.N.T.S. 240.

[15] Eur. T.S. No. 143 (1992).

(1970).[16] Another instrument to facilitate cooperation in the return and restitution of cultural material is the UN International Institute for the Unification of Private Law's Convention on the Return of Stolen or Illegally Exported Cultural Objects (1995), known as the "UNIDROIT" Convention.[17] These two instruments also help accomplish a third function of the emerging regime: rectification of wrongful activity. Rectification includes requirements of repatriation involving the return and restitution of cultural material and compensation for wrongfully acquired intangible heritage. A fourth function, criminal justice, is largely the province of domestic law and the international criminal tribunals. The fifth and weakest component of the emerging regime, dispute resolution, includes various processes for resolving civil disputes under both public and private law. This component relies on scattered provisions in regional and international instruments but mostly on arbitration, litigation in national courts, and intergovernmental judicial cooperation. In support of this legal regime, primarily by UNESCO and satellite organizations in cooperation with national governments, are programs of professional and public education, of technical assistance in improving national antiquities legislation, of promoting equitable exchange, and of facilitating international cooperation.

Finally, it should be noted that some normative instruments include multiple components, for example, the 1970 UNESCO Convention, the Buenos Aires Draft Convention on the Protection of the Underwater Cultural Heritage (1994),[18] the UNESCO Convention on the Protection of the Underwater Cultural Heritage (2001),[19] and the UNESCO

[16] Convention on the Means of Prohibiting and Preventing the Illicit Import, Export and Transfer of Ownership of Cultural Property, *adopted* Nov. 14, 1970, 96 Stat. 2350, 823 U.N.T.S. 231 [hereinafter the 1970 UNESCO Convention].

[17] Final Act of the Diplomatic Conference for the Adoption of the Draft UNIDROIT Convention on the International Return of Stolen or Illegally Exported Cultural Objects, June 24, 1995, 34 I.L.M. 1322 (1995) [hereinafter UNIDROIT Convention]. UNIDROIT is the official acronym in English that is derived from the French for the International Institute for the Unification of Private Law. For a detailed analysis of the UNIDROIT Convention, *see* LYNDEL V. PROTT, COMMENTARY ON THE UNIDROIT CONVENTION(1997); John H. Merryman, *The UNIDROIT Convention, Three Significant Departures from the Urtext*, 4 INT'L J. CULTURAL PROP. 11 (1996); Lyndel V. Prott, *UNESCO and UNIDROIT: A Partnership against Illicit Trafficking*, 1 UNIFORM L. REV. 59 (1996).

[18] *See* Buenos Aires Draft Convention on the Protection of the Underwater Cultural Heritage, *reprinted in* INT'L L. ASS'N, REPORT OF THE SIXTY-SIXTH CONFERENCE 432 (1994) [hereinafter Buenos Aires Draft Convention].

[19] UN Educational, Scientific and Cultural Organization, Convention on the Protection of the Underwater Cultural Heritage, art. 1(1)(a), Nov. 2, 2001, 41 I.L.M. 40 (2002) [hereinafter the 2001 UNESCO Convention]. The convention is based on the Buenos Aires Draft Convention that was adopted by the International Law Association and submitted to UNESCO in 1994 (*supra* note 18). For a summary of the UNESCO Convention, see James A.R. Nafziger, *The UNESCO Convention on the Protection of the Underwater Cultural Heritage*, IFAR J., Autumn 2001, at 22 (2001). For further background and analysis, *see* THE PROTECTION OF THE UNDERWATER CULTURAL HERITAGE: BEFORE AND AFTER THE 2001 UNESCO CONVENTION (Roberta Garabello & Tullio Scovazzi eds., 2003); *Draft Convention on the Protection of the Underwater Cultural Heritage, A Commentary*, UNESCO Doc. CLT-99/WS/8 (April 1999); Guido Carducci, *New Developments in the Law of the Sea: The UNESCO Convention on the Protection of the Underwater Cultural Heritage*, 96 AM. J. INT'L L. 419 (2002); and Craig Forrest, *A New International Regime for the Protection of the Underwater Cultural Heritage*, 51 INT'L & COMP. L.Q. 511, 535–36 (2002) (adding that "[t]he creation of an international legal regime that will be applicable to the recovery of [underwater cultural heritage,] based on historical importance, rather than the existence of marine peril, will replace the necessity of having to determine whether salvage law is applicable"). For an annotated commentary, *see* PATRICK J. O'KEEFE, SHIPWRECKED HERITAGE: A COMMENTARY ON THE UNESCO CONVENTION ON UNDERWATER CULTURAL HERITAGE (2002).

Convention on the Protection and Promotion of the Diversity of Cultural Expression (2005), noted earlier.

NOTE

The vast literature on cultural heritage law is spread over many sources. Several English-language periodicals, however, are particularly rich sources of pertinent news about legal developments and scholarly commentary. The following periodicals normally devote substantial attention to cultural heritage matters in every issue:

- *Archaeology* (popular monthly magazine of the Archaeological Institute of America), http://www.archaeology.org
- *Art Antiquity and Law* (quarterly scholarly journal), http://www.ial.uk.com/aal.php
- *The Art Newspaper* (monthly periodical with short news items), http://www.theartnewspaper.com
- *International Journal of Cultural Property* (quarterly scholarly journal), http://www.journals.cambridge.org/jcp
- *IFAR Journal* (quarterly journal of the International Foundation for Art Research, with shorter commentary on important developments), http://www.ifar.org

The Web sites of several prominent organizations in the sphere of cultural heritage law are as follows:

- American Association of Museums, http://www.aam-us.org
- Association of Art Museum Directors, http://www.aamd.org
- Canadian Museums Association, http://www.museums.ca
- International Council of Museums, http://icom.museum
- International Council on Monuments and Sites, http://www.icomos.org
- International Foundation for Art Research, http://www.ifar.org
- International Law Association, http://www.ila-hq.org
- United Kingdom Spoliation Advisory Panel, http://www.culture.gov.uk
- UNESCO, http://www.unesco.org
- United Nations Institute for the Unification of Private International Law (UNIDROIT), http://www.unidroit.org
- World Intellectual Property Organization, http://www.wipo.int/portal.index.html.en

4. Cultural Material: Protection and Cooperation

A. Protection

1. Threats to Cultural Resources

a. Archaeological

Ricardo J. Elia, *Looting, Collecting, and the Destruction of Archaeological Resources*, 6 Nonrenewable Resources, no. 2, at 85–86, 88–89, 91, 93, 95 (1997)

Archaeological resources are frequently described as nonrenewable resources. It is true that new archaeological sites are being formed every day by the same processes that created sites in the past – the disposal of refuse, the [abandonment] of living and working spaces, and natural causes like alluviation, flooding, and earthquakes. But archaeological resources from past epochs can never be renewed. The surviving stock (including recorded and as yet unrecorded sites) of Sumerian temples, early hominid sites, or Anasazi pithouses is all that we will ever have; the resource base of past sites may be preserved or diminished, but will never be augmented. To cite one specific example, historical records indicate that between 1492 and 1520, the period of European exploration of the Americas, slightly more than 50 vessels were lost in the New World. Considering that some of these ships were later stripped for parts and materials, the actual number is probably smaller. The result is a strikingly small potential database for underwater archaeologists who are interested in this important period of nautical history.

The physical remains of the past constitute a fragile and finite archaeological resource base that is regularly threatened with depletion, destruction, and disturbance from several causes, some deliberate and others unintentional. The principal causes of the attrition of the archaeological record are environmental forces, development, warfare, vandalism, and looting. Each factor varies in intensity and scope, but all produce the same result – a steady, irremediable erosion of the record of our life on the planet.

Environmental forces that destroy or damage archaeological resources include natural conditions like rain, wind, erosion, floods, and humidity, and harmful conditions caused by human agency, such as air pollution. The other threats – development, warfare, vandalism, and looting – are all the results of human activities. Of these, development is probably the most extensive and affects the most sites throughout the world. Development includes all construction, building, and earth-moving activities that are the consequence of human habitation, economy, and subsistence. The construction of buildings, shopping malls, industrial complexes, highways, pipelines, as well as other activities like agriculture, lumbering, and dredging of waterways, are common examples of development activities that can destroy archaeological sites if no measures are taken to discover sites and avoid impacts to them before the activity takes place.

Warfare frequently causes intensive damage and destruction to archaeological sites, monuments, collections, and records. Much of the loss results from the destructive forces of war, including weaponry and the movements of vehicles and troops. Often archaeological and cultural resources are plundered or deliberately destroyed during armed conflict. During World War II, for example, a massive and systematic campaign of looting of art treasures, including archaeological collections, was undertaken by the Nazis. Near the end of the war, Russian trophy brigades carted off artworks from Germany to Russia, including the famous "Priam's Treasure," excavated by Heinrich Schliemann at Troy in 1873. In the Gulf War, the contents of the Kuwait Museum were removed by the Iraqis, and the National Museum in Kabul was plundered in the course of the recent civil war in Afghanistan. [During the 1990s] in the Balkans, churches, museums, and libraries were regularly targeted by the combatants in a form of cultural genocide. Moreover, the collapse of civil and police authority during armed conflict frequently results in the plundering of archaeological sites, storerooms, and archives.

Vandalism is a relatively minor, though harmful, cause of damage to archaeological resources. Site vandals maliciously deface or damage archaeological sites, monuments, and objects. Examples of vandalism include the damaging of buildings and monuments from gunfire and the defacing of prehistoric rock paintings.

Looting is the deliberate, destructive, and non-archaeological removal of objects from archaeological sites to supply the demand of collectors for antiquities. Site looting is motivated by commercial factors and is stimulated by the international demand of collectors and museums for archaeological objects. In their efforts to supply marketable objects to collectors, looters remove objects from their archaeological context and in the process destroy or disturb the archaeological sites that contained them. Looting is both intensive in its damage to specific archaeological sites and global in its scale. It constitutes one of the gravest threats to the archaeological resource base, and, because looting is a deliberate activity, unlike development, where site damage is an unintentional consequence of an earth-moving project, archaeologists regard it as the most pernicious and difficult to control of all threats to the cultural heritage.

Scale of the Looting Problem

The looting of archaeological sites is a worldwide crisis. Few archaeological regions of the world are immune to the destructive removal of archaeological objects for sale in the antiquities market. Recent estimates put the volume of stolen art, including antiquities, at between [$2 billion and $6] billion dollars per year. Unfortunately, the clandestine nature of much of the antiquities market system makes it difficult to quantify the full extent of the problem. Two types of empirical data, from opposite ends of the system, may be used to document the scale of looting: first, the evidence of looted sites in the countries of origin; and second, the continuous surfacing of previously unrecorded and unprovenienced material on the market, in private collections, and museums.

Despite legal efforts to protect sites, looting continues unabated in many areas of the United States. In the Four Corners region of the Southwest, for example, a government study showed that almost one-third of all surveyed sites had experienced some looting.

Central and South America also suffer from a massive looting problem. The looting of Precolumbian sites increased dramatically in this century after previously unpopular antiquities suddenly became desirable to collectors.

The scale of looting in these areas almost defies description. Aerial photographs show entire river valleys in Peru pitted with tens of thousands of looters' holes; the scenes are reminiscent of a lunar landscape. In the Cara Sucia region of El Salvador, more than 5,000 looters' pits were counted by archaeologists. In Belize, a majority of recorded sites have experienced looting, and archaeologists report finding looters' camps with bulldozers and housing for 70–80 people. In Costa Rica, looting of archaeological sites was such a common activity that the looters were organized, for a time, in a legal trade union.

In Europe, especially in the Mediterranean countries, the tradition of looting of Greek and Roman antiquities goes back hundreds of years. In the 18th century, ancient tombs were opened so that wealthy collectors could obtain painted pottery. Before 1960, most of the tombs in several Etruscan cemeteries had already been looted; not only were the movable artifacts removed, especially the prized Greek pottery, but frequently the looters also damaged or destroyed fragile wall paintings. It was probably a looted Etruscan tomb that produced the Euphronios Vase, the famous million-dollar "hot pot" acquired by the Metropolitan Museum of Art in New York in 1972. Today the discovery of an unplundered Etruscan tomb is more likely to be the result of tombaroli (tomb robbers) than archaeologists. Several Italian tombaroli have even published their memoirs.

Greece and Turkey continue to be rich sources of looted antiquities, despite strong protective laws and aggressive policies of claiming stolen art in foreign courts, especially the United States. The countries of the Middle East have long been plundered, and political instability and war further hamper the ability of national authorities to protect sites. Egyptian archaeological sites have been looted for centuries to provide artworks for Western collectors and there is no indication that looting in Egypt has diminished. Since the dissolution of the Soviet Union, an upsurge in looting has been noted in Ukraine and the countries around the Black Sea. Asia is another region where looting is rife, and archaeological sites and monuments have been ransacked in the Indian subcontinent, Southeast Asia (e.g., Angkor Wat), and China as collectors accumulate artworks like Ghandara and Angkor sculptures, Chinese bronzes, painted pottery, and tomb fixtures. In China alone, 40,000 tombs were reported plundered in 1989 and 1990, and tens of thousands of objects destined for the international market have been intercepted since the early 1980s. Chinese antiquities are frequently smuggled into Hong Kong and Macau; between 1981 and 1989, customs officials in Guangdon Province alone reportedly recovered more than 70,000 smuggled artifacts. Treasure hunting and site looting went hand in hand with European colonization in Subsaharan Africa, and today the market in stolen African antiquities and ethnographic objects is thriving. Countries in West Africa have been particularly hard hit as peasants dig for terracotta sculptures that have become popular among Western collectors and museums. In the inland Niger Delta of Mali, for example, archaeological sites have been plundered by looters organized by local dealers and numbering up to 200 peasants.

The Consequences of Looting

The most serious consequence of the pillaging of archaeological resources is not the loss of individual objects to the illicit market, although the attention given to the aesthetic values of antiquities as "art," their treatment in law as cultural property, and the focus of countries of origin and possessors alike on the ownership of objects, all tend to reinforce that perspective. The most serious consequence is, instead, the destruction of the original archaeological context in which the looted objects were found. Once destroyed, archaeological context cannot be recovered and the loss of archaeological and scientific information is permanent.

The looting of archaeological sites both diminishes the informational value of the looted object and destroys or damages the surrounding archaeological resource. Little can be said about a looted object other than what may be gleaned from the physical object itself; often, the very authenticity of the object may be questioned in the absence of a verifiable find-spot. For example, several gold ornaments in the shape of peanuts surfaced on the market after an intact Moche tomb was looted in the Sipán region of Peru; one sold for $22,000. What can be learned from these objects? Nothing certain can be said about their date, function, symbolism, or placement in the grave; how can we be sure that they are even genuine? By contrast, we may compare the abundance of information that is being learned by the scientific excavation and study of unplundered tombs at the same Sipán site that followed the looting. Even though only preliminary analysis has been completed, and full study will take many years, unparalleled new information has been learned about the nature of Moche society, ritual, material culture, and technology. And, unlike the looted materials, which were ripped from their context and scattered among collectors throughout the world, the artifacts from the excavations are being curated as an assemblage and will be available for continuing study. Most importantly, the results are being made accessible to the scholarly community and the general public.

The removal of archaeological objects from their contexts and the destruction of archaeological resources in the search for archaeological objects are two of the most damaging consequences of looting. A third consequence is the uncertainty and corruption introduced into studies of ancient material culture and art as a result of the presence of fakes or forgeries of ancient objects. The development of a trade in fakes is an automatic by-product of any flourishing art market; it thrives in the antiquities market precisely because the overwhelming majority of objects acquired by collectors lack a documented archaeological provenience. Few types of material culture have not been the object of faking, and art historians who rely on stylistic and subjective criteria of authentication have regularly been duped by clever forgeries. Even scientific analysis of materials is not guaranteed to successfully spot the well-made fake.

How fakes corrupt studies of ancient culture and art is exemplified by the case of the Getty kouros, a marble statue of Archaic type acquired by the Getty Museum in the 1980s from a Swiss dealer for as much as $9 million. The statue of the male youth, if genuine, would be an extremely rare find, but in the absence of an archaeological provenience, the Getty had to consider the possibility that the piece was fake. It conducted a battery of art, historical and scientific tests and purchased the Kouros even after learning that the documentation showing that the statue was in a private collection in the 1930s had been forged. The Getty held a colloquium in Athens in 1992 to discuss the question of authenticity. A panel of distinguished art historians, sculptors, and scientists could not agree; some claimed the statue was a genuine masterpiece of Greek art while others derided it as an obvious fake. Today, the statue stands in art historical limbo: if genuine, it remains tainted with suspicion; if fake, then those who treat it as genuine run the risk of corrupting the study of Greek sculpture. The problem is one that is repeated in many areas and with many types of material culture, from Chinese bronzes to Precolumbian figurines, and is directly attributable to the willingness of collectors to acquire looted, or unprovenienced, objects. Looting, and the acceptance of looting by the market, allows fakes to proliferate; fakes, in turn, corrupt our ability to make reasoned statements about the past.

NOTES AND QUESTIONS

1. A leading marine archaeologist, James Delgado, has written the following about the threat that souvenir hunters pose to the underwater heritage:

> In Mexico, while studying the wreck of the brig *Somers* – the only ship in the U.S. Navy to suffer a mutiny and whose story inspired Melville to write *Billy Budd* – I discovered that souvenir hunters had ripped into the ship's stern, taking some of the small arms, swords and the ship's chronometer. We never got them back. They either crumbled into dust without treatment, or were treated and sold on the black market. This happens too often. I also have watched countless auctions of artifacts from shipwrecks, raised by treasure hunters and sold off to the highest bidder, usually not museums, as most museums will not participate in activities that turn archeological relics into commodities for sale. Our role is to encourage understanding and appreciation of the past, of other cultures and of who we are. We work to encourage science and knowledge. Wrenching a porthole off a wreck or digging into a ballast pile on the bottom to take a copper spike home is as wrong as systematically mining a wreck of its artifacts and then selling them off with some hype, often abetted by the media.

James P. Delgado, Adventures of a Sea Hunter 6 (2004).

How can the oceans be effectively policed? A partial answer to the problem of underwater looting may lie in the imposition and enforcement of controls over the market in artifacts. But how can such controls reach souvenirs that never enter the market?

2. Ricardo Elia's article emphasized that the most serious consequence of looting is the destruction of the original archaeological context in which looted objects were found. Similarly, James Delgado has lamented the loss of context that results from underwater souvenir hunting:

> A few years ago, I went on a trip to Bermuda, a graveyard of lost ships and home to one of the word's great maritime museums. In a souvenir shop, I saw a brick with a maker's stamp from San Francisco. I had only seen that stamp once before, in the ballast of a mid-nineteenth century wreck in the North Pacific that I was still trying to identify. I asked where the brick came from. "A shipwreck off the coast," I was told. Did they know what ship? Where had it come from? How old was it? How had this brick from far-off San Francisco reached the Caribbean? Where had the wrecked ship gone in her travels? The shopkeeper didn't know. A local diver had pulled it off the bottom a long time ago, and others had followed to strip the wreck clean. The souvenir shop, and other[s] like it, had been selling bits and pieces of the wreck to tourists for years. This was an opportunity lost, a story never told. The divers, the shops, the buyers who wanted a "piece of the past," had scattered the pieces of the puzzle all over the globe, and now the puzzle will never be assembled to reveal the whole picture.

James P. Delgado, Adventures of a Sea Hunter 6–7 (2004).

3. Typically, we think of looting as the dominant threat to archaeological heritage. But air and water pollution, armed conflict, construction projects, and urban

sprawl pose major threats, too. See, e.g., Jane Arraf, *Iraq's Urban Sprawl, Not Looting, Threatens Ninevah Antiquities*, CHRISTIAN SCI. MONITOR, Mar. 4, 2009, at 4 (noting that "urbanization is more of a threat than looting is" and that erosion from the elements is rapidly deteriorating the most excavated area of Ninevah, the palace of Sennacherib).

4. For a revealing, well-illustrated set of essays on endangered sites, see *10 Must-See Endangered Cultural Treasures*, SMITHSONIAN, March 2009, at 30.

b. Artistic

CARTER v. HELMSLEY-SPEAR, INC.,
71 F.3d 77 (2d Cir. 1995)

Cardamone, Circuit Judge:

Defendants 474431 Associates and Helmsley-Spear, Inc. (defendants or appellants), as the owner and managing agent respectively, of a commercial building in Queens, New York, appeal from an order of the United States District Court for the Southern District of New York . . . following a bench trial. The order granted plaintiffs, who are three artists, a permanent injunction that enjoined defendants from removing, modifying or destroying a work of visual art that had been installed in defendants' building by plaintiffs-artists commissioned by a former tenant to install the work. *See Carter v. Helmsley-Spear, Inc.*, 861 F. Supp. 303 (S.D.N.Y. 1994). Defendants also appeal from the dismissal by the trial court of their counterclaim for waste. Plaintiffs cross-appeal from the dismissal of their cause of action for tortious interference with contractual relations and from the denial of their requests to complete the work and for an award of attorney's fees and costs.

On this appeal we deal with an Act of Congress that protects the rights of artists to preserve their works. One of America's most insightful thinkers observed that a country is not truly civilized "where the arts, such as they have, are all imported, having no indigenous life." 7 Works of Ralph Waldo Emerson, Society and Solitude, Chapt. 2 *Civilization* 34 (AMS. ed. 1968). From such reflection it follows that American artists are to be encouraged by laws that protect their works. Although Congress in the statute before us did just that, it did not mandate the preservation of art at all costs and without due regard for the rights of others.

For the reasons that follow, we reverse and vacate the grant of injunctive relief to plaintiffs and affirm the dismissal by the district court of plaintiffs' other claims and its dismissal of defendants' counterclaim for waste.

BACKGROUND

. . . Plaintiffs John Carter, John Swing and John Veronis (artists or plaintiffs) are professional sculptors who work together and are known collectively as the "Three-Js" or "Jx3." On December 16, 1991, SIG entered into a one-year agreement with the plaintiffs "engag[ing] and hir[ing] the Artists . . . to design, create and install sculpture and other permanent installations" in [their] building, primarily the lobby. Under the agreement plaintiffs had "full authority in design, color and style," and SIG retained authority to direct the location and installation of the artwork within the building. The artists were to retain copyrights to their work and SIG was to receive 50 percent of any proceeds from its exploitation. On January 20, 1993 SIG and the artists signed an agreement extending the duration of their commission for an additional year. When Corporate Life became a general partner of the Limited Partnership, the Limited Partnership assumed the agreement with plaintiffs and in December 1993 again extended the agreement.

The artwork that is the subject of this litigation is a very large "walk-through sculpture" occupying most, but not all, of the building's lobby. The artwork consists of a variety of sculptural elements constructed from recycled materials, much of it metal, affixed to the walls and ceiling, and a vast mosaic made from pieces of recycled glass embedded in the floor and walls. Elements of the work include a giant hand fashioned from an old school bus, a face made of automobile parts, and a number of interactive components. These assorted elements make up a theme relating to environmental concerns and the significance of recycling.

. . . The property was surrendered to defendant Associates [as the owner of the property in bankruptcy] and defendant Helmsley-Spear, Inc., took over management of the property. Representatives of defendants informed the artists that they could no longer continue to install artwork at the property, and instead had to vacate the building. These representatives also made statements indicating that defendants intended to remove the artwork already in place in the building's lobby.

As a result of defendants' actions, artists commenced this litigation. On April 26, 1994, the district court issued a temporary restraining order enjoining defendants from taking any action to alter, deface, modify or mutilate the artwork installed in the building. In May 1994 a hearing was held on whether a preliminary injunction should issue. The district court subsequently granted a preliminary injunction enjoining defendants from removing the artwork pending the resolution of the instant litigation. *See Carter v. Helmsley-Spear, Inc.*, 852 F. Supp. 228 (S.D.N.Y.1994).

A bench trial was subsequently held in June and July 1994, at the conclusion of which the trial court granted the artists the permanent injunction prohibiting defendants from distorting, mutilating, modifying, destroying and removing plaintiffs' artwork. *Carter v. Helmsley-Spear, Inc.*, 861 F. Supp. 303, 337 (S.D.N.Y. 1994). The injunction is to remain in effect for the lifetimes of the three plaintiffs. Plaintiffs' other claims, including their cause of action for tortious interference and a request for an award of costs and attorney's fees and that they be allowed to continue to add to the artwork in the lobby, as well as defendants' counterclaim for waste, were all dismissed with prejudice. This appeal and cross-appeal followed.

DISCUSSION

I. Artists' Moral Rights

A. History of Artists' Moral Rights

Because it was under the rubric of the Visual Artists Rights Act of 1990 that plaintiffs obtained injunctive relief in the district court, we must explore, at least in part, the contours of that Act. In doing so it is necessary to review briefly the concept of artists' moral rights and the history and development of those rights in American jurisprudence, which led up to passage of the statute we must now examine.

The term "moral rights" has its origins in the civil law and is a translation of the French *le droit moral*, which is meant to capture those rights of a spiritual, non-economic and personal nature. The rights spring from a belief that an artist in the process of creation injects his spirit into the work and that the artist's personality, as well as the integrity of the work, should therefore be protected and preserved. . . . Because they are personal to the artist, moral rights exist independently of an artist's copyright in his or her work. . . .

While the rubric of moral rights encompasses many varieties of rights, two are protected in nearly every jurisdiction recognizing their existence: attribution and integrity.

. . . The right of attribution generally consists of the right of an artist to be recognized by name as the author of his work or to publish anonymously or pseudonymously, the right to prevent the author's work from being attributed to someone else, and to prevent the use of the author's name on works created by others, including distorted editions of the author's original work. . . . The right of integrity allows the author to prevent any deforming or mutilating changes to his work, even after title in the work has been transferred. . . .

In some jurisdictions the integrity right also protects artwork from destruction. Whether or not a work of art is protected from destruction represents a fundamentally different perception of the purpose of moral rights. If integrity is meant to stress the public interest in preserving a nation's culture, destruction is prohibited; if the right is meant to emphasize the author's personality, destruction is seen as less harmful than the continued display of deformed or mutilated work that misrepresents the artist and destruction may proceed. . . .

Although moral rights are well established in the civil law, they are of recent vintage in American jurisprudence. Federal and state courts typically recognized the existence of such rights in other nations, but rejected artists' attempts to inject them into U.S. law. *See, e.g., Vargas v. Esquire, Inc.*, 164 F.2d 522, 526 (7th Cir. 1947); *Crimi v. Rutgers Presbyterian Church*, 194 Misc. 570, 573–76 (N.Y. Sup. Ct. 1949). Nonetheless, American courts have in varying degrees acknowledged the idea of moral rights, cloaking the concept in the guise of other legal theories, such as copyright, unfair competition, invasion of privacy, defamation, and breach of contract. . . .

In the landmark case of *Gilliam v. American Broadcasting Companies, Inc.*, 538 F.2d 14 (2d Cir. 1976), we relied on copyright law and unfair competition principles to safeguard the integrity rights of the "Monty Python" group, noting that although the law "seeks to vindicate the economic, rather than the personal rights of authors . . . the economic incentive for artistic . . . creation . . . cannot be reconciled with the inability of artists to obtain relief for mutilation or misrepresentation of their work to the public on which the artists are financially dependent." *Id.* at 24. Because decisions protecting artists' rights are often "clothed in terms of proprietary right in one's creation," we continued, "they also properly vindicate the author's personal right to prevent the presentation of his work to the public in a distorted form." *Id.*

Artists fared better in state legislatures than they generally had in courts. California was the first to take up the task of protecting artists with the passage in 1979 of the California Art Preservation Act, Cal. Civ. Code § 987 *et seq.* (West 1982 & Supp. 1995), followed in 1983 by New York's enactment of the Artist's Authorship Rights Act, N.Y. Arts & Cult. Aff. Law § 14.03 (McKinney Supp. 1995). Nine other states have also passed moral rights statutes, generally following either the California or New York models.

B. Visual Artists Rights Act of 1990

Although bills protecting artists' moral rights had first been introduced in Congress in 1979, they had drawn little support. *See Copyright Law* at 1018 n. 1. The issue of federal protection of moral rights was a prominent hurdle in the debate over whether the United States should join the Berne Convention, the international agreement protecting literary and artistic works. Article 6bis of the Berne Convention protects attribution and integrity, stating in relevant part:

> Independently of the author's economic rights, and even after the transfer of the said rights, the author shall have the right to claim authorship of the work and to object to any distortion, mutilation or other modification of, or other derogatory action in relation to, the said work, which would be prejudicial to his honor or reputation.

Berne Convention for the Protection of Literary and Artistic Works, September 9, 1886, art. 6bis, S. Treaty Doc. No. 27, 99th Cong., 2d Sess. 41 (1986).

The Berne Convention's protection of moral rights posed a significant difficulty for U.S. adherence. *See Copyright Law* at 1022 ("The obligation of the United States to provide *droit moral* . . . was the single most contentious issue surrounding Berne adherence."); *Nimmer* at 8D-15 ("During the debate over [the Berne Convention Implementation Act], Congress faced an avalanche of opposition to moral rights, including denunciations of moral rights by some of the bill's most vociferous advocates."); H.R. Rep. No. 514, 101st Cong., 2d Sess. 7 (1990), *reprinted in* 1990 U.S.C.C.A.N.

6915, 6917 ("After almost 100 years of debate, the United States joined the Berne Convention. . . . [C]onsensus over United States adherence was slow to develop in large part because of debate over the requirements of Article 6bis.").

Congress passed the Berne Convention Implementation Act of 1988, Pub. L. No. 100-568, 102 Stat. 2853 (1988), and side-stepped the difficult question of protecting moral rights. It declared that the Berne Convention is not self-executing, existing law satisfied the United States' obligations in adhering to the Convention, its provisions are not enforceable through any action brought pursuant to the Convention itself, and neither adherence to the Convention nor the implementing legislation expands or reduces any rights under federal, state, or common law to claim authorship of a work or to object to any distortion, mutilation, or other modification of a work. *See id.* §§ 2, 3; *see also* S. Rep. No. 352, 100th Cong., 2d Sess. 9–10 (1988), *reprinted in* 1988 U.S.C.C.A.N. 3706, 3714–15.

Two years later Congress enacted the Visual Artists Rights Act of 1990 (VARA or Act), Pub. L. No. 101-650 (tit. VI), 104 Stat. 5089, 5128–33 (1990). Construing this Act constitutes the subject of the present appeal. The Act

> protects both the reputations of certain visual artists and the works of art they create. It provides these artists with the rights of "attribution" and "integrity." . . .
>
> These rights are analogous to those protected by Article 6bis of the Berne Convention, which are commonly known as "moral rights." The theory of moral rights is that they result in a climate of artistic worth and honor that encourages the author in the arduous act of creation.

H.R. Rep. No. 514 at 5 (internal quote omitted). The Act brings to fruition Emerson's insightful observation.

Its principal provisions afford protection only to authors of works of visual art – a narrow class of art defined to include paintings, drawings, prints, sculptures, or photographs produced for exhibition purposes, existing in a single copy or limited edition of 200 copies or fewer. 17 U.S.C. § 101 (Supp. III 1991). With numerous exceptions, VARA grants three rights: the right of attribution, the right of integrity and, in the case of works of visual art of "recognized stature," the right to prevent destruction. 17 U.S.C. § 106A (Supp. III 1991). For works created on or after June 1, 1991 – the effective date of the Act – the rights provided for endure for the life of the author or, in the case of a joint work, the life of the last surviving author. The rights cannot be transferred, but may be waived by a writing signed by the author. Copyright registration is not required to bring an action for infringement of the rights granted under VARA, or to secure statutory damages and attorney's fees. 17 U.S.C. §§ 411, 412 (1988 & Supp. III 1991). All remedies available under copyright law, other than criminal remedies, are available in an action for infringement of moral rights. 17 U.S.C. § 506

(1988 & Supp. III 1991). With this historical background in hand, we pass to the merits of the present litigation.

II. Work of Visual Art

Because VARA is relatively new, a fuller explication of it is helpful. In analyzing the Act, therefore, we will follow in order the definition set forth in § 101, as did the district court when presiding over this litigation. The district court determined that the work of art installed in the lobby of Associates' building was a work of visual art as defined by VARA; that distortion, mutilation, or modification of the work would prejudice plaintiffs' honor and reputations; that the work was of recognized stature, thus protecting it from destruction (including removal that would result in destruction); and that Associates consented to or ratified the installation of the work in its building. The result was that defendants were enjoined from removing or otherwise altering the work during the lifetimes of the three artists.

A. Singleness of the Work

As a preliminary matter, we must determine whether the trial court correctly found that the work is a single piece of art, to be analyzed under VARA as a whole, rather than separate works to be considered individually. This finding was a factual one reviewed under the clearly erroneous standard. For purposes of framing the issues at trial the parties entered into a joint stipulation relating to numerous facts, including a definition of "the Work." This stipulated definition contained a long, detailed list of all the sculptural elements contained in the building's lobby. The district court found that, with a few precise exceptions determined to be separate works of art, the artwork created by plaintiffs in the lobby was a single work. *See* 861 F. Supp. at 314–15. This finding was based on testimony, credited by the trial judge, of the artists themselves and of their expert witnesses.

The trial court found further support for its conclusion in the method by which the artists created the work – each additional element of the sculpture was based on the element preceding it so that they would mesh together. The result was a thematically consistent, inter-related work whose elements could not be separated without losing continuity and meaning. *See id.* at 315. The record evidence of singleness was confirmed at the request of the parties by the district court's own inspection of the work.

Appellants' primary contention is that the finding of singleness is inconsistent with a finding that certain works of art were separate from the work that is the subject of this appeal. This assertion rests on the mistaken belief that the parties' joint stipulation to a definition of "the Work" precluded an ultimate determination by the factfinder that most but not all of the work installed in the lobby was a single artwork. In other words, according to appellants, either every component in the stipulated definition is part of a single work or every component is an individual work; there is no middle ground. Appellants' goal is to have VARA applied to each element of the sculpture individually, so that components that may not be visual art standing alone cannot be considered visual art when they are combined by the artists to create a whole that has a nature different than the mere sum of its parts.

Appellants' goal is not attainable. The parties stipulated that when they used the term "the Work" it included a list of sculptural components. The result was that during the trial there was no dispute as to the parties' meaning when referring to "the Work." The trial court was free to find that a few items of "the Work" were separate works of art, while the remainder of "the Work" was a single, interrelated, indivisible work of art. The finding of singleness was based on determinations of witness credibility as well as the district court's own inspection of the artwork. We cannot say that such a finding was clearly erroneous.

B. The Statutory Definition

A "work of visual art" is defined by the Act in terms both positive (what it is) and negative (what it is not). In relevant part VARA defines a work of visual art as "a painting, drawing, print, or sculpture, existing in a single copy" or in a limited edition of 200 copies or fewer. 17 U.S.C. § 101. Although defendants aver that elements of the work are not visual art, their contention is foreclosed by the factual finding that the work is a single, indivisible whole. Concededly, considered as a whole, the work is a sculpture and exists only in a single copy. Therefore, the work satisfies the Act's positive definition of a work of visual art. We next turn to the second part of the statutory definition – what is not a work of visual art.

The definition of visual art excludes "any poster, map, globe, chart, technical drawing, diagram, model, applied art, motion picture or other audio-visual work." 17 U.S.C. § 101. Congress meant to distinguish works of visual art from other media, such as audio-visual works and motion pictures, due to the different circumstances surrounding how works of each genre are created and disseminated. *See* H.R. Rep. No. 514 at 9. Although this concern led to a narrow definition of works of visual art,

> [t]he courts should use common sense and generally accepted standards of the artistic community in determining whether a particular work falls within the scope of the definition. Artists may work in a variety of media, and use any number of materials in creating their works. Therefore, whether a particular work falls within the definition should not depend on the medium or materials used.

Id. at 11.

"Applied art" describes "two- and three-dimensional ornamentation or decoration that is affixed to otherwise utilitarian objects." *Carter*, 861 F. Supp. at 315, *citing Kieselstein-Cord v. Accessories By Pearl, Inc.*, 632 F.2d 989, 997 (2d Cir. 1980). Defendants' assertion that at least parts of the work are applied art appears to rest on the fact that some of the sculptural elements are affixed to the lobby's floor, walls, and ceiling – all utilitarian objects. Interpreting applied art to include such works would render meaningless VARA's protection for works of visual art installed in buildings. A court should not read one part of a statute so as to deprive another part of meaning. *See, e.g., United States Nat'l Bank of Or. v. Independent Ins. Agents of America, Inc.*, 508 U.S. 439, ___, 113 S. Ct. 2173, 2182, 124 L. Ed. 2d 402 (1993); *United States v. LaPorta*, 46 F.3d 152, 156 (2d Cir. 1994).

Appellants do not suggest the entire work is applied art. The district court correctly stated that even if components of the work standing alone were applied art, "nothing in VARA proscribes protection of works of visual art that incorporate elements of, rather than constitute, applied art." 861 F. Supp. at 315. VARA's legislative history leaves no doubt that "a new and independent work created from snippets of [excluded] materials, such as a collage, is of course not excluded" from the definition of a work of visual art. H.R. Rep. No. 514 at 14. The trial judge correctly ruled the work is not applied art precluded from protection under the Act.

III. Work Made for Hire

Also excluded from the definition of a work of visual art is any work made for hire. 17 U.S.C. § 1012(B). A "work made for hire" is defined in the Copyright Act, in relevant part, as "a work prepared by an employee within the scope of his or her employment." *Id.* § 101(1). Appellants maintain the work was made for hire and therefore is not a work of visual art under VARA. The district court held otherwise, finding that the plaintiffs were hired as independent contractors.

A. Reid Tests

The Copyright Act does not define the terms "employee" or "scope of employment." In *Community for Creative Non-Violence v. Reid*, 490 U.S. 730, 109 S. Ct. 2166, 104 L. Ed. 2d 811 (1989), the Supreme Court looked to the general common law of agency for guidance. It held that a multi-factor balancing test was required to determine if a work was produced for hire (by an employee) or was produced by an independent contractor. *Reid*, 490 U.S. at 751, 109 S. Ct. at 2178. The Court elaborated 13 specific factors:

> the hiring party's right to control the manner and means by which the product is accomplished[;] . . . the skill required; the source of the instrumentalities and tools; the location of the work; the duration of the relationship between the parties; whether the hiring party has the right to assign additional projects to the hired party; the extent of the hired party's discretion over when and how long to work; the method of payment; the hired party's role in hiring and paying assistants; whether the work is part of the regular business of the hiring party; whether the hiring party is in business; the provision of employee benefits; and the tax treatment of the hired party.

Reid, 490 U.S. at 751–52, 109 S. Ct. at 2178–79. While all of these factors are relevant, no single factor is determinative. *Id.* at 752. *See also Hilton International Company v. NLRB*, 690 F.2d 318, 321 (2d Cir. 1982). Instead, the factors are weighed by referring to the facts of a given case. *See Aymes v. Bonelli*, 980 F.2d 857, 861 (2d Cir. 1992).

The district court determined that the sculpture was not "work for hire" and therefore not excluded from the definition of visual art. The *Reid* test is a list of factors not all of which may come into play in a given case. *See Aymes*, 980 F.2d at 861. The *Reid* test is therefore easily misapplied. We are usually reluctant to reverse a district court's factual findings as to the presence or absence of any of the *Reid* factors and do so only when the district court's findings are clearly erroneous. By contrast, the ultimate legal conclusion as to whether or not the sculpture is "work for hire" is reviewed *de novo*. The district court correctly stated the legal test. But some of its factual findings, we think, were clearly erroneous. . . .

Our review . . . persuades us that the factors that weigh in favor of finding the artists were employees outweigh those factors supporting the artists' claim that they were independent contractors. . . .

. . . [W]hile the existence of payroll formalities alone would not be controlling, *see Reid*, 490 U.S. at 743 n. 8, 109 S. Ct. at 2174 n. 8, in combination with other factors, it may lead to a conclusion that a given work is one made for hire. Such other factors include:

> plaintiffs under their contract could be and were in fact assigned projects in addition to the work in the lobby; they were paid a weekly salary for over two years for a contracted 40 hours of work per week; they were furnished many of the needed supplies necessary to create the work; and plaintiffs could not hire paid assistants without defendants' consent. These factors, properly considered and weighed with the employee benefits granted plaintiffs and the tax treatment accorded them, are more than sufficient to demonstrate that the artists were employees, and the sculpture is therefore a work made for hire as a matter of law.

. . . [S]ince we have determined that the work is one made for hire and therefore outside the scope of VARA's protection, we need not discuss that Act's broad protection of visual art and the protection it affords works of art incorporated into a building. Also, as plaintiffs' sculpture was not protected from removal because the artists were employees and not independent contractors, we need not reach the defendants' Fifth Amendment takings argument.

Moreover, because the sculpture is not protected by VARA from removal resulting in its destruction or alteration, we do not address plaintiffs' contentions that VARA entitles them to complete the "unfinished" portion of the work, that they are entitled to reasonable costs and attorney's fees, and that appellants tortiously interfered with the artists' contract with SIG and the Limited Partnership. Finally, the district court dismissed defendants' counterclaim against the artists for waste, finding, *inter alia*, that such a cause of action under New York law may only be brought by a landlord against a tenant. *See* 861 F. Supp. at 334–36. Appellants have failed to persuade us that it was error to dismiss this counterclaim.

CONCLUSION

Accordingly, the district court's order insofar as it held the work was one not made for hire is reversed and the injunction vacated. In all other respects, the order of the district court is affirmed. Each party to bear its own costs.

NOTES AND QUESTION

1. VARA § 106A(c)(2) provides several exceptions to the ordinary protection, including one as follows:

   > (2) the modification of a work of visual art which is the result of conservation, or of the public presentation, including lighting and placement, or the work is not a destruction, distortion, mutilation, or other modification described in subsection (a)(3) unless the modification is caused by gross negligence.

   Was the removal of the work at issue in *Carter* a "modification" that was "the result of . . . the public presentation of the sculpture"?
2. Under Canadian law, moral rights are separate and independent from copyright. Although often viewed as continental in origin, moral rights have a long, though fragmentary, history in common law. They have been acknowledged in Canada since 1931, in anticipation of Canadian accession to the 1928 revision of the Berne Convention, which is discussed in *Carter.* Generally, the Canadian interpretation of moral rights, tracking the Berne Convention, is similar to VARA in the United States.

   In *Snow v. Eaton Centre Ltd.*, 70 C.P.R. (2d) 105 (Ont. H.J.C., 1982), the sculptor of some forty Canada geese on display at a shopping mall obtained an injunction to stop the mall operators from adding red Christmas ribbons to "decorate" his work. The remedy was granted on the ground that the modification of the work would harm the professional and artistic reputation of the artist by damaging the integrity of his work. O'Brien, J. stated that "[t]he plaintiff is adamant in his belief that his naturalistic composition has been made to look ridiculous by the addition of ribbons and suggests it is not unlike dangling earrings from the Venus de Milo." *Id.* at 106.

   Snow demonstrates what many regard as the most important aspect of moral rights law: the continuing protection it gives to the freedom of creative human expression, particularly by limiting purchasers of artistic works from treating such works in any way they wish. *Snow* is not, however, indicative of unequivocal support for moral rights in Canadian law. Such rights are not alienable (assignable), although they may be waived. This may mean that the inequality of bargaining power between artists, on the one hand, and buyers (galleries, publishers, collectors, and others), on the other hand, will effectively extinguish in practice those moral rights that may have existed.

   The civil law of Quebec emphasizes principles of natural justice. Accordingly, rights in a work arise from an act of personal creation and are part of the personality of the author for life. In addition to the rights of attribution and integrity contained in the Berne Convention, the civil law recognizes the right of publication (*le droit de divulgation*) and the right to withdraw or repent (*droit de retrait ou de repentir*) an artistic expression.

Short Guide to the European Convention on Human Rights 112–13 (Donna Gomien ed., 2005)

[T]he European Court of Human Rights has extended a wide margin of appreciation to States to restrict the freedom of expression of artistic ideas. In a case in which the "protection of morals" clause was at issue, the applicants complained that the Swiss Government's confiscation of several sexually explicit paintings and its fining of the artist for publishing obscene materials constituted a violation of Article 10 (*Müller and Others v. Switzerland* (1988)). In finding the State's actions justified under the second paragraph, the Court accepted that States have a wide margin of appreciation in determining what is "necessary" for the "protection of morals." However, in delivering its judgment, the Court noted that the term "expression" under Article 10 encompasses artistic expression, "which affords the opportunity to take part in the public exchange of cultural, political and social information and ideas of all kinds." The Court has also deferred to the States where the religious feelings of parts of the population might be offended by the exercise of artistic expression. In the cases of *Otto-Preminger-Institut v. Austria* (1994) and *Wingrove v. []United Kingdom* (1996), the Court found no violation of Article 10 where the respective governments prohibited the exhibition of films that presented irreverent images and interpretations of certain Christian figures and practices.

In recent years, the Court has considered a number of cases where authorities have prohibited the publication of literary works on the grounds that the literature in question expressed prohibited political views. As in other cases in which purely public interest or political expression was at issue, the Court has found violations of Article 10 in most of these cases, stressing such factors as the limited impact of literary works on national security, the failure of the State to show that negative views of the majority of the population could be equated with incitement to violence, armed resistance or uprising, and the severity of penalties imposed (see, for example, *Karatas v. Turkey* (1999) and *Arslan v. Turkey* (1999)).

NOTE

The threat to artistic expression is almost inextricably tied to cultural traditions. That is why the regional initiatives within the Council of Europe are so significant. Given the vast historical differences in traditions within Europe, the European

Court of Human Rights' judgments concerning sensitive moral and aesthetic issues of artistic expression testify to the progress in Europe of establishing standards of human rights that transcend otherwise deep-seated cultural differences.

c. Architectural

Architecture, which provides compelling examples of cultural change, is itself constantly threatened by change. The wheels of progress often become the treads of bulldozers. A historic building is razed; another is raised in its place. No other facet of the cultural heritage reflects the expression "here today, gone tomorrow" more clearly than architecture. Not surprisingly, therefore, historic preservation laws primarily address buildings and other architectural structures. The acceptability of replacing historic structures in the course of urban development and the pace of doing so are hotly debated.

A poignant example of the triumph of venture capital over architectural heritage involves the second Imperial Hotel in Tokyo. Completed in 1922 to replace another hotel of that name, it was designed by the preeminent American architect Frank Lloyd Wright. The building itself was perhaps the fullest expression of Wright's genius. It nevertheless was closed in 1967 and torn down shortly thereafter to make way for loftier real estate that would maximize economic efficiency and profits.

Japanese culture fascinated Wright throughout his career. His visit to the replica of a medieval Japanese chapel at the 1893 Columbian Exposition in Chicago strongly influenced his early prairie-style houses and organic architecture as well as his later works. He drew inspiration from Japanese literature and, after a visit to Japan in 1905, began to collect and trade in Japanese woodblock prints. Japanese architectural elements often influenced his designs. For example, the Dana House in Springfield, Illinois, which Wright completed in 1900, has turned-up ends on its roof eaves that were inspired by traditional Japanese construction. Several decades later, the layered roofing and taproot structure of Japanese temples found expression in his famous Research Tower for the Johnson Wax Company in Racine, Wisconsin. The same building features an open courtyard that is reminiscent of Japanese landscaping, and a revolving circular stage in the Dallas (Texas) Theater Center was modeled after Kabuki theaters.

Wright's acceptance of a commission to design the Imperial Hotel in 1916 as a gift to the people of Japan led to his residence of several years in that country. During that period of time, primarily 1919–22, he designed virtually all exterior and interior details of the building, from the woven exterior fabric of brick and volcanic *oya* stone to the carpeting, tableware, beverage mugs, and tea service inside. Traditional Japanese concepts of space and a Zen-like sense of personal exploration were evident throughout the interior partitioning and modular units of the hotel.

Wright took pride in the almost singular ability of the Imperial Hotel to withstand the devastating Kanto Earthquake of September 1, 1923, which obliterated much of Tokyo. Wright had carefully planned for such a disaster by supporting the hotel on thousands of concrete pins to a depth of eight fcct. Ironically, the formal opening of the hotel, which had been completed only the previous year, was scheduled for the very day of the earthquake.

The Japanese, in turn, took pride in Wright's integration of traditional Japanese and Western elements, not only in the Imperial Hotel but also in many other buildings he designed. This mutuality of influence continues even today as Tadao Ando and other contemporary Japanese architects draw on Wright's work. The centerpiece of this cross-cultural relationship was the Imperial Hotel.

NOTES AND QUESTIONS

1. One architectural expert has observed the following concerning the Imperial Hotel's demise: "What was really lost in the demolition of this great work of architecture will never be fully measured – certainly not by the careless instruments of land speculation." ROBERT MCCARTER, FRANK LLOYD WRIGHT 155 (1997).

   In contrast, a small portion of the Imperial Hotel, primarily the entrance lobby, was saved and transported to a theme park, Meiji Village, near Nagoya, Japan. Did this modest reconstruction of Wright's masterpiece strike a satisfactory compromise between the preservation of cultural heritage and the exigencies of real estate development?
2. Was the Imperial Hotel part of the Japanese national heritage alone, thereby justifying the Japanese, in their sovereign capacity, to dispose of the structure as they saw fit? Or was the hotel part of a transnational heritage? If so, what difference would that make? Would the responsible Japanese authorities then have had an obligation to consult with Wright's estate? (Wright himself died in 1959). Consider a description of the hotel as "probably the largest and most complex project of Wright's career." THOMAS HEINZ, THE VISION OF FRANK LLOYD WRIGHT 304 (2001). In view of such an accolade, should the United States, as the national state of Frank Lloyd Wright, have some sort of moral right (*droit moral*) to share in the preservation and disposition of the building?
3. The 1970 UNESCO Convention on illegal trafficking in cultural property defines important cultural material as a common heritage of humankind. Would the inclusion of the Imperial Hotel within this common heritage impose on Japan an obligation of preservation, *erga omnes*, to the world at large? Does such a cosmopolitan view of property raise any ethical, diplomatic, or legal issues?
4. What about the deliberate destruction of important material for cultural rather than commercial reasons? For example, in 2001 the Taliban government in Afghanistan deliberately blew up two colossal monuments, dating from between the second and fifth centuries CE, whose humanization of the Buddhist deities offended the Taliban's Islamic sensibilities. The statues were carved out of limestone at Bamiyan, along one of the branches of the Silk Road that linked medieval Europe and Asia. Would the fact that the statues represented a striking fusion of East Asian (Buddhist) and Western (late classical) cultural characteristics affect your analysis?
5. For further reading, from which the essay above was drawn, see FRANK LLOYD WRIGHT PRESERVATION TRUST, FRANK LLOYD WRIGHT'S FIFTY VIEWS OF JAPAN: THE 1905 PHOTO ALBUM (1996); THOMAS HEINZ, THE VISION OF FRANK LLOYD WRIGHT (2001); ROBERT MCCARTER, FRANK LLOYD WRIGHT (1997); JULIA MEECH, FRANK LLOYD WRIGHT AND THE ART OF JAPAN: THE ARCHITECT'S OTHER PASSION (2001); MERYLE SECREST, FRANK LLOYD WRIGHT (1992).

d. Archival

In December 2007, officials of the Biblioteca Ambrosiana in Milan, Italy, acknowledged that its famous *Codex Atlanticus*, a compilation of works by Leonardo da Vinci and the largest single collection of the Renaissance master's drawings and writings, was damaged, probably by mold, and would require expensive treatment. After a yearlong investigation, scientists concluded that the stains were more likely caused by mercury salt that had been used as a bacterial disinfectant. This development is a particularly poignant reminder of uncertainties about myriad threats to archival material despite the best prevention and precautionary efforts. In this instance, the codex had been kept in a vault in which temperature and humidity were constantly monitored.

Jutta Reed-Scott, Preserving Research Collections 4–6 (1999)

The print resources of the past 150 years constitute a significant portion of the nation's cultural legacy and are crucial to all areas of the humanities especially.... Virtually all post-1850 publications are at risk, because they are printed on paper manufactured from unbleached wood pulp – which is highly acidic – [or] treated with acidic sizing. Unbleached wood pulp paper deteriorates rapidly with the passage of time; the process can be slowed down but not reversed. Unless libraries take action, books printed on acidic paper may become unusable in the twenty-first century....

While the uncertainty of paper-based research collections is a stark reality, the growing reliance on information in electronic form poses the challenge of maintaining access to an even more volatile format. Magnetic media are especially subject to physical deterioration; hardware and software obsolescence presents a different but equally serious problem. Overshadowing these concerns is the complex intellectual question about which electronic information to save. The projected growth in digital information in the twenty-first century threatens to overwhelm libraries' capacity to select, manage, and preserve these new formats.

Preservation in the digital era presents challenges that are not only more complex, but also reach beyond the traditional boundaries of preservation programs. Preserving information in electronic form entails significant technical investments and structural institutional change. Files must be refreshed – that is, copied – and existing applications must be migrated repeatedly to new hardware and software platforms. As scholarship becomes increasingly reliant on digital collections, research libraries face the challenge of maintaining for long-term access resources created with the new technologies....

Virtually every medium used to record information is threatened by the natural forces of deterioration. The magnitude of preservation needs in a library is determined by the interplay of many factors; chief among them are the age, scope, and composition of the collections. Research library collections include a multiplicity of formats (e.g., monographs, journals, newspapers, maps, manuscripts, photographs, digital images) and media (e.g., paper, vellum, photographs, films, magnetic tapes, various types of disks). Among these diverse resources there is tremendous variation in life expectancy. Paper made from cotton fiber has lasted for more than a thousand years, preservation microfilm can have a life expectancy of hundreds of years, wood pulp newspaper pages deteriorate within decades, and some types of computer disks show loss of information after a few years....

One estimate based on a Library of Congress study shows that 77,000 volumes in that library's collection become "brittle" each year.

While the brittle books problem has dominated the preservation discourse, research libraries also hold vast collections of manuscripts, archives, and rare books printed on alkaline paper that require conservation treatments to restore them to usable condition. In addition, there are aging problems with motion picture films, sound recordings, and videotapes, all of which have limited life spans and require substantial preservation investment.

Electronic information and communications technologies are reshaping research libraries. At present, digital resources are a small percentage of total collections, but this situation will change dramatically. The amount of information that is created on computers is increasing exponentially, and the number of electronic collections is already huge. Not only will this upward trend continue, it is certain to accelerate. Information created in electronic form is presenting libraries with yet a new set of preservation challenges. The traditional preservation strategies used in the past to ensure the longevity of intellectual resources are not long appropriate in the digital environment. Not only are digital media short-lived, there are no warning signals when they are becoming unreadable. Long-term retention of digital resources requires systematic maintenance and monitoring of data integrity, with continued upgrading of system components. Migration to newer technologies will eventually occur, and new information technology standards will be implemented as they are developed. Ensuring long-term survival of digital information is a complex technical and economic problem that will consume an increasing portion of preservation investments in the twenty-first century.

NOTES AND QUESTIONS

1. Under the circumstances described in the foregoing, as a matter of fundamental policy in the public interest, should all public libraries be required to devote a percentage of their budgets to preservation and digitalization of their material? For an extensive exposition of the extent of the problem and the author's "desperate bid to save America's past," see Nicholas Baker, *Deadline*, NEW YORKER, July 24, 2000, at 42.
2. Another huge problem is that libraries and other archival deposits must be accessible in the public and scholarly interest. The public must be allowed to handle

and study material. Security measures, therefore, can go only so far. Moreover, surveillance is expensive, if it exists at all. Vulnerability to theft is therefore nearly impossible to overcome. Indeed, vulnerability is the other side of the coin of accessibility. For a detailed study of a well-established map dealer's use of X-Acto knives to excise and steal material from the Beinecke Rare Book and Manuscript Library at Yale University, see William Finnegan, *A Theft in the Library*, New Yorker, Oct. 17, 2005, at 64.

3. The digitalization of archives is a significant response to their deterioration as well as a powerful extension of public and scholarly access to materials. On the huge effort to digitalize archives and related issues of copyright, see Katie Hafner, *History, Digitalized (and Abridged)*, N.Y. Times, Mar. 11, 2007, § 3, at 1.
4. Among the most important cultural treasures in Africa are the severely threatened collections of more than one hundred thousand Islamic manuscripts, some of them a thousand years old, scattered among some twenty private libraries in storied Timbuktu, Mali. Written on paper, tanned gazelle skin, or tree bark, they offer an extraordinary historical record, including some testimony to bygone processes of conflict resolution and commitments to tolerance. The manuscripts have been threatened by the elements, human neglect, and a lack of protective funding. Until recently, the government of Mali had failed to extend its definition of the national patrimony beyond traditional sculpture and works of art so as to protect the manuscripts. Fortunately, after years of benign neglect, the treasures are being rescued by U.S. and South African funding as well as by the first cultural project of the Pan-African New Partnership for African Development. See Alex Ulam, *Elusive Libraries of Timbuktu*, Archaeology, July/August 2004, at 36; Christian Sci. Monitor, Feb. 5, 2008, at 1.

2. General Protections of the Cultural Heritage

a. United States Law

Regulation of the domestic heritage under U.S. law is generally limited to public lands, public projects, and Indian tribal culture. Privately owned, non-Indian heritage lies largely beyond protective regulation. The U.S. regime ranks among the least protective countries of its national heritage. In contrast, the United States cooperates broadly in international efforts to deter and respond to illegal trafficking and other threats to the foreign and global heritage, even where such efforts impinge on private interests. This peculiar imbalance of protection between the domestic and the international heritage sharply contrasts with the practice elsewhere.

A variety of historical, social, and political factors help explain the United States' distinctive regime of protection. Of particular significance is the influence of constitutionalism: a commonly shared set of principles, norms, and expectations concerning the ground rules of political and social organization. The U.S. Constitution barely explains the distinctive regime. Unlike some constitutions, it makes no reference whatsoever to cultural property or heritage. Beneath the surface of the formal document, however, are strata of constitutionalism in which the distinctive regime of cultural heritage law is embedded. It is not the constitutional text but constitutional tradition that makes the difference. Of greatest significance are principles of federalism, libertarianism, judicial review, inherent executive powers over foreign affairs, and collaboration with the Indian tribes.

The principal statutory law of the United States follows.

(i) Federal Law. The Antiquities Act of 1906 made it a crime to "appropriate, excavate, injure, or destroy any historic or prehistoric ruin or monument, or any object of antiquity" found on federal lands, without a permit from the federal government. Penalties are minor, however. Moreover, in *United States v. Diaz*, 499 F.2d 113 (9th Cir. 1974), the Ninth Circuit Court of Appeals, whose jurisdiction encompasses a major part of the indigenous cultural heritage, largely eviscerated the penal provisions of the Act. As a matter of due process, the court declared unconstitutional the vague definition of the terms "ruin," "monument," and "object of antiquity."

Despite the *Diaz* decision, however, the 1906 Act continues to have profound effects in protecting cultural heritage. For example, the Act authorizes the president, without legislative enactment, to establish national monuments to preserve "objects of historic or scientific interest that are situated upon the lands owned or controlled by the Government of the United States." Under this authority, Theodore Roosevelt established the Grand Canyon National Monument in 1908; Franklin D. Roosevelt designated the Jackson Hole National Monument in 1913; Jimmy Carter added fifteen more national monuments in Alaska in 1978; and, in 1996, Bill Clinton created the largest monument outside Alaska, the Grand Staircase-Escalante.

The National Historic Preservation Act of 1966 established the National Register of historically significant buildings, sites, and areas. It provides special tax benefits, such as income tax credits, deductions, and accelerated depreciation of designated property. The Act also provides for federal matching grants to the states to support local survey and preservation efforts. The Act requires all federally directed, funded, or licensed projects, public or private, to consider a project's impact on archaeologically significant resources and to take account of nonbinding comments by the Advisory Council on Historic Preservation.

The Archaeological Resources Protection Act of 1979 (ARPA) refines and largely supersedes the Antiquities Act of 1906. It reasserts federal control over archaeological resources on federal lands and provides stiff penalties for persons who knowingly excavate, sell, purchase, transport, exchange, receive, or remove those resources without a federal permit. The term "archaeological resources" is defined to include "any material remains of past human life or activities which are of archaeological interest" and are at least one hundred years old. A critical issue is whether ARPA applies to private land. The following case addresses this issue.

United States v. Gerber,
999 F.2d 1112 (7th Cir. 1993)

Posner, Circuit Judge.

Arthur Joseph Gerber pleaded guilty to misdemeanor violations of the Archaeological Resources Protection Act of 1979, 16 U.S.C. §§ 470aa *et seq.*, and was sentenced to twelve months in prison, reserving however his right to appeal on the ground that the Act is inapplicable to his offense.

What he had done was to transport in interstate commerce Indian artifacts that he had stolen from a burial mound on privately owned land in violation of Indiana's criminal laws of trespass and conversion. The section of the Archaeological Resources Protection Act under which he was convicted provides that "no person may sell, purchase, exchange, transport, receive, or offer to sell, purchase, or exchange, in interstate or foreign commerce, any archaeological resource excavated, removed, sold, purchased, exchanged, transported, or received in violation of any provision, rule, regulation, ordinance, or permit in effect under State or local law." 16 U.S.C. § 470ee(c). Gerber argues that despite the references in this section to state and local law, the Act is inapplicable to archaeological objects removed from lands not owned either by the federal government or by Indian tribes. His back-up argument is that the provisions, rules, regulations, and so forth of state or local law to which the Act refers are limited to provisions expressly protecting archaeological objects or sites, as distinct from laws of general application such as those forbidding trespass and theft. The issues are novel because this is the first prosecution under the Act of someone who trafficked in archaeological objects removed from lands other than either federal or Indian lands.

More than fifteen hundred years ago in the American [M]idwest[,] Indians built a series of large earthen mounds over prepared mound floors containing human remains plus numerous ceremonial artifacts and grave goods made of silver, copper, wood, cloth, leather, obsidian, flint, mica, quartz, pearl, shells, and drilled, carved, or inlaid human and bear teeth. This mound culture, the product of a civilization that included the beginnings of settled agriculture, an elaborate ceremonialism, and far-flung trading networks, has been dubbed the "Hopewell phenomenon." . . . In 1985 farmers sold General Electric a piece of untillable land in southwestern Indiana adjacent to one of its factories. The land contained a prominent knob on top of a ridge. Unbeknownst to anyone this knob was a Hopewell burial mound some 400 feet long, 175 feet wide, and 20 feet high. The mound and its contents (which included two human skeletons) were intact – even the perishable materials such as wood and leather artifacts were well preserved – and when discovered it would prove to be one of the five largest Hopewell burial mounds known.

A highway was planned to run through the ridge on which the knob was located. In the course of construction, in 1988, earth was removed from the knob to stabilize the roadbed. Workmen engaged in this removal discovered in the knob curious objects – turtleback-shaped rocks – which they showed to a heavy-equipment operator on the project, named Bill Way, who happened to be a collector of Indian artifacts. Recognizing the significance of the find, Way nosed his bulldozer into the knob and quickly discovered hundreds of artifacts, including copper axeheads, inlaid bear canines, and tooled leather. He loaded these items into his pickup truck and covered up the excavation he had made. An acquaintance put him in touch with Arthur Joseph Gerber, a well-known collector of Indian artifacts and promoter of annual Indian "relic shows." Gerber paid Way $6,000 for the artifacts and for revealing to Gerber the location of the mound. Way took Gerber to the site the same night, encountering other people digging for Indian artifacts. Gerber returned to the site several more times, excavating and removing hundreds of additional artifacts, including silver earspools, copper axeheads, pieces of worked leather, and rare silver musical instruments, some with the original reeds preserved. On Gerber's last visit to the site he was detected by a General Electric security guard and ejected. Shortly afterward Gerber sold some of the artifacts at his annual "Indian Relic Show of Shows" in Kentucky. He acknowledges that in entering upon General Electric's land without the company's permission and in removing, again without its permission, Indian artifacts buried there, he committed criminal trespass and conversion in violation of Indiana law. He also acknowledges having transported some of the stolen artifacts in interstate commerce.

The preamble of the Archaeological Resources Protection Act of 1979 states that "archaeological resources on public lands [defined elsewhere in the Act as federal public lands] and Indian lands are an accessible and irreplaceable part of the Nation's heritage" and that the purpose of the Act is "to secure, for the present and future benefit of the American people, the protection of archaeological resources and sites which are on public lands and Indian lands." 16 U.S.C. §§ 470aa(a)(1), (b). Consistent with this preamble, most of the Act is given over to the regulation, in the form of civil and criminal penalties, permit requirements, forfeiture provisions, and other regulatory devices, of archaeological activities *on federal and Indian lands*. The criminal penalties are for archaeological activities conducted on those lands without a permit and for trafficking in archaeological objects that have been removed from them in violation either of the Act's permit requirements or of any other federal law. §§ 470ee(a), (b). Gerber did not remove Indian artifacts from federal or Indian lands, however, and was therefore prosecuted under the third criminal provision (§ 470ee(c), quoted earlier), which is not in terms limited to such lands.

The omission of any reference in subsection (c) to federal and Indian lands was, Gerber argues, inadvertent. Not only the preamble of the Act, but its legislative history, shows that all that Congress was concerned with was protecting archaeological sites and objects on federal and Indian lands. This is indeed all that the preamble mentions; and a principal sponsor of the Act said that "it does not affect any lands other than the public lands of the United States and [Indian] lands." 125 Cong. Rec. 17,394 (1979) (remarks of Congressman Udall). The legislative history contains no reference to archaeological sites or objects on state or private lands. The Act superseded the Antiquities Act of 1906, 16 U.S.C. §§ 431–33, which had been expressly limited to federal lands. And if the Act applies to nonfederal, non-Indian lands, its provisions are at once overinclusive and underinclusive: overinclusive because the Act authorizes the federal court in which a defendant is prosecuted to order, in its discretion, the forfeiture of the archaeological objects involved in the violation *to the United States* (unless they were removed from Indian lands), §§ 470gg(b), (c); underinclusive because the provisions authorizing civil penalties and the payment of rewards to informers out of fines collected in criminal prosecutions under the Act are administered by officials who lack jurisdiction over nonfederal, non-Indian lands. §§ 470bb(2), 470ff, 470gg(a). (The artifacts stolen by Gerber were recovered and are being held by the United States as evidence in this case, but they have not been ordered forfeited.) Most scholarly commentators on the Act assume that it is limited to federal and Indian lands.... Gerber reminds us of the rule of lenity in interpreting criminal statutes and of the implied constitutional prohibition against excessively vague criminal statutes. He adds that subsection (c) of section 470ee would not be a nullity if the Act were held to be limited to sites and objects on federal and Indian lands. A number of state laws prohibit trafficking in stolen Indian artifacts regardless of their origin, and it has not been suggested that these statutes are preempted by the federal Act even with respect to artifacts stolen from federal or Indian lands. A person who trafficked in Indian artifacts in violation of state law would be subject to federal prosecution only under subsection (c) even if the artifacts had been removed from federal or Indian lands, if the removal happened not to violate federal law.

We are not persuaded by these arguments. That the statute, the scholarly commentary, and the legislative history are all focused on federal and Indian lands may simply reflect the fact that the vast majority of Indian sites – and virtually all archaeological sites in the Western Hemisphere are Indian – are located either in Indian reservations or on the vast federal public lands of the West. Subsection (c) appears to be a catch-all provision designed to back up state and local laws protecting archaeological sites and objects wherever located. It resembles the Mann Act, the Lindbergh Law, the Hobbs Act, and a host of other federal statutes that affix federal criminal penalties to state crimes that, when committed in interstate commerce, are difficult for individual states to punish or prevent because coordinating the law enforcement efforts of different states is difficult. The reference to interstate commerce would be superfluous if the subsection were limited to artifacts taken from federal or Indian lands, since either source would establish federal jurisdiction with no need to require proof that the artifacts were transported in interstate commerce. Probably the subsection was added as an afterthought, so one is not surprised that it does not jibe perfectly with the surrounding provisions; but that does not make it invalid, and it certainly is not vague. And we cannot see how the purposes of the Act would be undermined by our giving subsection (c) the interpretation that its words invite.

An amicus brief filed by several associations of amateur archaeologists claims that such an interpretation will infringe their liberty to seek to enlarge archaeological knowledge by excavating private lands. But there is no right to go upon another person's land, without his permission, to look for valuable objects buried in the land and take them if you find them. At common law General Electric would have been the owner of the mound and its contents regardless of the fact that it was unaware of them. . . . Although we have found no Indiana cases, we are given no reason to suppose that the Indiana courts would adopt a different rule. It would make no difference if they would. Whatever the rightful ownership of the mound and its contents under current American law, no one suggests that Way or Gerber obtained any rights to the artifacts in question. No doubt, theft is at the root of many titles; and priceless archaeological artifacts obtained in violation of local law are to be found in reputable museums all over the world. But it is almost inconceivable that Congress would have wanted to encourage amateur archaeologists to violate state laws in order to amass valuable collections of Indian artifacts, especially as many of these amateurs do not appreciate the importance to scholarship of leaving an archaeological site intact and undisturbed until the location of each object in it has been carefully mapped to enable inferences concerning the design, layout, size, and age of the site, and the practices and culture of the inhabitants, to be drawn. It is also unlikely that a Congress sufficiently interested in archaeology to impose substantial criminal penalties for the violation of archaeological regulations (the maximum criminal penalty under the Act is five years in prison plus a $100,000 fine, § 470ee(d)) would be so parochial as to confine its interests to archaeological sites and artifacts on federal and Indian lands merely because that is where most of them are.

We conclude that section 470ee(c) is not limited to objects removed from federal and Indian lands, but we must consider Gerber's alternative argument, that the section is limited to removals in violation of state and local laws explicitly concerned with the protection of *archaeological* sites or objects. Gerber argues that if it is not so limited all sorts of anomalies are created. Suppose he had bought an Indian artifact from its rightful owner but had failed to pay the applicable state sales tax, and had transported the artifact across state lines. Then he would, he tells us, be transporting in interstate commerce an archaeological object purchased in violation of state law. And likewise if he transported such an object in interstate commerce in a vehicle that exceeded the weight limitations imposed by state law.

These are poor examples. It is unlikely in either case that the state would consider the *transportation* of a good to be in violation of state law merely because sales tax had not been paid or an overweight vehicle had been used. But we agree with the general point, that the Act is limited to cases in which the violation of state law is related to the protection of archaeological sites or objects. A broader interpretation would carry the Act far beyond the objectives of its framers and create pitfalls for the unwary. But we do not think that to be deemed related to the protection of archaeological resources a state or local law must be *limited* to that protection. A law that forbade the theft of Indian artifacts "and any other objects having historical or artistic value" could not reasonably be thought a law unrelated to the protection of such artifacts merely because it had broader objectives. That is essentially what Indiana's laws forbidding trespass and conversion have: objectives that include but are not exhausted in the protection of

Indian artifacts and other antiquities. A law that comprehensively protects the owner of land from unauthorized incursions, spoliations, and theft could well be thought to give all the protection to buried antiquities that they need, making the passage of a law specially protecting buried antiquities redundant – and the passage of new laws is never costless and rarely easy. The interpretation urged by Gerber would if accepted compel states desiring federal assistance in protecting Indian artifacts in nonfederal, non-Indian lands within their borders to pass laws that might duplicate protections already adequate conferred on landowners sitting atop undiscovered archaeological sites by existing laws of general applicability. Granted, all fifty states have laws expressly protecting their archaeological sites; and in 1989, too late for this case, Indiana amended its law to forbid – redundantly – what Gerber had done. So the interpretation for which he contends might not actually impose a significant burden on the states. But Indiana may not have amended its law earlier because it thought its general criminal laws of trespass and conversion adequate – for all we know, it amended the law in response to Gerber's contention that the federal Act contains a loophole through which he and others like him might be able to squeeze.

We conclude that Gerber's conduct was forbidden by the Act. . . .

Affirmed.

The Convention on Cultural Property Implementation Act (1983) executes the United States' obligations under the 1970 UNESCO Convention on illicit trafficking of cultural property. The United States entered a reservation to the Convention through which it refused to enforce export controls of foreign countries solely on the basis of illicit trafficking of cultural property. Instead, U.S. cooperation relies heavily on another provision of the Convention, according to which other parties to the Convention can call upon the United States to prohibit import of a specified class or classes of items from their national patrimony if such items are jeopardized by illegal trafficking. The president may then enter into executive agreements with individual nations to restrict the importation from them of archaeological or ethnological materials threatened with "pillage" or to impose import restrictions on such materials in "emergency" situations.

The Abandoned Shipwreck Act of 1987 vests title in the United States to all shipwrecks of historic significance embedded in the submerged lands and coralline formations of a state. The Act simultaneously transfers title to the wrecks to the states in which they are located. State jurisdiction is subject to federal standards and planning requirements. In particular, these include a set of guidelines for managing underwater resources that seek to maximize the enhancement of cultural resources; foster a partnership among sport divers, fishermen, archaeologists, salvors, and other interests to manage shipwreck resources; facilitate access and utilization by recreational interests; and recognize the interests of individuals and groups engaged in shipwreck discovery and salvage. Most important, the Act alters traditional admiralty jurisdiction in the courts. In general, it transfers "management of and litigation over embedded shipwreck sites from the federal courts to the states," and to that extent, it displaces traditional admiralty jurisdiction and rules, such as those governing finders and salvors.

Until the Abandoned Shipwreck Act, legal protection of the underwater heritage consisted of limited state jurisdiction and admiralty decisions of federal courts. These decisions characteristically applied laissez-faire rules favorable to finders and salvors. They left largely unresolved such fundamental issues as the respective powers of state and federal authority, constructive possession of shipwrecks by state or federal governments, and federal preemption of state ownership rights.

A majority of federal courts have concluded that the Submerged Lands Act of 1953, which granted coastal states general jurisdiction over their offshore shelves, did not specifically assert U.S. title to shipwrecks or transfer that title to the states. Thus, under the supremacy clause of the Constitution, federal admiralty rules protecting finders and salvors of underwater heritage have generally preempted state laws of historic preservation. Only recently, however, has federal admiralty law begun to require a consideration of factors such as archaeological or historical value of shipwrecks.

The Native American Graves Protection and Repatriation Act of 1990 (NAGPRA) vests ownership and control of American Indian and native Hawaiian human remains and cultural objects from federal or tribal lands in the tribes and native Hawaiian groups, respectively. It also regulates excavation and removal of human remains and objects from federal or tribal lands and establishes criminal sanctions for certain unauthorized activities. The Act requires federal agencies and federally funded museums to furnish an inventory or summary of American Indian human remains and associated funerary objects, as well as a summary of unassociated cultural objects. The law provides for the repatriation to the tribes of such objects according to prescribed procedures and establishes a review committee to supervise its implementation. Alternatively, claims under NAGPRA may be brought in federal district court.

Other federal laws seek to protect archaeological resources only secondarily. For example, the National Environmental Policy Act of 1969 (NEPA) requires federal agencies to prepare an environmental impact statement whenever a proposed project might affect the quality of the environment. The NEPA specifically includes the historical and cultural heritage within the federal government's scope of responsibility under the Act.

The Department of Transportation Act and related regulations seek to avoid harm to historical sites threatened by federal highway and related projects. They also provide a means for recovery of archaeological material at impacted sites. The *Preservation of Historic and Archeological Data Act of 1974* seeks to ensure the preservation of archaeological material threatened by federal and federally assisted construction projects. *The American Indian Religious Freedom Act of 1978* protects access to sites, use and possession of sacred objects, and the practice of sacred ceremonies and rites by indigenous people. This Act has not had much effect because it is largely precatory and applies only to federal agencies, and courts have not interpreted it as establishing new rights. This legislation does remind government agencies, however, that they must consider the impact of proposed projects on indigenous religious sites and practices.

The Indian Arts and Crafts Act was initially enacted in 1935 during the Great Depression to encourage a legitimate market for Native American arts and crafts. Amendments in 1990 updated the purpose and scope of the Act to establish a procedure for certification of authentic work created by an enrolled member of a recognized tribe. The main purpose was to discourage if not foil counterfeit or bogus Native American art. The authenticity of a work refers not to its cultural representation but to the tribal status of its creator.

In other words, certified works eligible for protection under the Act need not bear any particular association with a particular tribe or its tradition.

(ii) State Law. State statutes within the United States generally protect cemeteries, human remains, American Indian religious and cultural objects, and archaeological resources on state lands. Some states require the reinterment of all Indian remains from private as well as public lands. Several states require permits for archaeological controls, prohibit burial desecration, or impose land-use and surveying controls over private land containing cultural relics. Other than those controls, private owners are generally entitled to free use and enjoyment of their archaeological and other cultural property.

Whitacre v. Indiana
619 N.E. 2d 605 (Ind. 1993)

Barteau, Judge.

Robert W. Whitacre appeals the trial court's judgment in favor of the Indiana Department of Natural Resources (IDNR) on Whitacre's petition for declaratory judgment. The sole issue on appeal is whether Indiana Code 14-3-3.4, the Indiana Historic Preservation and Archeology Act (the "Act"), is applicable to privately owned property. We conclude that it is and affirm the trial court.

FACTS

The facts are straightforward. Whitacre and his wife are amateur archeologists. In 1982, they discovered a Hopewell Indian site with artifacts dating to *circa* 150 A.D. on a 40-acre farm in Dearborn County, Indiana. With permission from the property owner, they began excavating areas of the site and removing artifacts. In 1987, the Whitacres purchased the farm and continued excavating and conducting investigations. In July 1989, after hearing that a new law had been passed, Whitacre inquired of an archeologist at IDNR about the necessity of a permit for conducting investigations on his own property. Whitacre was informed that he would need a permit. After investigating the law on his own, Whitacre determined that he did not need a permit and filed this declaratory judgment action.

The trial court concluded that Ind. Code 14-3-3.4 was applicable to private property and not just property owned or leased by the State of Indiana.

DISCUSSION

The thrust of this appeal is whether a person needs to have an archeological plan approved by the Indiana Department of Natural Resources before that person may disturb *private* property for the purpose of discovering artifacts or burial objects.

The Historic Preservation and Archeology Act, I.C. 14-3-3.4, established the division of historic preservation and archeology within the IDNR to administer and develop the programs and policies of the Act. I.C. 14-3-3.4-2. As gleaned from the Act, the policies to be furthered by the Division include encouraging the continuous maintenance and integrity of historic sites and structures and coordinating the activities of local historical associations, commissions and private individuals and organizations interested in the historic culture of Indiana. It has been stated that protecting our national and state heritage through the preservation of archeological sites is included in the broad spectrum of legitimate interests of government. *Indiana Dept. of Natural Resources v. Indiana Coal Council, Inc.* (1989), Ind., 542 N.E.2d 1000, 1005. "The information in these sites expands our knowledge of human history and prehistory and thus enriches us as a state, nation and as human beings." *Id.*

When construing a statute, this court is guided by several rules of statutory construction. First, it must be noted that when a statute is clear and unambiguous on its face, the court need not, and indeed may not, interpret the statute. *Economy Oil Corp. v. Indiana Dept. of State Revenue* (1974), 162 Ind. App. 658, 321 N.E.2d 215, 218. When a statute is ambiguous, the court must ascertain the intent of the legislature and interpret the statute to effectuate that intent. *Id.* When so doing, we read the statutes of an act as a whole and attempt to give effect to all provisions. *Id.* A statutory amendment changing a prior statute indicates a legislative intention that the meaning of the prior statute has been changed. *Wright v. Fowler* (1984), Ind. App., 459 N.E.2d 386. Another consideration in construing a statute is to give effect to the purpose of the statute. *State v. Adams* (1992), Ind. App., 583 N.E.2d 799, *trans. denied.*

With these guidelines in mind, we conclude that private property is included within the scope of I.C. 14-3-3.4 as amended. Unless the legislature intended to give the state the power to oversee and regulate the treatment of historical and archeological findings on private property, section 15 of the amended act is virtually meaningless, as a review of the old and new statutes shows. Prior to 1989, I.C. 14-3-3.4 restricted activities that affected historic sites or structures only within the boundaries of property owned or leased by the state. Indiana Code 14-3-3.4-7 provided:

> A person who knowingly, without a permit, conducts a field investigation or alters historic property within the boundaries of property owned or leased by the state commits a Class B misdemeanor.

Thus, prior to 1989, Whitacre was not required to have an archeological plan approved by the state in order to conduct archeological investigations and excavations on his own property.

In 1989, the legislature amended I.C. 14-3-3.4. Specifically, I.C. 14-3-3.4-7 was amended to provide:

> Except as provided in sections 14 through 16 [I.C. 14-3-3.4-14-14-3-3.4-16] of this chapter, a person who knowingly, without a permit, conducts a field investigation or alters historic property within the boundaries of property owned or leased by the state commits a Class A misdemeanor.

Sections 14 through 16 are new sections that provide for (1) the adoption of rules establishing standards for plans, I.C. 14-3-3.4-14, (2) the necessity of a plan, I.C. 14-3-3.4-15, and (3) steps to take when buried human remains are disturbed, I.C. 14-3-3.4-16. Of particular relevance to this appeal is section 15, which provides:

> (a) A person who disturbs the ground for the purpose of discovering artifacts or burial objects must do so in accordance with a plan approved by the department under section 14 [I.C. 14-3-3.4-14] of this chapter.
> (b) A person who recklessly, knowingly, or intentionally violates this section commits a Class A misdemeanor.

I.C. 14-3-3.4-15. "Plan" is defined as "an archeological plan for the systematic recovery, analysis, and disposition by scientific methods of material evidence and information about the life and culture in past ages." I.C. 14-3-3.4-1.

Nothing in chapter 3.4 explicitly states that the chapter applies only to property owned or leased by the state or that it applies to private property. However, section 13 does provide that the requirement of a plan when disturbing ground does not apply to (1) surface coal mining regulated under I.C. 13-4.1, (2) cemeteries and human remains subject to I.C. 23-14, (3) disturbing the earth for an agricultural purpose, and (4) collecting any object (other than human remains) that is visible on the surface of the ground. These activities are typically conducted on private property, not state owned or leased property; thus, section 13 is superfluous if the chapter applies only to state owned or leased property.

Further, prior to the amendments, I.C. 14-3-3.4-7 prohibited conducting field investigations or *altering historic property* within the bounds of property owned or leased by the state without a permit. "Historic property" is defined as "any historic site or structure," I.C. 14-3-3.4-1, and "historic site" or "historic structure" is any site or structure important to the "general, archeological, agricultural, economic, social, political, architectural, industrial, or cultural history of Indiana." *Id.* Thus, in effect, I.C. 14-3-3.4-7 already prohibited disturbing the ground of state owned or leased property without a permit if anything of historic significance was on the property. The new section 15 adds nothing to the chapter unless it is interpreted as expanding the scope of coverage by prohibiting the disturbance of *any* "ground" for purposes of discovering artifacts or burial objects without an approved plan. I.C. 14-3-3.4-15. The legislature specifically did not restrict this section to only "the ground" of state owned or leased property as it did in section 7. Thus, we conclude that the legislature intended to mean any ground within the State of Indiana, whether owned by the state or privately owned.

This construction of the statute effectuates the policies of the Act. The purpose of the Historical Preservation and Archeology Act is to further our understanding of the state's heritage and historical culture by preserving and studying what has been left behind. Obviously, not all sites of historical or archeological significance are located on property owned or leased by the state. Consequently, prior to the 1989 amendments, the state did not have the means to prevent the destruction, inadvertent or intentional, or share in the knowledge of possibly significant sites located on private property. The legislature, through the 1989 amendments, expanded the scope of the Act to include not only "historic sites" and "historic structures," as defined in I.C. 14-3-3.4-1, and located on state owned or leased property, but also to include any property where a person discovers or tries to discover "artifacts" or "burial objects," as defined in I.C. 14-3-3.4-1. Through the amendments, the state may regulate activities on private property that affect our historical and archeological culture; thus, the state is better able to discover and preserve more of our heritage. This is the purpose of the Act and is best effectuated by construing the Act to include private, as well as state owned, property.

We also find support for interpreting the statute to protect private as well as state owned property in a recent opinion from the Seventh Circuit Court of Appeals. In *United States of America v. Gerber* (7th Cir. 1993), 999 F.2d 1112, the Seventh Circuit had to decide if a conviction pursuant to the federal Archaeological Resources Protection Act of 1979 was valid where the Indian artifacts had come from privately owned land in Indiana. The Court interpreted the Act as applying to artifacts found on privately owned property as well as property owned by the federal government or by Indian tribes, even though the Act explicitly refers only to property owned by the federal government or by Indian tribes. The Court concluded that such an interpretation best furthered the purposes of the Act "to secure, for the present and future benefit of the American people, the protection of archaeological resources and sites. . . . " *Gerber*, 999 F.2d at 1114. It is also interesting to note that the Court assumed the amended Indiana statute at issue in our case applied to privately owned land. 999 F.2d at 1116 ("Granted, all fifty states have laws expressly protecting their archaeological sites; and in 1989, too late for this case, Indiana amended its law to forbid – redundantly – what Gerber had done [which was to disturb artifacts on private property]."). Consistent with the interpretation of the federal Act, we interpret the Indiana Act as applying to privately owned property.

The trial court's judgment is affirmed.

---

b. Canadian Law

Under the Canadian constitution, legislative jurisdiction over all types of property is divided between the federal and provincial levels of government. Provincial legislatures can enact laws concerning provincial government (Crown) land and in respect of property situated within their respective provinces. The federal Parliament can pass legislation respecting federal Crown land, Aboriginals (termed "Indians" in the Constitution), and the regulation of trade and commerce.

Most Canadian provinces have enacted heritage resource legislation. These laws usually establish heritage protection for various buildings and sites on a selective basis. For example, the British Columbia Heritage Conservation Act, R.S.B.C. 1996, c. 187, allows the province's government to register sites and objects as possessing heritage status. This is accomplished through a designation process that protects such designated heritage property from being destroyed, altered, or removed unless a permit is first obtained. Provincial heritage laws also protect archaeological resources through permit requirements for excavations.

Provincial parks are also established by provincial legislation in Canada (*see, e.g.*, Park Act, R.S.B.C. 1996, c. 344). Such laws allow for the establishment of parks and historic sites. Once established, ownership of such parklands is vested in the province concerned.

Alberta is the only Canadian province to have enacted legislation in respect of Aboriginal cultural property in the form of personalty. The First Nations Sacred Ceremonial Objects Repatriation Act, R.S.A. 2000, c. F-14, provides a mechanism for the return of "sacred ceremonial objects" whose return is requested by an Alberta First Nation from the Alberta government (including the two major provincial museum collections). Under this law a repatriation request can be refused on the basis that it is considered "inappropriate" (section 2(2)). Although it is of limited scope, the new Alberta repatriation law is the only one of its kind in Canada and the only Canadian law resembling the U.S. Native American Graves Protection and Repatriation Act.

Unlike the provinces, the Canadian Parliament has not enacted any comprehensive legislation concerning the protection of archaeological heritage on federal Crown lands. A draft federal law was tabled in 1991 (the Archaeological Heritage Protection Act) that would have established such a system, but it was not pursued. The draft law would have applied to wrecks, burial sites, and the export of archaeological objects.

The Canadian Parliament has, however, passed laws concerning the establishment and protection of parks and heritage sites on federal Crown land. Thus, the Canada National Parks Act, S.C. 2000, c. 32, largely mirrors the provincial legislation mentioned. The Historic Sites and Monuments Act, R.S.C. 1985, c. H-4, facilitates the designation and protection of nationally significant historic sites. In 2006 a federal program led to a Historic Places Initiative, which is the most important federal heritage conservation strategy in Canadian history. Other federal legislation relating to heritage conservation includes the Territorial Lands Act, R.S.C. 1985, c. T-7 (Crown land in the Northwest Territories, the Yukon, and Nunavut); the Canada Shipping Act, S.C. 2001, c. 26 (archaeological wrecks); and the Department of the Environment Act, R.S.C. 1985, c. E-10.

A discussion paper prepared by the Canadian Department of Communications by way of background to the proposed 1991 Archaeological Heritage Protection Act cited the following as perceived weaknesses in relation to Canada's archaeological heritage under federal jurisdiction (at 66):

- The full extent and nature of archaeological resources under federal jurisdiction [are] unknown. This is true of archaeological resources in the territories as well as of federal lands within the provinces.
- There is inconsistent implementation of impact assessments among government entities. Assessment criteria are not prescribed and the processes are not perceived to be effective.
- Some resources are more threatened than others. The most endangered resources are historic wrecks and surface artifacts on Crown land, particularly in some Arctic regions.

- There are inconsistencies with respect to when archaeologists have to apply for permits. They are only required for work on some federal Crown lands.
- Provincial measures to protect archaeological heritage are frustrated by lack of a remedy when an artifact has crossed the provincial boundaries.

The main reason the law, which was considered a remedy for these concerns, was not proceeded with appears to have been opposition to it from Aboriginal peoples. This opposition reflects the increasingly central role that indigenous concerns play in relation to the development of cultural heritage law in Canada. A major concern of Aboriginals in connection to the 1991 proposal was the issue of ownership and jurisdiction over Aboriginal archaeological resources.

The only federal law specifically addressing Aboriginal cultural property is section 91 of the Indian Act, R.S.C. 1985, c. 1–5, which is as follows:

> (1) "*Certain property on reserve may not be acquired* – No person may, without the written consent of the Minister, acquire title to any of the following property situated on a reserve, namely,
> (a) an Indian grave house;
> (b) a carved grave pole;
> (c) a totem pole;
> (d) a carved house post; or
> (e) a rock embellished with paintings or carvings.
>
> (2) *Saving* – Subsection (1) does not apply to chattels referred to therein that are manufactured for sale by Indians.
>
> (3) *Removal, destruction, etc.* – No person shall remove, take away, mutilate, disfigure, deface or destroy any chattel referred to in subsection (1) without the written consent of the Minister."

This provision is based on Parliament's jurisdiction over Indians. The removal of Aboriginal heritage objects from Canada is also controlled under the provisions of the Cultural Property Export and Import Act, R.S.C. 1985, c. c-51, which governs the export of cultural objects from Canada in general.

The Canadian constitution was amended in 1982 to entrench the recognition and affirmation of the "existing aboriginal and treaty rights" of the Aboriginal peoples of Canada. The effect of this provision (schedule B of the Constitution Act, 1982 (U.K.) 1982, c. 11) is that the provinces can no longer pass laws that have the effect of extinguishing the rights of Aboriginals protected under the section.

In a 2002 decision (*Kitkatla Band v. British Columbia (Minister of Small Business, Tourism and Culture)*, [2002] 2 S.C.R. 146, 2002 SCC 31), the Supreme Court of Canada dealt with an argument that the British Columbia Heritage Conservation Act (discussed earlier) was unconstitutional insofar as it applied to trees culturally modified by Aboriginals. The Court commented on the cultural heritage of British Columbia as follows:

> The history of the province means that its cultural heritage is in the vast majority of cases an aboriginal one, often going back to pre-contract times and prior to the establishment of the first non-native settlements and the creation of the British

> colonies on Vancouver Island and on the mainland. The [Heritage Conservation] Act was adopted to conserve and protect all forms of cultural property, objects and artifacts as well as sites in British Columbia which have heritage value to the province as a whole, to a community or to an aboriginal people. (Para. 42)

The Supreme Court went on to uphold the constitutionality of the provincial law on the ground that it struck an appropriate balance between the preservation of aboriginal heritage and the justifiable need to exploit provincial natural resources for economic reasons.

Other recent Supreme Court of Canada decisions have upheld the constitutional duty of Canadian governments, in making decisions that might adversely affect as-yet-unproven Aboriginal rights and title claims, to consult with and accommodate native peoples. Whether such a duty has been adequately fulfilled will be decided on a case-by-case basis (see *Taku River Tlingit First Nation v. British Columbia (Project Assessment Director)*, [2004] S.C.J. No. 69, 2004 SCC 74, and *Haida Nation v. British Columbia (Minister of Forests)*, [2004] S.C.J. No. 70, 2004 SCC 73).

In the absence of modern comprehensive federal legislation relating to the cultural heritage of the Aboriginal peoples of Canada, provincial laws play a somewhat-exaggerated role in relation to contemporary indigenous cultural heritage concerns in Canadian society. Once the Canadian Parliament enacts comprehensive laws dealing with Aboriginal cultural heritage issues, any inconsistent provincial laws will be overridden.

NOTES AND QUESTIONS

1. On the subject of Canadian cultural heritage law, especially in relation to Aboriginal peoples, see Catherine Bell, *Aboriginal Claims to Cultural Property in Canada: A Comparative Legal Analysis of the Repatriation Debate*, 17 AM. INDIAN L. REV. 457 (1992); CANADIAN DEPT. COMMC'NS, FEDERAL ARCHAEOLOGICAL HERITAGE PROTECTION AND MANAGEMENT: A DISCUSSION PAPER (April 1988); and Catherine Bell & Robert Paterson, *Aboriginal Rights to Cultural Property in Canada*, 8 INT. J. CULTURAL PROP. 167 (1999).
2. How would you compare Canadian with U.S. law to protect the cultural heritage? Do the states and provinces play the same or different roles within their respective national systems?
3. As we have seen, federal and state authority in the United States to regulate privately owned cultural heritage, though increasing, is still very limited. Moreover, this authority is fragmented among federal, state, and native tribal governments, and it is further divided among multiple agencies of the federal government. Do you favor further regulation? Less regulation? More systematic regulation that would avoid the jurisdictional fragmentation?

c. Swiss Law

An excellent example of a comprehensive European law is the Swiss Federal Act on the International Transfer of Cultural Property (CPTA). The following summary itemizes the CTPA's principal features in implementing the 1970 UNESCO Convention and amending the Swiss Civil Code.

- The CPTA enforces foreign export bans in Switzerland. It does not matter whether the illegal exported object is stolen. Objects that are *only* stolen abroad but not smuggled are not affected by the bilateral agreement that will be concluded between Switzerland and other signatories of the UNESCO convention.
- Claims in Switzerland for return of foreign illegally exported cultural property or claims before foreign courts for the return of illegally removed cultural property to Switzerland are only successful when there is an agreement (on the import and return of cultural property) between the forum state and the claiming foreign state. The agreement must be performed before the illegal export and illegal import occurred. Like Switzerland, the claiming state must be a member state of the UNESCO Convention of 1970.
- The CPTA does not change the duty of diligence for the art trade. It only codifies the preexisting rules that were created by case law and also stated in not binding self-regulations of public museums and private institutions such as art dealer associations. The demand on good faith is substantially high when it comes to the purchase of cultural property. The duties stipulated by the CPTA and CPTR only apply to certain categories of persons and, furthermore, only when the traded piece of art has a value of at least CHF 5,000.
- Derelict objects or antiquities of scientific value are the property of the canton where the items are found. Under current law it is undoubtful that the cantons [states] become the owner of archaeological objects in the moment of the discovery of the items.
- Registered cultural property that belongs to the Federal State and archaeological objects, which belong to the canton by law, can neither be acquired by prescription nor acquired in good faith. The claim for return is not subject to a statute of limitations. They are so-called *res extra commercium.*
- The claim for return of stolen cultural property is subject to a statute of limitations of 30 years after the property is lost.
- The return guarantee for foreign art loans may be issued if the object comes from both public and private institutions. The same is considered for artworks borrowed from private collections. As long as the art loan is located in Switzerland, no private party or authority may make legal claims to the cultural property.

Marc Weber, *New Swiss Law on Cultural Property,* 13 INT'L J. CULTURAL PROP. 99, 108 (2006) (reprinted with the permission of the Cambridge University Press).

d. International Law

The last section of Chapter 3 identified the international legal framework that expresses cultural heritage values and within which cultural heritage issues are addressed. The following section summarizes six of the principal legal instruments, each of which is further examined elsewhere in this chapter and in Chapter 5.

(i) The Hague Convention for the Protection of Cultural Property in the Event of Armed Conflict (1954). The 1954 Hague Convention arose out of the ashes of Dresden, the Nazi confiscation of art treasures, and massive looting on both sides of the Second World War. The agreement built on a foundation of international law, particularly the 1899 and 1907 Hague Conventions on the Laws of War and their annexed regulations, the Nuremberg and Tokyo prosecutions of war criminals, and the 1949 Geneva Convention Relative to the Protection of Civilian Persons in Time of War. Together, they forbid pillage; prohibit seizure or damage to monuments and works of art – subject to the customary rule of military necessity; and extend protective obligations to occupying powers.

The 1954 Hague Convention consolidated these and other rules; added substantial details such as to prohibit looting and any use of cultural property that would likely expose it to destruction or damage; required parties to prepare in time of peace against foreseeable effects of armed conflict; and established designated zones of protection for sites and material of very great importance to humanity. A distinctive emblem was devised for specially protected heritage. A 1977 Protocol to the 1949 Geneva Convention confirms what was already a rule of custom: that it is a war crime to destroy such sites and material. Although the 1954 Hague Convention did not originate in UNESCO, it has depended on the organization from the start. A 1954 Protocol to the agreement requires occupying powers to prevent the illegal export of cultural material and to seize and return illegal imports. A 1999 Protocol reinforces existing rules, mandates prosecution or extradition of violators, sets forth procedures to designate enhanced zones of protection, and establishes an implementing committee.

States have varying commitments to the 1954 Convention. The United States ratified the 1954 Convention in 2008.[1] Under international law, the Convention's specific rules therefore were not fully binding on the United States until then, but, as a signatory, it had to refrain from doing anything that would defeat the objects and purposes of the treaty. Thus, any substantial diversion of resources away from minimal protection of monuments and sites in occupied Iraq would run afoul of the country's obligations, even in the midst of chaos arguably brought on by others.

(ii) The Convention on the Means of Prohibiting and Preventing the Illicit Import, Export, and Transfer of Ownership of Cultural Property (1970). The 1970 Convention has well more than one hundred parties, of which the first major art-market party was the United States. It is a cornerstone of cultural heritage law, creating multilateral control over the movement of cultural property while seeking to promote its legitimate exchange and international cooperation in preparing national inventories of it. The UNESCO Convention defines cultural property as "property which on religious or secular grounds is specifically designated by each State as being of importance for archaeology, prehistory, history, literature or science." The Convention then lists rare collections and specimens

[1] Under the U.S. Constitution, the Senate must give its advice and consent to treaties by a two-thirds vote before the president may give notice of ratification on behalf of the United States. U.S. CONST. art II, § 2. *See generally* James A.R. Nafziger, *Treaties, in* THE OXFORD COMPANION TO AMERICAN LAW 809–11 (Kermit L. Hall ed., 2002). Most agreements binding on the United States, however, are executive agreements, which by constitutional practice do not require the Senate's advice and consent. *See* James A.R. Nafziger, *Executive Agreements, id.* at 282–83.

of fauna, flora, minerals, and anatomy, and objects of paleontological interest; property relating to history; products of archaeological discoveries; elements of artistic or historical monuments; antiquities such as coins that are more than one hundred years old; objects of ethnological interest; works of art such as paintings and sculpture; rare manuscripts and documents; postage stamps; archives; and articles of furniture and musical instruments that are more than one hundred years old.

The 1970 Convention's most important features are a system of export certification; an emergency measure permitting signatories to call on one another to help control the flow of jeopardized property of special significance; a requirement that parties return property within their jurisdiction stolen from museums, monuments, and other institutions; a requirement that, "consistent with national legislation," parties prevent museums and similar institutions from acquiring property illegally exported from other states; a commitment that parties impose penalties or other administrative sanctions for stipulated infringements; and a provision for international cooperation in identifying cultural property and developing national inventories. Contraband items are recoverable on demand by the state of origin, so long as just compensation is paid to innocent purchasers. This document strikes a compromise between the interests of art-importing and art-exporting states while requiring the importing state's cooperation in the recovery and retrieval of illicitly exported property.

(iii) The Convention for the Protection of the World Cultural and Natural Heritage (1972). The 1972 Convention established the evolving World Heritage List, whereby governments nominate natural and cultural properties – now numbering more than 800 – for designation as properties of "outstanding universal value." Parties to the Convention agree to undertake effective site management, the submission of periodic reports, and preparation of management plans for sustainable tourism. Fundamentally, they undertake to transmit World Heritage sites in good condition to future generations. The advantages to parties include international prestige, tourist income, and access to emergency assistance for World Heritage sites in danger.

A short list of World Heritage sites in danger identifies sites threatened by a natural disaster, war, pollution, or inadequate funding. These sites are entitled to emergency safeguarding that may entail international funding. Yellowstone National Park in the United States, for example, was on the danger list for eight years until nearby mining operations ceased, local building and road construction were modified, the full-facility tourist season was reduced, and the United States reported on plans to phase out snowmobile riding.

NOTES AND QUESTIONS

1. The UNESCO Conventions rely heavily on implementation by states as well as by the UNESCO and other designated bodies. The following commentary discusses additional implementation of the World Heritage Convention by private entities:

> The World Heritage Convention has become a focal point of a growing range of interactions that do not fit the standard interstate model of treaty engagement. Oil and gas and mining companies claim they are performing aspects

> of this treaty. Banks and insurance companies are imposing requirements of treaty performance on other corporations. The key treaty body, the World Heritage Committee, has also developed ways to interact directly with corporations, including in situations where state actors have been unwilling or unable to regulate behavior within the state's borders. Together, these direct interactions between companies and the World Heritage Convention highlight the need to extend our analysis of environmental treaties in new ways.
>
> . . .
>
> Extractive activity in and around World Heritage sites undermines the goals of the treaty. The World Heritage Committee each year, through its decision reports, criticizes those states that allow extractive activity to threaten the heritage values of listed sites. In cases where states have not acted to prevent extractive activity in or near a site, the committee has added the site to the List of World Heritage in Danger, or has threatened to do so. For the first time, the committee in 2007 entirely removed a site from the World Heritage List [the Arabian Oryx Sanctuary in Oman] because the state had failed to protect it from threats, including those posed by oil exploration and extraction.
>
> These threats to listed World Heritage sites reveal the limits of relying purely on states to give effect to the Convention. Some states are unwilling to treat World Heritage sites as no-go areas and allow extractive activity to affect such sites. Other states are unable to stop illegal mining from taking place in World Heritage sites within their territory. Recognizing that states may be unwilling or unable to protect such sites in this regard, environmental NGOs and the World Heritage Committee have each directly targeted corporate behavior. Against this backdrop of states' failure to prevent mining and oil and gas activity from undermining the integrity of World Heritage sites, and mining and oil and gas companies' efforts to evidence compliance with relevant international standards of environmental behavior, corporate claims of compliance with the Convention have emerged.

Natasha A. Affolder, *The Private Life of Environmental Treaties*, 103 Am. J. Int'l L. 510, 513–14 (2009).

2. For an excellent case study of the dynamics of compliance and noncompliance with the World Heritage Convention, within a complex structure of local, regional, national, and international governance, see Sabine von Schorlemer, *Compliance with the UNESCO World Heritage Convention: Reflections on the Elbe Valley and the Dresden Waldschlösschen Bridge*, 51 Ger. Y.B. Int'l L. 321 (2008).

(iv) The Convention on the Protection of the Underwater Cultural Heritage (2001). The 2001 Convention seeks to protect shipwrecks and related material and to regulate historic salvage beyond territorial waters. The agreement delineates jurisdiction and requires collaboration in protecting the heritage among flag states of sunken vessels, coastal states on whose continental shelves vessels may repose, and other interested states. Parties must also enforce a set of standards and requirements against salvors of wreck and others within their jurisdiction, engage in international information sharing and decision making concerning discoveries and protective measures, and respond to excavation and importation of underwater heritage that violate prescribed standards and requirements that form an annex to the treaty. These standards and requirements are modifications of provisions that had been adopted by the International Council on Monuments and Sites. A more detailed description and analysis of the Convention appears later in this chapter.

(v) The Convention for the Safeguarding of the Intangible Cultural Heritage (2003). The 2003 Convention embraces oral traditions, languages, social practices, rituals, festive events, folklore, craft skills, and traditional knowledge. The agreement, which entered into force in 2006, complements but does not fully square with the 1972 Convention for the Protection of the World Cultural and Natural Heritage. It calls on parties to prepare inventories of their intangible heritage as a basis for drawing up two lists, one of representative material and the other of material in urgent need of safeguarding. A list of "masterpieces" of intangible practice includes, for example, the Duduk music of Armenia, processional giants and dragons of Belgium, mask dances of Bhutan, shadow theater of Cambodia, and the ox-herding tradition of Costa Rica.[2]

(vi) The Convention on the Protection and Promotion of the Diversity of Cultural Expression (2005). The 2005 Convention recognizes that everyone profits from the free flow of diverse ideas, words, and images; encourages preservation of indigenous traditions and minority languages; and protects the cultures of rich and poor countries alike in an era of cultural homogeneity. Although the 2005 Convention's basic idea of promoting cultural diversity is admirable, it turned out to be quite controversial. The diplomatic debate centered on the extent to which the treaty was anything more than an elaborate means to protect national cultural industries, especially the media, from the foreign influences of Hollywood movies and television programs. The general economic stakes are obvious – American movies alone garner $16 billion at foreign box offices – but the specific implications of the Convention and its validity in international trade law are unclear.

The Convention's proponents, led by Canada and France, hailed it as an important means for protecting threatened cultures, particularly in developing countries, from the homogenizing effect of cultural globalization. Opponents, led by the United States, argued that the Convention simply promoted unwarranted restrictions of freedom of expression and free trade. The debate centered on conflicting interpretations of the phrase "protection and promotion of the diversity of cultural expression." To the French and Canadian governments, the phrase entails efforts to protect local culture from contamination and homogenization by outside cultural infiltration; to the American government, the phrase means nurturing freedoms of expression and choice.[3]

The UNESCO regime also includes nonbinding declarations and recommendations to supplement the treaty framework. For example, the 2003 Declaration Concerning the Intentional Destruction of Cultural Heritage largely responds to the demolition of two

[2] *See* Art Newspaper, May 2006, at 31.

[3] *See* Alan Riding, *A Global Culture War Pits Protectionists against Free Traders*, N.Y. Times, Feb. 5, 2006, at B9 (noting that "[b]ehind the idealistic screen of cultural diversity, weighty economic and political issues are at stake").

colossal Buddhist statues in Bamiyan, Afghanistan, by the Taliban government of that country. This declaration addresses the problem of intentional destruction in peacetime, wartime, and military occupation, thereby applying to acts related to both parties and nonparties to the 1954 Hague Convention, including acts occurring within their territories. The 2003 Declaration is premised on two conditions: a violation of international law or, under the catch-all Martens clause in the 1899 and 1907 Hague Conventions and Regulations on the laws of war, "an unjustifiable offense to the principles of humanity and dictates of public conscience."[4] The operative provisions of the 2003 Declaration establish state responsibility and individual criminal responsibility for intentional destruction of cultural heritage or for any failure to take appropriate protective measures. The declaration also instructs states to cooperate with each other in measures of protection and to organize public awareness-raising campaigns.

Other UNESCO declarations have called on states to help return stolen material even when they are not formally bound to do so. The organization's General Conference also adopts recommendations, such as the 2003 Recommendation on the Promotion and Use of Multilingualism and Universal Access to Cyberspace.

In 2004 UNESCO established a rapid reaction force, by agreement with Italy, to rescue cultural heritage threatened by natural catastrophe or armed conflict. Modeled after UN peacekeeping troops, the civilian and paramilitary specialists who comprise the force were quickly dubbed the "cultural blue berets." These specialists include engineers, geologists, seismologists, architects, art historians, restorers, book conservationists, and law enforcement experts on illegal trafficking in cultural heritage. Accordingly, a national government may request such assistance from UNESCO. If UNESCO agrees, it asks the Italian government to organize and deploy an emergency action group to assist the requesting government in its efforts to protect its heritage.

NOTES AND QUESTIONS

1. The Taliban government's intentional destruction of the colossal Buddhist statues at Bamiyan underscored the fragility of the protective regime and the inadequacy of legal rules alone to facilitate the kind of constructive discourse and supportive processes that would help deter and respond effectively to such vandalism in even the wildest precincts of the global village. After all, these were not just ordinary monuments. Situated at a crossroads between ancient European and Asian civilization, and reflecting an extraordinary blend of artistic traditions, Bamiyan was Afghanistan's most important cultural site. Ironically named "the Place of Shining Light," it was by far the most prominent victim of the Taliban's "spree of iconoclasm."[5]

[4] Preamble, Convention with Respect to the Laws and Customs of War on Land, July 29, 1899, 32 Stat. 1803, T.S. No. 403, 26 Martens Nouveau Recueil (ser. 2) 949, *reprinted in* 1 Am. J. Int'l L. 129 (1907); Preamble, Convention Respecting the Laws and Customs of War on Land, Oct. 18, 1907, 36 Stat. 2277 (1907), T.S. No. 539, 3 Martens Nouveau Recueil (ser. 3) 461, *reprinted in* 2 Am. J. Int'l L. 90 (1908).

[5] *See* Brendan Cassar & Ana Rosa Rodríguez García, *The Society for the Preservation of Afghanistan's Cultural Heritage: An Overview of Activities since 1994, in* Art and Archaeology in Afghanistan: Its Fall and Survival 15, 25 (Juliette van Krieken-Pieters ed., 2006) [hereinafter Afghanistan].

What caused the Taliban to destroy the Bamiyan statues, given that just two years earlier the Taliban's Mullah Omar had decreed an unqualified protection of the Afghan heritage, including a specific prohibition on destruction of the statues? What caused this wanton act of cultural suicide? The explanations for Mullah Omar's abrupt reversal of his own decrees range from his fundamentalist revulsion toward graven images to a messianic assertion of the Taliban's power to snub global opinion and diplomatic pressures. Some have suggested that the destruction may have been more carefully staged than appeared at the time.[6] The strategy was essentially one of cultural genocide against all blasphemous images. The tactics, however, were subtler, at least before the demolition itself. For example, an exhibit at the reopened Kabul Museum in 2000 may have been designed deliberately to elicit strong objections from fundamentalists and foment a campaign of religious cleansing.

Whatever may have been the motivations of the Taliban, its actions do not seem to have been dictated or even strongly encouraged by other Islamic authorities. Nine months after the Bamiyan obliteration, UNESCO, the Organization of the Islamic Conference, and the Arab League Educational, Scientific and Cultural Organization organized a conference in Doha, Qatar, to examine Islamic views on the protection of cultural heritage. Drawing on the Koran, the hadith, and traditions of Islamic jurisprudence, the assembled specialists expressed several schools of Islamic thought, concluding on a theme of cultural diversity within an Islamic religious framework.

The applicable hard international law is problematic. Any attempt to characterize the armed conflict as either international or noninternational is frustrating. Even so, the Taliban's intentional destruction of the statues arguably violated customary norms of cultural rights, *erga omnes*, and such monumental heritage is entitled to protection even if it does appear on the World Heritage List. In direct response to the Bamiyan destruction, UNESCO adopted the Declaration Concerning the Intentional Destruction of Cultural Heritage in 2003. As noted earlier, the Declaration affirms the global and intergenerational dimensions of intentional destruction and the extension of state responsibility to such acts regardless of whether a target is inscribed on a UNESCO list or similarly official roster of protected heritage. Cultural suicide is simply unacceptable.

The efficacy of these norms is, however, another matter. The reader cannot help but be struck by the sharp contradiction between the law's ambition and its futility in circumstances such as the looting of the Kabul Museum and the demolition of the Bamiyan statues. The problem seems to be our inability not only to use the right words at the right time but also to put those words into action. For example, a 1997 resolution of the World Heritage Committee gracefully confirmed the cultural significance of the Afghan heritage and invited Afghan authorities

6 "[T]he demolition was carefully planned, painstakingly announced to the media all over the world, and cynically documented in all its phases of preparation, bombing and ultimate destruction . . . an act of narcissistic self-assertion [and] of defiance." Indeed, the Bamiyan assault may have been the first ever that was directed specifically at the United Nations and the international community, coming as it did in the wake of antiterrorist sanctions against the Afghan government under UN Security Council resolutions in 1999 and 2000. Francesco Francioni & Federico Lenzerini, *Afghan Cultural Heritage and International Law: The Case of the Buddhas of Bamiyan, in* Afghanistan, at 265, 266, 267.

to cooperate with UNESCO and the Committee in helping ensure protection of the country's cultural and natural heritage. Unfortunately, however, the resolution failed to set in motion any enduring process to achieve the desired cooperation. It was essentially only words.

It is likely, of course, that the Taliban simply stonewalled efforts, or would have stonewalled efforts, to turn Mullah Omar's initial assurances into long-term commitments that would trump politics. But who knows for sure? What we can conclude is that a premise of condemnation in the legal and scholarly discourse about the Bamiyan demolition is inadequate. The unanswered questions about the Taliban provide yet another example of the need to improve the discourse concerning cultural heritage.

International institutions can help meet the challenges, but they suffer from their own limitations, as UNESCO's involvement in the endless Afghan imbroglio demonstrates. When the insecurity of the Afghan cultural heritage had become apparent in the years before the destruction at Bamiyan, UNESCO, working with a nongovernmental organization, the Society for the Preservation of Afghanistan's Cultural Heritage (SPACH) and other organizations, sought to safeguard it. On the one hand, UNESCO raised expectations of protection and even rescue of material; but, on the other hand, it abided by national export controls that inhibited efforts to remove heritage from harm's way. In explaining such dilemmas, it must be kept in mind that UNESCO is an intergovernmental organization.[7] It must therefore respect national laws. It has no mandate to provide criminal detection or custody of materials, not to mention to impose sanctions directly against delinquent national authority. At best, UNESCO can only mediate between states and enlist its own corps of professional expertise in the interest of protecting heritage in times of crisis. Fortunately, skillful negotiations and discreet arrangements eventually made the best out of an institutional predicament – and UNESCO's structure and status as an intergovernmental organization limits its powers of persuasion. Those powers therefore are apt to be secondary to initiatives by such nongovernmental organizations as SPACH.

Today the dilemma in the Bamiyan Valley is to decide what to do with the empty niches that once framed the statues. There are three basic issues. The first is whether the decision to restore the statues should be made exclusively by the Afghans or, if the statues are truly deemed part of a global heritage, in some sort of consultation with the international community, perhaps within UNESCO. The second issue is whether to restore the statues. Many other cultural treasures have been restored in the public interest. However, the empty niches may make a powerful statement that is more important than the healing quality of restoration. Moreover, Buddhist scruples may counsel a gentle acceptance of what has been done. What is done is done. Construction follows destruction follows construction in endless cycles. Assuming, however, that restoration is a viable option, the third issue would be how to do it. One proposal, for example, is to employ the technique of anastylosis, by which the statues would be rebuilt with both original and fabricated pieces assembled together but distinguishable from one another. As Afghanistan attempts

[7] *See* Lyndel Prott, *The Protection of Cultural Movables from Afghanistan: Developments in International Management, in* Afghanistan, at 189, 200.

to rebuild itself in the throes of conflict, ways must also be found to reconcile its developmental needs with the exigencies of protecting the heritage. Otherwise, economic development may threaten the heritage. Afghanistan, at the crossroads of civilizations, "deserves to be discovered not by bulldozers but by professional archaeologists."[8]

The experience in Afghanistan may teach us a rather unexciting but important lesson: the effectiveness of cultural heritage law requires the education and informed engagement of local communities. Indeed, there may be no better way of preventing the wanton destruction of heritage than to rely on local communities. That is, of course, problematic if a consensus of a community favors such destruction or is otherwise unprepared to prevent it physically or politically. Educational initiatives therefore will be essential in trying to improve all levels of discourse and action. Such initiatives will take plenty of hard work and money.

2. Some key questions arise from the experience in Afghanistan. Were the Taliban encouraged to participate actively in meetings of the World Heritage Committee, especially the one that adopted the resolution? Did the Committee or any other international institution attempt to assure the Taliban that they respected the sincerity of the Taliban's religious aversion to graven images? Was there any concerted effort whatsoever, until it was too late, to listen to the Taliban on an ongoing basis and thereby tame their fiery egos by simply paying serious attention to them? Was there any concerted effort, despite the obstacles, to engage them further in the kind of constructive dialogue that might have helped decouple the heritage from a combination of their religious zeal and xenophobia before it was too late to change their minds? If so, was there any follow-up effort to nudge them into a long-term commitment to protect Afghanistan's cultural heritage? Mullah Omar's temporary decrees were one thing, but a minimum level of genuine trust was quite another.
3. Numerous catastrophes and other circumstances may threaten cultural material, as in times of armed conflict (for example, Europe during the Second World War, the former Yugoslavia during its civil war, and currently Iraq and Afghanistan). Natural disasters may also imperil cultural material (for example, floods in Florence, Italy; New Orleans; and Dresden, Germany; volcanic eruptions in Italy and Indonesia; earthquakes in Pakistan and Iran; and fires in California, Greece, and Germany). Other threats include unauthorized excavations (for example, in Guatemala, Iraq, Italy, and Turkey) and public projects (for, example, dam construction in China, highway construction in Greece). Whatever the cause of a threat, cultural material may need to be removed temporarily to safe havens for safekeeping and proper preservation until its original site is safe again.

   In response to this need, the Guidelines for the Establishment and Conduct of Safe Havens for Cultural Material were adopted by the nongovernmental International Law Association in 2008. They are intended to provide a framework, setting the terms for the establishment and conduct of safe havens and for the return of cultural material held for safekeeping and preservation there. The initiator of the temporary relocation may be a state, a private owner, a museum, or another

[8] *See* van Krieken-Pieters, *Dilemmas in the Cultural Heritage Field: The Afghan Case and the Lessons for the Future*, in Afghanistan, at 201, 204.

entitled person or entity. A model contract for the establishment of a safe haven is attached to the Guidelines.

3. Protection of the Cultural Patrimony and Export Controls

a. Cultural Patrimony

Legal systems typically provide special protection for cultural heritage that falls within their national patrimonies. The term "cultural patrimony" refers to that part of a national, tribal, or other society's culture that is so fundamental to the society's identity and character that it is deemed inalienable from it. The term embraces tangible artistic, historic, and archaeological objects or sites, as well as intangible phenomena such as folklore, rituals, language, and craft skills. It is often associated with the broader term "cultural heritage"; the narrower terms "cultural objects" and "cultural material," which exclude intangible heritage; and the more technical legal term "cultural property," which connotes ownership.

One definition of the term "cultural patrimony" is found in the Native American Graves Protection and Repatriation Act of the United States (NAGPRA), as follows:

> an object having ongoing historical, traditional, or cultural importance central to the Native American group or culture itself, rather than property owned by an individual American, and which, therefore, cannot be alienated, appropriated, or conveyed by any individual whether or not such individual is a member of the Indian tribe or Native Hawaiian organization and such object shall have been considered inalienable by such Native American group at the time the object was separated from such group.

Clearly established examples of Native American patrimony include Zuni war gods and the confederacy wampum belts of the Iroquois. Often, however, a specific determination of cultural patrimony is difficult in the absence of an official registration of it, in the instance of competing claims to it between individuals and a larger society, or after the society has redefined the patrimony.

The term's definitional scope varies greatly among legal systems. On the one hand, several legal systems limit the term to registered, officially listed, or otherwise explicitly identified cultural heritage, whether in private or public hands. Mexico and other countries claim as patrimony all objects of a specified age and cultural affinity that originated within their territory, for example, all indigenous material that is found within sovereign territory or was exported after enactment of pertinent antiquities legislation. Such laws, by failing to differentiate between culturally important and less important material, pose difficult problems of acceptance and enforceability elsewhere. On the other hand, U.S. patrimony extends only to sites or objects that are located on federal and tribal lands or are specifically designated by historic preservation laws. Whatever form national patrimony laws assume, there is no consensus that sovereign designation of an object can by itself reconstitute the object as a *res extra commercium* that transcends the normal rules of private international law that would generally govern commercial dealings.

The legal consequences of designating heritage as cultural patrimony also vary among legal systems. Some countries with rich but endangered heritage assert blanket ownership and bar export of all patrimony. Other countries, such as Guatemala, claim entitlement over patrimony only on its export or attempted export, thereby allowing individual ownership within the sovereign territory but requiring it to stay there. The United Kingdom does not assert control over significant privately acquired cultural material until it is subject to an export permit. The state or a public institution may then exercise an option to gain entitlement to an item by matching its purchase price or ascribed value.

Several international agreements seek to protect cultural patrimony from plunder and illegal trafficking. For example, one of the operative provisions in the 1970 UNESCO Convention – article 9 – enables one treaty party to request another to impose trade controls or other concrete measures over "cultural patrimony" that is in jeopardy from pillage. The 1995 UNIDROIT Convention, however, uses the terms "cultural objects" and especially objects "of significant cultural importance" to describe patrimony.

In the absence of an international agreement, the designation of cultural heritage as patrimony may heighten the normal tensions resulting from claims by one country for the repatriation of cultural material from another. A frequently contentious issue is simply to define the patrimony. Take, for example, an icon of modern art. The well-known Dutch artist, Piet Mondrian, fled war-torn Europe in 1940 to spend the remainder of his life in New York. In 1942 he began work on his last and one of his most ambitious works, "Victory Boogie Woogie," based on his cultural experiences in the United States and the historical circumstances of the Second World War. This extraordinary example of plasticity and modernism is considered by some to be the culmination of Mondrian's acclaimed career. He was still working on the canvas in 1944 when he died. "Victory Boogie Woogie" now hangs in the Municipal Museum of The Hague, in the Netherlands, which has announced that it "will never be loaned," ostensibly "because the condition of the paint is too fragile." ART NEWSPAPER, July-Aug. 2009, at 18. But what is the painting's country of origin? Is it an American or a Dutch work? If it is either an American work or of ambiguous patrimony, shouldn't the Dutch Museum at least consult with the Association of American Museums or some other such American body before ruling out any loans of the painting? In the unlikely event that the U.S. government requested its "repatriation," the Dutch government would likely respond that Mondrian's Dutch nationality and the lawful circumstances of its acquisition by the Municipal Museum of The Hague should trump any equitable identification of the art with a constructed U.S. patrimony.

Another issue involves material whose acquisition is traceable to conquest, confiscation, or colonization. Among the most enduring claims have been those by Greece for return of the Elgin (Parthenon) Marbles from the British Museum and by European and African governments and institutions against the Louvre and other French institutions for the return of Napoleón's booty.

Civil litigation is a last resort for resolving repatriation claims. The most common arguments for retaining patrimony outside its country of origin are that it is in the possession of a bona fide purchaser protected by continental European-based civil law; that the allowable period for asserting a claim under a statute of limitations has expired; and that, regardless of the circumstances of its acquisition, an object has reposed in a second state long enough for it to become identified with that state. Conflicting statutes of limitations, rules of repose, and rules related to a bona fide purchaser often complicate dispute resolution.

Criminal prosecutions sometimes face troublesome issues, for example, whether to include any illegally exported material within the definition of stolen property. Although the United States does not normally enforce the foreign antiquities or export laws of another state, its courts have recognized them as bases for defining theft under the National Stolen Property Act so long as the state of origin or other claimant state has specifically declared ownership over regulated heritage.

Despite the legal issues, however, private collectors, museums, and other public institutions voluntarily return some cultural patrimony either unconditionally or on a shared basis, such as by agreement for alternating possession and display of an object. Countries of origin and tribal societies have been particularly willing to share an object where it is redundant as patrimony. Collaborative dispute resolution based on principles of mutual protection and exchange of cultural heritage, as opposed to adversarial processes, offers particular promise in reconciling competing claims to patrimony.

b. Export Controls

Many countries have enacted laws that restrict the freedom of persons to remove certain cultural property beyond their boundaries. These controls are significant in protecting the culture of individual nations. The earliest of them seem to have been imposed in 1464 by Pope Pius II in the Papal States.[9] Such laws, however, do not appear to have become common until around the turn of the last century. Most countries have adopted comprehensive export controls for cultural property. However, U.S. controls are largely limited to material taken from tribal or federal lands.

National export controls vary in scope from blanket prohibitions on the export of all objects of a certain age or other classification, without even the possibility of an official permit, to prohibitions on only well-defined material of great cultural importance. Japan, for example, prohibits export of all "national treasure" but allows "important cultural property" to be exported with a permit under exceptional circumstances.

(i) International Law. International law has become increasingly sympathetic to the removal of barriers to trade in movable property. Thus, article XI of the 1994 General Agreement on Tariffs and Trade (GATT) prohibits export quotas (quantitative restrictions). However, GATT 1994 does contain an exception to this prohibition. Article XX(f) allows measures that are "imposed for the protection of national treasures of artistic, historic or archaeological value." This provision has not been the subject of detailed analysis, but insofar as it is premised on items being national treasures, it establishes a standard that is similar to the systems of export controls already in place in such countries as the United Kingdom, Canada, and Japan.

A basic difference between this approach and that taken in some countries, such as Mexico, is that the latter seek to prohibit the export of a far wider range of indigenous cultural material – well beyond the normal "national treasure" category. To the extent that these export prohibitions exceed those allowed under Article XX(f) of GATT 1994, they risk attack under the dispute settlement procedures of the World Trade Organization (WTO).

Although resort to the WTO to determine the validity of cultural property export controls may seem improbable, similar initiatives have recently been made in regard to trade barriers imposed for environmental reasons (under article XX(b) and (g), invoking

[9] *See* PAUL M. BATOR, THE INTERNATIONAL TRADE IN ART 37 (1982).

other exceptions to article XI). In those cases, WTO and GATT dispute resolution panels have found that, to be valid, the impugned trade restrictions must be the "least trade restrictive" to achieve the desired legitimate environmental objectives. It could thus be argued that very broad cultural property export controls would fail to meet this standard and would open the country establishing them to WTO-sanctioned retaliatory measures from importing market countries such as the United States.

The 1970 UNESCO Convention (against illegal trafficking) relies in part on the following provision (article 6):

> The States Parties to this Convention undertake:
>
> (a) To introduce an appropriate certificate in which the exporting State would specify that the export of the cultural property in question is authorized. The certificate should accompany all items of cultural property exported in accordance with the regulations;
> (b) to prohibit the exportation of cultural property from their territory unless accompanied by the above-mentioned export certificate;
> (c) to publicize this prohibition by appropriate means, particularly among persons likely to export or import cultural property.

This provision not only has encouraged states to establish domestic processes of export certification but also is one of the cornerstones of the Convention's system for mutual enforcement of its provisions.

(ii) Regional Law. Several regional instruments to protect cultural material have operated in both hemispheres, the oldest of which predated the Second World War. The most important of these instruments operate within the European Union, based on article 36 of the 1957 Treaty of Rome that established the Common Market (later reconfigured as the European Community and eventually the European Union). Article 36 authorizes restrictions on movement between member states of all material designated as "national treasures."

Specifically, Directive 93/7, (1993), O.J. (L. 74) 7, responded to the problem that illegal trafficking in cultural material posed for the establishment of the European Single Market. As a Directive, this instrument prescribes national enforcement measures without specifying the content of the measures. It simply requires member states to take measures to effect the return of cultural objects unlawfully taken from the territory of another member state. A second instrument, Council Regulation 391/92, (1992), O.J. (L. 395) 1, requires member states to require licensing of all cultural material destined for export outside the European Community or Union. As a Regulation, the licensing requirement is specific, leaving no room for national variations.

(iii) Practical Problems of Implementation. Export control laws and regulations vary greatly from one legal system to another. As noted earlier, such variations include the type or amount of property that is subject to restrictions on export. Another major difference among national laws concerns the type of enforcement system. Many developing countries have comprehensive export control laws in their statute books but lack a system of enforcement that offers any real protection against widespread abuse. For many states, particularly those in Africa and parts of Oceania, the existence of such laws is itself largely irrelevant because so many objects of any major significance from both a cultural and an artistic perspective have already been taken abroad. The most serious situations arise in the case of developing countries with important sites where unexcavated material awaits discovery, such as in Guatemala and China. In these truly "art-rich" source countries, there is a pressing need for international assistance to prevent unsupervised illicit excavations. Even in developed countries, the enforcement system in place may fail to adequately protect against illegal export. For example, Canada's long-undefended border with the United States complicates the task of policing the unauthorized movement of newly excavated or otherwise unknown and undocumented objects between the two countries.

Related to these issues is the intangible factor of political will. Especially in the case of archaeological sites, the people (largely indigenous) whose material culture attracts illicit excavation may be represented only marginally in the contemporary government of a source state. Those people therefore may have little incentive to comply with export controls. It is even more likely that indigenous peoples whose material culture is at risk are a minority or have a history of being discriminated against by certain entrenched ruling groups. Any lack of commitment to the enforcement of export controls is likely to marginalize such laws or render them meaningless, as they are inherently difficult to enforce in the first place, short of the kind of customs and other police procedures that would be intolerable in most democratic systems.[10]

NOTES AND QUESTIONS

1. Some national customs offices, such as those of China, require all outgoing passengers, on their baggage-declaration form, to indicate whether they are taking out of the national territory any "cultural relics" (as well as large amounts of local currency, precious metals, endangered animals and plants, and so on). The declarations are backed up with criminal sanctions for misrepresentation. The United States does not have such a requirement for either outgoing or incoming passengers. Should it have such a check-off category? Would any of the common terms such as "cultural relics," "cultural material," or "cultural property" be clear to passengers? (You should weigh the efficacy and the *in terrorem* effect of such a requirement against the administrative burden of enforcing it.)
2. The Declaration Card of the Canada Border Services Agency gives notice to all persons seeking admission into Canada that cultural property, in addition to firearms, other weapons, drugs, and endangered species, may be restricted, controlled, or

[10] "Export controls are difficult to enforce and in many nations are easily evaded. By denying the opportunity for illicit export such laws drive the traffic underground, assuring the existence of an active, profitable and corrupting black market." John H. Merryman, *A Licit International Traffic in Cultural Objects*, FIFTH COLLOQUIUM ON LEGAL ASPECTS OF INTERNATIONAL TRADE IN ART: LICIT TRADE IN WORKS OF ART 1, 16–17 (1994). The accuracy of such opinions is well supported by comparing cultural property export controls with those that have been or are in place to control traffic in alcoholic beverages, narcotics, or sensitive technology and armaments. However, Professor Merryman cites British and Canadian export controls, which he concludes are admired because they are selective (many objects are freely exportable) but work well in practice because, for a small number of objects of outstanding importance, export permission is withheld for a short time to allow government and domestic institutions an opportunity to buy objects at their full price.

prohibited, or require a special permit. Does cultural property belong in the same category as firearms, other weapons, drugs, and endangered species?

PROBLEM

In 1921 France enacted a statute that has made it a crime to export works of fine art without an export permit. Request for a permit can be denied if the Council of Experts determines that the artwork is part of the French national cultural patrimony, based on an expansive definition by the Council. In 1967 a French national, Mme. X, without obtaining a permit, exported from France a drawing she owned by Leonardo da Vinci, the Italian artist who died while residing in France. The Council of Experts had previously determined that the drawing was part of the French national patrimony. In 1987 France amended its 1921 export law to provide that the export prohibition thereafter would be limited to works of art created by French citizens or created in France by French residents. In 1989 Mme. X. drove to nearby Geneva, Switzerland with a watercolor by the French artist Claude Monet. She was waved through customs at the border. In Geneva, she boarded a plane for New York where she sold the watercolor at auction to a well-known collector, B. F. Paley, for $19 million. After Mme. X took up residence in New York, the French government attempted but failed for technical reasons to secure her extradition from the United States in order to bring criminal charges against her. The French government then brought a federal court action in New York against her to recover the da Vinci and against her and Mr. Paley to recover the Monet. Both France and the United States are parties to the 1970 UNESCO Convention, but the United States has a reservation to article 6 (p. 300) and is therefore not bound by it.

Would the French government prevail in the action on the basis of a recognition of its national cultural patrimony and export laws? Are they entirely consistent? What questions about the facts might you want to ask? (Please assume that there are no statute-of-limitations or other such technical issues – these are examined in the next chapter.)

(iv) The Canadian Model. Canadian law controls the removal of what are deemed objects of nationally outstanding significance or importance. The law is based on earlier English legislation that originated in the 1952 English *Report of the Committee on the Export of Works of Art, etc.* (popularly known as the Waverley Report, after its chair, Lord Waverley). The "Waverley Criteria," as they are known, appear in section 11 of the Canadian law that follows here. It came into force in September 1977 and implements the 1970 UNESCO Convention against illegal trafficking.

Cultural Property Export and Import Act, R.S.C. 1985, c. C-51

Establishment of Control List

4. (1) The Governor in Council, on the recommendation of the Minister made after consultation with the Minister of Foreign Affairs, may by order establish a Canadian Cultural Property Export Control List.

Inclusions

(2) Subject to subsection (3), the Governor in Council may include in the Control list, regardless of their places of origin, any objects or classes of objects hereinafter described in this subsection, the export of which the Governor in Council deems it necessary to control in order to preserve the national heritage in Canada:

(a) objects of any value that are of archaeological, prehistorically, historical, artistic or scientific interest and that have been recovered from the soil of Canada, the territorial sea of Canada or the inland or other internal waters of Canada;

(b) objects that were made by, or objects referred to in paragraph (d) that relate to, the aboriginal peoples of Canada and that have a fair market value in Canada of more than five hundred dollars;

(c) objects of decorative art, hereinafter described in this paragraph, that were made in the territory that is now Canada and are more than one hundred years old:

(i) glassware, ceramics, textiles, woodenware and works in base metals that have a fair market value in Canada of more than five hundred dollars, and

(ii) furniture, sculptured works in wood, works in precious metals and other objects of decorative art that have a fair market value in Canada of more than two thousand dollars;

(d) books, records, documents, photographic positives and negatives, sound recordings, and collections of any of those objects that have a fair market value in Canada of more than five hundred dollars;

(e) drawings, engravings, original prints and water-colours that have a fair market value in Canada of more than one thousand dollars; and

(f) any other objects that have a fair market value in Canada of more than three thousand dollars.

Exclusions

(3) No object shall be included in the Control List if that object is less than fifty years old or was made by a natural person who is still living.

Export Permits

Immediate issue of export permit

7. A permit officer who receives from a resident of Canada an application for an export permit shall issue the permit forthwith if the person applying for the permit establishes to the satisfaction of the permit officer that the object in respect of which the application is made

(a) was imported into Canada within the thirty-five years immediately preceding the date of the application and was not exported from Canada under a permit issued under this Act prior to that importation;

(b) was lent to an institution or public authority in Canada by a person who was not a resident of Canada at the time the loan was made; or

(c) is to be removed from Canada for a purpose prescribed by regulation for a period of time not exceeding such period of time as may be prescribed by regulation for the purposes of this paragraph.

Where object included in Control List

11. (1) Where an expert examiner determines that an object that is the subject of an application for an export permit that has been referred to him is included in the Control List, the expert examiner shall forthwith further determine

(a) whether that object is of outstanding significance by reason of its close association with Canadian history or national life, its aesthetic qualities or its value in the study of the arts or sciences; and

(b) whether the object is of such a degree of national importance that its loss to Canada would significantly diminish the national heritage.

Review Board

Review Board established

18. (1) There is hereby established a board to be known as the Canadian Cultural Property Export Review Board, consisting of a Chairperson and not more than nine other members appointed by the Governor in Council on the recommendation of the Minister.

Members

(2) The Chairperson and one other member shall be chosen generally from among residents of Canada, and

(a) up to four other members shall be chosen from among residents of Canada who are or have been officers, members or employees of art galleries, museums, archives, libraries or other similar institutions in Canada; and

(b) up to four other members shall be chosen from among residents of Canada who are or have been dealers in or collectors of art, antiques or other objects that form part of the national heritage.

Review of applications for export permits

Request for review by Review Board

Object that does not meet criteria

29. (4) Where the Review Board determines that an object fails to meet one or more of the criteria set out in subsection (3), it shall direct

a permit officer to issue an export permit forthwith in respect of the object.

Object that meets criteria

(5) Where the Review Board determines that an object meets all of the criteria set out in subsection (3), it shall,

(a) if it is of the opinion that a fair offer to purchase the object might be made by an institution or public authority in Canada within six months after the date of its determination, establish a delay period of not less than two months and not more than six months during which the Review Board will not direct that an export permit be issued in respect of the object; or

(b) in any other case, direct a permit officer to issue an export permit forthwith in respect of the object.

Request for determination of an offer to purchase

30. (1) Subject to subsection (2), where the Review Board establishes a delay period under paragraph 29 (5)(a) in respect of an object and an offer to purchase the object is made by an institution or a public authority in Canada within that period, either the person who applied for an export permit in respect of the object or the institution or public authority making the offer to purchase may, where the offer is not accepted, by notice in writing given to the Review Board, request the Review Board to determine the amount of a fair cash offer to purchase.

Determination of the Review Board

(3) Where the Review Board receives a request under subsection (1), it shall determine the amount of a fair cash offer to purchase the object in respect of which the request is made and advise the person who applied for an export permit in respect of the object and the institution or public authority that offered to purchase the object of its determination.

Direction for export permit

(4) Where the Review Board establishes a delay period under paragraph 29 (5)(a) in respect of an object and does not receive a request under subsection (1) in respect of the object, it shall forthwith, after the expiration of the delay period and on the request of the person who requested the review under subsection 29(1), direct a permit officer to issue an export permit forthwith in respect of the object.

(v) The Enforcement of Export Controls.

(a) The Common Law of England and the United States. A vexing question in connection with foreign export controls is the readiness of importing states to recognize and enforce those controls when cultural objects have been illegally exported. Although there seems to be little doubt about the legitimacy of national cultural property export controls under international law, many common law countries refuse to recognize or enforce export controls on the basis that they are "penal or confiscatory" or foreign "public laws" of a regulatory nature, akin to tax and revenue statutes.[11] The following case, in particular, addressed this issue of private international law and emphasized the British rejection of extraterritorial enforcement of foreign laws.

Attorney-General of New Zealand v. Ortiz, [1982] 3 W.L.R. 570, 575–76, 580–82, 585 (Court of Appeal)

Lord Denning, M.R.

Years ago in New Zealand a great chief of the Maoris had a treasure house. In it there were stored such things as dried fish, special foods and valuables. At the entrance there was a great door. It was made of totaro wood, which is light, durable, tough, and of a dark red colour. This great door was four feet high and nearly five feet wide. It had five panels carved with exquisite skill. These depicted human figures with serpentine bodies and wide pointed heads.

This great door was lost for centuries in a swamp near Waitara in the province of Taranaki in North Island. Then in 1972 a Maori tribesman called Manukonga, whilst cutting a track through the swamp, came upon it and carried it to his home.

In the next year, 1973, there came to New Zealand Lance Entwhistle, the third defendant. He was from London and was a dealer in primitive works of art. He got to know of this carving and went to see it. He realised at once that it was of much value. It was of the highest importance to the study of Maori art and civilization and Polynesian sculpture. He persuaded Manukonga to sell it to him for the sum of $6,000. He took it up to Auckland and then across to New York. From there he telephoned to George Ortiz, the first defendant, who lived in Geneva. Now George Ortiz was a collector of African and Oceanic works of art. His collection was one of the finest in the world. Lance Entwhistle asked George Ortiz to inspect this carving. George Ortiz went to New York to see it. Lance Entwistle told him that it had been exported from New Zealand without a permit but nevertheless he was the owner of it and could pass a good title to it.

Thereupon, on April 23, 1973, George Ortiz bought this carving from Lance Entwhistle for US$65,000. It was sent to Geneva by air and was kept by George Ortiz in his collection there. In October 1977 the daughter of George Ortiz was kidnapped. In order to raise money for her release, he sent his art collection to Sotheby's, the second defendants, in London for sale by auction. Sotheby's prepared an attractive catalogue. It contained a fine coloured picture of this carving. It was the principal item in the sale. Sotheby's announced that the auction was to be held on Thursday, June 29, 1978.

[11] *See, e.g.*, Huntington v. Attrill, [1893] A.C. 150 (P.C.); Loucks v. Standard Oil Co. of N.Y., 120 N.E. 198 (1918).

This came to the notice of the New Zealand Government. Their Attorney-General at once on June 26, 1978 – three days before the sale – issued a writ claiming a declaration that this carving belonged to the New Zealand Government and an injunction to prevent the sale or disposal of it. In the face of this writ it was agreed that Sotheby's would not include this carving in the sale but would hold it pending trial or further order. The sale was held without this carving. Enough was realised from the other items to pay the ransom. So George Ortiz does not propose to sell it now. It is said to be worth £300,000.

The case may eventually require a hearing on disputed points of fact. But meanwhile this court has ordered that these two points be tried as preliminary issues:

> "(1) Whether . . . Her Majesty the Queen has become the owner and is entitled to possession of the carving . . . pursuant to the provisions of the [New Zealand] Historic Articles Act 1962 and the Customs Acts 1913 and 1966; and (2) whether in any event the provisions of the said Acts are unenforceable in England as being foreign penal, revenue and/or public laws."

The defendants have also made the following concessions:

> "The great majority of countries have legislation to forbid or control the export of antiquities and in many cases the sanction for any attempt to export an antiquity illegally is that the object may be confiscated."

Although this case concerns New Zealand law, I propose to consider first the English law. This is because New Zealand has inherited the common law of England; and also because its statutes and methods of interpretation are on much the same lines as our own. We use the same language – the English language – to express the same principles, to define the same concepts, and to give the same meaning.

The territorial theory of jurisdiction

It was said long ago by Story J. in the Supreme Court of the United States in *The Apollon* (1824) 9 Wheat. 362, 370: "The laws of no nation can justly extend beyond its own territories, except so far as regards its own citizens." And in his book, *Story's Conflict of Laws*, 2nd ed. (1841), p. 26, he said: "no state or nation can, by its laws, directly affect or bind property out of its own territory, or bind persons not resident therein," except that, see p. 28, "every nation has a right to bind its own subjects by its own laws in every other place."

In our present case the New Zealand Government invites us to interpret section 12 (2) of the Historic Articles Act 1962 as if it said: "An historic article which has been knowingly exported from New Zealand in breach of this Act shall be automatically forfeited to Her Majesty, and Her Majesty can recover it in any other country into which it may be imported." So interpreted, the Act seems to me to infringe the rule of international law which says that no country can legislate so as to affect the rights of property when that property is situated beyond the limits of its own territory. It is a direct infringement of the territorial theory of sovereignty which is most ably discussed by Dr. F. A. Mann in his *Studies in International Law* (1973), pp. 1 to 139.

If this Historic Articles Act 1962 provided for *automatic* forfeiture, that forfeiture would take place and would come into effect as soon as the historic article was *exported*, i.e. as soon as it left the territorial jurisdiction of New Zealand. That would be a piece of extra-territorial legislation which is invalid by international law.

Rather than suppose that the New Zealand Parliament would infringe international law, or would go beyond the limits of its own jurisdiction, I am quite clear that we should read section 12 (2), not as providing for automatic forfeiture, but as meaning "shall be liable to forfeiture."

A point of vast importance

The next preliminary point proceeds on the assumption that the Historic Articles Act 1962 provides for automatic forfeiture and then asks: should this law be enforced by the courts of England?

This point may become real when it is remembered that the Act of 1962 applies not only to *actual export* of an historic article, but also to *attempted export*. An *attempt* might be made to export an historic article. It might be taken to the airport and then prevented at the last moment from being loaded on to the aircraft. A New Zealand statute could well provide (within its territorial jurisdiction) for automatic forfeiture to the Crown on such an attempt being made. The owner makes a second attempt. Then, before it is seized by the authorities, he manages to export it. He gets it to England. The New Zealand Government seeks to recover it. Will the English courts enforce its claim?

This second point is of vast importance. Most countries have legislation to prevent the export of their historic articles unless permitted by licence. This legislation may provide for automatic forfeiture on export or attempted export. It might be very desirable that every country should enforce every other country's legislation on the point – by enabling such articles to be recovered and taken back to their original home. But does the law permit of this?

Recognition and enforcement

At the outset I must point out that we are here concerned with a suit by a foreign state to enforce its laws. I hope our New Zealand friends will forgive me calling them a "foreign state." I only use the term so as to bring home the fact that we are concerned with an independent sovereign government which exercises sovereign authority over its own territory, and which, by international law, has no right to exercise sovereign authority beyond its own territorial limits.

This suit by a foreign state to enforce its laws is to be distinguished altogether from a suit between private firms or individuals which raises a question as to whether a contract has been broken by one or the other or whether a wrong has been done by one to the other. In such a suit our courts will often recognize the existence of the laws of a foreign state. We will recognize the foreign law so much that we will refuse to enforce a contract which is in breach of the laws of the foreign state: see the Prohibition case of *Foster* v. *Driscoll* [1929] 1 K.B. 470, and the jute case of *Regazzoni* v. *K.C. Sethia (1944) Ltd.* [1956] 2 Q.B. 490 and [1958] A.C. 301.

This present case is different. It is a suit by a foreign state brought in the English courts here to enforce its laws. No one has ever doubted that our courts will not entertain a suit brought by a foreign sovereign, directly or indirectly, to enforce the penal or revenue laws of that foreign state. We do not sit to collect taxes for another country or to inflict punishments for it. Now the question arises whether this rule extends to "other public laws." *Dicey & Morris, The Conflict of Laws*, 10th ed. (1980), vol. 1, p. 90, rule 3[,] say it does. I agree with them. The term "other public laws" is very uncertain. But so are the terms "penal" and "revenue." The meaning of "penal" was discussed in *Huntington* v. *Attrill* [1893] A.C. 150 and *Loucks* v. *Standard Oil Co. of New York* (1918) 120 N.E. 198. The meaning of "revenue" was discussed in *Government of India* v. *Taylor* [1955] A.C. 491. But what are "other public laws?" I think they are laws which are eiusdem generis with "penal" or "revenue" laws.

Then what is the genus? Or, in English, what is the general concept which embraces "penal" and "revenue" laws and others like them? It is to be found, I think, by going back to the classification of acts taken in international law. One class comprises those acts which are done by a sovereign "jure imperii," that is, by virtue of his sovereign authority. The others are those which are done by him "jure gestionis," that is, which obtain their validity by virtue of his performance of them. The application of this distinction to our present problem was well drawn by Dr. F. A. Mann 28 years ago in an article "Prerogative Rights of Foreign States and the Conflict of Laws" in *Transactions of the Grotius Society (1954)* 40 Tr. Gro. Soc. *25*, reprinted in his *Studies in International Law* (1973), pp. 492 to 514.

Applied to our present problem the class of laws which will be enforced are those laws which are an exercise by the sovereign government of its sovereign authority over property within its territory or over its subjects wherever they may be. But other laws will not be enforced. By international law every sovereign state has no sovereignty beyond its own frontiers. The courts of other countries will not allow it to go beyond the bounds. They will not enforce any of its laws which purport to exercise sovereignty beyond the limits of its authority.

If this be right, we come to the question: what is meant by the exercise of sovereign authority?" It is a term which we will have to grapple with, sooner or later. It comes much into the cases on sovereign immunity and into the State Immunity Act 1978: see sections 3 (3) *(c)* and 14 (2) *(a)*. It was much discussed recently in *1 Congreso del Partido* [1981] 3 W.L.R. 328 and by Hazel Fox ("Stoke Immunity: The House of Lords' Decision in I Congreso del Partido" in the *Law Quarterly Review* [1982] 98 L.Q.R. 94).

It can provoke much difference of opinion as is shown by the differences amongst the Law Lords on the facts of that very case. But, difficult as it is, it must be tackled.

I suggest that the first thing in such a case as the present is to determine which is the relevant act. Then to decide whether it is of a sovereign character or a nonsovereign character. Finally, to ask whether it was exercised within the territory of the sovereign state – which is legitimate, or beyond it – which is illegitimate.

In solving the question, we can get guidance from the decided cases. I will take therefore the cases decided in the English courts about tangible things which have been confiscated – or attempted to be confiscated – by a sovereign government.

Conclusion

Returning to our present case, I am of opinion that if any country should have legislation prohibiting the export of works of art, and providing for the automatic forfeiture of them to the state should they be exported, then that falls into the category of "public laws" which will not be enforced by the courts of the country to which it is exported, or any other country, because it is an act done in the exercise of sovereign authority which will not be enforced outside its own territory.

On this point, therefore, I differ from the judge; but I would express my gratitude to him for his most valuable contribution to this important topic. He held that our courts should enforce the foreign laws about works of art by ordering them to be delivered up to the foreign government. He hoped that, if we did this, the courts of other countries would reciprocate and enforce our laws which prohibit the export of works of art. I regard this as too sanguine. If our works of art are sold to a dealer and exported to the United States without permission, as many have been, I doubt very much whether the courts of the United States would order them to be returned to England at the suit of our government, on the ground of forfeiture.

The retrieval of such works of art must be achieved by diplomatic means. Best of all, there should be an international convention on the matter where individual countries can agree and pass the necessary legislation. It is a matter of such importance that I hope steps can be taken to this end. I would answer the first preliminary issue, "No," and the second preliminary issue, "Yes." I would allow the appeal accordingly.

NOTES

1. The other court of appeals judges did not agree with Lord Denning that there was a category of foreign public laws that were unenforceable. Instead, they saw the New Zealand law simply as a foreign penal law that was unenforceable on that limited basis. On further appeal to the English House of Lords, the issue of enforceability of foreign penal or public laws was not discussed on the ground that New Zealand had not been able to establish its entitlement to or ownership of the carvings.

Attorney-General of New Zealand v. Ortiz [1983] 2 W.L.R. 809. The House of Lords upheld the Court of Appeal decision simply on the basis that the New Zealand statute required actual seizure of an object for title to vest in the Crown, and that had not occurred.

For courts, the type of situation that arose in *Ortiz* involves the extent to which they are generally prepared to give effect to foreign laws as a matter of private international law. When laws affecting private rights are involved, such as the law of tort or contract, few problems arise other than deciding which country's laws should apply according to well-established rules as to the applicable law. In the case of foreign legislation of a public character, such as income taxation, customs duties, and competition rules, the added dimension exists of whether the local court should facilitate the enforcement of government regulations of a public policy nature. Under the common law, foreign penal and revenue laws are not enforceable. One basis for this rule is that judicial assistance with the enforcement of such foreign laws represents an incursion into the role of the executive branch of government. Thus, in *Attorney-General (U.K.)* v. *Heinemann Publishers Australia Pty. Ltd. et al.*, 165 C.L.R. 30 (1988), a majority of the High Court of Australia thought that the nonenforcement rule applied to "claims enforcing the interests of a foreign sovereign which arise from the exercise of certain powers peculiar to government."

In *Ortiz*, the applicable New Zealand export control legislation purported to vest title to the Maori carvings in the New Zealand Crown on their being unlawfully exported from the territory of New Zealand. The issue for the English courts involved the extent to which they would give effect to this foreign law in respect of property now situated in England. The trial judge in *Ortiz* held that since the basis for the New Zealand government's claim that it had title to the Maori carvings was through forfeiture pursuant to the Historic Articles Act, the claim amounted to one of enforcement rather than recognition. He then went on to find that the New Zealand law was not penal in character and was therefore "enforceable" in England.

English common law is uncertain not only as to the content of "non-penal and non-revenue" public laws but also as to whether such laws should be enforced (as opposed to penal or revenue laws). It has been suggested that international public policy favors enforcement of national cultural property legislation on the basis of an emerging consensus that such domestic measures are desirable, as follows:

> Comity requires that we should respect the national heritage of other countries, by according both recognition and enforcement to their laws which affect the title to property while it is within their territory. The hope of reciprocity is an additional ground of public policy leading to the same conclusion.[12]

Although the relationship of international public policy to the common law is uncertain, there are solid examples of the incorporation of such policy into domestic law. For example, judicial interpretation of legislation to facilitate private arbitration of commercial disputes often diminishes the scope for judicial intervention. The basis for this approach has been judicial recognition of an increased

[12] *Ortiz*, [1982] 1 Q.B. 349, at 371–2 (Staughton, J.)

international acceptance and preference for private arbitration of international business disputes. The main problem with arguments based on a consensus about the desirability of domestic control measures is that they assume that all national cultural property export laws justify recognition on the same policy basis. This argument fails to take into account that some of these laws may be overrestrictive in prohibiting the export of all or almost all such property while others are more limited in scope. There may exist a supportive international public policy consensus in respect of the latter, but not necessarily the former.

2. In *Government of Iran v. The Barakat Galleries Ltd.*, [2007] EWCA Civ. 1374, [2009] Q.B. 22, Iran claimed in conversion to recover possession of a collection of antiquities that had originated in Iran but were in the possession of a private dealer and being offered for sale in England. The English court of appeal concluded that the laws under which Iran claimed title to the objects were not of a penal or public nature but simply laws that made the state the owner of the objects in question and therefore entitled to their immediate possession. The court thus avoided having to revisit the law concerning nonrecognition of cultural property export controls on the basis that they were public laws. The court did, however, make reference to the 1970 UNESCO Convention and other international agreements as evidence that Iran's claim was consistent with public policy and international recognition that states should assist each other to prevent the unlawful removal of cultural objects.
3. The common law rule that foreign export controls will not be enforced is applicable in some civil legal systems as well. For example, an Italian court refused to recognize or enforce French controls in the case of illegally exported tapestries. See KURT SIEHR, INTERNATIONAL ART TRADE AND THE LAW 188 (1993) (citing *Stato francese v. Ministerio dei beni culturali* (1987)). For a summary of national practices, see Kurt Siehr, *The Beautiful One Has Come – To Return, in* IMPERIALISM, ART AND RESTITUTION 114, 121 (John Henry Merryman ed., 2006).

(b) Enforcement under the 1970 UNESCO Convention. Despite the widespread judicial antipathy toward recognition and enforcement of foreign cultural property export controls, the 1970 UNESCO Convention provides a framework for enforcement. It prohibits acquisition by state-sponsored institutions of stolen cultural property; mandates the return of property stolen from museums, churches, and other cultural institutions; provides for export certification of cultural property; and requires parties to prohibit import of items that another party demonstrates to be a part of cultural patrimony in jeopardy.

The level of enforcement varies among parties to the agreement. For example, U.S. ratification of the agreement is conditioned by a reservation and six "understandings." When enacted into law as the Convention on Cultural Property Implementation Act (CPIA),[13] recognition of foreign export controls under the Convention was made contingent on either entry by the United States into a bilateral agreement with an individual requesting state or the existence of an "emergency condition" in respect of pillage of cultural property in a foreign country. Although the United States has thereby refused to provide blanket enforcement of foreign export certificates, it has actively cooperated in

[13] 19 U.S.C. §§ 2601–2613 (2002).

barring the import of patrimonial material in jeopardy, as determined by the Department of State's Cultural Property Advisory Committee.

Canada also is party to the UNESCO Convention and has implemented its provisions in the form of the Cultural Property Export and Import Act. Along with establishing a system of controls on the export from Canada of significant cultural property, this Act also deals with the importation into Canada of cultural property that has been exported from a State Party to the 1970 UNESCO Convention contrary to the laws of that state.

Under the Canadian legislation a foreign state that is party to the Convention may ask the minister of Canadian heritage to assist in the recovery and return of cultural property that has been illegally exported from the reciprocating state. If the property is located in Canada, the attorney general of Canada may bring action for recovery of such property on behalf of the reciprocating state. The court ordering return of an object may also order that compensation be paid to a bona fide purchaser for value or someone who otherwise has valid title to the object and was unaware of the illegality of its exportation. Thus, it is clear that under Canadian law it is not necessary for the enforcement of foreign cultural property export control laws that the source state claim title to the property involved. These provisions furnish a procedure whereby, in a case like *Ortiz*, a court could have ordered both the return of the carvings to New Zealand and the payment of compensation to an innocent party (whether or not residing in Canada). The provisions of the Act supersede considerations of public policy that are relevant in developing common law solutions. No matter how different Canadian export controls may be from the export controls of the reciprocating foreign state, the latter are enforceable.

No foreign representative has standing to institute recovery proceedings. It is possible that the attorney general of Canada could decline a foreign request to institute recovery proceedings if certain aspects of the request were deemed unreasonable or contrary to Canadian public policy. However, because there is no reported Canadian case involving a recovery proceeding under the Act, it cannot be predicted with certainty how Canada would assist in the enforcement of foreign export control laws whose scope might vastly exceed that of Canadian laws.

David Walden, *Canada's Cultural Property Export and Import Act: The Experience of Protecting Cultural Property* 203, 208–10, U. B.C. L. Rev. (Special Issue)(1995)

In July 1989, Canada Customs officials at Mirabel Airport near Montreal, Quebec, intercepted a shipment of Egyptian antiquities that had originated in Switzerland and was destined for an Egyptian citizen living in Canada. The shipment was discovered during a routine inspection of incoming goods, and after examining the antiquities, Customs officials became suspicious that they had been illegally exported from Egypt. The shipment was then detained pending further investigation.

Two months later the Royal Canadian Mounted Police (RCMP) searched the importer's Montreal home and seized additional artifacts that had been imported into Canada in 1988. Both the initial shipment and the items subsequently seized by the RCMP consisted of wood, gypsum and stucco masks, painted wood statuettes, bronze statuettes, limestone sculptures of animals, alabaster vases, beads, coins and inscribed wood fragments. The objects were variously described as being of Roman, Egyptian or Coptic origin from the Late Period, Ptolemaic Period or New Kingdom. The invoice from the vendor in Switzerland also described them as being of "archaeological value dating from the 13th century B.C. to the 10th century A.D."

The Movable Cultural Property Program of the government of Canada, which is responsible for administering the *Cultural Property Export and Import Act*, was notified of the detention and the seizure and asked to assist law enforcement officials to obtain the services of an expert in Egyptian antiquities to identify and authenticate the items. The curator of the Egyptian Department at a major Canadian museum examined the collection and advised that, of the 215 items, all but ten appeared to be genuine.

A delegation from Egypt examined the first shipment in August 1989 and concluded that the artifacts had been discovered as a result of clandestine excavations and then smuggled out of Egypt. Photographs and descriptions of the items in both shipments were sent to the Egyptian antiquities authorities, who in turn sent this information to museums throughout Egypt. With the exception of two of the objects, no records were found, which suggested that they had neither been registered with the authorities nor reported missing. The two objects with registration numbers were traced to the importer and records indicated that they had once been in his possession in Egypt. The same records also indicated that he had sold them in Egypt at an earlier, unspecified time.

The Egyptian authorities identified several of the artifacts as displaying markings that linked them to an archaeological site at the village of Sharouna. The site had been discovered in May 1978 but archaeological excavations had not begun until 1981. Egyptian officials argued that this demonstrated that the artifacts could not have been exported from Egypt prior to Canada becoming a signatory to the *1970 UNESCO Convention* (June 1978). The Egyptians subsequently acknowledged, however, that looting had been a problem at the Sharouna site since 1976. Finally, one other piece of circumstantial evidence provided an indication of when the export might have taken place: the antiquities in the first shipment were wrapped in Egyptian newspapers dated 4 October 1986. It was learned, however, that this same newspaper was readily available in major cities outside Egypt. As a result, the existence of the newspaper in the crates was considered to be circumstantial evidence that could not be used to conclusively establish the date of export or that the shipment had originated in Egypt.

From September 1989 until April 1990, the RCMP tried unsuccessfully to obtain further information about the whereabouts of these artifacts before their arrival in Switzerland. In the absence of sufficient evidence that they had been exported from Egypt after June 1978, legal counsel advised that there was insufficient evidence to lay charges for the illegal import of cultural property. The Ambassador of Egypt was advised of this evidentiary problem and advised that the antiquities would have to be released to the importer.

The Arab Republic of Egypt then launched a civil suit against the importer, challenging his ownership of the antiquities. The importer tried unsuccessfully to have this action quashed and while the court did deny his motion, it also determined that it required "security for costs" and gave the Arab Republic of Egypt sixty days to deposit the required money with the court. During this time the "Mirabel shipment" was still being detained in commercial warehouse space and, as costs were mounting, Customs officials were anxious to release the shipment. As the ownership of the collection was being disputed before the courts, however, it was not clear to whom it could or should be released. Further questions arose about where the antiquities would be stored pending resolution of the civil suit and what arrangements would be made for insurance during this time.

A museum in Montreal finally agreed to keep the collection in its environmentally controlled storage area and the Movable Cultural Property Program was able to assist both parties in obtaining a preferred premium for the insurance. The Egyptian Embassy and the importer agreed to share the cost of the insurance, and the collection was transferred to the museum where it remains today. Over five years later, the civil action to determine the ownership of the antiquities remains unresolved.

NOTES AND QUESTIONS

1. The legal and factual complexities associated with the enforcement of cultural property export controls defy simple solution. One starting point, however, might be an attempt to reach agreement on a model export control law. This not only would facilitate reciprocal recognition pursuant to such initiatives as the UNESCO Convention but also would provide a basis for legislation in the many countries that currently either have no such laws or whose existing laws are outmoded. Finally, a model cultural property export control law would constitute a major step toward the crystallization of international public policy in an area often characterized by acrimony and uncertainty. What, then, should such a law provide? See Robert K. Paterson, *A Proposed Strategy for the Multilateral Recognition of National Property Export Controls*, 8 ART, ANTIQUITY & L. 57 (2003).
2. What do you think are the main difficulties with using export controls as a method to protect a country's cultural heritage? What other alternatives can you suggest that would afford such protection less problematically?
3. Do you think the U.S. reservation to the UNESCO Convention was justified? What factors do you think may have led the country to enter the reservation?
4. If you were asked to draft a cultural property export control law for the United States, how would you go about formulating such a law, and what property would you seek to restrict from being freely exportable?

4. Protection of Underwater Cultural Heritage

Underwater cultural heritage has been a frontier of international legal authority. Only recently, as a result of technological advances, has the systematic exploration and excavation of this heritage become possible, leading inevitably to disputes and the need for some kind of a legal regime to help avoid and resolve them.[14] Because of the huge expense of the requisite technology, commercial salvors have been singularly able to exploit the opportunities for maritime excavation.[15] The high stakes of commercial salvage have offered new opportunities for litigation, too. Some of the cases are strictly domestic, but some raise important international issues. Claims of exclusive salvage rights and salvage awards have been particularly controversial. The scientific community and the public have also had to seek protection of their interests in admiralty courts – ordinary courts exercising jurisdiction and hearing disputes under the rules and procedures of common law-based admiralty rules – or other courts of maritime jurisdiction specifically. For them, salvage itself may be a threat to the heritage, as is looting by pirates and irresponsible recreational divers. Whatever the dispute, the legal regime of regulatory jurisdiction, protection, and international cooperation has been very much at sea until recently.

Maritime courts, applying a hybrid of national and international rules loosely called general maritime law, have struggled to resolve disputes involving the underwater cultural heritage. Because of the prominence of U.S. salvage interests in exploring and excavating underwater cultural heritage, it is instructive to focus on the U.S. experience. In the United States, the legal process has advanced through four stages in a little more than a quarter of a century.

At first, the federal courts, masquerading as agents of an international maritime custom, simply applied the common law of salvage and finds.[16] Accordingly, salvage claims, for example, are based on three well-established elements and the valuation of salvage

[14] *See* Gerard J. Mangone, United States Admiralty Law 223, 230 (1997). For commentary on the current impact and commercial underpinnings of treasure hunting on underwater sites, *see* Heather Pringle, *Profiteers on the High Seas*, Archaeology, July–Aug. 2007, at 20.

[15] *See* Council of Europe, Parliamentary Assembly, Maritime and Fluvial Cultural Heritage, Doc. 8867, at 7 (2000) [hereinafter Council of Europe Study].

[16] *See generally* Hener v. United States, 525 F. Supp. 350 (S.D.N.Y. 1981).

> Sharp theoretical differences exist between the law of salvage and the law of finds, although which one is applicable to a particular case may present some difficulty. The clear major premise of the law of salvage is that the property that is the object of the salvage act is owned by persons other than the salvor. The purpose and rules of the laws of salvage are designed to accord the salvor a right to compensation, not title. . . . The salvor has only superior right to possession, not title, until a court has passed on title and the salvage award.
>
> The law of finds is operative in admiralty as an adjunct to the law of salvage, with the same jurisdictional basis. The assumption of the law of finds is that title to the property may have been lost; this normally requires strong proof, such as the owner's express declaration abandoning title. The primary concern of the law of finds is title to the property. The finder can acquire title against all the world (except an owner who shows non-abandonment) by demonstrating the intent to acquire the property and possession (or a high degree of control).

Thomas J. Schoenbaum, Admiralty and Maritime Law 851–52 (3d ed. 2001) (footnotes omitted). "Nothing could be farther from the truth as far as the law of finds is concerned" than the childhood rhyme, "finders, keepers; losers, weepers." Mangone, *supra* note 14, at 223.

awards on six factors (the *Blackwall* rules).[17] Of particular interest is a seventh factor – archaeological supervision and documentation[18] – which began to be applied to salvage of historic wreck during the first stage in the evolution of admiralty court practice related to historic wreck.

Later, at a second stage, the Abandoned Shipwreck Act (ASA),[19] applicable to submerged lands of a state of the union, transferred authority over wreck from the admiralty courts to the federal executive for transfer to coastal states. The ASA thereby confined judicial discretion largely to factual issues of abandonment and compliance with the new authority vested in the states. A third stage of legal development involved a more complex analysis of issues relating to the salvage of wreck lying beyond coastal state jurisdiction and therefore beyond the scope of the ASA. Although even the early cases addressed issues of extraterritorial jurisdiction, the basis for such jurisdiction evolved during the third stage well beyond simplistic applications of traditional rules. Unfortunately, however, issues of competing salvage rights, jurisdiction to regulate salvage activities, and public access to such wreck began to fall between jurisdictional cracks. Admiralty courts sometimes took foreign and international interests into account, but they either ignored international law altogether or adopted a pseudointernational law to vindicate national interests.[20] The federal district court in the *R.M.S. Titanic* litigation,[21] for example, failed

[17] The three substantive elements of a valid salvage claim are as follows: (1) a marine peril, (2) service voluntarily rendered and not required as a preexisting duty, and (3) success in recovering imperiled maritime property. 8 Benedict on Admiralty § 8.03 (7th ed., rev. 2002).

Successful salvage gives rise to a lien in the rescued property in favor of the salvor. The value of the lien is set by an admiralty court. In *The Blackwall*, 77 U.S. 1, 14 (1870), the U.S. Supreme Court established the following factors: (1) the labor expended by the salvors in rendering the salvage service; (2) the promptitude, skill, and energy displayed in rendering the service and saving the property; (3) the value of the property employed by the salvors in rendering the service, and the danger to which such property was exposed; (4) the risk incurred by the salvors in securing the property from the impending peril; (5) the value of the property saved; and (6) the degree of danger from which the property was rescued.

[18] *See, e.g.*, Columbus-Am. Discovery Group v. Atl. Mut. Ins. Co., 974 F.2d 450, 468 (4th Cir. 1992); Klein v. The Unidentified, Wrecked and Abandoned Sailing Vessel, 758 F.2d 1511, 1515 (11th Cir. 1985); Marex Int'l Inc. v. The Unidentified, Wrecked and Abandoned Vessel, 952 F. Supp. 825, 829 (S.D. Ga. 1997); Titanic, Inc. v. The Wrecked and Abandoned Vessel, 924 F. Supp. 714 (E.D. Va. 1996) (imposing various requirements of archaeological protection). The effectiveness of this requirement is controversial. *See, e.g.*, Paul Fletcher Tomenius, Patrick O'Keefe & Michael Williams, *Salvor in Possession: Friend or Foe to Marine Archaeology?*, 9 Int'l J. Cultural Prop. 263, 292 (2000) (questioning the effectiveness of the requirement).

[19] 43 U.S.C. §§ 2101–2106 (2000).

[20] For instance, the court noted that "[r]estricting freedom of navigation over a few square miles of the vast North Atlantic Ocean is hardly a significant intrusion," *R.M.S. Titanic*, 9 F. Supp. 2d at 634–35, whereas the Geneva Convention on the High Seas, to which the United States is a party, prohibits such restrictions on freedom of navigation, Geneva Convention on the High Seas, art. 2, Sept. 30, 1962, 13 U.S.T. 2312, 450 U.N.T.S. 82.

[21] After a long court battle, the District Court for the Eastern District of Virginia granted exclusive salvage rights and the related rights of a salvor-in-possession to the R.M.S. Titanic, Inc., a Florida corporation. Order of June 7, 1994, *cited in* 924 F. Supp. at 716 n. 2. Later, the same court rejected a challenge to these rights and enjoined competing salvage. R.M.S. Titanic, Inc. v. The Wrecked and Abandoned Vessel, 924 F. Supp. 714 (E.D. Va. 1996). The court extended this injunction to prohibit virtually all activity, including photography, related to the *Titanic* that was not authorized by the exclusive salvor. R.M.S. Titanic, Inc. v. The Wrecked and Abandoned Vessel, 9 F. Supp. 2d 624 (E.D. Va. 1998). The case continued with a variety of motions, orders, and appeals. R.M.S. Titanic, Inc. v. Haver, 171 F.3d 943 (4th Cir. 1999), *cert. denied*, 120 S. Ct. 74 (1999) [hereinafter *Haver*], excerpts from which are set forth after this introduction, was

to apply the clear prescriptions of Congress,[22] executive policy,[23] and international law,[24] all of which manifested a new sensitivity to foreign and international interests. The district court's nonchalance about the legal authority, though partly reversed on appeal,[25] generated shock waves abroad. The court's interpretation of the normal jurisdiction it has vis-à-vis "the whole world" in an *in rem* action[26] seemed inappropriate as applied to wreck of historic foreign vessels, prompting English and Australian observers to write as follows: "Private property rights are being asserted by a national court in international waters over wreck of a foreign vessel in derogation of its own state's authority to conduct foreign policy and, albeit potentially, in direct contravention of a treaty recognized in international law."[27] The need was becoming clear for admiralty courts to reconcile conflicting national interests with newly acknowledged international interests.

Fortunately, a fourth stage of legal development has been characterized by a more sensitive interpretation of bilateral treaty law, a recognition of multilateral treaty law, and a new commitment to general principles of comity and international cooperation. The opinions of the Fourth Circuit Court of Appeals in the *Titanic*[28] and *Sea Hunt*[29] cases, in particular, have been watersheds in this development. The Fourth Circuit, which is often cited as one of the most conservative in the federal system, has nevertheless been at the vanguard of progressively redefining U.S. admiralty courts as emerging fora in litigation of internationally significant historic wrecks. Admiralty courts that are

the concluding phase of protracted litigation concerning the claims of competing salvors and the rights of access for nonsalvors, including tourists and photographers.

22 The court acknowledged but failed to apply the R.M.S. Titanic Memorial Act of 1986, U.S.C. §§ 450rr to 450rr-6 (2000) [hereinafter the 1986 Act]. As a Sense of Congress, the 1986 Act denies "sovereignty or sovereign *or exclusive rights of jurisdiction over*... the R.M.S. Titanic." *Id.* at § 450rr-6 (emphasis added). In providing for research and limited exploration activity, *id.* at § 450rr-5, the Act specifically provides that "no person should conduct any such research or exploration activity which would physically alter, disturb, *or salvage* the R.M.S. Titanic." *Id.* (emphasis added).

23 The 1986 Act established the parameters of executive policy. Accordingly, the secretary of the interior was committed to enter into negotiations with the United Kingdom, France, Canada, and other interested states concerning the *Titanic.* In carrying out the Sense of Congress, the executive was also committed to protect the *Titanic* against physical alteration, disturbance, or salvage. Later, President Clinton, in one of his final actions as president, concisely articulated the U.S. policy: "International law encourages nations to preserve objects of maritime heritage wherever located for the benefit of the public." Addressing the status of state craft (ships) (typically sunken naval vessels), President Clinton confirmed that "[t]he United States will use its authority to protect and preserve sunken State craft of the United States and other nations, whether located in the waters of the United States, a foreign nation, or in international waters." Statement on United States Policy for the Protection of Sunken Warships, 37 Weekly Comp. Pres. Doc. 195–96 (Jan. 19, 2001). Although the president was concerned primarily with the special status of state craft (ships), his statement articulated a broader, long-standing commitment to international cooperation, particularly in executing the 1986 Act.

24 *E.g.*, "Restricting freedom of navigation over a few square miles of the vast North Atlantic Ocean is hardly a significant intrusion." *R.M.S. Titanic*, 9 F. Supp. 2d at 634–35 (the Geneva Convention on the High Seas, Sept. 30, 1962, 13 U.S.T. 2312, 450 U.N.T.S. 82, to which the United States is a party, prohibits such restrictions on freedom of navigation, *id.* at art. 2).

25 *See Haver.*

26 *R.M.S. Titanic*, 9 F. Supp. 2d at 634.

27 Tomenius, O'Keefe & Williams, *supra* note 18, at 272.

28 *Haver.*

29 Sea Hunt, Inc. v. The Unidentified Shipwreck Vessel or Vessels, 221 F.3d 634 (4th Cir. 2000), *cert. denied*, 121 S. Ct. 1079 (2001). For a good analysis, *see* Carla J. Shapreau, *Extension of Express Abandonment Standard for Sovereign Shipwrecks in* Sea Hunt *et al., Raises Troublesome Issues Regarding Protection of Underwater Cultural Property*, 10 Int'l J. Cultural Prop. 276 (2001).

engaged in "unique developments of salvage law"[30] provide an alternative to outlawry on the frontier of underwater cultural heritage and thereby fill a void.

Current developments in the evolution of historic wreck litigation in admiralty courts have been creative rather than natural, teleological rather than incremental. The key features have been three efforts: to fashion a constructive *in rem* basis of adjudicatory jurisdiction, to apply the conventional international law more credibly and responsibly, and to redefine the general maritime law.

R.M.S. Titanic v. Haver,
171 F.3d 943 (4th Cir. 1999)

Niemeyer, Circuit Judge:

This appeal presents questions about the authority of a United States court to regulate the salvage rights in the wreck of the luxury liner, *R.M.S. Titanic*, which lies in international waters.

The *Titanic* was launched in 1912 as the "largest and finest steamship ever built" and with the claim that she was "unsinkable." On her maiden voyage from Southampton to New York, however, with 2,340 passengers on board, the *Titanic* collided with an iceberg in the North Atlantic and sank less than three hours later, on April 15, 1912. A nearby ship saved 745 persons and some lifeboats and took them to New York. Another ship recovered several hundred bodies and took them to Halifax, Nova Scotia.

In 1985, the wreck of the *Titanic* was discovered at the bottom of the North Atlantic in international waters, approximately 400 miles off the coast of Newfoundland in 12,500 feet of water. Salvage efforts began two years later. In 1994, the district court in the Eastern District of Virginia, exercising "constructive *in rem* jurisdiction" over the wreck and the wreck site of the *Titanic*, awarded exclusive salvage rights, as well as ownership of recovered artifacts, to R.M.S. Titanic, Inc. ("RMST"), a Florida corporation.

Two years later, the court rejected a challenge to the exclusive salvage rights of RMST, *see R.M.S. Titanic, Inc. v. The Wrecked and Abandoned Vessel* ("*Titanic I*"), 924 F. Supp. 714 (E.D. Va. 1996), and shortly thereafter, entered an injunction dated August 13, 1996, protecting the salvage rights of RMST against *any person* in the world "having notice of this Order," prohibiting any such person from "conducting search, survey, or salvage operations, or obtaining any image, photographing or recovering any objects, entering, or causing to enter" the area of the Atlantic Ocean surrounding the *Titanic* wreck site. On June 23, 1998, the court reaffirmed, "personalized and enforced" the 1996 injunction against new parties. *R.M.S. Titanic, Inc. v. The Wrecked and Abandoned Vessel* ("*Titanic II*"), 9 F. Supp. 2d 624, 626 (E.D. Va. 1998). In that order, the court enjoined the appellants, Christopher S. Haver, an Arizona resident, and Deep Ocean

[30] Tomenius, O'Keefe & Williams, *supra* note 18, at 264.

Expeditions ("DOE"), a British Virgin Islands corporation, as well as others from:

> (i) interfering with the rights of [RMST], as salvor in possession of the wreck and wreck site of the *R.M.S. Titanic*, to exclusively exploit the wreck and wreck site, (ii) conducting search, survey, or salvage operations of the wreck or wreck site, (iii) obtaining any image, video, or photograph of the wreck or wreck site, and (iv) entering or causing anyone or anything to enter the wreck or wreck site with the intention of performing any of the foregoing enjoined acts.

Id. at 640. . . . DOE had planned an expedition to view and to photograph the *Titanic* for the late summer of 1998, and Haver had planned to be a passenger.

DOE, never a party to the proceedings in the district court, and Haver, who filed a declaratory judgment action in the district court to challenge the court's jurisdiction over the wreck and over him, appealed to this court to challenge the June 1998 injunction. They claim (1) that the district court lacked jurisdiction over the wreck and wreck site, (2) that the court lacked personal jurisdiction over them, and (3) that the scope of the injunction is too broad. As they summarize their position,

> No theory of "constructive *in rem* jurisdiction" permits a court to adjudicate the rights of persons over which it lacks personal jurisdiction with respect to a vessel [in international waters] that has never been within the court's territory. Nor does any such theory authorize an injunction prohibiting persons from viewing and photographing a wreck when the salvor is not actively conducting salvage operations.

For the reasons that follow, we affirm in part and reverse in part the injunctions and remand the case to the district court with instructions to modify them in accordance with this opinion.

I

A procedural history, while somewhat involved, is nonetheless necessary for an understanding of the jurisdictional discussions that follow.

In 1985, a joint American-French expedition discovered the wreck of the *Titanic*. Two years later, in the summer of 1987, Titanic Ventures, a Connecticut limited partnership, in conjunction with the Institute of France for the Research and Exploration of the Sea, the French government's oceanographic institution, voluntarily undertook efforts to salvage the wreck. Titanic Ventures conducted 32 dives over 60 days, recovering approximately 1,800 artifacts. It thereafter sold both its interest in the salvage operation and the artifacts it recovered to RMST. RMST recovered another 800 artifacts during a second expedition to the *Titanic*'s wreck site in 1993.

In August 1993, RMST filed this action in the Eastern District of Virginia, requesting, among other things, that the district court exercise *in rem* jurisdiction over the *Titanic* to award it exclusive salvage rights. In support of its request, RMST presented the court with a wine decanter salvaged from the *Titanic* and stated that numerous other artifacts were physically within the Eastern District of Virginia. The court issued a warrant directing the United States Marshal to arrest the wreck and all artifacts already salvaged and yet to be salvaged from the wreck and, at the same time, ordered that RMST be substituted for the Marshal as custodian of the wreck, the wreck site, and the artifacts. Formal notice of the court's order appeared in three newspapers, *The Virginian-Pilot*, *The Wall Street Journal*, and *The Journal of Commerce*.

Only one party, Liverpool and London Steamship Protection and Indemnity Association ("Liverpool & London"), filed a claim asserting an interest in the wreck. After RMST and Liverpool & London entered into a settlement agreement, the district court dismissed Liverpool & London's claim on June 7, 1994. On the same day, the court entered a separate order granting RMST not only exclusive salvage rights over the wreck and the wreck site of the *Titanic*, but also "true, sole and exclusive owner[ship] of any items salvaged from the wreck."

In 1996, a competing salvor, John A. Joslyn, filed a motion in the action under Federal Rule of Civil Procedure 60(b), challenging RMST's status as exclusive salvor of the *Titanic* and requesting that the court rescind its June 1994 order. Joslyn claimed not only that RMST had failed diligently to salvage the *Titanic*, but also that RMST lacked the financial capacity to undertake future salvage operations. Following a hearing, the district court denied Joslyn's motion, finding that RMST had successfully undertaken a number of salvage operations and that its favorable prospects for ongoing and future salvage demonstrated that RMST deserved to remain the exclusive salvor-in-possession. *See Titanic I*, 924 F. Supp. at 722–24.

When Joslyn, nonetheless, expressed an intention to visit the wreck site for the sole purpose of taking photographs, the district court issued a temporary restraining order to prevent him from doing so. The court reasoned that "the need for R.M.S. Titanic, Inc. to have jurisdiction over the wreck site" brought with it a power to determine "who could enter the site for any purpose and who could photograph the ship and the locale." The district court converted the temporary restraining order to a preliminary injunction, dated August 13, 1996, enjoining Joslyn as well as "[a]ny other person having notice of this Order, actual or otherwise," from:

> conducting search, survey, or salvage operations, or obtaining any image, photographing or recovering any objects, entering, or causing to enter, anything on or below the surface of the Atlantic Ocean, otherwise interfering with operations conducted by plaintiff, or entering the wreck site for any purpose not approved by R.M.S. Titanic, Inc., within a ten (10) mile radius of [specific] coordinates....

In entering the injunction, the court reasoned that "allowing another 'salvor' to take photographs of the wreck and wreck site is akin to allowing another salvor to physically invade the wreck and take artifacts themselves."

In the spring of 1998, Deep Ocean Expeditions ("DOE"), a British Virgin Islands corporation headquartered on the Isle of Man, Great Britain, began marketing an expedition dubbed "Operation Titanic," planned for August 1998, that would allow members of the public to visit the wreck of the *Titanic.* The expedition was to be conducted with the assistance of the P. P. Shirshov Institute of Oceanology of the Russian Academy of Sciences in Moscow, using its research ship, the *R/V Akademik Keldysh,* and one of its two deep-sea submersibles, *Mir 1* or *Mir 2.* The Russian submersibles had conducted numerous earlier dives to the *Titanic.* DOE announced the cost of participating at $32,500 per person. One of the subscribers was Christopher S. Haver, an Arizona resident.

When RMST learned that DOE's "Operation Titanic" would result in persons' viewing and photographing the *Titanic* wreck, RMST filed another motion for a preliminary injunction in this action to prevent DOE, among others, from visiting and photographing the wrecksite. At the same time, Haver filed a separate action against RMST seeking a declaratory judgment that he had a right to enter the wreck site to observe, video, and photograph the *Titanic.* RMST filed a counterclaim in Haver's action, requesting a preliminary injunction to prohibit him from visiting the site. The district court consolidated Haver's action with the ongoing *in rem* action and conducted a hearing in the consolidated action on May 27, 1998. While Haver thus appeared by filing his own action to challenge the district court's jurisdiction over the wreck and the wreck site of the *Titanic,* as well as the court's personal jurisdiction over him, DOE did not appear, having not been served with any process.

Following the hearing, the district court disposed of all the issues before it in an order dated June 23, 1998. On the challenge to its exercise of *in rem* jurisdiction over the *Titanic,* the district court observed that while "[i]t is undisputed that the wreck lies in international waters . . . and no state may exercise sovereignty over any part of the high seas, . . . these rules must be harmonized with the internationally recognized rules of salvage." *Titanic II,* 9 F. Supp. 2d at 634. Observing that "internationally recognized principles governing salvage on the high seas encourage the exercise of *in rem* jurisdiction over a wreck site to facilitate the salvage operation itself," the court affirmed its exercise of "constructive *in rem* jurisdiction over the *R.M.S. Titanic* wreck site to facilitate RMST's salvage operations . . . under international law." *Id.* In reaching this conclusion, the court explained:

> It is in the interest of the whole world to have salvage claims decided in a single forum so that multiple, conflicting litigation is avoided. The whole world is placed on notice of the action in this Court by the publication of notice of the *in rem* arrest. Moreover, the recognized

> international rights at stake are minimally infringed upon. Restricting freedom of navigation over a few square miles of the vast North Atlantic Ocean is hardly a significant intrusion.

Id. at 634–35.

The district court also rejected Haver's claims that the court did not have personal jurisdiction over him and that a new complaint for a preliminary injunction needed to be filed and served on him. The court noted that Haver consented to the court's jurisdiction by filing a declaratory judgment action raising the same issues affirmatively asserted by RMST. *See id.* at 635.

The district court then addressed the merits of the question of whether RMST, as salvor-in-possession, had the right to exclude others from visiting the wreck site to photograph the wreck. In justifying the entry of the injunction, the court relied upon general safety concerns caused by the depth and darkness of the North Atlantic waters around the wreck site, the need to protect RMST's substantial investment to date in salvaging the *Titanic*, and the public's interest in preventing unorganized, piecemeal salvaging of the *Titanic*, a shipwreck of great historical significance. *See id.* at 635–36. The court also observed that those enjoined by its order from personally viewing the *Titanic* could enjoy future television broadcasts of RMST's salvage efforts. *See id.* at 638. Accordingly, the court enjoined not only DOE and Haver, but also "anyone else having notice" from obtaining any image, video or photograph of the wreck or the wreck site and from "entering or causing anyone or anything to enter the wreck or the wreck site with the intention of performing any of the foregoing enjoined acts." *Id.* at 640. The court defined the wreck site as encompassing a 168 square mile area of the North Atlantic surrounding the wreck of the *Titanic. See id.* The injunction, by its terms, was to remain in effect "[u]ntil further order of this Court." *Id.*

From the district court's June 23, 1998 order, Haver filed this appeal. While DOE was not made a party to the litigation below, it too appealed because the injunction entered by the district court was specifically directed against it. [The court then determined that the case was justiciable as a live controversy. The court further determined that it had constructive *in rem* jurisdiction over the *Titanic*, based on objects that had been salvaged from the wreck and brought into the judicial district. The court determined that it had personal jurisdiction over Haver but not DOE.]

. . .

V

Because the district court had personal jurisdiction over Haver, we must address his claim that the district court could not have exercised jurisdiction over the wreck and the wreck site of the *Titanic* because the wreck lay in international waters. Haver maintains that while the presentation of a wine decanter and other artifacts from the wreck to the district court in the Eastern District of Virginia might have enabled the district court to exercise *in rem* jurisdiction over those artifacts, there exists no principle that authorized the district court to exercise *in rem* jurisdiction over the wreck itself which is beyond the territorial waters of the United States. Without *in rem* jurisdiction, Haver argues, the district court had no power to adjudicate salvage rights and therefore had no power to enter an injunction giving effect to salvage rights.

Any analysis regarding the authority of a United States court to adjudicate salvage rights in shipwrecks in international waters requires inquiry first into several fundamental principles of admiralty: (1) the nature and scope of admiralty jurisdiction, (2) the applicability of salvage law as part of the common law of maritime nations, i.e., the *jus gentium*, and (3) the reach of an admiralty court's *in rem* jurisdiction. Only after we have explicated these principles can we address the existence and scope of authority of a United States court over the *Titanic*.

A

Article III of the Constitution extends the judicial power of federal courts to "all Cases of admiralty and maritime Jurisdiction." U.S. Const. art. III, § 2, cl. 1. And Congress implemented Article III by conferring on district courts exclusive, original jurisdiction of "[a]ny civil case of admiralty or maritime jurisdiction" and "[a]ny prize brought into the United States and all proceedings for the condemnation of property taken as prize." 28 U.S.C. § 1333. Maritime law was placed under national control "because of its intimate relation to navigation and to interstate and foreign commerce." *Panama R.R. Co. v. Johnson*, 264 U.S. 375, 386, 44 S. Ct. 391, 68 L. Ed. 748 (1924).

The body of admiralty law referred to in Article III did not depend on any express or implied legislative action. Its existence, rather, preceded the adoption of the Constitution. It was the well-known and well-developed "venerable law of the sea" which arose from the custom among "seafaring men," *see United States v. W.M. Webb, Inc.*, 397 U.S. 179, 191, 90 S. Ct. 850, 25 L. Ed. 2d 207 (1970), and which enjoyed "international comity," *see The Belgenland*, 114 U.S. 355, 363, 5 S. Ct. 860, 29 L. Ed. 152 (1885). Nations have applied this body of maritime law for 3,000 years or more. Although it would add little to recount the full history here, we note that codifications of the maritime law have been preserved from ancient Rhodes (900 B.C.E.), Rome (Justinian's *Corpus Juris Civilis*) (533 C.E.), City of Trani (Italy) (1063), England (the Law of Oleron) (1189), the Hanse Towns or Hanseatic League (1597), and France (1681), all articulating similar principles. And they all constitute a part of the continuing maritime tradition of the law of nations – the *jus gentium*.

The framers drafted Article III with this full body of maritime law clearly in view. This is not to say that the Constitution recognized an overarching maritime law that was to bind United States courts. On the contrary, the Constitution conferred admiralty subject matter jurisdiction on federal courts and, by implication, authorized the federal courts to draw upon and to continue the development of the substantive, common law of admiralty when exercising admiralty jurisdiction. *See The Lottawanna*, 21 Wall. 558, 88 U.S. 558, 572–78, 22 L. Ed. 654 (1874); *see also* 1 *Benedict on Admiralty* § 105, at 7–11 (7th ed. 1998). As Chief Justice Marshall observed:

> A case in admiralty does not, in fact, arise under the Constitution or laws of the United States. These cases are as old as navigation itself; and the law, admiralty and maritime, as it has existed for ages, is applied by our Courts to the cases as they arise.

The American Ins. Co. v. 356 Bales of Cotton, 26 U.S. (1 Pet.) 511, 544–45, 7 L. Ed. 242 (1828).

Since the Founding, federal courts sitting in admiralty jurisdiction have steadfastly continued to acquiesce in this *jus gentium* governing maritime affairs. Indeed, the Supreme Court has time and again admonished that "courts of this and other commercial nations have generally deferred to a non-national or international maritime law of impressive maturity and universality." *Lauritzen v. Larsen*, 345 U.S. 571, 581, 73 S. Ct. 921, 97 L. Ed. 1254 (1953); *see also United States v. W.M. Webb, Inc.*, 397 U.S. at 191, 90 S. Ct. 850 (1970) (observing that the "[m]aritime law . . . provides an established network of rules and distinctions that are practically suited to the necessities of the sea"). This body of maritime law "has the force of law, not from extraterritorial reach of national laws, nor from abdication of its sovereign powers by any nation, but from acceptance by common consent of civilized communities of rules designed to foster amicable and workable commercial relations." *Larsen*, 345 U.S. at 581–82, 73 S. Ct. 921. Thus, when we say today that a case in admiralty is governed by the general maritime law, we speak through our own national sovereignty and thereby recognize and acquiesce in the time-honored principles of the common law of the seas. *See Ex Parte Western Maid*, 257 U.S. 419, 432, 42 S. Ct. 159, 66 L. Ed. 299 (1922).

The exercise of admiralty subject matter jurisdiction has never been limited to maritime causes arising solely in the United States territorial waters. On the contrary, maritime causes arising from matters on the high seas anywhere in the world have traditionally been brought to courts of admiralty, subject only to a discretionary exercise of the doctrine of *forum non conveniens*. *See Offshore Logistics, Inc. v. Tallentire*, 477 U.S. 207, 218–19, 106 S. Ct. 2485, 91 L. Ed. 2d 174 (1986); *see also Mason v. Ship Blaireau*, 6 U.S. (2 Cranch) 240, 2 L. Ed. 266 (1804); *The Belgenland*, 114 U.S. at 362–63, 5 S. Ct. 860 (*in rem* admiralty jurisdiction proper in action arising out of collision on the high seas between two foreign vessels); *Treasure Salvors, Inc. v. The Unidentified Wrecked & Abandoned Sailing Vessel*, 640 F.2d 560, 567 (5th Cir. 1981) ("Since the admiralty jurisdiction of United States courts is not limited by the nationality of ships, sailors or seas involved and since the principles of the law of salvage are part of the *jus gentium*, i.e., the international maritime law, United States courts have long adjudicated salvage claims involving foreign vessels, alien salvors and salvage operations occurring on the high seas"); Grant Gilmore & Charles Black Jr., *The Law of Admiralty* § 1–19, at 51–52 (2d ed. 1975) (stating that "[t]he courts of the United States take jurisdiction, subject to some reservations imposed by their own application of the doctrine of *forum non conveniens*, of suits on maritime claims arising out of transactions and occurrences anywhere in the world" (footnotes omitted)).

Even though admiralty courts may adjudicate matters arising on navigable waters anywhere in the world, that recognition of subject matter jurisdiction does not imply that American courts in admiralty have the power to command that any person or any ship appear before a United States court sitting in admiralty. Stated differently, Article III of the Constitution and 28 U.S.C. § 1333 do not amount to an attempt by the United States to extend its sovereignty over persons (*in personam*) or things (*in rem*) beyond the territorial limits of the United States. While we note this important distinction between a broad subject matter jurisdiction and the limitation imposed by territorial jurisdiction, we discuss the territorial limitation in more detail, below.

B

The general maritime law of nations includes a law of finds and a law of salvage, and courts of admiralty apply one to the exclusion of the other, as appropriate, to resolve claims in property discovered and recovered in navigable waters by those other than the property's owners or those taking through them. *See Columbus-America Discovery Group v. Atlantic Mut. Ins. Co.*, 974 F.2d 450, 459–60 (4th Cir. 1992). Under the law of finds, a person who discovers a shipwreck in navigable waters that has been long lost and abandoned and who reduces the property to actual or constructive possession, becomes the property's owner. *See Martha's Vineyard Scuba Headquarters, Inc. v. The Unidentified, Wrecked and Abandoned Steam Vessel*, 833 F.2d 1059, 1065 (1st Cir. 1987); *Hener v. United States*, 525 F. Supp. 350, 354–57 (S.D.N.Y. 1981) (cited and quoted with approval in *Columbus-America Discovery*, 974 F.2d at 460).

Because the law of finds deprives the true owner of a property right, the courts of admiralty disfavor its application and prefer to apply the law of salvage in its stead. They have reasoned that the law of salvage better serves the needs of maritime commerce by encouraging the saving of property for the benefit of its owner rather than the secretive discovery of property in an effort to deprive the owner of title. *See Columbus-America Discovery*, 974 F.2d at 464; *Hener*, 525 F. Supp. at 354 ("salvage law assumes that the property being salved is owned by another, and thus that it has not been abandoned"). Accordingly, the law of finds is most often applied in the context of long-lost shipwrecks. *See, e.g., Treasure Salvors, Inc. v. The Unidentified Wrecked & Abandoned Sailing Vessel*, 569 F.2d 330, 337 (5th Cir. 1978) (applying the law of finds to the recovery of a Spanish vessel which sunk near the Florida Keys in 1622, stating that "disposition of a wrecked vessel whose very location has been lost for centuries as though its owner were still in existence stretches the fiction to absurd lengths"); *see also* 3A *Benedict on Admiralty* § 158, at 11–17 (7th ed. Supp. 1991) (recommending "limit[ing] the doctrine of 'find' relative to marine disasters to long-lost wrecks . . . or where the owners of maritime properties have publicly abandoned them" (footnote omitted)). Neither the parties nor the district court has urged the application of the law of finds in this case, leaving for application the law of salvage.

The principles of salvage law are intended to encourage persons to render prompt, voluntary, and effective service to ships at peril or in distress by assuring them compensation and reward for their salvage efforts. *See The Akaba*, 54 F. 197, 200 (4th Cir. 1893). Absent the promise of compensation and reward, we question whether a party, even one with the capacity to save the *Titanic* itself, would incur the costs to do so. *See M/V JA Orgeron*, 143 F.3d at 986 n. 12 (observing that "if the costs of performing a salvage are too high or the benefits to be derived are too low, the parties might well agree to call it a day and let the sea claim its prize"); *see also* William M. Landes & Richard A. Posner, *Salvors, Finders, Good Samaritans, and Other Rescuers: An Economic Study of Law and Altruism*, 7 J. Leg. Stud. 83, 100 (1978) (arguing that the law of salvage exists to "encourage rescues in settings of high transaction costs by simulating the conditions and outcomes of a competitive market").

The policies of salvage law have existed as an important part of the general maritime law of nations as long as there has been navigation. *See M/V JA Orgeron*, 143 F.3d at 985 ("This simple rule has been an integral part of maritime commerce in the western world since the western world was civilized"). Indeed, the 3,000-year old Rhodian Code provided:

> Article XLV. "If a ship be surprised at sea with whirlwinds, or be shipwrecked, any person saving anything of the wreck, shall have one-fifth of what he saves."

Reprinted in 3A *Benedict on Admiralty* § 5, at 1–8.

And as to salvage from shipwrecks, the Rhodian Code provided:

> Article XLVII. "If gold, or silver, or any other thing be drawn up out of the sea eight cubits deep, he that draws it up shall have one-third, and if fifteen cubits, he shall have one-half, because of the depth."

Id.

The Code also provided that those illegally pillaging a wreck would be required to restore fourfold. *See id.* The same principles of salvage were included in the Law of Oleron, codified about 2,000 years after the Rhodian Law and adopted in England in the 12th century. *See id.* § 8, at 1–11. And they continue to apply as part of the *jus gentium* today. *See, e.g., International Convention on Salvage, April 29, 1989*, preamble (providing that international salvage law should "ensure that adequate incentives are available to persons who undertake salvage operations in respect of vessels and other property in danger"); *see also United Nations Convention on the Law of the Sea*, Dec. 10, 1982, 21 I.L.M. 1245, 1326 art. 303 (providing that the Convention respects "the rights of identifiable owners, the law of salvage or other rules of admiralty").[31]

When providing salvage service, a salvor acts on behalf of the owner in saving the owner's property even though the owner may have made no such request or had no knowledge of the need. The law of salvage presumes that the owner desires the salvage service. And it is the assurance of compensation and reward that provides the "inducement to seamen and others to embark in such undertakings to save life and property." *The Blackwall*, 10 Wall. 1, 77 U.S. 1, 14, 19 L. Ed. 870 (1869) (citation omitted). As the Court in *Blackwall* explained, "Public policy encourages the hardy and adventurous mariner to engage in these laborious and sometimes dangerous enterprises, and with a view to withdraw from him every temptation to embezzlement and dishonesty, the law allows him, in case he is successful, a liberal compensation." *Id.* (footnote omitted). If the salvor fails in his salvage efforts, however, he can claim no compensation or reward.

To establish a salvage claim for compensation and award, a person must demonstrate (1) that he has rendered aid to a distressed ship or its cargo in navigable waters; (2) that the service was voluntarily rendered without any preexisting obligation arising from contract or otherwise to the distressed ship or property; and (3) that the service was useful by effecting salvage of the ship or its cargo, in whole or in part. *See The Sabine*, 101 U.S. 384, 384, 25 L. Ed. 982 (1879); *Brown v. Johansen*, 881 F.2d 107, 109 (4th Cir. 1989).

Upon rendering salvage service, a salvor obtains a lien in the saved property by operation of law to secure payment of compensation and award due from the property owner. *See The Sabine*, 101 U.S. at 386; *see also Amstar Corp. v. S/S Alexandros T.*, 664 F.2d 904, 909 (4th Cir. 1981). This lien attaches to the property to the exclusion of all others, including the property's true owner. And to facilitate enforcement of the lien, the salvor enjoys a possessory interest in the property until the salvor is compensated. *See S/S Alexandros T.*, 664 F.2d at 908–09. Because the salvor's lien is exclusive and prior to all others, so too, the salvor's possessory interest in the *res* is enjoyed to the exclusion of all others, including the *res*' [s] true owner.

By rendering salvage service, the salvor thus acquires a limited property interest in the goods saved – a first lien and exclusive possession – until the salvor has been paid or his right against the property has been enforced. *See The Emblem*, 8 F. Cas. 611, 614 (D. Me. 1840); 3A *Benedict on Admiralty* § 143, at 10–8 (quoting *The Emblem*). While this interest attaches only to saved property, to protect a salvor's general salvage rights, a court of admiralty will protect the inchoate right of salvors in yet-to-be salved property for a reasonable period. *See Treasure Salvors, Inc. v. The Unidentified Wrecked and Abandoned Sailing Vessel*, 546 F. Supp. 919, 929 (S.D. Fla. 1981).

[31] Although the United States signed the UN Convention in 1994, the Senate has not yet provided the necessary advice and consent for ratification.

Although a salvor may enforce its claim for salvage service by filing an *in personam* action against the owner, the salvor may also execute on the lien which attached to the ship and its cargo by filing an *in rem* action. The lien can be enforced only through the institution of an *in rem* action, and the admiralty court exercises *in rem* jurisdiction only to enforce a maritime lien. Thus, "[t]he lien and the proceeding *in rem* are . . . correlative – where one exists, the other can be taken, and not otherwise." *S/S Alexandros*, 664 F.2d at 909 (internal quotation marks omitted); *see also* Fed. R. Civ. P. Supp. R. C(1). To execute on the lien, the court may order the sale of the property, or, if a sale would yield an amount insufficient to fund an award to the salvor, the court may transfer title to the property to the salvor.

While the law of salvage provides substantial protection to salvors to encourage their saving of life and property at sea, it also imposes duties of good faith, honesty, and diligence in protecting the property in salvors' care. Thus, salvors have to exercise a trust over the property for the benefit of the owner and subject to any orders of a court. *See Cromwell v. The Bark Island City*, 66 U.S. (1 Black) 121, 17 L. Ed. 70 (1861). In this vein, salvors are not entitled to remove property from the wreck for their own use or to use the property for their own use. When a violation of this trust occurs, the salvage claim is forfeited. *See Danner v. United States*, 99 F. Supp. 880 (S.D.N.Y. 1951). Indeed, it has been held that even when salvors have mistakenly misunderstood their rights and have taken property for their own use, they forfeited their right to a salvage award. *See, e.g., id.*; *see also The Mabel*, 61 F.2d 537, 540 (9th Cir. 1932).

C

An *in rem* action, which is the most common process for enforcing a claim for salvage service, depends on the court's having jurisdiction over the *res*, the property which is named as defendant. *See Pennoyer*, 95 U.S. at 724. Only if the court has exclusive custody and control over the property does it have jurisdiction over the property so as to be able to adjudicate rights in it that are binding against the world. *See Darlak v. Columbus-America Discovery Group, Inc.*, 59 F.3d 20, 22–23 (4th Cir. 1995). Accordingly, to exercise *in rem* jurisdiction over a ship or its cargo, the ship or cargo must be within the district in which the *in rem* complaint is filed. *See The Brig Ann*, 13 U.S. (9 Cranch) 289, 291 3 L. Ed. 734 (1815); *see also Platoro Ltd., Inc. v. The Unidentified Remains of a Vessel*, 695 F.2d 893 (5th Cir. 1983); *see also* Fed. R. Civ. P. Supp. R. E(3) (providing that process *in rem* may only be served within the district).

While the *res* must be *in custodia legis* (in the court's possession), this possession may be actual or constructive. *See The Brig Ann*, 13 U.S. at 291. Constructive possession connotes something less than physical seizure of a *res* by a court. Just last term, for instance, the Supreme Court implicitly recognized the propriety of a district court's exercise of *in rem* admiralty jurisdiction over a shipwreck in California's territorial waters after a salvor presented "china, a full bottle of champagne, and a brass spike from the ship's hull" to the district court. *See California v. Deep Sea Research*, 523

U.S. 491, 118 S. Ct. 1464, 1467, 149 L. Ed. 2d 626 (1998). The propriety of exercising *in rem* jurisdiction over an entire shipwreck within the court's territorial jurisdiction when only part of that wreck is actually presented to a court rests upon the fiction that the *res* is not divided and that therefore possession of some of it is constructively possession of all. *See id.* at 1473.

But when the *res* is not in the court's actual or constructive possession, traditional principles of *in rem* jurisdiction dictate that the court may not adjudicate rights to the *res* and effectively bind others who may have possession. *See Pennoyer*, 95 U.S. at 724; *see also* Fed. R. Civ. P. Supp. R. E(3). Consequently, a court could not exercise *in rem* jurisdiction, as traditionally understood, so as to vest rights in property outside of its territory, such as in a shipwreck lying in international waters. This conclusion is compelled by a recognition of the sovereign limits of the United States and the open nature of the high seas.

The sovereign limits of a nation are defined by those territorial boundaries within which it exercises supreme and exclusive power. Where a nation has boundaries contiguous to the high seas, international law defines the nation's sovereign limits by dividing navigable waters generally into three categories "distinguished by the nature of the control which the contiguous nation can exercise over them." *United States v. Louisiana*, 394 U.S. 11, 22, 89 S. Ct. 773, 22 L. Ed. 2d 44 (1969) (footnote omitted).

Navigable waters that lie inland of a nation's borders are within the nation's complete control as with any real property within its borders. *See id.*; *see also Schooner Exchange v. McFaddon*, 11 U.S. (7 Cranch) 116, 136, 3 L. Ed. 287 (1812) (Marshall, C.J.) (stating that the "jurisdiction of the nation within its own territory is necessarily exclusive and absolute"). Likewise within the general sovereign sphere of a nation are its territorial waters, defined as those navigable waters lying up to 12 nautical miles beyond a nation's shoreline. *See United States v. California*, 332 U.S. 19, 35, 67 S. Ct. 1658, 91 L. Ed. 1889 (1947) (stating that the extension of our territorial jurisdiction "is but a recognition of the necessity that a government next to the sea must be able to protect itself from dangers incident to its location"). And beyond the territorial waters lie the high seas, over which no nation can exercise sovereignty. *See Louisiana*, 394 U.S. at 23, 89 S. Ct. 773; *see also United States v. Louisiana*, 363 U.S. 1, 33–34, 80 S. Ct. 961, 4 L. Ed. 2d 1025 (1960) (stating that the "high seas, as distinguished from inland waters, are generally conceded by modern nations to be subject to the exclusive sovereignty of no single nation"); *California*, 332 U.S. at 34, 67 S. Ct. 1658 (stating that the United States, "throughout its existence has stood for freedom of the seas, a principle whose breach has precipitated wars among nations"); *The Vinces*, 20 F.2d 164, 172 (E.D.S.C. 1927) (stating that the high seas "are the common property of all nations"). The mutual access to the high seas is firmly etched into the *jus gentium*. *See, e.g., United Nations Convention on the Law of the Sea*, Dec. 10, 1982, 21 I.L.M. 1245, 1286–87 arts. 87, 89 (providing that the high seas shall be open to all nations and that "no State may validly purport to subject any part of the high seas to its sovereignty").[32]

Any extension of jurisdiction into the high seas by a nation must be "subject to the consent of other nations." *See Louisiana*, 363 U.S. at 34, 80 S. Ct. 961; *see also California*, 332 U.S. at 35, 67 S. Ct. 1658 (stating that "whatever any nation does in the open sea, which detracts from its common usefulness to nations, or which another nation may charge detracts from it, is a question for consideration among nations as such, and not their separate governmental units" (footnote omitted)). We do, however, acknowledge that the law of nations sanctions limited extraterritorial exercises of jurisdiction. *See, e.g., Louisiana*, 363 U.S. at 34 n. 60, 80 S. Ct. 961 ("For example, the United States has long claimed the right to exercise jurisdiction over domestic and foreign vessels beyond the three-mile limit for purposes of customs control and for defense purposes and this practice is recognized by international law" (citations omitted)); *Hudson & Smith v. Guestier*, 10 U.S. (6 Cranch) 281, 284, 3 L. Ed. 224 (1810) (recognizing that a seizure of property on the high seas, beyond the territorial limits of all nations, for breach of a municipal revenue raising regulation is warranted by the *jus gentium*).

In sum, because the exercise of *in rem* jurisdiction depends on the court's exercise of exclusive custody and control over the *res*, the limits of *in rem* jurisdiction, as traditionally understood, are defined by the effective limits of sovereignty itself.

VI

In applying these principles to a wreck lying in international waters, obvious complexities emerge. *In rem* jurisdiction, which depends on sovereignty over property, cannot be given effect to property beyond a nation's boundaries of sovereignty. *See Pennoyer*, 95 U.S. at 722 (stating "that every State possesses exclusive jurisdiction and sovereignty over persons and property within its territory"). Where both persons and property are beyond a nation's zone of exclusive legal power, its ability to adjudicate rights as to them is limited, but not meaningless.

When nations agree on law to apply on the high seas, they agree to an order even beyond their sovereign boundaries which, while they hope will be honored on the high seas, can only be enforced completely and effectively when the people or property are brought within a nation's zone of power – its sovereignty.

[32] Under the 1982 UN Convention, an exclusive economic zone is recognized, beginning at the outer limit of the territorial waters and extending to two hundred nautical miles from the nation's shoreline. In this economic zone, a nation may exercise exclusive control over economic matters involving fishing, the seabed, and the subsoil but not over navigation. *See* United Nations Convention on the Law of the Sea, Dec. 10, 1982, 21 I.L.M. 1245, 1280, arts. 56(1), 57. Even though the United States has not yet ratified this treaty, *see supra* note 2, it generally recognizes this two-hundred-mile economic zone. *See* SCHOENBAUM,*supra* note 16,§ 2–16, at 35 (collecting legislation enacted by Congress in accordance with the Law of the Sea Convention).

So it must be with the *Titanic*. The *jus gentium*, the law of all maritime nations, is easy to define and declare. But its enforcement must depend on persons or property involved in such a declaration coming into the zone of power of participating nations. We now turn to observe how these intersecting principles operate in this case.

A

First, Haver presents us with no reason to upset the district court's findings that RMST (and its predecessors) represented the first party successfully to salvage the wreck of the *Titanic* and that RMST has continued and plans to continue its substantial efforts. As the district court recognized, salvaging the wreck of the *Titanic* has presented a challenge of unprecedented proportion. Because the wreck lies under 2.5 miles of water, where there is virtually no light, the water is frigid, and the water pressure beyond general comprehension, only the most sophisticated oceanographic equipment can explore the site and recover property. Doing so is time consuming, expensive, and dangerous.

Since 1993, RMST has overcome these challenges, conducting research and recovery expeditions in June 1993, July 1994, and August 1996. From these expeditions, it has been able to recover over 3,600 artifacts from the wreck and to gather thousands of photographs and hundreds of hours of video footage. As the district court observed, "RMST has exhibited considerable zeal as salvor in possession despite the fact that salvaging the wreck is extremely time consuming, dangerous, and expensive." *Titanic II*, 9 F. Supp. 2d at 627.

As the first successful salvor, RMST obtained an inchoate lien as a matter of law in the wreck as well as the artifacts from the wreck to enforce its claim for compensation and reward. And with its lien, RMST obtained the right to exclusive possession, not only of the artifacts removed from the wreck of the *Titanic*, but also of the wreck itself, so that no other person is entitled lawfully to intrude as long as salvage operations continue. *See Treasure Salvors, Inc.*, 640 F.2d at 567.

Because RMST has necessarily acted on behalf of the owners of the property even if the owners did not or could not know of RMST's efforts, its interest in the property is limited to an exclusive possessory right, not for its own use, but for the purpose of bringing the property within the jurisdiction of a court in admiralty to enforce its maritime lien securing its claim for compensation and reward. But once the property is brought in *custodia legis*, the court can execute on RMST's lien and sell the property, or if the sale of the property would prove insufficient to compensate RMST fairly, the court can award title in the property to RMST.

These conclusions reached by the district court about RMST's rights are consistent with the salvage law which is part of the *jus gentium*, and we expect that whether RMST had returned property from the *Titanic* to an admiralty court in England or France or Canada, the court would, by applying the same principles, have reached the same conclusions. The need for courts of admiralty to apply the law similarly is fundamentally important to international commerce and to the policies supporting order on the high seas. It is therefore prudent for us, as one such court sitting in admiralty, to assure enforcement in harmony with these shared maritime principles. And to this end, we are satisfied that to the extent the district court applied these principles, it acted in accordance with the *jus gentium* in awarding RMST exclusive salvage rights in the wreck of the *Titanic.*

B

Although the district court applied principles of the *jus gentium* to award RMST exclusive salvage rights in the *Titanic*, the question peculiar to this case remains how, if at all, can a court in admiralty enforce these salvage rights with respect to property that does not lie within its jurisdiction, nor, for that matter, within the jurisdiction of any admiralty court.

RMST argues, somewhat boldly and apparently without any direct legal authority, that an admiralty court can simply assert *in rem* jurisdiction over wrecks lying in international waters, beyond the territorial limits of the court's jurisdiction, and enter orders to enforce that jurisdiction. But this fails to account for the limits of courts' jurisdiction and, indeed, the limits of national sovereignty.

In rem jurisdiction is traditionally justified by the presence of the *res* within the jurisdiction of the court. Having exclusive legal custody over the *res*, whether actual or constructive, enables the court to issue orders respecting the *res* that are exclusive as against the whole world. With *in rem* jurisdiction, therefore, a court has the power, among others, to order the seizure, the sale, or the transfer of the *res.* It follows that when the *res* is outside the jurisdiction of the court, indeed, beyond the territorial limits of the United States, the court cannot exercise *in rem* jurisdiction over it, at least in the traditional sense.

In this case, the district court recognized this limitation and rested its authority over the wreck of the *Titanic* on what it called "constructive *in rem*" jurisdiction. Obviously, any power exercised in international waters through "constructive *in rem*" jurisdiction could not be exclusive as to the whole world. For example, a French court could presumably have just as well issued a similar order at the same time with no less effect. But this nonexclusive control over the *res* would not defeat the district court's first purpose of declaring salvage rights to the wreck as against the world. In fact, we believe that the *jus gentium* authorizes an admiralty court to do so, even though the exclusiveness of any such order could legitimately be questioned by any other court in admiralty. The ultimate resolution could only occur at such time as property is removed from the wreck and brought within the jurisdiction of an admiralty court, giving it exclusive *in rem* jurisdiction over the property or when the persons involved in any dispute over the property are before the court *in personam.*

But this limitation on the jurisdiction exercised by the district court does not mean that its declaration with respect to the *res* was ineffective. We believe that the district court has a "constructive" – to use the district court'[s] term – *in rem* jurisdiction over the wreck of the *Titanic* by having a portion of it within its jurisdiction and that this constructive *in rem* jurisdiction continues as long as the salvage operation continues. We hasten to add that as we use the term "constructive," we mean an "imperfect" or "inchoate" *in rem* jurisdiction which falls short of giving the court sovereignty over the wreck. It represents rather a "shared sovereignty," shared with other nations enforcing the same *jus gentium*. Through this mechanism, internationally recognized rights may be legally declared but not finally enforced. Final enforcement requires the additional steps of bringing either property or persons involved before the district court or a court in admiralty of another nation.

Testing the effect of a United States court's attempt to assert exclusive jurisdictional power over property located beyond the territorial limits of the United States quickly brings a pragmatic response. When a nation seeks to exert sovereignty through exclusive judicial action in international waters, the effort prompts the obvious question of how the jurisdiction is to be enforced. But even beyond this pragmatic consideration lies the yet more significant consideration that asserting sovereignty through a claim of exclusive judicial action beyond the territorial limits of a nation would disrupt the relationship among nations that serves as the enforcement mechanism of international law and custom. What would occur if an English or French court were to exercise similar power? The necessary response to probes such as these leads to the now well-established norm of international law that no nation has sovereignty over the high seas. *See, e.g., United Nations Convention on the Law of the Sea*, Dec. 10, 1982, 21 I.L.M. 1245, 1287 art. 89 (providing that "no state may validly purport to subject any part of the high seas to its sovereignty").

This conclusion that no nation has sovereignty through the assertion of exclusive judicial action over international waters does not leave the high seas without enforceable law. The law of salvage as shared by the nations as part of the *jus gentium* applies to the high seas, and we are satisfied that it will do no violence to the relationship among nations to enforce these rights to the extent generally recognized on a non-exclusive basis. For this reason, we conclude that the district court was correct in declaring that RMST has salvage rights in the wreck of the *Titanic* and that these rights include the right exclusively to possess the wreck for purposes of enforcing the maritime lien that RMST obtained as a matter of law. It also follows that the district court acted properly in entering an injunction against persons over whom it had jurisdiction, prohibiting them from interfering with the salvage efforts being pursued by RMST. We believe that these aspects of the district court's declaration and injunction would be recognized by all maritime nations and similarly be enforced by their courts.[33]

[33] In reaching this conclusion, we reject Haver's argument that the R.M.S. Titanic Maritime Memorial Act of 1986, 16 U.S.C. § 450rr *et seq.*, precluded the district court from exercising jurisdiction over the wreck of the *Titanic*. That statute, while recognizing the "major national and international cultural and historical significance" of the *Titanic*, 16 U.S.C. § 450rr(a)(3), merely exists to encourage the United States (or more specifically, the president) to coordinate cooperative international efforts "for conducting research on, exploration of, and if appropriate, salvage of the R.M.S. Titanic." 16 U.S.C. § 450rr(b)(3). The statute

We also refuse to construe the language in § 450rr-6 of the statute – "By enactment of sections 450rr to 450rr-6 of this title, the United States does not assert sovereignty, or sovereign or exclusive rights or jurisdiction over, or the ownership of, any marine areas or the R.M.S. Titanic" – as stripping the federal courts of jurisdiction over the wreck for purposes of recognizing, consistent with the *jus gentium*, RMST as the wreck's exclusive salvor. Read in the context of the entire R.M.S. Titanic Memorial Act, we believe that language has no bearing in this appeal.

But we hasten to point out, again, that the power of an American court to enforce such orders is effectively limited until persons and property are brought within its territorial jurisdiction. These are limits that any court faces, regardless of the nation involved. Shared rights to the high seas may be exercised by all nations, and the assertion by any nation of exclusive sovereignty over a portion would interfere with those rights. This notion of "shared sovereignty" does not, however, preclude all nations from enforcing the internationally recognized laws of salvage in courts with respect to persons and property within their jurisdiction, nor even from exercising this form of shared sovereignty for matters on the high seas.

If we were to recognize an absolute limit to the district court's power that would preclude it, or essentially any other admiralty court, from exercising judicial power over wrecks in international waters, then we would be abdicating the order created by the *jus gentium* and would return the high seas to a state of lawlessness never experienced – at least as far as recorded history reveals. We refuse to abdicate in this manner.

VII

While we affirm the district court's order enjoining Haver from interfering with the ongoing salvage operations of RMST, we must still address the additional terms to which he objects: (1) whether salvage rights include the right to exclude others from visiting, observing, and photographing the wreck; and (2) whether, in enjoining others from interfering with the ongoing salvage operations, the district court could exclude others from an area within a 10-mile radius (the 314-square-mile circular area protected by its August 1996 order) or a 168-square-mile rectangular area (protected by its June 1998 order), both of which lie entirely within international waters.

The June 1998 injunction provided in pertinent part:

> Until further order of this Court, these parties [including Haver] are ENJOINED from (i) interfering with the rights of RMST, as salvor in possession of the wreck and wreck site of the R.M.S. TITANIC, to exclusively exploit the wreck and wreck site, (ii) conducting search, survey, or salvage operations of the wreck or wreck site, (iii) obtaining

also specifically expresses Congress's sense that "research and limited exploration activities concerning the R.M.S. Titanic should continue for the purpose of enhancing public knowledge of its scientific, cultural, and historical significance" pending the consummation of such international efforts. 16 U.S.C. § 450rr-5.

> any image, video, or photograph of the wreck or wreck site, and (iv) entering or causing anyone or anything to enter the wreck or wreck site with the intention of performing any of the foregoing enjoined acts.

Titanic II, 9 F. Supp. 2d at 640.

This injunction was a reiteration of the court's August 1996 injunction in which it, for the first time, explicitly prohibited others from photographing the wreck or wreck site of the *Titanic.* In entering the 1996 order, the court expanded traditional salvage rights to include the right to exclusive photographing of the wreck and the wreck site. The court explained:

> [I]f R.M.S. TITANIC is not selling artifacts like traditional salvors, it must be given the rights to other means of obtaining income. The court finds that in a case such as this, allowing another "salvor" to take photographs of the wreck and wreck site is akin to allowing another salvor to physically invade the wreck and take artifacts themselves.

The court pointed out that photographs could be marketed like any other physical artifact and therefore that the rights to record images of the *Titanic* belonged to RMST, the salvor in possession of the wreck.

The district court's expansion of salvage rights to include the right exclusively to photograph or otherwise record images of the wreck for the purpose of compensating salvors for their effort is both creative and novel. We are aware of no case in the United States or in the body of *jus gentium*, however, that has expanded salvage rights to include this type of a right. More importantly, we are not satisfied that the law of salvage would be properly extended to give salvors exclusive image recording rights in yet to be saved property. The underlying policy of salvage law is to encourage the voluntary assistance to ships and their cargo in distress. *See, e.g., The Sabine*, 101 U.S. 384; *Columbus-America*, 974 F.2d at 459; *The Akaba*, 54 F. at 200. And the salvage service is useful to owners only when it effects *a saving of the specific property* at risk. The law does not include the notion that the salvor can use the property being salvaged for a commercial use to compensate the salvor when the property saved might have inadequate value. Traditionally, the inducement for salvage service is limited to the court's award of compensation and reward, which may be enforced *in personam* against the owner without regard to the property saved, or *in rem* against the property saved.

To award, in the name of salvage service, the exclusive right to photograph a shipwreck, would, we believe, also tend to convert what was designed as a salvage operation on behalf of the owners into an operation serving the salvors. The incentives would run counter to the purpose of salvage. Salvors would be less inclined to save property because they might be able to obtain more compensation by leaving the property in place and selling photographic images or charging the public admission to go view it.

Even if we were to assume that the salvors had full title to the yet to be recovered shipwreck, as would be the case if the law of finds were applied, it is doubtful that such title to property lying in international waters would include the right to exclude others from viewing and photographing it while in its public site. Exclusive viewing and photographing of property is usually achieved by exercising exclusive possession and removing the property to a private or controllable location where it cannot be viewed or photographed except under conditions controlled by the owner. But a property right does not normally include the right to exclude viewing and photographing of the property when it is located in a public place.[34]

In addition, if we were now to recognize, as part of the salvage law, the right to exclude others from viewing and photographing a shipwreck in international waters, we might so alter the law of salvage as to risk its uniformity and international comity, putting at risk the benefits that all nations enjoy in a well-understood and consistently-applied body of law. This risk is heightened when it is understood that such an expansion of salvage rights might not encourage salvage and might, additionally, discourage free movement and navigation in international waters.

For these reasons, we conclude that the district court erred in extending the law of salvage to vest in RMST exclusive rights to visit, view, and photograph the wreck and wreck site of the *Titanic* at its location in international waters.

The district court's August 1996 injunction also prohibited anyone from entering within a 10-mile radius of the wreck site to search, survey, or obtain any image of the wreck or wreck site, and the court's June 1998 order prohibited anyone from entering, for a similar purpose, a rectangular area around the wreck site computed to be 168-square miles. Neither prohibition is justified by the law of salvage or allowed by the law of free navigation on the high seas. For the same reasons that we gave in denying exclusive viewing and photographing rights – that to do so would alarmingly expand salvage law and interfere with the right of free navigation – we also reverse these aspects of the district court's orders. This does not mean, however, that a court may not enforce salvage rights by prohibiting a party over whom it has personal jurisdiction from conducting salvage operations or interfering with the first salvor's exclusive possession of the wreck for purposes of salving it.

VIII

In summary, we conclude that this appeal presents us with a case or controversy as understood under Article III of the Constitution. We also consider DOE's appeal of the June 1998 injunction directed against it, even though DOE was not a party to the district court proceedings, and agree with DOE that the injunction against it is not enforceable because it was never made a party through proper service of process nor was it in privity with the party. We reject, however, Haver's personal jurisdictional challenge. With

[34] For instance, even under U.S. copyright law, where an architect has a copyright in the design of a building that right does not extend to prevent the viewing and photographing of the building if it is located at a public site or is visible from a public place. *See* 17 U.S.C. § 120(a).

respect to Haver's challenge to the injunctions themselves, we affirm in part and reverse in part. We affirm the district court's injunctions insofar as they enjoin parties and persons in privity with them from conducting salvage operations of the *Titanic* wreck and interfering with the salvage operations of RMST. We reverse them insofar as they purport to prohibit the visiting, viewing, searching, surveying, photographing, and obtaining images of the wreck or the wreck site, as long as these activities do not constitute any salvage effort or interfere with RMST's salvage rights.

Affirmed in part, reversed in part, and remanded.

NOTES AND QUESTIONS

1. The technology that has made marine archaeology possible only in recent decades relies increasingly on remotely operated vehicles (ROVs).

> Originally developed more than half a century ago by the U.S. Navy to locate weapons and ships lost in depths beyond the reach of scuba divers, increasingly more sophisticated ROVs are now commonly used by world navies and natural-resource industries for deep-water exploration and construction. The first glimpse of robots' enormous potential in marine archaeology came in 1989, when a team led by Robert Ballard and Anna Marguerite McCann used an ROV to successfully investigate and sample a late Roman wreck more than 2,000 feet deep near Skerki Bank, off the coast of Sicily. Since then, engineers and archaeologists have endeavored to advance from mere visual survey and random removal of artifacts with ROVs, to full-blown robotic excavations.
>
> There were two major problems to solve in excavating underwater sites with ROVs. First the robots, which generally operate independently underwater, attached only by a tether to the command vessel, are bulky and weigh hundreds or thousands of pounds; there is a risk that they may disturb or even destroy the very sites they are sent to investigate. Second, accurate and delicate maneuvering of an ROV (which relies on powerful thrusters to maintain a steady position) on an archaeological site has been a challenge. "This is why most deep-sea archaeological operations have been limited to documentation, sampling, and digging trial trenches. . . . "[35]

2. The court of appeals in *Haver* cited the UN Convention on the Law of the Sea (UNCLOS) to support its cosmopolitan pronouncements, even though the United States was not a party to the Convention. Toward the end of the eight-year process of negotiating and drafting the treaty, however, the United States proposed and successfully secured support for the two provisions that seek to protect the underwater cultural heritage, as follows:

United Nations Convention of the Law of the Sea, *done* Dec. 10, 1982, U.N. Doc. A/CONF. 62/122, 1833 U.N.T.S 3 [hereinafter UNCLOS].

[35] Marianne Alfsen, *Digging Deep: Revolutionary Technology Takes Archaeologists to New Depths*, ARCHAEOLOGY, May–June 2006, at 29.

Article 149

Archaeological and historical objects

All objects of an archaeological and historical nature found in the [seabed] Area shall be preserved or disposed of for the benefit of mankind as a whole, particular regard being paid to the preferential rights of the State or country of origin, or the State of cultural origin, or the State of historical and archaeological origin. . . .

Article 303

Archaeological and historical objects found at sea

1. States have the duty to protect objects of an archaeological and historical nature found at sea and shall co-operate for this purpose.

2. In order to control traffic in such objects, the coastal State may, in applying article 33, presume that their removal from the sea-bed in the zone referred to in that article without its approval would result in an infringement within its territory or territorial sea of the laws and regulations referred to in that article.

3. Nothing in this article affects the rights of identifiable owners, the law of salvage or other rules of admiralty, or laws and practices with respect to cultural exchanges.

4. This article is without prejudice to other international agreements and rules of international law regarding the protection of objects of an archaeological and historical nature.

Article 303(2) makes reference to article 33 in the Convention, which reads as follows:

Article 33

Contiguous Zone

(1) In a zone contiguous to its territorial sea, described as the contiguous zone, the coastal State may exercise the control necessary to:

(a) prevent infringement of its customs, fiscal, immigration or sanitary laws and regulations within its territory or territorial sea;

(b) punish infringement of the above laws and regulations committed within its territory or territorial sea.

(2) The contiguous zone may not extend beyond 24 nautical miles from the baselines from which the breadth of the territorial sea is measured.

3. Articles 149 and 303, in association with Article 33, provide a foundation for a multilateral regime to govern the underwater heritage, but the provisions are jurisdictionally limited and provide no detailed regulatory guidance. Their limited jurisdictional scope is best understood within the UNCLOS regimes otherwise enshrined in customary international law, as the following commentary explains:

Like ripples from a stone thrown in a pond, national maritime jurisdictions encircle a state's land territory. These zones are measured from baselines; the "normal" baseline is "the low water line along the coast as marked on large-scale charts officially recognized by the coastal states," although there are

> special baselines permitted for, for example, deeply indented coasts and across river mouths and bays. Landward of the baselines are "internal waters," such as landlocked lakes and rivers, which are fully within the ordinary sovereignty of the coastal state. Measured seaward from the baselines is, first, the territorial sea, which may be as wide as 12 nautical miles and is subject, within some limits set by international law, to the sovereign jurisdiction of the coastal state. Second, and beyond the territorial sea, is the contiguous zone, which may not extend beyond 24 nautical miles from the baselines and within which the coastal state may enforce "customs, fiscal, immigration or sanitary law." A coastal state may, third, establish an "exclusive economic zone" in which it has "sovereign rights for the purpose of exploring and exploiting, conserving and managing the natural resources" up to 200 nautical miles from its coast. Fourth, and finally, a coastal state has rights to exploit its "continental shelf," that is, "the sea-bed and subsoil of the submarine areas that extend beyond its territorial sea throughout the natural prolongation of its land territory to the outer edge of the continental margin, or to a distance of 200 nautical miles from the baselines from which the breadth of the territorial sea is measured where the outer edge of the continental margin does not extend up to that distance." These four zones of national maritime jurisdiction, along with special regions permitted for archipelagic states, greatly expand state sovereignty in the oceans at the considerable expense of the traditional international regime.
>
> High seas freedoms are, however, still protected, not only in the greatly diminished area still outside national control. . . .
>
> The most controversial parts of the 1982 Law of the Sea Convention concern the seabed and ocean floor and subsoil thereof beyond the limits of national jurisdiction, territory referred to in the Convention as the "Area." Much of the Convention and several of its annexes are devoted to the Area and to the International Sea-Bed Authority (the "Authority"), which is envisioned as regulating the Area. The Area and its resources are declared "the common heritage of mankind." States are prohibited from exercising sovereign rights over the Area and from appropriating any of the Area's resources.

MARK W. JANIS, AN INTRODUCTION TO INTERNATIONAL LAW 220–21, 222–23 (4th ed. 2003) (reproduced with the permission of Aspen Publishers).

Should Article 303, in association with article 33, be interpreted to limit coastal state jurisdiction to twenty-four nautical miles or to enable the coastal state only to take the specific measures indicated within that zone without addressing coastal state jurisdiction beyond the contiguous zone?

4. In the UNCLOS framework and under international custom, as summarized previously, a substantial body of international law to govern the underwater heritage is gradually emerging. In particular, the UNESCO Convention on the Protection of the Underwater Cultural Heritage (2001),[36] which came into force in 2009, provides a comprehensive regime. In the meantime, both it and the Buenos Aires Draft Convention on the Protection of the Underwater Cultural Heritage (prepared by the International Law Association), on which the UNESCO Convention is based,

[36] 41 I.L.M. 40 (2000).

provide general principles to govern the heritage. The UNESCO Convention will have important implications for both parties and nonparties because it requires parties to apply new protective measures and pursue consultation and cooperation with other states regardless of their relationship with the Convention.

The UNESCO Convention's elaborate provisions for dispute resolution by international processes, however, are generally limited to interstate claims. Article 25 of the UNESCO Convention provides for peaceful settlement of disputes through "negotiations in good faith or other peaceful means of settlement of [the parties'] own choice." If these fail, the parties may agree to submit their dispute for mediation. If mediation fails, parties are bound by the provisions relating to settlement of disputes set out in UNCLOS. Nonparties to that Convention are free to choose any of several alternative means set forth in UNCLOS, including conciliation and arbitration.

Strictly private disputes, such as those between competing salvors, seem to lie beyond the treaty's competence even if a dispute raises important international issues. The prescribed regime will, however, indirectly affect private activities, and many otherwise-private disputes will rise to the surface of the Convention by virtue of state responsibility rules or by grace of a state's diplomatic protection of its nationals. Thus, even though some maritime courts may continue to focus on issues related to historic wreck that the Convention does not address, such as ownership and abandonment of a vessel, it is likely that the courts will also be instrumental as surrogates for dormant transnational authority.

5. In essence, the UNESCO Convention on the Protection of the Underwater Cultural Heritage:

   - Establishes objectives and general principles, within the terms of the UN Convention on the Law of the Sea (UNCLOS), to ensure and strengthen protection of the underwater cultural heritage
   - Requires parties to comply with detailed scientific rules concerning activities directed at heritage and to ensure compliance with these rules by their nationals
   - Provides that parties must cooperate with one another in protecting and reporting on underwater heritage discoveries and activities involving their offshore jurisdictions
   - Prescribes that parties seize and dispose of heritage recovered in violation of the Convention and impose effective sanctions for violations of measures under the Convention
   - Mandates scientific training, international cooperation, follow-up meetings, and peaceful settlement of disputes related to the Convention

   To launch its thirty-five articles and thirty-six annexed rules, the Convention defines "underwater cultural heritage" as "all traces of human existence having a cultural, historical or archaeological character which have been partially or totally under water, periodically or continuously, for at least 100 years." Parties to the Convention assume a responsibility to protect this heritage offshore. In some cases, consistent with international law, this may involve a coastal state jurisdiction out to 350 nautical miles offshore.

6. As a protective regime, the UNESCO Convention relies on a set of thirty-six detailed rules concerning activities directed at underwater cultural heritage that are

annexed to the Convention. For example, a qualified archaeologist must direct and control all such activities using "non-destructive techniques and survey methods in preference to recovery of objects." Also, the protection of heritage by on-site preservation must be considered as the first option, and public access to on-site heritage "shall be promoted, except where such access is incompatible with protection and management." The rules also encompass standards for project design and scope of activity, preliminary work on a proposed activity, funding and duration of the activity, required safety and environmental measures, conservation and site management, curation, reporting, and dissemination of information about discoveries.

7. On the critical issue of commercial exploitation, Rule 2 provides as follows:

> **Rule 2.** The commercial exploitation of underwater cultural heritage for trade or speculation or its irretrievable dispersal is fundamentally incompatible with the protection and proper management of underwater cultural heritage. Underwater cultural heritage shall not be traded, sold, bought or bartered as commercial goods.
>
> This Rule cannot be interpreted as preventing:
>
> (a) the provision of professional archaeological services or necessary services incidental thereto whose nature and purpose are in full conformity with this Convention and are subject to the authorization of the competent authorities;
>
> (b) the deposition of underwater cultural heritage, recovered in the course of a research project in conformity with this Convention, provided such deposition does not prejudice the scientific or cultural interest or integrity of the recovered material or result in its irretrievable dispersal; is in accordance with the provisions of Rules 33 and 34; and is subject to the authorization of the competent authorities.

This important Rule raises a number of interpretive questions. Does it bar all commercial activity involving underwater heritage? What about heritage that is traded, sold, bought, or bartered not as "commercial goods" but simply as the by-product of a scientifically organized excavation? Or is all traded material a commercial good regardless of any circumstances besides purchase and sale or barter of the material? In Rule 2(a), what is meant by "the provision of professional archaeological services?" Would provision of such services aboard a vessel that is engaged in underwater excavation recharacterize such activity as scientific and therefore exempt from the ban on commercial exploitation? Could such a strictly scientific expedition sell excavated material to finance its costs? Would Rule 2(b) enable any activity characterized as a research project to freely engage in commercial transfer of recovered material? Is the term "commercial goods" limiting so as to distinguish such goods from educational goods, artifacts, or even underwater cultural heritage? Or is all trading of the heritage commercial? If so, what was the purpose of adding the phrase "as commercial goods"? Or does the intended constraint on commercial use of underwater cultural heritage apply regardless of the nature or purpose of an excavation? In Rule 2(b), what is meant by "deposition" of the heritage "recovered in the course of a research project in conformity with this Convention"? In the same Rule, what is meant by "irretrievable dispersal"?

Would that include any transfer of excavated material? Is "deposition" the same as "dispersal"?

8. What is the status of the UNESCO Convention for states that have not ratified it? Is it the best evidence of customary international law? Does general acceptance of some or all of its provisions constitute *opinio juris* – that is, a recognition of the pertinent provisions as authoritative under international law? If some of the provisions are customary, representing a codification of international law, and others are innovative, representing a progressive development of international law, how would you describe the role of the Convention in the international legal system? If some of the Convention's provisions are not deemed to be customary, do they nevertheless serve as guidance or soft law to help standardize national rules and practices, as well as to encourage eventual acceptance of those provisions as general custom?
9. Despite such questions, the Convention establishes a clear set of basic requirements. Parties are obligated to ensure compliance with these requirements not only within their offshore jurisdiction but also by their nationals and flag vessels on the seabed beyond their jurisdiction or wherever they may be engaged in activity directed at the underwater heritage. In their territory, parties must take measures to prevent illicit import, trading, or possession of underwater cultural heritage. The Convention provides a detailed process of consultation and cooperation among coastal states and other parties that have declared an interest in particular heritage. Parties also agree to impose and enforce sanctions for violation of measures they have taken under the Convention, to seize and properly dispose of contraband property, and to cooperate in information sharing, public education, technical training, and follow-up meetings organized by UNESCO. Disputes that arise between parties are to be settled by prescribed procedures and institutions.

   The Convention takes no position on ownership of heritage or the precise manner in which parties should administer the Convention so long as they act as required. Thus, for example, should the United States become a party, it presumably would continue to rely on a combination of state authority under the Abandoned Shipwreck Act of 1987, some federal legislation applicable to marine sanctuaries and the like, and the decisions of federal admiralty courts.
10. Other treaties and national legislation supplement the emerging regime. For example, the Agreement Concerning the Shipwrecked Vessel R.M.S. Titanic[37] designates the famous shipwreck as an international maritime memorial. Parties to the agreement commit themselves to respect the scientific, cultural, and historical significance of the *Titanic* by regulating all activity in their jurisdiction that affects the vessel, including its hull, cargo, and artifacts at and strewn around the wreck site. On the level of domestic law, the Ronald W. Reagan National Defense Authorization Act for Fiscal Year 2005,[38] for example, contains a title with the popular name, The Sunken Military Craft Act (SMCA). It protects sunken military vessels and aircraft from any activity directed at them for which a permit has not been

[37] *See* Sarah Dromgoole, *The International Agreement for the Protection of the Titanic: Problems and Prospects*, 37 Ocean Dev. & Int'l L. 1 (2006). The United Kingdom signed the agreement in November 2003 and the United States signed it in June 2004.

[38] Pub. L. No. 108–375, §§ 1401–1408, 118 Stat. 1811 (2004), *to be codified at* 10 U.S.C. 113.

obtained. The SMCA provides for civil penalties and damages. It also encourages agreements with foreign countries to help implement the law.

11. In a further phase of the *Titanic* judicial saga after *Haver*, the same court rejected R.M.S. Titanic Inc.'s claim of actual entitlement to artifacts from the *Titanic*. The plaintiff salvor's claims were premised on the common law of finds and the award of title by a French administrative agency to R.M.S. Titanic's predecessor-in-interest that had preceded the plaintiff salvor's appointment by the U.S. district court as a salvor-in-possession of the wreck. The court also attempted, rather unconvincingly, to justify the fiction of historical salvage under what it described as a *jus gentium* based on U.S. judicial opinions. *R.M.S. Titanic v. The Wrecked and Abandoned Vessel*, 435 F.3d 521 (4th Cir. 2006). For earlier analysis of the *Titanic* saga, *see* James A.R. Nafziger, *Historic Salvage Law Revisited*, 31 OCEAN DEV. & INT'L L. 81 (2000); James A.R. Nafziger, *The Titanic Revisited*, 30 J. MAR. L. & COM. 311 (1999); James A.R. Nafziger, *Finding the Titanic: Beginning an International Salvage of Derelict Law at Sea*, 12 COLUM.–VLA J. L. & ARTS 339 (1988). *See also* James A.R. Nafziger, *The Evolving Role of Admiralty Courts in Litigation Related to Historic Wreck*, 44 HARV. INT'L L.J. 251, 256, 264, 267 (2003).
12. The definitive text in English on the underwater heritage before the UNESCO Convention is ANASTASIA STRATI, THE PROTECTION OF THE UNDERWATER CULTURAL HERITAGE: AN EMERGING OBJECTIVE OF THE CONTEMPORARY LAW OF THE SEA (1995).

PROBLEMS

1. Divers from XK-Vation, Inc., a Delaware Corporation, have just located a sunken Spanish ship twenty miles off the Florida coast. It is thought to be the *Santa María de Cartagena*, loaded with gold and silver en route to Spain when it was blown off course and lost during the Great Hurricane of 1597 in the Caribbean. The Spanish government, which has ratified the UNESCO Convention, has asked you to determine whether it has any legal rights to ensure appropriate scientific safeguards during excavation of the wreck and, more generally, to confirm its claim to the ship and its treasure. The Spanish government is interested in your interpretations of the Abandoned Shipwreck Act (ASA) of the United States and international law, including general maritime law, UNCLOS, and the UNESCO Convention.
2. In 1998, Odyssey Marine Exploration, a deep-sea treasure-hunting company chartered in the United States, began to search for the *HMS Sussex*. It is an eighty-cannon British warship that led a fleet, including ships from Spain and the Netherlands, leaving in 1694 from Gibraltar (then, as now, a British colony) for a naval battle against the French. Unfortunately, it sank during a violent storm in the Strait of Gibraltar. Three-hundred years later, in preparation for its search for the *Sussex*, Odyssey entered into agreements with both the United Kingdom, as the ship's flag state, and Spain, on whose continental shelf Odyssey planned to search. In 2001 Odyssey claimed that its side-scan sonar had located the *Sussex* somewhere east of Gibraltar and that the ship was full of gold and silver valued at up to $4 billion. Spain's autonomous region of Andalusia responded, however, by disputing the agreement between Odyssey and Spain, claiming that under Spanish

law, its regional authorization was required. Eventually, a settlement was reached by which Odyssey would allow Spanish-designated archaeologists to observe the treasure salvage in return for stipulated privileges. A subsequent development, as follows, suspended further activity directed at the *Sussex*, however.

In 2007, Odyssey acknowledged that it had recovered and transported to its base in Tampa, Florida, under cover of night, some seventeen tons of silver and gold coins (an estimated five hundred thousand pieces) and other artifacts. Odyssey estimated the value of the treasure at about $500 million but refused to reveal the location of its find or the name of the ship, instead giving it the code name "Black Swan." Speculation centered on the possibility that the vessel from which the treasure had been taken was the *Nuestra Señora de las Mercedes y las Animas*, a Spanish warship sunk in 1804 west of Gibraltar in the Atlantic Ocean. There was also speculation that Odyssey's announcement of the *Sussex* find had been only a bogus cover for its secretive excavation of the Black Swan. In any event, tensions flared between Odyssey and Spanish authorities because the Black Swan is quite likely a Spanish vessel and Odyssey initially refused to cooperate with the authorities. They forced Odyssey's two ships into Spanish ports, where they were searched by the Civil Garda. Odyssey then filed a federal admiralty action in Florida against the Spanish government, claiming full rights over the vessel. See John Colapinto, *Secrets of the Deep*, New Yorker, Apr. 7, 2008, at 44. In 2009, a federal magistrate judge in Florida dismissed the action on the basis that the defendant government enjoyed sovereign immunity from the court's jurisdiction. The court also refused to rule on an interpleaded "conditional claim" to the wreck brought by Peru against Spain. *Odyssey Marine Exploration, Inc. v. Unidentified Shipwrecked Vessel*, 675 F. Supp. 2d 1126 (M.D. Fla. 2009).

5. Protection of Cultural Heritage in Preparation for, during, and after Armed Conflict

The Stela of Matara,

Partial Award, Central Front, Eritrea's Claims 2, 4, 6, 7, 8, and 22 between the State of Eritrea and the Federal Democratic Republic of Ethiopia (April 28, 2004)

[In 2000 Eritrea and Ethiopia entered into a peace agreement that ended nearly three years of armed conflict concerning the border between the two countries. The peace agreement established two independent arbitral tribunals: the Eritrea-Ethiopia Claims Commission (EECC) and the Eritrea-Ethiopia Boundary Commission. In the following award, the EECC considered Eritrea's claim that the Ethiopian military had deliberately destroyed the Stela of Matara, a pre–Christian era obelisk that constituted the most significant archaeological monument in Eritrea.]

. . . 107. The stela is an obelisk that is perhaps about 2,500 years old. It is an object of great historical and cultural significance to both Eritrea and Ethiopia. It is located near the small village of Matara a few kilometers south of Senafe Town and off the main highway from Zalambessa to Senafe and Asmara. The stela stood alone on a plain 4.68 meters above ground, with another meter under ground. There were no houses or other structures near the stela.

108. The evidence indicates that the area where the stela is located was controlled by Ethiopian armed forces at least from May 28, 2000, and that those forces established a camp on high ground quite near the stela (perhaps as close as 100 meters). Witnesses who lived not far from the stela and regularly walked by it during the day stated that it was standing on the evening of May 30 and was lying on the ground on the morning of May 31. Some also described hearing an explosion during the night.

109. Eritrea presented an expert witness, highly experienced in the analysis and restoration of stone artifacts and structures, Mr. Laurent Bouillet, who inspected the stela in September 2002. Mr. Bouillet testified that a military type of explosive had been used to bring down the stela, pointing to the nature and areas of fragmentation of the stone and the white traces of explosive as proof of that conclusion. Eritrea's other expert witness, Mr. Arkin, also looked briefly at the stela a few weeks later than Mr. Bouillet, and testified that he saw no evidence of explosive damage. The Commission is satisfied that Mr. Bouillet's expertise is more directly related to the effects of explosives on stone than is Mr. Arkin's, and it is persuaded that the stela was damaged and toppled by an explosive charge of the type Mr. Bouillet described.

110. Ethiopia denied any knowledge about the damage inflicted on the stela. It submitted a statement by Brigadier General Berhane Negash, in which the only thing he said relevant to the damage to the stela of Matara was the following: "During this campaign, intense fighting occurred in the vicinity of the Eritrean locality of Matara. The only targets that were destroyed by Ethiopian forces in this locality were the barracks used by the Eritrean soldiers."

111. In effect, Ethiopia asserts that it is unclear what caused the stela to fall, that Eritrea has the burden of proof, and that it has not met that burden.

112. The Commission believes that Eritrea has proved that the stela was felled on the night of May 30–31, 2000, that it was felled by an explosive of a military type fastened at its base, and that an encampment of Ethiopian soldiers was quite near the stela when this occurred. In these circumstances, the Commission concludes that Ethiopia, as the Occupying Power in the Matara area of Senafe Sub-Zoba, is responsible for the damage, even though there is no evidence that the decision to explode the stela was anything other than a decision by one or several soldiers.

113. The Commission holds that the felling of the stela was a violation of customary international humanitarian law. While the 1954 Hague Convention on the Protection of Cultural Property was not applicable, as neither Eritrea nor Ethiopia was a Party to it, deliberate destruction of historic monuments was prohibited by Article 56 of the Hague Regulations, which prohibition is part of customary law. Moreover, as civilian property in

occupied territory, the stela's destruction was also prohibited by Article 53 of Geneva Convention IV and by Article 52 of Protocol I. The Commission notes that the applicability of Article 53 of Protocol I may be uncertain, given the negotiating history of that provision, which suggests that it was intended to cover only a few of the most famous monuments, such as the Acropolis in Athens and St. Peter's Basilica in Rome. However, given the clear applicability of the principles reflected in Article 56 of the Hague Regulations, the Commission need not attempt to weigh the comparative cultural significance of the stela.

114. Consequently, Ethiopia is liable for the unlawful damage inflicted upon the Stela of Matara in May 2000. Eritrea's request that Ethiopia also be obligated to apologize for that damage is dismissed. As the Commission stated in its Decision No. 3, in principle, the appropriate remedy for valid claims should be monetary compensation, except where other remedies can be shown to be in accordance with international practice and the Commission determines that another remedy would be reasonable and appropriate. No such showing was made here.

Three sets of treaties form the framework for protecting cultural heritage before, during, and after armed conflict.[39] These are the Hague Conventions of 1899 and 1907; the Geneva Convention of 1949 and its two Protocols; and the Hague Convention of 1954 and its two Protocols. Together, they require preparations for and responses to four threats to cultural heritage: deliberate attack, incidental damage, pillage, and outright theft. (Throughout the following discussion the term "cultural property" is used because of its use in the applicable treaties.)

a. The Hague Conventions of 1899 and 1907

The Hague Conventions of 1899 and 1907[40] with Respect to the Laws and Customs of War on Land, together with their Annexed Regulations, generally prohibit pillage and destruction or seizure of enemy property unless imperatively demanded by the necessity of war. Private property may not be confiscated. Attack or bombardment of undefended buildings, including cultural targets, is also prohibited. Three provisions of the two Conventions deal specifically with the protection of cultural property. Signatory states

[39] The treaty law, in turn, has generated rules of customary law. *See* Jean-Marie Henckaerts & Louise Doswald-Beck, I Customary International Humanitarian Law 127–38 (2005). *See generally* Wojciech W. Kowalski, Art Treasures and War (1998). The instant summary of the international legal framework draws on more extensive discussion, with greater attention to customary law, in M. Cherif Bassiouni & James A.R. Nafziger, *Protection of Cultural Property*, 1 International Criminal Law 949, 950–62 (2d ed. 1999) (with full citations of authority). *See also* Hays Parks, *Protection of Cultural Property from the Effects of War*, *in* The Law of Cultural Property and Natural Heritage ch. 3 (Marilyn Phelan ed., 1998).

[40] Convention with Respect to the Laws and Customs of War on Land, July 29, 1899, 32 Stat. 1803, T.S. No. 403, 26 Martens Nouveau Recueil (ser. 2) 949, *reprinted in* 1 Am. J. Int'l L. 129 (1907) [hereinafter 1899 Hague Convention]; Convention Respecting the Laws and Customs of War on Land, Oct. 18, 1907, 36 Stat. 2277 (1907), T.S. No. 539, 3 Martens Nouveau Recueil (ser. 3) 461, *reprinted in* 2 Am. J. Int'l L. 90 (1908) [hereinafter 1907 Hague Convention].

must take steps to spare buildings dedicated to art, science, and religion from attack, and, with respect to their own cultural objects, give notice to the enemy by marking such objects. An occupying power must act responsibly in administering all public institutions, including museums. All seizure or destruction with an intention to damage institutions and historic monuments of art, religion, science and charity or works of art and science is forbidden and subject to legal proceedings. The Convention of 1907 Concerning Bombardment by Naval Forces in Time of War (Hague Convention IX) requires that all necessary precautions be taken to spare historic monuments and edifices devoted to worship, art, science, and charity.

Unfortunately, the Hague Conventions of 1899 and 1907 failed to prevent widespread damage and destruction to cultural property during the First World War, including the bombing of the Rheims Cathedral and the burning of a renowned library in Louvain. There were no prosecutions for destruction of cultural property. Nevertheless, the experience in the Second World War prompted new efforts to update and refine the *jus in bello.* Although never formally adopted, the Hague Rules of Air Warfare (1922–23) reiterate that historic monuments and cultural institutions must be spared from aerial bombing during hostilities. Similarly, the Second World War witnessed the plunder by the Nazis of the European heritage. In the ensuing Nuremberg trials, however, the prosecutions of major Nazi war criminals firmly established confiscation, destruction, and damage to cultural property as a war crime subject to prosecution and punishment, and provided the first true international enforcement of cultural property law. In particular, Alfred Rosenberg, director of the notorious Einsatzstab Rosenberg, was found guilty of war crimes on the basis of his responsibility for the plunder of art treasures throughout Europe.

In an attempt to control looted articles after the Second World War, the United States, Great Britain, and France signed a statement of policy on control of looted articles that presaged the international response to the looting nearly six decades later in Iraq. The three nations agreed to take measures to seek out looted articles and prevent their exportation, to encourage liberated states to provide lists of looted articles not yet recovered, to disseminate the lists to art dealers and museums, and to alert the general public to help enforce the return of looted articles to their rightful owners.

b. The Geneva Convention IV of 1949 and Protocol I to the Convention

The Geneva Convention Relative to the Protection of Civilian Persons in Time of War (Geneva Convention IV),[41] one of four agreements that still define the conventional *jus in bello*, in general prohibits destruction of personal property, whether publicly or privately owned. In itself, the 1949 Convention does little to strengthen the protective regime applicable to cultural heritage. But Protocol I to the Convention, which was opened for signature in 1977, specifically prohibits acts of hostility against historic monuments, works of art, or places of worship that constitute the cultural or spiritual heritage of people and the use of such property for military efforts. Protocol I also prohibits direct reprisals against such property. Further, Geneva Convention IV and its Protocol I make it a "grave

[41] Geneva Convention Relative to the Protection of Civilian Persons in Time of War (Geneva Convention IV), *signed* August 12, 1949, 6 U.S.T. 3516, T.S. No. 3365, 75 U.N.T.S. 287 (effective Feb. 2, 1956) [hereinafter Geneva Convention IV].

breach" to destroy clearly recognized and specially protected historic monuments, works of art, or places of worship. As a "grave breach," the offense constitutes a war crime, and thus is an international crime subject to universal jurisdiction.

c. The 1954 Hague Convention

Increasing international pressure for an agreement that would specifically address the protection of cultural property during armed conflict resulted in negotiations that led to the 1954 Hague Convention for the Protection of Cultural Property in the Event of Armed Conflict.[42] It attempts to broaden the scope of the 1899 and 1907 Hague Conventions by taking into account the events of the First and Second World Wars, by premising the law in the need to protect the "cultural heritage of mankind," and by incorporating certain provisions of Geneva Convention IV to create a truly effective and comprehensive agreement on the protection of cultural property during hostilities, whether international or noninternational (civil war). The Convention covers both movable and immovable property, which parties to the agreement are encouraged to designate with a distinctive emblem.

Under the 1954 Hague Convention, parties must undertake preparations in time of peace against the foreseeable effects of armed conflict. This is called the precautionary rule. Parties must also prohibit any use of the cultural property in a manner that will likely expose it to destruction or damage in the event of an armed conflict; the commission of any acts of hostility or reprisal against cultural property except for reasons of military necessity; and any form of theft, pillage, or misappropriation of cultural property. To help enforce these provisions, parties agree to take steps to prosecute and impose sanctions upon offenders. The Convention also requires occupying states to help in safeguarding and preserving their cultural property and provides for return of property seized during a conflict.

In addition, the 1954 Hague Convention outlines procedures for the *special* protection of certain items of cultural property. To qualify for special protection, cultural property must be either immovable property of "*very great* importance" or a refuge to shelter movable property. It must also be situated at an "adequate distance" from an industrial center or important military objective. Finally, it may not be used for a military purpose, such as stationing military personnel or storing weapons. Once cultural property is placed under special protection, state parties must ensure its immunity by refraining from directing any hostilities against it. Special protection requires the use of distinctive markings and the property's subsequent entry in an international registry at UNESCO. To date, however, only a handful of states have registered property for special protection, and such property is limited to just a few works.

Protocol I[43] to the 1954 Hague Convention imposes additional obligations on a state party that is occupying the territory of another state. It requires an occupying state to prevent the export of cultural property from the occupied territory, seize all cultural property imported into its territory from any occupied territory, return the seized property to the formerly occupied territory at the close of hostilities, and pay an indemnity to the holders in good faith of any cultural property that has to be returned.

[42] *Signed* May 14, 1954, 249 U.N.T.S. 240.

[43] Protocol for the Protection of Cultural Property in the Event of Armed Conflict, *signed* 14 May 1954, 249 U.N.T.S. 358 [hereinafter Protocol I to the 1954 Hague Convention].

Perhaps the most successful implementation of the 1954 Hague Convention occurred during the Persian Gulf War of 1991, in which members of the coalition forces were either parties to the convention or, in the instance of nonparties such as the United States, accepted its rules, most notably by creating a "no-fire target list" of places where cultural property was known to exist.[44] The 1954 Hague Convention, however, was not effective in the breakup of Yugoslavia, as the disastrous bombardments of Dubrovnik, Croatia, and Mostar, Bosnia and Herzegovina, illustrate. Such wanton attacks on cultural property prompted efforts to amend the 1954 Hague Convention to prevent similar destruction and ensure greater individual and state accountability.

These efforts culminated in 1999 with the completion of a second protocol to the 1954 Hague Convention. Protocol II[45] contains a greater number of penal elements than any previous cultural property instrument, with specific articles on criminal jurisdiction, a duty to prosecute and extradite, and mutual legal assistance. In addition, going beyond the idea of special protection annunciated in the underlying 1954 Hague Convention, Protocol II includes a provision to define property under enhanced protection. This strengthening of the scope of protection represented frustration with the failure of the registration regime under the 1954 Convention to attract much interest. To qualify for enhanced protection, cultural property must meet three conditions: (1) it must be of the greatest importance to humanity, such as designated World Heritage sites; (2) it must be protected by adequate domestic legal and administrative measures, including existing UNESCO protections, recognizing its exceptional cultural and historic value; and (3) it must not be used for military purposes to shield military sites, and a declaration must have been made by the state that has control over the property that it will not be so used.

Protocol II to the 1954 Hague Convention expands on the provisions in the 1954 Hague Convention for preparatory actions in time of peace to safeguard cultural property against the "foreseeable effects" of an armed conflict. State parties must therefore prepare a national inventory, plan emergency measures for protection against fire and structural collapse, remove all movable cultural property from areas that are likely to be damaged during military action or prepare adequate *in situ* protections of such property, and designate competent authorities responsible for the safeguarding of cultural property.

The instrument also expands upon the precautionary measures in the 1954 Hague Convention that must be taken by state parties to prepare for and conduct military operations. All feasible measures must be taken to verify that the objects likely to be used for military purposes or likely to be attacked are not protected cultural property. Also, all feasible precautions must be made in the choice of targets and methods of attack with a view to protect cultural property and avoid losses and damage to it. Furthermore, a state must refrain from attack when either the objective is the destruction of protected cultural property or the attack might create incidental damage to cultural property that is excessive in relation to the anticipated military advantage of the attack. The underlying principle is one of military necessity. Protocol II to the 1954 Hague Convention also establishes individual criminal responsibility for violations. A state party therefore must either prosecute or extradite any person found in its territory who is deemed to have

[44] But *see* allegations of limited military damage in Richard L. Zettler, *Iraq's Beleaguered Heritage*, ARCHAEOLOGY, May–June 1991, at 38.

[45] Second Protocol to the Hague Convention of 1954 for the Protection of Cultural Property in the Event of Armed Conflict, *opened for signature* Mar. 26 1999, http://www.unesco.org [hereinafter Protocol II to the 1954 Hague Convention].

committed serious violations of the Hague/Protocol II rules. In addition, the instrument contains provisions for mutual legal assistance and the establishment of a committee to help implement the protocol and protect the specifically identified cultural property.

Protocol I for the Protection of Cultural Property in the Event of Armed Conflict

The High Contracting Parties are agreed as follows:

I

1. Each High Contracting Party undertakes to prevent the exportation, from a territory occupied by it during an armed conflict, of cultural property as defined in Article 1 of the Convention for the Protection of Cultural Property in the Event of Armed Conflict, signed at The Hague on 14 May 1954.

2. Each High Contracting Party undertakes to take into its custody cultural property imported into its territory either directly or indirectly from any occupied territory. This shall either be effected automatically upon the importation of the property or, failing this, at the request of the authorities of that territory.

3. Each High Contracting Party undertakes to return, at the close of hostilities, to the competent authorities of the territory previously occupied, cultural property which is in its territory, if such property has been exported in contravention of the principle laid down in the first paragraph. Such property shall never be retained as war reparations.

4. The High Contracting Party whose obligation it was to prevent the exportation of cultural property from the territory occupied by it, shall pay an indemnity to the holders in good faith of any cultural property which has to be returned in accordance with the preceding paragraph.

II

5. Cultural property coming from the territory of a High Contracting Party and deposited by it in the territory of another High Contracting Party for the purpose of protecting such property against the dangers of an armed conflict, shall be returned by the latter, at the end of hostilities, to the competent authorities of the territory from which it came.

---

d. Customary Humanitarian Law

The conventional (treaty) prescriptions generally codify customary practices despite the violations of the laws of war that commendably attract the media. A substantial body of customary law therefore mandates the protection of cultural material. The International Committee of the Red Cross, an organization chartered under Swiss law that is invested with international legal personality to implement the Geneva Conventions, has succinctly summarized this custom as black-letter rules followed by extensive commentary. International Committee of the Red Cross, I Customary International Humanitarian Law 127–42 (Jean-Marie Henckaerts & Louise Doswald-Beck eds., 2005). For example, apropos of the Iraqi conflict beginning in 2003, Rule 41 provides that "[t]he occupying power must prevent the illicit export of cultural property from occupied territory and must return illicitly exported property to the competent authorities of the occupied territory." *Id.* at 135.

e. The International War Crimes Tribunal for the Former Yugoslavia, the International Criminal Court, and Crises in Afghanistan and Iraq

The International War Crimes Tribunal for the Former Yugoslavia (ICTY) was established by Security Council Resolution 8727 on May 25, 1993. The establishment of the Tribunal was based on chapter VII of the UN Charter, which authorizes the Security Council to take such measures that it deems necessary to deal with threats to peace, breaches of the peace, and acts of aggression. The ICTY has jurisdiction over crimes committed in the territory of the former Yugoslavia after January 1, 1991.

The ICTY has handed out convictions for crimes against cultural property arising out of 1991 attacks on educational, cultural, and religious sites. These were mostly local mosques but also the famous Mostar bridge in Bosnia-Herzegovina and the old town of Dubrovnik, Croatia, which had been declared a UNESCO World Heritage site in 1979.

In 2000 the ICTY convicted General Tihomir Blaskic on charges related to Bosnian sites. In 2004 Vice Admiral Miodrag Jokic was convicted of targeting Dubrovnik. His seven-year jail sentence was upheld in 2005. Also in 2005, Pavle Strugar, the commander of the Yugoslav Peoples Army Forces, received an eight-year sentence for ordering attacks on targets in the Dubrovnik region and failing to prohibit attacks on the old town of Dubrovnik.

In *Strugar*, the Tribunal considered the defense of military necessity, saying:

> . . . the Chamber considers that the special protection awarded to cultural property itself may not be lost simply because of military activities or military installations in the immediate vicinity of the cultural property. In such a case, however, the practical result may be that it cannot be established that the acts which caused destruction of or damage to cultural property were "directed against" that cultural property, rather than the military installation or use in its immediate vicinity.[46]

The ICTY found, however, that there was no evidence that the destroyed buildings and structures in the Old Town had been used for military purposes at the relevant time. The tribunal concluded that the buildings were protected cultural property under the ICTY statute at the time they incurred damage, and because there were no military objectives, the defense of military necessity was unavailable.

[46] For ICTY decisions, *see* www.un.org/icty/index.html; Karine Lescure & Florence Trintignac, International Justice for Former Yugoslavia: The Working of the International Criminal Tribunal of the Hague (1996); Daryl A. Mundis, *Crimes of the Commander: Superior Responsibility under Article 7(3) of the ICTY Statute, in* International Criminal Law: Developments in the Case Law of the ICTY (Gideon Boas & William A. Schabas eds., 2003).

The principle of superior responsibility (or "command responsibility") led to Strugar's conviction. Article 7(3) of the ICTY Statute provides:

> The fact that any of the acts referred to in articles 2 to 5 of the present Statute was committed by a subordinate does not relieve his superior of criminal responsibility if he knew or had reason to know that the subordinate was about to commit such acts or had done so and the superior failed to take the necessary and reasonable measures to prevent such acts or to punish the perpetrators thereof.

Under this principle an accused may be convicted for failing to prevent a crime from occurring in the first place. In all three ICTY indictments the accused were prosecuted on this basis, along with allegations of individual responsibility. No conviction was upheld against Strugar based on his individual criminal responsibility as the ICTY was not satisfied that he knew there was a substantial likelihood of an unlawful attack. However, given its conclusion that Strugar had legal authority over the troops involved in the attack and knew that the attack was occurring and failed to stop it, he was found responsible for the actions of his subordinates under the doctrine of superior responsibility.

NOTES

1. For ICTY decisions, see http://www.un.org/icty/index.html; KARINE LESCURE & FLORENCE TRINTIGNAC, INTERNATIONAL JUSTICE FOR FORMER YUGOSLAVIA: THE WORKING OF THE INTERNATIONAL CRIMINAL TRIBUNAL OF THE HAGUE (1996); Daryl A. Mundis, *Crimes of the Commander: Superior Responsibility under Article 7(3) of the ICTY Statute, in* INTERNATIONAL CRIMINAL LAW: DEVELOPMENTS IN THE CASE LAW OF THE ICTY (Gideon Boas & William A. Schabas eds., 2003).
2. The International Criminal Court in The Hague is also available for prosecutions of individuals for war-related crimes against cultural heritage. Article 8 of the 1998 Rome Statute of the International Criminal Court gives the court jurisdiction over war crimes, which include crimes against cultural heritage. Specifically, articles 8(2)(a)(ix) of the Rome Statute that established the International Criminal Court, governing activity during international armed conflict, and 8(2)(e)(iv), governing activity during noninternational armed conflict, provide criminal sanctions for prohibited acts against cultural heritage. Article 28 also provides for command responsibility.
3. The cold war's end introduced prospects of a halcyon new world order. Once again, as happened every twenty years or so in the past century, the global community glowingly forecast a world ruled by right rather than might.[47] International law

[47] The first decade of the twentieth century witnessed the international codification of the modern laws of war and the establishment of the Permanent Court of Arbitration. In the 1920s the League of Nations opened its doors as the first worldwide mechanism for peaceful settlement of disputes, and the Kellogg-Briand Pact boldly outlawed all recourse to war. The 1940s introduced the United Nations and the Geneva Conventions of humanitarian law in time of armed conflict. The 1960s inaugurated major UN peacekeeping operations, and the late 1980s, the end of the cold war.

and institutions would protect persons and property around the world. Once again, however, the bubble of optimism soon burst in the heat of renewed warfare, ethnic cleansing, and collective terrorism. Iraq invaded Kuwait, removing some twenty thousand artifacts and objets d'art and, in the ensuing Gulf War, used cultural property to shield military objectives from attack. In particular, the destruction of Dubrovnik and the Old Bridge in Mostar during the bloody implosion of Yugoslavia heightened skepticism about the ability of the new world order to protect the cultural heritage.

In an era threatened by mass terrorism, the public has only limited confidence in the efficacy of either the *jus ad bellum* to avoid international terrorism and armed intervention or the *jus in bello* to protect persons and property.[48] Simultaneous acts of mass terrorism and sabotage, the preventive use of force, and selective avoidance of the Security Council by its permanent members pose new challenges. Skepticism about the efficacy of the laws of war should not obscure two important facts, however: (1) the unprecedented growth of international law and institutions during the cold war and (2) the impressive record of compliance with the *jus in bello* by coalition forces in the thick of battle during the Persian Gulf War of 1991. In general, the problems in protecting cultural heritage reflect not an inadequacy of the law of war itself,[49] but rather a lack of civic responsibility and inadequate commitment and training of military personnel, particularly in paramilitary operations and in times of civil war. The aftermath of the 2003 intervention in Iraq is a case in point.

4. In April 2003, as the dust began to settle on the Battle of Baghdad in one of the cradles of civilization, the world witnessed the horror of what appeared to be extensive looting of museums, libraries, and other institutions in Iraq. At first, the destruction of the world's finest collection of ancient Mesopotamian artifacts and a wealth of later material appeared to be of an unprecedented scale. Fortunately, the extent of the looting turned out to be considerably less than had been originally thought. Much of the lost material had been safely hidden away before the fighting began, and some looted items were soon recovered. The looting sparked renewed controversy about the adequacy of international law to protect cultural property during and after military conflict, the extent of the United States' obligations, and compliance by the United States with those obligations.
5. U.S. treaty obligations to protect cultural heritage during and after conflict are broad but lacking in detail. The United States ratified and therefore is a party to the Hague Conventions of 1899 and 1907, the Geneva Convention IV of 1949, and the 1954 Hague Convention, but it is not bound by the two Protocols to the 1949 Geneva Convention or the two Protocols to the 1954 Convention. Even

[48] On the general problem of looting in time of war or its aftermath, *see* Neil Brodie, *Spoils of War*, ARCHAEOLOGY, July–August 2003, at 16. Of course, destruction of cultural heritage is not limited to armed conflict, as the Taliban's obliteration of the Buddhist statues near Bamiyan, Afghanistan, attests, but despite the UNESCO Declaration Concerning the Intentional Destruction of Cultural Heritage (2003), it has to be acknowledged that such acts lie largely within the reserved domain of domestic jurisdiction and thus beyond the competence of international law.

[49] "Adequate law of war protection for cultural property exists." Parks, *supra* note 39, at 3–1, 3–26.

before the United States became a party to the 1954 Convention in 2009,[50] it took steps to comply with the Convention's conduct-regulating provisions under general principles of international law and international custom. These steps included signing the Convention (though not ratifying it for some thirty-four years), educating military personnel in it, and seeking to conform military operations to its requirements.

A concluding summary of U.S. obligations in the aftermath of its 2003 intervention in Iraq will illustrate the significance of both binding and nonbinding rules of warfare. The Hague Convention of 1907 requires military authorities to restore and ensure public order, including taking adequate measures to enforce a specific prohibition of pillage. As we have seen, the 1954 Hague Convention and its two Protocols impose additional obligations to safeguard and preserve property under military control, to prevent exportation of looted material, and to facilitate its return to countries of origin. Although the United States had not ratified and was therefore not fully bound by the 1954 Hague Convention at the time, it was nevertheless obligated as a signatory to act responsibly so as not to defeat the treaty's object and purpose of protecting cultural material.[51] Moreover, the 1970 UNESCO Convention prohibits the importation and acquisition of stolen material. This treaty obligation is a reminder that the protection of cultural heritage in the event of war and its aftermath depends on implementation in time of peace, especially efforts to increase public awareness and ensure education of military personnel.

6. Canada is a party to the 1954 Hague Convention and both of its Protocols. These have been implemented into Canadian law by the Crimes against Humanity and War Crimes Act, S.C. 2000, c. 24; amendments to the Cultural Property Export and Import Act; and the Criminal Code, R.S.C. 1985, c. C-46. Under these statutory provisions, various criminal offenses have been created under Canadian law, including those relating to theft and destruction of cultural material.
7. As we see in Chapters 4 and 5, the 1970 UNESCO Convention on illegal trafficking in cultural property is the primary, ongoing means by which the United States responds to appeals from foreign governments to bar imports of cultural heritage that they claim is in jeopardy. Under the Convention on Cultural Property Implementation Act (CCPIA), which implements the 1970 UNESCO Convention in U.S. jurisdiction, Congress enacted the following emergency measure in 2004 as a response to looting in Iraq:

Emergency Implementation of Import Restrictions

> (a) Authority. – The President may exercise the authority of the President under Section 304 of the Convention on Cultural Property Implementation Act (19 U.S.C. 2603) with respect to any archaeological or ethnological material of Iraq without regard to whether Iraq is a State Party under that Act,

[50] An explanation for this delay of more than a half-century lies in cold war anxieties, particularly about the implications of expected nuclear conflict, and, more recently, bureaucratic delays in ratifying the pertinent instruments.

[51] A rule of international custom to this effect is codified in article 18 of the Vienna Convention on the Law of Treaties, May 23, 1969, 1155 U.N.T.S. 331, *reprinted in* 8 I.L.M. 679 (1969). Although the United States is not a party to the Vienna Convention, it has accepted the articulated burden of international custom.

> except that, in exercising such authority, subsection (c) of such section shall not apply. [The cited provision imposes certain limitations and stipulates procedures for the proper exercise of the president's power to take measures and limits the duration of those measures.]
>
> (b) Definition. – In this section, the term "archaeological or ethnological material of Iraq" means cultural property of Iraq and other items of archaeological, historical, cultural, rare scientific, or religious importance illegally removed from the Iraq National Museum, the National Library of Iraq, and other locations in Iraq, since the adoption of United Nations Security Council Resolution 661 of 1990.

Miscellaneous Trade and Technical Corrections Act of 2004, Pub. L. No. 108-429, 118 Stat. 2434 § 3002 (2004).

This particular emergency apparently was deemed to have begun as early as a 1990 Resolution of the UN Security Council, to which the legislation makes reference, and no later than the massive looting of the Iraqi heritage after U.S. intervention in Iraq in the spring of 2003. Why, then, did it take Congress so long to respond to the problem of looting? Does section (b) of the measure permit the president to ban all importation into the United States of designated archaeological or ethnological material, even privately owned and transferred material, so long as it is "cultural property of Iraq"?

This measure and others directed at eliminating the art market for looted artifacts, coupled with increased military and police protection of sites, appear to have helped protect archaeological sites. See Martin Bailey, *Archaeological Sites in South Iraq Have Not Been Looted, Say Experts*, ART NEWSPAPER, July–Aug. 2008, at 4 (observing that there had been no evidence of looting at major sites since 2003). Unfortunately, however, Iraq's loss of control over border crossings has led to a steady stream of looted material on international markets. Stolen Iraq antiquities continue to show up in those markets or en route to them. In 2008, for example, Dubai customs authorities seized more than one hundred artifacts, and a pair of gold earrings dating back nearly ten thousand years, allegedly from the fabled treasures of Nimrud, became the focus of a legal dispute when Christie's auction house was preparing to put the earrings up for auction. Jane Arraf, *Iraq Bids to Stop Christie's Sale of Ancient Earrings*, CHRISTIAN SCI. MONITOR, Dec. 4, 2008, at 7.

8. In Afghanistan it is reported that "[n]early a quarter century of invasion and civil war have transformed archaeological sites into barren wastes of looters' pits, left ancient buildings in ruins, and destroyed or scattered thousands of statutes, carvings, and paintings. 'Illegal digging is going on in many provinces.... It's difficult to stop it. We have 2,800 known sites, but I think there are more than 4,000. Many sites have yet to be registered. We need to explore and survey these' (quoting the former Director of Afghanistan's Institute of Archaeology.)... While poppies may be Afghanistan's prime export, UNESCO officials warn that antiquities – looted and illegally spirited out of the country – may be second on that list. A single Buddha statute can bring tens of thousands of dollars in the art markets of London, Paris, New York, or Tokyo. And unlike poppies, antiquities are harvested in all seasons, and cannot be replanted." Andrew Lawler, *Saving Afghan Treasures*, NAT'L GEOGRAPHIC, Dec. 2004, at 28, 34.

Given the severe threats to the Afghan cultural heritage, Congress later provided protection of Afghan cultural heritage, too. But why did Congress initially limit emergency measures to looted material from Iraq? Why not Afghanistan, too? What does such emergency legislation accomplish that may not lie within the scope of the laws of war and normal import controls? (In the next chapter, we explore several types of import control, as well as international legislation applicable in times of armed conflict and peace alike.)

9. An important response to the risk of destruction of cultural material that is inherent in armed conflict has been international cooperation in providing a temporary safe haven elsewhere for the material. In 2008 the International Law Association adopted Guidelines for the Establishment and Conduct of Safe Havens for Cultural Material. These guidelines, which include an annexed Safe Haven Model Contract, provide for governmental establishment and supervision of safe havens, obligations of safe havens, obligations of source states or entities, contracting party autonomy to stipulate conditions of care, and implementation of the Guidelines within the framework of UNESCO and other international instruments and bodies. The Guidelines may be found at International Law Association, REPORT OF THE SEVENTY-THIRD CONFERENCE 380 (2008) and 16 INT'L J. CULTURAL PROP. 371 (2009).

B. Cooperation

Cooperation among museums and other institutions, normally involving loans of material, is well established. A more recent innovation has been the establishment of museum partnerships in museum building, collection building, and collection sharing. The Guggenheim Museum in New York and the Louvre in Paris, in particular, have been pioneers in this development. *See, e.g.*, ART NEWSPAPER, Feb. 2008, at 16.

Cooperation also plays an important role in dispute avoidance and resolution. The singularity and uniqueness of many cultural objects often make it futile or inappropriate to attempt to avoid or settle disputes surrounding them by conventional means. Laws surrounding the resolution of disputes involving ordinary personal property are usually premised on such property being fungible and on compensation in the form of damages being an acceptable form of relief.

The traditional legal approach often does not accommodate the positions of parties to a dispute involving cultural material. These parties may not want the publicity that court proceedings would generate. They may also seek an outcome that is beyond the scope of existing judicial forms of relief. Other problems with litigation include the unfamiliarity of many judges with cultural objects; the lack of special rules for cultural objects, as distinct from personal property generally; and the difficulty of examining disputes over material that was taken or otherwise lost by its original owners decades or even centuries ago.

Disputes concerning cultural material may involve parties from different countries, particularly as they relate to objects from former colonies of European powers. Most legal systems incorporate limitation periods that bar court proceedings after the passage of certain periods of time. These statutes of limitation have been especially problematic for claims surrounding works of art looted during the Holocaust. Although these laws are based on sound policies against the unreliability of stale evidence and the need for closure, the policies themselves often ring hollow in the face of the calamitous events that surrounded the loss of the material at issue. Perhaps the most well-documented instances of cooperative solutions to cultural property disputes have involved such claims by Jewish groups and individuals involving material looted during the Holocaust or otherwise stolen or lost in the period of the Second World War and claims by indigenous peoples for the return of objects from museum collections.

Holocaust-related claims have been litigated in the United States and elsewhere, but the number of such cases is still relatively small. Although claimants often do not necessarily want the objects themselves but rather a recognition of past illegality and misconduct, judges often cannot easily provide for that. Also, courts are often overwhelmed by considerations of historical wrongdoing, immorality, and fashioning remedies of appropriate financial or geographical scope. Claims by indigenous peoples have been pursued in various ways, but cooperative solutions have been the preferred approach in the United States, Canada, New Zealand, and elsewhere. These claims have often led to major changes in the museums involved and have sometimes involved a reorganization of museum management policy to include indigenous groups in the presentation of displays, conservation, and policy matters.

Apart from these two categories of cases, there are numerous examples in which issues involving cultural heritage transcend national boundaries so that no single state can fashion a solution on its own. A simple example is when a state prohibits the export of certain categories of cultural heritage. If an object is unlawfully removed from that state to another, the cooperation of authorities in the latter state is needed for the object to be returned to its state of origin. The easiest way to secure such cooperation on an ongoing basis is by an international agreement between the states concerned, the scope of which can be much wider than just securing the return of illegal exports. International agreements can also deal with a variety of cultural heritage concerns, such as exchanges of museum collections for exhibition purposes and the sharing of expertise on matters such as conservation, acquisitions, and display.

Cooperation can become a culture in its own right, one that fosters future productive outcomes including more amicable and productive resolutions to disputes. Eventually, this may secure the most desirable outcome of all: an increased level of protection of cultural heritage from whatever source and in whatever location.

1. Amicable Settlements and Partnerships

Amicable settlements to avoid and resolve claims for return or restitution of material are becoming more common. The substantive options are unlimited, ranging from outright formal conveyance of claimed material to long-term loans of it, exchange of it for other material, and rental arrangements for payment. Partnerships between and among otherwise litigious parties, fostered by public law and ethical codes, are also a promising development.

Claims by indigenous groups and individuals have often been made against museums in possession of human remains or cultural objects, sometimes of a sacred character. These claims become transnational whenever contested material was removed from its original location in colonial times and later ended up in a museum or other institution abroad. In pursuing claims, requirements such as collecting reliable evidence about the circumstances of the original acquisition and the length of time between the loss and the attempt at recovery suggest the advisability of less formal and more cooperative approaches, including those based on mutual trust and confidence.

Similarly, the complex factual, legal, moral, and ethical issues surrounding claims concerning art looted or otherwise lost during the Holocaust and otherwise in the period surrounding and during the Second World War have led to a number of difficult lawsuits – particularly in Europe and the United States – that might have been avoided on the basis of informal agreements. The set of Principles with Respect to Nazi-Confiscated Art, devised at the Washington Conference on Holocaust-Era Assets in 1998, offers guidance in resolving such disputes more informally, leading to agreements between otherwise litigious parties.

a. Indigenous Peoples and Museums

(i) Canada.

Turning the Page: Forging New Partnerships between Museums and First Peoples: A Report Jointly Sponsored by the Assembly of First Nations and the Canadian Museums Association (1991)

The mission of the Task Force has been to develop an ethical framework and strategies by which Aboriginal peoples and cultural institutions can work together to represent Aboriginal history and culture.... The three major issues identified were:

1) increased involvement of Aboriginal peoples in the interpretation of their culture and history by cultural institutions;
2) improved access to museum collections by Aboriginal peoples; and,
3) the repatriation of artifacts and human remains.

In order to ensure that consultation and research with regard to these issues would be as comprehensive as possible, the Task Force members worked as three regional committees, based on a traditional model proposed by a First Nations Task Force member. Each region was mandated with the responsibility to consult with First Peoples and other organizations, institutions, and communities within a specified area of Canada. The Western committee covered British Columbia and the Yukon, the Central Committee covered the Prairie Provinces and the Northwest Territories, and the Eastern Committee covered Ontario, Quebec and the Atlantic provinces....

IV. CREATING PARTNERSHIPS

Principles and Recommendations

If museums are to achieve their goal of "interpreting the past, explaining the present and thereby illuminating choices for the future," they must express accurately and in context the cultural heritage and spirit of the civilizations that they portray, in this regard. "The Spirit Sings" exhibition was a watershed in Canadian museology. It has served as a forum for identifying historical problems in the representation of Aboriginal peoples in museums and it has led to the present efforts toward establishing open and lasting partnerships between museums and Aboriginal communities.

Over the years museum exhibitions have usually been based on the assumption that Aboriginal peoples were extinct or on the verge of vanishing. A great portion of existing collections were gathered at the turn of the century when museums and private collectors rushed to collect cultural materials from Aboriginal communities, which according to the social, scientific and political philosophy of the time were believed to be well on the way to extinction. Some museum exhibitions reinforced a public perception that Aboriginal cultures existed only in the past and that they were incapable of change. Such perceptions continue to support the mistaken notion that Aboriginal cultures are inferior.

Museums have recognized the failings in such presentations and changes are being made. As well, a number of community-based Aboriginal cultural centres have been established instigating changes of far-reaching impact. Along with some museums, the latter have begun to develop new initiatives in cultural representation. However, a great deal remains to be done to set the record straight for a museum-going public accustomed to the old-style presentations.

In order to accurately reflect within museums the fundamental and unique contribution of First Peoples to Canada, as well as the spiritual and social values of their diverse contemporary cultures, it is necessary to develop new relationships with museums based on progressive principles and policy. To quote former AFN National Chief Georges Erasmus again, "We, the Aboriginal peoples, are well aware that many people have dedicated their time, careers and their lives showing what they believe is the accurate picture of indigenous peoples. We thank you for that, but we want to turn the page . . . "

In order to turn that page, and in the spirit of forging new partnerships, we offer the following principles and recommendations based on regional consultations, the many submissions received from organizations and concerned individuals combined with extensive and productive discussions at three national task force meetings.

A. Principles to Establish Partnerships between First Peoples and Canadian Museums.
   1. Museums and First Peoples will work together to correct inequities that have characterized their relationships in the past. In particular, the desire and authority of First Peoples to speak for themselves should be recognized and affirmed by museums.
   2. An equal partnership involves mutual appreciation of the conceptual knowledge and approaches characteristic of First Peoples and the empirical knowledge and approaches of academically-trained workers.

3. First Peoples and museums recognize mutual interests in the cultural materials and knowledge of the past, along with the contemporary existence of First Peoples.
4. First Peoples and museums must accept the philosophy of co-management and co-responsibility as the ethical basis for principles and procedures pertaining to collections related to Aboriginal cultures contained in museums.
5. Appropriate representatives of First Peoples will be involved as equal partners in any museum exhibition, program or project dealing with Aboriginal heritage, history or culture.
6. First Peoples and museums must recognize a commonality of interest in the research, documentation, presentation, promotion and education of various publics, including museum professionals and academics, in the richness, variety and validity of Aboriginal heritage, history and culture.
7. First Peoples must be fully involved in the development of policies and funding programs related to Aboriginal heritage, history and culture.

(ii) New Zealand. Examples of return to the Maori in New Zealand of significant Maori cultural objects have been relatively infrequent and have taken varying forms. In the absence of any clearly applicable statutory or common law rules, most returns have occurred as a result of drawn-out negotiations between the Maori and institutions or individuals. Sometimes these have occurred within New Zealand, and occasionally they have involved requests to foreign countries. One of the best-known instances of domestic repatriation was the agreement to return a Maori meeting house (*wharenui*) in New Zealand after lengthy negotiations between the New Zealand government and the Bay of Plenty Maori tribe (*iwi*) of Ngati Awa.

Mataatua is a Maori meetinghouse that was built by the Ngati Awa tribe between 1872 and 1875 at Whakatane, on the North Island of New Zealand. In 1879, the New Zealand government asked the chiefs of Ngati Awa to allow the house to be dismantled and sent to Sydney, Australia, for exhibition. From Australia, Mataatua was sent on to London and kept in storage at the Victoria and Albert Museum for some forty years. In 1924 it was reassembled for display at the Wembley Exhibition in London. In 1925 Mataatua was returned to its homeland for the Dunedin South Seas Exhibition of that year. Following that event, the house was given on permanent loan by the New Zealand government to the Otago Museum, in Dunedin, New Zealand, where it remained until 1996. During its stay at the Otago Museum, the house underwent reconstruction in the form of being shortened, and some of its original carvings were replaced.

It seems that the removal of Mataatua by the government in 1879 was done without consensus being reached among the Ngati Awa people. The carvers of the house protested its removal, and Maori women objected to its being dismantled for travel. It has also been suggested that the main reason the government was able to remove the house, despite these objections, was the fear and deprivation that characterized much of the Maori population during the period.

A request for the return of the house to the Ngati Awa people was made in 1983. In response to the request, the New Zealand minister of internal affairs, referring to the statute of limitations, advised the tribe to negotiate directly with the trustees of the Otago Museum. Subsequently, the New Zealand government suggested that the tribe include the house among issues affecting it that were already before the Waitangi Tribunal (a quasi-judicial body recommending solutions to Maori-related issues). The Ngati Awa considered commencing civil proceedings in conversion against the New Zealand government but eventually decided against bringing court action.

Negotiations between the Ngati Awa and the New Zealand minister of justice, Douglas Graham, began in 1995. In 1996, the Waitangi Tribunal recommended to the New Zealand government that Mataatua be returned. Eventually, a separate agreement was concluded that the house be returned. As part of this negotiating process, the New Zealand government agreed to pay the Otago Museum NZ$2.75 million for the house. An agreement dated August 30, 1996, was executed by both sides. Simultaneously, a deed of settlement and a covenant were signed between the government and Ngati Awa whereby title to Mataatua vested in the latter. A formal ceremony also took place at which two carved portions of the house were delivered to the Ngati Awa, who also received NZ$2 million from the government to help repair and reinstate the house and build a modern protective facility.

The former chair of the Otago Museum Trust Board, Dame Elizabeth Hanan, has stated that the board did not consider the return of Mataatua as constituting a precedent for the return of other parts of the collection of her museum. She has also been quoted as saying that neither the New Zealand Crown nor the Ngati Awa could definitively prove legal title to the house. The Otago Museum will apparently use the compensation it has received to build another meetinghouse.

It is difficult to predict how the Mataatua case would have been resolved had it come before the New Zealand courts. Rights based on the Treaty of Waitangi are difficult to enforce unless they have received support in the form of national legislation. A separate basis for upholding a Maori claim is for the courts to recognize aboriginal title as a common-law-based customary right. There have been some judicial statements in support of such a right based on the concept that indigenous rights continue after conquest by the imperial power, as part of the common law, unless expressly extinguished by legislation. It also may be that claims against the government have a greater likelihood of success than similar claims against private persons. This may arise from the idea that the Crown has the additional burden of having a fiduciary responsibility toward the Maori. This fiduciary duty has been referred to by the Waitangi Tribunal and the New Zealand courts.

(iii) United States. The Native American Graves Protection and Repatriation Act of 1990 (NAGPRA), which is discussed more thoroughly in Chapter 5, is the core of the emerging regime for repatriation of cultural heritage within the United States. In brief, the Act gives recognized indigenous groups ownership and control of American Indian and native Hawaiian human remains and certain cultural objects found on federal or tribal lands. NAGPRA also provides criminal sanctions for unauthorized excavation and removal of human remains and associated objects from federal or tribal lands. The law requires federal agencies and federally funded museums to furnish an inventory or summary of American Indian human remains and associated funerary objects as well as a summary of unassociated cultural objects. Also, NAGPRA provides for the repatriation to the tribes of certain classes of such objects according to prescribed procedures. To supervise implementation of these measures, NAGPRA established a review committee.

Because federally funded museums in the United States are often private and established at the state or local level, implementation of NAGPRA relies on federal-state cooperation. Critical issues under the Act may require resolution by state statutory or common law. Such issues include definitions of the ordinary ownership and disposition of property, as well as fiduciary duties imposed on museums and other institutions. The cooperation of state and local law enforcement agencies is also essential.

b. Holocaust-Related Claimants and Possessors

The complex factual, legal, moral, and ethical issues surrounding claims concerning art looted or otherwise lost during the Holocaust and in the period surrounding and during the Second World War have led to a number of lawsuits – particularly in the United States. Many, however, feel that the complexity and sensitivity of these claims are better suited to some more cooperative form of solution than that afforded by litigation.

M.J. Bazyler, Holocaust Justice: The Battle for Restitution in America's Courts 202–14, 249–62 (2003)

Between 1933 and 1945, the Germans stole approximately 600,000 pieces of art from both museums and private collections throughout Europe, including paintings, sculpture, objets d'art, and tapestries. When rare books, stamps, coins, and fine furniture are added, the figure goes into the millions. It took 29,984 railroad cars, according to records from the Nuremberg trials, to transport all the stolen art to Germany. The value of the art plundered during the Holocaust exceeded the total value of all the art in the United States in 1945: $2.5 billion at 1945 prices or $20.5 billion today. The Nazi art confiscation program was the greatest displacement of art in human history. As explained by one heir of a Holocaust victim who was killed and whose art was stolen: "You ask, did they kill? Yes, they killed. They killed for art, when it suited them. So killing Jews and confiscating art somehow went together."

Hitler, an unsuccessful art student, was obsessed with art.... Hitler "spent more on art then anybody in the history of the world," freely using state funds for this purpose. One of Hitler's grand plans was to build [the] Führermuseum in Linz, Austria, where many of his favorite paintings among the looted art would eventually be displayed. Professor Petropoulos estimates that "the Germans have today 1,532 paintings (1,076 of which hang in museums and the remainder in government offices and embassies) that came from the collections of Hitler, Hermann Goering, Martin Bormann, and other Nazi leaders, and were deemed not to have come from victims' collections."

After Hitler's rise to power and throughout the war years, there was a brisk market for works stolen by the Germans, as they did not keep all of what they stole. Much of what they considered "degenerate art" (modern art not favored by Hitler, works of Jewish artists, and art representing Jewish subjects) they "fenced" in order to obtain valuable foreign currency. Art dealers in Europe and even in the United States were not shy about trading in such art.... [A] list issued in 1946 by the U.S. Office of Strategic Services of persons involved in art trade with the Nazis... contains more than two hundred names....

Switzerland, along with other neutral countries – especially Spain and Portugal – became a favorite conduit for transferring art during the war, both art looted and art shipped off to safety from the Nazis. Holocaust historian Lynn Nicholas described this wartime trade in art:

> As the war widened, moving objects became much more difficult and neutral Switzerland became more prominent in the art trade.... The Nazi government went to Switzerland to sell the "degenerate" works it had purged from its own museums.... Many dealers fleeing Nazism took their stocks to Switzerland and continued trading. Therefore, it was natural, at the beginning of the occupation of Western Europe, for dealers to explore the possibilities of trading through Switzerland or using Switzerland as a route for sending works to the Americas.... All this did not affect Germans buying from Swiss nationals. Goering, through his curator, legally bought quite a number of works from Swiss dealers. The curators, of course, liked to be paid in Swiss francs, which was a problem for Goering. In order to circumvent this, he resorted to the barter system... trad[ing] "degenerate" works that were valueless in Germany for coveted, old, preferably Germanic, masters.
>
> All of these works had been confiscated. Most were confiscated from Jewish collections in France, Belgium, and Holland.

After the war, the Allies began the complicated task of returning art and other cultural objects to the country of those whose art had been recovered. While the effort was massive (for example, 60,000 artworks were returned to France, with 45,000 returned to their Jewish owners), it was only partially successful. "After the war, all art found that couldn't be identified went to checkpoints in Europe," Anita Difanis, executive director of Government Affairs for the Association of Art Museum Directors, pointed out. "The U.S. manned a checkpoint, and took all art that couldn't be identified and gave it back to the country of origin as best they could determine. Other armies did the same. Then things were sealed up after the war. Tons of research hasn't yet been tapped."

Although much of this art was returned between 1945 and 1949, since so much was stolen and also changed hands during the war years – and so many of its Jewish owners murdered by the Germans – [re-creating] the history of the owners (the technical term is *provenance*) of each piece stolen by the Nazis was impossible. The unstable postwar political climate in Europe, with entire cities reduced to rubble and millions of people displaced, made the job more difficult. The Soviet Union also aggravated the problem. As the Soviet army occupied eastern Germany and other areas liberated from Nazi Germany, they often sent home recovered artworks, claiming them as "war booty." Stalin even created special "trophy brigades" in the Soviet army for this purpose, and more than one million cultural objects were shipped to Soviet Russia between 1944 and 1947. While over the years the Soviets have returned some of these objects, no one knows today, not even the present Russian government, what Nazi-looted art still sits in dusty museum basements and warehouses throughout Russia. All these circumstances led to tens of thousands of artworks disappearing into a Soviet "black hole" at the conclusion of the war, with no trace of them after coming into German hands. . . .

According to one estimate, about 2,000 Holocaust looted artworks around the world have been returned since 1998, most from museums and public galleries. The efforts to restore art plundered during the Holocaust to its rightful owners, who today most often are heirs of the Jewish person or family from whom the Nazis stole the art, have been an important component of the Holocaust restitution campaign. As the following discussion reveals, these efforts began at the same time as the demands were being made on the Swiss banks to right the wrongs for their wartime and postwar behavior. The various Holocaust art restitution success stories and sometimes failures also came at the same time the other restitution claims were being settled.

This was not pure coincidence. As claimants, Jewish organizations, federal and state government officials, and other activists began in the late 1990s to look at the still-lingering wrongs committed by European corporate actors during World War II, they realized that the issue of missing Nazi-stolen art likewise needed to be addressed. Like the other property restitution claims, Holocaust art also was property stolen from Jews that had not been properly returned to its owners or their heirs after the war.

As with the other Holocaust restitution claims, especially the claims on the Swiss banks, books published in the late 1990s about the subject helped expose the extent of the problem. Especially important were Hector Feliciano's *The Lost Museum*, first published in France in 1996 and then in the United States in 1997, and Lynn Nicholas's *The Rape of Europa*, published in 1994. In his book, Feliciano, a Puerto Rican–born journalist living in Paris, described how many of the artworks stolen by the Nazis had turned up in French museums, with the museums simply turning a blind eye to their checkered provenance, never bothering to determine whether the prewar owners or any of their heirs were still alive. The book caused a sensation in France and led to a fresh look at the problem of Nazi-stolen artworks, not only in France, but around the world. Nicholas's earlier work also was critical, disclosing the location of many of the missing pieces. The Holocaust art cases helped drive the entire Holocaust restitution movement. Discoveries that valuable artworks hanging in public museums or in the private collections of prominent persons had been stolen by the Nazis make good stories and so were widely reported by the media. They covered these claims as part of the bigger Holocaust restitution picture, which kept the Holocaust restitution movement in the public eye.

The Holocaust art success stories – a claimant obtaining the return of a Holocaust artwork, through either litigation or mediation – emboldened the entire Holocaust restitution movement and helped those working on nonart Holocaust issues to continue their work. . . . At the same time, the corporate Holocaust restitution suits helped push along the Holocaust looted art claims. . . .

Because of the problem's complexity, at least five different organizations have been working on the issue. Since their efforts often overlap, these organizations have both worked together and also stumbled into each other.

In the United States, the World Jewish Congress (WJC) formed the Commission for Art Recovery (CAR), whose mission is to "identify and locate art stolen by the Nazis and their collaborators" and "register claims for the victims of Nazi art theft." CAR is chaired by Ronald Lauder, an art collector, philanthropist, heir to the Lauder cosmetics fortune, former U.S. ambassador to Austria, and chairman of New York's Museum of Modern Art (MoMA). Because of his two positions as chairman of MoMA and head of CAR, Lauder was pulled in opposite directions in [one] case. While CAR is concerned about restoring Nazi-stolen art to its former owners, MoMA was trying to return the [the art] to Austria.

A second organization in the United States involved with the issue is the Holocaust Art Restitution Project (HARP), formerly affiliated with the B'nai B'rith Klutznick National Jewish Museum in Washington, D.C. . . . HARP was critical to the restitution of one important work in the United States and has been involved behind the scenes in the restitution of a number of other artworks both in the United States and abroad.

A third body in the United States that is actively involved in the restitution of Holocaust looted art is the Holocaust Claims Processing Office (HCPO) of the New York State Department of Banking. The HCPO, established in 1997 as a division of the New York State Banking Department, does not limit its work to helping Holocaust claimants with banking issues or even to assisting only New York residents. Its deputy director, Monica Dugot, also has played an important role in the Holocaust looted art debate, and the office has been instrumental in the restitution of numerous looted artworks.

In Europe, the Commission for Looted Art in Europe (and using the acronym ECLA), founded in March 1999 in London by the European Council of Jewish Communities and the Conference of European Rabbis, is trying to trace Nazi-stolen art. Its director, Anne Webber, has been an important player in the field of recovering Nazi-stolen art in Europe.

Finally, the Art Loss Register (ALR), also based in London and founded in 1991 by auction houses to help retrieve all stolen art, not just that from the Holocaust, has also become actively involved in searching for art lost during the Holocaust and returning it to its rightful owners. ALR claims to have compiled the world's largest commercial database, nearly 100,000 items of stolen and missing art, antiques, and valuables. Although ALR is a commercial enterprise, it helps claimants searching for Holocaust looted art by listing their claims on its database free of charge. . . .

Many more Holocaust looted art claims have settled without resorting to litigation than through lawsuits. The lawsuits may dominate the headlines, but in the last seven years, quiet diplomacy and private negotiations have led to the return of some significant artworks to their rightful owners. Of course, while litigation may not have expressly led to the resolution of these claims, both in the United States and abroad, the threat of American litigation remains a powerful incentive for possessors of Holocaust looted art, whether they be museums, art galleries, or private collectors, to find an out-of-court resolution. Since the Holocaust restitution campaign began in the mid-1990s, more than two thousand artworks have been returned to their rightful owners around the world without litigation.

I will illustrate with one such successful resolution, because it presents a scenario unlike the bitterly fought battles just described.

In contrast to the position taken by the possessors of looted artworks in the preceding lawsuits, when the North Carolina Museum of Art (NCMA) was presented with a claim of having in its collection a Holocaust looted artwork, *Madonna and Child*, a 1518 painting by the German Renaissance artist Lucas Cranach, one of eighty-five artworks confiscated by the Nazis in 1940 from Dr. Philipp von Gomperz. The Nazis lionized Cranach as the quintessential Aryan painter. In the early 1950s, the painting ended up in Beverly Hills, California, bought by an unsuspecting collector who later donated it to the NCMA. In November 1999, two sisters living in Austria, the grandnieces of von Gomperz and his sole surviving heirs, laid claim to the painting. They filed a claim with both CAR and HCPO. CAR located the painting in the NCMA and informed HCPO of its discovery. The museum did not stonewall the claim. Instead, shortly after being informed that the painting might have been stolen, the North Carolina museum conducted with HCPO a thorough investigation of the provenance of the *Madonna and Child*, akin to the investigation conducted by HARP for the Seattle Art Museum regarding the *Odalisque*. In February 2000, when the investigation revealed the accuracy of the claim, the museum announced that it would return the painting to the Gomperz heirs, currently living in Austria. The sisters did not have to file suit or even hire an attorney. Instead, the agreement was negotiated by Monica Dugot, deputy director of New York State's HCPO. Even though the agreement had no connection to New York, Dugot, acting on behalf of the two Austrian nationals, settled the claim for them. Howard Spiegler [the claimant's attorney] summarized the surprising but happy ending to the story:

> The heirs were so taken with the Museum's beneficence that they agreed to sell the painting back to the Museum at substantially below the market price, reflecting what they called a "partial donation" because, as they put it, "the public should know that the heirs of Phillip Gomperz appreciate the sense of justice shown by the [museum's] decision

to restitute the painting." And the State of North Carolina was so impressed with the whole affair that it presented Ms. Dugot with a special state medal, never before given to a non-resident of North Carolina.

. . .

In 1998, the 170-member Association of Art Museum Directors (AAMD) in the United States created the Task Force on the Spoliation of Art during the Nazi World War II Era. The AAMD's press release announcing the creation of the task force declared:

> The Association of Art Museum Directors recognizes and deplores the systematic unlawful confiscation of art that was one of the many horrors of the Holocaust and World War II. The Association is committed to implementing a mechanism for coordinating full access to the newly available documentation on this wide-scale confiscation of art.
>
> In keeping with the AAMD's Code of Ethics, the Association reaffirms the commitment of its members to weigh, promptly and thoroughly, claims of title to specific works. . . . In order to achieve timely resolution of ownership claims relating to art alleged to have been stolen immediately before, during and immediately after World War II, the Association strongly recommends the creation of a mechanism for the resolution of these claims, such as mediation, arbitration or other forms of alternate dispute resolution.

The task force, in turn, issued guidelines to museums to expedite both the discovery and the handling of Nazi-stolen art. The guidelines, contained in a June 1998 report by the task force, mandate that museums respond to "legitimate" claims relating to illegal confiscation by "offer[ing] to resolve the matter in an equitable, appropriate and mutually agreeable manner." They also urge museums to take an active approach by reexamining the provenance of artworks in their collections that were assembled before 1945 and that changed hands between 1933 and 1953. Philippe de Montebello, director of New York's Metropolitan Museum of Art and chairman of the task force, claimed that "by adopting the report, America's museums place themselves on record as committed to acting swiftly and proactively to conduct the necessary research that will enable us to learn as much as possible about the history of works of art for which full ownership records have not been available."

Unfortunately, the AAMD's task force guidelines are vague, no more than statements of aspirations without any specifics or teeth for enforcement. For instance, while two of the guidelines urge resolution of "legitimate" claims, they offer no guidance as to which claims are to be considered legitimate. Another guideline recommends that museums "offer to resolve" the legitimate claim in "an equitable, appropriate, and mutually agreeable manner." Such language is meaningless, providing no specifics as to what a museum should do when faced with a claim that it possesses art stolen by the Nazis during World War II. Rather, the guidelines, and the creation of a museum task force, appear to be more a public relations exercise than a real attempt to deal with the problem. After the task force was created, Manhattan District Attorney Robert Morgenthau agreed that it was a matter of "too little, too late." Referring to his case against MoMA, Morgenthau stated, "I am pleased to learn that 53 years after the end of World War II, museum directors have established a task force to address the question of looted art. Would they have done so if it had not been for our investigation?" Lloyd P. Goldenberg, a Washington, D.C., art law specialist, added, "In the past the museums have clearly not complied with their legal and ethical responsibility to make appropriate title inquiry prior to acquisition." When confronted with a claim, the museums "most often resist." Goldenberg predicted that the guidelines could turn out to be little more than "a public relations effort to make the museums appear godly." Rabbi Abraham Cooper of the Simon Wiesenthal Center agreed:

> The energy to finally look at this issue didn't come from the art world. It came from the media, and human rights groups, and a few individuals who said, you know what, this was 50, 60 years ago, it didn't happen on my watch, but it's time to do the right thing. Something's got to be fixed. I'm sure that [museum] lawyers broke out in a sweat – but this is a very welcome development.

In April 2001, the AAMD task force issued a one-sentence addendum to its guidelines:

> It should be the goal of member museums to make full disclosure of the results of their ongoing provenance research on those works of art in their collections created before 1946, transferred after 1932 and before 1946, and which were or could have been in continental Europe during that period, giving priority to European paintings and Judaica.

The addendum, like the original guidelines, appears to be more empty verbiage. Member museums are given yet another goal rather than mandated requirements. To date, the guidelines have been ineffective in either uncovering any artworks or returning disputed works to their owners.

In late 1998 . . . a proposal began circulating in New York urging the creation of a central register of stolen art. Under the proposal, a victim of an artwork theft would have, in all instances, six years to file suit to recover the theft. The victim must also register the theft with the Art Loss Register (ALR), a privately owned, for-profit computerized database of 100,000 stolen and missing art-works. Failure by a victim to register the stolen artwork with ALR could immunize a good-faith purchaser from suit. Prospective buyers would also be required to check with ALR before making their purchase, to show their "due diligence" as a good-faith buyer. Holocaust victims would be allowed more time – ten years, according to some to make claims or be forever cut off from claiming looted art.

As the London-based *New Statesman* pointed out, the use of the ALR database has become more popular:

> Some in the art world have been reluctant to accept the register, because to do so would put their exalted business on a par with the second-hand car trade. The availability of stolen cars is so widespread that all reputable dealers, as a matter of course, check every motor vehicle passing through their premises with the police-operated register of stolen vehicles. The art trade seems finally to have accepted that, however sublime a Fragonard oil sketch, or a Matisse woodcut, in this regard they are no different from a 1988 Toyota with a dodgy clutch. In 1998, the register carried out barely 2,000 searches on behalf of dealers; by [2000] that had shot up to 15,000.

Nevertheless, the proposal was opposed by the various groups dealing with Nazi-stolen art, including HARP and CAR. A major practical problem, Constance Lowenthal of CAR pointed out, was

> how the register will make itself known. [T]heft victims could protect their rights in New York State only by knowing about this law and knowing about this registry. But there's nothing in the proposal about how the registry is going to inform someone who lives in Kiev or Ankara or Beijing or New Delhi that if they don't register their stolen object, and it turns up in New York, they have no chance of reclaiming it.

Another objection, voiced by Willi Korte, vice chairman of HARP, was to the idea that a single database would be adequate for researching Holocaust claims: "There are hundreds of thousands of missing art-works of all sorts. . . . The great majority of them will never be recovered and claimed because they can't be identified."

In January 1999, the Paris-based International Council of Museums (ICOM), a professional body in existence since 1946 with a membership of approximately fifteen hundred museums worldwide, issued its list of recommendations concerning how members should deal with "the issue of works of art confiscated from Jewish owners during the Second World War and kept in museums or public collections." The four recommendations are brief and seemed more in the nature of "we need to say something about the problem" rather than anything of substance. That is, member museums are to "actively investigate and identify all acquisitions . . . that might be regarded as of dubious provenance"; "make such relevant information accessible to facilitate the research and identification" of looted art; "actively address and participate in drafting and establishing procedures, nationally and internationally for disseminating information on these objects and facilitating their rightful return"; and "actively address the return of all objects of art that formerly belonged to Jewish owners . . . according to national legislation and where the legitimate ownership of these objects can clearly be established." The recommendations appear to be a shorter version of the guidelines issued more than a year earlier by the American museum directors' task force on Holocaust looted art. The last recommendation, and the only one to deal specifically with the issue, may in fact become an obstacle to returning a Holocaust looted art object. A museum faced with a claim of possessing a Holocaust looted artwork may argue that according to this recommendation, it need not return it because its domestic laws ("national legislation") makes the claim time barred or that the museum now holds clear title to the looted artwork under its domestic law because the artwork went though the hands of a good-faith purchaser before arriving at the museum. In addition, the museum could assert that in accordance with the ICOM recommendations, it can keep the looted artwork because legitimate ownership by the claimant to the artwork cannot be "clearly established" to the museum's satisfaction. As the HCPO's Dugot remarked,

> The reality is that few cases are . . . well documented and often, after much research has been done gaps in provenance still remain. While it is true that a gap in provenance does not necessarily suggest that a painting was looted in the Holocaust, the opposite cannot be inferred either. In other words, that same gap does not indicate that a painting was *not* looted. Absolute certainty in cases such as these can be elusive and inferences must be drawn on available information. Often, the quest for perfect and precise answers becomes an impossible barrier to just resolution of claims.

In December 1998, the U.S. State Department organized the Washington Conference on Holocaust-Era Assets. Delegates from forty-five countries and thirteen nongovernmental organizations (NGOs) met at the State Department over four days to discuss various Holocaust restitution issues, including looted art. Out of the conference came the so-called Washington principles, dealing specifically with World War II looted art.

Washington Conference on Holocaust-Era Assets, Principles with Respect to Nazi-Confiscated Art (1998) [The Washington Principles]

In developing a consensus on non-binding principles to assist in resolving issues relating to Nazi-confiscated art, the Conference recognizes that among participating nations there are differing legal systems and that countries act within the context of their own laws.

I. Art that had been confiscated by the Nazis and not subsequently restituted should be identified.

II. Relevant records and archives should be open and accessible to researchers, in accordance with the guidelines of the International Council on Archives.

III. Resources and personnel should be made available to facilitate the identification of all art that had been confiscated by the Nazis and not subsequently restituted.

IV. In establishing that a work of art had been confiscated by the Nazis and not subsequently restituted, consideration should be given to unavoidable gaps or ambiguities in the provenance in light of the passage of time and the circumstances of the Holocaust era.

V. Every effort should be made to publicize art that is found to have been confiscated by the Nazis and not subsequently restituted in order to locate its pre-War owners or their heirs.

VI. Efforts should be made to establish a central registry of such information.

VII. Pre-War owners and their heirs should be encouraged to come forward and make known their claims to art that was confiscated by the Nazis and not subsequently restituted.

VIII. If the pre-War owners of art that is found to have been confiscated by the Nazis and not subsequently restituted, or their heirs can be identified, steps should be taken expeditiously to achieve a just and fair solution, recognizing this may vary according to the facts and circumstances surrounding a specific case.

IX. If the pre-War owners of art that is found to have been confiscated by the Nazis, or their heirs, cannot be identified, steps should be taken expeditiously to achieve a just and fair solution.

X. Commissions or other bodies established to identify art that was confiscated by the Nazis and to assist in addressing ownership issues should have a balanced membership.

XI. Nations are encouraged to develop national processes to implement these principles, particularly as they relate to alternative dispute resolution mechanisms for resolving ownership issues.

Martha Lufkin, *The Increasing Role of the Market in Settling Claims*, Art Newspaper, December 2008, at 8.

In 1998, the question of art stolen by Nazis hit the U.S. art world in a dramatic way: the New York district attorney and the government sought to seize an allegedly Nazi-looted painting by Egon Schiele (*Portrait of Wally*, 1912), which was on loan from an Austrian museum to New York, where the heirs of a Jewish family claimed it . . .

[T]he case [later settled, on July 20, 2010] prompted worldwide calls for changes in dealing with Nazi-looted art. Attention bore down first on museums, accompanied by demands for Nazi-era provenance research of collections, a centralized provenance database and return of stolen art.

Rather than fizzling out, claims still keep coming, and now not only against museums. Instead, it appears that the shakeout of Nazi-looted art may increasingly occur in the marketplace, as new works come up for sale.

And rather than through litigation, a number of resolutions are quietly being facilitated by Sotheby's, Christie's, the Art Loss Register (ALR) and others.

Museums

In response to the Schiele uproar, in 1998 and 1999 U.S. museum groups called for Nazi-era provenance research for all acquisitions and loans, and encouraged the resolution of claims without court action. New guidelines from the American Association of Museums (AAM) allowed museums to return Nazi-looted art without raising every technical legal defense to keep it, such as invoking a statute of limitations to bar a claim. Many museums spent significant resources on provenance research. But after enormous expense, not much Nazi-stolen art has turned up at U.S. museums. About 32 claims have been made, with most items being returned.

Some museums have stepped forward after research, as in the case of the Virginia Museum of Fine Arts, which gave back *Portrait of a Courtier* (date unknown) by Jan Mostaert (around 1475–1555) to the descendants of the Polish Czartoryski family, in 2005. New museum websites showing provenance information have sparked some returns: the heirs of Jewish art dealer Max Stern regained a Nazi-confiscated work by Frans Snyders, *Still-life with Fruit and Game*, around 1615–20, from the National Gallery of Art in Washington, DC, after seeing it on the website. Museums elsewhere have also returned Nazi-stolen art, or paid compensation, including in the U.K., Netherlands, Israel, Austria and Germany.

. . .

In 2006, the Conference of Jewish Material Claims against Germany charged that U.S. museums had not adequately researched or published their collections. But museum representatives said at congressional hearings that museums had allocated significant resources to the problem, and would do so until the job was done.

Criticisms

Some have expressed concern that, with art prices high and more historical information available, financial backers are said to be putting up funds for research and legal fees, in exchange for a stake in sales proceeds. Others have criticized successful claimants for selling, saying that recovered art, or maybe at least one painting, should be given to a museum. But it is not clear why a person recovering stolen art should have less control over it than someone whose art was never stolen at all.

Where governments have been recalcitrant in giving up their art, lawyers have succeeded, in the U.S. and elsewhere. In 2005, the U.S. government agreed to an apology and a $225.5[million] settlement in a lawsuit over the notorious U.S. Army plundering of a train carrying valuables stolen by Nazis from Hungarian Jews. In 2006, Austria was forced to give back five Nazi-looted paintings by Gustav Klimt to the heirs of the Viennese Jewish collector Ferdinand Bloch-Bauer. The Dutch government, also in 2006, returned 202 Nazi-stolen paintings to the heir of the Jewish dealer Jacques Goudstikker.

In a ghostly reminder that much is not resolved, some governments have now posted websites seeking heirs in the Netherlands, Austria, Germany and the Czech Republic to Nazi art loot in their possession.

The trade

Before 1998, Nazi era provenance research was not on the radar screen of most dealers. The Art Dealers Association of America issued guidelines that year on the duties of dealers to conduct provenance research. "Dealers are much more careful and alert to this than they were ten or 12 years ago," Gilbert Edelson, administrative vice-president of the Art Dealers Association of America, told *The Art Newspaper*. "A careful dealer will not now buy or sell a work without being certain there is no problem involving the Holocaust."

At its February 2008 impressionist sale in London, Sotheby's included three stolen works whose resolution it had facilitated, two of them Nazi-loot claims: Degas's *Dancer Adjusting Her Slipper*, 1873, and Juan Gris's *The Bunch of Grapes*, 1924. Increasingly this is the case, Sotheby's and Christie's told *The Art Newspaper*. Each auction house said that it had facilitated scores of resolutions.

Both houses conduct their own provenance research and also use the ALR; if a Nazi-era problem is found, they alert the consignor. Sellers today tend to want to solve the problem, and may wish the auction house to start talking to heirs. "You're facilitating a discussion between two innocent parties," said Monica Dugot, Christie's director of restitution. Settlement terms vary, and have included sales with a division of the proceeds, or sellers returning art to heirs for some compensation.

Meanwhile, the ALR is the largest database that registers stolen art, including Nazi loot, and often facilitates resolutions. The ALR now vets most sales items for the major auction houses, 18 art fairs including Tefaf Maastricht and Aifaf Palm Beach, dealers and collectors, and museums which lack resources to check their entire collections.

The next generation

For Holocaust survivors, anguish may sap the strength to bring a claim, or sufficient facts may not be known. Many have let the question ride, possibly for a grandchild to pursue. Such claimants are now coming forward, at a time when more historical information is available.

Facts are irretrievably lost, in many cases. But perhaps not in all. And maybe art holders will come forward if private resolutions can now more easily be achieved without publicity. Many also wonder if Nazi-looted art is stashed in private collections owned by elderly war veterans or post-war buyers, whether in South America, Russia or Manhattan.

If so, collections will be passed on, and heirs may want to sell. The market may have a chance to do its work, so long as the vigilant keep watching.

Vineberg v. Bissonnette,
529 F. Supp. 2d 300 (D.R.I. 2007),
aff'd on other grounds, 548 F.3d 50 (1st Cir. 2008)

This is an action to recover personal property, for declaratory and injunctive relief, and for money damages. Plaintiffs, Robert S. Vineberg, Michael D. Vineberg, and Sydney Feldhammer, as Trustees of the Dr. and Mrs. Stern Foundation ("Plaintiffs" or "Stern Estate"), have moved for summary judgment on the replevin and conversion claims against Defendant Maria-Louise Bissonnette ("Defendant").

. . .

In or about 1913, Dr. Max Stern's ("Dr. Stern") father, Julius Stern, opened an art gallery in Dusseldorf, Germany. Julius Stern died in 1934, leaving the art gallery and its inventory to Dr. Stern. Dr. Stern was of Jewish descent and, under the Nuremberg laws, was subject to official persecution by the German government. In 1935, the Reich Chamber for the Fine Arts ("Reich Chamber"), an organization of the Nazi government, sent letters to Dr. Stern demanding that he liquidate his inventory and gallery. On or about September 13, 1937, Dr. Stern received a final order to sell his inventory immediately through a dealer approved by the Reich Chamber. Dr. Stern consigned most of his inventory and private collection, constituting hundreds of works, to the Lempertz Auction House ("LAH"), in Cologne, Germany. On or about November 13, 1937, LAH auctioned the items consigned to it by Dr. Stern, including the property that is the subject of the dispute in this matter, a nineteenth-century painting by Franz Xaver Winterhalter entitled "Mädchen aus den Sabiner Bergen" ("Girl from the Sabiner Mountains") ("the Painting"). The items consigned to LAH by Dr. Stern were sold at well below market value.

Dr. Stern fled Germany for Paris in December 1937. Upon discovering that Dr. Stern left Germany, the German government issued an order freezing his assets. Dr. Stern never received the proceeds of the LAH sale.[52] Dr. Stern eventually left Paris to join his sister in London prior to the outbreak of World War II. Dr. Stern later emigrated to Canada and became a preeminent art collector and dealer there.

LAH was heavily damaged in 1943 by wartime bombing and its Nazi-era records were destroyed. Post-war efforts to locate paintings from the LAH auction were hindered by the near-total destruction of LAH records. In spite of this, after the end of World War II, Dr. Stern made numerous attempts to locate his art collection. Immediately after the war, Dr. Stern recovered some paintings through his contact with the Canadian Military Mission and also filed a claim for restitution for artwork through the British military government in post-war Germany. In 1949, Dr. Stern and his wife traveled to Europe in an attempt to locate some of his art

[52] One commentator has suggested that Dr. Stern had to turn over the funds and several paintings from his private collection that he had left behind in Germany to secure an exit visa for his mother. Faculty of Fine Arts, Concordia University, *Auktion 392 Reclaiming the Galerie Stern, Dusseldorf*, at 14 & 24 n. 57 (2006).

collection. In 1948, and in 1952, Dr. Stern placed advertisements in two publications, "Canadian Art" and "Die Weltkunst." In 1958, Dr. Stern initiated proceedings in Germany for the recovery of paintings and other property seized by the Nazi government. In the early 1960s, Dr. Stern pursued claims for monetary compensation for his art losses through the German restitution courts. In 1964, a court in Germany awarded Dr. Stern partial damages for his loss of profits resulting from his being forced to sell his gallery's inventory at prices that were below market value. Upon his death in 1987, Dr. Stern bequeathed all residue of his estate to the Stern Estate. The Stern Estate primarily benefits three non-profit institutions: Concordia University and McGill University in Montreal, Canada, and the Hebrew University in Israel.

Dr. Karl Wilharm ("Wilharm") acquired the Painting through the LAH auction. Wilharm was Defendant's stepfather. Wilharm kept the Painting in his private collection except for one occasion, in 1954, when it was exhibited at a museum in Kassel, Germany. Defendant has had the Painting in her possession since 1959. Defendant inherited the Painting, from her mother's estate, in 1991. Defendant has resided in the United States since at least 1956 and in Rhode Island since at least 1991.

In April 2003, Estates Unlimited, Inc., received the Painting on consignment from Defendant. In April 2004, on behalf of the Stern Estate, the Art Loss Register ("ALR") agreed to list the lost inventory of Dr. Stern's gallery auctioned by LAH on its Holocaust related database. The Stern Estate also listed the Painting with Germany's Lost Art Internet Database. The Painting was to be auctioned by Estates Unlimited at a public auction scheduled for January 6, 2005. Just prior to the scheduled auction, however, the Stern Estate learned from ALR that the Painting was on consignment at Estates Unlimited. ALR contacted Estates Unlimited and informed Estates Unlimited of the Stern Estate's claimed ownership of the Painting. As a result, Estates Unlimited agreed to withdraw the Painting from the auction. Estates Unlimited then informed Defendant of the Stern Estate's claim of ownership.

In January 2005, the Stern Estate made a claim for restitution of the Painting with the Holocaust Claims Processing Office of the state of New York Banking Department ("HCPO"). In February 2005, HCPO sent a demand letter to Defendant through Estates Unlimited seeking restitution of the Painting. Defendant refused to return the Painting to the Stern Estate. From February 2005 through April 2006, HCPO and Defendant attempted to resolve the matter. On or about April 19, 2006, Defendant's former counsel notified the Stern Estate's counsel that the Painting had been sent to Germany "due to the institution of an action in German Courts to definitely determine title to the [P]ainting." Defendant's Opposition to Plaintiff's Statement of Undisputed Facts at 6. After the Painting arrived in Germany, Defendant obtained an appraisal of the Painting in the range of 50,000 to 70,000 [e]uros (approximately [US]$67,000 to $94,000). The instant action was instituted by the Stern Estate on May 8, 2006. The Stern

Estate has moved for summary judgment against Defendant on its claims for replevin and conversion.

III. Jurisdiction

This case is before the Court based on diversity jurisdiction. The named Plaintiffs are trustees of the Stern Estate and are citizens of Canada. Defendant is a citizen of the state of Rhode Island. Defendant does not dispute the parties' citizenship nor does she dispute that the amount in controversy exceeds $75,000. An exercise of this Court's diversity jurisdiction is, therefore, proper.

[Discussion of procedural aspects of the case are omitted.]

Replevin is an "action for the repossession of personal property wrongfully taken or detained by the defendant. . . . " As noted above, in Rhode Island, replevin is a statutory cause of action. [The statutory law] provides, in part, that "[w]henever any goods or chattels of more than [$5,000] value shall be unlawfully taken or unlawfully detained from the owner or from the person entitled to possession thereof . . . the owner or the other person may cause the same to be replevied by writ of replevin issuing from the superior court." Replevin is "available to persons claiming possession of goods or catties either wrongfully taken or wrongfully detained. Nothing more than the right of present possession, founded upon a general or special ownership of the goods or chattels, is necessary to enable a plaintiff to maintain the action." *Brunswick*, 389 A.2d at 1243. "An action in replevin merely adjudicates who has the *superior* right to possession of goods." The parties agree that to recover the Painting in a replevin action the Stern Estate must show that (1) it is the lawful owner of the Painting, (2) the Painting was taken from Dr. Stern, unlawfully, that is, without his permission, and (3) Defendant is in wrongful possession of the Painting.

1. Ownership of the Painting

In 1937, the LAH catalog for the auction of Dr. Stern's gallery inventory identified the Painting as being part of the auction. In addition to that evidence of ownership, in its 1964 decision, the restitution court in Germany cited and relied upon a list of the market value of the paintings at the Stern Gallery in 1937. That listing included the Painting. The restitution court awarded Dr. Stern compensation for lost profits on the artwork auctioned by LAH. Thus, the restitution court in Germany concluded that Dr. Stern was the owner of the Painting. At his death, Dr. Stern bequeathed all residue of his estate to the Stern Estate. The Court concludes that the Stern Estate is the lawful owner of the Painting.

2. Unlawful Taking of the Painting

In her opposition memorandum Defendant does not dispute the fact that the Nazi government forced Dr. Stern to liquidate inventory in his art gallery and controlled the manner of the forced sale. Dr. Stern fled the country before he realized any proceeds from the forced sale. It is clear that

Dr. Stern's relinquishment of his property was anything but voluntary. In support of its claim, the Stern Estate submitted a declaration from Lynn H. Nicholas ("Nicholas"), an expert in the field of World War II history relating to the Nazi party and its activities relating to the seizure of property. Nicholas concluded that the "methods used by the Gestapo and the Nazis to force Dr. Max Stern to sell the [P]ainting... amount to theft." "Dr. Stern's surrender of the [P]ainting to [LAH] for auction was ordered by the Nazi authorities and therefore the equivalent of an official seizure or a theft." In fact, the German restitution court found that the LAH auction was a "distress[ed] sale to which [Dr. Stern] was forced [to participate in] for reasons of persecution...." The Nazi party's actions in this instance are therefore properly classified as looting or stealing. *See generally Menzel v. List*, 49 Misc. 2d 300, 267 N.Y.S.2d 804, 811 (N.Y. Sup. Ct. 1966) (Nazi party could not convey good title to art taken during war because seizure of art during wartime constituted "pillage, or plunder... [which is the] taking of private property not necessary for the immediate prosecution of [the] war effort, and is unlawful"), *modified as to damages*, 28 A.D.2d 516, 279 N.Y.S.2d 608 (N.Y. App. Div. 1967), *rev'd as to modification*, 24 N.Y.2d 91, 298 N.Y.S.2d 979, 246 N.E.2d 742 (N.Y. 1969).

3. Wrongful Possession of the Painting

The Court acknowledges that Defendant acquired the Painting through no wrongdoing on her part. Defendant's predecessor-in-interest, Wilharm, however, as a result of the acquisition of the Painting through the forced sale, did not acquire good title to the Painting. "Where pillage has taken place, the title of the original owner is not extinguished." *Menzel*, 267 N.Y.S.2d at 811. [A] a thief "acquires not a semblance of right, title, or interest in his plunder." [T]he proposition that a thief has no "interest in the property as against the rightful owner" is "so well settled as to require no elaborate citation of authority in its support." *O'Keeffe v. Snyder*, 83 N.J. 478, 416 A.2d 862, 867 (1980) ("generally speaking, if the paintings were stolen, the thief acquired no title and could not transfer good title to others regardless of their good faith and ignorance of the theft"). Legal title to the Painting remained in Dr. Stern and was transferred to the Stern Estate upon Dr. Stern's death. Because Defendant's predecessor-in-interest did not have title to the Painting, Defendant cannot lay valid claim to ownership of the Painting. This Court concludes, therefore, that Defendant is in wrongful possession of the Painting.

...

In conclusion, the Court reiterates its findings:

1. The Stern Estate is the rightful owner of the Painting;
2. The Painting was taken unlawfully from Dr. Stern; and
3. Defendant is in wrongful possession of the Painting.

For the foregoing reasons, the Stern Estate's motion for summary judgment on the replevin claim is GRANTED. This Court therefore issues a writ of replevin. Defendant is ordered forthwith to turn over the Painting to the Stern Estate.

SO ORDERED.

NOTES AND QUESTIONS

1. Can the Washington Principles, which are expressed as moral commitments, ever be useful in resolving disputes or compelling restitution by governments, auction houses, galleries, museums, and individual museums? Does each of the principles apply to governments, institutions, and individuals? According to principle X, commissions or other bodies that are established to help give effect to the substantive requirements are to be "balanced." What does that mean? Is the balance intended to be the same as in other advisory bodies that must consider the interests of galleries, collectors, and governments?
2. Martha Lufkin's article reports that only about thirty-two claims have been made against museums in the United States, and most items have been returned. Especially given the high rate of return, what does the author think, and what do you think, accounts for so few claims? Insofar as technical barriers under private international law, such as statutes of limitations, offer at least a partial explanation for the paucity of claims, we return to the issue in the context of Holocaust-related claims in Chapter 5.
3. *Vineberg* was one of the first decisions to hold that a Nazi-forced sale of an artwork (typically at a depressed price) is tantamount to theft with the same consequences for bona fide purchasers and longtime possessors of the artwork. See also *Museum of Modern Art v. Schoeps*, 549 F. Supp. 2d 543 (2008) (denying motion to dismiss a declaratory judgment action to quiet title to paintings whose sale by a Jewish owner was claimed to have been forced by the Nazis); Andrew Adler, *Expanding the Scope of Museums' Ethical Guidelines with Respect to Nazi-Looted Art: Incorporating Restitution Claims Based on Private Sales Made as a Direct Result of Persecution*, 14 INT' J. CULTURAL PROP. 57 (2007).

2. International Agreements

Bilateral and multilateral agreements represent the most formal legal bases for cooperation in order to avoid and resolve disputes involving the status of cultural material. By their very nature, such agreements are based on a willingness on the part of one country to extend various legal guarantees to other countries on a reciprocal basis. These agreements, however, are mainly about the future. They establish foundations for resolving disputes that arise once cultural properties are unlawfully destroyed or removed. If this occurs, the provisions of these agreements furnish the basis for obliging parties to resolve disputes on a cooperative basis. The prescribed solutions are defined by the agreements themselves; to that extent they represent a certain level of certainty and predictability that is usually associated with judicial resolution of disputes.

Earlier we identified the principal multilateral agreements within UNESCO for protecting cultural heritage. Bilateral agreements are more numerous. The first bilateral agreements entered into by the United States predated its accession to the 1970 UNESCO

Convention on illegal trafficking in cultural property that was introduced in Chapter 3. These agreements sought to prevent the importation of officially designated objects into the United States, primarily from Latin American countries.[53] In 1995 the United States entered into its first bilateral agreement, under the 1970 Convention, with El Salvador,[54] to continue the protection of artifacts from the Cara Sucia archaeological site after the expiration of emergency measures under the Act that the United States had undertaken. In 1997 the United States and Canada entered into an agreement (which has since expired) to mutually restrict the import of a broad range of archaeological and ethnographic material, as well as material from shipwrecks and other underwater historic sites that are at least 250 years old.[55] The two neighbors also agreed to promote exchange of material for educational and scientific purposes. A third agreement, also in 1997, broadened the protection of Peruvian material to include Chavin, Paracas, Moche, Cuzco, Inca, and other material from 12,000 BCE to 1532 CE, as well as specific ethnological material from the colonial period (1532–1821), including paintings and sculptures used for evangelism among indigenous people.[56]

In 1982, the United States became a party to the 1970 UNESCO Convention. Since then, the United States has relied primarily on its provisions to cooperate with other countries in deterring and responding to illegal trafficking in cultural material. In contrast to other 1970 UNESCO Convention parties, however, the United States takes a selective and targeted approach to implementing the 1970 Convention. It has adopted a strategy that assesses the particular cultural property export control issues of individual countries and specific categories of cultural property. The Convention on Cultural Property Implementation Act (CPIA), which implements the 1970 UNESCO Convention, relies on article 9 of the Convention. Article 9 reads as follows:

> Any State Party to this Convention whose cultural patrimony is in jeopardy from pillage of archaeological or ethnological materials may call upon other States Parties who are affected. The States Parties to this Convention undertake, in these circumstances, to participate in a concerted international effort to determine and to carry out the necessary concrete measures, including the control of exports and imports and international commerce in the specific materials concerned. Pending agreement each State concerned shall take provisional measures to the extent feasible to prevent irremedial injury to the cultural heritage of the requesting State.

Accordingly, the United States has taken action to bar the importation of designated material in response to requests from numerous other states parties claiming that their cultural patrimony is in jeopardy from pillage of such material. Thus, under article 9 of

[53] *See, e.g.*, Treaty of Cooperation between the United States of America and the United Mexican States Providing for the Recovery and Return of Stolen Archaeological, Historical, and Cultural Properties, 22 U.S.T. 494 (1970).

[54] *See* 1995 Import Restrictions on Prehispanic Artifacts from El Salvador, 60 Fed. Reg. 13, 352 (1995).

[55] *See* U.S. Information Agency, News Release No. 031-97, Apr. 10, 1997, at 1–2.

[56] *See* U.S. Information Agency, News Release No. 048-97, June 9, 1997, at 1.

the 1970 UNESCO Convention, the United States has established a second, temporary but extendable type of bilateral agreement.

The CPIA sets up four conditions or "statutory determinations," as follows, for U.S. entry into a bilateral agreement under article 9:

> (A) that the cultural patrimony of a State Party is in jeopardy from pillage of archaeological or ethnological materials;
> (B) that the State Party has taken measures consistent with the Convention to protect its cultural patrimony;
> (C) that
> (i) the application of the most important restrictions . . . with respect to the archaeological or ethnological material of the State Party, if applied in concert with similar restrictions implemented, or to be implemented within a reasonable period of time, by those nations (whether or not State Parties) individually having a significant import trade in such material, would be of substantial benefit in deterring a serious situation of pillage, and
> (ii) remedies less drastic than the application of the restrictions set forth in such section are not available; and
> (D) that the application of the import restrictions . . . in the particular circumstances is consistent with the general interest of the international community in the interchange of cultural property among nations for scientific cultural, and educational purposes.

The Cultural Property Advisory Committee within the Department of State makes recommendations based on these four determinations. The president then has the option to negotiate a bilateral agreement with an initial lifespan of five years, subject to renewal. One such agreement, between the United States and Italy, was entered into in 2001 and renewed in 2006. The agreement is as follows:

Agreement between the Government of the United States of America and the Government of the Republic of Italy Concerning the Imposition of Import Restrictions on Categories of Archaeological Material Representing the Pre-Classical, Classical and Imperial Roman Periods of Italy, 40 I.L.M. 1031 (2001)

The Government of the United States of America and the Government of the Republic of Italy;

Acting pursuant to the 1970 UNESCO Convention on the Means of Prohibiting and Preventing the Illicit Import, Export and Transfer of Ownership of Cultural Property, to which both countries are States Party; and

Desiring to reduce the incentive for pillage of irreplaceable archaeological material representing the Pre-Classical, Classical and Imperial Roman periods of Italy's rich cultural heritage;

Have agreed as follows:

ARTICLE I

A. The Government of the United States of America, in accordance with its legislation entitled the Convention on Cultural Property Implementation Act, shall restrict the importation into the United States of the archaeological material ranging in date from approximately the 9th century B.C. to approximately the 4th century A.D., including categories of stone, metal, ceramic and glass artifacts, and wall paintings identified on a list to be promulgated by the United States Government (hereinafter known as the "Designated List"), unless the Government of the Republic of Italy issues a license or other documentation which certifies that such exportation was not in violation of its laws.
B. The Government of the United States of America shall offer for return to the Government of the Republic of Italy any material on the Designated List forfeited to the Government of the United States of America.
C. Such import restrictions shall become effective on the date the Designated List is published by the U.S. Customs Service in the U.S. Federal Register, the official United States Government publication providing fair public notice.

ARTICLE II

A. Representatives of the Government of the United States of America and representatives of the Government of the Republic of Italy shall take appropriate steps to publicize this Memorandum of Understanding.
B. Both Governments agree that in order for United States import restrictions to be fully successful in deterring pillage, the Government of the Republic of Italy shall use its best efforts to increase scientific research and protection of archaeological patrimony and protective measures for archaeological excavations at known sites, particularly in areas at greatest risk from looters. The Government of the United States of America acknowledges the efforts of the Government of the Republic of Italy in recent years to devote more public funds to guard archaeological sites and museums and to develop Italian tax incentives for private support of legitimate excavation. The Government of the Republic of Italy agrees to continue to pursue these efforts.
C. The Government of the Republic of Italy shall reinforce, with respect to the 1970 UNESCO Convention, the protection of its cultural patrimony. In particular, the Government of the Republic of Italy shall provide for:
   1. instituting more severe penalties and prompt prosecution of looters;

2. regulating the use of metal detectors;
3. providing additional training for the Carabinieri Special Unit for the Protection of Artistic Patrimony; and
4. intensifying the investigations by the Carabinieri Special Unit for the Protection of Artistic Patrimony on the looting of archaeological sites and on the routes of the smugglers of these artifacts.

D. Both Governments agree that, in order for United States import restrictions to be most successful in thwarting pillage, the Government of the Republic of Italy shall endeavor to strengthen cooperation among nations within the Mediterranean Region for the protection of the cultural patrimony of the region, recognizing that political boundaries and cultural boundaries do not coincide; and will seek increased cooperation from other art-importing nations to restrict illicit imports, in the effort to deter further pillage.

E. The Government of the United States of America recognizes that the Government of the Republic of Italy permits the interchange of archaeological materials for cultural, exhibition, educational and scientific purposes to enable widespread public appreciation of and legal access to Italy's rich cultural heritage. The Government of the Republic of Italy agrees to use its best efforts to encourage further interchange through:

1. promoting agreements for long-term loans of objects of archaeological or artistic interest, for as long as necessary, for research and education, agreed upon, on a case by case basis, by American and Italian museums or similar institutions, to include: scientific and technological analysis of materials and their conservation; comparison for study purposes in the field of art history and other humanistic and academic disciplines with material already held in American museums or institutions; or educational presentations of special themes between various museums or academic institutions;
2. encouraging American museums and universities jointly to propose and participate in excavation projects authorized by the Ministry of Culture, with the understanding that certain of the scientifically excavated objects from such projects could be given as a loan to the American participants through specific agreements with the Ministry of Culture; and
3. promoting agreements for academic exchanges and specific study programs agreed upon by Italian and American institutions.

F. The Government of the United States of America acknowledges the efforts by the Government of the Republic of Italy in recent years to review the laws concerning the export of archaeological artifacts and to improve the efficiency of the system to release certificates of exportation. The Government of the Republic of Italy will continue to examine new ways to facilitate the export of archaeological items legitimately sold within Italy.

G. The Government of the United States of America and the Government of the Republic of Italy shall use their best efforts to facilitate appropriate contacts between U.S. and Italian museums and institutions for the development of increased and extended loans of Italy's archaeological cultural patrimony to U.S. museums.

ARTICLE III

The obligations of both Governments and the activities carried out under this Memorandum of Understanding shall be subject to the laws and regulations of each Government, as applicable, including the availability of funds.

ARTICLE IV

A. This Memorandum of Understanding shall enter into force upon signature. It shall remain in force for a period of five years, unless extended.
B. This Memorandum of Understanding may be amended through an exchange of diplomatic notes.
C. The effectiveness of this Memorandum of Understanding shall be subject to review in order to determine, before the expiration of the five-year period of this Memorandum of Understanding, whether it should be extended.

IN WITNESS WHEREOF, the undersigned, being duly authorized by their respective Governments, have signed the present Memorandum of Understanding.

DONE at Washington, this 19th day of January, 2001, in the English and Italian languages, both texts being equally authentic.

Pending such agreements, the CPIA also allows the United States to respond to an "emergency condition" by imposing immediate prohibitions on the importation of designated material. In the words of article 9, these prohibitions constitute "provisional measures to the extent feasible to prevent irremediable injury to the cultural heritage of the requesting State." The measures are unilateral; they are never taken in response to a request by a foreign government. Under the CPIA, the term "emergency condition" means, with respect to any archaeological or ethnological material of any State Party, that such material is –

(1) a newly discovered type of material which is of importance for the understanding of the history of mankind and is in jeopardy from pillage, dismantling, dispersal, or fragmentation;

(2) identifiable as coming from any site recognized to be of high cultural significance if such site is in jeopardy from pillage, dismantling, dispersal, or fragmentation which is, or threatens to be, of crisis proportions, or
(3) a part of the remains of a particular culture or civilization, the record of which is in jeopardy from pillage, dismantling, dispersal, or fragmentation which is, or threatens to be, of crisis proportions; and
(4) application of the import restrictions . . . on a temporary basis would, in whole or in part, reduce the incentive for such pillage, dismantling, dispersal, or fragmentation.

Designated cultural heritage that is covered by either a bilateral agreement or unilateral import prohibition requires an export certificate from its country of origin to enter the United States.

The United States has also developed a practice not explicitly required by the Convention that takes account of the wider context in which returns of cultural property occur. Accordingly, bilateral agreements sometimes provide more broadly for cultural exchanges and museum exhibition loans. These so-called memoranda of understanding have been entered into as part of bilateral agreements with other parties to the UNESCO Convention, such as El Salvador and Italy.

Jane C. Waldbaum, *Opportunity Knocks*, Archaeology, Nov.–Dec. 2003, at 6

Before long, many Americans will have new opportunities to experience the ancient cultures of Italy, thanks to an agreement between the Italian and United States governments that specifies significant programs of legal cultural exchange, including long-term loans of archaeological materials for research and exhibition and a framework for scholarly and scientific cooperation between the countries. The agreement, which also restricts the import into the U.S. of a wide range of Italian archaeological materials . . . is the first one under the U.S. Convention on Cultural Property Implementation Act to mandate such broad exchange programs. . . . This is a win-win agreement. Italy benefits from the U.S. import restrictions that will protect its pre-classical, classical, and imperial Roman antiquities. Excavated material that has long lain unstudied and unpublished in Italian storerooms for lack of personnel will now be made available to American researchers for study, publication, and ultimately for exhibition. Meanwhile, American museums will be able to mount a variety of loan exhibitions of Italian archaeological materials, and the public will have new opportunities to see scientifically excavated artifacts whose known contexts will enhance the stories they have to tell. Several of these exhibitions will focus on less well-known regions and peoples such as ancient Liguria (the northwestern coast around Genoa), or types of materials not commonly seen in this country, like Etruscan gold jewelry. Exhibitions of looted artifacts seized by the Italian authorities are also proposed, to illustrate the consequences of illicit excavation and heighten public awareness of the gravity of this problem. Scholars, students and museum personnel will benefit from opportunities to collaborate with Italian colleagues on significant scholarly projects. They will be able to work on excavations, borrow excavated material on long-term loan for further research, study and publish previously unstudied archaeological material, and help organize exhibitions resulting from these projects.

These varied opportunities will allow a great many Americans to become better acquainted with the rich archaeological heritage of Italy. They will heighten public appreciation of the human past and increase public support for the protection of cultural heritage both at home and abroad. This enlightened plan should serve as a model for future agreements with other countries....

NOTES AND QUESTIONS

1. Bilateral agreements under the 1970 UNESCO Convention are normally extended for five-year periods. *See, e.g., United States Extends Agreements with Italy and Nicaragua on Protection of Cultural Property*, 100 AM. J. INT'L L. 460 (2006). An exception to this general practice was the agreement between the United States and Canada, which was allowed to expire in 2002.
2. On the efficacy of the provisions in the agreement between Italy and the United States, see Elisabetta Povoledo, *Italy and U.S. Museum Near Art Claim Deal*, INT'L HERALD TRIB., Nov. 24, 2005, at 2, as follows:

   > For all the saber-rattling before their grueling six-hour meeting on Tuesday, Italy's Culture Ministry and the Metropolitan Museum of Art in New York have mapped out a potential solution to Italy's claims on antiquities in the museum's collections, officials said Wednesday.
   >
   > In essence, Italy would officially own the works, which it asserts were looted within its borders, but the Met would get to keep them or receive objects of equal value on a long-term loan basis....
   >
   > Restitution, in any case, would not be an admission on the museum's part that it had knowledge of a potentially illicit provenance when it bought the pieces.

3. Aside from bilateral agreements, the United States has taken *unilateral* action under Article 9 of the 1970 UNESCO Convention. The list of emergency restrictions that have been imposed unilaterally under the CPIA gradually changes over the years. A few of the earliest examples include artifacts from the Cara Sucia Region of El Salvador; ceremonial textiles and other ethnological materials from Coroma, Bolivia; culturally significant archaeological objects from the [Sipán] Region of Peru; Mayan artifacts from the Petén Region of Guatemala; ethnographic and archaeological material from Mali; and looted material from Iraq.

   The following chart shows the cooperative action that has been taken by the United States under the CPIA in implementing Article 9 of the 1970 Convention (available at http://www.culturalheritage.state.gov; scroll down to "Chart of Current and Expired Import Restrictions"):

CHART OF EMERGENCY ACTIONS & BILATERAL AGREEMENTS

MOU = Memorandum of Understanding, or Bilateral Agreement.

See Chart in Chronological Order

COUNTRY	'87	'88	'89	'90	'91	'92	'93	'94	'95	'96	'97	'98	'99	'00	'01	'02	'03	'04	'05	'06	'07	'08	'09	'10	'11
Bolivia			March 14, 1989: Emergency Action on certain ethno. textiles.(expired Sept. 11, '96)												Dec. 7, '01: MOU on archaeo. & ethno. material (extended Dec. 4, '06).										
Cambodia													Dec. 2, '99: Emergency Action archaeo. material.				Sept. 22, '03: MOU on Khmer archaeo. material.								
Canada											April 22, '97: MOU on archaeo. and ethno. material. (exp. '02)														
Colombia																				March 15, '06: MOU on archaeo. & ethno. material.					
Cyprus Archaeo																July 19, 02: MOU on archaeo. material. Sept. 4, '06, amended to include prior protections.					July 16, '07: Amended Bilateral Agreement on archaeo. & ethno. material is extended.				
Cyprus Ethno													April 12, '99: Emergency Action on 'ethno. material (extended Aug. 29, '03).												
El Salvador	Sept. 11, '87: Emergency Action on Cara Sucia pre-Columbian material.								March 10, '95: MOU on pre-Columbian material. Continues protection for Cara Sucia material. (extended March 8, '00, and March 8, '05)																
Guatemala					April 15, '91: Emergency Action on pre-Columbian material from Petén.						Oct. 3, '97: MOU on pre-Columbian material. Continues protection for Petén material. (extended Sept. 29, '02); extended & amended Sept. 29, 07.														
Honduras																		March 12, '04: MOU on pre-Columbian material.							
Italy															Jan. 23, '01, MOU on certain archaeological material (extended on 19 January '06).										
Mali							Sept. 23, '93: Emergency Action on arch. material.				Sept. 23, '97: MOU on archaeo. material from the Niger River Valley and Bandiagara Escarpment. Continues previous protection (extended Sept. 19, '02; extended & amended Sept. 19, 07).														
Nicaragua														Oct. 26, '00: MOU on pre-Columbian material (extended 20 Oct '05).											
Peru				May 7, '90: Emergency Action on pre-Columbian material from Sipán.							June 11, '97: MOU on pre-Columbian material and Colonial ethnological material. Continues previous protection.(extended June 6, '02, and June 9, 07)														

4. For a more detailed discussion of the U.S. system implementing the 1970 UNESCO Convention, see PATRICK J. O'KEEFE, COMMENTARY ON THE UNESCO CONVENTION ON ILLICIT TRAFFIC (2000) *passim*; PATTY GERSTENBLITH, ART, CULTURAL HERITAGE, AND THE LAW: CASES and MATERIALS 556–68 (2004). For current information about U.S. measures to implement the 1970 UNESCO Convention, see http://exchanges.state.gov/heritage/index.html. See also *The Who, What, Why and How of the Cultural Property Advisory Committee (CPAC)*, 10 IFAR J., nos. 3 & 4, at 24–49 (2008–2009) (a symposium on the composition, process, and inner workings of the CPIA and divisive issues it has faced); Jeremy Kahn, *Is the U.S. Protecting Foreign Artifacts? Don't Ask*, N.Y. TIMES, Apr. 8, 2007, at 26 (on the work of the CPIA); Symposium, *Should the U.S. Grant China's Request for an Art Import Ban?* 7 IFAR J., nos. 3 & 4, at 20–59 (2004–2005).
5. For a commentary on a memorandum of understanding between the United States and Honduras under article 9 of the 1970 UNESCO Convention and its encouragement of dialogue among archaeologists, collectors, and the Honduran government, see Christina Luke, *Diplomats, Banana Cowboys, and Archaeologists in Western Honduras: A History of the Trade in Pre-Columbian Materials*, 13 INT'L J. CULTURAL PROP. 25–27, 47–49 (2006).

5. Cultural Material: Rectification, Criminal Justice, and Dispute Resolution

A. Rectification

1. International Return and Restitution

a. Introduction

Claims for the return or restitution of cultural heritage[1] are of central importance on both domestic and international levels of cultural heritage law. On the domestic level, for example, the historical and cultural identity of tribal and other indigenous groups may be at stake in efforts to reclaim significant artifacts from museums, art galleries, and private collections. On the international level, the recovery of stolen cultural material, whose value is estimated to be more than $3 billion annually, requires substantial diligence by customs officials and cooperation among governments, private institutions, and individuals.

Obligations to return cultural material to territories of origin date back at least to Greek and Roman times. Until recently, those obligations were addressed almost exclusively to military-related problems of plunder, the spoils of warfare, and occupation.[2] For example, the Hague Conventions of 1899 and 1907, followed by the reparation provisions of the Treaties of Versailles[3] and Saint-Germain[4] after the First World War, underscored the illegality of military plunder and articulated the remedy for victim states. Twenty-five years later, during the Second World War, a leading scholar,[5] urging moderation in dealing with the Germans after the war, referred to the Treaty of Saint Germain. Its provisions for the return of historical and cultural material took account,

[1] A distinction may be made between return of illegally exported material and restitution of material stolen from its owner in the traditional sense of criminal law. A third term, "repatriation," refers to the transfer of cultural material to the patrimonial state of origin or a recognized group such as an indigenous tribe or nation.

[2] Louis-Jacques Rollet-Andriane, *Precedents*, 31 Museum 4 (Special Issue: *Return and Restitution of Cultural Property*), no. 1 (1979).

[3] Treaty of Peace with Germany (Treaty of Versailles), June 28, 1919, 2 Bevans 43, 3 Malloy 3329–3522, at arts. 245–47.

[4] Treaty of Saint-Germain, Sept. 10, 1919, *reprinted in* A. Toynbee, 3 Major Peace Treaties of Modern History 1648–1967, at 1535 (1967).

[5] Douglas Rigby, *Cultural Reparations and a New Western Tradition*, 13 Am. Scholar 273 (1944).

on a reciprocal basis, of the cultural heritage of both the victor, Italy, and the loser, Austria:

> [The Treaty] stated, however incompletely, the reasonable principle that historical material belongs, wherever possible, to the land of its birth; and though it might prove highly impracticable to carry this principle through to its ultimate conclusion, the mere fact of its enunciation *on reciprocal terms*, while the smoke of the battle and revenge still clung to Europe, was a noble signal of growth.[6]

The spoils of war and occupation still threaten the world's cultural heritage, as in the wake of the 2003 military intervention in Iraq, but a booming art market has long since shifted much attention to peacetime trafficking as well. Some claims are the products of historical circumstances that address the status of plundered material resulting from conquest and colonization. For example, native peoples have brought claims for the return of heritage taken from them as a product of conquest. Newly independent states (former colonies) have brought claims against their parent states whose public institutions possessed property looted from the colonies. Nigeria, for example, claims to have lost more than half of its cultural heritage in this way.[7] The notorious punitive expedition of 1897 that was undertaken in Benin by British colonial officials involved the pillaging of tens of thousands of wood, ivory, and bronze objects. The British Museum and the Louvre in Paris, in particular, have generated controversy by exhibiting some of these bronze sculptures even after repeated, unsuccessful requests by Nigeria for them to return the loot. It is estimated that the British Museum alone may contain some ninety thousand African artifacts that came into its possession as the result of colonial plunder.

Countries of origin that were not under the domination of the state from which material was sought have also made demands. Examples include Greek demands for the return of the Elgin Marbles from the British Museum, Iraqi demands for the return of the Code of Hammurabi from France, and Mexican and Colombian demands for the return of pre-Columbian treasures. Sometimes, one former colony may demand restitution of cultural property from another former colony of the same parent state, as, for example, Malaysia's demands for ethnological and historical material from Singapore, as both states were British colonies.[8]

NOTE

> The succession of states, a complicated topic of international law, looms as an issue in current initiatives that would enable Ukraine, a former republic of the Soviet Union, to recover objects looted from Ukrainian territory, largely by Germany, during the Second World War. Ukrainian experts claim that much of the loot that was recovered during the Soviet period reposes in Russia. For some formal purposes, such as permanent membership on the UN Security Council, Russia has

[6] *Id.* at 280.

[7] Ekpo Eyo, *Nigeria*, 31 MUSEUM 18 (SPECIAL ISSUE: *Return and Restitution of Cultural Property*), no. 1 (1979).

[8] *See* RESTITUTION OF WORKS OF ART TO COUNTRIES VICTIMS OF EXPROPRIATION, REPORT OF THE SECRETARY-GENERAL, U.N. Doc. A/10244, at 3–4 (1975).

succeeded in its claim to be the sole successor state of the Soviet Union. But, for the most part, each of the former republics of the Soviet Union, including Ukraine, can rightfully claim to be the successor state in its own territory. The looting-related problem has been described as follows:

> The Nazis systematically looted Ukraine's cultural treasures, which by the end of the war accounted for about 55% of all Soviet cultural losses from museums. Losses included as many as 250,000 items missing from 21 major Ukrainian museums, and about 50 million books. Around 150 of Ukraine's 174 museums suffered severe physical damage.
>
> It was not only a matter of quantity. About 74% of the most valuable Soviet cultural losses came from Ukraine museums,. . .
>
> After the war, the Soviets recovered many works of art from Germany, but research shows that Germany was not alone in depriving Ukraine of its cultural heritage. According to Ms Grimsted, the Americans returned to the Soviets about 534,000 cultural items from 1945 to 1948, and about 167,000 of these items originated from Kiev. However, many items never made it home, and instead settled in cultural institutions in Leningrad and Moscow.

ART NEWSPAPER, June 2009, at 3.

b. The Adversarial Model (Internationalism versus Nationalism) and the Common Heritage Alternative

Until recently, rectification efforts relied essentially on an adversarial legal model expressed in either-or terms. The dichotomies included, for example, art-exporting versus art-importing countries (sometimes expressed as art-rich versus art-poor countries, or source nations versus market nations), common heritage versus national patrimony (and its siblings, cultural internationalism versus cultural nationalism), national retention versus free trade in heritage, underwater salvage versus preservation of the underwater heritage, property interests versus heritage interests, and so on. Dichotomies of this sort are, of course, normal if not essential as analytical constructs in developing any system of law and governance, but they have the effect of blinkering our vision of reality and inhibiting constructive discourse and action. At the end of this chapter, we explore alternative methods of resolving disputes.

Sterile debates based on the adversarial model have inhibited efforts to establish responsible procedures and rules for repatriation of material. A proposed division between cultural property internationalism and cultural property nationalism, though academically interesting, is highly questionable. According to this dichotomy, cultural heritage laws and policies fall into one or the other of two, more or less Manichaean categories: cultural internationalism (which, as defined in a controversial way, is said to be good) and cultural nationalism (which is said to be bad). This distinction is expressed in terms of a false dichotomy between free trade in cultural material (i.e., cultural property internationalism), on the one hand, and national constraints on trade to protect the integrity of a national patrimony (i.e., cultural property nationalism), on the other hand. This dichotomy is reminiscent of the seventeenth-century debate involving the fledgling law of the sea between the British and the Dutch. The British, represented by John Selden, argued for maritime states' strict (nationalist) controls over the use of the seas, whereas the Dutch, represented by Hugo Grotius, argued for free (internationalist) navigation and commerce. As Europe drifted away from mercantilist, statist economic policies toward the more laissez-faire, individualistic principles of Adam Smith, David Ricardo, and other classical economists, it was perhaps inevitable that the Dutch insistence on freedom of the seas prevailed.

In the mid-twentieth century, however, the old dichotomy between parochial, nationalist constraints and laissez-faire, internationalist freedoms, at least as applied to maritime commerce, gave way to a third concept: the common heritage of humankind. As part of the growing movement toward international cooperation whose first major experiment was the League of Nations, the common heritage approach rejected both nationalist and laissez-faire premises in favor of collaboration and functional cooperation among states toward common ends. Even the fundamental concept of free trade, based on a hidden economic hand and the economic law of comparative advantage, gave way to this third alternative of international cooperation through the General Agreement of Tariffs and Trade (GATT), the World Trade Organization (WTO), and such regional trade arrangements as the European Union (EU) and the North American Free Trade Agreement (NAFTA). In the specific context of cultural heritage, it follows that every human being may share in the expressions of other cultures but without compromising the integrity and commonality of those expressions.

The common heritage approach has inspired cultural heritage treaties and has served as an aspiration for the development, more generally, of cultural heritage law throughout its short history. It has become a premise of cultural heritage law. Indeed, the proponents of what might appear to be a cosmopolitan cultural property internationalism claim to have adopted the common heritage approach. But that claim is far from reality and far from cosmopolitan. What the cultural property internationalists seem to have in mind, akin to the unconstrained freedom of the seas, is a generally free trade in cultural heritage unfettered by cooperation among states. At the intergovernmental level, ironically, this interpretation of internationalism turns out to be fundamentally a disguised form of nationalism to protect a country's own collectors and collections. What is more, the rationale for cultural property internationalism turns out to be essentially commercial.[9]

To be sure, the artifice of cultural property internationalism forthrightly supports the restitution of stolen cultural material in the sense of ordinary theft under domestic criminal law. If the Louvre is looted, almost everyone agrees[10] – even the self-described

[9] *See* John Henry Merryman, *Cultural Property Internationalism*, 12 INT'L J. CULTURAL PROP. 11 (2005). Professor Merryman argues that the UNESCO Convention on the Protection of the Underwater Heritage exemplifies cultural nationalism because it expresses an "antimarket bias" in a "breathtaking provision" prohibiting commercial exploitation of underwater heritage. To the contrary, his criticism tilts at windmills. The provision in point, which is explicitly qualified, met with the satisfaction of responsible treasure salvors who participated in the drafting process. Far from having an antimarket bias, it is arguable that the provision not only helps protect the integrity of the market from looted contraband but also reconciles a general prohibition of commercial transactions involving heritage with an acceptance of scientifically sound deposition of underwater artifacts. (The term "deposition," however, is not clearly defined.) *But see* Lyndel V. Prott, *The International Movement of Cultural Objects*, 12 INT'L J. CULTURAL PROP. 225 (2005) (debunking the concept of cultural internationalism as defined by Professor Merryman).

[10] The qualifying adjective "almost" is used advisedly so as to take account of rare instances when states have supported self-help measures to seize and retain material stolen from the territory of other states. For

cultural property internationalists – that the stolen material should be restituted, and international criminal law and mutual cooperation treaties ought to provide as such. The controversial point, however, is that the "cultural property internationalists," in the interest of a generally free trade in artifacts, basically reject controls over trafficking in material that has been illegally exported (smuggled) from a country in violation of its antiquities laws or export controls even if it is significant to that country's cultural heritage. Significantly, such national controls and cooperation in their reasonable international enforcement by other governments and their courts of law are at the crux of any effective regime to protect the common cultural heritage of humankind.

The term "cultural property internationalism," then, cleverly pirates a commonly understood and venerated term – internationalism – to justify practices that actually defy the fundamental requirements of cooperation and collaboration underlying internationalism in the normal sense of the term. It is apparent that the old dichotomies, particularly that of internationalism versus nationalism, are unhelpful. They are simply rhetorical constructs. They must yield, and indeed are yielding, to more cooperative approaches for accommodating the many diverse interests in the cultural heritage of humankind. Foremost among these approaches, as we shall see in the concluding section of this study, are initiatives to establish principles for cooperation in the mutual protection and transfer of cultural material.

Shareen Blair Brysac, *The Parthenon Marbles Custody Case*, ARCHAEOLOGY, May–June 1999, at 74–76

The argument over the sculptures which once graced the Temple of Athena Parthenos on the Athenian acropolis has been unremitting since Thomas Bruce, the seventh earl of Elgin, carried off 56 pieces of its frieze, 15 metopes, and 17 pediment sculptures, plus a caryatid and a column from a nearby temple, the Erechtheion. This was accomplished during his tenure (1799–1802) as George III's ambassador to the Ottoman Empire. At that time Athens was a small, sleepy outpost of the sultan's empire, and Elgin was able to obtain firmans, or permits, for the removal and export of the sculptures by resorting to payments – he lists £21,902 in presents to local Turkish officials. One that survives in an Italian translation allowed him to take away "*qualche pezzi di pietra con iscrizioni e figure*" ("some pieces of stone with inscriptions or figures), which was interpreted by Elgin to include sculpture that until 1802 still decorated the building. Doubtless Elgin thought that he was performing an act of rescue, but from the beginning he was accused of vandalism and robbery. The attack was led by Lord Byron, who berated Elgin as "the last, the worst, dull spoiler" of the Parthenon.

example, in 1982 Mexico and France were involved in a dispute over the theft from the French National Library of a fifteenth-century codex consisting of colored drawings used as a horoscope. It is undisputed that a Mexican national absconded with the codex to Mexico and, on his arrest by Mexican authorities, turned it over to the Mexican government, which retained custody of it. The thief claimed that he had simply recovered stolen property from France even though the codex appears to have been in France, after a series of legitimate transactions, since the nineteenth century. Alan Riding, *Between France and Mexico: A Cultural Crisis*, INT'L HERALD TRIB., Aug. 31, 1982, at 1, col. 5.

In 1816 a series of personal misfortunes forced the earl to sell his collection to the British nation for the knock-down price of £35,000. The marbles were then deposited in the British Museum for safekeeping. Now the restitution dispute is taking a new turn with the revival of claims that the sculptures were mutilated by restorers on the orders of art dealer Lord Joseph Duveen. The British historian William St. Clair presented evidence . . . in his book, *Lord Elgin and the Marbles*. . . .

Long before their arrival in England, the Parthenon sculptures were battered by wars, fires, and earthquakes. In 1687, during a Venetian attack, a shell ignited Turkish gunpowder stored in the Parthenon, shattering the building and its sculpture. Although pilfering had started before their arrival, Elgin's minions contributed to the destruction by sawing off chunks of sculpture from the building. En route to England, one shipment containing 17 cases of antiquities aboard the earl's brig, *Mentor*, sank in 12 fathoms of water in the harbor of Kythera, where it remained for two years until it was retrieved at great expense. Reunited in London, the marbles languished in the courtyard of the earl's residence.

Originally the stones were painted with bright colors, but by the time Elgin acquired them the paint had almost vanished and the white Pentelic marble had aged to a honey brown. This natural patina was acceptable to the Romantics, but in the Victorian era aesthetics changed. The brown patina was at odds with the lustrous white demanded by cognoscenti weaned on the plaster casts of the period. According to St. Clair, Victorian restorers striving to make the marbles more "authentic" scrubbed the sculptures with fuller's earth, a claylike substance used to remove stains. . . .

In 1938 Lord Duveen, a trustee and benefactor of the museum, underwrote construction of a gallery bearing his name to house the marbles. Orders were given to prepare the sculptures for display, a task supervised by Duveen's workmen, who were notorious for freshening up masterpieces with paint thinner and varnish.

Copper tools and abrasive carborundum were used to remove not only two millennia of grime, but also the honey-brown patina, the remaining traces of original color, and the chisel marks of Pheidias'[s] workmen. . . .

What cannot be overlooked, in fairness, is that Greece itself has not been a perfect steward of the Acropolis monuments. In the 1920s architectural members remaining in situ were damaged by a Greek engineer who inserted iron clamps into the blocks in an attempt to restore the temple. The clamps subsequently rusted, swelling and cracking much of the marble. Damage to the structure was exacerbated by Athens' postwar pollution. . . .

David A. Walden, chairman of UNESCO's panel on returning cultural property, reported on efforts to mediate the return of the marbles. Walden was careful to point out that although UNESCO has received a request from the Greeks, the committee cannot initiate negotiations and at the moment, as both sides appear to have hardened their positions, there is no UNESCO-brokered dialogue with the British.

Elgin's booty is the source of the longest-running argument between Greece and Britain. The Greeks have campaigned for the marbles' restitution since the country gained independence in 1833, and some members of the British government have agreed – the first recorded proposal for their return was put before Parliament in 1816. Michael Foot and Neil Kinnock, successive heads of the Labour Party, have supported restitution. However, the party never adopted a policy on the matter and in 1997, when Tony Blair became prime minister, he differed with his predecessors. As one of his first acts in office, his minister Chris Smith claimed that the Parthenon Marbles were "an integral part" of the British Museum and would remain. Nonetheless, in January [1999], the European Union, which includes Britain, passed by a vote of 339 (of 626) a declaration urging the return of the marbles to Greece. . . .

The Greek government insists that aside from the marbles it is making no other demands for restitution. Yet the possibility of their return causes sleepless nights for curators the world over. If the marbles were returned to Greece, runs the argument, the halls of the western museums would be virtually emptied of their treasures. Where does one halt the chariot's plunge down a slippery slope? What if the world's ministers, deputies, and assorted local governments follow the lead of Samothrace's maverick mayor, who has called for the return of the Winged Victory from the Louvre?

John Henry Merryman, *Thinking about the Elgin Marbles*, 83 Mich. L. Rev. 1881 (1985)

The Greek case for return of the Marbles, like the cases of other 1881 nations seeking the return of cultural property, reduces to two propositions. One is that the Marbles were wrongly taken by Elgin and have never belonged, legally or morally,[11] to the British. The other is that, even if the Marbles became British property, they ought now to be returned to Greece. This seems to be an appropriate way to organize the inquiry. Accordingly, we can begin to think about the Elgin Marbles by examining the law and the ethics of the case. Was the removal illegal or immoral?

The British government bought the Marbles from Lord Elgin in 1816 after a full discussion in Parliament, in full knowledge of the facts. Accordingly, it seems fair, and is consistent with the law of all civilized jurisdictions, to suppose that the right of the Crown to the Marbles was no better than Elgin's right to them. . . . If Lord Elgin owned the Marbles, he could transfer ownership to the Crown. If his title was defective, then so was the Crown's title. How good was Lord Elgin's title to the Marbles? To answer that question we have to determine (1) whether the Ottoman authorities, who at

[11] There are several reasons morality enters the discussion. The Greek demand is based in part on moral grounds, and the attitude of people and governments throughout the world toward the case is based in large part on moral considerations. Further, although the international law applicable to the case is reasonably clear, international law derives much of its force from its moral authority. A legal argument that is morally offensive accordingly carries less weight in international than in municipal law. *See* 1 H. Lauterpacht, International Law 46 (1970); T. Nardin, Law, Morality, and the Relations of States 306 (1983); 1 L. Oppenheim, International Law 88 (H. Lauterpacht ed, 8th ed. 1955).

the time were the recognized government of Greece, had the authority to transfer property rights in the Marbles to Lord Elgin; (2) whether they did in fact authorize Lord Elgin to remove the Marbles and take them to England; and (3) whether Lord Elgin exceeded the authority given to him. Each of these major questions raises subsidiary questions.

We begin with the situation of the Greeks in 1801, when the crucial transaction took place. All of Greece was then a part of the Ottoman Empire, ruled from Constantinople, as it had been for nearly four centuries. Athens itself was conquered by the Ottomans in 1460 and had been under foreign rule since 1204. For most of the period of Turkish rule Athens had been the property of one of the numerous lesser dignitaries of the Ottoman court, the Chief of the "Black Eunuchs. . . ."[12] By 1800, "normal Turkish standards of administration had been reestablished,"[13] with the Grand Vizier, the head of the executive power of the Ottoman Government and second in command only to the Sultan, the internationally recognized authority governing Athens. The responsible local officials were the Voivode (the civil governor) and the Cadi (the chief judicial officer). The Acropolis of Athens was at that time the Citadel, or military fort, under the command of the Disdar. Under the international law of that time, the acts of Ottoman officials with respect to persons and property under their authority were presumptively valid. Even though their actions might seem regrettable, unsound, or unfeeling, one would not question their legality, except in the most unusual circumstances. In this instance the Ottomans had a solid claim to legal authority over the Parthenon because it was public property, which the successor nation acquires on a change of sovereignty.[14] It seems clear that under the international law of the time the Ottomans could give Elgin the right to remove the Marbles. Did they do so?

Elgin obtained from the Ottomans in Constantinople, where he was the British ambassador, a formal written instrument called a firman, addressed to the local authorities in Athens. The firman responded to Elgin's written request for permission and protection "in the following objects":

> (1) to enter freely within the walls of the Citadel, and to draw and model with plaster the Ancient Temples there.
> (2) to erect scaffolding and to dig where they may wish to discover the ancient foundations.

[12] [William St. Clair, Lord Elgin and the Marbles 50 (2d ed. 1983).] The author continues: "In 1760, however, [Athens] lost this privileged position and was henceforth auctioned by the Sultan to the highest bidder who then had the right to put the proceeds of taxation into his own pocket. Thirty-five years of unbelievable extortion . . . followed. . . . " *Id.* (footnote omitted).

[13] *Id.*

[14] *See* D. O'Connell, The Law of State Succession 226–27 (1956). It might be argued that the Parthenon was religious rather than state property, but the distinction seems difficult to sustain in the historical and factual context. What religious authority could have claimed ownership against the Ottoman temporal authority, if indeed the Ottomans recognized any such distinction at the time? The Ottoman civil and military authorities in Constantinople and in Athens certainly acted as though they had power to deal with the Parthenon, and there is no record of any religious protest.

(3) liberty to take away any sculptures or inscriptions which do not interfere with the works or walls of the Citadel.

The third of these could be interpreted as authority for what Elgin actually did, and if the firman had contained the same language, the case would be easier. We have only the Italian version of the firman. The original, in Turkish, was kept by the Ottoman officials in Athens and has been lost. The Italian version was given to Lord Elgin by the Turks and survives today. The following is a fair translation:

> [I]t is incumbent on us to provide that they [i.e., Elgin's artists] meet no opposition in walking, viewing or contemplating the pictures and buildings they may wish to design or copy; and in any of their works of fixing scaffolding, or using their various instruments; it is our desire that on the arrival of this letter you use your diligence to act conformably to the instances of the said Ambassador [Elgin] as long as the said five artists dwelling in that place shall be employed in going in and out of the citadel of Athens which is the place of observation; or in fixing scaffolding around the ancient Temple of the Idols, or in modelling with chalk or gypsum the said ornaments and visible figures; or in measuring the fragments and vestiges of other ruined buildings; or in excavating when they find it necessary the foundations in search of inscriptions among the rubbish; that they be not molested by the said Disdar nor by any other persons; nor even by you to whom this letter is addressed; and that no one meddle with their scaffolding or implements nor hinder them from taking away any pieces of stone with inscriptions and figures.[15]

The language of this last clause, even when taken in context with that of the third paragraph of Elgin's request to the Sultan, is at best ambiguous. While it is possible to read the firman as a flowery concession of everything for which Elgin asked, it is more reasonable to conclude that the Ottomans had a narrower intention, and that the firman provides slender authority for the massive removals from the Parthenon. The document appears to contemplate measuring, drawing, and making casts as the principal activity of Elgin's artists and workmen. The reference to 'taking away any pieces of stone' seems incidental, intended to apply to objects found while excavating. That was certainly the interpretation privately placed on the firman by several of the Elgin party, including Lady Elgin. Publicly, however, a different attitude was taken, and the work of dismantling the sculptures on the Parthenon and packing them for shipment to England began in earnest. In the process, Elgin's party damaged the structure, leaving the Parthenon not only denuded of its sculptures but further ruined by the process of removal. It is certainly arguable that Elgin exceeded the authority granted in the firman in both respects.

[15] St. Clair, *supra* note 12, at 90 (emphasis added) (quoting an English translation of the Italian version attributed to the Reverend D. P. Hunt, secretary to Lord Elgin). I have seen a photocopy of the Italian version and agree that the English translation here set out renders it faithfully.

Accordingly, it would seem that Elgin did not acquire property rights in the Marbles. It is the law everywhere, however, that an act in excess of the authority originally granted can be ratified, expressly or by implication, from conduct indicating acquiescence. There is evidence that the Ottomans twice ratified what Elgin had done. For one thing, it appears that Elgin caused the Sultan to issue additional firmans addressed to the Voivode and Disdar of Athens, in which the Sultan generally sanctioned what these local officials had done for Elgin and his party. For another, a large shipment of Marbles was held up in Piraeus (the port of Athens) because the Voivode, under pressure from the French, refused to give his permission for their embarkation. Eventually the Ottoman government gave written orders to the Athenian authorities to permit the shipment, and the Marbles were allowed to leave for England. Together these two events make a strong case for ratification of the removal, even if it exceeded the authority given in the original firman. If the removal was so ratified, then as a matter of international law the removal was legal, and Elgin was able to transfer title in the Marbles to the British Museum.

If similar events were to occur today, new principles of international law would apply.[16] As a result, the authority of the Ottoman government to dispose of Greek cultural property under its jurisdiction would be far less clear. In international law, however, as in domestic law, the rule is that the legal effects of a transaction depend on the law in force at the time.[17] The justice, as well as the practical necessity, of such a principle is obvious. It is both fair and practically advantageous that people be able to rely on the existing law to determine the legality of their actions. The most obvious applications of this principle occur in our own constitutional prohibition against ex post facto laws[18] and in our legal system's bias against retroactive legislation. Thus if the removal of the Marbles was proper under the then applicable international law, as it seems to have been, then the British are legally entitled to keep them.

It is possible that the Greeks would have lost their rights even if the removal were illegal, since it all happened long ago, between 1801 (the first removals from the Parthenon) and 1815 (the final shipment to England). The passage of time inevitably has an effect, and all legal systems recognize this fact in rules of prescription. Such rules respond to the difficulty of reconstructing ancient events and to the tendency of people to rely on the status quo. To allow old transactions to be questioned is to invite fraud

[16] Until this century, a treaty imposed on the loser by an aggressor was valid under international law. *See* M. Akehurst, A Modern Introduction to International Law 132 (5th ed. 1984). But with adoption of the Kellogg-Briand Pact, Aug. 27, 1928, 46 Stat. 2343, T.S. No. 796, 2 Bevans T.S. 732, by most nations, followed by U.N. Charter, art. 2, para. 4, and the Vienna Convention on the Law of Treaties, May 23, 1969, art. 52, U.N. Doc. A/Conf.3 9/27, *reprinted in* 63 Am. J. Intl. L. 875 (1969), the rule was changed. *Cf.* The Hague Convention of 1954 (Each party to the Convention is to "refrain from requisitioning movable cultural property" located in the territory of another party.). Under the new rule, it might be argued that the Ottoman occupation of Greece and the Ottoman permission to remove Greek antiquities were illegal, thus clouding Elgin's title to the Marbles.

[17] *See* Akehurst, *supra* note 16, at 150. [This is known as the intertemporal principle. – *Eds.*]

[18] U.S. Const. art. I, § 9, cl. 3.

and perjury and to unsettle the affairs of the present – hence what in the common law world are called "statutes of limitation" and elsewhere are referred to as rules of "prescription." In international law, of course, there is no statute of limitations, but the same considerations apply: witnesses die, memories fail, people rely on stable appearances, and so on. [In 1983, Minister of Culture Melina Mercouri] appears to have stimulated the first official request by Greece for return of the Marbles, although private approaches have undoubtedly been made over the years. If we take the date of Greek independence from the Ottoman Empire to be 1828 (1821 is sometimes used, but 1828 is the more widely accepted date), then the Greeks had 155 years during which to pursue their legal remedies before they finally demanded the return of the Marbles in 1983.

Prescription statutes run against one who fails to exercise an available judicial remedy, and it might seem unfair to apply the prescription principle in international law when no forum capable of definitively determining rights and providing remedies exists. In fact, however, Greece might have brought suit in an English court for return of the Marbles, on the theory that they were illegally taken by Elgin.[19] As we have already seen, the courts of most nations are open to an owner seeking the return of stolen property. Greece has accordingly been in a position to sue for the Marbles since 1828 and has never done so.[20] Nor has Greece aggressively pursued its diplomatic remedies, since the 1983 request for return of the Marbles is the first such official diplomatic demand. Unless some unusual exception were made, it seems clear that the Greeks have lost any right of action they might have had for the recovery of the Marbles before an English court, where the applicable statute of limitations is six years.[21]

Other legal questions can be raised about Elgin's actions: to what extent were the Ottomans induced by bribery to permit and condone the removal? Elgin and his party made numerous gifts to Ottoman officials in Constantinople and Athens. While many of these were offered and received in a ceremonial context, others were given and accepted in order to receive specific favors and would, by any standard, be understood as bribes. What shall we make of Elgin's ambiguous status as British ambassador and as

[19] Technically, the Marbles are the property of the Trustees of the British Museum, to whom they were transferred by act of Parliament. An Act to Vest the Elgin Collection of Ancient Marbles and Sculpture in the Trustees of the British Museum for the Use of the Public, 1816, 56 Geo. 3, ch. 99. Any action for their recovery would accordingly have to be brought against the Trustees who would, of course, have no better title to the Marbles than the British Government had at the time of transfer. The Trustees' enabling statutes prohibit them from conveying any of the property they hold. A bill to give them authority to convey the Marbles was introduced in Parliament and failed in 1984. *See* 444 Parl. Deb., H.L. (5th ser.) 399–422 (1983). An order of the court to deliver the Marbles to Greek authorities, however, would almost certainly be obeyed.

[20] Before January 1, 1948, the Greek Government would have had to employ the ancient Petition of Right, which was "the process by which property of any kind . . . was recoverable from the Crown." 11 Halsbury's Laws of England 747 (Lord Hailsham, 4th ed. 1976). Enactment of the Crown Proceedings Act, 10 & 11 Geo. 6, ch. 44 (1947), altered the procedure and extended the range of government liability. Now an ordinary proceeding may be brought in the County Court.

[21] *See* Limitation Act, 1939, 2 & 3 Geo. 6, ch. 21, § 2(1)(a).

private acquirer of the Marbles, at a time when the Ottoman court was eager to establish friendly relations with England?

On 17 June General Hutchinson received the surrender of Cairo and the success of the Egyptian expedition [against the French] was finally assured. On 6 July, Elgin obtained the firman he had asked for. These two events were intimately connected: indeed, allowing for the time news took to travel and the ceremoniousness of all Turkish business, one followed at once after the other. Elgin himself acknowledged that he was making little progress in the negotiations for a firman until the Ottomans suddenly began showering all kinds of favors on their British allies.

These are interesting questions, but it is difficult to turn their answer to the benefit of the Greek side in a legal dispute over the Marbles. The Ottomans who were bribed were the responsible officials. Whatever their motivation may have been, they had the legal authority to perform those actions. At a time and in a culture in which officials routinely had to be bribed to perform their legal duties (as is still true today in much of the world), the fact that bribes occurred was hardly a significant legal consideration.[22] As for the ambiguity of Elgin's position, there is a clear, if subtle, distinction between a gift of the Marbles to Elgin because he was a person of importance and influence in England, and a gift to the Crown in the person of its emissary Elgin. The Select Committee inquired whether Elgin got the Marbles as British Minister or in his personal capacity and decided the latter; hence the purchase by Parliament. If Elgin had acquired the Marbles as a representative of the British Crown they would already have been Crown property, and no purchase would have been necessary.

In brief, on the facts available to us, it appears that the law favors the British side of the case. Although the original firman provides only slender authority for the removals, subsequent ratification of Elgin's actions by the Sultan and the passage of time since Greek independence both support the proposition that the British own the Marbles. If Greece were to sue the Trustees of the British Museum today for their return, the remedy would be denied unless a quite different version of the facts were found.[23]

[The author then discusses the moral issues and concludes:]

[T]he legality of the removal of the Marbles is clearly established and that its immorality has not been demonstrated. The Greeks do not have a strong legal or moral case against Elgin. Minister Mercouri's and Byron's eloquence and art to the contrary notwithstanding, the British own the Marbles and, on balance, did not wrongly acquire ownership. For those who agree, that settles the legal and moral questions about the removal. There remains, however, the most difficult and interesting question of all:

[22] The text statement of course refers to the law in force at the time. Recent legal developments would make the use of bribery a more serious issue, at least in the United States. *See* Jimenez v. Aristeguieta, 311 F.2d 547 (5th Cir. 1962); Foreign Corrupt Practices Act, 15 U.S.C. § 78dd-2 (1982).

[23] It is possible that the facts are different, but none of the materials about the case that are available to the diligent researcher (in non-Greek-language publications) cast serious doubt on the version used here. There may be important additional sources in the Turkish archives, but those materials are in any practical sense inaccessible to me.

Should the British now return the Marbles to Greece? Independent of questions about the legality and morality of the removal is the argument that the Marbles should, on other grounds, be returned. Adequate analysis of this aspect of the case brings a new set of considerations into play, requiring us to consider the relative merits of nationalism and internationalism as guiding principles in the allocation of cultural property.

. . .

[C]ultural nationalism is a dubious argument at best, entitled to little weight. In any event, it supports both the Greek and the British cases and is inconclusive. Economic nationalism merely reargues the question of who has the legal property in the Marbles, and the British seem to win that one. Political nationalism is difficult to employ in a convincingly principled way, since it seems to urge values that are of dubious desirability. The values of cultural internationalism – preservation, integrity, and distribution/access – lead in different directions. The most powerful of them, preservation, does not under present circumstances advance the Greek cause, since there is no basis for arguing that the Marbles would be safer in Athens. The integrity argument favors reuniting the Marbles with the Parthenon, but at present that is not possible without exposing them to unacceptable hazards. There are no developed criteria for applying the distribution/access concern, but it does not appear that the present distribution of Greek antiquities argues strongly for returning the Marbles to Athens.

NOTES AND QUESTIONS

1. Professor Merryman concludes his careful legal analysis of the Greek claim for repatriation of the Elgin Marbles by asking whether, on the basis of contemporary values assigned to cultural heritage, the Marbles should nevertheless be restituted by the British Museum. He then weighs the values underlying cultural nationalism, which he rejects, against the values of cultural internationalism, which he favors. As we have seen in the introduction to this section, this dichotomy is controversial. If, however, we accept the dichotomy, do you agree with Professor Merryman that three values – preservation of the heritage, integrity of the cultural context, and distribution/access to cultural material – underlie the cultural internationalist inclination to protect collections outside countries of origin and to deny claims for repatriation of significant cultural heritage to its country of origin? Wouldn't those same values also support the claims of "nationalists," in Professor Merryman's terminology? And what about the third, cooperative alternative rooted in the common heritage of humankind?
2. In 2009 the British Museum made a first-ever offer to Greece whereby the museum would lend its collection of Elgin Marbles temporarily to Athens in return for which Greece would relinquish its claims to the items and acknowledge the museum as the rightful keeper of them. The Greek government replied that it was a "pleasing" development but rejected the offer. Anthee Carrassava, *Greece Rejects a British Proposal on Elgin Marbles*, Int'l Herald Trib., June 12, 2009, at 2.

3. A more extensive set of values, as follows, provides an alternative framework for addressing claims seeking the restitution and return of cultural heritage:
   (a) The preservation of archeological evidence, particularly in an on-site context
   (b) The association of art with its geographical-historical milieu
   (c) The preservation of the national patrimony for reasons of awakening the national conscience, fostering community pride, socializing youth, enhancing local scholarship, and elevating national civilization
   (d) The preservation of both individual objets d'art and, when significant, sets and collections of them
   (e) The enhancement of an exporting or loaning state's foreign policy and the financial resources of its museums
   (f) The enrichment of the importing state's civilization
   (g) The promotion of international understanding through diffusion of art
   (h) The respect for cultural diversity, acknowledgment of a global patrimony, and a shared heritage of significant art, as well as the elimination of parochialism
   (i) The widest possible visibility and accessibility of significant objects
   (j) The protection of significant objects, under the best possible circumstances, in both the country of origin and the importing country
   (k) The encouragement of respect for the law and the mutual development of shared controls
   (l) The enrichment of aesthetic and intellectual interests of individual collectors, museums, and museum viewers
   (m) Restraints on the production of forgeries

   Is this framework complete? Would you add any values? Do you question any of those listed? Is the framework workable or is it too complex to be effective?
4. Several principles emerge from this list of values and from the consensus of concerned states and professionals. First, every country should be allowed to possess that cultural material that is essential to an understanding of itself and its origins. Second, states that have acquired cultural material as the result of colonization or military occupation have a special obligation, as a matter of international solidarity, to cooperate in the return and restitution of at least some of that property to the former colony or territory of occupation. Third, special circumstances of acquisition ought to be considered, including understandings of donors and testators that might preclude return or restitution. Fourth, only that cultural material of a fundamental or genuine significance, privity, and cogency to a claimant state should be subject to return, restitution, or forfeiture. Fifth, return or restitution of foreign cultural material should not significantly dismantle collections of individuals or public institutions. Sixth, the relative importance to the target state of the cultural material ought to be considered, for example, the importance of Chinese vases to eighteenth-century European artists, the importance to France of particular African tribal objects in the development of modern French art, or the importance to Austria and Spain of pre-Columbian material identified significantly with the conquistadores. Seventh, the claimant state must ensure that conservation, safety, and security measures that meet international standards will protect the recovered property, and that the object will be adequately displayed and, normally, accessible to the public. Eighth, where restitution in kind is impossible,

there should be provision, under the *Chorzów Factory* rule, for "payment of a sum corresponding to the value which a restitution in kind would bear."[24] Ninth, the purposes of the return or restitution should not be defeated by a reappearance of the object on the international art market, as in the notorious case of the Afo-A-Kom statue.[25] Finally, there should be written evidence of the following measures before the return or restitution of an object or class of objects: an assessment of the losses suffered by the claimant state so as to prioritize the most significant objects; an inventory of objects preserved in the claimant state and a survey of measures taken on a national level to identify, preserve, and present them to the public; an inventory of all objects claimed in foreign collections; and precise provisions for compensation, or waiver of it, for objects whose return or restitution is requested but impossible.

5. The issue of proper disposition of material after its return extends well beyond the Afo-A-Kom debacle noted in note 4 here. For example, "one of the biggest antiquities-smuggling rings in history" had been broken and the alleged mastermind, Vaman Ghiya, was put on trial:

> It is not clear what will become of the thousands of art works that the police say Ghiya smuggled out of the country between the nineteen-seventies and his capture. A dispute between the Archaeological Survey and the state government in Rajasthan over who would underwrite the cost of returning the art seems to have stalled the prospect of recovery. Even if works are returned, it is not clear where precisely they would go. [It was] pointed out that, even after the Indian government spent enormous sums to secure the return of Norton Simons's bronze Nataraja in the seventies, the sculpture – which is considered one of the masterpieces of Indian art – was neither restored to the temple from which it had been stolen nor displayed in a museum.

Patrick Radden Keefe, *The Idol Thief*, New Yorker, May 7, 2007, at 58, 67.

Should an agreement to return or restitute a cultural object be conditioned on the terms for disposition of the object after its return or restitution? Wouldn't such a

[24] Case Concerning the Factory at Chorzów, 1928 P.C.I.J., ser. A, No. 13, at 47 (Judgment of Sept. 13).

[25] The Afo-A-Kom story is well told, as follows:

> In 1966, an African wood carving known as the Afo-A-Kom was taken from its ancestral home and transported to a New York Art Gallery where it appeared for sale. The events surrounding the transaction are cloudy, although members of the royal family of Kom appear to have been involved.
>
> The Afo-A-Kom is a statue which is said to embody the soul of the people of Kom. Its spiritual significance is such that it is the personification of the Kom belief in Animism, through which the spirits and souls of a rich cultural heritage communicate with present citizens of Kom. The effect of its disappearance on the people of Kom was profound. An integral part of their spiritual life was gone. Essentially a superstitious people, the Kom blamed any of their misfortunes on the loss of the Afo-A-Kom.
>
> When a Peace Corps volunteer located the statue in New York, Americans quickly registered their outrage. Some went so far as to threaten the dealer who had purchased the piece with physical violence, even though he did so without any knowledge of its tribal importance. Through the efforts of (a) the press, (b) public opinion, (c) a formal request from the Cameroon government, and (d) numerous public contributions, the Afo-A-Kom was returned to its ancestral home.

Leonard Du Boff, The Deskbook of Art Law 71–72 (1977). "Presumably, the Afo-A-Kom should remain in its country of origin, yet within a short period after its return the statue was again being offered for sale on the international market." *Id.* at 119.

qualification defeat the principle of rectification that underlies the rules for return and restitution?

6. In 2007 it appeared that Peru and Yale University had reached an agreement for the repatriation of some four thousand artifacts that the Yale archaeologist Hiram Bingham had excavated at Peru's renowned Machu Picchu. Bingham discovered this "lost" city of the Incas in 1911 and gave the Yale Museum several thousand artifacts from several expeditions. Yale returned only a limited amount of material from Bingham's last expedition, stipulating that it had done this *ex gratia*, free of any legal compulsion. It cited its interpretation of Peru's Civil Code of 1852 as a basis of its entitlement to the fruits of Bingham's several expeditions. As is often the case, however, the precise terms of Peru's grant of excavation rights to Bingham are uncertain. Yale and the National Geographic Society (NGS) cosponsored each of the expeditions. The latter understandably has no interest nowadays in offending Peru by supporting Yale's retention of the material – at the risk of prompting Peru to bar NGS from ongoing and future expeditions in that country.

   Peruvian statutory law proved less significant than the agreements by which the Peruvian government had granted excavation rights to Bingham. The agreement governing Bingham's 1914–15 expedition required him to return objects within eighteen months. Under a clause in the key agreement of 1912, however, Peru "reserves the right of requiring of Yale University and the National Geographical Society the restitution of single and duplicate artifacts that might be extracted and have been extracted." What issues of interpretation does this language raise?

   Under the 2007 agreement between Peru and Yale University, Yale would transfer title to most (but not all) of the objects from those expeditions but retain some minor material for research purposes. In addition, proceeds from a traveling exhibition of objects from the collection would be used to construct a new museum and research center in Cuzco, the former capital of the Inca Empire located near Machu Picchu. Peru's National Institute of Culture and Yale University would jointly curate the center. In December 2008, however, Peru filed an action in federal court, demanding return of the entire collection from the Bingham expeditions. The agreement was immediately suspended, pending further negotiations between the parties.

7. Both Peru and the United States are parties to the 1970 UNESCO Convention. What, if anything, should have been the U.S. response to the claims by Peru for return of material from Machu Picchu?

8. Cultural heritage issues are not only intense and emotional but also politically laden. For a fascinating examination of the politics surrounding the Machu Picchu controversy, see Arthur Lubow, *The Possessed*, N.Y. Times, June 24, 2007, at 42. The article concludes as follows:

   > Historic relics have pragmatic value: politically, for purposes of national pride and partisan advantage; economically, for display to tourists, museumgoers, magazine readers and TV-program watchers; scientifically, as research material for scholars pursuing academic careers; and, most nakedly, as merchandise for dealers in antiquities. In comparing the arguments and motivations of the different claimants to the Yale collection, I often identified with historians of the Inca trying to untangle those Spanish chronicles that were spun from

> the tales of native informants with their own purposes. The people at Yale say that they have preserved the collection as a legacy of a great civilization and they want to continue to study these artifacts to learn more about that culture. They are also paying tribute to one of the most colorful and glamorous figures in the university's history [the "discoverer" and excavator of the artifacts, Hiram Bingham]. The Peruvians celebrate their own legendary ancestor [Pachacuti] when they describe the urgency of their case, but they also have very down-to-earth political and commercial uses for the collection. "Cultural patrimony" – the phrase sounds so otherworldly. Bingham and Pachacuti were both very practical men. They would not have been fooled for a minute.

Id. at 83.

9. In recent years Italy and Greece have successfully reclaimed cultural material from foreign museums, other institutions, and private collectors. See, e.g., New Acropolis Museum, Repatriated Masterpieces Nostoi (2008) (cataloguing a display of seventy-four items returned to Italy and ten to Greece). For a detailed account of litigation brought by Italy against the J. Paul Getty Museum for return of an extraordinary bronze statue fashioned not in Italy but in ancient Greece, see *Italy Presses Its Fight for a Statute at the Getty*, N.Y. Times, Jan. 16, 2010, at C3.
10. The General Secretary of Egypt's Supreme Council of Antiquities has been particularly aggressive in seeking the return of cultural material long reposing in foreign museums, including the Rosetta Stone in the British Museum and the Bust of Nefertiti in Berlin's Neues Museum. His sometimes extravagant demands are often accompanied by threats to deny archaeological permits to scientists from museums that refuse to comply with his demands, and he has threatened to suspend cooperative ventures with those museums. "He has prevailed so often in getting pieces returned to what he calls their 'motherland' that museum curators are scrambling to appease him." John Tierney, *A Case in Antiquities for 'Finders Keepers,'* N.Y. Times, Nov. 17, 2009, at D1; *see also* Judy Dempsey, *A 3,500-Year-Old Queen Causes a Rift between Germany and Egypt*, N.Y. Times, Oct. 20, 2009, at A12. Given Egypt's vast storehouses full of duplicative material it is unable to display or even offer access to, as is widely known, what response should museums, individually and collectively, make to unreasonable demands accompanied by threats to cultural cooperation and exchange? Whatever the merits of claims for repatriation of cultural material, is there not a better means of resolving these kinds of disputes than by demands and threats?
11. For more on Lord Elgin and his travails, see Donald Dale Jackson, *How Lord Elgin First Won – and Lost – His Marbles*, Smithsonian, Dec. 1992, at 135 ("After 'saving' the stately Greek friezes by shipping them home, the unfortunate earl found himself pursued by the Furies.").

c. The UNESCO Convention on the Means of Prohibiting and Preventing the Illicit Import, Export, and Transfer of Ownership of Cultural Property (1970)

The 1970 UNESCO Convention on the Means of Prohibiting and Preventing the Illicit Import, Export and Transfer of Ownership of Cultural Property, which was introduced in Chapter 3, attempts to reconcile the concerns within the art market about freedom of movement for cultural material with those expressed by source countries. As we have seen, the Convention seeks to stem illicit trade in stolen or illegally exported cultural property and to encourage other cooperation to protect heritage. At first, few art market countries became parties to the treaty, with the notable exception of the United States, which joined the Convention in 1983. Recently, however, France (1997), the United Kingdom (2002), Japan (2002), Sweden (2003), and Switzerland (2003) have become parties.

Four provisions of the 1970 Convention merit particular emphasis in a discussion of rectification. Under article 2 of the UNESCO Convention, the parties agree that cooperation is an effective means to protect their cultural property and that "reparations" can constitute an effective outcome in certain instances. Article 7(a) obliges states to take measures to prevent museums and other institutions within their territories from acquiring illegally exported cultural property. Article 7(b) requires states to return stolen cultural property that has been properly inventoried, subject to payment of just compensation to innocent purchasers or holders of valid title to the material.

Also, under article 9 of the Convention, as we have seen, parties to the Convention can call on other parties to ban the importation of items that form a specific cultural element in their national patrimony if that element is in jeopardy. As a rule, a state will take such action only if similar action is taken by other states with a significant impact on trade in the particular material that is claimed to be in jeopardy.

Étienne Clement, *The Aims of the 1970 UNESCO Convention on the Means of Prohibiting and Preventing the Illicit Import, Export and Transfer of Ownership of Cultural Property and Action Being Taken by UNESCO to Assist in Its Implementation, in* Antiquities Trade or Betrayed: Legal, Ethical and Conservation Issues 38 (K.W. Tubb ed., 1995)

[Although most countries have adopted laws to protect their cultural heritage, many of them, particularly in developing countries and Eastern Europe, do not have sufficient resources to ensure compliance –*Eds.*].

According to the [1970] Convention it is the responsibility of each State to decide in full sovereignty on the nature of the measures to adopt to comply with the provisions of the Convention, taking into account compatibility with its own internal legal system. The States are invited:

- to create protection services;
- to draft legislative texts;
- to establish, on the basis of the national inventory, a list of important cultural property whose export would constitute an appreciable impoverishment of the national cultural heritage;
- to promote and develop institutions such as museums, libraries and archives;
- to supervise archaeological excavations;
- to establish rules of ethics for curators, collectors and antique dealers;

- to adopt educational measures to stimulate, and develop respect for, the cultural heritage;
- to ensure appropriate publicity for the disappearance of items of cultural property; and
- to institute a system for issuing export certificates which should accompany all items of cultural property exported, to prohibit export without the certificate and to publicise that prohibition, particularly among persons likely to export or import cultural property.

The State Parties are invited to request UNESCO's assistance in this respect.

One of the main provisions (Article 5) of the Convention deals with the importation of cultural property. Indeed, the States Parties undertake to:

- prevent museums and similar institutions from acquiring cultural property originating in another State Party which has been illegally exported after the entry into force of the Convention in the States concerned;
- prohibit the import of cultural property stolen from a museum or a religious or secular public monument or similar institution in another State Party after the entry into force of the Convention for the States concerned, provided that such property is in the inventory of that institution; and
- take steps, at the request of the State of origin, to recover and return any such cultural property imported after the entry into force of the Convention in both States concerned, provided that the requesting State shall pay just compensation to an innocent purchaser or to a person who has valid title to that property.

This is an essential provision of the Convention. It requests the States Parties to take measures for the return of cultural property to the country of origin even if it is in possession of someone who acquired it legally. Moreover there is no time limitation on that obligation. However, just compensation must be paid to the *bona fide* purchaser, namely, the one who did not know that the object was a stolen one. States who do not require holders of stolen cultural property to be compensated may make a reservation to that provision, as the United States has done.

In order to deal with the situation of archaeological objects illegally plundered from archaeological sites, which by definition are not registered in an inventory, the Convention contains a specific provision (Article 9) by which each State Party whose cultural patrimony is in jeopardy from pillage of archaeological or ethnological materials can call upon other affected States Parties and those States Parties undertake, in these circumstances, to participate in a concerted international effort to determine and to carry out the necessary concrete measures to redress the situation. Moreover, in another provision of the Convention (Article 13b), it is requested that competent services in all States Parties cooperate to facilitate the restitution of illicitly exported cultural property. A concrete example of such cooperation is illustrated by the law [the CPIA] adopted by the United States of America to implement the Convention. . . .

The Convention also provides (Article 8) that penalties should be imposed on any persons who have not respected the prohibition of exportation or importation. Moreover (Article 10a), the States must oblige antique dealers, subject to penal or administrative sanctions, to maintain a register recording the origin of each item, names and addresses of the supplier, and the description and price of each item sold. These persons should also inform the purchaser of the cultural property of the export prohibition to which such property may be subject.

. . .

The impact of the Convention on the acquisition of cultural property can be seen in the codes of ethics adopted by many museums in the industrialized countries, based on the code of professional ethics of the International Council of Museums (ICOM). Other examples are the codes of practice of antique dealers' associations such as the Code of Practice for the Control of International Trading in Works of Art adopted by members of the United Kingdom's Fine Art and Antiques Trade.

The role of UNESCO is essentially to encourage States to ratify the Convention and, once they have ratified it, to assist them in its implementation. This can be done by assisting in the drafting of national legislation, and in the organisation of regional and national workshops to develop regional cooperation and collaboration between museums, archaeologists, police and customs. . . . UNESCO also collects legislative texts on the matter and disseminates them widely. . . . A manual on export laws in force in more than 150 countries has also been published. . . . UNESCO also occasionally circulates notices on stolen cultural objects. However, in that field, UNESCO cooperates with other institutions such as INTERPOL, the Customs Cooperation Council, the International Council of Museums, national public institutions and, more recently, with existing private databases such as the International Foundation for Art Research (IFAR) or the Art Loss Register. As to the criminal aspect of the question, UNESCO cooperates with the United Nations Commission for the Prevention of Crimes . . . [on] the question of crimes against cultural property. . . .

The case of Cambodia

. . . [A]n example of what can be done to assist a country in implementing this Convention [is] UNESCO's response to the request by the Cambodian authorities for assistance. . . . Cambodia is facing a veritable hemorrhage of its cultural heritage. Statues, bas-reliefs, stone sculptures and entire lintels disappear each day from the famous monuments of Angkor and other lesser-known sites. Thieves attack by night and day, selling extremely valuable objects to unscrupulous traders who will pass them on through a number of hands before they end up gracing the shelves of private collectors in Europe, Japan and North America.

Having ratified the 1970 UNESCO Convention, Cambodia became the first signatory State to call upon UNESCO to assist in laying down a series of measures to combat a traffic which is gradually depriving the country of its exceptional cultural heritage, whose history is still largely unexplored. These measures were presented in a broad programme which was submitted in March 1992 to members of the Supreme National Council of Cambodia presided over by HM Prince Norodom Sihanouk. Before the recent elections which led to the designation of a new Government, the administrative structures of the country after several decades of instability did not allow it to struggle with efficiency against illicit traffic.

In order to define the steps that would have to be taken in cooperation with the national authorities, UNESCO organised a national workshop in July 1992 in Phnom Penh, capital of Cambodia, on the following subjects: education, public information, legislation, site and museum security, export controls by police and customs authorities, and preparation of inventories of cultural goods. More than 120 participants attended, including representatives of several components of the Supreme National Council, the United Nations, Interpol and the International Council of Museums (ICOM). High-level civil servants, police and customs officers, educators, journalists, jurists, conservators and students thus familiarised themselves with specific techniques and participated in short training sessions. Several government ministers took part in the workshop and in the small group sessions. The workshop ended by elaborating an action plan in four major target areas: training, communication, legislation and education. Completely financed by UNESCO, the meeting paved the way for a series of measures which began immediately afterward with the preparation of legislation for the protection of cultural property which was adopted in February 1993 by a decision of the Supreme National Council.

Action was also taken to strengthen security against theft in museums and storehouses, and an ICOM expert advised officials of the Museum of Phnom Penh on the organisation of a security service and the use of mechanical security devices. Security at the conservation storehouse at Angkor was also reinforced, however, the armed attacks on the building that took place in February and in April 1993 demonstrated that much more stringent measures are urgently required. . . .

. . . [T]o improve the level of awareness and the training of local agents in a variety of disciplines, . . . a number of initiatives have been undertaken. A poster competition was organised in cooperation with the University of Fine Arts and the prize-winning posters were distributed nationwide to various audiences: the general public, students and tourists. Tourists also receive brochures warning them against the export of cultural goods without appropriate export licenses.

UNESCO has also conducted a far-reaching information programme which has thus far included 120 customs officials, 24 Cambodian journalists, 450 Cambodian police officers responsible for guarding the monuments of Angkor (some of whom received practical training in cooperation with the French police in 1994), and a number of police officials of the United Nations Transitional Authority in Cambodia (UNTAC).

Alongside these measures UNESCO has supported the efforts of several institutions to compile inventories of movable cultural property, a costly and time consuming effort for which large-scale funding is being sought.

However, it must be recalled that the traffic in cultural goods cannot be stemmed simply by taking measures in the countries victimised by this practice; because the trade is international, action must also be taken in the receiving countries, and, in particular, those with flourishing art markets. This is, of course, the purpose of the 1970 UNESCO Convention, and in order to make its provisions better understood, a regional workshop was organised in Thailand in 1992 for 15 Asian countries, including Cambodia. On this occasion the Thai authorities announced that they were prepared to return to Cambodia cultural goods seized in Thailand. Discussions are under way with Thailand and France to encourage their ratification of the 1970 Convention.[26]

UNESCO, for its part, continues to inform the international media, and programmes and articles have appeared on Radio-France, the BBC, Australian television and in the Thai press. Most recently, the Organisation spearheaded a worldwide information effort with regard to the head of a statue stolen in Cambodia in February 1992. UNESCO also supported the publication of a booklet prepared by the International Council of Museums in cooperation with the École française d'Extrême-Orient which contains photographs and descriptions of 100 cultural objects stolen from Cambodia (ICOM, 1993). This is a very useful document which makes it difficult now to put on sale the objects presented in it. Major auction houses all over the world have received it and additional copies are available from the International Council of Museums.

The example of Cambodia, which must simultaneously confront a difficult political situation and the threat of losing a large part of its cultural heritage, demonstrates clearly the need for a genuine mobilization of the international community. UNESCO sincerely hopes that conferences such as *Conservation and the Antiquities Trade* and this volume will contribute to this movement of solidarity for the preservation of our cultural heritage.

---

d. The UNIDROIT Convention on Stolen or Illegally Exported Cultural Objects

In 1986 the UN International Institute for the Unification of Private Law (UNIDROIT) commenced a study of the international protection of cultural property and then responded to a request by UNESCO to prepare a convention to supplement its 1970 Convention in view of a number of significant gaps in it and the then small number of market-state parties. The aim was to focus on questions of private law associated with illicit trafficking that the 1970 UNESCO Convention did not address, and thereby to strengthen the protective regime. The assumption was that another agreement on illegal trade in cultural heritage might appeal to states that had concerns about the 1970

[26] [In 1997 France ratified the 1970 Convention. – *Eds.*]

UNESCO Convention as well as to those that had already become parties to it. The result was the UNIDROIT Convention on Stolen or Illegally Exported Cultural Objects.[27]

The UNIDROIT Convention uses the term "cultural objects" but adopts the same definition of such material as the definition of "cultural property" in article 1 of the UNESCO Convention. As with the UNESCO Convention, the UNIDROIT Convention applies prospectively only. It therefore does not apply to objects stolen or smuggled before the time it comes into force in particular states parties. Although the UNESCO Convention furnishes an opportunity for state parties to recognize export controls of other parties, this obligation is qualified by article 5 of the UNIDROIT Convention, to be discussed shortly.

Chapter 2 of the UNIDROIT Convention concerns the restitution of stolen cultural objects. Under article 3, the term "stolen cultural object" is extended to include objects unlawfully excavated or lawfully excavated but unlawfully retained. Claims for restitution of such objects expire three years after the claimant actually discovers where the object is located and who possesses it. All claims must be made within fifty years from the time of the theft. This rule of repose does not apply to objects belonging to public collections, forming part of identified monuments or archeological sites, or belonging to certain categories of tribal or indigenous cultural objects. A party to the agreement can declare, however, that a claim is subject to a time limitation of seventy-five years or longer under its law.

Persons required to restitute stolen cultural objects are entitled to compensation. This right is conditional on such persons being unaware that an object was stolen and exercising due diligence when acquiring such an object. Article 4(4) identifies factors that apply to the determination of whether this requirement of due diligence is satisfied, such as the price paid, whether registers of stolen objects were accessed, and "the character of the parties." It is not entirely clear who can be held liable to pay compensation, unless the claimant is required to do so.

Chapter 3 of the Convention concerns the return of illegally exported cultural objects. Such objects must be returned on the request of a state party to the courts of another state party. Significantly, there are separate criteria for such returns, apart from the laws of the source state. Article 5(3) provides that, unless the illegal export "significantly impairs" one of several interests, its return is not required under the Convention. This is an important concession to the reluctance of market states to recognize source state export controls regardless of their scope. Chapter 3 also includes a statute of limitations and repose provision similar to those under Chapter 2 concerning the restitution of stolen objects. Another paragraph provides for agreements between the requesting state and the possessor of an object providing for either the possessor's retention of an object or its transfer for payment or gratuitously.

NOTES AND QUESTIONS

1. The UNIDROIT Convention attempts to reconcile conflicting rules as between common law and civil law systems. For example, an express provision provides for payment by the requesting state of "fair and reasonable compensation" to a

[27] Final Act of the Diplomatic Conference for the Adoption of the Draft UNIDROIT Convention on the International Return of Stolen or Illegally Exported Cultural Objects, June 24, 1995, 34 I.L.M. 1322 (1995).

good-faith purchaser of an illegally exported object (more of a civil law idea). The purchaser's good faith involves whether he or she "knew or ought reasonably to have known at the time of acquisition that the object had been illegally exported" (article 6(1) – more of a common law idea).

2. The UNIDROIT Convention as a whole represents a major advancement in harmonizing and unifying otherwise conflicting national laws. It provides a detailed framework for international restitution of stolen objects and the return of illegally exported objects. It also provides a new vocabulary for international cooperation in the sphere of cultural property.
3. Unfortunately, some of the vocabulary of the conventional rules is subject to widely varying interpretation. For example, the core provision, article 5, lists four "interests" in cultural objects any one of which, if "significantly impair[ed]," may require a court of a state party to order return of an object to a requesting state.[28] This list of interests is subject to divergent interpretations. One might note, for example, the stipulated interest in "the preservation of information of, for example, a scientific or historical character." Would this support requests for return of poorly maintained colonial material from developing countries to Spain, France, and other former imperial powers? Would this language alone support claims, in the interest of restoring context and enhancing historical integrity, for the return to a country of origin of cultural material that forms part of a larger oeuvre? (An example would be one panel unhinged from a triptych and transported outside the triptych's country of origin.)
4. More generally, article 5's list of specific interests is followed by a catchall category for objects of "significant cultural importance for the requesting State."[29] This category limits the reach of overly expansive export controls of the sort we noted earlier in the book. In determining whether an object would fall within this catchall provision, it should be noted, first, that an item can easily be of significant cultural importance for more than one state, including the requested state. Which state gets the object in that case? It must also be noted that the UNIDROIT negotiators deliberately lowered the threshold language from material of "outstanding" cultural importance to that of "significant" cultural importance. The result of that unfortunate change in itself may be to open up a Pandora's box of disputes.

   In interpreting whether the cultural importance of a particular object may be merely "significant," the *travaux préparatoires* of the UNIDROIT negotiating

[28] In full, article 5(3) provides:

> The court or other competent authority of the State addressed shall order the return of an illegally exported cultural object if the requesting State establishes that the removal of the object from its territory significantly impairs one or more of the following interests:
> (a) the physical preservation of the object or of its context;
> (b) the integrity of a complex object;
> (c) the preservation of information of, for example, a scientific
> (d) or historical character;
> (e) the traditional or ritual use of the object by a tribal or
> (f) indigenous community, [sic] or establishes that the object is of significant cultural importance for the requesting State.
>
> UNIDROIT Convention, *supra* note 27.

[29] *Id.*

conference offer some guidance.[30] Several delegations argued that a claim for return of an object in itself indicated sufficient importance of the object to deny review by foreign authorities of that presumption. Art-importing countries responded that importance was not self-defining: a requesting state would have to prove its case to the authorities of the requested state. The UNIDROIT negotiating conference struck a compromise by holding open the possibility that foreign authorities could make their own determinations of an object's importance within the reasonable limits of that term. To an extent, these limits are more precisely defined by reference to an Annex to the UNIDROIT Convention that lists categories of objects as in the 1970 UNESCO Convention. Arguably, some of the language in this listing limits the discretion of the requested state to question the importance of an object to a requesting state. Qualifying language in the Annex – for example, "rare" and "more than one hundred years old" – would seem to clarify significance and thereby discourage extravagant claims to objects of little importance. Such limiting language is, however, helpful but not definitive in resolving issues of significance.

The 1970 UNESCO Convention on illegal trafficking provides an alternative litmus test of cultural significance, as follows:

> Official registration of the object by a national service, in an inventory of protected property whose export would constitute an appreciable impoverishment of the national cultural heritage, shall constitute prima facie evidence that the object is of outstanding cultural significance to the requesting state. Other evidence shall include, but not be limited to, published scholarship, scholarly testimony, and previous decisions of the competent authority of the State addressed.[31]

This more precise language was not transplanted into the UNIDROIT Convention, however. Some confusion may therefore arise, regardless of whether a state is party to both agreements or only one of them. Ultimately, of course, words are only words. The UNIDROIT framework for return of illegally exported objects must therefore rely less on constructions of conventional language than on the good faith and good will of states parties.

5. Even when there is no quarrel about the significance of a cultural object, it is questionable whether cultural material necessarily should be subject to mandatory return on the request of the country of origin, as the "shall order" language in article 5(3) of the UNIDROIT Convention indicates. Take, for example, two objects of the greatest cultural importance to the United States, one from its early history as an English colony and the other from its contemporary culture. Powhatan's mantle, from the early seventeenth century, consists of four deer skins sewn together with sinew thread and decorated with shells forming human and animal figures. The garment, or possibly wall hanging, is associated with a North American tribal chief who was the father of Pocahontas. The mantle has been described as "perhaps the most important North American Indian relic to survive

[30] *See, e.g.*, UNIDROIT Committee of Governmental Experts on the International Protection of Cultural Property, Report of the Second Session, Study LXX – Doc. 30, June 1992, at 26.

[31] Convention on the Means of Prohibiting and Preventing the Illicit Import, Export and Transfer of Ownership of Cultural Property, *adopted* Nov. 14, 1970, 96 Stat. 2350, 823 U.N.T.S. 231 [hereinafter the 1970 UNESCO Convention].

anywhere."[32] The contemporary object, created in 1952, is *Blue Poles* by Jackson Pollock, who has been described as America's greatest painter and is certainly one of the most innovative and celebrated artists of the twentieth century.[33] *Blue Poles* is the last, and perhaps the finest, of Pollock's monumental abstract paintings.

Both of these items are in foreign collections. Powhatan's mantle is the most famous exhibit in the Tradescant Collection that has formed a core of the Ashmolean Museum at England's Oxford University ever since the museum opened its doors in 1683. *Blue Poles* reposes in the National Gallery of Australia in Canberra. Although Powhatan's mantle certainly is as much a part of the English imperial heritage as it is the American colonial heritage, Pollock's masterpiece has nothing directly to do with the Australian heritage except that his work may have inspired that country's artists. Instead, the painting has everything to do with Native American elements, Thomas Hart Benton and the twentieth-century muralist traditions of the United States and Mexico, the tastes of American heiress Peggy Guggenheim, and the eccentricities of the New York art scene and American society.[34]

It is hard to imagine two more significant artifacts of U.S. cultural heritage, both of them located abroad. Even so, there has been no serious claim for a permanent return of the objects to the United States, nor should there be. Claims for the repatriation of even the most significant material to a country of origin should not be mandatory. Of course, the lack of any statutory basis under U.S. law for claiming return of the two objects would inhibit such a claim, but even when national laws support a claim for such objects or prohibit their export, international criteria are needed to strike a balance between the values of patrimonial retention and international dispersion of objects.

6. Canada and the UNIDROIT Convention: As we saw in Chapter 4, Canada is a party to the UNESCO Convention. Several factors have constrained Canada from becoming a party to the UNIDROIT Convention, however. First, the Cultural Property Export and Import Act goes beyond the UNESCO and UNIDROIT Conventions by setting up a procedure for the return of any foreign cultural property illegally exported from a UNESCO signatory state. Thus, Canada's ratification of the UNIDROIT Convention would have the effect of limiting Canada's obligations for the return of cultural material.

   Second, much of what UNIDROIT provides for is within provincial rather than federal jurisdiction. It is possible for provincial laws to enact an international agreement to which Canada is a party, but in this case, such laws would need to create a new category of property under provincial law (foreign cultural property), which would be an unusual development, to say the least. A further complication is that Canada has provinces with both civil law and common law systems. As noted earlier, the common law currently provides an unqualified right (except for limitations periods) on the part of the owner to recover stolen property. However, UNIDROIT would modify this right, though Canada could decline to implement the provisions.

[32] Ashmolean Museum (Oxford University), The Tradescant Room 4 (n.d.).

[33] *See* Museum of Modern Art (New York), Jackson Pollock, November 1, 1998-February 2, 1999, at 1, 4 [hereinafter Jackson Pollock].

[34] Jackson Pollock, *id.* at 2–3.

Third, private international law (or conflict of laws) poses problems in many international art law cases. One of the best-known cases involved an innocent English theft victim who was unable to recover his property in an English court because that court, by applying Italian law, concluded that an honest foreign purchaser had obtained good title by purchasing the controversial property in Italy, where the bona fide purchaser is protected (*Winkworth v. Christies*, [1980] 1 All E.R. 1121). The UNIDROIT Convention does not deal with the application of conflict of laws rules. If Canada were to consider enacting the UNIDROIT Convention, it would need to consider how the provisions of the Convention would relate to such rules. For example, how would a case like *Winkworth* be decided in Canada if article 3 on stolen objects were part of Canadian law?

Finally, of particular concern to Canada is how claims for the possession of Aboriginal objects are addressed. One of the grounds set out in article 5, on which the request for the return of an illegally exported cultural object might be based, is the significant impairment to its traditional or ritual use by a tribal or indigenous community. This applies even if the indigenous person who created the object is still alive (article 7(2)). Although enforcement of Canadian export controls in market countries is currently an unpredictable exercise, the provisions of articles 5 and 7 would only oblige market states to recognize a more limited range of indigenous cultural property export controls than currently exists under Canadian law. For stolen indigenous objects, international claims would be subject to limitation periods and rights to compensation that are more stringent than may otherwise be the case under foreign law.

7. Neither Canada nor the United States, for example, is a party to the UNIDROIT Convention. Taking account of the criticism in note 6, do you think either country or other nonparties should become parties?
8. For a detailed analysis of the UNIDROIT Convention, see LYNDEL V. PROTT, COMMENTARY OF THE UNIDROIT CONVENTION(1997); John H. Merryman, *The UNIDROIT Convention: Three Significant Departures from the Urtext*, 5 INT'L J. CULTURAL PROP. 11 (1996); Lyndel V. Prott, *UNESCO and UNIDROIT: A Partnership against Illicit Trafficking*, 1 UNIFORM L. REV. 59 (1996).

PROBLEMS

1. A series of stones with unusual carvings surfaces in New York and is offered for sale as Egyptian antiquities by a New York art gallery. Experts confirm that the unusual carvings on the stones are an unfamiliar form of hieroglyphics that may shed new light on ancient history. The Egyptian government brings a replevin action in a New York court to recover the stones, claiming that they are part of a sculpture of a sphinx that was recently unearthed in Egypt. Egypt has a statute that vests ownership in the state of all undiscovered movables and immovables found in Egyptian territory.
2. Instead of stones, substitute in the preceding problem a golden vase that bears the initials *OV*, which stands for Octavius Valinius, a Roman general who fought in the Roman army against Pompeii. Such vases are quite common in museums and private collections throughout the world. The Egyptian government claims that the vase was unearthed in Egypt and therefore should be returned there under

the patrimony statute referred to in problem 1. Please advise the gallery as to how it should respond to the two claims by the Egyptian government. What, if anything, is the responsibility in this case of the United States under the UNESCO Convention? If the UNIDROIT Convention were applicable, how might it affect the result? (Reprinted with Permission of the Association of the Bar of the City of New York).

e. UNESCO, UN, and ICOM Resolutions

In 1976 the General Conference of UNESCO expressed its support for exchange of cultural material by adopting the Recommendation to Member States on the International Exchange of Cultural Property, as follows:

> [That instrument] is based on the principle that a systematic policy for the exchange of cultural property will contribute to a better distribution and use of the cultural heritage on a world-wide scale and will be a means of combating illicit traffic and the rise in price of such property, which renders it inaccessible to the least-favoured countries and institutions.[35]

In 1978 the General Conference of UNESCO established an Intergovernmental Committee for Promoting the Return of Cultural Property to its Countries of Origin or its Restitution in Case of Illicit Appropriations. The Committee is entrusted with the task of promoting bilateral agreements for the return and restitution of cultural material, particularly that resulting from colonization and military occupation, to countries of origin. The Committee also seeks to assist countries in building representative collections of cultural material, preparing national inventories, informing public opinion, helping develop museum personnel, implementing the recommendation on international exchange, and advising UNESCO on pertinent issues.

Most significant, however, the UN General Assembly has adopted a series of resolutions since 1973. Although they have differed in wording, the essential provisions have been the following: to affirm the salutary implications of international cooperation in the restitution of cultural material to countries of origin; to invite states to take adequate measures to prohibit and prevent illicit trafficking in objets d'art; to invite states to prepare national inventories; to invite states to become parties to the UNESCO Convention; to strengthen museum infrastructures; and to marshal professional expertise, the media, and public opinion in favor of programs of restitution.

The work of nongovernmental organizations has also been influential. For example, the International Council of Museums (ICOM), as an affiliate of UNESCO, adopted the Study on Principles, Conditions and Means for Restitution or Return of Cultural Property in View of Reconstituting Dispersed Heritages. This study arrived at a number of interesting and controversial conclusions. One of these is that international cooperation in the reassembly of dispersed heritage through restitution or return of objects that are of major importance for the cultural identity and history of particular countries of origin is an ethical principle that international organizations recognize and affirm. The Study

[35] *A Brief History of the Creation by UNESCO of an Intergovernmental Committee for Promoting the Return of Cultural Property to its Countries of Origin or its Restitution in Case of Illicit Appropriation*, 31 MUSEUM 59 (SPECIAL ISSUE: *Return and Restitution of Cultural Property*) (1979).

optimistically forecast that this principle would soon become an element of *jus cogens* in international relations.

NOTE AND QUESTIONS

The ICOM Study, referred to previously, refers to the concept of *jus cogens.* An earlier reference in the Study (paragraph 8) even more ambiguously asserts, "[I]t is equally true that the community of nations now considers as an element of *jus cogens* the right of all peoples to recover cultural property which forms an integral part of their cultural identity." Article 53 of the Vienna Convention on the Law of Treaties explains the concept of *jus cogens* as follows:

> A treaty is void if, at the time of its conclusion, it conflicts with a peremptory norm of general international law. For the purposes of the present Convention, a peremptory norm of general international law is a norm accepted and recognized by the international community of States as a whole as a norm from which no derogation is permitted and which can be modified only by a subsequent norm of general international law having the same character.[36]

Although the identity of those peremptory norms is not perfectly clear, they would include, for example, restraints on the illegal threat or use of force under article 2(4) of the UN Charter; the principle of *pacta sunt servanda*; prohibitions on such egregious violations of human rights as apartheid, slavery, and the use by states of torture; and the principles of self-determination and minimum human welfare.

The ICOM Study, which helped shape international cooperation in the restitution and return of cultural material, was completed in 1979. Do you agree that the ethical principle requiring the reassembly of dispersed heritage did, indeed, "soon become an element of *jus cogens*"? Is there really an established "right of all people to recover cultural property which forms an integral part of their cultural identity"?

f. Codes of Ethics

In 1986 ICOM adopted the Code of Professional Ethics. As amended and revised in 2001 and 2004, the Code establishes basic expectations about the responsibility of museums to communities and sets minimum standards of conduct and performance to govern museum staff and collection management. Such codes of ethics adopted by museums, other institutions, and associations encourage compliance with legal requirements of return and restitution. They also serve to deter doubtful acquisitions that might be subject to such requirements.

Ellen Herscher, *Tarnished Reputations*, Archaeology, Sept.–Oct. 1998, at 66, 68, 75

... In 1969, Clemency Chase Coggins, of Boston University, published an article in *Art Journal* that is considered a milestone in the struggle to

[36] Vienna Convention on the Law of Treaties, *opened for signature* May 23, 1969, U.N. Doc. A/CONF. 39/27, at 291 (1969), *reprinted in* 8 Int'l Legal Materials 679 (1969).

curtail the illicit trade in antiquities and the plundering of archaeological sites. "Illicit Traffic in Pre-Columbian Antiquities" moved beyond general lamentation about the problem, providing specifics about looted pieces and naming names. In the article's most stunning disclosures, Coggins traced looted artifacts to some of America's best-known and most respected museums. With this, it became harder to ignore the museums' role in the acquisition of undocumented antiquities.

In the late 1960s, . . . the University of Pennsylvania Museum of Archaeology and Anthropology in Philadelphia also acquired a group of precious Bronze Age objects. George F. Bass, given the task of publishing the material, questioned the validity of doing so. If the items were indeed found together, as the dealer had assured the museum, they were extremely important evidence for ancient trade. If they were not found together, they were meaningless trinkets. A lot of history hung on a dealer's assertions.

These concerns, along with the inescapable evidence for the rapid destruction of sites by looting throughout the world, led to the Pennsylvania Declaration of 1970, the first institutional revolt against museum acquisition policies. This statement, issued by the University of Pennsylvania Museum, preceded by a few months the well-known UNESCO convention on the illicit trade in cultural property. It declared that the museum would purchase no more antiquities without a "pedigree" – that is, information about previous owners, country of origin, and legality of export – and it would make this information public. Several other, mostly smaller institutions soon followed suit with policy statements of their own.

It was a heavy time for those museums that underwent conversion. Thomas Hoving (director of the museum from 1967 to 1977) stated publicly that the [Metropolitan Museum of Art in New York] would henceforth respect other countries' export laws. The Harvard Report (1971), emphasizing the importance of preserving scientific information, made it official university policy not to acquire artifacts unless they had been legally exported from their country of origin. Similar policies were adopted by the Brooklyn Museum (1972), the Field Museum of Natural History (1972), the Smithsonian Institution (1973), and others.

Professional associations joined in as well. The Association of Art Museum Directors passed a resolution in 1973 pleading to "cooperate fully with foreign countries in their endeavors to prevent the illicit traffic in works of art." The American Association of Museums approved a comprehensive ethics code in 1978. The International Council of Museums (ICOM) adopted a stringent Code of Professional Ethics in 1986.

. . .

The ICOM Code of Ethics states that "museums should recognize the relationship between the market-place and the initial and often destructive taking of an object for the commercial market, and must recognize that it is highly unethical for a museum to support in any way, whether directly or indirectly, that illicit market." Indeed the direct linkage between looter and market has been documented frequently over the years. . . .

ARCHAEOLOGICAL INSTITUTE OF AMERICA, CODE OF ETHICS (1997)

The Archaeological Institute of America is dedicated to the greater understanding of archaeology, to the protection and preservation of the world's archaeological resources and the information they contain, and to the encouragement and support of archaeological research and publication.

In accordance with these principles, members of the AIA should:

1. Seek to ensure that the exploration of archaeological sites be conducted according to the highest standards under the direct supervision of qualified personnel, and that the results of such research be made public.
2. Refuse to participate in the trade in undocumented antiquities and refrain from activities that enhance the commercial value of such objects. Undocumented antiquities are those which are not documented as belonging to a public or private collection before December 30, 1970, when the AIA Council endorsed the UNESCO Convention on Cultural Property, or which have not been excavated and exported from the country of origin in accordance with the laws of that country;
3. Inform appropriate authorities of threats to, or plunder of archaeological sites, and illegal import or export of archaeological material.

Sharon Flescher, *AAMD Revises Guidelines for Acquisition of Antiquities – Again*, 10 IFAR J., no. 1, at 4 (2008) (reprinted with the permission of the International Foundation for Art Research)

For the third time in four years,[37] the Association of Art Museum Directors (AAMD) has published new guidelines for its member museums concerning the "Acquisition of Archaeological Materials and Ancient Art." The revised – and more stringent – 2008 guidelines, announced on June 4, come after a period when several U.S. museums have been embroiled in high profile claims by foreign countries to return works in their collections that were said by the countries to have been removed in violation of patrimony and export laws. Agreements to return works to Italy, for example, have recently been negotiated by the Metropolitan Museum, the Museum of Fine Arts, Boston, the Getty Museum, and the Princeton University Art Museum, among others.

AAMD is a membership organization comprised of 184 directors of the most important art museums in the United States, Canada, and Mexico. An accompanying press release noted that the Guidelines – which are not legally binding by member museums – were prepared by a task force of "more than twenty art museum directors representing a variety of art museums nationwide." They were then endorsed by the full membership.

[37] Previous AAMD Guidelines on the Acquisition of Archaeological Materials and Ancient Art were published in 2004 and 2006.

Although the new Guidelines will make it more difficult for museums to acquire antiquities – whether by purchase, gift, bequest, or exchange [–]they also reaffirm "the importance of collecting archaeological materials and ancient art." Collecting is *not* inconsistent with "protecting archaeological sites," the AAMD states, but for the dual goal to be accomplished, "enhanced cooperation" and "mutual understanding and respect" between source countries and museums will be necessary. On this point, some archaeologists might disagree. They believe that the very existence of a market encourages the looting of sites.

Highlights from the new Guidelines and accompanying Statement of Principles include:

- The establishment of November 1970 as a firm cut-off date for applying more stringent acquisition standards. This is the date of the UNESCO Convention[38] and is thirteen years prior to the January 1983 date when the U.S. enacted implementing legislation enforcing the Convention.
- The commitment to the principle of acquiring objects ethically and legally and in such a way that the acquisition doesn't "provide a direct and material incentive to looting." This includes requiring sellers and donors to provide all documentation and knowledge about the objects.
- A mandate for a museum to undertake provenance research to substantiate that an object was "outside its country of probable modern discovery before 1970 or was legally exported" after 1970.

Significantly, the new Guidelines encourage greater transparency in acquisitions:

- When museums do acquire archaeological materials and ancient art, they should "promptly publish acquisitions in print or electronic form," including an image of the object and its provenance.

Whereas previous AAMD Guidelines simply encouraged museums to do this, the AAMD is making this step a practical reality. It has established a new section of its Website – the AAMD Object Registry – for museums to post, and the public to search, acquisitions. The site (http://aamdobjectregistry.org) is searchable by "Object," "Object Type," "Institution," and "Country."...

On the thorny issue of acquiring objects lacking full provenance, and in recognition of the fact "that a complete ownership history may not be obtainable for all archaeological material and every work of ancient art," the new Guidelines allow members latitude in making "informed and defensible judgments about the appropriateness of acquiring" such objects. No doubt, this standard will not be sufficient for hard-liners who believe that a licit art market in antiquities is an oxymoron, but it is in line with those museum directors – such as Peter Marzio, James Cuno, and Philippe de Montebello – who have publicly stated that high quality artifacts whose provenance cannot be fully established still deserve to be

[38] [The 1970] UNESCO Convention on the Means of Prohibiting and Preventing the Illicit Import and Export and Transfer of Ownership of Cultural Property.

exhibited in public institutions, not only for their educational and esthetic value, but to give potential claimants the opportunity to see them.

Patrick J. O'Keefe, *Codes of Ethics: Form and Function in Cultural Heritage Management*, 7 Int'l J. Cultural Prop. 32 (1998)

The administrator of a historic monument considers that more than 100,000 visitors per year will cause damage to the fabric of the monument. He institutes a system of ticketing that will implement this limit. The government sees the monument as a major tourist revenue earner and orders that the number be increased to 300,000 per year.

An art historian is shown a statuette that the possessor claims is a long-lost work by a major medieval sculptor. The historian believes this to be correct and is prepared to endorse the attribution, despite knowing that many colleagues will disagree with the endorsement. The historian is offered ten percent of the sale price if the possessor can make public the endorsement.

The holder of a collection of material from a gravesite related to the local indigenous people offers a member of the provincial society of archaeologists a chance to study it. The material was excavated unlawfully and seized by the authorities and, at the urging of the indigenous people, is to be reinterred by the holder – a private owner – in six weeks['] time. The archaeologist is not to reveal any details of the work on the material until after the reburial takes place.

A bronze statuette is brought to a conservator for restoration before being offered for sale. There are particles of mud and wood on it, and the statuette appears to have been recently excavated. Stylistically and hagiographically it could only have come from one of a small group of countries – all of which have laws forbidding export of such an object. The possessor wants the work to be done rapidly. All defects are to be hidden as far as possible, and all material that is removed is to be destroyed.[39]

All of the above situations involve difficult choices for the persons indicated, if they have any concern for the well-being of the cultural heritage. To help in making the right choice, archaeologists, anthropologists, conservators, dealers, art historians, and historic preservationists have in recent decades sought guidance in codes of ethics. At their best, ethical codes provide a standard for making a choice and a shield against attack by those who would dispute that choice. When others disagree with the choice that has been made, a code can be the basis for criticism aimed at changing the decision. Reference to "right" and "wrong" indicates the moral element inherent in these decisions and the necessity for a standard of conduct.

. . .

Codes of ethics are not intended to be treated as legal documents where every nuance is considered, every comma checked for its effect on meaning. Rather they are guides prepared, in most cases, by persons concerned to

[39] *See* Fenna Schmidt, *Codes of Museum Ethics and the Financial Pressures on Museums*, 11 Museum Management and Curatorship 257, 259 (1992).

express their understanding of what members of their particular profession need in order to function successfully. Thus, the language may be imprecise, but it should be interpreted in the spirit in which it was written. For example, the Code of Ethics and Principles of the National Antique and Art Dealers Association of America contains a clause reading, "All bills of sale or invoices shall contain an accurate description of the articles sold and no representation that an article is genuine shall be made unless the article is truly genuine." The intent of this injunction is obvious, even though the language would not withstand scrutiny.

. . .

The precise legal implications [of ethical codes] will depend on the jurisdiction in which the matter is raised. . . . [I]n the Netherlands:

> Where the General Conditions of the Code of Ethics have been expressly stated to form part of the contract then they will form part of the contract. . . . Where the terms of the Code of Ethics have not been incorporated by "agreement between the parties" . . . Dutch Civil Code allows the Code of Ethics to be relevant, although not incorporated into the contract, because the terms of the Code of Ethics are a matter of "custom" or "reasonableness and fairness."[40]

[In the United Kingdom]:

> Anyone can publish a code of practice, but the codes most likely to be invoked in courts of law are those which purport to represent a consensus of respectable opinion in some community of skilled practitioners. The usefulness of such codes in furnishing guidance on the application of legal standards is undeniable.[41]

Consequently, the way in which a code of ethics has been drafted, the degree of consultation, its reflection of differing viewpoints, the extent of acceptance, and the standing of the sponsoring organization will all be relevant. . . .

[In *Kingdom of Spain v. Christie*,[42]] the auction house offered for sale [Francisco] Goya's painting[] *La Marquesa de Santa Cruz*. The Spanish Government claimed that this had been taken from Spain using forged export documents. Proceedings were begun in the English courts claiming declarations as to the falsity of the documents. In the course of his judgment, Sir Nicolas Browne-Wilkinson V-C. commented on the [U.K.] Code [of Practice for the Control of International Trading in Works of Art] and the interpretation of it postulated by Christie's:

> At first sight I thought that under . . . the Code, if it were established that the picture had been exported from Spain with the use of forged

[40] Caroline Forder, *The Civil Liability of Conservators under Dutch Law*, La Restauration Des Objets D'Art 63, 74–75 (Quentin Byrne-Sutton, Marc-Andre Renold & Beatrice Rötheli-Mariotti eds., Schulthess Polygraphiseher Verlag, Zurich 1995). Emphasis in original.

[41] R.B. Ferguson, *The Legal Status of Non-Statutory Codes of Practice*, J. Bus. L. 12, 19 (1988).

[42] Kingdom of Spain v. Christie, Mansen & Woods Ltd. [1986] 1 W.L.R. 1120, 1125.

> documents, Christie's, giving effect to that clause, would not have been prepared to auction it. That certainly was the view of the plaintiffs when they started these proceedings. However in the course of argument counsel for Christie's made it clear that even if it were to be declared by the court that the documents were forgeries, Christie's would feel free to continue with the sale. They take the view that [the Code] does not apply where the vendor has acquired the picture innocently (i.e., is not implicated in the illegal export) and that such a case falls to be dealt with under clause 4. Christie's also apparently take the view that the Spanish government [has] refused to agree [to "satisfactory reimbursement"].

Clause 4 of the code reads:

> Where a member of the U.K. fine art and antiques trade comes into possession of an object that can be demonstrated beyond reasonable doubt to have been illegally exported from its country of export and the country of export seeks its return within a reasonable period, that member, if legally free to do so, will take responsible steps to cooperate in the return of that object to the country of export. Where the code has been breached unintentionally, satisfactory reimbursement should be agreed between the parties.

[T]he interpretation urged by Christie's greatly narrows the scope of the code and is not one apparent on its face. . . .

> [t]he defendant appears to have argued that its obligation under the Code did not apply to any artefact entrusted to it by a purchaser in good faith, who has acquired it innocently of any involvement in illegal export. If that interpretation is correct, then the Code is of little practical consequence over and above existing common law obligations.[43]

The court was not able to rule on this interpretation:

> Whether Christie's are right on either of those views is not for this court to say. The fact is that Christie's are prepared to and will go ahead with the sale, even if the documents are found by the court to be forgeries. In any event the Code is not a document on which the Spanish Government can directly rely; it is not a party to the Code.[44]

Whether that interpretation is correct is precisely the problem. There is no way of establishing this apart from having the signatories come together again to redraft the code. . . .

Codes of ethics . . . are essential for persons dealing with cultural heritage material. They provide standards for conduct in day-to-day activities. Codes are also essential to reassure the public that those to whom the heritage is entrusted for safekeeping are indeed doing their duty, but codes will

[43] Antony Griffiths, *Codes of Conduct*, 2 Art, Antiquity and Law 173, 174 (1997).
[44] *Id.*

only perform these functions effectively if they are kept consonant with development in the various professions involved; if real efforts are made to deal with contentious issues; if interpretations are made on ambiguous points and freely distributed. Codes are capable of having a major educational impact, and this should be regarded as the primary objective in ensuring their distribution and understanding. Sanctions come after. The necessity for sanctions and the form they should take need careful deliberation before implementation. But, above all, codes need to be observed by those to whom they apply in a spirit of goodwill, not one of minute interpretation or in seeking loopholes.

NOTES AND QUESTIONS

1. The American Association of Museums (AAM) issued its Standards Regarding Archaeological Material and Ancient Art in 2008. Like the AAMD's Guidelines, the AAM's Standards require museums to research thoroughly the provenance of any prospective acquisitions, including any trade documents; procure from donors and sellers of prospective acquisitions all documentation and other information that they possess; ensure that any acquisition has been outside or legally exported from its probable country of modern discovery since November 1970; and address claims of ownership by third parties.

   The AAMD Guidelines go beyond the AAM requirements, however, in several respects. First, they require museums to notify third parties of their rights of ownership and to return material to them when the museums acquire information to that effect. Second, the Guidelines require museums to post images and information on the AAMD's Web sites about any acquisitions of uncertain provenance.

   In contrast, the AAM Standards extend beyond the AAMD Guidelines in requiring museums to open their records and undertake research with regard to any material of uncertain provenance. Also, the AAM Standards explicitly prohibit the acquisition of material that is known to have been illegally exported from its country of modern discovery or in which it had been owned, regardless of when that occurred, that is, either before or after 1970.
2. The Canadian Museums Association (CMA) and the Canadian Art Museum Directors Organization have published the Guidelines: Roles and Responsibilities of Museum Boards of Trustees, which are suggested as checklists for the development or improvement of internal museum policies and procedures with respect to board roles and responsibilities. As with similar statements elsewhere, the intention of the Guidelines is not to insulate museum trustees and directors from legal liability but instead to form a basis of support for higher professional standards and an improved administrative environment. The Guidelines address such specific issues as the hiring and monitoring of performance of trustees; policy development; and board recruitment orientation, development, evaluation, and conduct. They also deal with avoidance of conflict of interest and board-director and board-state relations. Boards of Canadian museums are urged to adopt their own codes of ethics or the CMA Guidelines.
3. Of the three codes of museum associations – the AAMD, the AAM, and the CMA – which do you like the best and why?

2. Indigenous Heritage

a. Introduction

Several national legal systems have mandated or otherwise facilitated the repatriation of indigenous cultural heritage. These frameworks for repatriating indigenous cultural heritage, all recently constructed, share several general characteristics. They have been inspired by international developments. In particular, the decolonization movement after the Second World War spurred claims by newly independent states for return from former colonial powers of looted material.[45] Frameworks for repatriation of indigenous heritage rely on either legislation or agreements between the state and indigenous groups. Second, they have encouraged creative partnerships between institutions and indigenous communities. Third, they have provided reliable bases for returning heritage to its original patrimony. Fourth, they have helped redefine the fiduciary role of museums and institutions. The most important message may be that national legislation or a systematic use of agreements is an effective means for avoiding and resolving issues related to the possession and repossession of cultural heritage within a single country.

Throughout the world, it is no longer a matter of whether to repatriate human remains and significant classes of sacred and other cultural material to indigenous cultures. What material should be repatriated? To whom or to what groups should it be repatriated? From whom? With what qualifications? Under what conditions? By what authority? Supported by what sanctions? In responding to these questions, voluntary dialogue and ad hoc agreements between institutions and indigenous groups may be useful. Legislation, however, is more reliable. Moreover, statutes demand more consistent practices and strongly encourage the establishment of genuine communities of interest. Legislation may thus provide the surest paths for the long journeys that remain and that objects may have to take as they find their way back to their indigenous resting places.

International law helped shape national legislation on repatriation of cultural material to natives and native groups. The 1970 UNESCO Convention, in particular, profoundly influenced the formation of the new national frameworks. That agreement protects entire indigenous cultures and groups rather than simply vindicating individual claims. What followed quite naturally from ratifications of this approach has been a greater sensitivity to claims by indigenous groups based on self-determination and group ownership of material, as these and other so-called third-generation human rights became more prominent. The ratifications of the 1970 Convention include, for example, six states with important, assertive indigenous groups: Mexico (1972), Canada (1978), the United States (1983), Australia (1989), Finland (1995), and New Zealand (2007). Thus, indigenous demands for repatriation of domestic heritage were far more persuasive once the national government had accepted the concept of group rights in a regime for international repatriation of cultural material. Although it is possible to exaggerate the role of the international regime as a model for strictly domestic repatriation, there is no doubt that the 1970 Convention helped inspire national legislation and, in the instance of the United States, state as well as federal laws.

[45] *See, e.g.*, Michael F. Brown & Margaret M. Buruchac, *NAGPRA from the Middle Distance: Legal Puzzles and Unintended Consequences*, *in* Imperialism, Art and Restitution 193 (John Henry Merryman ed., 2006).

National regimes have therefore come full circle. International and domestic regimes of cultural heritage law have been symbiotic. Protection of indigenous property on national and tribal lands broadened into international cooperation to protect related heritage. In turn, confidence in a process of repatriation of selective material to neighboring countries of origin contributed significantly to the establishment of the new domestic regimes of repatriation.

Australia, Canada, New Zealand, and the United States all have well-developed national regimes for the repatriation of heritage to indigenous groups. But these regimes differ considerably from one another. For example, unlike the strong federal and state laws of the United States, Canada has no federal legislation at all in this area and only one substantial provincial law, that of Alberta. Instead, Canada relies on a system of nonbinding practices between and among First Nation groups, museums, and other institutions. Ethical mandates of national professional organizations and management protocols of individual museums and institutions provide a partial substitute for legislation.

NOTES AND QUESTIONS

1. The UN Declaration on the Rights of Indigenous Peoples was adopted by the UN General Assembly in 2007. Article 12 of the Declaration provides as follows:

   > Indigenous peoples have the right to manifest, practice, develop and teach their spiritual and religious traditions, customs and ceremonies; the right to maintain, protect, and have access in privacy to their religious and cultural sites; the right to use and control of their ceremonial objects; *and the right to the repatriation of their human remains.*

   UN Declaration on the Rights of Indigenous Peoples, GA Res. 295, UN GAOR, 61st Sess., UN Doc. A/RES/61/295 (2007) art. 12.
2. In interpreting the UN Declaration and other instruments, a nagging issue is the lack of an agreed-on definition of "indigenous people." New Zealand, for example, has stated the following:

   > [W]e cannot accept the argument . . . that this declaration will only apply to countries that have significant or obvious indigenous populations. There is no definition of "indigenous peoples[.]" . . . The lack of definition or scope of application . . . means that separatist or minority groups, with traditional connections to the territory where they live – in all regions of the globe – could seek to exploit this declaration to claim the right to self-determination, including exclusive control of their territorial resources. . . .

   Contemporary Practice of the United States, 101 Am. J. Int'l L. 213 (2007). How would you define the protected class of indigenous peoples? Even if it is possible to establish the identity of groups whose ancestors were the first to settle national territory, why should that factor alone merit special protection? Should the term encompass all clearly defined cultural minority groups? What problems would that pose?
3. Does retention by public museums of disinterred human remains constitute a violation of human rights provisions in, for example, the International Covenant on Economic, Social and Cultural Rights and the European Convention on Human

Rights and Fundamental Freedoms, which require states parties to respect religious practices in general and religious and spiritual beliefs of racial minorities?

b. United States Law

(i) Federal Law: The Native American Graves Protection and Repatriation Act (NAGPRA). The most comprehensive national legislation is that of the United States. The Native American Graves Protection and Repatriation Act (NAGPRA)[46] is the keystone in the legal framework for protecting and repatriating indigenous heritage within the United States. Despite the limiting word "graves" in its title, NAGPRA substantially elaborates and broadens the framework of federal and state law to protect the indigenous heritage. Until NAGPRA, federal and state laws largely sought to protect historical and archaeological resources found on federal, tribal, or state land. Only a few state laws specifically regulated commercial or donative transactions in indigenous heritage or provided for return of material to indigenous sources. Export controls were, and still are, generally limited to cultural material that has been taken illegally from federal or tribal lands.

(a) Summary of Provisions. First, NAGPRA confirms indigenous ownership or control over native cultural items found on federal and tribal lands. The governing body of a pertinent Indian tribe or Native Hawaiian organization may, however, relinquish title or control to such items.[47] Ancillary provisions restrict the availability of permits for excavation and removal of Native American[48] human remains or cultural items and require notification of inadvertent discoveries of such material.[49] To enforce these provisions, NAGPRA amends the federal code by criminalizing illegal trafficking in Native American human remains and cultural items obtained in violation of the law's provisions.[50] Arguably, criminal sanctions against what would otherwise be normal dealing in cultural items might drive the market further underground and thereby imperil the public values and opportunities that inhere in open trading. Although NAGPRA does not seem to have produced this result, the risk of a black market bespeaks the need for vigilance, education of dealers and prospective collectors, strong professional and institutional codes of ethics, and improved recordation or registration of cultural items.

[46] 25 U.S.C. §§ 33001–33013 (1994). This law should be seen alongside a precursor, the National Museum of the American Indian Act, 20 U.S.C. §§ 80q-80q-15 (2002), which requires the Smithsonian Institution to inventory Native American remains and return identifiable remains to the tribes.

[47] 25 U.S.C. § 3002. In this and other respects, NAGPRA is closely related to the Archaeological Resources Protection Act of 1979 (ARPA), 16 U.S.C. §§ 470aa-470mm (1994), which reasserts federal control over archaeological resources on federal and tribal lands and provides stiff penalties for persons who knowingly excavate, remove, or engage in transactions involving those resources without a federal permit.

[48] 25 U.S.C. § 3002(c). "'Native American' means of, or relating to, a tribe, people or culture that is indigenous to the United States." 25 U.S.C. § 3001(9). The term therefore embraces Indian tribes and Native Hawaiian organizations.

[49] 25 U.S.C. § 3002(d).

[50] 53 U.S.C. § 1170 (1994). Penalties include fines and imprisonment up to five years in the case of a second or subsequent offense, for knowingly engaging in commercial transactions without the right of possession to human remains of a Native American or otherwise in violation of NAGPRA. It is unclear what constitutes a criminal "violation of NAGPRA." Presumably, violations would be limited to commercial transactions in material either taken without permit and against specific federal law from federal or tribal land or obtained from museums or federal agencies after NAGPRA's enactment.

The most innovative part of NAGPRA – some might say its heart – is a scheme for repatriation of Native American human remains and other cultural items from museums and federal agencies.[51] They are required to compile inventories or provide summaries[52] of Native American remains and cultural items[53] in their possession. A lineal descendant of a deceased Native American, a culturally affiliated Indian tribe,[54] a culturally affiliated Native Hawaiian organization, or a tribe or organization that can show ownership or control of an item may then request material listed in a specific inventory of human remains and associated funerary objects[55] or a general summary of unassociated funerary objects, sacred objects, and objects of cultural patrimony.[56] Under pain of civil penalty, museums and federal agencies must then expeditiously return any such material to a claimant that has established the requisite link of lineal descendancy, cultural affiliation, or ownership or control, as the case may be.[57] Most of the returns have been to U.S. tribes and Native Hawaiian groups, but NAGPRA has also encouraged museums to return remains and other material to foreign claimants. For example, in 2008 the American Museum of Natural History returned ancestral remains to the Tseycum First Nation in Canada.[58]

Determination of whether an object is properly classified, particularly as a "sacred object"[59] or an "object of cultural patrimony,"[60] poses particular difficulties of definition. Issues of classification have often been resolved by consultation and collaboration

[51] 25 U.S.C. § 3005. NAGPRA does not provide for the repatriation of cultural items from individuals or enterprises that are not museums, as defined, but the law's terms and process of repatriation have helped define claims beyond its scope. "[M]useum" means any institution or State or local government agency (including any institution of higher learning) that receives Federal funds and has possession of, or control over, Native American cultural items. Such term does not include the Smithsonian Institution or any other federal agency. 25 U.S.C. § 3001(8).

[52] The statute requires each institution to undertake a detailed, object-by-object inventory of all human remains and associated funerary objects in a collection. 25 U.S.C. § 3003(a). The statute also requires a more general summary of unassociated funerary objects, sacred objects, or objects of cultural patrimony. The summary is to describe the collection, its size, and the circumstances of its acquisition. 25 U.S.C. § 3004(a).

[53] Although the statutory definition of the term "cultural items" includes all material for which an inventory or summary is required, including human remains, NAGPRA regulations, reflecting objections to the classification of human remains as cultural items, eliminate the generic term "cultural items" and refer only to "human remains" and other specific categories of materials. 43 C.F.R. 10.1(3) (1998).

[54] The statutory definition of "cultural affiliation" refers to "a relationship of shared group identity which can be reasonably traced historically or prehistorically between a present-day Indian tribe or Native Hawaiian organization and an identifiable earlier group." 25 U.S.C. § 3001(2).

[55] 25 U.S.C. § 3003.

[56] 25 U.S.C. § 3004.

[57] 25 U.S.C. § 3005(a)(1), (2), (4), (5). 25 U.S.C. § 3007 allows the secretary of the interior to assess a civil penalty against "[a]ny museum that fails to comply with the requirements of this Act." *See* 43 C.F.R. § 10.12 (1998).

[58] Christian Sci. Monitor, June 12, 2008, at 3.

[59] The statutory definition of "sacred objects" includes "specific ceremonial objects which are *needed* by traditional Native American religious leaders for the practice of traditional Native American religions by the *present day* adherents." 25 U.S.C. § 3001(3)(C) (emphasis added).

[60] NAGPRA defines "cultural patrimony" as "an object having ongoing historical, traditional, or cultural importance central to the Native American group or culture itself, rather than property owned by an individual native American, and which, therefore, cannot be alienated, appropriated, or conveyed by any individual regardless of whether or not the individual is a member of the Indian tribe or Native Hawaiian organization and such object shall have been considered inalienable by such Native American group at the time the object was separated from such group." 25 U.S.C. § 3001(3)(D).

between native groups and museums or federal agencies. Aside from understandable delays that may result from having to resolve these kinds of issues, there are four statutory qualifications on the requirement of expeditious return of material. First, if an inventory or summary does not itself establish cultural affiliation of the item with a requesting tribe or organization, a federal agency or museum may retain an item until the requesting party can demonstrate cultural affiliation by a preponderance of evidence based on several factors. These factors include "geographical, kinship, biological, archaeological, anthropological, linguistic, folkloric, oral traditional, historical or other relevant information or expert opinion."[61] Second, if a cultural item is "indispensable for completion of a specific scientific study, the outcome of which would be of major benefit to the United States," repatriation may be delayed until no later than ninety days after completion of the study.[62] Third, the claimant of an unassociated funerary object, sacred object, or object of cultural patrimony must present evidence "which, if standing alone before the introduction of evidence to the contrary, would support a finding that the federal agency or museum did not have the right of possession."[63] In response, the particular museum or federal agency is given an opportunity to prove its right of possession to the item.[64] Finally, a museum or federal agency may retain an item disputed by multiple (competing) claimants until they agree on its disposition or until the dispute is otherwise resolved under either internal NAGPRA procedures or a court of competent jurisdiction.[65]

In addition, NAGPRA establishes the Review Committee within the U.S. Department of the Interior to monitor and review implementation of the inventory and identification process and repatriation activities.[66] Concluding sections of the legislation provide for grants of assistance by the federal government to Indian tribes, Native Hawaiian organizations, and museums[67]; require the secretary of the interior to promulgate regulations to carry out the law[68]; and establish the jurisdiction of federal district courts over alleged violations of NAGPRA.[69]

(b) Origins. The proper disposition of non-Indian remains in the American West has often been significant. For example, when William F. "Buffalo Bill" Cody, the legendary

This appears to be "NAGPRA's most difficult definition." Thomas H. Boyd & Jonathan Haas, *The Native American Graves Protection and Repatriation Act: Prospects for New Partnerships between Museums and Native American Groups*, 25 Ariz. St. L.J. 253, 265 (1992). "[I]dentifying cultural patrimony may require extensive inquiry into both the circumstances surrounding the alienation and the state of traditions and customs as they existed at the time of transfer." *Id.* at 266. Arguably, the result is to create a rebuttable presumption that an object belongs to a claimant tribe's cultural patrimony. Sarah Harding, *Justifying Repatriation of Native American Cultural Property*, 72 Ind. L.J. 723, 738 (1997). Regardless of this presumption, the interpretive task is demanding.

[61] 25 U.S.C. § 3005(a)(4).

[62] 25 U.S.C. § 3005(b).

[63] 25 U.S.C. § 3005(c). The statutory definition of a "right of possession" is elaborate. Essentially, it requires "possession obtained with the voluntary consent of an individual or group that had authority of alienation." 25 U.S.C. § 3001(13).

[64] 25 U.S.C. § 3005(c).

[65] 25 U.S.C. § 3005(e).

[66] 25 U.S.C. § 3006.

[67] 25 U.S.C. § 3008.

[68] 25 U.S.C. § 3011. The Review Committee is given the responsibility of consulting with the secretary of the interior in the development of regulations to carry out the law. 25 U.S.C. § 3006(c)(7). Current regulations appear at 43 C.F.R. § 10 (1998).

[69] 25 U.S.C. § 3013.

impresario of the American West, died in 1917, the location of his gravesite became a major controversy. On his widow's request, he was buried on Lookout Mountain near Denver rather than, as expected, in the town he founded, Cody, Wyoming. The circumstances remain unclear under which Buffalo Bill, on his deathbed, is said to have changed his preference of a gravesite from Cody to Lookout Mountain. What is clear is that resentment simmered in Cody for more than thirty years. In 1948, fearing removal of his bones under a bounty offered by the Cody American Legion Post, Denver city officials dug a new tomb, twenty feet deep, lined it with thick casing, installed steel support rails, and poured more than thirty tons of concrete over the grave to prevent its plunder.[70]

By contrast, Native American remains, even those of the greatest tribal chiefs, have enjoyed very little protection until recently. State laws criminalizing any disturbance or desecration of marked graves seldom barred excavation of Native American sites, either because they were usually unmarked[71] or because they did not otherwise satisfy definitions of protected graves or cemeteries. For example, the law failed to take into account such tribal practices as scaffold, canoe, or tree burials. It is no exaggeration to conclude that American law historically has "protect[ed] the sanctity of the non-Indian at all costs, while tolerating the promiscuous snatching of the Indian dead on a massive scale."[72] Science and human curiosity have normally trumped the sanctity and human dignity of Native American remains.

During the 1970s and 1980s, however, an Indian burial rights movement, which was opposed to the use of ancestral remains as scientific resources, began fighting for return of remains to the tribes for reburial.[73] It would no longer be acceptable to ignore Native American rights simply in the interests of physical anthropology. Native Americans also became more assertive about their entitlement to important cultural items, especially sacred objects. The Zuni, in particular, began to request the return of their Ahayu:da (wooden figures that represent twin gods).[74] More generally, the tribes demanded to be put on a more equal footing with science in the control of indigenous cultural material.

The normative origins of the burial rights movement are international.[75] They lie in the regime of human rights and self-determination that emerged after the Second World War. This regime, by confirming the dignity of individual human beings (and, by natural extension, their remains) inspired national claims for the protection of cultural heritage. A growing awareness of extensive looting and destruction of cultural material led to the establishment of a new regime, with rights vested in national patrimonies, to deter illegal trafficking and to return stolen and illegally exported objects to countries of

[70] *See* Stanley Zamonski, Buffalo Bill: The Man and the Museum 32–35 (1987).

[71] Jack F. Trope & Walter R. Echo-Hawk, *The Native American Graves Protection and Repatriation Act: Background and Legislative History*, 24 Ariz. St. L.J. 35, 46, 47 (1992).

[72] Robert M. Peregoy, *The Legal Basis, Legislative History, and Implementation of Nebraska's Landmark Reburial Legislation*, 24 Ariz. St. L.J. 329, 331 (1992).

[73] James Riding In, *Without Ethics and Morality: A Historical Overview of Imperial Archaeology and American Indians*, 24 Ariz. St. L.J. 11, 25 (1992). *See also* Francis P. McManamon, *The Reality of Repatriation: Reaching Out to Native Americans*, Fed. Arch., Fall–Winter 1995, at 2.

[74] William L. Merrill, Edmund J. Ladd, & T.J. Ferguson, *The Return of the Ahayu:da: Lessons for Repatriation from Zuni Pueblo and the Smithsonian Institution*, 35 Current Anthrop. 523 (1993); Fergus M. Bordewich, Killing the White Man's Indian 189 (1996).

[75] *See, e.g.*, Suzan Shown Harjo, *Native Peoples' Cultural and Human Rights: An Unfinished Agenda*, 24 Ariz. St. L.J. 321, 325; Rennard Strickland, *Implementing the National Policy of Understanding, Preserving, and Safeguarding the Heritage of Indian Peoples and Native Hawaiians: Human Rights, Sacred Objects, and Cultural Patrimony*, 24 Ariz. St. L.J. 175, 190 (1992).

origin.[76] Repatriation, restitution, or return of such objects and the concept of cultural patrimony, on a basis of general rights, became enshrined in international law. Moreover, the acknowledgment by this international law regime of a collective, so-called third-generation right of repatriation on behalf of nations and groups is noteworthy because it eased the way for the assertion within the United States of tribal and organizational claims under NAGPRA.

Four factors contributed to the extension of the international regime to the domestic indigenous heritage: U.S. leadership in establishing and implementing the international regime, the U.S. concentration on protecting the heritage of the Americas (including, eventually, the country's own indigenous heritage), diplomatic gains and public satisfaction derived from implementing the regime, and explicit acknowledgment by the United States of the applicability to Native Americans of human rights provisions such as those crystallized in the Helsinki Accords of 1976.[77] Consequently, by the late 1980s, the museum community, galleries, and individual collectors had become accustomed to constraints on questionable acquisitions and to the requirements of international return, restitution, or repatriation of cultural material.

Against this backdrop of international law and practice, the stage was set for translating into domestic law the aspirations of the native burial movement and claimants of significant cultural material. Native American activism played a major role in this process. In 1989 the World Archaeological Congress, led by tribal leaders and responding in part to a position paper prepared by the International Indian Treaty Council, adopted the Vermillion Accord (set forth later in this chapter) as a basis for protection and repatriation of human remains and sacred items. During the same year, the Smithsonian Institution, given the opportunity to acquire a major collection of Native American material, agreed to repatriate human remains and sacred objects in its possession to the tribes.[78] This agreement was incorporated into the National Museum of the American Indian Act.[79] The next year, the Report of the Panel for a National Dialogue on Museum/Native American Relations[80] proposed similar legislation to be binding on all federal agencies and federally funded institutions (museums). The result was NAGPRA.

(c) Legal Foundations. Essentially, NAGPRA is human rights law.[81] Its legislative history confirms this foundation: "Such human rights include religious, cultural, and group survival rights, as understood within the context of U.S. and international standards of

[76] The core international agreement, to which the United States is a party, is the UNESCO Convention on the Means of Prohibiting and Preventing the Illicit Import, Export, and Transfer of Ownership of Property, Nov. 14, 1970, 823 U.N.T.S. 231, 10 I.L.M. 289. On the development during the 1970s of general principles for repatriation of cultural property, *see* James A.R. Nafziger, *The New International Legal Framework for the Return, Restitution or Forfeiture of Cultural Property*, 15 N.Y. U. J. Int'l L. & Pol. 789, 799 (1983).

[77] Conference on Security and Cooperation in Europe: Final Act, Aug. 1, 1975, *reprinted in* 14 I.L.M. 1292 (1975). *See* Harjo, *supra* note 75.

[78] 135 Cong. Rec. S12388 (daily ed. October 3, 1989) (statement of Sen. Inouye).

[79] 20 U.S.C. §§ 80q to 80q-15 (1994).

[80] *Reprinted in* 24 Ariz. St. L.J. 487 (1992) [hereinafter Report on National Dialogue].

[81] *See, e.g.*, Trope & Echo-Hawk, *supra* note 71, at 59 ("NAGPRA is, first and foremost, human rights legislation"); Gene A. Marsh, *Walking the Spirit Trail: Repatriation and Protection of Native American Remains and Sacred Cultural Items*, 24 Ariz. St. L.J. 79, 96 (1992) ("NAGPRA is described by leaders in the Native American community as the most important human rights legislation for Native Americans ever passed by Congress.").

human rights and rights of self-determination."[82] In this regard, the United States is guided by the Universal Declaration of Human Rights,[83] as evidence of international custom, and the International Covenant on Civil and Political Rights,[84] as a party. Although neither of these instruments articulates a specific right of repatriation, reburial, or cultural patrimony, their provisions for "security of person,"[85] "[and] right to recognition everywhere as a person before the law,"[86] as well as for "self-determination,"[87] can be interpreted, at least in concert, to embrace a right to repose, that is, a right to noninterference with personal remains as well as associated cultural items. The collective right of self-determination established under international law has been repeatedly invoked to justify claims for repatriation of sacred objects and other significant cultural items. Also, as we noted earlier, the UN Declaration on the Rights of Indigenous Peoples, since its adoption in 2007, has confirmed for indigenous peoples "the right to the repatriation of their human remains."

In the U.S. constitutional order, NAGPRA manifests the historic relationship of entrustment between the federal government, on the one hand, and indigenous groups, on the other hand.[88] In practice, the underlying trust doctrine requires a liberal construction of public enactments to the benefit of native peoples.[89]

(d) Benefits. The most obvious benefit of NAGPRA is its systematic promotion of human rights, self-determination, and distributive justice on behalf of Indian tribes and Native Hawaiian organizations. Although private agreements and state legislation may serve the same purposes, they are inadequate for the complex task of providing for comprehensive protection and repatriation of indigenous heritage. Selective repatriation of sacred and other objects serves vital community needs, and repatriation of cultural items for such purposes as tribal museum development enhances the avowed national policy of tribal economic development and education. Also, as an expression of civil rights and ethnic reconciliation, NAGPRA, as implemented, helps redress historic grievances against the dominant culture and, in the long run, serves as a catalyst for cross-cultural understanding.

Required processes of inventorying, consultation, and reporting have had the beneficial effect of highlighting the history of what many regard as a form of colonialism in the

[82] Report on National Dialogue § D(1)(a), *reprinted in* 24 Ariz. St. L.J. 487, 494 (1992).

[83] G.A. Res. 217A (III), U.N. Doc. A/810, at 71 (1948) [hereinafter UDHR]. Although the UDHR was not intended to be legally binding, it became a basic component of international customary law. *See, e.g.*, Louis B. Sohn, *The New International Law: Protection of the Rights of Individuals Rather than States*, 32 Am. U. L. Rev. 1, 16–17 (1982).

[84] G.A. Res. 2200 A (XXI), U.N. Doc. A/6316 (1966), 999 U.N.T.S. 171, 6 I.L.M. 368 (1967) [hereinafter ICCPR]. The United States is not a party to a sister instrument that more directly protects cultural rights, the International Covenant on Economic Social and Cultural Rights, G.A. Res. 2200A (XXI), U.N. Doc. A/6316 (1966), 993 U.N.T.S. 3, 6 I.L.M. 360 (1967).

[85] UDHR, *supra* note 83, arts. 3, 6; ICCPR, *supra* note 84, arts. 9, 16.

[86] UDHR, *supra* note 83, art. 6; ICCPR, *supra* note 84, art. 16.

[87] ICCPR, *supra* note 84, art. 1. The specific right of self-determination to freedom of religion is not easily translated into a right to repatriation of sacred material. The right is defined to "include freedom to have or adopt a religion or belief of [one's] choice, and freedom . . . to manifest his religion or belief in worship, observance, practice and teaching." ICCPR, *supra* note 84, art. 18. The underlying language in the UDHR is similar. UDHR, *supra* note 83, art. 18.

[88] 25 U.S.C. § 3010.

[89] *See* Trope & Echo-Hawk, *supra* note 71, at 60.

United States.[90] It is NAGPRA that reveals this legacy and, at the same time, fundamentally alters the power dynamics between tribes and collecting institutions. Drawing from the international law of human rights and the international regime for protecting cultural property, NAGPRA recognizes "tribal property interests in various cultural resources," including property held by museums and institutions, and "group entitlement to cultural property that stems from tribal law and tradition."[91] The statute specifies that a right of possession must mean "possession obtained with the voluntary consent of an individual *or group that had authority of alienation*"[92] and by defining cultural patrimony as an object that should be considered "inalienable" by any individual, even a tribal member, because of its significance to the entire group.[93] Concomitantly, NAGPRA employs tribal law or custom to address the legal questions of voluntary consent and authority of alienation when establishing rights of possession.[94] It is important to note, however, that by giving this right only to federally recognized tribes, NAGPRA leaves unfinished the business of redressing power imbalances over the control of cultural property. In this way, NAGPRA reinforces the federal government's power to define, in legal terms, who is and is not an Indian tribe.

For museums, NAGPRA has had the benefit of encouraging closer communication with knowledgeable tribal historians and other members. It has also stimulated museums to undertake comprehensive reexamination and improved documentation of their collections.[95]

The NAGPRA requirements of consultation and cooperation between Indian tribes and Native Hawaiian organizations, on the one hand, and museums, on the other hand, foster broader respect and interchange.[96] Although the communication has sometimes been difficult or even acrimonious, it nevertheless has been essential. It has been observed,

[90] "Participating in repatriation necessarily brings one into contact with the historical gears of the process of colonization which ultimately give way to less mechanical and more personal strategies of assimilation, denigration, and/or creative transformation between people and nations." *See* Diana Drake Wilson, *California Indian Participation in Repatriation: Working toward Recognition*, 21 Am. Indian Culture & Res. J. 191, 191 (1997).

[91] Rebecca Tsosie, *Indigenous Peoples' Claims to Cultural Property: A Legal Perspective*, 21 Museum Anthrop. 5, 6 (1997).

[92] 25 U.S.C. § 3001(13) (emphasis added).

[93] 25 U.S.C. § 3001(3)(d).

[94] *See* Tsosie, *supra* note 91, at 6.

[95] *See, e.g.*, Barbara Isaac, *An Epimethean View of the Future at the Peabody Museum*, Fed. Arch., Fall–Winter 1995, at 18, 21 (resulting in a recalculation of the number of human remains from seven thousand to ten thousand and of cultural objects tenfold from eight hundred thousand to 8 million); Robert Pickering & R.L. Jantz, *Look Again before Repatriating: Avoiding a Moral and Legal Morass*, Fed. Arch., Fall–Winter 1995, at 36.

[96] *See* C. Timothy McKeown, *Inside the Act: Confessions of a Bureaucrat*, Fed. Arch., Fall–Winter 1995, at 4, 9 ("there has been a dramatic increase in dialogue among tribes, museums, and agencies"); Francis P. McManamon & Larry V. Nordby, *Implementing the Native American Graves Protection and Repatriation Act*, 24 Ariz. St. L.J. 217, 244 (1992) (noting NAGPRA's encouragement of collaborative agreements for access, use, care, and treatment of cultural items); Dean B. Suagee, *Tribal Voices in Historic Preservation: Sacred Landscapes, Cross-Cultural Bridges, and Common Ground*, 21 Vt. L. Rev. 145, 207 (1996); Martin Sullivan, *A Museum Perspective on Repatriation: Issues and Opportunities*, 24 Ariz. St. L.J. 283, 291 (1992); Rosita Worl, *NAGPRA: Symbol of a New Treaty*, Fed. Arch., Fall–Winter 1995, at 28, 29 (emphasizing meaningful consultation as an alternative to conflict between Indians and museums). "Now that it is a fact of life, the federal law on repatriation is forcing a degree of collaboration with Indian tribes that is new to many scholars and museum people – a partnership, some say, that can only benefit anthropology." E.K. Coughlin, *Returning Indian Remains*, Chron. Higher Educ., at A8 (16 March 1994).

for example, that NAGPRA's definitions of such terms as "cultural affiliation" and "cultural patrimony" virtually require consideration of indigenous views.[97] In this and other ways, the legislation provides a basis for enduring association and partnership.

Under state law and professional ethics, museums and other institutions are entrusted with fiduciary responsibility.[98] They must acquire, maintain, exhibit, and deaccession collections according to minimum enforceable standards. They must take care to protect material for the benefit of intended beneficiaries, which often include the public.

The NAGPRA-centered regime of repatriation has had the effect of enriching and extending the definition of this fiduciary duty. Today, institutions must take account not only of the interests of visitors and other users of their facilities but also of the tribes. This new duty may override normal principles of display as well as prohibitions on the depletion or deaccessioning of collections.

In discharging their responsibilities more effectively, museums have adopted alternatives to strictly in-house processing and display of objects. High technology has facilitated more rapid and widespread access to collections and scientific data. Museums can virtually universalize their displays, at least for professional viewing. Core museums have also helped develop tribal centers and museums. Such initiatives have given new meaning to the term "repatriation." As two prominent curators have concluded, "In a sense this effort to widely disseminate museum collection information is itself a form of repatriation; it expands and interconnects the roles of curators and Native American peoples, *bringing native voices into museums and taking objects beyond museum walls*."[99] In this way, federal and state legislation, by helping confirm an important mission of museums, has helped benefit both indigenous cultures and the public.

The conflicting views and tensions between scientific and indigenous communities that led in part to the enactment of NAGPRA are expressed in the following two readings:

Fergus M. Bordewich, Killing the White Man's Indian 172–74 (1996) (used with permission of Doubleday, a division of Random House, Inc.)

To many Indians, unredeemed artifacts and the bones of the ancestors had become potent symbols of conquest and cultural rape. In a sense, repatriation thus represents a campaign to regain contact with the dead, to draw strength from them and from the material remains of what idealistic traditionalists and others regard as an all-embracing way of life whose potency has been all but lost. As they see it, repatriation often means the "liberation" of still-living things that have been trapped in museum basements, in a limbo between the spirit world and the human. . . .

Indian spokesmen often define repatriation as an issue of fundamental religious freedom, asserting as a general principle, for example, that native bones remain imbued with the spirit of the dead even after hundreds or

[97] Gary D. Stumpf, *A Federal Land Management Perspective on Repatriation*, 24 Ariz. St. L.J. 303, 308 (1992).

[98] *See, e.g.*, Rowan v. Pasadena Art Museum, No. C-32287 at 6 (Cal. Sup. Ct. Sept. 22, 1981); Illinois v. Silverstein, 408 N.E. 2d 243 (Ill. Ct. App. 1980); Lefkowitz v. Museum of the American Indian, No. 41416175 (N.Y. Sup. Ct. June 27, 1975).

[99] J.D. Nason & R.K. Wright, *Sharing Heritage: Native American Exhibits*, Museum News, May–June 1994, at 43, 60 (emphasis added).

thousands of years, and that keeping bones in a museum is a permanent desecration that produces ongoing spiritual ailments among the living. Some go so far as to blame alcoholism, AIDS, and social disintegration on the wandering spirits of the unshriven dead. In this view, contemporary Indians are deemed to be responsible for the spiritual well-being of all deceased Indians, a moral duty that compels living Indians to ensure that the remains of their ancestors are buried in the ground, because retention of the remains in museums and elsewhere is regarded as disturbing to the ancestors' spirits. So long as the spirits are suffering, living Indians will continue to suffer a myriad of adverse consequences.

Beyond this, however, lies an often quite explicit, and for anthropologists unnerving, assault upon the customary right of free scientific inquiry. "The bone robber barons, as some archaeologists would be apprehended, are academic neocolonialists and racial technocrats who now seem to posture as liberal humanists," Gerald Vizenor, a Chippewa journalist and academic, has written. "These bone barons protect their 'rights' to advance science and careers on the backs of tribal bones. The tribal dead become the academic chattel, the aboriginal bone slaves to advance archaeological technicism and the political power of institutional science." Similarly, the Lakota author Vine Deloria, Jr., asserts that Western science has "always been available as apologists for the majority who wished to dehumanize minorities for commercial and political purposes." But only American Indians, he says, have "become the exclusive province (and property) of scholars to the extent that the bones of their dead can be disinterred with impunity to be displayed in museum cases or used in speculative scientific experiments." Like many activists, Deloria argues that the scholarly analysis of bones has no value for contemporary Indians, charging that "no explanation has been given regarding the peculiar characteristics which make Indian remains more valuable than the remains of other races. What could possibly be learned exclusively from Indian bones which could not also be learned from the bones of other races?"

"This is an issue of racism," asserts Bob Peregoy, an attorney for the Native American Rights Fund, which represented the Pawnee Tribe in its successful effort to recover some three hundred sets of its ancestors' bones and thousands of burial artifacts from the Nebraska State Historical Society in the mid-1980s. The Nebraska law that resulted from the Pawnee victory was the first of its kind in the United States. It soon became a model for similar laws and voluntary museum policies around the country, as well as for the federal legislation that imposed repatriation upon the Smithsonian Institution. Adds Peregoy, "Indian people have been treated in a very discriminatory manner by the anthropological community. No other groups were targeted for massive grave robbing. In Nebraska you've got to get a court order to open a non-Indian burial. But no archaeologist ever thought he had to get one to open an Indian grave."

Anthropologists attempt to counter Indian arguments by pointing out that individual Indians frequently sold their artifacts to collectors as a matter of individual choice or, concerned about their tribes dying out, willingly entrusted their ritual objects to whites to ensure that they survived into the future. Similarly, it is often noted that native beliefs about the sanctity of human remains varied quite widely; neither corpses nor graves held special significance for every tribe. At one extreme, some tribes simply disposed of remains in communal refuse heaps. Other did not bury their dead at all, but rather placed them ceremonially in trees or on raised platforms where, eventually, their bones would be devoured by animals. At times, Indians also showed appalling contempt for other tribes' dead; the historian Francis Parkman recorded an instance in which five corpses of Sioux placed in trees were thrown down and kicked into fragments by a war party of Crows, who then held the muzzles of their rifles against the skulls and blew them to pieces.

Tessie Naranjo, *Thoughts on Two Worldviews*, FED. ARCHAEOLOGY, Fall–Winter 1995, at 8

Traditional Native Americans believe that everyone and everything exist in an integrated and pervasive system of relationships. One resident of Santa Clara Pueblo puts it this way: "We are part of an organic world in which interrelationships at all levels of life are honored. Our relations to the place we live – the land, water, sky, mountains, rocks, animals, plants – is tangible. Our sense of social relationships leads us to respect all who have gone before and all who will follow, our elders as well as our youth."

Traditional Native Americans see an essential relationship between humans and the objects they create. A pot is not just a pot. In our community, the pots we create are seen as vital, breathing entities that must be respected as all other living beings. Respect of all life elements – rocks, trees, clay – is necessary because we understand our inseparable relationship with every part of our world.

This is why we honor our ancestors and the objects they created. This honoring allows us to remember our past and the natural process of transformation – of breathing, living, dying, and becoming one with the natural world. Not even in death are we unrelated.

My understanding of relationships has been hard to reconcile with the non-tribal view. Consider museums. Human remains and cultural items are treated as non-living entities. Unacknowledged are the enduring relationships that traditional Native Americans maintain with their ancestors and their world.

I have come to realize that the staffs of most museums and agencies do not share our basic values and philosophic views. Museums certainly have had a great impact on traditional Native Americans and our perceptions of who we are. But we do not share the assumptions underlying what museums do: collection, preservation, documentation, and exhibition.

This difference in view surfaces in most of the activities surrounding NAGPRA. Encouragingly, this has led to a growing awareness among all those with a stake in repatriation.

Nowhere is this more apparent than at meetings of the [NAGPRA Review Committee]. From the very first one – when six members were asked to nominate a seventh – decisions have been by consensus. This is the way of my people and the one with which I am most comfortable. The meetings are often more like open discussions than formal get-togethers. Decisions are made only after all members, as well as the public, get a chance to air their views. Thus far, all of our decisions have been unanimous. . . .

NAGPRA has brought together two completely different worldviews in a forum where people freely discuss their differences. This relationship, like any human relationship, is sometimes awkward, sometimes caring, and sometimes difficult. But it is a relationship that will continue.

[See also the debate on these issues between Clement W. Meighan, *Burying American Archaelology*, and Larry J. Zimmerman, *Sharing Control of the Past*, 47 ARCHAEOLOGY, Nov.-Dec. 1994, at 6.4. – *Eds.*].

NATIVE AMERICAN GRAVES PROTECTION AND REPATRIATION ACT, 25 U.S. § 3001 *et seq.*

§ 3005. REPATRIATION.

(a) REPATRIATION OF NATIVE AMERICAN HUMAN REMAINS AND OBJECTS POSSESSED OR CONTROLLED BY FEDERAL AGENCIES AND MUSEUMS. –

(1) If, pursuant to section 5 [providing for required inventories by museums of human remains and associated funerary objects], the cultural affiliation of Native American human remains and associated funerary objects with a particular Indian tribe or Native Hawaiian organization is established, then the Federal agency or museum, upon the request of a known lineal descendant of the Native American or of the tribe or organization and pursuant to subsections (b) and (e) of this section, shall expeditiously return such remains and associated funerary objects.

(2) If, pursuant to section 6 [providing for required summaries by museums of their collections of funerary objects, sacred objects, and cultural patrimony], the cultural affiliation with a particular Indian tribe or Native Hawaiian organization is shown with respect to unassociated funerary objects, sacred objects or objects of cultural patrimony, then the Federal agency or museum, upon the request of the Indian tribe or Native Hawaiian organization and pursuant to subsections (b), (c) and (e) of this section, shall expeditiously return such objects.

(3) The return of cultural items covered by this Act shall be in consultation with the requesting lineal descendant or tribe or organization to determine the place and manner of delivery of such items.

(4) Where cultural affiliation of Native American human remains and funerary objects has not been established in an inventory

prepared pursuant to section 5, or the summary pursuant to section 6, or where Native American human remains and funerary objects are not included upon any such inventory, then, upon request and pursuant to subsections (b) and (e) and, in the case of unassociated funerary objects, subsection (c), such Native American human remains and funerary objects shall be expeditiously returned where the requesting Indian tribe or Native Hawaiian organization can show cultural affiliation by a preponderance of the evidence based upon geographical, kinship, biological, archaeological, anthropological, linguistic, folkloric, oral traditional, historical, or other relevant information or expert opinion.

(5) Upon request and pursuant to subsections (b), (c) and (e), sacred objects and objects of cultural patrimony shall be expeditiously returned where –

(A) the requesting party is the direct lineal descendant of an individual who owned the sacred object;

(B) the requesting Indian tribe or Native Hawaiian organization can show that the object was owned or controlled by the tribe or organization; or

(C) the requesting Indian tribe or Native Hawaiian organization can show that the sacred object was owned or controlled by a member thereof, provided that in the case where a sacred object was owned by a member thereof, there are no identifiable lineal descendants of said member or the lineal descendants, upon notice, have failed to make a claim for the object under this Act.

(b) SCIENTIFIC STUDY. – If the lineal descendant, Indian tribe, or Native Hawaiian organization requests the return of culturally affiliated Native American cultural items, the Federal agency or museum shall expeditiously return such items unless such items are indispensable for completion of a specific scientific study, the outcome of which would be of major benefit to the United States. Such items shall be returned by no later than 90 days after the date on which the scientific study is completed.

(c) STANDARD OF REPATRIATION. – If a known lineal descendant or an Indian tribe or Native Hawaiian organization requests the return of Native American unassociated funerary objects, sacred objects or objects of cultural patrimony pursuant to this Act and presents evidence which, if standing alone before the introduction of evidence to the contrary, would support a finding that the Federal agency or museum did not have the right of possession, then such agency or museum shall return such objects unless it can overcome such inference and prove that it has a right of possession to the objects.

(d) SHARING OF INFORMATION BY FEDERAL AGENCIES AND MUSEUMS. – Any Federal agency or museum shall share what information it does possess regarding the object in question with the known lineal descendant, Indian tribe, or Native Hawaiian organization to assist in making a claim under this section.

(e) COMPETING CLAIMS. – Where there are multiple requests for repatriation of any cultural item and, after complying with the requirements of this Act, the Federal agency or museum cannot clearly determine which requesting party is the most appropriate claimant, the agency or museum may retain such item until the requesting parties agree upon its disposition or the dispute is otherwise resolved pursuant to the provisions of this Act or by a court of competent jurisdiction.

(f) MUSEUM OBLIGATION. – Any museum which repatriates any item in good faith pursuant to this Act shall not be liable for claims by an aggrieved party or for claims of breach of fiduciary duty, public trust, or violations of state law that are inconsistent with the provisions of this Act.

NOTES AND QUESTIONS

1. The widely shared observation that NAGPRA has helped forge good relationships between Native Americans and Native Hawaiians, on the one hand, and museums, on the other hand, has not been without its critics. For example, the curator emerita of the Milwaukee Public Museum, which has one of the most extensive collections of artifacts in the United States, concluded that "[a]lthough NAGPRA grew out of genuine instances of questionable and disrespectful practices in the country, the legislation created a confrontational climate when Indian people and museums were developing positive relationships." NANCY OESTREICH LURIE, WISCONSIN INDIANS 81 (2002). It is interesting to contrast that observation with the opposite view of two other experts on Indian burials in the same state of Wisconsin: "NAGPRA has provided new and exciting opportunities for dialogue and close cooperation between Native American tribes and American cultural and academic institutions. It has also led to increasing sensitivity on the part of the general public toward human remains and objects that Native Americans hold in great reverence." ROBERT A. BIRMINGHAM & LESLIE E. EISENBERG, INDIAN MOUNDS OF WISCONSIN 184 (2000).
2. W. Richard West, the first director of the Museum of the American Indian, has emphasized the significance to tribal cultures of repatriating their most sacred and important cultural heritage:

> Repatriation is the most potent political metaphor for cultural revival that is going on at this time. Political sovereignty and cultural sovereignty are linked inextricably, because the ultimate goal of political sovereignty is the protecting of a way of life. As separate polities, tribes can tax and regulate, and exercise jurisdiction. But it is equally important, perhaps even more important, to protect Indian ways of life and ways of thinking.

W. Richard West, *qtd. in* FERGUS BORDEWICH, KILLING THE WHITE MAN'S INDIAN 171–72 (1996).

What is meant by "cultural sovereignty?" Does that term necessarily imply a peremptory claim to all heritage by its creators? Might a preferred interpretation equate sovereignty with autonomy in the sense of ensuring cultures of their right to protect themselves from threats to their heritage as a whole? Would the term imply special protections to ensure cultural survival in what some claim to be an era of cultural imperialism (otherwise known as McDonaldization) brought on by rampant globalization and commodification of heritage?

3. The NAGPRA protection of human remains *in situ* is limited to federal or tribal land. See *Castro Romero v. Becker*, 256 F.3d 349 (5th Cir. 2001) (NAGPRA does not protect human remains on municipal land). Should NAGPRA be amended to protect remains on municipal and private land? *Castro Romero* also confirmed that NAGPRA does not provide a basis for recovery of monetary damages by individuals. However, NAGPRA does support standing for tribes and Native Hawaiian groups to seek injunctive relief, as does the National Historic Preservation Act, 16 U.S.C. § 470 *et seq.* (2000).
4. For an extraordinary account of bureaucratic delays, complexities, and other frustrations involved in properly reburying remains of Native Americans with no identifiable modern descendants ("culturally unidentifiable human remains"), see Jerald T. Milanich, *The Realities of Reburial*, ARCHAEOLOGY, March–April 2009, at 18.
5. In NAGPRA, there are two avenues for resolving disputes arising out of its implementation: its own Review Committee and federal court jurisdiction.

   The seven-person NAGPRA Review Committee, which was chartered in 1991, is an advisory group appointed by the U.S. secretary of the interior. The Committee comprises three members nominated by the indigenous community, three members nominated by national museum and scientific organizations, and a seventh member chosen by the other six members. In making recommendations to the secretary of the interior, the Committee is charged with nine responsibilities[100]:

   (a) Appointing one of its members as chair
   (b) Monitoring the inventory and identification process
   (c) On request of "any affected party," reviewing and making findings related to the identity or cultural affiliation of cultural items or the return of such items
   (d) Facilitating the resolution of disputes relating to return of cultural items, "including convening the parties to a dispute if deemed desirable"
   (e) Compiling an inventory of culturally unidentifiable human remains in the possession of federal agencies and museums and developing a process for disposing of them
   (f) Consulting with Indian tribes, Native Hawaiian organizations, and museums on pertinent matters
   (g) Consulting with the secretary of the interior in developing regulations to implement the law
   (h) Performing other functions assigned by the secretary of the interior
   (i) Making recommendations regarding future care of repatriated items

[100] 25 U.S.C. § 3006(c).

6. According to official minutes of its meetings, the Review Committee's agenda has spanned all nine of its responsibilities. Not surprisingly, its initial meetings were devoted to organizational tasks and review of proposed regulations, whereas substantive issues have dominated its later meetings. The most frequent discussions have focused on developing definitions and a process for the disposition of unidentifiable remains, monitoring implementation of the law, and reviewing regulations.

   In facilitating the resolution of disputes, the Committee may make recommendations and findings related to four general topics: the applicability of a definition of human remains and cultural items to a particular object, its cultural affiliation, its ownership, and its appropriate disposition. The Committee chair and the departmental consulting archaeologist in the National Park Service screen and coordinate all requests for review of a dispute.

   The Committee has attempted to facilitate the resolution of five disputes that have been brought to it for formal review. The first of these involved a request by a Native Hawaiian organization to the Phoebe Hearst Museum for the return of two sets of remains of uncertain ethnicity.[101] In an interesting application of the precautionary principle of environmental law, the museum emphasized the need to retain the remains until such a time as research tools might permit their identification. The claimant organization minimized the importance of close cultural affiliation, noting that reburial would benefit everyone by restoring a spiritual force. The Committee indicated that it would review three types of evidence: osteological (or physical anthropological), contextual (where and under what circumstances the bones were found), and spiritual. In regard to the last procedure, one member of the Committee normally reserved judgment until he could "go to the spirits for guidance." In applying NAGPRA's preponderance-of-evidence test, the Committee recommended that one set of remains be returned to the Native Hawaiian organization and the other be transferred to a museum in Hawaii (the Bishop Museum in Honolulu) for safekeeping and further analysis. Both parties to the dispute accepted the recommendations, and both sets of remains were eventually reburied.[102] Does this Solomonic judgment suggest the efficacy of collaborative dispute resolution by an open process of review by a representative committee?

7. The year 2006 marked the centennial of the controversial donation to the American Museum of Natural History in New York of the Willamette meteorite – or Tomonowos (in the Clackamas language) – the largest meteorite ever found in the United States and the sixth largest in the world. After coming to rest in the Willamette Valley of Oregon thousands of years ago, it eventually endured a questionable series of transactions and litigation early in the last century that resulted in the relocation of most, but not all, of it in what is now a specially built exhibit area at the museum. Meanwhile, the Grand Ronde tribe and others in Oregon requested return of the meteorite to the state. Eventually, negotiations took place to fashion an accommodation of interests. Since the year 2000, the meteorite in New York has been subject to an agreement that ensures special access to it by

[101] Minutes, NAGPRA Review Committee, Fourth Meeting, Feb. 26–28, 1993, at 4.

[102] *See* Edward Halealoha Ayau, *Rooted in Native Soil*, Fed. Arch., Fall–Winter 1995, at 24, 27.

members of the Grand Ronde community for cultural, religious, and historical purposes, including an annual ceremonial visit.

8. Federal cases involving NAGPRA have been infrequent. In *United States v. Corrow*,[103] the Tenth Circuit Court of Appeals affirmed the district court's criminal conviction of the defendant for illegal trafficking in Navajo masks and associated objects that constituted a medicine bundle or *jish*. Charges had been brought under both NAGPRA and the Migratory Bird Treaty Act.[104] The NAGPRA-related conviction involved the defendant's purchase and offer to sell items of cultural patrimony. The defendant claimed that the definition of this category of cultural items was constitutionally void for vagueness and that he had purchased the items from their individual owner, the widow of a spiritual chanter, thereby removing the transaction from the scope of NAGPRA. A core issue, however, was whether the *jish* had been individually owned by the widow from whom the defendant had purchased the items or communally owned and hence part of the Navajo patrimony.[105] The appellate court acknowledged that "the parameters of the designation 'cultural patrimony' might be unclear in some of its applications and at its edges."[106] It decided, however, that a jury could find beyond a reasonable doubt that the ceremonial adornments at issue had "ongoing historical, traditional or cultural importance central to the Native American group or culture itself, rather than [being] property owned by an individual Native American."[107]

A particularly troublesome constitutional issue in *Corrow* related to the prosecutor's examination in court of Navajo spiritual chanters concerning the religious nature of the masks.[108] In allowing such evidence, the court may have encouraged the jury to make its determination of ownership on the basis of its understanding and interpretation of divergent Navajo religious beliefs.[109] Moreover, the masks were never exhibited for the jury to see because of the court's acceptance of the plaintiff's claim that the spiritual nature of the objects did not allow them to be exhibited.[110] The appellate court declined to rule on the appropriateness of the lower court's reliance on religious belief.

The *Corrow* proceedings therefore left unanswered serious issues of doctrinal entanglement[111] by the federal government in violation of the establishment clause, providing for a separation of church and state, of the First Amendment to the U.S. Constitution.[112] In addition, NAGPRA's general protection of Native American but not other sacred material might be seen as an even more sweeping violation

[103] United States v. Corrow, 119 F.3d 796 (10th Cir. 1997), *cert. denied*, 118 S. Ct. 1089 (1998).

[104] 16 U.S.C. §§ 701–712 (1994).

[105] Because of the allegedly communal nature of ownership of the *jish*, equitable rather than normal common law principles shifted the burden of analyzing the original conveyance to the defendant. *See* Ralph W. Johnson & Sharon I. Haensly, *Fifth Amendment Takings Implications of the 1990 Native American Graves Protection and Repatriation Act*, 24 Ariz. St. L.J. 151, 158–59 (1992).

[106] *Corrow*, 119 F.3d 796 at 803.

[107] 25 U.S.C. § 3001(3)(D).

[108] United States v. Corrow, 941 F. Supp. 1553, 1561 n. 10, 1562 (D. N.M. 1996).

[109] Brief of the Antique Tribal Arts Dealers Association as *Amicus Curiae* in Support of the Petition at 13–16, Corrow v. United States, 118 S. Ct. 1089 (1998).

[110] *Id.* at 12.

[111] On the constitutional issue of doctrinal entanglement, *see generally* Laurence H. Tribe, American Constitutional Law 1231–42 (1988).

[112] U.S. Const. amend. I.

of the establishment clause. The apparent preference for Native American religion may be justified, however, as a rectification of past wrongs that resulted in wrongful takings of such items. It is quite another matter, however, for a court to become entangled in, and allow evidence to be based on, divergent interpretations of Navajo religious belief and practice by members of the same tribe and on a religious-based exclusion of otherwise-admissible evidence.

9. For an extensive bibliography on NAGPRA, see Nancy Carol Carter, *Native American Groves Protection and Repatriation Act: Law, Analysis, and Context*, 8 Int'l J. Cultural Prop. 285 (1999).

Bonnichsen v. United States,
357 F.3d 962 (9th Cir. 2004)

Gould, Circuit Judge:

I

In July 1996, teenagers going to a boat race discovered a human skull and bones near the shore of the Columbia River just outside Kennewick, Washington.[113] The remains were found on federal property under the management of the United States Army Corps of Engineers ("Corps") and, at the request of the county coroner, were removed for analysis by an anthropologist, Dr. James Chatters, pursuant to an Archaeological Resources Protection Act of 1979 ("ARPA"), 16 U.S.C. §§ 470aa-470mm, permit. Because of physical features such as the shape of the skull and facial bones, anthropologists at first thought the remains were those of an early European settler. But the anthropologists then found a stone projectile point embedded in the skeleton's upper hip bone. The object's design, when viewed with x-rays and CT scans of the hip, resembled a style that was common before the documented arrival of Europeans in the region. Further study of the remains revealed characteristics unlike those of a European settler, yet also inconsistent with any American Indian remains previously documented in the region. A minute quantity of metacarpal bone was radiocarbon dated. The laboratory estimated the age of the bones to be between 8,340 and 9,200 years old.[114]

The skeleton attracted attention because some of its physical features, such as the shape of the face and skull, differed from those of modern

[113] Our rendition of the facts is adapted from the district court's third published opinion in this case. *See* Bonnichsen v. United States, 217 F. Supp. 2d 1116 (D. Or. 2002). No party on appeal disputes the district court's findings of fact, which are supported by the administrative record.

[114] Human skeletons this old are rare in the Western Hemisphere, and most found have consisted of only fragmented remains. The record indicates that less than twelve securely dated human crania older than eight thousand years have been found in the United States. By contrast, about 90% of this skeleton was recovered in good condition. Dr. Chatters testified in an affidavit: "The Kennewick Man skeleton is virtually intact. It lacks only the sternum and a few small nondiagnostic bones of the hands and the feet. Although some of the ribs and other long bones are fragmented, they can be reconstructed. The skull and the lower jaw are complete and are not deformed. The bones of the skeleton are extremely well preserved, with only minor surface mineralization and little if any evidence of decay."

American Indians. Many scientists believed the discovery might shed light on the origins of humanity in the Americas. On August 31, 1996, Dr. Douglas Owsley, Division Head for Physical Anthropology at the Smithsonian Institution in Washington, D.C., made arrangements for Dr. Chatters to bring this important find to the Smithsonian's National Museum of Natural History for further study.[115]

Indian tribes from the area of the Columbia River opposed scientific study of the remains on religious and social grounds.[116] Four Indian groups (the "Tribal Claimants") demanded that the remains be turned over to them for immediate burial. The Tribal Claimants based their demand on the Native American Graves Protection and Repatriation Act ("NAGPRA"), 25 U.S.C. § 3001 *et seq.* The Corps agreed with the Tribal Claimants and, citing NAGPRA, seized the remains on September 10, 1996, shortly before they could be transported to the Smithsonian. The Corps also ordered an immediate halt to DNA testing, which was being done using the remainder of the bone sample that had been submitted earlier for radiocarbon dating. After investigation, the Corps decided to give the remains to the Tribal Claimants for burial. As required by NAGPRA, the Corps published a "Notice of Intent to Repatriate Human Remains" in a local newspaper on September 17, 1996, and September 24, 1996.

The scientists and others, including the Smithsonian Institution, objected to the Corps' decision, arguing that the remains were a rare discovery of national and international significance. In late September and early October 1996, several scientists asked Major General Ernest J. Herrell, Commander of the Corps' North Pacific Division, to allow qualified scientists to study the remains.

The scientists did not convince the Corps to permit them to study the remains, and commenced this litigation on October 16, 1996, in the United States District Court for the District of Oregon. In an opinion issued June 27, 1997, the district court denied the Corps' motion for summary judgment, finding that the Corps had "acted before it had all of the evidence," "did not fully consider or resolve certain difficult legal questions," and "assumed facts that proved to be erroneous." *Bonnichsen II*,

[115] The Smithsonian Institution in Washington, D.C., is the world's largest museum complex, with fourteen museums in the District of Columbia and more than ninety affiliate museums. The National Museum of Natural History, part of the Smithsonian Institution, was established in 1910 and "is home to about 185 professional natural history scientists, the largest group of scientists dedicated to the study of the natural and cultural history in the world." National Museum of Natural History Research & Collections Home Page, http://www.mnh.si.edu/rc/.

[116] For example, the Tribal Claimants urged that "[w]hen a body goes into the ground, it is meant to stay there until the end of time. When remains are disturbed and remain above the ground, their spirits are at unrest.... To put these spirits at ease, the remains must be returned to the ground as soon as possible." *Bonnichsen III*, 217 F. Supp. 2d at 1121 (quoting Joint Tribal Amici Memorandum (1997) at 4–5). We note that the Ethnic Minority Council of America, in its amicus brief, urges that: "Potential descendants [of Kennewick Man] may not be members of the Joint Tribal Claimants or believe in the expressed 'Indian' religious interpretations made by the political leaders of the tribes." Further, as suggested by *amicus* Ohio Archaeological Council, in the absence of a conclusive determination of cultural affiliation, the Tribal Claimants cannot establish that permitting Plaintiffs-scientists to study the Kennewick Man's remains offends their religious views or customs.

969 F. Supp. 628, 645 (D. Or. 1997). The district court vacated the Corps' earlier decision on disposition of the remains and remanded the case to the Corps for further proceedings. *Id.* at 644–45. The district court also denied, without prejudice, Plaintiffs' motion to study the remains and directed the Corps to consider, on remand, "whether to grant plaintiffs' request [under ARPA] for permission to study the remains." *Id.* at 632, 651.

On March 24, 1998, the Corps and the Secretary of the Interior entered into an agreement that effectively assigned to the Secretary responsibility to decide whether the remains were "Native American" under NAGPRA, and to determine their proper disposition. The Department of the Interior then assumed the role of lead agency on this case.

Almost two years after this matter was remanded, the Secretary's experts began to examine the remains in detail. The experts estimated that Kennewick Man was 5′9″ to 5′10″ tall, 45 to 50 years of age when he died, and 15 to 20 years old when the projectile point became embedded in his hip. The experts could not determine, from non-destructive examination of the skeleton alone, when Kennewick Man lived. However, analysis of sediment layers where the skeleton was found supported the hypothesis that the remains dated back not less than 7,600 years ago, and Kennewick Man could have lived more than 9,000 years ago (the date indicated by the initial radiocarbon dating of the skeleton). Further study of the sediment was recommended, but the Corps' decision to bury the discovery site in April 1998 prevented completion of those studies.[117]

The experts compared the physical characteristics of the remains – e.g., measurements of the skull, teeth, and bones – with corresponding measurements from other skeletons. They concluded that Kennewick Man's remains were unlike those of any known present-day population, American Indian or otherwise.

The Secretary's experts cautioned, however, that an apparent lack of physical resemblance between the Kennewick Man's remains and present-day American Indians did not completely rule out the possibility that the remains might be biologically ancestral to modern American Indians. Moreover, although Kennewick Man's morphological traits did not closely resemble those of modern American Indian populations, the Secretary's experts noted that Kennewick Man's physical attributes are generally consistent with the very small number of human remains from this period that have been found in North America.

[117] The Corps buried the discovery site of the remains under approximately 2 million pounds of rubble and dirt, topped with 3,700 willow, dogwood, and cottonwood plants. The lengthy administrative record that Defendants filed with the district court documents only a portion of the process by which the decision to bury the site was made. Nevertheless, that record suggested to the district court that the Corps' primary objective in covering the site was to prevent additional remains or artifacts from being discovered, not to "preserve" the site's archaeological value or to remedy a severe erosion control problem as Defendants represented. *Bonnichsen III*, 217 F. Supp. 2d at 1125. Burial of the discovery site hindered efforts to verify the age of Kennewick Man's remains and effectively ended efforts to determine whether other artifacts are present at the site that might shed light on the relationship between the remains and contemporary American Indians. *Id.* at 1126.

Relying solely on the age of the remains and the fact that the remains were found within the United States, on January 13, 2000, the Secretary pronounced Kennewick Man's remains "Native American" within NAGPRA's meaning. And on September 25, 2000, the Secretary determined that a preponderance of the evidence supported the conclusion that the Kennewick remains were culturally affiliated with present-day Indian tribes. For this reason, the Secretary announced his final decision to award Kennewick Man's remains to a coalition of the Tribal Claimants. The Corps and the Secretary also denied Plaintiffs' request to study the remains.

Plaintiffs filed an amended complaint in the district court challenging the Secretary's decisions. The district court again ruled in Plaintiffs' favor. As pertinent to this appeal, the district court vacated the Secretary's decisions as contrary to the Administrative Procedure Act, 5 U.S.C. § 706(2)(A) ("APA"), on the ground that the Secretary improperly concluded that NAGPRA applies.[118] *Bonnichsen III*, 217 F. Supp. 2d 1138–39. The district court also held that, because NAGPRA did not apply, Plaintiffs should have the opportunity to study Kennewick Man's remains under ARPA. Defendants and the Tribal Claimants appealed, and we stayed the district court's order granting Plaintiffs-scientists' study of the remains pending our decision herein.

[The Court then addressed issues of jurisdiction and standing, concluding that the district court was correct in taking jurisdiction over the matter and granting standing to the plaintiffs.]

III

Our review of the Secretary's decision to transfer Kennewick Man to the Tribal Claimants is governed by the APA, which instructs courts to "hold unlawful and set aside agency action, findings, and conclusions found to be . . . arbitrary, capricious, an abuse of discretion, or otherwise not in accordance with law." 5 U.S.C. § 706(2)(A).

NAGPRA vests "ownership or control" of newly discovered Native American human remains in the decedent's lineal descendants or, if lineal descendants cannot be ascertained, in a tribe "affiliated" with the remains. 25 U.S.C. § 3002(a). NAGPRA mandates a two-part analysis. The first inquiry is whether human remains are Native American within the statute's meaning. If the remains *are not* Native American, then NAGPRA does not apply. However, if the remains *are* Native American, then NAGPRA applies, triggering the second inquiry of determining which persons or tribes are most closely affiliated with the remains.

The parties dispute whether the remains of Kennewick Man constitute Native American remains within NAGPRA's meaning. NAGPRA defines

[118] The district court also held that even if NAGPRA applied: (1) the remains were not "culturally affiliated" with the Tribal Claimants; (2) only an individual Indian tribe – not a coalition of Indian tribes – could be a proper claimant under NAGPRA; and (3) the Tribal Claimants' alleged "aboriginal occupation" of the discovery site was not a proper reason to give the Tribal Claimants the remains. *Bonnichsen III*, 217 F. Supp. 2d at 1158. Because we conclude *infra* that NAGPRA does not apply to Kennewick Man's remains, we do not need to reach and we do not review these additional holdings of the district court.

human remains as "Native American" if the remains are "of, or relating to, a tribe, people, or culture that is indigenous to the United States." 25 U.S.C. § 3001(9). The text of the relevant statutory clause is written in the present tense ("of, or relating to, a tribe, people, or culture *that is* indigenous"). Thus the statute unambiguously requires that human remains bear some relationship to a *presently existing* tribe, people, or culture to be considered Native American.

It is axiomatic that, in construing a statute, courts generally give words not defined in a statute their "ordinary or natural meaning." *United States v. Alvarez-Sanchez*, 511 U.S. 350, 357, 114 S. Ct. 1599, 128 L. Ed. 2d 319 (1994); *see also Williams v. Taylor*, 529 U.S. 420, 431, 120 S. Ct. 1479, 146 L. Ed. 2d 435 (2000) (holding that courts "give the words of a statute their ordinary, contemporary, common meaning, absent an indication Congress intended them to bear some different import") (internal quotation marks omitted).

In the context of NAGPRA, we conclude that Congress's use of the present tense is significant. The present tense "in general represents present time." R. Pence and D. Emery, A Grammar of Present Day English 262 (2d ed. 1963). Congress, by using the phrase "is indigenous" in the present tense, referred to presently existing tribes, peoples, or cultures. We must presume that Congress gave the phrase "is indigenous" its ordinary or natural meaning. *Alvarez-Sanchez*, 511 U.S. at 357, 114 S. Ct. 1599. We conclude that Congress was referring to *presently existing* Indian tribes when it referred to "a tribe, people, or culture *that is* indigenous to the United States." 25 U.S.C. § 3001(9) (emphasis added).[119]

NAGPRA also protects graves of persons not shown to be of current tribes in that it protects disjunctively remains "of, or relating to" current indigenous tribes. Thus, NAGPRA extends to all remains that relate to a tribe, people, or culture that is indigenous to the United States, *see* 25 U.S.C. § 3001(9) (defining human remains as Native American if they are "of, *or relating to*, a tribe, people, or culture that is indigenous to the United States") (emphasis added).

Our conclusion that NAGPRA's language requires that human remains, to be considered Native American, bear some relationship to a presently existing tribe, people, or culture accords with NAGPRA's purposes. As regards newly discovered human remains, NAGPRA was enacted with two main goals: to respect the burial traditions of modern-day American Indians and to protect the dignity of the human body after death. NAGPRA was intended to benefit modern American Indians by sparing them the

[119] The secretary argues that "[i]n common parlance, the words 'is' and 'was' are appropriately used interchangeably when referring to tribes, peoples and cultures that existed in the past but are being spoken of in the present." Gov't Opening Brief at 31. The secretary offers no support for this assertion, and we decline to accept it as an accurate description of the intent of Congress in this case as we interpret NAGPRA. Our holding is limited to a determination that Congress was referring to *presently existing* Indian tribes when it referred to "a tribe, people, or culture *that is* indigenous to the United States." We do not foreclose the possibility that, in any other statute, Congress's use of the present tense, in the context of a different statute, with different statutory language, structure, and purposes, could implicate a time period other than the present.

indignity and resentment that would be aroused by the despoiling of their ancestors' graves and the study or the display of their ancestors' remains. *See* H.R. Rep. No. 101–877, at 4369 (1990) ("For many years, Indian tribes have attempted to have the remains and funerary objects of *their ancestors returned to them.*") (emphasis added).

Congress's purposes would not be served by requiring the transfer to modern American Indians of human remains that bear no relationship to them. Yet, that would be the result under the Secretary's construction of the statute, which would give Native American status to any remains found within the United States regardless of age and regardless of lack of connection to existing indigenous tribes.[120] The exhumation, study, and display of ancient human remains that are unrelated to modern American Indians was not a target of Congress's aim, nor was it precluded by NAGPRA.

NAGPRA was also intended to protect the dignity of the human body after death by ensuring that Native American graves and remains be treated with respect. *See* S. Rep. No. 101–473, at 6 (1990) ("The Committee believes that human remains must at all times be treated with dignity and respect."); H.R. Rep. No. 101–877, at 4372 (1990) ("Some Indian representatives testified that the spirits of *their ancestors* would not rest until they are returned to their homeland. . . . ") (emphasis added). Congress's purpose is served by requiring the return to modern-day American Indians of human remains that bear some significant relationship to them.

Despite the statute's language and legislative history, the Secretary argues that the district court's interpretation "improperly collapses" NAGPRA's first inquiry (asking *whether* human remains are Native American) into NAGPRA's second inquiry (asking *which* American Indians or Indian tribe bears the closest relationship to Native American remains). The Secretary is mistaken. Though NAGPRA's two inquiries have some commonality in that both focus on the relationship between human remains and present-day Indians, the two inquiries differ significantly. The first inquiry requires only a general finding that remains have a significant relationship to a presently existing "tribe, people, or culture," a relationship that goes beyond features common to all humanity. The second inquiry requires a more specific finding that remains are most closely affiliated to specific lineal descendants or to a specific Indian tribe. The district court's interpretation of NAGPRA preserves the statute's two distinct inquiries. Because the record shows no relationship of Kennewick Man to the Tribal Claimants, the district court was correct in holding that NAGPRA has no application.

[120] At oral argument, the government urged that its interpretation of remains as Native American when found within the United States would apply even to remains as old as 100,000 or 150,000 years, close to the dawn of *Homo sapiens*. Indeed, the government at oral argument even said that if remains of a mythical first man and woman, an "Adam and Eve," were found in the United States, those remains would be "Native American" under the government's interpretation of NAGPRA. Thus, the government's unrestricted interpretation based solely on geography, calling any ancient remains found in the United States "Native American" if they predate the arrival of Europeans, has no principle of limitation beyond geography. This does not appear to us to be what Congress had in mind. Nor does the legislative history support NAGPRA coverage of bones of such great antiquity.

The Secretary finally argues that, under *Chevron U.S.A. v. Natural Res. Def. Council*, 467 U.S. 837, 104 S. Ct. 2778, 81 L. Ed. 2d 694 (1984), we must defer to the Secretary's interpretation of "Native American." The Secretary by regulation has defined "Native American" to mean "of, or relating to, a tribe, people, or culture indigenous to the United States." 43 C.F.R. § 10.2(d). The Secretary's regulation, enacted through notice and comment rulemaking, defines Native American exactly as NAGPRA defines it, with one critical exception: the regulation omits the present tense phrase "that is." *Compare* 25 U.S.C. § 3001(9) ("*a culture that is indigenous* to the United States") (emphasis added) *with* 43 C.F.R. § 10.2(d) ("*a culture indigenous* to the United States") (emphasis added). We hold, for the reasons discussed above, that NAGPRA's requirement that Native American remains bear some relationship to a *presently existing* tribe, people, or culture is unambiguous, and that the Secretary's contrary interpretation therefore is not owed *Chevron* deference. *See Chevron*, 467 U.S. at 842–43, 104 S. Ct. 2778 ("If the intent of Congress is clear, that is the end of the matter; for the court, as well as the agency, must give effect to the unambiguously expressed intent of Congress.");[121] *see also Wilderness Soc'y v. United States Fish & Wildlife Serv.*, No. 01–35266, 353 F.3d 1051, 1061, 2003 WL 23025466, at *6 (9th Cir. Dec. 30, 2003) (en banc) ("If, under these canons, or other traditional means of determining Congress's intentions, we are able to determine that Congress spoke clearly . . . , then we may not defer to the [agency's] contrary interpretation."). Moreover, the Secretary's regulation conflicts with NAGPRA's plain language and so is invalid for that reason. *See Whitman v. Am. Trucking Ass'ns*, 531 U.S. 457, 481, 121 S. Ct. 903, 149 L. Ed. 2d 1 (2001) (holding that *Chevron* deference is due only to a "*reasonable* interpretation made by the administrator of an agency") (emphasis added) (internal quotation marks omitted); *Pub. Employees Ret. Sys. of Ohio v. Betts*, 492 U.S. 158, 171, 109 S. Ct. 2854, 106 L. Ed. 2d 134 (1989) ("[N]o deference is due to agency interpretations at odds with the plain language of the statute itself."). Finally, the common maxim of statutory construction that we must give effect, if possible, to every word Congress used is fatal to the Secretary's attempt to amend NAGPRA by removing the phrase "that is." *See Bennett*, 520 U.S. at 173, 117 S. Ct. 1154 ("It is the 'cardinal principle of statutory construction' [that courts must] give effect, if possible, to every clause and word of a statute. . . . "). We hold that, notwithstanding 43 C.F.R. § 10.2(d), NAGPRA requires that human remains bear a significant relationship to a *presently existing* tribe, people, or culture to be considered Native American. The district court did not err in reaching that conclusion.

The requirement that we must give effect, if possible, to every word Congress used supports our holding that human remains must be related to a currently existing tribe to come within NAGPRA's protection. Under

[121] Because this aspect of NAGPRA is unambiguous, we need not resort to the "Indian canon of construction," under which "doubtful expressions" in legislation passed for the benefit of Indian tribes are resolved in favor of the Indians. *See* South Carolina v. Catawba Indian Tribe, Inc., 476 U.S. 498, 506, 106 S. Ct. 2039, 90 L. Ed. 2d 490 (1986).

the Secretary's view of NAGPRA, all graves and remains of persons, predating European settlers, that are found in the United States would be "Native American," in the sense that they presumptively would be viewed as remains of a deceased from a tribe "indigenous" to the United States, even if the tribe had ceased to exist thousands of years before the remains were found, and even if there was no showing of any relationship of the remains to some existing tribe indigenous to the United States. Such an extreme interpretation, as was urged by the Secretary here . . . would render superfluous NAGPRA's alternative "relating to" method for establishing remains as "Native American" (i.e., if remains are "of, *or relating to*, a tribe that is indigenous to the United States"). If accepted, the Secretary's interpretation would mean that the finding of any remains in the United States *in and of itself* would automatically render these remains "Native American." This interpretation would leave no meaning for the "relating to" clause, unless we were to interpret the clause to cover remains found outside the United States. But we cannot conclude that Congress intended an absurd result, for Congress could not be considered to have jurisdiction over disposition of human remains found in some other country. By reading NAGPRA's definition of "Native American" literally, meaning is given to each of its terms. Some remains may be covered because they are remains of a tribe, people, or culture that is indigenous, while other remains may be covered because they are "related to" a currently existing indigenous tribe, people, or culture.

Our analysis is strengthened by contrasting the statutory definition of the adjective "Native American" to the statutory definition of the noun "Native Hawaiian." Under § 3001(9), "'Native American' means of, or relating to, a tribe, people or culture that is indigenous *to the United States*." (Emphasis added). Under § 3001(10), "'Native Hawaiian' means any individual who is a descendant of the aboriginal people who, prior to 1778, occupied and exercised sovereignty *in the area that now constitutes the State of Hawaii*." (Emphasis added).

The "United States" is a political entity that dates back to 1789. *Owings v. Speed*, 18 U.S. (5 Wheat.) 420, 423, 5 L. Ed. 124 (1820). This term supports that Congress's use of the present tense ("that *is* indigenous") referred to tribes, peoples, and cultures that exist in modern times, not to those that may have existed thousands of years ago but who do not exist now. By contrast, when Congress chose to harken back to earlier times, it described a geographic location ("the area that now constitutes the State of Hawaii") rather than a political entity ("the United States").

Our conclusion that NAGPRA requires human remains to bear some relationship to a presently existing tribe, people, or culture to be considered "Native American" is also reinforced by how NAGPRA defines "sacred objects." NAGPRA defines "sacred objects" as "specific ceremonial objects which are needed by traditional Native American religious leaders for the practice of traditional Native American religions *by their present day adherents*." 25 U.S.C. § 3001(3)(C) (emphasis added). A literal reading of this definition reveals that any artifact to be deemed a "sacred object" must be connected to the practice of an American Indian religion by *present-day* peoples. This reading is consistent with our reading of "Native American"; that is, just as there must be a relationship between an artifact and a presently existing peoples for the artifact to be a "sacred object" under NAGPRA, there must be a relationship between a set of remains and a presently existing tribe, people, or culture for those remains to be "Native American" under NAGPRA.

Although NAGPRA does not specify precisely what *kind* of a relationship or precisely *how strong* a relationship ancient human remains must bear to modern Indian groups to qualify as Native American, NAGPRA's legislative history provides some guidance on what type of relationship may suffice. The House Committee on Interior and Insular Affairs emphasized in its report on NAGPRA that the statute was being enacted with modern-day American Indians' identifiable *ancestors* in mind. *See, e.g.*, H.R. Rep. No. 101–877, at 4372 (1990) ("Indian representatives testified that the spirits of *their ancestors* would not rest until they are returned to their homeland. . . . " (emphasis added)); *id.* at 4369 ("For many years, Indian tribes have attempted to have the remains and funerary objects of *their ancestors* returned to them." (emphasis added)). Human remains that are 8340 to 9200 years old and that bear only incidental genetic resemblance to modern-day American Indians, along with incidental genetic resemblance to other peoples, cannot be said to be the Indians' "ancestors" within Congress's meaning. Congress enacted NAGPRA to give American Indians control over the remains of their genetic and cultural forebears, not over the remains of people bearing no special and significant genetic or cultural relationship to some presently existing indigenous tribe, people, or culture.

The age of Kennewick Man's remains, given the limited studies to date, makes it almost impossible to establish *any* relationship between the remains and presently existing American Indians. At least no significant relationship has yet been shown. We cannot give credence to an interpretation of NAGPRA advanced by the government and the Tribal Claimants that would apply its provisions to remains that have at most a tenuous, unknown, and unproven connection, asserted solely because of the geographical location of the find.

IV

Finally, we address the Secretary's determination that Kennewick Man's remains are Native American, as defined by NAGPRA. We must set aside the Secretary's decision if it was "arbitrary" or "capricious" because the decision was based on inadequate factual support. *See* 5 U.S.C. § 706(2)(A). We review the full agency record to determine whether substantial evidence[122]

[122] *See* Wileman Bros. & Elliott, Inc. v. Espy, 58 F.3d 1367, 1374–75 (9th Cir. 1995) ("When the arbitrary and capricious standard is performing that function of assuring factual support, there is no substantive difference between what it requires and what would be required by the substantial evidence test.") (internal quotation marks omitted), *rev'd on other grounds*, 521 U.S. 457, 117 S. Ct. 2130, 138 L. Ed. 2d 585 (1997). Substantial evidence means such relevant evidence as a reasonable mind might accept as adequate to support a conclusion. Richardson v. Perales, 402 U.S. 389, 401, 91 S. Ct. 1420, 28 L. Ed. 2d 842 (1971). We

supports the agency's decision that Kennewick Man is "Native American" within NAGPRA's meaning. Here, after reviewing the record, we conclude that the record does not contain substantial evidence that Kennewick Man's remains are Native American within NAGPRA's meaning.[123]

The administrative record contains no evidence – let alone substantial evidence – that Kennewick Man's remains are connected by some special or significant genetic or cultural relationship to any presently existing indigenous tribe, people, or culture. An examination of the record demonstrates the absence of evidence that Kennewick Man and modern tribes share significant genetic or cultural features.[124]

No cognizable link exists between Kennewick Man and modern Columbia Plateau Indians. When Kennewick Man's remains were discovered, local coroners initially believed the remains were those of a European, not a Native American, because of their appearance. Later testing by scientists demonstrated that the cranial measurements and features of Kennewick Man most closely resemble those of Polynesians and southern Asians, and that Kennewick Man's measurements and features differ significantly from those of any modern Indian group living in North America.[125]

Scant or no evidence of cultural similarities between Kennewick Man and modern Indians exists. One of the Secretary's experts, Dr. Kenneth Ames, reported that "the empirical gaps in the record preclude establishing cultural continuities or discontinuities, particularly before about 5000 B.C." Dr. Ames noted that, although there was overwhelming evidence that many aspects of the "Plateau Pattern" were present between 1000 B.C. and A.D. 1, "the empirical record precludes establishing cultural continuities or discontinuities across increasingly remote periods." He noted that the available evidence is insufficient either to prove or disprove cultural or group continuity dating back earlier than 5000 B.C., which is the case with regard to the Kennewick Man's remains, and that there is evidence that substantial changes occurred in settlement, housing, diet, trade, subsistence patterns, technology, projectile point styles, raw materials, and mortuary rituals at various times between the estimated date when Kennewick Man

consider the record as a whole, weighing both the evidence that supports and the evidence that detracts from the Secretary's decision. *See* Mayes v. Massanari, 276 F.3d 453, 459 (9th Cir. 2001).

[123] In so holding, we necessarily determine that no reasonable person could conclude by a preponderance of the evidence on this record that Kennewick Man is "Native American" under NAGPRA. *See* Allentown Mack Sales & Serv., Inc. v. NLRB, 522 U.S. 359, 366–67, 118 S. Ct. 818, 139 L. Ed. 2d 797 (1998) (holding that under the substantial evidence standard the reviewing court "must decide whether on this record it would have been possible for a reasonable jury to reach the [agency's] conclusion.").

[124] As pointed out by *amici* Texas Historical Commission, under the framework proposed by the government and the Tribal Claimants, as soon as any remains are determined to be pre-Columbian, any study or testing of such remains would have to stop. This blanket prohibition could result in improper disposition of remains to parties wholly unrelated to the remains.

[125] In a letter announcing his final decision that Kennewick Man is Native American, the secretary acknowledged this discontinuity:

> [T]hat the morphological characteristics of the remains differ from modern day Indian tribes may indicate a cultural discontinuity between the two groups, or may indicate that the cultural group associated with the Kennewick Man may have subsequently intermixed with other groups migrating into or through the region, leading to changes in the morphological characteristics of the group.

lived and the beginning of the "Plateau Culture" some 2000 to 3000 years ago.

Dr. Ames'[s] conclusions about the impossibility of establishing cultural continuity between Kennewick Man and modern Indians is confirmed by other evidence that the Secretary credited. For example, the Secretary acknowledges that the record shows that there were no villages or permanent settlements in the Columbia Plateau region 9,000 years ago and that human populations then were small and nomadic, traveling long distances in search of food and raw materials. The Secretary's experts determined, and the Secretary acknowledged, that it was not until 2,000 to 3,000 years ago that populations began to settle into the villages and bands that may have been the antecedents of modern Indian tribes something like those encountered by European settlers and colonists. As the Secretary summarized, "Cultural discontinuities are suggested by evidence that the cultural group existing 8500–9500 years ago was likely small in size and highly mobile while the Plateau culture consisted o[f] larger, more sedentary groups."

The Secretary also acknowledges that "there is very little evidence of burial patterns during the 9500–8500 period and significant temporal gaps exist in the mortuary record for other periods." So, even if we assume that Kennewick Man was part of a stable social group living in the area, it still would be impossible to say whether his group's burial practices were related to modern tribes' burial practices. The Secretary also noted that "the linguistic analysis was unable to provide reliable evidence for the 8500–9500 period."

The Secretary's only evidence, perhaps, of a possible cultural relationship between Kennewick Man and modern-day American Indians comes in the form of oral histories. One of the Secretary's experts, Dr. Daniel Boxberger, concluded that modern day Plateau tribes' oral histories – some of which can be interpreted to refer to ancient floods, volcanic eruptions, and the like – are "highly suggestive of long-term establishment of the present-day tribes." Stated another way, Dr. Boxberger noted that oral traditions showed no necessary tale of a superseding migration with newer peoples displacing older ones. But evidence in the record demonstrates that oral histories change relatively quickly, that oral histories may be based on later observation of geological features and deduction (rather than on the first teller's witnessing ancient events), and that these oral histories might be from a culture or group other than the one to which Kennewick Man belonged. The oral traditions relied upon by the Secretary's expert, Dr. Boxberger, entail some published accounts of Native American folk narratives from the Columbia Plateau region, and statements from individual tribal members. But we conclude that these accounts are just not specific enough or reliable enough or relevant enough to show a significant relationship of the Tribal Claimants with Kennewick Man. Because oral accounts have been inevitably changed in context of transmission, because the traditions include myths that cannot be considered as if factual histories, because the value of such accounts is limited by concerns of authenticity, reliability, and accuracy, and because the record as a whole does not show where historical fact ends and mythic tale begins, we do not think that the oral traditions of interest to Dr. Boxberger were adequate to show the required significant relationship of the Kennewick Man's remains to the Tribal Claimants. As the district court observed, 8,340 to 9,200 years between the life of Kennewick Man and the present is too long a time to bridge merely with evidence of oral traditions.

Considered as a whole, the administrative record might permit the Secretary to conclude reasonably that the Tribal Claimants' ancestors have lived in the region for a very long time. However, because Kennewick Man's remains are *so* old and the information about his era is *so* limited, the record does not permit the Secretary to conclude reasonably that Kennewick Man shares special and significant genetic or cultural features with presently existing indigenous tribes, people, or cultures. We thus hold that Kennewick Man's remains are not Native American human remains within the meaning of NAGPRA and that NAGPRA does not apply to them. Studies of the Kennewick Man's remains by Plaintiffs-scientists may proceed pursuant to ARPA.[126]

We remand to the district court for further proceedings consistent with this opinion.

AFFIRMED.

NOTES AND QUESTIONS

1. It may seem rather strained, if not macabre, to treat human remains as cultural. Three bases support this characterization: first, the historical display by museums of remains as cultural artifacts; second, legal authority such as NAGPRA that applies concepts such as cultural affiliation to remains; and third, both statutory and nonstatutory claims that remains are sacred or otherwise of cultural significance.
2. A fascinating essay on the scientific value of examining human remains is Kevin Krajick, *The Mummy Doctor*, New Yorker, May 16, 2005, at 66. Although remains that NAGPRA intends to protect are nearly always skeletal, mummies, if any, would also be covered, and many of the findings and implications of research on mummies apply to bones as well.
3. Should protection of Native American and Native Hawaiian claims be temporally limited so as to avoid the dilemma in *Bonnichsen* of establishing cultural affiliation between a tribe and prehistoric remains? One commentator, arguing that "NAGPRA needs to reflect a temporal limit to cultural affiliation," has proposed amending NAGPRA § 3005(b) (pertaining to scientific study of material subject to repatriation), largely on the basis of H.R. 28931, 105th Cong. (1997), as follows:

> Scientific Study and Retention of Remains: In situations where human remains cannot be culturally affiliated with a living group by a showing

[126] As pointed out by *amici* Texas Historical Commission, Plaintiffs-scientists plan to engage in the following general types of testing: (1) morphometric cranial and post-cranial measurements comparing the Kennewick Man's remains with other populations; (2) dental characteristic studies; (3) DNA studies; and (4) diet analysis.

> of shared group identity by a preponderance of the evidence, such remains should be held in stewardship by a museum or institution equipped to analyze them to the fullest extent possible using modern scientific methods. If, at any time, pursuant to such a study, cultural affiliation is identified, the relevant Native American group must be notified within 90 days, and that group's wishes as to the ultimate disposition of the remains must be fully accommodated. Additionally, such remains, should they remain unaffiliated following complete scientific analysis, should be maintained by the curating institution in perpetuity to allow for further analysis and examination as new methods are developed.

Ryan M. Seidemann, *Time for a Change? The Kennewick Man Case and Its Implications for the Future of the Native American Graves Protection and Repatriation Act*, 106 W. Va. L. Rev. 149, 171 (2003).

If a temporal limit is appropriate, would more of a bright-line temporal limit be preferable? For example, the cutoff date for Native American tribal material might be the approximate date of the Vikings' arrival in Newfoundland or perhaps 1492, when Christopher Columbus arrived in the West Indies. For Native Hawaiians, the cutoff date might be 1776, when Captain James Cook "discovered" Hawaii.

4. The unearthing of Kennewick Man occurred at a time when archaeologists were reconsidering the identity and origins of the first inhabitants of North America. In particular, doubts have multiplied about what was assumed to be an exclusive migration of the first inhabitant over a now-submerged land bridge across the Bering Strait. They were said to be the Clovis people (named after spearheads, dated to 12,500–13,500 years ago, that were first found in Clovis, New Mexico, and have been excavated throughout North America as far south as Costa Rica).

   Today, new evidence of earlier inhabitation as remote as the southern tip of South America, together with other circumstances of early settlement, suggest a far more complicated history. Alternatives to the land-bridge theory include maritime migration from both East Asia and Southeast Asia along the Pacific coast and even prehistoric settlement by Europeans. See, e.g., Evan Hadingham, *America's First Immigrants*, Smithsonian, Nov. 2004, at 91.

5. How do the new uncertainties and ambiguities about the identity and origins of "Native" Americans and "First" Nations complicate the various regimes for protection of indigenous heritage? One anthropologist has observed as follows:

> Anthropologists may be making peace with culture, but they are also beginning to question the validity and political implications of "the indigenous" as a category of people. In North and South America, indigenousness is easy to define, at least in principle: it refers to the descendants of the New World's original inhabitants. (Because of generations of intermarriage and cultural blending, however, the question of which individuals qualify as indigenous remains irksome.) In regions such as South Asia and Africa, in contrast, claims of prior occupation may be extremely divisive in political arenas already plagued by violence and instability. The rise of indigenism and the special rights that it typically advances – to say nothing of the romance and primal authenticity with which native culture is imbued in the popular imagination – have made it increasingly attractive to claim, or reclaim, an indigenous identity. Debates about indigenous identities seem destined to intensify in the coming years.

Michael F. Brown, *Heritage Trouble: Recent Work on the Protection of Intangible Cultural Property*, 12 Int'l J. Cultural Prop. 40 (2005).

As already noted, however, the identity of the "descendants of the New World's original inhabitants" – the "easy case" – has become unclear.

6. Overall, how would you rate NAGPRA? Do you agree with the following list of its strength and weaknesses? How would you revise this list?

   Strengths:
   (a) Basis for comprehensive, ongoing repatriation of cultural heritage
   (b) Mandate for enhanced protection of sites
   (c) Coherent structure for resolving disputes
   (d) Encouragement of centralized data collection and dissemination
   (e) Impetus for public awareness, education
   (f) Enhanced focus on Native Hawaiian claims
   (g) Basis for greater collaboration between tribes and museums

   Weaknesses:
   (a) Terminological issues (e.g., affected parties and their standing, repatriation, associated and unassociated funerary objects, cultural affiliation, cultural patrimony, Native American)
   (b) Related policy issues (e.g., accommodation of competing claims, status of claims from nonrecognized tribal groups, protection of information, disposition of unidentifiable remains and heritage, disposition of unclaimed remains and heritage)
   (c) Evidentiary issues (e.g., role of oral traditions, need for confidentiality, use of video recordings)
   (d) Gaps in the legislation (e.g., acceptability of replicas and virtual representations, digital and other recordation and information sharing, contamination of material, expectations about reburial or other final disposition of repatriated material by tribal groups)
   (e) Bureaucratic delays and conflicts of interest
   (f) Financial limitations
   (g) Exclusion of state and private lands

(ii) State Law. State statutes protecting Native American remains vary widely in scope.

Christopher A. Amato, *Digging Sacred Ground: Burial Site Disturbances and the Loss of New York's Native American Heritage*, 27 Colum. J. Envtl. L. 1 (2002)

Forty-six states (all but New Jersey, New York, Vermont, and Wyoming) have laws that either specifically protect Native American burial sites, or protect unmarked graves generally. These laws typically include provisions prohibiting intentional disturbance of unmarked graves, establish procedures for proposed excavation and/or inadvertent disturbance of such sites, and require reburial of excavated remains within a certain time period. In addition, the majority of these laws include criminal penalties for violations of their grave protection provisions.

Thirty-two states require as part of their statutory scheme that notice be provided to appropriate tribal groups when Native American remains are inadvertently discovered or may be intentionally excavated. In addition, twenty-eight states have created commissions or boards with Native American representation whose role is to facilitate state/tribal relations, provide notice to appropriate tribes in the event of excavation or discovery of Native American remains, and/or participate in the decision-making process for disposition of remains and artifacts from unmarked graves.

Thirteen states require some form of consent by, or agreement with, tribal representatives concerning the disposition of Native American remains that are either inadvertently discovered or intentionally excavated. In addition, eleven states have passed laws that specifically require repatriation of Native American human remains to appropriate tribal representatives. Of these, the laws of five states also require repatriation of cultural artifacts. Since these latter statutes represent the most comprehensive efforts by individual states to address the issue of burial site protection, it is worth examining them in some detail.

In 1990, Arizona passed a broad law mandating repatriation of human remains, funerary objects, sacred objects, and objects of tribal patrimony.[127] The law requires that the person in charge of any survey, excavation, construction or other activity on state or municipal lands promptly report to the director of the Arizona state museum the discovery of any human remains, funerary objects,[128] sacred ceremonial objects,[129] or objects of national or tribal patrimony.[130] In cases where such remains or items are Native American, the director of the state museum must provide notice of the discovery to "all groups that it is reasonable to believe may have a cultural or religious affinity to the remains or objects,"[131] and to "the tribes that occupy or have occupied the land on which the discovery is

[127] ARIZ. REV. STAT. 41–844(D) (2000). *See generally* Paul Bender, *1990 Arizona Repatriation Legislation*, 24 ARIZ. ST. L.J. 391 (1992).

[128] The Act defines "funerary object" as "an object discovered in proximity to human remains and intentionally buried or interred with the remains." ARIZ. REV. STAT. 41–844(M)(1) (2000).

[129] A "sacred ceremonial object" is defined as "an object traditionally utilized in religious observances." *Id.* 41–844(M)(6).

[130] An "object of national or cultural patrimony" is defined as "inalienable items of historical or cultural significance to tribal groups." *Id.* 41–844(M)(5).

[131] *Id.* 41–844(B)(2). The Act provides that a "group with cultural or religious affinity" means any of the following:

> (a) In the case of human remains or funerary objects, any tribe that has submitted a written claim of affinity . . . or any other group or tribe that has cultural affinity in light of all the relevant evidence.
> (b) In the case of a sacred ceremonial object, a group whose religious observances traditionally have utilized such object.
> (c) In the case of an object of national or cultural patrimony, a group whose past or present government or traditional cultural organization was or is associated with the object.

Id. 41–844(M)(2).

made and to the Arizona commission on Indian affairs and the intertribal council of Arizona."

Subsequent to notification, the director attempts to secure agreement among the notified parties regarding the appropriate disposition of the remains and/or objects. In the event an agreement cannot be reached, the remains and objects "shall be disposed of and treated in accordance with the wishes of the nearest relative with a direct kinship relationship, or with the wishes of the governing body of the group with cultural or religious affinity to the remains or objects if no relative exists."[132] With respect to remains or objects in the possession and ownership or control of an agency of the state, such remains and objects must be repatriated upon request of the government of an Indian tribe.[133] Furthermore, the Act requires that any repository charged with the care or custody of remains or objects "shall maintain them with appropriate dignity and respect and with consideration for the specific applicable cultural or religious traditions...."[134]

Maryland's law[135] places responsibility for disposition of human remains and associated funerary objects[136] in the state Historical Trust. If the cultural affiliation of remains and funerary objects can be established with a particular cultural group, the Trust may transfer possession of such remains and objects to "groups established as culturally affiliated with the deceased, including Native American tribes, bands, groups or clans."[137]

In 1989, Nebraska passed the Unmarked Human Burial Sites and Skeletal Remains Protection Act,[138] which requires all state-recognized museums to repatriate "reasonably identifiable"[139] remains and burial goods[140] to affiliated tribes upon request.

North Dakota's law[141] places responsibility for disposition of Native American human remains and burial goods[142] in the state's Intertribal

[132] *Id.* 41–844(G). If remains of American Indians are involved, in the event that no culturally affiliated tribe exists for discovered remains or objects, they may be reburied with the cooperation of the Indian tribe located nearest to the place where the remains were discovered and may, with the tribe's consent, be reburied on the tribe's reservation.

[133] "Tribe" is defined as "any federally recognized tribal government." *Id.* 41–844(M)(7).

[134] *Id.* 41–844(H).

[135] Ownership and Deposit of Submerged or Terrestrial Archaeological Objects and Materials. MD. CODE ANN. art. 83B, 5–627 (2001).

[136] "Associated funerary object" is defined as "an item of human manufacture or use that is intentionally placed with human remains at the time of interment in a burial site or placed later as a part of a death rite or ceremony of a culture, religion or group." *Id.* art. 27, 265(a)(2)(i).

[137] *Id.* art. 83B, 5–627(b)(2).

[138] NEB. REV. STAT. 12–1201 (1990); *see also* Peregoy, *supra* note 72, at 329.

[139] "Reasonably identifiable" is defined as "identifiable, by a preponderance of the evidence, as to familial or tribal origin based on any available archaeological, historical, ethnological, or other direct or circumstantial evidence or expert opinion." NEB. REV. STAT. 12–1204(6) (1990).

[140] "Burial goods" are defined as "any item or items reasonably believed to have been intentionally placed with the human skeletal remains of an individual at the time of burial and which can be traced with a reasonable degree of certainty to the specific human skeletal remains with which it or they were buried." *Id.* 12–1204(1).

[141] Protection of Human Burial Sites, Human Remains and Burial Goods, N.D. CENT. CODE 23–06–27 (2001); Protection of Prehistoric Sites and Deposits, *id.* 55–03 to –07 (2000).

[142] "Burial goods" are defined as "any objects or items interred with human remains at the time of burial." *Id.* 23–06–27(1)(a).

Reinterment Committee, comprised of representatives appointed by each tribal government to represent their respective tribe "in matters related to the deaccession and reinterment of human skeletal remains and associated grave goods."[143] Upon discovery of such remains or goods, or when a proposed undertaking may affect a site containing such items, the Committee attempts to determine the tribal identity or affiliation of the items and transfer them to the appropriate tribal government for reinterment.

South Dakota's law[144] directs the State Archaeologist to determine the direct relation to a tribal group[145] and to notify such group of the discovery of human remains and funerary objects.[146] The State Archaeologist must repatriate such remains and funerary objects upon request of the tribal group, provided such request is made within one year of notification.

Utah's statute, the Native American Graves Protection and Repatriation Act,[147] modeled after the federal law of the same name, is perhaps the most comprehensive state law dealing with Native American burial sites, remains, and cultural items. Utah's NAGPRA vests ownership and control of Native American remains that are discovered or excavated on state lands in the lineal descendants of the Native American. If the lineal descendants cannot be ascertained, ownership and control vests "in the Indian tribe that has the closest cultural affiliation[148] with the remains and that states a claim for the remains."[149] If the tribe with the closest cultural affiliation cannot be ascertained, ownership and control vests in the tribe that is recognized as aboriginally occupying the area in which the remains were discovered, if the tribe files a claim. Unclaimed remains are to be disposed of in consultation with Native American groups and other interested organizations.

The intentional removal or excavation of Native American remains on state lands is subject to a permit requirement, and such permits may only be issued after ownership and control have been determined. If Native American remains are inadvertently discovered during construction, agriculture, mining, logging, or other activity on state land, the activity must immediately cease, measures must be taken to protect the remains, and the appropriate state official must be notified. Scientific study of Native American remains may only be carried out with the consent of the owner of the remains as established under the Act. Utah's NAGPRA also establishes a Native American Remains Review Committee,[150] which is responsible

[143] N.D. Admin. Code 40–01–03–01(6) (2001).

[144] Cemeteries and Burial Records, S.D. Codified Laws Ann. 34–27–21 to –32 (Michie 2001).

[145] A "tribal group" is defined as "a federally recognized Indian tribe." *Id.* 34–27–21(4).

[146] "Funerary object" is defined as "any artifact or object which was intentionally placed with a deceased person, either at the time of burial or interment or at some subsequent time, and which is reasonably associated with human remains... or has been identified, through available evidence, as having been removed from a specific burial site in South Dakota." *Id.* 34–27–21(2).

[147] Utah Code Ann. 9–9–401–9–9–406 (1953).

[148] "Cultural affiliation" means that "there is a relationship of shared group identity that can be reasonably traced historically or prehistorically between a present day Indian tribe and an identifiable earlier group." *Id.* 9–9–402(2).

[149] *Id.* 9–9–403(1)(b).

[150] Like the NAGPRA Review Committee, the Utah Committee is composed of seven members. Four members are appointed by the director of the state Division of Indian Affairs on the basis of nominations submitted

for monitoring determinations concerning ownership of Native American remains, mediating disputes among lineal descendants, Indian tribes and state agencies relating to ownership or repatriation of remains, and consulting with Indian tribes concerning determinations of cultural affiliation, repatriation, care of remains, and other matters within the Committee's jurisdiction.

What happens when "little NAGPRA" laws of the states conflict with other state laws? That is the fundamental issue in the following opinion.

State Commissioner of Transportation v. Medicine Bird Black Bear White Eagle,
63 S.W.3d 734 (Tenn. 2001)

The Tennessee Department of Transportation sought to discontinue use of property, containing ancient Native American graves, as burial ground in order to widen an intersection of roads. The Chancery Court ruled that individual Native Americans, the Commission of Indian Affairs, and the executive director of the Commission were interested persons who could intervene in the proceeding. The following excerpts from the opinion discuss the jurisprudence pertaining to the human remains, with specific reference to the special status of Native American remains.

I.

COMMON-LAW PROTECTION OF BURIAL GROUNDS

We deal here with a most sensitive matter. Disputes regarding burial and disinterment touch deep-seated human emotions and evoke strongly held personal and religious beliefs. Where once persons looked to religion or custom for resolution of these disputes, now they look to the law to provide the neutral principles for resolving among the living disputes involving the disposition of the dead and the rights surrounding their remains.

A.

Since antiquity, most societies have held burial grounds in great reverence. *Memphis State Line R.R. v. Forest Hill Cemetery Co.*, 116 Tenn. 400, 418, 94 S.W. 69, 73 (1906) (observing that repositories of the dead are regarded with veneration); *see also In re Widening of Beekman Street*, 4 Bradf. Sur. R. 503, 522–23 (Sur. Ct. of N.Y. County 1856); *Mills v. Carolina Cemetery Park Corp.*, 242 N.C. 20, 86 S.E.2d 893, 898 (1955). The early common law protected the sanctity of the grave by recognizing the "right" to a decent burial and the "right" to undisturbed repose. *Carney v. Smith*, 222 Tenn. 472, 475, 437 S.W.2d 246, 247 (1969); *Thompson v. State*, 105 Tenn. 177, 180, 58 S.W. 213, 213 (1900). Accordingly, unless a good and substantial

by Indian tribes, and three members are appointed by the director on the basis of nominations submitted by museum representatives. *Id.* 9–9–405(2)(a).

reason existed, the common law strongly disfavored disturbing a body once it had been suitably buried. *Estes v. Woodlawn Mem'l Park, Inc.*, 780 S.W.2d 759, 763 (Tenn. Ct. App. 1989); *Mallen v. Mallen*, 520 S.W.2d 736, 737 (Tenn. Ct. App. 1974). In the words of Justice Cardozo, then a member of the New York Court of Appeals, "[t]he dead are to rest where they have been laid unless reason of substance is brought forward for disturbing their repose." *Yome v. Gorman*, 242 N.Y. 395, 152 N.E. 126, 129 (1926).

The right to undisturbed repose was not, however, absolute. *Mallen v. Mallen*, 520 S.W.2d at 737. The aphorism "Once a graveyard, always a graveyard" reflects custom only, not a rule of substantive law. *Trustees of First Presbyterian Church v. Alling*, 54 N.J. Super. 141, 148 A.2d 510, 514 (Ch. Div. 1959); Percival E. Jackson, *The Law of Cadavers* 395 (2d ed. 1950) ("Jackson"). Thus, American common law recognized that human remains could be disinterred and reinterred elsewhere when their burial place is no longer under the care of the living or has lost its character as a burial ground. *Hines v. State*, 126 Tenn. 1, 6, 149 S.W. 1058, 1060 (1911); *Memphis State Line R.R. v. Forest Hill Cemetery*, 116 Tenn. at 419, 94 S.W. at 73–74; *Boyd v. Ducktown Chem. & Iron Co.*, 19 Tenn. App. 392, 401, 89 S.W.2d 360, 365–66 (1935). The relatives of persons buried in an abandoned burial ground had only the right to due notice and the right to a reasonable opportunity to move their relative's body to some other place of their own selection. If the relatives declined to take responsibility for moving the human remains, others could see to it that the remains were disinterred and reinterred in a decent manner. *Dutto v. Forest Hill Cemetery*, 8 Tenn. C.C.A. (Higgins) 120, 133 (1917) (quoting *Bessemer Land & Improvement Co. v. Jenkins*, 111 Ala. 135, 18 So. 565 (1895)).

The common law permitted the disinterment of human remains when the demands of the living outweighed the right of undisturbed repose. Henry Y. Bernard, *The Law of Death and Disposal of the Dead* 4 (2d ed. 1979) ("Bernard"); Jackson, at 111. Accordingly, the common law did not place burial grounds beyond the power of eminent domain. *United States v. Unknown Heirs of All Persons Buried in Post Oak Mission Cemetery*, 152 F. Supp. 452, 453 (W.D. Okla. 1957) (authorizing the reinterment of the widow and children of the last chief of the Comanche Indians); *In re Widening of Beekman Street*, 4 Bradf. Sur. R. at 503; Bernard, at 4; Jackson, at 404; C.J. Polson et al., *The Disposal of the Dead* 205–06 (1953) ("Polson"). . . .

B.

Prehistoric humans showed indifference to the dead by abandoning their bodies where they died. Polson, at 3. As time passed, the fear of death, the belief in life after death, and the unclean nature of dead bodies began to shape human burial practices. Superstition and religion played a significant role. Sir James G. Frazier, *The Golden Bough*, preface vii (1 vol. abridged ed. 1996); Polson, at 4–5; Note, *Criminal Law – Right to Autopsy in Murder Prosecutions*, 24 Tenn. L. Rev. 385, 385 (1956). The first active burials amounted to placing a pile of stones over the body or placing the body in a cave when one was available. These practices were later replaced by burial in the earth which has continued to be the principal method of disposing of human remains throughout the world. Polson, at 3.

In pre-Christian England, the dead were buried far from towns and cities. With the arrival of Christianity came the custom of burial in and around church buildings. Prominent persons were buried in the churches themselves. Eventually, every person in England, except executed felons, heretics, and persons who took their own lives, had a right to be buried in the consecrated ground of a parish churchyard. *In re Widening of Beekman Street*, 4 Bradf. Sur. R. at 518; Jackson, at 12–13, 24, 57–58.

Between the sixth and thirteenth centuries, as the custom of burial in churchyards became more widespread, the church's ecclesiastical courts gradually extracted jurisdiction over all matters relating to burial from the common-law courts. Eventually, the ecclesiastical courts exercised exclusive temporal jurisdiction over these matters. *In re Widening of Beekman Street*, 4 Bradf. Sur. R. at 518; Jackson, at 22. Disinterring human remains without lawful authority was a common-law misdemeanor and was also an ecclesiastical offense. Polson, at 187. For human remains buried in consecrated ground, permission to disinter could be obtained only from the bishop of the diocese having jurisdiction over the burial ground and then only if the remains were to be reinterred in consecrated ground. For human remains not buried in consecrated ground, permission had to be obtained from the coroner, and the coroner granted permission only for the purpose of conducting an inquest. The ecclesiastical courts' jurisdiction did not begin to wane until Parliament enacted the Burial Acts of 1855 which invested the Crown's Principal Secretaries of State with authority over human remains buried in unconsecrated ground and any other exhumation for purposes other than reburial in consecrated ground. Polson, at 187–205; *see also* Anne R. Schiff, *Arising from the Dead: Challenges to Posthumous Procreation*, 75 N.C. L. Rev. 901, 923 (1997).

Many of the English burial customs found their way to America. Even though the colonists did not have the same right to be buried in a churchyard that their counterparts in England had, interment in churchyards was the most common mode of burial, followed by family burial grounds and, later, public cemeteries. Jackson, at 14. The states did not incorporate the English ecclesiastical law when they incorporated the common law. . . .

In this country today, the civil courts have unquestioned jurisdiction to resolve disputes involving the burial and reinterment of human remains. *Wolf v. Rose Hill Cemetery Ass'n*, 832 P.2d 1007, 1008 (Colo. Ct. App. 1991); *Louisville & Nashville R.R. v. Wilson*, 123 Ga. 62, 51 S.E. 24, 25–26 (1905); *Sherman v. Sherman*, 330 N.J. Super. 638, 750 A.2d 229, 233 (1999); *Whitehair v. Highland Memory Gardens, Inc.*, 327 S.E.2d at 441. It is now commonly said that human remains, after interment, are in the custody of the law, and are subject to the control and discretion of the courts applying equitable principles. *Estes v. Woodlawn Mem'l Park, Inc.*, 780 S.W.2d at 762–63; *see also In re Estate of Medlen*, 286 Ill. App. 3d 860, 222 Ill.

Dec. 220, 677 N.E.2d 33, 36 (1997); *Harris v. Borough of Fair Haven*, 317 N.J. Super. 226, 721 A.2d 758, 762 (1998).

The courts must employ neutral legal principles to resolve disputes among the living involving the disposition of human remains. *Mallen v. Mallen*, 520 S.W.2d at 737. In the search for these principles, the courts should not close their eyes to the customs and necessities of civilizations in dealing with the dead and the sentiments connected with the decent care and disposal of human remains. *Mallen v. Mallen*, 520 S.W.2d at 737; *see also Louisville & Nashville R.R. v. Wilson*, 51 S.E. at 25; *Goldman v. Mollen*, 168 Va. 345, 191 S.E. 627, 632 (1937). However, while the courts should respect the rights of persons to freely exercise their religion, *Wolf v. Rose Hill Cemetery Ass'n*, 832 P.2d at 1009, they must not permit the civil law to be circumscribed or superceded by the canon law of any particular religion. *Mallen v. Mallen*, 520 S.W.2d at 737. Religious customs, laws, and beliefs regarding the disposition of human remains are to be considered only for the purpose of producing an equitable result. . . .

The late 1940s and early 1950s marked dramatic growth in the construction of roads in the nation and in Tennessee. In 1949, most likely to facilitate the construction of an expanded network of rural roads, the General Assembly expanded the power of public authorities to condemn real property containing burial grounds, to relocate the human remains in the burial grounds, and to put the property to other uses.

In 1990, both the General Assembly of Tennessee and the Congress enacted additional statutes governing Native American human remains and funerary objects. First, the Tennessee General Assembly strengthened the State's protection of these artifacts. This legislation added three Native American members to the Archeological Advisory Committee [Tenn. Code Ann. § 11–6–103(c)(4) (1999)] and outlawed the display of Native American human remains except when used as evidence in judicial proceedings [Tenn. Code Ann. §§ 11–6–104(b), – 117 (1999)]. It also required prompt reporting of the discovery of human remains to the Department of Environment and Conservation [Tenn. Code Ann. § 11–6–107(d)(3) (1999)] and gave Native Americans the right to be present during the excavation of Native American human remains [Tenn. Code Ann. § 11–6–116(a)].

Unlike statutes in other states giving Native Americans veto power over the disinterment of Native American remains, Tennessee's statutes envision that human remains and funerary objects may be removed and appropriately reinterred.[151] Tenn. Code Ann. § 11–6–107(d)(4) requires the State to

[151] Every state has enacted statutes pertaining to ancient or historic human remains, including Native American remains. Only one state, Washington, prohibits relocation of ancient human remains altogether. Most states require notice to some government commission or agency such as a state museum, state archeologist or archeological society, the department of anthropology at a state university, or a Native American board or commission. Thirty-four of these states require some sort of governmental approval before relocating the human remains. Seventeen states require permission of the landowner. Five states, Idaho, Massachusetts, Minnesota, Missouri, and Oregon, give a Native American tribe veto power over the removal and reinterment of the human remains.

take control of Native American human remains and that they be reinterred as provided in Tenn. Code Ann. § 11–6–119 (1999) or Tenn. Code Ann. §§ 46–4–101, –104. Tenn. Code Ann. § 11–6–116(c) requires persons intending to close a burial ground containing Native American human remains to give ten days written notice to the State Archeologist and requires the State archeologist to promptly notify the Native American members of the Archeological Advisory Commission and the chair of the Commission of Indian Affairs. Finally, Tenn. Code Ann. § 11–6–119 provides that Native American human remains and funerary objects "shall be properly reburied . . . in accordance with procedures formulated by the advisory council which are appropriate to Native American traditions."[152]

---

c. Other Approaches: South Africa, Australia, New Zealand, and Canada

Ryan M. Seidemann, *Bones of Contention: A Comparative Examination of Law Governing Human Remains from Archaeological Contexts in Formerly Colonial Countries*, 64 La. L. Rev. 545 (2004)

South Africa

As with many other previously colonial nations, South Africa has begun to take an interest in the disposition and protection of its indigenous dead derived from archaeological contexts. Prior to 1999, South African legislation dealing directly with human remains was limited to the National Monuments Act (NMA). This legislation only provided protection for the graves of individuals who lived before 1652.[153] The NMA further protected "all graves of people who died in wars up to 1914, and gravestones older than 50 years." Rather bizarre crenulations in the law left post-1652 graves (other than the graves of war dead) and their contents unprotected unless they were independently declared a national monument. Thus, as noted by Deacon, "[o]ddly, if a grave is marked by a gravestone older than 50 years, the gravestone is protected as a 'historic site,' but the human remains are not."

This rather counterintuitive approach to grave protection changed in 1999 with the passage of the National Heritage Resources Act (NHRA). Such a drastic change in the law regarding the protection of old graves, as NHRA is, should be viewed in light of a general increase in the interest

[152] The Department has promulgated regulations intended to ensure that Native American human remains are properly reinterred in accordance with "original and/or traditional customs." When documentation exists that specifies the original manner of burial, reburial must be carried out in the same manner. Tenn. Comp. R. & Regs. r. 0400–9–1-.01(1) (1999). When documentation does not exist, reburial must be done in subsurface grave pits at such a depth to prevent further disturbance, and the human remains must be placed directly into the soil. Tenn. Comp. R. & Regs. r. 0400–9–1.01(2). These reburial areas must be as close to the original burial area as possible, Tenn. Comp. R. & Regs. r. 0400–9–1-.02 (1999), and must be suitably recorded and demarcated. Tenn. Comp. R. & Regs. r. 0400–9–1-.02, – 03.

[153] The time of the arrival of European settlers. H.J. de Blij & Peter O. Muller, Geography: Realms, Regions, and Concepts 362 (1997).

in protecting and establishing a national heritage in many post-colonial African nations at about the same time.[154]

Unlike the NAGPRA legislation in the United States, the South African NHRA is not specifically aimed at the protection of indigenous graves. Rather, it is directed at the general protection of "heritage resources," including archaeology, architecture, graves, and other items of "cultural significance." There are, however, several parts of the NHRA that specifically address the disposition of excavated and curated human remains.

The lax protections of the NMA, discussed *supra*, have been bolstered by the NHRA that provides a blanket protection of all graves older than 60 years. Indeed, section 35(2) reserves all archaeological resources as state property and, if culturally significant, they are to be administered by heritage resource authorities. This is certainly broader than the NAGPRA legislation, which is limited to federal property only. Not only does the NHRA apply to archaeological resources yet to be excavated, but section 35(7)(a) also requires resources held by those other than museums or universities who did not obtain the resources pursuant to NHRA, NMA, or similar provincial legislation, to register a list of the items with a governmental heritage resources authority. This provision reaches deeply into the private realm, presumably to identify the whereabouts of years' worth of looted materials. Despite these protections, Deacon and Deacon point out that "[t]he descendants of the indigenous people . . . have no particular legal claim to [heritage objects and sites] and have an equal status regarding the protection of this heritage with any other interested party." Thus, while new protections exist in South Africa, they do not empower the indigenous population in the protection of their heritage, but rather reduce remains to objects to be dealt with under property rights regimes. Although this lack of indigenous control (beyond anyone else's control) is present in the disposition of existing collections, as will be demonstrated, indigenous groups are not so powerless as to the protection of remains discovered in situ.

More specific to the topic of this study are the contents of section 36, the rules for burial grounds and graves. This section vests in SAHRA the authority to protect and conserve any burial grounds and graves not covered by another authority. This section distinguishes between two types of burials: victims of conflict and other graves older than 60 years. Section 36(3) protects both categories from destruction, damage, alteration, exhumation, removal, or even disturbance from above in the form of excavation equipment or metal detection. Such areas can only be disturbed, in any capacity, if SAHRA (or a provincial heritage resources authority)

[154] Scott MacEachern notes substantial activity in the development of archaeology and national heritage construction in such nations as South Africa, Zimbabwe, Namibia, and Mozambique with the ending of colonial rule in the latter twentieth century. Indeed, MacEachern notes that "[c]olonial ideologies that belittled African cultural achievements and distorted Africa's history to political ends have gradually been discarded." Scott MacEachern, *Cultural Resource Management and Africanist Archaeology*, 75 Antiquity 866, 868 (2001). Presumably, such a revolution in cultural awareness prompted a reexamination of the protections of cultural heritage such as those contained in the NMA.

issues a permit for such work subject to the requirement of reasonable arrangements being in place for exhumation and reburial. More importantly, section 36(5) mandates that, prior to the issuance of a permit, SAHRA must ensure that the applicant for the permit has:

(a) made a concerted effort to contact and consult communities and individuals who by tradition have an interest in such grave or burial ground; and
(b) reached arrangements with such communities and individuals regarding the future of such grave or burial ground.

This section gives indigenous groups a unique amount of control over the disposition of the remains of their ancestors, discovered in situ, that they do not have with remains that have already been excavated.

Finally, NHRA section 36(6) requires notice to SAHRA and local law enforcement authorities if an unmarked burial is discovered in the course of development. The NHRA requires an identification investigation of the remains to occur in order to decide the ultimate disposition of the find.

With respect to the remains of "victims of conflict," SAHRA is charged with further duties. "Victims of conflict" is defined in section 2(xviii) as:

(a) persons who died in any area now included in the Republic as a result of any war or conflict . . . , but excluding victims of conflict covered by the Commonwealth War Graves Act, 1992;
(b) members of the forces of Great Britain and the former British Empire who died in active service in any area now included in the Republic prior to 4 August 1914;
(c) persons who, during the Anglo-Boer War (1899–1902) were removed as prisoners of war from any area now included in the Republic to any place outside South Africa and who died there; and
(d) certain persons who died in the 'liberation struggle' . . . in areas included in the Republic as well as outside the Republic.

For these individuals, not only is SAHRA charged with protecting their final resting places as discussed *supra*, but they are also responsible for "assist[ing] other State Departments in identifying graves in a foreign country of victims of conflict connected with the liberation struggle." Following such identification, SAHRA, with the permission of the next of kin, "may re-inter the remains of that person in a prominent place in the capital of the Republic."

While the NHRA appears to provide more substantial protection than the United States' NAGPRA legislation with respect to in situ remains, NHRA's provisions concerning the repatriation of remains curated in museums and institutions is a bit more vague than those of NAGPRA and the National Museum of the American Indian Act (NMAIA). Section 41(1) reads:

> When a community or body with a bona fide interest makes a claim for the restitution of a movable heritage resource which is part of the national estate and is held by or curated in a publicly funded

> institution, the institution concerned must enter into a process of negotiation with the claimants regarding the future of the resource.

Although this section does not directly address human remains, it appears that, through a four-step process beginning with section 41(1), interested groups can make a NAGPRA-like claim to such remains or other materials. From section 41(1), one must look to section 2(xvi) to find the definition of a "heritage resource." A "heritage resource" is defined as "any place or object of cultural significance." "Object" is defined in section 2(xxix) as:

> any movable property of cultural significance which may be protected in terms of this Act including
>
> (a) any archaeological artifact;
> (b) palaeontological and rare geological specimens;
> (c) meteorites; and
> (d) other objects referred to in section 3.

Among the other objects referred to in section 3 are:

> graves and burial grounds, including
>
> (i) ancestral graves;
> (ii) royal graves of traditional leaders;
> (iii) graves of victims of conflict;
> (iv) graves of individuals designated by the Minister by notice in the Gazette;
> (v) historical graves and cemeteries; and
> (vi) other human remains which are not covered in terms of the Human Tissue Act, 1983.

Thus, from section 41(1), through sections 2(xvi) and 2(xxix), to section 3(2)(g), it appears that South Africa's NHRA allows for repatriation of remains and objects of cultural patrimony in much the same way as the United States' NAGPRA legislation does. However, repatriation is not mandatory under NHRA, only negotiation for repatriation. Interestingly, although NHRA requires registration of privately held resources and protects graves on private property, like NAGPRA, it has no power to repatriate items from private possessors.

New Zealand

The interest by New Zealand's indigenous population, the Maori, in the repatriation of the remains of their ancestors has surfaced much more recently than similar movements in Australia and the United States. In the early to mid-1990s, a "rise in Maori ethnic consciousness" forced the New Zealand government to reassess its treatment of its indigenous population. Cultural ties of modern Maori people (when considered as a culturally homogeneous group) to the remains currently held in museums around the world as well as those potentially unearthed during construction or other excavations are temporally closer than many of those in the United

States and Australia.[155] Much of the repatriation activity over the past five years by the Maori has focused on the return of toi moko [preserved tattooed human heads] from museums abroad. However, more recent efforts have resulted in the return of skeletal remains to New Zealand.

With respect to the disposition of human remains of Maori affiliation within New Zealand, the situation is somewhat different. The law that governs such materials is the Historic Places Act (HPA). The HPA is more powerful than the United States' federal legislation that protects areas of historic significance because it applies its protections equally to Crown property as well as private property. However, in contrast to NAGPRA that protects things regardless of age, New Zealand's HPA only protects archaeological sites "associated with human activity that occurred before 1900." It is likely that this 100-plus-year gap in protection, at least of human remains, is covered by the other acts mentioned above. At a minimum, it seems that [the] Maori could assert property interests in remains positively identified to be of Maori origin through the Treaty of Waitangi. The Treaty of Waitangi, still partially in force, was signed by the British Crown and various Maori tribes in 1840. The Treaty established British sovereignty over all New Zealand, but retained to the Maori "full, exclusive, and undisturbed possession of their Lands and Estates, Forests, Fisheries, and other properties which they may collectively or individually possess. . . . " Human remains may, arguably, fall under the "other properties" portion of the Treaty of Waitangi. A literal translation of the Maori version of the Treaty seems to give stronger support to this notion. The literal translation reads: "The Queen of England agrees to protect the chiefs, the subtribes and all the people of New Zealand in the unqualified exercise of their chieftainship over their lands, villages, and all their treasures."

In situ human (and archaeological) remains are protected from destruction, damage, or modification before archaeological and Maori values of the site can be determined. Where an application for the destruction or alteration of an archaeological site is submitted to the New Zealand Historic Places Trust, and the site is considered to be of Maori interest, "the Trust shall refer that application to the Maori Heritage Council to make such recommendations as the Council may consider appropriate." Such requirements vest substantial power regarding the protection of in situ remains in the Maori, a factor not always present in current United States legislation. This also applies to the conduct of legitimate archaeological investigations.

[155] This is because the culturally distinct Maori arrived on New Zealand circa 1000 CE as compared to the culturally unidentifiable (at least in terms of analogues to modern peoples) populations of the United States (circa 13,000 BP) and Australia (circa 40,000 BP). For recent radiocarbon dating information on old New World and Pacific sites, *see* Thomas D. Dillehay, The Settlement of the Americas: A New Prehistory 295–321 (2000); Geoffrey Irwin, The Prehistoric Exploration and Colonisation of the Pacific 5, 78 (1992). "BP" here refers to years before present, where present is defined by the radiocarbon present of 1950 CE. *See generally* Minze Stuiver & Paula J. Reimer, CALIB 4.1 Manual, available at http://depts.washington.edu/qil/calib/manual/ (last visited Oct. 9, 2002).

Despite the broad reach of the Maori voice in the protection of relevant in situ archaeological remains, there is no legislation in New Zealand that provides for the repatriation of human remains or other archaeologically derived materials from any museum to affiliated Maori groups, [but New Zealand museums appear to] respect any Maori request for the return of such material.

Australia

In much the same atmosphere as NAGPRA was passed in the United States in 1990, the Australian Parliament passed the Aboriginal and Torres Strait Islander Heritage Protection Act of 1984 (ATSIHPA). The sentiments of the Aboriginal people, generally, include a desire for research on Aboriginal remains to cease and for a return of curated collections to the indigenous communities. This long-held assertion for the return of Aboriginal remains has not wavered over the past twenty or so years, resulting in the return of collections of ancient remains.

As is the case in NAGPRA, the ATSIHPA has no temporal limit on protections of graves and curated museum collections. This similarity marks a significant encroachment onto the understanding and interpretation of all human history, as the remains of individuals potentially as old as 40,000 years are subject to repatriation. Successful claims have already been asserted by Aboriginal groups to remains dated to 15,000 years old. Such claims to remains that are 40,000 years old begin to reach into the realm of paleoanthropology, thus putting Aboriginal property claims on the order of modern Europeans claiming repatriation rights to Neandert[h]al skeletal material.

This claim to ancient remains is based largely on Aboriginal religious beliefs that their people have inhabited the continent of Australia since the Dreamtime,[156] and thus have a cultural claim to any human remains, regardless of age. The Aboriginal community is generally unimpressed "by assertions that 'some heritage is universal property,'" thus rejecting scientific beliefs that ancient remains should be studied as belonging to a broader community of all humanity as part of our common heritage as Homo sapiens.

It was within this social atmosphere in 1984 that Australia passed ATSIHPA. ATSIHPA works much like NAGPRA in that it is a federal law that preempts any state or territory law on the subject of Aboriginal heritage protection. Although never overtly referring to the "protection" and "repatriation" of Aboriginal human remains, ATSIHPA provides a substantial range of protection for such materials from "injury or desecration" throughout the Commonwealth. This protection occurs via several provisions of ATSIHPA, namely: sections 3(1), 12, 20, and 21. Section 12 deals with the protection of "significant Aboriginal objects." "Significant

[156] "The Dreamtime is the era of creation, the time of the great Spirit Ancestors, who have profoundly influenced the traditional pattern of life as Aborigines know it today. The myths tell the story of human origins in Australia." Josephine Flood, Archaeology of the Dreamtime: The Story of Prehistoric Australia and its People 9 (1990).

Aboriginal object" is defined in section 3(1) as "an object (including Aboriginal remains) of particular significance to Aboriginals in accordance with Aboriginal tradition." "Aboriginal remains," also defined in section 3(1):

> means the whole or part of the bodily remains of an Aboriginal, but does not include:
>
> (a) a body or remains of a body:
> (i) buried in accordance with the law of a State or Territory; or
> (ii) buried in land that is, in accordance with Aboriginal tradition, used or recognized as a burial ground. . .

For purposes of clarification, "Aboriginal" is defined in §3(1) as "a member of the Aboriginal race of Australia, and includes a descendant of the indigenous inhabitants of the Torres Strait Islands."

Under section 12, in situ or curated Aboriginal remains are eligible for a "declaration" if they are in danger of "injury or desecration." Such a declaration provides for "the protection and preservation of the object or objects from injury or desecration" and may provide for the delivery of the remains to "an Aboriginal . . . entitled to, and willing to accept, possession, custody or control of the remains in accordance with Aboriginal tradition." A declaration will only be made by the Minister after receipt of an application "made orally or in writing by or on behalf of an Aboriginal or a group of Aboriginals seeking the preservation or protection of a specified object or class of objects from injury or desecration." The issuance of such a declaration is also subject to a consideration of non-Aboriginal interests in the object(s). In terms of "injury or desecration," section 3(2)(b) defines such mistreatment of an object as an occasion when "it is used or treated in a manner inconsistent with Aboriginal tradition." Under the objections to scientific research discussed *supra* by the Aboriginal community, it is not a substantial leap to expect declarations to issue against museums or other institutions curating or excavating Aboriginal remains under the guise that such activity is "inconsistent with Aboriginal tradition."

Under section 20, the inadvertent discovery of remains suspected to be Aboriginal is covered. These materials are protected by a requirement of reporting the discovery to the Minister and a requirement that the Minister consult with relevant Aboriginal peoples. Section 21 covers the ultimate disposition of remains delivered to the Minister. Such remains are to be returned "to an Aboriginal or Aboriginals entitled to, and willing to accept, possession, custody or control of the remains in accordance with Aboriginal tradition." In instances where no such return is possible, the remains are to be dealt with "in accordance with any reasonable directions of an Aboriginal or Aboriginals referred to in paragraph (a)"; or in the event that no such people exist, the remains are to be transferred "to a prescribed authority for safekeeping."

The regulations of human remains in Victoria largely follow the provisions for the rest of the Commonwealth, discussed *supra*. However, section

21L provides for the taking of such remains from private individuals. Local Magistrates also have relatively broad powers to enter and search for remains. Section 21X of ATSIHPA specifically and explicitly addresses the repatriation of Aboriginal remains from "a university, museum, or other institution." This section, much more broad in scope than the United States' NAGPRA, does not require any showing of cultural affiliation in order to reclaim remains so held. The only restriction is a spatial one. The remains must have been found or have come from the area around the claiming Aboriginal community. Like NAGPRA, there is also no mention of any temporal restriction to such claims.

Canada

Canada has not escaped the worldwide surge of indigenous civil rights. Confrontations between the archaeological and indigenous communities in Canada have occurred much the same as in the previously discussed nations. The anger among the First Nations[157] communities regarding the disposition of skeletal remains has been directed at the archaeological community, developers, and the government. Baikie points out the unjust discrepancy between these interested groups in Canada:

> A few years back, skeletal remains of some American soldiers were found in southern Canada. Upon their discovery, a full military burial was planned and initiated. Why are Aboriginal remains held in storage or displayed, and what is the purpose of this? What would the reaction be if Inuit were to come to St. John's, go down to one of the local burial grounds, and dig up some remains, bring them back to northern Labrador and display some of the skeletons and put the rest in storage in the name of archaeological research?

Although some of the confrontations and negotiations between the First Nations communities and archaeologists have ultimately resulted in the reburial of skeletal remains, Canada's indigenous peoples have a reputation for being much more interested in involvement and in benefiting from Western scientific analyses of their ancestors' remains than those groups in the United States and Australia.

Canada presents a unique legal situation in terms of laws relating to the protection and repatriation of indigenous human skeletal remains. There is no national law governing such remains in Canada. Neal Ferris, an archaeologist in Ontario's Ministry of Culture, suggests that this absence of federal law "is in part due to jurisdiction issues (provinces like states, are responsible for heritage off federal lands) . . . partly due to the lack of willingness [of the federal government] to grapple with such a complex issue, and partly due to major research institutions . . . being proactive and developing their own repatriation policies in [t]he absence of legislation."

[157] [The term] First Nations, and sometimes First Peoples, [is] used by indigenous groups and the Canadian government (Constitution Act §35(2)) to refer to the Indian and Inuit groups that originally inhabited Canada and their descendants. Catherine Bell, *Aboriginal Claims to Cultural Property in Canada: A Comparative Legal Analysis of the Repatriation Debate*, 17 Am. Ind. L. Rev. 457, 522 n.3 (1992).

Part of this void in legislation is also filled by ethical mandates of national professional organizations such as the Canadian Archaeological Association and the Canadian Museums Association.

Many of the individual provinces and territories have developed their own management legislation to deal with human remains. It is outside of the scope of this paper to undertake a province-by-province examination of legislation dealing with the protection and repatriation of indigenous skeletal remains.

The absence of some minimum national standard is disconcerting to both the indigenous and archaeological communities. Out of respect for the First Nations, it is past time for Canada to promulgate federal legislation aimed at the protection of indigenous skeletal remains. The lack of certainty about the outcome of a particular situation makes it virtually impossible for these communities to effectively deal with situations as they arise. Indeed, Ferris notes that "[i]t is . . . generally less than satisfying to either archaeologists or First Nations . . . how an individual case of burial discovery and disposition of those remains goes is as wide a spectrum as you can imagine." As asserted by Baikie, "[b]oth federal and provincial legislation should change to enhance [indigenous] involvement in archaeology." At an absolute minimum, federal legislation is needed to establish a universal minimum standard for dealing with repatriation issues so as to avoid protracted legal battles between scientists and First Nations communities.

Vermillion Accord on Human Relations

Following a suggestion by the International Law Association's Committee on Cultural Heritage Law, another avenue for independently addressing the problems of drafting national or international laws dealing with repatriation may be to consider codes of ethics of professional organizations. The Vermillion Accord on Human Remains (Vermillion Accord), created by the World Archaeological Congress (WAC), represents the only international agreement among the anthropological and indigenous communities on the issue of human remains.

World Archaeological Congress, The Vermillion Accord on Human Remains(1989)

1. Respect for the mortal remains of the dead shall be accorded to all, irrespective of origin, race, religion, nationality, custom and tradition.
2. Respect for the wishes of the dead concerning disposition shall be accorded whenever possible, reasonable and lawful, when they are known or can be reasonably inferred.
3. Respect for the wishes of the local community and of relatives or guardians of the dead shall be accorded whenever possible, reasonable and lawful.
4. Respect for the scientific research value of skeletal, mummified and other human remains (including fossil hominids) shall be accorded when such value is demonstrated to exist.

5. Agreement on the disposition of fossil, skeletal, mummified and other remains shall be reached by negotiation on the basis of mutual respect for the legitimate concerns of communities for the proper disposition of their ancestors, as well as the legitimate concerns of science and education.
6. The express recognition that the concerns of various ethnic groups, as well as those of science are legitimate and to be respected, will permit acceptable agreements to be reached and honoured.

NOTES AND QUESTIONS

1. Despite strong protest from scientists, the Canadian Museum of Civilization decided to allow the Algonquin First Nation in Quebec to rebury remains from ninety skeletons dating back at least five thousand years. The bones were excavated in the 1960s from the Morrison Island encampment near Ottawa, one of North America's most significant Stone Age sites. Museum officials contended that the remains could not be reliably affiliated with any modern-day native group and that reburial would constitute a serious scientific loss including an opportunity for DNA analysis. The museum nevertheless agreed to turn them over to the First Nation group because "our museum depends on good relationships with aboriginal communities." See Randy Boswell, *Reburial of Aboriginal Bones a Grave Loss to Science*, EDMONTON J., June 12, 2005, at A2. Do you agree that the need for an institution to maintain good relations with an indigenous group should outweigh the interests of the scientific community and the public? However, wasn't forty years or so, since excavation of the Canadian remains, long enough for scientific analysis? Or should human remains be made available to scientists for as long as new scientific techniques, such as DNA analysis, become available?
2. We have now looked at five national approaches to indigenous claims of repatriation. How do they differ from one another? As compared with NAGPRA, do the approaches taken in South Africa, New Zealand, Australia, and Canada have any particular strengths or weaknesses?

B. Criminal Justice

UNITED STATES v. LIGON, 440 F.3d 1182 (9th Cir. 2006)

Defendants John Ligon and Carroll Mizell appeal their felony convictions under 18 U.S.C. § 641 for theft of government property. They contend, inter alia, that the government did not prove that the property had a "value" within the meaning of § 641. We agree and reverse the convictions.

I. Factual Background

The United States Forest Service ("USFS") posted a reward for information concerning the theft of several Native American petroglyphs that had been removed from an unmarked site on the side of a mountain in northwest Reno. Acting on a tip received under a "secret witness" program, Reno police found two of the petroglyphs prominently displayed in the front yard of Ligon's home, and a third in the back of his Suburban vehicle parked at his home.

USFS special agents then interviewed Ligon and Mizell. Ligon explained that he drove out to the mountainside and used a winch and a roller device to pull the three "rocks" out. He admitted that he never sought permission or advice before taking the rocks, and that he excavated them after dark. He claimed that he took the rocks in order to protect them from being "bowled over" by an encroaching construction development, and to display them in his front yard. Mizell stated that he went to the mountainside with Ligon, and he corroborated that the winch and roller device had been used to extract the petroglyphs and move them to Ligon's yard. A USFS special agent found a pry bar on the mountainside near where the petroglyphs had been, but neither Ligon nor Mizell mentioned using this tool.

A grand jury indicted Ligon and Mizell for removing archaeological resources in violation of 16 U.S.C. § 470ee (Count I), and stealing United States government property in violation of 18 U.S.C. § 641 (Count II). Count I charged that each defendant "did knowingly excavate, remove, damage and otherwise alter and deface archaeological resources located on public lands . . . without having a permit to do so, and commercial and archaeological value and the cost of restoration and repair of said resources exceed[ed] the sum of $500." Count II charged that the defendants "did willfully and knowingly steal . . . three petroglyph rocks . . . having a value in excess of $1,000, and which was then and there the property of the United States[.]" The jury acquitted Ligon and Mizell of Count I, but found them both guilty of knowingly stealing property valued at more than $1,000 under Count II.

Before trial, a USFS archaeologist prepared a report that included an estimate of "commercial or fair market value" by Mark Bahti, the owner of "Bahti Indian Arts," a commercial art gallery in Tucson, Arizona. Bahti's report was based on photographs of the petroglyphs. Noting that they had been "badly scarred in the removal process," Bahti estimated their retail value at $800 or $900. He "conservatively" estimated that they could be sold for $1,500 if they were in good condition.

The government did not introduce Bahti's report at trial. In fact, the government introduced no evidence at all of market or other monetary value of the petroglyphs. For both Counts I and II, it relied only on "archaeological value," a valuation concept that considers the worth of archaeological information. A USFS archaeologist testified that the petroglyphs had an archaeological value in the $8,000 range, and a USFS special agent testified that she could not determine a "commercial value" for the petroglyphs, even after contacting numerous sources. The jury instruction on property value for Count II provided: "On the valuation issue as to Count Two, the government relies on archaeological value."

At the close of evidence, the defendants moved for judgments of acquittal on Count II under Federal Rule of Criminal Procedure 29(a) on the ground that the government had introduced no evidence of value within the meaning of § 641. The district court took the motions under advisement and submitted the cases to the jury. After the jury returned verdicts of guilty on Count II, defendants renewed their motions for acquittal, now as Rule 29(c) motions. Defendants attached copies of Bahti's report to their renewed motions. The district court denied the motions.

II. Discussion

[1] Section 641 criminalizes the theft of a "thing of value of the United States." 18 U.S.C. § 641. The statute provides two tiers of penalties depending on the value of the stolen property. If the value exceeds $1,000, the court can sentence the defendant to a maximum of ten years in prison. *Id.* Since this offense is "punishable" by a term of imprisonment "exceeding one year," it constitutes a felony. 18 U.S.C. § 1(1). If the value is $1,000 or less, however, the maximum sentence is one year, 18 U.S.C. § 641, which makes the offense a misdemeanor. 18 U.S.C. § 1(2). Regardless of whether the government charges a felony or a misdemeanor, value is an element of the offense, and the government must prove that the property stolen had "value." *United States v. Seaman*, 18 F.3d 649, 650 (9th Cir. 1994) (noting that "value" is an element of a § 641 offense).

Section 641 defines "value" as "face, par, or market value, or cost price, either wholesale or retail, whichever is greater." 18 U.S.C. § 641. The historical and statutory notes to § 641 indicate that the 1948 drafters adopted this definition "to conform with that provided in section 2311 of this title." Construing § 2311, we have found that "where goods have no readily ascertainable market value, 'any reasonable method may be employed to ascribe an equivalent monetary value to the items.'" *United States v. Drebin*, 557 F.2d 1316, 1331 (9th Cir. 1977) (quoting *United States v. Lester*, 282 F.2d 750, 755 (3d Cir. 1960)). In a more recent § 641 case, we interpreted "market value" to include value in a so-called "thieves' market":

> In the absence of face or par value, property value is determined by market forces which establish the price at which a buyer is willing to offer the property to a willing seller. As there is no commercial market for [the property in question in this case], however, comparisons with similar transactions in a conventional market do not exist to assess the value of this particular sale. In such cases, the property's value in an illegal market may be considered. This gives § 641 its obvious, and certainly its practical, meaning, namely, the amount the goods may bring to the thief.

United States v. Bigelow, 728 F.2d 412, 413–14 (9th Cir. 1984) (citations and internal quotation marks omitted).

[2] The government did not rely on the definition of "value" in § 641. Instead, it entirely relied on "archaeological value," as that term is used in 16 U.S.C. §§ 470ee(d) and 470ff(a)(2)(A), for proof of value under 18 U.S.C. § 641. The following colloquy between the district court and the

government during the discussion of the defendants' Rule 29(a) motions makes this clear:

> THE COURT: Is there evidence in this case on the market value?
> MR. GIFFORD[for the government]: No, Your Honor.
> . . . .
> MR. GIFFORD: We only presented archaeological value, Your Honor. And that's all we're –
> THE COURT: Okay. Is there anything here on par value?
> MR. RACHOW[for the government]: Your Honor, there's no definition of par value.
> THE COURT: Is there anything on face value?
> MR. GIFFORD: No, Your Honor.
> THE COURT: Okay. So what you're relying on is the archaeological value and asking that that be extrapolated and used for purposes of Count Two in establishing the value, is that correct?
> MR. GIFFORD: Yes, Your Honor.

Congress coined the term "archaeological value" when it passed the Archaeological Resources Protection Act ("ARPA") in 1979. ARPA protects "archaeological resources and sites which are on public lands and Indian lands." 16 U.S.C. § 470aa(b). Violators of ARPA are subject to penalties that vary depending on the "commercial or archaeological value of the archaeological resources involved" and the "cost of restoration and repair." *Id.* §§ 470ee(d), 470ff(a)(2).

[3] Regulations promulgated pursuant to ARPA define "archaeological value" as the value of archaeological information rather than the value of archaeological artifacts. These regulations share the following definition:

> Archaeological value. For the purposes of this part, the archaeological value of any archaeological resource . . . shall be the *value of the information associated with the archaeological resource.* This value shall be appraised in terms of the costs of the retrieval of the scientific information which would have been obtainable prior to the violation. These costs may include, but need not be limited to, the cost of preparing a research design, conducting field work, carrying out laboratory analysis, and preparing reports as would be necessary to realize the information potential.

18 C.F.R § 1312.14(a); 32 C.F.R. § 229.14(a); 36 C.F.R. § 296.14(a); 43 C.F.R. § 7.14(a) (emphasis added). "Archaeological value" is based on an analysis that "go[es] back in time before the violation occurred and estimate[s] what it would have cost the United States to engage in a full-blown archaeological dig at the site" in order to obtain the archaeological information. *United States v. Quarrell*, 310 F.3d 664, 679 (10th Cir. 2002) (citation omitted).

"Archaeological value," so defined, is not the equivalent of, nor is it encompassed by, "face, par, or market value, or cost price, either wholesale or retail," as those terms are used to define "value" in § 641. Moreover, our case law is clear that acceptable alternative methods of calculating value under §§ 2311 and 641 are permissible only where market value is not readily ascertainable. *See Bigelow*, 728 F.2d at 414; *Drebin*, 557 F.2d at 1331. Here, the government had evidence of the petroglyphs' market value but did not introduce that evidence at trial.

We recognize that for theft offenses involving "archaeological resources," the Sentencing Guidelines impose an enhancement that is tied to "archaeological value," irrespective of whether the government obtains the conviction under § 641 or ARPA. *See* U.S.S.G. app. C, amend. 638; U.S.S.G. §§ 2B1.1(c)(4), 2B1.5(b)(1) & cmt. n. 1(C), n. 2(A)(i), n. 2(C)(i). But the Sentencing Guidelines do not apply until the government secures a conviction under a statute such as § 641 in accordance with the statutory terms.

The government's choice not to introduce any evidence of "value" within the meaning of § 641 unfortunately leaves us little choice. It is clear that Ligon and Mizell stole the petroglyphs. It is equally clear that the petroglyphs had a market value, as evidenced by Bahti's report. But the government did not introduce that report into evidence, or indeed anything else that might have served as evidence of "value" within the meaning of § 641, although it obviously could have done so. We therefore are constrained to reverse the district court's denial of the defendants' Rule 29(c) motions.

Conclusion

"Archaeological value," as that term is used in 16 U.S.C. §§ 470ee(d) and 470ff(a)(2)(A), and in the regulations promulgated thereunder, does not come within the definition of "value" as that term is used in 18 U.S.C. § 641. Because the government introduced no evidence other than "archaeological value" to prove that Ligon and Mizell stole something of "value" belonging to the government in violation of § 641, the district court should have granted their motions for acquittal.

REVERSED.

QUESTIONS

> Did the federal prosecutors simply botch their work, as the appellate court suggests? Or did the court fail to take account of the value of the archaeological information – estimated at $8,000 – in defining the requisite value under section 641? Is the outcome of this decision sensible?

By the twentieth century, the practice of Elginism had become discredited.[158] Looting in time of peace or war was no longer tolerable. Law was brought to bear on looters. The

[158] "Elginism," named after the infamous exportation by Lord Elgin of marbles from the Parthenon on the Acropolis in Ottoman Greece, is "the dismemberment of an historical monument, so as to export fragments of it or remove the whole piece by piece." Sharon Williams, The International and National Protection of Movable Cultural Property: A Comparative Study 1, 9 (1977).

conviction in 1924 of André Malraux on a charge of filching some stones and bas-reliefs from a Khmer temple was a rather memorable example of an aroused reaction to foreign plunder. Illicit trafficking in antiquities nevertheless remains brisk. By one estimate, some 170,000 cultural objects are missing today. It is all too easy to smuggle cultural contraband across national boundaries. Hidden caches in cargo shipments, personal luggage, and motor vehicles are not the only means. Blatant use of the mail, couriers, and parcel services, and laundering of items through third-world countries are also common practices.

Unfortunately, but understandably, customs services are often too hard pressed dealing with the drug trade and money laundering to devote adequate resources to combat illegal trafficking in antiquities. Never mind that it involves billions of dollars each year and ranks in profitability with illegally imported weapons, though well behind drugs, as contraband. Sometimes drugs, money laundering, arms smuggling, and trafficking in antiquities are closely related, as Operation Dinero, directed against the Locatelli crime syndicate and the Cali drug cartel, revealed.[159]

The following examples of penal law, applicable to crimes against cultural heritage, are drawn from the United States and treaties to which it is a party. Federal authorities in the United States, for example, may detain or seize cultural property on any of six legal bases.[160]

First, Customs agents, acting under general powers, may seize any item that is smuggled, improperly declared, or undervalued upon its entry into the country.[161] False entry declarations, invoicing, or valuations can also constitute the federal offense of commercial fraud. In the absence of a seizure or investigation, Customs has no power to detain property once it has received and processed entry documents, classified and valued the property, and assessed a duty.[162] Otherwise, the powers of Customs to seize and detain restricted merchandise are broad, extending even to bona fide purchases.

After Customs has seized and detained cultural property, its Office of Enforcement normally undertakes an investigation. If the Office can determine the country of origin, it will notify that country's embassy. If necessary, enforcement proceedings may include a criminal action, forfeiture proceedings, or an interpleader action on the status of the contested property. On completion of any such action, an illegally imported object may then be returned, if requested, to the country of origin.

[159] *See* Anna J. Kisluk, *DEA Operation Nets 3 Pictures*, 16 IFAR Rep., Dec. 1995, at 6. In December 1994, the Drug Enforcement Agency completed its investigation into the money-laundering operations of the Cali, Columbia, drug cartels. The operation led to eighty-eight arrests and the seizure of nine tons of cocaine and more than $650 million in cash and property. The seized property included paintings by Pablo Picasso, Peter Paul Rubens, and Sir Joshua Reynolds.

[160] The criminal laws of states of the Union also provide, of course, for seizure of stolen and illegally excavated cultural property. Typically, the state role is confined to strictly local trafficking. For a discussion of federal preemption of state laws in this context, *see* John Henry Merryman & James A.R. Nafziger, *The Private International Law of Cultural Property in the United States*, 42 Am. J. Comp. L. 221, 222–23 (1994).

[161] *See* 18 U.S.C. § 545 (2002) (discussing smuggling goods into United States); 19 U.S.C. § 1497 (1994) (discussing penalties for failure to declare); 19 U.S.C. § 1595 (1994) (discussing searches and seizures of merchandise on cause to suspect failure to pay duties on it or if it "has been otherwise brought into the United States contrary to law").

[162] *See* Azurin v. Von Raab, No. CIV.A.86–50189, 1986 WL 10700 (D. Haw. June 6, 1986) (holding that Customs could not detain property when "all entry requirements have been discharged"), *rev'd on other grounds*, 803 F.2d 993 (9th Cir. 1986).

An interesting case arose in 1994 when a New York art dealer consigned three works of pre-Columbian art to Sotheby's for inclusion in an auction.[163] On the basis of information in the catalog for the auction, Customs seized the artifacts, claiming that they had been either imported in violation of the CPIA or smuggled into the country. While a grand jury was convening in the matter but before any indictment, the dealer moved to recover his property on the ground that it had been illegally seized.[164] The court, however, denied the motion for failure to make the showing of requisite harm. Although the government conceded that the artifacts did not fall within the protection of the CPIA, the allegation of smuggling was sufficient to justify detention of the property by Customs.

Second, the National Stolen Property Act (NSPA)[165] prohibits the transportation in interstate or foreign commerce of any article with a value of $5,000 or more that is known to be stolen.[166] Occasionally, Interpol and foreign governments initiate requests for detention or seizure of objects. With or without such a request, federal law enforcement agencies may seize objects under the general customs law; however, the NSPA does not itself authorize seizure or detention of objects. The NSPA does provide a basis for prosecution and return of illegally imported objects to countries of origin. Ordinarily, the return of such objects is coordinated with foreign embassies.

In 1996, a federal grand jury indicted a retired art history professor on four counts of possessing and transporting several leaves from a rare manuscript in the Vatican that had once belonged to the fourteenth-century humanist Petrarch.[167] As usual in a federal case, Customs had been deeply involved in investigating and seizing the material even though it had reposed in the clutches of the acquisitive professor for a substantial period of time after the manuscript leaves had been smuggled into the United States.

The cases of *United States v. Hollinshead*[168] and *United States v. McClain*[169] established that the term "stolen property" (theft) in the NSPA may be defined by the law of the country of origin. Even if a foreign state has not reduced an illegally exported object

[163] *See In re* Search Warrant Executed February 1, 1995, No. M 18–65 (RJW), 1995 WL 406276 (S.D.N.Y. July 7, 1995).

[164] Federal Rule of Criminal Procedure 41(e) states:

> A person aggrieved by an unlawful search and seizure or by the deprivation of property may move the district court for the district in which the property was seized for the return of the property on the ground that such person is entitled to lawful possession of the property. The court shall receive evidence on any issue of fact necessary to the decision of the motion. If the motion is granted, the property shall be returned to the movant, although reasonable conditions may be imposed to protect access and use of the property in subsequent proceedings. If a motion for return of property is made or comes on for a hearing in the district of trial after an indictment or information is filed, it shall be treated also as a motion to suppress under Rule 12.

[165] 18 U.S.C. §§ 2311–2319 (2002).

[166] *Id.* § 2314. This section states in part:

> Whoever transports, transmits, or transfers in interstate or foreign commerce any goods, wares, merchandise, securities or money, of the value of $5,000 or more, knowing the same to have been stolen, converted, or taken by fraud, shall be fined under this title or imprisoned not more than ten years, or both.

[167] *See Indictment in Case of Leaves from Petrarch's Manuscript in the Vatican*, 17 IFAR Rep., Jan.–Feb. 1996, at 5.

[168] United States v. Hollinshead, 495 F.2d 1154 (9th Cir. 1974).

[169] United States v. McClain, 593 F.2d 658 (5th Cir. 1979). Excerpts of this case appear later in this chapter.

to its possession, it may validly claim ownership over the property so long as it has previously declared so by law.[170] In these circumstances, the item constitutes "stolen property" under the NSPA. *United States v. Pre-Columbian Artifacts*[171] extended its "prior declaration rule" to include objects over which a country, namely Guatemala, had claimed ownership effective only as of the time of their illegal export – that is, only on their departure from the country. The court held that, "while traveling in foreign commerce, the articles were stolen [under the NSPA definitions] in that they belonged to the Republic, not the person who unlawfully possessed the artifacts."[172] It is important to note that the court was enforcing foreign antiquity legislation, not an export law. Even so, this decision comes close to ignoring the old taboo against even selectively enforcing foreign export laws.

Third, the Pre-Columbian Monumental or Architectural Sculpture or Mural Statute (Pre-Columbian Statute)[173] prohibits the import of any designated pre-Columbian stone carvings or wall art into the United States unless they are accompanied by sufficient documentation showing that their export either complied with the laws of the country of origin or occurred before 1972, when the Pre-Columbian Statute came into force.[174] The secretary of the treasury has the responsibility of preparing the list of designated protected items after consulting with the secretary of state. On detention of listed objects by Customs, articles are stored at a storage facility or bonded warehouse at the risk of a consignee until sufficient documentation is presented. If no certification of legitimate export is presented within ninety days, the item is to be seized, forfeited, and returned to the country of origin, so long as that country agrees to bear all expenses incident to the return. A bona fide owner or other successful claimant receives no compensation under this legislation.

Fourth, bilateral treaties with Ecuador, Guatemala, Mexico, and Peru provide for mutual cooperation, with various arrangements for detention and seizure, to recover and return stolen cultural property to the country of origin.[175] An official request from one country automatically triggers enforcement procedures in the requested country.

[170] *See* Republic of Turkey v. OKS Partners, 797 F. Supp. 64 (D. Mass 1992) (allowing Turkey to assert cause of action over coin collection allegedly smuggled out of country); *McClain*, 593 F.2d at 664 (confirming that definition of stolen property under the NSPA may rely on foreign patrimonial legislation). *But see* Peru v. Johnson, 720 F. Supp. 810 (C.D. Cal. 1989), *aff'd. sub nom.*, Peru v. Wendt, 933 F.2d 1013 (9th Cir. 1991) (establishing that unless a state had effectively declared ownership, it could not claim that an illegally exported object had been "stolen" under the NSPA).

[171] United States v. Pre-Columbian Artifacts, 845 F. Supp. 544 (N.D. Ill. 1993).

[172] *Id.* at 547.

[173] Act on the Regulation of Importation of Pre-Columbian Monumental or Architectural Sculpture or Murals, 19 U.S.C. §§ 2091–2095 (2000). For a summary, *see* Kifle Jote, International Legal Protection of Cultural Heritage 162–65 (1994).

[174] 19 U.S.C. §§ 2091–2095.

[175] *See* Agreement for the Recovery and Return of Stolen Archaeological, Historical and Cultural Properties, Jan. 14, 1987, U.S.-Ecuador, T.I.A.S. No. 11075; Agreement for the Recovery and Return of Stolen Archaeological, Historical and Cultural Properties, May 21, 1984, U.S.-Guat., T.I.A.S. No. 11077; Treaty of Cooperation Providing for the Recovery and Return of Stolen Archaeological, Historical and Cultural Properties, July 17, 1970, U.S.-Mex., 22 U.S.T. 494; Agreement for the Recovery and Return of Stolen Archaeological, Historical and Cultural Properties, Sept. 15, 1981, U.S.-Peru, 33 U.S.T. 1608.

Judicial proceedings, such as in the treaty with Mexico, are among several avenues of implementation provided by the treaties.

More recent arrangements with the Czech Republic, Romania, and Ukraine provide for cooperation in the protection of certain Jewish-owned property in those countries.[176] A treaty with Greece[177] provides, in part, for cooperation between Customs of both countries to combat illicit trafficking of artifacts. Forfeiture is one type of mutual assistance. The government of Greece brought a claim in federal court for the return of a collection of rare Mycenaean gold jewelry and ornaments in the possession of a New York art dealer.[178] In 1996 the dealer agreed to donate the collection to a foundation for eventual return to the government of Greece. This marked the first repatriation of significant cultural objects from the United States to Greece.[179]

Fifth, the Archaeological Resource Protection Act also provides for seizure and forfeiture of cultural materials, as the following commentary explains:

> In 1996, the United States government seized and forfeited a set of Etruscan pottery, alleged by the Italian government to have come from an archaeological site, the Etruscan necropolis of Crustumerium, near Rome, and dated approximately to the 7th century B.C. The U.S. government's forfeiture complaint was filed under § 470ee(c) of ARPA, which bars interstate and international trafficking in archaeological resources in violation of state and local law. The local law on which the government relied was New York Penal Law § 165.45, which prohibits knowingly holding stolen property. The gallery which had possession of the artifacts waived any claim to them and the pottery was ultimately returned to Italy. The government's legal theory was thus never contested.... This same provision of ARPA was used to prosecute a Virginia dealer who possessed a collection of antiquities from Peru. The defendant pled guilty and so the case did not come to trial. What advantages and disadvantages does an ARPA prosecution have in comparison to prosecution under other federal statutes, such as the National Stolen Property Act? The National Stolen Property Act prohibits the possession, receipt, sale, disposal and transport of any goods or merchandise worth $5000 or more that has crossed a state or United States boundary. 18 U.S.C. §§ 2314–15.

Patty Gerstenblith, Art, Cultural Heritage and Law 649 (2004).

[176] *See* Agreement for the Protection and Preservation of Cultural Properties, Mar. 17, 1992, U.S.-Czech Rep., Hein's No. KAV 3167, State Dep't No. 92–63; Agreement for the Protection and Preservation of Certain Cultural Properties, July 29, 1993, U.S.-Rom., Hein's No. KAV 3641, State Dep't No. 93–156; Agreement for the Protection and Preservation of Cultural Heritage, Mar. 4, 1994, U.S.-Ukr., Hein's No. KAV 3795, State Dep't No. 94–81.

[177] *See* Agreement Regarding Mutual Administrative Assistance between Their Customs Administrations, Jan. 17, 1993, U.S.-Greece, Hein's No. KAV 3085, State Dep't No. 93–33.

[178] *See* Irvin Molotsky, *20 Years after Thievery, Rare Gold Ornaments Will Return to Greece*, N.Y. Times, Jan. 31, 1996, at C16.

[179] *See id.* The art dealer, Michael Ward, was a member of the Cultural Property Advisory Committee of the U.S. Information Agency (USIA) when the incident first came to light. *See id.* He was, therefore, a kind of fox in the chicken coop of the federal government's principal agency to protect threatened cultural property.

Sixth, under the Convention on Cultural Property Implementation Act (CPIA),[180] any designated or stolen property is subject to seizure and forfeiture pursuant to a warrant from a magistrate or judge.[181] The possessor of any seized article has an opportunity to be heard. If the possessor loses, the government first offers a forfeited article to the country of origin if that country agrees to bear all expenses incident to its return, including compensation to any claimant who can demonstrate that he or she is a bona fide purchaser. Otherwise, the item may be returned to the claimant on proof of valid title and status as a bona fide purchaser for value.

The CPIA also provides for repose from litigation. That is, it excludes from seizure and return all material that has been held for periods of at least three to twenty years and, depending on the precise threshold period, has been displayed, reported in an appropriate publication, or cataloged for public scrutiny.[182] Another statute, which is cross-referenced in the Act, holds immune from seizure any cultural property imported into the United States for temporary exhibit or display and designated by the president for such immunity.[183]

The United States' reservation to the 1970 UNESCO Convention, through which it has refused to enforce export controls of foreign countries solely on the basis of illicit trafficking of cultural property,[184] has nevertheless been qualified by a willingness of U.S. courts to define the crime of theft in accordance with foreign export controls.

As we have seen, the United States entered a reservation to the 1970 UNESCO Convention through which it refused to enforce export controls of foreign countries solely on the basis of illicit trafficking of cultural property.[185] Instead, under article 9 of the Convention, the United States has agreed that other parties to the Convention can call on it to ban the importation of items that form a specific cultural element in their national patrimony if that element is in jeopardy. As a rule, the United States will take such action only if similar action is taken by other states with a significant impact on trade in the particular material to be protected. The CPIA also provides for official cooperation in returning property stolen from a museum, religious or secular public monument, or similar institution in a requesting state.[186]

This mechanism does not justify seizure of property merely on the basis that it appears to meet the general definition of cultural property common to the 1970 UNESCO Convention and the CPIA. Rather, an item may be seized under the CPIA only if it has been specifically identified in the Federal Register or if it is already inventoried property stolen from a museum, religious or secular public monument, or similar institution in a requesting party to the agreement.[187] For specific cultural property to be listed in the Federal Register, the president must either order emergency import restrictions to protect the property or enter into a bilateral agreement with the requesting country to the same

[180] 19 U.S.C. §§ 2601–2613 (2002).

[181] *See* 19 U.S.C. §§ 2601–2613 (2002).

[182] *See id.* § 2611.

[183] *See* 22 U.S.C. § 2459 (2002).

[184] *See* S. Rep. No. 97–564, at 21 (1982).

[185] *See* S. Rep. No. 97–564, at 21 (1982).

[186] *See* 19 U.S.C. 2607 (2002).

[187] *See id.* Article 7(b)(i) of the UNESCO Convention provides, in pertinent part, that the parties to the Convention undertake to prohibit the import of stolen cultural property "provided that such property is documented as appertaining to the inventory of that institution."

effect.[188] As we have seen, the president does so only on the request of a foreign country and with the advice of the Cultural Property Advisory Committee that was established for this purpose within the U.S. Department of State.[189]

Throughout the world, illegal trafficking in cultural property is rampant, and the legal regime is still weak. The trend, however, is encouraging, as courts and government agencies gradually learn to apply the law more effectively. The hunt for cultural contraband is becoming better organized.

United States v. McClain, 593 F.2d 658 (5th Cir. 1979)

Gee, Circuit Judge:

Again, before us come Patty McClain, Mike Bradshaw, Ada Simpson, and William Simpson, challenging their second round of convictions for having received, concealed, and/or sold stolen goods in interstate or foreign commerce and also for conspiracy to do the same, violations of 18 U.S.C. §§ 371, 2314, and 2315. The goods in which they dealt are pre-Columbian artifacts, and in neither this nor the prior trial was there evidence that the appellants or anyone else had taken the items from the personal possession of another. The legal theory under which the case was tried was that the artifacts were "stolen" only in the sense that Mexico generally has declared itself owner of all pre-Columbian artifacts found within its borders. Thus, anyone who digs up or finds such an item and deals in it without governmental permission has unlawfully converted the item from its proper owner.[190]

By various formulations, appellants and the amicus curiae, the American Association of Dealers in Ancient, Oriental & Primitive Art, raise basically three issues in this appeal. They challenge: (1) the propriety of the application of the National Stolen Property Act (NSPA), 18 U.S.C. §§ 2314, 2315, to dealings in pre-Columbian artifacts; (2) the correctness and sufficiency of the jury instructions regarding the Mexican law of pre-Columbian artifacts; and (3) the sufficiency of the evidence to support the convictions as measured under their view of the Mexican law.

. . .

II. Application of N.S.P.A. to Dealings in Pre-Columbian Artifacts

Appellants attack the application of the N.S.P.A. to their conduct under two different theories. They first argue that Congress never intended the

[188] *See* 19 U.S.C. § 2607.

[189] *See id.* § 2603.

[190] *See generally* United States v. McClain, 545 F.2d 988 (5th Cir.), *reh'g denied*, 551 F.2d 52 (5th Cir. 1977).

Only one other reported conviction has resulted from application of the National Stolen Property Act to dealings in pre-Columbian artifacts. In *United States v. Hollinshead*, 495 F.2d 1154 (9th Cir. 1974), Clive Hollinshead of Los Angeles was successfully prosecuted for transporting into the United States a known and cataloged Guatemalan stela. Hollinshead was on probation for this offense during the events leading to the instant prosecution. At least [two of the appellants] knew Hollinshead and were aware of his conviction and probation. Hollinshead was to have supplied several of the artifacts that appellants were selling when they were arrested.

N.S.P.A. to reach items deemed "stolen" only by reason of a country's declaration of ownership. In any event, they claim, the N.S.P.A. was superseded from the 1972 Law on Importation of Pre-Columbian Monumental or Architectural Sculpture or Murals, 19 U.S.C. §§ 2091–95, which provides only the civil penalty for forfeiture[191] for importation of certain types of pre-Columbian artifacts.[192]

We view appellants' first argument as foreclosed by our doctrine of law of the case. Under that doctrine it is our practice to apply a rule of law enunciated by the court to the same issues in subsequent proceedings and appeals in the same case. Unlike the rule of res judicata, the doctrine applies only to issues that were decided in the former proceeding but not to questions that might have been decided but were not. Carpa, Inc. v. Ward Foods, Inc., 567 F.2d 1316, 1320 (5th Cir. 1978). Though appellants articulated their theories in a slightly different manner in the first appeal, they provoked a square holding that, in addition to the rights of ownership as understood by the common law, the N.S.P.A. also protects ownership derived from foreign legislative pronouncements, even though the owned objects have never been reduced by possession by the foreign government. United States v. McClain, 545 F.2d 988, 994–97 (5th Cir. 1977). Moreover, the earlier panel had considered evidence of the 1972 statute, its legislative history and UNESCO negotiations, holding nevertheless that neither statute nor treaty nor our historical policy of encouraging the importation of art more than 100 years old had the effect of narrowing the N.S.P.A. so as to make it inapplicable to artifacts declared to be the property of another country and illegally imported into this country. 545 F.2d at 996–97. Appellants' attempt to raise these points again on appeal is therefore foreclosed unless

> (1) the evidence on a subsequent trial was substantially different, (2) controlling authority has since made a contrary decision of the law applicable to such issues, or (3) the decision was clearly erroneous and would work manifest injustice.

...

Our study of the statute and its scant legislative history persuades us that appellants' reading of it is not correct. Both the Report by the House Ways and Means Committee and the Report by the Senate Finance Committee

[191] 19 U.S.C. § 2093 details the only penalties contained in the 1972 Importation Act. It provides that any object imported in violation of the Act shall be seized and subject to forfeiture under the customs law.

[192] This statute prohibits importation into the United States, unless the country of origin has certified exportation, if "stone carvings and wall art which are pre-Columbian monumental or architectural sculpture or murals." The latter term is defined in § 2095(3) as any stone carving or wall art (or fragment or part thereof) that (1) is the product of pre-Columbian Indian culture of Mexico, Central America, South America, or the Caribbean Islands; (2) was an immobile monument or architectural structure or was a part of, or affixed to, any such monument or structure; and (3) is subject to export control by the country of origin.

Though some of the artifacts seized in San Antonio and Los Angeles seem to come within this definition, the majority of the pieces are movable items such as ceramic dishes, pots, or figurines that may not have been part of or affixed to monuments or walls within the apparent meaning of the statute.

explicitly refer to the presence of other unspecified sanctions: "While legal remedies for the return of such objects are available in U.S. courts in some cases, these procedures can be extremely expensive and time consuming and do not provide a meaningful deterrent to the pillage of pre-Columbian sites now taking place." . . . Moreover, the Act covers objects imported from all the countries of Latin America. These countries may have acted quite differently to protect their cultural heritage, some by declaring national ownership and others merely by enacting stringent export restrictions. Since it covers artifacts from such a large number of countries, the Act is better seen not as an indication that other available penalties were thereby precluded, but rather as a recognition that additional deterrents were needed. We cannot see in this congressional intent any desire to prevent application of criminal sanctions for dealing in items classified as stolen because a particular country has enacted national ownership of its patrimony.[193]

Appellants' second challenge is not so easily resolved. It is elementary that criminal statutes must give notice of the acts they prohibit before valid penalties may be imposed thereunder. In their first appeal, appellants argued broadly that a reference to any foreign law for the purpose of determining what is or is not "stolen" would "inject an unacceptable degree of uncertainty into the administration" of the N.S.P.A. This argument drew a firm ruling that application of the N.S.P.A. to foreign exportation did not render that statute void for vagueness. 545 F.2d at 1001, 1002 n.30. The court reasoned that the statute's specific scienter requirement eliminates the possibility that a defendant is convicted for an offense he could not have understood to exist. In support, the court cited *Boyce Motor Lines v. United States*, 342 U.S. 337, 340, 72 S. Ct. 329, 331, 96 L. Ed. 367 (1952), for the proposition that it is not "unfair to require that one who deliberately goes perilously close to an area of proscribed conduct shall take the risk that he may cross the line." The court finally noted that it would have been impossible for the statute to have explicitly described every type of theft that might fall within its broad purview. *Id.*

In assessing whether the law of the case doctrine precludes further challenge under a void-for-vagueness theory, we first observe that the panel's holding was in response to a challenge about reference to foreign law generally and not to a challenge about the specific Mexican statutes. Moreover, we think it very significant that the panel's response was made in the context of its independent review of the relevant Mexican statutes. Its study of those statutes led the court to conclude that Mexico had not unequivocally declared national ownership of all artifacts until 1972.[194]

[193] "As the earlier panel observed, the fundamental rule, absent modification as by the 1972 statute, is that it is not a violation of law to import an item of art or anything else simply because it has been illegally exported from another country. 545 F.2d at 996. But that generalized principle does not preclude federal criminal liability for concealing, selling, or transporting across state or international borders items that are not only illegally exported from a country such as Mexico, but are also incapable of being privately owned or conveyed. Dealing in such items is dealing in stolen goods and may be punished accordingly, irrespective of import regulations."

[194] [The applicability of Mexican statutes before a 1972 law was a critical issue in the case because it was unclear whether the alleged criminal acts of bringing the artifacts into the United States occurred before

545 F.2d at 997–1000. Entailed in the proposition that criminal penalties on the basis of the 1972 declaration of ownership are proper is the probable corollary that criminal penalties on the basis of, for instance, the 1897 Mexican statute alone would have been improper because that statute did not declare the nation's ownership of movables with sufficient clarity.[195] The panel's opinion is consistent with the view that, had there been no subsequent enactments that declared ownership with enough specificity to be accessible to and understandable by our citizenry, criminal penalties may well have violated our fundamental standards of due process. We are therefore convinced that, insofar as criminal liability in the second trial may possibly have been predicated on a conclusion that the 1897 Act declared Mexican ownership of all artifacts, appellants' precise due process challenge was not decided before and therefore survives. Because the due process challenge is so closely linked with the issue of the proper view of Mexican law, further discussion of this issue will be postponed until we have described and assessed the record on that point.

III. Jury Instructions Regarding Mexican Law, Sufficiency of Evidence

At appellants' first trial a deputy attorney general of Mexico testified as an expert witness, and the trial court subsequently instructed the jury that Mexico had, since 1897, vested itself with ownership of all pre-Columbian artifacts found in that country. As mentioned above, its independent review of translations of the various Mexican statutes convinced the earlier panel that Mexico had not unequivocally claimed ownership of all such artifacts until 1972. The earlier Mexican statutes seemed only to have claimed national ownership of immovable monuments and such movable artifacts as were found on, and possibly in, the immovable objects.[196] Movable objects not in the above classes seemed capable of being privately owned and conveyed, though the Mexican government required that such objects be registered and retained the right to acquire items of great cultural or archaeological value by purchase at a fair price. Certain other provisions referred to in the petition for rehearing seemed to have established a presumption against private ownership of any movable not registered within

or after the 1972 law. A series of subsequent transactions in the United States apparently began in 1973. – *Eds.*]

[195] Article 1 of the Law on Archaeological Monuments, May 11, 1897 (Diario Oficial de 11 de Mayo de 1897, See XIV Annario de Legislacion y Jurisprudencia (1897)) of the nation, but "archaeological monuments" were defined in article 2 as "ruins of cities, Big Houses (Casas Grandes), troglodytic dwellings, fortifications, palaces, temples, pyramids, sculpted rocks or those with inscriptions, and in general all the edifices that in any aspect may be interesting for the study of civilization and history of the ancient settlers of Mexico." There was no corresponding declaration of ownership of movable artifacts such as codices, idols, or amulets, though exportation of such items was forbidden unless legally authorized. Art. 6.

[196] For instance, the Law for the Protection and Preservation of Archaeological and Historical Monuments, Typical Towns and Places of Scenic Beauty, January 19, 1934 (82 Diario Oficial 152, 19 de enero de 1934), broadened the definition of "monuments" to include "all vestiges of the aboriginal civilizations dating from before the completion of the Conquest." Art. 3. But art. 4 clearly declared national ownership of artifacts in more limited categories "immovable archaeological monuments" and "objects which are found (in or on) immovable archaeological monuments." *See McClain*, 545 F.2d at 998–99, including n. 20, which explains the dispute over movable items found in immobile monuments.

the applicable time limits.[197] In view of the complicated and gradual nature of Mexico's apparent declarations of ownership, the earlier panel ruled that the defendants were entitled to a new trial because of the prejudice that may have resulted from the erroneous instruction that Mexico owned all artifacts as early as 1897. Its analysis of the changes in Mexican law convinced the panel that the jury should have been told to determine when the artifacts had been exported from Mexico and to "apply the applicable Mexican law to the exportation." 545 F.2d at 1003.

When the additional complication of the statutory presumptions was raised in the petition for rehearing, the court explained that its earlier discussion of Mexican law had not been "an exegesis of every relevant statutory clause or a holding on every issue that was or might have been raised." Rather, the court contemplated that on remand "objective testimony" on the meaning of the relevant Mexican enactments would be introduced, so as to lighten the burden of both the district court and the reviewing court. The court reiterated that the earlier instructions had been "clearly in error" as to Mexican law but added that at any subsequent trial "experts will have an opportunity to correct any misconstruction of which this Court may have been guilty in venturing forth in the arcane field of the Mexican law of pre-Columbian artifacts." United States v. McClain, *on petition for rehearing*, 551 F.2d 52, 54 (5th Cir. 1977).

Pursuant to these instructions, at the second trial the judge admitted testimony from several government and defense witnesses about the relevant Mexican law. Only two of the witnesses were accepted by the court as experts specifically on the Mexican law of archaeological monuments. The first, Javier Andres Oropeza-Secura, is the Director of the Judicial Branch of the National Institute of Anthropology and History of Mexico, the office in charge of the official registry for ancient artifacts. The second was Ricardo de los Rios, an attorney who currently works at the Ministry of Labor and who formerly worked in the Attorney General's office, where he prosecuted about 150 cases under the Mexican laws regulating artifacts. Since each of these men is an employee of the Mexican government and was challenged by defendants as possibly biased, the government introduced other witnesses to corroborate their testimony. Carlos Schon, an attorney in Mexico City with a general practice and a heavily American clientele, was allowed to testify as a licensed practitioner of the general laws of Mexico from whom one may seek legal opinions. His testimony on

[197] Article 9 of the 1934 statute "created a Register of Private Archaeological Property ("Propriedad") with which private individuals were to register movable monuments in their 'control' or 'ownership.'" (Translation of any terms suggestive of private ownership was hotly disputed at trial.) Article 12 of that statute prescribed that objects not registered within the period stipulated in the Act's transitory articles "shall be presumed to come from archaeological monuments which are real property." Because the Act had earlier declared national ownership of all immovable monuments, . . . the force of this presumption seems to nationalize all movable artifacts not registered by the end of the transitory period.

There is a similar presumption in the statute that superseded the 1934 Act, the Federal Law Concerning Cultural Patrimony of the Nation, December 16, 1970 (303 Diario Oficial 8, 16 de diciembre de 1970). See art. 55 thereof, which provides that movable objects not registered within the allowed time limits are presumed "the property of the nation" ("propriedad").

archaeological law was based on his review of the various statutes and the Mexican Constitution. Though the testimony of these witnesses varied on a specific point here and there, the weight of their testimony as a whole indicated a general opinion that the Mexican government owned all pre-Columbian artifacts at least as early as 1897. Rights of private individuals were limited to the right of possession, but only if the particular artifact had been properly registered, and the mere right to possess does not confer the right to sell an item or to give it as security for a loan.

[At the second trial on remand, the district court heard extensive testimony overwhelmingly in support of application of the 1897 law.]

. . . [T]he question of whether the right to a jury trial in criminal matters requires submission of a question of foreign law to the jury, because it can be found as a matter of fact, has never been definitively laid to rest. . . . In the absence of compelling evidence of prejudice, we would be loath to reverse a conviction such as this where the evidence of guilt and of intent to violate both foreign and domestic law is near overwhelming. We believe, nevertheless, that reversal of at least the substantive count [namely of having received, concealed, and/or sold stolen goods in interstate or foreign commerce] is required here because the most likely jury construction of Mexican law upon the evidence at trial is that Mexico declared itself owner of all artifacts at least as early as 1897. And under this view of Mexican law, we believe the defendants may have suffered the prejudice of being convicted pursuant to laws that were too vague to be a predicate for criminal liability under our jurisprudential standards.

It may well be, as testified so emphatically by most of the Mexican witnesses, that Mexico has considered itself the owner of all pre-Columbian artifacts for almost 100 years. If so, however, it has not expressed that view with sufficient clarity to survive translation into terms understandable by and binding upon American citizens.[198] Neither the early statutes nor the Constitution of 1917 clearly declare national ownership of the sort of pre-Columbian movable artifacts in which appellants dealt. One of the government experts testified that a literal translation of the Mexican statutes into English would mislead those not familiar with Mexican law into thinking that such movables had been capable of being privately owned.[199] Another admitted that there were "confusions" in the 1934

[198] Because of our disposition of the claims in this appeal largely on the ground of unconstitutional vagueness and harmless error, we need not now undertake the delicate task of deciding the meaning of the Mexican statutes and the manner in which the various provisions interact. We leave that task to subsequent courts should the government prosecute others by reference to pre-1972 Mexican statutes, either directly or as incorporated by article 4 of the 1972 Transitory. . . .

[199] "He especially objected to translating the word 'propriedad' as 'ownership' or 'property,' though he conceded that that rendering was proper in some of the statutory passages. He said that only one familiar with the Mexican law could decide when to translate the word as 'ownership' because in many instances regarding artifacts the law limits 'propriedad' to connoting mere possessory rights. Translation of 'propriedad' as 'property' might incorrectly lead those unfamiliar with Mexican law to believe some artifacts could be 'outright property.' He further testified that 'translacion de dominion' could be translated as 'acts of conveyance,' provided the latter term was not understood to include 'transfer of property or outright ownership.' The literal translation, 'transfer of dominion,' would also be misleading, since the correct meaning of the law does not go beyond allowing 'transfer of possession.'"

statute caused by the lack of technical language and that subsequent statutes had been designed to clarify the legal situation. . . .

The 1972 statute, on the other hand, is clear and unequivocal in claiming ownership of all artifacts.[200] Deferring to this legitimate act of another sovereign, we agree with the earlier panel that it is proper to punish through the National Stolen Property Act encroachments upon legitimate and clear Mexican ownership, even though the goods may never have been physically possessed by agents of that nation. Nor does the infirmity of vagueness attach to the 1970 and possibly the 1934 statute insofar as they established presumptions that unregistered movables belong to the sovereign. Had these theories alone (either post-1972 exportation or post-1934 appropriation, coupled with failure to register) been presented to the jury, our appellate task would have been much simpler.[201] There is no doubt that the evidence is sufficient to have sustained convictions under either theory, and there would have been little prejudice involved in letting the jury decide the appropriate Mexican law to apply. But the expert testimony in the main allowed the jury to conclude that Mexico had long owned all these items outright. There was thus little need for the jury to consider legal and factual technicalities such as the probable date of exportation or the effect of the presumptions upon appellants' unregistered items. Unfortunately, under this broad view of Mexican law, our basic standards of due process and notice preclude us from characterizing the artifacts as "stolen." Though the National Stolen Property Act is not void for vagueness because the general class of offenses to which it is directed is plainly within its terms, it cannot properly be applied to items deemed stolen only on the basis of unclear pronouncements by a foreign legislature. The principle from *Boyce Motor Lines*, employed in the earlier appeal, cannot be used to deflect the vagueness charges directed at the early Mexican statutes.

. . .

By contrast, the requisite degree of prejudice for reversal is lacking as to the conspiracy count. The evidence presented to the jury amply showed that appellants' Conspiracy was much broader than an intent to deal in the single collection already in the United States for an unspecified length of time. It is abundantly clear that they conspired to bring in at least one other load, and most likely a continuing stream of articles that, owing to a broken drive shaft and appellants' subsequent arrest, never arrived. Their plans regarding those loads and the conduit itself were clearly illegal under any view of Mexican law, including that presented by their own witnesses. The evidence is massive that appellants knew and deliberately ignored Mexico's post-1972 ownership claims. In addition, the continuing nature of their enterprise was highlighted in the closing arguments to the jury by the government and the defendants alike. . . . Moreover, the instructions

[200] "The 1972 statute also contains a grandfather clause under which rights gained under previous statutes are preserved. . . . Thus, if private persons were allowed ownership as opposed to mere possessory rights under the earlier laws, those rights would be retained provided the owner complied with the requirements of those laws."

[201] We express no opinion regarding the claim, made by amicus in its brief in the earlier appeal, that predicating criminal liability on a presumption contained in a foreign statute also would infringe due process.

regarding the conspiracy count were separated from the instructions regarding the substantive count and, in outlining the required elements of the offense, the judge made no reference back to the jury's role regarding Mexican law. He correctly charged that the defendants need never have completed the illegal object of their conspiracy to be found guilty and also correctly instructed that none of the overt acts need themselves be illegal.

. . .

Given the strength of this evidence regarding the continuing illegal purpose of appellants which, if effectuated, would necessarily entail dealing in "stolen" property under any view of Mexican law, we hold that the dubious shifting of the determination of Mexican law constituted harmless error as to the conspiracy count. . . . Accordingly, appellants' convictions on the conspiracy count are AFFIRMED, and the convictions on the substantive court are REVERSED.

One Lucite Ball Containing Lunar Material, 252 F. Supp. 2d 1367 (S.D. Fla. 2003)

The United States seeks civil forfeiture *in rem* of one lucite ball containing lunar material, that is, a moon rock, and one 10 inch by 14 inch wooden plaque. It asserts that the moon rock and plaque are stolen property that were introduced into the United States in violation of 19 U.S.C. § 1595a(c)(1)(A). The claimant, Alan Rosen – who purchased the items from a retired Honduran colonel for $50,000 – argues that he is entitled to the return of the property because, among other things, the government has failed to establish probable cause.

On March 3, 2003, the parties presented evidence (through testimony and matters already in the record) at a bench trial. As explained below, I find that the United States is entitled to forfeiture because the items were stolen from the Republic of Honduras and then introduced into the United States.

I. Facts

The moon rock was originally retrieved from the surface of the moon by astronauts on a NASA mission. In 1973, President Nixon, on behalf of the United States, made a gift of the moon rock and plaque to the government and people of the Republic of Honduras. . . .

C. Honduras' Request

On May 4, 1999, Juan Alberto Lara Buesco, the Acting Vice-Secretary of State of Honduras, sent a letter to Customs Commissioner Raymond Kelly to seek the return of the moon rock and plaque, to identify it as the patrimony of the government and people of Honduras, and to confirm that it was illegally taken from Honduras. According to Jany del Cid Martinez, a Special Prosecutor for Ethnic Groups and Cultural Heritage, Office of the Public Prosecutor of Honduras, the items were stolen from the government and the people of Honduras in violation of several laws of Honduras, specifically, Article 223 and Article 225 of the Criminal Code; Article 2, paragraph 2, and Article 4 of the Law on the Protection of the Nation's Cultural Heritage; and Article 194 and Article 195 Number 5 of the National Tax Code.

II. Honduran Law

[1] "[F]ederal law controls the question of whether an item is stolen," but "local law" – i.e., the law of the place from where the item was taken – governs "whether any person or entity has a property interest in the item such that it can be stolen and whether the receiver of the item has a property interest in it." *United States v. Portrait of Wally*, 105 F. Supp. 2d 288, 292 (S.D.N.Y. 2000) (*Wally I*) (forfeiture under 19 U.S.C. § 1595a(c) and 22 U.S.C. § 401(a)). Because the issue of title to the moon rock and plaque must be determined by reference to Honduran law, *see United States v. An Antique Platter of Gold*, 991 F. Supp. 222, 231–32 (S.D.N.Y. 1997) (forfeiture under 19 U.S.C. § 1595a(c) and 18 U.S.C. §§ 981(a)(1)(C) & 545), *aff'd on other grounds*, 184 F.3d 131 (2d Cir. 1999), I make the following determinations pursuant to Federal Rule of Civil Procedure 44.1.

A. Professor Rosenn's Report

With the agreement of the parties, and pursuant to Federal Rule of Evidence 706(a), I appointed Professor Keith S. Rosenn, Esq., an expert in Honduran law and a law professor at the University of Miami School of Law, to conduct research on and analyze the issues of Honduran law as they related to the cultural patrimony of historic artifacts, and particularly as they related to the moon rock and wooden plaque. Professor Rosenn, who is no relation to the claimant, Mr. Rosen, was also authorized to conduct research into collateral matters of Honduran law to the extent he found necessary to prepare his report. Professor Rosenn issued his preliminary report in the form of a letter on March 25, 2002, was deposed on April 25, 2002, by both parties, and subsequently issued a revised report on October 10, 2002.

B. The Moon Rock and Plaque Were Taken from the Presidential Palace between 1990 and 1994

Professor Rosenn determined that the moon rock and plaque became the property of the Republic of Honduras in 1973, when they were donated to that nation by President Nixon. Though the gift was accepted by the nation's then *de facto* leader, President Oswaldo Lopez Arellano, Honduras, like most of Latin America, treats the acts of *de facto* governments as having the same force and effect as those of *de jure* governments. The moon rock and plaque were placed in the Presidential Palace, and viewed by the public. President Lopez Arellano was ousted by a military coup in 1975, as was his successor, Colonel Juan Alberto Melgar Castro. In 1981, General Paz Garcia, the leader of the military junta which ousted Colonel Castro, called for free elections, and since then Honduras has had a series of six democratically elected presidents.

Nothing in the record establishes exactly when the moon rock and plaque disappeared. Professor Rosenn reviewed articles that appeared in *La Prensa*, the main Honduran newspaper, to try to establish some sort of time frame for the disappearance. According to an article published in *La Prensa* on January 19, 1999, the moon rock and plaque disappeared during the administration of President Rafael Lonardo Callejas (1990–1994). Two other articles published in *La Prensa* in 1999 indicated that the Honduran prosecutor investigating the disappearance focused on the testimony of various ex-employees of the Presidential Palace during President Callejas'[s] term, as well as on Pompeyo Bonilla, a former member of the military who served in the Casa de Gobierno and was then a member of the Chamber of Deputies.

[2] As noted earlier, Mr. Rosen testified that Colonel Argurcia told him that he was given the moon rock and plaque as a gift sometime around 1973. Hearsay is admissible for some purposes in a forfeiture proceeding (such as establishing probable cause), *see, e.g., Nnadi v. Richter*, 976 F.2d 682, 686 (11th Cir. 1992), but even if I were to credit Mr. Rosen's testimony about what he was told, I do not find Colonel Argurcia's statement about the date of acquisition credible. Colonel Argurcia had every incentive to lie about when he obtained the moon rock and plaque, did not have any documents establishing his ownership, first offered to sell the items for $1 million, and reduced his asking price to $50,000 just one year later.

Based upon the evidence in the record, and the fact that Mr. Rosen was offered the moon rock and plaque in 1994, I find, consistent with Professor Rosenn's report, that these items disappeared from the Presidential Palace in Honduras sometime between 1990 and 1994.

C. The Moon Rock and Plaque Became Part of the Patrimony of the Republic of Honduras by Virtue of a Completed Gift from President Nixon in 1973

A donation effectively transfers title to property when accepted by the donee under Honduran law. Articles 1296 and 1297 of the Civil Code provide as follows:

> Art. 1296. An *inter vivos* gift is an act by which one person transfers gratuitously and irrevocably all or part of property to another, who accepts it.
>
> Art. 1297. Those who can enter into contracts have the capacity to make and to accept donations except in cases in which the law expressly provides to the contrary.

When President Lopez Arellano accepted the gift on behalf of the Honduran government and people and placed it in the Presidential Palace, the lunar rock and plaque became part of the patrimony of the Republic of Honduras. That President Lopez Arellano was a *de facto* and not a *de jure* leader is immaterial under Honduran law, and his act of acceptance of the gift on behalf of Honduras has the same effect as if he had been a constitutionally elected head of state.

D. The 1984 and 1997 Honduran Laws for the Protection of Cultural Patrimony Do Not Apply to the Moon Rock and Plaque

Though Honduras has enacted two Laws for the Protection of Cultural Patrimony, Decree No. 81–84 of May 30, 1984, and Decree No. 220–97 of December 29, 1997, neither law is applicable to the moon rock and plaque.

The 1997 law, which repealed the 1984 law, defines cultural patrimony to include moveable property (*bienes muebles*) such as engravings, paintings, sculptures, furnishings, jewelry, currency, weapons, dress items, machinery, tools, and other objects of anthropological and historic interest. The moon rock and plaque, which fit squarely into the category of objects of anthropological and historic interest, would therefore be non-exportable under the second sentence of Article 4 of the 1997 law, which prohibits exportation of any type of cultural good, except a part of cultural interchanges with express authorization. The difficulty lies, however, in the fact that the statute was not effective until the date of its publication in the Official Gazette, which was February 21, 1998.

Both the Constitution and the Civil Code of Honduras prohibit retroactive application of laws, unless they favor a criminal defendant. Article 96 of the Honduran Constitution provides that no law has retroactive effect, except in criminal matters when the new law favors the accused. Article 7 of the Civil Code includes an identical bar on such retroactive application. Because the moon rock and plaque disappeared from Honduras and were transported into the United States before February of 1998, the 1997 law is inapplicable.

The 1984 law was in effect at the time of the disappearance of the moon rock and plaque, but its language [is] problematic. It provides:

> Art. 172. All the anthropological, archeological, historical and artistic wealth of Honduras forms part of the cultural patrimony of the Nation.
>
> The law shall establish the rules that will serve as the basis for its conservation, restoration, maintenance and restitution, as the case may be.
>
> It is the duty of all Hondurans to safeguard their [cultural patrimony] and to prevent its unlawful removal.
>
> Sites of natural beauty, monuments, and reserved zones shall be under the protection of the State.

Article 17 of the 1984 law prohibits the donation or sale of cultural property, and Article 28 prohibits such property from being alienated or taken out of the country. Article 5 defines six categories of cultural patrimony, but the only category relevant to the moon rock and plaque is "moveable property." Unlike the 1997 law, however, the 1984 law only includes objects of anthropological or historic interest if they were manufactured before 1900. Article 5 characterizes moveable property (*bienes muebles*) as

> [e]ngravings, paintings, sculptures, furnishings, jewelry, currency, weapons, dress items, machinery, tools and other objects of anthropological and historic interest, manufactured before 1900.

Because the moon rock is not something that was manufactured, but is rather a work of nature, I agree with Professor Rosenn that the 1984 law cannot apply to it. And though the plaque is of course manufactured, there is no evidence that it was manufactured before 1900. Thus, the 1984 law does not apply to the moon rock and plaque.

E. The Lunar Rock and Plaque Constitute National Property of Public Use under the Civil Code

Title III of Book II of the general provisions of the Honduran Civil Code deals with national property. Article 617 of the Civil Code provides:

> Art. 617. Property whose dominion belongs to the whole nation is called national property. If its use belongs to all the inhabitants of the nation, such as the streets, plazas, bridges and roads, the adjacent sea and its beaches, it is called national property of public use or public property. National property whose use does not belong generally to the inhabitants is called State property or government property.

Thus, the Honduran Civil Code separates national property into two categories: (1) national property of public use (*bienes nacionales de uso público o bienes públicos*), and (2) state property (*bienes del Estado o bienes fiscales*). . . .

H. Professor Rosenn's Conclusions

. . . [After an extensive review of Honduran legislation], Professor Rosenn concluded that the moon rock and plaque became inalienable national property of public use of the Republic of Honduras in 1973, as a result of a completed gift by President Nixon. Special legislation was necessary to alienate these items, and no such legislation was enacted. Thus, whoever took the items from the Presidential Palace committed larceny, making the rock and plaque stolen property. I agree with Professor Rosenn's interpretation of Honduran law, and note that Mr. Rosen has not presented any persuasive argument to challenge those conclusions.

Thus, neither Mr. Rosen nor any of his Honduran associates could have acquired good title to the moon rock and plaque under Honduran law. Although good title to stolen property can sometimes be acquired by prescription, the statute of limitations does not run against national property of public use. Even assuming that the moon rock and plaque are merely state property, which can be acquired by prescription, good title could not have been acquired unless the items were possessed for 20 years (or at least 14 years). The moon rock and plaque, missing from the Presidential Palace since no earlier than 1990, could not have been lawfully possessed by Mr. Rosen or any of his Honduran associates in the mid-1990s.

The exportation of the moon rock and plaque from Honduras under such circumstances would have been unlawful because they were stolen property. For example, Honduran law makes it a criminal offense "to procure the disappearance of evidence of a crime." Honduran Penal Code, Art. 388. The moon rock and plaque are indeed evidence of a crime, and their exportation to the United States is an act that procures their disappearance as evidence for any Honduran authorities investigating their theft.

III. Forfeiture under 19 U.S.C. §§ 1595A(C)(1)(A) & 1615

[3] The United States seeks forfeiture pursuant to 19 U.S.C. § 1595a(c)(1)(A), which provides that

> [m]erchandise which is introduced or attempted to be introduced into the United States contrary to law shall be treated as follows:
>
> (1) The merchandise shall be seized and forfeited if it –
> (A) is stolen, smuggled, or clandestinely imported or introduced. . .

This statute is procedurally governed by 19 U.S.C. § 1615, which provides in pertinent part that [i]n all suits or actions . . . brought for the forfeiture of any . . . merchandise . . . seized under the provisions of any law relating to the collection of duties on imports or tonnage, where the property is claimed by any person, the burden of proof shall lie upon such claimant . . . *Provided*, that probable cause shall be first shown for the institution of such suit or action, to be judged by the court. . . .

Thus, once the government establishes probable cause, the burden shifts to the claimant to rebut the probable cause showing or to establish an affirmative defense by a preponderance of the evidence. *See Nnadi*, 976 F.2d at 686; *United States v. A Single Family Residence and Real Property*, 803 F.2d 625, 629 (11th Cir. 1986); *United States v. One 1975 Ford F100 Pick-up Truck*, 558 F.2d 755, 756 (5th Cir. 1977); *United States v. One Defender Lobster Vessel Named Betty II*, 606 F. Supp. 32, 36 (S.D. Fla. 1984).

Unlike other forfeiture statutes, § 1595a(c) does not contain a so-called "innocent owner" defense. *See An Antique Platter of Gold*, 991 F. Supp. at 232 ("[§] 1595a(c) does not provide for an innocent owner defense"). *See also One 1975 F100 Ford Pick-up Truck*, 558 F.2d at 757 (holding, in case involving forfeiture under 49 U.S.C. § 782 and the former version of § 1595a, that "good faith or innocence on the part of an owner of property subject to forfeiture is immaterial in a seizure under the narcotics laws"). Although many forfeiture statutes now have an innocent owner defense under the CAFRA, *see* 19 U.S.C. § 983(d), the CAFRA does not apply to forfeiture proceedings under § 1595a(c). *See* n.4 (explaining that the CAFRA does not apply to provisions under Title 19).

A. Mr. Rosen's Standing

[4] The government contends that Mr. Rosen lacks standing because the agreement he presented is not for the purchase of the moon rock and plaque, but instead specifically provides for Mr. Rosen to take possession of the items in order to market them and sell them to a third party. If the sale is not effectuated within 90 days, the items are to be returned to Colonel Argurcia. Mr. Rosen testified to the contrary, however, explaining that he had actually purchased the items. In addition, at the time the items were seized, Mr. Rosen had been in possession of them for a year and a half – well over the 90-day period within which he had to effectuate a sale under the agreement. Accordingly, I find that Mr. Rosen has established by a preponderance of the evidence that he has standing to assert a claim for the items. *See United States v. Carrell*, 252 F.3d 1193, 1201 (11th Cir. 2001) ("To have standing to contest a . . . forfeiture, a claimant must have an ownership or possessory interest in the property seized.") (internal quotation marks omitted).

B. Probable Cause

[5][6][7][8] Probable cause is defined as a reasonable ground for belief of a fact supported by less than *prima facie* proof, but more than mere suspicion. *See United States v. $242,484.00*, 318 F.3d 1240, 1243 (11th Cir. 2003); *A Single Family Residence*, 803 F.2d at 628; *United States v. One 1978 Chevrolet Impala*, 614 F.2d 983, 984 (5th Cir. 1980). The existence of probable cause is judged not with clinical detachment, but with a common sense view toward real life. *See A Single Family Residence*, 803 F.2d at 628. Additionally, probable cause in a civil forfeiture proceeding may be established by circumstantial or hearsay evidence. *See id.* at 628–29.

[9][10] An item is "stolen" under federal law when there is a felonious taking with intent to deprive the owner of the rights and benefits of ownership, regardless of whether the taking constitutes larceny at common law. *See United States v. Turley*, 352 U.S. 407, 417, 77 S. Ct. 397, 1 L. Ed. 2d 430 (1957). Stated differently, "in order for property to be considered 'stolen,' the property must rightfully belong to someone other than the person who has it." *United States v. Portrait of Wally*, 2002 WL 553532, *19 (S.D.N.Y. 2002) (*Wally II*).

The government's evidence amply establishes probable cause that the moon rock and plaque were stolen for purposes of § 1595a(c) and then introduced into the United States.

First, Honduras has title to the moon rock and plaque under its law, and it has in no way authorized the transfer of those items, which were a gift to the country from President Nixon in 1973. Honduran law does not allow for the alienation of such items absent some special legislation, and no such legislation has been enacted. And, as explained earlier, it would be impossible under Honduran law for anyone to acquire title to these items through other means such as prescription. To the extent that title prescription were theoretically possible, no such title was acquired because the items were taken from the Presidential Palace between 1990 and 1994. In addition to Professor Rosenn's conclusions about the illegal taking of the items, there is additional evidence that the items were stolen. Most significant is that Colonel Argurcia was "quite anxious" to sell the items (without any papers establishing his ownership) for a mere $50,000 when he had been seeking $1 million just a year earlier. Apparently Colonel Argurcia was having trouble moving items with a questionable provenance. At about the same time, Mr. Rosen estimated the value of the items at $500,000 (and later at $5 million). Although Mr. Rosen still owes $15,000, apparently neither Colonel Argurcia nor Mr. Bayardo have demanded return of the items or sued Mr. Rosen for the balance, suggesting that the sale was not a normal arms' length commercial transaction. Furthermore, Mr. Rosen's own web site obscured the Honduran flag and the presentation plaque, suggesting that he knew or believed that the items were illegally obtained. Finally, Mr. Rosen's statements to the undercover agents – that dealings were done under the table or in dark alleys, that possession of lunar material was illegal, and that he was concerned that the agents might be working for the federal government and be trying to seize the items – show that he knew (or at least suspected) that he did not have lawful possession of the items. *See, e.g.*, *United States v. McClain*, 545 F.2d 988, 1003 n. 33 (5th Cir.) (*McClain I*) ("illegal exportation constitutes a sufficient act of conversion to be deemed a theft"), *on rehearing*, 551 F.2d 52 (5th Cir. 1977).

Second, it is uncontested that the moon rock and plaque were introduced into the United States. The items were delivered to Honduras in 1973, and Mr. Rosen took possession of the items in Miami more than two decades later.

Accordingly, the United States has met its burden of showing probable cause under §§ 1595a(c) and 1615. In order to prevail, Mr. Rosen must therefore present evidence sufficient to rebut the government's probable cause showing by a preponderance of the evidence. *See United States v. 1948 S. Martin Luther King Dr.*, 270 F.3d 1102, 1114 (7th Cir. 2001) (holding that self-serving assertions, unsupported by records or witnesses, are insufficient to rebut a showing of probable cause); *United States v. Parcels of Property*, 9 F.3d 1000, 1005 (1st Cir. 1993) ("[D]enials alone, unaccompanied by offers of proof, [are] insufficient to rebut a showing of probable cause."). Mr. Rosen has failed to do so.

C. Mr. Rosen's Evidence and Arguments

Mr. Rosen initially contends that Professor Rosenn's report is flawed because it was based in part on the incorrect assumption that Mr. Rosen did not have a bill of sale. Mr. Rosen has in fact produced a document – the assignment agreement – which he says became a bill of sale from Colonel Argurcia for the moon rock and plaque. Nevertheless, his argument is flawed. The fact that Mr. Rosen was in possession of a bill of sale does not alter Professor Rosenn's conclusion or my determination of Honduran law. The only way the items at issue could be alienated would be by authorization of the Honduran government through special legislation, and no such legislation exists. In any event, the bill of sale does little to establish that Colonel Argurcia was lawfully in possession of the items when he sold them to Mr. Rosen.

[11] Next, Mr. Rosen faults Professor Rosenn's classification of the moon rock and plaque as national property of public use under Honduran law. He notes that the Civil Code's exemplars of this type of property are streets, bridges, plazas, beaches, and the adjacent sea. Mr. Rosen contends that I should apply American statutory construction principles to this Honduran provision and exclude the items from its scope. *See, e.g., Beecham v. United States*, 511 U.S. 368, 371, 114 S. Ct. 1669, 128 L. Ed. 2d 383 (1994) ("That several items in a list share a common attribute counsels in favor of interpreting the other items as possessing that attribute as well."). He then argues that the essential characteristics of national property of public use are real property used by the public at large. Because the moon rock and plaque are not real property, he continues, they do not fall within this category. His argument fails for two reasons.

First, Article 617 of the Civil Code provides that national property of public use is property that "belongs to all the inhabitants of the nation." Although Article 617 cites the examples mentioned by Mr. Rosen, Honduran authority (cited by Professor Rosenn) indicates that the list is merely descriptive, and not all-inclusive, *see* Reinaldo Cruz Lopez, Los Bienes: Apuntes De Derecho Civil 27 (3d ed. 1989), so there is no basis for importing American principles of statutory construction into the analysis. The moon rock and plaque were a gift from the United States to the people of Honduras, as evidenced by the inscription on the plaque, which reads that the items were "[p]resented to the people of the Republic of Honduras from the people of the United States of America." The gift was intended for the use of all the inhabitants of Honduras, and its lack of real property characteristics, therefore, does not exempt it from inclusion in the category of national property of public use.

[12] Second, even assuming that the moon rock and plaque are not considered national property of public use, Mr. Rosen still fails to rebut the government's showing of probable cause. Article 617 of the Civil Code provides that "[n]ational property whose use does not belong generally to the inhabitants is called State property." If the moon rock and plaque are not national property of public use, they are state property. Like national property of public use, state property also may not be alienated absent special legislation. And although state property may be acquired by prescription, the earlier discussion of Honduran law indicates that to do so in this case would take 20 years (or at least 14 years). The moon rock and plaque have been missing from the Presidential Palace for, at most, 12 years.

In a related argument, Mr. Rosen contends that the United States has failed to show that the Republic of Honduras owned the moon rock and plaque. The lone authority he cites in support of his position is *Government of Peru v. Johnson*, 720 F. Supp. 810. In *Johnson*, the district court concluded that the government of Peru could not establish that it was the legal owner of certain artifacts seized by the United States government. *See id.* at 815. The court reached this decision based on several factors. First, the court could not determine in what country the artifacts were found. Second, it could not determine when they were found. Third, it had no way of knowing whether the artifacts were the possessions of a private person. Fourth, Peru's claim of ownership was not supported by its domestic law. *See id.* In my view, *Johnson* is distinguishable because it does not appear to involve forfeiture under 19 U.S.C. § 1595a(c) – it is unclear from the opinion what substantive law governed or was applied – and because all of the factors identified by the district court in that case are absent here.

Mr. Rosen further suggests, citing *United States v. McClain*, 593 F.2d 658 (5th Cir. 1979) (*McLain II*), that the application of ambiguous foreign law in this civil forfeiture proceeding is prejudicial to him. In that opinion, the Fifth Circuit held that, in a criminal prosecution under 18 U.S.C. § 2314, it is error to permit the jury to interpret and decide issues of foreign law. *See id.* at 667–70. This case, however, is a civil forfeiture proceeding (with a probable cause standard and no jury), and not a criminal prosecution (which requires proof beyond a reasonable doubt). But even if the concerns articulated in *McClain II* were relevant here, there is no ambiguity about Honduran law.

Focusing on the fact that admiralty rules sometimes govern civil *in rem* forfeiture proceedings, Mr. Rosen next requests that I allow for an equitable division of the items so that the competing claims – his and those of the United States and/or Honduras – can be satisfied. Although Mr. Rosen does cite authority indicating that courts have some equitable powers in a forfeiture cases, *see One Single Family Residence*, 932 F.2d 1433, 1434 (11th Cir. 1991) (forfeited house was sold at an interlocutory auction pursuant to a stipulation between the parties), the facts of this case do not indicate that any such equitable division is justified. Mr. Rosen also relies on [a case] where the subject property was sold at a Sotheby's auction and the proceeds were divided between the claimant and the government. Although Mr. Rosen suggests that Judge Hallerstein ordered the property sold at an auction in that case, a telephone conversation with Judge Hallerstein reveals that the parties in the *Double Eagle* case agreed to such a disposition and entered into a stipulation to that regard. Judge Hallerstein therefore never ordered any equitable division. Accordingly, in both cases where an equitable apportionment occurred, it was because the parties agreed to it. In this case, the United States has not agreed to an equitable division, and indeed, vehemently opposes it.

In sum, Mr. Rosen has failed to rebut the government's showing of probable cause by a preponderance of the evidence. Accordingly, the United States is entitled to judgment in its favor.

IV. Conclusion

The moon rock and plaque are forfeited to the United States under 19 U.S.C. §§ 1595a(c) and 1615. A final judgment will be issued separately.

United States v. Schultz,
333 F.3d 393 (2d Cir. 2003)

Schultz was a successful art dealer in New York City. On July 16, 2001, he was indicted on one count of conspiring to receive stolen Egyptian antiquities that had been transported in interstate and foreign commerce, in violation of 18 U.S.C. § 371. The underlying substantive offense was a violation of 18 U.S.C. § 2315, the National Stolen Property Act (NSPA).

Schultz moved to dismiss the indictment, asserting that the items he was charged with conspiring to receive were not stolen within the meaning of the NSPA. Specifically, Schultz contended that the Egyptian antiquities he allegedly conspired to receive were not owned by anyone, and therefore could not be stolen. The prosecution asserted that the antiquities were owned by the Egyptian government pursuant to a patrimony law known as "Law 117," which declared all antiquities found in Egypt after 1983 to be the property of the Egyptian government. After an evidentiary hearing, the district court denied the motion to dismiss in a written memorandum and order. *See* United States v. Schultz, 178 F. Supp. 2d 445 (S.D.N.Y. 2002). Schultz was tried before a jury. . . . The jury found Schultz guilty on the sole count of the indictment, and on June 11, 2002, Schultz was sentenced principally to a term of 33 months' imprisonment. This appeal followed.

. . .

I. Application of the NSPA to Cases Involving Patrimony Laws

In order to preserve its cultural heritage, Egypt in 1983 enacted a "patrimony law" which declares that all antiquities discovered after the enactment of the statute to be the property of the Egyptian government. The law provides for all antiquities privately owned prior to 1983 to be registered and recorded, and prohibits the removal of registered items from Egypt. The law makes private ownership or possession of antiquities found after 1983 illegal. Schultz' primary argument is that the NSPA does not apply to cases in which an object was "stolen" only in the sense that it was possessed or disposed of by an individual in violation of a national patrimony law, as opposed to "stolen" in the commonly used sense of the word – for instance, where an object is taken from a museum or a private collection. The government contends that the plain language of the NSPA indicates that the NSPA applies to *any* stolen property, regardless of the source of the true owner's title in the property. The question, in other words, is whether an object is "stolen" within the meaning of the NSPA if it is an antiquity that was found in Egypt after 1983 and retained by an individual (and, in this case, removed from Egypt) without the Egyptian government's consent.

. . .

[The NSPA] is unambiguous. It applies to goods that are "stolen, unlawfully converted, or taken." *Id.* Goods that belong to a person or entity and are taken from that person or entity without its consent are "stolen" in every sense of that word. *See, e.g., Black's Law Dictionary* 989–90 (6th ed. Abr. 1991) (defining "stolen" as "[a]cquired or possessed, as a result of some wrongful or dishonest act or taking, whereby a person willfully obtains or retains possession of property which belongs to another, without or beyond any permission given, and with the intent to deprive the owner of the benefit of ownership (or possession) permanently"); *Webster's New International Dictionary* 2248 (1971) (defining "stolen" as "obtained or accomplished by theft, stealth, or craft"). Accordingly, Schultz's actions violated the NSPA if the antiquities he conspired to receive in the United States belonged to someone who did not give consent for Schultz (or his agent) to take them. That "someone" is the nation of Egypt.

In 1983, Egypt enacted Law 117. The law, which is entitled "The Law on the Protection of Antiquities," reads, in pertinent part, as follows:

> Article 1
>
> An "Antiquity" is any movable or immovable property that is a product of any of the various civilizations or any of the arts, sciences, humanities, and religions of the successive historical periods extending from prehistoric times down to a point one-hundred years before the present, so long as it has either a value or importance archaeologically or historically that symbolizes one of the various civilizations that have been established in the land of Egypt or that has a historical relation to it, as well as human and animal remains from any such period....
>
> Article 6
>
> All antiquities are considered to be public property – except for charitable and religious endowments.... It is impermissible to own, possess or dispose of antiquities except pursuant to the conditions set forth in this law and its implementing regulations.
>
> Article 7
>
> As of [1983], it is prohibited to trade in antiquities....
>
> Article 8
>
> With the exception of antiquities whose ownership or possession was already established [in 1983] or is established pursuant to [this law's] provisions, the possession of antiquities shall be prohibited as from [1983].

Law 117 includes a chapter entitled "Sanctions and Penalties" detailing the criminal penalties to be imposed on persons found to have violated the law.

...

Schultz contends that in spite of its plain language, Law 117 is not a "real" ownership law, and that Egypt does not truly claim ownership over all antiquities, but merely seeks to restrict their export. The district court disagreed, finding, based substantially on the testimony and other evidence presented at the hearing, that the plain language of Law 117 accurately reflects its purpose and effect: to vest absolute and true ownership of all antiquities found in Egypt after 1983 in the Egyptian government. *See Schultz*, 178 F. Supp. 2d at 448.

"Issues of foreign law are questions of law," *Fed. R. Crim. P. 26.1 (2003)*, and accordingly we should review the district court's findings regarding Law 117 *de novo. See* Curley v. AMR Corp., 153 F.3d 5, 11 (2d Cir. 1998) ("[A] court's determination of foreign law is treated as a question of law, which is subject to *de novo* review." (*citing* parallel rule *Fed. R. Civ. P. 44.1*)).

Schultz failed to present any evidence at the hearing or at trial that Law 117 is not what its plain language indicates it is – that is, an ownership law. [One expert witness's] opinion that the law is ambiguous cannot overcome the combination of (1) the plain text of the statute, and (2) the testimony of two Egyptian government officials to the effect that the statute is a true ownership law and is enforced as such. Although [the third witness] testified that he believed it would be *possible* for Egyptian authorities to leave antiquities in the possession of private individuals who discovered them, Schultz offered no evidence that the authorities ever *actually* had permitted an individual to retain an antiquity found after 1983. The Egyptian government officials testified that there was no legal way for a private individual to retain possession of an antiquity discovered after 1983, and that all such antiquities are seized by the government.

Law 117 defines "antiquity" and prescribes the procedure to be followed by persons in possession of antiquities at the time the Law takes effect, and by persons who discover antiquities thereafter. It sets forth serious criminal penalties for the violation of its provisions. It provides for licensure of certain foreign archaeological missions, and for circumstances under which antiquities may be donated by the government to foreign museums in appreciation of those missions' work. The Law's provisions are directed at activities within Egypt as well as export of antiquities out of Egypt. Law 117 makes it clear that the Egyptian government claims ownership of all antiquities found in Egypt after 1983, and the government's active enforcement of its ownership rights confirms the intent of the Law. Accordingly, we conclude that Law 117 is clear and unambiguous, and that the antiquities that were the subject of the conspiracy in this case were owned by the Egyptian government.

The question thus becomes whether Schultz's actions in conspiring to take antiquities owned by the Egyptian government pursuant to Law 117 out of Egypt violate the NSPA. Schultz argues that even if Law 117 does intend to vest true ownership of all antiquities with the Egyptian government, that sort of "ownership" should not be recognized by the United States for purposes of prosecution under the NSPA.

Schultz urges us to adopt a narrow reading of the NSPA. However, the Supreme Court and this Court have acknowledged that the NSPA has a "broad purpose," McElroy v. United States, 455 U.S. 642, 655, 102 S. Ct. 1332, 71 L. Ed. 2d 522 (1982), and that "the statute should be broadly construed." United States v. Wallach, 935 F.2d 445, 469 (2d Cir. 1991) (*citing* Moskal v. United States, 498 U.S. 103, 113, 111 S. Ct. 461, 112 L. Ed. 2d 449 (1990)). We have held that the language of the NSPA "is broad enough to justify the federal courts in applying the statute whenever they determine that the [property was] stolen in another country." United States v. Greco, 298 F.2d 247, 251 (2d Cir. 1962); *see also* United States v. Parness, 503 F.2d 430, 440 n. 14 (2d Cir. 1974) (*citing Greco* with approval). Accordingly, there can be no doubt that if the antiquities involved in the conspiracy were stolen in Egypt and then shipped to the United States, the NSPA would be violated.

Just as the property need not be stolen in the United States to bring the NSPA into play, the fact that the rightful owner of the stolen property is foreign has no impact on a prosecution under the NSPA. *See* Untied States v. Frazier, 584 F.2d 790, 794 (6th Cir. 1978) ("The court ruled that even if it were conceded that the defendants would be able to prove beyond a reasonable doubt that" the victim was a foreign company, the NSPA would still apply. "This was clearly a correct interpretation of the statute."). Furthermore, this Court has held that the NSPA applies to stolen property even where the person from whom the property was stolen may not have been the true owner of the property, and that the validity of the victim's title in the property is sometimes "irrelevant." United States v. Benson, 548 F.2d 42, 46 (2d Cir. 1977).[202] Accordingly, it does not matter that the antiquities at issue here were stolen in a foreign country, or that their putative owner is a foreign entity.

. . .

[The court then reviewed *Hollinshead, McClain*, and the following authority to establish that violations of Egyptian Law 117, which brought antiquities within the national patrimony, constituted stolen property under the NSPA.]

. . .

iii. Steinhardt

Schultz also contends that our decision in *Steinhardt* indicates that we have rejected the holding of *McClain*. In *Steinhardt*, the district court had found that an Italian antiquity should be forfeited by Steinhardt, who had imported it into the United States, because (1) Steinhardt had made material misrepresentations on a customs form, or (2) in the alternative, the antiquity was properly owned by the Italian government pursuant to a patrimony law and was therefore stolen property within the meaning of the NSPA and subject to forfeiture. *See Steinhardt*, 184 F.3d at 134.

[202] *Benson* involved a prosecution under a different section of the NSPA, 18 U.S.C. § 2314, which prohibits the transport of stolen property, as opposed to the receipt of stolen property, which is prohibited by § 2315. Our precedent interpreting § 2314 is persuasive in considering § 2315, as the two sections merely address different aspects of the same type of criminal behavior – namely, dealing in stolen property – and both are part of the same legislative scheme.

On appeal, we concluded that Steinhardt had made a material misstatement on a customs form when he represented that the antiquity was from Switzerland, not Italy. *See id.* at 137. Accordingly, the Court concluded that the antiquity was subject to forfeiture.[203] See *id.* at 138. The Court declined to reach the alternative ground relied on below, stating: "We need not . . . address whether the NSPA incorporates concepts of property such as those contained in the Italian patrimony laws." *Id.* at 134.

It is irrelevant that we previously reviewed a case in which it was not necessary to reach the question now before us. It is not at all uncommon for us to decline to reach an issue when the case before us can be resolved on other grounds. *See, e.g.,* Wexner v. First Manhattan Co., 902 F.2d 169, 175 (2d Cir. 1990) ("[I]n light of our determination that the district court should be affirmed on other grounds, we find it neither necessary nor appropriate to reach this issue today."). Our failure to address a question that is not necessary to the outcome of a case is simply a wise exercise of our discretion. *See* United States v. United States Gypsum Co., 333 U.S. 364, 402, 68 S. Ct. 525, 92 L. Ed. 746 (1948) (Frankfurter, J., concurring in part) ("Deliberate dicta, I had supposed, should be deliberately avoided. Especially should we avoid passing gratuitously on an important issue of public law where due consideration of it has been crowded out by complicated and elaborate issues that have to be decided.").[204] We find Schultz's reliance on *Steinhardt* unpersuasive.

B. United States Policy

Schultz contends that it is United States policy not to enforce the export restrictions of foreign nations. Schultz offers no evidence in support of this assertion, but even if his assessment of United States policy is accurate, the outcome of this case is unaffected. We have already concluded, based on the plain language of Law 117 and the evidence in the record, that Law 117 is an ownership law, not an export-restriction law. Two Egyptian officials testified under oath that the law is used in Egypt to prosecute people for

[203] *Steinhardt* involved the application of *18 U.S.C. § 545.* As we explained:

> *Section 545* prohibits the importation of merchandise into the United States "contrary to law" and states that material imported in such a manner "shall be forfeited." 18 U.S.C. § 545. The government claims that the importation of [the Italian antiquity] was illegal because it violated 18 U.S.C. § 542, which prohibits the making of false statements in the course of importing merchandise into the United States.

Steinhardt, 184 F.3d at 134–35 (internal footnote omitted).

[204] The dangers inherent in a court's reaching out to decide issues not essential to the outcome of the case before it were perhaps most colorfully described by the nineteenth century English jurist Lord Justice Bowen, who has been quoted by our Supreme Court as saying:

> I am extremely reluctant to decide anything except what is necessary for the special case, because I believe by long experience that judgments come with far more weight and gravity when they come upon points which the Judges are bound to decide, and I believe that obiter dicta, like the proverbial chickens of destiny, come home to roost sooner or later in a very uncomfortable way to the Judges who have uttered them, and are a great source of embarrassment in future cases. Darr v. Burford, 339 U.S. 200, 214, 70 S. Ct. 587, 94 L. Ed. 761 (1950), *overruled in part on other grounds* by Fay v. Noia, 372 U.S. 391, 83 S. Ct. 822, 9 L. Ed. 2d 837 (1963).

trafficking in antiquities *within Egypt's borders.* Law 117 provides for a minimum five-year prison term and a fine of 3,000 pounds for persons convicted of "[t]heft or concealment of a state-owned antiquity." Persons convicted of smuggling an antiquity out of Egypt face "a prison term with hard labor and a fine of not less than 5,000 and not more than 50,000 pounds." Clearly, theft or concealment of an antiquity within Egypt is a different offense than smuggling an antiquity out of Egypt, and *both are* prohibited by Law 117. Accordingly even if Schultz's interpretation of American policy is accurate, it is not relevant here. While Law 117 does restrict exportation of cultural objects, its scope is not limited to export restrictions. Law 117 is more than an export regulation – it is a true ownership law.

C. The CPIA[205]

Schultz contends that the adoption of the CPIA shows that Congress did not intend the NSPA to apply to objects such as the ones he conspired to bring to the United States. The CPIA implements a United Nations [sic] convention that was ratified by the United States in 1982, the purpose of which was to achieve "greater international cooperation towards preserving cultural treasures that not only are of importance to the nations whence they originate, but also to greater international understanding of our common heritage." S. Rep. No. 97–564, at 21 (1982).

The CPIA provides a mechanism for the American government to establish import restrictions on "cultural property" at the request of another signatory nation and after a determination by the President that (1) "the cultural patrimony of [the requesting nation] is in jeopardy from the pillage of archaeological or ethnological materials of [that nation]," (2) the requesting nation "has taken measures . . . to protect its cultural patrimony," (3) the import restrictions are necessary and would be effective in dealing with the problem, and (4) the restrictions are necessary in the "general interest of the international community." 19 U.S.C. § 2602(a)(1)(A)-(D) (2003).

Schultz argues that the CPIA was intended to be the only mechanism by which the United States government would deal with antiquities and other "cultural property" imported into the United States. However, nothing in the language of the CPIA supports that interpretation, and the legislative history shows that exactly the converse is true. As the district court correctly noted, *Schultz,* 178 F. Supp. 2d at 449, the Senate Report on the CPIA expressly states that the CPIA "neither pre-empts state law in any way, nor modifies any Federal or State remedies that may pertain to articles to which [the CPIA's] provisions . . . apply." S. Rep. No. 97–564, at 22 (1982). Furthermore, the Senate Report states that the CPIA "affects neither existing remedies available in state or federal courts nor laws prohibiting the theft and the knowing receipt and transportation of stolen property in

[205] [The Convention on Cultural Property Implementation Act (CPIA) was enacted after *Hollinshead* and *McClain* and therefore was not discussed in those cases. – *Eds.*]

interstate and foreign commerce (*e.g., National Stolen Property Act, Title 18, U.S.C. Sections 2314–15).*" *Id.* at 33 (emphasis added).

The CPIA also bars the importation of items that have been stolen from a museum or other cultural institution in a foreign signatory nation. *See* 19 U.S.C. § 2607. Schultz argues that because only those items that are stolen *from specified places* are covered by the CPIA, Congress never intended in any way to limit the import of items "stolen" only in the sense that they were taken in violation of patrimony laws. This argument is unpersuasive. The CPIA does not state that importing objects stolen from somewhere *other than* a museum is legal. If, for instance, an artifact covered by the CPIA were stolen from a private home in a signatory nation and imported into the United States, the CPIA would not be violated, but surely the thief could be prosecuted for transporting stolen goods in violation of the NSPA.

The CPIA is an import law, not a criminal law; it is not codified in *Title 18* ("Crimes and Criminal Procedure"), with the NSPA, but in *Title 19* ("Customs Duties"). It may be true that there are cases in which a person will be violating both the CPIA and the NSPA when he imports an object into the United States. But it is not inappropriate for the same conduct to result in a person being subject to both civil penalties and criminal prosecution, and the potential overlap between the CPIA and the NSPA is no reason to limit the reach of the NSPA. *See, e.g.*, Hudson v. United States, 522 U.S. 93, 98–99, 118 S. Ct. 488, 139 L. Ed. 2d 450 (1997) (holding that a person may be subjected to civil and criminal penalties for the same conduct without violating the Double Jeopardy Clause).

For the reasons set forth above, we conclude that the passage of the CPIA does not limit the NSPA's application to antiquities stolen in foreign nations.[206]

D. Common-Law Definition of "Stolen"

Schultz argues that the Court must look to the common law definition of "stolen" to determine whether the antiquities at issue are covered by the NSPA.[207] Schultz cites *United States v. Turley*, 352 U.S. 407, 77 S. Ct. 397, 1 L. Ed. 2d 430 (1957), in which the Supreme Court considered the meaning of the term "stolen" in the context of the statute that served as the precursor and model for the NSPA. *See id.* at 410–11, 77 S. Ct. 397. The Supreme

[206] *Schultz* notes that Senator Moynihan stated, after the adoption of the CPIA, that part of the compromise reached in passing that law included an agreement to later amend the NSPA to overrule *McClain. See* 131 Cong. Rec. S2598–03 (Mar. 6, 1985). Senator Moynihan introduced legislation on two occasions that would have done just that; however, neither bill passed. Accordingly, although it may have been Senator Moynihan's belief that the Congress intended to overrule *McClain* in separate legislation after the adoption of the CPIA, that never actually happened. We note that this history further supports our holding that the CPIA itself did nothing to overrule *McClain* or alter the effect of the NSPA with regard to foreign antiquities.

[207] *Schultz* also argues that because a thing can only be "stolen" if it is already owned, then the term "ownership" is implied in the NSPA (although that word never appears anywhere in the text of the NSPA), and accordingly, we must determine the common law meaning of "ownership." We decline to accept this invitation to delve into the meaning of a term that is not even present in an unambiguous statute.

Court stated: We recognize that where a federal criminal statute uses a common-law term of established meaning without otherwise defining it, the general practice is to give that term its common-law meaning." *Id.* at 411, 77 S. Ct. 397. Schultz contends that interpreting the NSPA to apply to items that are "stolen" in the sense that they are possessed by a defendant in violation of a foreign patrimony law would be in derogation of the common law. However, in *Turley*, the Supreme Court explicitly recognized that "'stolen' (or 'stealing') has no accepted common-law meaning." *Id.* If "stolen" has no common law meaning, we cannot look to the common law to assist us in interpreting that term.

The Supreme Court also stated in *Turley* that the term "stolen" included "all felonious takings . . . regardless of whether or not the theft constitutes common-law larceny." *Id.* at 417, 77 S. Ct. 397. In other words, according to the Supreme Court, the precursor to the NSPA – and by extension the NSPA – covers a broader class of crimes than those contemplated by the common law. Accordingly, we find this argument unpersuasive.

E. Summary

In light of our own precedents and the plain language of the NSPA, we conclude that the NSPA applies to property that is stolen in violation of a foreign patrimony law. The CPIA is not the exclusive means of dealing with stolen artifacts and antiquities, and reading the NSPA to extend to such property does not conflict with United States policy. We believe that, when necessary, our courts are capable of evaluating foreign patrimony laws to determine whether their language and enforcement indicate that they are intended to assert true ownership of certain property, or merely to restrict the export of that property. In this case, the district court carefully evaluated the language of Law 117. The court also heard testimony from one academic expert and two Egyptian government officials. This evidence was sufficient to inform the court of the nature of Egypt's interest in the antiquities that were the subject of the conspiracy.

Although we recognize the concerns raised by Schultz and the *amici* about the risks that this holding poses to dealers in foreign antiquities, we cannot imagine that it "creates an insurmountable barrier to the lawful importation of cultural property into the United States." Our holding does assuredly create a barrier to the importation of cultural property owned by a foreign government. We see no reason that property stolen from a foreign sovereign should be treated any differently from property stolen from a foreign museum or private home. The *mens rea* requirement of the NSPA will protect innocent art dealers who unwittingly receive stolen goods, while our appropriately broad reading of the NSPA will protect the property of sovereign nations.

II. Defense of Mistake of United States Law

Schultz argues on appeal that the district court erred in refusing to allow him to present a defense of mistake of law. Specifically, Schultz sought to argue to the jury that he did not know that importing antiquities owned by the Egyptian government pursuant to Law 117 violated the NSPA.[208] The government contends that the district court was correct to bar this defense, relying on "the venerable principal that ignorance of the law generally is no defense to a criminal charge." Ratzlaf v. United States, 510 U.S. 135, 149, 114 S. Ct. 655, 126 L. Ed. 2d 615 (1994). [The court determined that several exceptions to this rule are inappropriate.]

...

In addition, the record demonstrates that Schultz's actions were not "innocent" or merely "negligent." This is not a case in which the defendant believed that he was doing something lawful, and was surprised to find that his conduct could result in criminal sanctions. To the contrary, Schultz was conspiring to *smuggle* antiquities out of Egypt and into the United States. He was defrauding (or attempting to defraud) potential buyers.

...

We conclude that the district court did not err in denying Schultz's request to present a defense of mistake of American law. The jury did not have to find that Schultz knew what he was doing was illegal. As long as the jury found beyond a reasonable doubt that Schultz knew the antiquities were "stolen," the jury, following the law, would have been required to convict Schultz even if it believed he had misunderstood American law.

...

Conclusion

We conclude that the NSPA applies to property that is stolen from a foreign government, where that government asserts actual ownership of the property pursuant to a valid patrimony law. We find the remainder of Schultz's claims [related to jury instructions and admission of evidence] to be without merit. Accordingly, the judgment of the district court is hereby affirmed....

---

[208] [This footnote is taken from later text in the opinion – *Eds.*]

The jury heard substantial evidence indicating that Schultz was actually aware that the NSPA had been applied to objects stolen in violation of a patrimony law. Specifically, it appears that Schultz was aware of the *McClain* decision.

In 1994, Schultz was contacted by the Turkish government. The Turkish government requested that Schultz detail the provenance of several items in his gallery that the Turkish authorities believed to be of Turkish origin. In this correspondence, the Turkish government noted that all antiquities found in Turkey are the property of the Turkish government under a patrimony law. Schultz, acting through counsel, refused to cooperate with Turkey in this inquiry, claimed that Schultz had no knowledge that any Turkish artifacts in his possession were stolen, and referred to the *McClain* case.

Schultz concedes in his appellate brief that the *McClain* decision was "well publicized." Schultz was an owner of a gallery dealing in antiquities, and was once the president of the National Association of Dealers in Ancient, Oriental and Primitive Art, suggesting that he would be aware of all significant developments in the field.

Accordingly, even if Schultz had been permitted to present this defense, it is unlikely that the jury would have credited it.

NOTES AND QUESTIONS

1. Should criminal prosecutions for theft of cultural heritage be subject to statutes of limitations? Should the ends of justice outweigh the problem of stale evidence and unavailable witnesses that may otherwise necessitate limitations to actions after a number of years? The following commentary raises this question in a notorious case involving theft by a soldier of priceless heritage in occupied Germany at the end of the Second World War.
2. The Italian government, after massive national and transnational criminal investigations, took action early in the twenty-first century to recover important objects that allegedly had been looted by *tombaroli* (tomb raiders) and acquired illegally by major museums around the world. See PETER WATSON & CECILIA TADESCHINI, THE MEDICI CONSPIRACY: THE ILLICIT JOURNEY OF LOOTED ANTIQUITIES, FROM ITALY'S TOMB RAIDERS TO THE WORLD'S GREATEST MUSEUMS (2006). A critical review of this book appears as Hugh Eakin, *Notes from Underground*, 53 N.Y. REV. BOOKS, May 25, 2006, at 49, and letters in response by the book's coauthors, 53 N.Y. REV. BOOKS, July 13, 2006, at 56. On the fallout of the Italian initiative, see also Elisabetta Povoledo, *Prosecutors Bet Big on Antiquities Trial in Italy*, N.Y. TIMES, Nov. 16, 2005, at B-1; Lee Rosenbaum, *Truth in Booty: Coming – and Staying – Clean*, WALL ST. J., Feb. 28, 2006, at D8.
3. In *Government of Iran v. The Barakat Galleries Ltd.*, [2007] EWCA Civ. 1374, [2009] Q.B. 22 (C.A.), which we noted in Chapter 4 on the issue of enforcement of foreign law, the English Court of Appeal upheld Iran's title and right to possession of antiquities from Iran now located in England. In so doing, the English court reflected the changing international climate of opinion and applied both binding and nonbinding norms, writing that it was "certainly contrary to public policy for such claims to be shut out." (*Id.* at ¶ 154). The court also referred specifically to the 1970 UNESCO Convention and the 1995 UNIDROIT Convention, though neither applied to the case, because "they do illustrate the international acceptance of the desirability of protection of the national heritage. A refusal to recognize the title to a foreign State, conferred by its law, to antiquities unless they had come into the possession of such State, would in most cases render it impossible for this country to recognize any claim by such a State to recover antiquities unlawfully exported to this country." (*Id.* at ¶ 163).

   Despite the different legal framework from *Schultz*, the *Barakat* court displayed a remarkably similar attitude toward foreign laws concerning illegally excavated cultural property. See Matthias Weller, Iran v. Barakat: *Some Observations on the Application of Foreign Public Law by Domestic Courts from a Comparative Perspective*, 12 ART, ANTIQUITY & LAW 279 (2007).

Ruth Redmond-Cooper, *Quedlinburg Indictment Comes Too Late*, ART ANTIQUITY & L., Sept. 1998, at 307

This infamous saga of the Quedlinburg treasures has ended in a sorry fashion. In April 1998, the U.S. Court of Appeals, Fifth Circuit, held (by a majority) that the criminal proceedings against the defendants, two of whom had inherited the treasures from their brother, was time-barred as having been commenced 24 hours too late.[209]

Background

The background to the case begins at the end of World War Two when Joe T. Meador, a young American serviceman, was part of the Allied force posted to maintain the peace in Quedlinburg, Germany, a town which dates back to medieval times. Various precious items had been placed for safekeeping in an abandoned mine near the town, but when the US troops withdrew from the area, a number of important items were missing, including the "Samuhel Evangeliar" (the Samuhel Gospels), a ninth-century medieval manuscript written entirely in gold and the "Evangelistar aus St. Wiperti," a sixteenth-century prayer book (the "Prayer Book"). Letters sent by Meador to his family appeared to indicate that these items had also been sent by him to them. When Joe Meador died, his brother, Jack Manning Meador, and his sister, Jane Meador Cook, inherited his possessions, including the Samuhel Gospels and the Prayer Book. When they later decided to sell the treasures, they sought the advice of a Houston attorney, Torigian, who assured them that they had good title to the treasures under the Texas laws of inheritancy. They proceeded, with the help of Torigian, to sell the manuscripts. The Samuhel Gospels were acquired for $3 million dollars on behalf of the Cultural Foundation of the States in Berlin; the last transaction in this regard took place on 9th May 1990.

The Investigation

The United States Government then began investigating the transactions involving the two manuscripts with a view to bringing criminal proceedings against the brother and sister and the attorney for conspiring to receive, possess, conceal, store, barter, sell and dispose of stolen goods and for receiving, possessing, concealing, storing, bartering, selling and disposing of stolen goods. Before proceedings could be commenced, it was necessary to enlist the assistance of the German Ministry of Justice, as much of the evidence was located in Germany. Under the applicable statute of limitations, the limitation period for such US criminal proceedings was five years; it therefore *prima facie* expired on 9th May 1995. However, in a case such as this, where evidence relating to the commission of a criminal offence is located in a foreign country, the running of the limitation period may be suspended, with the period of suspension starting on the date on which an official request for information is made to the other State, and ending on the date on which the foreign court or authority takes final action on the request.[210] The term "final action" is not defined in the section and the present proceedings turned on this point.

[209] United States v. Meador, 138 F.3d 986 (1998).

[210] 18 U.S.C. § 3292 (enacted as part of the Comprehensive Crime Control Act 1984) provides:

§ 3292 Suspension of limitations to permit United States to obtain foreign evidence

(a) (1) Upon application of the United States, filed before return of an indictment, indicating that evidence of an offense is in a foreign country, the district court before which a [G]rand [J]ury is impaneled to investigate the offense shall suspend the running of the statute of limitations for the

The indictment against the defendants was returned by the grand jury on January 4th 1996. The defendants pleaded that it was time-barred.

Period of Suspension of the Limitation Period

There were a number of possible dates put forward for the date of "final action." The first of these was June 7th 1995, the date on which all the interviews relevant to the proceedings had been conducted in Germany and all documents handed over; that would have given a period of suspension of the limitation period of 97 days (from March 2nd 1995, the date of the official request, to June 7th 1995). Alternatively, if the final action occurred on the date on which the German Ministry of Justice informed the United States Department of Justice's Office of International Affairs that it considered that the request for assistance had been completely satisfied,[211] the period of suspension would have been 239 days, from March 2nd 1995 to October 27th 1995, and would have caused the limitation period to expire on January 3rd 1996, one day before the indictment was returned. It was argued for the US Government that the date of "final action" was either the date when certain additional documents were sent to the FBI by the Secretary General of the body which had bought the Samuhel Gospels (January 31st 1996), or even the date (31st March 1996) when the German Government officially notified the United States about the production of those documents. The US Government argued that "final action" does not occur in such a case until it is itself satisfied that all the evidence that may be responsive to its official request for assistance has been produced.

The Meaning of "Final Action"

There is surprisingly little case law on the meaning of the term "final action" in this context. The only case to consider the issue is United States

offense if the court finds by a preponderance of the evidence that an official request has been made for such evidence and it reasonably appears, or reasonably appeared at the time the request was made, that such evidence is, or was, in such foreign country.

(2) The court shall rule upon such application not later than thirty days after the filing of the application.

(b) Except as provided in subsection (c) of this section, a period of suspension under this section shall begin on the date on which the official request is made and end on the date on which the foreign court or authority takes final action on the request.

(c) The total of all periods of suspension under this section with respect to an offense:

(1) shall not exceed three years; and

(2) shall not extend a period within which a criminal case must be initiated for more than six months if all foreign authorities take final action before such period would expire without regard to this section.

(d) As used in this section, the term 'official request' means a letter rogatory, a request under a treaty or convention, or any other request for evidence made by a court of the United States or an authority of the United States having criminal law enforcement responsibility, to a court or other authority of a foreign country.

18 U.S.C. § 3292 (1995). Under subsection (b), the period of suspension ends when "the foreign court or authority takes final action on the government's official request." 18 U.S.C. § 3292(b) (1995).

211 "I have the honor of transmitting to you the following items in satisfaction of the above request which have turned up in Bavaria . . . according to my documentation, the request has now been completely satisfied. I therefore consider my function to be concluded."

v. Bischel[212] where the U.K. Government, in accordance with a request from the US Government, handed over all the records requested by the US, but delayed certifying their authenticity. In that case, the Ninth Circuit agreed with the argument put forward by the US Government that the "final action" for the purposes of ending the suspension of the limitation period did not occur until the foreign authority has not only supplied all the information requested by the U.S., but has also communicated its belief that it has fully complied with the request for information.

The argument of the U.S. Government in this case that "final action" occurs only when it is satisfied with the evidence was rejected by the court as untenable: it would provide an almost open-ended suspension period, tempered only by the three-year maximum laid down by section 3292(c)(1). Similarly, the fact that later evidence was found to be relevant did not detract from the fact that the request for information had, objectively, been fulfilled. Again, to allow later information would mean that the period of suspension was potentially open-ended.

Expiry of the Limitation Period

The majority therefore held that the period of suspension ended on the date when the German Ministry of Justice declared that it had complied with all requests. The limitation period consequently expired on January 3rd 1996, just 24 hours before the indictment. The criminal proceedings against the defendants were therefore time-barred as having been commenced 24 hours too late.

Comment

Section 3292 performs a useful function in suspending the running of the limitation period in cases where evidence relevant to criminal proceedings is located overseas.[213] The court can take account of the delays inherent in such proceedings by disregarding the time taken to acquire such necessary evidence. However, the protective nature of a limitation period must remain paramount: limitation periods exist to encourage the speedy resolution of disputes, and to protect defendants from the prospect of legal proceedings hanging over them indefinitely. Any provision which allows for the suspension of the limitation period must be interpreted restrictively in order to ensure that the aims of the legislation are met. Although in a case such as this, the instinctive arguments are clearly in favour of interpreting the legislation in the manner most appropriate to achieving "justice" in the particular circumstances, the wider picture must not be ignored and a clear, certain rule must be applied.[214]

---

[212] United States v. Bischel, 61 F.3d 1429 (9th Cir. 1995).

[213] English law does not generally provide a limitation period in criminal proceedings: *nullum tempus currit regi* (time does not run against the Crown).

[214] A "'bright-line" rule. It has been said that "criminal limitations statutes are 'to be liberally interpreted in favor of repose.'" (Toussie v. United States, 397 U.S. 112, 115, 90 S. Ct. 858, 860, 25 L. Ed. 2d 156 (1970), *quoting* United States v. Scharton, 285 U.S. 518, 522, 52 S. Ct. 416, 417, 76 L. Ed. 917 (1932).

NOTE

Some legal systems provide for immunity from seizure of cultural objects on loan from foreign sources. As you read the following, consider whether such immunity should be criminal as well as civil.

> One of the most high profile events in the history of immunity for seizure came in January 1998 when the New York County District Attorney ("DA") issued a subpoena to the Museum of Modern Art in New York ("MOMA") for the production of two paintings exhibited from 8th October 1997 to 4th January 1998. The exhibition was on loan from the Leopold Museum in Austria and was part of a three-year worldwide tour of the Austrian expressionist painter Egon Schiele. The heirs of two European Jews claimed ownership of the paintings, which they alleged were looted by the Nazis from their ancestors during the Second World War. No federal immunity protection was sought for the paintings and MOMA instead relied on the New York statute in their defence.
>
> The case hinged on the interpretation of the New York statute and whether it was intended to apply only to civil cases and therefore excluded criminal acts, such as theft, as falling under the jurisdiction of the law. MOMA argued to the contrary in the trial court and successfully moved to quash the subpoena. [MOMA argued that "the success of New York's museums in presenting first class exhibitions on a consistent basis is dependent, in part, on their ability to provide assurances to art lenders that their works will be safely returned."] The success was short lived however and the Appellate Division of the State of New York reversed the trial court's ruling, finding the statute did not immunize loans seized pursuant to criminal investigations. MOMA asked the highest court, the Court of Appeals, to review the lower court's finding and the NY State Court of Appeals quashed the Appellate Court's ruling on finding that the New York statute applies to criminal as well as civil proceedings.
>
> Despite MOMA's court victory, the seizure of the two paintings by the New York DA had an immediate and profound effect on the museum community. Suddenly the assurance that works would be returned was thrown into question. One month after the seizure of the Schiele paintings, two lenders backed out of an agreement to loan paintings to the museum for a Pierre Bonnard retrospective. One of the lenders wrote to the exhibition curator saying "the news of the arrest of the two Schiele paintings in your museum made me very anxious and unsure and you certainly will understand that I'm not in a position to lend you my painting under such circumstances."
>
> In December 1998, the French authorities decided to re-route a Monet painting away from the UK because of the lack of any 'safe conduct' legislation. The painting in question, Monet's *Waterlilies 1904*, had been loaned to the 'Monet in the Twentieth Century' exhibition at the Boston Museum of Fine Art and was due to return to the Musée des Beaux Arts at Caen via an exhibition at the Royal Academy in London. [The painting had been in the collection of Adolf Hitler's foreign minister Joachim von Ribbentrop (who had selected it from the Jeu de Paume Museum in Paris) and had been claimed by the heirs of its owner Paul Rosenberg and registered on the Art Loss Register as a

stolen work by his daughter and widowed daughter-in-law. Through the Art Loss Register, the painting was eventually returned to the Rosenberg family in April 1999, per Sarah Jackson, historic claims director, Art Loss Register. – *Eds.*]

In 2000, the New York statute was amended so that protection applies only to civil, not criminal seizures. In the words of the presiding Governor Pataki:

> the legislation is intended to assist in the recovery of stolen property and help keep our promise to help New York's Holocaust survivors and others whose property was taken from them unlawfully.

To address concerns raised by museum representatives, a sunset clause was introduced to allow the law to expire on 1st June 2002 so that the New York statute of 1968 currently applies to all civil and criminal seizures.

Anna O'Connell, *Immunity from Seizure: An Overview*, 11 Art, Antiquity & L., Mar. 2006, at 1, 6–7. *See also* Manlio Frigo, *Protection of Cultural Property on Loan – Anti-Seizure and State Immunity Laws: An Italian Perspective*, 14 Art, Antiquity & L., Apr. 2009, at 49 (examining a draft bill in the Italian Parliament on immunity from seizure of artworks on loan to Italy in the context of regional and international law, especially the UNIDROIT Convention).

PROBLEM

The director of a small art gallery in New York has asked you, as outside counsel, to summarize the legal authority for seizure and forfeiture of cultural property by the U.S. and New York State governments. The gallery specifically wants to protect itself against any risks resulting from acquisitions of new material.

C. Dispute Resolution

1. Litigation: The Core Issues

Litigation related to the transfer of cultural material often involves a conflict of laws and thereby raises issues of private international law. Accordingly, a claimant must be prepared to establish the requisite standing to bring an action in a chosen forum and to ensure that the forum has jurisdiction over the subject matter of the litigation and the parties to it. Also, a claim for transfer of material that originated in one country but is located in another creates the possibility that a law other than that of the country of origin governs the resolution of a dispute. Furthermore, a claim for cultural material may be challenged on the basis that too long a period of time has elapsed since the property was originally lost or taken, even if it had gone missing in times of great social upheaval such as the Holocaust. A statute of limitations or repose as well as the equitable doctrine of laches therefore may apply. The state of origin or of the owner or bona fide purchaser of an object may be unwilling to enforce the decision of a foreign court that violates the enforcing forum's public policy. Such issues in private international law are explored in the following sections.

a. Standing

The term "standing" describes a party's right to make a legal claim or seek judicial enforcement of a duty or right. The standing of a plaintiff to pursue a claim in a court of law may be at issue, however, if the party has a legal character unrecognized by the forum's law (*lex fori*), but that is seldom the case. In Chapter 4, the *Mullick* and *Bumper* decisions established that cultural material itself may have standing in British courts. The same chapter introduced the *Goldberg* case, involving a claim by the established Orthodox Church of Cyprus for return of Byzantine mosaics in the possession of an Indiana art dealer, Peg Goldberg. We return to that case several times in this chapter, beginning with the following excerpt from the majority opinion that addresses the issue of whether the plaintiff church can bring an action in a U.S. district court, given the jurisdictional requirement of a full diversity of citizenship between the parties. This opinion thus straddles issues of standing and jurisdiction, a topic that is explored more fully in the next section.

AUTOCEPHALOUS GREEK-ORTHODOX CHURCH OF CYPRUS AND THE REPUBLIC OF CYPRUS v. GOLDBERG, 917 F. 2d 278 (7th Cir. 1990)

Cyprus, for its part, asserted in its jurisdictional statement that "the Church of Cyprus is a citizen and subject of the Republic of Cyprus, and is a religious corporation under Cypriot law, maintains its principle [sic] place of business in Cyprus, and is empowered to own, regulate and administer property." . . . Goldberg has since filed an "Amendment to Jurisdictional Statement and Suggestion of Jurisdictional Issue," stating that she "has now concluded that the record does not appear to support diversity jurisdiction because the record does not address the legal status and the citizenship of [the Church of Cyprus]." . . . She alleges that, because "she has been unable to locate evidence in the record to establish that the Church of Cyprus is incorporated under the laws of any foreign state or that the Church should be considered a 'citizen or subject' of a foreign state," the Church should be considered an unincorporated association whose citizenship includes all jurisdictions of which its members are citizens. *Cf. Hummel v. Townsend*, 883 F.2d 367 (5th Cir. 1989). Goldberg recommends at least a remand for further proceedings as to the citizenship of all of the Church's members (if any are domiciled in Indiana, the argument goes, diversity is destroyed), and at best a remand with directions to dismiss for lack of jurisdiction. Neither option is warranted.

. . .

Goldberg's argument substantially misstates the issue. The primary question here is not whether the Church of Cyprus is incorporated under the laws of Cyprus. Proving that it is incorporated under Cypriot law is indeed one method for the Church to establish that it is a "citizen or subject" of Cyprus; . . . but it is only one method. The primary issue here is whether the record contains sufficient evidence that, under the laws of the Republic of Cyprus, the Church is considered a juridical entity distinct from its members, regardless of its corporate status. *See Puerto Rico v. Russell & Co.*, 288 U.S. 476, 479–82, 77 L. Ed. 903, 53 S. Ct. 447 (1933); *Cohn v. Rosenfeld*, 733 F.2d 625, 628–30 (9th Cir. 1984). We stress that the citizenship status generally attributed to religious organizations under American law, as well as the characteristics of and requirements for the corporate form under American law, are irrelevant. As we stated in *Sadat v. Mertes*, 615 F.2d 1176, 1183 (7th Cir. 1980):

> The generally accepted test for determining whether a person is a foreign citizen for purposes of 28 U.S.C. § 1332(a)(2) is whether the country in which citizenship is claimed would so recognize him. This is in accord with the principle of international law that "it is the inherent right of every independent nation to determine for itself, and according to its own constitution and laws, what classes of persons shall be entitled to citizenship."

(quoting *United States v. Wong Kim Ark*, 169 U.S. 649, 668, 42 L. Ed. 890, 18 S. Ct. 456 (1898))....

Cyprus presented the following evidence to the district court: 1) the Constitution of the Republic of Cyprus recognizes the existence of the Autocephalous Greek-Orthodox Church of Cyprus and grants to it the "exclusive right of regulating and administering its own internal affairs and property in accordance with the Holy Canons and its Charter;" 2) under the "Immovable Property (Tenure, Registration and Valuation) Law" of the Republic of Cyprus, a "religious corporation" – defined as a "religious establishment or religious institution belonging to any denomination and any throne, church, chapel, monastery, mosque, tekye, shrine or synagogue" – may own and register property; and 3) the Church of Cyprus registered the Kanakaria Church in the Land Registry Office of the Republic of Cyprus pursuant to this statute.... We conclude that this evidence sufficiently established that the Church is recognized under and by the laws of the Republic of Cyprus as a distinct juridical entity, and thus is a "citizen or subject" of that state....

---

b. Jurisdiction

A claimant of cultural material ordinarily will commence proceedings in the legal system where the material is currently located. Sometimes, as in the following case, an issue may arise if the country where the material is located appears to have little connection with the material.

H.R.H. Maharanee Seethadevi Gaekwar of Baroda v. Wildenstein, [1972] 2 Q.B. 283 (C.A.)

Lord Denning M.R. The Maharanee of Baroda lives in France, but she has lived in England for long periods, and has had many flats and large houses in this country. She is intimately connected with English social life. She frequently visits England for considerable periods, and has horses in training here. She has a stud farm in Ireland.

M. Daniel Wildenstein lives in Paris. He is an art dealer of international repute. In September 1970, the *Paris Match* published an article about him. It describes him as the greatest art dealer in the world. The business was founded by his grandfather in Paris and New York. It was extended to London by his father, who had a gallery in New Bond Street and a small flat above it. Daniel Wildenstein himself succeeded to it. He was at all material times a director of Daniel Wildenstein Ltd., the important art dealers of 147 New Bond Street in London. Daniel Wildenstein is also connected with the important New York house of Wildenstein Inc. He has another great interest, racehorses. He has a stud farm in Ireland, and he comes over to England from time to time for the races here.

Both the Maharanee and M. Wildenstein speak perfect English. In 1965, the Maharanee's son, the Prince of Baroda, was invited to go to the house of M. Daniel Wildenstein at 57 rue de La Boètie, Paris. He was told there were some beautiful old masters which the Maharanee might like to purchase. At the house he was shown a painting called *La Poésie.* It was said to be by a great French artist, François Boucher. After some negotiation, the picture was purchased by the Maharanee at a sum which in English money was put at £32,920. It was delivered to the Maharanee there in Paris – a purchase by her from M. Daniel Wildenstein.

In July 1966, M. Daniel Wildenstein gave a certificate of authenticity and value. It was on the notepaper of the English company – Wildenstein & Co. Ltd., 147 New Bond Street, London. W.l. The directors were named as M. Daniel Wildenstein (French) and Mr. Hunter, F.C.A. The certificate says (translated into English):

> "I, the undersigned, Daniel Wildenstein, director of Wildenstein & Co. Ltd., certify that the painting by Francois Boucher, *D'Etude ou la Poésie,* 0.95 × 1.25 m., belonging to Her Highness the Maharanee of Baroda, has this day a value of 450,000 French francs. July 20, 1966. Daniel Wildenstein."

The Maharanee brought the picture to England. On December 6, 1967, it was put up for sale by Sotheby's in a catalogue of important old master paintings. At the beginning of the catalogue Sotheby's set out a glossary saying that if the forename and surname of the artist [are] given, it means that, in the opinion of Sotheby's, it is a work by the artist. There is a photograph of the picture. It says: *La Poésie* by François Boucher. It describes it as: "the property of Her Royal Highness the Maharanee of Baroda – *La Poésie,* a girl in pale blue and white drapery reclining, holding a book and a lyre." That catalogue is a representation by Sotheby's that, in their opinion, it was a work by François Boucher.

The painting was not sold by Sotheby's at that sale. I presume it did not reach the reserve price. Perhaps some people had doubts about its authenticity. A little later, the picture was shown to Mr. Francis Watson, who is the Surveyor of Her Majesty's Works of Art, but not of her pictures. He only saw it for a few minutes, but he is said to have expressed the view that it was not a Boucher. In July 1968 it was put in the hands of Christie's, who are art dealers equal in repute to Sotheby's. On October 18, 1968, Christie's wrote to the Maharanee's solicitors:

> In confirmation of our telephone conversation. I am writing to say that in our opinion the painting of a female allegorical figure representing poetry, which was sent to us on July 26, cannot be regarded as an autograph work by François Boucher, but would appear to be a work from his immediate circle of followers. We think that it might make about *£750* at auction and in the event of the owner deciding to sell we would not recommend a reserve of more than about £500/£600.

On September 3, 1969, the solicitors for the Maharanee issued a writ against M. Daniel Wildenstein. The statement of claim set out the circumstances in which she bought the picture, saying that it was represented to be by Boucher, but alleging that it was not by Boucher. She claimed rescission and repayment to her of the money which she had paid.

In the writ, the Maharanee gave her address as Claridge's in Brook Street – the hotel where she was staying at the time. M. Daniel Wildenstein's address was given as 147 New Bond Street, because he was at that time a director of the English company.

The writ was not served on M. Wildenstein at that time, because he was not in London. Those advising the Maharanee waited till he came over here. In June 1970 M. Daniel Wildenstein came over for the Ascot races. On Saturday, June 20, 1970, the writ was served on him at the racecourse at Ascot. His solicitors entered an appearance. They now seek to set the writ aside. The master and the judge have set it aside. The Maharanee appeals to this court.

In this case the writ has been properly served on the defendant in this country. This makes the case very different from those in which the defendant is in a foreign country and the plaintiff has to seek leave to serve him out of the jurisdiction. It is also different from those cases in which the plaintiff has already started an action in another country, and the question is whether he should be allowed to start another action in this country on the same subject matter. In this case the plaintiff has validly invoked the jurisdiction of our courts in this, the one and only action she has brought.

QUESTIONS

Do you agree that a service of process on a defendant should be adequate to establish the personal jurisdiction of a court over the defendant? Such a basis – so-called tag jurisdiction – is well established in the United Kingdom and United States but controversial elsewhere. Should it matter that the defendant in *Baroda* had multiple connections with the United Kingdom and was a director of an

English company, or would it be enough that the defendant was simply present in the United Kingdom? What if the defendant had never before been to the United Kingdom and was only changing planes in London when the process was served?

c. Choice of Law

Every legal system has either a body of rules – choice-of-law rules – or other established practice that enables its courts to apply either local law or that of a foreign jurisdiction to resolve a case before it. The premise underlying the seemingly unusual possibility of applying foreign law is that it may be more appropriate, for example, when an issue or dispute bears a closer connection to foreign territory than the forum's territory or local legal interest.

(i) Alternative Approaches.

Winkworth v. Christie Manson and Woods Ltd., [1980] 1 Ch. 496, 497

[The plaintiff had certain works of art stolen from him in England, where he was domiciled. The artworks were then taken to Italy and sold to the second defendant under a contract made in Italy and governed by Italian law. The second defendant then sent the artworks to the first defendants for sale at auction in London. On becoming aware of the whereabouts of his stolen property the plaintiff brought an action seeking, *inter alia*, a declaration that the artworks were his property. In response, the second defendant argued that, under Italian law, he had acquired a good title to the artworks. – *Eds.*]

This is an action in detinue and conversion. The general rule is that the title which must be established by a person bringing an action for detinue or conversion of goods in an English court consists of proof not so much of absolute ownership, as proof that he had at the time of the detention or conversion, either actual possession of the goods or the immediate right to possession of them. On the agreed facts the second defendant has on no footing violated any actual possession of the goods by the plaintiff, who, by reason of the theft, had already lost such possession before the time when the contract of sale was concluded in Italy. As against the second defendant therefore the plaintiff must establish the immediate right to possession of the goods. It is accordingly common ground between counsel that the phrase "title to," as appearing in the question of law formulated for the decision of this court, must lie construed as meaning "the immediate right to possession of." The distinction may have little or no practical significance on the facts of this case, but must be recorded for the sake of accuracy.

It is common ground that at the time of the theft the plaintiff was the owner of the goods, and that they were in his lawful possession. It is also common ground that he neither knew of nor consented to their removal to Italy or any subsequent dealing with or movements of them up to the time when the undertakings were given by Christie's. There is no suggestion in the agreed facts or on the pleadings that any person not a party to these proceedings ever acquired a title to the goods which would have destroyed the plaintiff's immediate right to possession of them. It is therefore plain that, on any footing, at least until the sale in Italy, nothing had occurred which destroyed such right.

On the other hand, if the effect of the subsequent sale in Italy was to confer on the second defendant a title to ownership of the goods which is valid even against the plaintiff and is of such a nature that it must now be recognized by the English court, it would necessarily follow that, in the events which have happened, the plaintiff has lost and the second defendant has acquired, the immediate right to possession of them.

In the circumstances, a crucial issue in the present case must be: was the effect of the sale in Italy to confer on the second defendant a title to ownership of the goods which is valid even against the plaintiff? And the question of law now before the court resolves itself to the question whether this issue falls to be determined in concordance with English domestic law or Italian domestic law. The question is one of practical importance for the parties. For, while the point has not been argued before me and I do not purport to decide it, it seems probable that, if English domestic law alone applies, the second "defendant," who does not claim to have been a purchaser "in market overt," within the meaning of section 22(1) of the Sale of Goods Act 1893, would not have acquired a title to these stolen goods, which was valid vis-à-vis the plaintiff. On the other hand, the second defendant in paragraph 6 of his defence pleads, inter alia:

> Under Italian law a purchaser of movables acquires a good title notwithstanding any defect in the seller's title or in that of prior transferors provided that (1) the purchaser is in good faith at the time of delivery, (2) the transaction is carried out in a manner which is appropriate, as regards the documentation effecting or evidencing the sale, to a transaction of the type in question rather than in some other manner which is irregular as regards documentation and (3) the purchaser is not aware of any unlawful origin of the goods at the time when he acquires them. The second defendant will rely on articles 1153 and 1154 of the Italian Civil Code in relation to the foregoing.

In paragraph 7 of his defence, the second defendant goes on to plead, as matters of fact, that he was in good faith at the time of the Italian contract; that he was not aware of any defect of title of the vendor in Italy; that the transaction of purchase was carried out in the suitable and appropriate manner as regards documentation, and that he had reasonable grounds for believing that his vendor was entitled to dispose of the goods to him. If, therefore, the crucial issue which I have mentioned fails to be determined in accordance with Italian law and the second defendant can establish that its relevant contents is as pleaded in paragraph 6 of his defence and that the facts are as pleaded in paragraph 7, suppose that he may well have acquired a title to the goods, which must be recognized by the English court as being valid, even vis-à-vis the plaintiff.

The grounds upon which Mr. Gilman, on behalf of the second defendant, submitted the crucial issue falls to be determined in accordance with Italian law are essentially very simple. There is, he submits, a general rule of private international law that the validity of a transfer of movable property and its effect on the proprietary rights of any persons claiming to be interested therein are governed by the law of the country where the property is situated at the time of the transfer ("lex situs").

. . .

Accordingly, it is submitted that the general rule of private international law, which it is claimed governs the effect of transfers of movable property, must apply in the present case. It is common ground that at the time of the sale and transfer of the goods by the third party to the second defendant, the goods were situated in Italy. Accordingly, Mr. Gilman submits, in effect the English court is bound to apply Italian law for the purpose of determining whether the second defendant has acquired ownership of the goods, not only vis-à-vis the transferor, but also vis-à-vis the plaintiff – in other words, for the purpose of determining whether the plaintiff can prove the title necessary to enable him to succeed in these proceedings or whether his title has been divested by the sale in Italy.

Mr. Mummery, on behalf of the plaintiff, accepted that as a general rule the validity of a transfer of movables is governed by the lex situs and that accordingly the principle of *Cammell v. Sewell* would have the effect of rendering Italian law the relevant law for the purpose of determining the rights of the second defendant and the vendor in Italy, from whom he purchased, as between themselves and their respective successors in title. He pointed out, however, that the present case is, in contrast, concerned with the respective proprietary rights of the second defendant and the plaintiff. He pointed out the many circumstances which cumulatively give this case a strong association with England, at least if it be regarded solely from the standpoint of his client. At the time of the theft, the goods were situated in England, in the ownership and lawful possession of a person who was domiciled in England. The plaintiff neither knew of nor consented to the removal of the goods from England or anything which made such removal more probable. The goods have now been voluntarily redelivered to England where they or their proceeds of sale still remain. Finally, it is an English court which is now hearing the matter.

Laying emphasis on what may be called these English connecting factors, Mr. Mummery advanced two main propositions as possible avenues of escape from the principle of *Cammell v. Sewell.* Briefly, the first was that for the purpose of applying this principle to determine the respective rights of the plaintiff and the second defendant in the peculiar circumstances of this case, the lex situs should be treated as being English, rather than Italian law. The second was that if, contrary to his first submission, the application of the principle of *Cammell v. Sewell* would result in the relevant issue being determined according to Italian law, then the exceptional facts of the case bring it outside this principle.

. . .

In support of the first of them, he referred to a general statement in *Halsbury's Laws of England* 4th ed., vol. 8 (1974), para. 632 p. 433, to the effect that the location of property is a matter for English law and that it is possible for property to be regarded as having different locations for different purposes. He accepted that, for the purpose of determining the respective rights in the goods of the Italian vendor and the second defendant as between themselves, the situs of the goods must be regarded as Italian. In his submission, however, it does not follow that the situs of the goods must be regarded as Italian for the purpose of determining the respective proprietary claims of the plaintiff and the second defendant. For the latter purpose, he suggested, on the particular facts of the present case, the court is entitled and obliged to hold that the situs of the goods remained English throughout. They were in England at the date of the theft; they are still here; they never left England with the plaintiff's consent; there was never any voluntary act on his part which connected or was even likely to connect the goods with any foreign system of law. In these circumstances, Mr. Mummery submitted, the alleged connection of the situs with Italy, for the purpose of determining the plaintiff's rights, is a spurious connection which should be disregarded by the court.

This line of argument was supported by no relevant authority and, though attractively presented by Mr. Mummery, in my judgment does not itself avail the plaintiff for these short reasons. It is in my judgment abundantly clear from the authorities already cited that, in appropriate circumstances, the court is prepared to follow the principle of *Cammell v. Sewell* by applying the law of country A, in favour of a person who acquires title to personal property under the law of that country, even though the effect of such application is to destroy the proprietary rights of a former owner, who never himself possessed the property in country A and never consented, expressly or implicitly, to its going to country A. This was the situation in *Cammell v. Sewell* itself, where, as Cockburn C.J. pointed out in argument, 5 H. & N. 728, 735: " . . . the goods were wrecked on the coast of Norway and came there without the owner's assent." It was the situation also in *Embiricos v. Anglo-Austrian Bank* [1905] 1 K.B. 677, where the court applied Austrian law so as to divest the title of the injured original owners, even though they had done nothing to consent to the cheque finding its way to Austria. Furthermore, the plaintiff's English domicile cannot avail him in this context, any more than it availed the English plaintiffs in *Cammell v. Sewell*. Nor can presence of the goods, or their proceeds, in England at the date of the hearing entitle the plaintiff to assert that their situs should be treated as English for the purpose of any application of the principle of that decision. As Crompton J. there said, 5 H. & N. 728, 742–743: " . . . we do not think that the subsequent bringing the property to England can alter the position of the parties."

Accordingly, I think it clear that, if the principle of *Cammell v. Sewell* applies at all on the facts of the present case, then the lex situs of the relevant disposition cannot be treated as being English rather than Italian. Intolerable uncertainty in the law would result if the court were to permit the introduction of a wholly fictional English situs when applying the principle to any particular case, merely because the case happened to have a number of other English connecting factors.

It therefore follows that, if the plaintiff is to succeed, he must satisfy the court that the second principal submission made on his behalf is correct, namely that the principle of *Cammell v. Sewell* does not apply to this case, because the particular circumstances bring it within exception to that principle.

I have already mentioned that Mr. Gilman, on behalf of the second defendant, accepted that there are a number of well-recognized exceptions to this principle. For present purposes the most significant of them is that based on public policy. As is stated in *Halsbury's Laws of England* 4th ed., vol. 8 (1974), para. 418, p.315:

> Exceptionally, the English court will not enforce or recognize a right conferred or a duty imposed by a foreign law where, on the facts of the particular case, enforcement or, as the case may be, recognition, would be contrary to a fundamental policy of English law. The court has, therefore, refused in certain cases to apply foreign law where to do so would in the particular circumstances be contrary to the interests of the United Kingdom or contrary to justice or morality.

If therefore a case arose where, by reference to the principle of *Cammell v. Sewell*, a person claimed a title to goods in an English court, which he would not be able to establish by reference to English law alone, and the content of the particular foreign law on which he relied was so outrageous that this court regarded it as wholly contrary to justice and morality, then it would, I conceive, probably refuse to recognize the rights conferred on the claimant by the relevant foreign law.

...

I turn now to the remaining consideration urged on me by Mr. Mummery, namely that, on the facts of his hypothetical case, country A is justified in making an exception to the general principle of *Cammell v. Sewell* for the purpose of securing a title recognized by its own system of law. This, I think, is by far his strongest point. In principle any court must surely regard, with some initial sympathy, the position or blameless person, such as the plaintiff in the present case, who, if attention is paid solely to the law of the country of that court, has at all material times had and retained good title to the goods which are the subject of his claim.

On the other hand, there are other equally powerful – I think more powerful – counter-balancing considerations. Security of title is as important to an innocent purchaser as it is to an innocent owner when goods have been stolen from him. Commercial convenience may be said imperatively to demand that proprietary rights to movables shall generally be determined by the lex situs under the rules of private international law. Were the position otherwise, it would not suffice for the protection of a purchaser of any valuable movables to ascertain that he was acquiring title to them under the law of the country where the goods were situated at the time of the purchase; he would have to effect further investigations as to the past title, with a view to ensuring, so far as possible, that there was no person who might successfully claim a title to the movables by reference to some other system of law and in many cases even such further investigations could result in no certainty that his title was secure. In these circumstances, there are, in my view, very strong grounds of business convenience for applying the principle of *Cammell v. Sewell* even in a case such as the present. Maugham J. said in *In re Anziani* [1930] 1 Ch. 407, 420, with reference to the principle: "Business could not be carried on if that were not so." This was putting the point very strongly. I think, however, that most undesirable uncertainty in the commercial world would result if the choice of the system regulating the validity of a disposition of chattels were to depend not only on the situation of the goods at the time of the disposition, but also on the additional factors suggested on behalf of the plaintiff.

It must be accepted that exclusive reference to the lex situs must cause hardship to a previous owner in some cases, particularly if his goods have been moved to and sold in a foreign country without his knowledge or consent. Crompton J., however, in the passage already quoted, from 5 H. & N. 728, 744–745, in the majority judgment in *Cammell v. Sewell*, expressly recognized that the English law as to stolen goods acquired by a purchaser under sale in market overt might seem harsh to a former foreign owner, but expressed the view that it made no difference that such owner did not intend them to be sent to the country where they were sold. . . .

I must therefore accept the second defendant's submission that the relevant question of title falls to be determined in accordance with Italian law. This decision, however, must be subject to one proviso. I have heard no evidence as to the content of Italian law. Though the plaintiff's counsel has not sought to submit that either of these things is likely to occur, it is theoretically possible that the trial judge, on hearing such evidence, could form the view that the particular content of the relevant Italian law was such that the public policy of this country required him to disregard any rights asserted by the second defendant by reference to such law. Alternatively, it is theoretically possible that the evidence as to Italian law would show that the Italian court would itself apply English law, on the particular facts of the present case, for the purpose of determining the rights of the second defendant vis-à-vis the plaintiff and vice versa. In this event I suppose it would be open to the plaintiff to argue that English law should, in the final result, be applied by the English court by virtue of the doctrine of renvoi. By this judgment I do not intend to deprive the plaintiff of the right to argue either of these two points at the trial.

In all the circumstances I propose to declare, in answer to the questions put to me, that, upon the basis of the agreed facts set forth, in the schedule to the order of March 16, 1979, but without prejudice to any submissions which any party may wish to put forward at the trial based on evidence as to the particular content of the relevant Italian domestic law, Italian domestic law is to be applied to the issue whether the plaintiff or the second defendant has the immediate right to possession of the goods with which the action and the counterclaim are concerned. I will, however, hear counsel as to the precise form which this declaration should take.

NOTES

1. Two of the three main topics of private international law, jurisdiction and choice of law, are specifically addressed by the judicial opinions in this section. As to the third topic, enforcement of foreign judgments, notice that *Winkworth*, by recognizing the applicability of the Italian law, almost certainly would have enforced a foreign judgment had the Italian court heard the same issues.
2. The decision in *Winkworth* has been criticized on many grounds, including the following: the court insufficiently considered that it was through no fault of the English owner that his stolen property was removed to a civil law system such as Italy, a country whose laws might uphold good title on the part of a subsequent bona fide purchaser; though the goods had not only been stolen in England and had been returned there for the purpose of sale, the court was unwilling to uphold the applicability of English law to the issue of their ownership; and the court failed to consider England's proximity to the continental European systems in which a bona fide purchaser can acquire good title to stolen property under certain conditions, thus, in a sense, suggesting a *modus operandi* for an art thief wishing to facilitate an effective market for his stolen goods. Despite these and other arguments, an English court applied the principle in *Winkworth* in *Federal Republic of Germany v. Sotheby's and Cobert Finance*, H.C. 9, Sept. 1998, where German law was held to apply to the issue of title to a painting smuggled out of Russia (although the object had originated in the German ducal estate of Saxe-Coburg-Gotha).

Autocephalous Greek-Orthodox Church of Cyprus and the Republic of Cyprus v. Goldberg, 917 F. 2d 278 (7th Cir. 1990)

B. Choice of Law

As a federal court sitting in diversity, the district court was obligated to (and did) apply the law of the state in which it sat – Indiana. *See Erie R.R. Co. v. Tompkins*, 304 U.S. 64, 82 L. Ed. 1188, 58 S. Ct. 817 (1938). This included Indiana law as to which body of substantive law to apply to the case, i.e. Indiana's choice of law rules. *See Consolidated Rail Corp. v. Allied Corp.*, 882 F.2d 254, 255 (7th Cir. 1989) (citing *Klaxon Co. v. Stentor Elec. Mfg. Co.*, 313 U.S. 487, 85 L. Ed. 1477, 61 S. Ct. 1020 (1941)). From his analysis and application of Indiana rules and decisions regarding choice of law, Judge Noland concluded that Indiana would choose to apply its own substantive law to this case. *Autocephalous*, 717 F. Supp. at 1393–95. This ruling actually contained two parts. First, Judge Noland applied the two-step "most significant contacts" test used by Indiana courts for choice of law in Indiana tort cases. *See Hubbard Mfg. Co., Inc. v. Greeson*, 515 N.E.2d 1071 (Ind. 1987). Second, with the help of the trial testimony of an expert in the law of Switzerland, Judge Noland looked to Swiss choice of law principles and determined that they, too, dictate that Indiana substantive law should control. On appeal, Goldberg claims that both of these determinations were in error. Because we find Judge Noland's analysis under Indiana law to be free of error, we affirm his conclusion that Indiana law applies without reaching his discussion of Swiss law.

...

The district court properly considered Cyprus'[s] suit to recover the mosaics a replevin action, long recognized in Indiana law as the proper legal action for the recovery of wrongfully detained personal property. *See* 25 Indiana Law Encyclopedia ("I.L.E.") *Replevin* §§ 1, 2 & 11 (West 1960). The district court could find no Indiana case dealing specifically with choice of law in replevin actions, nor can we. Thus, we will look (as did Judge Noland) to the choice of law principles Indiana generally applies in tort cases.

...

In *Hubbard*, 515 N.E.2d 1071, the Indiana Supreme Court modified Indiana's traditional *lex loci delicti commissi* rule for choice of law in tort cases. Under the traditional rule, the court chose the law of the state in which occurred "the last event necessary to make an actor liable," most times meaning the place of injury. *Id.* at 1073. *See also Consolidated Rail*, 882 F.2d at 256. Citing the often anomalous results that can obtain from the rigid application of this rule, as well as the recent trend away from it, the court in *Hubbard* declared that the *lex loci* rule should be applied only when the place of the tort is also the place with the most significant contacts. When the place of the tort bears little connection to the legal action, the court declared, the following factors should be considered:

1) the place where the conduct causing the injury occurred;
2) the residence or place of business of the parties; and
3) the place where the relationship is centered.

Id. at 1073–74 (citing Restatement (Second) of Conflicts of Laws § 145(2) (1971)). *See also Tompkins v. Isbell*, 543 N.E.2d 680 (Ind. App. 1989) (discussing and applying *Hubbard* approach). Thus, the court established a two-step test, the first inquiry focusing on the contacts between the place of the wrong and the legal action. If these contacts are significant, the *lex loci* rule should be applied; if not, the court should move to the second inquiry, which focuses on which jurisdiction has the most significant contacts.

In this case, Judge Noland first determined that Switzerland – "the place of the wrong" because it was at the Geneva airport that Goldberg took possession and control of the mosaics – bears little connection to Cyprus'[s] cause of action. *Autocephalous*, 717 F. Supp. at 1393–94. He reached this conclusion based on his findings regarding the following facts: no Swiss citizen has or ever had an interest in this action, as none of the parties, actors in the transaction, or past or current interest-holders are Swiss citizens; and the temporal and geographical connection between the mosaics and Switzerland were "fortuitous and transitory," as the mosaics were on Swiss soil for only four days, never passed through Swiss customs (they remained in the "free port" area of the Geneva airport), and never otherwise entered the Swiss stream of commerce. Goldberg has failed to establish error in either these factual findings or the conclusion based thereon, choosing instead to reiterate Swiss "connections" considered and rejected by Judge Noland (e.g. the money Peg Goldberg paid for the mosaics was wired to her through a Swiss bank), and to cite us to an Indiana court's application of the *lex loci* doctrine in a factually inapposite case. *Tompkins*, 543 N.E.2d at 681–82 (law of place of tort applied in auto collision case where "the place of the tort has extensive connection with the legal action"). Thus, we agree that in this case an Indiana court would find Switzerland's contacts too attenuated to apply the *lex loci* rule, and thus would proceed to the second step of the analysis. *Cf. Hubbard*, 515 N.E.2d at 1074 (events in Illinois unrelated to the action do not equal significant contacts).

Moving to step two of the *Hubbard* approach, the contacts between the action and the two contending jurisdictions (Indiana and Switzerland) must be reviewed, with special attention given to the Second Restatement factors. Applying this approach, Judge Noland noted the following facts that weigh in favor of applying Indiana law: the defendants, those who financed and effected the transfer of the mosaics, and those who now hold the principal monetary interests in the mosaics are all Indiana citizens; the money used to purchase the mosaics came from an Indiana bank; the agreement among Goldberg, Fitzgerald, van Rijn and Faulk stipulates that Indiana law will apply, indicating Goldberg's reliance on the law of her home state; and the mosaics are presently being held in Indiana, where they have been stored since they entered the U.S. in July, 1988. Based on our review of these and other facts as found by Judge Noland, we agree with his conclusion that Indiana has the more significant contacts with and interest in this action. Thus, Indiana law and rules govern every aspect of this action, from the statute of limitations issues through the application of the substantive law of replevin.

D. The Merits of the Replevin Claim

Under Indiana law, replevin is an action at law "whereby the owner or person claiming the possession of personal goods may recover such personal goods where they have been wrongfully taken or unlawfully detained. . . . The gist of the action is the defendant's unlawful detention of the plaintiff's property. The issue litigated is the present right to the possession of the property in controversy, and the purpose of the action is to determine who shall have possession of the property sought to be replevied." . . . To recover the item sought to be replevied, . . . the plaintiff must establish three elements: his title or right to possession, that the property is unlawfully detained, and that the defendant wrongfully holds possession.

Judge Noland [the trial judge] applied these elements to the facts of this case and determined that Cyprus had met its burden as to each. . . . Our review of this application of Indiana law to the facts convinces us that it is free of error: 1) the Kanakaria Church was and is owned by the Holy Archbishopric of the Church of Cyprus, a self-headed (hence "Autocephalous") church associated with the Greek-Orthodox faith; 2) the mosaics were removed from the Kanakaria Church without the authorization of the Church or the Republic (even the TRNC's unsuccessful motion to intervene claimed that the mosaics were improperly removed); and 3) Goldberg, as an ultimate purchaser from a thief, has no valid claim of title or right to possession of the mosaics.

. . .

We note that Judge Noland again backstopped his conclusion, this time conducting an alternative analysis under Swiss substantive law. . . . Briefly, the court concluded that the Church had superior title under Swiss law as well, because Goldberg could not claim valid title under the Swiss "good faith purchasers" notion having only made a cursory inquiry into the suspicious circumstances surrounding the sale of the mosaics. Under Indiana law, such considerations are irrelevant because, except in very limited exceptions not applicable here, a subsequent purchaser (even a "good faith, *bona fide* purchaser for value") who obtains an item from a thief only acquires the title held by the thief; that is, *no* title. . . . As we state above, Indiana law controls every aspect of this action. Thus, Judge Noland's extensive (and quite interesting) discussion of Swiss law, as well as Goldberg's lengthy attack thereon, need not be reviewed. Cyprus adequately established the elements of replevin under Indiana law, on which ground alone we affirm the district court's decision to award the possession of the mosaics to the Church of Cyprus.

E. The Effect of the TFSC Edicts

Finally, Goldberg argues that several decrees of the TFSC (the entity established in northern Cyprus by the Turkish military immediately after the 1974 invasion) divested the Church of title to the mosaics. Goldberg asks us to honor these decrees under the notion that in some instances courts in the United States can give effect to the acts of nonrecognized but "*de facto*" regimes if the acts relate to purely local matters. . . . (Under Soviet law, U.S.S.R. nationalization decree effective to pass title to oil within Russia despite fact that U.S.S.R. was not yet recognized by the U.S.). The TFSC decrees at issue, all propagated in 1975, are principally these: 1) the "Abandoned Movable Property Law," which provided that all movable property within the boundaries of the TFSC abandoned by its owner because of the owner's "departure" from northern Cyprus "as a result of the situation after 20th July 1974" now belongs to the TFSC "in the name of the Turkish Community" and that the TFSC "is responsible for the possession and control of such property"; and 2) the "Antiquities Ordinance," which provided that all religious buildings and antiquities, including specifically "synagogues, basilicas, churches, monasteries and the like," located north of the Green Line, as well as any and all "movable antiquities" contained therein, are now the property of the TFSC. . . . Because these decrees were enacted before the Kanakaria Church was looted and its mosaics stolen, the argument concludes, the Church cannot here claim to hold title to the mosaics.

. . .

It is helpful to note at the outset what is *not* being claimed here. First, Goldberg does not (and cannot) suggest that this court should pass on the validity of the Turkish administration in northern Cyprus. We repeat here precepts that are well-established in the law of this country:

> The conduct of foreign relations was committed by the Constitution to the political departments of the government, and the propriety of what may be done in the exercise of this political power [is] not subject to judicial inquiry or decision, . . . [and] who is the sovereign of a territory is not a judicial question, but one the determination of which by the political departments conclusively binds the courts[.] . . .

Indeed, Goldberg herself supports the district court's decision to deny the TRNC's motion to intervene in this case, which decision was based on the TRNC's continued status as a nonrecognized entity. . . .

Second, this is not a case in which one party is claiming title under the laws of a state that has been entirely displaced, and the other is claiming title under the laws of the new, displacing regime. All Goldberg can hope to gain from the invocation of these TFSC edicts is a finding that the Church's claim of title is defective; she has no plausible claim of valid title in herself based on these edicts. This fact sets this case apart from the cases cited by Goldberg, including *Salimoff*, 262 N.Y. 220, 186 N.E. 679 (plaintiff Russian nationals claimed title to property under laws of the old Russian Empire and defendant U.S. companies claimed title due to purchase from Soviet government, which seized the property pursuant to nationalization decree); and *The Denny*, 127 F.2d 404 (3d Cir. 1942) (dispute between Lithuanian citizens wherein both claimed right to possess property as agents under Lithuanian law, one relying on the effect of nationalization decrees of the Lithuanian Soviet Socialist Republic, the other on pre-nationalization law). . . .

What Goldberg is claiming is that the TFSC's confiscatory decrees, adopted only one year after the Turkish invasion, should be given effect by this court because the TFSC and its successor TRNC should now be viewed as the "*de facto*" government north of the Green Line. This we are unwilling to do. We draw on two lines of precedent as support for our decision. First, we note that, contrary to the New York court's decision in *Salimoff*, 262 N.Y. 220, 186 N.E. 679, several courts of the same era refused to give effect to the nationalization decrees of the as-yet-unrecognized Soviet Republics. These courts relied on a variety of grounds, including especially the fact that the political branches of our government still refused to recognize these entities.... Similarly, as regards the Turkish administration in northern Cyprus, the United States government (like the rest of the non-Turkish world) has not recognized its legitimacy, nor does our government "recognize that [the Turkish administration] has functioned as a de facto or quasi government..., ruling within its own borders."...

Second, we are guided in part by the post-Civil War cases in which courts refused to give effect to property-affecting acts of the Confederate state legislatures. In one such case,... the Supreme Court drew a helpful distinction between two kinds of "*de facto*" governments. The first kind "is such as exists after it has expelled the regularly constituted authorities from the seats of power and the public offices, and established its own functionaries in their places, so as to represent in fact the sovereignty of the nation."... This kind of *de facto* government, the Court explained, "is treated as in most respects possessing rightful authority,... [and] its legislation is in general recognized."... The second kind of *de facto* government "is such as exists where a portion of the inhabitants of a country have separated themselves from the parent State and established an independent government. The validity of its acts, both against the parent State and its citizens or subjects, depends entirely upon its ultimate success.... If it succeed, and become recognized, its acts from the commencement of its existence are upheld as those of an independent nation."... Goldberg argues that the TFSC and its successor TRNC have achieved the level of "ultimate success" contemplated by this standard, because they have maintained control of the territory north of the Green Line for over fifteen years. We will not thus equate simple longevity of control with "ultimate success." The Turkish forces, despite their best efforts, did not completely supplant the Republic nor its officers. Instead, the TFSC and the TRNC, neither of which has ever been recognized by the non-Turkish world, only acceded to the control of the northern portion of Cyprus. The Republic of Cyprus remains the only recognized Cypriot government, the sovereign nation for the entire island. Rejecting Goldberg's invitation to delve any further into facts and current events which are not of record in this proceeding, we conclude that the confiscatory decrees proffered by Goldberg do not divest the Church of its claim of title.

III. Conclusion

As Byron's poem laments, war can reduce our grandest and most sacred temples to mere "fragments of stone." Only the lowest of scoundrels attempt to reap personal gain from this collective loss. Those who plundered the churches and monuments of war-torn Cyprus, hoarded their relics away, and are now smuggling and selling them for large sums, are just such blackguards. The Republic of Cyprus, with diligent effort and the help of friends like Dr. True, has been able to locate several of these stolen antiquities; items of vast cultural, religious (and, as this case demonstrates, monetary) value. Among such finds are the pieces of the Kanakaria mosaic at issue in this case. Unfortunately, when these mosaics surfaced they were in the hands not of the most guilty parties, but of Peg Goldberg and her gallery. Correctly applying Indiana law, the district court determined that Goldberg must return the mosaics to their rightful owner: the Church of Cyprus. Goldberg's tireless attacks have not established reversible error in that determination, and thus, for the reasons discussed above, the district court's judgment is AFFIRMED.

Lest this result seem too harsh, we should note that those who wish to purchase art work on the international market, undoubtedly a ticklish business, are not without means by which to protect themselves. Especially when circumstances are as suspicious as those that faced Peg Goldberg, prospective purchasers would do best to do more than make a few last-minute phone calls. As testified to at trial, in a transaction like this, "All the red flags are up, all the red lights are on, all the sirens are blaring." . . . In such cases, dealers can (and probably should) take steps such as a formal IFAR search; a documented authenticity check by disinterested experts; a full background search of the seller and his claim of title; insurance protection and a contingency sales contract; and the like. If Goldberg would have pursued such methods, perhaps she would have discovered in time what she has now discovered too late: the Church has a valid, superior and enforceable claim to these Byzantine treasures, which therefore must be returned to it.

Cudahy, Circuit Judge, concurring:

Although I concur in all respects in the excellent majority opinion, there are two points that I believe merit elucidation. The first of these involves the difficult problem of the time of accrual of the cause of action in replevin. The majority opinion affirms the holding of the district court, based on its interpretation of Indiana law, that the plaintiff's cause of action does not accrue until it has, *or reasonably should have*, discovered the location of the stolen property – in this case the Cypriot mosaics. Although we accept the district court's construction of Indiana law, it is unnecessary to rely solely upon this application of the discovery rule. For, . . . whenever the possessor of lost or stolen personal property commits "fraud in the concealment," the statute of limitations does not run against the original owner until that owner has *actual knowledge* of the location of the property and of the identity of the possessor.

This concept is analogous to the requirement that one who asserts a statute of limitations defense against an action for the recovery of *real* property must have possessed the property in an "open and notorious" manner. Because it is difficult to assess openness of possession in the realm of personal property, courts have required good faith on the part of the possessor to satisfy, or substitute for, the openness requirement. Most courts considering this problem have thus concluded that the statute of limitations should not run against an original owner who lacks the facts necessary to institute suit as long as the property is held by the original thief or by a subsequent holder acting in bad faith.

If a good faith requirement were applied to the facts of the case before us, the statute of limitations would not have begun to run so long as the mosaics were in the hands of Dikman, the original thief. Nor would Goldberg's purchase of the mosaics in July 1988 have triggered the running of the statute. As Judge Noland pointed out, Goldberg undertook only a cursory inquiry into Dikman's ability to convey good title under circumstances which should have aroused the suspicions of a wholly innocent and reasonably prudent purchaser. She thus does not appear to have been a good faith purchaser. Under the foregoing analysis, the cause of action would not have accrued until later in 1988, when Cyprus first ascertained the location of the mosaics and the identity of the current possessor. This approach, which seems equitable to me, thus poses no bar to a cause of action for replevin of the mosaics. An owner should not be at risk under the statute of limitations until she has actual knowledge or the property has passed into innocent hands.

II.

A second and unrelated, but important, aspect of this case involves the treatment of the cultural heritage of foreign nations under international and United States law. The United States has both acceded to international agreements and enacted its own statutes regarding the importation of cultural property. These regulatory efforts have encompassed transfers of property during both wartime and peacetime and apply whether the property was originally stolen or "merely" illegally exported from the country of origin. The two most significant international agreements that attempt to protect cultural property are the 1954 Convention on the Protection of Cultural Property in the Event of Armed Conflict (the "1954 Hague Convention"), 249 U.N.T.S. 215 (1956), and the UNESCO Convention on the Means of Prohibiting and Preventing the Illicit Transport, Export and Transfer of Ownership of Cultural Property (the "UNESCO Convention"), 823 U.N.T.S. 231 (1972). Under both these multinational treaties, as well as under the United States' Convention on Cultural Property Implementation Act, 19 U.S.C. § 2601 *et seq.* (1983), the Cypriot mosaics would be considered cultural property warranting international protection. For example, Article I of the UNESCO Convention defines cultural property as "property which, on religious or secular grounds, is specifically designated by each State as being of importance for archaeology, prehistory, history, literature, art or science and which belongs to one or more of the following categories:

(d) elements of artistic or historical monuments or archaeological sites which have been dismembered;
(e) antiquities more than one hundred years old . . . ;
(f) property of artistic interest, such as:

> (i) pictures, paintings and drawings produced entirely by hand on any support and in any material. . . . "

The 1954 Hague Convention may be applicable to the case before us given the incursion of Turkish armed forces into Cyprus in 1974 and our ongoing refusal to recognize the government established in the northern part of Cyprus. The 1954 Hague Convention, which is but the most recent multilateral agreement in a 200-year history of international attempts to protect cultural property during wartime, prohibits the destruction or seizure of cultural property during armed conflict, whether international or civil in nature, and during periods of belligerent occupation. The Hague Convention also applies to international trafficking during peacetime in cultural property unlawfully seized during an armed conflict. The attempt of the government established in northern Cyprus by the Turkish military to divest the Greek Cypriot church of ownership of the mosaics might be viewed as an interference of the sort contemplated by the 1954 Hague Convention. If this were the case, the acts and decrees of the northern Cyprus government divesting title to this cultural property would not demand the deference of American courts.

The second international agreement, the UNESCO Convention, focuses on private conduct, primarily during peacetime, and thus is also applicable to the theft and removal of the mosaics from Cyprus. Article 7 of that Convention requires signatory nations:

> (a) To take the necessary measures, consistent with national legislation, to prevent museums and similar institutions within their territories from acquiring cultural property originating in another State Party which has been illegally exported . . . ;
>
> (b)(i) to prohibit the import of cultural property stolen from a museum or a religious or secular public monument or similar institution in another State Party . . . , provided that such property is documented as appertaining to the inventory of that institution;
>
> (ii) at the request of the State Party of origin, to take appropriate steps to recover and return any such cultural property . . . , provided, however, that the requesting State shall pay just compensation to an innocent purchaser or to a person who has valid title to that property. . . .

It is clear that the mosaics in the case before us were stolen (under any reasonable definition of that word) from a religious institution and that the mosaics were extensively documented by the Dumbarton Oaks publication as belonging to the Kanakaria Church. While the UNESCO Convention seems to contemplate primarily measures to be implemented by the executive branch of a government through its import and export rules and policies, the judicial branch should certainly attempt to reflect in its decisionmaking the spirit as well as the letter of an international agreement to which the United States is a party.

The UNESCO Convention, although ratified by Congress in 1972, was not formally implemented in the United States until the enactment of the Cultural Property Implementation Act in 1983. The Cultural Property Implementation Act, 19 U.S.C. §§ 2601–2613, focuses primarily on implementation of Articles 7(b) and 9 of the UNESCO Convention, which call for concerted action among nations to prevent trade in specific items of cultural property in emergency situations. The delay in the enactment of the Cultural Property Implementation Act apparently was caused, in part, by pressure from art dealers and traders, who argued that if the United States undertook unilateral import controls, illegal cultural property would simply be sold to those art market countries lacking similar import controls. In fact, the Cultural Property Implementation Act was perhaps finally enacted only because it was perceived as a restraint of sorts on certain Customs officers. These officials had deemed all archaeological materials that a foreign country had claimed were "stolen" to be subject to seizure under the National Stolen Property Act, 18 U.S.C. § 2311 *et seq.* (1934). The Cultural Property Implementation Act, therefore, emphasized the need for concerted action and, in particular, seemed to prefer action resulting from bilateral treaties between the United States and the affected source countries. Such treaties have now been put into effect with a few countries, including Mexico, Guatemala and Peru.

As indicated, the Cultural Property Implementation Act addresses primarily the question of import controls and, in section 2607, prohibits the importation into the United States of any "cultural property documented as appertaining to the inventory of a museum or religious or secular public monument or similar institution in any State Party which is stolen from such institution. . . . " This section is not directly applicable here, first, because the mosaics were stolen after the effective date of the statute and, second, because the statute is directed at import controls rather than replevin suits. Nonetheless, the policy that the Act embodies is clear: at the very least, we should not sanction illegal traffic in stolen cultural property that is clearly documented as belonging to a public or religious institution. This is particularly true where this sort of property is "important to the cultural heritage of a people because of its distinctive characteristics, comparative rarity, or its contribution to the knowledge of the origins, development, or history of that people." 19 U.S.C. § 2601(2)(C)(ii)(II).

Focusing on a relatively short segment of what might otherwise be considered its "history," the United States chooses sometimes to ignore the ancient cultural heritage of the land which it now occupies. But a short cultural memory is not an adequate justification for participating in the plunder of the cherished antiquities that play important roles in the histories of foreign lands. The UNESCO Convention and the Cultural Property Implementation Act constitute an effort to instill respect for the cultural property and heritage of all peoples. The mosaics before us are of great intrinsic beauty. They are the virtually unique remnants of an earlier artistic period and should be returned to their homeland and their rightful owner. This is the case not only because the mosaics belong there, but as a reminder that greed and callous disregard for the property, history and culture of others cannot be countenanced by the world community or by this court.

NOTES AND QUESTIONS

1. In common law jurisdictions a property owner cannot lose title to his or her property if it is stolen and sold to an innocent purchaser. Often presented in terms of the Latin maxim *nemo plus juris ad alium transferre potest quam ipse habet*, the rule means that owners of stolen art can usually resist any claim to entitlement by a bona fide purchaser from a thief. The rule is normally the opposite in countries whose civil law systems are more directly based on Roman law. These legal systems, in particular of continental Europe, allow a bona fide purchaser of stolen goods to assert good title against their original owner subject to varying conditions. Thus, in *Winkworth*, unlike *Goldberg*, once the English court decided that it should apply the civil (Italian) law, it found that the bona fide purchaser had good title.
2. It is clear that Indiana's minimum-contacts test, which the federal court applied to govern its choice of law, made it easier to apply the law of the forum rather than that of Cyprus or Switzerland. The court reinforced its choice of Indiana law, however, by asking whether application of Swiss law would have produced the same result. The answer was yes, according to an expert witness on Swiss law, Professor Arthur von Mehren of Harvard Law School. He concluded that in a questionable situation where the only connection between Switzerland and the mosaics was their temporary storage and passage through the Geneva airport, the purchaser would lose the normal protection of a bona fide purchaser under Swiss law. The *Goldberg* court's choice of Indiana law was therefore backstopped by Swiss law, which conveniently led to the same result because of an exception in Swiss law to the normal protection that it and other civil law systems would give to the bona fide purchaser. The defendant, Goldberg, was thereby barred from claiming that she had acquired better title to the mosaics she had purchased as against the original owner of them – that is, the church.
3. Do you think the U.S. approach to determining the applicable law is preferable to the UK approach as represented by *Winkworth*? Could the English court's willingness to apply Italian law encourage the use of Italy as a place to sell stolen art to unsuspecting buyers?
4. To what extent do you think choice-of-law rules reliably lead to application of the most appropriate law for resolving a claim or particular issue? Do you think the court in *Goldberg* was influenced in deciding to apply Indiana law by the fact that the mosaics had been looted in Cyprus?
5. Symeon Symeonides, a leading choice-of-law scholar, has argued that the *Goldberg* court reached the right result but with the wrong choice-of-law reasoning. See Symeon C. Symeonides, *A Choice-of-Law Rule for Conflicts Involving Stolen Cultural Property*, 38 Vand. J. Transnat'l L. 1177, 1182 (2005). Professor Symeonides argues that the court should have chosen the law of Cyprus rather than that of Indiana or Switzerland. He bases his argument on the need to achieve *material* (substantive) justice as well as *conflicts* (procedural) justice in choosing

the applicable law. He has proposed a choice-of-law rule to govern "the rights of parties with regard to a corporeal thing of significant value." First read the rule, as follows; then read the next subsection on the *lex rei extra commercium* in the civil law. Is the proposed rule an elaboration of the "outside of commerce" rule?

1. Except as otherwise provided by an applicable treaty or international or interstate agreement, or statute, the rights of parties with regard to a corporeal thing of significant cultural value (hereinafter "thing") are determined as specified below.
2. A person who is considered the owner of the thing under the law of the state in which the thing was situated at the time of its removal to another state shall be entitled to the protection of the law of the former state (state of origin), except as specified below.
3. The owner's right may not be subject to the less protective law of a state other than the state of origin,
   (a) unless:
      (i) the other state has a materially closer connection to the case than the state of origin; and
      (ii) application of that law is necessary in order to protect a party who dealt with the thing in good faith after its removal to that state; and
   (b) until the owner knew or should have known facts that would enable a diligent owner to take effective legal action to protect those rights.

Id. at 1183.

6. Notice that *Goldberg* involved choice-of-law issues both in the main substantive action, based on a theory of wrongful conversion of property, and in Peg Goldberg's procedural claim that a decree of the Turkish occupying authority in Northern Cyprus had divested the plaintiff church of its title to the mosaics. In addition, Judge Cudahy's concurring opinion argues for the applicability of international treaty law even when the forum state, the United States, was not a party to one of the treaties (the 1954 Hague Convention).

(ii) The *Lex Rei Extra Commercium* in the Civil Law. The common law of English-speaking countries has never developed special rules or principles of private international law limited to cultural objects. Such material is treated differently from more fungible chattels only when it is the subject of specific legislation such as the Native American Graves Protection and Repatriation Act in the United States or the Cultural Property Export and Import Act (export controls) in Canada. Otherwise, the ordinary, judicially created rules of personal property apply.

Civil law systems, however, sometimes characterize cultural objects as *res extra commercium*, the effect of which is to render the objects unmerchantable in the ordinary sense. In France and the Canadian province of Quebec, for example, the term *objets hors de commerce* is used for public and private property that is unmerchantable or inalienable in certain ways because of its special character. Which particular property is subject to differentiated treatment varies somewhat among civil law systems. Typically, assets such as historical monuments and archives that belong to a state, department of a state, or municipality are not subject to trade. They are simply outside of commerce, hence *extra commercium.*

The following discussion of a Quebec case confirms that religious cultural objects can also be seen as unmerchantable according to canon law. Unlike secular objects that might constitute a *res extra commercium*, the objects in dispute were private (church) property (*res sacrae*). The Quebec courts therefore applied canon law to the issue of their transferability. They did not, therefore, conclude that the objects were inalienable under Quebec law, but rather that Quebec law would recognize the special character accorded them by canon law.

B. Pelletier, *The Case of the Treasures of L'Ange Gardien: An Overview*, 2 Int'l J. Cultural Prop. 371 (1993)

1. Abstract

It is clearly defined, in Quebec civil law, that "sacred things are excluded from being objects of commerce." However, we might ask the following question: In order to determine how an object gets or loses its sacred character, do we have to refer to the internal rules of the various religious societies or instead, to the rules of civil law? It is that precise but difficult question, on which Quebec civil law does not say a word, that is raised principally by the case of the treasures of l'Ange-Gardien.

2. Introduction

The case of the treasures of l'Ange-Gardien, as referred to in Quebec, was at the very source of one of the most widespread awareness campaigns ever known in Quebec, if not in Canada, for the protection of the religious patrimony. In order to fully understand this case, we have to go back to the social and cultural context of the sixties and to the aftermath of Vatican II. At that particular time, the Roman Catholic Church was in the midst of a total transformation of its liturgy and so in order to answer the new call for simplicity, most parishes had to remake their environment. Unfortunately, this cleanup often became a ruinous adventure. The parish priests, as most of the population, did not have a clear understanding of the artistic and patrimonial importance of what they owned and did not hesitate to get rid of these objects at very low prices to the benefit of well-informed collectors and national and international museums who rejoiced at these bargains.

It is in this very precise context that a former parish priest of l'Ange-Gardien, Joseph-Henri Gariépy, sold a bunch of "old-fashioned things," apparently without any value but now worth more that CDN$100,000, to a sculptor for a sum of money for lower than their true worth.

Finally, after more than eleven years of lawsuits and the intervention of three Canadian courts, the sculptures and silversmiths' religious objects were given back to the parish of l'Ange-Gardien by those who were then in their possession: the National Gallery of Canada, the Musée du Quebec and a certain number of private collectors. Those objects had been depossessed from the parish some 25 years earlier under circumstances which will be discussed later on.

The return of the treasures of l'Ange-Gardien to the parochial patrimony put an end to a case that made the headlines more than once in Quebec. Curiously enough, this case, which captured the general public, did not seem to warrant the attention of jurists. The only scholarly studies to be found on this subject are the interesting commentaries of Ernest Caparros, a professor of canon law and an expert in this field. In addition, the Canadian jurisprudence did not make a great deal of the case of the treasures of l'Ange-Gardien, but it must be admitted that the opportunity has not presented itself until recently. One of the most tangible consequences of this case was that it determined with much clarity the rights and obligations of the Church Council in matters of alienation of sacred objects and resulted in the end of the "bleeding" which, in the past, emptied churches of their treasures and which enriched so many museums and personal collections.

3. The Legislative Context

It comes out from certain provisions particular to Quebec civil law that sacred objects are, as long as their destination has not been changed, *imprescriptibles, non-seizable* and *excluded from being objects of commerce.* Obviously, being excluded from commerce, they cannot be bought or sold and a right of ownership cannot be obtained towards them by the sole passing of time as they are imprescriptibles.

Furthermore, it comes out from Quebec civil law that objects are considered to be sacred if they are used for religious worship. Some of these objects are sacred by nature (i.e., dead bodies), whereas others are classified by their destination only. In the latter case, however, it is obvious that the destination of worship can be changed. Being the case, the objects will lose their sacred character and will then be subject to commerce, unless, of course, the change of destination was brought about by "encroachment," in which case, nevertheless, the objects will be reputed not to have lost their sacred character.

But we also notice that these legislative measures do not answer a certain number of questions: When is a thing sacred and when does it lose this sacred character? Who can change the destination of a sacred object and how is this change of destination to be carried out? Do we have to refer to canon law in order to answer the preceding questions or do we have to refer strictly to the general rules already established by Quebec civil law in regard, notably, to the change of destination of movable things?

It is precisely all these questions, and a few others including the application of the "*Law of Church Councils*" of Quebec, that the courts had to address in the case of the treasures of l'Ange-Gardien.

4. The Facts of the Case and the Points of Contention

In 1962, Joseph-Henri Gariépy was appointed parish priest of l'Ange-Gardien with, among other duties, the task of renovating and rejuvenating the church and the presbytery. In order to finance a part of the works and within the spirit of renewal and simplicity put forth by the recent reforms of the Vatican II Council, Gariépy decided to sell a few objects belonging to the Church Council. These objects were bought by a sculptor-gilder, Roger Prévost, for the modest sum of $800 CDN. An important fact is to be noted: the cheques given by Prévost were made payable to the Church Council of the parish and were effectively deposited into its account. Another important fact to keep in mind is that parish priest Gariépy sold the objects in question without the previous consent of the parish churchwardens nor the authorization of the diocese bishop. Finally, the last important fact to take into consideration is that Gariépy acted in good faith; he really thought that the objects he sold had no particular value at the time.

Shortly afterwards, Prévost sold most of the objects to various antique dealers, who in turn sold the objects to the Musée du Québec, the National Gallery of Canada and to various private collectors. The objects stayed peacefully in the hands of these various collectors until 1973, when Gariépy left the parish of l'Ange-Gardien. Then his successor, Marc Leclerc, decided to question the sale of the objects which had taken place several years earlier, relying on the Quebec civil law principle that sacred objects are imprescriptible and thus excluded from being objects of commerce. He relied on the point that the objects in question had not been desacralized before being alienated. More precisely, according to Mr. Leclerc, his predecessor should have respected the rules of canon law in regard to desacralization, which specify that a written authorization from the archbishop of the diocese has to be obtained before alienating the objects in question. According to Leclerc, the objects were still of a sacred nature when they were alienated since Gariépy had not obviously prescribed to the above-mentioned requirement. Therefore, the alienation was illegal in regard to Quebec civil law.

Then, in 1976, the Church Council of the parish of l'Ange-Gardien decided to bring proceedings against Roger Prévost and those in possession of the objects in question.

The lawsuit instituted by the Church Council took the form of a claim and its main purpose was to have the transactions by which it was illegally dispossessed of the objects in question declared null and void and to obtain the return of the objects into the parochial patrimony.

In this lawsuit, the plaintiff, the Church Council of l'Ange-Gardien, essentially invoked certain provisions of the *Civil Code of Lower Canada* and held that the objects of contention were sacred things at the time of their alienation and, therefore, were imprescriptibles and excluded from being objects of commerce. Furthermore, the plaintiff put forward the view that only the relevant religious authorities could decide the sacred character of an object belonging to them and that only the ecclesiastical authority which was declared competent by Canon law, the bishop of the diocese, could desacralize an object – which had not occurred in the case of the objects of contention. Finally, the Church Council claimed that Gariépy did not have the right, according to the *The Fabrique Act (Law of Church*

Councils), to sell the objects in question before obtaining its authorization in the form of a resolution duly adopted by its board.

As for the defendants, they denied categorically that the objects in question were still sacred at the time of their alienation. They added that, in any case, canon law could not be applied in civil matters unless the legislator expressly referred to it, which was not the case in the provisions of the *Civil Code of Lower Canada* relied upon [by] the plaintiff. Finally, the defendants asserted that according to the rules of Quebec civil law, the parish priest of l'Ange-Gardien was a competent authority and had the power to change the destination of the objects of contention, which he did when he sold them.

In brief, it seems that the disputed questions in the case of l'Ange Gardien could be put under the two following major categories:

(1) the definition of a sacred object, the loss of its sacred character and the application of canon law in the matter and,
(2) the terms of the alienation of the goods of a Church Council once they have been desacralized.

But before examining more closely the details of the decisions reached by the different courts that intervened in this case, it would be useful to provide a description of the disputed objects and to say a few words about the artists that created them.

5. The Disputed Treasures and their Manufacture

The parish of l'Ange-Gardien is one of the oldest parishes in Quebec, even of all Canada. Located on the coast of Beaupré, near Quebec City, it was founded in 1664 and was granted authority of a Church Council in 1678. Without a doubt it was one of the parishes that formed the cradle of New France. Thus, following the example of numerous Quebec parishes during the nineteen century, the parish of l'Ange-Gardien was enriched with several art objects devoted to the cult. These liturgical objects, either sculpted or crafted with materials like silver or wood, were the works of sculptors and silversmiths well renowned for the beauty and delicacy of their work. In fact, the meticulous inventory undertaken by Gérard Morisset enables us today to appreciate the historical and artistic value of these objects that were sold, in all likelihood, in good faith by the parish priest of l'Ange-Gardien. . . .

6. The Decisions

6.1 The Quebec Superior Court

. . .

Judge Paul-Étienne Bernier [of the Quebec Superior Court] pronounced the court decision on January 18, 1980, in a thorough document of more than 135 pages. The Judge concurred with the Church Council, declared void of absolute nullity all acts that brought about the dispossession of the disputed goods and declared that the Church Council was the sole owner of the objects of contention. He then ordered the defendants to return the objects in their possession, without indemnity, or, failing that, to compensate the plaintiffs. In order to nullify the transactions in question, the first instance judge pointed out the essential imprescriptible character of the objects of contention and the fact that, as sacred objects, they were excluded from being objects of commerce. He also emphasized the total absence of a change of destination of these goods at the time of their alienation, the omission by the parish priest of the necessary formalities by canon law, not only for a change of destination of sacred things, but also for the alienation of ecclesiastic goods and, finally, the absence of authorization from the Church Council in regard to the said alienation. It should be noted that in order to reach his findings, judge Bernier had to recognize the application of canon law.

Applying these principles in the case in point, judge Bernier concluded that the evidence revealed that the objects of contention had not lost their sacred character because the competent authorities of the diocese of Quebec had not sanctioned their desecralization. Therefore, these objects were still sacred at the time of their alienation and thus, were imprescriptible and excluded from being objects of commerce. Furthermore, judge Bernier came to the conclusion that Gariépy did not have the mandate to act on behalf of the Church Council of the parish, sole owner of the parochial properties, and therefore did not have the authority to sell them. The sale of the objects in question was thus illegal from all points of view.

6.2 The Quebec Court of Appeal

The decision of the Quebec Superior Court was appealed by some of the defendants: the National Museums of Canada, the Musée du Québec and three private collectors: Roger Prévost, Jean Soucy and Jean-Paul Lemieux. Seven years later, the Court of Appeal unanimously confirmed, with a bench of three judges, the decision rendered by the Superior Court. However, only judges Malouf and L'Heureux-Dubé submitted written opinions; judge Rothman only subscribed to them.

Judge Malouf shared the opinion of the first instance judge in regard to the application of canon law in this case. He also agreed with the definition of sacred things given by the Superior Court, which were objects used for religious purposes. Furthermore, judge Malouf rejected the defendants' argument that claimed that the objects of contention were no longer sacred at the time of their alienation. On the contrary, he confirmed in this respect the conclusion of judge Bernier which stated that the alienated goods were indeed sacred at the time of their alienation as their destination has not been properly changed according to the procedure requested by canon law.

In interpretation of ecclesiastic as well as civil law, judge Malouf also examined the question of whether the parish priest, Gariépy, could have had the authority to alienate the objects of contention if they had been no longer sacred at the time of their alienation. In this regard, judge Malouf recalled that in civil law, a Church Council is a corporation not only formed of the parish priest but also of the churchwardens and that it is by virtue of official resolutions that all decisions regarding the parish are taken. As for canon law, it requires a written estimate from experts, a just cause or a reason of piety and the permission of the legitimate superior in order to alienate an ecclesiastic object. Judge Malouf concluded that Gariépy acting on his own initiative, without the authorization of neither the Church Council nor that of the bishop of the diocese, had violated the provisions of civil law as well as those of canon law and, consequently, did not have the necessary authority to sell the goods belonging to the Church Council as he had done.

Judge L'Heureux-Dubé also agreed with the reference to canon law by the Superior Court in order to determine the destination and sacred character of the objects of contention. She asserted that the relevant sections of the *Civil Code of Lower Canada* could be construed according to the norms pertaining to the particular belief, whether that of canon law for the Catholic religion, of the Torah for Judaism or the Koran for the Muslim faith. In fact, according to judge L'Heureux-Dubé, there had not been an introduction of these religious codes into the civil law but merely a reference to the prescriptions of the different religious denominations in their sovereign realm their beliefs.

Judge L'Heureux-Dubé shared the opinion of the first judge who stated that the goods of contention were still sacred when alienated. She also ruled that Gariépy had unduly bestowed upon himself the power to alienate the objects in question.

The Quebec Court of Appeal rejected the appeal in its judgment of May 28, 1987 and consequently ordered the defendants to remit the objects in their possession to the Church Council.

6.3 The Supreme Court of Canada

The Musée du Québec yielded to the decision of the Court of Appeal, but the National Museums of Canada, as well as the defendants Jean-Paul Lemieux and Roger Prévost, requested from the Supreme Court of Canada the right to appeal. This request was rejected by the Court on December 17, 1987. The decisions of the Quebec Superior Court and of the Quebec Court of Appeal being confirmed, the National Gallery of Canada, Roger Prévost and Jean-Paul Lemieux complied with the ruling and returned the "treasures" to the Church Council of the parish of l'Ange-Gardien.

NOTES AND QUESTIONS

1. Although the concept of *res sacrae* has never been part of the common law, there are indications of a growing sensibility in many legal systems toward sacred objects. As we have seen, the Native American Graves Protection and Repatriation Act, 25 U.S.C. §§ 3001–3013 (2000), provides for the return of sacred objects to American Indians and Native Hawaiians. This suggests that religious objects may enjoy special rights in certain contexts. With the reception of indigenous customary laws into

national legal systems such as that of Canada, this process is becoming a reality. Recently, the Association of Art Museum Directors' report of its Task Force on the Acquisition and Stewardship of Sacred Objects (June 1, 2006) has urged its members to be aware of the special character of sacred cultural material in museum collections.

2. Do you think the common law should embrace rules that give special status or protection to religious or culturally significant objects? If so, what do you think the form and scope of such rules should be? Is it ever appropriate for any legal system to apply religious law as an exception to state law? How can such rules be reconciled with constitutional and legislative prohibitions on religious establishment as in the First Amendment of the U.S. Constitution?
3. Although *res extra commercium* is a civil code principle, the same general concept is highlighted by a series of lawsuits involving attempts to seize Iranian cultural material owned by or on loan to museums and other institutions in the United States. Federal law permits U.S. citizens, with some qualifications, to sue an officially designated "state sponsor of terrorism" for providing "material support" for acts of terrorism (28 U.S. at § (1605(a)(7) (2006)). Successful litigants under that statute have then sought to attach Iranian cultural material in the United States, sell it at judicial auction, and use the proceeds in satisfaction of their multimillion-dollar judgments. The institutions against whom actions to enforce judgments have been made include the Oriental Institute at the University of Chicago, the Field Museum of Natural History in Chicago, Harvard University, and the Museum of Fine Arts in Boston. One of the cases involves the interesting question of whether Iran's expansive cultural patrimony law establishes Iranian "ownership" of certain items at risk of seizure in the United States. The Persepolis and Chogha Mish collections at the Oriental Institute are two of the most famous collections at risk. The federal government has filed several briefs in support of Iran's position against seizure of cultural material. See Laina Catherine Wilk Lopez, *Should Cultural Heritage Be on the Judicial Auction Block?*, 75 KEY REPORTER, Spring 2010, at 8.

   Do you think that cultural material should be exempt from seizure as ordinary "assets" of a judgment debtor, or do you think such material should be treated like any other property? If some, but not all, "cultural material" is considered to be special and thereby protected from seizure to satisfy judgments, how should such material be defined?
4. A leading commentary on the *res extra commercium* is Kurt Siehr, *Kulturgüter als res extra commercium im internationalen Rechtsverkehr, in* LEBENDIGES REICHT – VON DEN SUMERERN BIS ZUR GEGENWART 703 (1995).

d. Statutes of Limitation

Lawrence M. Kaye, *The Statute of Limitations in Art Recovery Cases: An Overview*, 1 IFAR J., Autumn 1998, at 22 (reprinted with the permission of the International Foundation for Art Research)

There is perhaps no legal rule as much debated in claims for the recovery of stolen art as the Statute of Limitations. The Statute of Limitations embodies the policy of giving repose to human affairs and was enacted to protect defendants against stale claims asserted long after the events at issue occurred. The policy of repose behind the Statute of Limitations protects defendants by preventing surprises caused by the revival of stale claims that have been allowed to slumber until evidence has been lost, memories have faded, and witnesses have disappeared.

The Statute of Limitations begins to run when the claim "accrues," that is, when a suit may be maintained on that claim. The New York Statute of Limitations governing actions for the recovery of property requires that suit be brought within three years of the time the action accrued. In most cases it is not difficult to determine the moment of accrual; where an owner pursues a party who wrongfully took his property, the three-year period begins to run when the property was taken. But art recovery claims can present a myriad of problems in this regard.

First of all, claims for the recovery of stolen art often seek the recovery of unique and irreplaceable objects, where money damages will not suffice and only the return of the object itself will do. Where one is dealing with a clearly identifiable object, particularly one stolen from a documented or catalogued public or private collection, both the object and the date of the theft may be easy to identify. The plot thickens, however, when the objects are pillaged from unexcavated archaeological sites and have been removed from the country of origin before archaeologists or museum officials have been able to view, much less document, them. In such cases, both the date of the theft and exact descriptions of the objects may be difficult to ascertain, resulting in delays in locating the property and creating obvious Statute of Limitations issues.

In addition, stolen art may surface long after the initial theft, and often only after it has passed into the hands of an asserted good faith purchaser who has no privity at all to the thief and, indeed, may pass from one good faith purchaser to another. Under the common law in effect in the United States and Canada, no one, not even a good faith purchaser, can acquire good title to stolen property, and a claim can therefore be brought against the good faith purchaser by the true owner. But, by necessity, such claims often cannot be brought until years or even decades after the original theft, i.e., after the owner first learns that the property has surfaced. This will often be the situation with Holocaust era art claims, which are so much in the news at this time.

Yet another complicating factor is that Statutes of Limitations vary in length and type from one jurisdiction to another in the United States and are strikingly different in most European countries, which, unlike the United States and Canada, are governed by Civil Codes (one exception being the United Kingdom, which is a common law jurisdiction). Different jurisdictions even apply different rules as to when a claim accrues, and the potential for uncertainty is heightened by the variety of limitations rules employed. In an action for replevin, that is, an action to recover possession of the property taken, the limitations period will normally run against the original owner from the time the taking occurred. Exceptions have been made, however, for situations where the possessor has committed fraud or otherwise concealed the object.

Moreover, especially when confronted with claims of lost or stolen cultural property, the legislatures and courts often devise special rules to meet the specific circumstances pertaining to such cases. Thus, three major rules for such cases have been developed in the United States: the "discovery rule," now being used in one form or another in a number of states; a special statute for art objects adopted in California; and the "demand and refusal" rule employed in New York and a few other states.

THE DISCOVERY RULE

Many states utilize the discovery rule, which provides that the Statute of Limitations begins to run when the claimant knew, or with reasonable diligence should have known, the location and identity of the possessor of its property.

O'Keefe v. Snyder

In New Jersey the landmark art case is *O'Keefe v. Snyder* in which the artist Georgia O'Keefe commenced a replevin action against a bona fide purchaser in 1976 for the return of three paintings that had been stolen from an exhibition in 1946. O'Keefe had not publicly advertised the loss, but she had discussed it with associates in the art world and in 1972 she had reported the loss to the Art Dealers Association of America. In September 1975 she learned that the paintings were in a gallery in New York, and in February 1976 she learned that they had been sold to the defendant, Barry Snyder. The trial court had granted summary judgment for the defendant on the ground that O'Keefe's action was barred by the Statute of Limitations.

Concluding that works of art pose special problems because they are readily moved and easily concealed, the Supreme Court of New Jersey reversed the lower court and formulated a discovery rule in actions for replevin: [the] cause of action accrued when she first knew, or reasonably should have known through the exercise of due diligence, of the cause of action, including the identity of the possessor of paintings. . . . For example, under the discovery rule, if an artist diligently seeks the recovery of a lost or stolen painting, but cannot find it or discover the identity of the possessor, the statute of limitations will not begin to run.

The court acknowledged that the meaning of due diligence will vary with the facts of each case and that the equitable claims of all parties must be considered in applying the discovery rule.

THE "CALIFORNIA" RULE

California has a special accrual rule applicable to objects of historical or artistic significance. The rule, which went into effect in 1983, provides that actions to recover such property do not accrue until the actual discovery of the whereabouts of the object. [California confusingly has a different statute for claims to recover artwork stolen or converted before 1983].

. . .

THE "DEMAND AND REFUSAL" RULE

New York employs the "demand and refusal" rule, pursuant to which a claim to recover stolen property from a good faith purchaser does not accrue until the possessor refuses to return the object upon demand. The owner has three years thereafter to commence suit. The rule has been a mainstay of New York law since the last century, when the Court of Appeals held: The rule is a reasonable and just one that an innocent purchaser of personal property from a wrongdoer shall first be informed of the defect in his title and have an opportunity to deliver the property to the true owner before he shall be made liable as a tort feasor for wrongful conversion.

Weimar v. Elicofon

One of the best illustrations of the application of the "demand and refusal" rule is the landmark case of *Kunstammlungen zu Weimar v. Elicofon.* The *Weimar* case involved two extraordinary Fifteenth Century portraits by Albrecht Dürer stolen from the collections of the Weimar Museum. The paintings had been stored in the Schwarzburg Castle, where they had been moved for safekeeping during World War II. During the occupation of the castle by American troops, the paintings disappeared. They were discovered some twenty years later in the possession of a Brooklyn attorney, Edward I. Elicofon, who had purchased them in 1946 for $450 from an American serviceman who showed up at Elicofon's home, claiming that he had bought the paintings in Germany. The discovery of the identity of the paintings was fortuitous – a friend of Elicofon's who had seen them in his house recognized them in a newly published book on German art works stolen during World War II.

Under New York's "demand and refusal rule" the limitations period began to run in 1966, when Elicofon, after allegedly learning of the paintings' true identity for the first time, held a press conference to announce his discovery and was immediately confronted with demands for their return from three parties: the Weimar Museum (which was later found by the court to be an instrumentality of what was then the Government of East Germany); the hereditary Grand Duchess of Saxony-Weimar-Eisenach, who claimed that her husband, the Grand Duke, owned the paintings in his private capacity; and finally, the Government of West Germany, which claimed to be the sole representative of all the German people pending unification. Elicofon rejected all of these demands.

Elicofon sought to discredit the demand and refusal rule, claiming that it was unfair because the demand upon a bona fide purchaser "indefinitely postpones commencement of the action," while the thief would have long since gained immunity from suits. The court disagreed, citing the principle that a thief who conceals his possession and thereby makes it impossible for the true owner to locate the property and initiate a suit would be barred from asserting the Statute of Limitations as a defense. After some 13 years of hard-fought litigation, Elicofon's position was soundly rejected by the courts and the paintings were returned to the Weimar Museum. The *Weimar* case is a perfect example of how the Statute of Limitations issue can inject an enormous amount of time and expense into art recovery cases.

. . .

HOLOCAUST CLAIMS AND THE NEW YORK STATUTE OF LIMITATIONS

No discussion of the Statute of Limitations and its relationship to the claims of innocent victims of theft would be complete without some reference to the growing number of claims asserted by the heirs of Holocaust victims against good faith purchasers of artworks previously confiscated from their owners by the Nazi regime. As should be clear from the above discussion, New York's "demand and refusal" rule, which favors original owners, will provide an enormous benefit to such heirs in connection with claims asserted against good faith purchasers of art confiscated during the Holocaust. Under the New York rule, these claims accrue only when the heirs first make a demand for the artwork and it is refused, and they should therefore be able to withstand any challenge of untimeliness under the New York Statute of Limitations.

[There has been] concern that New York's "borrowing statute" could have a "devastating effect" on claims for Nazi-confiscated art and prevent the heirs of Holocaust victims from enjoying the benefits of New York's "demand and refusal" rule. Simply put, his concerns are unfounded.

The "borrowing statute" – Section 202 of the New York Civil Practice Law and Rules – basically provides that where a non-resident sues in New York on a claim that arises in a foreign jurisdiction, the court will apply either the Statute of Limitations of New York or of the jurisdiction where the claim accrues, whichever is shorter. Feldman concludes that whenever Holocaust claims are brought in New York, the New York court will be required to apply the Statute of Limitations of the foreign jurisdiction (e.g., Germany) where the theft occurred. But, particularly in Holocaust cases, a New York action to recover stolen art will typically, if not always, be brought against a collector, dealer or museum who claims to be a good faith purchaser and not against the original thief. Under New York's "demand and refusal" rule, the claim will accrue in New York (not the place of the theft) when the purchaser refuses the claimant's demand to return the stolen work. The borrowing statute would therefore not be implicated and the fact that the original theft may have occurred in Germany fifty years before would be irrelevant to the limitations issue. As the New York Court of Appeals in Guggenheim made clear, demand and refusal are substantive elements of a claim for the recovery of property and must occur before any such claim can be deemed to have accrued.

. . .

As the Court of Appeals acknowledged, the best way to protect victims of art theft and not only Holocaust victims is to safeguard New York's demand and refusal rule: "While the demand and refusal rule is not the only possible method of measuring the accrual of replevin claims, it does appear to be the rule that affords the most protection to the true owners of stolen property.... There is no reason to obscure its straightforward protection of true owners by creating a duty of reasonable diligence. As the Court also maintained, New York's position as the preeminent art center of the world and the need to prevent it from becoming a haven for stolen art requires that the demand and refusal" rule be retained, because it protects the true owner – "the shifting of the burden onto the wronged owner is inappropriate... and the better rule gives the owner relatively greater protection and places the burden of investigating the provenance of a work of art on the potential purchaser." In some, to change the rules in the midst of the rising tide of Holocaust claims would obviously harm – not help – the heirs of Holocaust victims.

(i) The Demand-and-Refusal Rule

Guggenheim v. Lubell,
569 N.E. 2d 426 (N.Y. 1991)

The backdrop for this replevin action is the New York City art market, where masterpieces command extraordinary prices at auction and illicit dealing in stolen merchandise is an industry all its own. The Solomon R. Guggenheim Foundation, which operates the Guggenheim Museum in New York City, is seeking to recover a Chagall gouache worth an estimated $200,000. The Guggenheim believes that the gouache was stolen from its premises by a mailroom employee sometime in the late 1960s. The appellant Rachel Lubell and her husband, now deceased, bought the painting from a well-known Madison Avenue gallery in 1967 and have displayed it in their home for more than 20 years. Mrs. Lubell claims that before the Guggenheim's demand for its return in 1986, she had no reason to believe that the painting had been stolen.

On this appeal, we must decide if the museum's failure to take certain steps to locate the gouache is relevant to the appellant's Statute of Limitations defense. In effect, the appellant argues that the museum had a duty to use reasonable diligence to recover the gouache, that it did not do so, and that its cause of action in replevin is consequently barred by the Statute of Limitations. The Appellate Division rejected the appellant's argument. We agree with the Appellate Division that the timing of the museum's demand for the gouache and the appellant's refusal to return it are the only relevant factors in assessing the merits of the Statute of Limitations defense. We see no justification for undermining the clarity and predictability of this rule by carving out an exception where the chattel to be returned is a valuable piece of art. Appellant's affirmative defense of laches remains viable, however, and her claims that the museum did not undertake a reasonably diligent search for the missing painting will enter into the trial court's evaluation of the merits of that defense. Accordingly, the order of the Appellate Division should be affirmed.

The gouache, known alternately as *Menageries* or *Le Marchand de Bestiaux (The Cattle Dealer)*, was painted by Marc Chagall in 1912, in preparation for an oil painting also entitled *Le Marchand de Bestiaux.* It was donated to the museum in 1937 by Solomon R. Guggenheim.

The museum keeps track of its collection through the use of "accession cards," which indicate when individual pieces leave the museum on loan, when they are returned and when they are transferred between the museum and storage. The museum lent the painting to a number of other art museums over the years. The last such loan occurred in 1961–1962. The accession card for the painting indicates that it was seen in the museum on April 2, 1965. The next notation on the accession card is undated and indicates that the painting could not be located.

Precisely when the museum first learned that the gouache had been stolen is a matter of some dispute. The museum acknowledges that it discovered that the painting was not where it should be sometime in the late 1960s, but claims that it did not know that the painting had in fact been stolen until it undertook a complete inventory of the museum collection beginning in 1969 and ending in 1970. According to the museum, such an inventory was typically taken about once every 10 years. The appellant, on the other hand, argues that the museum knew as early as 1965 that the painting had been stolen. It is undisputed, however, that the Guggenheim did not inform other museums, galleries or artistic organizations of the theft, and additionally, did not notify the New York City Police, the FBI, Interpol or any other law enforcement authorities. The museum asserts that this was a tactical decision based upon its belief that to publicize the theft would succeed only in driving the gouache further underground and greatly diminishing the possibility that it would ever be recovered. In 1974, having concluded that all efforts to recover the gouache had been exhausted, the museum's Board of Trustees voted to "deaccession" the gouache, thereby removing it from the museum's records.

Mr. and Mrs. Lubell had purchased the painting from the Robert Elkon Gallery for $17,000 in May of 1967. The invoice and receipt indicated that the gouache had been in the collection of a named individual, who later turned out to be the museum mailroom employee suspected of the theft. They exhibited the painting twice, in 1967 and in 1981, both times at the Elkon Gallery. In 1985, a private art dealer brought a transparency of the painting to Sotheby's for an auction estimate. The person to whom the dealer showed the transparency had previously worked at the Guggenheim and recognized the gouache as a piece that was missing from the museum. She notified the museum, which traced the painting back to the defendant. On January 9, 1986, Thomas Messer, the museum's director, wrote a letter to the defendant demanding the return of the gouache. Mrs. Lubell refused to return the painting and the instant action for recovery of the painting, or, in the alternative, $200,000, was commenced on September 28, 1987.

In her answer, the appellant raised as affirmative defenses the Statute of Limitations, her status as a good-faith purchaser for value, adverse possession, laches, and the museum's culpable conduct. The museum moved to compel discovery and inspection of the gouache and the defendant cross-moved for summary judgment. In her summary judgment papers, the appellant argued that the replevin action to compel the return of the painting was barred by the three-year Statute of Limitations because the museum had done nothing to locate its property in the 20-year interval between the theft and the museum's fortuitous discovery that the painting was in Mrs. Lubell's possession. The trial court granted the appellant's cross motion for summary judgment, relying on *DeWeerth v. Baldinger* (836 F.2d 103), an opinion from the United States Court of Appeals for the Second Circuit. The trial court cited New York cases holding that a cause of action in replevin accrues when demand is made upon the possessor and the possessor refuses to return the chattel. The court reasoned, however, that in order to avoid prejudice to a good-faith purchaser, demand cannot be unreasonably delayed and that a property owner has an obligation to use reasonable efforts to locate its missing property to ensure that demand is not so delayed. Because the museum in this case had done nothing for 20 years but search its own premises, the court found that its conduct was unreasonable as a matter of law. Consequently, the court granted Mrs. Lubell's cross motion for summary judgment on the grounds that the museum's cause of action was time barred.

The Appellate Division modified, dismissing the Statute of Limitations defense and denying the appellant's cross motion for summary judgment. The Appellate Division held that the trial court had erred in concluding that "delay alone can make a replevin action untimely." . . . The court stated that the appellant's lack of diligence argument was more in the nature of laches than the Statute of Limitations and that as a result, the appellant needed to show that she had been prejudiced by the museum's delay in demanding return of the gouache. . . . The court also held that summary judgment was inappropriate because several issues of fact existed, including whether the museum's response to the theft was unreasonable, when the museum first realized that the gouache was missing, when the museum should have realized that the gouache had been stolen, whether it was unreasonable for the museum not to have taken certain steps after it realized that the gouache was missing but before it realized that it had been stolen, and when the museum learned of the defendant's possession of the gouache. . . . The Appellate Division granted leave to this Court, certifying the following question: "Was the order of this Court, which modified the order of the Supreme Court, properly made?" We answer this certified question in the affirmative.

New York case law has long protected the right of the owner whose property has been stolen to recover that property, even if it is in the possession of a good-faith purchaser for value. There is a three-year Statute of Limitations for recovery of a chattel. . . . The rule in this State is that a cause of action for replevin against the good-faith purchaser of a stolen chattel accrues when the true owner makes demand for return of the chattel and the person in possession of the chattel refuses to return it. . . . Until demand is made and refused, possession of the stolen property by the good-faith purchaser for value is not considered wrongful. . . . Although seemingly anomalous, a different rule applies when the stolen object is in the possession of the thief. In that situation, the Statute of Limitations runs from the time of the theft . . . even if the property owner was unaware of the theft at the time that it occurred. . . .

In *DeWeerth v Baldinger*, which the trial court in this case relied upon in granting Mrs. Lubell's summary judgment motion, the Second Circuit took note of the fact that New York case law treats thieves and good-faith purchasers differently and looked to that difference as a basis for imposing a reasonable diligence requirement on the owners of stolen art. Although the court acknowledged that the question posed by the case was an open one, it declined to certify it to this Court, . . . stating that it did not think that it "[would] recur with sufficient frequency to warrant use of the certification procedure." . . . Actually, the issue has recurred several times in the three years since *DeWeerth* was decided, . . . including the case now before us. We have reexamined the relevant New York case law and we conclude that the Second Circuit should not have imposed a duty of reasonable diligence on the owners of stolen art work for purposes of the Statute of Limitations.

While the demand and refusal rule is not the only possible method of measuring the accrual of replevin claims, it does appear to be the rule that affords the most protection to the true owners of stolen property. Less protective measures would include running the three-year statutory period from the time of the theft even where a good-faith purchaser is in possession of the stolen chattel, or, alternatively, calculating the statutory period from the time that the good-faith purchaser obtains possession of the chattel (*see generally*, Weil, *Repose*, 8 IFAR Rep., at 6–7 [Aug.–Sept. 1987]). Other States that have considered this issue have applied a discovery rule to these cases, with the Statute of Limitations running from the time that the owner discovered or reasonably should have discovered the whereabouts of the work of art that had been stolen. . . .

New York has already considered – and rejected – adoption of a discovery rule. In 1986, both houses of the New York State Legislature passed Assembly Bill 11462-A (Senate Bill 3274-B), which would have modified the demand and refusal rule and instituted a discovery rule in actions for recovery of art objects brought against certain not-for-profit institutions. This bill provided that the three-year Statute of Limitations would run from the time these institutions gave notice, in a manner specified by the statute, that they were in possession of a particular object. Governor Cuomo vetoed the measure, however, on advice of the United States Department of State, the United States Department of Justice and the United States Information Agency (see *3 U.S. Agencies Urge Veto of Art-Claim Bill*, N.Y. TIMES, July 23, 1986, at C15, col. 1). In his veto message, the Governor expressed his concern that the statute "[did] not provide a reasonable opportunity for individuals or foreign governments to receive notice of a museum's acquisition and take action to recover it before their rights are extinguished." The Governor also stated that he had been advised by the State Department that the bill, if it went into effect, would have caused New York to become "a haven for cultural property stolen abroad since such objects [would] be immune from recovery under the limited time periods established by the bill."

The history of this bill and the concerns expressed by the Governor in vetoing it, when considered together with the abundant case law spelling out the demand and refusal rule, convince us that that rule remains the law in New York and that there is no reason to obscure its straightforward protection of true owners by creating a duty of reasonable diligence. Our case law already recognizes that the true owner, having discovered the location of its lost property, cannot unreasonably delay making demand upon the person in possession of that property (see, e.g., Heide v. Glidden Buick Corp., 188 Misc. 198). Here, however, where the demand and refusal is a substantive and not a procedural element of the cause of action, . . . it would not be prudent to extend that case law and impose the additional duty of diligence before the true owner has reason to know where its missing chattel is to be found.

Further, the facts of this case reveal how difficult it would be to specify the type of conduct that would be required for a showing of reasonable diligence. Here, the parties hotly contest whether publicizing the theft would have turned up the gouache. According to the museum, some members of the art community believe that publicizing a theft exposes gaps in security and can lead to more thefts; the museum also argues that publicity often pushes a missing painting further underground. In light of the fact that members of the art community have apparently not reached a consensus on the best way to retrieve stolen art (see Burnham, Art Theft: Its Scope, Its Impact and Its Control), it would be particularly inappropriate for this Court to spell out arbitrary rules of conduct that all true owners of stolen art work would have to follow to the letter if they wanted to preserve their right to pursue a cause of action in replevin. All owners of stolen property should not be expected to behave in the same way and should not be held to a common standard. The value of the property stolen, the manner in which it was stolen, and the type of institution from which it was stolen will all necessarily affect the manner in which a true owner will search for missing property. We conclude that it would be difficult, if not impossible, to craft a reasonable diligence requirement that could take into account all of these variables and that would not unduly burden the true owner.

Further, our decision today is in part influenced by our recognition that New York enjoys a worldwide reputation as a preeminent cultural center. To place the burden of locating stolen artwork on the true owner and to foreclose the rights of that owner to recover its property if the burden is not met would, we believe, encourage illicit trafficking in stolen art. Three years after the theft, any purchaser, good faith or not, would be able to hold onto stolen art work unless the true owner was able to establish that it had undertaken a reasonable search for the missing art. This shifting of the burden onto the wronged owner is inappropriate. In our opinion, the better rule gives the owner relatively greater protection and places the burden of investigating the provenance of a work of art on the potential purchaser.

NOTES AND QUESTIONS

1. On remand, the parties in *Guggenheim v. Lubell* settled their case in 1993. They agreed that Mrs. Lubell could keep the painting, but that she and the two dealers who sold it to her would pay an undisclosed sum to the Guggenheim Museum. For a discussion favoring the claim of the original owners, see Steven A. Bibas, *The Case against Statutes of Limitation for Stolen Art*, 103 YALE L.J. 2437 (1994).
2. In the excerpts above, Lawrence Kaye writes further, as follows:

> [T]he New York limitations rule has been criticized by some as providing no limitations period at all. The critics point out that plaintiffs have been able to prevail even though the demand was not made until many years after the theft, and, just as in [*Weimar v. Elicofon*], they argue that the rule favors the thief over the bona fide purchaser. The parties, however, are not equally innocent victims. As one expert has pointed out, "the purchasers with whom we are dealing – and museum purchasers in particular – are not for the most part unsophisticated.... In an extreme case we might even question whether [such a purchaser] really is a 'good faith' purchaser at all."

In the final analysis, the New York demand-and-refusal rule does strike a fair balance, "one that is protective of both parties but inclines somewhat more toward the original owner than the subsequent purchaser. They are both victims, but the former would appear to be the more innocent victim than the latter." After reading the *Guggenheim* case, do you agree that parties in these kinds of cases are "not equally innocent victims"?

(ii) The Discovery Rule and the Doctrine of Fraudulent Concealment. The discovery rule is a much more popular approach in the United States for divining when a cause of action accrues under a statute of limitations. The rule seeks to balance the equities between the innocent owner and theft victim, on the one hand, and the bona fide purchaser for value, on the other hand. The Seventh Circuit Court of Appeals in the *Goldberg* case approached the issue of the timeliness of the Cypriot complaint based on the discovery rule as adopted in Indiana law.

Autocephalous Greek-Orthodox Church of Cyprus and the Republic of Cyprus v. Goldberg, 917 F.2d 278 (7th Cir. 1990)

C. Statute of Limitations

With great zeal, Goldberg has from the beginning of this action challenged the timeliness of Cyprus'[s] complaint. Under Indiana's statute of limitations for replevin actions, Cyprus had six years from the time its cause of action accrued in which to sue for the recovery of the mosaics. Ind. Code § 34–1–2–1 (1982). Though the exact date of the looting of the Kanakaria Church is unknown, it is agreed that Cyprus first learned of the theft of their mosaics in November 1979. It is also agreed that Cyprus first learned that the mosaics were in Goldberg's possession in late 1988. If Cyprus'[s] cause of action accrued on the former date, their complaint, filed in March, 1989, was untimely. If, on the other hand, it accrued on the latter date (or at any other point after March, 1983), their complaint was timely. Thus, the dispositive determination is when did Cyprus'[s] cause of action "accrue" within the meaning of Indiana's limitations statute.

The determination of when Cyprus'[s] cause of action accrued involves the interpretation of Indiana authorities and their application to the facts of this case.... [W]e give substantial deference to the district court's resolution of such issues, as we assume that the district court has greater expertise in interpreting and applying the law of the state in which it sits. Our review of Judge Noland's statute of limitations analysis convinces us that he has here proved true that assumption.

...

Apart from but related to the discovery rule, Indiana recognizes, by both statute and case law, the doctrine of fraudulent concealment. Under this doctrine, a defendant who has by deceit or fraud prevented a potential plaintiff from learning of a cause of action cannot take advantage of his wrongdoing by raising the statute of limitations as a bar to plaintiff's action. *See* Ind. Code § 34–1–2–9 (1982); *Burks*, 534 N.E.2d at 1104 n.11.

...

Central to both the discovery rule and the doctrine of fraudulent concealment is the determination of the plaintiff's diligence in investigating the potential cause of action. *See Burks*, 534 F.2d at 1104 (under discovery rule, statute begins to run when damage was "ascertained or ascertainable by due diligence"); *Guy v. Schuldt*, 236 Ind. 101, 138 N.E.2d 891, 896 (1956) (despite fraudulent concealment, if plaintiff was not reasonably diligent in discovering fraud "the statute will run from the time discovery ought to have been made").

Applying these Indiana rules and principles to this case, and unguided by any directly analogous Indiana precedent, Judge Noland concluded that an Indiana court would find that Cyprus'[s] action was timely filed. *Autocephalous*, 717 F. Supp. at 1388–93. His primary ground for so concluding was his determination that, under a discovery rule, Cyprus'[s] cause of action did not accrue until Cyprus learned from Dr. True that the mosaics were in Goldberg's possession in Indiana. In so holding, he looked not only to Indiana cases but also to general discovery rule principles, see 51 Am. Jur. 2d *Limitation of Actions* § 146 (1970); 54 C.J.S. *Limitation of Actions* § 87 (1987); and to *O'Keefe v. Snyder*, 83 N.J. 478, 416 A.2d 862 (1980), a decision of the New Jersey Supreme Court addressing the accrual of a cause of action in the context of a replevin action involving a work of art. (In *O'Keeffe*, the court held that artist Georgia O'Keeffe's cause of action for replevin of three paintings stolen from a gallery in 1946 accrued "when she first knew, or reasonably should have known through the exercise of due diligence, of the cause of action, including the identity of the possessor of the paintings." 416 A.2d at 870). Further, Judge Noland found, as a necessary pre-condition to the application of the discovery rule, that Cyprus exercised due diligence in searching for the mosaics. Thus, Judge Noland ruled that Cyprus was not, nor reasonably should have been, on notice as to the possessor or location of the mosaics until late 1988. *Autocephalous*, 717 F. Supp. at 1389–91.

Goldberg attacks Judge Noland's discovery rule analysis on two grounds. First, she charges that in applying the discovery rule in this case Judge Noland "announced a new rule of Indiana law in conflict with established Indiana limitations principles." Not so. Judge Noland applied legal principles set out in Indiana cases, and generally accepted elsewhere, to a new situation not yet addressed by the Indiana courts, exactly what a district court sitting in diversity is obligated to do when presented with a novel issue under state law. *See* 19 C. Wright, A. Miller & E. Cooper, *Federal Practice and Procedure: Jurisdiction* § 4507 (1984). Further, his conclusion that in this case the operative "discovery" had to include the identity of the holder of the mosaics is eminently sound. In the context of a replevin action for particular, unique and concealed works of art, a plaintiff cannot be said to have "discovered" his cause of action until he learns enough facts to form its basis, which must include the fact that the works are being held by another and who, or at least where, that "other" is. *See O'Keeffe*, 416 A.2d at 869–70. Further, we note that any "laziness" this rule might at first blush invite on the part of plaintiffs is heavily tempered by the requirement that, all the while, the plaintiff must exercise due diligence to investigate the theft and recover the works.

Second, Goldberg attacks Judge Noland's due diligence finding. Specifically, she argues that Cyprus failed to contact several organizations it should have, particularly IFAR [the International Foundation for Art Research in New York] and Interpol [in Lyon, France]. She also repeats the argument she made to Judge Noland that events occurring before the end of 1983 should have started the clock ticking on Cyprus'[s] cause of action, with particular emphasis on an article that appeared in a Turkish newspaper. We note first that the due diligence determination is, as Judge Noland noted, highly "fact-sensitive and must be decided on a case-by-case basis." *Autocephalous*, 717 F. Supp. at 1389. Although Goldberg cites some support for a *de novo* standard of review on this issue, *see DeWeerth v. Baldinger*,

836 F.2d 103, 110 (2d Cir. 1987), *cert. denied*, 486 U.S. 1056, 108 S. Ct. 2823, 100 L. Ed. 2d 924 (1988), we ordinarily review determinations such as this, which involve the application of law to facts, under the "clearly erroneous" standard. . . . *See also Mucha v. King*, 792 F.2d 602, 604–06 (7th Cir. 1986). Further, in this case the assessment of Cyprus'[s] diligence necessarily involves a contextual analysis of "a particular and nonrecurring set of historical events," *Mucha*, 792 F.2d at 605, as well as an assessment of the credibility of the various witnesses who testified as to what Cypriot officials knew and when they knew it. Thus, there is substantial support for a very deferential standard of review. *Cf. Louis Dreyfus Corp. v. 27,946 Long Tons of Corn*, 830 F.2d 1321, 1325–27 (5th Cir. 1987) (due diligence finding reviewed under clearly erroneous standard). Under any standard of review, however, Judge Noland's due diligence determination must be affirmed.

. . .

The record evidence (summarized above) makes it clear that, although the Republic of Cyprus may not have contacted all the organizations Goldberg in hindsight would require, it took substantial and meaningful steps, from the time it first learned of the disappearance of the mosaics, to locate and recover them. The efforts by the Republic's officials, targeted at the likely points of sale of the mosaics, were sweeping and consistent with trade practices. Indeed, one expert, a curator from The Walters Art Gallery in Baltimore, Maryland, testified at trial that Cyprus "stands apart" in its efforts to recover stolen cultural properties. *Autocephalous*, 717 F. Supp. at 1389 (quoting testimony of Dr. Vikan). As to Goldberg's repetition here of her arguments regarding the article in the Turkish publication and the other events, the record adequately supports Judge Noland's conclusion that these events did not nor should not have put Cyprus on notice as to a possible cause of action. The article, which fingered Dikman as a man wanted in Cyprus and Turkey for smuggling artifacts and later mentioned the mosaics from the Kanakaria Church, did not reveal that Dikman might be in possession of the mosaics from the Kanakaria Church. What's more, the record reveals that, upon learning of such Turkish press reports, Cyprus redoubled its efforts at notification and recovery. In sum, then, Judge Noland's conclusion that Cyprus was duly diligent and should not have discovered its cause of action before late 1988 stands on firm factual footing. Goldberg's fervent attack on this conclusion at most establishes that an alternative view of the evidence was plausible, which is not enough to merit our disturbing it.

Judge Noland backstopped his discovery rule analysis by also applying the doctrine of fraudulent concealment to the facts of this case. From that application, Judge Noland concluded that the statute of limitations on Cyprus'[s] action was tolled until at least the end of 1983, and thus Cyprus'[s] March, 1989 complaint was timely. *Autocephalous*, 717 F. Supp. at 1391–93. Goldberg takes issue with this conclusion, arguing, *inter alia*, that it is counter to Indiana law as expressed in *Landers v. Evers*, 107 Ind.

App. 347, 24 N.E.2d 796 (1940), a case Judge Noland distinguished on the ground that, in *Landers*, the court found that the plaintiff did not exercise due diligence. Because we find no error in Judge Noland's analysis and application of the discovery rule, we need not and will not pass on the fraudulent concealment issue. Similarly, because we find no error in Judge Noland's determination that Cyprus was duly diligent and their action timely filed, we agree with his decision to reject without further discussion Goldberg's laches and estoppel arguments, and we follow the same prudent course.

NOTE

See Stephen L. Foutty, Autocephalous Greek-Orthodox Church of Cyprus v. Goldberg & Feldman Fine Arts Inc.: *Entrenchment of the Due Diligence Requirement in Replevin Actions for Stolen Art*, 43 VAND. L. REV. 1839 (1990). A similar approach to that in *Goldberg* was adopted by the U.S. district court in *Erisoty v. Rizik*, 1995 U.S. Dist. LEXIS 2096.

ERISOTY v. RIZIK,
1995 U.S. Dist. LEXIS 2096

Plaintiffs in this case seek declaratory and injunctive relief awarding them title to and possession of "Winter," an eighteenth-century masterpiece painted by Corrado Giaquinto (hereinafter "Winter" or "the Painting"), currently possessed by defendants. Alternatively, plaintiffs seek an award of damages on a quantum meruit theory based on their restoration of the painting. I granted the parties' request to bifurcate this action in order to resolve title to the painting first. A non-jury trial limited to this issue was held on October 11 and 12, 1994.

Mr. and Mrs. Rizik (the defendants' parents) owned four paintings by Corrado Giaquinto (1703–1763), an Italian artist. One of these was "Winter." Mr. Rizik acquired the paintings around 1940. In 1960 three Giaquinto paintings were stolen from his widow's home in Washington, D.C. The theft was reported to the Washington, D.C. Police Department and the FBI who both conducted investigations. The FBI also informed INTERPOL of the burglary. Mrs. Rizik received $15,000 in compensation for the loss of three stolen paintings (including "Winter") from Maryland Casualty company.

In 1988 the painting was discovered (in five pieces) by a house remover (Karl Kern) while he was removing the contents of a house in Philadelphia. Mr. Kern sought assistance from an antique dealer who took the painting to the Philadelphia Museum of Art (the museum). The museum could not find out any information about the painting's provenance but it expressed interest in purchasing it. In March 1989, Mr. Kern consigned the painting for sale by Barry S. Slosberg Inc., a Philadelphia auction house. He told the auctioneers that the painting had been attributed to Corrado Giaquinto by the museum. The sale was extensively advertised and the painting was available for public viewing.

Steven Erisoty (one of the plaintiffs) learnt of the auction and was told by the auctioneers that the painting had been attributed to Giaquinto. Dreama Erisoty purchased the painting (on behalf of her family) at auction in April, 1989, for $29,050. The Erisotys intended to restore the painting and resell it. Stephen Erisoty then spent over four years restoring the painting.

In 1992, a member of the Rizik family (Jacqueline Rizik) learnt of the existence of the International Foundation for Art Research;

> The International Foundation for Art Research ("IFAR") is a nonprofit organization dedicated to preventing the circulation of stolen, forged, and misattributed works of art. IFAR was established in 1976, and since that date, owners of stolen art have been able to register their losses with IFAR.
>
> IFAR publishes a magazine known as *IFARreports*, which reports on stolen or lost art and publishes articles relating to art law, cultural property, and authentication. The magazine circulates to art dealers, law enforcement officials, insurance agencies, museums (including the PMA), and private collectors throughout the world. *IFARreports* is published ten times a year. The circulation of *IFARreports* is approximately 1200.
>
> The Art Loss Register, established by IFAR in 1991, is an international clearinghouse for information on stolen art, which maintains an image database of nearly 40,000 stolen items.

Jacqueline Rizik filed an Art Theft Report with the Art Loss Registry at IFAR which reported the theft of the three Giaquinto paintings and offered a reward for information leading to their recovery. The September 1992 issue of *IFARreports* included an announcement of the 1960 theft of the paintings. Subsequently, the Executive-Director of IFAR (Dr. Constance Lowenthal) was contacted by the museum who had received information from one of its former curators who recalled seeing the painting while he was working at the museum. Dr. Lowenthal was also informed of the sale of the painting at auction in 1989.

In April 1993, IFAR disclosed the information it had about the painting to the FBI in Philadelphia. The FBI contacted Slosberg's who confirmed that the painting had been purchased by the Erisotys. The FBI then demanded that Steven Erisoty hand the painting over to them and he did so. After Jacqueline Rizik had been informed by the FBI of the seizure of the painting, she provided the FBI with the insurance claim documents. On September 10, 1993 Gregory Erisoty sent a letter to the FBI stating that the Erisotys were the lawful owners of the painting and demanding its return. On September 13, 1993, the insurers (Maryland Casualty) agreed to release the painting to the Riziks[] in exchange for $5,000 (the amount paid by them in 1960 for the loss of the painting). The painting was returned the next day to the Riziks by the FBI in Washington DC.

On September 20, 1993 the Erisotys demanded the Riziks' return the painting to them. The Riziks refused this demand. The Riziks retained possession of the painting which was appraised in 1993 as having an estimated fair market value of $200,000.

. . .

III. Discovery Rule

Under the discovery rule, an original owner's cause of action does not accrue "until the injured party discovers, or by exercise of reasonable diligence and intelligence should have discovered, facts which form the basis of a cause of action." O'Keeffe, 416 A.2d at 869 (citing *Burd v. New Jersey Telephone Co.*, 76 N.J. 284, 386 A.2d 1310 (N.J. 1978). In the stolen art context, such facts include "the identity of the possessor of the paintings." *Id.* at 870 (citation omitted). In *O'Keeffe*, the Supreme Court of New Jersey articulated the focus of the discovery rule as follows:

> The discovery rule shifts the emphasis from the conduct of the possessor to the conduct of the owner. The focus of the inquiry will no longer be whether the possessor has met the tests of adverse possession, but whether the owner has acted with due diligence in pursuing his or her property.

O'Keeffe, 416 A.2d at 872. In stolen art cases, where a court finds that an owner has diligently searched for a painting "but cannot find it or discover the identity of the possessor, the statute of limitations will not begin to run."...

As an aside, it should be noted that the process of analyzing the factual and procedural aspects of this case as it relates to the discovery rule is not unlike the process of examining a work of art: the view of the beholder varies depending upon the distance from the subject. When one stands too close, the details predominate; the farther away one moves, the greater the appreciation for the overall significance of the work. Upon stepping back from the factual litany set forth above in the findings of fact, one realizes that what happened from the time of the theft of the Painting in 1960 until its recovery by the Riziks in 1993 is unique indeed.

Factually, the case is an anomaly in that the Painting was probably not susceptible to discovery for nearly three decades after its theft. Rather than drifting in the international art community, the Painting may well have remained all the while in a trash bag – torn in five pieces – in the house on Catherine Street, not to see the light of day from 1960 until 1988. Unlike the more usual scenario in which an art work has been resting comfortably with a new owner for many years before the original owner arrives on the scene, in this case the Painting was with the Erisotys a relatively brief four years before the efforts of the Riziks bore fruit and the whereabouts of the Painting became known.

It is tempting to think that this factual distinction impacts the application of the discovery rule – namely, that I should not be concerned with the efforts made to locate the Painting until it could have been discovered in 1988. Yet the focus must be on the nature of the Riziks' efforts, as measured by the standard of reasonable due diligence, not by a standard of discoverability. If anything, the probable difficulty of discovery before 1988 gives rise to unverifiable speculation absent in many cases where discoverable works were not discovered, notwithstanding the original owner's efforts; here, query whether the painting – if out of hiding – would have been located through the Riziks,' F.B.I.'s, and Interpol's actions. These observations are interesting but, in the end, largely irrelevant to the legal rights of the parties, and perhaps only of some marginal import in considering the equities discussed below.

. . .

Of greater legal concern is the unusual procedural posture of the case. Rather than suing to recover their lost chattel, the original owners recovered the Painting through the efforts of the F.B.I., and here seek to defend their ownership as against plaintiffs, the putative bona fide purchasers of the Painting. Notwithstanding this unique scenario, neither party has challenged the applicability of the doctrine of replevin, and I therefore analyze this dispute in the context of that doctrine so as to determine whether or not defendants may retain possession of the Painting, and, relatedly, whether they may claim title to it.

Defendants do contend, however, that, in light of the fact that plaintiffs herein seek to regain possession of the Painting from its original owners (and thus use the discovery rule as a sword rather than shield), the burden of proof as to the sufficiency of defendants' efforts to locate the Painting should rest with the plaintiffs. The burden of proving due diligence under the discovery rule logically rests with the original owner as the party "seeking the benefit of the rule to establish facts that would justify deferring the beginning of the period of limitations." *O'Keeffe*, 416 A.2d at 873. This case is no different. Notwithstanding the fact that defendants currently possess the Painting, it is they who rely on the discovery rule as grounds for preserving their claim to title to the Painting beyond the normal two-year statutory period. As such, the burden of proof as to this issue properly rests with defendants.

Two precedents provide a helpful basis for applying the discovery rule to the facts at hand. In *O'Keeffe*, wherein the artist Georgia O'Keeffe commenced a replevin action against a bona fide purchaser seeking possession of three paintings that she claimed had been stolen in 1946 from an art gallery operated by her late husband, the purported crime was never reported to the authorities nor to an insurance company, as the paintings were uninsured. In 1972, O'Keeffe reported the theft to the Art Dealers Association of America, which had then recently begun maintaining a registry of stolen art work. 416 A.2d at 866. The whereabouts of the paintings remained unknown to O'Keeffe until September of 1975, when she discovered that they were in a New York art gallery.

The *O'Keeffe* court recognized that "the meaning of due diligence will vary with the facts of each case, including the nature and value of the personal property." 416 A.2d at 873. Thus, the court explained, "with respect to jewelry of moderate value, it may be sufficient if the owner reports the theft to the police. With respect to art work of greater value, it may be reasonable to expect an owner to do more." *Id.*

In *Autocephalous Greek-Orthodox Church*, the Seventh Circuit followed *O'Keeffe* and also adopted the discovery rule. In that case, which involved stolen mosaics, the court emphasized that an original owner's obligation to search for missing property is a continuing one:

> We note that any "laziness" this rule might at first blush invite on the part of plaintiffs is heavily tempered by the requirement that, all the while, the plaintiff must exercise due diligence to investigate the theft and recover the works.

917 F.2d at 289. Notwithstanding this command, the court deemed plaintiff's search efforts reasonable despite its failure to contact several organizations such as IFAR and Interpol. The court observed: "Although the Republic of Cyprus may not have contacted all the organizations Goldberg in hindsight would require, it took substantial and meaningful steps, from the time it first learned of the disappearance of the mosaics, to locate and recover them." *Id.* at 290.

The discovery rule is "highly 'fact-sensitive,'" *id.* at 289 (quoting trial judge), and flexible; it thus permits the court to consider the relative equities of the rival claimants to the art work. One commentator has explained:

> In determining whether to apply the [discovery] rule, all relevant factors should be considered including, but not limited to, the following: (1) the nature of the injury; (2) the availability and quality of witnesses and physical evidence; (3) the lapse of time since the initial wrongful act; (4) whether the circumstances permit the inference that the delay has been intentional or deliberate; and (5) whether the delay has unusually prejudiced the defendant.

John G. Petrovich, Comment, *The Recovery of Stolen Art: Of Paintings, Statues, and Statutes of Limitations*, 27 U.C.L.A. L. Rev. 1122, 1152 (1980).

IV. Application of Discovery Rule to Facts

After careful consideration of the law and the very unique facts of this case, I find that defendants' search efforts were reasonably diligent for discovery rule purposes. Several factors contribute to this conclusion. First, the evidence demonstrates that defendants did make an affirmative, sustained effort to locate the Painting. Foremost in this effort was defendants' reporting of the theft to the F.B.I. and continued contact with the F.B.I. through the late-1970s. It was not unreasonable for defendants to conclude, either on their own as well as on the advice of their insurer and the police, that the F.B.I. and Interpol's involvement constituted the best investigative channels available for locating their missing art work. Indeed, in light of Philip

Rizik's status as a government official, and the highly responsive service he received from the F.B.I. culminating in their personal delivery of the Painting in 1993, defendants' reliance on that agency is, in my view, all the more reasonable.

Nor was defendants' apparent lack of contact with the F.B.I. after 1979 necessarily unreasonable. The evidence indicates that defendants and the F.B.I. communicated with each other from time to time over a nineteen-year period, generally occurring when either came into possession of potentially relevant information. Presumably no leads arose after 1979 until subsequent to the publication of the IFAR report in 1992. That assumption aside, it is quite understandable, in my view, that one's efforts to search for a lost item would wane somewhat as the years passed. Indeed, I believe it would be unusual for theft victims such as the defendants to keep in frequent contact with law enforcement officials twenty to thirty years after the fact. Rather, it seems the more plausible approach for victims in defendants' position [is] to keep eyes and ears open, and to expect that the police or F.B.I. would be in touch should any leads arise.

Furthermore, that defendants did not discover IFAR sooner should not be fatal to their claim. Notably, the court in Autocephalous Greek-Orthodox Church affirmed the lower court's holding that the Republic of Cyprus had satisfied the discovery rule despite the Republic's failure to inform IFAR or Interpol. 917 F.2d at 289–90. Here, defendants are neither a government entity nor even serious art collectors; rather, they are merely a family in search of lost art work that decorated the walls of their family home. I choose to focus on defendants' exercise of diligence after discovering the IFAR registry – namely, their registering the Painting in 1992 – rather than their arguable lack of diligence in discovering IFAR's existence.

Plaintiffs contend that providing "notice to the world" is fundamental to compliance with the demands of the discovery rule. While *O'Keeffe* includes this factor as a variable for consideration, . . . it does not, nor does any of the case law reviewed, make compliance with such factor prerequisite to satisfaction of the discovery rule. Further, in light of defendants' lack of familiarity with the art world, as well as the fact that IFAR was not created until some sixteen years after the theft, I find that defendant's reliance on law enforcement agencies constituted the giving of reasonable notice under the circumstances of this case.

Additionally, the balance of equities weighs in defendants' favor. Plaintiffs purchased the Painting without inquiring as to the painting's prior ownership or the identity of the consignor, or making any inquiry of art or law enforcement agencies, and with the knowledge that the Painting was in five pieces – suspicious circumstances to say the least. They took the risk that an original owner could appear at any time. In short, plaintiffs took a gamble – they combined their savings to purchase what they felt was a masterpiece, hoping to reap tremendous benefits in the long run. While plaintiffs' intentions will not ultimately be realized, any detrimental reliance suffered by them as the result of their purchase of the Painting may be remedied by pursuit of their quantum meruit claim against defendants and any claims they may have against Slosberg.

Defendants, on the other hand, suffered an intrusive crime, subsequently contacted the F.B.I. and remained in contact with that agency for many years and, finally, set in motion the process of recovering the Painting through their diligence in contacting IFAR when they became aware of its existence. The fact that the Painting was located within a few years of purchase, yet many years after being stolen, was specifically due to the revived efforts of the Riziks in 1992; this constitutes, in my view, a continuing vigilance rather than an attenuated effort that lapsed in 1979. . . .

The discovery rule is fact-sensitive so as to adjust the level of scrutiny as is appropriate in light of the identity of the parties; what efforts are reasonable for an individual who is relatively unfamiliar with the art world may not be reasonable for a savvy collector, a gallery, or a museum. While defendants could certainly have been more aggressive in their search – for example, making inquiries at galleries and museums rather than merely visiting them – it is my considered view that defendants' occasional visitations to galleries and museums, follow-up on tips, and reliance on the services of the F.B.I. (and, through them, Interpol) constitute a reasonable search effort under the discovery rule. Notably, the standard is not whether defendants did everything that might have been done with the benefit of hindsight, but whether their efforts were reasonable given the facts of the case.

. . .

There are admittedly numerous vagaries associated with the discovery rule. It would be helpful to resolution of these disputes if a more definite approach were adopted, such as, as one commentator has proposed, a rule providing that statutes of limitations do not apply to art theft victims who promptly report thefts to the police and a computerized theft database. *See* Sevven A. Bibas, Note, *The Case against Statutes of Limitations for Stolen Art*, 103 YALE L.J. 2437 (1994). Given the flexibility of the standard as currently applied in the case law, it should not be required of individual victims, unschooled in the ways of the art community, that they leave no stone unturned in order to recover their stolen art.

In light of all factors considered above, I find that defendants exercised reasonably due diligence in searching for the Painting and as such have satisfied the demands of the discovery rule. Accordingly, the governing statute of limitations did not begin to run in this case until 1993 when defendants discovered the whereabouts of the Painting and the identity of the possessors. *O'Keeffe*, 416 A.2d at 870. Their claim to title of the Painting is thus timely and will be honored by this Court. . . .

NOTES

1. Compare *Erisoty* with *DeWeerth v. Baldinger*, 836 F.2d 103 (2d Cir. 1987), where the Court faulted the original owner for not carrying out even the most basic investigation as to the whereabouts of her lost artwork.

2. The discovery rule involves an analysis of due diligence on the part of the bona fide purchaser. What this means is determined by the circumstances of each case. Article 4(4) of the 1995 UNIDROIT Convention on Stolen or Illegally Exported Cultural Objects lists the following factors as relevant to determining due diligence:

> . . . the character of the parties, the price paid, whether the possessor consulted any reasonably accessible register of stolen cultural objects, and any other relevant information and documentation which it could reasonably have obtained, and whether the possessor consulted accessible agencies or took any other step that a reasonable person would have taken in the circumstances.

(iii) Characterization: Procedural or Substantive? In most U.S. jurisdictions, statutes of limitation are characterized as procedural. Thus, even if choice-of-law rules provide for applying the law of another country or state, the statute of limitations of the forum will govern. See, e.g., *Charash v. Oberlin College*, 14 F.3d 291 (6th Cir. 1994), and *Sun Oil Co. v. Wortman*, 486 U.S. 717 (1987). In some instances, however, a foreign statute of limitations may be applied where it is considered a condition of the enforceability of a foreign right and thus as substantive in nature. *Bournias v. Atlantic Maritime Co.*, 220 F.2d 152 (2d Cir. 1955). Also, most states have enacted borrowing statutes, which provide that a cause of action will be barred in a forum if it is barred where it arose, accrued, or originated.

In recent years, several states have characterized statutes of limitations as substantive, in accordance with the Uniform Conflict of Laws-Limitation Act. The courts of those states therefore apply their normal choice-of-law rules to resolve conflicts between statutes of limitations. All tolling and accrual provisions are treated as parts of the limitations law of the state whose substantive law applies to the underlying claim.

The Supreme Court of Canada in *Tolofson v. Jensen*, [1994], 120 DLR (4th) 289 (SAC), characterized statutes of limitation as substantive. In that case, Justice LaForest said:

> To permit the court of the forum to impose its views over those of the legislature endowed with power to determine the consequences of wrongs that take place within its jurisdiction would invite the forum shopping that is to be avoided if we are to attain the consistency of result an effective system of conflict of laws should seek to foster.

A similar approach has also been taken in Australia; see *John Pfeiffer Pty. Ltd. v. Rogerson*, [2000], 203 CLR 503 (High Court of Australia).

In 2002 the state of California extended its statute of limitations, as part of a policy of providing a reasonable opportunity for claimants to commence actions in respect of wrongfully taken Holocaust-era artworks. CAL. CODE CIV. PROC. § 354.3 (2005) provides as follows:

> § 354.3 Action to recover Holocaust-era artwork.
>
> (a) the following definitions govern the construction of this section:
> (1) "Entity" means any museum or gallery that displays, exhibits, or sells any article of historical, interpretive, scientific, or artistic significance.

(2) "Holocaust-era artwork" means any article of artistic significance taken as a result of Nazi persecution during the period of 1929 to 1945, inclusive.

(b) Notwithstanding any other provision of law, any owner, or heir or beneficiary of an owner, of Holocaust-era artwork, may bring an action to recover Holocaust-era artwork from any entity described in paragraph (1) of subdivision (a).

(c) Any action brought under this section shall not be dismissed for failure to comply with the applicable statute of limitation, if the action is commenced on or before December 31, 2010.

Orkin v. Taylor,
487 F.3d 734 (9th Cir. 2007), *cert. denied*, 128 S. Ct. 491 (2007)

Thomas, Circuit Judge.

Descendants of Jewish art collector Margarete Mauthner (collectively, "the Orkins") claim that their ancestor was wrongfully dispossessed of a painting during Hitler's Nazi regime, entitling them to ownership of the painting, which was later purchased by actress Elizabeth Taylor. In this appeal, we conclude that the Holocaust Victims Redress Act does not create a private right of action and that the Orkins' state law claims are barred by the statute of limitations. We affirm the judgment of the district court, dismissing the complaint.

I

Vincent van Gogh is said to have reflected that "paintings have a life of their own that derives from the painter's soul." The confused and perhaps turbulent history of his painting *Vue de l'Asile et de la Chapelle de Saint-Rémy* may prove the truth of his observation.

In 1889, a few months after cutting off the lower part of his left ear following a dispute with Paul Gauguin, van Gogh entered the Saint-Paul-de-Mausole asylum near the town of Saint-Rémy-de-Provence. During this period of his life, he produced over 150 paintings, including some of his most famous works, such as *The Starry Night*. In the summer or fall of 1889, he painted *Vue de l'Asile et de la Chapelle de Saint-Rémy*, which may have been part of a series that he described to his brother Theo as "Sketches of Autumn." The painting portrays either the Church of Labbeville near the town Auvers, a few miles from the asylum, or a monastery that was part of the asylum. Within a year of completing the painting, van Gogh died from a self-inflicted gunshot wound.

Van Gogh sold only one painting during his lifetime. Since his death, however, his works have indeed had lives of their own. After Vincent's death in 1890, and his brother Theo's death six months later, ownership of *Vue de l'Asile et de la Chapelle de Saint-Rémy* passed to Theo's widow, Johanna. The German art dealer Paul Cassirer, an early promoter of the works of van Gogh and other post-impressionist artists, purchased the painting in 1906 or 1907. Shortly thereafter, Cassirer sold the picture to Margarete Mauthner, an early collector of van Gogh's works. The parties vigorously dispute the circumstances under which Mauthner parted with the painting, and that dispute forms the basis of the current controversy between the parties. We need not, and we do not, resolve those factual disputes in this appeal because the issues before us are purely legal in nature. However, a description of the general factual background of the case – highlighting where appropriate the factual disputes – is helpful to frame the legal issues presented.

One of the tools used by art historians to trace ownership is an artist's *catalogue raisonné*. A *catalogue raisonné* is an annotated, illustrated book of a particular artist's works, usually prepared by art historians, scholars, and dealers, which constitutes "a definitive listing and accounting of the works of an artist." *DeWeerth v. Baldinger*, 836 F.2d 103, 112 (2d Cir. 1987). A *catalogue raisonné* published in 1928, *L'oeuvre de Vincent Van Gogh Catalogue Raisonné*, shows Margarete Mauthner as the owner of the painting. J.B. de la Faille's *catalogue raisonné* of van Gogh, published in 1939, also identifies Mauthner as the owner.

From the time of Adolf Hitler's election as Chancellor of Germany in 1933 until the end of World War II, Hitler's Nazi regime engaged in a systematic effort to confiscate thousands of works of art throughout Europe. Hector Feliciano, The Lost Museum: The Nazi Conspiracy to Steal the World's Greatest Works of Art 3 (Basic Books 1997). Within Germany, the enactment of the Ordinance for the Attachment of the Property of the People's and State's Enemies and the Ordinance for the Employment of Jewish Property gave Nazi officials the authority to seize artwork from Jewish owners under color of law. Jonathan Petropoulos, Art as Politics in the Third Reich 190 (University of North Carolina Press 1996).

As the Nazis' persecution accelerated, Mauthner fled Germany to South Africa in 1939, leaving her possessions behind. She remained there until her death in 1947, at the age of 84. What happened to *Vue de l'Asile et de la Chapelle de Saint-Rémy* during that time is not clear from the record. A 1970 *catalogue raisonné* prepared by a committee of scholars in the Netherlands lists the next owner as Alfred Wolf, a Jewish businessman who left Germany for Switzerland in 1934 and ultimately relocated to South America. The auction catalogue prepared by Sotheby & Co. in 1963 lists the provenance, or chain of title, as including three owners prior to Wolf. The Sotheby's catalogue traces the ownership of the painting from Mauthner to Paul Cassirer, to Marcel Goldschmidt, and then to Alfred Wolf. The Orkins contend that this chain of ownership cannot be correct because Paul Cassirer had committed suicide in 1926, two years before the 1928 *catalogue raisonné* was published, listing Mauthner as the owner.

Notably, the Orkins do not contend that the painting was confiscated by the Nazis. Rather, they allege economic coercion, contending that Mauthner sold the painting "under duress." They note that laws promulgated by the Allied Forces after the conclusion of World War II established a presumption that any transfer or relinquishment of property by a persecuted person within the period January 30, 1933 to May 8, 1945 was an act of confiscation. Military Government Law No. 59 § 375(b).

Taylor contends that, at best, the record shows that the painting was sold through two Jewish art dealers to a Jewish art collector, with no evidence of any Nazi coercion or participation in the transactions.

In short, the parties agree that Mauthner once owned the painting and that it was later possessed by Alfred Wolf. At this point in the development of the case, the rest of what transpired with the painting during the 1930s in Berlin is clouded in uncertainty. Sometime in the early 1960s, the Estate of Alfred Wolf commissioned Sotheby's to sell by auction a number of Impressionist and Post-Impressionist paintings, including *Vue de l'Asile et de la Chapelle de Saint-Rémy.*

With the help of her father, who was an art dealer, Elizabeth Taylor began collecting art in the 1950s, acquiring works of Degas, Renoir, Pissarro, Monet, Cassatt and other prominent artists. She had long wanted to acquire a van Gogh. While living in London with her husband, Richard Burton, Taylor learned that *Vue de l'Asile et de la Chapelle de Saint-Rémy* would be offered at a Sotheby's auction in April 1963. She authorized her father to bid for her at the auction, and he was successful in purchasing the painting on her behalf for £ 92,000.

Taylor's acquisition was publicized at the time. Subsequently, the 1970 *catalogue raisonné* referenced Taylor's ownership. From November 1986 until March 1987, the painting was exhibited publicly at the Metropolitan Museum of Art in New York, in an exhibition entitled *Van Gogh in Saint Rémy and Auvers.*

In 1990, Taylor offered the painting for sale through Christie's auction house in London. The provenance for the sale lists Taylor as the current owner, with the prior owners being Alfred Wolf (of Stuttgart and Buenos Aires), Marcel Goldschmit & Co. (of Frankfurt), Margarete Mauthner (of Berlin), Paul Cassirer (of Berlin), and Johanna van Gogh-Bonger (of Amsterdam). The work did not sell at the auction.

In 1998, Congress enacted three statutes pertaining to victims of Nazi persecution: the Holocaust Victims Redress Act ("Act"), Pub. L. No. 105–158, 112 Stat. 15 (1998), the Nazi War Crimes Disclosure Act of 1998, Pub. L. No. 105–167, 114 Stat. 2865 (1998), and the United States Holocaust Assets Commission Act of 1998, Pub. L. No. 105–186, 112 Stat. 611 (1998). The Orkins allege that their inquiry into whether their ancestor, Mauthner, may have lost her art collection due to Nazi persecution began upon the passage of these acts. They retained a law firm in 2001 and claim that, until their attorneys completed their investigation, they did not discover the basis of their current claim. The Orkins allege that, before they began that investigation, they did not know that Mauthner had owned *Vue de l'Asile et de la Chapelle de Saint-Rémy*, that she had lost the painting as a result of Nazi persecution, that Taylor had bought the painting, or that there was a legal basis for recovering the painting. They also claim that they first learned of Taylor's ownership in 2002, through a rumor on the internet that Taylor was interested in selling the painting.

In December 2003, the Orkins wrote a letter to Taylor, demanding that she return the painting to them. After some discussion of settlement, Taylor wrote a response letter declining settlement and asserting that the Orkins' claim to the painting was untimely. Taylor then filed a complaint for declaratory relief to establish her title. . . .

II

The district court properly dismissed the Orkins' federal claims on the ground that the Holocaust Victims Redress Act did not create a private right of action against private art owners. In determining whether a federal statute creates a private right of action, congressional intent is the cornerstone of the analysis. The Supreme Court has established a four-factor test for discerning whether a statute creates a private right of action. *Cort v. Ash*, 422 U.S. 66, 95 S. Ct. 2080, 45 L. Ed. 2d 26 (1975). Under that test, we must ask: (1) whether the plaintiff is a member of a class that the statute especially intended to benefit, (2) whether the legislature explicitly or implicitly intended to create a private cause of action, (3) whether the general purpose of the statutory scheme would be served by creation of a private right of action, and (4) whether the cause of action is traditionally relegated to state law such that implication of a federal remedy would be inappropriate. 422 U.S. at 78.

[The court reviews the evidence, concluding that] the Act does not satisfy any of the *Cort* factors; none of the relevant indicia of intent supports the conclusion that Congress intended to create an implied private right of action in this case. The Act is a precatory announcement of the "sense of the Congress," which neither confers rights nor creates duties. Given the absence of congressional intent to create a private right of action, the Orkins' assertion of a federal right of action must fail.

III

The district court also properly concluded that the Orkins' state-law claims were time-barred. California provides a three-year statute of limitations for any action arising from the "taking, detaining, or injuring" of any "goods or chattels." Cal. Civ. Proc. Code § 338(c). In 1983, the statute of limitations was amended to specify that a "discovery rule" governs accrual of causes of action for recovery of "any article of historical, interpretive, scientific, or artistic significance." In other words, under the new law, an action for recovery of artwork accrues when the rightful owner discovers the whereabouts of the artwork. Before 1983, the statute did not specify when a cause of action for theft would accrue.

The Orkins do not argue that the 1983 amendment applies retroactively to their allegations of a 1939 theft and a 1963 conversion. Rather, they contend that the discovery rule applies even under pre-1983 law. . . .

"The task of a federal court in a diversity action is to approximate state law as closely as possible in order to make sure that the vindication of the state right is without discrimination because of the federal forum." *Ticknor v. Choice Hotels Intern., Inc.*, 265 F.3d 931, 939 (9th Cir. 2001) (quoting *Gee v. Tenneco, Inc.*, 615 F.2d 857, 861 (9th Cir. 1980)). If the state's highest appellate court has not decided the question presented, then we must predict how the state's highest court would decide the question. In doing so, we take state law as it exists without speculating as to future changes in the law.

The California Supreme Court has never confronted the question of what rule governs accrual of pre-1983 causes of action for theft and conversion. The California Supreme Court has, however, specifically held that the discovery rule, whenever it applies, incorporates the principle of constructive notice. In *Jolly v. Eli Lilly & Co.*, the California Supreme Court held that, under California's discovery rule, "[a] plaintiff is held to her actual knowledge as well as knowledge that could reasonably be discovered through investigation of sources open to her." 44 Cal.3d 1103, 1109, 245 Cal. Rptr. 658, 751 P.2d 923 (1988). In other words, under the discovery rule, a cause of action accrues when the plaintiff discovered *or reasonably could have discovered* her claim to and the whereabouts of her property. In assessing California law, we conclude that it is highly unlikely that the California Supreme Court would abandon the *Jolly* rule, much less adopt a new rule that eschewed the concept of constructive notice.

Under *Jolly*, the latest possible accrual date of the Orkins' cause of action was the date on which they first reasonably could have discovered, through investigation of sources open to them, their claim to and the whereabouts of the van Gogh painting. From the face of the Orkins' complaint, it is apparent that Taylor's acquisition of the painting was certainly discoverable at least by 1990, when she held it out for sale in an international auction, and most probably as early as 1963, when she acquired the painting in a highly publicized international auction. In fact, the complaint alleges – and demonstrates by attachment – that Taylor bought the painting at a publicized auction in 1963, that Taylor was listed as the owner of the painting in a publicly available 1970 *catalogue raisonné*, and that Taylor publicly offered the painting for sale in 1990. Had the Orkins investigated any of those publicly-available sources, they could have discovered both their claim to the painting and the painting's whereabouts long before the 2002 internet rumor was posted.

We therefore affirm the district court's conclusion that the Orkins' state-law claims are time-barred. Even under the most generous possible rule for accrual of the causes of action, the claims expired in or before 1993 – three years after the last public announcement of Taylor's ownership. The district court correctly held that the Orkins' state law claims were untimely filed.

NOTES

1. It is important to note, as a litigation strategy, that the possessor of the disputed painting, Elizabeth Taylor, filed this action for a declaratory judgment to quiet title

to the painting. "This can be a particularly attractive strategy if the facts set forth in the restitution demand reveal that the claim is barred by the applicable statute of limitations, which can allow the case to be resolved without the need to determine the precise circumstance of the work's loss or transfer decades earlier (which, given the passage of time, may be elusive)." Steven Alan Reiss & Jonathan Bloom, *The Good Faith Owner and the Tardy Heir*, 10 IFAR J., no. 2, at 13 (2008).

2. *Toledo Museum of Art v. Ullin*, D.N.D. Ohio, W. Div. 2006, applied the same constructive discovery rule as in *Orkin*. There, insofar as the plaintiff museum's ownership and possession of a Paul Gauguin painting were public knowledge, the defendant's claim was held to be time barred.

e. The Doctrine of Laches

Quite apart from any applicable statutes of limitation, the equitable doctrine of laches can still bar a cause of action on the separate ground that under certain circumstances it may be unfair for a bona fide purchaser to be deprived of property in its possession for a substantial period of time. The laches defense requires the purchaser to establish the unreasonableness of the owner's delay in bringing proceedings and resulting prejudice to the purchaser. Thus, in *Guggenheim v. Lubell*, the appellate court, applying New York's demand-and-refusal rule, rejected the defendant's argument that an original owner of a painting, the Guggenheim Museum, had an obligation to exercise due diligence to maintain its action within the terms of a statute of limitations. The court held, however, that the demand-and-refusal rule did not bar a laches defense against an owner. This argument failed for lack of evidence to establish which party the equities favored. See also *Republic of Turkey v. Metropolitan Museum of Art*, 762 F. Supp. 44, 45 (S.D.N.Y. 1990). The doctrine of laches is of special significance in jurisdictions that have adopted the demand-and-refusal rule instead of the discovery rule. In the following case, the court weighed the equities between the original owner and present possessor.

Sanchez v. Trustees of the University of Pennsylvania, 2005 U.S. Dist. LEXIS 636 (2005)

Plaintiffs, the grandchildren and heirs of Pablo Isaias Sanchez, seek to obtain from the Trustees of the University of Pennsylvania and the University of Pennsylvania Museum of Archeology and Anthropology (collectively, "the University") a valuable collection of pre-Columbian gold art objects that they allege was stolen from their grandfather over eighty years ago and ultimately transferred to the University. For the reasons that follow, defendants' motion for summary judgment is granted.

...

The pertinent facts, either undisputed or, where disputed, taken most favorably to the plaintiffs, show that in or around 1909, Pablo Isaias Sanchez discovered on his land a valuable collection of pre-Columbian gold art objects (the "Collection"), which he kept at his family hacienda in Tumaco,

Columbia. At some point thereafter, but no later than 1920, the Collection disappeared. While plaintiffs believe the collection was stolen, their only evidence to that effect is inadmissible hearsay at best and rank speculation at worst.

...

In any event, by 1920 the Collection was in the possession of Amsinck, a New York joint venture company, which sold it to the University for $5,000.

Following discovery, each side has moved for summary judgment, raising a number of interesting legal issues. Only one such issue need here be addressed, however, and that is the issue of laches, which is dispositive.

Under the doctrine of laches, a suit will be dismissed when a plaintiff has engaged in unreasonable delay in bringing suit and defendant has suffered prejudice as a result of the delay. See Robins Island Preservation Fund v. Southold Development Corp., 959 F.2d 409, 423 (2d Cir. 1992). In the context of suits over allegedly stolen artwork, a plaintiff can establish that he has not engaged in unreasonable delay by establishing that he engaged in a diligent search for the missing artwork during the period between the alleged theft and the institution of the lawsuit. See, e.g., Solomon R. Guggenheim Foundation v. Mrs. Jules Lubell, 77 N.Y.2d 311, 315–321, 569 N.E.2d 426, 567 N.Y.S.2d 623 (N.Y. 1991); Greek Orthodox Patriarchate v. Christie's, Inc., 1999 U.S. Dist. LEXIS 13257 (S.D.N.Y. 1999). For example, in DeWeerth v. Baldinger, 836 F.2d 103 (2d Cir. 1987), the owner of a Monet painting engaged in an insufficiently diligent search when she reported the theft of the painting shortly after she discovered it was missing, engaged an attorney and an art professor to help find it, and then gave up her search for twenty-four years. In Wertheimer v. Cirker's Hayes Storage Warehouse, Inc., 300 A.D.2d 117, 752 N.Y.S.2d 295 (N.Y. App. Div. 1st Dep't 2002), plaintiffs were insufficiently diligent when they reported the theft of the artwork in 1947 but thereafter took no steps to recover the painting for fifty years, even though the artwork was offered publicly for sale in 1951 in New York City, where plaintiff's grandfather, the original owner, lived.

...

Applying the principles of laches to the instant case, no reasonable fact-finder could find that plaintiffs' efforts were diligent. Plaintiffs have offered no evidence that their grandfather, from whom the collection was allegedly stolen, undertook any search or made any effort whatever to recover the Collection. The only evidence they provide of any search conducted by their father and oldest brother is inadmissible hearsay in the form of vague second-hand accounts of unproduced letters. Moreover, even if such evidence were admissible, it only serves to demonstrate how inadequate, by contrast, have been the efforts of the instant plaintiffs in the decades following cessation of the letter-writing by their father and brother. Indeed, of all the plaintiffs, only Luis Sanchez conducted any search, and the only things he did in the thirty-two years between arriving in this country and retaining his current lawyer were walking into the Metropolitan Museum of Art (and, occasionally, other, unspecified galleries) to look for the Collection and asking two lawyers he never retained, and some unspecified United Nations persons, about the Collection. He never wrote any letters or placed any telephone calls to any museums; never hired any investigator; never consulted any experts; never reported the theft; and never even conducted any research on where the collection might be found.

Plaintiffs argue that Luis'[s] trivial efforts were nonetheless legally sufficient given Luis'[s] and the other plaintiffs' income and education level. None of the siblings has any post-secondary education, and Luis never made more than $28,000 per year. But how much money or education does it take to write letters, do a little research in the relevant literature, ask a librarian at the New York Public Library (whose main branch is close to Luis'[s] apartment) to help do such research, or, in more recent years, do an internet search? The desultory efforts Sanchez engaged in between 1970 and the present are not remotely enough to satisfy the requirements of a diligent search.

By contrast, the prejudice to defendants in allowing such a suit to proceed more than 80 years after the events in issue is real and substantial. See Robins, 959 F.2d at 424. The long delay has resulted in "deceased witness[es], faded memories, lost documents, [and] hearsay testimony of questionable value," Solomon R. Guggenheim Foundation v. Jules Lubell, 153 A.D.2d 143, 550 N.Y.S.2d 618, 621 (N.Y. App. Div. 1st Dep't 1990), making it extremely difficult for defendants to establish either that the collection was not stolen or that they conducted a vigilant effort to make sure the transaction was legally appropriate. Any depositions or other inquiries of the grandfather, father, or older brother are no longer possible; any records of these individuals are no longer in existence or available; and the original parties to the University's 1920 purchase are long deceased.

. . .

Because defendants have established as a matter of law both prongs of their laches defense, the Court need not reach the other issues raised by counsel. Accordingly, defendants' motion for summary judgment is hereby granted, plaintiff's cross-motion for summary judgment is hereby denied, and the action is dismissed with prejudice. Clerk to enter judgment.

---

f. The Doctrine of Repose

The doctrine of repose – that certain cultural objects that have been in the same location for a substantial period of time should be exempt from claims that they be returned to their places of origin – is akin to the policy behind limitation statutes insofar as it seeks to bring closure and certainty to the possessors of such material. The UNIDROIT Convention establishes periods of repose for both stolen and illegally exported material.

A federal bill in the U.S. Congress would have provided for a nationwide period of repose for cultural property. S. 1523, 131 Cong. Rec. 10, 288, 1st Sess. 99th Cong (1985). This initiative failed, along with a subsequent bill introduced in the New York State legislature. See James A.R. Nafziger, *Repose Legislation: A Threat to the Protection of the World's Cultural Heritage*, 17 CAL. WEST. INT'L L.J.250 (1987).

QUESTIONS

The doctrine of repose is particularly controversial as applied to long-dormant claims arising during the Holocaust as well as claims by indigenous peoples for return or restitution of cultural objects in Western museums. Do you think these sorts of claims should be exempt from the doctrine of repose? If so, how should the exemption be expressed?

PROBLEM

A Fragonard chalk drawing was stolen from the Beaux Arts Museum in Paris in July 1972. The theft attracted some, but not wide, publicity. *Le Monde*, other French papers, and some art magazines reported the theft. There was no mention of the theft in any other newspapers or periodicals. Within France, the police were formally notified of the theft. Although UNESCO was not formally notified, the museum director mentioned the theft to a colleague in the Cultural Heritage Division of UNESCO. In May 2008, the drawing was recognized in the living room of Benjamin Fitt Payne, a New York art collector, who claims to have purchased it from the Receleur Gallery, a gallery that went out of business in 1996. The bill of sale indicates that the drawing is by Fragonard but is silent as to its provenance. No witnesses are available to testify with respect to the circumstances of the gallery's acquisition of the drawing. Mr. Payne has produced a copy of the canceled check that he used to pay the gallery for the drawing and has the receipt and bill of sale provided by the gallery. Mr. Payne admits that, although he inquired into the authenticity of the picture at the time he purchased it, he did not inquire into its provenance. He has stated that it never even occurred to him that Receleur might not have been the true owner of the drawing because they specialized in French art of the eighteenth and early nineteenth centuries.

The Beaux Arts Museum has instituted a replevin action against Payne to recover the drawing. The action is filed in a New York state court. What are the issues? What more information will you seek? With the information you have, what result in the replevin action would you expect?

(Reproduced with permission of the Association of the Bar of the City of New York.)

g. Foreign Sovereign Immunity

The Foreign Sovereign Immunities Act, 28 U.S.C. § 1602 *et seq.* (2000) grants foreign states immunity from suit in federal and state courts in certain instances. The statute has been the subject of two important recent cases insofar as it affects claims against foreign states arising out of appropriation of artworks during the Holocaust era by the Nazis and others.

Republic of Austria v. Altmann,
541 U.S. 677 (2004)

Justice Stevens delivered the opinion of the Court.

In 1998 an Austrian journalist, granted access to the Austrian Gallery's archives, discovered evidence that certain valuable works in the Gallery's collection had not been donated by their rightful owners but had been seized by the Nazis or expropriated by the Austrian Republic after World War II. The journalist provided some of that evidence to respondent, who in turn filed this action to recover possession of six Gustav Klimt paintings. Prior to the Nazi invasion of Austria, the paintings had hung in the palatial Vienna home of respondent's uncle, Ferdinand Bloch-Bauer, a Czechoslovakian Jew and patron of the arts. Respondent claims ownership of the paintings under a will executed by her uncle after he fled Austria in 1938. She alleges that the Gallery obtained possession of the paintings through wrongful conduct in the years during and after World War II.

The defendants (petitioners here) – the Republic of Austria and the Austrian Gallery (Gallery), an instrumentality of the Republic – filed a motion to dismiss the complaint asserting, among other defenses, a claim of sovereign immunity. The District Court denied the motion, 142 F. Supp. 2d 1187 (CD Cal. 2001), and the Court of Appeals affirmed, 317 F.3d 954 (CA9 2002), as amended, 327 F.3d 1246 (2003). We granted certiorari limited to the question whether the Foreign Sovereign Immunities Act of 1976 (FSIA or Act), 28 U.S.C. § 1602 *et seq.* [28 USCS §§ 1602 *et seq.*], which grants foreign states immunity from the jurisdiction of federal and state courts but expressly exempts certain cases, including "cases in which rights in property taken in violation of international law are in issue," § 1605(a)(3), applies to claims that, like respondent's, are based on conduct that occurred before the Act's enactment, and even before the United States adopted the so-called "restrictive theory" of sovereign immunity in 1952. 539 U.S. 987, 156 L. Ed. 2d 703, 124 S. Ct. 46 (2003).

I.

Because this case comes to us from the denial of a motion to dismiss on the pleadings, we assume the truth of the following facts alleged in respondent's complaint.

Born in Austria in 1916, respondent Maria V. Altmann escaped the country after it was annexed by Nazi Germany in 1938. She settled in California in 1942 and became an American citizen in 1945. She is a niece, and the sole surviving named heir, of Ferdinand Bloch-Bauer, who died in Zurich, Switzerland, on November 13, 1945.

Prior to 1938 Ferdinand, then a wealthy sugar magnate, maintained his principal residence in Vienna, Austria, where the six Klimt paintings and other valuable works of art were housed. His wife, Adele, was the subject of two of the paintings. She died in 1925, leaving a will in which she "ask[ed]" her husband "after his death" to bequeath the paintings to the Gallery. The attorney for her estate advised the Gallery that Ferdinand intended to comply with his wife's request, but that he was not legally obligated to do so because he, not Adele, owned the paintings. Ferdinand never executed any document transferring ownership of any of the paintings at issue to the Gallery. He remained their sole legitimate owner until his death. His will bequeathed his entire estate to respondent, another niece, and a nephew.

...

On March 12, 1938, in what became known as the "Anschluss," the Nazis invaded and claimed to annex Austria. Ferdinand, who was Jewish and had supported efforts to resist annexation, fled the country ahead of the Nazis, ultimately settling in Zurich. In his absence, according to the complaint, the Nazis "Aryanized" the sugar company he had directed, took over his Vienna home, and divided up his artworks, which included the Klimts at issue here, many other valuable paintings, and a 400-piece porcelain collection. A Nazi lawyer, Dr. Erich Fuhrer, took possession of the six Klimts. He sold two to the Gallery in 1941 and a third in 1943, kept one for himself, and sold another to the Museum of the City of Vienna. The immediate fate of the sixth is not known. 142 F. Supp. 2d, at 1193.

...

In 1946 Austria enacted a law declaring all transactions motivated by Nazi ideology null and void. This did not result in the immediate return of looted artwork to exiled Austrians, however, because a different provision of Austrian law proscribed export of "artworks . . . deemed to be important to [the country's] cultural heritage" and required anyone wishing to export art to obtain the permission of the Austrian Federal Monument Agency. Seeking to profit from this requirement, the Gallery and the Federal Monument Agency allegedly adopted a practice of "forc[ing] Jews to donate or trade valuable artworks to the [Gallery] in exchange for export permits for other works."

The next year Robert Bentley, respondent'[s] brother and fellow heir, retained a Viennese lawyer, Dr. Gustav Rinesch, to locate and recover property stolen from Ferdinand during the war. In January 1948 Dr. Rinesch wrote to the Gallery requesting return of the three Klimts purchased from Dr. Fuhrer. A Gallery representative responded, asserting – falsely, according to the complaint – that Adele had bequeathed the paintings to the Gallery, and the Gallery had merely permitted Ferdinand to retain them during his lifetime.

Later the same year Dr. Rinesch enlisted the support of Gallery officials to obtain export permits for many of Ferdinand's remaining works of art. In exchange, Dr. Rinesch, purporting to represent respondent and her fellow heirs, signed a document "acknowledg[ing] and accept[ing] Ferdinand' declaration that in the event of his death he wished to follow the wishes of his deceased wife to donate" the Klimt paintings to the Gallery. In addition, Dr. Rinesch assisted the Gallery in obtaining both the painting Dr. Fuhrer had kept for himself and the one he had sold to the Museum of the City of Vienna. At no time during these transactions, however, did Dr. Rinesch have respondent's permission either "to negotiate on her behalf or to allow the [Gallery] to obtain the Klimt paintings."

. . .

In 1998 a journalist examining the Gallery's files discovered documents revealing that at all relevant times Gallery officials knew that neither Adele nor Ferdinand had, in fact, donated the six Klimts to the Gallery. The journalist published a series of articles reporting his findings, and specifically noting that Klimt's first portrait of Adele, "which all the [Gallery] publications represented as having been donated to the museum in 1936," had actually been received in 1941, accompanied by a letter from Dr. Fuhrer signed "'Heil Hitler.'"

In response to these revelations, Austria enacted a new restitution law under which individuals who had been coerced into donating artworks to state museums in exchange for export permits could reclaim their property. Respondent – who had believed, prior to the journalist's investigation, that Adele and Ferdinand had "freely donated" the Klimt paintings to the Gallery before the war – immediately sought recovery of the paintings and other artworks under the new law. A committee of Austrian government officials and art historians agreed to return certain Klimt drawings and porcelain settings that the family had donated in 1948. After what the complaint terms a "sham" proceeding, however, the committee declined to return the six paintings, concluding, based on an allegedly purposeful misreading of Adele's will, that her precatory request had created a binding legal obligation that required her husband to donate the paintings to the Gallery on his death.

Respondent then announced that she would file a lawsuit in Austria to recover the paintings. Because Austrian court costs are proportional to the value of the recovery sought (and in this case would total several million dollars, an amount far beyond respondent's means), she requested a waiver. The court granted this request in part but still would have required respondent to pay approximately $350,000 to proceed. *Ibid.* When the Austrian Government appealed even this partial waiver, respondent voluntarily dismissed her suit and filed this action in the United States District Court for the Central District of California.

II.

Respondent's complaint advances eight causes of action and alleges violations of Austrian, international, and California law. It asserts jurisdiction under § 2 of the FSIA, which grants federal district courts jurisdiction over civil actions against foreign states "as to any claim for relief in personam with respect to which the foreign state is not entitled to immunity" under either another provision of the FSIA or "any applicable international agreement." 28 U.S.C. § 1330(a) [28 USCS § 1330(a)]. The complaint further asserts that petitioners are not entitled to immunity under the FSIA because the Act's "expropriation exception," § 1605(a)(3), expressly exempts from immunity all cases involving "rights in property taken in violation of international law," provided the property has a commercial connection to the United States or the agency or instrumentality that owns the property is engaged in commercial activity here.

...

Petitioners filed a motion to dismiss raising several defenses including a claim of sovereign immunity. Their immunity argument proceeded in two steps. First, they claimed that as of 1948, when much of their alleged wrongdoing took place, they would have enjoyed absolute immunity from suit in United States courts. Proceeding from this premise, petitioners next contended that nothing in the FSIA should be understood to divest them of that immunity retroactively....

The District Court rejected this argument, concluding both that the FSIA applies retroactively to pre-1976 actions and that the Act's expropriation exception extends to respondent's specific claims. Only the former conclusion concerns us here. Presuming that our decision in *Landgraf* v. *USI Film Products*, 511 U.S. 244, 128 L. Ed. 2d 229, 114 S. Ct. 1483 (1994), governed its retroactivity analysis, the court "first consider[ed] whether Congress expressly stated the [FSIA's] reach." 142 F. Supp. 2d, at 1199. Finding no such statement, the court then asked whether application of the Act to petitioners' 1948 actions "would impair rights [petitioners] possessed when [they] acted, impose new duties on [them], or increase [their] liability for past conduct." *Ibid.* Because it deemed the FSIA "a jurisdictional statute that does not alter substantive legal rights," the court answered this second question in the negative and accordingly found the Act controlling. *Id.*, at 1201. As further support for this finding, the court noted that the FSIA itself provides that "[c]laims of foreign states to immunity should *henceforth be decided* by courts of the United States... *in conformity with the principles set forth in this chapter.*" *Ibid.* (quoting 28 U.S.C. § 1602 [28 USCS § 1602]) (emphasis in District Court opinion). In the court's view, this language suggests the Act "is to be applied to all cases decided after its enactment regardless of when the plaintiff's cause of action may have accrued." 142 F. Supp. 2d, at 1201.

The Court of Appeals agreed that the FSIA applies to this case. Rather than endorsing the District Court's reliance on the Act's jurisdictional nature, however, the panel reasoned that applying the FSIA to Austria's alleged wrongdoing was not impermissibly retroactive because Austria could not legitimately have expected to receive immunity for that wrongdoing even in 1948 when it occurred. The court rested that conclusion on an analysis of American courts' then-prevalent practice of deferring to case-by-case immunity determinations by the State Department, and on that Department's expressed policy, as of 1949, of "reliev[ing] American courts from any restraint upon the exercise of their jurisdiction to pass upon the validity of the acts of Nazi officials." 317 F.3d at 965 (quoting Press Release No. 296, Jurisdiction of United States Courts Re Suits for Identifiable Property Involved in Nazi Forced Transfers (emphasis deleted)).

. . .

We granted certiorari, 539 U.S. 987, 156 L. Ed. 2d 703, 124 S. Ct. 46 (2003), and now affirm the judgment of the Court of Appeals, though on different reasoning.

III.

Chief Justice Marshall's opinion in *Schooner Exchange v. M'Faddon*, 7 Cranch 116, 11 U.S. 116, 3 L. Ed. 287 (1812), is generally viewed as the source of our foreign sovereign immunity jurisprudence. In that case, the libellants claimed to be the rightful owners of a French ship that had taken refuge in the port of Philadelphia. The Court first emphasized that the jurisdiction of the United States over persons and property within its territory "is susceptible of no limitation not imposed by itself," and thus foreign sovereigns have no right to immunity in our courts. *Id.*, at 136, 11 U.S. 116, 3 L. Ed. 287. Chief Justice Marshall went on to explain, however, that as a matter of comity, members of the international community had implicitly agreed to waive the exercise of jurisdiction over other sovereigns in certain classes of cases, such as those involving foreign ministers or the person of the sovereign. Accepting a suggestion advanced by the Executive Branch, see *id.*, at 134, 11 U.S. 116, 3 L. Ed. 287, the Chief Justice concluded that the implied waiver theory also served to exempt the *Schooner Exchange* – "a national armed vessel . . . of the emperor of France" – from United States courts' jurisdiction. *Id.*, at 145–146, 11 U.S. 116, 3 L. Ed. 287.

. . .

In accordance with Chief Justice Marshall's observation that foreign sovereign immunity is a matter of grace and comity rather than a constitutional requirement, this Court has "consistently . . . deferred to the decisions of the political branches – in particular, those of the Executive Branch – on whether to take jurisdiction" over particular actions against foreign sovereigns and their instrumentalities. *Verlinden B. V. v. Central Bank of Nigeria*, 461 U.S. 480, 486, 76 L. Ed. 2d 81, 103 S. Ct. 1962 (1983) (citing *Ex parte Peru*, 318 U.S. 578, 586–590, 87 L. Ed. 1014, 63 S. Ct. 793 (1943); *Republic of Mexico v. Hoffman*, 324 U.S. 30, 33–36, 89 L. Ed. 729, 65 S. Ct. 530 (1945)). Until 1952 the Executive Branch followed a policy of requesting immunity in all actions against friendly sovereigns. 461 U.S., at 486, 76 L. Ed. 2d 81, 103 S. Ct. 1962. In that year, however, the State Department concluded that "immunity should no longer be granted in certain types of cases." In a letter to the Attorney General, the Acting Legal Adviser for the Secretary of State, Jack B. Tate, explained that the Department would thereafter apply the "restrictive theory" of sovereign immunity:

> A study of the law of sovereign immunity reveals the existence of two conflicting concepts of sovereign immunity, each widely held

> and firmly established. According to the classical or absolute theory of sovereign immunity, a sovereign cannot, without his consent, be made a respondent in the courts of another sovereign. According to the newer or restrictive theory of sovereign immunity, the immunity of the sovereign is recognized with regard to sovereign or public acts (*jure imperii*) of a state, but not with respect to private acts (*jure gestionis*).... [I]t will hereafter be the Department's policy to follow the restrictive theory... in the consideration of requests of foreign governments for a grant of sovereign immunity.

As we explained in our unanimous opinion in *Verlinden*, the change in State Department policy wrought by the "Tate Letter" had little, if any, impact on federal courts' approach to immunity analyses: "As in the past, initial responsibility for deciding questions of sovereign immunity fell primarily upon the Executive acting through the State Department," and courts continued to "abid[e] by" that Department's "suggestions of immunity." 461 U.S., at 487, 76 L. Ed. 2d 81, 103 S. Ct. 1962. The change did, however, throw immunity determinations into some disarray, as "foreign nations often placed diplomatic pressure on the State Department," and political considerations sometimes led the Department to file "suggestions of immunity in cases where immunity would not have been available under the restrictive theory." *Id.*, at 487–488, 76 L. Ed. 2d 81, 103 S. Ct. 1962. Complicating matters further, when foreign nations failed to request immunity from the State Department:

> [T]he responsibility fell to the courts to determine whether sovereign immunity existed, generally by reference to prior State Department decisions.... Thus, sovereign immunity determinations were made in two different branches, subject to a variety of factors, sometimes including diplomatic considerations. Not surprisingly, the governing standards were neither clear nor uniformly applied.

Ibid.

In 1976 Congress sought to remedy these problems by enacting the FSIA, a comprehensive statute containing a "set of legal standards governing claims of immunity in every civil action against a foreign state or its political subdivisions, agencies, or instrumentalities." *Id.*, at 488, 76 L. Ed. 2d 81, 103 S. Ct. 1962. The Act "codifies, as a matter of federal law, the restrictive theory of sovereign immunity," *ibid.*, and transfers primary responsibility for immunity determinations from the Executive to the Judicial Branch. The preamble states that "henceforth" both federal and state courts should decide claims of sovereign immunity in conformity with the Act's principles. 28 U.S.C. § 1602 [28 USCS § 1602].

The Act itself grants federal courts jurisdiction over civil actions against foreign states and over diversity actions in which a foreign state is the plaintiff, § 1332(a)(4); it contains venue and removal provisions, §§ 1391(f), 1441(d); it prescribes the procedures for obtaining personal jurisdiction over a foreign state, § 1330(b); and it governs the extent to which a state's property may be subject to attachment or execution, §§ 1609–1611. Finally, the Act carves out certain exceptions to its general grant of immunity, including the expropriation exception on which respondent's complaint relies. These exceptions are central to the Act's functioning: "At the threshold of every action in a district court against a foreign state, . . . the court must satisfy itself that one of the exceptions applies," as "subject-matter jurisdiction in any such action depends" on that application. *Verlinden*, 461 U.S., at 493–494, 76 L. Ed. 2d 81, 103 S. Ct. 1962. . . .

IV.

The District Court agreed with respondent that the FSIA's expropriation exception covers petitioners' alleged wrongdoing, 142 F. Supp. 2d, at 1202, and the Court of Appeals affirmed that holding, 317 F.3d at 967–969, 974. As noted above, however, we declined to review this aspect of the courts' opinions, confining our grant of certiorari to the issue of the FSIA's general applicability to conduct that occurred prior to the Act's 1976 enactment, and more specifically, prior to the State Department's 1952 adoption of the restrictive theory of sovereign immunity. We begin our analysis of that issue by explaining why, contrary to the assumption of the District Court, 142 F. Supp. 2d, at 1199–1201, and Court of Appeals, 317 F.3d at 963–967, the default rule announced in our opinion in *Landgraf v. USI Film Products*, 511 U.S. 244, 128 L. Ed. 2d 229, 114 S. Ct. 1483 (1994), does not control the outcome in this case.

In *Landgraf* we considered whether § 102 of the Civil Rights Act of 1991, which permits a party to seek compensatory and punitive damages for certain types of intentional employment discrimination, Rev Stat § 1977A, as added, 105 Stat 1072, 42 U.S.C. § 1981a(a) [42 USCS § 1981a(a)], and to demand a jury trial if such damages are sought, § 1981a(c), applied to an employment discrimination case that was pending on appeal when the statute was enacted. The issue forced us to confront the "'apparent tension'" between our rule that "'a court is to apply the law in effect at the time it renders its decision,'" 511 U.S., at 264, 128 L. Ed. 2d 229, 114 S. Ct. 1483 (quoting *Bradley v. School Bd. of Richmond*, 416 U.S. 696, 711, 40 L. Ed. 2d 476, 94 S. Ct. 2006 (1974)), and the seemingly contrary "axiom that '[r]etroactivity is not favored in the law'" and thus that "'congressional enactments . . . will not be construed to have retroactive effect unless their language requires this result,'" 511 U.S., at 264, 128 L. Ed. 2d 229, 114 S. Ct. 1483 (quoting *Bowen v. Georgetown Univ. Hospital*, 488 U.S. 204, 208, 102 L. Ed. 2d 493, 109 S. Ct. 468 (1988)).

Acknowledging that, in most cases, the antiretroactivity presumption is just that – a presumption, rather than a constitutional command . . . – we examined the rationales that support it. We noted, for example, that "[t]he Legislature's . . . responsivity to political pressures poses a risk that it may be tempted to use retroactive legislation as a means of retribution against unpopular groups or individuals," *Landgraf*, 511 U.S., at 266, 128 L. Ed. 2d 229, 114 S. Ct. 1483, and that retroactive statutes may upset settled expectations by "tak[ing] away or impair[ing] vested rights acquired under existing laws, or creat[ing] a new obligation, impos[ing] a new duty, or attach[ing] a new disability, in respect to transactions or considerations already past," *id.*, at 269, 128 L. Ed. 2d 229, 114 S. Ct. 1483 (quoting *Society for Propagation of the Gospel v. Wheeler*, 22 F. Cas. 756, 767, F. Cas. No. 13156 (No. 13,156) (CCNH 1814) (Story, J.)). We further observed that these antiretroactivity concerns are most pressing in cases involving "new provisions affecting contractual or property rights, matters in which predictability and stability are of prime importance." 511 U.S., at 271, 128 L. Ed. 2d 229, 114 S. Ct. 1483.

. . .

In contrast, we sanctioned the application to all pending and future cases of "intervening" statutes that merely "confe[r] or ous[t] jurisdiction." *Id.*, at 274, 128 L. Ed. 2d 229, 114 S. Ct. 1483. Such application, we stated, "usually takes away no substantive right but simply changes the tribunal that is to hear the case." *Ibid.* (internal quotation marks omitted). Similarly, the "diminished reliance interests in matters of procedure" permit courts to apply changes in procedural rules "in suits arising before [the rules'] enactment without raising concerns about retroactivity." *Id.*, at 275, 128 L. Ed. 2d 229, 114 S. Ct. 1483.

Balancing these competing concerns, we described the presumption against retroactive application in the following terms:

> When a case implicates a federal statute enacted after the events in suit, the court's first task is to determine whether Congress has expressly prescribed the statute's proper reach. If Congress has done so, of course, there is no need to resort to judicial default rules. When, however, the statute contains no such express command the court must determine whether the new statute would have retroactive effect, *i.e.*, whether it would impair rights a party possessed when he acted, increase a party's liability for past conduct, or impose new duties with respect to transactions already completed. If the statute would operate retroactively, our traditional presumption teaches that it does not govern absent clear congressional intent favoring such a result.

Id., at 280, 128 L. Ed. 2d 229, 114 S. Ct. 1483.

Though seemingly comprehensive, this inquiry does not provide a clear answer in this case. Although the FSIA's preamble suggests that it applies to preenactment conduct, that statement by itself falls short of an "expres[s] prescri[ption of] the statute's proper reach." Under *Landgraf*, therefore, it is appropriate to ask whether the Act affects substantive rights (and thus would be impermissibly retroactive if applied to preenactment conduct) or addresses only matters of procedure (and thus may be applied to all pending cases regardless of when the underlying conduct occurred). But the FSIA defies such categorization. To begin with, none of the three examples of retroactivity mentioned in the above quotation fits the FSIA's clarification of the law of sovereign immunity. Prior to 1976 foreign states had a justifiable expectation that, as a matter of comity, United States courts would grant them immunity for their public acts (provided the State Department did not recommend otherwise), but they had no "right" to such immunity. Moreover, the FSIA merely opens United States courts to plaintiffs with pre-existing claims against foreign states; the Act neither "increase[s those states'] liability for past conduct" nor "impose[s] new duties with respect to transactions already completed." 511 U.S., at 280, 128 L. Ed. 2d 229, 114 S. Ct. 1483. Thus, the Act does not at first appear to "operate retroactively" within the meaning of the *Landgraf* default rule.

That preliminary conclusion, however, creates some tension with our observation in *Verlinden* that the FSIA is not simply a jurisdictional statute "concern[ing] access to the federal courts" but a codification of "the standards governing foreign sovereign immunity as an aspect of *substantive* federal law." 461 U.S., at 496–497, 76 L. Ed. 2d 81, 103 S. Ct. 1962 (emphasis added). Moreover, we noted in *Verlinden* that in any suit against a foreign sovereign, "the plaintiff will be barred from raising his claim in *any* court in the United States" unless one of the FSIA's exceptions applies, *id.*, at 497, 76 L. Ed. 2d 81, 103 S. Ct. 1962 (emphasis added), and we have stated elsewhere that statutes that "*creat[e]* jurisdiction" where none otherwise exists "spea[k] not just to the power of a particular court but to the substantive rights of the parties as well," *Hughes Aircraft Co. v. United States ex rel. Schumer*, 520 U.S. 939, 951, 138 L. Ed. 2d 135, 117 S. Ct. 1871 (1997) (emphasis in original). Such statutes, we continued, "even though phrased in 'jurisdictional' terms, [are] as much subject to our presumption against retroactivity as any other[s]." *Ibid.*

Thus, *Landgraf*'s default rule does not definitively resolve this case. In our view, however, *Landgraf*'s antiretroactivity presumption, while not strictly confined to cases involving private rights, is most helpful in that context. Cf. 511 U.S., at 271, 128 L. Ed. 2d 229, 114 S. Ct. 1483, n. 25 ("[T]he great majority of our decisions relying upon the antiretroactivity presumption have involved intervening statutes burdening private parties"). The aim of the presumption is to avoid unnecessary *post hoc* changes to legal rules on which parties relied in shaping their primary conduct. But the principal purpose of foreign sovereign immunity has never been to permit foreign states and their instrumentalities to shape their conduct in reliance on the promise of future immunity from suit in United States courts. Rather, such immunity reflects current political realities and relationships, and aims to give foreign states and their instrumentalities some *present* "protection from the inconvenience of suit as a gesture of comity." *Dole Food Co. v. Patrickson*, 538 U.S. 468, 479, 155 L. Ed. 2d 643, 123 S. Ct. 1655 (2003). Throughout history, courts have resolved questions of foreign sovereign immunity by deferring to the "decisions of the political branches . . . on whether to take jurisdiction." *Verlinden*, 461 U.S., at 486, 76 L. Ed. 2d 81, 103 S. Ct. 1962. In this *sui generis* context, we think it more appropriate, absent contraindications, to defer to the most recent such decision – namely, the FSIA – than to presume that decision *inapplicable* merely because it postdates the conduct in question.

. . .

This leaves only the question whether anything in the FSIA or the circumstances surrounding its enactment suggests that we should not apply it to petitioners' 1948 actions. Not only do we answer this question in the negative, but we find clear evidence that Congress intended the Act to apply to preenactment conduct.

To begin with, the preamble of the FSIA expresses Congress' understanding that the Act would apply to all postenactment claims of sovereign immunity. That section provides:

> *Claims* of foreign states to immunity should *henceforth* be decided by courts of the United States and of the States in conformity with the principles set forth in this chapter.

28 U.S.C. § 1602 [28 USCS § 1602] (emphasis added).

Though perhaps not sufficient to satisfy *Landgraf's* "express command" requirement, 511 U.S., at 280, 128 L. Ed. 2d 229, 114 S. Ct. 1483, this language is unambiguous: Immunity "claims" – not actions protected by immunity, but assertions of immunity to suits arising from those actions – are the relevant conduct regulated by the Act; those claims are "henceforth" to be decided by the courts. As the District Court observed, this language suggests Congress intended courts to resolve *all* such claims "in conformity with the principles set forth" in the Act, regardless of when the underlying conduct occurred. . . .

The FSIA's overall structure strongly supports this conclusion. Many of the Act's provisions unquestionably apply to cases arising out of conduct that occurred before 1976. In *Dole Food Co. v. Patrickson*, 538 U.S. 468, 155 L. Ed. 2d 643, 123 S. Ct. 1655 (2003), for example, we held that whether an entity qualifies as an "instrumentality" of a "foreign state" for purposes of the FSIA's grant of immunity depends on the relationship between the entity and the state at the time suit is brought rather than when the conduct occurred. In addition, *Verlinden*, which upheld against constitutional challenge 28 U.S.C. § 1330's [28 USCS § 1330's] grant of subject-matter jurisdiction, involved a dispute over a contract that predated the Act. 461 U.S., at 482–483, 497, 76 L. Ed. 2d 81, 103 S. Ct. 1962. And there has never been any doubt that the Act's procedural provisions relating to venue, removal, execution, and attachment apply to all pending cases. Thus, the FSIA's preamble indicates that it applies "henceforth," and its body includes numerous provisions that unquestionably apply to claims based on pre-1976 conduct. In this context, it would be anomalous to presume that an isolated provision (such as the expropriation exception on which respondent relies) is of purely prospective application absent any statutory language to that effect.

Finally, applying the FSIA to all pending cases regardless of when the underlying conduct occurred is most consistent with two of the Act's principal purposes: clarifying the rules that judges should apply in resolving sovereign immunity claims and eliminating political participation in the resolution of such claims. We have recognized that, to accomplish these purposes, Congress established a comprehensive framework for resolving any claim of sovereign immunity:

> We think that the text and structure of the FSIA demonstrate Congress' intention that the FSIA be the sole basis for obtaining jurisdiction over a foreign state in our courts. Sections 1604 and 1330(a) work in tandem: § 1604 bars federal and state courts from exercising jurisdiction when a foreign state *is* entitled to immunity, and § 1330(a) confers jurisdiction on district courts to hear suits brought by United States citizens and by aliens when a foreign state is *not* entitled to immunity. As we said in *Verlinden*, the FSIA "must be applied by the district courts in every action against a foreign sovereign, since subject-matter jurisdiction in any such action depends on the existence of one of the specified exceptions to foreign sovereign immunity."

Argentine Republic v. Amerada Hess Shipping Corp., 488 U.S. 428, 434–435, 102 L. Ed. 2d 818, 109 S. Ct. 683 (1989) (quoting *Verlinden*, 461 U.S., at 493, 76 L. Ed. 2d 81, 103 S. Ct. 1962).

The *Amerada Hess* respondents' claims concerned conduct that postdated the FSIA, so we had no occasion to consider the Act's retroactivity. Nevertheless, our observations about the FSIA's inclusiveness are relevant in this case: Quite obviously, Congress' purposes in enacting such a comprehensive jurisdictional scheme would be frustrated if, in postenactment cases concerning preenactment conduct, courts were to continue to follow the same ambiguous and politically charged "'standards'" that the FSIA replaced.

We do not endorse the reasoning of the Court of Appeals. Indeed, we think it engaged in precisely the kind of detailed historical inquiry that the FSIA's clear guidelines were intended to obviate. Nevertheless, we affirm the panel's judgment because the Act, freed from *Landgraf's* antiretroactivity presumption, clearly applies to conduct, like petitioners' alleged wrongdoing, that occurred prior to 1976 and, for that matter, prior to 1952 when the State Department adopted the restrictive theory of sovereign immunity.

We conclude by emphasizing the narrowness of this holding. To begin with, although the District Court and Court of Appeals determined that § 1605(a)(3) covers this case, we declined to review that determination. Nor do we have occasion to comment on the application of the so-called "act of state" doctrine to petitioners' alleged wrongdoing. Unlike a claim of sovereign immunity, which merely raises a jurisdictional defense, the act of state doctrine provides foreign states with a substantive defense on the merits. Under that doctrine, the courts of one state will not question the validity of public acts (acts *jure imperii*) performed by other sovereigns within their own borders, even when such courts have jurisdiction over a controversy in which one of the litigants has standing to challenge those acts. See *Underhill v. Hernandez*, 168 U.S. 250, 252, 42 L. Ed. 456, 18 S. Ct. 83 (1897); *Banco Nacional de Cuba v. Sabbatino*, 376 U.S. 398, 401, 11 L. Ed. 2d 804, 84 S. Ct. 923 (1964) ("The act of state doctrine in its traditional formulation precludes the courts of this country from inquiring into the validity of the public acts a recognized foreign sovereign power committed within its own territory"). Petitioners principally rely on the act of state doctrine to support their assertion that foreign expropriations are public acts for which, prior to the enactment of the FSIA, sovereigns expected immunity. Brief for Petitioners 18–20. Applying the FSIA in this case would upset that settled expectation, petitioners argue, and thus the Act "would operate retroactively" under *Landgraf*. 511 U.S., at 280, 128 L. Ed. 2d 229, 114 S. Ct. 1483. But because the FSIA in no way affects application of the act of state doctrine, our determination that the Act applies in this case in no way affects any argument petitioners may have that the doctrine shields their alleged wrongdoing.

...

Finally, while we reject the United States' recommendation to bar application of the FSIA to claims based on pre-enactment conduct, Brief for United States as *Amicus Curiae*, nothing in our holding prevents the State Department from filing statements of interest suggesting that courts decline to exercise jurisdiction in particular cases implicating foreign sovereign immunity. The issue now before us, to which the Brief for United States as *Amicus Curiae* is addressed, concerns interpretation of the FSIA's reach – a "pure question of statutory construction well within the province of the Judiciary." *INS v. Cardoza-Fonseca*, 480 U.S. 421, 446, 448, 94 L. Ed. 2d 434, 107 S. Ct. 1207 (1987). While the United States' views on such an issue are of considerable interest to the Court, they merit no special deference. See, *e.g.*, *ibid.* In contrast, should the State Department choose to express its opinion on the implications of exercising jurisdiction over *particular* petitioners in connection with *their* alleged conduct, ... that opinion might well be entitled to deference as the considered judgment of the Executive on a particular question of foreign policy. *See, e.g.*, *Verlinden*, 461 U.S., at 486, 76 L. Ed. 2d 81, 103 S. Ct. 1962; *Am. Ins. Ass'n v. Garamendi*, 539 U.S. 396, 414, 156 L. Ed. 2d 376, 123 S. Ct. 2374 (2003) (discussing the President's "'vast share of responsibility for the conduct of our foreign relations'"). We express no opinion on the question whether such deference should be granted in cases covered by the FSIA.

...

The judgment of the Court of Appeals is affirmed.
It is so ordered.

Malewicz v. City of Amsterdam,
362 F. Supp. 2d 298 (U.S. D.C. 2005)

This lawsuit attempts to correct an alleged wrong committed by the City of Amsterdam, a political subdivision of the Kingdom of the Netherlands, when it expropriated eighty-four (84) works of art created by Kazimir

Malewicz. Brought by heirs of Mr. Malewicz, who died in 1935 (the "Malewicz Heirs"), the suit arises in replevin, rescission and conversion and seeks the return of the artwork as well as damages. The first question is whether this Court has jurisdiction to hear the merits of the complaint. Having before it a fully-briefed motion to dismiss on jurisdictional grounds, and a Statement of Interest filed by the United States to which both parties have filed responses, the Court concludes that it cannot determine on this record whether the City of Amsterdam's contacts with the United States were "substantial" within the meaning of the Foreign Sovereign Immunities Act, 28 U.S.C. § 1603(e), to support jurisdiction.

I. BACKGROUND

A. The Malewicz Collection

Kazimir Malewicz was a world-renowned Russian artist in the years before World War II; "he founded the Suprematist Movement, which had an enormous influence on abstract art." Mr. Malewicz took more than one hundred of his works of art to Berlin for exhibition in 1927. When he had to return unexpectedly to Russia, he entrusted his art pieces to four friends in Germany: Gustav von Riesen, Hugo Haring, Hans Richter, and Dr. Alexander Dorner. When the exhibition closed, the art works were packed in crates and shipped to Dr. Dorner for safekeeping and storage since they could not safely be returned to Russia because "Stalinist condemnation of abstract art would undoubtedly have led to their confiscation and destruction."

...

The art works were stored in the basement of the *Landesmuseum* in Hannover, Germany, of which Dr. Dorner was the director. Alfred Barr, then-director of the Museum of Modern Art in New York ("MoMA"), visited Dr. Dorner in 1935 and persuaded him to ship some of the works to MoMA to be held on loan. Kazimir Malewicz died in May of 1935. Dr. Dorner fled Nazi Germany in 1937, taking two other works by Mr. Malewicz with him. Because the Malewicz works would not have been acceptable for display to the governments of either Russia or Germany, Dr. Dorner sent the crates of Malewicz paintings and drawings to Mr. Haring who, alone of the original group of friends, remained in Berlin, Germany. Mr. Haring safeguarded the works in Berlin until that city was bombed in 1943, and then removed them to his native town, Biberach. Mr. Haring died in Biberach in 1958.

Dr. Dorner died in November 1957. He bequeathed the two Malewicz works that he had taken out of Germany to the Busch-Reisinger Museum at Harvard University in Cambridge, Massachusetts, to be held on loan and for the benefit of "the rightful owners." Upon demand from the Malewicz Heirs, MoMA has resolved their demands by returning one of the Malewicz works and the Busch-Reisinger Museum returned both works to the Heirs.

The Malewicz Collection at issue is housed, when not on exhibit elsewhere, at the Stedelijk Museum in Amsterdam. Between the years of 1951 and 1956, Dr. W.J.H.B. Sandberg, then-director of the Stedelijk, and other museum directors tried to persuade Mr. Haring to send the Malewicz Collection to the Stedelijk for restoration and exhibition. Mr. Haring refused to do so and repeatedly "emphasized that he was only a custodian of the works, responsible for their safekeeping and that he had no right to convey ownership of them to anyone." Mr. Haring took the same position with anyone who attempted to purchase any works from the Malewicz Collection. When Mr. Sandberg attempted to acquire a Malewicz painting that Mr. Haring had loaned for an exhibition at the Stuttgart Staatsgalerie, he was advised that Dr. O. Domnick of Domnick Verlag of Stuttgart had attempted to buy a Malewicz painting, but that Mr. Haring had refused to sell it, declaring "that he could not sell it to me because he is not the owner and only considers himself to be the trustee of the Malewicz works." Mr. Sandberg visited Mr. Haring in a hospital in Biberach in February 1956, where Mr. Haring "was recovering from many illnesses." Mr. Haring explained again that "he was not the owner and that therefore he could not sell anything." This time, however, Mr. Haring finally agreed to lend the works to the Stedelijk.

Mr. Sandberg prepared a short proposal stating the terms of the contemplated loan of the Malewicz Collection, which he left with Ms. Margot Aschenbrenner, Mr. Haring's trusted secretary. The note read:

> Proposal of Mr. Sandberg, Director, Stedelijk Museum, Amsterdam
>
> Mr. Hugo Haring suggested to me that the pictures and studies by Kazimir Malewicz in his possession should be made available against an annual annuity of DM 12,000. At the moment it is not possible to guarantee such an annuity over a period of many years because the people expected to contribute to it are not sufficiently familiar with the collection. For that reason, may I suggest that the collection initially be lent to the Stedelijk Museum in Amsterdam for a year for purposes of exhibition in various other museums, with an option for extending it for further years.
>
> For this purpose, I would guarantee DM 12,000. – to Mr. Hugo Haring for this year (the first payment of DM 4,000. – would take place immediately as soon as the pictures are sent to Amsterdam).
>
> During said year we would make Malewicz's work well-known and thus glean the possibility of guaranteeing a similar annuity to Mr. Hugo Haring for further years.
>
> Dated: Biberach, February 29, 1956
> signed: Sandberg
> Director, Stedelijk Museum Amsterdam

Id. P 20.

The response sent by Ms. Aschenbrenner, dated May 8, 1956, for the first time suggested the possible sale of the Malewicz Collection for DM 120,000 (less the sum of annual rental payments made during the loan period).

Mr. Sandberg readily agreed to the terms of the loan but, by letter dated June 4, 1956, he asked, "On what conditions can we purchase the collection since Mr. Haring can transfer possession but not ownership. Nemo plus juris in alium transferre potest quam ipse habet. [One cannot transfer to another a right which he has not.]." In response, a letter dated June 23, 1956, signed "on behalf" of Mr. Haring but not by him, "announced that, under German law, ownership of the Malewicz works had passed to Haring in 1955; that Haring had in his possession a notarial exposition of his acquisition of ownership based on a purported gift *causa mortis* by Malewicz to Haring of the works left in Berlin; and that Haring thus had the power to sell the works to Amsterdam." Plaintiffs' amended complaint alleges that these documents were obvious frauds and were known by Mr. Sandberg to be frauds because of his prior direct conversations with Mr. Haring, who never claimed that Mr. Malewicz intended to transfer the collection to Mr. Haring upon Mr. Malewicz's death.

Based on these communications, however, the City of Amsterdam, through Mr. Sandberg and other representatives, entered into a loan contract with Mr. Haring in November 1956 that contained an option to purchase the Malewicz Collection. "Thereafter, in 1958, [the City] purported to exercise that option in the face of its awareness that Haring had no authority to convey title and that he had consistently denied that he had any such authority. . . . " The amended complaint further alleges that Amsterdam and the Stedelijk concealed the nature of the acquisition of the Malewicz Collection in its Annual Report for 1958, in catalogues on the collection, and through a lack of customary publicity for this kind of acquisition.

"It took several years after the fall of the Iron Curtain for all of Malewicz's living heirs to locate and contact each other and begin the difficult process of recovering the family's property. . . . " Plaintiffs comprise the 35 living heirs of Kazimir Malewicz, two of whom are citizens of the United States and none of whom resides in, or is a citizen of, The Netherlands. The Malewicz Heirs first asked Amsterdam to return the Malewicz Collection to them in 1996. A formal response from Amsterdam in September 2001 stated that:

> its purported acquisition of the Malewicz Collection was valid and that it became the owner of the Malewicz Collection at that time, but that if this were not so, it nevertheless became the owner on January 1, 1993, through acquisitive prescription under Article 3:105 of the Dutch Civil Code in connection with Article 93 of the Transitory Act.

The Malewicz Collection continues to be housed at the Stedelijk.

B. The Malewicz Collection in the United States

Fourteen of the eighty-four pieces in the Malewicz Collection were exported to the United States in 2003 to be part of a temporary exhibition of artwork at the Solomon R. Guggenheim Museum in New York

City (from May 22, 2003, until September 7, 2003) and the Menil Collection in Houston (from October 2, 2003, until January 11, 2004). These exhibitions were arranged under the terms of the Mutual Educational and Cultural Exchange Program administered by the U.S. Department of State ("State Department"). *See* 22 U.S.C. Chapter 33; Statement of Interest of the United States ("U.S. Statement") at 1. Following a request by Amsterdam that the artwork be granted immunity from legal process while in this country, and an objection filed by counsel for the Malewicz Heirs, the State Department determined that the objects were of cultural significance and that their temporary exhibition was in the national interest. *See* 68 Fed. Reg. 17852–01, April 11, 2003. The State Department therefore granted immunity from seizure to the 14 Malewicz pieces. U.S. Statement at 1. Pursuant to 22 U.S.C. § 2459, these artworks were immune from seizure and other forms of judicial process that might have had the purpose or effect of depriving the Guggenheim or the Menil Collection (or any carrier) of custody or control of the artworks while in this country.

The Malewicz Heirs filed this action two days before the exhibit in Houston closed. The artwork was returned to Amsterdam in accordance with the prearranged schedule, and before Amsterdam was served with notice of this suit.

The City of Amsterdam filed a motion to dismiss the complaint on April 30, 2004. That motion became ripe after full briefing on September 24, 2004. However, the United States filed a Notice of Possible Interest on November 15, 2004, and then a Statement of Interest on December 22, 2004. The Malewicz Heirs and the City of Amsterdam filed responses to the U.S. Statement on January 24, 2005, and February 16, 2005, respectively. The United States subsequently filed a Supplemental Statement of Interest on March 17, 2005. The matter is now ready for decision.

. . .

The foreign owner of works of art who is willing to have them exhibited by a museum in this country can, under specified circumstances, obtain immunity from any court process that would interfere with the custody or control of the foreign works while in the hands of the American institution, as provided by 22 U.S.C. § 2459:

> (a) Whenever any work of art or other object of cultural significance is imported into the United States from any foreign country, pursuant to an agreement entered into between the foreign owner or custodian thereof and the United States or one or more cultural or educational institutions within the United States providing for the temporary exhibition or display thereof within the United States at any cultural exhibition, assembly, activity, or festival administered, operated, or sponsored, without profit, by any such cultural or educational institution, no court of the United States, any State, the District of Columbia, or any territory or possession of the United States may issue or enforce any judicial process, or enter any judgment, decree, or order, for the purpose or having the effect of depriving such institution, or any

> carrier engaged in transporting such work or object within the United States, of custody or control of such object if before the importation of such object the President or his designee has determined that such object is of cultural significance and that the temporary exhibition or display thereof within the United States is in the national interest, and a notice of that effect has been published in the Federal Register.

. . .

IV. Analysis

The City of Amsterdam is clearly a "political subdivision" of The Kingdom of the Netherlands and is therefore a "foreign state" within the meaning of FSIA, 29 U.S.C. § 1603. FSIA is the "sole basis for obtaining jurisdiction over a foreign state in our courts." *Republic of Austria v. Altmann*, 541 U.S. 677, 159 L. Ed. 2d 1, 124 S. Ct. 2240, 2253 (2004) (citation omitted); *see also Millen Industries, Inc. v. Coordination Council*, 272 U.S. App. D.C. 240, 855 F.2d 879, 884 (D.C. Cir. 1988) ("FSIA is the exclusive means of exercising jurisdiction over the foreign sovereigns. . . . "). The City is therefore "immune from the jurisdiction of the courts of the United States," 28 U.S.C. § 1604, unless one of the FSIA statutory exceptions applies. . . .

The exception upon which the Malewicz Heirs rely, 28 U.S.C. § 1605(a)(3), allows a suit against a foreign sovereign when (1) rights in property were taken in violation of international law, (2) the property is present in the United States, and (3) the property has a connection to a commercial activity in the United States conducted by the foreign state. See 28 U.S.C. § 1605(a)(3). The City of Amsterdam moves to dismiss, in part because it argues that none of these three factors under § 1605(a)(3) can be met. These arguments will be examined in turn. As the Defendant here, the City "bears the burden of proving that the plaintiff[s]' allegations do not bring [their] case within a statutory exception to immunity." *Phoenix Consulting*, 216 F.3d at 40 (citations omitted). Because the City challenges only the legal sufficiency of the allegations in the amended complaint, the factual allegations must be taken as true for the purpose of ruling on the motion to dismiss.

A. Violation of International Law

The City argues that the Malewicz Heirs cannot claim an expropriation in violation of international law in this Court because they have failed to exhaust their remedies in the courts of The Netherlands. The City essentially concedes that a taking without compensation violates international law. *See Crist v. Republic of Turkey*, 995 F. Supp. 5, 10–11 (D.D.C. 1998) ("An expropriation is a violation of international law if the taking . . . does not provide for just compensation. At the jurisdictional stage, a court is not required to determine whether a taking or expropriation actually violated international law. The claim must merely be substantial and non-frivolous to provide a sufficient basis for jurisdiction") (citations omitted). However, "as a threshold matter, a claimant cannot complain that a taking, or other economic injury has not been fairly compensated, and hence violates international law unless the claimant has first pursued and exhausted domestic remedies in the foreign state that is alleged to have caused the injury." *Millicom International Cellular v. Republic of Costa Rica*, 995 F. Supp. 14, 23 (D.D.C. 1998); *see also Altmann*, 124 S. Ct. at 2262–2263 (Breyer, J., concurring) ("A plaintiff who chooses to litigate in this country in disregard of the postdeprivation remedies in the expropriating state may have trouble showing a taking in violation of international law.'").

The Malewicz Heirs threatened to sue the City in the courts in The Netherlands and even presented the City with a draft writ of summons to commence such an action.... There is no doubt about the general adequacy of the legal system in The Netherlands to address the Plaintiffs' claims.... Nonetheless, Plaintiffs have not filed suit in The Netherlands, which, according to the City, dooms their lawsuit here.

...

B. Present in the United States

The 14 Malewicz works at issue here were temporarily present in the United States for exhibition at the Guggenheim and the Menil Collection. They were shipped back to Amsterdam when the second exhibition closed and actually left this country before the City was served with the complaint.... The City argues that the artwork was not "present in the United States" as a matter of fact when the City was served and was not "present in the United States" as a matter of law during the course of the exhibitions.

It is undisputed that the 14 works were physically present in the United States when the Malewicz Heirs filed the first complaint in this matter. The City understandably likens FSIA § 1605(a)(3) to an *in rem* action and points out that jurisdiction in an *in rem* action vests only upon assertion of judicial authority over the *res* and not upon the filing of opening papers. *Republic National Bank v. United States*, 506 U.S. 80, 84–85, 121 L. Ed. 2d 474, 113 S. Ct. 554 (1992), indicates that the assertion of authority over the *res* is ordinarily accomplished by seizure, which is "regarded as equivalent to the particular service of process in the courts of law and equity." 506 U.S. at 85 (*quoting Taylor v. Carryl*, 61 U.S. 583, 599, 15 L. Ed. 1028 (1857)). "Seizure" in this instance would be unavailable because of the Immunity from Seizure Act. The problem with the City's argument is that it ignores the salient history and purpose of FSIA.

"Foreign sovereign immunity is a matter of grace and comity rather than a constitutional requirement...." *Altmann*, 124 S. Ct. at 2248. From the earliest years of the Republic until 1976, U.S. courts "consistently... deferred to the decisions of the political branches – in particular, those of the Executive Branch – on whether to take jurisdiction..." over actions involving foreign sovereigns. *Id.* (*quoting Verlindin B. V. v. Central Bank of Nigeria*, 461 U.S. 480, 486, 76 L. Ed. 2d 81, 103 S. Ct. 1962 (1983)). In 1952, the State Department officially adopted the "restrictive theory" of sovereign immunity, whereby a sovereign acting "with regard to sovereign or public acts (*jure imperii*) of a state" would be granted immunity, but no immunity would be recognized "with respect to private acts (*jure gestionis*)." *Id.* Because of inconsistent standards in applying restrictive theories of sovereign immunity between the Executive and Judicial Branches, Congress passed FSIA in 1976 to codify the restrictive theory of sovereign immunity and to place primary responsibility for interpreting and applying FSIA standards in the Judiciary and away from political pressures in the Executive. *Id.* at 2249; *see also Cicippio-Puleo v. Islamic Republic of Iran*, 359 U.S. App. D.C. 299, 353 F.3d 1024, 1034 (D.C. Cir. 2004) (FSIA "was intended to preempt other federal or state law that accorded sovereign immunity, and to discontinue the practice of judicial deference to suggestions of immunity from the executive branch."). Critically for this point, FSIA intentionally overrode the common-law requirement that a plaintiff obtain *in rem* jurisdiction over property before suit could be filed against a foreign sovereign. *See* U.S. Statement at 6 ("Section 1605(a)(3) of the FSIA, first effective in 1977, provides for the possibility of *in personam* jurisdiction over foreign states in expropriation cases without the need for the prior attachment of the property in question.") (citing H.R. Rep. 94–1487, 94th Cong., 3d Sess. at 8, *reprinted in* 1976 U.S.C.C.A.N. 6604, 6606)). It would be anomalous to re-insert the jurisdictional requirements of an *in rem* action when Congress so clearly intended to remove them from consideration. The Court concludes that Plaintiffs' filing of the complaint while the artworks were physically present in this country was sufficient to meet the "present in the United States" factor of FSIA without regard to later service of the complaint.

...

Whether the artworks were present in the United States for purposes of legal process raises a different question and is one of the points on which the United States has indicated its Interest.

...

The Department of State administers the Mutual Educational and Cultural Exchange Program, pursuant to 22 U.S.C. § 2459 ("§ 2459"), which protects imported artworks and cultural objects by making them immune from seizure and other forms of judicial process. It is undisputed that the Malewicz Heirs could not seek to seize the artwork while it was in this country under a grant of such § 2459 immunity. Pls.' Opp. at 6–7. Plaintiffs do not contend that they could have filed this FSIA suit prior to the importation of the works or following their departure. Compl. PP 3–7. As described by the United States, "Plaintiffs are therefore using the window of opportunity afforded by the Malewicz exhibition[s] as the jurisdictional hook for their claims." U.S. Statement at 4. Plaintiffs do not disagree. Pls.' Response at 5.

There is no doubt that § 2459 fulfills an important role in fostering the exchange of art and cultural works between this country and other nations. In the past ten years alone, the State Department has published immunity notices under § 2459 for more than 600 exhibits. U.S. Statement at 4, 5 n.3.

The United States informs the Court that § 2459 was enacted to protect such exchanged works because the Second Hickenlooper Amendment, 22 U.S.C. § 2370(e)(2), adopted one year before § 2459, had exposed such works to seizure. U.S. Statement at 5. The Second Hickenlooper Amendment "sharply restricted application of the Act of State doctrine as a bar to jurisdiction over claims to property allegedly taken in violation of international law." *Id.* at 5–6. Section 2459 was passed to address this "threat to cultural exchange" and specifically to address situations in which "as a condition to the loan, [a foreign nation] insisted on a grant of immunity from seizure as protection against [its] former . . . citizens who had valid claims to the title of the works." *Id.* at 6 (*quoting* Rodney M. Zerbe, *Immunity from Seizure for Artworks on Loan to United States Museums*, 6 NW. J. Int'l L. & Bus. 1121 n.21 (1985)).

The United States argues that § 1605(a)(3) of FSIA "requires a sufficient nexus with the United States to provide fair notice to foreign states that they are submitting themselves to U.S. jurisdiction and abrogating their sovereign immunity." The connection under § 1605(a)(3) is, of course, that the foreign state is carrying on a commercial activity in this country and not conducting itself as a sovereign. According to the United States, "foreign states are unlikely to expect that this standard is satisfied by a loan of artwork for a U.S. Government-immunized exhibit that must be carried out by a borrower on a non-profit basis." The United States urges the Court to give its concerns "great weight as the considered judgment of the Executive on a particular question of foreign policy." *Id.* (*quoting Altmann, 124 S. Ct. at 2255*). Because it expresses no opinion on the resolution of this specific case, the United States does not address the arguments of the parties as to whether these exhibitions were or were not "commercial" in nature.

The City, of course, supports the Statement from the United States and its expression of concerns that a confluence of FSIA expropriation jurisdiction and cultural exchanges will reduce such exchanges. Further, it argues that the 14 Malewicz works at issue were protected by the immunity from judicial process provided by § 2459 and therefore were not "present in the United States" for legal purposes. Def. Mem. at 4; Def. Reply at 5.

The U.S. Statement presents the Court with something of a dilemma. The opinions of the United States are entitled to "great weight," especially when speaking in the realm of foreign policy as the Statement does with respect to cultural exchanges and interpreting the statutory terms that affect the Mutual Educational and Cultural Exchange Program. However, the Court concludes that § 2459 granting immunity and § 1605(a)(3) establishing jurisdiction for certain claims against a foreign sovereign are both clear and not inconsistent. The Court is bound to the plain meaning of these statutes. *See Suburban Transit Corp. v. I.C.C.*, 251 U.S. App. D.C. 325, 784 F.2d 1129, 1130 (D.C. Cir. 1986). The relationship between the two statutory provisions is more clearly perceived by the Malewicz Heirs: in fact, they are unrelated except that a cultural exchange might provide the basis for contested property to be present in the United States and susceptible, in the right fact pattern, to a FSIA suit.

Clearly, as the United States and the City argue, § 2459 protects loaned artworks and cultural items from seizure or judicial process "for the purpose or having the effect of depriving such [U.S. cultural] institution . . . of custody or control of such object." 22 U.S.C. § 2459. A litigant with a claim against a foreign sovereign may *not* seize that sovereign's property that is in this country on a cultural exchange and the litigant may *not* serve the receiving museum with judicial process to interfere in any way with the physical custody or control of the artworks. The Malewicz Heirs have tried to do neither. They have sued the City of Amsterdam, not the Guggenheim or the Menil Collection. Had this lawsuit begun and concluded before the Malewicz Collection left this country, no order of this Court would have, or could have, affected the custody or control that the museums (and carriers) exercised over the artworks. The Immunity from Seizure Act deprives all U.S. courts from taking any action to obtain physical custody of the Malewicz Collection or other cultural icons granted immunity while in this country.

Instead, the happenstantial presence in this country of 14 pieces by Kazimir Malewicz fulfilled one requirement for FSIA jurisdiction: that the contested property be "present" in this country at the time of suit. The current absence of the artworks from the United States might make a court order to return the works to the Malewicz Heirs only as valuable as their ability to persuade a Dutch court to enforce it but, because of § 2459, the presence or absence of the property makes no difference during the litigation, as long as it was "present" when suit was filed.

Because the Malewicz Heirs are not seeking judicial *seizure* of the artworks, the City's and the United States' reliance on § 2459 is misplaced. Immunity from seizure is not immunity from suit for a declaration of rights or for damages arising from an alleged conversion if the other terms for FSIA jurisdiction exist. *See generally Magness v. Russian Fed'n*, 84 F. Supp. 2d 1357, 1358–59 (S.D. Ala. 2000) (noting that while the cultural artifacts at issue were immune from seizure, plaintiffs who obtained judgment against defendants for expropriation of the artifacts in violation of international law could recover on their judgment in some other fashion).

The United States argues that FSIA requires "fair notice to foreign states that they are submitting themselves to U.S. jurisdiction" and that "foreign states are unlikely to expect" that a loan of artwork could be deemed commercial activity by the foreign state. Whether the United States does or does not recognize a foreign state's sovereign immunity "reflects current political realities and relationships" among nations and provides "protection from the inconvenience of suit as a gesture of comity." *Altmann*, 124 S. Ct. at 2252 (*quoting Dole Food Co. v. Patrickson*, 538 U.S. 468, 155 L. Ed. 2d 643, 123 S. Ct. 1655 (2003)). "Fair notice" is not part of the equation for court consideration. ("The principal purpose of foreign sovereign immunity has never been to permit foreign states and their instrumentalities to shape their conduct in reliance on the promise of future immunity from suit in United States courts.")

The Court concludes that the 14 Malewicz artworks were "present in the United States" for purposes of FSIA jurisdiction.

C. Commercial Activity by the Foreign State

Plaintiff's amended complaint states without elaboration that the 14 Malewicz pieces were "in the United States in connection with a commercial activity carried on in the United States by Amsterdam, namely loaning the 14 works for exhibitions in the United States starting in May 2003." The United States advises that "the possibility that such a minimal level of contact will necessarily suffice to provide jurisdiction threatens to chill the willingness of sovereign lenders to participate in the section 2459 program." The City of Amsterdam agrees and states that it would not have loaned the Malewicz artworks if it had known that it could face litigation. It also protests that it was merely a lender from a distance and not engaged in commercial activity here.

In determining whether a foreign state has engaged in "commercial activity" in the United States, the Congress has done us no favors by its choice of words. "We do not, however, have the option to throw up our hands. The term has to be given some interpretation, and congressional diffidence necessarily results in judicial responsibility to determine what a commercial activity is for purposes of the Act." *Saudi Arabia v. Nelson*, 507 U.S. 349, 359, 123 L. Ed. 2d 47, 113 S. Ct. 1471 (1993). "Congress deliberately left the meaning open and . . . put [its] faith in the U.S. Courts to work out progressively, on a case-by-case basis . . . the distinction between commercial and governmental." *Millen Industries*, 855 F.2d at 884 n. 6 (*quoting Texas Trading & Milling Corp. v. Federal Republic of Nigeria*, 647 F.2d 300, 308–09 (2d Cir. 1981)).

Before beginning that effort, it is critical to appreciate the real issue here: the Malewicz Heirs are not suing the City of Amsterdam "based on" alleged "commercial activities" of the City in this country. Many of the cases that address FSIA's definition of "commercial activity" do so in the context of whether that activity was (a) "commercial" and (b) whether the cause of action was "based on" that activity. *See id. at 884.* In the context of this lawsuit, Plaintiffs' claims are not "based on" the alleged commercial activity of Amsterdam in the United States at all; thus, the analysis is subtly, but importantly, different. At 28 U.S.C. § 1605(a)(3), FSIA allows suits against foreign states over "rights in property taken in violation of international law . . . [when] that property . . . is present in the United States in connection with a commercial activity carried on in the United States by the foreign state."

At 28 U.S.C. § 1603(e), we are instructed that "commercial activity carried on in the United States by a foreign state" means "commercial activity carried on by such state and having substantial contact with the United States." Our Circuit has essentially adopted the "rule of thumb" suggested by the Second Circuit in *Texas Trading*: "If the activity is one in which a private person could engage, it is not entitled to immunity." *Practical Concepts, Inc. v. Republic of Bolivia*, 258 U.S. App. D.C. 354, 811 F.2d 1543, 1549 (D.C. Cir. 1987) (*quoting Texas Trading*, 647 F.2d at 309). "Congress did indeed contemplate that courts would regard as key the question whether the foreign sovereign's contract issue is of the same character as a contract which might be made by a private person." *Id.* (citing H. Rep. No. 1487, 94th Cong., 2d Sess. 16 (1976), *reprinted in* 1976 U.S. Code Cong. & Admin. News 6604, 6615); *see Millen Industries, 855 F.2d at 884* ("A useful inquiry . . . is whether the essence or central elements of an agreement made by a foreign state might be made by a private person."). It is the "nature of [the] activity, *e.g.*, purchase contract, not its purpose, *e.g.*, providing food for the needy, [that] determines whether activity is commercial." *Practical Concepts*, 811 F.2d. at 1551 n. 18.

The use of the word "commercial" in § 1605(a)(3) of FSIA leads one to a detour from the statutory purpose by thinking of distinctions between activities that are for-profit, not-for-profit, educational, cultural, philanthropical, etc. However, as noted by the Supreme Court in *Republic of Argentina v. Weltover, Inc.*, 504 U.S. 607, 119 L. Ed. 2d 394, 112 S. Ct. 2160 (1992):

> Because the Act provides that the commercial character of an act is to be determined by reference to its "nature" rather than its "purpose," the question is not whether the foreign government is acting with a profit motive or instead with the aim of fulfilling uniquely sovereign objectives. Rather, the issue is whether the particular actions that the foreign state performs (whatever the motive behind them) are the *type* of actions by which a private party engages in "trade and traffic or commerce."

Id. at 614 (emphasis in original). In large measure, the terms "commercial" and "sovereign" are merely opposites: if an act is something only sovereigns do, it is not "commercial." Similarly, if an act is something that a private person or entity *can* do, it is not "sovereign." "Commercial" means only "not sovereign," as long as there is some example of private action of a similar type connected with "trade and traffic or commerce." *Id.*; *see Millen Industries*, 855 F.2d at 884 n. 6 (The court must parse "the distinction between commercial and governmental") (quoting *Texas Trading*, 647 F.2d at 308–09).

With this understanding, it is clear that the City of Amsterdam engaged in "commercial activities" when it loaned the 14 Malewicz works to museums in the United States. There is nothing "sovereign" about the act of lending art pieces, even though the pieces themselves might belong to a sovereign. Loans between and among museums (both public and private) occur around the world regularly. The City resists this conclusion, asserting that the exchange of artworks between not-for-profit organizations in different countries does not constitute "trade and traffic or commerce." . . . There is force to the argument and the Court has considered it with great care. Ultimately, because the international loan of artworks between museums can and does occur with potential sales of the works contemplated by the parties (which is undoubtedly "commerce" in the traditional sense), and because it is the *type* of activity – not its purpose – that must guide the analysis, the Court finds the City's argument unpersuasive.

The record is replete with evidence that artwork is loaned internationally and domestically on a frequent basis. The parties appear to agree that this particular loan was for purely educational and cultural purposes – certainly, the Stedelijk Museum entered into the loan without any intention of offering the Malewicz works for sale. Does that remove this kind of sovereign loan from "commerce," even though loans for purely educational or cultural purposes are also conducted by private parties? The distinction Amsterdam wishes the Court to draw would depend on the *purpose* of a loan: if a loan promotes only educational or cultural goals it would be exempt from the reach of FSIA while a loan that has additional attributes more in line with traditional concepts of "commerce" would not. FSIA itself dooms the distinction because the Court is not to consider the purpose of the activity. *See* 28 U.S.C. § 1603(d) ("The commercial character of an activity shall be determined by reference to the nature of the course of conduct or particular transaction or act, rather than by reference to its purpose."); *see Weltover*, 504 U.S. at 614; *Practical Concepts*, 811 F.2d. at 1551 n. 18.

An example might make this point clear. Suppose the Stedelijk agreed with the Guggenheim and the Menil Collection to loan the museums specific Malewicz paintings that have great fame and have never traveled away from Amsterdam. Suppose the American museums advertised heavily that these great works would be seen for the first time outside of The Netherlands and, as a result, developed significant corporate and other support. Then suppose the Stedelijk became concerned over the safety of the paintings and sent, instead, lesser works of Malewicz that had earlier been displayed in this country. Would the Guggenheim or the Menil Collection be able to sue the Stedelijk for breach of contract or would sovereign immunity protect the Dutch museum? The example is fantastic and would likely never happen. But it clearly demonstrates the logic of finding that the Stedelijk was not engaging in a "sovereign" act when it loaned artworks that it asserts properly belong to the sovereign.

...

There is one further critical point. The City of Amsterdam and the United States argue that the City's contacts with this country are insubstantial and insufficient to expose it to FSIA jurisdiction ("Indeed, as expected and intended in such an act of courtesy, the loan-handling fees received from the American museums were nominal and did not cover even the administrative and other costs incurred by the Stedelijk Museum, causing the Stedelijk Museum to lose money."); U.S. Statement at 7 ("Foreign states are unlikely to expect that this standard [presence in the United States in connection with a commercial activity] is satisfied by a loan of artwork for a U.S. Government-immunized exhibit that must be carried out by a borrower on a non-profit basis. The possibility that such a minimal level of contact will necessarily suffice to provide jurisdiction threatens to chill" the entire international exchange program.). This is not an insubstantial point and it requires a detailed factual analysis of the nature and extent of such contacts. *See Saudi Arabia v. Nelson*, 507 U.S. 349, 356, 123 L. Ed. 2d 47, 113 S. Ct. 1471 (1993); *Burnett v. Al Baraka Invest. and Develop. Corp.*, 292 F. Supp. 2d 9, 21 (D.D.C. 2003); *Sealift Builders, Inc. v. Republic of Armenia*, 965 F. Supp. 81, 85 (D.D.C. 1997) (noting the constitutional parameter to the question).

The existing record does not permit the Court to ascertain the substantiality of the City's contacts or activities with or in the United States in connection with the loan of the Malewicz artworks. Apart from the presence of the artworks themselves, what were the terms of the loan agreements? Did the Stedelijk send any representatives to this country to work out arrangements, to travel with the art, or to oversee its safety and display? What consideration did the Guggenheim or Menil Collection offer for the loan – money, a future loan of American art to The Netherlands, a share in any receipts from visitors, catalogue sales, and the like – or was this only a courtesy between professionals in the art world, as the City argues? The extent and the nature of the City of Amsterdam's contacts with this country must be identified and addressed before the Court can determine its own jurisdiction, or lack thereof, over Plaintiff's amended complaint.

V. Conclusion

For the foregoing reasons, the City of Amsterdam's motion to dismiss will be DENIED. The Court will convene a status conference to determine whether the parties wish to proceed by way of affidavits or limited jurisdictional discovery to develop record evidence on whether, through its immunized loan of cultural and educational artworks, the City of Amsterdam had "substantial contact with the United States" within the meaning of 28 U.S.C. § 1603(e). At that time, the Court will also inquire of the City whether it and the courts of The Netherlands will waive any potential statute-of-limitations defenses. A memorializing order accompanies this memorandum opinion.

NOTES

1. The U.S. Supreme Court decision in *Altmann*, although it was in general in accord with the district court and Ninth Circuit Court of Appeals decisions that follow, did not endorse the Circuit Court's denial of immunity to Austria because of its complicity in, and perpetration of, the expropriation of the paintings. The circuit court had also found that the seizures violated Austrian and German obligations under the 1907 Hague Convention on the Laws and Customs of War on land. See *Altmann v. Republic of Austria*, 317 F. 3d 954 (9th Cir. 2002).

2. After the decision of the U.S. Supreme Court, Maria Altmann discontinued proceedings against Austria in California, after Austria agreed to abide by the outcome of a ruling on her claim to the Klimt paintings by a court of arbitration in Vienna. When that court issued an award in her favor, she offered to sell the paintings to Austria, but that country declined to purchase them. She then sent the paintings to the United States where they were temporarily on view at the Los Angeles County Museum of Art and Neue Gallerie in New York. Mrs. Altmann sold one of the paintings, *Adele Block-Bauer II*, for $135 million to the cosmetics heir Ronald Lauder. In adding the painting to his collection in the Neue Gallerie, Lauder described it as "our Mona Lisa." See April Austin, *Complex Justice in a Nazi-Looting Case*, Christian Sci. Monitor, Nov. 1, 2006, at 15; Michael Kimmelman, *Klimt's Adele Has Her New York Debut*, N.Y. Times, July 18, 2006; Christopher Reynolds, *Yours for a Price*, L.A. Times, June 21, 2006, at E1. The remaining four Klimt paintings were sold at auction at Christie's in New York on November 8, 2006, for a total of $192.2 million, part of "the biggest in auction history, netting almost half a billion dollars." See Carol Vogel, *$491 Million Sale Shatters Art Auction Record*, N.Y. Times, Nov. 9, 2006.
3. See also *Aqudas Chasidei Chabad v. Russian Fed'n*, 466 F. Supp. 2d 6 (D.D.C. 2006). There the court held that the Foreign Sovereign Immunities Act (FSIA), which provides the exclusive basis of jurisdiction over a foreign state in a U.S. court, did not bar a claim for Russia's return of an archive of handwritten teachings, correspondence, and records of a Jewish rabbi that had been expropriated illegally by the Nazis during World War II and by the Soviet army's seizure of the items from the Nazis at the end of the war. Also, under the doctrine of *forum non conveniens*, the court's jurisdiction was appropriate. However, under the act of state doctrine the court had no jurisdiction over the plaintiff's claim for return of a library of Jewish material that had been seized by the Soviet predecessors of the Russian government.
4. See also Mark J. Chorazak, *Clarity and Confusion: Did* Republic of Austria v. Altmann *Revise State Department Suggestions of Foreign Sovereign Immunity?*, 55 Duke L.J. 373 (2005); A. Gupta, Note, *A Portrait of Justice Deferred: Retroactive Application of the FSIA and Its Implications for Holocaust-Era Art Restitution*: Republic of Austria v. Altmann, 30 U. Dayton L. Rev. 373 (2005).
5. In 2007, the *Malewicz* court ruled that the city of Amsterdam did have "substantial" contact in the United States so as to satisfy the definition of the commercial-activity exception to the city's immunity under the FSIA. The controlling evidence took the form of financial payments by U.S. museums for the defendant city's loan of the Malewicz works and the presence in the United States of the city's employees to oversee the safety of the paintings. The court further held that the act of state doctrine did not shield the city because its activity was not essentially sovereign. Although the court did not rule on the applicability of a statute of limitations, it did acknowledge that a defense under the statute did have merit. In the end, the city was therefore subject to the court's jurisdiction. *Malewicz v. City of Amsterdam*, 517 F. Supp. 2d 322 (D.D.C. 2007). The effect of this decision was to encourage a settlement of the dispute, which eventuated in 2008. The settlement agreement split the ownership of the collection (seventy-nine paintings to be retained by the Stedelijk Museum and five to be transferred to the plaintiff family).

6. A very different question of sovereign immunity involved the attempted attachment of cultural material in satisfaction of an unrelated judgment. Several survivors of a suicide bombing in Jerusalem in 1997 sued the government of Iran. Having won a default judgment from the federal district court in Washington, D.C., the plaintiffs sought to attach for execution on the judgment a valuable collection of Persian artifacts, including the Persepolis Fortification Archive, on long-term loan from Iran, in the Oriental Institute at the University of Chicago.

h. Remedies

Claimants are interested primarily in recovering an object itself rather than receiving damages for injury. In common law systems, however, a bona fide purchaser of stolen art who cannot rely on a statute of limitations, the doctrine of laches, or some other defense can seek to recover the purchase price of the object from the seller, under a warranty theory, providing the seller is still in business. See Uniform Commercial Code § 2–312(1)(a) (1988), and Note, *Uniform Commercial Code Warranty Solutions to Art Fraud and Forgery*, 14 Wm. & Mary L. Rev. 409 (1972).

Hoelzer v. City of Stamford,
972 F. 2d 495 (2d Cir. 1992), *cert. denied*, 506 U.S. 1035 (1992)

Lumbard, Circuit Judge:

The City of Stamford, Connecticut, appeals from a judgment of the District Court for the Southern District of New York, Louis L. Stanton, Judge, awarding Hiram Hoelzer $557,200 as quantum meruit compensation for art restoration services he performed on six murals belonging to the City, in the belief that they belonged to him. In this action to quiet title in October 1989, Judge Stanton entered partial judgment holding that title to the murals rested in the City. We affirmed and remanded the case for trial to determine whether Hoelzer was entitled to any compensation. After taking additional evidence, the district court awarded Hoelzer $557,200. On appeal, the City contends that Hoelzer is not entitled to equitable relief because he did not perform the restoration work in good faith and that the damages exceed the benefits conferred and that they were excessive. We affirm but direct modification of the judgment to allow the City of Stamford to satisfy the award by returning the murals to Hoelzer, within a reasonable time to be set by the district court.

In 1934, the Works Progress Administration (W.P.A.) commissioned James Daugherty, a nationally known artist, to paint a set of six murals, each over 8 feet high and with a combined length of over 100 feet, on canvas affixed to the walls of the Stamford High School. In 1970, when the school was renovated, workers removed the murals from the walls and placed them outside with other construction debris. Frank Bowne, a recent graduate of the school, discovered the murals and took them home, where he stored them in the garage.

. . .

In 1971, Bowne gave the murals to Karel Yasko, supervisor of the Fine Arts Inventory Project of the U.S. General Services Administration (G.S.A.), who placed the murals with Hiram Hoelzer, a noted art restorer in New York. In April of 1972, Hoelzer wrote to Yasko to explain the wet, dirty and damaged condition of the murals and the scope of the restoration project. Although Yasko did not respond, Hoelzer nevertheless began working to stabilize and restore the murals.

Throughout the 1970s and early 1980s, Hoelzer continued work on the murals, periodically requesting direction and compensation from Yasko, who made no response. The City did not know the whereabouts of the murals and took no steps to locate them during the 1970s. Sometime in the 1980s, at the insistence of Daugherty's son, the City contacted Hoelzer about the possibility of returning the murals to their original place in the Stamford High School.

Hoelzer then telephoned the G.S.A. seeking title to the murals. Meanwhile, Yasko had died, and the G.S.A. disclaimed any interest in the murals, telling Hoelzer to resolve the issue with the City. In subsequent correspondence, Hoelzer and the City each claimed to own the murals, which have been appraised by Deborah Coy Ahearn of Sotheby's at $1,250,000.

Finally, on January 10, 1989, Hoelzer brought suit in New York Supreme Court, Westchester County, seeking declaratory judgment awarding him title or alternatively recovery, in quantum meruit, for the value of his services in restoring and safeguarding the murals. The City then removed the case to federal court.

On October 16, 1989, Judge Stanton found that the City never abandoned the murals and still owned them. Hoelzer v. City of Stamford, 722 F. Supp. 1106 (S.D.N.Y. 1989). We affirmed, noting that Hoelzer could "pursue whatever claim exists for equitable compensation" for his restoration services. Hoelzer v. City of Stamford, 933 F.2d 1131, 1139 (2d Cir. 1991). Subsequently, on January 29, 1992, Judge Stanton found that Hoelzer had performed the restoration work in the good faith belief the murals belonged to him. Accordingly, Hoelzer was entitled to equitable compensation for his efforts. Judge Stanton heard the testimony of experts and accepted their valuation of the work done at a reasonable hourly rate, arriving at the total of $557,200. This appeal followed.

The City contends that Hoelzer performed the restoration work in the face of an adverse claim of title and thus his efforts did not meet the good faith requirement for equitable relief and that the court erred in awarding damages of $557,200 for murals which have little or no market value. The City conceded, however, in its brief and at oral argument that Hoelzer was entitled to be paid for his restoration services. The City now asks that we vacate the judgment and remand to the district court for a new trial.

Whatever the merits of Stamford's claim that Hoelzer's work in the restoration was not performed in the good faith belief that the murals belonged to him, the conduct of the City and its representatives during the years when most of the restoration was being done, indicates that the City was quite willing to have Hoelzer proceed with the restoration.

Representatives of the City visited Hoelzer's workshop from time to time in the years from 1980 through 1986. They knew of the work that Hoelzer had done and was doing to restore the murals. The City made no objection to Hoelzer's work nor did anyone ask Hoelzer the total cost of the restoration work. We have previously recognized that an "equitable remedy . . . may be granted . . . to prevent one party, at the expense of another, from retaining a benefit to which he is not entitled." *See United States v. Bedford Assoc.*, 713 F.2d 895, 903–04 (2d Cir. 1983).

Hoelzer, for his part, continued his work in the expectation that he would be compensated, but never spoke to anyone of what had to be done or how much the project would cost. In 1972, he had written Yasko of the G.S.A. that the restoration of approximately 900 sq. feet of canvas would cost $6,400. Later in 1980, Hoelzer told Mr. Nerreau, a Stamford teacher who wanted his help, that the work on a particular panel of 100″ × 5′ would cost about $3,000, which would, assuming uniform deterioration, suggest an amount of approximately $63,000 for all of the panels. These estimates are a small fraction of the $557,200 which Hoelzer eventually claimed at the 1992 trial before Judge Stanton.

We find no error in Judge Stanton's finding that the value of the restoration of the murals was $557,200. *See Lemon v. Kurtzman*, 411 U.S. 192, 200, 36 L. Ed. 2d 151, 93 S. Ct. 1463 (1973) (plurality opinion) ("In shaping equity decrees, the trial court is vested with broad discretionary power; appellate review is correspondingly narrow."). The district court, acting in equity, has the discretionary power to fashion a remedy to do complete justice, *including a monetary award if necessary.* An appellate court will set aside such an exercise of discretion only if it is arbitrary. *Goldberg v. Medtronic, Inc.*, 686 F.2d 1219, 1229 (7th Cir. 1982) (emphasis added). Judge Stanton accepted the testimony of the experts at trial. One of them, Eugene Bechtel, a noted art restorer, had recently agreed to payment of $452,700 by the City of Norwalk for restoration of murals in the nearby city high school. This work was less complex and time consuming than Hoelzer's restoration work for Stamford. Judge Stanton's award of $557,200 is supported by substantial evidence. *See United States v. Bedford Assoc.*, 713 F.2d at 902 (equitable remedy rests in the sound discretion of the district court); *Liberty Nat'l Bank and Trust Co. v. Life Ins. Co. of Cincinnati*, 901 F.2d 539, 547 (6th Cir. 1990); *United States v. City of Chicago*, 631 F.2d 469, 472 (7th Cir. 1980).

Nevertheless, from a review of the evidence, it is clear that the City of Stamford could have had no idea that the cost of restoring the murals would come to as much as $557,200. When it claimed ownership of the murals and conceded that Hoelzer should receive some compensation for his labors, the City could not reasonably have expected that Hoelzer would claim nearly as much as $557,200. Equitable compensation should not unduly prejudice the party which would otherwise receive the benefit. *See Alden Auto Parts Warehouse, Inc. v. Dolphin Equip. Leasing Corp.*, 682 F.2d 330, 333 (2d Cir. 1982). On the equities, we cannot say that Stamford should be compelled to pay any such amount unless it is willing to do so.

Accordingly, we hold that the City may satisfy the judgment by abandoning its ownership of the murals and returning them to Hoelzer within a reasonable time to be fixed by the district court. If the City elects to retain the murals, the judgment against it for $557,200 is affirmed.

NOTE

The *Hoelzer* case demonstrates that a good-faith purchaser who fails to acquire valid title of property against a true owner may nevertheless have a remedy for damages in *quantum meruit* if the purchaser has incurred costs to protect or restore the artwork. In *Hoelzer*, the costs amounted to the equivalent of almost half the value of the artworks. When the market value of the murals declined precipitously after the court's decision, the city decided to return them to Hoelzer rather than pay in compliance with the order against it.

2. Alternative Dispute Resolution

a. Background

As we have seen, the origins of international cultural heritage law often lie in the battlegrounds of conflict and the underworld of crime. In particular, claims for restitution and return of cultural heritage are typically the legacy of armed combat, imperial conquest, and theft. It should not be surprising, therefore, that the normative framework to protect the cultural heritage has been essentially adversarial. Efforts in the late twentieth century to develop an effective body of cultural heritage law emphasized formal remedies for past wrongs. In procedural terms, litigation has been a preferred means of resolving pertinent disputes,[215] despite the voices of experienced litigators urging greater recourse to mediation and other informal means of dispute resolution when that is feasible.[216] In substantive terms, considerable emphasis is placed on exclusive rights of ownership and the elaboration of rules for the return or restitution of stolen or illegally exported property.

The availability of adjudication and the articulation of applicable rules are essential, of course. A growing infusion of international norms into the adjudication of claims by national courts attests to the importance of effective rules.[217] Conversely, an absence of detailed rules may inhibit the resolution of cultural property disputes. We have seen this problem, for example, in our examination of efforts to resolve issues related to confiscation of material during the European Holocaust. We have also noted the impasse in German-Russian negotiations over mutual return of Second World War loot and plunder, in part attributable to a lack of effective rules.

[215] *See* Daniel Shapiro, *Litigation and Art-Related Disputes, in* Resolution Methods for Art-Related Disputes 17, 18 (Quentin Byrne-Sutton & Fabienne Geisinger-Mariéthoz eds., 1999) [hereinafter Resolution Methods](offering explanations for this preference, ranging from inertia – "it is what everyone is used to" – to vindictive passions).

[216] *See* Resolution Methods, at 24; Lawrence Kaye, *Disputes Relating to Ownership and Status of Cultural Property*, in Resolution Methods, at 35, 44.

[217] *See, e.g.*, James A.R. Nafziger, *The Evolving Role of Admiralty Courts in Litigation of Historic Wreck*, 44 Harv. Int'l L.J. 251 (2003).

In particular, private international law has helped shape the emerging regime of cultural heritage law.[218] The trend in the development of this body of law, though slow, is toward harmonization or unification of such troublesome rules of municipal law as those of the bona fide purchaser, formalities for valid transfer of title, and statutes of limitations.[219] Over time, private international law, equipped with its general rules of jurisdiction, choice of law, and enforcement of foreign judgments, has helped and will continue to help stabilize expectations concerning the outcome of dispute resolution within the constraints of public law. Despite this favorable appraisal and forecast, however, some basic premises of the emerging regime should be reconsidered, if not reformed. For example, the development of private international law rules to govern cultural heritage issues continues to be handicapped by the description of cultural heritage as "property." As a result, such entrenched rules as the *lex rei sitae* of an object, regardless of its origin, inhibit the growth of concepts such as that of a *res extra commercium*[220] that may be better suited to the cultural heritage.

Even more fundamentally, however, it is questionable whether an adversarial process should so fully define the process for protecting and properly allocating the cultural heritage of humankind. As a leading African scholar has pointed out, a reliance on adversarial processes, particularly litigation, "is bedeviled by two intractable problems"[221]: evidentiary issues and refusals by some legal systems to recognize or enforce foreign export controls, in addition to often prohibitive costs of litigation. Also, in addressing the claims of indigenous people, it is apparent that formal rules, scientific theories and academic practices – the legacy of what Roger Echo-Hawk calls conquest archaeology – have inherent limitations in constructing our views of ancient human history.

It may be advisable, instead, to rely more heavily on such alternatives as negotiation, mediation, and arbitration. This, however, requires a greater emphasis on the concept of commonality, the principle of sharing, and the technique of open, well-informed collaboration.[222]

b. Advantages of Collaboration

The advantages of collaboration, whenever it is possible, are evident. One is reminded of the parable of the two sisters, each of whom wants a single orange.[223] How should it be allocated? One solution is to award the orange to the sister with the greater rights to

[218] *See, e.g.*, Kurt Siehr, *International Art Trade and the Law*, 243 Recueil Des Cours 9 (1993-VI); Lyndel V. Prott, *Problems of Private International Law for the Protection of the Cultural Heritage*, 217 Recueil Des Cours 215 (1989-V).

[219] *But see* Prott, *supra* note 218, at 217 ("The prospect of achieving a harmonization of these rules is not good.").

[220] *See* Kurt Siehr, *Kulturgüter als res extra commercium im internationalen Rechtsverkehr*, *in* Lebendiges Recht – Von Den Sumerern Bix Zur Gegenwart 703 (1995).

[221] Folarin Shyllon, *The Recovery of Cultural Objects by African States through the UNESCO and UNIDROIT Conventions and the Role of Arbitration*, 2002–2 Uniform L. Rev. 219, 221.

[222] *See* Patrick J. O'Keefe, Trade in Antiquities: Reducing Destruction and Theft 99 (1997) ("As part of the formulation of a common approach to the issues involved in preventing the destruction of sites and monuments and theft from collections, it is absolutely essential that dealers, auction houses, archaeologists, collectors (both public and private) and government officials come together in a spirit of cooperation.").

[223] This parable is retold in Alan Scott Rau, *Mediation in Art-Related Disputes*, *in* Resolution Methods, at 153, 157.

the orange. That is the strictly adversarial approach that often characterizes the formal resolution of cultural property disputes today. A second solution is to award half of the orange to each sister, an appealing compromise until it becomes apparent that one sister wants the orange only to eat its pulp whereas the other wants only the orange peel for cooking. Thus, although compromises may often be preferable to either-or solutions, they typically fail to take full account of contending interests as opposed to stated positions. A third, better informed allocation of the disputed orange would be to encourage the sisters to express their respective interests in the orange and then to work out a mutually productive, more-than-zero-sum solution to a dispute. (One sister can have the pulp, which is all she wants, and the other can have the peel, which is all she wants.)

Moreover, disputes involving art and cultural material often create unique challenges for those involved. The singular nature of art and cultural objects and the often-strong emotions surrounding their ownership, custody, and care may mean that conventional forms of dispute resolution (e.g., litigation) are inappropriate. Over the past twenty years or more, there has been an overall increase in the use of alternative forms of dispute resolution, including negotiation, mediation, and arbitration. This has noticeably arisen in international commercial practice and family law, where the deficiencies of litigation outcomes have often been measurable. As we have seen, the outcome of the Austrian arbitration in 2006 that upheld Marie Altmann's Holocaust-related claim to several Gustav Klimt paintings possessed by Austria highlighted the efficacy of methods other than litigation for resolving disputes involving cultural material.

Effective negotiation can lead to win-win solutions by mutually educating disputing parties and thereby broadening their options for reaching an agreement. When direct negotiations break down, however, third-party alternative dispute resolution may be the best alternative. Sometimes, when a dispute is particularly heated, it may be necessary to call on a third party simply to bring the disputing parties to the bargaining table. We call this preliminary step good offices. A mediator can then facilitate communication between the parties and, if asked to do so, articulate a solution to what would otherwise be an impasse.

Quentin Byrne-Sutton, *Resolution Methods for Art-Related Disputes*, 7 Int'l J. Cultural Prop. 249, 250–55 (1998)

[W]orks of art are distinguishable from everyday objects in that they not only have financial, but also cultural and immaterial value. The cultural value is linked to the fact that countries, regions, and sometimes even the whole of mankind attribute a special cultural importance to certain objects, which is translated into the law by the adoption of international treaties and special national rules, some of which are protective in nature. For example, nearly every country in the world has a set of rules protecting its national treasures by means of export restrictions and other measures – while other rules such as wealth-tax exemptions for art collectors, tax rebates for donations to museums, the right to give works of art in lieu of taxes as well as favourable customs and VAT regimes for art transactions are in the nature of incentives. The immaterial value is linked to the importance our Western societies attach to the individuality and originality of artists' works. This immaterial value is legally recognized by giving copyright, moral rights and *droit de suite* to artists and is also invoked by litigants in contractual disputes each time there is an issue of authenticity or attribution.

Thus, no matter what legal issue is under dispute in an art-related matter, it is very often the particular nature of a work of art that lies at the heart of the litigation. Furthermore, when the cultural or immaterial value of a work is in question, the financial stakes are frequently high. For example, a work of art that has been purchased for several million dollars may become worthless simply because a committee or a "mandarin" refuses to include it in a *catalogue raisonné.* To take another example, the financial value of a work may also be considerably reduced because it is deemed a national treasure and blocked from sale on the international market, as was illustrated recently in a French case concerning a painting by van Gogh.

A second feature that art-related disputes have in common is the market within which they arise. By its very nature, this market is international and highly specialized, with a limited number of passionate players who often have conflicting interests as well as particular habits, customs and codes of conduct.

Arguments for and against [Alternative Dispute Resolution (ADR)]

Bearing in mind the particular nature of the objects and of the market, some of the frequently cited advantages of arbitration and mediation could be attractive for the resolution of certain art-related disputes. Among those that spring to mind are confidentiality, less formal and more compromise-oriented proceedings, the possibility of having a tribunal or mediator that is not part of the legal apparatus of a given country, and the freedom to select specialized persons who understand the art market.

...

[T]here is much room for negotiation for mutual gain in art-related disputes (a process sometimes referred to as "expanding the pie" or "logrolling" in U.S. mediation terminology)....

> [t]he potential for such "logrolling" seems particularly fertile in art-related disputes, because such disputes are usually likely to involve a number of different issues and concerns – tangible and intangible, short term and long term. A mediator – or, again, a wise negotiator – has to be skilled at developing an inventory of the various interests on the part of the parties: The greater the variety of interests that can be identified, the more likely it is that the parties value them differently, or attribute different priorities to them – and in consequence, the more likely it is that they can trade one off against the other for "mutual gain." Perceiving that such trades are possible often makes an agreement possible, when it earlier had appeared to the parties that there was no basis for a deal at all.

...

A real-life example is provided by the celebrated case involving Norton Simon's acquisition of an Indian sculpture depicting Shiva, with regard to which the government of India filed a claim for restitution. The case was settled on the agreement that Simon would give up all right and title to the sculpture in exchange for the Simon Foundation's receiving from India a ten-year loan of the sculpture. It is interesting to note in this connection that article 6, paragraph 3, of the 1995 UNIDROIT Convention on the International Return of Stolen or Illegally Exported Cultural Objects actually recognizes the possibility of "expanding the pie" by providing for a converse solution whereby the good faith purchaser of an illegally exported cultural object can remain the owner, on condition that the object is returned to the territory of the requesting State. Experience teaches that art transactions are indeed rich in potential for these types of arrangements, which can be facilitated by a mediator (or negotiator) whose knowledge allows him or her to imagine mutually beneficial solutions.

...

[A]ny dispute-resolution method that could account for the parties' emotions would be helpful in art-related disputes, where the parties – be they artists, collectors, galleries, or States – are often very emotionally involved. In this respect, arbitration is usually less formal than court proceedings, thus promoting more self-liberating discussion between the parties, while mediation offers the opportunity for the mediator to listen to the parties separately, in "caucus," where they may be more apt to express their feelings.

From an ethical point of view, such types of constructive solution – which prevent having to decide in terms of "right" and "wrong" – are welcome, since art disputes quite often involve conflicting yet legitimate interests. For example, the owner of a work of art has a property interest that may come into conflict with the moral rights of an artist, the copyright of an artist may hamper certain not-for-profit uses of his works (raising the question of where to draw the line of "fair use"); a collector may find his freedom of movement hindered by a country's right to retain within its borders given cultural objects, or more generally the need to allow international exchange and dissemination of cultural objects may come into conflict with needs of physical preservation, and so on. Furthermore, when issues of attribution and authenticity are involved, it needs to be borne in mind that judgments are often very subjective and that the more objective foundations underlying them (for example, historical and scientific knowledge) are liable to change with time. Consequently, what seems legally right today may appear wrong tomorrow. Because of the uncertainty surrounding such issues and the varied importance different individuals attach to authenticity/attribution at any given moment, this is also a fruitful terrain for seeking negotiated or mediated solutions that better preserve at least certain interests of all the parties involved.

[T]here may be factual situations in which a State has much to gain from engaging in arbitration and where it may rather be resisted by the defendant, for example, if the cultural object is situated in a country whose courts do not easily apply foreign public laws or are reticent in accepting jurisdiction over foreign State claims in general, or in which the forum is in a country that for political, historical, cultural, or other reasons might not be favorable to the claim in question. There may also be circumstances in which, all aspects carefully considered, both the claiming State and the defendant believe for different reasons that their respective chances of prevailing are likely to be higher in arbitration than before a national court – a call that an experienced litigator, understanding and comparing the various possibilities, will have to help the client make and that may be a fundamental tactical decision.

> Notwithstanding the obstacle presented by the need for the parties to agree on arbitration in connection with a restitution claim, there are a number of reasons that make arbitration theoretically attractive in such an area, notably from an ethical point of view where questions of national cultural policy are involved. First, notwithstanding the principle of separation of powers that exists to varying degrees around the world, an arbitration panel is more detached from a given State than a national court. Under modern rules on international arbitration, the arbitrators hold their immediate authority from the parties who select them, rather than representing the legal system of a given country; for this very reason, the tribunal is free (under the parties' control) to sit in any country, the parties usually choosing the place of arbitration. . . .

Thus, as it does not represent a national forum, an arbitration tribunal appears at first sight to be in a more neutral position than a national court to pronounce itself on a State claim that, among other issues, involves assessing issues of sovereignty and national cultural policy and law.

Second, under certain circumstances, arbitration of restitution claims could lead more easily to a body of coherent case law, for example, where the application of a given treaty such as the 1995 UNIDROIT Convention was repeatedly examined by panels of arbitrators selected from lists established by an arbitration center. In the long run, this could work in the interest of better justice, by allowing more predictability as well as decision-making by more experienced and specialized persons.

A skillful mediator can develop an extensive inventory of implicated interests, thereby increasing the probability that parties to a dispute, each attributing different values and priorities to the implicated interests, will "trade one off against the other for 'mutual gain.'"[224]

For example,[225] difficult issues of ownership, long-standing adverse possession and repose, good faith purchase, and the like arise in very different contexts. The precise context can help define a particular mediated solution, on a case-by-case basis. The dispute between the Norton Simon Museum and the Government of India over Nataraja, an Indian bronze sculpture, was resolved when the museum agreed to recognize India's

[224] *Id.* at 160.

[225] Professor Rau has made a "partial list" of some fifteen types of art-related interests that could be traded off against each other for mutual gain. What follows in the text is his first example. *Id.* at 160–61.

entitlement to the sculpture in return for a ten-year loan of it to the museum. A mirror-image solution confirmed the entitlement of the Cleveland Museum to a Poussin painting in return to an extended loan of the work to the claimant museum, the Louvre.

In thinking about a loan of an object as a basis for resolving a dispute over entitlement to it, the following matrix of considerations may be helpful[226]:

Reasons to Lend

1. Contributing to an important exhibition.
2. Adding to the knowledge of a particular work.
3. Making an object available for an interesting educational purpose and reaching out to new audiences.
4. Temporarily reuniting ensembles or parts of objects that have drifted apart in time.
5. Showing objects (or works of artists) that seldom or never leave the reserves and thereby give access to them for pleasure or study.
6. Introducing and interpreting other culture.
7. An opportunity to conserve an object to an exhibition standard.
8. Sharing and improving museum staff working practices.
9. Repaying other museums' generosity.
10. Introducing and interpreting other cultures.

Reasons Not to Lend

1. Legal restrictions placed on the object by the owner, donor or museum's statute.
2. The subject of the exhibition is too limited or too commercial to let an object travel.
3. Purpose of the object in the proposed exhibition is unclear or necessity for inclusion of a particular object is not sufficiently demonstrated by the request. There is no confidence in the added value of lending the object.
4. Fragility of the object or sensitivity to exposure to light (works on paper, textiles) or the fact that it has traveled too often in recent times.
5. Efforts and costs required for conservation or restoration (making it fit for travel) not in reasonable proportion to the quality of the object.
6. Object not available, because already promised to another exhibition or because it is a key-work in the display of the museum or central to a specific educational program.
7. Object of great actual symbolical, historical, or religious value for the own community, only to be lent under exceptional circumstances or outside the tourist season.
8. Object asked at too short notice to process the preparations for the loan in a responsible way.
9. Borrowing museum not up to standard: security, fire prevention system, climate control, conditions for display, poor scholarly or educational standing.
10. Unstable political situation, threat of terrorism, or risk of a third-party claim.

[226] *See* Lending in Europe, Recommendations on Collection Mobility For European Museums (A Report Produced by an Independent Group of Experts, Set up by Council Resolution 13839/04 (April 2005) (EU) (edited by the authors)).

Even a hypothetical agreement for the return to Greece of the Elgin Marbles in the British Museum need not be simply a transfer from one museum management to another. The two governments and parliaments could devise new forms of trusteeship that are tailor-made to the needs of the monument in the twenty-first century. A new trusteeship could, for example, lay specific duties on the trustees with regard to conservation, display, access, record-keeping, needs of scholars, consultation, and accountability. Such a new form of trusteeship could draw on expertise and resources from other countries besides Greece who share in the Hellenic heritage, including international organizations. That would be real universalism.[227]

A more collaborative and eclectic approach, moving beyond binary classifications and black-letter injunctions, will require a simple framework. To achieve a greater measure of uniformity among states, it was deemed advisable to formulate a set of principles for consultation and collaboration that both national authorities and private parties could adopt.

c. The Principles for Cooperation in the Mutual Protection and Transfer of Cultural Material

The Principles for Cooperation in the Mutual Protection and Transfer of Cultural Materials[228] provide a substantive framework for helping to avoid and resolve disputes arising out of requests for the transfer of cultural material, usually involving its return or restitution to countries of origin or indigenous groups. Adopted in 2006 by the International Law Association (ILA), the nine Principles were drafted by the ILA's Committee on Cultural Heritage Law after several years of research, preliminary reports, and review sessions.[229]

The Principles begin with a preamble, followed by definitions of requesting party or requesting parties, for the transfer of cultural material, and recipient or recipients of requests for such transfers. The topics of the nine Principles are as follows: requests and responses to requests for the transfer of cultural material, alternatives to the transfer of cultural material, cultural material of indigenous peoples and cultural minorities, human remains, registers of cultural material, notification of newfound cultural material, considerations for negotiations concerning requests, dispute resolution, and a concluding Principle that takes the form of a reservation-of-rights clause and is titled "Other Rights and Obligations." All but the concluding Principle are followed by explanatory notes.

The preamble to the Principles emphasizes the need for a guiding spirit of partnership among private and public actors through international cooperation. The Principles are therefore intended for use by a broad range of interested parties: governments, museums,

[227] William St. Clair, *Imperial Appropriations of the Parthenon, in* IMPERIALISM, ART AND RESTITUTION (John Henry Merryman ed., 2006).

[228] International Law Association, REPORT OF THE SEVENTY-SECOND CONFERENCE 338 (2006) [hereinafter Principles].

[229] For a summary of the Draft Principles before they were put in final form, *see* Robert K. Paterson, *The "Caring and Sharing" Alternative: Recent Progress in the International Law Association to Develop Draft Cultural Material Principles*, 12 INT'L J. CULTURAL PROP. 62 (2005). The text in this section draws on a commentary about the Principles, and a copy of them as adopted, in James A.R. Nafziger, *The Principles for Cooperation in the Mutual Protection and Transfer of Cultural Materials*, 8 CHI. J. INT'L L. 147 (2007); for additional background, *see* James A.R. Nafziger, *A Blueprint for Avoiding and Resolving Cultural Heritage Disputes*, 9 ART, ANTIQUITY & LAW 3, 14–18 (2004).

other institutions, persons, and groups of persons. By fostering mutually acceptable agreements for the careful disposition and possession of such material, the Principles are intended to avoid the unnecessary litigation of competing claims. They are intended not to replace litigation of issues but simply to facilitate collaboration between competing claimants in a process of first resort. To facilitate the desired spirit of partnership among such a broad range of actors and potential issues, the Principles are simple and specific. Their guidance in handling transfer requests is fundamentally a technique for mutual protection of cultural material. The Principles are therefore tools for good stewardship.

NOTES

1. The director of restitution at Christie's, a leading auction house, has described the mediating role of Christie's in responding to restitution issues related to objects consigned for auction, as follows:

   > To the extent that Christie's can act as a neutral intermediary, helping to seek a resolution that is fair to both parties, we do so. Where issues arise, we strive to act as an "honest broker" amongst the parties. Presently, there is no viable dispute resolution mechanism to resolve claims that arise as an alternative to avoiding lengthy judicial proceedings. To be sure, Christie's role is not to adjudicate these claims but where we discover a problem and find ourselves in a situation where we can encourage a dialogue between consignor and claimant, assisting the parties in reaching a settlement is a service we can provide. Where the original owner is a private individual, a dialogue often results in restitution, some monetary compensation or the sale going forward. Where the original owner is a Government or museum, a deal often results in the object being returned.
   >
   > Although we ask our sellers to warrant that they have good title to the property, as well as warrant that the property is free from third party claims, this alone is no longer sufficient because of the complexities of these issues. Most often, sellers legitimately believe that the work in their possession is free and clear of claims. Christie's generally sells as agent rather than as principal. This means that we are not the owners of the property that we sell and often have or start off with incomplete provenance information when an object is consigned to us.

   Monica Dugot, *International Law Weekend Panel on Litigating the Holocaust in U.S. Courts*, 12 ILSA J. Int'l & Comp. L. 389 (2006).

   Should an auction house, as a consignee of material, assume even greater responsibility by blowing the whistle on objects of suspect provenance or objects that likely have been exported from their country of origin? If not, should an auction house blow the whistle at least when it knows an object to be stolen? If so, when should the auction house notify the appropriate authorities? Which authorities? Or, as a third alternative, should the auction house simply refuse to accept such material on consignment?
2. During the 1990s, a Norwegian collector, Martin Schøyen, began purchasing manuscripts, manuscript fragments, and microfragments from the Bamiyan Valley in Afghanistan. These items, dating from the late first to the early eighth century

CE and written on palm leaves, birch bark, and vellum, constitute an important source of information about the spread of Buddhism on the Silk Road. They have been dubbed the "Buddhist Dead Sea Scrolls." Together they are "one of the jewels"[230] of what is thought to be the world's largest private collection of manuscripts assembled in the past century.

Despite well-documented objections that the provenance of the material was seriously tainted, the Norwegian National Library and University of Oslo cooperated with Schøyen in conducting research on the manuscripts, storing some of the material, and publishing an online presentation of selected objects in the collection. Vigorous lobbying against retention of the material in Norway prompted those institutions to suspend their cooperation and also led to a restitution of seven manuscripts in Afghanistan, with the promise of some forty-three or forty-four more fragments by the end of 2007. Most of the thousands of items in contention remained in place, however, not so much because their return to Afghanistan was risky but because of the priority given to ownership entitlements and research opportunities. Even more to the point, it became clear by early 2007 that the owner of the collection wished to sell his entire manuscript collection to Norway, almost certainly for repose in the Norwegian National Library if the requisite funding were available.

Neither hard law nor soft law proved very effective in challenging the retention of the controversial manuscripts in the Schøyen collection. As to hard law, Norway did not become a party to the 1970 UNESCO Convention until 2007. Even though it was a party to the 1954 Hague Convention,[231] the Norwegian government apparently failed to undertake a thorough investigation of the material's provenance, despite the ongoing armed conflict in Afghanistan for many years. Nor did Oslo exercise its investigative or restitutive authority as a matter of international comity. Soft law proved disappointing, too. Because the Norwegian National Library (the intended purchaser of the Schøyen collection) was not a member of ICOM, it was not bound by ICOM's Code of Ethics.[232] Thus, when the vice chancellor of the University of Oslo asked for guidance from the National Committee for Research Ethics, that body expressed disagreement with the zero tolerance of the ICOM Code and criticized the university for provisionally stopping research in response to a media debate concerning the Schøyen collection. To be sure, the Ethics Committee did set forth recommendations to improve research ethics and reminded Norwegian institutions of their obligation to exercise due diligence in deciding whether to associate themselves with questionable material. The Ethics Committee's bottom line, however, was to prioritize autonomous research above caution in responding to the serious claims that had been leveled against the integrity of the Schøyen collection.[233] Had the research focused on the provenance of the manuscripts rather than a general historical inquiry, the Ethics Committee's criticism of the decision by the university to suspend the inquiry would have been commendable. This

[230] *See* Atle Omland, *Claiming Gandhara: Legitimizing Ownership of Buddhist Manuscripts in the Schøyen Collection, Norway, in* Art and Archaeology in Afghanistan: Its Fall and Survival 229 (Juliette van Krieken-Pieters ed., 2006).

[231] *Signed* May 14, 1954, 249 U.N.T.S. 240.

[232] Omland, *supra* note 230, at 236.

[233] *Id.* at 245–46.

controversy demonstrates the difficulty of applying norms, rules, and procedures in the absence of a collaborative ethos. The Principles for Cooperation in the Mutual Protection and Transfer of Cultural Material help define this ethos.

3. Collaborative solutions to issues of repatriation are nothing new. For example, a large and valuable collection of paintings donated by Hugh Lane, an Englishman who moved to Dublin, Ireland, formed the core of Dublin's Municipal Gallery of Modern Art when it opened in 1908. Unfortunately, the collection generated controversy:

> Most famously, of course, there is the saga of Hugh Lane's bequest. Disgusted by political opposition to plans to provide a purpose-built gallery, Lane withdrew some 39 paintings from Dublin and willed them to London's National Gallery instead. Although he later relented, the codicil he wrote was unwitnessed, so that when he was killed after the *Lusitania* was torpedoed off Cork in 1915, the validity of his amendment was open to question. Dublin's moral claim to the pictures was set against London's legal rights. After much wrangling, a co-operative deal eventually emerged involving the loan of the majority of the works to the Hugh Lane and the alternate exhibition, four at a time, in London and Dublin, of the eight French Impressionist paintings that are generally regarded as the cream of the crop.

Aiden Dunn, *Revisiting a Controversial Collection*, IRISH TIMES, July 2, 2008, at 16.

4. Collaborative solutions are becoming more common. Accordingly, long-term loans of disputed material in return for transfer of title to foreign sovereigns and institutions have been worked out, such as by the Boston Museum of Fine Arts, the J. Paul Getty Museum in Los Angeles, and the Metropolitan Museum of Art in New York. Howard Blume, *Italy Lending Bernini Art to the Getty*, L.A. TIMES, Feb. 2, 2008, at B4; Elisabetta Povoledo, *Returning Stolen Art: No Easy Answers*, N.Y. TIMES, Oct. 27, 2007, at B13; Eti Bonn-Muller & Eric A. Powell, *A Tangled Journey Home*, ARCHAEOLOGY, Sept.–Oct. 2007, at 34.
5. For detailed discussions of alternate dispute resolution methods in art disputes, see Isabelle Fellrath Gazzini, *Cultural Property Disputes: The Role of Arbitration in Resolving Non-Contractual Disputes* (2004); PERMANENT COURT OF ARBITRATION, RESOLUTION OF CULTURAL PROPERTY DISPUTES (2004).

6. Intangible Cultural Heritage

A. Introduction

For the past two or three decades the phrase "intangible cultural heritage" has increasingly been used to focus attention on the vulnerability of cultural phenomena that do not assume tangible form (for example, a painting or a book) but are manifest in myriad other ways that often present challenges of definition and protection for lawyers and others. The 2003 UNESCO Convention for the Safeguarding of the Intangible Cultural Heritage[1] defines the phrase "intangible cultural heritage" as follows (article 2):

> For the purposes of this Convention,
>
> 1. The "intangible cultural heritage" means the practices, representations, expressions, knowledge, skills – as well as the instruments, objects, artefacts and cultural spaces associated therewith – that communities, groups and, in some cases, individuals recognize as part of their cultural heritage. This intangible cultural heritage, transmitted from generation to generation, is constantly recreated by communities and groups in response to their environment, their interaction with nature and their history, and provides them with a sense of identity and continuity, thus promoting respect for cultural diversity and human creativity. For the purposes of this Convention, consideration will be given solely to such intangible cultural heritage as is compatible with existing international human rights instruments, as well as with the requirements of mutual respect among communities, groups and individuals, and of sustainable development.
> 2. The "intangible cultural heritage," defined in paragraph 1 above, is manifested inter alia in the following domains:
>   (a) oral traditions and expressions, including language as a vehicle of the intangible cultural heritage;
>   (b) performing arts;
>   (c) social practices, rituals and festive events;
>   (d) knowledge and practices concerning nature and the universe;
>   (e) traditional craftsmanship;

[1] *Adopted* Oct. 17, 2003, UNESCO Doc. Misc/2003/CLT/CH14.

The breadth of this definition underlines the challenges that protecting various manifestations of intangible cultural heritage may present. Most legal systems – especially Western ones – tend not to see the aspects of culture set out in the UNESCO Convention as susceptible to analysis and protection within established legal principles and rules. This vacuum has only reinforced the determination of individuals and groups who fear that a lack of legal protection will lead to such risks as commodification, appropriation, and even extinction of their heritage. A major focus in this debate has been on what is usually described as "traditional knowledge," which is usually seen as insufficiently protected under existing international and domestic intellectual property regimes. The suggestion that intellectual property norms should afford protection for traditional knowledge has also met resistance in the form of various arguments – such as freedom of speech and expression and the protection of established commercial interests. The scholarship tracing this debate is profuse and often polarized. Its outcome, however, has special urgency not only for indigenous peoples but also for others, such as cultural minorities and individual artists who are arguably at particular risk.

B. Traditional Knowledge

It is difficult to separate the definition of "traditional knowledge" from that of "intangible cultural heritage." The respective purposes of each of these terms may best describe what differentiates them. "Intangible cultural heritage" is a phrase mainly used to distinguish elements of culture that are not of a material nature – in other words, characteristically incorporeal. "Traditional knowledge," however, usually refers to cultural expressions that are part of the traditions of a particular community. Thus, the term includes things that take tangible form, such as naturally occurring species of plants or animals with which a particular people have long been connected. Despite this distinction, the two terms both relate to cultural phenomena that are unique to particular indigenous and local communities around the world. Typically, these include medicinal knowledge, folklore, legends, rituals, laws, languages, and agricultural practices, most of which are communally based.

Daniel J. Gervais, *Spiritual but Not Intellectual? The Protection of Sacred Intangible Traditional Knowledge*, 11 CARDOZO J. INT'L & COMP. L., 467, 471–72 (2003)

"Traditional knowledge" is used in a broad sense, similar to the definition proposed in the WIPO Report, where it is basically defined as a subset of the broader concept of "heritage." According to the Chairperson of the United Nations Working Group on Indigenous Populations, heritage itself may be defined as:

> [E]verything that belongs to the distinct identity of a people and which is theirs to share, if they wish, with other peoples. It includes all of those things which contemporary international law regards as the creative production of human thought and craftsmanship, such as songs, music, dances, literature, artworks, scientific research and knowledge. It also includes inheritance from the past and from nature,

> such as human remains, the natural features of the landscape, and naturally occurring species of plants and animals with which a people has long been connected.

And according to WIPO, the subset of "heritage" referred to as traditional knowledge comprises:

> Tradition-based literary, artistic or scientific works; performances; inventions; scientific discoveries; designs; marks, names and symbols; undisclosed information; and all other tradition-based innovations and creations resulting from intellectual activity in the industrial, scientific, literary or artistic fields.

In the above definition, "tradition-based" "refers to knowledge systems, creations, innovations and cultural expressions that have generally been transmitted from generation to generation, are generally regarded as pertaining to a particular people or its territory, have generally been developed in a non-systematic way, and are constantly evolving in response to a changing environment.

Characteristically traditional knowledge is thus knowledge that:

- is traditional only to the extent that its creation and use are part of the cultural traditions of a community – "traditional," therefore, does not necessarily mean that the knowledge is ancient or static;
- is representative of the cultural values of a people and thus is generally held collectively;
- is not limited to any specific field of technology or the arts.

Because traditional knowledge encompasses several forms of cultural expressions, it also applies to religious and sacred arts, customs and other expressions of faith and ancient beliefs. To quote again from the WIPO Report,

> Intertwined within practical solutions, traditional knowledge often transmits the history, beliefs, aesthetics, ethics, and traditions of a particular people. For example, plants used for medicinal purposes also often have symbolic value for the community. Many sculptures, paintings, and crafts are created according to strict rituals and traditions because of their profound symbolic and/or religious meaning.

Christoph Antons, *Traditional Knowledge and Intellectual Property Rights in Australia and Southeast Asia, in* New Frontiers of Intellectual Property Law 37, 40–41 (Christopher Heath & Anselm Kamperman eds., 2008)

It is obvious from the definition of traditional knowledge that the definition is written by people concerned with intellectual property law. At the same time, however, the definition crosses the entire range of intellectual property rights. It makes no distinction between copyrights, patents, trade marks or other forms of intellectual property. The definition does, however, distinguish intellectual property related forms of traditional knowledge from other forms of real or moveable property and from heritage protection in a broader sense.

[T]he shift away from the term "folklore" occurred after it was criticized for its Eurocentric content and lack of capability to express the holistic conception of many non-Western communities with regards to knowledge and the transmission of knowledge. The term ["]folklore["] was regarded as giving the impression of dealing with static rather than evolving traditions and it gave the communities an inferior status in comparison with the dominant culture. The view of indigenous Australian representatives was prominent in this criticism. In her report "Our Culture: Our Future," written in 1998 for the Aboriginal and Torres Strait Islander Commission (ATSIC), Terri Janke preferred to use the term "indigenous cultural and intellectual property rights" introduced a few years earlier by Ms. Erica Daes, the Special Rapporteur of the UN Sub-Commission on Prevention of Discrimination and Protection of Minorities.

The WIPO definition is narrower than the definition of "indigenous cultural and intellectual property" used in the report drafted by Terri Janke. This report's definition includes indigenous ancestral remains, sacred indigenous sites, so-called "cultural environment resources" such as minerals and species and even languages as far as they are relevant for "cultural identity, knowledge, skill and the teaching of culture." On the other hand, the WIPO definition is much wider than the previously predominant term of "folklore," which clearly focused on copyright-related artistic expressions such as handicrafts, dances and music. WIPO has illustrated the new approach with a picture of overlapping circles. The WIPO term is, therefore, narrower than heritage, but wider than both "expressions of folklore" and "indigenous knowledge," because the material in question may be produced by indigenous people, but that is not necessarily the case.

QUESTIONS

1. Do you think the character of traditional knowledge as part of a communal tradition justifies it receiving a higher level of legal protection than other intangible cultural phenomena that lack such a connection? Do existing property laws provide sufficient protection for the latter? Should the protection of traditional knowledge be considered part of the protection of the human rights of those cultures to whom it belongs? See Erica-Irene Daes, Final Report on the Protection of the Heritage of Indigenous Peoples, 26 U.N. Doc. E/CN.4/sub.z/(1995), U.N. Sales.
2. Do you prefer the WIPO definition of "traditional knowledge" to that in the reports of Terri Janke and Erica Daes, which include elements of a tangible nature (for example, sacred sites, ancestral remains)? Are these best addressed by separate methods of legal protection?

C. International Regimes

Several governmental and nongovernmental bodies have engaged the issues surrounding traditional knowledge. The most significant of these, apart from UNESCO, are the World Intellectual Property Organization (WIPO) and the World Trade Organization (WTO), which administers the Agreement on Trade Related Aspects of Intellectual Property Rights (TRIPs).[2] The activities of these organizations have been supplemented by various declarations at international meetings and fora. In addition, a number of conventions and declarations speaking to the rights of indigenous peoples, such as the UN Declaration on the Rights of Indigenous Peoples, in general support the intangible cultures of such groups.

The Uruguay Round of multilateral trade negotiations saw the United States argue in favor of greater protection for intellectual property than was being afforded by the existing treaty and organizational framework. This effort culminated in the establishment of TRIPs, as part of the Agreement Establishing the WTO. Although TRIPs does not require that national intellectual property regimes be modeled on those of the United States or Europe, it does mandate that national laws comply with certain minimum standards set out in the Agreement (Parts II and III). In effect, TRIPs establishes minimum standards for national intellectual property regimes among all WTO members. What gives TRIPs added significance is that the well-established and effective trade dispute mechanisms of the WTO are available to WTO members alleging noncompliance on the part of other WTO members with their TRIPs obligations. Thus, in 1996 the United States alleged that India had failed to comply with certain TRIPs obligations concerning patent protection, and the WTO (panel and appellate body) decided in favor of the United States. If India had not implemented this ruling, the United States could have been authorized by the WTO to take retaliatory measures to neutralize the adverse effects of Indian noncompliance with the TRIPs Agreement.

1. The Convention on Biological Diversity

The Convention on Biological Diversity[3] is a multilateral treaty, adopted in Rio de Janeiro in 1992, which came into force in 1993. It now has some 190 states parties. The United States and Canada have signed the convention but not yet ratified it. The Convention focuses on the sustained use, conservation, and equitable sharing of the benefits arising out of the use of genetic resources. The Convention represented a compromise between the interests of industrialized Western countries and those in the developing world. The latter wanted to secure technological and economic benefits in exchange for allowing access to their biological assets. The Convention has served as a platform for governments to involve indigenous and local communities in strategies to protect traditional knowledge through legal and nonlegal strategies – including respect for indigenous customary laws.

Of particular significance to indigenous peoples is article 8(j) of the Convention, which states that parties to the Convention are to:

> respect, preserve and maintain knowledge, innovations and practices of indigenous and local communities embodying traditional lifestyles relevant for the conservation

[2] 33 I.L.M. 1197 (1994).

[3] *Opened for signature* June 5, 1992, 31 I.L.M. 822 (1992).

> and sustainable use of biological diversity and promote the wider application with approval and involvement of the holders of such knowledge, innovations and practices and encourage the equitable sharing of the benefits arising from the utilization of such knowledge, innovations and practices.

Graham Dutfield, Intellectual Property Rights, Trade and Diversity 35–37 (2000) (reprinted with the permission of Earthscan, Ltd.)

Use of the terms "knowledge," "innovations" and "practices" in addition to "traditional" is very significant. There is a tendency to assume that "traditional" implies any or all of such notions as "time-honoured," "historical," "inflexible" and "static." On the contrary, "traditional innovations" would not be an oxymoron in this context. Perhaps the most significant word of all, though, is "holders," which arguably implies ownership but minimally seems to indicate the existence of legal entitlements.

The Article seems to affirm, then, that the holders ("subject to national legislation") have *rights* over their knowledge, innovations and practices, *whether or not they are capable of being protected by IPRs* [intellectual property rights]. If they are not capable of being protected by the existing IPR system, there is still an obligation for governments to safeguard these entitlements either through a new IPR law or by other legal or policy measures. These duties should also extend to users of traditional knowledge, innovations and practices. Minimally giving effect to these obligations should be through prior informed consent and observation of codes of conduct, such as those developed by some scientific organizations.

This interpretation that these communities have legal entitlements over their knowledge, innovations and practice just as companies have over their inventions is reinforced by Article 18.4, which affirms the need for Contracting Parties to "encourage and develop models of cooperation for the development and use of technologies, including traditional and indigenous technologies . . . ". Since it is agreed that indigenous and traditional technologies have a role to play in biodiversity conservation, there is no justification for assuming (as many tend to do) that such technologies have a lower status than other technologies relevant to the Convention; nor should they be any less morally entitled to legal protection.

It is very important, though, that the requirement to respect, preserve and maintain traditional knowledge not be justified *solely* by its instrumental value. Traditional knowledge should not be respected, preserved and maintained merely *because* it is relevant to biodiversity conservation and sustainability; even less because some of it has industrial application. A great deal of traditional knowledge has no commercial potential whatsoever, but this does not make it any less worthy of respect or protection. The disappearance of traditional knowledge may be a tragedy for the world, but above all, it is a tragedy for those peoples and communities of the world that depend upon the integrity of their knowledge systems for their cultural and even physical survival.

In 2002 the Parties to the Convention adopted the *Bonn Guidelines on Access to Genetic Resources and the Fair and Equitable Sharing of Benefits Arising out of Their Utilization.*[4] The Bonn Guidelines are designed to assist the development of access and benefit-sharing strategies respecting genetic resources. They are further evidence of a multilateral commitment to advance the policies behind the Convention itself. Despite such initiatives, international efforts to extend protection for aspects of traditional knowledge face many systematic problems. The two most significant of these are, first, that several major states in this process have only limited or qualified participation and, second, that (as things stand) national measures to protect traditional knowledge may experience effective annulment under WTO dispute settlement mechanisms or through simply not being recognized by other states.

2. The WTO Agreement on TRIPs

Olufunmilayo B. Arewa, *TRIPs and Traditional Knowledge: Local Communities, Local Knowledge, and Global Intellectual Property Frameworks*, 10 Marq. Intel. Prop. L. Rev., 155, 164–80 (2006)

1. Treatment of Local Knowledge under TRIPs

What is often termed "traditional knowledge" is in many respects a negative category that is typically applied to types of knowledge found to a greater extent in the Third World and among indigenous peoples. The term "local knowledge" will be used herein to refer to traditional knowledge and other types of knowledge typically subsumed within the categories of knowledge that fall within the rubric of WIPO's Intergovernmental Committee on Intellectual Property and Genetic Resources, Traditional Knowledge and Folklore (IGC). This knowledge within the IGC's rubric includes a broad range of knowledge that is most united in having the common characteristic of not being protected under existing intellectual property frameworks. As a result of the negative nature of the definition of traditional knowledge, a wide range of cultural knowledge falls within its rubric, including "biological and other materials for medical treatment and agriculture, production processes, designs, and literature, music, rituals and other techniques and arts." Local knowledge also plays a vital role in much of the Third World for medicinal treatment and other purposes. The breadth of the material falling within the category of local knowledge at times makes discussions

[4] Conference of the Parties to the Convention on Biological Diversity, 6th mtg., Apr. 7–19, 2002, Bonn Guidelines to Genetic Resources and Fair and Equitable Sharing of the Benefits Arising out of Their Utilization, Annex I, Decision VI/24/A, at 262, U.N. Doc. UNEP/CBD/COP/6/20.

about protection of local knowledge complex and the goals of those who seek protection for local knowledge potentially quite varied.

The adoption of the TRIPs Agreement and common minimum global standards for intellectual property frameworks for Members of the WTO has led to increasing debate and dialogue about the lack of protection for local knowledge under TRIPs. Current global dialogue about intellectual property treatment of local knowledge is taking place at WIPO. WIPO was established in 1967 as a specialized United Nations agency and now administers a number of intellectual property treaties, including the Berne and Paris Conventions. In 2000, WIPO established the IGC. The IGC is intended to deal with the range of cultural material falling under the rubric of local knowledge. The choice of WIPO as a forum for local knowledge discussions may reflect the general lack of consensus about how local knowledge should be treated under existing intellectual property frameworks. Placing this forum at WIPO may also represent a potential effort to divert discussion of local knowledge from the WTO. This is particularly true because the WTO was chosen as a forum for TRIPs, at least in part because the WTO had greater enforcement power through international trade mechanisms than WIPO. WIPO was formerly the dominant arena for international intellectual property matters.

2. TRIPs and Commercial Interests

The negotiation, implementation, and substantive content of TRIPs reflect the influence of its beneficiaries. Primary among those are private and public interests in countries such as the United States, the member states of the European Union and Japan. Commercial interests in such countries played a critical role in the shaping of provisions of the TRIPs Agreement and provided a significant impetus for its implementation. Such commercial interests were also motivated by the increasing value of knowledge assets protectable by intellectual property in the post-industrial digital era. The role of commercial interests in the adoption of TRIPs reflects an ongoing relationship between such interests and intellectual property rights frameworks.

In addition, an important part of the post-TRIPs turmoil concerning local knowledge relates to the commercialization of knowledge that is currently not protected under global intellectual property frameworks. This has led to the development and intensification of narratives of appropriation in discussions of local knowledge and intellectual property that outline in detail what are seen as inappropriate uses of local knowledge. These narratives of appropriation also highlight the extent and nature of uses of such knowledge by commercial actors, most of which are located in the North.

3. Intellectual Property and Scientific, Technological, and Institutional Capacity

Underlying narratives of appropriation is yet another asymmetry: relative scientific, technological, and institutional capacity between North and

South. Although not a homogeneous group, an immense technological disparity exists between North and South. Consequently, many countries in the South do not have extensive internal technological and scientific capacity to enable them to transform local knowledge into knowledge that might be protected under current intellectual property frameworks. Without the establishment of structures within current global intellectual property frameworks intended to help the development of such capacity, TRIPs has the potential to exacerbate existing disparities in technological and scientific capacity. This is partly a result of the relative inflexibility of TRIPs for Third World countries. In addition, the existence of technological and scientific disparities means that some countries in the South are less likely to experience the benefits that are supposed to accompany free trade in the intellectual property arena.

4. The Uncertain Short-Term Benefits of TRIPs for Third World Countries

TRIPs is based on an assumption that technological capacity fosters development. Despite this assumption, the relative scientific and technological disparity between North and South means that countries in the South may, in the aggregate, suffer a net loss as a consequence of TRIPs. As a result, in the short-run, developing countries are worse off under TRIPs. The extent to which countries in the South continue to experience losses under TRIPs may depend in part on how global intellectual property frameworks treat resources found in greater abundance in the South. The business practices of companies that use local knowledge and the circumstances and relative terms of such usage will also be important.

II. TRIPs, Local Communities, and Local Knowledge

Local knowledge is in many respects a negative category, shaped as much by history and culture as by the composition of the actual knowledge contained in this category. How global intellectual property frameworks treat local knowledge today is in part a function of how local communities interface with intellectual property systems. Local communities include both people in the South as well as indigenous groups in both the North and South. Local knowledge is an acknowledged and important resource in many such local communities. At least partly as a result of the globalization of intellectual property frameworks under TRIPs, local communities today have far less flexibility to craft intellectual property frameworks to help develop technological capacity. This contrasts with the development experience of other countries, such as the United States in the nineteenth century as well as countries in East Asia in the twentieth century.

A. TRIPs, Local Communities, and Development

Global intellectual property frameworks should to a greater extent allow for more flexibility for local communities. In cases of local knowledge, this means that local communities should have some ability to participate in decisions regarding uses of local knowledge as well as the development of intellectual property frameworks that influence the treatment of such knowledge. Such steps may help encourage the development of technological, scientific, and institutional capacity that could help local communities realize more broadly the benefits of free trade. The current imbalances in scientific and technological capacity and the distribution of short-term benefits of TRIPs have contributed to the opposition to TRIPs in the Third World. Part of the opposition to TRIPs is evident in the development of narratives of appropriation in which the uses of resources of the South are characterized as misappropriation or even "biopiracy."

B. TRIPs and Narratives of Appropriation of Local Knowledge

Narratives of appropriation are typically told with respect to three broad categories: Agriculture and medicinal and other plants, expressive culture, and other commercial uses. A significant number of such narratives are becoming increasingly part of the discourse with respect to global intellectual property frameworks. These narratives also reflect the tensions inherent in the broader application of a global intellectual property framework that developed in a particular historical and cultural context. The section that follows outlines some of the narratives of appropriation of local knowledge that are mentioned in discussions of intellectual property. These narratives relate to a wide variety of types of knowledge in varied regions of the world.

1. Agriculture and Medicinal and Other Plants

One of the most prominent narratives of appropriation involves the neem tree. Called the "curer of all ailments" in Sanskrit, the neem tree is used for medicinal, agricultural, pesticidal, contraceptive, cosmetic and dental applications. From 1992 to 1995, W.R. Grace & Co. received several U.S. and European patents for applications relating to the neem seed. Although the U.S. Patent & Trademark Office (PTO) has permitted neem patents to stand, the European Patent Office has revoked its neem patent on the basis of biopiracy. The neem tree case highlights the fact that varying national patent standards can lead to different outcomes when patents based on local knowledge are challenged. The neem tree is perhaps the most prominent of a number of cases involving local knowledge in India. In addition to the basmati rice, turmeric, and arogyapaacha cases discussed below, karela juice and *Phyllanthus amarus* are cases mentioned in discussions of local knowledge in India.

The basmati rice case demonstrates that revocation of patents based on local knowledge does not always adequately secure rights with respect to the contested knowledge. In 1997, the U.S. firm RiceTec, Inc. received a patent relating to plants and seeds with a relationship to basmati rice. Basmati, long grown in India and Pakistan, is a major export crop with estimated annual export revenues of $300 million. India requested reexamination of the basmati patent in 2000. In response, RiceTec withdrew its claims relating to basmati-type rice. The debate over basmati then moved to use of the name basmati and whether basmati could be deemed a generic term, which would mean that rice grown outside of India and Pakistan could be marketed as basmati rice. The United States has found basmati to be a generic term.

In yet another case involving local knowledge in India, a patent involving turmeric was successfully revoked based on prior art. Turmeric is used in India for cooking, dy[e]ing, cosmetics, and medicinal purposes. In 1995, a U.S. patent was granted to two Indian national researchers at the University of Mississippi Medical Center for use of turmeric in wound healing. The Indian Center for Scientific and Industrial Research asked for reexamination of the turmeric patent based on prior art in ancient Sanskrit texts and in a 1953 article in the *Journal of the Indian Medical Association.* The PTO then revoked the patent.

The arogyapaacha plant of India is a case that shows the potential prospects of benefit-sharing agreements for uses of local knowledge. The arogyapaacha plant is used by the Kani in South India for medicinal purposes. An anti-stress and anti-fatigue sports drug named Jeevani has been developed based on the arogyapaacha plant. The active compounds in arogyapaacha were isolated by scientists at the Tropical Botanic Garden and Research Institute in India. Patents were filed based on Kani know-how and the technology licensed to Arya Vaidya Pharmacy, Ltd., an Indian pharmaceutical manufacturer. A benefits-sharing arrangement was established to share any benefits with the Kani from commercialization of Kani traditional knowledge.

A number of cases of uses of African local knowledge are also mentioned in narratives of appropriation, including rosy periwinkle, Hoodia cactus, and rooibos tea. The case of rosy periwinkle illustrates the potential difficulty of sorting out proprietary claims to some types of local knowledge. As the narrative is typically told, rosy periwinkle was originally native to the island of Madagascar. The rosy periwinkle was used to develop two pharmaceutical drugs for treating Hodgkin's disease and juvenile leukemia. The rosy periwinkle used to develop these drugs was eventually grown almost entirely in Texas and not in Madagascar. Eli Lilly and Co. has profited from the sale of the anticancer drugs vinblastine and vincristine extracted from the rosy periwinkle. Although Eli Lilly earned millions of dollars per year from these drugs, no compensation has been given to Madagascar. As anthropologist Michael Brown has pointed out, however, the story of the rosy periwinkle may not be quite as simple as is sometimes presented and illustrates the potential difficulties in ascribing ownership rights with respect to certain types of cultural knowledge.

Hoodia cactus is an appetite-suppressant used by the San of Southern Africa. A patent for P57, the active ingredient in Hoodia, was granted to the South African Council for Scientific and Industrial Research (SCIR) based on San local knowledge about Hoodia. This patent was then licensed to a British pharmaceutical company. Pfizer then acquired the rights to develop and market drugs based on P57. After the San threatened to sue under the Convention on Biodiversity (CBD), the CSIR entered into a benefit-sharing arrangement with the San. The CBD reflects the use of non-intellectual property frameworks as a source of authority in discussions of local knowledge.

Reflecting some of the issues that have arisen in the basmati rice case with respect to uses of names, the rooibos case involves naming rights with respect to tea derived from a bush that grows in South Africa. The rooibos tea case involves a U.S. trademark acquired by an American company from a South African company for the mark ROOIBOS. Rooibos, which means "red bush," is a plant indigenous to South Africa that is used to make a number of products, including tea. A recent settlement has been made with respect to this case and the trademark has been abandoned by the U.S. company that had purchased it. Other cases discussed in the African context include *Maytenus buchananii*, the endod berry, Monellin, and Thaumalin.

A number of narratives of appropriation are also discussed in the South American context. Quinine, a treatment for malaria, is derived from cinchona bark, which has long been used by indigenous groups in the Andes as a cure for fevers. In 1630, Peruvian indigenous peoples gave Jesuit priests information about the use of chichona bark to treat fevers and malaria. Since the initial disclosure of this knowledge, a number of pharmaceutical drugs have been developed, including quinine (isolated in 1820), its synthetic derivative, and quinidine for treating arrhythmia.

The ayahuasca vine is native to the Amazon rain forest and is used by shamans and healers for medicinal and spiritual purposes. In 1986, an American scientist was granted a patent on a strain of the ayahuasca vine. In 1999, a council representing some four hundred indigenous groups was successful in having the ayahuasca patent cancelled by the PTO.

Pozol is used by the Maya in Mexico for nutritional purposes and prevention of intestinal ailments, including giardia and amoebas. In 1999, Quest International, a Dutch corporation, and the University of Minnesota were granted a patent for the active component in pozol, giving no acknowledgement or recognition to knowledge upon which the patent was based.

Two Colorado State University researchers acquired a patent for quinoa based upon knowledge of Bolivian farmers, who shared seeds from their quinoa crop with the researchers. The researchers abandoned the quinoa patent after confronting global opposition to their attempt to assert proprietary rights, including a plea at the UN General Assembly. The researchers failed to pay a fee to the PTO, thus allowing the patent to lapse.

The tamate, a small cylindrical tomato, was used by Amazonian Indians in Ecuador for its cancer-fighting properties. The active ingredient in the tamate, lycopene, was isolated by a multi-national pharmaceutical company that now sells lycopene as a cancer treatment.

2. Expressive Culture

Although many cases involving uses of local knowledge [involve medicinal plants and agriculture], other cases involve expressive culture. These include the Ami "Song of Joy," the album "Deep Forest," and other cases.

The Ami "Song of Joy" involves use for a commercial recording of a sample made from the voices of indigenous people in Taiwan. In 1996, "Return of Innocence," a song by "ethno-techno" artist Enigma, was licensed for use in the 1996 Atlanta Olympics. The song included a sampling from a recording made in 1988 of a live performance of members of the Ami, Taiwan's largest indigenous group. The French cultural organization that made the original recording licensed the sample to Enigma without any authorization or license from any Ami or representatives of the Ami. Five million copies of "Return of Innocence" were sold worldwide. Following a lawsuit that settled out of court, the defendant record companies gave formal thanks and full credit to the Ami in future releases of "Return of Innocence" and established a foundation with the proceeds of the settlement.

As was the case with the Ami "Song of Joy," "Deep Forest" involved the use of samples of indigenous people in commercial recordings. "Deep Forest" was a techno-house dance rhythm album created in 1992 that fused digital samples from Ghana, the Solomon Islands, and African pygmies. "Deep Forest" sold over two million copies by May 1995, received a Grammy nomination, and remained on Billboard Magazine's "top album" chart for twenty-five weeks. A number of companies, including Porsche, Sony TV and Coca-Cola have used music from "Deep Forest" in advertising campaigns. The musicians sampled do not appear to have received any benefit from the proceeds of commercialization of their music.

A final case that should be noted relates to blues and rock-and-roll music. A number of commentators have noted a longstanding use of blues traditions in commercial popular music in the United States. Particularly noteworthy are uses of blues music by rock-and-roll performers. In a case that eventually settled out of court, blues singer Willie Dixon sued the rock group Led Zeppelin, alleging that Led Zeppelin's song "Whole Lotta Love" constituted copyright infringement of Dixon's song "I Need Love." Although the uses of blues music do not involve Third World countries or indigenous peoples, they do illustrate the ways in which hierarchies of power can influence the operation and beneficiaries of intellectual property protection.

3. Other Commercial Uses: Images of Indigenous Peoples

A number of other uses connected to discussions of misappropriation of local knowledge relate to the images of indigenous peoples. Also relevant is the use of unauthorized symbols of indigenous peoples for commercial benefit.

The use of Native American words and symbols by sports teams is an issue of continuing debate and dialogue. Native American sports team logos such as those of the Washington Redskins, Cleveland Indians, Atlanta Braves, Chicago Blackhawks, and Kansas City Chiefs remain a point of continuing tension and debate in the United States. . . .

Similar cases have arisen in other countries, such as New Zealand. In one case, Air New Zealand removed the Maori-derived koru logo from its floor mats. This removal was a result of complaints about situating the logo in a place where people would walk on it (although the koru symbology was retained in the airline logo).

Another New Zealand case involved Maori images. The Lego Corporation received letters from lawyers representing Maori indigenous non-governmental organizations concerning the use of Maori words and historical figures in "Bionicle" action toys that were combined with terms and figures from Easter Island and Polynesian cultures. After receiving these letters, the Lego Corporation agreed to "engage Maori advisors as consultants in the development of a code of conduct for governing the use of traditional knowledge in the manufacture of toys."

C. TRIPs and "Biopiracy"

Narratives of appropriation are often closely related to discourse that terms use of local knowledge as "biopiracy." Such talk of "biopiracy" reflects the increased property-based rights talk that characterizes intellectual property discourse today. It also clearly responds to the property-based rights talk that was integral to the process of negotiating and adopting TRIPs. The discourse of TRIPs proponents, focused on property-based rights talk, emphasized the "piracy" of a wide range of actors, even when activities fell within the applicable legal boundaries. Between accusations of "piracy" and counter-accusations of "biopiracy" stands a range of uses for which such characterizations are inaccurate, including uses that borrow from existing materials and resources.

Conclusion

TRIPs raises a number of issues of significant concern with respect to local knowledge. How global intellectual property frameworks address local knowledge is of critical importance to many local communities. Such frameworks have the potential to be a source of wealth creation for local communities to the extent that they are designed in a flexible manner. Such flexible frameworks may enable the flow of resources to be reversed and local communities to benefit to a greater extent from the potential benefits of global trade frameworks.

NOTE AND QUESTION

Professor Arewa suggests that "local communities," including developing country populations and indigenous peoples in general, suffer from having become aware of their rights only after the global intellectual property regime had been erected to the advantage of (mostly) Western industrialized states. Can or should this historical circumstance be redressed, and, if so, how? See M. Geuze & H. Wager, *WTO Dispute Settlement Practice Relating to the TRIPS Agreement*, 2 J. Int'l Econ. L. 347 (1999); F. Gurry, *The Dispute Resolution Services of the World Intellectual Property Organization*, 2 J. Int'l Econ. L. 385 (1999). The issues surrounding the relationship of local communities to the different fora that engage intellectual property rights have been explored in Chidi Oguamanam, *Local Knowledge as Trapped Knowledge: Intellectual Property, Culture, Power and Politics*, 11 J. World Intell. Prop. 29 (2008); Chidi Oguamanam, *Regime Tension in the Intellectual Property Rights Arena: Farmers' Rights and Post-TRIPS Counter Regime Trends*, 29 Dalhousie L.J. 413 (2006).

3. The UNESCO Convention for the Safeguarding of the Intangible Cultural Heritage

The UNESCO Convention for the Safeguarding of the Intangible Cultural Heritage came into force in 2006 and had 114 state parties in 2009, not including the United States and Canada. It obliges parties to take necessary measures to safeguard the intangible cultural heritage in their respective territories, including an official identification of the elements of such heritage that includes the participation of communities, groups, and nongovernmental organizations. Consistent with UNESCO's educational mandate, the Convention requires that the intangible cultural heritage of member states be inventoried and that measures be put in place to raise awareness and the likelihood of preservation concerning such local heritage. The Convention also establishes the Intangible Cultural Heritage Fund to assist members to carry out their obligations under the Convention.

The Convention established the Intergovernmental Committee for Safeguarding of the Intangible Cultural Heritage comprising twenty-four representatives of states parties. The functions of the Committee are to promote and provide guidance concerning the implementation of the Convention. In particular, the Committee supervises the publication of the Representative List of the Intangible Cultural Heritage of Humanity and the List of Intangible Cultural Property in Need of Urgent Safeguarding. The Committee has met several times and finalized the first draft Operational Directives for the Implementation of the Convention.

The most controversial aspect of the UNESCO Convention is its relationship to other international agreements, particularly those developed under WIPO or WTO auspices. Article 3(b) of the Convention provides that nothing in the Convention "may be interpreted as affecting the rights and obligations of State Parties deriving from any international instrument relating to intellectual property rights or to the use of biological and ecological resources to which they are parties." This is a significant condition on the scope of the Convention insofar as it, in effect, preserves intellectual property rights under such agreements and, in doing so, significantly reduces the scope of the Convention.

There have been ongoing efforts to address concerns about the intangible cultural heritage that had emerged before the 1989 UNESCO Recommendation on the Safeguarding of Traditional Culture and Folklore. After the UNESCO/WIPO World Forum on the Protection of Folklore, held in Thailand in 1997, the two organizations embarked on regional consultations aimed at promoting folklore protection at the national and regional level. It can be assumed that similar meetings will continue, but the systemic problems of how to reconcile intellectual proprietary rights with broader concerns about the protection of traditional culture seem to be as intractable as ever.

Despite these limitations, the UNESCO Convention does represent a commitment to recognize and protect cultures at their own level rather than by states on their behalf. The Convention may lack the certainty of a property or rights-based accord, but it could provide a foundation for the development of such a document.

D. The Limits of Intellectual Property Laws

1. Introduction

Although modern indigenous artists have been able to resort to traditional property rights concerning movable cultural property, many native peoples have found their claims to ownership of their intangible cultural property, such as motifs, songs, prayers, ceremonies, music, legends, and folklore, frustrated by the limits of established intellectual property and other legal regimes. Especially frustrating for these groups are the difficulties faced by collectives, as opposed to individuals, when trying to establish elements of traditional intellectual property protection.

One of the consequences of the assertion of traditional intellectual property rights (IPRs) is the commodification of intangible cultural property. In this case, "commodification" can be defined as the conversion of intangible cultural property into items of economic worth that can be traded for commercial gain by such means as license, rental, or sale. The exploitation of this reified intangible property is often referred to as commercialization. The desirability of this consequence for indigenous people is controversial. Transmogrifying songs and legends, chants and rituals, and collective heritage into products of trade has been seen by some as diminishing the inherent spirituality or dignity of native heritage. The very notion of such collective experience being turned into "property" (with all its connotations of individual or exclusive ownership) has been identified by many as a misappropriation or at least an inappropriate use. Yet the denial or withholding of traditional IPRs concerning cultural property has been identified by others within the indigenous community as denying indigenous peoples control over their own cultural property.

In many cases, legitimate concerns of indigenous people can be accommodated without going to the extreme of recognizing new intellectual property rights. This can be done through modest reinterpretation of existing legal regimes concerning contract, privacy, and unfair competition law; carefully tailored but general statutory amendments; or incrementally developed common law principles aimed to level what might otherwise be seen as an unfair playing field. This approach to cultural property has a number of advantages. First, it affords protection not just to indigenous claimants, though it may be especially suitable for their needs, but also to any person or group whose needs, arising from similar causes, justify specific legal recognition and protection. Second, it avoids the need for its claimants to define their legal rights in terms of a preexisting category of property rights, thus avoiding charges of debasement and commercialization that have adhered to such claims in the past. Finally, it respects the fundamental human rights and social values of democratic traditions and the carefully articulated social policy balances embodied in intellectual property law for both indigenous and nonindigenous people.

2. Problems Resulting from the Failure to Protect Indigenous Cultural Heritage

A number of problems that have been identified in the literature call for more, better, or different legal protection of the cultural heritage of indigenous peoples. One such problem is the use of indigenous knowledge to develop a commercial product, especially a valuable drug. Many feel that the group that first discovered, say, a medicinal use for a plant and conveys that knowledge to outside scientists should share in the profits when that knowledge serves as the basis for a commercial pharmaceutical. The circumstances in which the knowledge is conveyed can add force to the claim. Where an outsider obtains knowledge by fraudulent or deceptive means concerning, say, which plants are effective against what or the location of mineral or plant resources, there is a clear element of unfairness, even where the outsider takes nothing tangible from the group supplying the knowledge. The knowledge might also be acquired by taking advantage of the ignorance of indigenous peoples concerning Western intellectual property traditions and contract norms, thereby openly depriving the knowledge suppliers of the return that someone more familiar with those Western institutions could have negotiated.

The use by outsiders of tribal names or other identifiers, sacred symbols or images, or artistic designs generally is also problematic. Use of sacred symbols or rituals may offend the beliefs of the people from whom they were taken, and all the more so if they are corrupted or used out of context. If the group has sought to maintain secrecy in its rituals, using unfair means to learn about them offends basic notions of privacy. The use of artistic designs may occur without attribution to the group from which they sprang, or a corrupted version may be attributed to that group without its permission or against its will. A related problem concerns use of these names, symbols, or designs by authentic members of the group but in ways that assertedly run contrary to the group's traditional use. Similarly, even when the group does not object to the commodification of, say, an artistic design, people outside the group may be confused as to whether a given object is authentic, and that can harm the group's ability to profit from commercial sales.

Another problem is the disturbance of an embedded landscape, in which indigenous knowledge is so intimately tied to nature that it cannot be removed without either detracting from its original environment or rendering the knowledge less useful. The notion is that local ecological knowledge belongs to the community as a whole and should be considered inalienable from it. It is also asserted that indigenous people should have the right to restrict research on indigenous knowledge or biological resources when the integrity of a natural or cultural patrimony is threatened.

3. Indigenous Cultural Heritage and IPRs

To what degree can intellectual property law be successful in addressing some of the identified problems? Given the intangible nature of much indigenous culture, intellectual property rules seemed, at first, the most promising for the protection of indigenous cultural traditions against inappropriate use. Early optimism, however, quickly gave way to the view that, without elaborate modification, existing intellectual property laws were likely an inadequate basis to protect indigenous cultural property.

a. Copyright

Because copyright is designed to prevent unauthorized reproduction of artistic works, it immediately springs to mind as a potential tool for the protection of indigenous cultural traditions from inappropriate use. This initial impression, however, fades once certain characteristics of indigenous culture are tested against the requisite elements of copyright protection. Ironically, as one indigenous writer has pointed out, "In fact, copyright is used to protect non-Aboriginal people who appropriate and exploit [Aboriginal] oral tradition."

Copyright requires, among other things, that a literary, dramatic, musical, or artistic work originate from an author. Although a new work can be based on the earlier works of others, the new work must constitute a new expression to receive protection. Indigenous cultural heritage often emphasizes and reiterates the incrementally evolving expressions of past generations. In their desire to preserve the past, indigenous authors may unwittingly limit their eligibility for copyright privileges. Of course, at least in theory, works that are in a constant state of development should be considered derivative works based on the public domain expression handed down from the past, and nothing in copyright law limits the number of joint authors of a given work. Nevertheless, the reality is often that no one today knows just who was involved in creating the innovative expressive aspect that theoretically remains under protection, and the nearly universal absence of clearly defined ownership agreements among the joint authors makes reliance on this approach difficult.

In some countries, such as the United States and Canada, attachment of copyright protection also requires that works be fixed in material form. Indigenous cultural traditions are mostly oral and may have never been recorded in any material form whatsoever. Indigenous material expressions that do occur are often intended to be temporary, such as those connected with ceremonies and celebrations. Many indigenous oral traditions have been translated and published in printed form by nonindigenous authors, who then themselves receive the benefits of copyright protection. Similarly, a photograph of an indigenous person in traditional attire confers copyright on the photographer but not the subject of the photograph. The copyright requirement of fixation often demands a change in indigenous cultural tradition that may itself amount to a kind of forced assimilation of that tradition into Western culture.

In Berne Convention countries such as Canada, the United States, and some 120 others, the minimum term of copyright protection is the life of the author and fifty (or even more) years. This long but limited term derives from Lockean theory that individual property rights are based on the addition of labor and must be reconciled with the competing demands of the public domain. Indigenous cultural traditions, which are usually seen as requiring indefinite protection, contradict the whole notion of a finite term or life span.

The notion of perpetual cultural property rights is linked to another characteristic of indigenous cultures, that of collectivity. Unlike Western concepts of the romantic solitary genius, indigenous cultures tend to value the collective efforts of a community that, in turn, reveres the significance of the past. Copyright law recognizes joint authorship only when it is the clear intention of the authors that authorship be so held. In the Australian decision of *Yumbulul v. Reserve Bank of Australia*, an Aboriginal artist sued the Reserve Bank of Australia for copyright infringement regarding its use of an image of his sculpture *Morning Star Pole* on a new ten-dollar bank note. The action was dismissed, and the court did not address the argument that permission to reproduce the sculpture had to be obtained from the relevant tribal owners. The case, however, is a good illustration of the dilemma of using copyright law in an attempt to meet indigenous concerns. As one writer has pointed out, the *Morning Star Pole* motif used in the banknote design will eventually enter the public domain so that others can base their own designs on it. Copyright eventually frees up underlying work to encourage continuing individual innovation. Indigenous cultures put a premium on the preservation and control of the underlying work. They want to prevent future artists from basing their work on the cultural symbols of indigenous groups.

b. Moral Rights

In Chapter 4, we saw that moral rights offer a kind of adjunctive protection to that afforded by copyright. With its focus on the rights of creators, moral rights law has sometimes been seen to be sympathetic to the concerns of indigenous peoples. They may think that the right to integrity may offer protection against distortion through inaccurate or unauthorized use of their cultural symbols. The right of attribution may also be able to afford protection against claims by nonindigenous persons to original authorship. Despite its potential advantage for indigenous persons, however, moral rights law remains focused on the individual author and not the community as a whole. Although the Berne Convention and the copyright laws of all countries provide for some notion of joint authorship, the limited term comes into play for traditional works of indigenous peoples, even if the original (joint) authors could be known. Without significant modification to address these sorts of concerns, moral rights, like copyright, will remain inadequate as a legal basis to address indigenous concerns.

c. Patent Law

In protecting artistic designs, symbols, literature, or music, patent law simply does not apply because these types of works are not technological and are therefore not patent subject matter. The potential relevance of patent law to traditional knowledge of herbal or other medicines, which can result in processes or medicines for treating human disease or other physical ailments, is equally clear, but it does not often lead to the result desired by advocates for indigenous peoples. For example, in the paradigmatic case in which a scientist learns that an indigenous group has found a particular plant effective in treating a human health problem, subsequent isolation of the active ingredient and its development into a useful drug by a modern pharmaceutical company may well result in a patent for the company, but nothing in the patent law requires that the company share any of the profits with the source of the information that led to the discovery. In principle, there would be nothing to stop the indigenous group from doing what the drug company did, but in practice, such groups are not equipped to engage in the complex and very expensive process of determining scientifically which elements of the plant are active, creating an industrial process for manufacturing the drug, and proving its effectiveness and safety.

4. Appropriateness of IPR Protection

Several commentators have attributed the inability of copyright to deal with problems of cultural heritage protection to a supposed copyright focus on the individual author. More generally, some might feel that traditional intellectual property law, especially copyright, is based on natural rights of authorship, pursuant to which an author's (or perhaps an inventor's) rights are grounded in the moral Lockean principle that the creator of something should have exclusive ownership rights to his or her creation. Eminent copyright scholars have, indeed, pointed out that the notion of the romantic author in copyright theory is often used as a political tool by forces seeking stronger, longer, and broader copyright protection. Yet no matter how appealing claims to natural rights might seem at a casual glance, no country follows a pure natural rights theory for intellectual property. Natural rights theory, for example, does not and cannot incorporate limitations on either the duration or the scope of the right. How do natural rights justify a very long copyright term while maintaining a relatively short period of protection for patents? Many inventions are at least as intellectually creative as the bulk of copyright-protected works. Nor would a pure natural rights perspective distinguish between idea and expression in determining the scope of copyright protection. Often the most creative aspect of a work is its underlying idea, yet nothing in pure natural rights theory can tell us where to draw the line between protected and unprotected elements of works. Thus, concern for the romantic author, whether individual or communal, is not a true policy basis for patent and copyright legislation. Vague appeals to the natural rights of authors are almost invariably a political smoke screen aimed to reduce the public benefits of a copyrighted idea in favor of greater monetary returns to copyright owners.

The real policy basis for recognizing exclusive IPRs derives from the public goods problem; namely, failure to protect the fruits of intellectual creativity would result in fewer creative and socially desirable works being produced and made available to the public because the effort involved in first producing the works is much greater than that involved in simply copying works already made. However, protection that is too strong or too long also has a deleterious effect on the social availability of desirable works, because later authors and inventors depend and build on works that have come before them. The goal of intellectual property law is to balance these two tensions to optimize the works made available to the public. Thus, all countries have concluded that the free use of ideas results in more works from subsequent authors than are lost by failing to protect ideas. In other words, they apply a public-benefit, or instrumentalist, philosophy in setting limits on intellectual property rights. Many believe that IPRs have become too strong in that further rights do not add any incentive for the creation of socially desirable works. Adding (unlimited) cultural rights to the mix would only increase the pressure from interest groups to extend traditional IPRs, especially copyright.

An appropriate balance in copyright law is also vital for maintaining and enhancing basic freedoms in a democratic society. Thus, copyright serves as an incentive for the creation and dissemination of original expression that is free of government regulation, supporting basic concepts of individual liberty. In contrast, overly strong copyright protection can stifle rather than promote expressive diversity:

> All authors draw upon existing works in creating new ones. For that reason, a democratic copyright must provide considerable leeway for creative transformations of protected expression. At least to some extent, authors must be free to adapt, reformulate, quote, refer to, and abstract from existing expression without having to obtain copyright owner permission. Absent that breathing space, authors would be severely fettered in their ability to participate in public discourse, whether by building upon literary or artistic traditions, laying bare the contradictions in venerable cultural icons, or challenging prevailing modes of thought.

We must therefore be cautious in too rapidly seizing on the notion of IPRs as a general mode of protection for intangible knowledge arising out of a given cultural heritage. It is important that our economically dominant Western culture not take by stealth or deception that which a particular indigenous group wishes and has sought to keep secret. However, it is also important that indigenous groups recognize the fundamental role of individual freedom (from government regulation) in modern democratic societies. The emphasis on a broad and growing public domain is not simply utilitarianism, unless that term is defined in the broadest sense to include the utility of a growing and diverse cultural environment. Our culture greatly benefits when Pablo Picasso brings elements of African art into his own or Vincent van Gogh similarly employs Japanese art. Indigenous cultures also benefit from the broad and vibrant public domain that has resulted from the time-limited nature of our IPRs. Many drugs, tools, and industrial processes that were once patented are now free all over the world for use or further adaptation by others, including indigenous peoples. A whole canon of cultural works from the Greek playwrights to early-twentieth-century composers remains free for the taking by anybody. People all over the world, from nearly every culture, benefit from this rich public domain of intellectual property. We must at least pause before reducing the public domain solely on the ground that some of it "belongs" to a specifically identifiable cultural heritage.

Treating intangible cultural property under the intellectual property regimes of patent and copyright would raise practical problems as well. The absence of specified authors or inventors raises the question of who should have powers of enforcement. In general, the incentive or instrumentalist basis for IPRs cannot serve as a basis for IPRs in intangible works that have already been created, and any justification based on natural rights must be squared with the inapplicability of that justification for IPRs in general. In the United States, there are, in addition, specific constitutional problems with recognizing IPRs in intangible cultural heritage.

Moreover, and putting aside for the moment questions like defamatory uses of sacred symbols and objects by outsiders, denying IPRs in intangibles associated with indigenous cultural heritages does not deprive those cultures of their own continued use of that knowledge. We must be careful to distinguish between physical cultural artifacts and intangible cultural property. It is one thing to take an archaeological artifact that represents an important part of a group's heritage and quite another simply to remember the design of the artifact and create a copy or derivative work based on it. As long as the new work is not attributed to the original group, how is indigenous culture harmed when an outsider takes a design and commodifies the work?

The failure to recognize that knowledge is not depleted by use can easily lead to misarticulation of claims and even to results that nobody, indigenous or otherwise, would likely seek. Some commentators seeking more protection for traditional knowledge seem to favor actions by indigenous groups to limit or deny patents in developed countries where the invention in question is based on folk knowledge that has long been available in traditional cultures elsewhere. But what purpose is served by denying patents in these cases? The traditional culture from which the knowledge derives may still make full traditional use of it. And if the knowledge is only the starting point for costly research to isolate, extract, and develop the active ingredient of a traditional herbal remedy into a useful product such as a drug, how can we be sure the investment will be made to engage in this research without the patent incentive? If patents are uniformly denied in these cases, valuable medical and other advances may well simply not be made at all. How can this possibly help the culture that was the original source for the knowledge? It seems that the real complaint in these situations is that the traditional culture often does not share in the profits from a product derived from their knowledge base. To the extent that complaint is based on fraudulent inducements to transfer the knowledge, breach of a confidential relationship, or even unequal knowledge or bargaining power, it is something that must be addressed. Simply arguing for denial of patent rights in developed countries does not do this.

In short, IPRs under patent and copyright are in the nature of exclusive property rights. They reward intellectual creativity and recognize the human creative spirit, but they are potent weapons. They can provide a necessary incentive for a flowering of new and valuable works, but when they are made too strong or too long, they can inhibit growth and diversity. There are better ways to handle the legitimate claims made on behalf of indigenous peoples seeking protection for their cultural heritages.

Given the fundamental inadequacy and contradiction of using IPRs to resolve indigenous concerns, it is necessary to look elsewhere for a solution to what is in a real sense a conflict of the traditional and the modern. This step also involves a more sophisticated appreciation of the various interests and perspectives within indigenous and other communities. Once the dilemma is conceded of choosing between a kind of protective freezing of indigenous culture and an opening up of it to new interpretations and market forces, then the opportunity arises to develop a fresh basis for the legal protection of indigenous culture. This task will not be a simple one, and it may take courts and legislatures many years to determine the form of such protection and its appropriate extent.

a. Contract, Privacy, Trade Secret, and Trademark Law

The preceding discussion shows that no existing legal regime, whether one directly creating IPRs like patent and copyright or others aimed more specifically at cultural property, appears capable of solving the perceived abuses of indigenous people's interests in their cultural heritages. Moreover, expanding the IPR regimes to cover such abuses would raise new practical problems and create even more fundamental conflicts between cultural heritage protection and the basic notions of free expression in democratic societies that are the underlying policy basis for the limitations we find in the current IPR regimes. It will therefore be helpful to turn our attention to a more modest approach that might be helpful in solving at least some of the problems associated with the perceived abuses while creating less tension with underlying IPR policies. This approach takes each of the identified problems, outlined in the foregoing, and tries to see how modest variations of current legal doctrine might achieve at least acceptable, if not perfect, results.

(i) Contract Law. The problem of taking indigenous people's information concerning the medicinal effects of a plant and developing it into a patented and popular drug by large pharmaceutical companies has, in fact, parallels that lie wholly outside the arena of cultural heritage protection. It is the basic problem that someone has an idea for, say, a movie script that he or she divulges in the hope of receiving some recompense if the idea is turned into a profitable film. The policy tensions are the same as well: our sense that justice requires some recompense to the supplier of a good inspiration for a film is tempered by the notion that ideas, at least in general, must remain free for the taking unless they fall squarely within one of the traditional categories of protection, such as copyright, patent, or trade secret.

An express contract specifying the idea communicated and stating the rights and duties of the parties will be enforceable, of course. The "idea person" can also rely to some extent on theories of an implied contract and quasi-contract claims, as well as claims for breach of a confidential relationship. There seems to be little reason in principle that indigenous peoples who are aware of Western norms of contract law could not similarly agree to condition their transfer of information on some degree of participation in any resulting profits, perhaps supplemented with approaches taken or borrowed from trademark that would allow indigenous people exclusive rights to use their name or other identifiers that the public comes to associate with quality in the product.

The problem with contract notions is that many indigenous peoples are presumably unaware both of their rights under Western contract law and of the commercial value of the information they are communicating. Although courts are sometimes willing to find an implied contract in the case of the idea person for a movie, based on industry custom, it is much more difficult conceptually to rely on implied contract in which one party to the supposed contract is essentially unaware of the underlying principle. Quasi-contract, an equitable notion of unjust enrichment related to breach of a confidential relationship, is another possible theory, especially when one party takes undue advantage through unfair conduct, such as a breach of confidence or other reprehensible means of obtaining valuable information without compensation. However, it is heavily fact dependent, and in the case of indigenous communities, it may not be easy to prove exactly who said what to whom to establish the background for deeming the conduct unfair. Moreover, judges do not apply this theory uniformly even in the more established situation between the idea person and the entertainment industry user. The theory also contains no built-in limitations to resolve the apparent contradiction that the claimant seeks compensation for something, an idea, that fundamental property law principles leave free for the taking.

Notwithstanding numerous problems surrounding the protection of information flowing from indigenous peoples' cultural heritage, the various contract theories outlined herein do hold at least some theoretical promise for the assertion of claims based on subsequent profitability arising from information taken from an indigenous group. The apparent contradiction between ideas as free-for-all property and compensation to the group supplying the information can be resolved by treating the disclosure of the information as a service that, in fairness, should be paid for, especially when it results in a highly profitable product. This could be effected by courts directly, but that is not always a coherent process.

A statutory solution along these same lines would likely be preferable, provided that the statute is carefully tailored to limit compensation to circumstances in which the disclosure of information is an important service to a commercial activity. The law should probably defer to express contracts between the parties when they are made from roughly equal bargaining positions, but it could supply default rules concerning liability for compensation where no express or implied contract exists. The key feature of such a statute would be its definition of the groups with respect to which the law would presume, absent fair bargaining, a right to compensation for knowledge transferred that is later developed into a commercial product. A statute of this sort could resolve a commonly cited problem involved in taking the cultural heritage of indigenous peoples without raising any of the fundamental difficulties that would result from using traditional IPRs to achieve the desired goal.

(ii) Privacy and Trade Secret. Fairness dictates that some sort of legal protection would be appropriate when symbols or rituals that the peoples treat as sacred are publicized against their will. Applying modern technology to gain access for recording such works, such as filming a sacred dance from an airplane, is a standard example. Acts of this type are analogous to invasions of privacy, where the privacy in question is that of the group rather than any particular individual. Trade secret law is another branch of Western law that comes close to addressing the core problem. Trade secret law does not afford full-scale property rights like patent and copyright, but it does seek to protect valuable business information that has been conveyed in confidence to employees and others for the purposes of carrying out the business of an enterprise. A general requirement of trade secret law is that the information must have commercial value in a business, which means that it cannot be applied directly to sacred symbols and rituals. Again, however, a modest statutory approach might be effective that is modeled on trade secret law and aimed, as in the case for contracts, at symbols and rituals that people legitimately seek to maintain in private. The statute could, perhaps, continue to apply even after the information is once wrongfully disclosed to the public. The goal here is different from that of trade secret, because it is not so much knowledge of the information that the group wishes to confine but rather the use of that knowledge outside the sacred circumstances for which it is intended. The aim is a mixture of trade secret and privacy notions.

(iii) Trademark. Trademark law is often included in the intellectual property constellation, but, like trade secret law, it does not afford the full-fledged property rights that cause so many problems in using IPRs to right some of the perceived wrongs in the use by outsiders of intangibles taken from the cultural heritage of indigenous peoples. At its core, trademark law protects the investment of a commercial operation in names or symbols that identify a commercial product as coming from that source. Any member of the public who prefers to buy from A and not from B will be able rapidly and easily to do so simply by noting A's mark on the product, which B is prohibited from using. Thus, trademark law helps assure consumers of authenticity as to the source of particular products.

Authenticity has already been recognized as an important tool in the protection of intangible goods as well as moral rights. Just as a very good copy of a Rembrandt or a van Gogh, even one indistinguishable to all but the most highly trained eye, will sell for only a tiny fraction of the original, purchasers of copies of artistic works purporting to come from a particular cultural heritage often want authentic products and not simply products that look very much the same even though made by outsiders. The notion of certification marks to assure the consuming public that a product originates where the mark says it originates is not at all new to Western law. It is now a major feature of international trade law, where TRIPs now requires members to prevent the use of false indications of the geographic region from which a product originates. Where traditional trademark law proves insufficient, a modest statutory provision along the lines of the TRIPs agreement – aimed to identify the kinds of groups that legitimately could claim certification rights to protect them as the source of products attributed to the group – would seem possible without resorting to the blunderbuss approach of applying IPRs to the problem. U.S. law has already made a step in this direction with the Indian Arts and Crafts Act of 1990, which is discussed in Chapter 4. It provides for criminal penalties and authorizes civil actions against persons who offer or sell goods "in a manner that falsely suggests it is Indian produced, an Indian product, or the product of a particular Indian or Indian tribe or Indian arts and crafts organization." In 1996 the Department of the Interior published regulations defining the nature and Indian origin of products protected by the statute from false representations and specifying how the Indian Arts and Crafts Board would interpret certain conduct for enforcement purposes.

b. Cultural Heritage Rights in Domestic Law

The concerns of indigenous peoples about effective legal recognition and protection of their intangible cultural heritage often overlap with demands for sovereignty or self-government. These broader pressures have led to new legal frameworks allowing for the recognition of expanded indigenous rights (including sovereignty over land and natural resources). This has been the pattern in countries such as Australia, Canada, and New Zealand. As these broader based rights regimes expand, they may include, or at least give room for, cultural heritage protection. It is not possible to explore these trends in any detail here because they depend on individual national situations. What can be said, however, is that any cultural heritage protection developed in this manner will require carefully crafted legislation or incremental judicial definition.

New cultural heritage protection for indigenous culture may not necessarily be proprietary in nature. Instead, it may recognize that cultural rights are a separate category of rights with their own unique characteristics. Given the inevitable comparison of such rights with IPRs, questions may arise regarding the appropriate basis for limits on such rights. Just as IPRs are qualified by the concept of the public domain, cultural heritage rights are compromised by competing interests in appropriate instances. One methodology for accommodating such pressures might be to place the onus for establishing justifiable exceptions on those seeking to rely on them. Because the appropriation of accessible intangible culture is less likely to cause harm to source communities than commodification of cultural heritage, it may justify commensurately less legal protection. While much will depend on individual national characteristics, the scope of legislation or even incrementally developed judicial definition of cultural heritage rights must involve a careful balance between the legitimate interests of source communities to maintain a degree of control over their cultural heritage and the legitimate concerns of global society as a whole to maintain a rich and growing public domain that promotes basic values of free thought and expression in all individuals.

Any rules in respect of intangible property will always present difficulties for lawyers and judges. The whole IPR system in Western law was a response to the complexity of industrialization and, now, postindustrialization. Accommodating concerns of a noneconomic nature in relation to the characteristics of different cultures is likely to be no less simple. Legal theories such as the civil law concept, *choses hors commerce* – things outside of commerce – as well as contract and unfair competition furnish useful precedent, or at least bases for the creation of statutory solutions that are general in scope but do not carry with them the many problems that would result from application of an IPR regime. The development of cultural heritage rights along these lines will need to recognize the unique character and legitimacy of the rights to be protected. Both statutory and judicial common law solutions will have to recognize the special character of cultural heritage rights, especially that commercial value will not always, or indeed often, be at the core of a legitimate claim. Cultural heritage rights claimants will need to rely on judicial deference to religious or indigenous beliefs and practices. The challenge for courts will be to differentiate between legitimate and illegitimate statements of such beliefs and practices and to afford legal protection that accommodates respect for the past with the pressures of the present.

The dilemma indigenous people face is that the characteristics of their culture require them to make demands that may be attacked as special treatment or privileges. If they refrain from making such claims, however, they face the impairment of the very culture that defines them as indigenous peoples in the first place. The answer to this problem seems to be to seek or create legal rights that meaningfully apply to the perceived abuses of indigenous peoples' cultural heritage but that also apply, at least in principle, to anyone, whether or not indigenous, who can satisfy the requirements flowing from the rights. Rights in cultural heritage that are developed on this basis will have enhanced credibility and compatibility with existing property rights and liability systems. The existence of a civil law category of *choses hors commerce*, as well as common law notions of contract and unfair competition or trademark, is evidence that such rights need not be seen as novel or discriminatory in character.

The net result of this complex approach will not be the recognition of all the claims that have been asserted on behalf of indigenous peoples. Direct use of indigenous artistic designs without attribution is legitimately analogous to a trademark issue, but the creation of derivative works based on public domain indigenous designs, absent false attribution, is not. Just as indigenous artists can adapt techniques and styles from outside their group and incorporate them into new designs based on their cultural heritage without harming artistic traditions outside their group, indigenous culture is not harmed when an outsider takes one of its publicly known designs and commodifies it, assuming no misattribution or other misfeasances. Where privacy and confidentiality are legitimately present, there is nothing in the Western legal tradition antithetical to protection carefully tailored to these concerns. However, where knowledge of old works no longer protected by copyright is publicly available, the creation of new exclusive rights somehow restricting the use of those designs, and all designs based on them, to a single group is fundamentally antithetical to basic notions of free expression and the overall dissemination and development of culture. In the end, indigenous cultural tradition may have to give way to the modern creative spirit.

NOTES AND QUESTIONS

1. Do you agree that extending IPRs to afford protection for the intangible culture heritage of indigenous peoples raises serious, perhaps intractable, problems in relation to the protection of freedom of speech and expression?
2. Is there validity in the argument that recognition of cultural rights on the part of traditional knowledge holders might give rise to pressure from interest groups to extend existing IPR protection such as copyright?
3. Do you think that the development of specialized modes of legal protection for traditional knowledge might have the unforeseen result of stifling the development of existing traditional cultures? Should there be some limits on the forms that specialized protection might take, such as term limitations. If so, what factors should be determinative?

4. In February 2009, as part of the settlement of a Waitangi Treaty claim by the Ngati Toa Rangatira (Maori tribal chiefs), the New Zealand government agreed to acknowledge the tribe's authorship and the significance of the haka. The Ka Mate haka is a world-famous Maori dance ceremony usually associated with its pregame performance by the New Zealand All Blacks rugby team. The settlement agreement did not express any redress in the form of royalties for the use of the dance or even any right on the part of the tribe to veto its use. There were reports that several earlier attempts to trademark the dance had failed.

   The limits of any attempt to prevent what could be seen as culturally inappropriate use of the dance immediately became clear when objections were raised to the incorporation of a version of the dance in a contemporary English production of *The Taming of the Shrew* by the Royal Shakespeare Company. See *All Black's Haka Challenge Gets Protection*, INT'L HERALD TRIB., Feb. 11, 2009. The avoidance by the Ngati Toa treaty settlement of any meaningful attempt to give effective legal protection to the haka is striking evidence of how difficult it is to afford legal protection to indigenous culture that has long been in the public domain.
5. Some legal systems ban so-called hate speech to protect vulnerable minorities such as gays and ethnic minorities. Is this a better, though more general, limitation on free expression of indigenous heritage than trying to carve out some form of selective protection for the cultural sensitivities of indigenous peoples? Or do indigenous peoples possess sufficiently differentiated cultural characteristics that would call for special protection under a rights-based approach?
6. The discussion on the limits of intellectual property laws was drawn from Robert K. Paterson & Dennis S. Karjala, *Looking beyond Intellectual Property in Resolving Protection of the Intangible Cultural Heritage of Indigenous Peoples*, 11 CARDOZO J. INT'L & COMP. L. 633 (2003).

E. *Sui Generis* Protection

Sui generis protection is extremely diverse in its manifestation and remains elusive in the absence of any comprehensive legal framework. Its main defining characteristic is that it seeks to afford legal protection to traditional knowledge outside traditional legal rules (principally IPRs). Since a 1971 amendment, the Berne Convention has explicitly authorized the adoption by signatories of *sui generis* protection. The WIPO has also produced a comprehensive survey of national *sui generis* protection. *See* World Intellectual Property Organization, Intergovernmental Committee on Intellectual Property and Genetic Resources, Traditional Knowledge and Folklore, *Comparative Summary of Sui Generis Legislation for the Protection of Traditional Cultural Expressions*, WIPO/GRTKF/IC/5/INF/3 (Geneva: WIPO, 2003) [hereinafter Comparative Summary].

There have been a number of efforts to create model laws with a *sui generis* approach. *See*, in particular, the Tunis Model Law on Copyright for Developing Countries (1976), the WIPO-UNESCO Model Provisions for National Laws on the Protection of Expressions of Folklore against Illicit Exploitation and Other Prejudicial Actions (1982), and the Pacific Regional Framework for the Protection of Traditional Knowledge and Expressions of Culture (2002). The WIPO Intergovernmental Committee on Intellectual Property and Genetic Resources, Traditional Knowledge and Folklore has prepared a summary of existing *sui generis* measures and laws for the protection of traditional knowledge. See Comparative Summary.

Under the Convention on Biological Diversity, the Working Group on article 8(j) of the Convention has described the purpose of *sui generis* protection of traditional knowledge as follows:

> 5. The overall purpose of *sui generis* system could be to put in place a set of measures that would respect, [and] preserve the knowledge, innovations and practices of indigenous and local communities embodying traditional lifestyles relevant for the conservation and sustainable use of biological diversity (hereinafter referred to as "traditional knowledge") and to ensure that they derive fair and equitable benefits from its utilization and that such utilization is based on their prior informed consent.
> 6. More particularly, *sui generis* systems could provide the means for indigenous and local communities to:
>   (a) Control access to, disclosure and use of traditional knowledge;
>   (b) Exercise the right to require prior informed consent for any access to or disclosure and use of traditional knowledge;
>   (c) Ensure that they derive fair and equitable benefits from the wider application of their traditional knowledge, innovations and practices;
>   (d) Ensure continued customary use of traditional knowledge, innovations and practices and avoid negative effects thereon.
> 7. *Sui generis* systems could provide safeguards against claims of third parties to intellectual property rights over traditional knowledge. Exceptions to this general protection would be clearly defined and any consent to use would follow principles of prior informed consent, benefit sharing and other principles of customary law of the affected communities. The safeguarding of knowledge from intellectual property claims from third parties could extend to protection against unauthorized disclosure, culturally offensive or unauthorized use of traditional knowledge.
> 8. *Sui generis* systems could also promote a clear, transparent and effective system of traditional knowledge protection, which increases legal certainty and predictability to the benefit not only of knowledge holders, but also of society as a whole, including firms and research institutions, who are potential partners of knowledge holders. By promoting such transparency and efficiency, *sui generis* systems would aim to lower transaction costs for local and indigenous communities for protecting their traditional knowledge or for those using it for commercial or non-commercial purposes.
> 9. Economic development and poverty alleviation are also both possible subsidiary purposes of *sui generis* systems. In particular, a system could work to increase access to capital for indigenous and local communities, thus facilitating the establishment of commercial ventures within traditional communities. While promoting economic development, if they so choose, *sui generis* systems would need to carefully balance the goal of

protection of traditional knowledge as against the goal of promotion of use.

10. Finally, given the holistic nature of traditional knowledge and the need to respect its cultural context, *sui generis* systems should not require the separation and isolation of the different elements of traditional knowledge, but rather take a systematic and comprehensive approach.

F. Comparative Approaches to Protection

In the absence of international norms to provide significant protection for the intangible cultural heritage, individual countries have developed *ad hoc* initiatives to afford such protection on a localized basis. These developments have often been of international interest, but they have been largely shaped by political, legal, and policy factors peculiar to individual countries. Even so, they can provide models for adoption outside the countries of origin. Some selected examples follow.

1. United States: Nonregistrable Subject Matter under the Lanham Trademark Act

In the United States, the Lanham Trademark Act, 15 U.S.C. § 1052, provides that the U.S. Patent and Trademark Office (PTO) must deny registration to marks that, among other things, "may disparage or falsely suggest a connection with persons, living or dead, institutions, beliefs or national symbols, or bring them into contempt, or disrepute." Section 1064(3) provides that if a mark is registered in violation of section 1052, any person who believes he or she is or will be damaged by the registration may petition to cancel it. These provisions were the subject of a petition by seven Native Americans to cancel the registration of six trademarks that included the word "Redskin." The trademarks were owned by Pro-Football, Inc., the owner of the Washington Redskins football team.

Harjo v. Pro-Football, Inc., 50 U.S.P.Q.2d 1705 (1999)

The Pleadings

Petitioners allege that they are Native American persons and enrolled members of federally recognized Indian tribes. As grounds for cancellation, petitioners assert that the word "redskin(s)" or a form of that word appears in the mark in each of the registrations sought to be canceled; that the word "redskin(s)" "was and is a pejorative, derogatory, denigrating, offensive, scandalous, contemptuous, disreputable, disparaging and racist designation for a Native American person"; that the marks . . . "also include additional matter that, in the context used by registrant, is offensive, disparaging and scandalous"; and that registrant's use of the marks in the identified registrations "offends" petitioners and other Native

Americans. Petitioners assert, further, that the marks in the identified registrations "consist of or comprise matter which disparages Native American persons, and brings them into contempt, ridicule, and disrepute" and "consist of or comprise scandalous matter"; and that, therefore, under Section 2(a) of the Trademark Act, the identified registrations should be canceled.

Respondent, in its answer, denies the salient allegations of the petition to cancel and asserts that "through long, substantial and widespread use, advertising and promotion in support thereof and media coverage, said marks have acquired a strong secondary meaning identifying the entertainment services provided by respondent in the form of professional games in the National Football League"; and that "the marks sought to be canceled herein cannot reasonably be understood to refer to the Petitioners or to any of the groups or organizations to which they belong [as] the marks refer to the Washington Redskins football team which is owned by Respondent and thus cannot be interpreted as disparaging any of the Petitioners or as bringing them into contempt or disrepute."

Summary of the Arguments of the Parties

Petitioners state that the issues in this cancellation proceeding are whether petitioners have standing to file these petitions to cancel and whether, at the time respondent's registrations issued, the registered marks consisted of or comprised scandalous matter, or matter which may disparage Native Americans, or matter which may bring Native Americans into contempt or disrepute.

Petitioners contend that the subject registrations are *void ab initio* and that the word "redskin(s)" "is today and always has been a deeply offensive, humiliating, and degrading racial slur." Petitioners contend that "a substantial composite of the general public considers 'redskin(s)' to be offensive" and that "the inherent nature of the word 'redskin(s)' and Respondent's use of [its marks involved herein] perpetuate the devastating and harmful effects of negative ethnic stereotyping." Petitioners contend, further, that Native Americans "have understood and still understand" the word "redskin(s)" to be a disparaging "racial epithet" that brings them into contempt, ridicule and disrepute.

Petitioners contend that the Board must consider "the historical setting in which the word 'redskin(s)' has been used." In this regard, petitioners allege that "the history of the relationship between Euro-Americans and Native Americans in the United States has generally been one of conflict and domination by the Euro-Americans"; that "[b]eneath this socioeconomic system lay an important cultural belief, namely, that Indians were 'savages' who must be separated from the Anglo-American colonies and that Anglo-American expansion would come at the expense of Native Americans"; that, in the 1930s, government policies towards Native Americans began to be more respectful of Native American culture; that, however, these policies were not reflected in the activities and attitudes of the general public, who continued to view and portray Native Americans as "simple 'savages' whose culture was treated mainly as a source of amusement for white culture"; and that it was during this time that respondent first adopted the name "Redskins" for its football team.

. . .

Petitioners allege the following:

The term "redskin(s)" rarely appears in formal writing, such as judicial decisions, scholarly dissertations, government documents, or papers of diplomacy, where such terms as 'uncivilized' and 'savages' frequently appeared. The term has been reserved for informal writing as a slur of the most demeaning sort and as an epithet to influence the sensibilities of the general public. American newspapers . . . reveal vivid examples of the offensive and disparaging use of "redskin(s)" as a term associated with violence, savagery, racial inferiority, and other negative ethnic stereotypes.

Petitioners argue that the frequency with which the word "redskin(s)" appears in the context of savagery, violence and oppression is explained by the negative connotation of that word which is not conveyed by such terms as "Indian," "Native American," or "American Indian"; and that the repeated appearance of "redskin(s)" in this context reinforces its derogatory character. Petitioners' evidence in this regard includes newspaper articles, film excerpts, dictionaries and encyclopedias. Petitioners' linguistics expert, Dr. Nunberg, testified, *inter alia*, that "lexicographers consider[ed] the word 'redskin' from the '60s onward as a disparaging word which is variously labeled contemptuous, offensive, disparaging"; and that newspaper writers avoid using the word "redskin(s)," not because it is "too informal for use, even in the popular press," but because it is "a loaded pejorative term."

Petitioners contend that sports team names are chosen to reflect the team's location or to sound "fierce . . . so as, in a symbolic way, to strike fear into the hearts of opponents." Petitioners' expert witness, Dr. Nunberg, states that "Redskins," as part of respondent's team's name, falls into the latter category and is intended to "evoke the sense of an implacable and ferocious foe"; that this association derives from the otherwise negative connotations of savagery and violence attributable to the word "redskin(s)"; and that the word "redskin(s)" as it appears in the team name "Washington Redskins" has not acquired "a meaning that somehow is divorced from or independent of its use in referring to Native Americans."

. . .

Respondent contends that the word "redskin(s)" has throughout history, been a purely denotative term, used interchangeably with 'Indian.'" In this regard, respondent argues that "redskin(s)" is "an entirely neutral and ordinary term of reference" from the relevant time period to the present; and that, as such, "redskin(s)" is "[synonymous] with ethnic identifiers such as 'American Indian,' 'Indian,' and 'Native American.'" Respondent also states that, through its long and extensive use of "Redskins" in connection with professional football, the word has developed a meaning, "separate and distinct from the core, ethnic meaning" of the word "redskin(s)," denoting the "Washington Redskins" football team; and that such use by respondent "has absolutely no negative effect on the word's neutrality – and, indeed, serves to enhance the word's already positive associations – as football is neither of questionable morality nor *per se* offensive to or prohibited by American Indian religious or cultural practices."

Respondent states that while "the term 'redskin,' used in singular, lower case form references an ethnic group, [this] does not automatically render it disparaging when employed as a proper noun in the context of sports."

In response to petitioners' contentions, respondent argues that while "'redskin' may be employed in connection with warfare, [this] is but a reflection of the troubled history of American Indians, not of any negative connotation inherent in the term itself." Respondent argues that "'redskin' is not always employed in connection with violence"; that, when "redskin" appears in a violent context, the neutrality of the word "redskin" is apparent from the fact that, as it appears in the evidence of record, the word "Indian" or "Native American" can be substituted therefor without any change in meaning; and, further, that it is often the negative adjective added to this neutral term that renders the entire phrase pejorative.

Respondent contends, further, that its evidence establishes that Native Americans support respondent's use of the name "Washington Redskins"; and that Native Americans "regularly employ the term 'redskin' within their communities."

Respondent concludes that its marks "do not rise to the level of crudeness and vulgarity that the Board has required before deeming the marks scandalous," nor do its marks disparage or bring Native Americans into contempt or disrepute. Respondent argues that disparagement requires intent on the part of the speaker and that its "intent in adopting the team name was entirely positive" as the team name has, over its history, "reflected positive attributes of the American Indian such as dedication, courage and pride." Similarly, respondent notes that third-party registrations portraying Native Americans and the United States nickel, previously in circulation for many years, portraying a Native American are similar to respondent's "respectful depiction in the team's logo"; and that petitioners have not established that this logo is scandalous, disparaging, or brings Native Americans into contempt or disrepute.

Section 2(a)

The relevant portions of Section 2 of the Trademark Act provide as follows:

No trademark by which the goods of the applicant may be distinguished from the goods of others shall be refused registration on the principal register on account of its nature unless it –

(a) Consists of or comprises immoral, deceptive, or scandalous matter; or matter which may disparage or falsely suggest a connection with persons, living or dead, institutions, beliefs, or national symbols, or bring them into contempt, or disrepute;

Scandalous Matter

The vast majority of the relevant reported cases involving that part of Section 2(a) with which we are concerned in this case were decided principally on the basis of whether the marks consisted of scandalous matter. We begin with a review of this precedent.

Faced with a "paucity of legislative history," to aid in interpreting the term "scandalous" in Section 2(a), one of the predecessor courts of our primary reviewing court found that it must look to the "ordinary and common meaning" of that term, which meaning could be established by reference to court and Board decisions, and to dictionary definitions. In particular, the Court looked to dictionary definitions extant at the time of the enactment of the Trademark Act in 1946, and noted that "scandalous" was defined as "'Giving offense to the conscience or moral feelings; exciting reprobation, calling out condemnation.... Disgraceful to reputation... ' [and] 'shocking to the sense of truth, decency, or propriety; disgraceful, offensive; disreputable, as *scandalous* conduct.'" In a case predating the Trademark Act of 1946, the Court had looked to similar dictionary definitions of "scandalous," and concluded that the use of the mark MADONNA upon wine which is not limited to a religious use was "scandalous" under the relevant provision of the 1905 Trademark Act.

...

Disparagement

As stated previously herein, our analysis is essentially a two-step process in which we ask, first: What is the meaning of the matter in question, as it appears in the marks and as those marks are used in connection with the services identified in the registrations? Second, we ask: Is this meaning one that may disparage Native Americans? As previously stated, both questions are to be answered *as of the dates of registration of the marks herein.*

...

1. Meaning of the Matter in Question

We agree that there is a substantial amount of evidence in the record establishing that, since at least the 1960s and continuing to the present, the term "Redskins" has been used widely in print and other media to identify respondent's professional football team and its entertainment services. But our inquiry does not stop here. Our precedent also requires us to consider the manner in which respondent's marks appear and are used in the marketplace. In this regard, while petitioners concede that, from at least the 1960s to the present, the word "Redskins," in the context of professional sports, identifies respondent's football team, petitioners contend, essentially, that all professional football teams have themes that are carried through in their logos, mascots, nicknames, uniforms and various paraphernalia sold or used in connection with their entertainment services. Petitioners point to the Native American theme evident in respondent's logos and the imagery and themes used by respondent in connection with its football team and games. This imagery is also evident in the writings and activities of the media and in the activities and writings of the team's fans. Petitioners contend that, in view of the team's Native American theme, one cannot separate the connotation of " redskin(s)" as a reference to Native Americans from the connotation of that word as it identifies respondent's football team and is used in connection with respondent's entertainment services.

[7] Respondent correctly notes that the evidence herein establishes that the vast majority of uses of the word "redskin(s)" in the press and other media, since at least the 1960s, refer to respondent's professional football team, rather than to Native Americans. At the same time, we find that, in determining the meaning of the term "redskin(s)" as it appears in respondent's registered marks, it would be both factually incomplete and disingenuous to ignore the substantial evidence of Native American imagery used by respondent, as well as by the media and respondent's fans, in connection with respondent's football team and its entertainment services. Respondent admits that it "does not claim that its marks bear no association with American Indians, nor that when the team name was *first adopted* in 1933 it connoted anything other than an ethnic group." However, the evidence simply does not support respondent's further contention that, in view of its use since 1933, the meaning of the word "Redskins," as part of its registered marks, is as "a purely denotative term of reference for the professional football team [with] no connotative meaning whatsoever." As used by respondent in connection with its professional football team and entertainment services, the word "Redskins," as it appears in the marks herein, clearly carries the allusion to Native Americans.

Two of the registered marks include a portrait that respondent acknowledges is a profile of a Native American and a spear that we presume is a Native American spear. We believe these two elements reinforce the allusion to Native Americans that is present in the word "Redskins" in both marks. Because of the manner of use of respondent's marks in connection with Native American themes and imagery, as discussed herein, this same allusion is also present in the marks that include the word "Washington," to indicate the full name of the football team, *i.e.*, "Washington Redskins." Further, the registered mark, REDSKINETTES, clearly consists of the root word "redskin" with the diminutive or feminine "ettes" added as a suffix. Thus, our conclusions regarding the word "Redskins" are equally applicable to the mark REDSKINETTES.

We note that, in considering the meaning of the matter in question, respondent misunderstands the issue when it states, in reaction to newspaper headlines in the record, such as "Skins Scalp Giants, 23–7," that "no Redskins fan truly believes that the players huddled on the ten yard line are in fact tribal bounty hunters primed to scalp their opponents upon scoring a touchdown." Clearly, the connection being made between the quoted headline and respondent's football team by the media, fans, and respondent itself is metaphorical rather than literal, as acknowledged by respondent's written statement . . . that states in part, "Over the long history of the Washington Redskins, the name has reflected positive attributes of the American Indian such as dedication, courage and pride."

This is not a case where, through usage, the word "redskin(s)" has lost its meaning, in the field of professional football, as a reference to Native Americans in favor of an entirely independent meaning as the name of a professional football team. Rather, when considered in relation to the other matter comprising at least two of the subject marks and as used in connection with respondent's services, "Redskins" clearly both refers to respondent's professional football team and carries the allusion to Native Americans inherent in the original definition of that word. This conclusion is equally applicable to the time periods encompassing 1967, 1974, 1978 and 1990, as well as to the present time.

2. Whether the Matter in Question May Disparage Native Americans.

We turn, now, to the second part of our analysis, the question of whether the matter in question may disparage Native Americans. We have found that, as an element of respondent's marks and as used in connection with respondent's services, the word "redskin(s)" retains its meaning as a reference to Native Americans, as do the graphics" of the spear and the Native American portrait. In view thereof, we consider the question of whether this matter may disparage Native Americans by reference to the perceptions of Native Americans. Our standard, as enunciated herein, is whether, as of the relevant times, a substantial composite of Native Americans in the United States so perceive the subject matter in question. In rendering our opinion, we consider the broad range of evidence in this record as relevant to this question either directly or by inference.

Several of petitioners' witnesses expressed their opinions that the use of Native American references or imagery by non-Native Americans is, essentially, *per se* disparaging to Native Americans or, at the very least, that the use of Native American references or imagery in connection with football is *per se* disparaging to Native Americans. We find no support in the record for either of these views. Consequently, we answer the question of disparagement based on the facts in this case by looking to the evidence regarding the views of the relevant group, the connotations of the subject matter in question, the relationship between that matter and the other elements that make up the marks, and the manner in which the marks appear and are used in the marketplace.

We find petitioners have clearly established, by at least a preponderance of the evidence, that, as of the dates the challenged registrations issued, the word "redskin(s)," as it appears in respondent's marks in those registrations and as used in connection with the identified services, may disparage Native Americans, as perceived by a substantial composite of Native Americans.

In particular, we find that, based on the record in this case, petitioners have not established by a preponderance of the evidence that the marks in respondent's challenged registrations consist of or comprise scandalous matter. We find that the evidence, as discussed above, *does* establish that, during the relevant time periods, a substantial composite of the general population would find the word "redskin(s)," as it appears in the marks herein in connection with the identified services, to be a derogatory term of reference for Native Americans. But the evidence *does not* establish that, during the relevant time periods, the appearance of the word "redskin(s)," in the marks herein and in connection with the identified services, would be "shocking to the sense of truth, decency, or propriety" to, or "giv[e] offense to the conscience or moral feelings [of,] excit[e] reprobation, [or] call out for condemnation" by, a substantial composite of the general population.

. . .

Decision: As to each of the registrations subject to the petition to cancel herein, the petition to cancel under Section 2(a) of the Act is granted on the grounds that the subject marks may disparage Native Americans and may bring them into contempt or disrepute. As to each of the registrations subject to the petition to cancel herein, the petition to cancel under Section 2(a) of the Act is denied on the ground that the subject marks consist of or comprise scandalous matter. The registrations will be canceled in due course.

NOTES

1. After the decision of the Trademark Trial and Appeal Board (TTAP), the owner appealed to the U.S. District Court for the District of Columbia, which overturned the board's cancellation of the trademark, partly on the ground that the TTAP lacked substantial evidence to find disparagement. The Native Americans then appealed to the U.S. Court of Appeals for the District of Columbia, which remanded the case to the District Court on a procedural matter. *Pro-Football, Inc. v. Harjo*, 415 F.3d 44 (D.C. Cir. 2005). Eventually, the U.S. Supreme Court denied certiorari, 130 S.Ct. 631 (2009) (mem.).
2. Tribes and tribal members sometimes support American Indian mascot and logos as, for example, the Florida State University Seminoles and University of North Dakota Fighting Sioux. On the legal and other aspects of the "Fighting Sioux" mascot and logo, which have divided Native Americans, see Monica Davey, *In Twist, Tribe Fights for College Nickname*, N.Y. Times, Dec. 9, 2009, at A16.
3. A member of the Oklahoma Choctaw Nation has suggested that an alternative to the comprehensive prohibition on Indian mascot usage advocated by the U.S. Commission on Civil Rights might be to allow tribes to treat their identities

as cultural assets, which could then be licensed when culturally appropriate. See Galvin Clarkson, *Racial Imagery and Native Americans: A First Look at the Empirical Evidence behind the Indian Mascot Controversy*, 11 Cardozo J. Int'l & Comp. L. 393 (2003). See Note, *A Public Accommodations Challenge to the Use of Indian Team Names and Mascots in Professional Sports*, 112 Harv. L. Rev. 904 (1999) (advocating use of the Civil Rights Act of 1964 to challenge the use of Indian nicknames and mascots); Kimberly A. Pace, *The Washington Redskins Case and the Doctrine of Disparagement: How Politically Correct Must a Trademark Be?*, 22 Pepperdine L. Rev. 7 (1994); Ethan G. Zlotchew, *"Scandalous" or "Disparaging"? It* Should *Make a Difference in Opposition and Cancellation Actions: Views on the Lanham Act's Section 2(a) Prohibitions, Using the Example of Native American Symbolism in Athletics*, 22 Colum.-VLA J.L. & Arts 217 (1998).

4. An offensive mark might also be challenged as a violation of a privacy right so as to protect collective tribal identities. In *Estate of Tasunke Witko a/k/a Crazy Horse v. Hornell Brewing Co.*, 165 F. Supp. 2d 1092 (D.S.D. 2001), the plaintiff sued a brewer for using the name of Crazy Horse in connection with the sale of a malt liquor product. The case was settled out of court, but Congress then enacted a law banning the use of the name Crazy Horse. Subsequently, a New York federal court overturned the law on the basis of the brewer's right to free speech. See Molly Torser, *"Anonymous, Untitled, Mixed Media": Mixing Intellectual Property Law with Other Legal Philosophies to Protect Traditional Cultural Expressions*, 54 Am. J. Comp. L. 173, 194–95 (2006).

2. New Zealand: The Regulation of Offensive Marks under the Trade Marks Act 2002

New Zealand has been a fertile source for a variety of responses to pressures for changing laws and policies to address ongoing concerns about the level of protection of both the tangible and intangible facets of Maori culture. The 1993 Mataatua Declaration on the Cultural and Intellectual Property Rights of Indigenous Peoples highlighted the inadequacy of existing intellectual property rules and the need for new initiatives. One of the recommendations contained in the Declaration was that indigenous peoples should "define for themselves their own intellectual and cultural property." Two years earlier, six Maori tribes (*iwi*) had filed a claim with the country's Waitangi Tribunal, alleging that various New Zealand intellectual property laws violated the 1840 Treaty of Waitangi, which had marked the establishment of British sovereignty over New Zealand and purportedly guaranteed its Maori inhabitants certain basic rights. In 1975 the Waitangi Tribunal was established as a quasi-judicial body to make recommendations to the New Zealand government concerning allegations of Treaty violations. In 1982, for instance, the Tribunal concluded that the New Zealand government had not adequately protected the Maori language (*te reo Maori*), a decision that led to the recognition, by the Maori Language Act 1987, of Maori as an official New Zealand language. There is an important claim now pending before the Waitangi Tribunal that covers cultural and intellectual property rights relating to flora and fauna that are native to New Zealand. Known as the WAI 262 claim, it alleges, among other things, that the New Zealand government is in breach of the Treaty of Waitangi in entering into several international intellectual property agreements without first engaging in proper consultation with Maori.

In 2002 New Zealand enacted legislation dealing with offensive trademarks. The Trade Marks Act 2002 prevents trademarks from being registered if their registration or use is likely to be offensive to a significant section of the community, including the Maori. A person who claims to be "culturally aggrieved" can apply to have a registered mark declared invalid. Under the law, the Maori Trade Marks Advisory Committee has been established to advise the commissioner of trademarks on whether trademarks based on Maori text and imagery are likely to be considered offensive to the Maori. Members of the Committee must be qualified in Maori culture and protocols. See Owen Morgan, *Protecting Indigenous Signs and Trade Marks – The New Zealand Experiment,* 1 INTELL. PROP. Q.58 (2004). The 2002 law has been interpreted as a self-imposed restraint that the government imposed on itself in deference to Maori self-determination of its own imagery; see Graeme W. Austin, *Re-Treating Intellectual Property? The WAI 262 Proceeding and the Heuristics of Intellectual Property Law,* 11 CARDOZO J. INT'L & COMP. L. 333, 360 (2003).

3. Canada: The Recognition of Aboriginal Custom in Constitutional Law

The revised Canadian constitution that became effective in 1982 ushered in a series of Supreme Court of Canada decisions that explore the meaning of section 35(1) of the Constitution Act, 1982. That provision reads as follows: "The existing aboriginal and treaty rights of the aboriginal peoples of Canada are hereby recognized and affirmed." The Supreme Court of Canada has identified the steps needed to establish Aboriginal rights under section 35 and has developed criteria for claimants. One of the most important of its decisions, *Delgamuukw v. British Columbia,* comments on the *sui generis* nature of Aboriginal title in Canada and the admissibility of indigenous oral history in relation to establishing such title.

DELGAMUUKW v. BRITISH COLUMBIA, [1997] 3 S.C.R. 1010

[The Court, Chief Justice Lamer, Justices Cory and Major, and Justice McLachlan concurring, discussed the general features and content of Aboriginal title in Canadian common law.]

(a) General Features

112 The starting point of the Canadian jurisprudence on aboriginal title is the Privy Council's decision in *St. Catherine's Milling and Lumber Co. v. The Queen* (1888), 14 A.C. 46, which described aboriginal title as a "personal and usufructuary right" (at p. 54). The subsequent jurisprudence has attempted to grapple with this definition, and has in the process demonstrated that the Privy Council's choice of terminology is not particularly helpful to explain the various dimensions of aboriginal title. What the Privy Council sought to capture is that aboriginal title is a *sui generis* interest in land. Aboriginal title has been described as *sui generis* in order to distinguish it from "normal" proprietary interests, such as fee simple. However, as I will now develop, it is also *sui generis* in the sense that its characteristics cannot be completely explained by reference either to the common law

rules of real property or to the rules of property found in aboriginal legal systems. As with other aboriginal rights, it must be understood by reference to both common law and aboriginal perspectives.

113 The idea that aboriginal title is *sui generis* is the unifying principle underlying the various dimensions of that title. One dimension is its *inalienability*. Lands held pursuant to aboriginal title cannot be transferred, sold or surrendered to anyone other than the Crown and, as a result, is inalienable to third parties. This Court has taken pains to clarify that aboriginal title is only "personal" in this sense, and does not mean that aboriginal title is a non-proprietary interest which amounts to no more than a license to use and occupy the land and cannot compete on an equal footing with other proprietary interests: see *Canadian Pacific Ltd. v. Paul*, 1988 CanLII 104 (C.S.C.), [1988] 2 S.C.R. 654, at p. 677.

114 Another dimension of aboriginal title is its *source*. It had originally been thought that the source of aboriginal title in Canada was the *Royal Proclamation, 1763*: see *St. Catherine's Milling*. However, it is now clear that although aboriginal title was recognized by the *Proclamation*, it arises from the prior occupation of Canada by aboriginal peoples. That prior occupation, however, is relevant in two different ways, both of which illustrate the *sui generis* nature of aboriginal title. The first is the physical fact of occupation, which derives from the common law principle that occupation is proof of possession in law: see Kent McNeil, *Common Law Aboriginal Title* (1989), at p. 7. Thus, in *Guerin, supra*, Dickson J. described aboriginal title, at p. 376, as a "legal right derived from the Indians' historic occupation and possession of their tribal lands." What makes aboriginal title *sui generis* is that it arises from possession *before* the assertion of British sovereignty, whereas normal estates, like fee simple, arise afterward: see Kent McNeil, "The Meaning of Aboriginal Title", in Michael Asch, ed., *Aboriginal and Treaty Rights in Canada* (1997), 135, at p. 144. This idea has been further developed in *Roberts v. Canada*, 1989 CanLII 122 (S.C.C.), [1989] 1 S.C.R. 322, where this Court unanimously held at p. 340 that "aboriginal title pre-dated colonization by the British and survived British claims of sovereignty." . . . What this suggests is a second source for aboriginal title – the relationship between common law and pre-existing systems of aboriginal law.

115 A further dimension of aboriginal title is the fact that it is held *communally*. Aboriginal title cannot be held by individual aboriginal persons; it is a collective right to land held by all members of an aboriginal nation. Decisions with respect to that land are also made by that community. This is another feature of aboriginal title which is *sui generis* and distinguishes it from normal property interests.

(b) The Content of Aboriginal Title

116 Although cases involving aboriginal title have come before this Court and Privy Council before, there has never been a definitive statement from

either court on the *content* of aboriginal title. In *St. Catherine's Milling*, the Privy Council, as I have mentioned, described the aboriginal title as a "personal and usufructuary right", but declined to explain what that meant because it was not "necessary to express any opinion upon the point" (at p. 55). Similarly, in [other cases], the issues were the extinguishment of, the fiduciary duty arising from the surrender of, and statutory easements over land held pursuant to, aboriginal title, respectively; the content of title was not at issue and was not directly addressed.

117 Although the courts have been less than forthcoming, I have arrived at the conclusion that the content of aboriginal title can be summarized by two propositions: first, that aboriginal title encompasses the right to exclusive use and occupation of the land held pursuant to that title for a variety of purposes, which need not be aspects of those aboriginal practices, customs and traditions which are integral to distinctive aboriginal cultures; and second, that those protected uses must not be irreconcilable with the nature of the group's attachment to that land.

. . .

93 [Earlier in the opinion, the Court discussed the admissibility of indigenous oral history to establish aboriginal title, as follows:] The adaawk and kungax of the Gitksan and Wet'suwet'en nations, respectively, are oral histories of a special kind. They were described by the trial judge, at p. 164, as a "sacred 'official' litany, or history, or recital of the most important laws, history, traditions and traditional territory of a House." The content of these special oral histories includes its physical representation totem poles, crests and blankets. The importance of the adaawk and kungax is underlined by the fact that they are "repeated, performed and authenticated at important feasts" (at p. 164). At those feasts, dissenters have the opportunity to object if they question any detail and, in this way, help ensure the authenticity of the adaawk and kungax. Although they serve largely the same role, the trial judge found that there are some differences in both the form and content of the adaawk and the kungax. For example, the latter is "in the nature of a song . . . which is intended to represent the special authority and responsibilities of a chief. . . . " However, these differences are not legally relevant for the purposes of the issue at hand.

94 It is apparent that the adaawk and kungax are of integral importance to the distinctive cultures of the appellant nations. At trial, they were relied on for two distinct purposes. First, the adaawk was relied on as a component of and, therefore, as proof of the existence of a system of land tenure law internal to the Gitksan, which covered the whole territory claimed by that appellant. In other words, it was offered as evidence of the Gitksan's historical use and occupation of that territory. For the Wet'suwet'en, the kungax was offered as proof of the central significance of the claimed lands to their distinctive culture. As I shall explain later in these reasons, both use and occupation, and the central significance of the lands occupied, are relevant to proof of aboriginal title.

95 The admissibility of the adaawk and kungax was the subject of a general decision of the trial judge handed down during the course of the trial regarding the admissibility of all oral histories (incorrectly indexed as *Uukw v. R.*, reflex, [1987] 6 W.W.R. 155 (B.C.S.C.)). Although the trial judge recognized that the evidence at issue was a form of hearsay, he ruled it admissible on the basis of the recognized exception that declarations made by deceased persons could be given in evidence by witnesses as proof of public or general rights: see Michael N. Howard, Peter Crane and Daniel A. Hochberg, *Phipson on Evidence* (14th ed. 1990), at p. 736. He affirmed that earlier ruling in his trial judgment, correctly in my view, by stating, at p. 180, that the adaawk and kungax were admissible "out of necessity as exceptions to the hearsay rule" because there was no other way to prove the history of the Gitksan and Wet'suwet'en nations.

96 The trial judge, however, went on to give these oral histories no independent weight at all. He held, at p. 180, that they were only admissible as "direct evidence of facts in issue . . . in a few cases where they could constitute confirmatory proof of early presence in the territory." His central concern that the adaawk and kungax could not serve "as evidence of detailed history, or land ownership, use or occupation." I disagree with some of the reasons he relied on in support of this conclusion.

97 Although he had earlier recognized, when making his ruling on admissibility, that it was impossible to make an easy distinction between the mythological and "real" aspects of these oral histories, he discounted the adaawk and kungax because they were not "literally true," confounded "what is fact and what is belief," "included some material which might be classified as mythology," and projected a "romantic view" of the history of the appellants. He also cast doubt on the authenticity of these special oral histories (at p. 181) because, *inter alia*, "the verifying group is so small that they cannot safely be regarded as expressing the reputation of even the Indian community, let alone the larger community whose opportunity to dispute territorial claims would be essential to weigh." Finally, he questioned (at p. 181) the utility of the adaawk and kungax to demonstrate use and occupation because they were "seriously lacking in detail about the specific lands to which they are said to relate."

98 Although he framed his ruling on weight in terms of the specific oral histories before him, in my respectful opinion, the trial judge in reality based his decision on some general concerns with the use of oral histories as evidence in aboriginal rights cases. In summary, the trial judge gave no independent weight to these special oral histories because they did not accurately convey historical truth, because knowledge about those oral histories was confined to the communities whose histories they were and because those oral histories were insufficiently detailed. However, as I mentioned earlier, these are features, to a greater or lesser extent, of all oral histories, not just the adaawk and kungax. The implication of the

trial judge's reasoning is that oral histories should never be given any independent weight and are only useful as confirmatory evidence in aboriginal rights litigation. I fear that if this reasoning were followed, the oral histories of aboriginal peoples would be consistently and systematically undervalued by the Canadian legal system, in contradiction of the express instruction to the contrary in *Van der Peet* that trial courts interpret the evidence of aboriginal peoples in light of the difficulties inherent in adjudicating aboriginal claims.

(c) Recollections of Aboriginal Life

99 The trial judge also erred when he discounted the "recollections of aboriginal life" offered by various members of the appellant nations. I take that term to be a reference to testimony about personal and family history that is not part of an adaawk or a kungax. That evidence consisted of the personal knowledge of the witnesses and declarations of witnesses' ancestors as to land use. This history had been adduced by the appellants in order to establish the requisite degree of use and occupation to make out a claim to ownership and, for the same reason as the adaawk and kungax, is material to the proof of aboriginal title.

100 The trial judge limited the uses to which the evidence could be put. He reasoned, at p. 177, that this evidence, at most, established "without question, that the plaintiff's immediate ancestors, for the past 100 years or so" had used land in the claimed territory for aboriginal purposes. However, the evidence was insufficiently precise to demonstrate that the more distant ancestors of the witnesses had engaged in specific enough land use "far enough back in time to permit the plaintiffs to succeed on issues such as internal boundaries." In the language of *Van der Peet*, the trial judge effectively held that this evidence did not demonstrate the requisite continuity between present occupation and past occupation in order to ground a claim for aboriginal title.

101 In my opinion, the trial judge expected too much of the oral history of the appellants, as expressed in the recollections of aboriginal life of members of the appellant nations. He expected that evidence to provide definitive and precise evidence of pre-contact aboriginal activities on the territory in question. However, as I held in *Van der Peet*, this will be almost an impossible burden to meet. Rather, if oral history cannot conclusively establish pre-sovereignty (after this decision) occupation of land, it may still be relevant to demonstrate that current occupation has its origins prior to sovereignty. This is exactly what the appellants sought to do.

(d) Territorial Affidavits

102 Finally, the trial judge also erred in his treatment of the territorial affidavits filed by the appellant chiefs. Those affidavits were declarations of the territorial holdings of each of the Gitksan and Wet'suwet'en houses

and, at trial, were introduced for the purposes of establishing each House's ownership of its specific territory. Before this Court, the appellants tried to amalgamate these individual claims into collective claims on behalf of each nation and the relevance of the affidavits changed accordingly. I have already held that it is not open to the appellants to alter fundamentally the nature of their claim in this way on appeal. Nevertheless, the treatment of the affidavits is important because they will be relevant at a new trial to the existence and nature of the land tenure system within each nation and, therefore, material to the proof of title.

103 The affidavits rely heavily on the declarations of deceased persons of use or ownership of the lands, which are a form of oral history. But those declarations are a kind of hearsay and the appellants therefore argued that the affidavits should be admitted through the reputation exception to the hearsay rule. Although he recognized, at p. 438, that the territorial affidavits were "the best evidence [the appellants] could adduce on this question of internal boundaries," the trial judge held that this exception did not apply and refused to admit the declarations contained in the affidavits.

104 I am concerned by the specific reasons the trial judge gave for refusing to apply the reputation exception. He questioned the degree to which the declarations amounted to a reputation because they were largely confined to the appellants' communities. The trial judge asserted that neighbouring aboriginal groups whose territorial claims conflicted with those of the appellants, as well as non-aboriginals who potentially possessed a legal interest in the claimed territory, were unaware of the content of the alleged reputation at all. Furthermore, the trial judge reasoned that since the subject-matter of the affidavits was disputed, its reliability was doubtful. Finally, the trial judge questioned, at p. 441, "the independence and objectivity" of the information contained in the affidavits, because the appellants and their ancestors (at p. 440) "have been actively discussing land claims for many years."

105 Although he regretted this finding, the trial judge felt bound to apply the rules of evidence because it did not appear to him (at p. 442) "that the Supreme Court of Canada has decided that the ordinary rules of evidence do not apply to this kind of case." The trial judge arrived at this conclusion, however, without the benefit of *Van der Peet*, where I held that the ordinary rules of evidence must be approached and adapted in light of the evidentiary difficulties inherent in adjudicating aboriginal claims.

106 Many of the reasons relied on by the trial judge for excluding the evidence contained in the territorial affidavits are problematic because they run against this fundamental principle. The requirement that a reputation be known in the general community, for example, ignores the fact that oral histories, as noted by the Royal Commission on Aboriginal Peoples, generally relate to particular locations, and refer to particular families and communities and may, as a result, be unknown outside of that community, even to other aboriginal nations. Excluding the territorial affidavits

because the claims to which they relate are disputed does not acknowledge that claims to aboriginal rights, and aboriginal title in particular, are almost always disputed and contested. Indeed, if those claims were uncontroversial, there would be no need to bring them to the courts for resolution. Casting doubt on the reliability of the territorial affidavits because land claims had been actively discussed for many years also fails to take account of the special context surrounding aboriginal claims, in two ways. First, those claims have been discussed for so long because of British Columbia's persistent refusal to acknowledge the existence of aboriginal title in that province until relatively recently, largely as a direct result of the decision of this Court in *Calder*, *supra*. It would be perverse, to say the least, to use the refusal of the province to acknowledge the rights of its aboriginal inhabitants as a reason for excluding evidence which may prove the existence of those rights. Second, this rationale for exclusion places aboriginal claimants whose societies record their past through oral history in a grave dilemma. In order for the oral history of a community to amount to a form of reputation, and to be admissible in court, it must remain alive through the discussions of members of that community; those discussions are the very basis of that reputation. But if those histories are discussed too much, and too close to the date of litigation, they may be discounted as being suspect, and may be held to be inadmissible. The net effect may be that a society with such an oral tradition would never be able to establish a historical claim through the use of oral history in court.

(e) Conclusion

107 The trial judge's treatment of the various kinds of oral histories did not satisfy the principles I laid down in *Van der Peet.* These errors are particularly worrisome because oral histories were of critical importance to the appellants' case. They used those histories in an attempt to establish their occupation and use of the disputed territory, an essential requirement for aboriginal title. The trial judge, after refusing to admit, or giving no independent weight to these oral histories, reached the conclusion that the appellants had not demonstrated the requisite degree of occupation for "ownership." Had the trial judge assessed the oral histories correctly, his conclusions on these issues of fact might have been very different.

---

4. Australia: Constraints on Appropriation of Aboriginal Culture

As in New Zealand, the recognition of indigenous culture in Australia has occurred in the context of more prominent issues such as land rights and self-determination. Perhaps because of its traditions of nomadism, Australian Aboriginal culture has presented opportunities for Australian law to address issues surrounding intangible indigenous culture that tend to be more pronounced than elsewhere. A number of Australian court decisions have explored remedies for alleged misappropriation of Aboriginal images and designs. Although these decisions have been grounded in intellectual property norms, they have sometimes been particularly sensitive to Aboriginal cultural perspectives.

Milpurrurru v. Indofurn Pty. Ltd., (1994) 54 FCR 240

This is a claim for remedies under the *Copyright Act 1968* for copyright infringement and under the *Trade Practices Act* for alleged contraventions of *ss. 52*, *53*(c) and (d) and *55*.

2. The first three applicants are Aboriginal artists. The fourth applicant, the Public Trustee, represents the estates of five deceased Aboriginal artists. The skill of each of the artists is recognised nationally and internationally as exceptional; their works are represented in national, State and other major collections of Australian artworks. The pleadings allege that since about October 1992 the respondents have manufactured, imported into Australia, offered for sale and sold woolen carpets which reproduce artwork, or substantial parts thereof, of each of the artists without the licence of the owners of the copyright.

3. In accordance with Aboriginal custom, and out of respect for the deceased artists, their names have not been spoken in the course of the trial. They have been referred to throughout by their appropriate skin names. It is however necessary to adequately identify the artworks in question to refer once in the judgment to these artists by name, but having done so the skin names will be used thereafter.

...

4. The first four artists are from Central Arnhem Land. The artworks in question are bark paintings. The first three paintings are presently owned by the Australian National Gallery ("the ANG"). In 1993 in recognition of the International Year for the World's Indigenous People the ANG held the first solo exhibition of the works of an Aboriginal artist. The exhibition was a retrospective look at the works of Mr. Milpurrurru, and included the Goose Egg Hunt which is also featured in the publication "The Art of George Milpurrurru" which was published by the ANG at the same time. As part of the program for the 1993 International Year for the World's Indigenous People, Goose Egg Hunt was adopted as the design for the 85 cents Australian stamp issued on 4 February 1993. A large number of these stamps were put into circulation, perhaps as many as two to three million.

...

9. In both the ANG portfolio, and the AIS [Australian Information Services] publications the reproduction of the artworks were published over the name of the artist. Amongst the carpets the subject of this action seven of the eight artworks were reproduced in virtually identical form and colour. It is common ground that the source of the artwork reproduced was these publications.

10. The reproduction of the artworks in the ANG and AIS portfolios and on the postage stamp followed formal approval and royalty agreements with the artists or their representatives. The evidence is to the effect that reproductions of this kind are permitted by Aboriginal artists, including those involved in this case, and by traditional owners, where the reproduction is in a prestigious publication for the purposes of educating members of the white community about Aboriginal culture. In each of the ANG and AIS publications the artworks were accompanied by brief descriptions of the subject matter of the artist's work. With one qualification, the descriptions made it plain that the subject matter concerned creation stories of spiritual and sacred significance to the artist. The one qualification is in respect to the Seven Sisters Dreaming where the description at the foot of the AIS reproduction does not spell that out expressly. However the introduction page to the 1986 calendar makes the following clear statement about the significance of the works in that publication:

> The paintings have been acclaimed as "statements of great value to the people who made them." They express concepts that are intensely personal. These are very often private expressions concerned with ownership, ownership of land, ownership of stories, stories of the Dreamtime, that indefinable period of past time which to the Aboriginals is the source of all knowledge and of all living things.
>
> Sacred ceremonies, generally restricted to the initiated members of the tribe or those undergoing initiation, and their related celebrations in dance, song and design, form the basis of what may seem nothing more than complex abstract patterns in the paintings.
>
> The patterns in fact represent explicit visual descriptions, stylised maps of identifiable locations and myths, though the full meaning of each painting may not be clear to non-Aboriginal viewers. Nevertheless, the paintings are eloquent witnesses to the rich and enduring nature of Aboriginal culture.

11. The evidence led at trial, including the evidence of an Aboriginal artist, Mr. Bruce Wangurra, called by the respondents, explained the importance of the creation stories and dreamings in the cultures of the clans to which they relate. Those stories are represented in ceremonies of deep significance, and are often secret or sacred, known only to a few senior members of the clan chosen according to age, descendence, sex, initiation, experience in the learning of the dreamings and ceremonies, and the attainment of skills which permit the faithful reproduction of the stories in accordance with Aboriginal law and custom. Painting techniques, and the use of totemic and other images and symbols are in many instances, and almost invariably in the case of important creation stories, strictly controlled by Aboriginal law and custom. Artworks are an important means of recording these stories, and for teaching future generations. Accuracy in the portrayal of the story is of great importance. Inaccuracy, or error in the faithful reproduction of an artwork can cause deep offence to those familiar with the dreaming.

12. The right to create paintings and other artworks depicting creation and dreaming stories, and to use pre-existing designs and well recognised totems of the clan, resides in the traditional owners (or custodians) of the stories or images. Usually that right will not be with only one person, but with a group of people who together have the authority to determine whether the story and images may be used in an artwork, by whom the artwork may be created, to whom it may be published, and the terms, if any, on which the artwork may be reproduced. The evidence in this case about these aspects of traditional collective ownership was similar to the account recently published in "Unauthorised Reproductions of Traditional Aboriginal Art," Dean A. Ellinson (1994) 17 UNSW Law Journal 327.

13. If unauthorised reproduction of a story or imagery occurs, under Aboriginal law it is the responsibility of the traditional owners to take action to preserve the dreaming, and to punish those considered responsible for the breach. Notions of responsibility under Aboriginal law differ from those of the English common law. If permission has been given by the traditional owners to a particular artist to create a picture of the dreaming, and that artwork is later inappropriately used or reproduced by a third party, the artist is held responsible for the breach which has occurred, even if the artist had no control over or knowledge of what occurred. The evidence of Ms Marika, which I accept without hesitation, illustrates the severe consequences which may occur even in a case where plainly the misuse of the artwork was without permission, and contrary to Australian statute law. In times past the "offender" could be put to death. Now other forms of punishment are more likely such as preclusion from the right to participate in ceremonies, removal of the right to reproduce paintings of that or any other story of the clan, being outcast from the community, or being required to make a payment of money; but the possibility of spearing was mentioned by Mr. Wangurra as a continuing sanction in serious cases.

14. Ms Marika has endeavoured to conceal the unauthorised reproduction on carpets of Djanda and the Sacred Waterhole from her community as she will be held responsible. Her artwork expresses pictorially the creation when her ancestral creator Djang'Kawu and his two sisters, the Wagilag sisters, at the end of their journey from Burralku, landed at Yelangbara, south of Port Bradshaw, the site of their first journey. The image which she utilised in the artwork is associated with this place. Her rights to use the image arise by virtue of her membership of the land owner group in that area, and is an incident arising out of land ownership. She explained in an affidavit:

> As an artist whilst I may own the copyright in a particular artwork under western law, under Aboriginal law I must not use an image or story in such a way as to undermine the rights of all the other Yolngu (her clan) who have an interest whether direct or indirect in it. In this way I hold the image on trust for all the other Yolngu with an interest in the story.

15. Her creation of the artwork contemplated that it would be displayed with appropriate sensitivity in art galleries and for education purposes to help bring about a greater awareness of Aboriginal culture. The reproduction of the artwork in circumstances where the dreaming would be walked on, is totally opposed to the cultural use of the imagery employed in her artwork.

16. This misuse of her artwork has caused her great upset. If it had become widely known in her community at the time, she believes that her family could have ordered her to stop producing any works of art; they might have stopped her participating in ceremonies; they might have outcast her, and they may have sought recompense from her – nowadays in money terms. So far these possibilities have not eventuated – and now that she has taken action to prevent further misuse and to seek a public recognition of the past misuse through the courts, she is hopeful that the community reaction, when it learns what has happened, will be more forgiving. I note in passing the observation in the paper "Aboriginal Designs and Copyright" Stephen Gray, Copyright Reporter Vol. 9 No. 4, p. 8 at 11 that punishment of the Aboriginal law breaker may to a large extent be determined by the success or failure of action in the Anglo-Australian Courts.

17. It is a feature of the style of the artworks in question that the artist will encode into the artwork secret parts of the dreaming that will be recognised and understood only by those who are initiated into the relevant ceremonies, or at least have a close knowledge of the cultural significance of the story. This adds to the sensitivity and risk of offending the traditional owners involved in the reproduction of Aboriginal artwork, unless the reproduction is accurate in every respect and done with full and proper permission.

18. The extent to which Aboriginal law and culture imposes limitations on the reproduction of Aboriginal artwork will vary according to the clans concerned and the significance of the imagery and dreaming which is reflected in the particular artwork. Where the artwork concerns a public story or ceremony there may be few restrictions on reproduction. This is plain from the quantity and variety of artwork presently produced by Aborigines for the commercial market. Again, depending on the subject of the artwork there may be no restriction on an artist creating a work for use under appropriate copyright licence in the mass productions of items such as clothing and wall-hangings. The licence agreement which the respondents have with Mr. Wangurra and other artists provide examples. Evidence in this case indicates that there is continuing uncertainty in some sections of the Aboriginal community as to the appropriateness of the use of traditional images on products which utilise non-traditional mediums, and on carpets designed to be walked upon.

19. The reproduction of paintings which depict dreaming stories and designs of cultural significance has been a matter of great concern to the Aboriginal community. Pirating of Aboriginal designs and paintings for

commercial use without the consent of the artist or the traditional owners was common for a long time. The recognition of the sacred and religious significance of these paintings, and the restrictions which Aboriginal law and culture imposes on their reproduction, is only now being understood by the white community.

...

20. These papers also discuss a problem perceived to exist at one time in relation to the application of the *Copyright Act* to Aboriginal artworks based on pre-existing tradition and images. That problem was whether works incorporating them satisfied the requirement of originality so to attract copyright protection. In the present case that issue has not arisen, and by the end of the trial the copyright ownership of the artists in each of the eight works was admitted. Although the artworks follow traditional Aboriginal form and are based on dreaming themes, each artwork is one of intricate detail and complexity reflecting great skill and originality.

21. It is against this background that the conduct of the respondents in question in the present case falls to be considered.

...

126. I turn now to the remedies sought by the applicants.

127. In the event of an established infringement the *Copyright Act* relevantly provides remedies to the copyright owner. The statutory remedies do not recognise the infringement of ownership rights of the kind which reside under Aboriginal law in the traditional owners of the dreaming stories and the imagery such as that used in the artworks of the present applicants. That is a matter which has been commented on in the course of the trial, as the evidence discloses the likelihood that the unauthorised reproduction of the artworks has caused anger and offence to those owners, and the potential for them to suffer humiliation and repercussions in their cultural environment. It will be necessary to return to that topic.

128. Where a number of people join together as applicants in the one action as they have done here, and successfully prosecute for separate remedies for invasions of their separate rights, the order of the Court would normally specify separate judgments in favour of each applicant, assessed according to the loss and damage which each suffered.

129. On express instructions from the applicants, counsel has informed the Court that Aboriginal law and custom would treat each of the applicants in a case like the present one equally so that the fruits of the action would be shared equally between the named parties. Some anecdotal evidence of this custom was led through Mr. McGuigan who was involved as director of AAMA [Aboriginal Arts Management Association] in the Johnny Bulun Bulun case. Counsel for the applicants acknowledged that to treat the invasion of the rights of each artist (or those of his estate) on the basis of equality would not be in accordance with the principles of assessment of damages for infringement under the *Copyright Act*. Whilst not suggesting

that the Court should assess the liabilities of each respondent otherwise than according to those principles, counsel invited the Court to express its judgment in terms which defined the aggregate liability of each respondent to the applicants as a group, rather than as individual judgments in favour of each applicant. A judgment so expressed would enable the applicants, including the Public Trustee in consultation with those entitled by Aboriginal law and custom to the proceeds of each estate, to agree upon a division of the damages which met with their cultural and other wishes. Under *Part III*, Division 4 A, of the Administration and Probate Act 1969 (NT), the estate of an intestate Aboriginal may, on order of the Supreme Court of the Northern Territory, be distributed in accordance with the traditions of the community or group to which the intestate Aboriginal belonged. Whilst the *Copyright Act* only recognises the rights of the copyright owner, in a practical way it appears that there may be scope, even in the case of the estates administered by the Public Trustee, for the distribution of the proceeds of the action to those traditional owners who have legitimate entitlements according to Aboriginal law to share compensation paid by someone who has without permission reproduced the artwork of an Aboriginal artist.

130. So far as the procedural rules and practice of the Court permit, I consider this Court should accommodate the applicants' request. In so doing, the reasons for judgment must indicate the basis of assessment according to the established requirements of copyright law so that the respondents' liability is patently established according to the municipal law of Australia. In what follows, I have had regard both to this need, and to the request of the applicants.

...

144. Principles discussed in the authorities on the assessment of damages under s.115(2) [of the Copyright Act] concentrate upon aspects of monetary loss likely to flow from the impaired commercial potential of the copyright. That is hardly surprising as infringement actions usually arise in the commercial context of our market economy. In the circumstances of this case the damages sustained, at least by the living artists, extend beyond the commercial potential for monetary return from the copyright. The assessment of damages under s.115(2) may include compensation for personal suffering, for example for insulting behaviour: Beloff v. Pressdram Ltd and Anor (1973) 1 All ER 241 at 268; and for humiliation: Nichols Advanced Vehicle Systems Inc. and Others v. Rees and Others (1979) RPC 127 at 140. In the present case the infringements have caused personal distress and, potentially at least, have exposed the artists to embarrassment and contempt within their communities if not to the risk of diminished earning potential and physical harm. The losses arising from these risks are a reflection of the cultural environment in which the artists reside and conduct their daily affairs. Losses resulting from tortuous wrongdoing experienced by Aborigines in their particular environments are properly to be brought to account: Napaluma v. Baker (1982) 29 SASR 192;

Weston v. Woodroffe (1985) 36 NTR 34, and Dixon v. Davies (1982) 17 NTR 31.

145. The applicants contend that the unauthorised use of the artwork was in effect the pirating of cultural heritage. That is so, but under copyright law damages can be awarded only insofar as the "pirating" causes a loss to the copyright owner resulting from infringement of copyright. Nevertheless, in the cultural environment of the artists the infringement of those rights has, or is likely to have, far reaching effects upon the copyright owner. Anger and distress suffered by those around the copyright owner constitute part of that person's injury and suffering: Williams v. Settle (1960) 1 WLR 1072 at 1086–87.

146. If these matters of personal and cultural hurt are to be the subject of compensatory damages assessed under s.115(2), the damages awarded would vary from artist to artist. In the case of the artists who died before the infringement occurred, I do not think the copyright owner, the Public Trustee, has suffered any losses beyond the commercial considerations arising from the depreciation in the value of the copyright. (No attempt was made in the proceedings to advance an argument that beneficiaries of the estates held interests as equitable owners in the copyright sufficient to support claims by them for personal harm suffered in their communities, being claims which the Public Trustee as legal owner could bring on their behalf). In the case of the artists who were alive when the infringement occurred but died at about the time that the proceedings were commenced or shortly thereafter, the damages would cover the harm actually suffered by them up to the date of death. In the case of the other applicants the damages would be considerably higher, covering harm already suffered and the potential for further harm in the future. Assessments along these lines, artist by artist, would not be in accordance with the principles of equality which the Court has been invited by the applicants to follow.

147. There is in the circumstances of this case another avenue by which damages over and above the depreciation in the commercial value of the copyright can be awarded, namely as additional damages for flagrant infringement under s.115(4). That avenue may not be available in other cases, but I am satisfied that this is an appropriate case to make an order of additional damages, having regard to the matters referred to in s.115(4)(b). In Williams v. Settle the Court of Appeal upheld a substantial award of "vindictive" damages under the English equivalent provision in a case where purely commercial considerations dictated only a minimal level of loss. A commercial photographer had been commissioned to take photographs of the plaintiff's wedding. Two years later, when the plaintiff's wife was expecting a child, her father was murdered in circumstances which attracted publicity. The defendant, without authority, sold certain of the wedding photographs to a publisher who subsequently published one prominently in two national newspapers. The trial judge awarded $1,000 damages. The Court of Appeal upheld the verdict.

. . .

148. In Ravenscroft v. Herbert and New English Library Ltd at 208, Brightman J described "flagrancy" as implying "the existence of scandalous conduct, deceit and such like; it includes deliberate and calculated copyright infringements." Wilcox J applied this description in Autodesk Australia Pty Ltd v. Cheung at 17 IPR 76, 94 ALR 478. In the present case the copyright infringement was plainly deliberate and calculated by Beechrow and Mr. Bethune. From the outset the source of the imagery on the carpets was known. Even if that were not sufficient in itself to cause Mr. Bethune to have actual knowledge of the likelihood of infringement, he gained that knowledge upon his return to Australia after ordering the samples when first his friends and later Mr. Horrocks brought the true situation to this attention. With that knowledge it was a calculated decision on his part to proceed with the manufacture and import of the carpets in the hopeful expectation that copyright permission would be granted. Without any reason to suspect that permission had been granted, the exhibition was held at the Guildford Hotel. On the day of the exhibition the seriousness of the infringement was stressed by Mr. Horrocks. Nevertheless the promotion, distribution and sale of carpets continued for the obvious economic benefit of Beechrow. Then, when copyright permission was not immediately forthcoming through AAMA, Beechrow through Mr. and Mrs. Bethune, instead of complying with the law, and apologising to the copyright owners, sought to question the authority of AAMA and to accuse it of acting otherwise than in the interests of the artists. Thereafter they continued importing and distributing the snake, the green centre and the waterholes carpets, even after service of the proceedings. I cannot accept their assertion that they did not realise these carpets were alleged to be infringements. In my opinion they realised the scope of the allegations but chose to rely on the argument that the carpets did not reproduce a substantial part of the artworks.

149. The degree of flagrancy involved is a matter to be assessed having regard to the circumstances of the case, and it will vary from case to case. Beechrow and Mr. Bethune point out that they did not seek to hide the activities of Beechrow from AAMA, on the contrary they first instructed Mr. Horrocks to seek permission, and then in November 1992 Mrs. Bethune forwarded photographs of the carpets and certain of the reproductions of the artwork from which the design had been taken. Moreover offers to enter into licence agreements were repeated thereafter. Beechrow and Mr. Bethune also draw attention to the fact that an apology was offered to Ms Marika through officers of AAMA at a conference with them in September 1993 (some months after the proceedings were issued), and oral apologies were also extended to both Ms Marika and Mr. Milpurrurru during the trial. (The latter apologies were offered after attention had been drawn by the Court to the apparent absence of contrition on the part of the respondents, and had the appearance of being motivated rather by desire to mitigate the assessment of damages than for any other reason.)

150. These matters are to be taken into account, and the early attempts to obtain permission render the flagrancy of the conduct less serious than it would otherwise have been.

151. There are however other factors to be taken into account. The acquisition of the carpets was, according to Mr. Bethune's evidence, initially undertaken to curry favour with a potential customer in Vietnam with complete disregard for the potential copyright issues. Then, when the marketing of the carpets commenced they were promoted as Aboriginal artworks, and that promotion implied endorsement or approval of prominent artists of the carpet venture. That representation became more obvious as the business developed and a swing tag printed with the Beela Art business name was attached to each carpet.

152. Whilst benefits initially flowed to Beechrow and Mr. Bethune, I consider they should now be treated as extinguished by the proposed orders under s.116.

153. The Court is also directed by s.115(4)(b) to have regard to "all other relevant matters." It is upon this consideration that the cultural issues which are so important to the artists and their communities assume great importance.

154. If an award of additional damages under s.115(4) is made to reflect culturally based harm, the particular losses of the artists who were alive at the time of the infringement which might otherwise be assessed under s.115(2) can be subsumed within the additional damages. Upon an assessment of the cultural aspects of the harm as additional damages a position of equality between the artists can more easily be rationalised. Nevertheless there is a plain distinction between the living artists and those who are deceased. In the case of the latter some died before the infringement and some after, but those that died after the infringement did so only shortly after they became aware of the infringement and probably before their communities did so. In these circumstances I see force in the applicants' submission that all the deceased artists should be treated equally but that there must be some differential between them and the first three applicants.

NOTES AND QUESTIONS

1. In *Milpurrurru*, does the flagrant infringement provision of Australia copyright law serve the same, essentially punitive, purpose of treble damages in U.S. antitrust actions? Why did the court apply it in a case of intangible cultural heritage?
2. *Mulpurrurru* is one of a number of cases in which Australian courts have used their discretionary powers (e.g., to award damages) in a way that accords with Aboriginal customs and cultural beliefs. Thus, in *Yumbulul v. Reserve Bank of Australia* 211 P.R 481 (1991), which was discussed earlier in this chapter, Aboriginal customary law concerning title was applied to various designs; and in *Bulun Bulun* v. *R&T Textiles*

Pty. Ltd. 157 A.L.R. 193 (1998), traditional Aboriginal designs were accorded copyright protection.

Barbara T. Hoffman, *Exploring and Establishing Links for a Balanced Art and Cultural Heritage Policy, in* Art and Cultural Heritage: Law, Policy, and Practice 1, 8–9 (Barbara T. Hoffman ed., 2006) (reprinted with the permission of the Cambridge University Press)

[The] tension between private rights of ownership created by western intellectual property systems such as copyright and communal ownership held by artists and their communities is an issue that has received attention by various scholars, policy makers, and courts. Recognizing a link between the spiritual and the material causes us to focus on the relationship between an individual artist/author as a possessor of intellectual property rights and collective ownership rights. Different conceptions of "ownership" within copyright law, on the one hand, and customary laws and protocols, on the other, may intersect, particularly in those cases in which an indigenous artist is entitled to assert copyright to prevent infringement of his creation and is simultaneously subject to parallel customary rules and regulations. Although intellectual property laws confer private rights of ownership, in customary discourse, to "own" does not necessarily or only mean "ownership" in the Western nonindigenous sense. It can convey a sense of stewardship or responsibility for the traditional culture, rather than the right to exclude others from certain uses of expressions of the traditional culture, which is more akin to the nature of many intellectual property rights systems.

The issue was directly addressed in the Australian case of *John Bulun Bulun v. R and T Textiles*. Mr. Bulun Bulun is a well-known artist from Arnhemland, Ganalbingu, and his work *Magpie Geese and Water Lilies at the Waterhole* was altered and copied by a textile company. In 1996, Mr. Bulun Bulun commenced action against the textile company for copyright infringement.

The Ganalbingu people are the traditional indigenous owners of Ganalbingu country. They have the right to permit and control the production and reproduction of the artistic work under the law and custom of the Ganalbingu people. The artwork of *Magpie Geese and Water Lilies at the Waterhole* depicts knowledge concerning Djulibinyamurr. Djulibinyamurr, along with another waterhole site, Ngalyindi, are the two most important cultural sites in Ganalbingu country for the Ganalbinju people. Mr. Bulun Bulun noted that, under Ganalbingu law, ownership of land has corresponding obligation to create artworks, designs, songs, and other aspects of ritual and ceremony that go with the land.

The pertinent aspect of the case related to a claim by the clan group to which Mr. Bulun Bulun belonged that, it, in effect, controlled the copyright in the artwork, and that the clan members were the beneficiaries of the creation of the artwork by the artist acting on their behalf. Accordingly, they claimed to be entitled to assert a collective right with respect to the copyright in the work, over and above any issue as to authorship.

Justice Von Doussa said, "Whilst it is superficially attractive to postulate that the common law should recognize communal title, it would be contrary to established legal principle for the common law to do so." The court looked at the relevance of customary law and decided that evidence of customary law may be used as a basis for the foundation of rights recognized within the Australian legal system. After finding that Mr. Bulun Bulun's customary law obligations gave rise to a fiduciary relationship between himself and the Ganalbingu people, Justice Von Doussa stated:

> The conclusion does not treat the law and custom of the Ganalbingu people as part of the Australian legal system. Rather, it treats the law and custom of the Ganalbingu people as part of the factual matrix which characterizes the relationship as one of mutual trust and confidence. It is that relationship which the Australian legal system recognizes as giving rise to the fiduciary relationship, and to the obligations that arise out of it.

The Australian cases may not mean that Aboriginal customary law has been unequivocally incorporated into Australian law, but, at a minimum, they enforce Aboriginal law through the means of interpreting and applying Australian law. See Colin Golvan, *Aboriginal Art and Copyright – An Overview and Commentary Concerning Recent Developments*, 1 MEDIA & ARTS L. REV. 151 (1996); Christoph Antons, *Folklore Protection in Australia: Who Is Expert in Aboriginal Tradition? in* EXPERTS IN SCIENCE & SOCIETY 85 (E. Kurz-Milcke & Gerd Gigerenzer eds., 2004).

5. Taiwan: Act for the Protection of the Traditional Intellectual Creations of Indigenous Peoples

Taiwan's initiative takes the form of a unique piece of legislation, the Act for the Protection of the Traditional Intellectual Creations of Indigenous Peoples, Executive Yuan No. 05128, Dec. 27, 2007:

Article 1

(Legislative Purpose)

> In order to protect the traditional intellectual creations of indigenous peoples (hereinafter referred to as "Intellectual Creations"), and to promote the cultural development of indigenous peoples, this Act is set forth according to Article 13 of the Native Peoples Basic Law.

Article 2

(Competent Authority)

> The competent authority referred to herein shall mean the Council of Indigenous People, Executive Yuan.

Article 3

(Definition of Intellectual Creations)

The intellectual creations referred to in this Act shall mean traditional religious ceremonies, music, dance, songs, sculptures, weaving, patterns, clothing, folk crafts or any other expression of the cultural achievements of indigenous peoples.

Article 4

(Recognition Registration)

Intellectual creations shall be recognized by and registered with the competent authority so as to be protected by the Act. The criteria for recognizing intellectual creations mentioned in the previous paragraph shall be determined by the competent authority.

Article 5

(Recruitment of Personnel)

The competent authority shall recruit (assign) personnel of related institutions, specialists, scholars and aboriginal representatives to undertake the recognition of intellectual creations in addition to any matters stipulated in other regulations.

Article 6

(Documents Required for Registration Application and Selection of Representatives)

The applicant for any intellectual creation shall provide a written application, a specification, necessary graphics, images and related documents or provide audiovisual creations in order to apply for registration with the competent authority.

The applicant mentioned in the previous paragraph is limited to aboriginal groups or tribes and a representative shall be elected to take care of all matters arising. The regulations of electing representatives shall be determined by the competent authority.

Article 7

(Obtaining Exclusive Rights to Use Intellectual Creations)

Upon being recognized as intellectual creations, the exclusive right to use such intellectual creations shall be obtained according to the following rules:

1. Once the applicant is confirmed to be the owner of an intellectual creation, registration shall be approved. And starting from the date of registration, the applicant shall obtain the exclusive right to use such intellectual creations.
2. If an intellectual creation is confirmed to belong to the applicant and other specific aboriginal groups or tribes, the applicant and other specific aboriginal groups or tribes shall jointly obtain the exclusive right to use the intellectual creation starting from the date of registration.
3. If an intellectual creation cannot be confirmed to belong to any specific aboriginal group or tribe, the rights shall be registered under the entire

indigenous peoples. The entire indigenous peoples will obtain the exclusive right to use such intellectual creation starting from the date of registration.

...

Article 10

(Definition of the Exclusive Right to Use Intellectual Creations)

The exclusive right to use intellectual creations shall mean the property rights and moral rights of intellectual creations
The owner of an exclusive right to use intellectual creations enjoys the following moral rights of intellectual creations:

1. the moral right to publicly release the work.
2. the moral right to indicate the name of the exclusive user.
3. the moral right to prohibit others from distorting, mutilating, modifying, or otherwise changing the content, form, or name of the work, thereby violating the author's reputation.

The owner of the exclusive right to use intellectual creations shall exclusively use and profit from the property rights of such intellectual creations on behalf of specific ethnic groups, tribes or the entire indigenous peoples, unless otherwise stipulated by law or agreement, and shall exercise the rights mentioned in the previous paragraph.

Indigenous peoples themselves are entitled to use and profit from the intellectual creations of ethnic groups, tribes or the entire indigenous peoples and shall not be subject to the limitations stipulated in Article 14.

...

Article 17

(Remedy for Infringement on the Exclusive Right to Use Intellectual Creations)

An exclusive user of an intellectual creation may demand removal of infringement of its rights. Where there is likelihood of infringement, a demand may be made to prevent such infringement.

Article 18

(Damage Compensation Liability)

Parties infringing on the exclusive right of intellectual creations willfully or negligently shall be liable for damage compensation. When there is more than one infringer, all infringers shall be held jointly and severally liable.

The right to make claims as mentioned in the previous paragraph shall be terminated if not exercised within two years after learning of the existence of parties liable for damages and compensation. The same shall apply if not exercised within ten (10) years of infringement.

...

Article 21

(Protection of Intellectual Creations of Foreigners)

If there exist any intellectual creation protection treaties or agreements between the government of the Republic of China and foreign governments, such treaties or agreements shall be followed.

NOTES AND QUESTIONS

1. These examples of how national laws have responded to concerns surrounding aspects of the intangible cultural heritage all involve efforts to protect the cultures of indigenous peoples. Two of the examples focus on IPRs, reinforcing the generally held view that such rights are not conceptually suited to address most of the cultural concerns of indigenous peoples. See J.C. Weiner, *Protection of Folklore: A Political and Legal Challenge*, 18 INT'L REV. INDUS. PROP. & COPYRIGHT 67 (1987); Russel L. Barsh, *How Do You Patent a Landscape? The Perils of Dichotomizing Cultural and Intellectual Property*, 8 INT'L J. CULTURAL PROP. 14 (1999); Susan Scafidi, *Intellectual Property and Cultural Products*, 81 B.U. L. REV. 793 (2001); Christine H. Farley, *Protecting Folklore of Indigenous Peoples: Is Intellectual Property the Answer?*, 30 CONN. L. REV. 1 (1997); Cynthia Callison, *Appropriation of Aboriginal Oral Traditions*, 1995 U. B.C. L. REV. S165; Isabella Alexander, *White Law, Black Art*, 10 INT'L J. CULTURAL PROP. 185 (2001).
2. The 2007 Taiwanese law is a rare attempt at a comprehensive national system to afford legal protection for the cultural heritage of indigenous peoples. Do you consider it a *sui generis* solution or an attempt to extend IPRs in a new and different manner? Is it the sort of *sui generis* method of protection envisaged by the UN Convention on Biological Diversity? What would be the solution to a competing assertion of copyright by the owner of a film or video of an indigenous dance or ceremony that had been recognized and registered under the law? Do these kinds of laws unrealistically raise expectations about the levels of national and international legal protection they purport to create?
3. Another legal perspective on the intangible cultural heritage, at least that of indigenous peoples, is one based on human rights law. Although cases like *Delgamuukw* show how national laws of individual states can develop to accord such rights, there is growing evidence of a similar international consensus as well. Chapter 5 introduced the 2007 United Nations Declaration on the Rights of Indigenous Peoples, which contains the following provisions:

Article 11

1. Indigenous peoples have the right to practice and revitalize their cultural traditions and customs. This includes the right to maintain, protect and develop the past, present and future manifestations of their cultures, such as archaeological and historical sites, artefacts, designs, ceremonies, technologies and visual performing arts and literature.
2. States shall provide redress through effective mechanisms, which may include restitution, developed in conjunction with indigenous peoples, with respect

to their cultural, intellectual, religious and spiritual property taken without their free, prior and informed consent or in violation of their laws, traditions and customs.

Article 12

1. Indigenous peoples have the right to manifest, practice, develop and teach their spiritual and religious traditions, customs and ceremonies; the right to maintain, protect, and have access in privacy to their religious and cultural sites; the right to the use and control of their ceremonial objects; and the right to the repatriation of their human remains.
2. States shall seek to enable the access and/or repatriation of ceremonial objects and human remains in their possession through fair, transparent and effective mechanisms developed in conjunction with indigenous peoples concerned.

Article 13

1. Indigenous peoples have the right to revitalize, use, develop and transmit to future generations their histories, languages, oral traditions, philosophies, writing systems and literatures, and to designate and retain their own names for communities, places and persons.
2. States shall take effective measures to ensure that this right is protected and also to ensure that indigenous peoples can understand and be understood in political, legal and administrative proceedings, where necessary through the provision of interpretation or by other appropriate means.

The UN Declaration, as soft law, is still only evidence of the present state of international law on the subject of the human rights of indigenous peoples, but it is part of a growing body of evidence that such rights are gathering legal force. Although the focus of most Western legal systems is on the protection of tangible and intangible cultural phenomena in terms of proprietary rights, there is also growing support for a different approach in terms of traditional cultures. See James Anaya, Indigenous Peoples In International Law 101 (1996); Claire Charters, *Reparation for Indigenous Peoples: Global International Instruments and Institutions*, *in* Reparations for Indigenous Peoples: International and Comparative Perspectives 163 (Federico Lenzerini ed., 2008); Robert K. Paterson, *Resolving Material Culture Disputes: Human Rights, Property Rights and Crimes against Humanity*, 14 Willamette J. Int'l L. & Disp. Resol. 155 (2006); Dean B. Suagee, *Human Rights and the Cultural Heritage of Indian Tribes in the United States*, 8 Int'l J. Cultural Prop. 48 (1999); Rosemary J. Coombe, *Intellectual Property, Human Rights and Sovereignty! New Dilemmas in International Law Posed by the Recognition of Indigenous Knowledge and the Conservation of Biodiversity*, 6 Ind. J. Global Legal Stud. 59 (1998).

4. Do you think that developing a comprehensive understanding about the human rights of indigenous peoples and other minorities might be an effective basis for adequate protection of their traditional knowledge and customs, or do you think more specific forms of *sui generis* protection should be developed to protect the intangible cultural heritage? Would the *sui generis* approach perhaps offer greater

certainty as to the scope of rights conferred? One of the criticisms of the Canadian Supreme Court decision in *Delgamuukw* has been that it allows Canadian courts to continually modify the scope of the constitutionally protected rights of Canada's First Nations according to what sometimes are perceived as countervailing social values and policies, such as environmental and resource protection.

7. Museums

A. Introduction

Once largely seen as institutions catering to school visits and elite scholarship, museums have been reinventing themselves. As Western countries embrace multiculturalism and as financial support for the arts dwindles, museums have become both more sensitive to their diverse communities and alive to the challenges of fund-raising and commercial ventures. These developments have spurred reexaminations of the laws and policies surrounding museum governance – as we have seen, for example, in the return of objects to indigenous peoples and victims of Nazi-era confiscations. Museums have also been engaged in debates about controversial exhibitions and the appropriate missions they should pursue.

There is no definitive legal or even factual definition of a museum. Nevertheless, although the basic concept of a museum has changed over time, it retains the scholarly cast of the word's origin in the Greek *mouseion*, meaning "seat of the Muses." It is also understood that modern museums have two basic dimensions: a physical manifestation – usually a building enclosing objects of certain kinds – and an intellectual dimension that expresses the purposes for which the objects in the building's collection are preserved and complemented over time.

The International Council of Museums' (ICOM) Code of Ethics for Museums, which was introduced in Chapter 5, defines a museum as

> a non-profit making permanent institution in the service of society and its development, open to the public, which acquires, conserves, researches, communicates and exhibits, for purposes of study, education and enjoyment, the tangible and intangible evidence of people and their environment.

Museums, in this sense, can be either private or public, but these terms are themselves ambiguous. Many museums were originally established by private initiative but have grown to become more dependent on government subsidies. Moreover, all museums are public in the sense that their purpose is to benefit the public at large through exhibitions, educational activities, and other programs. Some museums, once dependent on public resources, have been weaned from such support as public coffers have dwindled. Still other museums have always been private. Regardless of whether a museum is public or private, similar issues concerning collection management and accountability tend to arise.[1]

Since 2002 the Constitution of Museums Australia Incorporated has included a new definition of "museum" based on concerns about what the organization views as deficiencies in the ICOM definition, such as its focus on enjoyment, which may exclude Holocaust museums and other institutions that are custodians of distressing material. In addition, the organization was concerned that the ICOM museum definition, though workable, was dated in failing to include virtual museums or collections of intangible cultural heritage. The Museums Australia definition is as follows:

> A museum helps people understand the world by using objects and ideas to interpret the past and present and explore the future. A museum preserves and researches collections and makes objects and information accessible in actual and virtual environments. Museums are established in the public interest as permanent, not for profit organisations that contribute long-term value to communities.
>
> Museums Australia recognises that museums of science, history and art may be designated by many other names (including gallery and Keeping Place). In addition, the following may qualify as museums for the purposes of this definition:
>
> (a) natural, archaeological and ethnographic monuments and sites of a museum nature that acquire, conserve and communicate material evidence of people and their environment;
> (b) institutions holding collections of and displaying specimens of plants and animals, such as botanical and zoological gardens, herbaria, aquaria and vivaria;
> (c) science centres;
> (d) cultural centres and other entities that facilitate the preservation, continuation and management of tangible or intangible heritage resources (living heritage and digital creative activity);
> (e) such other institutions as the council considers as having some or all of the characteristics of a museum.

NOTES AND QUESTIONS

1. In the Constitution of Museums Australia Incorporated, as set forth in the foregoing, what "other institutions" might qualify as museums under subparagraph (e)? Why is it important to have a working definition of a museum other than to establish a basis for membership in a museum association?
2. For an analysis of the evolving purposes and policies of several museums in the United States, the United Kingdom, and Australia during the past century and a half, see ANA FELIPA VRDOLJAK, INTERNATIONAL LAW, MUSEUMS, AND THE RETURN OF CULTURAL OBJECTS (2008).
3. In September 2008 the Smithsonian Institution's National Museum of African American History and Culture opened eight years ahead of schedule in the form

[1] *See* MARIE C. MALARO, A LEGAL PRIMER ON MANAGING MUSEUM COLLECTIONS (2d ed. 1998).

of an interactive Web site (http://nmaahc.si.edu). Would such Web sites fall within national regulation of museums? If so, what state or states would have regulatory authority? Only the state in whose territory such a cyberspace museum is projected?

4. For other definitions of the term "museum" by national museum associations, see the American Association of Museums' Web site, at http://www.aam-us.org/aboutmuseums/whatis.cfm; the Association of Art Museum Directors' Web site, at http://www.aamd.org/about/#Members; and the Canadian Museums Association's Web site, at http://www.museums.ca/en/info_resourcesreports_guidelines/museum_definition/.

B. The Museum Culture through History

1. General Observations

Alan Ullberg, Patricia Ullberg, Ann Hofstra Grogg & Robert Lind, *A Short History of the Museum, in* Art and Museum Law: Cases and Materials 425–31 (Robert C. Lind, Robert M. Jarvis & Marilyn E. Phelan eds., Carolina Academic Press 2002)

The traditions that govern the behavior of the caretakers of public treasures began in ancient Greece. Although collecting and hoarding state treasures and documents [have] been recorded in other cultures, the Athenians refined this social and religious area of public life. They built special additions to their sanctuaries and temples to house and display the statues, armor, and objects in precious metals, bone, and glass presented as votive offerings by individuals or groups of private citizens. The collections in temples also included relics of heroes. Pausanias, a second-century A.D. traveler to Greece, reported that the sword of Achilles was preserved in the Sanctuary of Athena at Phaselis and the sword of Memnon in the Temple of Aesculapius at Nicomedia. In Athens the Pinakotheka, a picture gallery in the Propylaea at the west end of the Acropolis exhibited paintings by the finest artists of the time commemorating important events in the history of Athens. They were regarded as sacred treasures belonging to all citizens and were viewed and enjoyed by the entire populace, much as art museums are visited today.

Custodians of temple collections, called *hieropoei*, were responsible for guarding the temples and caring for the treasuries. Annual inventories recorded advances of temple properties from one board of custodians to the next. In addition to keeping records of the treasures, the *hieropoei* made sure that the collections were appropriately housed and displayed, and that the objects were maintained in good condition. At a change in magistery, the collection was reviewed. The position of *hieropoei* entailed obligations to the gods and the state – and thus to the public.

This emphasis on the public nature of collections, with corresponding high ethical standards for their care, did not pass from Greece to Rome.

The trend in imperial Rome was toward secular collecting by private persons. Collections became a means of social prestige. Private individuals and amateurs amassed huge collections, and selling, trading, and speculating in art [were] brisk. Provincial officials and military leaders routinely made free with the sacred and secular treasures of the countries they administered. Art objects, antiques, and fakes changed hands for fabulous sums unrivaled until modern times. The Latin word museum came to mean a country villa housing a private collection, unlike the Greek *mouseion*, a shrine to the Muses that began as a place of contemplation and developed into a repository of man's cultural heritage and finest creative art.

In their private villas Romans displayed artifacts and curiosities for their own enjoyment and for their friends and other collectors, but the practice came under criticism. Julius Caesar sought to set precedent by dedicating his collections to temples, and Agrippa, the son-in-law of Augustus, argued in a speech to the Roman Senate that all confiscated paintings and statues be rendered to the Roman people rather than exiled to country houses. This and similar exhortations by men such as Cicero prompted large-scale public donation of plunder. Eventually, even many private collections and libraries were opened to the public.

An example of the emerging public interest in art concerned a scandal surrounding Lysippus'[s] *Apoxyomenos*, a bronze of a youth. The emperor Tiberius was so taken with the statue that he had it removed from the Baths of Agrippa to his bedchamber, only to be forced to return it, to quiet the public outcry that ensued. But Roman ideas of private initiative in the collecting and donating of art to the temples were far removed from the Athenian ideal of individuals in service at temples and sanctuaries holding objects in trust for religious and community or state purposes. They were also vastly different from the dedication to knowledge of the great Mouseion of Ptolemy Philadelphus at Alexandria, which during the Hellenistic era maintained a library and scientific collections, and supported scholars in collaborative research.

As Rome entered its final phase and converted to Christianity, there was less interest in collecting art. By the fifth century A.D. the arms and legs of statues in Rome were being hacked off for sale to bronze foundries and lime burners. Many collections, both Roman and imported, fell into the hands of the Teutonic tribes that sacked Rome. They valued these objects only as spoils of war, and not as sacred objects of public ownership.

In the Middle Ages there was no mass appreciation or display of art. The precious metals and stones hoarded by ruling families merely provided a means to increased economic and political power. Art and precious objects, however, were primarily the property of the religious community, and the church used them to enhance religious experience and embody expressions of divine omniscience. They were not valued for esthetic or historical reasons. The church, under the influence of Augustinian teaching, actively opposed estheticism and virtually ignored history. It did not occur to the medieval mind that collections might further the appreciation of art or the education of the greater community; or even be held in trust as cultural heritage. Medieval treasures may have paralleled the temple collections of ancient Greece and Rome in location but not in purpose.

Even in the Middle Ages, Italians lived in the midst of "the grandeur that was Rome." They never entirely abandoned the idea that great art belonged to the people. Scholars date the first attempt to preserve an historical monument to an edict of the Roman Senate in 1162 declaring that the Column of Trajan "should never be destroyed or mutilated but should remain as it stands to the honor of the Roman people as long as the world endures." Renewal of interest in classical antiquity became, in time, the Italian Renaissance. As its notion of humanism spread northward, it revived an appreciation of works of art as esthetic and historic objects and an interest in the natural sciences for their own sakes. In the sixteenth and seventeenth centuries personal collecting by scholars and amateurs (from the Latin for "to love") became something of a mania. The great collections amassed in these years by royal and noble connoisseurs would later become the nuclei of Europe's modern museums.

Perhaps the most outstanding collectors were the Medicis of Florence, with wide-ranging interests in books, intaglios, precious stones, medals, tapestries, Byzantine icons, Flemish paintings, contemporary sculpture, Etruscan artifacts, and natural history specimens. They built additions to palaces to house their collections and founded the first public library in Europe since Roman times. The first recorded use of the term museum, in fact, described a Medici collection at the time of Lorenzo the Magnificent. But these and other early collections throughout Europe were all privately owned, incorporated as galleries or "cabinets of curiosities" into houses and palaces. Royal collections, such as that of Charles V of Spain, were represented to be the property of the state. Some were available to visitors, often on payment of a small fee, but public access was not actively encouraged.

In various locations, however, municipal corporations began to accumulate art. In 1629 the city of Zurich established a library and a gallery. In 1638 the municipality of Amsterdam commissioned Rembrandt to paint the civic guard – the result was *The Night Watch*. The first known public purchase of a private collection occurred in 1661 when the council of Basel decided to buy the "cabinet" assembled by Basilius Amerbach. Ten years later it was made accessible to the public as part of the new university.

By the eighteenth century Enlightenment notions of equality were beginning to broaden the meaning of Renaissance humanism even among the aristocracy. In Rome, Pope Clement XII turned a palace over to the people in 1734. The Museo Capitolino is often regarded as the first public art museum. Nine years later the last of the Medicis – Grand Duchess Anna Maria Ludovica – bequeathed all the great Medici collections to the state of Tuscany. She provided that "none of these collections should ever be removed from Florence," and they should be "for the benefit of the public of all nations." By mid-century a selection of paintings from the Louvre could be viewed at the Palais du Luxembourg on certain mornings and afternoons. Even in autocratic Russia, Peter the Great established a *Kunstkammer* with the words: "I want people to look and learn." In Kassel, the Museum Fridericianum was designed specifically to hold the vast collections of the landgraves of Hesse-Kassel. Completed in 1779, the building was open to the public from 9 to 10 in the morning and again from 2 to 3 in the afternoon. By the end of the eighteenth century even the collections of the Austrian Museum were available at a set time to anyone "with clean shoes."

The first great public museum to be created with government revenues was initiated in mid-century when, in 1753, the House of Commons purchased the scientific collection of Sir Hans Sloane and joined it to the Cottonian library and Harleian manuscripts. Parliament set up a board of trustees and allowed funds for the housing and maintenance of the British Museum, which was to be opened "to all studious and curious persons." The library had a reading room, and a guided tour of the museum could be had on approval of a written application.

Symptomatic of the emerging public character of museum collections was a new concern with the arrangement and presentation of objects in a way that would make sense even to the uninitiated. A few early scientific collections in Renaissance Italy had been conceived as instruments "for the comprehension and exploration of the natural world." To facilitate study, cupboards were numbered and labeled with the contents. Specimens were carefully recorded and examined.

During the Enlightenment principles of arrangement and display were incorporated into the very nature of collecting and the function of museums. Following the model of scientific collections, all fields of collecting were now rationally structured and subdivided. The objects in the Dresden *Kunstkammer*, for example, were classified as artistic, scientific, or technical; and each field of collecting had its own subdivisions. Paintings in galleries were often arranged by artist and school. They literally covered the walls from top to bottom, and their keepers debated the best lighting to ensure their visibility. Keepers also imposed order through the records they maintained, records that no longer were mere lists or inventories but, through classification, were developing into catalogs.

At the same time there were advances in the fields of restoration and conservation. With the excavations near Mount Vesuvius in Italy's Campania came the application of scientific study to artifacts of ancient cultures and the analysis of materials to establish authenticity. The reconditioning of paintings, practiced since the sixteenth century, became enough of a science and skill to warrant the establishment of centers for its study. One such center in Venice was supported with public funds.

The era of museums as instruments of public edification was dawning. Learned societies, especially in the sciences, formed collections for the benefit of their members. In the next century these would contribute to the founding of public museums. When Chrétien de Mechel reorganized the Austrian Imperial collections in Vienna's Schloss Belvedere, he arranged the paintings by school and period "so that one learns at a brief glance infinitely more than one could if the same paintings were hung without regard to the period which has made them."

With the French Revolution the royal collections of the French Bourbons became, all at once, the property of the people. The National Assembly created a new national museum to which the public was admitted without charge the last three days of each *decade* (ten-day period). Artists were given special preference, however, as the display of art was considered a primary interest to them. French troops marching across Europe took their public ideas with them. Throughout the continent, royal collections were made public property. Under Napoleon, French troops also brought a great many European masterpieces back to Paris, where the French philosophes' dream of a truly encyclopedic collection was realized in the Musee Napoleon. When, in 1815, many of these works of art were returned, they went into large, centralized, often national museums that were open to, and the pride of, all citizens. As a result, museums became an important element of the modern State.

With the rise of national consciousness in the nineteenth century, museums became preservers of cultural and ethnic heritage. In Copenhagen and in German states such as Bavaria, ethnological museums traced the development of a people, especially its social classes, industries, and handicrafts, through examples of its decorative arts. In Sweden, museums of folklore, in outdoor settings, preserved old trades, dress, and building styles. Museums were especially important for peoples with a shared sense of nationalism but, as yet, no nation-state. In Norway, Hungary, and Czech-speaking lands, for example, museums promoted national identity and played active roles in their respective movements for independence. In England, the Victoria and Albert Museum combined national pride with educational purposes. Displays of the useful arts served as examples for artisans, and the museum circulated exhibitions, books, and lecture materials. It also accommodated public comfort with the world's first museum restaurant.

Museums in the United States began with the ideas that had taken centuries to evolve in Europe. From the first they were public in character, even if not in support, and dedicated to the dissemination of knowledge. They reflected the American belief that education is necessary to human welfare. To this day the most noteworthy American addition to the museum idea has been the expansion of the museum as an educational institution. The museum becomes a center for learning that pushes beyond mere exposure, to an active communication with the visitor through lectures, concerts, films, circulating exhibitions, publications, and special programs for children and adults. Museum exhibitions are planned and set up to encourage the visitor to learn as well as to enjoy.

Predictably, the first museum in the colonies was established by a learned society, the Library Society of Charleston, South Carolina. Other early museums were adjuncts of scientific societies. Charles Willson Peale's famous museum in Philadelphia initially received support from the

American Philosophical Society. Though eclectic in content – with fossils, shells, wax figures, models of machines, and portraits by the artist himself of the great men of the American Revolution – it was clearly didactic in purpose. Unless diverse objects "are systematically arranged and the proper modes of seeing and using them attended to," Peale wrote, "the advantage of such a store will be of little account to the public." Peale argued that his museum was a national institution deserving of public patronage, but he failed to receive the government support he required. After his death parts of the collection were sold off until the museum no longer existed.

Most early museums, like the Wadsworth Athenaeum, continued to be privately owned and primarily scholarly. In the 1870s, however, the city of New York set an important precedent by granting land and constructing buildings for the Metropolitan Museum of Art and the American Museum of Natural History. The city later agreed to annual appropriations for these museums. Other cities followed suit, and municipal support for museums became a key factor in museum development and funding in the United States. County and state governments also have participated in the establishment and funding of many museums.

Most American museums, however, have been made possible primarily by private philanthropy. Gifts from wealthy patrons such as J. Pierpont Morgan in the nineteenth century and Andrew W. Mellon in the twentieth established major museums. The nineteenth century in particular, with its emphasis on national pride and strong sense of obligation to public welfare, inspired many founders of American fortunes to give their fabulous collections of European Old Masters and antiquities to public museums. This pattern has been repeated throughout the nation to found and endow museums of all sizes and types. Tax and tariff laws in the United States also encouraged collecting and donating objects to nonprofit museum organizations. As a result, American museums have diverged from the European museum in organization and funding. While European museums principally have been state-managed and supported enterprises, American museums have been mostly self-supporting organizations operated by groups of private citizens who serve as trustees for the museum and its operations. Trustees often are major supporters through regular gifts of money and the donation of objects. Additional groups of individuals may provide financial and other support for a museum in their roles as members or "friends."

In addition to the support for museums in the United States through tax benefits for donors and supporters, governments waive federal, state, county and municipal taxes because museums are nonprofit organizations. Beyond special tax relief, governments at all levels may provide support for museums through grants for special exhibitions and other educational projects. Governments often provide additional support by making old or new buildings available to museums at little or no cost. Funding from governments may come in the form of museum staff salaries, often by placing museum staff on the government payroll. There are many variations of government support for museums in the United States, and for the legal arrangements under which museums are established, managed, and funded. These often are ingenious working partnerships between a government and a nonprofit organization or other groups that manage and support the museum.

As museums take on more tasks as cultural and educational institutions, they usually need more funding than can be supplied by supporting governments and private benefactors. Museums traditionally looked to private foundations, and in recent decades to business corporations for grants to fund exhibitions and other programs. Sponsors usually are required to leave the final version of the story line of an exhibit or the content of a program to museum staff, but the subjects chosen may represent the interests of the funders. Although museums may obtain funding for exhibitions and programs from a wide range of outside sources, a heightened professionalism of museum staff allows museums to maintain considerable independence and intellectual integrity. A number of universities operate museum studies or management programs applicable to museums. They have graduated thousands of individuals trained to serve as professionals in museums: curators, historians, exhibition designers, collection managers and administrators. Codes of ethics reinforce autonomy on the part of museums and professional staff.

Until recent years museums in the United States were described as "America's cathedrals." They were viewed as the expression of community values, as both community center and monument, as a "university for the general public, an institution of learning and enjoyment for all men," as a "social instrument," or "the midwife of democracy." The ancient idea of the *mouseion* was echoed in historian Niels von Holst's observation that for some of the twentieth century, art became our religion, museums our temples, and museum managers the keepers of our sanctuaries. Museums have attained high status in our society; museum exhibitions were viewed by many members of the public as official or authoritative pronouncements on the subjects covered by their exhibits.

With the increased cultural and intellectual diversity in American society in recent decades, museums have oriented exhibitions and programs to wider and different audiences and publics. Less and less are museum exhibitions categorical declarations of monolithic points of view. Exhibitions are more likely to present complex and diverse interpretations of the subjects covered. Museums are thus becoming more like community educational centers, encouraging pluralistic learning from multiple cultural and scholarly points of view.

In the past two decades there have been a number of large, well-financed and publicized museum exhibitions attracting visitors numbering in the many hundreds of thousands. These "blockbuster" shows, such as the exhibition in the 1980s of the objects from Tutankamen's tomb, often are heavily advertised on television and in other media by their corporate sponsors. Resulting large visitations, including by many who are not regular museum visitors, have further democratized museums as popular institutions. No longer are museums perceived either as cathedrals or as dull, musty depositories of specimens. Increasingly they are thought of as glamorous places to see interesting objects and programs and have fun. By now museums have become essential institutions in a culture focused on continuous learning for all.

NOTES

1. The following summary highlights the immensity of the museum industry in just the United States:

   > According to the Commerce Department, the nation's 6,651 museums, historic sites and nature centers – most of them tax-exempt nonprofits – generated \$8.6 billion in revenue in 2002, the latest year for complete figures. The nation's 4,535 museums form the largest share of the cultural attraction industry, generating \$5.9 billion in annual revenue and employing nearly 82,000 people.
   >
   > Some museum stores are gold mines. The Metropolitan Museum of Art in New York, which manages its own retail division, had \$79.7 million in merchandise sales in 2003, according to its federal income tax filing, with profits of \$39 million. The Museum of Modern Art's retail sales, also managed in house, reached \$25.7 million in 2004, with profits of \$12.5 million.

   Keith Schneider, *Adding Profits to the Gift Shop*, N.Y. Times, Mar. 29, 2006, at 31.

2. On the history of museums, see Museum Revolutions: How Museums Change and Are Changed (Simon J. Knell, Suzanne MacLeod, & Sheila Watson eds., 2007); Julian Spalding, The Poetic Museum: Reviving Historic Collections (2002); E. Hooper-Greenhill, Museums and the Shaping of Knowledge (1992); The Origins of Museums: The Cabinets of Curiosities in Sixteenth and Seventeenth-Century Europe (O. Impey & A. MacGregor eds., 1985); A. Wittlin, Museums (1970); G. Bazin, The Museum Age (1969).

2. The Ritual of the Secular

The past twenty-five years have witnessed a relentless drive to establish new museums, sometimes through the reinvention of old ones. This development often has accompanied efforts to enhance a new sense of cultural sophistication in a particular city, region, or country as well as efforts to attract tourist dollars. Some people see the modern museum as a new sort of secular temple that asserts itself as a replacement for the temples and churches of history. The reading that follows explores these concepts.

Carol Duncan, *Art Museums and the Ritual of Citizenship, in* Exhibiting Cultures: The Poetics and Politics of Museum Display 90–92 (Ivan Karp & Steven D. Lavine eds., 1991)

The Museum as Ritual

. . . In referring to museums as ceremonial monuments, my intention is to emphasize the museum experience as a monumental creation in its own right, a cultural artifact that is much more than what we used to understand as "museum architecture." Above all, a museum is not the neutral and transparent sheltering space that it is often claimed to be. More like the traditional ceremonial monuments that museum buildings frequently emulate – classical temples, medieval cathedrals, Renaissance palaces – the museum is a complex experience involving architecture, programmed displays of art objects, and highly rationalized installation practices. And like ceremonial structures of the past, by fulfilling its declared purposes as a museum (preserving and displaying art objects) it also carries out broad, sometimes less obvious political and ideological tasks.

Since the Enlightenment, our society has distinguished between the religious and the secular. We normally think of churches and temples as religious sites, different in kind from secular sites such as museums, courthouses, or state capitols. We associate different kinds of truths with each kind of site. The distinction, rooted in Enlightenment struggles against authoritative religious doctrines, makes religious truth a matter of subjective belief, while the truths belonging to museums, universities, or courts of law claim to be self-evident to reason, rooted in experience, and empirically verifiable. According to this tradition, we think of religious truth as addressed to particular groups of voluntary believers, while secular truth has the status of objective or universal knowledge and functions in our society as higher, authoritative truth. As such, it helps bind the community as a whole into a civic body, identifying its highest values, its proudest memories, and its truest truths. Art museums belong decisively to this realm of secular knowledge, not only because of the branches of scientific and humanistic knowledge practiced in them – conservation, art history, archaeology – but also because of their status as preservers of the community's cultural heritage.

In contrast, our concept of ritual is normally associated with religious practices, with real or symbolic sacrifices or spiritual transformations. Clearly, such events can have little to do with so secular a place as a museum. But, as anthropologists now argue, our supposedly secular culture is full of ritual situations and events. Once we recognize the ideological character of our Enlightenment vocabulary and question the claims made for the secular – that its truths are lucid, rationally demonstrable, and objective – we may begin to conceptualize the hidden (or perhaps the better word is *disguised*) ritual content of secular ceremonies. We can also consider the advantages of a ritual that passes as a secular, and therefore objective and neutral, occurrence.

The very architecture of museums suggests their character as secular rituals. It was fitting that the temple façade was for two hundred years the most popular signifier for the public art museum. The temple façade had the advantage of calling up both secular and ritual associations. The beginnings of museum architecture date from the epoch in which Greek and Roman architectural forms were becoming the normal language for distinctly civic and secular buildings. Referring to a pre-Christian world of highly evolved civic institutions, classical-looking buildings could well suggest secular, Enlightenment principles and purposes. But monumental classical forms also brought with them the space of rituals – corridors scaled for processionals and interior sanctuaries designed for awesome and potent effigies.

Museums do not simply resemble temples architecturally; they *work* like temples, shrines, and other such monuments. Museumgoers today, like visitors to these other sites, bring with them the willingness and ability to shift into a certain state of receptivity. And like traditional ritual sites, museum space is carefully marked off and culturally designated as special, reserved for a particular kind of contemplation and learning experience and demanding a special quality of attention – what Victor Turner called "liminality."

In all the ritual sites, some kind of performance takes place. Visitors may witness a drama – often a real or symbolic sacrifice – or hear a recital of texts or special music; they may enact a performance themselves, often individually and alone, by following a prescribed route, repeating a prayer or certain texts, reliving a narrative relevant to the site, or engaging in some other structured experience that related to the history or meaning of the site. Some individuals may use ritual sites more knowledgeably than others; they may be more educationally prepared to respond to their symbolic cues. Ritual is often regarded as transformative; it confers identity or purifies or restores order to the world through sacrifice, ordeal, or enlightenment.

So visitors of a museum follow a route through a programmed narrative – in this case, one or another version of the history of art. In the museum, art history displaces history, purges it of social and political conflict, and distills it down to a series of triumphs, mostly of individual genius. Of course, what the museum presents as the community's history, beliefs, and identity may represent only the interests and self-image of certain powers within the community. Such deceit, however, does not necessarily lessen the effectiveness of the monument's ritual structure as such.

NOTES

1. The economic aspects of museum collections provoke different reactions and theories. Although the market value of many artworks regularly attracts front-page attention, some professionals associated with museums eschew an economic perspective on the contents of their institutions. To archaeologists and indigenous peoples, in particular, assigning monetary value to objects in museums encourages theft and looting and dishonors the sacred significance that some objects are deemed to possess.
2. Arguably, because the contents of a country's museums are an important part of that country's national wealth, they should not be repatriated to peoples and countries of origin. See Stephen K. Urice, *The Beautiful One Has Come – To Stay*, 135, 151–52, IMPERIALISM, ART AND RESTITUTION (John Henry Merryman ed., 2006). Professor Urice refers to the literature on the "value of culture and

cultural capital," including DAVID THROSBY, ECONOMICS AND CULTURE (2001). See also Bruno Frey, *Evaluating Cultural Property: The Economic Approach*, 6 INT'L. J. CULTURAL PROP. 231 (1997); THE ECONOMICS OF ART MUSEUMS (Martin Feldstein ed., 1991).

3. The wealth and other resources of certain prominent institutions, such as the J. Paul Getty Museum and the Metropolitan Museum of Art, tend to draw attention away from the financial plight that many less well-known museums face as a result of declining attendance, reduced government grants, and rising operational costs. See Stephen E. Weil, *The Multiple Crises in Our Museums*, *in* BEAUTY AND THE BEASTS: ON MUSEUMS, ART, THE LAW AND THE MARKET 3 (1983).
4. The problems of funding have been exacerbated in the United States by declining appropriations to the National Endowment for the Arts. The following is an excerpt from the March 13, 2007, written testimony of Robert L. Lynch, president and chief executive officer of Americans for the Arts, to the House Appropriations Subcommittee on Interior, Environment and Related Agencies:

> Despite the economic and societal potential of the arts, the federal government has not kept pace with its government partners at the state and local level. Except for declines in funding after 9/11, local and state government budgets for the arts have collectively and steadily increased, respectively representing a 32 percent and 45 percent increase since 1994. On the other hand, federal support for the National Endowment for the Arts took a deep 40 percent cut in 1995 and has had only modest increases in the subsequent years, representing a 27 percent decrease.
>
> During the mid-90s when Congress decided to cut funding for the arts, one rationale was that private sector charitable giving would easily make up for the funding gap. Unfortunately, the problem became worse. The matching requirement that is prerequisite in NEA grants acts as a powerful funding magnet for the arts. Despite record increases in total philanthropy for charities over the last decade, the market share of private giving to the arts has rapidly decreased, perhaps not so coincidentally around the same time as the cuts in federal funding for the arts.
>
> Last October, the *Wall Street Journal* ran a major article on this topic, "Hunger vs. the Arts," which described the challenges that arts organizations are facing as this market share of private sector support for the arts declines. Expressed in real dollars, if the nonprofit arts had merely maintained the 8.4 percent market share of total philanthropic giving that it enjoyed back in 1992, instead of the 5.2 percent market share it has today, there would have been an additional infusion of $8.4 billion for the arts this year alone. The federal government can help reverse this trend by bringing back national attention and incentives for giving to the arts in America.

In light of uncertainty over public assistance, museums increasingly look to private sources to support their missions. Although gifts of art by collectors confer tax advantages on donors, more ambiguous forms of support from private sources have recently given rise to controversy. For example, a retrospective of the work of Takashi Murakami at the Los Angeles Museum of Contemporary Art received significant financial support from galleries who sell the artist's work, raising serious ethical issues. See Jori Finkel, *Dealers' Money Nudges Museums*, N.Y. TIMES, Nov. 18, 2007, at 2.1.

3. The Culture of Collecting

As we have seen, most museums, whether privately or publicly sponsored, have their origins in the collecting activities of individuals. Recent examples of private initiatives include the J. Paul Getty Museum and the Norton Simon Museum, both in Los Angeles, and the Neue Galerie in New York. Chapter 3 introduced the role of the collector in the cultural heritage regime. We return here to that theme in the context of museum acquisitions. Private collecting remains controversial to some, but its motivation seems to be an inherent aspect of human nature. In the following reading, the activities of the book's hero evoke insightful comments on the motives of collectors generally.

SUSAN SONTAG, THE VOLCANO LOVER 25, 144, 201 (1992) (reprinted with permission of Farrar, Straus, and Giroux, LLC)

To collect is to rescue things, valuable things, from neglect, from oblivion or simply from the ignoble destiny of being in someone else's collection rather than one's own. But buying a whole collection instead of chasing down one's quarry piece by piece – it was not an elegant move. Collecting is also a sport, and its difficulty is part of what gives it honor and zest. A true collector prefers not to acquire in bulk (any more than hunters want the game simply driven past them) [and is] not fulfilled by collecting another's collection: mere acquiring or accumulating is not collecting. But the Cavaliere was impatient. There are not only inner needs and exigencies. And he wanted to get on with what would be but the first of his Neapolitan collections." . . .

. . . Of course to show off one's possessions may seem like boasting, but then the collector did not invent or fabricate these things, he is but their humble servant. He does not praise himself in exhibiting them, he offers them humbly for the admiration of others. If the objects a collector has were of his own making, or even if they were a legacy, then it would indeed seem like boasting. But building a collection, the anxious activity of inventing one's own inheritance, frees one from the obligation of reticence. For the collector to show off his collection is not bad manners. Indeed, the collector, like the impostor, has no existence unless he goes public, unless he shows what he is or has decided to be. Unless he puts his passions on display.

. . . Every collector feels menaced by all the imponderables that can bring disaster. Which is to say that every collection – itself an island – needs an island. And grandiose collections often inspire grandiose ideas of proper storage and safekeeping. An indefatigable collector in southern Florida, who travels about on his buying expeditions in the last private train in the United States, has acquired a gigantic castle in Genoa to store his vast assemblage of decorative objects; and the Nationalist Chinese who in

1949 packed up in rice grass and cotton all the portable masterpieces of the fine arts in China then above ground (silk paintings, small sculpture, jades, bronzes, porcelain, and calligraphy) to take with them to Taiwan, keep[ing] them in tunnels and vaults hollowed out of a mountain next to a huge museum with room to display no more than a tiny fraction of their booty. Most storage places need not be so fanciful or fortress-like to be safe. But stored in a place that does not feel secure, the collection is a constant source of anxiety. Pleasure is haunted by the phantom of loss.

Hermione Waterfield & J.C.H. King, Provenance: Twelve Collectors of Ethnographic Art in England 1760–1990, 111 et seq. (2007)

[The remarkable story that follows, about a great English collector of ethnographic objects, highlights the characteristic fixations of collectors. The second reading raises serious cross-cultural and ethical issues related to collecting. It is oriented toward the implications of the Native American Graves Protection and Repatriation Act (NAGPRA) of the United States, which was extensively discussed earlier in the book. – *Eds.*]

James Hooper was the last Englishman to form a great private collection of tribal art. This was dispersed, some of it during his lifetime through sale or exchange and after his death by sales and donations to places of origin and in a series of auctions.

Born in North Wraxall, Wiltshire, James Hooper was the third child and eldest son of six children. His grandfather was a surgeon who was also an amateur taxidermist and minor collector of paintings and furniture. His father, Thomas Race, inherited both his father's interests, but forsook a career in medicine to join the police and move to London. After spells in Greenwich and Clapham they settled in Kingston-upon-Thames in 1911, where he was appointed a Sub-divisional Inspector, and he continued to collect – or rather amass – objects of all kinds.

Thomas gave his young son a spear in about 1912, which he cleaned and hung on his bedroom wall. James later related how the original spear aroused his curiosity to search the shops for curios and weapons, and read the relevant books. Thomas continued to give James weapons – for instance a Maori *tewhatewha* in 1931.

. . .

After [World War I] James spent time on a farm before obtaining qualifications and a job with the Thames Conservancy in 1922 as Assistant Inspector for the Oxford area. His interest in tribal artefacts had not diminished and he realized that the way of life for most of the peoples who had made them was changing fast, so he hastened to preserve what he could find. He determined to form a collection of material from the Pacific Islands, Africa and the Indians of North America. Happily for him the Oxford area included the Pitt River Museum in Oxford, with its distinguished curator, Henry Balfour, who became a friend and who bought many objects for the museum. The Hooper labels may still be seen on the relevant objects on display today.

The Hooper family has his ledger which he apparently began in 1920 and which he continued until September 1952, although the entries became increasingly sporadic. The title written in James'[s] hand is "Ethnographical Collection [James Thomas Hooper]" and the first entry reads: North American Indian dress and Japanese spears £1 6s.od. The first twenty-one entries are registered by Roman numerals but thereafter in Arabic. The first mention of a date is on page 7 when, in January 1924, Hooper found in Oxford a Kota reliquary figure (#153) for 15s.od. On 31 March he discovered in Oxford a model boat from the Solomon Islands (#158) for 2s.6d. For a shilling each he could buy a Gilbert Islands spear, a Maori *tewhatewha*, a Fiji club with ivory inlay, a bowl with pearl-shell inlay, a tooth necklace, a fish hook, a Maori mat, an Aborigine spear thrower, two New Guinea breast ornaments and an African axe. A New Ireland *tatanua* mask cost £1, as did a Plains Indian stone-headed club, an African axe, a *patu onewa*, a Solomon Islands canoe prow ornament and an old claymore. The workmanship on a Raivavae paddle in Windsor which cost him £1 10s.od. seemed to fascinate Hooper because he drew a sketch on the opposite page. There are random sketches throughout the ledger. Hooper did not have independent means, so he had to subsidise his acquisitions by making sales, which he recorded on six pages at the back of the ledger until May 1934 – again the entries become increasingly sporadic.

In August 1923 he married Ivy Dale and they moved to Littlemore, outside Oxford, in 1927. The walls became covered with spears and clubs while the stairs remained uncarpeted. Their daughter, Babette, was born in 1926 and a son, Kenneth, in 1929. Hooper became increasingly serious about his ambition to form a major collection of tribal art, and in August 1931 he started another list which is headed "Catalogue of the Ethnographical Collection of James T. Hooper." He continued the general ledger but entered in his second volume (henceforth referred to as the catalogue) the items he planned to keep from his purchases, and marks what he believed were the actual values of his acquisitions. Thus a Marquesas Island club which had cost him £5 with a group of other things from Surbiton is marked at £20. A Yoruba mask from the same source for 5s.od. is valued at £8, and a New Ireland mask for £1 at £8.

...

In 1935 Hooper moved to Banbury and in 1939 to South Hertfordshire where the house on New Road, Croxley Green, was named "The Totems." He remained there throughout World War II, refusing to move despite bombs in the area falling close enough to shatter the windows. He published a book in 1953 entitled *The Art of Primitive Peoples* for which Cottie Burland of the British Museum wrote the first half. This is a lengthy preamble which includes a short chapter on his friend who "felt it a duty to preserve something of the past for the sake of the future. It is a collection of things of beauty, which will never be made again, of which the ancient inspiration has fled. In the many years through which the collection has grown,

Mr. Hooper has built up his knowledge of Ethnology and speaks as an expert and careful recorder of information, but all the time he has chosen with artistic judgment, selecting the works best suited to show the real quality reached by the 'primitives.' There is no doubt that the collection is among the finest in private hands in Europe both from the point of view of quality of specimens and of careful documentation." In the second half of the book, James Hooper gives a brief description of the geography, history and art of the peoples of Polynesia, Melanesia, the Northwest coast and Arctic North America, West Africa and Congo, with some mention of their customs and which he illustrates with items from his collection.

Hooper retired from the Thames Conservancy in 1957 and opened "The Totems Museum" in the High Street, Arundel, Sussex in May of that year. . . . "The Totems" consisted of two large rooms, one for American Indian material, the other for Pacific and African, later expanded to a third room as the Pacific holdings increased. There was also a "witch doctor's hut" under the stairs, viewed through a window with a step provided for children. Hooper wished to entertain as well as to inform his visitors, so the contents of the hut were from various parts of the world chosen for dramatic effect rather than ethnographic content.

. . .

Hooper died intestate, so, with few other assets, the collection had to be dispersed to settle the estate. . . . The collection was then sold as five sales over the years 1976–1980 and some items in a sale on 3 July 1990.[2] As a result of these sales, material has returned to museums and collections in New Zealand, Canada, Solomon Islands, Vanuatu, Fiji, Tahiti and America, including Hawaii. Private sales were arranged with the Tahiti and Fiji museums and family donations were also made to both museums. A number of major items were transferred to British national collections in lieu of tax.

Elizabeth A. Sackler, *The Ethics of Collecting*, 7 INT'L J. CULTURAL PROP. 132, 134–40 (1998)

Amassing is part of the European heritage of contemporary American culture and the foundation upon which our competitive economy rests. It is also the fertile soil out of which collecting, in all arenas, has blossomed.

Today, consumerism is the food of the United States' most powerful educational vehicle – television. It is estimated that the average television viewer watches five hours each day – this means that every year an average viewer is bombarded with 21,000 commercials; the message 21,000 times a year is to buy more, to have more. According to *Advertising Age*, 75 percent of commercial network advertising is paid for by only 100 corporations of more than 450,000 corporations in America. Have more, know more,

[2] The Hooper collection appears in STEVEN PHELPS, ART AND ARTEFACTS OF THE PACIFIC, AFRICA AND THE AMERICAS (1976).

be more. The relatively nascent Indian art market benefited from this consumer mentality. Once solely comprised of paintings, sculpture, and so forth, the art market expanded to include antiquity and artifact.

Fine American Indian Art, as it is referred to by auction houses, now fetches excellent prices on the block; dealers sell to collectors who savor the pieces on walls and mantels; anthropologists covet artifacts to enhance scholarship; museums and historical societies create educational and cultural exhibitions.

However, even in [pre–Native American Graves Protection and Repatriation Act (NAGPRA)] 1989, debate around collecting was heated. Phyllis Mauch Messenger edited *The Ethics of Collecting Cultural Property: Whose Culture? Whose Property?* Brian Fagan (University of California at Santa Barbara) posed a series of provocative questions in the foreword. Do people have the right to collect artifacts for personal profit and gratification? Who owns the archaeological record? Should all objects be deposited in museums for common enjoyment? Karen J. Warren's introduction to Messenger's book reminds us:

> For persons in a cultural context where "the past" is not viewed as property, perhaps not even as "past" (e.g., some Native American cultures), or where talk of property ownership, utility and right do not capture important conceptions of the past (e.g., communal kinship with the "living past") . . . *parties to the debate must take enormous care not to see as inferior, irrelevant or of less significance the sorts of concerns that indigenous peoples raise.* (author's emphasis)

From the worldview of many Indigenous Peoples, collecting is unnatural and conclusions deduced from decontextualized accumulated items inaccurate. In addition, the insatiable, passionate exploitation of American Indian culture is painfully offensive.

There is an innate intercultural tension around the ethic of collecting. It is but one of a long list of cultural differences between Western and Indigenous cultures. The separation of spirituality from daily life, dead relatives regarded as gone rather than present, time measured by machine rather than awareness, private ownership as opposed to communal ownership, environment as resource rather than deliberate subsistence, and, of course, amassing as opposed to giving.

NAGPRA is an unusual meeting of White Man's law and Indigenous law. The American Indian Ritual Object Repatriation Foundation arose from the need for a place where people of disparate worldviews could meet to discuss issues surrounding the collecting of American Indian ceremonial material of living cultures. That place, that intersection, has proven to be fertile ground and has provided advocacy resulting in new understandings between individuals as well as Native Nations and public institutions.

NAGPRA raises the question of whether it is appropriate for non-Natives to possess sensitive American Indian objects and raises the issue of questionable provenance. Recognizing the distinction between sensitive material as commodity and its spiritual connection to living cultures has been central to the Foundation's success in influencing a change of ethics in the private sector.

Living cultures is a key phrase. Foremost, the Repatriation Foundation is engaged with *living* peoples and cultures on this continent. It is part of the continuing chronicle of the conquest of the Western Hemisphere and the endurance of the two million survivors whose reculturalization is often dependent on the return of ceremonial material. The manner in which intercultural interaction unfolds determines the diversity of this continent and the future of the First Peoples.

Value: A Conceptual Construct

Dealers in American Indian art are delighted that what were originally considered curios used in anthropological study are now recognized as sophisticated, aesthetic pieces appealing to art collectors. As we have seen, one of the primary goals of the collection-gathering modality is determining and explaining the *value* of objects. Value includes not only monetary value and aesthetic value, but informational value, cultural value, and historical value.

What is the *source* of value? At this time museums are concerned with the contextualization of objects they hold as opposed to their long-accepted approach of positioning all objects as isolated instances of a timeless global patrimony. For museums and collectors there is a polemic between the arguments of contingent and intrinsic value.

In 1993, the Brooklyn Museum's Native American Exhibition *Of Myth and Memory* included a cutting-edge symposium exploring the collecting and exhibiting of ethnographic materials. [Professor Richard Handler] argued in favor of a contingent (or relativistic) position: objects have no intrinsic value or meaning as isolated masterpieces. To have meaning, objects must be surrounded by other objects, by words, by human activity.

In order to provide maximum information to the viewer regarding the cultures, individual items are labeled. Text relating geography and/or general use is on walls, and sometimes audio recordings are available to enlighten the viewer, or scholarly catalogs, or docent tours. All have become a part of daily museum life and a visitor's experience.

Handler supports the relativizing of positivist constructs. Specifically, he argues that labels including "title," "provenance," and "date" – are *interpretive* information.

> Of these three, surely date – the "time" or historical moment at which an object was produced – would seem to be something that is intrinsic to the object and not a function of our interpretation of it. Yet, an intricate system of interpretive presuppositions is built into the innocuous date.... That system of presuppositions is the modern Western conception of time... that conception is not universally shared among all peoples. Western time is homogeneous... enumerating time to objects emerging out of vastly different cultural contexts brings them all into

> a universalized game of reference constructed from the perspective of modern Western historiography.

In short, a fictional time-creation of the objects and the peoples from which they come is artificially created.

Referring to identification of objects through collective labeling, Handler states, "[O]ur own theories of collective and social boundaries [have been imposed] on peoples and places that fell under Western control . . . the ethnic or collective labels we attach to exotic museum objects would not always be recognized by the peoples who are deemed to be their creators." If this is true, labels are as irrelevant to the cultures whose works they "describe" as they are relevant to interpretive Western frameworks. What value do they hold?

Tom Hill notes in his introduction to *Creation's Journey, Native American Identity and Belief* that museums and universities are beginning to support the cultural self-determination of Native Peoples. New theories in anthropology now question "once-assumed objectivity," art history is less hierarchical and "emerging scholarship more closely reflects Native Americans' traditional notions of artistic expression, in which art is an integral element of life."

Extending Handler's and Hill's observations to private collections of Native American artifact, it follows that the value attached to an object is not intrinsic to it but solely meaningful within a Western conceptual framework of "collecting," since the material has been contextually severed from function and culture of origin.

NAGPRA is a door to legal revolution in that it not only requires Western institutions to honor the rights of Native Americans to manage their own cultural patrimony, but also summons scholars and collectors to review their conceptual frameworks and assumptions.

The meaning of collecting and the value of interpreting ethnographic material are no longer as obvious as they were in the past, and the practices not as clearly defined. This is a hard pill to swallow for conservative collectors and scholars, yet this is where we are.

Conclusion: New Ethic

Museums, scholars, and collectors still discuss the relevance of "comprehensive" Native American collections in order to satisfy educational, applied, and aesthetic passions. The question of whether NAGPRA is creating an obstacle or even destroying the possibility for comprehensive collections has been posed in any event.

We know that the limitations of NAGPRA negate the possibility for a museum to possess a "complete" collection. But, what is the loss? From a scholarly point of view, it has been argued, an object's decontextualization can provide neither complete nor accurate information. What value is there in amassing objects under the pretext of knowledge and scholarship when the methodology is faulty at its core? Is it possible for collectors to amass a "valuable" body of artifacts or American Indian art? Can one put together a collection ethically?

You *cannot* put together a collection ethically *if* you confine yourself to the conceptual framework of traditional scholarship and connoisseurship and an antiquated ethic of collecting. Until recently, *comprehensive* collections attempted to include Indigenous materials relating to *all* aspects of lifeways. Yet knowledge about them has been limited to anthropological and archaeological field notes, or dealers and auction house provenance, if any.

I must ask, then, if one cannot possess a comprehensive collection as defined above, what is the loss? What is the *value* of amassing objects under the pretext of aesthetic or love of culture when we *know* that an item is acquired despite the protestations of its original cultures? Is that not a contradiction, in addition to being morally untenable?

On the other hand, you can achieve a collection of "value" if you create new standards and approaches toward acquisition of material and its relevant data. A new ethic of collecting that includes reciprocity and the proactive participation on the part of the collector in identifying from primary sources, such as Native Americans, what it is appropriate to possess. Native Americans do have select items of sensitivity. The repatriation of masks, wampum, pipes, ceremonial regalia, and cultural patrimony, such as the Zuni War Gods, has become the backbone of reculturalization for surviving cultures. Museum personnel across the nation are discovering the excitement of the *new* information forthcoming as a result of interpersonal communications and relationships with Native representatives; this is a requirement of NAGPRA.

Vine Deloria points out that the "ethical systems are notorious for having the ability to relate concepts and doctrines to every abstract consideration except the practical situation with which we become involved. Ethics seems to involve an abstract individual making clear, objective decisions that involve principles but not people."

Possessing "objects" is not the only means to a goal of fulfillment. NAGPRA invites the possibility that objects are *not* more important than human dignity. Assisting in the revitalization of living cultures through communication and repatriation is a greater purpose that provides even greater pleasure than possessing even the most beautiful mask. It also nets a collection of knowledge and wisdom.

Regardless of whether or not "comprehensive" collections are currently a viable possibility, the questions of validity and value echo. In the face of what is understood as offensive decontextualization, the resounding question remains: Are scholarly endeavors, aesthetic appreciation, or monetary gains acceptable motives?

In addition, we know that without proper care, feeding, and use, certain objects are unable to fulfill their function in preserving the life cycle. This information has been told to personnel in scores of museums across the country by Native representatives from scores of Nations visiting their material in museums under NAGPRA guidelines. The meaning of preservation is a worldview: different cultures, different assumptions, different conclusions. To Indigenous People, objects kept in a museum are not being preserved; to the contrary, their life-giving purpose is obliterated.

I propose that museums, institutions, scholars, and collectors abandon the idolization of objects whose richest values are within the cultures that created and use them. And instead, embrace the spirit of the NAGPRA legislation by supporting the human rights of the First Peoples, whose cultures they profess to revere and to whom the objects belong.

From this flows the possibility for Western culture, whose history is scarred with the guilt of conquest and suppression, to relinquish its hold and collect knowledge and wisdom from Indigenous Peoples of this continent out of which a triumphant hybrid of legitimacy, respect and integrity might emerge.

NOTES AND QUESTIONS

1. The collecting impulse is perhaps as old as civilization itself. Few laws relate specifically to collectors. In New Zealand, under the Protected Objects Act of 1975, the sale of Maori objects (*nga taonga tuturu*) to anyone other than a registered collector is prohibited. Residents of the country who possess one or more Maori objects more than fifty years old must register as collectors if they want to purchase additional objects. In many countries, newly discovered antiquities are deemed to belong to the state. Such laws seem less aimed at the practice of collecting *per se* than at discouraging illegal excavations of vulnerable archeological sites. In the United States, for example, one of the purposes of NAGPRA is to regulate the discovery of cultural material on federal or tribal lands.
2. Elizabeth Sackler, the author of the preceding reading, was the sponsor of a unique initiative to acquire American Indian objects in the open art market with the intention of returning them to originating populations. Do you find her interpretation of the motives of traditional collectors convincing? What steps does she argue should be taken to change the freedoms collectors currently enjoy? Would the regulation of collecting cultural objects face any constitutional barriers? What about material of cultures that are extinct?
3. For further discussion of collecting as a phenomenon, review Chapter 3.B.1, and see HERMIONE WATERFIELD, PROVENANCE: TWELVE COLLECTORS OF ETHNOGRAPHIC ART IN ENGLAND 1760–1990 (2007); PHILIPP BLOM, TO HAVE AND TO HOLD: AN INTIMATE HISTORY OF COLLECTORS AND COLLECTING (2003); COLLECTORS, INDIVIDUALS AND INSTITUTIONS (Anthony Shelton ed., 2001); THE CULTURES OF COLLECTING (John Elsner & Roger Cardinal eds., 1994); WERNER MUENSTERBERGER, COLLECTING: AN UNRULY PASSION (PSYCHOLOGICAL PERSPECTIVES) (1994); R. POMIAN, COLLECTORS AND CURIOSITIES: PARIS AND VENICE, 1500–1800 (1990); *Journal of History of Collections* (1989 to date); SUSAN M. PEARCE, OBJECTS OF KNOWLEDGE (London, 1988); S. JOHNSTON & T. BEDDOW, COLLECTING, THE PASSIONATE PASTIME (1986).

4. The Global Museum

Largely in the context of controversial claims for the return of objects from major museum collections – the classic example of which is the Greek claim for the return of the Elgin or Parthenon Marbles from the British Museum – several directors of major museums in Europe and North America have advocated a special role for their museums as custodians of world heritage and culture.

James Cuno, *View from the Universal Museum, in* Imperialism, Art and Restitution 18–21 (John Henry Merryman ed., 2006) (reprinted with the permission of Cambridge University Press)

I should be clear. I am convinced of the values of the Enlightenment museum – call it the "Universal" museum, if you like – just as I am convinced of the humanist values of such recent scholars as Edward Said, who in his preface to the 2003 edition of his groundbreaking work *Orientalism* wrote [about] "those of us who by force of circumstance actually live the pluri-cultural life as it entails Islam and the West" – but the same is true of those of us who live the pluricultural life as it entails any combination of cultures. [Edward Said also said:] "I think it is incumbent upon us to complicate and/or dismantle the reductive formulae and the abstract but potent kind of thought that leads the mind away from concrete human history and experience and into the realms of ideological fiction, metaphysical confrontation and collective passion. . . . Our role is to widen the field of discussion, not set limits in accord with the prevailing authority." Museums have an important role to play in this regard. Those that include works of art from multiple periods and cultures have the opportunity and obligation to present their visitors with experiences that encourage looking for connections between apparently disparate works and cultures rather than reaffirming distinctions that often are, as Said notes, the result of ideological fictions.

As Patrick Geary wrote in *The Myth of Nations: The Medieval Origins of Europe*, which explores the role the academic discipline of history has played in defining nations and substantiating their nationalist claims:

> Modern history was born in the nineteenth century, conceived and developed as an instrument of European nationalism. As a tool of nationalist ideology, the history of Europe's nations was a great success, but it has turned our understanding of the past into a toxic waste dump, filled with the poison of ethnic nationalism, and the poison has seeped deep into popular consciousness. Clearing up this waste is the most daunting challenge facing historians today.

And facing museums, too, I would propose. At their best, museums do not affirm but complicate and challenge the easy and dangerous reliance on such simplistic definitions. They expand rather than narrow our view of the world and the history of its – and our common – artistic patrimony. And as Neil MacGregor, director of the British Museum, wrote recently: "All great works of art are surely the common inheritance of humanity. . . . [T]his is a truth that is surely more important to proclaim now than ever before. In a world increasingly fractured by ethnic and religious identities, it is essential that there are places where the great creations of all civilizations can be seen together, and where the visitor can focus on what unites rather than what divides us. And as Said said, "Rather than the manufactured clash of civilizations, we need to concentrate on the slow working together of cultures that overlap, borrow from each other, and live together in far more interesting ways than any abridged or inauthentic mode of understanding can allow." But for that kind of wider perception we need time and patient and skeptical inquiry, supported by faith in communities of interpretation that are difficult to sustain in a world demanding instant action and reaction."

Museums are, or should be, instruments for encouraging our skeptical inquiry into the simplistic notions of cultural identities. And national policies and laws should respect this all-important contribution by the world's museums by encouraging a licit trade in antiquities and cultural property. Increasingly, in my view, such policies and laws are doing just the opposite.

Historically, the United States government takes an internationalist position with regard to culture. It presumes that exposing our citizens to works of art from the world's many cultures is in their best interest and promotes cultural understanding.

. . .

Our government believes that citizens of other countries benefit from exposure to American works of art just as we benefit from exposure to works of art from other cultures. This is why I so forcefully disagree with the recent decision by the United States government to fund a special exhibition of American art to tour around the United States. At this time especially, when the United States is in military, political, and ideological conflict with high-profile elements in the Islamic world, when much of that world – its glorious past and present, its historic and current internal political and religious conflicts – is almost totally unknown, and certainly too little understood, by almost all Americans, the Bush administration should have been funding and touring across the United States exhibitions of Islamic art, not American art. We Americans do not need to celebrate more our identity as Americans. We need much more to know better and come to appreciate more fully the beauty, sophistication, subtleties, and complexities of the art and culture of that part of the world in which our government, in our name, is engaged in military conflict.

Largely in response to claims for return of objects from museums to Italy, Greece, Egypt, and other states, eighteen directors of major museums in Europe and North America issued the following declaration in December 2002:

Declaration on the Importance and Value of Universal Museums, ICOM NEWS, no. 1, at 4 (2004)

The international museum community shares the conviction that illegal traffic in archaeological, artistic, and ethnic objects must be firmly discouraged. We should, however, recognize that objects acquired in earlier times must be viewed in the light of different sensitivities and values, reflective of that earlier era. The objects and monumental works that were installed decades and even centuries ago in museums throughout Europe and America were acquired under conditions that are not comparable with current ones.

Over time, objects so acquired – whether by purchase, gift, or partage – have become part of the museums that have cared for them, and by extension part of the heritage of the nations which house them. Today we are especially sensitive to the subject of a work's original context, but we should not lost sight of the fact that museums too provide a valid and valuable context for objects that were long ago displaced from their original source.

The universal admiration for ancient civilizations would not be so deeply established today were it not for the influence exercised by the artifacts of these cultures, widely available to an international public in major museums. Indeed, the sculpture of classical Greece, to take but one example, is an excellent illustration of this point and of the importance of public collecting. The centuries-long history of appreciation of Greek art began in antiquity, was renewed in Renaissance Italy, and subsequently spread through the rest of Europe and to the Americas. Its accession into the collections of public museums throughout the world marked the significance of Greek Sculpture for mankind as a whole and its enduring value for the contemporary world. Moreover, the distinctly Greek aesthetic of these works appears all the more strongly as the result of their being seen and studied in direct proximity to products of other great civilizations.

Calls to repatriate objects that have belonged to museum collections for many years have become an important issue for museums. Although each case has to be judged individually, we should acknowledge that museums serve not just the citizens of one nation but the people of every nation. Museums are agents in the development of culture, whose mission is to foster knowledge by a continuous process of reinterpretation. Each object contributes to that process. To narrow the focus of museums whose collections are diverse and multifaceted would therefore be a disservice to all visitors.

Hector Feliciano, The Lost Museum: The Nazi Conspiracy to Steal the World's Greatest Works of Art 16, 21 (1997)

Between 1939 and 1944, the Nazis systematically confiscated, stole, or bought works from a number of European collections, or from private collections belonging to wealthy Jewish families, Freemasons, and political opponents. In the end, hundreds of thousands of paintings, priceless sculptures, and drawings by the great masters – as well as millions of books, manuscripts, and other cultural artifacts – were taken from across Europe. These were the spoils of war. Holland and Belgium were heavily hit by this plundering, but of all of the Western European countries it was France that suffered the most. Eastern Europe, of course, presented a different case; it was the victim of the Nazis' iron will to shamelessly annihilate its cultural heritage. There, the Nazis undertook to destroy its identity, folklore, architecture, and even its language through mass murder and forced Germanization.

...

According to Hitler's grand scheme, Linz, a provincial capital in Alpine Austria, where Hitler had spent part of his childhood and his adolescence, was to be, along with Munich, N[u]remberg, and Berlin, one of the Reich's crowning glories, a showpiece of Nazism. The monumental museum was to be made up of a series of colossal buildings housing the most important European works from prehistoric times to the present day. Every European master of painting and sculpture (recognized as such by Nazi ideology, of course) would be represented.

Jonathan Petropoulos, Art as Politics in the Third Reich 245, 248 (1996)

Sonderauftrag Linz, the cultural complex planned for Hitler's childhood hometown that had the Führermuseum as its center, expressed Hitler's megalomania and style of self-promotion. Everything about the project was to set new records for size and grandeur – from the number of works in the galleries to the sculptural frieze that he planned for the central gallery, which at 660 feet in length would be the largest in Europe, if not the world. Yet the Linz Project, which Hitler launched in 1938 when he was securely in power, was not intended to glorify the Führer only at that historical moment but also to constitute a lasting and transcendent monument to his rule.

...

Sondrauftrag Linz, however, represented more than an effort to control the artistic products of the German nation; it constituted the clear expression of Hitler's plans to dominate Europe. The creation of the largest museum in the world would serve as a symbol of Germany's cultural hegemony.

NOTES AND QUESTIONS

1. The 2002 Declaration by the eighteen major museum directors is an unusual example of a united professional front against the return of material in their collections. See James Cuno, Whose Culture? The Promise of Museums and the Debate over Antiquities (2009); Stephen K. Urice, *The Beautiful One Has Come – To Stay*, *in* Imperialism, Art and Restitution 135 (John Henry Merryman ed., 2006) (arguing that the preservation of existing collections can promote ongoing creativity and broader benefits to the public). Most museums, however, have been more receptive to concerns raised by indigenous groups and

others about certain material in their collections. See Willard L. Boyd, *Museums as Centers of Cultural Understanding, id.* at 47, 55–58; Geoffrey Lewis, *The Universal Museum: A Case of Special Pleading? in* Art and Cultural Heritage: Law, Policy and Practice 379 (Barbara T. Hoffmann ed., 2006); Christine K. Knox, *They've Lost Their Marbles: 2002 Universal Museum's Declaration, The Elgin Marbles and the Future of the Repatriation Movement*, 29 Suffolk Transnat'l L. Rev. 315 (2006) (arguing that the Declaration was intended to change the way people view the role of museums in society).

2. Many see the Declaration as a reactionary response by wealthy established institutions that are concerned about their vulnerability to claims. Do you agree? The universality principle guided assemblages of objects from the seventeenth into the twentieth century on the basis of a mission that complemented parallel developments in the arts and sciences. Should these collections be vulnerable to disassembly merely because of different contemporary values and priorities? Is the intertemporal doctrine of international law discussed in Chapter 5 applicable to the rights of indigenous peoples?
3. Was Adolf Hitler's plan for the world's largest museum in Linz, Austria, an early example of the universal museum advocated by the eighteen major museum directors? Did its general limitation to Western art and its exclusion of what was deemed "degenerate art," according to Nazi standards, distinguish it materially from the contemporary idea of a universal museum or not? Were the purposes of the respective kinds of projects similar? Different? What else distinguishes the two kinds of projects?

5. Biculturalism and Museums

a. Introduction

Over the past twenty years, a principle known as biculturalism has been developed in connection with some museum exhibitions and their governance in general. The concept of biculturalism seems associated with that of multiculturalism, especially in such countries as Australia, Canada, New Zealand, and the United States, where movements for self-determination and recognition of indigenous rights have led to new concepts of diversity and the recognition of ethnic and other differences. How this principle manifests differs widely among institutions, but its adoption has resulted in significant changes in the definition of a museum's fiduciary duty, in the way museum exhibitions are presented, and in other aspects of museum activities. Salient examples are the National Museum of the American Indian in Washington, D.C., and New York and hundreds of other museums in the United States affected by NAGPRA. The following commentary focuses on the concept of biculturalism as it has been applied in two other countries: New Zealand and Canada.

b. New Zealand Museums

A good example of a museum reinventing itself occurred in 1998, when the Museum of New Zealand (Te Papa Tongarewa) in Wellington opened as a reincarnation of the former National Museum of New Zealand. The institution had begun in 1865 as the Colonial

Museum, whereas the new museum represents an attempt at a genuine partnership between Maori and non-Maori (*pakeha*) in the operation of a national museum.

Te Papa Tongarewa represents an example of the implementation of "biculturalism" that has been developed in several New Zealand museums. In this context, biculturalism means some form of Maori partnership with non-Maori, not only in the management and governance of a museum but also in such matters as employment, exhibitions, loans, and other museum services.

Te Papa Tongarewa displays a broad range of policies and practices that reveal its commitment to the concept of biculturalism. One example is the tribal (*iwi*) exhibition program. This is a program of short-term exhibitions that the museum develops with identified *iwi* partners. Through such exhibitions, *iwi* can present cultural treasures (*taonga*), art, and narratives from their own collections and those of Te Papa Tongarewa or other museums whereby the museum acknowledges, in effect, that cultural knowledge does not always lie with museum experts. Another example of biculturalism in action is Rongomaraeroa, which is a functioning ritual courtyard (*marae*) within the museum building. Although it is a Maori institution, its placement inside the museum is symbolic of the strength of the commitment of that institution to the recognition of Maori values and beliefs.

In its role as the national museum of New Zealand, Te Papa Tongarewa also administers Te Paerangi National Services, which is a program supporting regional museums and offering partnership programs with other museums in areas such as biculturalism and exhibition development. Given the extensive financial and human resources of Te Papa Tongarewa, it is appropriate that it use these to expand the work of other museums around New Zealand. To that end, Te Paerangi National Services has organized several conferences on bicultural developments at New Zealand museums.

The Auckland War Memorial Museum Act 1996 specifically provides for Maori representation on the board of trustees of that museum – now renamed Tamaki Paenga Hira. The law also establishes the Maori Advisory Committee (Taumata-a-Iwi), which comprises representatives of Maori from the Auckland area. The Committee has five members (three of whom are from the Ngati Whatua tribe, and one each from the Tainui and Ngati Paoa tribes). Unlike Te Papa Tongarewa, the Auckland Museum's version of biculturalism (or what it prefers to call integrated Maori values) focuses on a relationship with local tribes and relies on them to represent the interests of Maori outside the region. It appears that the Auckland Museum policy emphasizes that both Maori and non-Maori alike should seek to uphold Maori values and concerns in the governance of the museum.

c. Canadian Museums

The past decade has witnessed several controversies concerning museum exhibitions in Canada. One such instance led to fundamental changes in the political and professional relationships between Canadian museums and First Nations. In 1988, the Glenbow Museum in Calgary, Alberta, organized an exhibition titled "The Spirit Sings" in conjunction with the Winter Olympic Games, which took place in the city that year. The exhibit contained a number of masks lent by foreign museums. The Lubicon Lake First Nation objected to the masks' exhibition in public and organized a boycott of the display.

Several Mohawk bands then sought an interim injunction to prevent the display of a "false face" mask at the exhibition. The trial judge decided not to issue an interim injunction pending trial. Justice Shannon thought that, although the claim to ownership of tribal cultural property was a serious issue to be tried, the applicants were unable to show that irreparable harm would result from the continued display of the mask. He supported this view by noting that the mask had been on display at various museums for many years without any objections from the Mohawks.

The Lubicon Cree were supported by the Assembly of First Nations, which agreed to cosponsor a national conference of the Canadian Museums Association on issues connected with the relationship between Canadian museums and Aboriginal peoples. The conference was held in Ottawa in November 1988 and led to the establishment of the Task Force on Museums and First Peoples whose mission was to develop a framework for a new relationship between the two groups. The outcome went far beyond questions of repatriation by calling for improved Aboriginal access to museum collections as well as increased Aboriginal involvement in their management.

In February 1992, the Task Force on Museums and First Peoples released its report titled *Turning the Page: Forging New Partnerships Between Museums and First Peoples*, which outlined principles and recommendations for change. Following the report, an application was made to the Canadian federal government to fund the Council for Museums and First Peoples, which would work to further the partnership ideals envisaged in the Task Force's report. This approach was unsuccessful, and the implementation of the report was then left to individual museums, regional museum associations, and the Canadian Museums Association, working with Aboriginal groups. In contrast to the United States, therefore, Canada has lacked a centralized system to administer and monitor the recommendations of the Task Force. Most significant, the Task Force's recommendations lack any force of law. Instead, their observance or implementation relies on the individual discretion of museums and museum associations.

The Task Force acknowledged that the spark leading to its work had been the Glenbow Museum exhibition of 1988, which had returned to the assumptions behind many exhibitions of Aboriginal cultural property in Canadian museums: that Aboriginal people were either extinct or on the verge of being so and that there was no need to involve Aboriginal people in the preparation of exhibitions of their own culture. The report cites Chief George Erasmus (former Assembly of First Nations national chief): "We [the Aboriginal peoples] are well aware that many people have dedicated their time, careers and their lives to showing what they believe is the accurate picture of indigenous peoples. We thank you for that, but we want to turn the page." The Task Force went on to develop principles and recommendations that could form the basis for establishing new relationships between Aboriginal peoples and Canadian museums. The specific recommendations in the Task Force's report deal with interpretation, access, repatriation, and training. The report recommends that Aboriginal peoples be involved in preparing exhibitions and other projects that include Aboriginal culture. It goes on to recommend that increased opportunities be made available by museums and galleries for the employment of Aboriginal peoples and their representation on management organizations – such as boards of directors. It suggests that museums disclose more information about their Aboriginal collections and allow Aboriginal people access to objects and relevant documentation. The report also recommends that funding be provided for professional and technical training of Aboriginal people in connection with Aboriginal initiatives, such as cultural centers. It also urges that museums recognize the legitimacy of the credentials of Aboriginal individuals and groups who possess knowledge of particular cultures.

Since its publication, the report has played a significant role as a framework for newly emerging forms of partnership between museums and Aboriginal peoples in Canada. Many museums and museum associations have adopted the report as a basis for developing their own relationships with Aboriginal peoples. First Nations individuals are now members of the boards of directors of several Canadian museums and are routinely involved in the preparation and presentation of exhibitions. In the absence of any umbrella or national organization, detailed information about the interpretation and application of the Task Force's recommendations is unavailable. This may not be as much of a problem in Canada, given the relatively small size of the country's museum community, as it might be elsewhere, but it clearly compromises the scope for the successful implementation of the Task Force's recommendations.[3]

NOTES AND QUESTIONS

1. The approach of the Canadian Task Force on Museums and First Peoples, as in the implementation of NAGPRA in the United States, is one of partnership between Canadian museums and First Nations. What sorts of problems do you think such partnerships may encounter? Should there be a similar obligation to respond to the concerns of communities and ethnic groups outside the country where the museum is located? What if a First Nation group is part of a larger indigenous group based in the United States?
2. Do you think museum trustees could be in a position of conflict of interest if they respond to the demands of particular groups within their community in ways that might not be considered in the interest of the community as a whole? Should they be legally accountable in such instances?
3. For general commentary on biculturalism, see ANA FELIPA VRDOLJAK, INTERNATIONAL LAW, MUSEUMS, AND THE RETURN OF CULTURAL OBJECTS (2008); Timothy W. Luke, *Inventing the Southwest: The Fred Harvey Company and Native American Art, in* MUSEUM POLITICS: POWER PLAYS AT THE EXHIBITION 82 (Timothy W. Luke ed., 2002); James A.R. Nafziger, *The New Fiduciary Duty of United States Museums to Repatriate Cultural Heritage: The Oregon Experience,* U. B.C. L. REV. (SPECIAL ISSUE) 37 (1995).

   For additional background on biculturalism specifically in New Zealand museums, see Arapata Hakiwai, *Maori Taonga-Maori Identity, in* ART AND CULTURAL HERITAGE: LAW, POLICY AND PRACTICE, 409 (Barbara T. Hoffman ed., 2006); Merata Kawharu, *Indigenous Governance in Museums: A Case Study, the Auckland War Memorial Museum, in* THE DEAD AND THEIR POSSESSIONS: REPATRIATION IN PRINCIPLE, POLICY AND PRACTICE 293 (Cressida Fforde, Jane Hubert, & Paul Turnbull eds., 2002); David Butts, *Maori and Museums: The Politics of Indigenous Recognition,* in MUSEUMS, SOCIETY, INEQUALITY 225 (Richard Sandell ed., 2002); GERALD O'REGAN, BICULTURAL DEVELOPMENTS IN MUSEUMS OF AOTEAROA: WHAT IS THE CURRENT STATUS? (1997).

[3] The editors thank Professor Catherine Bell for her coauthorship of an earlier version of this commentary.

On the Canadian experience, see *Mohawk Bands* v. *Glenbow-Alberta Institute* [1988], 3 C.N.L.R. 70 (Alta. Q.B.); TASK FORCE REPORT ON MUSEUMS AND FIRST PEOPLES (TURNING THE PAGE: FORGING NEW PARTNERSHIPS BETWEEN MUSEUMS AND FIRST PEOPLES) (2d ed. 1992). See also Barbara H. Winter, *New Futures for the Past: Cooperation between First Nations and Museums in Canada*, U. B.C. L. REV. (SPECIAL ISSUE) 29 (1995).

C. Museum Organization and Governance

1. Introduction

In the United States, most museums are established as nonprofit corporations under state law. Usually incorporation occurs under a statute that allows the process for all nonprofits, but occasionally an individual statute incorporates a particular institution, as is also possible in Canada. Examples of the latter include the Smithsonian Institution (20 U.S.C. §§ 41–80 (2000)) and the National Gallery of Canada (Museums Act, S.C. 1990, c. 3).

There is ordinarily no legal requirement that a museum be a corporation, but that form of organization is usually chosen for the same reasons that appeal to businesses; centralized management, separate legal personality, perpetual succession, and limited liability. If a museum chooses not to incorporate, it can operate as a charitable trust or other form of association. These various forms of organization have different rules of both statutory and common law that are applicable to them, but none arises peculiarly from the fact that an institution is a museum. Other laws and regulations may apply only to museums, such as immunity of collections from seizure. Unlike for-profit businesses, whether or not incorporated, nonprofit organizations such as museums cannot return any profits they accrue to their members except in the form of salaries, reimbursement of expenses, and the like; instead, they must use such funds for the pursuit of institutional objectives. In this sense, the dividends, if any, accruing through the operations of a museum belong to the institution and not to its members or employees.

An institution established as a museum is deemed in law to hold its property for a charitable purpose for the benefit of the public. Thus, all museums are governed by state laws that apply to property held in trust for charitable purposes. According to the *Restatement Second of the Law of Trusts*: "A purpose is charitable if its accomplishment is of such social interest to the community as to justify permitting the property to be devoted to the purpose in perpetuity."[4] The Second Restatement lists the methods by which a charitable trust may promote education, including the establishment of art museums or other museums. See *People ex rel. Scott v. George F. Harding Museum*, 374 N.E. 2d 756 (Ill. App. Ct. 1978). Museums, as charitable enterprises, usually enjoy certain tax relief and are exempt from the rule against perpetuities. Let us, then, ask: when is a museum a charity? In the following opinion, the English Court of Appeal considered whether a valid charitable trust had been created by a testator who gave his studio and its contents to trustees and directed that his residual estate be used to endow the studio as a museum for the display of his collection.

[4] RESTATEMENT (SECOND) OF TRUSTS, § 368, comment b, at 248 (1957).

In Re Pinion,
[1965] 1 Ch. 85 (C.A.)

Harman, L.J.

This appeal concerns the testamentary dispositions of Arthur Watson Hyde Pinion, who died in the year 1961, having, by his will made in 1956 as varied by a codicil made in 1961, sought to devote almost the whole of his not inconsiderable estate to a project designed to keep himself and his family for all time before the public eye by allowing the public to view without cost his studio, situated at 22A, Pembridge Villas, Notting Hill, intact with its entire contents. These treasures are to be entrusted to a custodian, first his sister and subsequently a blood relation of his, who are to be paid and housed out of his estate. The question is whether he was entitled to saddle his property with this [chimera] to the deprivation of his next-of-kin and this, the judge has held, he was entitled to do at the instance of the Attorney-General, who persuaded him, though hardly, that the testator has created a valid charitable trust.

The will and codicil are rambling and half coherent documents reduced to some semblance of order by the judge but his summary is, I think, perhaps too neat and logical and the actual words should be read to convey its authentic flavour. It starts by conferring a life interest in the whole estate on his sister, the first defendant, who is also his sole next-of-kin, and proceeds. [Lord Justice Harman then read those passages of the will and codicils set out in the statement of facts, referred to the fact that the testator had revoked the life estate of his sister, had given her an annuity, and continued.] I construe this farrago as meaning that the entire contents of the studio, which housed all the articles referred to, are to be exhibited as a whole and, as he says, "to be kept "intact in the studio." The only exception is that articles "not of an antique nature" may be disposed of. I assume that the revocation of the sister's life interest accelerated the gift to the National Trust, which has refused the bequest, and that the authority to his executors to appoint a trust to carry out the bequest is in fact mandatory, the contrary not having been argued.

In this court the Attorney-General did not seek to support the gift as being beneficial in a general sense to the public, but confined his plea to that head of charity which is characterized as the advancement of education. He argued both here and below that no evidence was receivable on this subject. A museum, he said, is a place which the law assumes to have an educational value and purpose. The cases on this subject to be found in *Tudor on Charities*, 5th edition (1929), are not very satisfactory. It would appear that a gift to an established museum is charitable: see *British Museum Trustees v. White*. In *In re Holburne*, a gift to trustees of objects of art to form an art museum in Bath open to the public and a fund to endow it was held a valid charitable gift as being of public utility or benefit. No question was there raised as to the merit of the collection. It must have been agreed that such merit existed, for everyone assumed it, including the judge. I conclude that a gift to found a public museum may be assumed to be charitable as of public utility if no one questions it. So in a case about religion, such as *Thornton v. Howe*, the case about Joanna Southcote, the court will assume without inquiry that the teaching may do some good if not shown to be subversive of morality. Where the object is to found a school the court will not study the methods of education provided that on the face of them they are proper: *In re Shaw's Will Trusts*. A school for prostitutes or pickpockets would obviously fail. A case about education is *In re Hummeltenberg*, where the headnote reads: "to be valid a charitable bequest must be for the public benefit, and the trust must be capable of being administered and controlled by the court. The opinion of the donor of a gift or the creator of a trust that the gift or trust is for the public benefit does not make it so, the matter is one to be determined by the court on the evidence before it."

The bequest in that case was connected with spiritualism and the point to which I draw attention is that the judge (the late Lord Russell of Killowen, then Russell J.) said it must be decided on the evidence. There is a passage in his judgment as follows: "It was contended" (says he) "that the court was not the tribunal to determine whether a gift or trust was or was not a gift or a trust for the benefit of the public. It was said that the only judge of this was the donor of the gift or the creator of the trust. For this view reliance was placed on the views expressed "by the Master of the Rolls" [Porter M.R.] and by some members of the Court of Appeal in Ireland in *In re Cranston*. Reliance was also placed on a sentence in the judgment of Chitty J. in *In re Foveaux*. So far as the views so expressed declare that the personal or private opinion of the judge is immaterial, I agree; but so far as they lay down or suggest that the donor of the gift or the creator of the trust is to determine whether the purpose is beneficial to the public, I respectfully disagree. If a testator by stating or indicating his view that a trust is beneficial to the public can establish that fact beyond question, trusts might be established in perpetuity for the promotion of all kinds of fantastic (though not unlawful) objects, of which the training of poodles to dance might be a mild example. In my opinion the question whether a gift is or may be operative for the public benefit is a question to be answered by the court by forming an opinion upon the evidence before it."

Where a museum is concerned and the utility of the gift is brought in question it is, in my opinion, and herein I agree with the judge, essential to know at least something of the quality of the proposed exhibits in order to judge whether they will be conducive to the education of the public. So I think with a public library, such a place if found to be devoted entirely to works of pornography or of a corrupting nature, would not be allowable. Here it is suggested that education in the fine arts is the object. For myself a reading of the will leads me rather to the view that the testator's object was not to educate anyone, but to perpetuate his own name and the repute of his family, hence perhaps the direction that the custodian should be a blood relation of his. However that may be, there is a strong body of evidence here that as a means of education this collection is worthless. The testator's own paintings, of which there are over 50, are said by competent persons to be in an academic style and "atrociously bad": and the other pictures without exception worthless. Even the so-called "Lely" turns out to be a 20th century copy.

Apart from pictures there is a haphazard assembly – it does not merit the name collection, for no purpose emerges, no time nor style is illustrated – of furniture and objects of so-called "art" about which expert opinion is unanimous that nothing beyond the third-rate is to be found. Indeed one of the experts expresses his surprise that so voracious a collector should not by hazard have picked up even one meritorious object. The most that skilful cross-examination extracted from the expert witnesses was that there were a dozen chairs which might perhaps be acceptable to a minor provincial museum and perhaps another dozen not altogether worthless, but two dozen chairs do not make a museum and they must, to accord with the will, be exhibited stifled by a large number of absolutely worthless pictures and objects.

It was said that this is a matter of taste, and *de gustibus non est disputandum*, but here I agree with the judge that there is an accepted canon of taste on which the court must rely, for it has itself no judicial knowledge of such matters, and the unanimous verdict of the experts is as I have stated. The judge with great hesitation concluded that there was that scintilla of merit which was sufficient to save the rest. I find myself on the other side of the line. I can conceive of no useful object to be served in foisting upon the public this mass of junk. It has neither public utility nor educative value. I would hold that the testator's project ought not to be carried into effect and that his next-of-kin is entitled to the residue of his estate.

NOTES

1. In the United States, following the English practice, the traditional responsibility to enforce charitable trusts or gifts has rested not with private parties but with the attorney general of the state where the charity is located. These officials have brought most of the small number of cases against museum trustees. See Marie C. Malaro, A Legal Primer on Managing Museum Collections 22–26 (2d ed. 1998); Uniform Supervision of Trustees for Charitable Purposes Act §§ 1, 6, and 8 (1954).

   In light of growing concern about the standards of management of many charitable organizations, however, the extent to which attorneys general should in effect dominate legal challenges involving those standards has been subject to reconsideration. See *Hardman v. Feinstein*, 240 Cal. Rptr. 483 (Ct. App. 1987); *Owens v. Magill*, 419 S.E.2d 786 (S.C. 1992). There may be scope for those with permission from the attorney general to sue as relators. *Wiegand v. Barnes Found.*, 97 A.2d 81 (Pa. 1953); *Dickey v. Volker*, 11 S.W.2d 278 (Mo. 1928), *cert. denied*, 279 U.S. 839 (1929). See also R. Kusiak, *The Case for the A.U. (Accountable Universities): Enforcing University Administrators Fiduciary Duties through Student Derivative*

Suits, 56 AM. U. L. REV. 129 (2006); MARIE C. MALARO, A LEGAL PRIMER ON MANAGING MUSEUM COLLECTIONS 27–33 (2d ed. 1998).

2. Few museums have experienced problems as complex and protracted as has the Barnes Foundation. It owns one of the world's valuable collections of impressionist and post-impressionist art, located in the township of Merion, outside Philadelphia. The collection includes 181 Renoir paintings, 69 Cezannes, 59 Matisses, 46 Picassos, 18 Rousseaus, 11 Degas, 7 Van Goghs, 6 Seurats, 4 Manets, and 4 Monets. In recent years, the foundation experienced serious financial difficulties that led to various proposals, such as authorization to lend some of the collection for touring exhibition purposes and the sale of some of the artworks. In 2004 a Pennsylvania court ruled that the Foundation could move to downtown Philadelphia, to attract more entrance revenue but contrary to the founder's will that the collection remain in Merion. Even as the ground was broken for the new museum in Philadelphia, the dispute continued. See Richard L. Feigen, *The Barnes Collection Is Not Being Saved, It Is Being Stolen*, ART NEWSPAPER, JAN. 2010, at 32 (describing the move to Philadelphia as the "biggest heist in history [involving] some US $20–30 billion"). On the move itself and the ground-breaking, see Kate Taylor, *Barnes Museum Pushes Forward Move Downtown*, ART NEWSPAPER, JAN. 2010, at 14. For further background, see *Pennsylvania v. Barnes Foundation*, 159 A.2d 500 (Pa. 1960); *Barnes Foundation v. Keely*, 171 A. 267 (Pa. 1934); *Wiegand v. Barnes Foundation*, 97 A.2d 81 (Pa. 1953); JOHN ANDERSON, ART HELD HOSTAGE: THE BATTLE OVER THE BARNES COLLECTION (2003); HOWARD GREENFELD, THE DEVIL AND DOCTOR BARNES: PORTRAIT OF AN AMERICAN ART COLLECTOR (2006); Ilana H. Eisenstein, Comment: *Keeping Charity in Charitable Trust Law: The Barnes Foundation and the Case for Consideration of Public Interest in Administration of Charitable Trusts*, 151 U. PA. L. REV. 1747 (2003).

The following judicial opinion, during protracted litigation, highlights issues of standing to sue and the public interest.

IN RE BARNES FOUNDATION,
684 A.2d 123 (Pa. Super. Ct. 1996)

[The Barnes Foundation appealed an order refusing a settlement it had proposed. The appealed order had granted various parties intervenor status. These included certain students of the Barnes Foundation (for the purpose of providing the court information about the educational process and curriculum of the foundation's art department from the perspective of current and future students); the de Mazia Trustees (which included Violette de Mazia, who had served as director of education of the foundation's art education program for fifty years before her death in 1987 and had, under her will, established a charitable trust for the benefit of the Barnes Foundation); and the Friends of the Barnes Foundation (an unincorporated nonprofit association whose membership is comprised of present and former students of the art department of the Barnes Foundation and their spouses) – *Eds.*].

Kelly, J.

After considering the testimony and arguments of the parties, Judge Ott entered the following order:

> AND NOW, this 10th day of July, 1995, after hearing and consideration of briefs of counsel, the Petition filed on behalf of the de Mazia Trust seeking to amend the charitable trust established under the will of Violette de Mazia is DENIED on the grounds that the doctrine of deviation is inapplicable and no other bases for allowing the amendments have been demonstrated. The joint Petition filed on behalf of the Barnes Foundation and the de Mazia Trust is hereby rendered moot.

The Order was founded upon Judge Ott's conclusion that "[t]he Barnes Foundation continues to meet the criteria required of a 'support organization' as defined in Miss de Mazia's will." *Barnes Foundation-deMazia Trust, supra* at 337. As a result, the court held that the sanctity of the donor's written intent should be upheld, and that the proposed settlement and amendment would violate the intent of the de Mazia trust.

This appeal followed. It was initiated by the Barnes Foundation. However, the trustees of the de Mazia trust, although technically designated as appellees, are also seeking a reversal of the trial court's order. It is only the aforementioned "Students" who have filed a brief in support of the order. Unfortunately, the Students have nowhere established their entitlement to standing in this particular dispute, and based on our review of the record, and the prior litigation involving these parties, we see no foundation for affording standing to the Students in this particular dispute.

Standing requires a substantial, direct and immediate interest in the subject matter of the litigation. *William Penn Parking Garage* v. *City of Pittsburgh*, 464 Pa. 168, 846 A.2d 269 (1975).

> A "substantial" interest is an interest in the outcome of the litigation which surpasses the common interest of all citizens in procuring obedience to the law. A "direct" interest requires a showing that the matter complained of caused harm to the party's interest. An "immediate" interest involves the nature of the causal connections between the action complained of and the injury to the party challenging it, and is shown where the interest the party seeks to protect is within the zone of interests sought to be protected by the statute or constitutional guarantee in question.

South Whitehall Twp. Police Service v. *South Whitehall Twp.*, 521 Pa. 82, 86–87, 555 A.2d 793, 795 (1988) (citations omitted).

Given the respective disputes of the de Mazia trust and the Barnes Foundation, we fail to see how the "Students," however that body is constituted, have standing in contesting the proposed settlement. They have demonstrated no harm that would accrue to them if the settlement were affirmed. In fact, if the settlement were permitted, the Barnes' students would immediately benefit in two ways: the Foundation would no longer be dissipating assets and the Foundation would receive a total of 2.75 million dollars dedicated to promoting and teaching the Barnesian method. Moreover, their arguments both here and in the court below are directed to presuming to act in the interest of the public, an interest which is already represented by the Attorney General, and which this Court has previously held affords them no standing. *See In re Barnes Foundation; Appeal of Tinari*, 443 Pa. Super. 369, 378, 661 A.2d 889, 894 (1995). Hence, the group designated as "Students of the Barnes Foundation" is dismissed from this litigation on the basis of lack of standing.

Turning our attention to the decision of Judge Ott, and his opinion in support thereof, the judge refused to "sanction the requested amendments to the trust provision of Miss de Mazia's will," because he believed that these amendments ran directly counter to the express will of Violette de Mazia and that there were no legal exceptions upon which to alter the terms of the will. We disagree.

. . . In his opinion in support of his decision, Judge Ott stated that he would not permit the requested deviation from the terms of the de Mazia trust because in his view "the sanctity of the donors' written intent [was] more compelling than the immediate but short-sighted benefits of approving the agreements *sub judice*." *Barnes Foundation, supra* at 338. Although we agree in principle with Judge Ott that the sanctity of the donor's intent should be honored and upheld whenever possible, we are convinced that the benefits of approving the present settlement will go further to advance Ms. De Mazia's intent than forcing the parties to continue in what has obviously become a bad marriage: a marriage which threatens to damage or destroy one or both parties' respective abilities to benefit the citizens of this Commonwealth. This latter concern was obviously at the heart of the position taken by the Attorney General, the statutorily designated guardian of the interest of the general public, who stated: "[T]he public interest would best be served by allowing each [party] to pursue its own program independently rather than be tied to the other with the resultant disharmony, disagreement, and litigation that has ensued." We are compelled to agree. *Cf. In re Little Estate*, 403 Pa. 534, 170 A.2d 106 (1961) (court may not approve family settlement agreement affecting residuary charities without participation of Office of Attorney General).

Accordingly, the order of the Court of Common Pleas is reversed. The requested modifications to the Trust of Violette de Mazia are granted and the Court of Common Pleas is directed to accept the settlement as affirmed by the parties.

Order reversed. Jurisdiction relinquished.

---

2. The Fiduciary Duties of Museum Managers

The trustees and directors of a museum, whether or not the museum is incorporated, stand in a fiduciary relationship toward their institution and must not place themselves in a position of real or potential conflict between their personal interests and those of the institution. This responsibility includes an obligation not to appropriate to themselves any opportunity for personal profit or benefit that might arise in connection with the execution of their responsibilities (sometimes described as a duty of loyalty) and a duty of care regarding the performance of their role as trustees. Furthermore, liability for breach of fiduciary duty is strict and therefore does not depend on proof of actual harm or loss to the institution.

We have seen that a museum can usually choose its particular form of organization and governance. It is unclear whether this choice affects the standard of care applicable to those who manage the museum, whatever their actual title as a director or trustee may be. See, e.g., Maurice C. Cullity, *The Charitable Corporation: A "Bastard" Legal Form Revisited*, 17 PHILANTHROPIST 17 (2002); Steven L. Katz, *Museum Trusteeship: The Fiduciary Duty Applied*, J. ARTS MGMT. & L., Winter 1987, at 57. The preferred view, however, is that the structural choice does not and should not affect the standard of care. It may be, however, that directors of a museum, whether it is organized as a charitable trust or as a nonprofit corporation, are not to be held to as high a fiduciary standard as trustees of a private trust. Instead, they are subject to a fiduciary standard that lies somewhere between that of a private trust and a business corporation. Given the complexity and magnitude of the tasks facing trustees of large museums, compared with those of a traditional trustee – such as someone whose responsibilities include the care of only a single incapacitated individual – it would be unrealistic to expect museum trustees to acquit themselves "of the punctilio of an honor the most sensitive" (per Chief Justice Cardozo, in *Meinhard v. Salmon*, 164 N.E. 545, at 546 (1928)). Many museum trustees are wealthy collectors who may owe their position to an expectation that they will eventually give items from their collections to the museum. This can lead to acts by museum managers, such as hiring a relative of a trustee whose motivation may be clear enough but whose legitimacy may be questionable.

In re Charles M. Bair Family Trust, 183 P.3d 61 (Mont. 2008), is a rare instance in which a court unambiguously ruled that members of a museum board had breached their fiduciary duty. The case involved allegations that a board of advisers created under a family trust had breached its obligations by, among other things, closing the Charles M. Bair Family Museum, in Martinsdale, Montana. The court, rejecting an argument that the court should not interfere with the exercise of the board's discretion, stated:

> The Board's and the Trustee's arguments emanate from their fundamental misunderstanding of the Trust Agreement. The Board and the Trustee share the misconception that the Museum did not constitute the Trust's primary purpose; as discussed . . . the Museum constituted the Trust's primary purpose. Further, the plain language of the Trust Agreement contradicts the Board's claim of "absolute discretion." The Trust Agreement provides that the Board "is directed to use whatever principal and income of the [Trust] *that is necessary* to establish, improve and maintain the museum, and shall have full discretion and authority to administer and manage the same." [Emphasis added.] Though the Trust Agreement grants the Board discretion to administer and manage the Museum, it grants the Board no discretion regarding the amount of principal and income to use in establishing,

> improving, and maintaining the Museum. On the contrary, the Trust Agreement directs the Board to use the amount of principal and income that actually is necessary to establish the Museum. In carrying out this directive, the Board was required to give the Museum a fair opportunity to succeed; the Board was required to exercise the "care, skill, prudence, and diligence" of a prudent person.

Id. at para. 53.

The Montana court also found that the board had failed in its duty to administer the trust according to the trust instrument, as follows:

> The Board breached its duty to administer the Trust according to the trust instrument and breached its duty to administer the trust . . . with the "care, skill, prudence and diligence" of a prudent person when it failed to install a fire-prevention system, failed to install a proper air-handling system, failed to maintain an appropriate security system, and when it failed to build additional structures for the Museum. Although the Board considered the Bair Ranch's inadequate systems and buildings as factors supporting its decision to close the Museum, the Board's initial failure to address these limitations, especially in light of [professional architectural and engineering] recommendations, more accurately demonstrates the Board's failure to comply with its fiduciary duties to the Trust. The Board's failures to address the non-existent fire-sprinkler system, the deficient air-handling system, the insufficient security system, and the Museum's space limitations constitute breaches of the Trust Agreement's directive to "use whatever principal and income of the [Trust] that is necessary to establish, improve and maintain the museum. . . . " As the Board chairman so aptly observed in his 2003 email to the Trust members regarding repairs, the Museum "was never really made 'museum ready' in 1995 when it opened." We agree with the Board chairman's assessment.

Id. at para. 60.

Finally, the court found that the board had breached its fiduciary duties in closing the museum without first concluding that it had ceased to serve its scholarly, educational, and historical purposes.

> Additionally, the Board and the Trustee both acknowledge that the Museum enjoyed more than 4,000 visitors in every year that it was open. Though the Board is correct to address the Museum's declining attendance, the record fails to support the Board's claim that the Museum's declining attendance is "irreversible." Both [consultants] offered suggestions to address the declining attendance, including hiring a professional museum administrator to give year-round attention to marketing and fund-raising, as well as to handle other responsibilities; underwriting public radio programs; creating traveling exhibits throughout Montana; and expanding the educational outreach by negotiating with the Montana State University to offer courses related to the Museum's collection and exhibits. Further, at no point has the Board set forth a level of attendance at which the Museum would cease to serve its scholarly, educational, and historical purposes. Although the Board justifiably may be concerned with the Museum's declining attendance, a museum that

> educates 4,000 visitors a year has not yet ceased to serve its purposes under any standard.

Id. at para. 81.

The court instructed the successor trustee (U.S. Bank) to appoint a new board pursuant to the trust agreement. Because the Montana attorney general, supported by amicus briefs filed by thirteen states, had intervened in the case as a matter of right, the court did not find it necessary to rule on whether the community group Friends of the Bair had standing to intervene.

The fiduciary obligations just described do not apply only to the trustees or directors of a museum. As with business associations, others with senior management responsibilities, such as general counsels or senior executives, may also be subject to fiduciary obligations toward their institutions. The uncertainty of who in a museum may be subject to these responsibilities argues for the adoption by museums of protocols and procedures that limit the possibilities of any breach of duty occurring in the first place.

In Canada, where there are fewer private-funded museums than in the United States, many government-controlled institutions have been adopting the corporate form of legal association. The federal Museums Act, S.C. 1990, c.3, establishes several national museums as Crown (government) corporations, including the National Gallery of Canada and the Canadian Museum of Civilization. The corporate form has aroused concern about the risk that directors and officers of such institutions might compromise their obligation to further the public interest through commercial activities aimed at increasing economic efficiency. As long as commercial activities – such as corporate sponsorships and licensing agreements – are seen as furthering the long-term interests of the museum, they should not amount to a breach of fiduciary duty. Because Canadian museums are also charitable institutions, the federal or provincial attorneys general would have standing to bring such claims. See Robert K. Paterson, *Totems and Teapots: The Royal British Columbia Museum Corporation*, 40 U. B.C. L. Rev. 421 (2007).

a. Deaccessioning: Selling the Family Silver

One of the most controversial aspects of museum governance in recent years has been the practice of deaccessioning, whereby a museum sells or otherwise parts with possession of objects forming part of its collection. Though such transfers are usually legal, they can sometimes engender heated controversy and debate. A striking recent example involves a painting (*The Gross Clinic*) by the American artist Thomas Eakins that belongs to Thomas Jefferson University in Philadelphia. The university announced in November 2006 that it had agreed to sell the painting for US$68 million to the National Gallery of Art and the Crystal Bridges Museum of American Art, a museum founded by Wal-Mart heiress Alice L. Walton, due to open in 2009. The university gave local institutions until December 26, 2006, to match the offer. On December 21, 2006, the mayor of Philadelphia, who had said that the painting "belongs in Philadelphia as much as the Liberty Bell and our sports teams," announced that the required funds had been raised and the painting would stay in Philadelphia. Although the significance of the painting in American art history cannot be denied, some questioned the expenditure of so much money when three-quarters of

Eakins's works were already in Philadelphia and there were other pressing causes needing financial support in the city.

Much of the controversy surrounding deaccessioning by museums seems to arise from the perception that they are public institutions impressed with the role of protecting and preserving their collections intact for future generations. The enormous market prices for certain works of art in recent years, however, have created tempting options for museums to raise funds by selling objects from their collections despite objections to sales of objects based purely on their market value. An instructive example arose in 2007 when the Albright-Knox Art Gallery in Buffalo, New York, decided to auction off dozens of objects in its collection as part of a new plan to focus on modern and contemporary works of art. Several members of the Buffalo Fine Arts Academy (the so-called Buffalo Art Keepers), challenging the decision of its board to do so, sought an injunction to stop the sales. A New York Supreme Court judge dismissed the claim as follows:

> The petitioners' third claim [that the board misappropriated and wasted assets] is unlikely to succeed, because the [Academy's] Board did not act in bad faith in deciding to sell the items and they did not violate the donors' intent. The Board did not misappropriate or waste the items donated to them. The Board reasonably and honestly exercised their judgment to determine that deaccession was necessary for the continued existence and notoriety of the Albright-Knox. Thus, their decision is unreviewable by the court under the business judgment rule. . . .
>
> The third and final requirement for imposition of a preliminary injunction further moves this court to find for the respondents. A court must balance the equities to determine if a preliminary injunction is a just and fair result. Other than petitioners' arguments that certain pieces of artwork will be forever lost from the Academy's collection, petitioners offer no other discussion of the reasons that the balance of the equities should fall in their favor. On the other hand, respondents, particularly respondent Sotheby's, have come forward with evidence that the company has expended nearly $200,000 solely from the marketing of the auction. Petitioners do not contest that delay of the auction will cost respondents estimates in the millions of dollars.

Dennis v. Buffalo Fine Arts Academy, No. 50520(u), slip. op. at 3, 836 N.Y.S.2d 498 (Table) (Sup. Ct. Erie Cty., March 21, 2007).

Although the petitioners vehemently objected to the sales, they were a huge financial success for the gallery. A single Roman antiquity (the sculpture *Artemis and the Stag*) sold for more than $28 million – a record price for an antiquity at auction. Though artworks that many thought should remain the kernel of the gallery's collection were sold, the proceeds multiplied its endowment several times over. The court made no reference to nonbinding museum codes of ethics, which may condemn significant museum sales whose purpose is to buy new objects.

Deaccessioning can be justified for a variety of reasons. An institution may face rising costs for storage, conservation, and insurance or may want to dispose of items unrelated to its core collection strengths. Because it is often unpredictable when very desirable objects will become available for purchase, sales of objects may give museums a quick way to purchase items that they may never again have an opportunity to acquire. The recent sale of the Dundas collection of Canadian First Nations objects at auction in the United States is a good example of the problems facing Canadian museums in this respect. The collection comprised several dozen outstanding objects collected by the Reverend Robert J. Dundas at Metlakatla, British Columbia, in 1863. The English owners of the collection, who were descendants of Dundas, had decided to sell the collection at auction, but it appears few Canadian museums were able to raise sufficient funds quickly enough to make purchases of any of the major items in the collection, which realized a total of more than US$7 million. It was only through the purchase of many of the auctioned items by the wealthy Thomson family of Canada that the return of these culturally important objects to Canada was secured.

In the few cases of deaccessioning to have reached courts in the United States, judges have been reluctant to second-guess the decisions of museum trustees, as in *Dennis v. Buffalo Fine Arts Academy*. Instead, the issue of deaccessioning has been addressed primarily in nonbinding codes of ethics. The Canadian Museums Association's Ethical Guidelines, for example, contain detailed provisions on what it calls disposals. The Guidelines acknowledge that, although disposals can strengthen and refine the quality of a museum collection, "*there is a strong presumption against* the disposal of accessioned collections to which the museum has acquired title...." A number of desirable conditions for deaccessioning or disposal of cultural objects are set out, including consent by the public or private sources of the objects, the desirability of disposed material remaining in public institutions, and the publication of the intention to dispose of material at least three months in advance. In particular, a museum must ensure that it is legally free to act; that it has clear title to the objects proposed for disposal; in the case of undocumented material, that it has made a serious, diligent, and documented effort to locate owners; that there are no restrictions associated with the material when it was acquired; that the transaction is fully approved by the governing authority; and that objects for which a request for return, restitution, or repatriation could reasonably be expected to arise in the future are not to be considered for disposal by other means.

The Guidelines specify what has become a commonly accepted ethical and professional standard for museums: funds generated by disposals may not be used to provide for any other purposes besides the acquisition or direct care of museum collections. What remains unclear, however, is when such expenditures are a breach of fiduciary duty. See Jennifer L. White, *When It's OK to Sell the Monet: A Trustee-Fiduciary Duty Framework for Analyzing the Deaccessioning of Art to Meet Museum Operating Expenses*, 94 MICH. L. REV. 1041 (1996) (arguing that museums that use funds generated from the sale of objects in their collections should not be stigmatized as long as they otherwise act in accordance with their fiduciary obligations).

Patricia Ainslie, *The Deaccessioning Strategy at Glenbow, 1992–97*, 15 MUSEUM MGMT. & CURATORSHIP 21 (1996) (reprinted with the permission of Taylor and Francis Ltd.)

[The Glenbow Museum, operated by the Glenbow-Alberta Institute in Calgary, Alberta, was the subject of controversy as a result of its sale of some thirty thousand objects from its collection between 1980 and 1992. – *Eds.*]

Early in June 1992, Glenbow's senior management team reviewed a five-year budget forecast. All of our revenues from the public and private sector were decreasing, but we were not sure what were the [long-]term implications. The shocking news was that at the current rate of expenditure we would be bankrupt in five years, with an accumulated deficit of 7.7 million dollars. Recognizing that one of our fiduciary responsibilities is to ensure the continuity of the museum for the community, this situation created a need for immediate action. In late June we spent a weekend off site to plan. We developed many ideas which were refined to six strategies intended to guide us into a healthy future. It was in this context that deaccessioning, one of the six strategies, was seen as a way to augment income to care for the collections, while at the same time refining and focusing our collections. We felt that deaccessioning was a prudent, responsible and realistic approach given our current situation and the nature of our collections.

Glenbow is the largest museum in Western Canada, with a collection of approximately 1.2 million objects and three floors of exhibition space totaling over 93,000 square feet. The diverse collections include the disciplines of art, cultural history, military history, ethnology and mineralogy, consisting of 240,000 objects. In addition, Glenbow has the largest library of Western Canadiana and the largest non-government archives in Canada. Glenbow's primary mandate is to document and preserve the history and development of the northwest quadrant of North America, and secondly, to provide a national and international context for these core collections. However, Glenbow is unique in Canada due to our history and the way in which some of our collections were acquired. Eric L. Harvie, Glenbow's founder, was a philanthropist with eclectic tastes and wide-ranging interests. He built two major collections: the Glenbow Collection of over 120,000 objects, plus books, archives and photographs, which was given to the people of Alberta in 1966, and the Riveredge Collection of over 37,000 objects, plus books, archives and photographs, gathered from 1966 to 1979, when it was given to the Province of Alberta. Glenbow holds both of these collections in trust. Over the years, other donations and purchases have been added to these collections.

. . .

The Glenbow-Alberta Institute was established 15 April 1966, through an Act passed by the Alberta Legislature. The departments of cultural and military history, ethnology, art, mineralogy, library and archives were amalgamated, and the collections were housed under one roof beginning in 1976 when Glenbow moved to its Ninth Avenue S.E. location in Calgary. Two years later, in May 1978, Glenbow developed a policy for deaccessioning and this policy has been updated over the years. Deaccessioning became an active part of professional collections management at Glenbow through the 1980s. Collections care involves maintenance and ongoing expense and we can no longer justify retaining material which is not germane to our purposes. In the 1980s, objects were deaccessioned primarily because they were reproductions, were not of museum quality, were duplicates inferior to material remaining in the collection, or lacked provenance. Most of this deaccessioned material was sold at auction in Calgary and the proceeds were put into the acquisition fund. Up to 1992 and the beginning of the current Deaccessioning Strategy, we had deaccessioned 18,256 items from the Glenbow Collection and 12,491 items from the Riveredge Collection.

The current plan will allow us to continue to refine parts of the collections not central to our mandate, as well as to raise funds for the preservation and future stability of the collections. It will allow Glenbow to define more closely its mandate regarding the international collections and to focus these collections more clearly, but we will remain committed to keeping selected international collections. It is with this current Deaccessioning Strategy that we depart from tradition. We planned to deaccession collections of high value and of museum quality, but which we felt were outside our core purposes. We also planned to expand the use of funds earned from the sale of nine collections to allow us to use the income generated by the Collections Endowment Fund for care and maintenance of the collection. This involves:

- conservation and preservation
- registration,
- documentation and cataloguing,
- storage,
- research of objects, and
- acquisition of new material.

This also includes salaries of staff dedicated to the above activities. Excluded are exhibitions, programming and publications, and all other activities not directly related to the care of the collections. The central principle of this Deaccessioning Strategy was that Glenbow's curatorial staff would make the selection based on their knowledge of the collection and their field. The process for all deaccessioning involves selection of material by the curator responsible for the collection, approval by the Director of Collections and by the Executive Director, then recommendation for approval by the Collections Management Committee, and approval by the Board of Governors. There are clear policies, procedures, and a system of checks and balances to guide Glenbow's deaccessioning.

. . .

There was agreement that we must focus the collections and make appropriate decisions in *each* collection area without applying any kind of blanket deaccessioning policy. There was consensus that only *income* from monies raised would be used for the direct care and maintenance of the collections and that this should be strictly defined. There was agreement that material would be sold in the manner most appropriate to the specific collection. Auction would be preferable to private sale as it is the most public method. We decided that for donated items, we would approach donors and obtain their agreement to any proposed deaccessioning. In fact, when we reviewed the collections, there were very few privately donated objects, and we decided to exclude them altogether. Most of the 3,000 items that were subsequently selected were from the Glenbow Collection, the major public gift made by Eric Harvie to the people of Alberta in 1966. Not more than 20 other items, purchased after 1966, were deaccessioned. We also realized that if the process was to be credible, the whole deaccessioning program would have to be communicated very carefully and clearly to the public. We had to be prepared to deal with adverse public reaction if it materialized. As a result, we decided that Glenbow's name would be used in the sale of all deaccessioned objects. Overall, it was acknowledged that deaccessioning was a healthy practice for Glenbow; it had been important through the 1980s to focus our collections and this current Deaccessioning Strategy was necessary to guarantee the future care of the collections. This special meeting and the ongoing team meetings built support for the process among staff, while one of the first things we did was to draft a preliminary communications statement, in case the news of our deaccessioning activity became known before we were ready. It was important to us that the public understood what we were doing and why, and as the work progressed this statement was refined.

...

By mid-September of 1993, the press became interested in Glenbow's deaccessioning and we gave more than a dozen print, radio and TV interviews including *Maclean's* magazine, the *Calgary Herald* and CBC's *Morningside* with Peter Gzowski. The press was very fair in their reporting, although some of the headlines were provocative, and there were very few negative responses as a result of this media coverage. The Government of Alberta is our partner, providing just less than half of our funding. During 1993 we had regular discussions with the Provincial Government, explaining our six strategies, including deaccessioning. In the late summer, Glenbow's deaccessioning had become controversial and members of Cabinet were concerned about the use of the funds realized from deaccessioning. In addition, some people believed that deaccessioned collections should stay in the public domain and be donated to other institutions in Alberta. We subsequently did a presentation to the Standing Policy Committee of the Provincial Government in Edmonton and, on 13 December 1993, we received formal approval to proceed with our plan.

...

We intend to be strict in the use of the income from the endowment funds raised from deaccessioning. The income from the Collections Endowment will be applied only to collections care and documentation, and the endowment will be indexed to protect it from inflation for future purchases for the collections. All of Glenbow's deaccessioning is thoroughly documented, and catalogue records have been changed to reflect the disposal of objects. Over the course of the past two and a half years, we have received positive comments on our Deaccessioning Strategy from professional colleagues and members of the public. We have also had some criticism including two letters to Glenbow from members of the public, and we have heard of other criticism second-hand. The community is certainly not silent in this matter! However, due to our responsible approach, careful planning and consultation, this criticism has not had a negative impact on Glenbow. Donors have not been adversely affected by the deaccessioning and we continue to receive important gifts of material related to our core mandate.

Deaccessioning of collections is not about lowering standards. It is dependent on good judgement and responsibility, and on being true to core values and beliefs. These are the same attitudes which should guide our acquisitions. In the past, there has been a great deal of mindless collecting along with poor documentation and inadequate care in public collections. Deaccessioning is about making difficult but realistic decisions in the interests of the museum and its community. Stewardship means being entrusted with the management of another's property and preserving that inheritance. It does not mean keeping everything in a collection for all time. As Sir Roy Strong, former Director of the Victoria and Albert Museum in London, said, "How can museums function properly if they are going to carry on collecting from here to eternity?" He went on to say, "What we should be doing instead is assessing our collections, refusing some, closing others, and even more important, putting what we have in good order." We no longer have the resources for the proper long-care and management of collections not germane to our purpose. Through deaccessioning, we believe in ensuring the prudent application of our resources and maintaining public confidence.

Attorney General v. Trustees of the British Museum
[2005] Ch. 397

[Famously, as revealed in the context of the claim by Greece for return of the Elgin Marbles to Athens, the British Museum is expressly prohibited by statute from disposing of objects in its collections. The position of the British Museum is that until this legislation is amended, the trustees of the institution cannot respond to claims to return objects. Recently, however, the U.K. attorney general sought a judicial opinion on whether the trustees of the museum could lawfully return four old master drawings to the heirs of pre–Second World War owners from whom they had been stolen by the Nazis. This request was based on the trustees' expressed wish that the objects be returned if it would be lawful for them to do so. – *Eds.*]

Sir Andrew Morritt V-C:

Introduction

1 The trustees of the British Museum were incorporated by section 14 British Museum Act 1753 (26 Geo 2, c 22). By section 9 of the same

Act it was provided that the "several collections, additions and library" of the museum "shall remain and be preserved . . . for public use to all posterity." Subject to various powers of disposal conferred on the trustee by subsequent enactments, none of which is presently relevant, the obligation imposed by section 9 of the 1753 Act remained in force until the enactment of the British Museum Act 1963.

2 In 1946 the trustees bought at auction at Sotheby's for the aggregate sum of nine guineas three old master drawings, namely *The Holy Family* by Niccolò dell'Abbate, *An Allegory on Poetic Inspiration with Mercury and Apollo* by Nicholas Blakey and *Virgin and Infant Christ, adored by St. Elizabeth and the infant St. John* by Martin Johann Schmidt. At about the same time the Keeper of Prints at the British Museum, Mr. Campbell Dodgson, acquired a fourth, *St. Dorothy with the Christ Child* by a follower of Martin Schongauer. This drawing was part of the bequest made by Mr. Dodgson in favour of the British Museum which took effect in 1949. Since 1946 and 1949 respectively those drawings have been held by the trustees as part of the collections of the British Museum.

3 On 30 September 1963 the British Museum Act 1963 came into force in the place of inter alia the 1753 Act. It provided for the trustees to continue as a body corporate (section 1) and conferred on them power, subject to the restrictions imposed on them by virtue of any enactment (whether contained in that Act or not) to enter into contracts and other agreements, to acquire and hold land and other property, and to do all other things that appear to them necessary or expedient for the purposes of their functions (section 2). Section 3(1) to (3) require the trustees to keep the objects comprised in the collections at the places and in the manner there specified. Section 3(4) provides:

> Objects vested in the trustees as part of the collections of the museum shall not be disposed of by them otherwise than under section 5 or 9 of this Act or section 6 of the Museums and Galleries Act of 1992.

Section 5 authorises the trustees to dispose of duplicates, objects made after 1850 and objects unfit to be retained in the collections of the museum. It also entitles the trustees to destroy useless objects. Section 9 of that Act and section 6 of Museums and Galleries Act 1992 entitle the trustees to transfer objects comprised in the collections of the British Museum to the trustees of any other of the specified national museums.

4 In 1970 Cross J determined that the court or the Attorney General may authorize

> a payment . . . out of charity funds which is motivated simply and solely by the belief of the trustees or other persons administering the funds that the charity is under a moral obligation to make the payment": see In re Snowden, decd [1970] Ch 700, 709.

5 In 2002 the trustees considered a claim advanced by the Commission for Looted Art in Europe ("CLAE") on behalf of the heirs of the late Dr. Feldmann that each of the four drawings had been the property of Dr. Feldmann in Brno, Czechoslovakia and had been stolen from him on 15 March 1939 by the Gestapo. The claim was and is for restitution not compensation alone. At a meeting of the trustees held on 27 July 2002 it was agreed that:

> 6.4.3 Having regard to the cogency of the evidence adduced within the context of what were acknowledged to be the exceptional atrocities committed during the 1933–1945 era, the claimant's request for the return of these drawings ought to be acceded to if and to the extent permissible by law.
>
> 6.4.4 With the agreement of the claimants and [Department for Culture, Media and Sport], this case should be referred to the Spoliation Advisory Panel for an opinion on the appropriate action to take in response to the claim given the fact that the claim is solely for restitution.

6 Before the claim was put before the Spoliation Advisory Panel the trustees sought the advice of counsel and in implementation of that advice wrote to the Attorney General on 29 August 2003. The trustees expressed the view that

> If the Attorney General were to take a positive view of his powers to sanction Snowden-type action [see paragraph 4, supra] in relation to objects now comprised in a national collection and subject to an acknowledged holocaust restitution claim, he would offer a straightforward solution to the debate in the present case, in respect of which equity requires a swift solution.

7 The Attorney General was concerned whether as a matter of statutory construction the express prohibition contained in section 3(4) of the British Museum Act 1963 on the disposal of objects comprised in the collections of the British Museum prevents the objects to which that prohibition applies from being disposed of under the *In re Snowden* principle.

. . .

36 It is appropriate to acknowledge at the outset the evident sincerity of all parties to these proceedings. The circumstances give rise to a dilemma for each of them. It is in precisely those circumstances that it is essential to ascertain the relevant principles of law and to apply them so that the dilemmas are resolved by the law and not otherwise. It is convenient to start with a series of propositions, many of them elementary.

37 First, neither the Crown nor the Attorney General as a minister of the Crown has any power to dispense with due observance of Acts of Parliament. The pretended power of dispensing with or suspending Acts of Parliament was emphatically rejected by the Bill of Rights 1689 (1 Will

& Mary, sess 2, c 2). Similarly the courts and the judges are committed to upholding the law, not sanctioning departures without lawful authority. Accordingly the first essential step is to ascertain what is prohibited by section 3(4) of the British Museum Act 1963.

38 Second, section 3(4) applies to "Objects vested in the trustees as part of the collections of the museum." There is no doubt that given the basis on which this application is made, each of the four drawings is such an object. It is, of course, possible that in other proceedings the heirs of Dr. Feldmann may establish title to the drawings with the consequence that they will never have been "part of the collections of the museum." In that event section 3(4) will not preclude a disposition by the trustees in their favour. This conclusion leads to two further propositions.

39 Third, the compromise of a claim by the heirs of Dr. Feldmann to be entitled to the drawings does not involve any breach of section 3(4). A bona fide compromise of the issues of fact involved in the claim is as binding as the decision of the court to that effect, see *Binder v. Alachouzos* [1972] 2 QB 151. It may involve a recognition that the drawings have never been part of the collections. For this reason I reject the argument which suggests that the power to compromise is somehow an unexpressed exception to section 3(4). It is not an exception but the consequence of the limited application of section 3(4) only to objects which are part of the collection.

40 Fourth, for similar reasons I reject the argument that as moral considerations may be relevant to an exercise of the power to compromise they may alone justify the non-observance of section 3(4) in relation to objects which are part of the collections. They are, alone, incapable of disapplying section 3(4) or justifying a failure to observe its terms.

41 Fifth, it follows that any disposition by the trustees in favour of the heirs of Dr. Feldmann can be justified, if at all, only by reference to a statutory exception to section 3(4). It is not suggested that the drawings fall within any of the express exceptions provided for in section 5 or 9 of the British Museum Act 1963 or in section 6 of the Museums and Galleries Act 1992. It was submitted that cases falling within the Snowden jurisdiction constitute an implied exception. I reject that submission. The very existence of the express exceptions negatives the recognition of further but implied exceptions. It is true that at the time the British Museum Act 1963 was before Parliament Cross J. had not decided in re Snowden, decd [1970] Ch 700. But the enactment of the Museums and Galleries Act 1992 provided a parliamentary opportunity to insert a further exception if that had been thought desirable.

42 Sixth, if the drawings are part of the collections of the museum and there is no express or implied exception in the British Museum Act 1963 itself it would require some other statutory authority to justify ignoring the prohibition on dispositions. None has been suggested in this case.

There are provisions in the Charities Act 1993 whereby schemes in relation to the funds of a charity regulated by statute may be made subject to obtaining the requisite parliamentary approval, see sections 15(3) and 17. Similarly there is the jurisdiction to authorize applications to Parliament described by Lord Cottenham LC in In re Shrewsbury Grammar School 1 Mac & G 324,333. Though such jurisdiction is rarely exercised now its existence demonstrates that nothing less than some statutory authority is required to justify a departure from statutory obligations imposed on trustees.

43 Seventh, section 3(4) prohibits any disposition by the trustees. The word "disposition" is not defined. It is of its nature a word of wide import. The context in which it is used does not require a restrictive interpretation; quite the reverse. I see no reason, and none was suggested in argument, to limit its operation to acts so as to exclude omissions.

Property in goods may be passed by a failure to act as well as by an active delivery. Consequently I consider that a failure to rely on relevant provisions of the Limitation Acts 1939 and 1980, otherwise than on legal advice, in order to effect a transfer of the drawings to the heirs of Dr. Feldmann is as prohibited by section 3(4) as in a delivery by the trustees. I did not understand the trustees in the oral argument of their counsel to contend otherwise.

...

45 For all these reasons I conclude that no moral obligation can justify a disposition by the trustees of an object forming part of the collection of the Museum in breach of section 3(4). There is nothing in the decision of Cross J in In re Snowden, decd [1970] Ch 700 to suggest otherwise. The fact, if it be one, that the four considerations which led Cross J to decide that case in the way that he did apply in this case cannot justify a breach of section 3(4). What is required is some statutory authority by way of exception. There is none and it is beyond the power of the Attorney General to provide one. It follows that I reject the submission that section 3(4) only becomes relevant at the stage when the Attorney General decides whether or not to exercise the Snowden jurisdiction. The existence of section 3(4) excludes any such jurisdiction in relation to acts or omissions it prohibits.

...

In my judgment only legislation or a bona fide compromise of a claim of the heirs of Dr. Feldmann to be entitled to the four drawings could entitle the Trustees to transfer any of them to those heirs.

NOTES AND QUESTIONS

1. In the United Kingdom, similar legislation also restricts deaccessioning by other major museums and galleries, such as the National Gallery and the Tate gallery.

See *Museums and Galleries Act*, 1992 (U.K.), c. 44, s. 4. The *Holocaust (Return of Cultural Objects) Act*, 2009 (U.K.), c. 16, now allows for the return of objects from museums in the United Kingdom, including the British Museum, when claims for such return are based on Nazi-era circumstances and are supported by recommendations of the U.K. Spoliation Advisory Panel or its equivalent. No federal laws in the United States specifically bar museums from outright deaccessioning. The charters of particular museums, however, may prevent sales or returns of items in collections. See, e.g., Re the Barnes Foundation, 684 A.2d 123 (Pa. Sup. Ct. 1996).

2. The sale of artwork from a museum's permanent collection, known as deaccessioning, is not illegal in the United States, provided that any terms accompanying the original donation of artwork are respected. In Europe, by contrast, many museums are state financed and prevented by national law from deaccessioning.

   But under the code of ethics of the American Association of Museums, the proceeds should be "used only for the acquisition, preservation, protection or care of collections." The code of the Association of Art Museum Directors is even stricter, specifying that funds should not be used "for purposes other than acquisitions of works of art for the collection." . . .

   [One expert saw] no reason for strict rules about deaccessioning, other than telling the truth to the public and not selling to international trafficking mafias. . . .

   [Another expert] said her position had softened over the years. "If it's really a life-or-death situation, if it's a choice between selling a Rauschenberg and keeping the museum doors open, I think there's some justification for selling the painting," she said.

   But several directors drew a much harder line, noting that museums get tax-deductible donations of art and cash to safeguard art collections for the public. Selling off any holdings for profit would thus betray that trust, they say, not to mention rob a community of art, so no exceptions for financial hardships should be allowed. . . .

   It's a classic slippery slope, this thinking goes: Letting one museum sell off two paintings paves the way for dozens of museums to sell off thousands of artworks, perhaps routinely.

Jori Finkel, *Whose Rules Are These, Anyway?* N.Y. Times, Dec. 28, 2008, at AR 28 (describing the ethical issues and recent controversies concerning deaccessioning).

What is your position?

3. In December 2008, the Association of Art Museum Directors (AAMD) publicly censured one of its members, the National Academy Museum and School of Fine Arts in New York, for selling four valuable paintings from its collection to finance its operations. The AAMD statement of December 5, 2008, reads in part as follows:

   It is . . . a fundamental professional principle that works can only be deaccessioned to provide funds to acquire works of art and enhance a museum's

> collection.... The National Academy is now breaching one of the most basic and important of AAMD's principles by treating its collection as a financial asset, rather than the cornerstone of research, exhibition, and public programming, a record of human creativity held in trust for people now and in the future. In the notification of its decision to AAMD last evening, the National Academy voluntarily withdrew from membership in the organization. It is not, however, membership in AAMD per se, but rather a broader commitment to ethical museum practice that demands adherence to the principles governing deaccessioning.

See Jason E. Kaufman, *First Ever Censure over Sales: National Design Academy to Be Boycotted on Collaboration*, ART NEWSPAPER, Jan. 2009, at 15.

4. Museum managers and trustees may be governed by different laws and policy considerations when pondering the return of objects to a country, group, or individual outside the national territory of the museum. If a claimant can prove that title to an object or its return is mandated by an international convention, the situation may be resolved purely by the application of legal principles. It is more likely, however, that a museum must consider whether to return material on moral or ethical grounds.

   This has been the background, for example, to a significant number of returns of preserved tattooed Maori heads (*toi moko*) to New Zealand from museums and other institutions abroad. The heads were originally treasured as memorial relics but began to be collected by Europeans during the nineteenth century. It may have been this foreign interest that led to the practice of preserving the heads of enemies as objects of trade. These preserved heads were long displayed openly in New Zealand and foreign museums, as well as being sold at auction or privately. This practice came to public attention in the 1988 decision of the High Court of New Zealand in *Re Estate of Tupuna Maori*, P580/88 High Court of New Zealand, Wellington, May 19, 1988, Greig J. (unreported). That probate decision enabled the president of the New Zealand Maori Council to take possession of a head that had been privately consigned for sale by auction in London. Following this case and growing outrage at the trade in Maori ancestral remains, leading international auction houses declined to accept *toi moko* for sale and they were withdrawn from open display by many foreign and all New Zealand museums. In 2003, the New Zealand government approved a repatriation policy regarding Maori ancestral remains (the Karanga Aotearoa Repatriation Programme) and mandated the Museum of New Zealand (Te Papa Tongarewa) to be the authorized agent of the government to implement the new policy. Pursuant to this program, returns of *toi moko* have included those from the Kelvingrove Art Gallery and Museum in Glasgow, Scotland; the Übersee Museum in Bremen, Germany; and the Field Museum of Natural History in Chicago.

5. In October 2007, the mayor of Rouen, France, agreed to return to New Zealand a *toi moko* held in the French city's Museum of Natural History. The French Ministry of Culture, however, blocked the return on the grounds that the object was an "inalienable" work of art under French law. A French administrative court subsequently ruled that the attempted return was invalid on the grounds that the

city of Rouen had failed to consult a scientific committee – the head was, after all, a body part – before withdrawing the head from the museum's collection. See Robert K. Paterson, *Administrative Tribunal of Rouen, Decision No. 702737, December 27, 2007 (Maori Head Case)*, 15 Int'l J. Cultural Prop. 223 (2008); Olivier Amiel, *A Maori Head: Public Domain?* 15 Int'l J. Cultural Prop. 371 (2008). The case raises questions about the scope of the inalienability of French museum collections and whether human remains can properly be regarded as part of such collections in the first place.

6. When the law permits deaccessioning, what do you think should be the limits on it, if any, by museums? Should courts defer to the judgment of museum professionals, or are there some sales, such as those of major items which a museum has owned for decades or more, that should never be permitted? If you agree with the last proposition, would such a rule bar most international returns of hotly contested objects such as the Elgin (Parthenon) Marbles?
7. Do you think deaccessioning deters donors from giving objects to institutions for fear that they might dispose of them some time in the future? Might there not be pressure on an institution seeking buyers for objects in its collection to sell only its most valuable or significant pieces?
8. Do you think that the Glenbow Museum's policies regarding deaccessioning strike a good balance between those in favor of the practice and those who are highly critical of it? Do you think a museum should ever be allowed to sell material from its collections to generate funds for museum maintenance and upkeep?
9. Does deaccessioning place museum trustees and directors in a potential conflict of interest situation when sales from collections are made to the same dealers from whom the museum has earlier purchased items for its collection? In one case at the Brooklyn Museum, it was alleged that a former curator of primitive art had exchanged items in the collection with a dealer for similar but inferior pieces. See Michael Twaddle, *Acquisitions and Disposition of Art Objects*, 4 Art & L. 67 (1979).
10. On deaccessioning, see *Hammond Museum, Inc. v. Harshbarger*, No. 92E-0067-G1 (P. & 6 Fam. Ct. Essex County, Mass., Oct. 5, 1992); *Eilstach Estate*, 1 Pa D. & C.2d 197 (Pa. Orph. Ct. 1954); *Conway v. Emeny*, 96 A.2d 221 (Conn. 1953); David R. Gabor, Comment, *Deaccessioning Fine Art Works: A Proposal for Heightened Scrutiny*, 11 Vill. Sports & Ent. L.J. 383 (2004); Jason R. Goldstein, *Deaccession: Not Such a Dirty Word*, 15 Cardozo Arts & Ent. L.J. 213 (1997); A Deaccession Reader (Stephen E. Weil ed., 1997).

b. Conservation of Cultural Material and the Duty of Care

As part of their overall legal responsibilities, museum fiduciaries such as trustees and directors have a duty to exercise reasonable care and skill in the management of the collections for which they are responsible. This obligation is part of their equitable duty so that any remedies for its breach are also equitable rather than legal in nature. Thus, damages are not an appropriate remedy for a breach of a fiduciary's duty of care, but equitable relief, such as compensation, may be appropriate. In the case of museums, the duty of care leads to several responsibilities, such as ensuring the security of objects in collections and taking out proper insurance against loss through theft or damage. In the past, courts seem to have been fairly lenient in their assessment of whether museum managers have breached their duty of care. See *Attorney-General* v. *Olson*, 191 N.E. 2d 132 (Mass. 1963). This attitude may undergo change, but a problem for courts lies in substituting their judgment concerning appropriate management practices for that of museum fiduciaries, who are assumed to have the necessary expertise to run their institutions.

A crucial facet of museum management is, of course, the conservation of objects in collections. In *Parkinson* v. *Murdock*, 332 P.2d 273 (1958), 183 Kan. 706, one issue was whether the trustees of a collection had implied authority to employ a conservator to evaluate the care and condition of art in the collection. The Supreme Court of Kansas concluded as follows:

> As a necessary incident to the carrying out of the expressed intention to provide an art collection that would last throughout the years, the trustees also have the duty to see that the objects of art purchased are properly housed and cared for so as not to deteriorate after a relatively short period of time. To achieve this end, the trustees have the power, with the approval of the court, to use all reasonable and necessary means to ascertain the condition of the objects of art. . . .
>
> We think that the employment of an expert, a conservator, to inspect the objects of art to determine if they are being properly housed and cared for is a necessary and appropriate exercise of power conferred upon the trustees by the terms of the decedent's will. The ruling of the district court that a conservator be employed should not be disturbed.

Another problem that plagues the issue of conservation is uncertainty about its very meaning. In 1984 the ICOM Committee for Conservation adopted the following definition of "conservator-restorer":

> 2.1 The activity of the conservator-restorer (conservation) consists of technical examination, preservation, and conservation-restoration of culture property: Examination is the preliminary procedure taken to determine the documentary significance of an artefact; original structure and materials; the extent of its deterioration, alteration, and loss; and the documentation of these findings. Preservation is action taken to retard or prevent deterioration of or damage to cultural properties by control of their environment and/or treatment of their structure in order to maintain them as nearly as possible in an unchanging state. Restoration is action taken to make a deteriorated or damaged artefact understandable, with minimal sacrifice of aesthetic and historic integrity.
>
> 2.2 Conservator-restorer[s] work in museums, in official heritage protection services, in private conservation enterprises or independently. Their task is to comprehend the material aspect of objects of historic and artistic significance in order to prevent their decay and to enhance our understanding of them so as to further the distinction between what is original and what is spurious.

See http://icom-cc.icom.museum/About/DefinitionofProfession/.

Sarah E. Botha, *Art Conservation: Problems Encountered in an Unregulated Industry*, 26 Colum. J. L. & Arts 251, 259–60 (2003)

In order to understand how these problems emerged and why they persist, it is necessary to consider the manner in which the art conservation profession has developed. The practice of retouching works of art has been occurring for centuries, if not millennia. In Russia, painting restoration dates back to at least the Middle Ages, with the earliest rules for restoration of icons being established by Metropolitan Illarion in the eleventh century. At times, retouching was done to accommodate changing tastes in art, as when loincloths were painted over several of Michelangelo's figures in the *Last Judgment.* At other times, it became necessary soon after the completion of a particularly delicate work to intervene in order to assure its continuing survival, as was the case with Leonardo's *Last Supper.* One commentator explains that the motivation for restoration has often been aesthetic: to counter "the effects of aging, accidental damage, or vandalism on works of art [that] reduce their aesthetic appeal." Interventions often took the form of "improver" restorations, which resulted in a new surface being applied to the original work. Early critics of this practice included Eug[è]ne Delacroix, who wrote: "Each so-called restoration is an injury far more to be regretted than the ravages of time, for the result is not a restored picture but a different picture by the hand of a miserable dauber who substitutes himself for the author of the original who has disappeared under his retouching." Delacroix himself lamented the darkening of the paintings of the old masters, however, and Sir Joshua Reynolds likewise commented on the negative effects of dirt and varnish over time.

Although a desire to maintain the original appearance of a masterpiece is understandable, disastrous results were attained when restoration proceeded without any understanding of the scientific qualities of the artwork. During a mid-nineteenth century restoration of a [Diego] Vel[á]zquez painting, a restorer ironed the back of the canvas as part of the relining procedure. The heat applied was so strong that a great deal of the paint blistered, and a large portion of the canvas that was laid bare had to be repainted. Several events in the eighteenth and nineteenth centuries resulted in a growing appreciation of the need for a more scientific approach to restoration: the scientific optimism of the Enlightenment; the increased pollution in the atmosphere brought on by industrialization; and the increasing collections of archaeological objects for which traditional restoration methods proved useless. The damage inflicted by the events of World War I acted as a catalyst in the formation of a research laboratory at the British Museum. Furthermore, a conference in Rome in 1930 organized by the International Museums Office of the League of Nations focused attention on preventive conservation, making utilization of scientific methods an international priority. This increased focus on science is one of the primary factors that distinguishes modern-day conservation from traditional restoration.

Marie C. Malaro, A Legal Primer on Managing Museum Collections 412–13 (2d ed., 1998)

The approach to conservation has changed radically in many U.S. museums – and with good reason. Historically, the conservator was trained to focus on the individual objects: the object in serious need of treatment or the object that warranted special attention because it was to go on exhibit. Within the museum the conservators' talents were usually limited to this type of service. But by the mid-1970s a number of museums in the United States began to take a more holistic approach to the management of their collections. The early emphasis was on the quality of documentation and record-keeping. Standards were established in these areas within the museum as a whole, and the authority to implement and oversee these standards was centralized in one individual or office. This change reflected the heightened consciousness of those governing museums, who now realized that they had a trustlike responsibility to see that collections were managed prudently for the benefit of the public. And when standards were being established for documentation and record-keeping, a major goal was to prevent problems. In other words, a central test was the following question: "Based on our experience to date, are these standards designed to avoid problems now and in the future?" Using this holistic approach, museums made dramatic advances in gaining control over collections.

All of this was not lost on some conservators. If problems could be avoided in the areas of documentation and record-keeping through coordinated effort within the museum, why could not this approach be used to prevent or mitigate damage to collection objects? These conservators began to look at collections as a whole and to identify steps that could be taken to slow deterioration, to prevent damage, or to control loss. This new approach is commonly called "preventive conservation." "Preventive conservation can be defined as any measure that prevents damage or reduces the potential for it. It focuses on collections rather than individual objects, nontreatment rather than treatment. In practical terms, the handling, storage, and management of collections (including emergency planning) are critical elements in a preventive conservation methodology."

Catherine Sease, *Codes of Ethics for Conservation*, 7 Int'l J. Cultural Prop. 98, at 106–08 (1998)

Cultural Sensitivity

A similar situation has occurred with cultural sensitivity. Over the past five years or so, indigenous groups, especially Native Americans, have come to play a significant role in how conservators handle and care for ethnographic collections. Spurred on by the Native American Graves Protection and Repatriation Act of 1990 (although many institutions had taken the initiative long before this), museums have entered into active dialogues with Native American and other indigenous groups, which has resulted in these groups providing input on appropriate methods for handling, storing, and exhibiting their cultural patrimony in museum collections. This interaction has forced ethnographic conservators to acknowledge the feelings and sensitivities of the people from whose culture their collections come; more important, to recognize that people connected culturally to objects in their collections may have values and priorities that differ significantly from how we have been practicing conservation to date. As a result, they may want these objects to be cared for in ways other than what has traditionally been done. For example, many groups on visiting collections may wish to "feed" certain objects, which involves performing ritual ceremonies to provide sustenance for them. In the course of these ceremonies, cornmeal may be sprinkled on the objects or tobacco smudged or placed on the shelves next to the objects. Once placed on objects or shelves, the cornmeal or tobacco is not to be removed. This practice presents the conservator with a conflict. By respecting the spiritual integrity of some objects, one can jeopardize the well-being of others, as tobacco and cornmeal are extremely attractive to pests that can do considerable damage to collections.

Severe conflicts arise when an object needs interventive treatment for its physical survival, but to carry out such treatment is against the wishes of the particular cultural group that made the object. Preservation might not be seen as desirable, as illustrated by Edmund Ladd's statement, "Everything for ceremonial, religious and ritual purposes that my culture [Zuni] makes is meant to disintegrate . . . to go back into the ground. Conservation is a disservice to my culture."

Increasingly, ethnographic conservators spend considerable time trying to determine how far to go in placing priorities on being sensitive to Native American or other indigenous groups and their concerns at the expense of their own professional standards as conservators. The balance is by no means obvious and will take time to be worked out. The ultimate goal, of course, is to do what is in the best interest of the object.

One result of this interaction is that ethnographic conservators have been forced to reassess the purpose of conservation and rethink their priorities as well as their approach. In essence, ethnographic conservators are redefining conservation for ethnographic materials, and this is an area where the codes of ethics have not been terribly effective in providing guidelines, especially since these issues of cultural sensitivity are complex and question the validity of our assumptions and philosophies. As codes set forth generalized and idealized standards of behaviour that are applicable to the profession as a whole, they have not been able to handle such specific problems that have so radically changed our attitudes and practices.

> The recent revisions of the various codes have gone a little way toward meeting some of these issues.... While all of these codes could be seen to recognize that alternate ways of treating and caring for objects exist and may at times be appropriate, they are not helpful to conservators in resolving conflicts that arise out of these issues. For example... respecting the intangible or conceptual integrity of an object might well conflict with the preservation of other aspects of the object. Perhaps the definition of the term *preservation* needs to be changed and broadened in light of these issues; all codes currently are based on the Western understanding of the word. While it is appropriate that the codes reflect our Western conservation point of view, they must also openly acknowledge the validity of other cultural approaches to the preservation of objects. They need to recognize that in some instances, conservation as we currently practice it will be only one of many options that might be chosen for a given object. As a result, these issues are forcing some conservators to recognize and accept that museum conservation as we know it may not be the only ethical form of conservation, a concept that is not addressed by the codes of ethics in their present form.

Miriam Clavir, Preserving What Is Valued: Museums, Conservation and First Nations 119–20, 125–26, 135–37, 139 (2002) (reprinted with the permission of UBC Press. All rights reserved.)

(a) Preservation and Conservation:

Every [Canadian] First Nations person I talked to supported the view that the preservation of the intangible cultural aspects of an object is very significant – that it is as essential as is the preservation of the tangible object itself.

> I think it's important to preserve objects because of the dances that they go with, the songs that go with them. The dances and songs still belong to people; they're still part of people's rights and privileges. Maybe those people don't know that right now, but some day they will, and they'll go back to the objects. I think if they can see it in a physical sense, it seems more real to them. If they see the mask that goes with the dance or song, then they're more excited about it, and want to learn more. In general, I think people really like objects... [;] people really want to work with objects and they want to come to museums to see the pieces, they don't want to see a picture of it. (Juanita Johnston)
>
> A few years ago, I interviewed an elder from Katzie about the "From Under the Delta" exhibit at [the University of British Columbia

> Museum of Anthropology]. The exhibit was about materials recovered from archaeological wetsites and I asked her why she thought the objects are important. She said they are important because every object tells a story; they tell stories of our people. They illustrate our histories. Sometimes, those objects offer the only opportunity for young First Nations people to see a visual representation of those stories and to be introduced to our histories. The objects may even initiate further conversation. If elders have passed on and are no longer available to answer questions (for example, when I mentioned losing my grandmother) then those objects can help to tell some of our stories. They can help to maintain some of that knowledge in the community. As I understood, she was reminding me that the objects are tangible evidence of those who came before us. They are markers of our history. Our communities have persevered through a great deal of oppression and devastation; often the objects form a crucial link to our histories, our traditions, and our culture. (Dena Klashinsky)

(b) The Use of Modern Science in Preservation?

People were asked whether they felt modern scientific materials were appropriate to use in repairing or restoring heritage objects.

. . .

> [Miriam Clavir:] Some people don't like the fact that objects from First Nations are being preserved by Western scientific methods. They don't feel that's appropriate. What do you think about that?
>
> [Gloria Cranmer Webster:] Well, I think that some of the people who are saying that are carvers who use power tools. We're living in the nineties. Museums are part of our world now and the kinds of things museums are able to do are also part of our world and I think if those objects are owned by those museums, I think those museums have a responsibility to preserve those objects in whatever way works. However, if the people who make this kind of criticism prefer not to preserve their own treasures with Western means, that's fine.
> [On the use of twentieth-century chemicals to preserve old pieces:] Some people might say it's not appropriate. But I think some people also might say, "Well it's that or lose it forever" . . . but I think some people might object . . . it's old and that's not the way we do it. (Juanita Johnston)

Another person who had worked for many years in conjunction with museums stated that she considered that any methods, including Western scientific methods, that successfully preserved objects were worthwhile. She said that many of the pieces she had seen in people's homes were not well cared for. Several others commented on hazards, such as theft and fire, that are a constant worry when one has something valuable at home.

The above comments on science reveal a general acceptance, particularly by people who have been responsible for collections, of its use in the preservation of material culture. However, it is interesting that other people had no opinion on this matter. In fact, their hesitation in answering showed that this issue was new to them. The impression that questions about the preservation of objects [were] not a topic of much concern to several of the people with whom I talked was reinforced in some of the other conversations. It is not surprising that the issues of interest to conservators are not widely shared; the profession of conservator and the details with which it is concerned represent a small circumscribed world. Although all of the First Nations people to whom I spoke were involved in cultural or educational areas, the preservation of objects was not necessarily something they had to concern themselves with, and museum-style conservation of collections was even less important.

(c) Completing the Natural Cycle of Objects: Preservation versus Use:

[The relationship between people can be as important as the logistics of preservation on which conservators focus.]

> I can see the value in [the argument against preservation], particularly if an object is no longer useable and it doesn't have an important history associated with it, or if its history is unknown. It may be possible to have another object created, one that serves the same function. The new object might even function better than the old one! Under those conditions, a new, fully functioning object would have more value than an old one that can't be used. It seems crazy to spend your energy on preserving an object that . . . is lifeless. (Dena Klashinsky)

. . .

So, regarding the question of what attributes of an object must be preserved, First Nations clearly place a high value on usability. There are a number of reasons for this, one being that use reflects what the originators intended for the objects.

. . .

If a family is actively participating in their cultural ceremonies, the use of a ritual object can be a matter of necessity rather than choice:

> The same kind of rights are not associated with pieces of jewelry. You treasure a gold bracelet your grandmother gave you. You don't ever have to wear it like we have to once in a while wear a mask that's been passed down to us. (Gloria Cranmer Webster)

Use is also seen as crucial to the transmission of the culture.

> I suppose for kids in the city the business of touching may be more important. Potlatches are so much a part of kids' lives here in Alert Bay. (Gloria Cranmer Webster)

Even with regard to archaeological objects, where the question of current use does not come up, knowing about how they were used is still important in transmitting culture. Transmitting culture means passing on a positive cultural identity.

. . .

Use is also indicative of rights and privileges, as, for example, in the case of cultural prerogatives being displayed and witnessed at a potlatch or other ceremonial occasion.

. . .

To further underline the First Nations perception of "use," it should be noted that certain kinds of wear are mitigated by the passing on of cultural values. In other words, there exists a traditional cultural connection between the use of objects and the proper care of these objects. Values such as these can be found in Western as well as indigenous societies. For example, Western musicians take great physical care of the old musical instruments that they use because they respect them and because their sound (i.e., their inherent meaning) depends on their condition.

NOTES AND QUESTIONS

1. Do you think that museum trustees who ignore indigenous concerns such as those discussed in the foregoing readings can or should be held liable for breaches of their duty of care as fiduciaries?
2. How do you think museum trustees should address the sorts of indigenous perspectives outlined herein? Are there other constituencies that relate to the material in their collections with which museums might seek to engage? If a museum's conservation practices are challenged in court as constituting a breach of a fiduciary duty, could deference to the concerns of the indigenous peoples from whom objects in its collection originated be relied on as a defense?
3. An integral aspect of the duty of care expected of directors and officers of business corporations is the so-called business judgment rule. This rule provides that, where there is no evidence of fraud, illegality, or lack of loyalty in respect of actions involving business judgment, directors are presumed to have acted in good faith and reasonably. *Shlensky v. Wright*, 237 N.E. 2d 776 (Ill. App. 1968). A major rationale for the rule is that there are no defined professional standards for business managers, at least in the sense that there exist for doctors and engineers. Conversely, should this rule be interpreted to mean that museum management must be held to a higher standard in respect of matters such as conservation and deaccessioning where professional minimum standards arguably do exist? See Denise Ping Lee, Note, *The Business Judgment Rule: Should It Protect Nonprofit Directors?* 103 Colum. L. Rev. 925 (2003) (arguing against the application of the business judgment rule to nonprofit directors on the basis of the limited level of accountability they presently face).
4. Several nonbinding conservation standards and practices have been designed for general application by museums. In 1950 the International Institute for Conservation of Historic and Artistic Works (IIC) was established, and it was followed by

national associations of conservators, such as the American Institute for Conservation of Historic and Artistic Works, which developed the first code of conservation standards in 1963 (*Report of the Murray Pease Committee: IIC American Group Standards of Practice and Professional Relations for Conservators*). In 1967 the IIC-American Group also adopted the Code of Ethics and Standards of Practice for Art Conservators. *See* http://aic.stanford.edu/about/coredocs/coe/index.html. Other conservation-focused organizations include the International Centre for the Study of the Preservation and Restoration of Cultural Property, with 110 member states; the Getty Conservation Institute; and the Canadian Conservation Institute.

Despite these developments at the international and national level there is still concern that the conservation profession lacks enforceable standards. See *City of Amsterdam v. Daniel Goldreyer, Ltd.* 882 F. Supp. 1273 (E.D.N.Y. 1995), where a conservator was sued for a botched restoration of a Barnett Newman painting that had been vandalized. Some states such as California have art-preservation laws that are designed to protect artworks from destruction, including that which arises from grossly negligent conservation and restoration efforts. See Heidi Stroh, Comment: *Preserving Fine Art from the Ravages of Art Restoration*, 16 ALB. L.J. SCI. & TECH. 239 (2006). These and other laws may afford additional remedies in cases of negligent conservation.

3. Ethical Constraints

In Chapter 5 we examined codes of ethics, a topic to which it is appropriate to return in concluding this chapter on museums. The material that follows focuses on the specific role of ethics in museum decisions and the resolution of museum-related disputes. There is clearly a relationship between dispute resolution and codes of ethics. Essentially, the rarity of judicial decisions on deaccessioning and other crucial issues involving museums and the resulting lack of legal guidance for officers and trustees help explain why numerous museums have adopted ethical codes as a substitute in recent decades. Another explanation for this burgeoning adoption of codes may lie in changing attitudes and norms of museum leaders as they expand and modify institutional agendas to respond better to public expectations. As the public demands greater transparency and accountability, codes of ethics can be seen as a means to legitimize evolving practices of museum management and deflect criticism that museums otherwise might attract.

Such codes are essentially voluntary and nonenforceable, however. As in other forms of self-regulation affecting professional activities, the primary, though not exclusive, sanction for noncompliance is some form of institutional discipline – such as expulsion from membership. Sometimes, however, the sanctions become more public when courts use them to gauge professional standards in cases of alleged negligence or other misfeasance. Codes may even gain the force of law when, taken together, they embody professional custom and thereby inform the content of enforceable fiduciary and other standards. See *Re Porter*, 890 P.2d 1377 (Or. 1995).

The ICOM's Code of Ethics for Museums, as summarized in Chapter 5, is a model for the codes of individual museums and national associations. These associations include, for example, the American Association of Museums, the Association of Art Museum Directors, and the Canadian Museums Association.

ROSENBERG v. SEATTLE ART MUSEUM, 70 F. Supp. 2d 1163 (W.D. Wa. 1999)

[The following case, involving a museum's only painting by Henri Matisse, raises significant questions about the role of ethics in the adjudication of cultural heritage claims. – *Eds.*]

LASNIK, District Judge.

Third-Party Defendant Knoedler-Modarco, Inc., moves the Court for summary judgment against Third-Party Plaintiff Seattle Art Museum (SAM) on its claim of fraud, and moves for dismissal of SAM's other claims for lack of personal jurisdiction. Having considered the materials filed in support and opposition, the Court hereby grants partial summary judgment and dismisses this case.

The facts of the case are well known. *See, e.g., Rosenberg v. Seattle Art Museum*, 42 F. Supp. 2d 1029, 1031–32 (W.D. Wash. 1999). A 1928 painting by Henri Matisse, known as "L'Odalisque," was purchased by Virginia and Prentice Bloedel from Knoedler in 1954. In 1991, the Bloedels gave the painting to SAM; L'Odalisque, it now appears, was stolen by German Nazis from French art collector Paul Rosenberg during World War II. Rosenberg's heirs discovered the whereabouts of L'Odalisque and filed this suit against SAM for its return. SAM, in turn, sued the Knoedler gallery for breach of title, fraud, and negligent misrepresentation. SAM has agreed that the Rosenberg heirs are the rightful owners of the painting and have given it to them. The question remaining is who in L'Odalisque's postwar chain of possession will suffer the loss.

SAM claims Knoedler defrauded the Bloedels when it sold them the painting in 1954, by lying to them about the painting's provenance, or chain of title. SAM presents evidence that Knoedler knew that the painting belonged to Rosenberg, but assured the Bloedels that Knoedler had good title to it. Knoedler argues on this motion that SAM cannot prove this claim, and that if this claim is dismissed, its other claims should also be dismissed because the Court would lack personal jurisdiction over Knoedler.

Summary judgment is appropriate only where there are no genuine issues of material fact and the moving party is entitled to judgment as a matter of law. Fed. R. Civ. P. 56(c). The moving party bears the burden of establishing that it is entitled to summary judgment.

. . .

Establishing fraud requires clear and convincing proof of nine elements: (1) representation of an existing fact; (2) materiality; (3) falsity; (4) the speaker's knowledge of its falsity; (5) intent of the speaker that it should be acted upon by the plaintiff; (6) plaintiff's ignorance of the falsity; (7) plaintiff's reliance on the truth of the representation; (8) plaintiff's right to rely upon it; and (9) damages suffered by the plaintiff. . . . Knoedler argues that it made no representation regarding L'Odalisque's title; that neither the Bloedels nor SAM relied upon, or had a right to rely upon, any such representation; and that Knoedler did not intend the Bloedels or SAM to rely upon any such representation.

If it were necessary to resolve this motion, the Court would find SAM has presented sufficient evidence of fraud to avoid summary judgment. Looking at the evidence in a light most favorable to SAM, the letter written by Knoedler's Lelia Wittler to Virginia Bloedel on December 21, 1954, touches on L'Odalisque's title, and appears to be a response to an inquiry about title by the Bloedels.[5] Combined with evidence that Knoedler possessed information that showed that the painting belonged to Paul Rosenberg before World War II, and that much of Rosenberg's collection had been looted during the Nazi occupation of Paris, there is a genuine dispute whether Knoedler defrauded the Bloedels.[6]

However, SAM presents no evidence that Knoedler defrauded the museum. In particular, there is no evidence SAM relied upon anything Knoedler ever said about L'Odalisque's title. Therefore, the question is whether SAM has the right to recover for an alleged fraud upon the Bloedels. Knoedler claims that this right can never be asserted by a third party, but this is incorrect. *See Harvey v. Cleman*, 65 Wash. 2d 853, 857–58, 400 P.2d 87 (1965) ("all causes of action" survive death since passage of RCW 4.20.046, and thus are assignable) [but] SAM is certainly not a personal representative of either of the Bloedels.

. . .

In the absence of any other basis upon which SAM may be entitled to assert the rights of the Bloedels in tort, the Court must grant Knoedler's motion for summary judgment.

. . .

Accordingly, Knoedler's motion for partial summary judgment and dismissal is granted, and this case is ordered dismissed. Seattle Art Museum's motion to compel is stricken as moot.

NOTES AND QUESTIONS

1. The Seattle Art Museum (SAM) agreed that the Rosenbergs were the proper owners of the Matisse painting, given its questionable pedigree, as reflected in the

[5] The letter reads in substance as follows:

> I am sorry there was any question left unanswered in your mind, but the thing was so clear to us although we do not know the name of the former owner. The Paris dealer from whom we bought the Matisse would not give out the name of the former owner, as they always hoped to get more pictures from the same source.
>
> This picture, as you know, was painted in 1928 and was exhibited at the Salon des Tuileries that same year; and in 1937 it was exhibited in the Independent show when it was loaned by the artist. In 1938 he again exhibited it in the International Exhibition at Carnegie Institute in Pittsburgh. It was without doubt in his possession through 1938. As it was published in a Swedish publication in 1938, it may have gone to Sweden and was in some Swedish collection. However, from then on it was owned privately by this collection, from which it now comes, and whose identity we are unable to get from the Paris dealer. The document, of which you have a photostat, comes directly from Madame Matisse, which leaves, of course, no doubt as to the authenticity of the picture.

[6] While SAM's strong advocacy of its position is understandable, the Court is very aware of how difficult it is to determine what really happened 45 years ago, since all the participants are deceased. Indeed, one can imagine an observer in 2041 persuasively arguing that SAM must have known L'Odalisque was a stolen painting some time in the mid-1990s, particularly after the appearance of Hector Feliciano's book identifying the painting as missing. . . .

footnoted letter from Knoedler to Virginia Bloedel. The court discussed SAM's actions against the Knoedler gallery from which the donors of the Matisse, the Bloedels, had purchased it. The court reasoned that, although the gallery may have defrauded the donors, the museum had not been defrauded and had not acquired a right to the donor's cause of action when it acquired the painting. The murkiness of the pedigree clearly casts doubt on the chain of possession prior to SAM's acquisition of the painting. Aside from the strictly legal considerations that emerged in the course of the *Rosenberg* litigation, as well as SAM's deaccession of the Matisse, what were SAM's ethical responsibilities to ensure that the chain of possession was clean, before it accepted the painting and, later, when the Rosenbergs sought its return? After all, the painting, which had clearly been confiscated by the Nazis from the Rosenbergs, had been proudly displayed by SAM for several years before and after Héctor Feliciano's exposé. With reference to the discussion of ethical codes and guidelines in Chapter 5, would any provisions in either the AAM Code of Ethics for Museums or the Washington Principles for return of Holocaust-related material stolen by the Nazis have helped to determine the museum's actions?

2. After this phase of *Rosenberg*, the Bloedels' personal representative assigned their claim to SAM. In a subsequent action, the federal district court vacated its order granting summary judgment to the Knoedler gallery and ordered the parties to prepare for further proceedings. *Rosenberg v. Seattle Art Museum*, 124 F. Supp. 2d 1207 (W.D. Wash. 2000). In the end, the case was settled before the perfected claim was heard. What ethical responsibilities might then be at issue, taking into account that Knoedler, a commercial art gallery, was not subject to codes of ethics in the museum industry? As between Knoedler and SAM, both of which may have had unclean hands, should ethical considerations have played any role at all in subsequent litigation?
3. The Devil's Island Museum in French Guiana tells the history of that wretched prison of last resort in the French criminal justice system, from the mid-nineteenth to the mid-twentieth century. The museum's exhibits are described in both English and French. One prisoner, Charles de Rudio, goes down as a rare escapee from Devil's Island. He had been convicted of participation in a plot to assassinate Napoléon III in 1858 and, after his miraculous escape from Devil's Island in 1859 – having survived that living hell – he fled first to England and then the United States, where he was one of the last survivors of the Battle of the Little Bighorn in 1876. In the museum exhibit in French Guiana, his biography ends abruptly in English as follows: "He died many years later in Los Angeles." The French version, however, ends as follows: "De Rudio est consideré par les Americains comme une grande figure de leur histoire" ("De Rudio is considered by the Americans as a great figure in their history"). Do museums operate under any ethical constraints on their narrative license (e.g., De Rudio's asserted prominence in U.S. history)? Might cultural or political factors explain the completely different versions of De Rudio?
4. The U.K. Spoliation Advisory Panel was established in 2000 to assist claimants and institutions concerning property lost during the Nazi era and held in national institutions. The panel provides an alternative to litigation and is not a judicial body, although its chair is a retired lord justice of appeal. In a report recommending the

introduction of legislation to allow the British Library to return a twelfth-century manuscript in its collection to Beneveto Cathedral in Italy, the panel acknowledged its reliance on the Statement of Principles and Proposed Actions issued by the National Museum Directors Conference regarding the moral considerations the panel was obliged to uphold. See STATIONERY OFFICE (U.K.), REPORT OF THE SPOLIATION ADVISORY PANEL IN RESPECT OF A 12TH-CENTURY MANUSCRIPT NOW IN THE POSSESSION OF THE BRITISH LIBRARY 16–17 (2005); Norman Palmer, *Spoliation and Holocaust-Related Cultural Objects: Legal and Ethical Models for Resolution of Claims*, 12 ART, ANTIQUITIES & L. 1 (2007).

8. Sports

In this chapter, we examine the exciting cultural activity of sports competition. Before we turn to the legal framework, it will be useful to place sports in a larger context of play, games, and recreation. It also is useful to ask about the consequences of classifying a particular activity as a recreation or sport by contrast to some other form of activity. We will see that a classification we may take for granted is actually culturally conditioned.

A. Characteristics

David Parlett, *The Arts of Contest, in* Asian Games: The Art of Contest 23–24, 27 (Asia Society 2004) (reprinted with the permission of the Asia Society)

We might begin by asking[,] "What is a game?" . . . [A] glance at any substantial dictionary will uncover a long list of intuitively but not analytically related usages. They include triviality ("This isn't a game"), scheme or intrigue (So that's your little game!"), pursuit ("The game's afoot, Watson!"), object of pursuit ("Big game hunter"), prostitution ("On the game"), performance of a game ("My game's a bit off today"), and target score ("Game is 121 points"). Eric Berne's book *Games People Play* is a psychological study of "social transaction"; James Carse's *Games Finite and Infinite* is an exercise in theology. "Game theory" started life as a mathematical model of economic behavior, and has been extended to a variety of practical and academic studies, but offers little of interest to the players of real games like faro or football. About the only thing these uses have in common is some underlying concept of purposeful activity, except in ironic mode, when with equal facility they come to connote purpose*less* activity.

. . .

Essentially, a game is a particular session of play ("We had a game of tennis yesterday"), or a particular species of play ("Tennis is an international game").

. . .

As "play" itself covers more than just "games," a way of clarifying the meaning of "games" might be to explore the meanings of "play" and deduct those definitions to which the term "game" is not normally applied. Even this proves to be problematic.

. . .

The underlying connotation of *play* is that of repeated movement or activity, a sense reinforced by the image of sunlight playing over the waves, or of fingers over a keyboard. In addition, and more essentially, it implies *voluntary* activity or *freedom* of movement, as in the play of a wheel or piston in a machine – that is, the area in which that component has a limited freedom to operate. The freedom and voluntary nature of play means that, by definition, it does not serve a conscious utilitarian function in the individual playing, unlike other human activities such as eating, reproducing, keeping warm, finding shelter, and so on. We engage in play not because we have to, but because we want to. Play is a self-validating, self-actualizing activity.

Just as all art constantly aspires toward the condition of music (as asserted by the nineteenth-century art critic Walter Pater), so might it be said that all human activities aspire toward the condition of play. Johan Huizinga, in *Homo Ludens* (Man the Player), goes further, arguing that all major manifestations of civilized culture have their roots in the urge to play. Play is a universal human activity, and therefore presumably has some sort of survival value for the human species; nevertheless, as Huizinga states, the need for play is only urgent to the extent that the enjoyment of it makes it a need. The same thought is more pithily expressed by theologian James Carse: "Whoever *must* play cannot [really] *play*."

Play therefore belongs to the superior field of activities that define us as spiritual beings, together with religion and the arts. Huizinga goes so far as to characterize art as a form of play in itself – music is playing with sounds, painting is playing with paint, poetry is playing with words, and so on (which is not to say, nor does Huizinga assert, that these are nothing but play). He traces the civilizing function of play on warfare, for example, as expressed in the ethical rules and ceremonials of the tournament and the duel. Turning to law, he notes that *jeopardy* derives from *jeu parti*, meaning (literally) an evenly balanced game; furthermore,

> That an affinity may exist between law and play becomes obvious to us as soon as we realize how much the actual practice of the law, in other words a lawsuit, properly resembles a contest whatever the ideal foundations of the law may be.

. . .

Unlike play in general, a game is a structured set of procedures defined by a code of rules to which the players, by an act of free will, agree faithfully to submit. Disagreements may arise as to what the rules actually are (it is well known that hardly anyone plays Monopoly exactly in accordance with the published instructions), but the very arousal of heated disagreement demonstrates how earnestly the players expect there to be some sort of ultimate authority that will command their allegiance and bring them all to heel.

> The agreement of the players to the applicable rules constitutes the ultimate validation of those rules.... There are no rules that require us to obey rules. If there were, there would have to be a rule for those rules, and so on.

Even the cheat acknowledges the existence of rules: he merely tries to win unfairly by circumventing them. The real bane of the game-player's life is not the cheat but the spoilsport – the one who doesn't really care what the rules are or whether he wins or loses, because, when all is said and done, "It's only a game."

There is a Western misperception about games that must be corrected before rules can be understood properly; namely, that authority resides within the covers of a book, or at least within a printed rules sheet. It cannot be overemphasized that the vast majority of games played throughout the world are not book games but folk games. Games are no exception to the rule that every local community imposes its own personality on its cultural heritage, a rule more readily observed in costume and cuisine, or in song and dance. Games certainly require submission to a code of rules, but the rules of folk games exist only in the collective mind of a circle of players in constant contact with one another. Such rules are transmitted primarily by observation and word of mouth, and can only be arbitrated, when necessary, by consultation with older or more experienced players. Neighboring areas may play games that, although apparently identical to the outside observer, nevertheless incorporate subtle differences of layout or rules of play – a circumstance well illustrated today by the vast range of similar race and hunt games played throughout India.

Book games belong to highly urbanized, literate, and administratively centralized nation states. Besides proprietary games such as Monopoly, Scrabble, and Trivial Pursuit, which can be credited to named inventors and publishers, they include traditional games such as chess, bridge, and backgammon, which originated as folk games of unknown authorship but have been transformed subsequently into book games, equipped with a code of "official rules" available in print emanating from an authoritative body, such as the World Bridge Federation or the Fédération Internationale des Echecs. The growth of computer games and online play has further strengthened the urge to regulation, thus reinforcing the misperception of universal fixity. Yet as a matter of fact, most nonproprietary Western games are themselves folk games. Nobody learns tic-tac-toe/noughts and crosses, for example, from a book (though this is partly because it is so simple). Such "folk" as students and soldiers play many card games that have yet to reach the pages of a book, and may never come to enjoy the dubious luxury of official regulation. Nevertheless, Westerners do have a marked tendency to expect "real" games to have "official rules" and are largely unaware of the existence and widespread popularity of such folk games as are born, thrive, and die at a subliterary level.

Jerry L. Anderson, *Comparative Perspectives on Property Rights: The Right to Exclude*, 56 J. Legal Ed. 539, 544–48 (2006)

Chai Vang and Laotian Hunting Rights on Communal Lands

In November 2004, Chai Vang, an immigrant from Laos, was hunting deer in Wisconsin. He apparently got lost, wandered onto a 400-acre piece of private property, found an empty tree stand and climbed up. Not long thereafter, the landowner, accompanied by a group of hunters, discovered Vang, confronted him, and asked him to leave. According to Vang, the confrontation was hostile and aggressive. One hunter angrily shouted profanities at him and used racial slurs. Vang also claimed that another hunter fired a shot at him. We don't know if Vang's version of the events is true, unfortunately, because most of the witnesses are dead – Vang opened fire on them with a semi-automatic rifle, killing six of the hunters and wounding the other two. . . .

. . . [S]omewhere at the bottom of this conflict – in both the hostility that Vang claimed he encountered and his extreme reaction to it – is a lesson about how different cultures view private property rights and why it matters.

In Laos, especially among the Hmong people to which Vang belonged, the community owns the forests and much other land. Thus, every member of the public has abundant land, typically nearby, on which to hunt freely. Many Hmong are avid hunters and depend on game as a vital source of their sustenance. To the Hmong, the "right to hunt" might be seen as a basic human right, perhaps roughly like the American view of communal rights to navigable waters. If hunting is seen as a necessity rather than a sport, depriving a Hmong of access to hunting land might be somewhat equivalent to depriving Americans of access to breathable air.

Given this background of free access to hunting lands, Hmong immigrants may find it difficult to comprehend a system comprised of mostly private lands, on which an almost absolute right to exclude is fiercely protected. In many areas of the United States, communal hunting lands are extremely hard to find. In the upper Midwest, where Vang lived, most huntable land is in private hands. . . . In Wisconsin, where the shootings occurred, over 80 percent of land is private and most of the government land is not open for hunting. Of course, many private landowners will give permission to hunt on their land, and it is possible to rent land for hunting, but Laotian hunters would confront significant financial, language, and cultural barriers in striking such a bargain. Moreover, the mostly urban Laotian community probably just doesn't know many people in rural areas with suitable acreages.

In Laos, the balance of public and private rights to land is struck much differently. Whereas we value the property owner's right to privacy and want to protect against unwanted intrusion, in Laos the right of the community to access the fruits of the land is paramount. Again, while differing property norms can scarcely excuse murder, at least some of the fuel for this hunter's fury may have arisen from the frustration of adjusting to a culture that declares wild animals – the deer, the birds, even the bear – as *res nullius* and therefore available for capture by anyone but then makes it very difficult for the public to get at them. . . .

Interestingly, even in the Wild West, the right to exclude has not always been so absolute. In South Dakota, from 1899 to 1973, hunters could enter and hunt on the private land of others without permission. Land was off limits only if it was fenced with woven wire, had standing crops, or was near livestock, dwellings, schools, or churches. This "right to hunt" reflected, perhaps, the importance of hunting to the frontier culture and relatively larger tract sizes, which would lessen privacy concerns. Even today, landowners in the region are significantly less likely to post their property to keep out hunters, indicating that the public's right of access may be valued differently in various areas of the country.

Private property protection will naturally be weaker in a country like Laos, one of the few remaining Communist regimes. . . . But even in capitalist democracies, the right to exclude has been significantly tempered by giving the public access rights over private lands. As the next section illustrates, even Madonna found that property norms change and that the right to exclude may not be absolute.

Madonna and the Right to Roam

. . . [In the United Kingdom], Parliament recently enacted a statutory "right to roam" giving the public access to millions of acres of privately owned land. The Countryside and Rights of Way Act of 2000 (CRoW) declares private land that contains mountains, moorland, heath, or downland to be "open country," on which the public is now free to walk. The private landowner may not bar the public from wandering over these lands. . . .

Even Madonna has been affected by CRoW. In 2001, Madonna and her husband, Guy Ritchie, bought Ashcombe House in south Wiltshire – over 1000 acres – for £9 million (about $16.5 million). Thereafter, the Countryside Agency announced it planned to classify about 350 acres of their estate as downland, which would have opened the property to public access. The famous couple objected at a public inquiry into the matter, arguing that the land was not suitable as open country and that free access would violate their privacy rights under the European Convention on Human Rights. Ultimately, an independent inspector appointed to resolve the matter decided that only 130 acres, all of which was out of sight of Madonna's home, should be opened to access.

Timothy R. Pauketat, *America's First Pastime*, ARCHAEOLOGY, Sept./Oct. 2009, at 20-21, 22, 23, 25

The chief standing at the summit of the black, packed-earth pyramid raises his arms. In the grand plaza below, a deafening shout erupts from 1,000 gathered souls. Then the crowd divides in two, and both groups run across the plaza, shrieking wildly. Hundreds of spears fly through the air toward a small rolling stone disk. Throngs of cheering spectators gather along the sidelines and root for the two teams as they play *chunkey*, a game that had a significant role in organizing social and political life at Cahokia, the great prehistoric city that arose around A.D. 1050 near present-day St. Louis, Missouri.

When Europeans began exploring the vast expanse of eastern North America, they encountered many tribes of farmers that still played the last, lingering versions of this once great game, which involved hurling spears or sticks at a rolling disk called a chunkey stone. The stories these Native Americans told of its history imply chunkey was significant to their Cahokian forbears. It's possible the Cahokians used this game, which was much more than a way of passing time, to win the hearts and minds of distant people.

Many, possibly most, Midwestern, Southern, and Plains Indians were in one way or another entangled in a history that began at Cahokia. The evidence is often indirect, but it is compelling, and points toward a singular history-changing moment 1,000 years ago, when social life, political organization, religion, art, and culture were all utterly transformed in the middle of the Mississippi River Valley. At the epicenter of events was a radical new kind of social and political experiment: a planned capital city. Someone – or some governing body – designed one from scratch at Cahokia. The leaders superimposed a new plan directly over an old village and supervised the construction of great earthen pyramids, open plazas, and huge wooden buildings. Then they gained control over people living throughout the region, an unprecedented move in the history of ancient America north of Mexico.

A new culture developed at the city, perhaps inspired by Mesoamerican models.... Archaeologists refer to the culture as Mississippian, after the river that flows by many of its known sites.

One of the primary vehicles for the growth of this new civilization may have been Cahokian envoys who carried chunkey stones in one hand and war clubs in the other as they ventured into the hinterlands with the purpose of making peace or political alliances. These emissaries seem to have established and enforced a region-wide peace of sorts, a veritable *Pax Cahokiana*, an important element of which may have been the game of chunkey.

....

Not only was chunkey an important event, as attested by its prominent venue on town grounds, but there were other possible associations, direct or indirect, with warfare and enemy executions. In historic times chunkey was also a gambling game par excellence. It seems to have been addictive for both players and spectators.

....

Chunkey meant a lot to its participants, who would have learned the game as children. Archaeologists have found both child-sized disks, made of stone or baked clay, and the more finely made, adult-sized stones. The latter were presumably the prized heirlooms of whole families, clans, or even entire towns, as described by the Anglo explorers. "The hurling stones they use at present," [one observer] wrote, were from "time immemorial rubbed smooth on the rocks, and with prodigious labor; they are kept with the strictest religious care. From one generation to another, and are exempted from being buried with the dead. They belong to the town where they are used, and are carefully preserved."

Some archaeologists suspect that the politicians of the biggest southern towns infused the play with political or religious associations that served tribal interests. At a minimum, this might have included a sense of team loyalty and community identity. Players from different towns would have faced off, and the cheering and wagering would split along community lines. Just as in modern sports leagues, there would have been challengers and a home team, perhaps mortal enemies who came together to settle a dispute or prove a point. Individuals or entire communities would have developed reputations for winning or losing, placing their very identities at stake.

Those identities, in turn, were tethered to deeper cultural meanings, memories, aesthetic sensibilities, and religious reliefs, many of which probably came from Cahokia. The game's sticks and stones, moreover, reaffirmed the relationship between the sexes and reflected the cosmos. Throwing a stick at a rolling disk was understood by adults to be a virtual sexual act. Thus, chunkey was also linked to certain creation-and-rebirth stories. The rolling chunkey stone was sometimes specifically likened to the sun moving across the daytime sky, reflecting the belief that the cosmos was in constant motion, balanced between the two extremes that could be represented by male and female, day and night, sky and earth, and life and death. As if to accentuate the idea that chunkey was a microcosm of the greater cosmos, crosses were occasionally engraved on chunkey disks representing the four directions or quarters of the universe.

. . .

But by the 19th century . . . the most popular competitive sport was not chunkey, but stickball, or lacrosse. Over the years, chunkey fell out of favor, probably because of the disappearance of Mississippian ideals and political organizations that attended the population loss caused by the spread of European diseases in North America.

Stickball was a more violent team sport, played by up to 1,000 people at a time. The game was like hand-to-hand combat, which is why some called it the "Little Brother of War." . . . The new, more violent realities of post-contact North America made stickball more relevant than chunkey to the lives of Native Americans.

NOTES AND QUESTIONS

1. We generally think of hunting and hiking more as recreation, a generic term, than as sport, a specific form of recreation associated with competition and agreed-on

rules of play. But whether we call them recreation or sport, hunting and hiking are culturally relative. A recreational hunting season in one culture may be a year-round pursuit of livelihood in another, and open hiking on private land in one culture may be trespassing in another. Notice that classification of an activity as recreation or sport (rather than as a means of livelihood, for example) may import a property-generated quality of exclusiveness to that activity and generate territorial imperatives. An example involved the cultural assumptions of the Wisconsin landowner and accompanying hunters that led to the hunting tragedy involving the immigrant hunter from Laos, who had very different cultural assumptions about the nature of hunting. However, classifying an activity as recreation (witness the British hiking legislation) may have the opposite effect of importing a quality of inclusiveness and public entitlement to what would otherwise fall within the exclusive domain of private property rights. For a fascinating article on the British hunting heritage, see Garry Marvin, *English Foxhunting: A Prohibited Practice*, 14 Int'l J. Cultural Prop. 337 (2007). See generally the special issue of that journal "Hunting as Heritage": 14 Int'l J. Cultural Prop. 279–398 (2007).

2. For an insightful presentation of scientific findings and theory concerning the importance (but not idealization) of play in children's lives, see Robin Marantz Henig, *Taking Play Seriously*, N.Y. Times Mag., Feb. 17, 2008, at 38.
3. In *America's First Pastime*, how many political and social functions of chunkey can you identify? Even a single sport can perform many different social functions and yet, like chunkey, disappear or at least fade in prominence under new physical, political, or social conditions. What led to the demise of chunkey?
4. The role of sports in society is culturally conditioned, and divergent sports cultures in different national societies are illuminating. Japanese baseball is an example: "Even visitors who aren't particularly interested in the sport itself will find that attending a baseball game in Japan provides an illuminating peek into Japanese culture." Ingrid K. Williams, *Root, Root, Root and Buy Me Some Eel*, N.Y. Times, July 5, 2009, at TR5 (noting, for example, the spectators' avoidance of booing and jeering of questionable calls by officials and errors by players).
5. In 2006 a large contingent of police in Rostov-on-Don, Russia responded to a report that a brawl had gotten out of control in a local field. After the police arrested several suspects, they were promptly released when it was discovered that they had simply been playing a game of rugby in a culture whose citizens were not familiar with the sport or its scrums.
6. Given such cultural relativities, what are the general characteristics of sports competition in today's world and around the world? It seems to be distinguishable, for example, from musical and theatrical performances that are forms of scripted entertainment. Sports competition, by contrast, is unscripted, relying instead on the opposite principle of unpredictability. It is only when a sports event is corrupted that it becomes truly predictable. What else characterizes sports? Does competition require spectators? Binding rules subject to private sanctions for noncompliance? Public sanctions with due process protections? Recognition and legitimation by established nongovernmental or governmental authority?

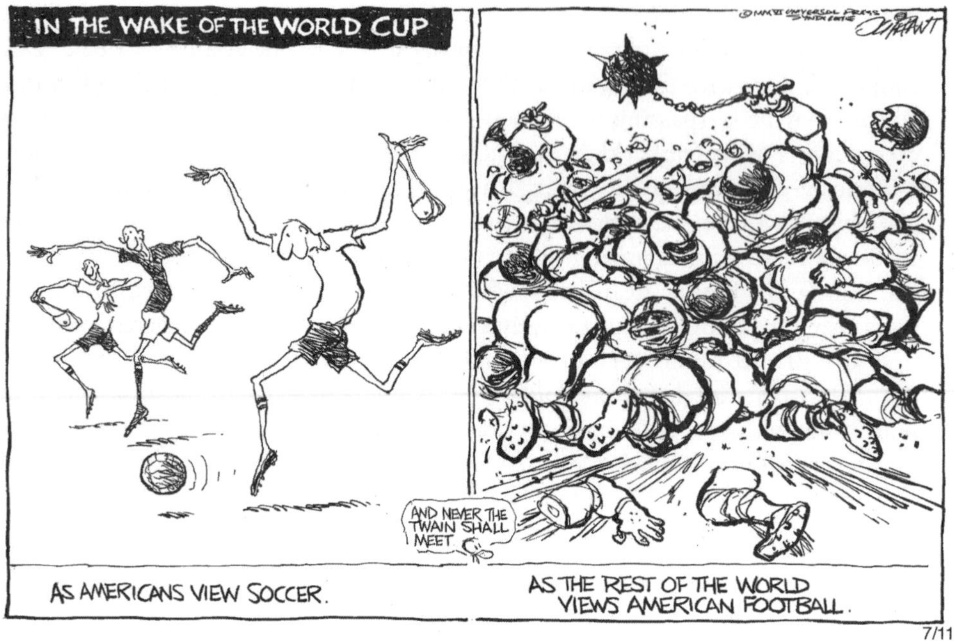

René Lefort & Jean Harvey, *What's in a Game?*, UNESCO Courier, Apr. 1999, at 19

Sport does not speak with a single voice. It is not monolithic. It holds different meanings for different social groups, partly depending on what they want to get out of it. For the well-heeled, sport can be a way of advertising their social status. Playing at exclusive golf, tennis or cricket clubs can be an opportunity to display membership of a privileged group. Amateur sport was controlled for a long time by such people.

At the other end of the spectrum, sport practiced with the most rudimentary facilities can be a great form of self-expression for disadvantaged young people the world over, and may – in exceptional cases – offer them a way out of poverty and deprivation. Here the myth of sport as a ticket to upward mobility can be seen in its quintessential form. . . .

The kaleidoscope of sport also includes the big-time spectacular events which have become first and foremost a commodity whose economic importance and presence in the media are growing non-stop. And finally there's sport as it is enjoyed by so many people around the world – a pastime that helps to keep them fit and brings them together in a convivial setting. But here too the competition can be intense, and the atmosphere may turn sour. It's among amateur sportsmen and sportswomen that drug-abuse is rife and where on-the-field clashes can be the most violent.

Sport is something more than a mirror of the societies in which it is played. It is not a carbon copy of their inequalities and problems. It is a world in its own right, with its own life and its own contradictions.

Through the medium of sport, countless volunteers, for example, organize activities and events that make a positive contribution to their communities.... Through sport, a strong feeling of comradeship develops among athletes at all levels. In short, major social issues influence sport, just as sport can play a big part in helping to solve them.

In a world in which all gifted young athletes were talent-spotted and given equal opportunities to develop their skills, sporting encounters really would take place on a level playing field. But we do not live in an ideal world. The great myth surrounding sport is that it abolishes social divisions, or at least that its symbolic force gives it a greater capacity to do so than any other social activity. But the fact remains that the essence of sport is competition, and competition means making comparisons, setting up hierarchies and separating winners from losers.

James H. Frey & D. Stanley Eitzen, *Sport and Society*, 17 Ann. Rev. Soc. 503, 508–10 (1991) (reprinted with permission of Annual Reviews)

Play is viewed as an activity where entry and exit are free and voluntary, rules are emergent and temporary, fantasy is permitted, utility of action is irrelevant, and the result is uncertain. Play has no formal history nor organization; motivation and satisfaction are intrinsic; and the outcome does not have serious impact beyond the context of the activity. On the other hand, modern sport as represented by the Olympic Games, big-time college athletics, and professional sports exhibits the opposite profile. This type of sport is hardly voluntary; rules are formal, generalizable, and enforced by formal regulatory bodies (e.g. National Collegiate Athletic Association – NCAA); the outcome is serious for individuals and organizations not actually participating in the physical activity, and winning (the outcome) is more important than participation (the process).

As sport becomes institutionalized, particularly at the highest levels of amateur and professional competition, it has come to reflect the corporate/commodity model. Sport is more like work than play. The locus of control has moved from the player/participant to the manager and audience. Morality and ennoblement are replaced by spectacle and entertainment. Play is replaced by display. Attracting spectators and media sponsorships becomes more important than the playing process because sport is now driven by profit and the market. The ethics of the business and corporate world tend to guide sport, not the principles of play and enjoyment. We should not be surprised that high-level sport has been transformed into a commercialized, commodified, and massified phenomenon. Since the business organization has replaced the family as the basic unit coordinating economic activity, and monopoly capital has promoted consumer markets as the preeminent factor in economic organization, many institutions, including sport, in America have been rationalized and corporatized. The commercial factor is so prominent that even a Gross National Sports Product (GNSP) has been calculated.... This places the sport GNP twenty-second on the list of the top 50 industry GNP, ahead of the automobile, petroleum, and airline industries.

The consequences of the commercialization of sport are significant. First, changes may be made in the game format or rules. In football, for example, the forward pass and the narrowing of the hash marks were changes designed to make football more appealing to viewers and spectators. Second, the orientation or values of the participants may change from those based on self-development and satisfaction to those of entertainment and self-interest. [It is] a change from an *aesthetic orientation* that emphasizes the beauty and pleasure of movement, skill and ability, and lifelong activity to a *heroic orientation* that emphasizes danger and excitement, style, and a short-term commitment to victory. There is a developing industry of sport sciences for the primary goal of performance enhancement. The emphasis is on strategies, technical improvement, nutritional and psychological intervention, or any technique to manipulate or engineer the athlete to perform better. This has been called the "scientization" of athletic sport; it is a trend consistent with the instrumental goals of corporate sport. Third, control and influence are largely in the hands of persons and organizations who are not direct participants. Leagues, regulatory groups like the NCAA, media, event sponsors, owners in professional sports, athletic departments and alumni in collegiate programs are examples of the centers of influence. This has forced professional athletes to take measures to enhance their own impact on decision-making; these include labor unionization, representation by agents, and recourse to legal challenges. The fourth consequence of commercialization is the decline of amateurism and the rise of professionalism. Elite amateur sport is corporate sport, whether it is related to the Olympic Games or to collegiate sports. True, amateur sport is characterized by participation for the love of the sport, not the extrinsic rewards. Intrinsic motivation and reward are still relevant, but their significance seems to be devalued by the rising importance of monetary rewards (legal and illegal) for athletes, the exaggerated importance of winning that translates into treating athletes as interchangeable parts, the increase in the incidence of athletes using performance enhancing drugs, and the association of athletic success with outcome goals of profit, visibility, entertainment, and community/organization prestige.

The commercialization of sport is strongly influenced by the role of the media, particularly television, in programming the sports product and in the monies paid to sports organizations for broadcasting rights. The role of the media has increased rapidly in recent years. . . .

The athletic establishment covets television coverage of its events because of the contribution the media make to profits and to exposure to a mass audience. The media pursue sports programming because it is cheaper to produce than other types of programs and it enables the media to reach a normally difficult-to-reach audience of young, college-educated males with disposable income. This makes sports programming attractive to certain advertisers. Thus, the media and sport emerge in a symbiotic relationship, particularly economically. It is important to understand that the media play a dominant role because sport is primarily directed by commercial guidelines.... However, once a sports entity has been displayed on television and received the financial support from television, the sports organization is forever changed.... Many changes in the nature of sport have resulted from media's influence and the desire of *both* media entrepreneurs and representatives of the sport establishment to enhance the appeal of their sport product to maintain profit margins. Thus, the media sometimes glorify violence, create heroes and heroines, demand that athletic schedules be shifted, and that rule changes be made to enhance the product, increase the audience, and generate greater revenues from advertisers.

The preeminent role of media in sport means that TV media's presentation of sport is "mediated." That is, viewers see a representation of sport as it is depicted by commentary, shot or scene selection, and editorialization.... Because the public rarely questions the media's construction of reality, particularly that created by the press and television, the media play a role in shaping images and opinions regarding sport.... The media's representation of an event is taken as reality, overlooking the reality that it is a staged event mediated by commentary. What is presented is generally consistent with the commercial and entertainment agendas of media and sport establishment.

One of the sport-related behaviors that has been projected as a result of media's definition of sport is gambling. Not only do media outlets provide the information a gambler needs, they also are a source of legitimation of gambling. The inclusion of point-spreads and injury reports in descriptions of upcoming games and the promotion of gambling celebrities and analysts together communicate the message that gambling is an acceptable activity and that gambling on sport is a natural accompaniment of sport, even though it is legal in only two states. Thus, the symbiotic relationship of sport and the media is enhanced by the provision of gambling information that appeals to viewers and readers.

It is apparent that the media have redefined the culture of sports, keeping spectators home in front of their TV sets and encouraging their participation in off-field gambling, for example. Even so, spectators continue to flock to the stadiums and playing fields. The following essay attempts to explain the sub-culture of spectators:

Barbara Ehrenreich, *Where the Wild Things Are: A Defense of Cheeseheads, the Chop, and Ecstatic Religion in the Stands*, Civilization, June–July 2000, at 84, 86

Sports fans don't usually attract much attention unless they get violent – hurling missiles at "enemy" players, rushing the field, brawling after the game. But in the last three decades, in a trend almost unnoticed by sports commentators and sociologists, fans have been expressing themselves in more colorful and peaceable ways, potentially even upstaging the games themselves. Soccer fans worldwide were generally the trendsetters, having been the first to paint their faces and decorate themselves head to toe in masks, ribbons, scarves, and massive headgear. These fans often bring music to the game – samba bands or African drums – and they sometimes march to stadiums in organized masses or leave in parades of heavily festooned, loudly honking cars. Most spectacularly, they engage in synchronized displays during the game, like the British "synchro-clap," in which the fans, as if schooled in the task, intersperse their songs and chants with precisely timed rhythmic clapping. Spectators don't get much respect, at least compared to athletes, but you can't call them passive anymore.

In the last two decades, the trend toward participation has spread to American sports events, especially football, baseball, and basketball. Take face painting: Only a few years ago, ardent fans had to use magic markers or even housepaint to lend their allegiances epidermal expression. Now there are at least half a dozen purveyors of skin-compatible colored makeup – and spokespersons for these companies describe the business as "really surprising" and "huge."

You can buy "team spirit" kits with colors appropriate to almost every known team, or you can be painted professionally at concessions located at stadium entrances. There are other forms of personal decoration, too, and these now go well beyond the team-colored scarf or sweatshirt to include color-coordinated nail polish, earrings, headgear – Cheeseheads, in the case of Green Bay Packer fans – and a new line of team-colored Afro wigs.

Americans have made their own unique contribution to the spectacle in the form of "the Wave," which was invented in 1981 – though where, exactly, is a matter of intense dispute – and moved quickly from football to baseball and basketball. Another distinctly American mode of synchronized crowd display, much criticized by Native Americans, is "the chop" and its accompanying war chant, popularized by fans of the Atlanta Braves.

What motivates fans to become part of the show? Is this a case of team ardor run amok, or could there be deeper psychological forces at work? Sheer exhibitionism might explain some forms of display in their earliest stages – a painted bare chest, for example, can still catch the attention of cameras – but this cannot explain the thousandth painted face or the massed synchronized activities. Nor, in a climate increasingly marked by free agency, is it easy to explain the ever-more flamboyant behavior of fans in terms of mounting team loyalty. With elite players free to market themselves to the highest bidder, and owners free to change lineups and move teams to new cities, fans may indeed be left with nobody to get excited about – except each other. In fact, Americans have been known to indulge in, say, face painting even when they have no direct stake in the game, as at soccer matches between teams representing foreign nations.

One possibility is that the fans are rebelling, however unconsciously, against their appointed role as spectators in sports that were once much more participatory. Medieval European football pitted whole villages against each other and involved "everyone . . . male and female, adult and child, rich and poor, laity and clergy," as Amherst College sports historian Allen Guttmann has written. He has speculated that today, "as sports become more commercialized and bureaucratized, fans may feel the need to say[,] 'We're part of this, too.'"

But the specific forms of display undertaken by modern fans recall a tradition even broader and more ancient than sports: the organized festivities, both secular and religious, of preindustrial societies throughout the world. Almost universally, these have involved masking, costuming, dancing, and feasting, all of which are in chaotic abundance at today's sports stadiums. Face painting is a form of masking; synchronized motions like the Wave a kind of dance. Medieval Europe boasted an especially robust tradition of communal festivity, with carnivals and other feast days taking up, in some regions as much as one day out of every four in the year. When commentators complain that today's demonstrative fans are turning the game into a "carnival," they only betray their ignorance of history: Carnival was in fact the traditional setting for medieval sports such as wrestling, bull running, and archery.

Only scattered remnants of the European festive tradition survived into the modern era. Beginning in the 16th century, both secular and religious authorities, representing the Protestant Reformation and the Catholic Counter-Reformation, moved to suppress popular festivities on the grounds that they were disorderly, indecent, un-Christian, and, especially as the Industrial Revolution gained ground, an extravagant waste of time. Feast days were canceled, carnivals denied a venue, raucous celebrations were transformed into sober prayer vigils. Sports, at least the ones seen as plebeian, fell under the same attack: In 1608, a Manchester ordinance prohibited football, complaining of the harm done by a "company of lewd and disordered persons usinge that unlawfulle exercise of playing with the ffotebale in ye streets."

The result today is a global culture fairly desolate of joyous communal ritual. Sports enjoyed a revival in the late 19th century, but only because they were seen as a fine source of manly, nationalistic values; later they were encouraged largely as a tame form of "entertainment." In today's multi-billion-dollar sports industry, it no longer takes a village to score a touchdown.

We do a lot of complaining about the lack of "community" in modern societies, but few have noted the absence of public and participatory festivities that can, however briefly, unite total strangers in ecstatic communion. Emile Durkheim called this experience "collective effervescence," which he discerned in the ritual dances of Australian aborigines and postulated to be the emotional basis of all religion. A few religious denominations – Pentecostalism, for example – still offer a collective ecstatic experience, as did rock culture at its height. But the ecstatic religions tend to be marginal, and rock has been tamed for commercial consumption or driven into clubs as "raves." Hence, perhaps, the attempts by fans to transform sports events into an occasion for communal festivity – where else, in a culture of cubicles and malls, can you lose yourself so completely in a transient community of like-minded others?

Unfortunately, English lacks a word, or even a graceful phrase, for the desire for ebullient self-expression and excited merger with the crowd. Call it primitive religiosity or some sort of "carnival instinct": What today's demonstrative fans are telling us is that it cannot be suppressed forever.

NOTES

1. Violence in the sports arena, aided and abetted by spectators hungry for action, remains a serious problem. Although most amateurs and professional sports leagues impose heavy fines for fighting, the National Hockey League (NHL) is a major exception. Brawls occur in 43% of all regular season games. An estimated twenty-four thousand fights have broken out in NHL history, with five hundred each season, according to a Web site (http://www.hockeyfights.com) that rates fights and posts videos of them. Ice hockey's reliance on gate receipts (80% of NHL revenue) over media payments encourages teams to turn a blind eye to staged fights by prior agreement between players and to spontaneous bullying. New rules would triple the five-minute penalty for fighting in staged fights. An interesting cultural dimension is that the expansion in the number of NHL players from Europe, where violence is less common, has helped constrain the greater Canadian proclivity to brutality on ice.
2. Should all violence be prohibited in sports competition? If so, how should we define "violence"? Would your definition permit or prohibit boxing, kick boxing, North American-style football, and other violence-prone sports?
3. Should player violence result in both criminal prosecution and league or team sanctions against an offending athlete or just one or the other of these responses? What standards should apply to league or team sanctions? Should such sanctions be uniform among different teams and leagues? To what extent should the context of an offense be relevant – for example, between professional and amateur competition and among various locations of the offense (for example, on the field of play, during practice, or outside the sports arena between athletic personnel)?
4. Spectator violence has also been a serious issue for many years, centering largely on international football/soccer contests. The causes range from hypernationalism to political protests to the use of alcohol. Sometimes the cause is mixed. For example, after a Japanese national team had beaten a Chinese team at a 2004 Asian Cup game in Beijing, Chinese fans, apparently inflamed by both long-standing national resentments as well as recent revelations of Japanese hiring of Chinese female "companions," chanted "kill, kill, kill" to the victorious Japanese. "Spectators in the stadium booed during the Japanese national anthem, and the

few Japanese fans who ventured into Beijing to attend the game were pelted with garbage. 'Death to the Japanese,' read the signs. 'Bomb Tokyo,' 'Exterminate the Jap midgets.'" JOHN POMFRET, CHINESE LESSONS 267 (2007) (describing this incident in the larger contexts of a historic animosity among some Chinese toward the Japanese, particularly since the Japanese occupation of China during the 1930s and 1940s, and a growing significance of football/soccer in China's process of modernization).

5. In Europe, a Convention on Spectator Violence provides for football stadium controls, judicial cooperation and extradition of apprehended spectators. *European Convention on Spectator Violence and Misbehaviour at Sports Events and in Particular at Football Matches, E.T.S. no. 120 (1985).*

James H. Frey & D. Stanley Eitzen, *Sport and Society,* 17 ANN. REV. SOC. 503, 511–12 (1991) (reprinted with the permission of Annual Reviews)

Two major motives govern a country's political and economic activity. The first is that of building an efficient but dynamic modern state. In other words, the country should exhibit an acceptable standard of living, a stable political order, an equitable system of social justice and social behavior governed by controlled, rational, not impulsive, procedures. The second national motive is to be recognized as a responsible actor in the international community of nations. In other words, nations seek internal stability and external status. Sport is commonly viewed as a vehicle to achieve both.

The integrative role of sport for a nation is similar to the structural-functional role assigned to sport in communities. . . . Integration to counteract internal racial, ethnic, regional and class diversity and conflict is a major reason that nations promote participation in highly visible international events. [A] study of soccer in Brazil documented the way that sport gave a diverse population something to share in the name of national solidarity. Thus, sport can contribute to a national identity or sense of nationalism that temporarily overrides differences. The world rugby championships provide an interesting example. Annually when national teams are selected, the warring factions in Ireland and Northern Ireland lay aside their bitter animosities, combining players to form the Irish national team which members of both nations cheer. Governments will often encourage international competition in acknowledgment of the unifying role of sport. However, critics employing a conflict perspective assert that the use of sport to encourage the homogenization of a population represents an effort to control that population by instilling certain dominant values, which reduce the likelihood of a challenge against those in power.

Involvement in international sport requires participation in networks of organizations that are transnational in scope. Before this participation can be effective, an organizational base staffed by competent personnel must be developed. Sport provides a mechanism to link organizations and to develop managerial and administrative skills among the local population. Several Latin American countries, including Cuba, have done this. Nicaragua used baseball as a mechanism to rebuild internal institutions after a revolution and to reinstitute regional and intranational communication and coordination. In some cases, Cuba and the Dominican Republic, for example, the use of sport to enhance the human capital of an indigenous population serves to reduce the dependency of a nation of smaller size and limited resources on the larger nations.

The primary role of sport in international relations is one of public diplomacy. That is, sport serves to articulate secondary national interests (e.g. visibility, ideological expression, status enhancement, legitimacy), to test foreign relations initiatives (e.g. ping-pong diplomacy between the United States and China), to enhance cultural exchange and understanding, and to reduce the potential for actual conflict by playing out hostilities in a restricted and controlled setting. Thus, sport is an activity of international cooperation and interaction, but it is peripheral to the survival of a state political system. Olympic record performances are irrelevant to hard-core negotiations over primary national interests that if unresolved could lead to war.

Nevertheless, status in the community of nations is ultimately related to success in athletic events. The gold medal count in the Olympics is important precisely because that count becomes a measure of political legitimacy, of modernization, or of a people's resolve.

Stephen Weatherill, *Sport as Culture in EC Law, in* Culture and European Union Law 113, 145 (Rachael Craufurd Smith ed., 2004) (reprinted with the permission of the Oxford University Press)

Participation even as a television viewer in a football World Cup or an Olympic games, both of which are staged only once every four years, could be taken to contribute to the construction of a shared sense of identify and of history, and as an indispensable basis for social communication. One may optimistically hope that, in so far as minority sections of a nation's population enjoy a disproportionately high representation among the cream of a country's sporting performers, the sight of the team or individual athletes in action may promote tolerance and respect for diversity in society. This appealing vision may be illustrated by the successful exploits of the multi-ethnic French national football side of recent years. But in response to every example of sport as a force for cohesion, it is not hard to paint a less agreeable picture. In 2001, two friendly football matches between countries with a troubled recent shared history, France and Algeria, and Portugal and Angola, were abandoned without reaching their allotted duration of 90 minutes as a result of violence among players and/or supporters. And in the uniquely odious case of the English national football team it is regrettably easy to reflect that scenes of young white men who travel in aggressive celebration of a deeply intolerant culture do nothing to foster social cohesion. Patriotism is too often transformed from allegiance to one's own country into disrespect or even hatred of other countries, and national representative sport has no special claim to be able successfully to achieve or promote the benefits of intercultural dialogue without suffering the burdens of sustained or deepened division.

NOTES AND QUESTIONS

1. On the whole, sports activity is more a microcosm of global society and its problems than a palliative for them. Clearly, it is a fundamental aspect of modern cultures. At the end of Chapter 1 we noted the use of sport to promote legal relationships and more generally to foster cooperation between states. For example, the "ping-pong diplomacy" between China and the United States in 1971 famously served to signal a rapprochement and eventual opening of diplomatic relations between the two countries. It is not so clear, however, whether sports activity can effectively play a loftier role as an agent of national and global harmony. That aspiration has always motivated major international competition. "One World, One Dream" was the theme of the 2008 Games in Beijing, for example. The power of the dream has inspired myriad major initiatives, from Baron Pierre de Coubertin's organization of the modern Olympic Movement to Nelson Mandela's vigorous promotion of the 1995 Rugby World Cup in South Africa to reassure white Afrikaners of the continued importance of their culture in the new society while also encouraging blacks to use that culture to advance themselves. See John Carlin, Playing the Enemy: Nelson Mandela and the Game That Made a Nation (2008).

   One cannot ignore, however, the profound political tensions in the sports arena: for example, the reciprocal cold war boycotts of the 1980 Moscow Olympic Games and 1984 Los Angeles Olympic Games, the armed conflict between Honduras and El Salvador after a football/soccer match, and the tragedy of war-torn Sarajevo just a decade after it hosted the Winter Olympics. One also cannot ignore the general displacement of world-order values by commercialization and the demands of the broadcast media.

   Sadly, Russia's attack in 2008 on neighboring Georgia, ostensibly as a response to Georgia's military action in two of its own ethnic Russian regions violated a cherished rule of the Olympic Movement. Known in ancient times as the *ekecheiria* and in the modern era as the sacred truce, the rule requires cessation of all armed conflict during the course of the Olympic Games. Enshrined in UN resolutions and international custom, the sacred truce has seldom been violated. It is, of course, more symbolic than functional, but it serves as a reminder of Olympic aspirations to promote global harmony and as an opportunity for belligerents or prospective belligerents to take stock of the devastation of warfare. What made the Russian attack on Georgia especially troublesome was its coincidence on August 8 with the opening ceremony of the Olympic Games. See Charles King, *The Five-Day War*, Foreign Aff., Nov./Dec. 2008, at 2.

2. For a fascinating discussion of the aspirations and implication of sports in entire societies, particularly in South Africa, *see* Simon Kuper, *Mixed Evidence on Team Colours*, Fin. Times, July 21, 2007, Life & Arts, at 2. Undoubtedly, the global boycott of South African teams was instrumental in helping eliminate apartheid there. But as that country geared up to host the 2010 World Cup in football/soccer, it was far from clear that sport had helped change attitudes toward race or national origin, either in South Africa or, for that matter, in England and France. "If policymakers reviewed the evidence, they might conclude that harnessing sport to build nations is not worth the time. Though it might boost national pride, that doesn't seem to do countries much good. Nor does sport appear to help integrate ethnic minorities, although it might provide evidence, as in England, that minorities have become more integrated." *Id.* Do you agree or disagree? Can you give examples to support your conclusion?
3. In 2007 the International Olympic Committee invited Sochi, Russia, to host the 2014 Winter Olympics. President Vladimir Putin, an avid skier who had himself actively sought the Olympic invitation, responded as follows: "This is, without a doubt not only a recognition of Russia's achievements in sports, it is, there is no doubt, an assessment of our country.... This is an acknowledgement of its growing capabilities, first and foremost in the economic and social spheres." Int'l Herald Trib., July 6, 2007, at C15. Likewise, the 2008 Olympic Games in Beijing were described as "China's global coming out party." Allen Carlson, *China's Conflicted Olympic Movement*, Current Hist., Sept. 2007, at 252; *see also* Howard W. French, *Pushed to Limit, and Beyond, for Gold: Chinese Athletes Put Health at Risk in Drive for Olympic Glory*, Int'l Herald Trib., June 20, 2008, at 1. What price national glory? To look its best, China launched an ambitious program to clean up its notoriously polluted environment, having promised to host a "green" Olympics. Measures included massive tree plantings, hybrid taxis and buses, relocation of factories, installation of solar energy panels, drastic restrictions on the use of private motor vehicles, and the temporary suspension of industrial activity. Elizabeth Economy, *The Great Leap Backward?* Foreign Aff., Sept.–Oct. 2007, at 38, 49.
4. The prospect of hosting the Olympic Games has also spurred political reform, as when the Korean public used the run-up to the Seoul Games in 1988 as a vehicle for demonstrations that transformed the authoritarian government into a fledgling democracy. Likewise, plans to host major competition may influence foreign policy. For example, China's tolerance of Sudan's atrocities against its own minority people in the Darfur region, underpinned by its stake in that country's oil reserves, quickly changed to support for UN peacekeeping in Darfur in response to a campaign against the so-called genocide Olympics in the run-up to the Beijing Games in 2008.
5. In 2007 the national team from war-ravaged Iraq, coached by a Brazilian, won the Asian Cup, 1–0. A Sunni Muslim scored the winning goal on a pass from a Kurd. The Iraqi goalkeeper was a Shiite Muslim. Does the continuation of interethnic bloodshed in that country after the unprecedented national victory confirm the inability of sports competition to foster societal integration, or, to the contrary, does it inspire hope that sport can play a role in gradually easing interethnic and other societal tensions?

B. Legal Framework

"Look, I'm not saying it's going to be today. But someday—someday—you guys will be happy that you've taken along a lawyer."

1. An Overview

Sport is unique in creating physical competition and conflict that are strictly controlled by rules, procedures, and sanctions (rules of the game) administered by designated referees who are charged with the responsibility of applying the rules of the game consistently. Also, sports competition, unlike ritual warfare, relies on institutionalized control systems that enlist cooperation, association, and collaboration among athletes.

A secondary rule system (rules of law) governs broader questions involving sport and its participants. These rules may address a vast array of issues – for example, the eligibility and participation of athletes, liability for accidental and intentional injury to them on the playing field, spectator violence, player contracting, collective bargaining rights of professional athletes, antitrust implications of sports organization, testing and sanctioning of athletes for using performance-enhancing agents, and taxation of typically mobile athletes. Moreover, the secondary rules may regulate the display of commercial logos on uniforms and impose sanctions for their misuse. These legal rules also address the problem of competing claims by rival sports clubs and associations vying to govern particular sports, and they provide complex processes for resolving sports-related disputes.

Historically, laws covering general topics have supplied the secondary rules of law for sports. For example, legal issues involving player injuries have been addressed not by rules specific to sport but by general tort law or the codified law of obligations in the civil code tradition. Similarly, procedures for drug testing of athletes are subject to general provisions of constitutional law. The secondary rule system traditionally was more one of law and sports than of an integrated sports law.

What has reconfigured the legal process in sports is the rapid growth of a distinctive regime of sports law, particularly on the international level. In this chapter, we examine the most significant legal issues that have arisen within national and regional (European) legal systems, as well as the broader process of international sports law. A focus of the concluding material in this chapter is the Court of Arbitration for Sport (CAS) and the growth of a CAS-based *lex sportiva.*

Until the 1990s, the principal focus within this process was on political issues, such as boycotts of the Olympic Games or competition involving athletes from apartheid South Africa, and on issues of eligibility based on a player's financial relationship with sport, given what used to be a sharp distinction between professionals and amateurs. Today, however, the focus of international sports law has shifted toward the organization and judging of competitions, use of performance-enhancing agents by athletes (doping), violence in sports, and commercialization of the sports arena and athletes.

The nongovernmental foundation of international sports law is unusual. It is noteworthy that the constituent organizations of the modern Olympic Movement, as it is formally called – the International Olympic Committee (IOC) and international sports federations (IFs) for each sport – are nongovernmental organizations, each with international legal personality whose normative instruments, such as the Olympic Charter, have binding force. The development of this process is striking insofar as the constituent organizations were intended to be not only strictly nongovernmental but also limited to the staging of specific events exclusively for the class of supposedly aspiring and elite athletes known as amateurs. As the events became the peak of aspiration for young athletes and as open competition blurred the distinction between professional and amateur athletes, however, the process of international sports law rooted in the Olympic Movement began to influence professional athletes and purely domestic competition.

National legal systems, for example, that of the United States, have strengthened this process. Courts have normally refused to review decisions of nongovernmental sports bodies such as the IOC and the IFs. Moreover, they have characterized the Olympic Charter as a binding international agreement. The Olympic and Amateur Sports Act, 36 U.S.C. § 220501 (2000), as revised in 1998, designates the U.S. Olympic Committee and constituent national bodies for each sport as the bodies to govern Olympic, Pan American, and Paralympic competition in the United States; participation of U.S. athletes in international competition; and the resolution of related disputes. The Act applies to all participants in designated competition regardless of their earnings from sport, thereby extending the process of international sports law beyond specific competitions to regulate athletes and athletic activity, at least minimally, in all sports that are fully recognized by the IOC. Even sports that the IOC has not formally recognized, such as golf and North American–style football, are influenced by secondary rules of sports such as uniform testing requirements, procedures, and sanctions related to athletes' use of performance-enhancing agents, otherwise known as doping.

The resolution of sports-related disputes is complex, involving administrative facilities within sports associations and IFs, national and international arbitration, and courts of law. The Court of Arbitration for Sport (CAS), headquartered in Lausanne, Switzerland, is a particularly effective tribunal of both first instance and last resort. Its jurisdiction extends, for example, to competing claims for accreditation of sports bodies, Olympic judging controversies, commercial and intellectual property right disputes, and appeals from antidoping sanctions.

As numerous cases that follow in this chapter indicate, the use of performance-enhancing drugs by athletes (and horses in equestrian events) has been a particularly troublesome issue. In general, the term "doping" is used internationally to describe prohibited uses of performance-enhancing drugs as well as methods such as blood packing to increase oxygen levels in the bloodstream. Until recently, efforts to provide a level playing field of competition by sanctioning and excluding abusers suffered from a lack of uniformity among national regulatory systems and in different sports. Now, however, the World Anti-Doping Authority (WADA), assisted by constituent national organizations, has established uniform rules, sanctions, and testing procedures in the form of the World Anti-Doping Code. The WADA Code is distinctive in combining both nongovernmental and governmental parties to it. In 2005, UNESCO adopted the International Convention against Doping in Sport that is now in force. We return to this topic later in this chapter.

Regional law, particularly within the European Union, has played an increasingly important role in shaping sports activity at both international and domestic levels. In *Union Royale Belge des Sociétés de Football Ass'n v. Bosman*, Case C-415/93, [1990 ECR I-4921], for instance, the European Court of Justice instituted new rules for free agency of football (soccer) players and imposed restrictions on national formulas for the constitution of football (soccer) teams. Regional sports organizations have also been influential in the international sports arena, for example, the Supreme Council for Sports in Africa, whose imposition of boycotts directed against teams from South Africa helped precipitate the end of apartheid in that sports-minded country.

2. National Litigation

The following case reveals the special but limited legal status of sports bodies and IFs in national litigation. As we shall see, the IFs, though nongovernmental, enjoy a substantial autonomy within the process of international sports law but must share their authority with national legal systems. The case also exemplifies the futility of relying on litigation to resolve issues that transcend national competence. Here the issue is one of a professional athlete's right to compete. The complex issues of jurisdiction in the case provoke broader insights into federal court jurisdiction in the United States.

a. Doping

Reynolds v. International Amateur Athletic Federation, 23 F.3d 1110 (1994)

Harry "Butch" Reynolds is a world-class sprinter who regularly participates in international track and field meets. Reynolds currently holds the individual world record in the 400 meters, is a member of the world record holding 4 × 400 relay team, and is a gold and silver medalist from the 1988 Olympics.

On August 12, 1990, Reynolds ran in the "Hercules '90" meet in Monte Carlo, Monaco. Immediately after the competition, Reynolds was tested for illegal performance-enhancing drugs as part of a random drug test conducted after all international track meets. Two different samples of Reynolds'[s] urine were sent to Paris for analysis. Each sample contained trace amounts of the steroid Nandrolone, a drug banned by international track regulations created by the [International Amateur Athletic Federation (IAAF)].

The IAAF is an unincorporated association based in London, England, and is made up of track and field organizations representing 205 nations and territories. Its purpose is to coordinate and control track and field athletes and competitions throughout the world. The IAAF has no offices in the United States, and holds no track meets in Ohio, where Reynolds brought this action. One member of the IAAF is the Athletics Congress of the United States, Inc. (TAC), the United States national governing body for track and field.

After Reynolds'[s] positive drug test, the IAAF banned him from all international track events for two years, thereby eliminating his hopes for competing in the 1992 Olympics in Barcelona. The IAAF issued a press release on November 5, 1990, stating that Reynolds was tested following the Monte Carlo meet and that "[t]he Paris laboratory revealed metabolites of the banned substance Nandrolone and a second analysis carried out on the 12th October 1990 confirmed their presence." The release went on to say that Reynolds had been suspended and offered a hearing by TAC, the date of which had not been set. American sports publications and newspapers picked up the release and reported Reynolds'[s] suspension as news items.

B.

Reynolds immediately brought suit in the Southern District of Ohio, arguing that the drug test was given negligently, and provided an erroneous result. The court dismissed one claim and stayed the remainder of the case after finding that Reynolds failed to exhaust administrative remedies provided by the Amateur Sports Act, 36 U.S.C. §§ 371–396 (1988) and TAC. Reynolds appealed the district court's decision. This court agreed with the exhaustion requirement but vacated the judgment and directed that the entire case be dismissed for lack of subject matter jurisdiction. *Reynolds v. TAC*, 935 F.2d 270 (6th Cir. 1991) (Table).

In an attempt to exhaust his administrative remedies, Reynolds participated in an independent arbitration before an [American Arbitration Association (AAA)] panel in June of 1991. Reynolds took this action under the Amateur Sports Act and the United States Olympic Committee Constitution. The AAA arbitrator rendered a decision fully exonerating Reynolds; the arbitrator found strong evidence that the urine samples provided to the Paris laboratory were not Reynolds'[s]. However, the IAAF refused to acknowledge the arbitrator's decision because the arbitration was not conducted under IAAF rules. Accordingly, the IAAF refused to lift Reynolds'[s] two-year suspension.

Reynolds then appealed his suspension to TAC, as required by IAAF rules. TAC held a hearing on September 13, 1991. After thoroughly examining the evidence and deliberating for two weeks, the TAC Doping Control Review Board completely exonerated Reynolds, stating that after hearing the matters before it, the testimony of witnesses and expert witnesses of both sides, documents and exhibits, "[we] find that Mr. Harry "Butch" Reynolds has cast substantial doubt on the validity of the drug test attributed to him."

Still not satisfied, the IAAF reopened Reynolds'[s] case pursuant to IAAF Rule 20(3)(ii), which allows the IAAF to conduct an independent arbitration where it appears that one of its member foundations such as TAC has "misdirected itself." The IAAF arbitration was held on May 10 and 11, 1992, in London, England (the London Arbitration). The parties to the arbitration proceeding were the IAAF and TAC. Reynolds attended and testified at the hearing, and Reynolds'[s] attorneys participated in the proceedings before the IAAF arbitration board, including examining and cross-examining witnesses. At the conclusion of the hearing, the IAAF arbitral panel found that the drug tests were valid, and that there was "no doubt" as to Reynolds'[s] guilt. As a result, the panel upheld Reynolds'[s] two-year suspension.

II.

A.

Soon after the IAAF made its final decision, Reynolds filed the present action in the Southern District of Ohio alleging four different state law causes of action: breach of contract, breach of contractual due process, defamation, and tortious interference with business relations. Reynolds sought monetary damages, and a temporary restraining order that would allow him to compete in races leading to the U.S. Olympic trials on June 20, 1992. The IAAF refused to appear in the case, stating in a letter to Reynolds'[s] attorney that the district court had no jurisdiction over the IAAF. The district court issued a temporary restraining order that prevented the IAAF from interfering with Reynolds'[s] attempt to make the Olympic tryouts. Despite IAAF threats to both Reynolds and TAC, Reynolds ran in a few races and qualified to compete in the U.S. Olympic trials in New Orleans.

On June 17, 1992, the district court held a preliminary injunction hearing to decide if Reynolds should compete in the June 20 Olympic trials. The IAAF refused to appear, but TAC intervened to oppose Reynolds. On June 19, the district court issued a preliminary injunction after finding that it had personal jurisdiction over the IAAF and that Reynolds was likely to succeed on the merits of his claims. That afternoon, TAC filed a motion with the Sixth Circuit Court of Appeals, asking for an emergency stay of the district court's decision. At 7:00 that evening, Judge Siler granted the stay. *Reynolds v. IAAF*, 968 F.2d 1216 (6th Cir. 1992) (Table). The next morning, Reynolds filed an emergency motion with Supreme Court Justice John Paul Stevens, asking for an order vacating Judge Siler's emergency stay. Justice Stevens granted Reynolds'[s] request, finding that the District Court's opinion was "persuasive." *Reynolds v. IAAF*, 505 U.S. 1301, 112 S. Ct. 2512, 120 L. Ed. 2d 861 (1992).

Despite these rulings, the IAAF announced that every athlete who competed with Reynolds at the U.S. Olympic trials would be ineligible to compete in the Barcelona Olympics. Reynolds'[s] events were temporarily postponed while TAC filed an application to the full Supreme Court to vacate Justice Stevens'[s] stay. The Court denied TAC's request, and

Reynolds was eventually allowed to compete in the Olympic trials, after an agreement was reached between the U.S. Olympic Committee and the IAAF. Reynolds made the Olympic team as an alternate for the 400[-] meter relay. However, the IAAF refused to let Reynolds compete at the 1992 Olympics, and TAC removed him from the U.S. Olympic team roster. Moreover, the IAAF increased Reynolds'[s] two-year suspension by four months as punishment for participating in the U.S. Olympic trials.

B.

On September 28, 1992, Reynolds filed a supplemental complaint with the district court, outlining the above events. The IAAF did not respond to Reynolds'[s] complaint and TAC did not appear in the default proceedings. After the IAAF was given full notice, the court entered a default judgment in Reynolds'[s] favor. Soon afterward, the district court held a hearing to determine damages. Again, the IAAF was provided notice but refused to appear. On December 3, 1992, the district court issued an opinion awarding Reynolds $27,356,008, including treble punitive damages. The district court found that the IAAF "acted with ill will and a spirit of revenge towards Mr. Reynolds." Particular acts by the IAAF cited by the district court included "the suppression of evidence, threats levied against Reynolds and his fellow athletes, and the extension of Reynolds'[s] suspension for an additional four months." More than $20,000,000 of the award was punitive damages for these acts.

The district court found that it had diversity jurisdiction in this case because Reynolds is a citizen of Ohio and the IAAF is a foreign association. The IAAF is an unincorporated association, and the district court reasoned that the IAAF is deemed to be a citizen of all states where its members are domiciled. *United Steelworkers of America v. R.H. Bouligny, Inc.*, 382 U.S. 145, 149–53, 86 S. Ct. 272, 274–76, 15 L. Ed. 2d 217 (1965). The court held that diversity jurisdiction was proper because no IAAF members are citizens of Ohio.

The district court also found that it had personal jurisdiction over the IAAF. The court held that the Ohio long-arm statute was satisfied because the IAAF transacted business with Reynolds in Ohio, and the IAAF's public announcement of Reynolds'[s] positive drug test adversely affected Reynolds in Ohio. The court held that the IAAF had the required minimum contacts with Ohio after finding that TAC acted as the IAAF's agent in the United States. *Behagen v. Amateur Basketball Ass'n*, 744 F.2d 731 (10th Cir. 1984), *cert. denied*, 471 U.S. 1010, 105 S. Ct. 1879, 85 L. Ed. 2d 171 (1985) (a question of fact whether American member of international amateur basketball association is the agent of the international association).

C.

On February 17, 1993, Reynolds began garnishment proceedings against four corporations with connections to the IAAF. The IAAF finally appeared at a garnishment hearing before the district court, and later filed a "Motion to Quash Garnishment Proceedings and To Vacate the Default Judgment" pursuant to Fed. R. Civ. P. 60(b)(4). In its motion, the IAAF contended that the court lacked personal and subject matter jurisdiction. Before the motion was decided, the IAAF filed a recusal motion, arguing that previous opinions by the court put the district judge's impartiality into question.

The district court denied all motions on July 13, 1993. The court found that it had jurisdiction to overturn the IAAF's arbitration decision despite the United States' participation in the United Nations Convention on the Recognition and Enforcement of Foreign Arbitral Awards (the Convention). *See* 9 U.S.C. § 201, *et seq.* The text of the Convention appears following 9 U.S.C.A. § 201 (West 1993). The Convention provides that recognition and enforcement of an award may be refused if it "has been set aside or suspended by a competent authority of the country in which, or under the law of which, that award was made." Convention, Article v. 1(e). The district court found that the Convention only applies where an agreement to arbitrate is in writing and signed by both parties – preconditions not present in the instant case.

The IAAF appeals from denial of its motions. Because it contends that the district court lacked jurisdiction in the earlier proceedings, the IAAF seeks to reverse the money judgment and injunction as well.

III.

Because we have concluded that the district court lacked personal jurisdiction over the IAAF, the sole defendant in this case, it is not necessary to consider the other issues presented and argued by the parties.

A.

The district court found that it had personal jurisdiction over the IAAF under Ohio's long-arm statute. Under this statute a nonresident may be sued in an Ohio court on a cause of action arising from the nonresident's:

> (1) Transacting any business in this state;
> * * *
> (3) Causing tortious injury by an act or omission in this state;
> (4) Causing tortious injury in this state by an act or omission outside this state if he regularly does or solicits business, or engages in any other persistent course of conduct . . . in this state;
> * * *
> (6) Causing tortious injury in this state to any person by an act outside this state committed with the purpose of injuring persons, when he might reasonably have expected that some person would be injured thereby in this state. . . .

Ohio Revised Code (O.R.C.) § 2307.382. The district court found the IAAF amenable to suit under subsection (1) on Reynolds'[s] contract claims and under subsections (3) and (6) on his claims of defamation and tortious interference with business relations.

Without elaboration, the district court held that a contract existed between Reynolds and the IAAF, which the IAAF breached. This was the basis for personal jurisdiction under subsection (1), "transacting business" in Ohio. The court referred to correspondence between the IAAF's counsel and Reynolds'[s] counsel and the appearance of a professor Donike who testified at the Doping Control Review Board hearing in Ohio that the tests upon which the suspension was based were valid. The district court also found that TAC was the IAAF's agent and that officers of TAC had repeatedly transacted business in Ohio.

With respect to the tort claims, the district court held that although the IAAF had issued the press release in Europe, it should reasonably have expected it to be disseminated in Ohio and should have anticipated that it would injure Reynolds in the state of his residence. Thus, according to the court, the IAAF should reasonably have expected to be "haled into court" in Ohio.

The district court recognized that, regardless of other considerations, a court's exercise of jurisdiction over a nonresident must satisfy due process. The district court found that the IAAF had "minimum contacts" with Ohio both through its own acts and those of its "agent" TAC. Referring to rules developed by this court in dealing with the due process issue in cases against nonresident defendants, the court held that the IAAF "purposefully directed" defamatory statements to Reynolds, knowing that he was a resident of Ohio and would suffer injury there. The court further held that Reynolds'[s] cause of action arose in Ohio, reasoning that the breach of contract and financial consequences to Reynolds (loss of endorsements and appearance payments) were brought about solely by the IAAF's "transaction of business with Plaintiff in Ohio." Thus, according to the court, the IAAF "purposefully availed" itself of Ohio privileges by subjecting Ohio athletes to its rules and by gaining substantial financial rewards from the performances of these athletes.

The district court also held that the IAAF failed to make a timely objection to personal jurisdiction, thereby waiving the defense. Under F.R.C.P. 12(h), a party waives the right to contest personal jurisdiction by failing to raise the issue when making a responsive pleading or a general appearance.

B.

When determining whether there is personal jurisdiction over a defendant, a federal court must apply the law of the state in which it sits, subject to constitutional limitations. *Welsh v. Gibbs*, 631 F.2d 436, 439 (6th Cir. 1980). A court, therefore, must satisfy a two-pronged test: the defendant must be amenable to suit under the forum state's long-arm statute and the due process requirements of the Constitution must be met. *In-Flight Devices Corp. v. Van Dusen Air, Inc.*, 466 F.2d 220, 224 (6th Cir. 1972). As stated, the district court found that the IAAF was amenable to suit in Ohio under both the "transacting business" and "tortious injury" clauses of the Ohio long-arm statute.

1. *Transacting Business*

The question of whether the IAAF submitted to personal jurisdiction through its alleged Ohio business transactions requires us to examine those transactions in light of due process principles because "it is a settled proposition of Ohio law that . . . the [transacting business clause] was intended to extend to the constitutional limits of due process. . . . " *Creech v. Roberts*, 908 F.2d 75, 79 (6th Cir. 1990).

Under the Constitution, personal jurisdiction over a defendant arises from "certain minimum contacts with [the forum] such that maintenance of the suit does not offend 'traditional notions of fair play and substantial justice.'" *International Shoe Co. v. Washington*, 326 U.S. 310, 316, 66 S. Ct. 154, 158, 90 L. Ed. 95 (1945) (citations omitted). Depending on the type of minimum contacts in a case, personal jurisdiction can be either general or specific. *Third Nat'l Bank v. Wedge Group Incorporated*, 882 F.2d 1087, 1089 (6th Cir. 1989). Reynolds relies on specific jurisdiction because he claims that jurisdiction arose out of the IAAF's alleged wrongful acts in Ohio. *Id.* at 1089.

The Sixth Circuit has established a three-part test for determining whether specific jurisdiction may be exercised:

> First, the defendant must purposefully avail himself of the privilege of acting in the forum state or causing a consequence in the forum state. Second, the cause of action must arise from the defendant's activities there. Finally, the acts of the defendant or consequences caused by the defendant must have a substantial enough connection with the forum to make the exercise of jurisdiction over the defendant reasonable.

In-Flight Devices, 466 F.2d at 226; *LAK, Inc. v. Deer Creek Enterprises*, 885 F.2d 1293, 1299 (6th Cir. 1989), *cert. denied*, 494 U.S. 1056, 110 S. Ct. 1525, 108 L. Ed. 2d 764 (1990).

(a)

Jurisdiction is proper under the purposeful availment requirement where "the contacts proximately result from actions by the defendant *himself* that create a 'substantial connection' with the forum State." *Burger King Co. v. Rudzewicz*, 471 U.S. 462, 475, 105 S. Ct. 2174, 2184, 85 L. Ed. 2d 528 (1985). Additionally, the defendant's conduct and connection with the forum must be of a character that he or she "should reasonably anticipate being haled into court there." *Id.* at 474, 105 S. Ct. at 2183 (quoting *World-Wide Volkswagen Corp. v. Woodson*, 444 U.S. 286, 297, 100 S. Ct. 559, 567, 62 L. Ed. 2d 490 (1980)). The district court found that the IAAF had created a "substantial connection" with Ohio through its "contract" with Reynolds and because of letters, calls and other incidental contacts made by the IAAF in Ohio.

The calls and letters from the IAAF consisted of a response to Reynolds'[s] request for information and a letter sent to Reynolds stating that the IAAF did not accept the district court's jurisdiction. Also,

Ollan Cassell, a TAC official who is a Vice-President of the IAAF, traveled to Ohio and repeatedly communicated with Reynolds regarding his suspension; and Professor Manfred Donike, a member of the IAAF Medical and Doping Commission, also appeared at a TAC Doping Control Review Board hearing against Reynolds in Ohio. Finally, Mark Gay, the IAAF's counsel, contacted Reynolds with regard to an IAAF hearing in May 1992. All of these contacts occurred after the issuance of the alleged defamatory statement and imposition of the suspension.

The district court gave no details of the "contract" between Reynolds and the IAAF other than the fact that all athletes who compete in international events are subject to IAAF rules, and the IAAF advances travel and expense money to those athletes. The record contains no evidence of any such advances to Reynolds, however.

(b)

Even if the IAAF purposefully availed itself of Ohio privileges, the claims against the IAAF must arise out of the IAAF's activities in Ohio. The controversial urine sample was taken in Monaco, analyzed in France, and confirmed by an arbitration hearing in England. The district court found that the IAAF breached Reynolds'[s] contract in Ohio, without conducting the analysis of this contractual relationship as required by *Burger King*.

(c)

Finally, the exercise of personal jurisdiction must comport with "traditional notions of fair play and substantial justice." *Asahi Metal Industry Co. v. Superior Court*, 480 U.S. 102, 113, 107 S. Ct. 1026, 1033, 94 L. Ed. 2d 92 (1987). In exceptional circumstances, this consideration may serve to establish the reasonableness of jurisdiction with a lesser showing of minimum contacts. *Burger King*, 471 U.S. at 477, 105 S. Ct. at 2184. A court should consider

> the burden on the defendant, the interests of the forum State, and the plaintiff's interest in obtaining relief. It must also weigh in its determination 'the interstate judicial system's interest in obtaining the most efficient resolution of controversies; and the shared interest of the several states in furthering fundamental substantive social policies.'

Asahi Metal, 480 U.S. at 113, 107 S. Ct. at 1033 (citing *World-Wide Volkswagen*, 444 U.S. at 292, 100 S. Ct. at 564).

The IAAF contends that holding it amenable to suit in an Ohio court would offend principles of international comity and put international cooperation at risk. Under this theory, the IAAF should not be required to bear the expense of litigating cases around the world when its only contact with a forum is an athlete's residence. Instead, the IAAF argues that only the courts of England, where it is located, have jurisdiction to review its arbitral proceedings. Reynolds counters that his interest in a convenient forum substantially outweighs the inconvenience to the IAAF. Over half of the IAAF's four-year $174.5 million budget is received from United States corporations, one of the IAAF's officers resides in the U.S., and its other officers regularly visit the U.S.

2. *Tortious Injury*

Reynolds claimed that the false IAAF drug report was both [sic] defamatory and interfered with his contractual relationships. He contends that he lost three Ohio corporate endorsement contracts worth over $2,500,000, and appearance fees in Ohio worth over $1,500,000. For the IAAF to be amenable to suit in Ohio, the IAAF's tortious acts must satisfy both the Ohio long-arm statute and the three constitutional requirements discussed above.

The district court found the Ohio long-arm statute satisfied by the IAAF's tortious acts in Europe. Reynolds claims to have lost over $4,000,000 in Ohio because of the IAAF's allegedly false press release. Also, the district court specifically found that the injury to Reynolds was in Ohio, finding that "[t]he IAAF intentionally and purposefully directed their tortious acts toward Plaintiff, and such acts had a devastating effect upon Plaintiff."

The district court also held that the alleged defamatory statement that the IAAF made in England created minimum contacts in Ohio. Reynolds argues that his claims arose out of the IAAF's contacts with Ohio because the IAAF intentionally defamed him and interfered with his Ohio business relationships. Under this theory, the IAAF knew that the worldwide media would carry the report and that the brunt of the injury would occur in Ohio. *See Hugel v. McNell*, 886 F.2d 1, 5 (1st Cir. 1989), *cert. denied*, 494 U.S. 1079, 110 S. Ct. 1808, 108 L. Ed. 2d 939 (1990) (information given to *Washington Post* with intent to disseminate nationwide creates personal jurisdiction in New Hampshire, where the plaintiff lived and had an established reputation).

IV.

This court reviews issues of personal jurisdiction de novo. *Conti v. Pneumatic Products Corp.*, 977 F.2d 978, 985 (6th Cir. 1992). Nevertheless, this appeal is from denial of the IAAF's Rule 60(b) motion to set aside a default judgment. We review the denial of that motion under the abuse of discretion standard. *Amernational Industries, Inc. v. Action-Tungsram, Inc.*, 925 F.2d 970, 973 (6th Cir.), *cert. denied*, 501 U.S. 1233, 111 S. Ct. 2857, 115 L. Ed. 2d 1024 (1991).

A.

The district court held that TAC was the agent of the IAAF and that TAC had sufficient minimum contacts with Ohio to bring the IAAF under the "transacting business" provisions of the Ohio long-arm statute. The IAAF insists that TAC, though a member of the IAAF, is an autonomous body that acts for itself within the United States. The record is to the contrary. TAC represents the IAAF in dealings with American athletes who participate in international events. Its bylaws state that "[t]he purposes of this Congress are to act as the national governing body for athletes in the United States, and to act as the IAAF member in the United States." TAC's president, Frank Greenberg, testified that TAC is "the exclusive representative of [the IAAF] in this country," and that "part of that obligation, part of being the named representative is that [TAC] must follow [IAAF] rules."

Furthermore, the facts in this case demonstrate the IAAF's control over TAC. After receiving the results of the two urine tests and after suspending Reynolds, the IAAF did not notify Reynolds. Instead it told TAC to notify Reynolds and look into the matter, even though the meet involved was sponsored by the IAAF. Reynolds requested documents directly from the IAAF, but the IAAF told Reynolds that all document requests must be made through TAC. As a result, all IAAF documents that Reynolds received came through TAC. Moreover, after the Supreme Court held that Reynolds could compete in the U.S. Olympic Trials, the IAAF told TAC to "take all necessary steps to ensure that Mr. Reynolds does not so compete." While it is true that TAC supported Reynolds at the London Arbitration, it was not there on his behalf, but as a member of the IAAF that was responding under the IAAF's rules. Thus, we agree with the district court that TAC is an agent of the IAAF.

Nevertheless, unless TAC had minimum contacts with Ohio in relation to the "contract" between the IAAF and Reynolds, the court erred in premising jurisdiction of TAC's agency.

B.

The Supreme Court has spoken with respect to the significance of a contractual relationship between an in-state plaintiff and an out-of-state defendant. The Court has held that a contract with an out-of-state party, standing alone, is not sufficient to establish minimum contacts. *Burger King*, 471 U.S. at 478, 105 S. Ct. at 2185. Instead, to determine whether a party purposefully availed itself of a forum a court must evaluate "prior negotiations and contemplated future consequences, along with the terms of the contract and the parties' actual course of dealing. . . . " *Id.* at 479, 105 S. Ct. at 2185. In the instant case, there were no negotiations between Reynolds and the IAAF prior to "execution" of the contract. The IAAF arguably had a minimal course of dealing with Reynolds in Ohio, providing money to Reynolds in Ohio to travel to track events. However, there is no real evidence that a contract was negotiated in Ohio, created in Ohio, performed in Ohio, or breached in Ohio. *See Lak, Inc. v. Deer Creek Enterprises*, 885 F.2d 1293, 1300 (6th Cir.1989) (place where contractual obligation is incurred is important factor for determining personal jurisdiction), *cert. denied*, 494 U.S. 1056, 110 S. Ct. 1525, 108 L. Ed. 2d 764 (1990).

Without further evidence concerning the purported contract, we are unable to agree that the district court had personal jurisdiction over the IAAF on the contract claims, either based on its own activities or those of TAC.

Moreover, the IAAF could not reasonably anticipate being sued in Ohio because of its alleged business dealings with Reynolds. It did not regularly transact or solicit business in Ohio or engage "in any other persistent course of conduct" there. O.R.C. § 2307.382(A)(4). The IAAF cannot foresee being required to defend in every forum where one of its athletes is present. Reynolds'[s] Ohio residence is merely fortuitous and "unilateral activity of [the plaintiff] is not an appropriate consideration when determining whether a defendant has sufficient contacts with a forum State to justify an assertion of jurisdiction." *Helicopteros Nacionales de Colombia, S.A. v. Hall*, 466 U.S. 408, 417, 104 S. Ct. 1868, 1873, 80 L. Ed. 2d 404 (1984). Instead, minimum contacts can only be formed by "an action of the defendant purposefully directed toward the forum State." *Asahi Metal Industry*, 480 U.S. at 112, 107 S. Ct. at 1032.

The IAAF's contact with Ohio through letters and phone calls was also insufficient to support jurisdiction. Reynolds asked the IAAF for information, but such unilateral action by a plaintiff does not render the defendant amenable to suit in the plaintiff's home forum. *Lak*, 885 F.2d at 1301; *American Greetings Corp. v. Cohn*, 839 F.2d 1164, 1169 (6th Cir. 1988). Moreover, "[t]he use of interstate facilities such as the telephone and mail is a 'secondary or ancillary' factor and 'cannot alone provide the minimum contacts required by due process.'" *Id.* (quoting *Scullin Steel Co. v. National Railway Utilization Corp.*, 676 F.2d 309, 314 (8th Cir. 1982)) (interior quotation marks omitted). Although various IAAF officials sent correspondence or made telephone calls to Ohio, these communications are insufficient to establish purposeful availment. *See, e.g.*, *Market/Media Research v. Union Tribune Pub.*, 951 F.2d 102, 105 (6th Cir. 1991), *cert. denied*, 506 U.S. 824, 113 S. Ct. 70, 121 L. Ed. 2d 43 (1992) (telephone calls and mail sent to Ohio insufficient for personal jurisdiction); *Capital Dredge & Dock Corp. v. Midwest Dredging Co.*, 573 F.2d 377, 380 (6th Cir. 1978) (same). It is the "quality" of such contacts, "not their number or their status as pre- or post-agreement communications" that determines whether they constitute purposeful availment. *Lak*, 885 F.2d at 1301 (quoting *Stuart v. Spademan*, 772 F.2d 1185, 1194 (5th Cir. 1985)). That quality is missing here.

In short, the IAAF is based in England, owns no property and transacts no business in Ohio, and does not supervise U.S. athletes in Ohio or elsewhere. Its contacts with Reynolds in Ohio are superficial, and are insufficient to create the requisite minimum contacts for personal jurisdiction.

Even if the IAAF purposefully availed itself of Ohio privileges, the claims against the IAAF must arise out of the IAAF's activities in Ohio. In general, "[a]n action will be deemed not to have arisen from the defendant's contacts with the forum state only when they are unrelated to the operative facts of the controversy." *Creech v. Roberts*, 908 F.2d 75, 80 (6th Cir. 1990). The controversial urine sample was taken in Monaco, analyzed in France, and confirmed by an arbitration hearing in England. The district court found that the IAAF breached Reynolds'[s] contract in Ohio, but there is no evidence of a contract made, performed, or breached in Ohio. Accordingly, Reynolds'[s] contract claim did not arise out of the IAAF's contacts with Ohio. All of the activities relied upon by the district court as taking place in Ohio occurred after the activities in Europe upon which Reynolds bases his contract claims. These activities do not constitute a basis for finding personal jurisdiction under subsection (1) for "transacting business" in Ohio.

V.

The district court found that the IAAF was subject to personal jurisdiction under the provision of the Ohio long-arm statute which provides that a party is amenable to suit by "causing tortious injury in this state . . . by an act outside this state." O.R.C. § 2307.382(A)(6). A tort action can be brought in the location where the injury is suffered. *Lachman v. Bank of Louisiana*, 510 F. Supp. 753 (N.D. Ohio 1981). Reynolds claimed a loss of more than $4,000,000 in Ohio because of the IAAF's false press release and the district court specifically found that the injury to Reynolds was in Ohio, holding "[t]he IAAF intentionally and purposefully directed their tortious acts toward Plaintiff, and such acts had a devastating effect upon Plaintiff." More needs to be demonstrated, however. The question remains whether the IAAF, in making the alleged defamatory statement in England, had minimum contacts with Ohio.

The leading case on this issue is *Calder v. Jones*, 465 U.S. 783, 104 S. Ct. 1482, 79 L. Ed. 2d 804 (1984). In *Calder*, a professional entertainer sued the writers and editors of a Florida magazine for libel in a California court. In concluding that the California court had personal jurisdiction, the Supreme Court reasoned that

> [t]he allegedly libelous story concerned the California activities of a California resident. It impugned the professionalism of an entertainer whose television career was centered in California. The article was drawn from California sources, and the brunt of the harm . . . was suffered in California. In sum, California is the focal point both of the story and the harm suffered.

Id. at 788–89, 104 S. Ct. at 1486. Because the defendants' intentional actions were aimed at California and the brunt of the harm was felt there, the Court concluded that the defendants could reasonably anticipate being haled into court in California. *Id.* at 789, 104 S. Ct. at 1487.

We find *Calder* distinguishable for several reasons. First, the press release concerned Reynolds'[s] activities in Monaco, not Ohio. Second, the source of the controversial report was the drug sample taken in Monaco and the laboratory testing in France. Third, Reynolds is an international athlete whose professional reputation is not centered in Ohio. Fourth, the defendant itself did not publish or circulate the report in Ohio; Ohio periodicals disseminated the report. Fifth, Ohio was not the "focal point" of the press release. The fact that the IAAF could foresee that the report would be circulated and have an effect in Ohio is not, in itself, enough to create personal jurisdiction. *World-Wide Volkswagen Corp.*, 444 U.S. at 295, 100 S. Ct. at 566. Finally, although Reynolds lost Ohio corporate endorsement contracts and appearance fees in Ohio, there is no evidence that the IAAF knew of the contracts or of their Ohio origin. *Calder* is a much more compelling case for finding personal jurisdiction.

Reynolds argues, however, that his claims arose out of the IAAF's connection with Ohio because the IAAF intentionally defamed him and interfered with his Ohio business relationships. Under this theory, the IAAF knew that the worldwide media would carry the report and that the brunt of the injury would occur in Ohio.

Even accepting that the IAAF could foresee that its report would be disseminated in Ohio, however, the IAAF would not be subject to personal jurisdiction in Ohio. *Madara v. Hall*, 916 F.2d 1510, 1519 (11th Cir. 1990) (defendant's knowledge that independent publisher might publish defamatory statements in California does not create personal jurisdiction). The press release that the IAAF issued in London did not directly accuse Reynolds of using forbidden substances. It recited the fact that the Paris laboratory had reported a positive drug test and that Reynolds had been suspended and offered a hearing. We cannot hold that this act of the IAAF satisfied the requirements of the Ohio statute, or that permitting the IAAF to be sued in Ohio for the press release would comport with due process.

VI.

Relying on F.R.C.P. § 12(h)(1) (waiver of defenses), the district court found that the IAAF waived its right to contest personal jurisdiction. See *Insurance Corp. of Ireland, Ltd. v. Compagnie des Bauxites de Guinee*, 456 U.S. 694, 703, 102 S. Ct. 2099, 2105, 72 L. Ed. 2d 492 (1982) (failure of timely objection to personal jurisdiction can result in waiver of objection). We do not agree. Under F.R.C.P. 12(h), a party waives the right to contest personal jurisdiction by failing to raise the issue when making a responsive pleading or a general appearance. *See, e.g., In Re Wolverine Radio Co.*, 930 F.2d 1132, 1137 n.5 (6th Cir. 1991). However, courts have generally held that "[d]efects in personal jurisdiction . . . are not waived by default when a party fails to appear or to respond." *Williams v. Life Saving and Loan*, 802 F.2d 1200, 1202 (10th Cir. 1986). *See also Hugel v. McNell*, 886 F.2d 1, 3 n.3 (1st Cir. 1989) ("[defendants] made no appearance prior to final judgment and thus never waived the defense of lack of personal jurisdiction"); *Pacific Atlantic Trading Co. v. M/V Main Exp.*, 758 F.2d 1325, 1331 (9th Cir. 1985) (default judgment entered without personal jurisdiction is void). The IAAF did not file a responsive pleading or enter a general appearance. Accordingly, the district court incorrectly decided that the IAAF waived its personal jurisdiction defense by failing to appear until after the default judgment was entered.

The district court also held that the IAAF waived its objection to personal jurisdiction by reason of TAC's intervention in this action. After Reynolds lost in the London arbitration proceeding, he filed a motion for [a] preliminary injunction to let him race in the United States Olympic Trials. The IAAF did not respond and did not appear at the injunction hearing, but TAC intervened as a defendant.

The key to determining whether the IAAF waived its personal jurisdiction defense through TAC's intervention is whether the IAAF authorized TAC to appear in its place. *Federal Deposit Ins. Corp. v. Oaklawn Apts.*, 959 F.2d 170, 175 (10th Cir. 1992). In its request to intervene, TAC argued that it was required to uphold IAAF regulations, and contended that TAC, a member of the IAAF . . . is bound by the decision declaring plaintiff ineligible; and thus under the Amateur Sports Act, TAC may not permit him to participate in the Olympic Trials.

TAC was carrying out its statutory duty under the Amateur Sports Act and was not acting as the IAAF's agent when it intervened. There is no indication that the IAAF authorized or even requested TAC to appear. Indeed, the IAAF had consistently refused to appear and had taken the position that the district court lacked jurisdiction over the entire proceeding. We conclude that TAC appeared solely in its role as the national governing body under the Amateur Sports Act.

CONCLUSION

In conclusion, we do not believe that holding the IAAF amenable to suit in an Ohio court under the facts of this case comports with "traditional notions of fair play and substantial justice." *Asahi Metal Industry*, 480 U.S. at 113, 107 S. Ct. at 1033. The IAAF stated in its brief and at oral argument that it will not challenge the jurisdiction of English courts to determine the validity of the London Arbitration award if Reynolds seeks to have it set aside in the courts of that country. Our decision renders the IAAF's recusal motion moot.

The district court abused its discretion by denying the IAAF's Rule 60(b)(4) motion for relief. The judgment of the district court is reversed. Upon remand the district court will dismiss this action for lack of personal jurisdiction over the IAAF.

As the next case demonstrates, a plaintiff may be confronted with an issue of standing to assert a private claim even when personal jurisdiction over the defendant is not at issue:

Walton-Floyd v. U.S. Olympic Committee,
65 S.W.2d 35 (Tex. App. 1st Dist. 1998)

The [U.S. Olympic Committee (USOC)] coordinates the United States's participation in international amateur athletic competitions. It resolves disputes among athletes and sports organizations or between competing sports organizations, and provides uniformity in the area of amateur athletics, thereby protecting the rights of amateur athletes to compete. The USOC has the power to sue and be sued. 36 U.S.C.A. § 375(a)(1), (5), (6) (West 1988).

The USOC selects the United States's governing bodies for every sport in the Olympics and Pan-American games. 36 U.S.C.A. § 375(a)(4) (West 1988). In track and field, the USOC recognizes The Athletic Congress (TAC) as the national governing body. TAC coordinates and conducts track and field competitions to ensure competitions comply with the rules and regulations of the International Amateur Athletic Federation (IAAF). The IAAF rules provide for punishment or suspension of athletes who use certain performance enhancing drugs. The IAAF publishes a list of the banned substances.

The USOC issued the appellant a card listing many of the more common substances on the banned list. The card warns:

> This list is not complete. It is the athlete's responsibility to check the status of all medications. CALL THE USOC HOTLINE 1-800-233-0393.

The appellant's husband, who was also her trainer, obtained a box of Sydnocarb. He testified the box appeared to be labeled in Russian, he could not read the writing, and he did not have it translated. The box had no instructions and did not list ingredients.

The appellant's husband testified that he called the USOC hotline to inquire about Sydnocarb's status and that the USOC operator told him Sydnocarb was a carbohydrate supplement not on the banned list. He admitted, however, that the hotline operator did not specifically tell him that Sydnocarb was safe to use, nor did she give any other assurances. The appellant called the hotline, with similar results, then began using Sydnocarb. She and her husband testified they called the hotline on subsequent occasions to inquire about the status of Sydnocarb, and that each time, the USOC's operator told them it was not on the banned list.

After the appellant's semi-final heat at the IAAF World Championships, she provided meet officials with a urine sample, which they divided into two samples. The first sample tested positive for amphetamines, a prohibited substance. IAAF officials told her the test results and invited her to attend a testing of the second sample, which also tested positive for amphetamines. The IAAF relayed the results to TAC, which suspended her from further competition. The appellant eventually discovered that Sydnocarb was the apparent source of the amphetamines.

The appellant alleges the following USOC acts and omissions were negligent:

(a) providing her with erroneous and false information through the hotline;
(b) not properly informing and warning her of the possible effect of ingesting Sydnocarb;
(c) not advising her that the use of Sydnocarb would result in the failure of the IAAF drug test;
(d) providing her with information that Sydnocarb was a carbohydrate supplement and not a substance on the banned list;

(e) not informing and educating its hotline personnel concerning Sydnocarb and the risk involved in using it;
(f) not keeping its list of banned substances up to date to include Sydnocarb despite actual knowledge and industry knowledge concerning Sydnocarb and the fact that it represented an amphetamine derivative;
(g) not testing or researching Sydnocarb despite calls from athletes inquiring whether the drug could be used; and
(h) not maintaining a system that would accurately identify the composition of drugs brought to its attention by athletes inquiring through the hotline.

Furthermore, she alleges the USOC negligently breached various duties prescribed by the Amateur Sports Act of 1978 (the Act). 36 U.S.C.A. §§ 371-396, 392(a)(3), (5), (6), (8), (9) (West 1988). She also alleges that the USOC owed her a duty, because the USOC represented itself as an expert in the field of illegal substances, instructed athletes to use its hotline to obtain information on those substances, provided her with inaccurate information, and intentionally or negligently misled her regarding the risk of taking Sydnocarb.

Private Right of Action under the Amateur Sports Act

The appellant maintains the Act provides for an implied private cause of action for monetary damages when the USOC fails to comply with the duties imposed by Congress. She further maintains that Congress would not have included a specific provision allowing the USOC to be sued if it did not intend to create a private cause of action. 36 U.S.C.A. § 375(a)(6) (West 1988). The USOC argues the Act's legislative history, underlying purposes, and caselaw contravene the appellant's interpretation.

The United States Supreme Court prescribes four factors to consider in finding an implied cause of action: (1) whether the plaintiff is a member of a class for whose special benefit the statute was enacted; (2) whether there is an indication of Congressional intent to create or deny a private remedy; (3) whether a private remedy would be consistent with the statute's underlying purposes; and (4) whether the cause of action traditionally is relegated to state law. *Cort v. Ash*, 422 U.S. 66, 79, 95 S. Ct. 2080, 2088, 45 L. Ed. 2d 26 (1975). The factors need not be equal in weight, and the central inquiry remains whether Congress intended to create, either expressly or by implication, a private cause of action. *Touche Ross & Co. v. Redington*, 442 U.S. 560, 576, 99 S. Ct. 2479, 2489, 61 L. Ed. 2d 82 (1979); *accord Merrill Lynch, Pierce, Fenner, & Smith v. Curran*, 456 U.S. 353, 377–78, 102 S. Ct. 1825, 1838–39, 72 L. Ed. 2d 182 (1982); *Transamerica Mortgage Advisors, Inc. v. Lewis*, 444 U.S. 11, 15–16, 100 S. Ct. 242, 245–46, 62 L. Ed. 2d 146 (1979). Once Congressional intent is determined, there is no need to work through all four of the *Cort* factors. *Merrill Lynch*, 456 U.S. at 388, 102 S. Ct. at 1844.

Because no Texas court has considered this issue, we turn to federal cases for guidance. Federal courts have interpreted the Act and its legislative history not to imply private causes of action against the USOC.[1] *Oldfield v. The Athletic Congress*, 779 F.2d 505, 506–08 (9th Cir. 1985); *Michels v. United States Olympic Committee*, 741 F.2d 155, 157–58 (7th Cir. 1984); *DeFrantz v. United States Olympic Committee*, 492 F. Supp. 1181, 1190–92 (D.D.C. 1980); *Martinez v. United States Olympic Committee*, 802 F.2d 1275, 1281 (10th Cir. 1986).

Intervention is appropriate only in the most extraordinary circumstances, where the association has clearly breached its own rules, the breach will imminently result in serious and irreparable harm to the plaintiff, and the plaintiff has exhausted all internal remedies. *Harding*, 851 F. Supp. at 1479. As a general rule, courts should not intervene in the merits of the underlying dispute, but if they do, then they should limit injunctive relief to correcting the breach of the rules. *Id.*

In analyzing the Act's legislative history, the courts have looked to four factors to determine Congress did not intend a private cause of action:

1) The Act strongly favors athletes resolving their disputes through the internal mechanisms provided by the USOC rather than the judicial system.
2) The Act expressly provides causes of actions for certain violations set out within the Act.
3) The USOC's Constitution, which is not part of the Act and was not approved by Congress, establishes the right to a private cause of action against the USOC.
4) The original Act was designed to settle disputes between organizations seeking recognition as national governing bodies for a particular sport and to shield amateur athletes from suffering harm because of internal conflicts. When rechartered in 1978, the Act added internal grievance procedures for athletes.

In *Oldfield*, TAC denied a shot putter's attempt to reestablish amateur status four years after he signed a professional contract. 779 F.2d at 506. Because of his professional status, TAC deemed Oldfield ineligible to compete in the Olympic Trials. *Id.* Oldfield brought suit for an injunction and damages against TAC and the USOC, alleging the two organizations had arbitrarily denied him the right to compete in violation of the Act. *Id.* While the plaintiff conceded no express right existed, he contended that an inferred right allowing a private cause of action existed. *Id.* at 507.

The Ninth Circuit denied Oldfield's motion for injunctive relief, but the court did not enjoin his damages claim. *Id.* at 506. However, the district court granted summary judgment on the damages claim, and the Ninth Circuit affirmed. *Id.* at 508.

[1] Actions against the USOC have proven successful in two scenarios: (1) disputes between organizations and the USOC, *U.S. Wrestling Fed'n v. Wrestling Div. of the AAU, Inc.*, 545 F. Supp. 1053, 1061 (N.D. Ohio 1982); Edward E. Hollis, III, Note, *The United States Olympic Committee and the Suspension of Athletes: Reforming Grievance Procedures Under the Amateur Sports Act of 1978*, 71 Ind. L.J. 183, 188; and (2) breach of contract allegations. *Harding v. U.S. Figure Skating Ass'n*, 851 F. Supp. 1476, 1480 (D. Or. 1994); *Reynolds v. Int'l Amateur Athletic Fed'n*, 841 F. Supp. 1444, 1448 (S.D. Ohio 1992).

The Ninth Circuit noted that the Act, as originally proposed, contained a provision referred to as the "Amateur Athletes' Bill of Rights," which expressly granted athletes the power to contest in federal court the actions of any sports organization that threatened to deny them the opportunity to participate. *See* S. 2036, 94th Cong. § 304(a) (1977); *Oldfield*, 779 F.2d at 507. The final version of the Act excluded the provision allowing athletes to sue in federal court and inserted it in the USOC's Constitution. *Oldfield*, 779 F.2d at 507. The court in *Oldfield* explained that the USOC's Constitution is not part of the Act, and thus, the provision did not allow private individuals to litigate in federal court. *Id.*

In *Michels*, the International Weightlifting Federation (IWF) suspended a weightlifter for two years because drug test results revealed an impermissible testosterone level. 741 F.2d at 156. The plaintiff brought suit against the IWF, the U.S. Weightlifting Federation, and the USOC, contending the USOC violated the Act. The plaintiff claimed the test results were invalid and he had a right to a hearing on the matter. *Id.* Based on the Act's legislative history, the Seventh Circuit held that the Act contained no private right of action to require the USOC to hold a hearing. The court noted that Congress's refusal to insert the bill of rights provision into the final version indicates that it considered and then rejected a cause of action for athletes to enforce the Act's provisions. *Id.* at 158. In concurrence, Judge Richard Posner suggested that in light of the Act's provisions to resolve disputes internally, the USOC is better equipped to handle disputes involving athletes. *Id.* He continued, "There can be few less suitable bodies than the federal courts for determining the eligibility, or the procedures for determining eligibility, of athletes to participate in the Olympic Games." *Id.*

The court in *DeFrantz* considered the case of 25 athletes and one executive member of the USOC who sought an injunction prohibiting the USOC from implementing USOC's House of Delegates' resolution to decline an invitation to 1980 Moscow Summer Olympics. 492 F. Supp. at 1183. The Court held the Act did not confer an enforceable right to an amateur athlete to compete in Olympic competition as the Act confers the broad authority to the USOC to make all decisions regarding competitions and participation. *Id.* at 1188. Furthermore, even if such a right to compete existed, the court noted that the Act does not imply a private cause of action to enforce such a right. *Id.* at 1192. The court noted that the Act sought to protect the opportunity for athletes to compete and prevent rivalries between sports organizations. *Id.* The court looked to 36 U.S.C. § 395 (1988) and found established procedures for the internal consideration and resolution of jurisdictional and eligibility issues. *Id.* The court also cited 36 U.S.C. § 395(c)(1), which grants any aggrieved party the right to review by arbitration after exhaustion of other USOC remedies, as confirming the Act's intent to handle disputes internally. *Id.*

Finally, in *Martinez*, a personal representative of the estate of an amateur boxer, who died from injuries sustained in a boxing tournament, filed a wrongful death action against the USOC and other various organizations responsible for the event. 802 F.2d at 1275. The Tenth Circuit, relying on the analysis of the Act's legislative history in *DeFrantz*, dismissed the suit for failure to state a federal cause of action. *Id.* at 1281. The Court found no indication in the Act that Congress intended the USOC to be liable to athletes injured while competing in events not fully controlled by the USOC. *Id.*

The appellant attempts to distinguish the above cases on the basis of the remedy sought by the plaintiff and scope of USOC control of the events. First, the appellant asserts that, with the exception of *Martinez*, all the cases cited by the USOC stand only for the proposition that Congress did not intend to create an implied right of action in favor of an athlete *to enjoin* the USOC or one of the National governing bodies from restricting that athlete's right to participate in amateur sporting events. The appellant argues that she seeks damages, not participation. The appellant does not present any cases in support of her position; instead, she directs the Court's attention to certain alleged duties conferred upon the USOC by the Act and to the fact that the USOC may be sued.

To permit the appellant to bring forth a private claim for damages would directly contravene *Oldfield*, wherein the Ninth Circuit expressly denied the plaintiff a cause of action for his damages claim. The legislative history of the Act indicates that Congress did not intend to provide individual athletes a private cause of action. If Congress had so intended, then it would not have removed the bill of rights from the original version of the Act. Moreover, if Congress desired to differentiate between monetary claims and injunctions, then it could have so provided in the Act. Congress promulgated the Act, including its emphasis on internal dispute mechanisms, and has expressly reserved the right to amend it. *See* 36 U.S.C.A. § 382 (West 1988).

Though the court in *Martinez* rejected an implied right of action for damages, the appellant contends that the court limited its holding to "athletes injured while competing in events that were *not fully controlled* by the USOC." *Martinez*, 802 F.2d at 1281 (emphasis added). Though the court alludes to the notion of control in disposing of this case, the court does not indicate control is a determining factor in claims seeking damages. Moreover, the courts neither make the issue of control into a determining factor in *Oldfield*, where the plaintiff sought damages, nor in the other aforementioned cases, where the USOC exercised complete control. The judiciary's silence in no way produces an inference that plaintiffs injured while competing in events not within exclusive USOC control [may] maintain a private cause of action.

Voluntary Assumption of a Duty under State Law

The appellant argues the Act imposes a duty upon the USOC or a duty exists through voluntary assumption of the hotline service. Since we have held there is no private cause of action under the Act, we must determine whether the USOC assumed a duty under state tort law. The appellant maintains that even absent a statutory duty under the Act, the USOC voluntarily undertook an affirmative course of action for her benefit. She asserts the USOC assumed the obligation to exercise reasonable care. The USOC claims it does not owe the appellant any duty under Texas tort law, because: (1) statutory goals and objectives cannot form the basis of a common law negligence action; (2) the USOC did not voluntarily assume a duty to the appellant; and (3) the Act pre-empts any common-law negligence action.

In determining whether a private cause of action existed under state tort law, the Appellate Division of the New Jersey Superior Court felt bound to follow federal case law. *Dolan v. U.S. Equestrian Team, Inc.*, 257 N.J. Super. 314, 608 A.2d 434, 437 (App. Div. 1992). The court noted:

> [W]e believe the Act should be uniformly interpreted; that it would be inappropriate to attribute different or unique meanings to its provisions in New Jersey and thus create a jurisdictional sanctuary from the Congressional determination that these types of disputes should be resolved outside the judicial process.

Id. 608 A.2d at 437.

We agree with *Dolan.* The interest of maintaining consistent interpretations among jurisdictions requires the Act to pre-empt claims asserted under state tort law. To hold a common law duty exists outside the scope of the Act, thereby enabling an individual athlete to bring suit, threatens to override legislative intent and opens the door to inconsistent interpretations of the Act.

We hold that the USOC did not owe the appellant a duty under any of the theories pleaded. Accordingly, . . . [w]e affirm.

NOTES AND QUESTIONS

1. The *Reynolds* saga involved some twelve stages of arbitration and litigation over a period of four years. It was worthy of Charles Dickens's *Bleak House.* In the end, the plaintiff's case was dismissed, and he received none of the $27 million plus that a lower court had earlier awarded him. Do you think the decision to dismiss the action was fair? As Reynolds' lawyer, what steps might you have taken to avoid or at least mitigate the penalty of suspension from competition that he received? Failing that, could you have better ensured a hearing on the merits of his claim for damages?
2. Consider the alternative to specific jurisdiction over the IAAF, namely, general jurisdiction, which requires not that the critical issue in a case must arise out of or relate to the jurisdiction of the disputed territory (Ohio, in *Reynolds*) but only that the defendant have a systematic and continuous presence in the particular territory whose court jurisdiction is at issue. Didn't the IAAF maintain a systematic and continuous presence in Ohio through the TAC and its control over the eligibility of all Ohio athletes in sanctioned international competition and over all sanctioned competition in Ohio? Ironically, the theory of general jurisdiction emerged from an Ohio-related decision by the U.S. Supreme Court: *Perkins v. Benguet Consolidated*

Mining Co., 342 U.S. 437 (1952). For an anatomy of the case, see James A. R. Nafziger, *International Sports Law as a Process for Resolving Disputes*, 45 INT'L & COMP. L.Q. 130, 134–40 (1996). We turn later to a key issue raised in the article, namely, the role that international sports law should play in determining both jurisdiction and a decision on the merits in cases such as *Reynolds*.

3. Note the *Walton-Floyd* court's citation to Judge Posner's famous observation that "[t]here can be few less suitable bodies than the federal courts for determining the eligibility, or the procedures for determining eligibility of athletes to participate in the Olympic Games." In *Harding v. U.S. Figure Skating Ass'n*, 851 F. Supp. 1476 (D. Or. 1994), a world-class figure skater, Tonya Harding, was implicated in a vicious attempt to maim a rival skater. On the eve of the 1994 Winter Olympic Games, her apparent complicity nearly cost her the right to participate in them. (At the last minute, she was allowed to compete but did not medal.) She then sought to enjoin her governing sports bodies from conducting a postcompetition disciplinary hearing that might lead to such sanctions as a lifetime suspension from sanctioned international competition. The court cautioned that "[t]he courts should rightly hesitate before intervening in disciplinary hearings held by private associations, including the defendant United States Figure Skating Association. Intervention is appropriate only in the most extraordinary circumstances, where the association has clearly breached its own rules, that breach will imminently result in *serious* and irreparable harm to the plaintiff, and the plaintiff has exhausted all internal remedies. Even then, injunctive relief is limited to correcting the breach of the rules. The court should not intervene in the merits of the underlying dispute." The court nevertheless concluded, "This is one of those rare cases where intervention was appropriate."

   Do you agree with these skeptical observations about the role of courts in deciding sports-related disputes? Are the alternative methods of dispute resolution adequate substitutions for courts? If so, do you think courts should always defer to the processes of private sports association organizations? Should courts decline to review the decisions of sports bodies even when procedural due process (natural justice) or simple fairness may be at issue? If you think that courts should always have the power of review in such cases, can you think of cases in which we would want them to be instrumental in protecting athletes?

4. What was the original purpose of the Amateur Sports Act of the United States? Is that still its primary purpose or has the legislation evolved beyond its original purpose?

5. English courts have also defined the parameters of judicial review narrowly. For discussion of the baseline rule against judicial review of sports-related decisions, see *Breen v. AEU*, [1972] 2 Q.B. 175, 190, and *McInnes v. Onslow-Fane*, [1978] 3 All E.R., at 223 ("Courts are reluctant to review the decisions of private sports bodies even where those bodies are concerned with the means of livelihood of those who take part in those activities"); *accord Law v. National Greyhound Racing Club Ltd.* [1983] 1 W.L.R. 1302, 1307. Normally, then, judicial review is very limited. Judges have often refused to review the decisions of private or domestic tribunals, such as review panels within sports organizations. In the words of one court, the rules of approved sports organizations are said to be "more than a contract: they are a legislative code laid down to be obeyed by the members."

English courts do, however, accept jurisdiction whenever a plaintiff has been denied an appropriate hearing or has been confronted with bias, whenever a sports organization has exercised a monopolistic position over its members, and whenever a professional athlete's livelihood is at stake. Also, courts have limited jurisdiction whenever a sports organization's administrative tribunal exercises public law functions (for example, to impose sanctions against gambling activity in a sports arena) and whenever its decision would violate statutory law or threaten the public order. As a matter of overriding public law, at least when an athlete's livelihood is at stake, the English High Court hinted at a restraint-of-trade exception to the normal requirement that domestic courts recognize and enforce otherwise-valid arbitral awards. *See Gasser v. Stinson*, [1998] High Court of Justice, No. CH-88. In another case, the High Court denied relief to an athlete who had been suspended from competition after testing positive for banned substances but suggested that, if an arbitral award deprives an athlete of his or her livelihood, the reasonableness of the award may be reviewable by a court. See *Nagle v. Feilden*, [1966] 2 Q.B. 633.

6. As both the *Reynolds* and *Walton-Floyd* cases attest, and as we will continue to observe throughout this chapter, athletes' use of performance-enhancing agents (doping) is a pervasive and highly contentious problem. The World Anti-Doping Code, within the organizational framework of the World Anti-Doping Agency, and UNESCO's International Convention against Doping in Sport, noted earlier in this chapter, together provide a promising international framework. The UNESCO Convention requires state parties to comply with the principles of the Code, to support the World Anti-Doping Agency that administers the Code, and to undertake educational programs against doping. The Code, however, is not an integral part of the Convention. Nor does it create binding obligations under international law for state parties except as specifically provided in the cooperative terms of the Convention.
7. The World Anti-Doping Code itself is based on a definition of doping, an evolving list of prohibited substances, testing requirements, a schedule of sanctions for use of those substances or related violations (see later discussion), and laboratory standards for handling and maintaining specimens. The general testing practice has been to take two samples of urine from athletes. If sample A is positive, the athlete involved may appeal the finding, as a result of which sample B is analyzed. If it is negative, the athlete is cleared of a testable doping violation. If sample B is also positive, however, the athlete is subject to sanctions but given the opportunity to present counterevidence in a hearing. Sample B must always be carefully sealed and stored for later review. See Richard H. McLaren, *WADA Drug Testing Standards*, 18 Marq. L. Rev. 1 (2007). The Code identifies eight violations subject to sanctions – namely, the presence of a prohibited substance or its metabolites or markers in an athlete's urine; the use or attempted use of a prohibited substance or a prohibited method; refusing, failing to submit to, or evading sample collection; violations of requirements regarding athlete availability for out-of-competition testing, including missed tests or failures to provide required out-of-competition information about an athlete's whereabouts; tampering or attempted tampering with any part of doping control; possession of prohibited substances and methods;

trafficking in them; and administration or attempted administration of them. For a succinct discussion of the Code and issues related to it, see Klaus Vieweg, *The Definition of Doping and the Proof of a Doping Offense (an Anti Doping Rule) Violation under Special Consideration of the German Position*, 15 MARQ. L. REV. 37 (2004).

8. The use by athletes and others of performance-enhancing substances and methods that are undetectable or difficult to detect in the laboratory further complicates efforts to ensure a level playing field of sports competition. Alternative techniques include nonanalytical positive evidence of doping by athletes in the form of e-mail communications with prohibited drug distributors, canceled personal checks for payment of drugs, and other extrinsic evidence. Such circumstantial evidence is, however, controversial, as is athletic profiling to establish violations on the basis of significant changes in an athlete's prototypical physical features over time. Frontier issues of genetic splicing and replacement already merit serious attention. See James A.R. Nafziger, *Circumstantial Evidence of Doping: BALCO and Beyond*, 16 MARQ. SPORTS L. REV. 45 (2005).

PROBLEM

Roderick "Red" Sangre is a young Canadian hockey player with the semi-professional Portland Winter Hawks. He has been on the team for just three months. Six months ago, a day after winning a silver medal in Canadian amateur competition, he tested positive for the presence of pseudo-erythropoietin, a substance that is closely related to erythropoietin (EPA), a peptide hormone, which is on the list of prohibited substances in the World Anti-Doping Code. Pseudo-erythropoietin is itself not on the prohibited list. The Code has been adopted by the International Hockey Federation (FIH). The FIH has decided that, if a hockey player's hematocrit (the percentage of red blood cells of total blood volume) is greater than 50%, he will be automatically suspended from FIH-sanctioned competition for two years. Sample A of Sangre's blood indicated a hematocrit of 51%, but sample B indicated only 49%. Thanks to sample B, Sangre was relieved from the penalty of suspension but had to forfeit his silver medal.

There is no evidence that any testing procedures at the accredited laboratory facility were defective or unfair. Sangre contends, however, that he naturally produces an unusually large amount of the hormone. (It is known that levels as high as 55% can be produced naturally, but such naturally produced levels are rare.)

Yesterday, the hockey league asked Sangre to take another doping test. He asks you, as his lawyer, whether he should simply refuse to take the test. He also asks you whether, if he should take the test, his defense of an abnormally large natural production of the hormone would be effective. Having heard something about strict liability for a positive test, he asks you whether he would have any chance of avoiding a very serious repeater's sanction if his hematocrit again is found to be more than 50%. He wants to know, too, whether the Amateur Sports Act is relevant to his situation. Finally, he asks you what his chances are of getting his silver medal back from the Canadian amateur league.

b. Discrimination

Kuketz v. Petronelli,
821 N.E.2d 473 (Mass. 2005)

Cordy, J.

In this case, we hold that a fitness club's refusal to permit a wheelchair racquetball player to compete in a club league under the condition that the wheelchair player receive two bounces and his able-bodied (referred to by the parties as "footed" player) opponents receive one bounce is not an act of discrimination on the basis of physical disability in violation of Federal and State antidiscrimination laws. . . .

The official rules of racquetball (rules), which govern league play, provide that the "objective" of the game is "to win each rally" and that a player loses a rally when he is "unable to hit the ball before it touches the floor twice." The rules further provide for a modification to the "standard rules" for wheelchair competition, and establish five different levels or "divisions" for such competition. Wheelchair players competing within these divisions must return the ball before the third bounce (i.e., "[t]he ball may hit the floor twice before being returned"), except in the "Multi-Bounce Division," where the "ball may bounce as many times as the receiver wants though the player may swing only once to return the ball to the front wall." These modified rules also provide that a player "can neither intentionally jump out of his chair to hit a ball nor stand up in his chair to serve the ball." The rules have no provision governing competitive play between a wheelchair player and a footed player.

In February 1995, the general manager of the club, Roslyn Petronelli, after consulting with other players in the league, informed Kuketz that he would not be allowed to play in the men's "A" league. Petronelli cited safety concerns as the primary reason and offered Kuketz two alternative options: he could play in a lower-level league under the one-bounce rule or he could play in a wheelchair league that she would assist him in organizing. Kuketz declined both offers.

Kuketz subsequently filed a complaint with the Massachusetts Commission Against Discrimination (commission) against the club, charging that it violated Title III of the Americans with Disabilities Act of 1990 (ADA), 42 U.S.C. §§ 12101 et seq. (2000); G.L. c. 151B, § 5; and G.L. c. 272, § 98, by refusing to allow him to participate in the men's "A" league. In defense of their actions, the club contended that Kuketz was denied the accommodation he requested for safety reasons and because to grant it would fundamentally change the nature of the game.

The ADA was enacted in 1990 for the express purpose of providing "a clear and comprehensive national mandate for the elimination of discrimination against individuals with disabilities." 42 U.S.C. § 12101(b)(1). Title III of the ADA confers rights to disabled patrons of places of public accommodation, "thus enabling individuals with disabilities to participate more fully in the mainstream of society with improved access to hotels, convention centers, entertainment and sporting events, and commercial establishments." 1 H.H. Perritt Jr., Americans with Disabilities Act Handbook § 6.01, at 389 (2003). Section 12182 of Title III of the ADA sets out the general rule:

> No individual shall be discriminated against on the basis of disability in the full and equal enjoyment of the goods, services, facilities, privileges, advantages, or accommodations of any place of public accommodation by any person who owns, leases (or leases to), or operates a place of public accommodation.

The statute then defines discrimination to include:

> [A] failure to make reasonable modifications in policies, practices, or procedures, when such modifications are necessary to afford such goods, services, facilities, privileges, advantages, or accommodations to individuals with disabilities, unless the entity can demonstrate that making such modifications would fundamentally alter the nature of such goods, services, facilities, privileges, advantages, or accommodations.

Id. at § 12182(b)(2)(A)(ii).

It is undisputed that Kuketz is an individual with a disability as defined in the ADA. There is also no dispute that the club was a place of public accommodation covered under Title III of the ADA. The issue we must decide is whether the club unlawfully discriminated against Kuketz when it refused to modify its policies and practices to allow Kuketz to play in the men's "A" league under a two-bounce rule.

The United States Supreme Court has noted that Title III of the ADA "contemplates three inquiries: whether the requested modification is 'reasonable,' whether it is 'necessary' for the disabled individual, and whether it would 'fundamentally alter the nature of' the competition.... Whether one question should be decided before the others likely will vary from case to case, for in logic there seems to be no necessary priority among the three." (Citation omitted.) *PGA Tour, Inc. v. Martin*, 532 U.S. 661, 683 n. 38, 121 S. Ct. 1879, 149 L. Ed. 2d 904 (2001) (*Martin*).

[2][3] The defendants do not contest that Kuketz's requested modifications – to play in a wheelchair and to be given two bounces – are "necessary" for Kuketz to play in the men's "A" league. There is significant dispute, however, as to the reasonableness of the modifications sought in light of the safety concerns raised by the defendants. There is also disagreement on whether the modifications would fundamentally alter the nature of the game. Because we conclude that affording Kuketz two bounces against footed players in league play would fundamentally alter the nature of the competition, we need not otherwise address the reasonableness of Kuketz's requested modifications. *School Bd. of Nassau County v. Arline*, 480 U.S.

273, 287 n. 17, 107 S. Ct. 1123, 94 L. Ed. 2d 307 (1987) (finding accommodation for employee unreasonable if it requires fundamental alteration in nature of program). See *Ganden v. National Collegiate Athletic Ass'n*, No. 96C 6953, 1996 WL 680000 (N.D. Ill. Nov. 21, 1996) ("modification is unreasonable if it . . . requires a 'fundamental alteration' in the nature of the privilege or program").

The "fundamental alteration" inquiry was the central issue before the United States Supreme Court in *Martin.* Casey Martin, a professional golfer afflicted with a degenerative circulatory disorder that made walking an eighteen-hole golf course a physical impossibility, requested permission to use a golf cart during the final stage of a professional tour qualifying tournament. *Martin, supra* at 668–669, 121 S. Ct. 1879. PGA TOUR, Inc., the sponsor of the tournament, refused to waive its walking rule. *Id.* at 669, 121 S. Ct. 1879. At trial and subsequently on appeal, the PGA TOUR argued that walking constituted a substantive rule of golf and that waiving this rule in any circumstances would fundamentally alter the nature of the competition. *Id.* at 670. The Supreme Court disagreed, deciding, inter alia, that permitting Martin to use a golf cart would not work a fundamental alteration of the game of golf. *Id.* at 683, 121 S. Ct. 1879. According to the Court:

> [A] modification of [the PGA TOUR's] golf tournaments might constitute a fundamental alteration in two different ways. It might alter such an essential aspect of the game of golf that it would be unacceptable even if it affected all competitors equally; changing the diameter of the hole from three to six inches might be such a modification. Alternatively, a less significant change that has only a peripheral impact on the game itself might nevertheless give a disabled player, in addition to access to the competition as required by Title III, an advantage over others and, for that reason, fundamentally alter the character of the competition.

Id. at 682–683, 121 S. Ct. 1879. The Court concluded that the PGA TOUR's walking rule, which was "based on an optional condition buried in an appendix to the Rules of Golf," was neither an essential element of the game nor "an indispensable feature of tournament golf." *Id.* at 683, 685, 121 S. Ct. 1879 ("essence of the game has been shot-making"). The Court also rejected the PGA TOUR's contention that Martin would gain an unfair advantage over his competitors if permitted to use a golf cart. *Id.* at 686–688, 121 S. Ct. 1879.

Applying these principles to the present matter, we find that summary judgment was properly granted. *Commonwealth v. One 1987 Mercury Cougar Auto.*, 413 Mass. 534, 536, 600 N.E.2d 571 (1992) ("order granting . . . summary judgment will be upheld if the trial judge ruled on undisputed material facts and his ruling was correct as a matter of law"). Unlike the use of carts in golf, the allowance for more than one bounce in racquetball is "inconsistent with the fundamental character of the game."

Martin, supra at 683, 121 S. Ct. 1879. The essence of the game of racquetball, as expressly articulated in the rules, is the hitting of a moving ball with a racquet before the second bounce. Giving a wheelchair player two bounces and a footed player one bounce in head-to-head competition is a variation of the official rules that would "alter such an essential aspect of the game . . . that it would be unacceptable even if it affected all competitors equally." *Id.* at 682, 121 S. Ct. 1879. The modifications sought by Kuketz create a new game, with new strategies and new rules. The club is certainly free to establish or enter into a league that plays this variation of racquetball, but it is not required by the ADA to do so.

Finally, Kuketz contends that the defendants' refusal to accommodate his needs is unjustified when the defendants previously have accommodated the needs of less skilled players through the practice of "spotting" points. That practice, however (just as a handicap in golf), does not change an essential aspect of how the game is played. Fitness and athletic clubs open to the public may choose to "level the playing field" in any number of ways, and such practices are not to be discouraged, but the law does not require modifications that change the fundamental rules of the sport.

Akiyama v. U.S. Judo, Inc.,
181 F. Supp. 2d 1179
(W.D. Wash. 2002)

[Judo competitors and a judo training center brought an action against United States Judo Inc. (USJI) seeking] an end to defendants' requirement that they bow to inanimate objects such as portraits and tatami mats prior to judo matches. Plaintiffs assert that such practices violate their religious beliefs and discriminate against them in violation of Title II of the Civil Rights Act of 1964 (42 U.S.C. § 2000a), the Washington Law Against Discrimination ("WLAD," RCW 49.60.010 *et seq.*), the Washington Consumer Protection Act ("CPA," RCW 19.86.010 *et seq.*), and the Amateur Sports Act ("ASA," 36 U.S.C. § 391(b)).

On May 13, 1997, the Court required plaintiffs to follow the administrative grievance procedure provided in the ASA and stayed the remaining claims until the administrative process was exhausted. In order to permit the individual plaintiffs to continue competing during the interim, the Court entered a preliminary injunction against defendants, prohibiting them from excluding the individual plaintiffs from judo tournaments based on their refusal to bow outside the contest area.[2] Thereafter, plaintiffs filed an administrative complaint with USJI, the national governing body for judo under the ASA. *See* 36 U.S.C. § 391. USJI appointed a panel to hear plaintiffs' complaint and both parties presented witnesses

2 The IJF bowing regulation at issue, which has been adopted by USJI and its members, USJF and USJA, requires that contestants stop and bow in a prescribed manner prior to entering the competition area, immediately before entering onto the tatami mat, and at their "mark" just before the start of the match. At the conclusion of the match, contestants are required to perform the same bows in reverse.

and submitted evidence. The administrative panel found no religious discrimination or any other ASA violations and, on June 21, 1997, dismissed plaintiffs' administrative complaint. Plaintiffs appealed to the Commercial Arbitration Tribunal of the American Arbitration Association, as required by USJI procedures. Following a second evidentiary hearing, the arbitrator rejected plaintiffs' claims under the ASA.

Plaintiffs then appealed to the United States Olympic Committee ("USOC"), the corporation empowered to oversee organized amateur sports in the United States. *See* 36 U.S.C. §§ 374, 395(a)(1). Although there were significant procedural irregularities in the way plaintiffs' appeal was handled by the USOC, it ultimately concluded "that the ceremonial bowing requirements of USJI do not rise to the level of proscribed racial, religious or national origin discrimination and are not violative of the obligations of a National Governing Body." In order to exhaust their administrative remedies, plaintiffs once more initiated arbitration proceedings under 36 U.S.C. § 395(c).

On June 21–23, 2000, a three-person tribunal of the American Arbitration Association held another evidentiary hearing on plaintiffs' ASA claims. The arbitration panel made findings of fact and conclusions of law before entering a final and binding decision in favor of defendants. Defendants then moved for confirmation of the arbitration award and summary judgment on the remainder of plaintiffs' claims. Defendants argued that a judo tournament and the rules associated therewith are not subject to judicial scrutiny under either Title II or WLAD. Two days before defendants filed their initial reply brief, however, the United States Supreme Court decided *PGA v. Martin*, 532 U.S. 661, 121 S. Ct. 1879, 149 L. Ed. 2d 904 (2001), in which the Court found that the Americans with Disabilities Act prevents discrimination against participants in a sporting activity. Although defendants' motion for confirmation of the arbitration award was granted, their motion for judgment as a matter of law was denied in order to give the parties an opportunity to evaluate and brief the impact of *Martin* on plaintiffs' Title II and WLAD claims. Defendants now seek the dismissal of all of plaintiffs' remaining claims.

. . .

A. Impact of *PGA v. Martin*

Defendants have abandoned their argument that Title II does not apply to sporting events, a change necessitated by the Supreme Court's analysis in *Martin*. Both the Americans with Disabilities Act ("ADA"), 42 U.S.C. § 12182(a), and Title II prohibit discrimination in places of public accommodation. In *Martin*, the Supreme Court held that the ADA's protections apply not only to the spectators at a public sporting event, but also to the participants if the competition is open to members of the general public.

. . .

In the case at hand, as in *Martin*, members of the general public are welcome to test their skills and talents in preliminary tournaments designed to identify the best competitors. In such circumstances, *Martin* compels the conclusion that the event organizers may not discriminate against potential competitors because of protected characteristics. The Supreme Court has also made clear that there is no "rules of competition" exception to the anti-discrimination laws: such rules are not immune from judicial review and may be subjected to the appropriate tests for identifying "discrimination."

Defendants argue, however, that the remainder of the *Martin* decision is irrelevant in the context of this case because its ultimate findings turn on a definition of "discrimination" which is not applicable under Title II. What constitutes "discrimination" under Title II, and how the facts of this case measure up under the applicable test, are hotly contested. Plaintiffs argue that Title II protects religious adherents from both intentional discrimination (*i.e.*, disparate treatment) and the adverse effects of facially neutral policies (*i.e.*, disparate impact). Defendants maintain that Title II encompasses only disparate treatment claims and that plaintiffs' claim, which is based solely on the disparate impact analysis, fails as a matter of law.

. . .

Whatever Title II's reach in cases involving racial discrimination,[3] the Court finds that, where the complaint is based on allegations of religious discrimination, intent must be an element of the claim. Unlike the class-wide characteristics which make up a particular race, the contours and tenets of one's religious beliefs are generally non-public and are highly individualized. Virtually any restriction or regulation imposed by a public accommodation could impinge on a person's religious beliefs because such beliefs, being both malleable and subjective, are of the individual adherent's own making. Absent more, the fact that a proprietor has decided to offer his or her services to the public in a way which could impact a religious practice or belief, whether it be by conducting business only on Sundays, by failing to keep a Kosher kitchen, by failing to include fish on the menu during Lent, or by prohibiting smoking, raises no inference of discrimination or other conduct which Congress sought to censure through the enactment of Title II.

The language and legislative history of Title II support the imposition of an intent requirement. Congress clearly knows how to preclude all adverse impacts on an individual's practice of religion, whether intended or unintended. *See* Religious Freedom Restoration Act, 42 U.S.C. § 2000bb, *et seq.* (invalidated by *City of Boerne v. Flores*, 521 U.S. 507, 117 S. Ct. 2157, 138 L. Ed. 2d 624 (1997)). In contrast, Title II precludes private and public actors from segregating or depriving individuals of services on account of their religion, a formulation which is more consistent with an intent to prevent disparate treatment than to prevent unintended adverse effects. As stated in the legislative history, the primary purpose of the Act was to remove "the humiliation, frustration, and embarrassment that a person must surely feel

[3] As discussed [herein], the language and legislative history of the Act suggest that intent should be required for all claims brought under Title II.

when he is told that he is unacceptable as a member of the public because of" a protected characteristic. S. Rep. No. 88–872 (1964), *reprinted in* 1964 U.S.C.C.A.N. 2355, 2370. *See also* H.R. Rep. No. 88–914 (1964), *reprinted in* 1964 U.S.C.C.A.N. 2391, 2393 (Title II will "make it possible to remove the daily affront and humiliation involved in discriminatory denials of access to facilities ostensibly open to the general public").[4] Such emotions and the overall insult to human dignity with which Congress was so clearly concerned arise in the context of intentional conduct, such as segregation and/or the denial of admission because of a patron's race or religion. The Senate Report specifically discusses the scourge of "differential treatment" and "differentiated services," both of which involve intent. S. Rep. No. 88–872 (1964), *reprinted in* 1964 U.S.C.C.A.N. at 2369. In fact, the only mention of facially neutral policies with unintended consequences recognizes that uniform practices may adversely impact religious adherents but strongly implies that such consequences do not run afoul of Title II. S. Rep. No. 88–872 (1964), *reprinted in* 1964 U.S.C.C.A.N. at 2377 (a seemingly reluctant legislator questioned whether Title II "could serve as the forerunner for legislation requiring the sale of kosher foods or fish on Friday").

. . .

The only court to specifically consider a religious discrimination claim under Title II struggled with the disparate treatment/disparate impact issue facing this Court and, while not making any findings on the matter, apparently concluded that disparate treatment, not disparate impact, is the appropriate analysis under the Act. In *Boyle v. Jerome Country Club*, 883 F. Supp. 1422 (D. Idaho 1995), a golfer alleged that his club discriminated against him by scheduling golf tournaments on Sundays because the Church of Jesus Christ of Latter-Day Saints, of which he is a member, counsels against engaging in recreational activities on Sunday. The court noted that "Congress enacted Title II of the Civil Rights Act of 1964 to 'vindicate the deprivation of personal dignity that surely accompanies denials of equal access to public establishments.'" *Boyle*, 883 F. Supp. at 1428 (quoting *Heart of Atlanta Motel, Inc. v. United States*, 379 U.S. 241, 250, 85 S. Ct. 348, 13 L. Ed. 2d 258 (1964) (quoting S. Rep. No. 88–872)). After considering the legislative history and the language of the statute, the court adopted the disparate treatment analysis of *Texas Dept. of Cmty. Affairs v. Burdine*, 450 U.S. 248, 101 S. Ct. 1089, 67 L. Ed. 2d 207 (1981), which, as plaintiffs point out, applies only where intentional discrimination is at issue. The court ultimately concluded that no rational trier of fact could find that defendant country club had discriminated against plaintiff on account of his religion.

[4] Even more poignantly, the Senate Report notes the heartbreak that must accompany a parent's "inability to explain to a child that regardless of education, civility, courtesy, and morality he will be denied the right to enjoy equal treatment, even though he be a citizen of the United States and may well be called upon to lay down his life to assure this Nation continues."

C. Proof of Adverse Impact

In addition, the circumstances presented in this litigation, in which each of the plaintiffs has his or her own belief system, highlight the difficulties that would arise were the Court to fashion a disparate impact claim for religious discrimination under Title II. The essence of a disparate impact claim is that facially neutral requirements or limitations adversely affect a protected group. Plaintiffs have assumed that because religion is a uniquely personal thing with every adherent free to make his or her own interpretation of what is holy and what is profane, the relevant "group" or "class" upon which a disparate impact analysis should focus consists of a single believer. Thus, any imposition on an individual's professed religious beliefs would constitute a 100% impact rate and prove disparate impact.

Identifying the relevant "group" or "class" in religious discrimination cases will, in many cases, be dispositive. For example, if plaintiff Drangeid is considered a Christian, there are hundreds-of-thousands of judo competitors with similar belief systems who are not adversely impacted by defendants' bowing requirement. A disparate impact claim brought by plaintiff Drangeid would, therefore, fail at the initial hurdle. The same is true if plaintiff Drangeid is considered a Lutheran. If, however, plaintiff Drangeid is considered a Christian/Lutheran who interprets the Bible to preclude bowing to inanimate objects, he may be able to show that defendants' bowing regulation discriminates against him, as the only member of this specially-defined class. These practical difficulties in identifying a protected class and determining whether there has been a statistically significant adverse impact are simply another reason to require a showing of intentional discrimination under Title II.[5]

Having considered the language of Title II, the relevant case law, and the legislative history, the Court finds that there is no claim under Title II where a proprietor or event organizer has set up facially neutral regulations governing the provision of its services, with no indication of discriminatory motive or intent. Absent some evidence that the regulation was aimed at a particular religious belief and/or that the proprietor adopted the regulation as a pretext for intentional discrimination on the basis of religion, Title II is not implicated.[6]

[5] The religious discrimination claims brought by plaintiffs Leilani Akiyama and the U.S. Judo Training Center are also defective in that, regardless of whether they are analyzed under a disparate treatment or a disparate impact standard, the objections of these plaintiffs are not religious in nature. As found by the arbitration panel after a full evidentiary hearing, plaintiff Leilani Akiyama is not a member of any particular religion, does not adhere to any particular religious faith, and was unable to identify any religious belief held by her which the bowing requirement offends. Rather, plaintiff Leilani Akiyama's firmly stated objection to bowing reflects her parents' objections, all of which are culturally based and none of which involves an adverse impact on a religious belief. Arbitration Award at 7. The U.S. Judo Training Center, as a corporation, is completely non-denominational and has no religious beliefs. Because there is no indication that the Center is being discriminated against because of the religion of its principle(s), it cannot maintain a claim for religious discrimination.

[6] By way of example, if a restauranteur's facially neutral prohibition against hats were shown to be a surrogate for a rule excluding Sikhs, Hasidic Jews, and/or Muslims, a disparate treatment claim under Title II would be appropriate. In determining whether such a claim should go to the jury, the *McDonnell Douglas Corp. v.*

D. Legitimate, Non-Discriminatory Justification

Even if the Court were to assume that Title II encompasses a disparate impact claim and that plaintiffs could establish an adverse effect on a protected group, defendants have met their burden of establishing a legitimate, non-discriminatory justification for the bowing requirement which bears a manifest relationship to their objectives. *See Watson v. Fort Worth Bank and Trust*, 487 U.S. 977, 996–99, 108 S. Ct. 2777, 101 L. Ed. 2d 827 (1988). Although disparaged by plaintiffs, the arbitration panel found defendants' interests to be as follows:

> U.S.J.I. did not make its decision to adopt the IJF Contest Rules, which include the mandatory bowing protocol . . . , because it intended to discriminate against anyone based on religion, national origin, race, or any of the other factors referenced in 36 U.S.C. § 220522(a)(8). U.S.J.I. made that decision because it reasonably believed and intended that adoption of those rules would promote the following useful, legitimate and non-discriminatory purposes:
>
> A) Promoting the fair and safe start of matches, particularly where participants and officials may not all speak the same language;
> B) Reflecting, highlighting and preserving the etiquette and traditions of judo;
> C) Promoting the dignity and unique identity of the sport, which U.S.J.I. regards as distinct from "wrestling";
> D) Promoting the effective presentation of the sport to spectators attending matches in person as well as those viewing matches on television or by similar visual presentation;
> E) Enhancing the ability of U.S. amateur athletes to compete effectively and competitively in Olympic and other international competitions;
> F) Enhancing the ability of U.S.O.C. and U.S.J.I. to perform their statutory duty under 36 U.S.C. § 22503(4) to secure for the United States the most competent amateur representation possible for Olympic and other international competitions; and
> G) Assuring uniform and consistent administration of one set of rules that are applied in the same way to all contestants at U.S.J.I.-sanctioned tournaments.
>
> These are the true and actual reasons for U.S.J.I.'s decision to adopt the IJF Contest Rules, are sincerely and reasonably held by U.S.J.I., and constitute legitimate, non-discriminatory reasons for U.S.J.I.'s decisions and for the rules themselves.

Green, 411 U.S. 792, 93 S. Ct. 1817, 36 L. Ed. 2d 668 (1973), burden shifting analysis would guide the Court in its attempts to root out discriminatory policies while permitting business owners to regulate the types and manner of services offered based on legitimate, non-discriminatory considerations.

While the aesthetic considerations associated with the pre- and post-match bowing are not related to the competition itself and are only tangentially related to defendants' formal objective of promoting the sport of judo, defendants' collective ability to generate legitimate representatives of the United States in international competition is one of their primary purposes and is clearly furthered by the mandatory bowing requirement. A ruling abolishing the bowing ritual in this country would have no force over international organizations who are not parties to this litigation or in international competitions such as the Olympics and World Championships. Thus, defendants have, as a matter of law, justified the mandatory bowing requirement and overcome any inference of discrimination that could possibly have arisen from the fact that the requirement adversely, although unintentionally, impacts plaintiffs' religious practices.

[The court also decided, on other grounds, that the alternative claims based on the WLAD and CPA also failed. The court therefore granted the defendants' motion for summary judgment and dissolved a preliminary injunction against it.]

NOTES AND QUESTIONS

1. Although the issues of unlawful discrimination against athletes arise largely in contexts of national statutes and can be considered intrinsically culturally bound, broader human rights law is clearly applicable. Indeed, an emerging theme of international sports law involves acts of national, racial, and gender discrimination in particular. We shall see, therefore, that uniform prohibitions against unwarranted discrimination in sports competition, at least at the international level, are gradually replacing arguments protecting such discrimination on the basis of cultural tradition. In this regard, note the language in the last paragraph of the *Akiyama* opinion: "A ruling abolishing the bowing ritual in this country would have no force over international organizations who are not parties to this litigation or in international competitions as the Olympics and World Championships."
2. In *Martin*, which is described in *Kuketz* and also cited in *Akiyama*, Justice Antonin Scalia, dissenting, wrote as follows:

   > [T]he very *nature* of competitive sport is the measurement, by uniform rules, of unevenly distributed excellence. This unequal distribution is precisely what determines the winners and losers – and artificially to "even out" that distribution, by giving one or another exemption from a rule that emphasizes [an athlete's] particular weakness, is to destroy the game.

   PGA Tour v. Martin, 532 U.S. 661, 703–04 (2001) (Scalia, J., dissenting).

   If, as Justice Scalia suggests, competition relies on the physical inequalities among athletes (in addition to other factors), should paraplegics with mechanical replacement limbs be allowed to compete in normal sanctioned competition? Suppose it can be shown that the equipment actually gives them an advantage. What does the *Kuketz* opinion teach in this regard, at least under the Americans with Disabilities Act?

3. At the international level, the Court of Arbitration for Sport (CAS) overturned a ban by the International Association of Athletic Federations (IAAF) on the use by disabled runners of prosthetic devices. As a result of the CAS decision, a double-amputee sprinter from South Africa, Oscar Pistorius, was allowed to compete in sanctioned international competition (in addition to Paralympic events) even though his prosthetic devices enabled him to expend an estimated 25% less energy than competitors without the devices. The arbitral award ruled that the IAAF had failed to produce sufficient evidence that the prosthetic device gave Pistorius an unfair net advantage. *Pistorius v. I.A.A.F.*, CAS 2008/A/1480.
4. A recurring issue is the slow pace of adding, and sometimes failing to add, women's events in the Olympic Games and other international competition that correspond to established men's sports. See *Sagen v. Vancouver Organizing Committee*, 2009 BCCA 522 (unsuccessful claim brought in a British Columbia court by women ski jumpers who sought to require the addition of their sport to the 2010 Olympic Winter Games in Vancouver); see also *Martin v. Int'l Olympic Comm.*, 740 F.2d 670 (9th Cir. 1984) (unsuccessful claim brought in a U.S. federal court by two women distance runners who sought to require the addition of their events to the 1984 Olympic Summer Games in Los Angeles).
5. A particularly visible vestige of the cultural exception is the blanket discrimination in some societies – for example, in some Islamic states – against women athletes and their participation in international competition.
6. The issue of gender-testing of women athletes, based on sampling of chromosomal material, dates back to the 1968 Olympic Games in Mexico City, when the testing was introduced in response to claims that some Eastern European athletes were either men disguised as women or women transformed by testosterone and steroids. Once barred from women's events, transsexuals are now eligible for competition when they produce evidence of sex-reassignment surgery and post-operative hormone replacement therapy. Gender-testing otherwise continues. See Jennifer Finney Boylan, *The XY Games*, N.Y. Times, Aug. 3, 2008, at 10.
7. Caster Semenya, a South African runner, won the women's 800-meter World Championship in 2009. During the competition, the International Amateur Athletics Federation (IAAF), which organized the competition, revealed that testing before the competition had indicated that Semenya had registered unusually higher-than-average levels of apparently naturally-produced testosterone, thereby raising questions about her gender. Leaving aside the propriety of the IAAF's public revelation and the political brouhaha it generated in South Africa, the issue of mixed-gender athletes is perplexing. Given that gender is a hallmark of competitive classification, better rules and legal controls will be essential. Unfortunately,

> [t]he current policies of the International Association of Athletics Federation are vague, incomplete and contradictory. For example, one states that some women with some male-typical aspects (including, in some cases, a Y chromosome and testes) can play as women, but it doesn't specify which combinations disqualify an athlete. This means a woman like Semenya can't really know for sure, in advance of competition, if she should show up.... [The IAAF] allows born-females with adrenal tumors to compete as women, even

> though their bodies may have higher levels of testosterone than the average male. Not too consistent.
>
> Simply stating which conditions disqualify an athlete would be a step in the right direction, especially if the list is based on standardized principles. But even that may not seem fair for some conditions, because two women with the same diagnosis may have different anatomies and physiologies.

Alice Dreger, *Seeking Simple Rules in Complex Gender Realities*, N.Y. Times, Oct. 25, 2009, at Sports 8; see also Alice Dreger, *Swifter, Higher, Stronger? Science Adds a Variable*, N.Y. Times, Sept. 13, 2009, at 10 (noting IAAF waivers, known as therapeutic-use exemptions, for men athletes who can demonstrate lower-than-average levels of testosterone – as in the case of men born with XXY chromosomes – to enable them to raise their levels artificially). In the end, "[t]he fundamental problem is that the science of sports has outpaced the philosophy of sport." *Id.* What do you think can be done to respond to the perplexing issue of gender identification?

3. The Process of International Sports Law

The term "international sports law" refers to a process that comprises a more or less distinctive body of rules, principles, institutions, and procedures to govern important consequences of transnational sports activity. As a body of international law, it draws on the general sources of law, including provisions of international agreements; international custom, as evidence of a general practice accepted as law; general principles (including equity and general principles articulated in the resolutions of international organizations); and, as subsidiary sources, judicial decisions (including those of both international and national tribunals) and scholarly writings.

As open competitions have become standard, thereby blurring, if not erasing, the traditional line between amateurism and professionalism, commercial issues have become more prominent in the emerging process. Related issues now loom large, such as broadcasting rights, taxation of athletes, and trademark infringements. What began as a limited framework to govern essentially amateur sports activity within the then-restrictive rules of the Olympic Movement has grown into an expansive framework that increasingly embraces professional sports as well.

The process of international sports law, though coherent, is nevertheless still quite new and as yet incomplete. Numerous sports-related problems – commercial transactions for the sale of sports equipment, antitrust implications of sports organizations and constraints on the freedom of athletes, questionable employment practices affecting athletes, personal injuries on the playing field, and so on – remain largely the province of domestic law. Sometimes other bodies of international law fill the gap. For example, the issue sometimes arises whether domestic antitrust law and taxing authority should be applied extraterritorially to reach professional teams, athletes, and events abroad. Such issues have generally been resolved under international agreements, such as double taxation treaties, or under the normal rules of private international law that govern jurisdiction, choice of law, and enforcement of foreign judgments.

Of particular significance is the Olympic Charter, which codifies general principles, custom, and authoritative decisions applicable to international sports competition ranging well beyond the Olympic Games. The Olympic Charter thereby forms the normative foundation of international sports law. Although the acceptance of its authority in all spheres of sports activity is not universal, and violations of its rules occur, most of the fundamental principles and operational rules of the Olympic Charter satisfy the requirements of international custom – repetition, duration, and universality of practice, together with an adherence to the rules as legal authority (*opinio juris*).

Many of the Charter's principles and rules are sufficiently detailed to operate without further interpretation – for example, specific rules on the organization of international competition. Other Charter provisions, particularly a set of principles it incorporates, require interpretation by national, regional, and international bodies – for example, the simple pronouncement of a human right to participate in sport. The idea that athletic participation is a human right is reflected in many different ways, such as when it is cited in statutes and judicial decisions as a basis for combating racial and gender discrimination. Still, such a broad human right of participation necessarily has been qualified in practice, often for cultural, economic, or institutional reasons. European and North American courts have refused to establish an unqualified right to compete regardless of an athlete's physical competence and ethical character. Similarly, the Court of Arbitration for Sport, to be discussed later in this chapter, has refused to adopt a general right of eligibility to protect its reputation as a case-specific tribunal.

In the process of international sports law, the dominant institutional framework is the Olympic Movement, which, according to the Olympic Charter, "encompasses organizations, athletes and other persons who agree to be guided by the Olympic Charter." Its structure and scope of authority embrace the International Olympic Committee (IOC), international sports federations (IFs), national Olympic committees (NOCs), the organizing committees of the Olympic Games (OCOGs), national associations, clubs, athletes, judges, referees, coaches, sports technicians, and "other organizations and institutions as recognized by the IOC" such as the International Paralympic Committee.

The supreme authority of the Olympic Movement is the IOC, headquartered in Lausanne, Switzerland. It is defined for legal purposes as an "international non-governmental non-profit organization of unlimited duration, in the form of an association with the status of a legal person, recognized by the Swiss Federal Council." The IOC's mission is "to lead the Olympic Movement in accordance with the Olympic Charter." The charisma and high visibility of the Olympic Games help explain the IOC's unusual influence and scope of authority in the legal process (as well as its vulnerability to public criticism as a sort of scapegoat of sports competition).

The IOC is a leading example of the role of a few nongovernmental organizations in the functional process of international integration and progressive development of international law. Even though the IOC is technically a nongovernmental organization with only limited competence outside the Olympic arena, its special status under international law is well established. States acquiesce in its decisions and conduct diplomacy with it. National courts defer to its authority. For example, a federal appeals court in the United States confirmed the special status of the Olympic Charter and the Games under international law. Cautioning that "a court should be wary of applying a state statute to alter the content of the Olympic Games," the court observed as follows: "The Olympic Games are organized and conducted under the terms of an international agreement – the Olympic Charter. We are extremely hesitant to undertake the application of one state's statute to alter an event that is staged with competitors from the entire world under the terms of that agreement."[7]

The U.S. Supreme Court has established that, although the U.S. Olympic Committee is nongovernmental, Congress officially adopted Rule 1 of the Olympic Charter's aim "to spread the Olympic principles."[8] Four justices of the Court described the IOC as "a highly visible and influential international body."[9] A Swiss statute accords the IOC special international status under Swiss tax and labor laws in view of its "universal vocation . . . in the world of sport."[10] Belgian and French courts, as well as the Council of Europe and the Court of Justice of the European Union, have established that the international rules of sport supersede conflicting national policies and laws in particular contexts. The Second Conference of European Sports Ministers long ago adopted a resolution that explicitly ratified the authority of the Olympic Charter.[11]

The centrality of Olympic aspirations in the commitment and training of athletes at all levels of development is an essential point in understanding the expansive role of international sports law. In today's high-tech world of sports, improved performance typically requires professional assistance and money. In response, grassroots management and funding of training and competition are made available to aspiring athletes through local and national sports associations. These associations operate at the base of a pyramid of authority with the IFs and the IOC at the top. This structure for transmitting the authority and legitimacy of international sports law thereby ensures its influence on schoolyard and sandlot activities whenever aspiring athletes receive support from sanctioned sports organizations that are even indirectly assisted or governed by institutions within the Olympic Movement. Sometimes the funding of athletes, particularly from developing countries, comes directly from such sources as Olympic Solidarity. National governments, committed to the Olympic Movement or influenced by it, often assist directly in this transmission of rules and decisions.

The agencies of transmission vary among countries. In some, the process is confined to a strictly nongovernmental hierarchy, from the IOC down through IFs and NOCs to national federations and finally to local associations. In other states, national legislation, pronouncements of sports ministries or national commissions, and judicial decisions may involve governments more directly. Through these various channels, Olympic rules and decisions normally constitute either a semiautonomous regime to which national governments defer or a body of international custom practiced by them.

Although international sports law crystallized around an Olympic nucleus, other institutions have also contributed to the formation of the law. An example of the ability of even a very loosely organized nongovernmental governance of sport is in sailing, where the dominant America's Cup competition is based on a cryptic nineteenth-century deed of gift whose interpretation and implementation are constantly evolving among a

[7] Martin v. Int'l Olympic Comm., 740 F.2d 670, 677 (9th Cir. 1984).

[8] San Francisco Arts & Athletes, Inc. v. U.S. Olympic Comm., 483 U.S. 522 (1987).

[9] *Id.*

[10] Olympic Rev., Nov. 1981, at 641. "The IOC, "a private entity governed by Swiss civil law, has been accorded some fiscal privileges. Furthermore the IOC is exempt to a certain extent from laws providing for limits on the issuance of working permits for foreign nationals." Letter from Jürg Leutert, Legal Adviser to the Embassy of Switzerland in the United States (Aug. 28, 1983).

[11] For background, *see* Bondoux, *Law and Sport*, Olympic Rev., Aug.–Sept. 1978, at 494, 501–02; Garrigues, *The Impact of Community Law on Physical and Sports Activities*, Olympic Rev., June 1979, at 345.

changing sailing elite. More formal institutions include the sports ministries and other agencies of national governments, whose sports policies often aggregate into custom and thereby influence the formation of law. Intergovernmental organizations, such as UNESCO and other specialized agencies of the United Nations, have been instrumental in combating forms of discrimination such as apartheid in South Africa and in promoting education, health, and a safe environment for athletes.

NOTES AND QUESTIONS

1. During actual competition, the IFs and the IOC repeatedly confront difficult issues requiring interpretation of the IF Constitutions and Bylaws and the Olympic Charter. The Charter serves as both a set of specific rules for Olympic-related competition and a source of customary law. In the 2008 Games in Beijing, for example, medal-winning Chinese women gymnasts appeared to all the world to be significantly under the minimum age of sixteen for eligibility in sanctioned international competition. It was claimed that the Chinese Olympic Committee and the General Administration of Sport of China had conspired to falsify their age certifications. Following the Games, an investigation by the International Gymnastics Federal (FIG) cleared the gymnasts and the Chinese authorities of wrongdoing, but doubts remained, and the FIG announced that, in the course of its investigation, it had uncovered evidence that the Chinese may have falsified documentation concerning the ages of women gymnasts in the 2000 Games. See Sports Illustrated, Oct. 13, 2008, at 20; Juliet Macur, *I.O.C. Is Seeking Proof of Chinese Gymnasts' Ages*, N.Y. Times, Aug. 23, 2008, at B13; George Vecsey, *A Hint of Doubt in Every Shiny Medal*, N.Y. Times, Aug. 23, 2008, at B11; *Gymnast Only 13, Xinhua Said in '07*, Int'l Herald Trib., Aug. 16–17, 2008, at 27.
2. Rules on the nationality of athletes are fundamental in the organization of international competition and the requisite generation of popular support for it. The IOC, for example, imposes a three-year waiting period for acquisition of a new nationality but will grant a waiver – as it often does – with the approval of a migrant athlete's IF and native Olympic committee. Despite substantial litigation and arbitration of such issues, the trend is toward a relaxation of such IF rules as those governing the duration of residence to confirm a new nationality and the prohibition of dual nationality. It has become difficult even to question "quickie" grants of nationality and their outright purchases to enhance a country's competitive position. In the United States, the practice of expedited naturalization of prize athletes, based on special bills in Congress, is common. See, e.g., Peter Berlin, *Frenchman Navigates the Waters for Togo's First Medal*, N.Y. Times, Aug. 13, 2008, at C17; Duff Wilson & Andrew W. Lehren, *Swapping Passports in Pursuit of Olympic Medals*, N.Y. Times, June 15, 2008, at Sports 1.
3. Courts and arbitral tribunals have generally adhered to a noninterference rule against hearing complaints about the enforcement by referees of rules of the game or in-play rules, except in rare instances of extreme bias or unfairness. In international dispute resolution, for example, the CAS drew a line between nonreviewable rules of the game and reviewable rules, procedures, and practices with legal status. The CAS consequently refused to hear an appeal arising out of an incident during the 1996 Olympic Games that involved a referee's disqualification of "Boxer M" for

landing a below-the-belt punch on his opponent. Applying international custom, particularly from the United States, France, and Switzerland, the CAS concluded that a technical decision, standard, or rule – in other words, a nonreviewable game rule – is shielded from arbitral or judicial scrutiny unless the rule or its application by sports officials is arbitrary, illegal, or the product of a wrong or malicious intent against an athlete. In such egregious instances, the rule or its application is reviewable. Sanctions appearing to be excessive or unfair on their face are also reviewable. The rationale for the *Boxer M* decision was twofold: that IFs have the responsibility to enforce rules, and referees or ring judges are in a better position than arbitrators to decide technical matters. See also *Lindland v. U.S. Wrestling Association, Inc.*, 230 F.3d 1036, 1038 (7th Cir. 2000) (considering the issue of whether a referee's decision should be countermanded on the basis of evidence taken from videotapes of a controversial match to select a member of the 2000 U.S. Olympic team).

4. A later case involved an administrative review by the international federation for swimming (Fédération Internationale de Natation, or FINA) of the use of full-body ("long john") swimsuits. The highly elastic suits, which were first marketed by Speedo, attempted to simulate natural sharkskin. The suits were designed to increase a swimmer's speed and endurance, to reduce drag, and possibly to enhance the buoyancy of the swimmer. The FINA Bureau, after lengthy discussion, ruled that "the use of these swimsuits does not constitute a violation of the FINA Rules." In response to this ruling, the Australian Olympic Committee (AOC), nervous about possible claims of unfairness at the Sydney Games in 2000, asked the CAS for an advisory opinion. The AOC inquired whether the FINA ruling had complied with FINA's own rules and whether, in any event, use of the suits would raise contestable issues of fairness. The CAS concluded that FINA's ruling, which was tantamount to approval of full-body suits, was in compliance with its own rules and did not raise any reviewable issues of unfair procedure, bad faith, conflict with general principles of law, or unreasonableness.
5. During the 2004 Olympic Games in Athens, a U.S. gymnast, Paul Hamm, won the all-around gold medal. The Korean silver medalist, Yang Tae Young, challenged the judges' decision, claiming that it had been based on a mistaken assignment of degree-of-difficulty points. The CAS, after hearing the claim according to its normal procedures and taking account of the noninterference rule of international sports law, upheld the award of the medal to Hamm primarily on the technical basis that the Korean Olympic Committee had failed to file a timely claim of unfairness immediately after the disputed decision. The decision is noteworthy not only because of the publicity the dispute generated but also because of the pronouncement by the CAS that athletes are entitled to "honest 'field of play' decisions, not necessarily correct ones." Do you agree?
6. Thus far in this chapter, how many types of constraints on litigation of athlete eligibility issues in U.S. courts can you identify?

4. European (EC) Law

Regional, notably European, law and legal institutions also govern sports activity. For example, the European Convention on Human Rights and Fundamental Freedoms, within the framework of the Council of Europe, defines and seeks to protect a limited range of athletes' rights. Article 6, for example, requires member states to ensure the right to a fair trial. Arguably, that protection extends to formal disciplinary proceedings if they involve a "determination of [an athlete's] civil rights and obligations." Article 8, which proscribes interference by member states in personal matters, protects athletes' personality assets, privacy, and employment rights within an increasingly intrusive sports industry.

The most significant vindication of athletes' rights by a regional court has been made not by the European Court of Human Rights under the European Convention on Human Rights and Fundamental Freedoms but by the European Court of Justice (ECJ). The ECJ is the judicial organ of the European Community (EC), as it has matured into the European Union (EU). The ECJ is fundamentally concerned with helping ensure the economic integration of European states. That raises critical issues, in an era of commercialization, of what is economic and what, to the contrary, is within the reserved domain of sporting activity. This issue has arisen repeatedly within the cultural parameters of the European Sports Model, which is discussed later.

The next case is the most famous in the history of European sports law. It specifically addresses the question, which remains a critical one in Europe, of the extent to which sport constitutes a cultural exception to the economic regulation of the EU.

Union Royale Belge des Societes de Football Association v. Bosman, 1990 E.C.R. 1-4921

Mr. Bosman, a professional footballer of Belgian nationality, was employed from 1988 by RC Liege, a Belgian first division club, under a contract expiring on 30 June 1990, which assured him an average monthly salary of BFR 120,000, including bonuses. On 21 April 1990, RC Liege offered Mr. Bosman a new contract for one season, reducing his pay to BFR 30,000, the minimum permitted by the [Union Royale Belge des Sociétés de Football Association (URBSFA)] federal rules. Mr. Bosman refused to sign and was put on the transfer list. The compensation fee for training was set, in accordance with the said rules, at BFR 11,743,000. Since no club showed an interest in a compulsory transfer, Mr. Bosman made contact with US Dunkerque, a club in the French second division, which led to his being engaged for a monthly salary in the region of BFR 100,000 plus a signing-on bonus of some BFT 900,000. On 27 July 1990, a contract was also concluded between RC Liege and US Dunkerque for the temporary transfer of Mr. Bosman for one year, against payment by US Dunkerque to RC Liege of a compensation fee of BFR 1,200,000 payable on receipt by the Federation Française de Football ("FFF") of the transfer certificate issued by URBSFA. The contract also gave US Dunkerque an irrevocable option for full transfer of the player for BFR 4,800,000.

Both contracts, between US Dunkerque and RC Liege and between US Dunkerque and Mr. Bosman, were however subject to the suspensive condition that the transfer certificate must be sent by URBSFA to FFF in time for the first match of the season, which was to be held on 2 August

1990. RC Liege, which had doubts as to US Dunkerque's solvency, did not ask URBSFA to send the said certificate to FFF. As a result, neither contract took effect. On 31 July 1990, RC Liege also suspended Mr. Bosman, thereby preventing him from playing for the entire season.

On 8 August 1990, Mr. Bosman brought an action against RC Liege before the Tribunal de Premiere Instance (Court of First Instance), Liege. Concurrently with that action, he applied for an interlocutory decision ordering RC Liege and URBSFA to pay him an advance of BFR 100,000 per month until he found a new employer, restraining the defendants from impeding his engagement, in particular by requiring payment of a sum of money, and referring a question to the Court of Justice for a preliminary ruling. By order of 9 November 1990, the judge hearing the interlocutory application ordered RC Liege and URBSFA to pay Mr. Bosman an advance of BFR 30,000 month and to refrain from impeding Mr. Bosman's engagement. He also referred to the Court for a preliminary ruling [on] a question (in Case C-340/90) on the interpretation of Article 480 in relation to the rules governing transfers of professional players ("transfer rules").

In the meantime, Mr. Bosman had been signed up by the French second-division club Saint-Quentin in October 1990, on condition that his interlocutory application succeeded. His contract was terminated, however, at the end of the first season. In February 1992, Mr. Bosman signed a new contract with the French club Saint-Denis de la Reunion, which was also terminated. After looking for further offers in Belgium and France, Mr. Bosman was finally signed up by Olympic de Charleroi, a Belgian third-division club. According to the national court, there is strong circumstantial evidence to support the view that, notwithstanding the 'free' status conferred on him by the interlocutory order, Mr. Bosman has been boycotted by all the European clubs which might have engaged him.

On 28 May 1991, the Cour d'Appel, Liege, revoked the interlocutory decision of the Tribunal de Premiere Instance in so far as it referred a question to the Court of Justice for a preliminary ruling. But it upheld the order against RC Liege to pay monthly advances to Mr. Bosman and enjoined RC Liege and URBSFA to make Mr. Bosman available to any club which wished to use his services, without it being possible to require payment of any compensation fee. By order of 19 June 1991, Case C-340/90 was removed from the register of the Court of Justice. On 3 June 1991, URBSFA, which, contrary to the situation in the interlocutory proceedings, had not been cited as a party in the main action before the Tribunal de Premiere Instance, intervened voluntarily in that action. On 20 August 1991, Mr. Bosman issued a writ with a view to joining UEFA to the proceedings which he had brought against RC Liege and URBSFA and bringing proceedings directly against it.

[After the subsequent litigation in Belgian courts,] the Cour d'Appel decided to stay the proceedings and refer the following questions to the Court of Justice for a preliminary ruling: "Are Articles 48 [on freedom of movement], 85 and 86 [on competition law] of the Treaty of Rome of 25 March 1957 to be interpreted as:

(i) prohibiting a football club from requiring and receiving payment of a sum of money upon the engagement of one of its players who has come to the end of his contract by a new employing club [and]
(ii) prohibiting the national and international sporting associations or federations from including in their respective regulations provisions restricting access of foreign players from the European Community to the competitions which they organize? . . .

. . .

Application of Article 48 to rules laid down by sporting associations

It is first necessary to consider certain arguments which have been put forward on the question of the application of Article 48 to rules laid down by sporting associations.

URBSFA argued that only the major European clubs may be regarded as undertakings, whereas clubs such as RC Liege carry on an economic activity only to a negligible extent. Furthermore, the question submitted by the national court on the transfer rules does not concern the employment relationships between players and clubs but the business relationships between clubs and the consequences of freedom to affiliate to a sporting federation. Article 48 of the Treaty is accordingly not applicable to a case such as that in issue in the main proceedings.

UEFA argued, inter alia, that the Community authorities have always respected the autonomy of sport, that it is extremely difficult to distinguish between the economic and the sporting aspects of football and that a decision of the Court concerning the situation of professional players might call in question the organization of football as a whole. For that reason, even if Article 48 of the Treaty were to apply to professional players, a degree of flexibility would be essential because of the particular nature of the sport.

The German Government [which had intervened in the action] stressed, first, that in many cases a sport such as football is not an economic activity. It further submitted that sport in general has points of similarity with culture and pointed out that, under Article 128(1) of the EC Treaty, the Community must respect the national and regional diversity of the cultures of the Member States. Finally, referring to the freedom of association and autonomy enjoyed by sporting federations under national law, it concluded that, by virtue of the principle of subsidiarity, taken as a general principle, intervention by public, and particularly Community, authorities in this area must be confined to what is strictly necessary.

In response to those arguments, it is to be remembered that, having regard to the objectives of the Community, sport is subject to Community law only in so far as it constitutes an economic activity within the meaning of Article 2 of the Treaty (see Case 36/74 Walrave v. Union Cycliste Internationale [1974] ECR 1401, paragraph 4). This applies to the activities of professional or semi-professional footballers, where they are in gainful employment or provide a remunerated service (see Case 13/76 Dona v. Mantero [1976] ECR 1333, paragraph 12). . . .

Application of Article 48 of the Treaty is not precluded by the fact that the transfer rules govern the business relationships between clubs rather than the employment relationships between clubs and players. The fact that the employing clubs must pay fees on recruiting a player from another club affects the players' opportunities for finding employment and the terms under which such employment is offered.

As regards the difficulty of severing the economic aspects from the sporting aspects of football, the Court has held (in Dona, cited above, paragraphs 14 and 15) that the provisions of Community law concerning freedom of movement of persons and of provision of services do not preclude rules or practices justified on non-economic grounds which relate to the particular nature and context of certain matches. It stressed, however, that such a restriction on the scope of the provisions in question must remain limited to its proper objective. It cannot, therefore, be relied upon to exclude the whole of a sporting activity from the scope of the Treaty.

With regard to the possible consequences of this judgment on the organization of football as a whole, it has consistently been held that, although the practical consequences of any judicial decision must be weighed carefully, this cannot go so far as to diminish the objective character of the law and compromise its application on the ground of the possible repercussions of a judicial decision. At the very most, such repercussions might be taken into consideration when determining whether exceptionally to limit the temporal effect of a judgment (see, inter alia, Case C-163/90 Administration des Douanes v. Legros and Others [1992] ECR I-4625, paragraph 30).

The argument based on points of alleged similarity between sport and culture cannot be accepted, since the question submitted by the national court does not relate to the conditions under which Community powers of limited extent . . . may be exercised but on the scope of the freedom of movement of workers guaranteed by Article 48, which is a fundamental freedom in the Community system (see, inter alia, Case C-19/92 Kraus v. Land Baden-Wuerttemberg [1993] ECR I-1663, paragraph 16).

As regards the arguments based on the principle of freedom of association, it must be recognized that this principle, enshrined in Article 11 of the European Convention for the Protection of Human Rights and Fundamental Freedoms and resulting from the constitutional traditions common to the Member States, is one of the fundamental rights which, as the Court has consistently held and as is reaffirmed in the preamble to the Single European Act and in Article F(2) of the Treaty on European Union, are protected in the Community legal order.

However, the rules laid down by sporting associations to which the national court refers cannot be seen as necessary to ensure enjoyment of that freedom by those associations, by the clubs or by their players, nor can they be seen as an inevitable result thereof. . . . Consequently, the transfer rules constitute an obstacle to freedom of movement for workers prohibited in principle by Article 48 of the Treaty. It could only be otherwise if those rules pursued a legitimate aim compatible with the Treaty and were justified by pressing reasons of public interest. But even if that were so, application of those rules would still have to be such as to ensure achievement of the aim in question and not go beyond what is necessary for that purpose.

. . .

Existence of justifications

First, URBSFA, UEFA and the French and Italian Governments have submitted that the transfer rules are justified by the need to maintain a financial and competitive balance between clubs and to support the search for talent and the training of young players. In view of the considerable social importance of sporting activities and in particular football in the Community, the aims of maintaining a balance between clubs by preserving a certain degree of equality and uncertainty as to results and of encouraging the recruitment and training of young players must be accepted as legitimate.

As regards the first of those aims, Mr. Bosman has rightly pointed out that the application of the transfer rules is not an adequate means of maintaining financial and competitive balance in the world of football. Those rules neither preclude the richest clubs from securing the services of the best players nor prevent the availability of financial resources from being a decisive factor in competitive sport, thus considerably altering the balance between clubs.

As regards the second aim, it must be accepted that the prospect of receiving transfer, development or training fees is indeed likely to encourage football clubs to seek new talent and train young players.

However, because it is impossible to predict the sporting future of young players with any certainty and because only a limited number of such players go on to play professionally, those fees are by nature contingent and uncertain and are in any event unrelated to the actual cost borne by clubs of training both future professional players and those who will never play professionally. The prospect of receiving such fees cannot, therefore, be either a decisive factor in encouraging recruitment and training of young players or an adequate means of financing such activities, particularly in the case of smaller clubs. . . .

The answer to the first question must therefore be that Article 48 of the Treaty precludes the application of rules laid down by sporting associations, under which a professional footballer who is a national of one Member State may not, on the expiry of his contract with a club, be employed by a club of another Member State unless the latter club has paid to the former club a transfer, training or development fee.

Interpretation of Article 48 of the Treaty with regard to the nationality clauses

By its second question, the national court seeks in substance to ascertain whether Article 48 of the Treaty precludes the application of rules laid down by sporting associations, under which, in matches in competitions which they organize, football clubs may field only a limited number of professional players who are nationals of other Member States.

Existence of an obstacle to freedom of movement for workers

. . . Article 48 of the Treaty applies to rules laid down by sporting associations which determine the conditions under which professional sports players may engage in gainful employment. It must therefore be considered whether the nationality clauses constitute an obstacle to freedom of movement for workers, prohibited by Article 48. Article 48(2) expressly provides that freedom of movement for workers entails the abolition of any discrimination based on nationality between workers of the Member States as regards employment, remuneration and conditions of work and employment. . . . Here, the nationality clauses do not concern specific matches between teams representing their countries but apply to all official matches between clubs and thus to the essence of the activity of professional players.

In those circumstances, the nationality clauses cannot be deemed to be in accordance with Article 48 of the Treaty, otherwise that article would be deprived of its practical effect and the fundamental right of free access to employment which the Treaty confers individually on each worker in the Community rendered nugatory (not this last point, see Case 222/86 Unectef v. Heylens and Others [1987] ECR 4097, paragraph 14). None of the arguments put forward by the sporting associations and by governments which have submitted observations detracts from that conclusion. [A] football club's links with the Member State in which it is established cannot be regarded as any more inherent in its sporting activity than its links with its locality, town, region or, in the case of the United Kingdom, the territory covered by each of the four associations. Even though national championships are played between clubs from different regions, towns or localities, there is no rule restricting the right of clubs to field players from other regions, towns or localities in such matches. . . . It follows from the foregoing that Article 48 of the Treaty precludes the application of rules laid down by sporting associations under which, in matches in competitions which they organize, football clubs may field only a limited number of professional players who are nationals of other Member States.

Meca-Medina & Majcen v. Comm'n,
Case C-519/04 P, July 18, 2006

Judgment

By their appeal, Mr Meca-Medina and Mr Majcen ("the appellants") ask the Court to set aside the judgment of the Court of First Instance of the European Communities of 30 September 2004 in Case T-303/02 *Meca-Medina and Majcen v. Commission* [2004] ECR II-3291 ("the contested judgment") by which the latter dismissed their action for annulment of the decision of the Commission of the European Communities of 1 August 2002 rejecting the complaint – lodged by them against the International Olympic Committee ("the IOC") – seeking a declaration that certain rules adopted by the IOC and implemented by the Fédération internationale de natation (International Swimming Federation; "FINA") and certain practices relating to doping control were incompatible with the Community rules on competition and freedom to provide services (Case COMP/38158 – Meca-Medina and Majcen/IOC) ("the decision at issue").

Background to the dispute

The Court of First Instance summarized the relevant anti-doping rules ("the anti-doping rules at issue") in paragraphs 1 to 6 of the contested judgment:

The [IOC] is the supreme authority of the Olympic Movement, which brings together the various international sporting federations, among which is [FINA]). FINA implements for swimming, by its Doping Control Rules ("the DCR," cited here in the version in force at the material time), the Olympic Movement's Anti-Doping Code. DCR 1.2(a) states that the offence of doping "occurs when a banned substance is found to be present within a competitor's body tissue or fluids." That definition corresponds to that in Article 2(2) of the abovementioned Anti-Doping Code, where doping is defined as the presence in an athlete's body of a prohibited substance or the finding that such a substance or a prohibited technique has been used.

Nandrolone and its metabolites, Norandrosterone (NA) and Norethiocholanolone (NE) (hereinafter together called "Nandrolone"), are prohibited anabolic substances. However, according to the practice of the 27 laboratories accredited by the IOC and FINA, and to take account of the possibility of endogenous, therefore innocent, production of Nandrolone, the presence of that substance in a male athlete's body is defined as doping only if it exceeds a limit of 2 nanogrammes (ng) per milliliter (ml) of urine.

For a first offence of doping with an anabolic substance, DCR 9.2(a) requires the suspension of the athlete for a minimum of four years, which may however be reduced . . . if the athlete proves that he did not knowingly take the prohibited substance or establishes how that substance could be present in his body without negligence on his part.

The penalties are imposed by FINA's Doping Panel, whose decisions are subject to appeal to the Court of Arbitration for Sport ("the CAS") under DCR 8.9. The CAS, which is based in Lausanne, is financed and administered by an organization independent of the IOC, the International Council of Arbitration for Sport ("the ICAS"). The CAS's rulings are subject to appeal to the Swiss Federal Court, which has jurisdiction to review international arbitration awards made in Switzerland.

. . .

The applicants are two professional athletes who compete in long-distance swimming, the aquatic equivalent of the marathon. In an anti-doping test carried out on 31 January 1999 during the World Cup in that discipline at Salvador de Bahia (Brazil), where they had finished first and second respectively, the applicants tested positive for Nandrolone. The level found for Mr. D. Meca-Medina was 9.7 ng/ml and that for Mr. I. Majcen 3.9 ng/ml. On 8 August 1999, FINA's Doping Panel suspended the applicants for a period of four years. On the applicants' appeal, the CAS, by arbitration award of 29 February 2000, confirmed the suspension.

In January 2000, certain scientific experiments showed that Nandrolone's metabolites can be produced endogenously by the human body at a level which may exceed the accepted limit when certain foods, such as boar meat, have been consumed. In view of that development, FINA and the applicants consented, by an arbitration agreement of 20 April 2000, to refer the case anew to the CAS for reconsideration. By arbitration award of 23 May 2001, the CAS reduced the penalty to two years' suspension. The applicants did not appeal against that award to the Swiss Federal Court.

By letter of 30 May 2001, the applicants filed a complaint with the Commission. . . . In their complaint, the applicants challenged the compatibility of certain regulations adopted by the IOC and implemented by FINA and certain practices relating to doping control with the Community rules on competition and freedom to provide services. First of all, the fixing of the limit at 2 ng/ml is a concerted practice between the IOC and the 27 laboratories accredited by it. That limit is scientifically unfounded and can lead to the exclusion of innocent or merely negligent athletes. In the applicants' case, the excesses could have been the result of the consumption of a dish containing boar meat. Also, the IOC's adoption of a mechanism of strict liability and the establishment of tribunals responsible for the settlement of sports disputes by arbitration (the CAS and the ICAS) which are insufficiently independent of the IOC strengthens the anti-competitive nature of that limit.

According to that complaint, the application of those rules (hereinafter "the anti-doping rules at issue") leads to the infringement of the athletes' economic freedoms, guaranteed inter alia by Article 49 EC and, from the point of view of competition law, to the infringement of the rights which the athletes can assert under Articles 81 EC and 82 EC. [By decision of August 1, 2002,] the Commission, after analyzing the anti-doping rules at issue according to the assessment criteria of competition law and concluding that those rules did not fall foul of the prohibition under Articles 81 EC and 82 EC, rejected the applicants' complaint.

. . .

It is to be remembered that, having regard to the objectives of the Community, sport is subject to Community law in as far as it constitutes an economic activity within the meaning of Article 2 EC (see Case 36/74 *Walrave and Koch* [1974] ECR 1405, paragraph 4; Case 13/76 *Donà* [1976] ECR 1333, paragraph 12; Case C-415/93 *Bosman* [1995] ECR I-4921, paragraph 73; Joined Cases C-51/96 and C-191/97 *Deliège* [2000] ECR I-2549, paragraph 41; and Case C-176–96 *Lehtonen and Castors Braine* [2000] ECR I-2681, paragraph 32). Thus, where a sporting activity takes the form of gainful employment or the provision of services for remuneration, which is true of the activities of semi-professional or professional sportsmen (see, to this effect, *Walrave and Koch*, paragraph 5, *Donà*, paragraph 12, and *Bosman*, paragraph 73), it falls, more specifically, within the scope of Article 39 EC et seq. or Article 49 EC et seq. These Community provisions on freedom of movement for persons and freedom to provide services not only apply to the action of public authorities but extend also to rules of any other nature aimed at regulating gainful employment and the provision of services in a collective manner.

. . .

The Court has, however, held that the prohibitions enacted by those provisions of the Treaty do not affect rules concerning questions which are of purely sporting interest and, as such, have nothing to do with economic activity (see, to this effect, *Walrave and Koch*, paragraph 8). With regard to the difficulty of severing the economic aspects from the sporting aspects of a sport, the Court has held (in *Donà*, paragraphs 14 and 15) that the provisions of Community law concerning freedom of movement for persons and freedom to provide services do not preclude rules or practices justified on non-economic grounds which relate to the particular nature and context of certain sporting events. It has stressed, however, that such a restriction on the scope of the provisions in question must remain limited to its proper objective. It cannot, therefore, be relied upon to exclude the whole of a sporting activity from the scope of the Treaty (*Bosman*, paragraph 76, and *Deliége*, paragraph 43).

In light of all of these considerations, it is apparent that the mere fact that a rule is purely sporting in nature does not have the effect of removing from the scope of the Treaty the person engaging in the activity governed by that rule or the body which has laid it down. If the sporting activity in question falls within the scope of the Treaty, the conditions for engaging in it are then subject to all the obligations which result from the various provisions of the Treaty. It follows that the rules which govern that activity must satisfy the requirements of those provisions, which, in particular, seek to ensure freedom of movement for workers, freedom of establishment, freedom to provide services, or competition. Thus, where engagement in the sporting activity must be assessed in the light of the Treaty provisions relating to freedom of movement for workers or freedom to provide services, it will be necessary to determine whether the rules which govern that activity satisfy the requirements of Articles 39 EC and 49 EC, that is to say do not constitute restrictions prohibited by those articles (*Delìège*, paragraph 60).

Likewise, where engagement in the activity must be assessed in the light of the Treaty provisions relating to competition, it will be necessary to determine, given the specific requirements of Articles 81 EC and 82 EC, whether the rules which govern that activity emanate from an undertaking, whether the latter restricts competition or abuses its dominant position, and whether that restriction or that abuse affects trade between Member States. Therefore, even if those rules do not constitute restrictions on freedom of movement because they concern questions of purely sporting interest and, as such, have nothing to do with economic activity (*Walrave and Koch* and *Donà*), that fact means neither that the sporting activity in question necessarily falls outside the scope of Articles 81 EC and 82 EC nor that the rules do not satisfy the specific requirements of those articles.

However, in paragraph 42 of the contested judgment, the Court of First Instance held that the fact that purely sporting rules may have nothing to do with economic activity, with the result that they do not fall within the scope of Articles 39 EC and 49 EC, means, also, that they have nothing to do with the economic relationships of competition, with the result that they also do not fall within the scope of Articles 81 EC and 82 EC. In holding that rules could thus be excluded straightaway from the scope of those articles solely on the ground that they were regarded as purely sporting with regard to the application of Articles 39 EC and 49 EC, without any need to determine first whether the rules fulfilled the specific requirements of Articles 81 EC and 82 EC, as set out in paragraph 30 of the present judgment, the Court of First Instance made an error of law. Accordingly, the appellants are justified in asserting that, in paragraph 68 of the contested judgment, the Court of First Instance erred in dismissing their application on the ground that the anti-doping rules at issue were subject to neither Article 49 EC nor competition law. The contested judgment must therefore be set aside, and there is no need to examine either the remaining parts of the first plea or the other pleas put forward by the appellants.

Substance

. . .

The appellants contend that in rejecting their complaint the Commission wrongly decided that the anti-doping rules at issue were not a restriction of competition within the meaning of Article 81 EC. They submit that the Commission misapplied the criteria established by the Court of Justice in *Wouters and Others* in justifying the restrictive effects of the anti-doping rules on their freedom of action. According to the appellants, first, those rules are, contrary to the Commission's findings, in no way solely inherent in the objectives of safeguarding the integrity of competitive sport and athletes' health, but seek to protect the IOC's own economic interests. Second, in laying down a maximum level of 2 ng/ml of urine which does not correspond to any scientifically safe criterion, those rules are excessive in nature and thus go beyond what is necessary in order to combat doping effectively.

. . .

Next, the compatability of rules with the Community rules on competition cannot be assessed in the abstract. . . . Not every agreement between undertakings or every decision of an association of undertakings which restricts the freedom of action of the parties or of one of them necessarily falls within the prohibition laid down in Article 81(1) EC. For the purposes of application of that provision to a particular case, account must first of all be taken of the overall context in which the decision of the association of undertakings was taken or produces its effects and, more specifically, of its objectives. It has then to be considered whether the consequential effects restrictive of competition are inherent in the pursuit of those objectives (*Wouters and Others*, paragraph 97) and are proportionate to them.

As regards the overall context in which the rules at issue were adopted, the Commission could rightly take the view that the general objective of the rules was, as none of the parties disputes, to combat doping in order for competitive sport to be conducted fairly and that it included the need to safeguard equal chances for athletes, athletes' health, the integrity and objectivity of competitive sport and ethical values in sport. In addition, given that penalties are necessary to ensure enforcement of the doping bank, their effect on athletes' freedom of action must be considered to be, in principle, inherent itself in the anti-doping rules. Therefore, even if the anti-doping rules at issue are to be regarded as a decision of an association of undertakings limiting the appellants' freedom of action, they do not, for all that, necessarily constitute a restriction of competition incompatible with the common market, within the meaning of Article 81 EC, since they are justified by a legitimate objective. Such a limitation is inherent in the organization and proper conduct of competitive sport and its very purpose is to ensure healthy rivalry between athletes.

While the appellants do not dispute the truth of this objective, they nevertheless contend that the anti-doping rules at issue are also intended to protect the IOC's own economic interests and that it is in order to safeguard this objective that excessive rules, such as those contested in the present case, are adopted. The latter cannot therefore, in their submission, be regarded as inherent in the proper conduct of competitive sport and fall outside the prohibitions in Article 81 EC.

It must be acknowledged that the penal nature of the anti-doping rules at issue and the magnitude of the penalties applicable if they are breached are capable of producing adverse effects on competition because they could, if penalties were ultimately to prove unjustified, result in an athlete's unwarranted exclusion from sporting events, and thus in impairment of the conditions under which the activity at issue is engaged in. It follows that, in order not to be covered by the prohibition laid down in Article 81(1) EC, the restrictions thus imposed by those rules must be limited to what is necessary to ensure the proper conduct of competitive sport. . . .

Rules of that kind could indeed prove excessive by virtue of, first, the conditions laid down for establishing the dividing line between circumstances which amount to doping in respect of which penalties may be imposed and those which do not, and second, the severity of those penalties. Here, that dividing line is determined in the anti-doping rules at issue by the threshold of 2 ng/ml of urine above which the presence of Nandrolone in an athlete's body constitutes doping. The appellants contest that rule, asserting that the threshold adopted is set at an excessively low level which is not founded on any scientifically safe criterion. However, the appellants fail to establish that the Commission made a manifest error of assessment in finding that rule to be justified.

It is common ground that Nandrolone is an anabolic substance the presence of which in athletes' bodies is liable to improve their performance and compromise the fairness of the sporting events in which they participate. The ban on that substance is accordingly in principle justified in light of the objective of anti-doping rules. It is also common ground that that substance may be produced endogenously and that, in order to take account of this phenomenon, sporting bodies, including the IOC by means of the anti-doping rules at issue, have accepted that doping is considered to have occurred only where the substance is present in an amount exceeding a certain threshold. It is therefore only if, having regard to scientific knowledge as it stood when the anti-doping rules at issue were adopted or even when they were applied to punish the appellants, in 1999 the threshold is set at such a low level that it should be regarded as not taking sufficient account of this phenomenon that those rules should be regarded as not justified in light of the objective which they were intended to achieve.

It is apparent from the documents before the Court that at the material time the average endogenous production observed in all studies then published was 20 times lower than 2 ng/ml of urine and that the maximum endogenous production value observed was nearly a third lower. While the appellants contend that, from 1993, the IOC could not have been unaware of the risk reported by an expert that merely consuming a limited quantity of boar meat could cause entirely innocent athletes to exceed the threshold in question, it is not in any event established that at the material time this risk had been confirmed by the majority of the scientific community. Moreover, the results of the studies and the experiments carried out on this point subsequent to the decision at issue have no bearing in any event on the legality of that decision.

In those circumstances, and as the appellants do not specify at what level the threshold in question should have been set at the material time, it does not appear that the restrictions which that threshold imposes on professional sportsmen go beyond what is necessary in order to ensure that sporting events take place and function properly. Since the appellants have, moreover, not pleaded that the penalties which were applicable and were imposed in the present case are excessive, it has not been established that the anti-doping rules at issue are disproportionate.... In light of all the foregoing considerations, the action brought by the appellants challenging the decision at issue must therefore be dismissed.

NOTES AND QUESTIONS

1. In *Bosman*, why did the ECJ rule that "[t]he argument based on points of alleged similarity between sport and culture cannot be accepted"? After *Bosman* and *Meca-Medina & Majcen*, what is left of the argument that sport is special – the so-called

rule of specificity – within the European Union? See also *Motosykletistiki Omospondia Ellados NPID v. Elliniko Dimosio,* [E.C.J.] Case C-49/07, Judgment of July 1, 2008 (refusing to allow the Greek motorcycling federation to serve monopolistically as both a government-designated regulator and authorizing authority of competition in that sport as well as a competitor of the petitioner in organizing motorcycling events).

2. After the *Bosman* and *Meca-Medina & Majcen* cases, decided by the ECJ, what can be done to protect the cultural values of equality of teams and unpredictability of competition in European sports that the ECJ endorsed?
3. A Declaration of Sport is annexed to the Treaty of Amsterdam Amending the Treaty on European Union and the Treaties Establishing the European Communities and Certain Related Acts, Oct. 2, 1997, 1997 O.J. (C340) 1 (1997), 37 I.L.M. 56 (1998). The Declaration outlines the European Sports Model, which is based on the presumption that sports activity is special and that football/soccer and other major European sports are part of an open system of sports organization. This system is said to entail a pyramidal structure of professional and nonprofessional clubs; annual promotion and relegation of teams between, respectively, superior and inferior divisions on the basis of win-loss records; encouragement of national and community identities in sports; and a reliance on voluntarism. For a commentary, see Stephen Weatherill, *Resisting the Pressures of "Americanization": The Influence of European Community Law on the "European Sports Model,"* 8 Willamette J. Int'l L. & Disp. Resol. 37 (2000).
4. Although Professor Weatherill has been a leading proponent of the European Sports Model, as the cited article discloses, he more recently concluded as follows:

> The EC in general and the Commission and the Court in particular possess limited competence in the field of sport. Elaboration of the social and cultural functions of sport belongs with the public authorities in the Member States and with sports federations. The Community's competence in these realms is lacking, but there is no compelling case for extending it. Below the professional level, EC action would add no evident value. In its economic manifestations, sport is subject to EC trade law. Given the burgeoning commercial significance of sport there is no convincing reason why this should not be so, provided that the peculiar economic interdependence of participants is taken into account – which it is, both by the Court and by the Commission. A wider "cultural" aspect to professional sport is, however, hard to discern and such submissions by the industry deserve a sceptical hearing. 'Vertical solidarity' in European sport is under threat, but it is leading clubs, not the Court or the Commission, that are responsible.... And ultimately, sport in Europe today encompasses a great many different activities and motivations, to the point where pursuit of a "Policy on Sport" may involve a misguided quest for uniformity.

Stephen Weatherill, *Sport as Culture in EC Law, in* Culture and European Union Law 113, 152 (Rachael Craufurd Smith ed., 2004).

Does this suggest a change in Professor Weatherill's attitude or perhaps simply a recognition that because of the "burgeoning commercial significance of sport" and the growing difficulty of discerning a "wider 'cultural' aspect to professional sport," claims by the sporting industry should be viewed as essentially economic in nature and therefore ordinarily subject to EC or EU regulation in the absence of compelling evidence (as in *Meca-Medina & Majcen*) of an overriding cultural exception for nonregulation?

5. Article 165 of the Lisbon Treaty of 2009 is intended to strengthen the institutional structure and decision making of the European Union. It establishes, inter alia, that "[t]he Union shall contribute to the promotion of sporting issues, while taking into account the specific nature of sport, its structure based on voluntary activity and its social and educational function." Among other provisions, the same Article emphasizes the aim of "developing the European dimension in sport." What, exactly, is that dimension? Is it simply a geographical reference or also a functional and sociological reference?
6. How, exactly, does the ECJ's decision in *Meca-Medina & Majcen* affect the European Sports Model's presumption that sports is special and therefore generally *extra commercium* – that is, outside the bounds of commerce and commercial regulation? The decision reaffirms the applicability of EC competition law to sports and rejects the hallowed notion of pure sporting rules immune from public regulators. The decision also establishes that only a case-by-case assessment can determine whether a particular sports rule or practice breaches EC law or pursues a legitimate sports objective whose anticompetitive effects are inherent in the pursuit of those objectives and are proportional and necessary to them. Does *Meca-Medina* thereby blur or sharpen the line between the characteristic economic and cultural aspects of professional sports? Is the distinction itself a cultural one, based on shared European values about the role of sports in society?
7. The Fédération Internationale de Football Association (the International Federation of Association Football, or FIFA) formulated the 6 + 5 rule as a compromise between the inclusion of talented nonnationals (often non-Europeans) in clubs and the responsibility of professional clubs, in terms of the European Sports Model, to provide preparation of local players for national teams. The 6 + 5 rule would require a football club to begin a game with at least six players entitled to play for the national team of the country in which the club is located. Thus, a maximum of five players could be used at the beginning of the match who are not entitled to play for that national team. An alternative approach in the English Premier League of football/soccer, beginning in the 2010–11 season, establishes a squad cap of 25 players, of whom at least eight must be "home grown." The definition of "home grown" is a player who has been registered and thereby trained in either the English or Welsh professional associations for a period of three years under the age of 21, regardless of his nationality. Do such formulas strengthen or weaken the cultural concept of the European Sports Model?
8. An entirely different national sports model is China's Sports Law, enacted in 1995, in response to the country's regulated privatization of social and economic activity and a series of embarrassing doping-related scandals. The pace of implementing these two purposes of the law, respectively, has been quite different. Although privatization of sports has proceeded very slowly – the organization of Chinese sports remains highly centralized and government-controlled rather than becoming effectively privatized – the Chinese Sports Law now animates an aggressive, even harsh campaign to deter if not eliminate doping. See, e.g., Mark McDonald, *Sprinter is Banned in Latest Scandal for China*, N.Y. Times, Oct. 28, 2009, at B14

(noting a continuing problem but routine, drastic suspensions of athletes who have failed drug tests, including a lifetime ban from sanctioned competition of China's fastest woman sprinter in 2009 and the suspension of most of the country's best distance runners from the 2000 Olympic Games).

Much of China's Sports Law, which is a product of the country's transitional policy of Market-Leninism, is in the style of a declaration. Essentially, it modernizes and codifies extant rules and procedures within an established framework of bureaucratic control. The legislative provisions and style in their socialist orthodoxy are old-fashioned. Vaguely expressed responsibilities, prohibitions and sanctions provide very little actual checks on administrative discretion. The style of the law may be somewhat deceptive, however. In name and practice, China's Sports Law has vested administration of sports activities in nongovernmental associations and clubs, including their competence to impose sanctions against doping and other threats to fair play. It has also been instrumental in encouraging private sponsorship and other market mechanisms to finance and promote sports. In 2009, for example, Mercedes-Benz became the first corporate sponsor to acquire naming rights for an indoor sports facility in China – an 18,000-seat arena in Shanghai.

China's Sports Law also has accorded individual athletes many privileges and a measure of autonomy from the bureaucracy as members of the newly empowered sports association. It is noteworthy, however, that the legislation rejects any recognition of the adjudicable rights of athletes, although it does entitle them to financial, educational, and other privileges. In lieu of recourse to adjudication of individual claims, China's Sports Law prescribes mediation and arbitration by a special, presumably nongovernmental body to be established for the purpose.

9. In resolving the controversy regarding the disputed age of Chinese women gymnasts, discussed previously, should China's own Sports Law have played a role? Article 34, speaking of "fair competition" and "sports morality," forbids organizers of sports competition from "resorting to deception or engaging in improper practices for selfish ends"; and Article 49 provides that "[v]iolations of sports etiquette and rules in athletic contests, such as fraud and deception, shall be punished by sports associations in accordance with their respective rules." Even if the Sports Law would not govern the outcome of the dispute, should not its ethical prescriptions help define the burden imposed upon the Chinese authorities to produce credible age documentation?

5. The Court of Arbitration for Sport

The Court of Arbitration for Sport (CAS) was created in 1983 and formally established in 1984 by the IOC for resolving disputes related to international sports. Like the IOC, its headquarters are in Lausanne, Switzerland. The CAS also maintains offices in Sydney and New York to facilitate its work.

The purpose of the CAS is to provide a central, specialized authority to decide sports-related disputes. Its jurisdiction is broad, extending to "all activities pertaining to sport and whose settlement is not otherwise provided for in the Olympic Charter." The Charter itself provides that "[a]ny dispute arising on the occasion of, or in connection with, the Olympic Games must be submitted exclusively to the CAS." According to the CAS Rules of Procedure, the applicable law to decide a dispute is that chosen by the parties or, in the absence of such a choice, Swiss law. In the instance of a dispute between an athlete and an IF where the parties have not chosen the governing law, Swiss choice-of-law rules will refer to the statutes and regulations of the IF. The parties may also authorize the CAS to decide a dispute *ex aequo et bono*, that is, on the basis of equitable principles without recourse to legal rules. Arbitration by CAS involves both written and oral arguments that are typically presented to panels of three arbitrators but occasionally to a single arbitrator.

In deciding hundreds of disputes, the CAS has not resolved technical questions such as those related to the rules of the game, scheduling of competition, or prescribed dimensions of the playing field or ball court. Instead, it addresses such important issues as the eligibility and suspension of athletes, the adequacy of protections for individual athletes during drug testing, breaches of contract between an athlete and a sports club, the validity of contracts for the sale of sports equipment, television rights, licensing, sponsorship, and the nationality of athletes for purposes of competition. Basically, the CAS hears three kinds of disputes: disciplinary, eligibility, and commercial.

The CAS arbitrates disputes brought by individual athletes as well as by IFs and national governing bodies. The CAS is empowered to review IF decisions if any of the following are at issue: the IF's constitution, its powers over an individual athlete's person or property, its adherence to the principles of good faith, its rights and obligations under general contract law, and its compliance with procedural fairness. The interests of individual athletes are fundamental. On the issue of an athlete's strict liability for doping, for example, "the interests of the athlete take precedence over those of the federation."

The advantages of the CAS arbitral procedures have been described as "confidentiality, specialization of the arbitrators, flexibility and simplicity of the procedure, speed, reduced costs and international effectiveness of the arbitration award." The CAS awards are final and binding on the parties but may be appealed to the Swiss Federal Tribunal exclusively. They can be enforced internationally through the New York Convention on the Recognition and Enforcement of Foreign Arbitral Awards.

With one exception, all IFs require clauses in contracts between athletes and national governing bodies by which the contracting parties agree to submit disputes between them to mandatory arbitration. The exception is FIFA, which has its own arbitral tribunal but recognizes a right of appeal to CAS. Athletes selected for the Olympics and other international competition must now sign a waiver form by which they agree to the exclusive jurisdiction of either the CAS or (for football/soccer players) the FIFA tribunal to resolve disputes involving doping and other issues of eligibility. Such waivers establish a basis for enforcing awards against individual athletes even when their future livelihood may be at issue. This has become highly significant as the distinction between amateur and professional athletes has faded and open competition has become common.

Reforms effective in 1994 created an umbrella organization, the International Council of Arbitration for Sport (ICAS), entirely independent of the IOC. Its purpose is to administer and finance the CAS. The 1994 reforms also restructured the CAS by creating two principal arbitration divisions: an Ordinary Arbitration Division and an Appeals Arbitration Division so as to distinguish disputes of the first instance from those arising on appeal of decisions by sports bodies, including IFs. In addition to contentious cases, the Code's procedural rules provide for the two arbitration divisions to render advisory opinions. The CAS also offers a mediation procedure, but it has no competence to resolve doping and disciplinary disputes on the premise than an athlete should not be allowed to negotiate a settlement of those issues. Mediation follows the parties' own procedural stipulations, failing which the CAS mediator determines the appropriate procedure. Constituents of the Olympic Movement may also request consultation proceedings concerning any legal issue with respect to the practice or development of sports or any activity related to sports.

Beginning with the Atlanta Games in 1994, the CAS established an ad hoc division to conduct expeditious on-site arbitration of decisions involving issues that arise during major competition. Normally, CAS must render a decision within twenty-four hours from the time an athlete has filed a claim challenging an eligibility, disqualification, or other time-sensitive decisions by the IOC, an IF, or other sports authority during competition. Since 1996, these ad hoc proceedings have addressed issues at all of the Olympic Games, the Commonwealth Games, and the European Football Championship. Because of the near impossibility of achieving instant agreement on the applicable law by the parties to ad hoc arbitration, as would be necessary during competition, the special rules for the ad hoc proceedings provide for "the applicable regulations, general principles of law and the rules of law, the application of which [a CAS panel] deems appropriate."

A. v. Federation Internationale des Luttes Associées (FILA), CAS 2000/A/317

The Appellant admits that he took Pyrovate 500 [a nutritional supplement] during the time preceding his doping test and that – according to the findings of the IOC accredited laboratory in Cologne – this product contained anabolic-androgenic-steroids although this was not declared on the label. No challenge has been brought forward with respect to the conduct of the doping test, the chain of custody of the sample or the laboratory analysis.

The parties differ in their interpretation of the FILA rules and the consequences to be drawn from them. According to the Appellant, "[I]t is clear that athletes, who have not broken the rules of doping with intent or negligently, cannot be punished" (statement of Appeal dated 5 December 2000), while the Respondent is of the opinion that: "[T]he doping definition resulting from the applicable FILA Regulations is a strict liability definition. If the presence of a doping agent is established, then the sanction applies. No intention has to be shown."

If, indeed, under the FILA rules no subjective element, i.e.[,] no intent or negligence on the part of the athlete were required for a doping offence to have been committed the Panel would in principle have to apply the two-year sanction provided for in Annex D, Section 2[,] of the FILA Doping Regulations and would be limited to evaluating whether there are "specific and exceptional attenuating circumstances which will enable the sanctions to be reduced" (Art. 26, Section 5[,] of the FILA Doping Regulations).

However, the Panel is of the opinion that as a matter of principle and irrespective of "specific and exceptional circumstances" an athlete cannot be banned from competition for having committed a doping offence unless he is guilty, i.e.[,] he has acted with intent or negligence. Even if the rules and regulations of a sports federation do not expressly provide that the guilt of the athlete has to be taken into account the foregoing principle will have to be read into these rules to make them legally acceptable.

CAS panels have to interpret the rules in question in a way "which seeks to discern the intention of the rule maker, and not to frustrate it" (A.C. *v/* FINA, CAS 96/149, Award of March 13, 1997, CAS Digest I p. 251, 259). In interpreting the FILA rules the Panel does not find any indication that they intended to ignore the subjective elements as such. Since the Panel is of the opinion that under Swiss law an athlete cannot validly be banned in the absence of any fault (see *infra*), an interpretation to the contrary would lead to the rules being void which would frustrate the objective of the fight against doping pursued by the entire sporting world.

Before explaining the reasons for the principle of guilt the Panel wishes to clarify that this principle does not apply to the disqualification of a "doped athlete" from the event at which the doping test was conducted. It is therefore perfectly proper for the rules of a sporting federation to establish that the results achieved by a "doped athlete" at a competition during which he was under the influence of a prohibited substance must be cancelled irrespective of any guilt on the party of the athlete. This conclusion is the natural consequence of sporting fairness against the other competitors. The interests of the athlete concerned in not being punished without being guilty must give way to the fundamental principle of sport that all competitors must have equal chances. . . .

The Panel comes to a different conclusion with regard to the suspension of an athlete from future competition. The so-called "strict liability" rule, i.e. a rule as advocated by the Respondent according to which the mere presence of a prohibited substance in an athlete's body justifies his suspension, does not, in the Panel's opinion, sufficiently respect the athlete's right of personality ("*Persönlichkeitsrecht*") as established in Articles 20 and 27 et seq. of the Swiss Civil Code which CAS panels are required to apply (Art. 58 of the Code of Sports-related Arbitration). In fact, under Swiss law also sporting federations are under a duty to respect the framework established by Articles 20 and 27 et seq. Swiss Civil Code (Baddeley, L'association sportive face au droit (1994), p. 227).

As a preliminary remark the Panel wishes to clarify that the legal relations between an athlete and a federation are of a civil nature and do not leave room for the application of principles of criminal law. This is particularly true for the principles of *in dubio pro reo* and *nulla poena sine culpa* and the presumption of innocence as enshrined in Art. 6 ECHR (Swiss Federal Tribunal, ASA Bull. 1993, p. 398, 409 *et seq.* [G. *v/* FEI] and Swiss Federal Tribunal judgment of March 31, 1999 [5P. 83/1999], unreported, p. 12, see also Baddeley, L'association sportive face au droit (1994) p. 220; Scherrer in: Fritzweiler (ed.) Doping-Sanktionen, Beweise, Ansprüche (2000, p. 119, 127).

When deciding whether a "strict liability" rule is proper under Swiss law, the Panel has to weigh the interests of the federation against those of the athlete, in particular his right of personality (see Baddeley, L'association sportive face au droit (1994) p. 239).

In recent times the fight against doping has become sport's most burning problem. At times, public attention and, in particular, that of the media are focused more on whether the athletes are under the influence of doping substances than on the sporting event itself and its results. This development is a very serious threat to the entire sporting movement and, indirectly, to an industry which accounts for an important percentage of the world economy.

It is obvious that it would be an important weapon in the fight against doping if the federations were able to impose sanctions on athletes who have tested positive, without having to establish any element of guilt on the part of the athlete. However, this argument, which is one of prevention and deterrence, loses sight of the general objective of doping sanctions, namely the punishment of the athlete for having violated the rules (Baddeley, L'association sportive face au droit (1994), p. 219).

On the other hand, it has to be recognized that in professional sport doping sanctions have the effect of restraining the athlete from carrying out his chosen trade and thus from earning a living for a certain period of time. In addition, doping sanctions clearly affect the honour and social standing of the athlete concerned and are a stigma on his future.

When weighing up the interests of both sides the Panel is of the view that the interests of the athlete take precedence over those of the federation to enforce a rule of "strict liability." The contrary view would only be acceptable if a strict liability rule were the only meaningful weapon in the fight against doping (see Baddeley in: Fritweiler (ed.) Doping Sanktionen, Beweise, Ansprü (2000), p. 9, 22; Scherrer in Fritweiler (ed.), id. at p. 119, 127; see also CAS 95/142, L. *v/* FINA, CAS Digest, p. 225, 231). As will be shown below, there are other means, in particular when allocating the burden of proof, to ensure an effective fight against doping without accepting the risk of sanctioning an athlete who is not guilty of an offence or whose level of guilt does not justify the full extent of the sanction.

The Panel further notes that in a recent decision the Court of Appeals of Frankfurt/Main, Germany also held that liability without fault was incompatible with the rights of the athlete and German law (OLG Frankfurt/Main, judgment of May 18, 2000, 13W29/00 [B. *v/* DLV] p. 15).

Having established the principle that the suspension of an athlete for a doping offence requires fault on his/her part, this does not, in the Panel's view, mean that it is for the federation to provide full proof of every element of the offence, as is necessary in respect of a criminal act for which a presumption of innocence operates in favour of the accused. There is no doubt that the federation has to establish and – if contested – to prove the objective elements of the offence, in particular, for example, that the sample was taken properly, that there was a complete chain of custody of the sample on its way to the laboratory and that the analysis of the sample was state-of-the-art. This follows from the general rule that a person who alleges a fact has the burden of proof. . . .

However, it would put a definite end to any meaningful fight against doping if the federations were required to prove the necessary subjective elements of the offence, i.e.[,] intent or negligence on the part of the athlete. . . . In fact, since neither the federation nor the CAS has the means of conducting its own investigation or of compelling witnesses to give evidence, means which are available to the public prosecutor in criminal proceedings, it would be all too simple for an athlete to deny any intent or negligence and to simply state that he/she has no idea how the prohibited substance arrived in his/her system (see CAS 96/156, F. *v/* FINA).

For this reason the Panel believes that, with regard to the subjective elements of a doping offence, when weighing the interests of the federation to combat doping and those of the athlete not to be punished without fault, the scales tip in favour of the fight against doping. In fact, doping only happens in the sphere of the athlete: he/she is in control of his/her body, of what he/she eats and drinks, of who has access to his/her nutrition, of what medication he/she takes, etc. In these circumstances it is appropriate to presume that the athlete has knowingly or at least negligently consumed the substance which has led to the positive doping test (see also: *Baddeley*, L'association sportive face au droit, (1994), p. 243; *Beloff*, Drugs, Laws and Versapaks, in: O'Leary (ed.), Drugs and Doping in Sport, Cavendish 2000, p. 39, 49; *Steiner*, Doping aus verfassungsrechtlicher Sicht, in Röhricht/Vieweg (eds.) Doping Forum (2000), p. 125, 134; *Baddeley* in: Fritzweiler (ed.) Doping Sanktionen and Beweise (2000), p. 9, 22).

Therefore, if the federation is able to establish the objective elements of a doping offence, there is a presumption of guilt against the athlete.

The principle of presumed fault on the part of the athlete does not, however, leave him without protection because he/she has the right to rebut the presumption, i.e. to establish that the presence of the prohibited substance in his/her body was not due to any intent or negligence on his/her part (CAS 95/141, C. *v/* FINA, CAS Digest, p. 215, 220 *et seq.*; CAS 98/214, B. v. FIJ, CAS Digest II, p. 319). The athlete may for example provide evidence that the presence of the forbidden substance is the result of an act of malicious intent by a third party. . . .

It is noteworthy that the Swiss Federal Tribunal has accepted an interpretation of doping rules to the effect that it is admissible to presume an athlete's guilt if he/she has been tested positive for a prohibited substance. The athlete is then accorded the opportunity to rebut the presumption (Swiss Federal Tribunal, CAS Digest, p. 561, 575 [G. *v/* FEI]; Swiss Federal Tribunal, 5P 83, 1999 [W.C.Z.W. *v/* FINA], p. 12.

The principle of presumption of guilt and rebuttal thereof by the athlete has also been applied by several CAS decisions, not only with respect of the rules of the FEI which expressly provide for a presumption of guilt, but also in connection with regulations which appear to follow a system of liability without fault. . . . On the other hand, the Panel is conscious of the fact that there have been CAS decisions where the Panel was prepared to apply a strict liability standard with respect to suspensions and was not willing to take into account the subjective elements of the case in questions. . . . However, it should be noted that all these decisions took account of the level of "guilt" on the part of the athlete when establishing the duration of the suspension. It can also be taken from these awards that their reasoning was often based on arguments invoked to justify a simple disqualification. They did not consider the very purpose of suspensions as opposed to a mere disqualification and the differences between them. For these reasons the Panel is not prepared to follow these decisions.

The Panel recognises that the opinions of the courts and legal authorities differ as to whether the reversal of the burden of proof puts too much burden on the athlete. As an example the OLG Frankfurt in its decision of 18 May 2000 (see above) is in favour of a rule pursuant to which the presence of a prohibited substance in an athlete's body provides prima facie evidence of guilt on the part of the athlete; this leaves the athlete with the burden of proving that, in his/her particular case, the facts were different from the normal sequence of events. In many cases the practical results of both scenarios – a reversal of the burden of proof or the rebuttal of prima facie evidence – will be the same, but the Panel does recognise that the burden on the athlete is slightly less in the latter case. The Panel does, however, believe that, as a matter of principle, the reversal of the burden of proof and thus the burden being on the athlete to provide full proof of the absence of intent or negligence, is adequate and appropriate when weighing the interests of both sides.

In the case in hand, at which none of the objective elements of the offence is in dispute, the Appellant is thus presumed to have intentionally or negligently committed the offence. As has been shown above, the burden is on the Appellant to prove that he is not guilty of a doping offence. To this end, the Panel took the testimony of several witnesses proffered by the Appellant.

It is the opinion of the Panel that the Appellant has not succeeded in proving that he was without fault. The Appellant contends that he was not aware that Pyrovate 500 contained a substance which was the source of his positive doping test in Sydney. In fact, the Panel accepts, in the Appellant's favour, that he did not intentionally take a prohibited substance, in other words, that he did not know that Pyrovate 500 contained precursors of nandrolone. The Panel further assumes, in the Appellant's favour, that his use of Pyrovate 500 was in fact the cause for his positive doping test in Sydney. However, the Panel is of the opinion that under the circumstances the Appellant acted negligently when he took Pyrovate 500 without making certain that it did not contain a prohibited substance.

As a general remark, the Panel observes that the sporting world has, for quite some time even before the 2000 Sydney Games, been well aware of the risks in connection with using so-called nutritional supplements, i.e.[,] the risk that they may be contaminated or, in fact, "spiked" with anabolic steroids without this being declared on the labels of the containers. There have been several cases of positive tests for nandrolone which have been attributed to nutritional supplements and which have been widely publicised in the sports press. This fact was the likely motive for the IOC press releases in October 1999 and February 2000 (II.2.2 above) which give an unequivocal warning about the use of imported and unlicensed nutritional supplements and their possible mislabeling.

Under these circumstances it is certainly not a valid excuse for an athlete to contend that he/she – personally – was not aware of these warnings. In fact, athletes are presumed to have knowledge of information which is in the public domain. In this context, the Panel notes that there is CAS case law to the effect that athletes are themselves solely responsible for, inter alia, the medication they take and that even a medical prescription from a doctor is no excuse for the athlete (CAS 92, 73, N. v/ FEI, CAS Digest, p. 153, 158). Furthermore an athlete cannot exculpate himself/herself by simply stating that the container of the particular product taken by him/her did not specify that it contained a prohibited substance. It is obvious that the sale of nutritional supplements, many of which are available over the internet and thus sold without an effective governmental control, would go down dramatically if they properly declared that they contain (or could contain) substances prohibited under the rules governing certain sports. Therefore, to allow athletes the excuse that a nutritional supplement was mislabeled would provide an additional incentive for the producers to continue that practice. In summary, therefore, it is no excuse for an athlete found with a prohibited substance in his/her body that he/she checked the label on the product he took and that the label did not specify that the product contained a prohibited substance.

The Panel can leave open the question whether a "doped athlete" can be sanctioned on the basis alone that he/she knew (or is presumed to have known) the risk involved in taking nutritional supplements which may contain a prohibited substance not declared on the label. In the case in hand there are additional elements which establish negligence on the Appellant's part:

In his statement before this Panel the Appellant admitted that during his training camp before the Olympic Games he had been informed that a weightlifter had tested positive for nandrolone and that nutritional supplements were suspected to be the cause of his positive test. At that point in time at the very latest the Appellant should have ceased taking a nutritional supplement which, it should be noted, was not prescribed to him by a medical doctor but was supplied by his "sponsor," a wholesaler of health products with a direct economic interest in marketing (and testing) these products in the sports world.

The rules and regulations of the Respondent (and of the IOC) provide for a two-year sanction in the case of a positive doping test for nandrolone. Even though it is well established that a two-year suspension for a first-time doping offence is legally acceptable, there are several CAS decisions according to which a sanction may not be disproportionate and must always reflect the extent of the athlete's guilt. . . . Therefore, this Panel in its capacity as an appeals body enjoys the same discretion in fixing the extent of the sanction as the Respondent's internal instances (Art. 26.5 of the FILA Doping Regulations, see above). In fact, the Panel would enjoy this discretion even if there were no "exceptional attenuating circumstances."

When taking into consideration all the elements of this case, in particular the fact that the Appellant acted negligently but without intent to indulge in doping, the Panel is of the view that, based on the evidence produced, there are mitigating circumstances which warrant a reduction of the maximum penalty allowed under the rules and regulations of the Respondent. As a result, the Panel is of the opinion that it is adequate and appropriate to suspend the Appellant for 15 months. As regards the date upon which the suspension should begin, the Panel takes note of the fact that the sanction imposed by the Respondent started to run on the date the test was carried out (27 September 2000). The Panel sees no reason why it should change this date. Therefore, the Appellant's suspension will last until 26 December 2001. . . .

Edita Daniute v. International Dancesport Federation, CAS 2006/A/1175

Ms. Edita Daniute (hereinafter referred to as the "Dancer" or the "Appellant") is a Lithuanian ballroom dancer, born in 1979.

The International DanceSport Federation (hereinafter referred to as the "IDSF" or the "Respondent") is the international federation, recognized by the International Olympic Committee, governing all aspects of DanceSport worldwide, either directly through its own organs, or through its national member bodies, or by administrative agreements with other persons and organisations. IDF is a legal entity under Swiss law and has its headquarters in Lausanne, Switzerland.

The Dancer is registered with the Lithuanian Dance Sport Federation (hereinafter referred to as the "LDSF"), which in turn is a member of the IDSF. As a result, the Dancer is subject to and bound by the applicable rules and regulations of IDSF, including its anti-doping rules.

1.2 The Dispute between the Parties

On 19 August 2006, the Dancer participated, with her dance partner, Mr. Arunas Bizokas, in an IDSF Grand Slam Standard competition in Stuttgart, Germany. On that occasion, the Dancer underwent a doping control according to the IDSF anti-doping rules. In a letter of 14 September 2006, the Anti-Doping Director of the IDSF informed the Dancer of her positive test result. The WADA-accredited German laboratory (the "Institut für Dopinganalytic und Sportbiochemie Dresden") had in fact detected in the A-sample of urine provided by the Dancer the presence of Sibutramine, which is a prohibited substance of the category: "S6: Stimulants" under the 2006 IDSF Anti-Doping Code (hereinafter referred to as the "IADC"). In the same letter, the Anti-Doping Director of the IDSF informed the Dancer of her provisional suspension from any further competition as from 14 September 2006 according to Article 5(IV)(1) of the IADC.

On 14 September 2006 the Dancer requested the analysis of the B-sample of urine she had provided. On 8 October 2006, the IDSF Disciplinary Council (hereinafter referred to as the "DC") decided to temporarily lift the provisional suspension until the B-sample was analyzed. The adoption of his decision was communicated to the Dancer on the same day by phone and on 10 October 2006 by e-mail. The formal written decision, dated 16 October 2006, was received by the Dancer on 18 October 2006. In a letter dated 10 October 2006 the Anti-Doping Director of the IDSF informed the Dancer that "the analysis of the B-sample confirmed the analysis of the A-sample." The Dancer was therefore charged with a doping offence under Article 1(VII)(1) of the IADC. By e-mail of 18 October 2006, the Dancer was informed that, as a consequence of the B-sample analysis, her provisional suspension from any further competition had re-entered into force with immediate effect until the case was decided by the DC. In the same e-mail, the Dancer was informed of the composition of the Chamber of the DC in charge of dealing with her case (hereinafter referred to as the "Chamber").

On 26 October 2006, the Dancer submitted to the Chamber her statement of defence. In substance, the Dancer indicated that the positive test was caused by her ingestion of a herbal slimming remedy, called "Meizitang," which she had bought for beauty purposes in a spa in Lithuania in August 2006 and began to ingest on a daily basis since this date until 19 August 2006. In this connection the Dancer emphasized that scientific examination, performed by the "Medicines Control Laboratory of the State Medicines Control Agency at the Ministry of Health of the Republic of Lithuania," had established that the tablets contained in the particular package of "Meizitang" contained Sibutramine, despite the fact that it was not mentioned on the ingredients list of the packet. As a result, the Dancer submitted, primarily, that she had to be held at "No Fault or Negligence" pursuant to Article 5(I)(1) of the IADC, and thus suffer no period of ineligibility, and, subsidiarily, that the sanction should be limited to a minimum level pursuant to Article 5(V)(2) of the IADC, Sibutramine being a "Specified Substance."...

The [Chamber's] Decision, in substance, confirmed that the presence of a prohibited substance in the urine samples provided by the Dancer constituted a doping offence pursuant to the IADC, and indicated that the "circumstance [inadvertent doping] that modifies responsibilities cannot be applied to this case...: the Athlete cannot claim ignorance as after carrying out the relevant investigations we have noted that the information on the substance, effects of the substance, on the combination specifically with Meizitang are easily accessible to any person and of course much more accessible to an Athlete who should be informed about the drugs and other substances she takes."

At the same time, however, the Chamber acknowledged that Sibutramine was a "Specified Substance" with the ensuing applicability of Article 5(V)(2) of the IADC, "that enables... replacing the sanction of two years of ineligibility by that set out in this regulation." Therefore, the

Chamber considered that the sanction of 3 months of ineligibility was appropriate.

. . .

On 21 November 2006, the Appellant filed an appeal with the Court of Arbitration for Sport (hereinafter referred to as the "CAS"), pursuant to the Code of Sports-related Arbitration (hereinafter referred to as the "Code"), to challenge the Decision, seeking the following relief:

(a) A cancellation of the sanction imposed on the athlete on the grounds that the athlete was at No Fault or Negligence; or alternatively
(b) A reduction in the period of ineligibility imposed on Ms. Daniute to 2 months or less, as this would be consistent with the relevant caselaw.

. . .

3.1 Jurisdiction

CAS has jurisdiction to decide the present dispute between the parties. The jurisdiction of CAS, which is not disputed by either party, is based *in casu* on Article 6(VI) of the IADC, and Article 11 of the DC Code, which provide for an appeal to CAS against any decision made by the DC or one of its chambers.

. . .

According to Article R58 of the Code, the Panel is required to decide the dispute "according to the applicable regulations and the rules of law chosen by the parties or, in the absence of such a choice, according to the law of the country in which the federation, association or sports-related body which has issued the challenged decision is domiciled or according to the rules of law, the application of which the Panel deems appropriate. In the latter case, the Panel shall give reasons for its decision."

In this case, the parties have not agreed on the application of any particular law. Therefore, IDSF rules and regulations have to be applied primarily, with Swiss law applying subsidiarily.

. . .

In this respect the Panel notes that, according to Article R57 of the Code, it has full power to review the facts and the law. The Panel consequently hears the case de novo and is not limited to considerations of the submissions before the DC: the Panel can consider all new arguments produced before it. This implies that, even if a violation of the principle of due process (such as the alleged "unfairness," "lack of independence," "risk of a conflict of interest," or lack of motivation) occurred in prior proceedings, it may be cured by a full appeal to the CAS (CAS 94/129, *USA Shooting & Q. v/ UIT, CAS Digest* I, p. 187 at 203; CAS 98/211, *B. v/ Fédération Internationale de Natation, CAS Digest* II, p. 255 at 257; CAS 2000/A/274, *S. v/ Fédération Internationale de Natation, CAS Digest* II, p. 398 at 400; CAS

2000/A/281, *H. v/ Fédération Internationale de Motocyclisme, CAS Digest* II, p. 410 at 415; CAS 2000/A/317, *A. v/ Fédération des Luttes Associés, in CAS Digest* III, p. 159 at 162; CAS 2002/A/378, *S. v/ Union Cycliste Internationale & Federazione Ciclistica Italiana*, in *CAS Digest* III, p. 311 at 315). In fact, the virtue of an appeal system which allows for a full rehearing before an appellate body is that issues relating to the fairness of the hearing before the tribunal of first instance "fade to the periphery" (CAS 98/211, *B. v/ Fédération Internationale de Natation, CAS Digest* II, p. 255 at 264, citing Swiss doctrine and case law).

The Appellant has had and has used the opportunity to bring the case before the CAS, where all of the Appellant's fundamental rights have been duly respected. At the end of the hearing, the Appellant expressly confirmed that she had no objections in respect of her right to be heard and to be treated equally in the CAS arbitration proceedings. Accordingly, even if any of the Appellant's rights had been infringed upon by the DC, the *de novo* proceedings before the CAS would be deemed to have cured any such infringements.

In the same way, the CAS Panel, by using its full power to review the facts and the law, can consider all the elements of the dispute, and review the exercise of the power of evaluation vested in the Chamber, indicated as flawed by errors, so to determine whether an anti-doping rule violation has been committed by the Dancer and, in the event an infringement is found, whether the proper sanction has been applied.

. . .

The members of disciplinary commissions of any sports federation are in fact ordinarily appointed by other bodies of the same federation: disciplinary proceedings, however intended to take place by paying due respect to the right to be heard of the parties involved, lead to decisions which can be imputed to the same federation. In other words, the existence of a functional and organizational link between a disciplinary commission and the sport federation is the result of the very nature and purpose of disciplinary adjudication. As recently confirmed by the Swiss Federal Tribunal (decision 5 January 2007, *Rayo Vallecano v/ FIFA*, 4).240/2006), Swiss law allows an association to sanction the associates for their breach of the association on the rules, so as to secure the observance of those rules. Disciplinary commissions are actually intended to serve this purpose. In this framework, the Panel therefore finds that any reproach for the way specific disciplinary proceedings are organized should not be limited to an overall criticism about an alleged lack of independence or of a conflict of interest between the association and the associates, or the functional or organizational position of the disciplinary committee, but concern identified violations of the internal rules of the association, or mandatory rules of the applicable law, governing the composition and the activity of the chamber in charge of hearing the given case.

In this context, the Panel finds that no violation of specific rules of the DC Code – or any other rule applicable within the IDSF, including mandatory rules of Swiss law – has been committed: the position of the members of the Chamber and their relation with IDSF in the constitution of the Chamber [and] its member associations do not lead to the setting aside of the Decision, failing a legal ground. In fact, it is not disputed that the components of the Chamber had the skills and qualities to meet the requirements of "*good standing and reputation*" set by Article 7 of the DC Code to act as adjudicators, and that the specific circumstances of ineligibility indicated in Article 18 para. 2 of the IDSF Statutes did not occur. In the same way, the Panel finds that the alleged existence of an interest of the IDSF to disqualify the Dancer is not supported by any factual element.

The main question, therefore, to be dealt with in these arbitration proceedings concerns the commission by the Dancer of an anti-doping rule violation pursuant to the IADC and the determination, and if it is the case, of the proper sanction to be applied. The issues raised by the Appellant (with respect to the errors committed by the DC in rendering the Decision, including the alleged failure to apply the principle of proportionality, whatever their "cause") have to be considered in this framework.

...

The Panel agrees with the Appellant and the Decision that Article 5(V)(2) of the IADC applies. The Panel remarks that Article 5(V)(2), in order to allow a replacement of the sanctions applicable pursuant to Article 5(V)(1) with those therein contained, requires the concurrent satisfaction of two conditions:

i. the anti-doping rule infringement should involve the use of a Prohibited Substance identified by the List of Prohibited Substances and Methods attached to the IADC as a "Specified Substance"; and
ii. the athlete can establish that the use of such a Specified Substance was not intended to enhance the performance of the sport.

The first condition is certainly met. The List of Prohibited Substances and Methods attached to the IADC, in fact, mention Sibutramine among the Specified Substances for the purposes of Article 5(V)(2) of the IADC. As a result, no further evaluation is requested in order to establish whether Sibutramine is particularly susceptible to unintentional doping. The inclusion of Sibutramine in the list [of] the Specified Substances is a conclusive element on the point.

The Panel is satisfied, in the same way as the Chamber was when it rendered the Decision, that the second condition is also met. More specifically, the Panel holds that the Dancer has adduced sufficient elements, which are based on the characteristics of DanceSport, as well as on scientific indications that have not been specifically contradicted, to confirm that Sibutramine could not enhance her sport performance, and therefore justify the conclusion of the lack of her intention to achieve that effect.

Such elements are not reversed by the contrary submissions of the Respondent, which claims now that the Dancer did intend to enhance her sport performance. According to IDSF, the Dancer, by taking Meizitang, i.e. the product that contained Sibutramine, in order to achieve "slimming" benefits, intended to increase her performance by influencing the aesthetic and artistic evaluation by the adjudicators. The Panel, in fact, taking into account the overall criteria according to which couples participating in IDSF events are judged, does not find that the "slimming" effects of Sibutramine amount to an improvement of the sport performance of a dancer. The general purpose to achieve a "slimming" benefit, by use of a product not mentioning on the label the presence of a Specified Substance, cannot be equated to the specific intention to enhance the sport performance within the meaning of Article 5(V)(2) of the IADC. The findings of the Decision on this point are therefore confirmed.

The next question, then, is whether the sanction imposed by the Chamber in the Decision is appropriate. In this respect, the Panel notes that according to Article 5(V)(2) of the IADC, the Chamber had the discretion to set the sanction in a scale ranging from a warning and a reprimand and no period of ineligibility to one year's ineligibility. The Chamber used that discretion to impose a sanction of three months of ineligibility, by taking into account all the elements of the case it heard.

The parties dispute the measure of such sanction. According to the Appellant, the sanction imposed is excessive, as it disregards, without any motivation, the case-law adduced by the Dancer, does not respect the principle of proportionality, and does not take into account general mitigating factors, as well as the lack of a proper anti-doping environment within the IDSF. On the other side, the Respondent submits, by way of a subordinate counterclaim . . . that the sanction should be increased to at least eight months' ineligibility.

The Panel finds the measure of the sanction appropriate and does not require adjustments. This conclusion is justified by several elements. In general terms, the Panel underlines that it is willing to enforce a strict approach in the definition of its power reviewing the exercise of the discretion enjoyed by the disciplinary body of an association to set a sanction. To the extent the exercise of such discretion does not run against the internal rules of the association, the mandatory provisions of the law applicable or even fundamental general principles of law, the Panel finds itself limited by the respect to be paid to the freedom of the association to set the way to secure observance by its associates of the association rules.

As a result this Panel adheres, in relation to proportionality, to CAS's jurisprudence, which makes it clear that the sanction imposed must not be evidently and grossly disproportionate to the offence (see CAS 2004/A/690, *Hipperdinger v/ ATP Tour, Inc.*, para. 86; CAS 2005/A/830, *Squizzato v/ FINA*, para. 10.26; CAS 2005/C/976 & 986, *FIFA & WADA*, para. 143). To [the] extent the sanction is not evidently and grossly disproportionate to the offence, therefore, it is appropriate to let the sanction remain as determined by the Chamber.

The Panel, in this respect, does not find the sanction imposed on the Dancer to be evidently and grossly disproportionate to the offence, taking into account all the elements of the case, and chiefly those indicated by the Appellant as general mitigating factors, including the duty of care which could be expected of a top-level athlete such as the Appellant. The fact that a major sporting event is to take place within the period of ineligibility of an athlete found responsible of an anti-doping rule violation does not affect the measure of the sanction. A different solution would create a high degree of uncertainty in the anti-doping system, particularly because it can be expected that doping practices are often undertaken in preparation for major events. The unfortunate fact that the ineligibility period imposed on the Dancer deprived her of the possibility to win (as she then did) the title of world champion does not render the sanction imposed evidently and grossly disproportionate to the offence. A different reasoning, taking into account the actual result achieved in the world championship, and therefore based on an ex post evaluation, is clearly not admissible.

The above conclusion is not refuted by the case law invoked by the Appellant, which refers to different cases heard [by] various sports federations. Contrary to the Appellant's submission, in fact, those decisions imposed sanctions similar to – or not conflicting with – that imposed on the Dancer, thereby confirming that the latter is not evidently and grossly disproportionate to the offence.

In the same way, the Panel finds that any deficiency in the anti-doping environment and culture with the IDSF system, even if existing, does not excuse practices contrary to rules in force and specifically accepted. Well to the contrary, the lower the degree of observance of the rules, the stronger the need of enforcement of those rules. At the same time, however, the Panel wishes to encourage the IDSF to take further steps, in addition to the necessary repression of doping violations, to develop, directly or through its member associations, the awareness by all the athletes of anti-doping values, and to create a proper anti-doping environment preventing the commission of anti-doping rule violations.

NOTES AND QUESTIONS

1. Do you agree with the CAS in its reluctance to impose strict liability for doping violations aside from the time-sensitive decisions during competition that cannot wait for detailed mitigating evidence? Are there cultural considerations to support the CAS view?
2. The CAS opinions are typically detailed in their reasoning. The two CAS opinions you have just read demonstrate the importance of both detailed procedural standards (for example, the proper imposition of a burden of proof) and an openness to the reception of evidence and substantive requirements (for example, the proportionality test to determine the validity of sanctions imposed against athletes for outside-of-event infractions of rules). But overall, do you think there are sufficient safeguards to protect the rights of athletes? Would the CAS opinions benefit from more explicit application of the World Anti-Doping Code, as referenced by UNESCO's International Convention against Doping in Sport?

3. Arbitral awards are normally binding only in the cases and on the parties to which they are addressed. Unlike judicial decisions in common law systems, arbitral awards therefore have no currency as *stare decisis*. At the most, they may sometimes constitute a special law in a case (*lex specialis*). If CAS awards are *lex specialis* and thus have no value as precedent, how can the Panel in *Daniute* speak of "CAS's jurisprudence"? Doesn't that require adherence to the common law principle of *stare decisis*? To what extent, from your reading of the two cases, do you think that, despite a restrictive characterization of all arbitral awards as *lex specialis*, CAS awards actually do establish *stare decisis*? Isn't it true that, in practice, the awards and opinions of the CAS and other arbitral tribunals provide guidance in later cases, strongly influence later awards, and often function as precedent? (Please keep your conclusion in mind when you read the remaining commentary in this chapter on *lex sportiva*.)
4. For a summary of the CAS's role in the development of international sports law, see James H. Carter, *The Law of International Sports Disputes*, 2007–2008 PROC. AM. BRANCH INT'L L. ASS'N 7 (2008). See also Christoph Vedder, *The IAAF Arbitration Panel: The Heritage of Two Decades of Arbitration in Doping-Related Disputes, in* 3–4 INT'L SPORTS L.J. 16 (2005).

PROBLEM

Roy Keane, the superstar of Ireland's national football team, got into a huge row with his coach after the team's arrival in Asia for the 2006 World Cup. During one heated exchange, Keane allegedly threatened the coach physically. Keane was promptly suspended from the team and sent home to Manchester, England, where he plays for Manchester United.

After the World Cup, Keane seeks to restore his place on the Irish national team. During a trial match organized by the Irish Football Association (IFA), Keane is twice carded for physical assault on another player. In each instance the other player falls to the ground in apparent agony but, after the carding, quickly rallies and returns to active play. As a result of being carded and putting in an average performance, Keane is denied a place on the Irish national team. He is very angry and has claimed that he was unfairly carded. He insists that in each instance the other player simply feigned injury without any actual physical contact.

Keane asks you to represent him in appealing the IFA's decision based on his performance in the trial match. The entire match was videotaped, but IFA policy excludes videotaped evidence from internal administrative hearings. You are under considerable time pressure because the regional competition will take place in two weeks. You have (wisely) decided against litigation in the Irish courts. Instead, you are looking into bringing an action before the Court of Arbitration for Sport (CAS). Keane and the IFA have entered into an agreement by which the CAS will hear all disputes between them and its decisions are to be final and binding. What issues of procedure and competence of the tribunal will you need to consider in evaluating your chances of success before the CAS? What presumptions against Keane's action will you have to overcome, aside from the presumption that he is a hothead? Will Keane be able to appeal a CAS decision in a court of law? If not, why not? If so, where?

6. The *Lex Sportiva*

By applying, reinforcing, and helping elaborate established rules and principles of international sports law, as we have just seen, CAS awards and opinions as well as those of other arbitral bodies provide a fertile source of law called the *lex sportiva*. The *lex sportiva* has been identified with the *lex mercatoria* (or merchant law), a venerable source of law going back to the customary practices at medieval fairs, which is said to form the foundation of international commercial practice and commercial arbitration. Strictly commercial issues bearing on sports but not directly affecting athletes ordinarily do not form part of the *lex sportiva*, however.

An example of a rule of the *lex sportiva* is the right of athletes to be heard in *de novo* proceedings that are empowered to review both the law and the facts in a case against a national sports body, IF, or other sports authority. Another rule of the *lex sportiva* is that all ambiguities in the rules of eligibility are to be construed in favor of athletes.

Do such issues as the arbitrability of a dispute, the validity of an arbitration agreement, or judicial remedies against awards fall within the scope of the *lex sportiva*? The secretary-general of the CAS has suggested that they ordinarily do not; instead, they fall within the *lex arbitrii* of Swiss law, as would most arbitral pronouncements on labor, antitrust (competition), and other regulatory law. That is so regardless of the actual location of a CAS hearing and award because the seat of the CAS for legal purposes is always in Lausanne, Switzerland. Consequently, all awards must conform to mandatory Swiss law and policy. Also, to the extent that the parties to arbitration have not exercised party autonomy, the Swiss Federal Act on Private International Law governs issues within its competence in all CAS arbitrations even when one or more of the parties is domiciled or has its registered office outside Switzerland. Whatever the applicable law, the CAS and other arbitral tribunals are gradually shaping a body of rules, the *lex sportiva*, within the larger process of international sports law.

9. Religion

A. The Setting: Globalization of Religion

Toby Lester, *Oh, Gods!* Atlantic Monthly, February 2002, at 37

Contemporary theories of social and political behavior tend to be almost willfully blind to the constantly evolving role of religion as a force in global affairs. The assumption is that advances in the rational understanding of the world will inevitably diminish the influence of that last, vexing sphere of irrationality in human culture: religion. Inconveniently, however, the world is today as awash in religious novelty, flux, and dynamism as it has ever been – and religious change is, if anything, likely to intensify in the coming decades. The spectacular emergence of militant Islamist movements during the twentieth century is surely only a first indication of how quickly, and with what profound implications, change can occur.

It's tempting to conceive of the religious world – particularly when there is so much talk of clashing civilizations – as being made up primarily of a few well-delineated and static religious blocs: Christians, Jews, Muslims, Buddhists, Hindus, and so on. But that's dangerously simplistic. It assumes a stability in the religious landscape that is completely at odds with reality. New religions are born all the time. Old ones transform themselves dramatically. Schism, evolution, death, and rebirth are the norm. And this doesn't apply only to religious groups that one often hears referred to as cults. Today hundreds of widely divergent forms of Christianity are practiced around the world. Islam is usually talked about in monolithic terms (or, at most, in terms of the Shia-Sunni divide), but one almost never hears about the 50 million or so members of the Naqshabandiya order of Sufi Islam, which is strong in Central Asia and India, or about the more than 20 million members of various schismatic Muslim groups around the world. Think, too, about the strange rise and fall of the Taliban. Buddhism, far from being an all-encompassing glow radiating benignly out of the East, is a vast family of religions made up of more than 200 distinct bodies, many of which don't see eye-to-eye at all. Major strands of Hinduism were profoundly reshaped in the nineteenth century, revealing strong Western and Christian influences.

The fact is that religion mutates with Darwinian restlessness. Take a long enough view, and all talk of "established" or "traditional" faith becomes oxymoronic: there's no reason to think that the religious movements of today are any less subject to change than were the religious movements of hundreds or even thousands of years ago. History bears this out. Early Christianity was deemed pathetic by the religious establishment: Pliny the Younger wrote to the Roman Emperor Trajan that he could get nothing out of Christian captives but "depraved, excessive superstition." Islam, initially the faith of a band of little-known desert Arabs, astonished the whole world with its rapid spread. Protestantism started out as a note of protest nailed to a door. In 1871 Ralph Waldo Emerson dismissed Mormonism as nothing more than an "after-clap of Puritanism." Up until the 1940s Pentecostalists were often dismissed as "holy rollers," but today the World Christian Encyclopedia suggests that by 2050 there may be more than a billion people affiliated with the movement. In the period after World War II so many new religious movements came into being in Japan that local scholars of religion were forced to distinguish between *shin-shukyo* ("new religions") and *shin-shin-shukyo* ("new new religions"); one Western writer referred to the time as "the rush hour of the gods." The implication is clear: what is now dismissed as a fundamentalist sect, a fanatical cult, or a mush New Age fad could become the next big thing.

Pauletta Otis, *Religion and War in the Twenty-First Century, in* Religion and Security: The New Nexus in International Relations 11, 15–16 (Robert A. Seiple & Dennis R. Hoover eds., 2004)

The twenty-first century will be a time of religious violence and warfare. Indeed, as religious zealots and opportunists use the power inherent in religious ideology to escalate the forms, levels, and types of violence, there is potential for devastation and destruction previously unknown in human history. Although religion has long been recognized as one factor, among many, relevant to discussions of security and warmaking (for example, the *jus ad bellum* and *jus in bello* criteria of just war theory), it is now emerging (or rather, re-emerging) as the single most important political-ideological default mechanism in global conflict. Yet the Western world has had trouble coming to terms with this reality. Some scholars maintain that the West has often been self-blinded to the reality of global religious issues because it is beholden to an ahistorical version of a "secular" state and therefore unable to provide a full explanation of contemporary warfare. Conversely, others contend that the Western world is only too aware of history – but it merely shudders at the tragic mistakes of past generations without taking proactive steps to learn from them.

. . .

It is apparent that religion plays a critical role in human security, both in preventing and provoking various forms of conflict – from conventional state-vs-state warfare to unconventional forms of political violence carried out by individuals or groups. More specifically, we must bear in mind that:

- Religion is relevant to all conflict, as it concerns life and death, just war, and justice in war.
- Religious conflicts tend to have higher levels of intensity, severity, brutality, and lethality than other forms of war.
- Wars are longer in duration when religion is a major factor.
- Over half of all contemporary conflicts have a significant religious dimension.
- Religious leaders emerge as primary authority figures under conditions of state failure.
- Religious factors are invariably related to ethnic group identity, language, territory, politics, and economics.
- Religious factors are an essential component of effective conflict management and resolution.

Currently, religious factors play a role in conflicts on all continents and between all major religions. The Hindu and Muslim strains are apparent in Gujarat. The Shi'a-Sunni divisions continue to factor in the Iraq conflict. The Lord's Revolutionary Army in Uganda pits Christians against Christians. In Sudan, the Muslims are said to repress and enslave Christians and animists. In Nigeria, the many ethnic groups have gradually polarized and redefined the ethnic-tribal conflict as basically religious. Aum Shinrikyo in Japan was responsible for the use of chemical weapons in a terrorist attack in a Tokyo subway. The conflict between Israel and Palestine is often held to be a religiously complicated war between Jews and Muslims. Lebanon pits groups identified as religious – Druze, Maronite, Catholic, and Shi'a – against one another. In Eastern Europe, various Christian groups – Orthodox, Catholic, Protestant – have evidenced levels of hatred and hostility not seen since the seventeenth century.

Why now? Religion's emergence as a critical dimension of twenty-first century warfare is a result of at least three principal dynamics: (1) the seeming failure of other ideologies and institutions; (2) the power of religion in providing ideological resources supporting social justice; and (3) the power of religion in providing an ideological basis for social coherence and comprehensiveness.

Mark W. Janis, *Introduction, in* Religion and International Law xi (Mark W. Janis & Carolyn Evans eds., 1999) (Martinus Nijhoff Publishers)

The connection between religion and international law is close but nowadays surprisingly little studied or analyzed. This lack of attention has, I think, two causes. First is the effort made in the 19th and 20th centuries to turn international law into a "science." Those who do this often feel that doing law "scientifically" means keeping religion entirely out of the discipline. Second is the addition to recent decades of more than a hundred new mostly non-Western states to the international political community. Conscious that Western values are not necessarily shared with other cultures, many international lawyers are unwilling to discuss religion, ethics and morals for fear of excluding those whose beliefs may be very different from their own.

I must admit to having little sympathy with the first cause of the modern scholarly separation between religion and international law. I doubt that the expectations for making international law or any law a "science" were ever or are now very realistic. Indeed, as Thomas Kuhn among others has pointed out, even science is a lot less "scientific" than we used to think. In any event, I conceive of international law or any law not as a science but as an art or a humanistic endeavor, which is at best descriptive, evaluative and predictive of human attitudes and styles. For international lawyers, in the name of "science," to reject religious, moral and ethical concerns is to curtail any objective attempt to adequately account for the actual nature and aspects of our discipline.

With the second cause of neglect, I am however fully sympathetic. One of the great tasks, perhaps the greatest task, weighing on modern international lawyers is to craft a universal law and legal process capable of ordering relations among diverse people with differing religions, histories, cultures, laws and languages. In so doing, we need to take the world's people as we find them and not pretend out of existence their wide variety. This proper respect cuts two ways. We should neither be presumptuous about Western religions, morals and ethics, nor should we avoid them. Given their real importance, we ought to pay them, as well as the religions, morals and ethics of other traditions, due regard.

Binoy Kampmark, *The Cartoon Riots: A New Cultural Diplomacy*, 7 Whitehead J. Dipl. & Int'l Rel., Summer–Fall 2006, at 69–72, 76

In September 2005, riots erupted, diplomatic relations with much of the Muslim world were ruptured, two embassies were destroyed, and several lives were lost. In Syria, the Danish and Norwegian embassies were burned. In Gaza, Danish flags were set alight. In Yemen, 100,000 women marched in protest. This mayhem was the result of a Danish newspaper's publication of caricatures (commissioned illustrations for a children's book) depicting the Prophet Muhammad. The images were not flattering. One pictured Muhammad with a bomb-shaped turban. Another mocked Islam's purported ambivalence towards women's rights: heaven was apparently running short of virgins for suicide bombers. They were hardly humorous and the Danish Government, led by a stubborn Anders Fogh Rasmussen, defended the publication of the cartoons on the grounds of free speech.

. . .

It is an incontrovertible fact that religion has been the subject of diplomacy for centuries. While religion has ceased to be a putative feature of diplomatic engagement between most power blocs in the world (Europe, the Americas, Asia), religion as a feature of international relations has not entirely disappeared. Islam, as a case in point, acknowledges no such exclusion of religion from diplomatic practice, despite the acceptance by most Muslim states of a "secular approach to the conduct of international relations." Historically, European states often employed the use of religion and culture in foreign affairs. Even after the Protestant-Catholic confrontation of the devastating Thirty Years War (1618–1648), when a nominally secular idea of the nation-state came into being after the Treaty of Westphalia, the existence of clauses protecting religious minorities were still part and parcel of treaty law. The secularization of diplomacy in the West has not precluded the use of religion for the sake of political gain or the use of religion in forcing a respect of cultural values in another state. The presence of religious and cultural values in interstate relations, in short, is a historically consistent process.

In the age of imperialism, it was not unheard of to legislate protective clauses for religious minorities. New scholarship has furnished a previously unexamined example from the 1860s. England and Italy sought a commercial agreement that would go on to become one of many marking the first push for a "common market" in Europe. The particular agreement is notable because British representatives inserted a religious clause protecting the rights of Protestants in Italy in an otherwise commercial treaty. To retain such a clause was perceived as potentially insulting by the Italians. The religious liberties of Protestants, so claimed Italian officials, were sufficiently protected under the Italian constitution. But, it was not inconsistent with London's desire to import Protestant values into a militant doctrine of free trade.

Islam acknowledges no official separation between diplomacy and religion, just as it recognizes no official division between governance and faith. As has been pointed out in some scholarship on the subject, classical Muslims saw Islam as the "one, true, final and universal religion" and central to their concept of the international system. The division between the Islamic and non-Islamic world would be ultimately overcome by "the movement from *Dar al-Harb* (abode of war encompassing unbelievers; Land of War) to *Dar al-Islam* (the abode of peace, encompassing all Muslims).

. . .

Perhaps it should come as no surprise that the objections of Muslim governments to attacks on Islam should transcend the conventional limits of the State. Islam has been affronted and requires defense; it faces a world of conflict beyond its borders, which constantly presents challenges that are difficult to overcome. Scholars argue that Western nations have been insensitive. Such humor masks old ethnocentric insensitivities, eschewing cultural difference and tolerance. Muslim delegations have been sent to Denmark and they have complained of being "hurt." Islam is affronted; the Prophet is inviolable, beyond representation, beyond parody.

The charge of being "hurt" should be taken seriously. Cultural hurt is the inevitable outcome of humor and parody. Parody is a weapon, recognized in cultures across the globe. Humor liberates. It attacks conventions and dogmas, subverting oppressive social structures. But the question to ask here is not whether the global village is humorless, but whether new international conventions have arisen, modifying cultural behavior within and beyond nation-states. Religion has again entered the equation of international relations, challenging the way states, notably those with Muslim immigrants, deal with their culturally diverse citizenry. Such citizens have affinities not merely with their adopted homeland, but with the countries of their faith. The protests caused by the cartoons must themselves be rationalized as part of this evolution. After all, there are representations of Muhammad in other parts of the Western world, too numerous to enumerate here. The U.S. Supreme Court embosses the Prophet in its façade and still stands without a murmur of protest. An understanding of the cultural diplomacy that has developed is useful to such ends. How, for instance, were these protests instigated?

A New Diplomacy

There is a fundamentally new strain of international engagement that has arisen from the globalization of cultural debates. We think of the sensitivities posed by the question of the Holocaust, and the sensitivities associated with its commemoration or denial. As common citizens gradually break out of the cage of sovereignty, the individual is far more significant, not merely from the viewpoint of rights, but from the viewpoint of expression. The field of religious expression is one feature of this revolution.

The closest parallel to the current crisis is the controversy that surrounded the publication of *The Satanic Verses* by the British author Salman Rushdie. With the release of the book in 1988, global tremors were felt. In October 1988, Islamic diplomacy (or rather, belligerent statesmanship) entered the fray, with Saudi Arabia taking up the cause in protesting against the book. As happened in the Danish case, local Muslim representatives organized protests. Muslim representatives in Britain drummed up support for their cause by emphasizing the blasphemous quality of the work. . . . In February 1989, Iran's Ayatollah Khome[ini] decreed that a bounty be put on Rushdie's head for having written a work he considered blasphemous.

The historical parallels between the Rushdie case and the Danish cartoons incident are striking. There were first protests in India, rather than the country of Rushdie's residence, Great Britain. Muslim members of the Indian parliament campaigned to have the book banned after excerpts and reviews in *India Today* and *Sunday* came to their attention. Book burnings took place and there was a violent protest in Islamabad on February 12, outside the American Cultural Center. There were six casualties in all.

The reaction toward the cartoons in the Danish case was similar. The difference, if anything, was the effectiveness of the agitation and the speed with which the message against their publication was disseminated. The

Muslim community in Denmark spread the word by telephone and the blogosphere was filled with discussion. Boycotts of Danish goods took place, first in Saudi Arabia, where text messaging spread the word with incredible speed. Arla Foods, a Danish dairy company with a highly profitable cheese business in the Middle East, suffered losses amounting to £1.5 million per day. But the key factor [was] the effective mobilization of low-level organizations and activists.

. . .

We have, in the final analysis, a departure from the norms of diplomatic engagement in the way Muslims in their non-Muslim settings reacted to the cartoons of the Prophet. International diplomacy is no longer exclusively fueled by conflicts of secular ideology (a free-market versus a command economy; liberalism versus communism). Religion, with its complex cultural, cross-border considerations, has become a paramount consideration in making policy. This requires that states realize how the highly mobile nature of the modern Muslim activists, operating from their adopted homes within the *Dar al-Harb*, may voice their grievances in the *Dar al-Islam*. A new diplomacy, aware of the cultural pitfalls brought on by this change of circumstances, is required. The twenty-first century, as the Gaullist Minister for Culture André Malraux posed, may indeed be an age of religion.

Martin E. Marty, *Fundamentalism and the Scholars*, Key Rep., Spring 1993, at 1, 3–4, 6

The dream, at least as old as World War II, of "one world" has been shattered. "Many worlds," worlds of religious and ethnic and cultural tribes – can we call them that? – are at war with each other. The bipolar world of the cold war is gone. In its place are many convulsive movements of people against each other. The "new world order" went before it came, and a new world disorder finds a chaos of ethnic cleansings, terrorism, and extremisms. The notion that religion, often a source of holy wars and lesser conflicts, would progressively disappear was misconceived. Religion is back in full force, often fueling the tribal movements and militancies. A parallel concept that surviving religion would be progressive and tolerant was also misguiding: the religions that prosper are hardline, dogmatic, and disciplined.

Not all the extremisms and belligerent forces are religious, and not all the religious forces are fundamentalist. But many of them are, and they make daily headlines.

. . .

There is no point here in getting out the atlas to point to all the fundamentalisms. They seem to be least vivid in Western Europe, but some are growing there thanks to immigrations from Eastern Europe and Africa. Eastern Europe in Soviet days was not seen to be a home for any (but Leninist?) fundamentalisms, but the fall of the Iron Curtain and the breaking down of the Wall reveal some more hardline, potentially fundamentalist-like movements taking shape. They trouble all of Islamic northern Africa, having been prime agents of unrest in the Middle East and the Gulf area. They take form in the central Asian republics and are likely to be tribal presences in Afghanistan and Pakistan as they are acquiring geopolitical importance in Sikh-, Hindu-, or Muslim-dominated areas on Asia's sub-continent. Protestant pentecostalisms and evangelicalisms in many South and Central American countries are taking on fundamentalist-like political characteristics and, of course, remain potent forces in the United States.

. . .

Religion has a side different from the one code-named "fundamentalism," and many members of fundamentalist movements know and cherish this. Religion can be used for counsel and consolation, for healing and reconciliation. Whether the religious people and their leaders can draw on some of these resources to bring about measures of concord is a question that will demand answers in the years to come. For the moment, it is the threatening side of religious passion that dominates. In a crowded world where weapons are cheap, the risks and the stakes remain high.

NOTES AND QUESTIONS

1. All of the foregoing readings emphasize the profound significance of religion in today's world. *See also* RICHARD FALK, RELIGION AND HUMANE GLOBAL GOVERNANCE (2001). The readings also underscore the global culture of religions and their impact on sovereignty and security. The interaction among religious traditions is at the heart of the controversial thesis discussed in Chapter 1 that security and international relations – indeed, the global structure itself – will be the product of cultural clashes between civilizations.
2. Given the significance and intensity of religious interaction, what explains the historical lack of attention to it in the description and analysis of international relations and law? Pauletta Otis, in her study in these readings, *supra* at 13, suggests four reasons for this neglect, at least in the context of U.S. national security: "(1) a preference for the 'wall of separation' at both a legal and cultural level; (2) traditional realpolitik analysis; (3) the inherent level of risk in the topic (which makes some rigid institutions avoid the issue); and (4) the potential for political backfire given the sensitivities and sensibilities of the American public."
3. Do you agree that "U.S. diplomacy should move resolutely to make the defense and expansion of religious freedom a core component of U.S. foreign policy"? Thomas F. Farr, *Diplomacy in an Age of Faith*, FOREIGN AFF., March/April 2008, at 110, 111. Wouldn't that just be asking for trouble? Shouldn't the conduct of U.S. foreign policy be wholly secular? Or should promotion and protection of fundamental human rights always be an essential component of a responsible foreign policy?
4. The International Court of Justice ruled on the legal aspects of a wall that Israel erected in the occupied territory of Palestine to protect itself from Palestinian-based intervention and hostility. The Court, holding that several aspects of the

wall violated international law, confirmed that Israel had agreed with Jordan to maintain "freedom of access to places of religious and historical significance," places whose access was either denied or significantly obstructed by the wall. Interestingly, the Court applied this law, *sua sponte*, without specific presentation of that argument by either Palestine or Jordan in their statements to the court. Legal Consequences of the Construction of a Wall in the Occupied Palestinian Territory, Advisory Opinion, 2004 I.C.J. 2 (July 7). See discussion in Geoffrey R. Watson, *The "Wall" Decisions in Legal and Political Context*, 99 AM. J. INT'L L. 6, 14 (2005).

5. On the Danish cartoon crisis, see David Keane, *Cartoon Violence and Freedom of Expression*, 30 HUM. RTS. Q. 845 (2008).

B. The Definitional Problem

WELSH v. UNITED STATES,
398 U.S. 333 (1970)

The petitioner, Elliott Ashton Welsh II, was convicted by a United States District Judge of refusing to submit to induction into the Armed Forces in violation of 50 U.S.C. App. § 462(a), and was on June 1, 1966, sentenced to imprisonment for three years. One of petitioner's defenses to the prosecution was that § 6(j) of the Universal Military Training and Service Act exempted him from combat and noncombat service because he was "by reason of religious training and belief... conscientiously opposed to participation in war in any form." After finding that there was no religious basis for petitioner's conscientious objector claim, the Court of Appeals, Judge Hamley dissenting, affirmed the conviction. 404 F.2d 1078 (1968). We granted certiorari chiefly to review the contention that Welsh's conviction should be set aside on the basis of this Court's decision in *United States v. Seeger*, 380 U.S. 163, 85 S. Ct. 850, 13 L. Ed. 2d 733 (1965).... For the reasons to be stated, and without passing upon the constitutional arguments that have been raised, we vote to reverse this conviction....

We certainly do not think that § 6(j)'s exclusion [from conscientious objector status] of those persons with "essentially political, sociological, or philosophical views or a merely personal moral code" should be read to exclude those who hold strong beliefs about our domestic and foreign affairs or even those whose conscientious objection to participation in all wars is founded to a substantial effect upon considerations of public policy. The two groups of registrants that obviously do fall within these exclusions from the exemption are those whose beliefs are not deeply held and those whose objection to war does not rest at all upon moral, ethical, or religious principle but instead rests solely upon considerations of policy, pragmatism, or expediency. In applying § 6(j)'s exclusion of those whose views are "essentially political, sociological, or philosophical" or of those who have a "merely personal moral code," it should be remembered that these exclusions are definitional and do not therefore restrict the category of persons who are conscientious objectors by "religious training and belief." Once the Selective Service System has taken the first step and determined under the standards set out here and in *Seeger* that the registrant is a "religious" conscientious objector, it follows that his views cannot be "essentially political, sociological, or philosophical." Nor can they be a "merely personal moral code." See *United States v. Seeger*, 380 U.S., at 186, 85 S. Ct. at 864.

Welsh stated that he "believe[d] the taking of life – anyone's life – to be morally wrong." In his original conscientious objector application he wrote the following:

> "I believe that human life is valuable in and of itself; in its living; therefore I will not injure or kill another human being. This belief (and the corresponding 'duty' to abstain from violence toward another person) is not 'superior to those arising from any human relation.' On the contrary: it is essential to every human relation. I cannot, therefore, conscientiously comply with the Government's insistence that I assume duties which I feel are immoral and totally repugnant."

Welsh elaborated his beliefs in later communications with Selective Service officials. On the basis of these beliefs and the conclusion of the Court of Appeals that he held them 'with the strength of more traditional religious conviction,' 404 F.2d at 1081, we think Welsh was clearly entitled to a conscientious objector exemption. Section 6(j) requires no more. That section exempts from military service all those whose consciences, spurred by deeply held moral, ethical, or religious beliefs, would give them no rest or peace if they allowed themselves to become part of an instrument of war.

W. Cole Durham Jr., *Facilitating Freedom of Religion or Belief through Religious Association Laws, in* Facilitating Freedom of Religion or Belief: A Deskbook 352–55 (Tore Lindholm, W. Cole Durham Jr. & Bahia G. Tahzib-Lie eds., 2004) (Martinus Nijhoff Publishers)

The Need for a Broad Definition of Religion

"*Religion.*" It is incumbent on officials administering religious association laws to take a broad approach that avoids discrimination by definitional fiat. Religion and a variety of other terms that may become relevant in applying norms governing freedom of religion or belief (e.g., conscience, belief, sect, clergy, confession and countless others) are notoriously difficult to define. This is in part because what counts as religion or religious is inherently vague, and the variation in the range of phenomena potentially described in these terms is so vast. But it is also in part because insensitive definitions by the state may themselves be inherently discriminatory and may have the practical effect of imposing limitations on beliefs that individuals and groups sincerely believe to be religious. While these definitional problems may be ultimately unsolvable at the level of theory, in the overwhelming majority of cases they are relatively easy to resolve in fact. The approach promulgated by the UN Human Rights Committee in its General Comment No. 22 in 1993 is sound and should be followed. Specifically, paragraph 2 of that document provides:

> Article 18 [of the International Covenant on Civil and Political Rights] protects theistic, non-theistic and atheistic beliefs, as well as the right not to profess any religion or belief. Article 18 is not limited in its application to traditional religions or to religions and beliefs with institutional characteristics or practices analogous to those of traditional religions. The Committee therefore views with concern any tendency to discriminate against any religion or belief for any reasons, including the fact that they are newly established, or represent religious minorities that may be the subject of hostility by a predominant religious community.

This provision recognizes the incredible diversity of religious phenomena that must be taken into account in protecting freedom of religion or belief. Religious association laws need to be drafted with the reality of this virtually boundless pluralism in mind. Whatever else religious freedom means, it is not limited to protecting "traditional religions" with which a state is comfortable. It clearly extends to similar groups, to newly established groups, to dissenting groups within a denomination, to schismatic groups, to extremist or fundamentalist groups – in short, to all the kinds of groups that test our ability to show genuine tolerance and respect.

Unfortunately, many countries ignore the foregoing counsel and are too specific in their legal definitions of "religion." In China definitions are so strict that even traditional religions do not fit within the set of religious organizations recognized by the state. More generally, the narrowness of the established criteria for a legitimate religious organization in many countries often excludes nonconventional religious organizations, whose characteristics may differ in some ways from the legal definition. For example, in the Belarusian Law the definition mentions "religious associations, monasteries, religious brotherhoods and sisterhoods, religious missions, and spiritual educational institutions." This implies a structured organization of only specific types, while there are other kinds of religious associations that are not even mentioned in the provision. Estonia provides another example: it dedicates three paragraphs in its religious law to a definition of religious organizations, with rigid rules that imply structured hierarchical organizations. In 2000 a Hungarian draft law on religious freedom proposed narrowing down possible legitimate religions by identifying them as "a structured set of beliefs" and also went further, adding to the definition a specific requirement of "focus on reality as a whole." Such a provision could prevent registration and thus legitimacy of nonstructured religious associations that focus their teachings on the afterlife or a different kind of reality. Fortunately, this restrictive draft was not adopted. In Armenia an association can only be recognized as religious if it "is based on any historically canonized Holy Scriptures," if its doctrine "forms part of the international contemporary religious-ecclesiastical communities," and if "it is free from materialism and is intended for purely spiritual growth." These definitions presuppose traditional religious organizations with clearly defined scriptures and familiar organizations.

In Peru it is not so much the term "religion" itself that has caused the problem, but instead unduly narrow interpretations of the terms "convents" and "monasteries." This is a useful reminder that definitional problems can extend to other types of terminology that may have a particular meaning in one religion, but rather different meanings (or counterparts) in other religions.

It should be clear that the term "religion" as used in the international instruments includes "religious sects." It has become all too common in recent years to stigmatize some groups by referring to them as sects. Intentional use of such terminology with the intent to disparage is itself a violation of religious freedom norms. Any claim that "sects" are not "religions" for purposes of ascertaining religious freedom claims adds injury to insult.

Note that inclusion of a group in the category of religion does not automatically lead to the conclusion that every religious claim it asserts will automatically be vindicated. Extreme claims that threaten others with imminent and palpable injury will clearly justify state intervention. More generally, religious claims may be subjected to limitations in the narrowly described situations articulated in the relevant limitation clauses. But what occurs in such situations is justifiable state intervention that overrides a religious freedom claim, not state regulation of nonreligious conduct.

NOTES AND QUESTIONS

1. Does *Welsh v. United States* attempt to define "religious belief" in the military conscription law? If not, why not and how was the Court able to apply the conscientious objector provision to exonerate Welsh?
2. A precise definition of religion is not only difficult but also may not always be necessary, as Professor Durham argues in his reading. In the context of constitutional law and practice, with which both of the preceding readings are concerned, a precise definition may even be unconstitutional as an unwarranted intervention by courts. See James M. Donovan, *God Is as God Does: Law, Anthropology, and the Definition of Religion*, 6 Const. L.J. 25, 28 (1995) (citing, *inter alia*, Edward McGlynn Gaffney, *Governmental Definition of Religion: The Rise and Fall of the IRS Regulations on an "Integrated Auxiliary of a Church,"* 25 Val. U. L. Rev. 203, 222 (1991), and noting that "[t]he issue is how far a religious organization can stray from stereotypical religious activities before it attracts the attention of the IRS. Should the government be empowered to ascertain which activities of a body are religious, and which are not?" *Id.* at 28.

3. Many scholars have concluded that no acceptable definition of religion for U.S. constitutional purposes is possible. That is because the Supreme Court has been stymied by a paradox presented by the coexistence of the establishment of religion and free exercise clauses of the First Amendment to the Constitution. One might nevertheless expect the Court to assume the responsibility of defining religion – just as it ordinarily interprets all constitutional language – so as to identify those beliefs and practices for which their free exercise merits constitutional protection and that may not be established by governmental action. The problem is that by defining religion explicitly, the Court itself would risk violating the First Amendment by establishing religious parameters that are either too exclusive or too inclusive. Noting that a definition is a delicate question, the Court has simply concluded that the concept of ordered liberty cannot permit individuals to make their own standards to govern conduct in which society as a whole has important interests.
4. The U.S. Congress has shared the Supreme Court's caution. For example, the Civil Rights Act of 1964 provides as follows with respect to nondiscrimination in employment: "The term 'religion' includes all aspects of religious observance and practice, as well as belief, unless an employer demonstrates that he is unable to reasonably accommodate to an employee's or prospective employee's religious observance or practice without undue hardship on the conduct of the employer's business." 42 U.S.C. § 2000e(j). Is such a definition simply circular and therefore without meaning, or does it accomplish a legislative purpose? Congress also abandoned the quest for a definition of religion long ago when it amended military service legislation to strike an earlier premise for conscientious objector status on a "belief in relation to a Supreme Being."
5. Statutory and regulatory definitions of religion may vary with the legal context. For example, U.S. immigration law defines a "religious organization" with precision for purposes of visa issuance to members of such organizations. Accordingly, such an organization must itself be or be part of a "religious denomination" that the Department of Homeland Security and the State Department define as "a religious group or community of believers," indicia of which include some form of ecclesiastical government, a creed or statement of faith, some form of worship, a formal or informal code of doctrine and discipline, religious services and ceremonies, established places of worship, and religious congregations. Nontraditional denominations normally must provide more supporting documentation than well-established denominations. Is this definition culturally conditioned? Do you understand the need for a flexible but generally clear set of criteria, expressed as indicia, for determining eligibility to receive a visa for admission into a country? Do foreign fines and imprisonment of persons on the basis of their religious practices constitute "persecution" within the legally binding definition of a refugee? See *Cañas-Segovia v. INS*, 970 F.2d 599 (9th Cir. 1992) (foreign punishment of Jehovah's Witnesses for refusing to perform required military service does not constitute "persecution" within the conventional definition of a refugee).
6. Notice that, to avoid unnecessarily sensitive constitutional or other issues, the term "religion" is often used in conjunction with "belief" or other nontheistic expressions. This is an essentially cultural approach that has been criticized, however, particularly in a constitutional context. See, e.g., Phillip E. Johnson, *Concepts and Compromise in First Amendment Religious Doctrine*, 72 Cal. L. Rev. 817 (1984),

arguing, for example, that "[s]uch formulations make the category of 'religion' seem so all-inclusive that it is doubtful whether any system of beliefs that people treat as important can be excluded." Could a commitment to agnosticism or atheism constitute a religious practice? If not, could the U.S. government, thereby freed of any unconstitutional entanglement with religion, endorse atheism? See R. Kent Greenawalt, *Religion as a Concept in International Law*, 72 CAL. L. REV. 753 (1984).

7. Why is religion so difficult to define? The following readings may help answer that question by offering highly contrasting perspectives about the nature of religion. The notes and questions after these observations refocus attention on a broad consideration of the definitional problem beyond the U.S. Constitution and statutory contexts that we have just examined.

James M. Donovan, *God Is as God Does: Law, Anthropology, and the Definition of "Religion,"* 6 CONST. L.J. 23, 98 (1995)

Clearly, there is no definitive definition of religion. The bulk of jurists faced with the task of developing a definition of religion, favor the functional interpretation over simple performative and organizational criteria. Expecting a functional definition to be also generative, future opinions should be able to tie the psychological function of religion more meaningfully to performative and exterior indicators than has thus far been the case.

The social sciences and the field of law have independently co[n]verged toward some sort of functional understanding of religion, allowing both fields to rest more secure in their conclusions. Both, however, have had difficulty operationalizing this intellectual understanding of a psychological function into objective and reliable indicators.

Anthropology, however, seems better equipped to resolve this problem. By combining the tools of psychology, sociology and sociolinguistics, for example, anthropology can investigate both the objects of true belief, and the effects of that belief upon the individual and society. Law, on the other hand, has no such tools or methods to investigate these problems. Instead, law can only decide what research outcomes produced by others, such as anthropologists, will be appropriate for resolving legal issues.

The first step, then, is for the social sciences to study these questions further. The legal discipline will then have to evaluate the results, and decide how they might be applied to resolve legal problems. Continued communication between the two disciplines will allow lawyers to enjoy the benefits of others' research, and thereby resolve many of the law's conundrums.

JOHN STEINBECK, THE LOG FROM THE *SEA OF CORTEZ* 216–17 (Viking Press ed., 1962) (© 1941, 1951, and 1969 by John Steinbeck and Edward F. Ricketts, Jr. Used with permission of Viking Penguin, a division of Penguin Group (USA) Inc.)

[I]t seems apparent that species are only commas in a sentence, that each species is at once the point and the base of a pyramid, that all life is relational to the point where an Einsteinian relativity seems to emerge. And then not only the meaning but the feeling about species grows misty. One merges into another, groups melt into ecological groups until the time when what we know as life meets and enters what we think of as non-life: barnacle and rock, rock and earth, earth and tree, tree and rain and air. And the units nestle into the whole and are inseparable from it. Then one can come back to the microscope and the tide pool and the aquarium. But the little animals are found to be changed, no longer set apart and alone. And it is a strange thing that most of the feeling we call religious, most of the mystical outcrying which is one of the most prized and used and desired reactions of our species, is really the understanding that the attempt to say that man is related to the whole thing, related inextricably to all reality, known and unknowable. This is a simple thing to say, but the profound feeling of it made a Jesus, a St. Augustine, a St. Francis, a Roger Bacon, a Charles Darwin, and an Einstein. Each of them in his own tempo and with his own voice discovered and reaffirmed with astonishment the knowledge that all things are one thing and that one thing is all things – plankton, a shimmering phosphorescence on the sea and the spinning planets and an expanding universe, all bound together by the elastic string of time. It is advisable to look from the tide pool to the stars and then back to the tide pool again.

Shankar Vedantam, *Are Religious Experiences Just a Side Effect of Brain Chemistry?*, INT'L HERALD TRIB., June 18, 2001, at 1, 4 (© *The Washington Post.* All Rights Reserved)

Using power brain imaging technology, researchers are exploring what mystics call nirvana and what Christians describe as a state of grace. Scientists are asking whether spirituality can be explained in terms of neural networks, neurotransmitters and brain chemistry.

What creates that transcendental feeling of being one with the universe? It could be the decreased activity in the brain's parietal lobe, which helps regulate the sense of self and physical orientation, research suggests. How does religion prompt divine feelings of love and compassion? Possibly because of changes in the frontal lobe, caused by heightened concentration during meditation. Why do many people have a profound sense that religion has changed their lives? Perhaps because spiritual practices activate the temporal lobe, which weights experiences with personal significance. Some scientists readily say the research proves there is no such thing as God. But many others argue that they are religious themselves and that they are simply trying to understand how our minds produce a sense of spirituality. . . .

[One] experiment consisted of taking brain scans of Tibetan Buddhist meditators as they sat immersed in contemplation. After giving them time to sink into a deep meditative trance, he injected them with a radioactive dye. Patterns of the dye's residues in the brain were later converted into images. [The researcher] found that certain areas of the brain were altered during deep meditation. Predictably, these included areas in the front of the brain that are involved in concentration. But he also found decreased activity in the parietal lobe, one of the parts of the brain that helps orient a person in three-dimensional space. [According to the researcher,] "When people have spiritual experiences, they feel they become one with the universe and lose their sense of self," he said. "We think that may be because of what is happening in that area – if you block that area you lose that boundary between the self and the rest of the world. In doing so you ultimately wind up in a universal state."

. . .

Could the flash of wisdom that came over Siddhartha Gautama – the Buddha – have been nothing more than his parietal lobe quieting down? Could the voices that Moses and Mohammed heard on remote mountaintops have been just a bunch of neurons – an illusion? Could Jesus' conversations with God have been a mental delusion? Those who believe the new science disproves the existence of God say they are holding a mirror to society about the destructive power of religion. They say that religious wars, fanaticism and its tolerance spring from dogmatic beliefs.

"But religion is more than that," said John Haught, a professor of theology at Georgetown University in Washington. "It involves commitments and suffering and struggle – it's not all meditative bliss. It also involves moments when you feel abandoned by God." Belief and faith, believers argue, are larger than the sum of their brain parts. "The brain is the hardware through which religion is experienced," said Daniel Batson, a University of Kansas psychologist. "To say the brain produces religion is like saying a piano produces music."

Richard Madsen, *China's Confounding Religious Revival*, Current Hist., Sept. 2007, at 288–91 (reprinted with permission from *Current History Magazine*)

Until the death of Mao Zedong in 1976, the People's Republic of China suppressed – and, during the Cultural Revolution, violently persecuted – virtually all forms of religion. Most secular China scholars in the West as a result assumed that Chinese religion was dead. Thus, one of the biggest surprises of China's reform era (beginning in 1979) has been the resurgence of religious belief and practice. All across the country, old forms are being revived and new forms invented. These unexpected developments call into question not only our ability to understand China, but also many of the assumptions that social scientists hold about the secularization of the modern world.

Such confusion, however, is not really new. Chinese religion has confounded Western scholars for hundreds of years. In the late sixteenth century, the Jesuit missionary Matteo Ricci and his colleagues claimed that China had no religion. As Ricci saw it, the Chinese were guided by a very rich and profound moral philosophy derived from the teachings of

Confucius, and this philosophy was completely compatible with the best moral philosophy in Christian Europe. The Chinese did not worship any supernatural deities that would be incompatible with worship of the one true Christian God. They could thus accept Christianity without having to modify any aspect of their moral life.

But what was one to make, then, of the elaborate rituals that Chinese emperors carried out to worship heaven and to ensure that the world maintained its proper place within the cosmic order? Or the complicated funeral rituals that people at all levels of Chinese society undertook to send their deceased family members to another world and to maintain contact with them? Or the temples that dominated practically every kind of community? The Jesuits said that the rituals of the imperial cult were only expressions of moral aspiration; they were not really religious. Likewise, the life-cycle rituals of family life were simply an expression of admirable filial piety. The temple worship of the common people, on the other hand, was "superstition" – *mixin*, a term introduced into Chinese by the Jesuits. Such superstition was the product of ignorance, just as it was when it appeared among the common people in Europe, and it would steadily be eliminated through the teaching and guidance of China's enlightened leadership.

Rival missionaries, who argued that Chinese rites were indeed practices of an idolatrous religion, of course challenged the Jesuit claims. The resultant "rites controversy" ended in the early eighteenth century with a papal edict against the Jesuit position. In response, the Chinese emperor in 1724 declared Christianity to be a heterodox teaching.

At the root of this problem was a lack of fit between European categories for understanding religion, on the one hand, and Chinese realities, on the other. Because of this mismatch, there was no clear way for Western missionaries to determine whether Chinese rituals were religious or not. Since the resulting controversy within the Catholic church could not be resolved through reason, it could only be resolved through papal authority. The incommensurability of China with Western categories of thought thus led to bitter political infighting, not to fruitful debate.

Similar problems persist to this day, and are highlighted in the difficulties that scholars face when they try to comprehend Chinese ritual life through categories based on Western religious experience. One difference between our predicament and that of European Catholic missionaries and theologians at the time of the rites controversy is that analytic categories rooted in Western religious experience have now been transmitted to China and dominate the discourse of Chinese intellectuals as well. So not only do Western scholars have a difficult time understanding Chinese ritual life, but Chinese scholars have a hard time as well.

Lost in Translation

For Western scholars of religion, religion is usually defined in terms of beliefs in supernatural realities. Rituals are symbolic ways of expressing these beliefs. The beliefs and rituals are preserved, developed, and enacted through religious institutions. Modern scholars of religion have a somewhat different understanding of the relationship between religious institutions and society than did the Jesuits and their rivals in the sixteenth century. We usually place our analysis of religion against the backdrop of secularization. In present usage, the categories of religion and secularization grow out of a narrative of the modernization of Western societies over the past four centuries.

The narrative goes something like this: In the middle ages, European culture was dominated and unified by a common Christian faith and by a Catholic church that was in practice tightly intertwined with – although in theory potentially separate from – European politics and economics. The Protestant Reformation shattered the unity of the Catholic faith. The resulting intra-European warfare was brought to an end by political arrangements that "secularized" politics – that separated religion from politics, legitimated public life on the basis of reason rather than faith, and relegated religion to the sphere of private life. Modern European nation-states are based on common cultures, which are connected to a common European culture that at one time was based on Christianity and to some degree, for better or worse, still bears the marks of its Christian origins. But contemporary political life is based on secular rationality, though there are "fundamentalist" political forces that would like to once again impose Christian principles on public life.

This way of thinking about religion defines it in terms of individual, subjective belief. It makes clear distinctions between religion, on the one hand, and science, economics, and politics on the other. And it sees as problematic the attempt by people of faith to impose their private faith on public life. Scholars like José Casanova and Talal Asad have recently argued that this account of religion in Western cultural history is, in important respects, misleading. However, for many generations of scholars, these categories have worked reasonably well in making sense out of Western cultural history, and in my view this demonstrates a rough correspondence between these categories and Western historical realities.

Between these categories and Chinese cultural history, however, there is not even a rough correspondence. If we apply the concepts drawn from European historical experiences to the history of modern China, we get a mass of confusion and a host of anomalies. First of all, imperial China was full of "teachings" (*jiao*) and "rituals" (*ji*), but these do not correspond to what Westerners have come to call "religion." As Kristofer Schipper has put it, "The very notion of religion as we define it in the West is an obstacle [to understanding Chinese society], and a great number of observers have fallen into the trap of failing to see that in a society so dissimilar from ours the religious system must also be very different."

For one thing, the various Chinese teachings (whether derived from Confucian, Taoist, or Buddhist texts) were not simply a matter of subjective belief. They consisted of stories, discourses, and practices that formed a comprehensive framework for understanding the nature of social relations and the proper ways to live a good life. They did not concern "supernatural" matters, supposedly separate from material life. They sometimes explained parts of ordinary life visible to the senses by reference to forces invisible to ordinary observation, but this is not different in principle (though it is different in substance) from how modern science explains empirical phenomena. For example, teachings in the Taoist tradition held that everything was made up of a primordial matter/energy called *qi* – including dead people, who continued to exist in an invisible form. Included among the still-existent dead were the *shen* that in Western tradition are called "gods." The *jiao* that we translate as "teachings" produced a kind of "knowledge" that lumped together and did not differentiate among what we would call scientific, moral, and religious learning.

The teachings during imperial times were intertwined with a rich and varied array of rituals, the meaning of which was only partly explained by the teachings. But the rituals were not segregated into specifically religious institutions. The great state rituals were an integral part of imperial politics. Community festivals, centered on local temples, combined commerce and local politics with enactment of legends and imprecations of the gods – so much so that it is almost impossible to tell where one begins and the other ends. Family rituals, such as funerals, were expressions of status, wealth, and power as well as expressions of belief in a world beyond the present. And the rebellious activities of "heterodox" sects were motivated as much by economic and social discontent as by heterodox teachings (*xiejiao*).

Losing Their Religion

Not only did the realities of "traditional" Chinese teachings fail to fit into Western categories for thinking about religion, but the history of China's passage to modernity fails to match the Western narrative of secularization. At the beginning of the twentieth century, for example, Chinese modernizing reforms did not seek to banish religion to the private sphere but actually "discovered" within their tradition new religious bases for public life. Thus, in 1906 the emperor elevated worship of Confucius to the level of a Grand Sacrifice at the imperial court. (Before this, Confucian sacrifice was only a Middle Sacrifice. The Grand Sacrifices were reserved for worshiping heaven and earth and the imperial ancestors.) Around the same time, rituals for worshiping Confucius were made part of newly reformed government schools. Immediately after the 1911 revolution, Chinese leaders began to create new nationwide Taoist, Buddhist, Confucian, and Muslim associations organized along the model of Christian denominations in the West.

. . .

The Sociology of Cults

During the ongoing reform era, which began in 1979, the problem has been further complicated by the adoption of categories from Western European social science. For example, the practice of physical, moral, and spiritual exercise known as *qigong* was encouraged during the Maoist era because it was seen as a kind of science based on the traditional wisdom of the masses. It was promoted and developed, along with traditional Chinese medicine, as part of a policy to combine Western and Chinese technologies. It continued to be promoted as such in the 1980s and early 1990s.

But then certain aspects of *qigong* came to be seen as incompatible with modern science and therefore religious or superstitious. When the Falun Gong and some similar *qigong* movements began to engage in activities that appeared to the government to threaten social stability (notably when Falun Gong mobilized 10,000 protesters in front of the Communist Party's leadership compound in April 1999), these movements were defined as purveyors of heterodox teaching, and the state launched a fierce campaign to exterminate them. (Although the Falun Gong has gone underground in China – it is hard to tell how much strength it has left there – it remains active worldwide and carries out vigorous protests against China from international safe havens.)

This term "heterodox teaching" (*xiejiao*) was commonly cited during the imperial era but had not been widely used in the twentieth century. By the year 2000 it had become defined in terms of the Western sociology of "cults." Although "cult" is now given a universal definition, so as to encompass groups like the Branch Davidians in the United States and Aum Shinrikyo in Japan, the sociological term "cult" bears the marks of the Christian background of the Western sociologists who first used it. The term "cult" in Western sociology usually refers to religious groups that are far removed from the dominant religion of a given society. In the United States, for example, cults are new religious groups that do not base their teachings on commonly recognized interpretations of the Hebrew or Christian Bible. In China, on the other hand, *qigong* groups – even innovative ones like the Falun Gong – are drawn from powerful currents of Chinese tradition. So the term "cult" does not seem to capture the realities of their practices. This lack of fit makes it difficult for Westerners concerned about religious freedom to fully accept Chinese government claims that the Falun Gong needed to be suppressed. . . .

Seval Yildirim, *Expanding Secularism's Scope: An Indian Case Study*, 52 Am. J. Comp. L. 901, 910–12 (2004)

Articles 25 through 28 [of the Constitution of India] describe the right to freedom of religion. Article 25 grants all persons the "freedom of conscience and the right freely to profess, practice and propagate religion." This right, however, is not without limitation and is "[s]ubject to public order, morality and health and to the other provisions." Section 2 of Article 25 gives the State the right to regulate or restrict "any economic, financial, political or other secular activity which may be associated with religious practice."

. . .

Although the Constitution does not define what is meant by the word "religion," the Supreme Court of India has expressed divergent views on the meaning of religion. In cases such as Commissioner of Hindu Religious Endowments v. Sri Lakshimdra Thirtha Swamiar, the Supreme Court took an inclusive approach to religion:

> Religion is certainly a matter of faith with individuals or communities and it is not necessarily theistic. . . . A religion may not only lay down a code of ethical rules for its followers to accept, it might prescribe rituals and observances, ceremonies and modes of worship which are regarded as integral parts of religion, and these forms and observances might extend even to matters of food and dress.

On the other hand, some Supreme Court cases have taken a narrower view of religion. For instance in *S.P. Mittal v. Union of India*, the Supreme Court took a restricted view of religion and held that Sir Aurobindo's teachings were a philosophy, not a religion, despite his followers' belief that it was a religion.

. . .

The *Quareshi* cow-slaughter case put to test what practices are essential to a religion. The *Quareshi* case involved a legal challenge by Muslim butchers to state legislation prohibiting the slaughter of cows. The state legislation was partly motivated by the strong religious sentiment of Hindus against the slaughter of cows because the cow is a sacred animal in Hinduism. The Muslim butchers, on the other hand, argued that their inability to continue their practice of sacrificing a cow on Bakr Id Day interfered with their religious beliefs. The Supreme Court held that the state law banning cow slaughter did not violate the religious rights of Muslims. The Court reasoned that the Quran did not mandate the sacrificing of cows and that there were economic (and therefore, secular) reasons for the legislation. In a subsequent case, the Supreme Court emphasized that the religious practices included in the freedom of religion are those which are "essential."

NOTES AND QUESTIONS

1. In the *Quareshi* case in the reading on Indian constitutional provisions and practices, the Supreme Court of India found that the Quran (Koran) of Islam did not require slaughtering of cows. That conclusion may have been correct, but by way of comparison, would an American or Canadian court have been able to reach a similar determination? If not, are there cultural explanations for the different competences of the courts? (We return shortly and more precisely to the topic of religious freedom and establishment.)
2. The reading by Richard Madsen goes on to describe the issues related to the practice of religion in China. The article concludes as follows:

   > In fact, revivals of all forms of religion pose difficult challenges for the Chinese government. It does not have an adequate system for understanding and categorizing the many subtle and complex forms of religiosity that are

intertwined with modern Chinese society. Begrudgingly accepting the fact that religion (whatever it is) is not quickly going to go away, government officials have developed a clumsy one-size-fits-all policy for co-opting and controlling it.

The policy seems to satisfy almost no one. It offers enough religious freedom to stimulate demand for religious practices, but it imposes enough restrictions to make satisfying the demand fully in a legitimate way impossible. Hence the proliferation of extralegal forms of religion – with often only an arbitrary and constantly shifting line separating legitimate from illegitimate religious activity. The government at times tolerates such activities (sometimes simply because officials are lazy or are paid bribes), but then, as in the case of the "evil cult" Falun Gong, it lashes out in overreaction. Yet heavy-handed suppression often creates religious martyrs, which makes some believers even more defiant.

Since the resurgence of religion is caused at least in part by a collapse in the credibility of the government's official Marxist ideology, the Communist Party is trying to fashion more effective ideological substitutes for religion. One strategy is to better formulate and explain Marxism. Another – which has been gaining some support lately – is to propagate a state-sponsored Confucianism, shorn of any mystical or metaphysical elements, as a distinctively Chinese version of moral order. It is hard to predict how far either of these strategies will go.

Almost by definition, religion is the aspect of society that most eludes rational control. When it interacts with such factors as ethnicity or when it inflames long-repressed memories of oppression, its effects become even harder to predict and control. Moreover, in an era of globalization, the Chinese government's attempts to grapple with religion expose it to international sanctions – which themselves are unpredictable, because it is difficult for foreign governments to understand Chinese religion and difficult to make sense of the Chinese government's response to it.

Id. at 295.

After considering all of the material thus far in this chapter, how would you advise the Chinese government on a more stable and globally acceptable approach to regulating (and possibly registering) religious associations? Might you be handicapped by your own cultural mindset, whether Chinese or non-Chinese?

3. Do forms of Australian and Native American/First Nation totemism that are based on the essence of carved and other images rather than on a belief in God constitute religion? The great pioneer in sociology Émile Durkheim argued in his masterpiece THE ELEMENTARY FORMS OF RELIGIOUS LIFE (1912) that such totemism is religion. He did so by dividing experience into two, diametrically opposed categories: the sacred and the profane. On that basis, Durkheim classified totemism as sacred on the basis of the shared sense of oneness or togetherness that a totemic image generates within a community. Durkheim went further in developing the sacred-profane distinction by equating God, in a theistic culture, with society itself, whereby individuals in such a culture are aware of society as an acceptable impersonal force surrounding them. Social ties and a sense of community are everything. Religion

therefore makes no sense without the personalization of society in the form of a cosmic deity. It is therefore easy to see how Durkheim's theory underpins the entire program of social action and communitarianism that is so characteristic of contemporary Western religious life.

4. Whether or not one agrees with Émile Durkheim's theoretical construct, it is a powerful reminder of what many perceive as a need at the international level to develop a working definition of religion that is as globally acceptable as possible. Any definition of religion is apt to be inadequate and culturally biased, but analysis of the role of religion in the international legal system requires some basis for distinguishing it from other belief systems, especially ideologies. To do so, it is necessary to take off any constitutional and other national cultural blinders. Instead, the need is apparent to seek, if not to find, a common definition of religion in the interest of global human rights and a more stable cultural environment for reconciling religious differences with the imperatives of world order. As Professor Durham noted in an earlier reading, for example, Article 18 of the International Covenant on Civil and Political Rights, to which we return later in this chapter, establishes a right to profess any religion or belief as well as the right not to do so. As we have seen, intolerance and religious zealotry present formidable barriers to the effective implementation of these rights. But the implementation of these rights has also been handicapped at intercultural and international levels by the fundamental problem of determining what constitutes a religious practice. To be sure, any attempt to convert something as personal and culturally conditioned as religion into a legal term has proved frustrating at best and perhaps unnecessary. Still, the process itself of seeking a common understanding of what we mean by "religion" is worthwhile. A significant benefit of conducting constructive dialogue within the established legal framework is educational – that is, simply to increase professional and public awareness of divergent perspectives as a predicate of tolerance and collaboration.
5. Ultimately, any attempt to define religion may run up against the fact that, at least in modern societies, religion is personal, whatever one's views of religion or religious views.[1] At the international level, as at the domestic level, the diversity and controversial nature of religious belief have further complicated the search for a definition. The famous psychologist William James grappled with this problem to the following conclusion: "The warring gods and formulas of the various religions do indeed cancel each other," he wrote.

> But there is a certain uniform deliverance in which religions all appear to meet, [based on] an uneasiness . . . that there is *something wrong about us* as we naturally stand [the solution to which] is a sense that *we are saved from the wrongness* by making proper connection with the higher powers.

Although this generalization may be historically and culturally biased, and perhaps is most properly viewed in the historical context of the late nineteenth and early twentieth centuries, it nevertheless seems to crystallize a shared feeling and concern,

[1] Notes 5, 6, 7, and 8, together with the commentary in Section C on functions of religion in the international legal system, draw on observations in James A.R. Nafziger, *The Functions of Religion in the International System, in* Religion and International Law (Mark W. Janis & Carolyn Evans eds., 1999). Further commentary, explanations, and examples are found in this source.

even anxiety, about the human condition. In pragmatic terms, according to James, the positive experience of deliverance from that anxiety helps verify religious belief.

James concludes that shared religious experience demonstrates "that we can experience union with *something* larger than ourselves and in that union find our greatest peace. . . . All that the facts require is that the power should be both other and larger than our conscience selves." What is that "other and larger"? James responds that each person's experience brings an answer. Thus, religion is "the feelings, acts, and experiences of individual men in their solitude, so far as they apprehend themselves to stand in relation to whatever they may consider the divine." This sense of individual inadequacy or anxiety and consequent need for connection with something greater than the self as an explanation for religious practice was reflected more parochially and radically in Judge Augustus Hand's famous opinion in *United States v. Kauten.*[2] Recognizing that religion "is incapable of compression into a few words," he nevertheless wrote that religious belief

> arises from a sense of the inadequacy of reason as a means of relating the individual to his fellow-men and to his universe. . . . It is a belief finding expression in a conscience which categorically requires the believer to disregard elementary self-interest and to accept martyrdom in preference to transgressing its tenets.[3]

Martyrdom would seem to be an excessive, if not objectionable, element in any attempt today to define religious belief.[4] Judge Hand's reference to martyrdom nevertheless reminds us that in today's world religious militancy and sacrifice transcend cultures and confound politics. The global community has become all too familiar with zealotry. We may be inclined to dismiss the urge toward martyrdom among Muslims, Sikhs, and others as "fundamentalist" aberrations, but this phenomenon is too widespread in current events to be taken lightly. Fundamentalism varies widely among religious cultures throughout the world. Because fundamentalism is not monolithic, the global order might best respond in the face of its militant forms with open-mindedness and imagination.

6. The dynamics of existence and anxiety also troubled the eminent theologian Paul Tillich. He defined religion as "the state of being concerned about one's own being and being universally . . . the state of being grasped by an infinite concern." Paul Tillich, *The Lost Dimension of Religion, in* ADVENTURES OF THE MIND (Richard Thruelsen & John Koblen eds., 1959). For Tillich, infinite or "ultimate" concerns define religious experience as follows:

> Being religious means asking passionately the question of the meaning of our existence and being willing to receive answers, even if answers hurt. Such an idea of religion makes religion universally human, but it certainly differs from what is usually called religion. It does not describe religion as the belief in the

[2] *United States v. Kauten*, 133 F.2d 703 (2d Cir. 1943).

[3] *Id.* at 708.

[4] *Kauten* was, after all, a wartime case involving an appeal of a criminal conviction against a conscientious objector.

> existence of gods or one God, and as a set of activities and institutions for the sake of relating oneself to these beings in thought, devotion and obedience. No one can deny that the religions which have appeared in history are religious in this sense. Nevertheless, religion in its innermost nature is more than religion in this narrower sense.

The "dimension of depth," according to Tillich, is "the distinctively religious dimension in man's nature." Tillich has been criticized, however, for inadequately distinguishing more or less "traditional" religion from nontraditional, functional equivalents of belief, ideology, and practice.

The teachings of another theologian, Joachim Wach, help elaborate a more precise definition. Wach described the parameters of religion as a holy or sacred experience that is expressed in thought (a theoretical dimension), action (a practical dimension), and fellowship (a social dimension).

7. Shankar Vedantam's commentary suggests that spirituality may be the product of neural networks, neurotransmitters, and brain chemistry. Another scientific explanation is based on evolutionary theory, as follows:

> Religion has the hallmarks of an evolved behavior, meaning that it exists because it was favored by natural selection. It is universal because it was wired into our neural circuitry before the ancestral human population dispersed from its African homeland.
>
> . . .
>
> What evolution has done is to endow people with a genetic predisposition to learn the religion of their community, just as they are predisposed to learn its language. With both religion and language, it is culture, not genetics, that then supplies the content of what is learned.

Nicholas Wade, *The Evolution of the God Gene*, N.Y. Times, Nov. 15, 2009, at Wk 3.

Do you agree? What scientific evidence would be relevant or even persuasive if it were available?

8. Taking account of these reflections, one working definition of the term "religion" is "the practice of ultimate concern about our nature and obligations as human beings, inspired by experience and typically expressed by members of a group or community sharing myths and doctrines whose authority transcends both individual conscience and the state." Such a broad definition of religion would be consistent with many of the main currents of twentieth-century theology hinted at previously, as well as that proposed by the special rapporteur for the UN Sub-Commission on Prevention of Discrimination and Protection of Minorities.

Of course, the suggested definition, as a sort of least common denominator to facilitate discourse, could be interpreted away or at least interpreted so broadly as to embrace Marxism, fascism, liberal democracy, the hidden hand of free enterprise, witch cults, fortune-telling, or any other belief systems based on *a priori* historical or natural forces that are supposed to transcend human control. The suggested definition can be interpreted also to include any ethical or moral code. Institutions devoted to specific principles or public values, such as economic justice, the inherent dignity of the individual, or the essential equality among human beings – which may be religiously based but not necessarily themselves religious in a traditional sense – might also fall within the scope of such a definition.

The suggested definition is intended, however, to focus attention on the most readily accepted systems of belief – transcendental partisan ideologies (often but not always institutionalized or at least ritualized) – such as Buddhism, Taoism, Shintoism, religious forms of Confucianism, Animism, Islam, Judaism, and Christianity.

9. There is no acceptable definition of religion under the UN Declaration on the Elimination of all Forms of Intolerance and of Discrimination Based on Religion or Belief or other international instruments. It was thought not only that any comprehensive definition in the Declaration would run the risk, paradoxically, of encouraging intolerance by including either too much or too little within the scope of its protection but also that it might establish a kind of orthodoxy contrary to religious freedom. Also, compliance with the Declaration and mutual enforcement of it by states might degenerate into just a harmful game of words. The *travaux préparatoires* of the Declaration, however, do indicate consensus that it embraces "theistic, non-theistic and atheistic belief and some understanding that belief systems which are fundamentally political, philosophical, historical, scientific, or aesthetic should be excluded, but no real definition emerged during drafting sessions. Within the Commission on Human Rights, a special rapporteur of the Sub-Commission on Prevention of Discrimination and Protection of Minorities issued a report that suggested a working definition of religion as follows: "an explanation of the meaning of life and how to live accordingly." Every religion has at least a creed, a code of action and a cult."
10. What is your own thinking in general about the need for a definition of religion and, if so, its content? Do you agree or not on the need, in some transnational legal contexts, for a definition of religion? If you agree, does your concept of the nature of religion shape your own working definition? If, however, you conclude that a working definition is impossible, isn't it nevertheless true that one of the lawyer's main tasks is to articulate and apply acceptable definitions when they can be of practical value in addressing and resolving issues? Do any of the definitions discussed herein appeal to you?
11. In struggling to define the elusive term "religion," which may seem to be all things to all people, we may be consoled by recalling both the frustrations and the rewards of trying to establish a universally acceptable definition of law itself.

C. Functions of Religion in the International System

Religious inspiration and religious institutions in today's world perform at least five positive functions in the international legal system: creative, aspirational, didactic, custodial, and mediative. They can, and sometimes do, promote global order, just as religious animosity so frequently and dramatically seems to disrupt it. In a later section, we return to the theme of religion's contributions to global disorder. Here, however, we note a few examples of the principal positive functions of religion in the international system.

1. Creative

a. Institutions

Religious institutions and doctrine have helped shape and develop modern international law. Certain denominations – for example, the Society of Friends (Quakers), the Brethren in Christ (Mennonites), the Church of the Brethren, the United Society of Believers in Christ's Second Appearing (Shakers), and Bahaism – have accorded a central role to peace and the development of global order since their establishment. The Quakers, in particular, were instrumental in the establishment of the modern peace movement, as were other Protestants such as the founding members and leaders of David L. Dodge's Christian Friendly Society (1808), Dodge's New York Peace Society (1815), and William Ladd's American Peace Society (1828). The Bahai, who have ironically borne the brunt of religious persecution in Asia, maintain that "[n]o serious attempt to achieve world peace can ignore religion." Many other denominations and ecumenical institutions, such as the World Council of Churches, influenced by third-world churches, actively pursue programs for the progressive development and implementation of international law. Witness the strong role played by the Vatican and Holy See through papal pronouncements and diplomacy regarding the use of force, the educational program of the United Methodist Church during the Third Conference of the United Nations on the Law of the Sea, and the Church of England's role in response to colonialism and racism.

b. Doctrine

The eighth-century Islamic scholar Shaybani derived the principle of *pacta sunt servanda*, as well as certain rules of war and postliminy, from religious doctrine. Later, the Jesuit missionaries Francisco de Vitoria, Francisco Suárez, and other initiators engraved the principle of *pacta sunt servanda* in the cornerstone of the international legal system. In doing so, they drew less on Roman law than on church thinking. Bartolus de Sassoferrato and other commentators of the fourteenth and fifteenth centuries had introduced what common lawyers would call the equitable remedies of the ecclesiastical courts, including the enforceability of contracts that were *nuda pacta* under the Roman law. The initiators or innovators of modern international law borrowed the expansive canon law maxim of *pacta sunt servanda.*

Lex talionis – the eye for an eye of the Babylonian and Mosaic codes – is reflected in the modern law of counterforce. Rules of reprisal and retorsion, as well as the requirement of proportionality in applying them, are thus rooted in biblical prescription. As early as 634 CE, Caliph Abu Bakr established rules of humanitarian warfare based on religious prescription to govern the conduct of his Islamic army against Syrian Christians.

Religious thinking, rooted in both religious and secular concepts of natural law, has also encouraged the growth of human rights law. Although the concept of inherent rights possessed by each and every human being is essentially the secular product of the Enlightenment rather than of religion, it must be seen against the backdrop of the Protestant Reformation and its reliance on individual conscience. Indeed, the story is even older. Although the vocabulary may have changed from Scripture to strictly secular declarations and conventions, the religious impulses are ancient and widespread. Most major religious traditions can lay legitimate claim to having fathered human rights law.

Whatever the parentage, modern religion has helped mature the growth of human rights law. The records indicate that in drafting and redrafting the Universal Declaration of Human Rights, leaders of the Commission on Human Rights invoked religious-ethical thinking. For example, in the 1940s, Vice Chair P. C. Chang of China cited the teachings of Confucius, Rapporteur Charles Malik of Lebanon quoted St. Thomas Aquinas, and Monsignor Roncalli (later Pope John XXIII) assisted René Cassin and Eleanor Roosevelt in drafting the Declaration.

2. Aspirational

Religious thinking has helped orient international law to the emerging needs of humankind by strengthening its aspirational or precatory content, which may also be considered an expression of ethics. It has helped counter the tendency of Austinian positivism and extreme versions of legal realism to equate law with power politics. It therefore helps ensure that international law is more than a mere reflection of power politics or a crystallization of custom. Often, religious thinking incorporated into the law has encouraged a progressive, moral development of international relations.

Ordinarily, aspirational or precatory language in international instruments is given short shrift. It seems soft. It is compromising, not forthright, and demanding. Often, however, such language is not only the best that can be expected to address important issues in a contentious world but also, in the long run, an effective means to entice states and other international actors gradually to take on binding obligations. The visibility and growing effectiveness of the more or less aspirational provisions of the International Covenant on Economic, Social and Cultural Rights are an example. Aspirational language introduced by religious doctrine has helped shape not only humanitarian law but other areas of international law as well. For example, qualifications on the freedom of states to exclude aliens have their roots in early and modern theology, as does the principle of good-neighborliness in environmental law.

3. Didactic

Religious institutions sometimes help socialize the public in international principles and law. For example, in his encyclical *Pacem in terris*, Pope John XXIII identified the Universal Declaration of Human Rights as a central tenet of Catholic dogma; Pope Paul VI continued to emphasize human rights; and Pope John Paul II reaffirmed the central role of the Declaration in his encyclical *Solicitudo rei socialis* and in repeated invocations of international human rights law by him and Benedict XVI. Jewish and Protestant support for human rights has also been significant. For example, one publication of the World Council of Churches describes the Universal Declaration of Human Rights as a modern version of the Ten Commandments because it presents "an easily understood standard of conduct whose respect alone already constituted in large part fulfillment." Mounting support for human rights law by some forms of Islam has been particularly significant, for the move not only represents a willingness to accept an ecumenical axiology but also redefines fundamental social values to an extent.

4. Custodial

Bishop Desmond Tutu's unceasing efforts in South Africa to vindicate ethical and human rights prescriptions in the long battle against apartheid is an example of the custodial function of religion in the international legal system. Another example is the role of religious institutions as guardians of conscience in protecting refugees from inhumane expulsion by states. Religious institutions also perform a custodial function by more directly implementing international law. Examples include the important role they play in processing and advocating immigration applications, in resettling refugees, and in undertaking and coordinating disaster relief. Conversely, and unfortunately, the lack of an explicitly religious foundation for a particular rule or principle of international law may deter institutional support for it. Saudi Arabia abstained from voting in favor of the Universal Declaration of Human Rights because it does not explicitly acknowledge God as the source of all rights.

5. Mediative

Religious institutions may play a mediative function in keeping the peace and maintaining global order. They can, first of all, offer their good offices to bring disputing parties together or more directly mediate disputes. In 1965 the Papal Nuncio in Santo Domingo arranged a cease-fire to end strife in the Dominican Republic that had become internationally complicated. Pope John Paul II successfully resolved the Beagle Channel territorial imbroglio between Argentina and Chile.[5] A distant mirror of the Beagle Channel mediation was Pope Alexander VI's mediating bull, issued in 1493, which divided the non-Christian world into Spanish and Portuguese zones of influence; the bull was codified with modifications as the Treaty of Tordesillas (1494). Nearly five hundred years later, the Vatican's temporary protection of deposed President Manuel Antonio Noriega in Panama and its advice to him served to mediate between his personal interests as a former head of state (and alleged drug runner wanted on narcotics charges in the United States) and the political realities that foreclosed a legalistic response to Noriega's quest for asylum.

6. Summary

It appears that, roughly speaking, these five general functions of religion in the international legal system have been effective and active in approximately the order in which they have been presented here. Certainly, religion has had a profound influence in the creation of international law, but for the most part, it has had only a limited role in mediating conflict.

[5] *See* M.C. Mirow, *International Law and Religion in Latin America: The Beagle Channel Dispute*, 28 Suffolk Transnat'l L. Rev. 1 (2004) (noting that "[t]he Church's main goal in intervention and mediation was the preservation of peace between countries claiming a common faith. Making peace is central to the religious mission of the Church. Beyond reaching a peaceful solution, the Church may have had other things to gain by successful mediation. A successful resolution would have greatly increased the international stature of both the Vatican and the new Pope, John Paul II. During the time of the dispute in the region, the Church's social conscience had been brought under close scrutiny by the rise of liberation theology. By maintaining peace between the countries and asserting its position against military governments of questionable validity, the Church expanded its activities in the region. The Church's actions may have even risen to the level of institutional atonement to these countries' poor who suffered most under Argentina and Chile's purges of communists and dissidents."). [In 1991 Oregon made the religious use of peyote defensible. Or. Rev. Stat. § 475.992 (2007). – *Eds.*]

D. Governmental Establishment of Religion

In Section E, we focus on the issues related to freedom of religion and freedom from religion. In this section, we consider several examples of religious establishment – that is, the formal identity between religion and the state in some legal systems – constraints on establishment, and views about it.

Dinah Shelton & Alexandre Kiss, *A Draft Model Law on Freedom of Religion with Commentary, in* Religious Human Rights in Global Perspective 572 (Johan van der Vyver & J. Witte eds., 1996) (reprinted with permission of Martinus Nijhoff)

The constitutions of some states establish the primacy of a religion over the state, granting privileges that are incompatible with religious liberty and non-discrimination. Even in states with excellent human rights records, links between religion and state pose problems. In Norway, the king and a majority of the cabinet are required to be members of the state church. Christianity is still a mandatory subject in the Norwegian public schools. Nonconformists have been permitted to teach it since 1969 as long as they do so in accordance with evangelical Lutheran doctrine. Only in 1964 was the constitution amended to guarantee all inhabitants the free exercise of religion. A 1969 Law Concerning Religious Denominations extends the right to form denominations and stipulates that groups registered with the Department of Justice may receive financial aid from both the national and municipal governments on the same basis as parishes of the state church in proportion to their membership statistics. The majority remains opposed to disestablishment of the state church. It is seen as "a public institution in which membership does not require a commitment of faith and which presently has approximately equal number of atheists and 'personal Christians' on its rolls."

In England, the Anglican Church remains at the center of public policy and has substantial support from the state. Prime ministers appoint bishops and the House of Lords contains 26 Anglican bishops who are the lords spiritual. The Parliament can rule on doctrinal and liturgical matters – most recently on the issue of ordination of women. Although there may be little real intervention in the internal affairs of the church, its strongly privileged position can be seen to discriminate against minority religions.

State budgets provide for some religious denominations in Spain, Italy, Greece, Belgium, and Luxembourg. Religious taxes exist in Austria, Switzerland, Denmark, Germany, Norway, and Finland. Indirect support is provided in France, Great Britain, the Netherlands, and Sweden.

Established religions exist in all parts of the world. In Africa, the constitutions of the Comor[o]s, Mauritania, Libya, and Somalia proclaim Islam as the religion of the state. Libya also declares that "the Holy Koran is the constitution of the Socialist People's Libyan Arab Jamahiriya." In the Sudan, all legislation must conform to Islamic prescriptions. The head of state must be a Muslim, and non-Muslims are incompetent to testify against

Muslims. Propagation of heretical beliefs is a crime. Similar justifications are put forward by other states that ban specific religions. In Pakistan, the Ahmadis are prevented by law from calling themselves Muslims and using Muslim practices in worship or in the public manifestations of their faith.

Both bans and restrictions may be imposed when the state is viewed as the beneficiary or object of religious liberty. The Saudi Arabian government states "[o]ur view is that freedom of religion (which is a basic issue in the Universal Declaration of Human Rights) has double edges: (a) The freedom *of any country* to adhere to, protect and preserve its religion. (b) The respect and tolerance towards religious minorities of the country's citizens as long as they respect the constitutional tenets of their country."

. . .

In contrast, the constitution of Botswana specifically recognizes the individual's right to propagate his religion. Proselytizing or converting others is permissible.

Subordination of religion to the state can have pernicious effects on religious liberty equal to those in states where the government is subordinate to religion. Revolutionary governments sometimes repress religious activities, providing that no one may invoke religious liberty "to hinder the state in its work of establishing the socialist order."

Some states limit the political activities of clergy or religious officials, on the pretext of maintaining the separation of religion and state. Such exclusionary laws have sometimes placed legislatures or courts in the position of deciding who constitutes "clergy" or officials of religion.

Mexico's constitution contains some of the more restrictive provisions. Its articles provide that no minister of any faith may be a candidate for elected office. Article 130 provides that ministers cannot form associations for political purposes or rally in favor of or against any candidate, political party or association. Neither can they oppose the laws of the country or its institutions, or attack in any way the patriotic symbols in their public meetings, religious ceremonies, religious propaganda or publications. It is strictly forbidden to establish any kind of political associations. It is also forbidden to hold political meetings in the churches.

Alan Wolfe, *And the Winner Is . . .*, Atlantic Monthly, Mar. 2008, at 56, 60–61

Religious monopolies or near-monopolies, such as state-sponsored churches, generally throttle religious practice over time, especially as a country becomes wealthier; the European experience amply demonstrates this. Lacking any incentive to innovate, churches atrophy, and their congregations dwindle. But places with a free religious marketplace witness something very different: entrepreneurs of the spirit compete to save souls, honing their messages and modulating many of their beliefs so as to appeal to the consumer. With more options to choose from, more consumers find something they like, and the ranks of the religious grow.

The key precondition for this sort of marketplace is the presence of rudimentary secular views. This may sound odd, since the secular has been thought the opposite of the religious; the First Amendment to the U.S. Constitution, the 1905 French law establishing *laïcité*, or the removal of religion from public affairs, and the creation of modern Turkey were once seen as the replacement of religious orthodoxy by Enlightenment principles. Secularism is still commonly understood in this way: a secular society is viewed as one with large numbers of freethinkers choosing science over superstition and reason over revelation.

But secularism is not the opposite of belief; nonbelief is. Indeed, secularism has religious, specifically Christian, roots; it renders unto Caesar what is Caesar's, while leaving to God what properly belongs in his realm. John Locke argued as much in *A Letter Concerning Toleration*, first published in 1689: genuine salvation, he wrote, can never be achieved through governmental coercion. In contemporary societies influenced by Lockean ideals, then, religion's priority of belief and secularism's commitment to individual rights are not in opposition; rather, they complement each other. It was once thought that the First Amendment was written to protect public life from the depredations of religious orthodoxy. It is now commonly accepted that the Founders also separated church and state in order to protect religion from government.

Remarks of Moshe Halbertal, *in* Religion and State 12–14 (Harvard Law School Human Rights Program, 2004)

My introductory comments concern the similarities and differences between Western conceptions of establishment and those that emerge from Islam and Judaism. I will focus primarily on Jewish conceptions, though they are relevant in many ways to Islam as well. And I speak more broadly about religion and "politics," rather than simply religion and the state.

In any discussion of religion and politics, we need to consider the nature of the religion or religions that must be accommodated. The American conception of religion is deeply supported by Protestant assumptions about religion, one of the principal features of which is voluntariness: for a religious act to have any meaning it must be done freely, out of conscious choice. So freedom itself – this great legal idea – is actually a condition for genuine religion. Tolerance follows. Another assumption of the American – perhaps also the larger Western – conception of religion is that the realm of intense religious experience is private. Religion is a matter of the spirit, of inwardness.

These two ideas, voluntariness and inwardness, help to shape a certain conception of separation and guide the debate over establishment of religion. The state guarantees a certain kind of freedom to enable genuine religious moments. Freedom does not contradict religion. Rather, it is separation of the private from the public, the creation and maintenance of a neutral public space – the very neutrality of the state vis-à-vis any form of religion or religious expression – that is a condition for the flourishing of this type of religious sensibility.

This is a very particular attitude and it permeates the relationship between religion and the state in America. For Judaism and Islam, I think both underlying assumptions are deeply questioned. As a result, we need a more complex model to understand the relationship of "establishment" to religion. Consider first the issue of voluntarism. In the United States, education is intended to produce a chooser who can make the voluntaristic act that renders religion meaningful. This is alien to both Islam and Judaism, which see education as the reproduction of a certain tradition, of a certain conscience. Your identity is prior to any choice. To say that a religiously-coerced act is empty of meaning may be a very straightforward Protestant statement, but it is complicated in the Jewish and Islamic traditions. These are very historically-oriented religions; they have very high stakes in politics. In the Jewish faith, for example, there is an eschatology of political salvation; redemption is not a matter of the individual overcoming sin so much, but a dramatic change in the very political structure. I don't think either Judaism or Islam permits privatization in a simple way.

Another aspect of this theme is that both religions are law-oriented religions. For them, a very important part of religion consists in setting norms and applying them to human activity; restructuring human behavior. As law-oriented religions, they seek to be manifested in the public sphere. Religious ideas and religious vision infuse political debate and affect the conduct of the community as a whole.

There is also the question of the demarcation between public and private spheres. It is not enough for the state to remain neutral vis-à-vis religious faiths that require their own public space. The issue raises complicated questions of community rights versus individual rights. Jerusalem provides excellent examples. It is at once the most international city in the world and the least cosmopolitan, separated into balkanized groups with little willful interaction. There is also the problem of the Sabbath, which is not perceived by religious Jews to be a private matter. People want to have a public *Shabbat* experience, which they see as a fulfillment of their religious expression, rather than simply a right to observe *Shabbat* in a public space. There is the issue of sexuality, which leads to a clash between secular ideas of eroticism and religious conceptions of modesty.

Here we are addressing the issues of how different communities establish a public sphere of their own. Once we accept the concept, we are faced with questions of governmental regulation and coercion, questions of exit. For example, what levels of force can the dominant communities use within those spheres against individuals who do not conform?

There are other conflicts with human rights – for example, on the issue of gender. Can a state subsidize synagogues where women play a secondary role? Does it matter that the women are there by choice? But, then, what constitutes genuine choice? Do they have to be exposed to other states' different solutions to state-religion relationships before genuine choice is possible?

These are all issues that arise out of traditions that do not maintain a distinction between the public and private sphere.

Remarks of Mordechai Kremnitzer, *in* Religion and State 14 (Harvard Law School Human Rights Program, 2004)

Moshe Halbertal's comments challenge us to look at the issues from the perspective of religion rather than the state. Most of us take the liberal state as a given, and we look at the issue of religion from its political point of view. But Moshe's comments challenge us to start with religion; then the state becomes the question rather than the given. Religion has a say about the existence of the state, its identity and structure. We cannot do justice to the topic of religion and state if we always assume the existence of a liberal, democratic state.

NOTES AND QUESTIONS

1. The cultural differences between Israeli and American expectations about the role of religion in the public sphere manifest in constitutional practices. In the United States,

 > the Constitution's religious protections are incorporated into precedent-setting U.S. Supreme Court decisions. Exceptions to religious neutrality have sometimes been made in such matters as tax exemption for churches; the use of chaplains in state legislatures, Congress, and the military; the display of the motto In God We Trust on currency; and the use of the phrase "one nation under God" in the Pledge of Allegiance. And, of course, we don't prohibit public fire departments from fighting church fires. Generally, though, the high court has held that for statutes to meet the requirements of the First Amendment, they must have "a secular purpose": their primary intent must be to neither help nor hurt church organizations, and they must avoid "excessive entanglement" with religion.

 Ethan Fishman, *Unto Caesar*, 76 Am. Scholar, Supp., at 36, 44 (2007) (the article as a whole contrasts the tradition of religious freedom, led by Roger Williams in the colonial era, with the less separatist policies and practices of the more recent George W. Bush administration).
2. In the United States, the separation of church and state emphasized in the previous readings has been analyzed, as follows, in terms of rational choice theory:

 > The essence of the idea is this: People act rationally in choosing their religion. If they are believers, they make a constant cost-benefit analysis, consciously or unconsciously, about what form of religion to practice. Religious beliefs and practices make up the product that is on sale in the market, and current and potential followers are the consumers. In a free-market religious economy there is a healthy abundance of choice (religious pluralism), which leads naturally to vigorous competition and efficient supply (new and old religious

> movements). The more competition there is, the higher the level of consumption. This would explain the often remarked paradox that the United States is one of the most religious countries in the world but also one of the strongest enforcers of a separation between Church and State.

Toby Lester, *Oh, Gods!* ATLANTIC MONTHLY, Feb. 2002, at 37, 43.

Do you agree with this analysis?

3. Is religion in the public sphere or public square necessarily a good thing? The constant tensions between Palestinians and Israelis would seem to challenge culturally conditioned expectations in Israel of a robust role for religion in the public sphere to the extent that religious intolerance is one factor contributing to those tensions. Such expectations presume a rational, constructive role of religion in the political process. Consider, however, the following observation on the "dark side" of religion with "the potential to be a powerfully destructive political force":

> It may, for example, harm the process of political decisionmaking. A believer who sees those who oppose or question her beliefs as aligned with the "powers of chaos" is likely to treat the public square as a battleground rather than as a forum for debate. Religion, if unleashed as a political force, may also lead to a particularly acrimonious divisiveness among different religions. Those religions that are accused of representing the powers of chaos are likely to react with similar vehemence in denouncing their attackers. Finally, and most problematically, religion's participation in the political process can produce dangerous results: Fervent beliefs fueled by suppressed fear are easily transformed into movements of intolerance, repression, hate, and persecution. There are, in short, substantial reasons for exercising caution with respect to religious involvement in the public square.

William P. Marshall, *The Other Side of Religion*, 44 HASTINGS L.J. 843, 859 (1993).

4. What role, if any, should religious courts and law play in the public sphere of secular societies? Should a secular judicial system ever defer to religious tribunals and religious law? For example, to what extent should traditional Islamic rules of the Sharia governing marital relations, inheritance, and banking practices coexist with modern secular requirements? To what extent should certain religious cultures enjoy a measure of autonomy that other cultures in the same secular legal system do not? In 2008, the archbishop of Canterbury created a stir when he commented that integration of the Islamic Sharia in the English legal system, at least in matters of family law (primarily divorce), was unavoidable. He made his remarks against a history of limited deference by Western secular courts to religious law and courts but drew a sharp rebuke from some English citizens. Consider the following summary of the context in the United States and Canada:

> The archbishop's proposal was groundbreaking only in extending to Islamic tribunals in Britain a role that Jewish and Christian ones have long played in the judicial systems of secular societies. Courts in the United States have endorsed all three kinds of tribunals.
>
> In 2003, for instance, a Texas appeals court referred a divorce case to a local tribunal called the Texas Islamic Court. In 2005, the federal appeals

> court in New Orleans affirmed an award in an employment arbitration by the Institute for Christian Conciliation, which uses Biblical teachings to settle disputes. And state courts routinely enforce the decisions made by a Jewish court, known as a *bet din*, in commercial and family law cases.
>
> [The notion of deferring to religious tribunals] has met resistance where Islam is involved. After the authorities in Ontario raised the possibility that arbitrators might use Shariah to settle family disputes, formal recognition of all religious arbitrations there, including existing Catholic and Jewish ones, was withdrawn. "There will be one law for all Ontarians," Dalton McGuinty, the province's premier, said in 2005.

Adam Liptak, *When God and the Law Don't Square*, N.Y. Times, Feb. 17, 2008, (Wk. in Rev.), at 3.

5. Is a voluntary submission to adjudication of disputes by religious tribunals by adherents to a particular religion any different from routine private arbitration of disputes? The discussion in Chapter 1 about the cultural defense in secular litigation suggests that the deliberate allocation of autonomous decision making is common throughout the world. What issues inhere in the allocation of authority to subgroups in matters of strictly intragroup dispute resolution? Prime examples include the exclusive systems of the Roma people (Gypsies), the Israeli religious courts, Native American tribal courts, and the special tribunals in the United States and United Kingdom that were noted previously. Suppose, though, that a party has a change of mind about its religious convictions. Can the party then opt out of an ongoing process or an adverse judgment by a religious tribunal? For example, suppose that in a divorce action a tribunal applies religious law that discriminates against women. Should a woman's consent to the adjudication bar her from later contesting an adverse enforcement of a judgment on grounds of discrimination?
6. The following readings continue our consideration of the controversial role of religious tribunals and law in the secular legal systems of multicultural societies. The relationship between religious and secular authority is particularly critical in developing countries during their ongoing processes of modernization.

Abdulmumini Adebayo Oba, *The Sharia Court of Appeal in Northern Nigeria: The Continuing Crisis of Jurisdiction*, 52 Am. J. Comp. L. 859–61, 892–93, 896–97 (2004)

The Sharia Court of appeal is perhaps the most controversial court in Nigeria. The court was first established, amidst much controversy, by the colonial authorities on the eve of their departure in 1960, and it replaced the Moslem Court of Appeal. The court came to light again during the making of the 1979, 1989 and 1999 Constitutions, respectively. The court is now a subject of fresh controversies following the revival of Islamic penal sanctions in some parts of northern Nigeria. The controversy surrounding the court is due mainly to the pluralistic nature of the Nigerian legal terrain and the conflicting approach thereto preferred by various groups in the country.

The Nigerian State is a state steeped in pluralism. There is ethnic pluralism with over 250 tribes in the country. There is religious pluralism with Islam, Christianity and a wide range of traditional belief systems as the dominant religions. There is also a multifaceted legal pluralism in the country, consisting of English-style laws, Islamic law and a wide variety of customary laws operating against the background of a three-tier federal system. Religious and legal pluralism are particularly relevant to the controversies that have dogged the Sharia Court of Appeal.

Legal pluralism has always been a prominent feature of law in Nigeria. In the pre-colonial era, the legal system included Islamic law and customary law. Islamic law was dominant in the north, but there were also many communities which were non-Islamic and in which customary laws dominated. In the south, there were a variety of customary laws. These laws enjoyed unfettered application of their areas of influence. In the northern part of the country, where Islam had taken root since the ninth century, courts manned by Qadis (judges) administering Islamic law were in existence as far back as 1463, when the first Qadis were appointed for Kano and Katsina. In those areas, which consisted of the Sokoto and Kanem-Bornu Caliphates, these courts were highly organized and formalized, and the Qadis were men of great respectability and considerable learning. The courts were in place at the time of the advent of colonialism. In the south, although there were large numbers of Muslims in the southwest among the Yoruba speaking peoples, the administration of Islamic law was not as organized as was the case in the north. Chiefs administered customary law while the administration of Islamic law was done informally by learned Islamic scholars who were consulted for the purpose by Muslims on voluntary basis. There were, however, prior to and during the colonial era, isolated instances of organized administration of Islamic law in towns such as Epe, Ikirun, Iwo, and Ede. These attempts were not encouraged by the colonial authorities, who encouraged the imposition of customary law on all Yoruba persons who had not "opted for" common law. In the east, consisting mostly of acephalous societies, customary law administered by elders held sway.

Colonialism itself brought into the country a third system, the common law, together with its system of administration of justice. The colonial authorities added another complication by defining customary law as including Islamic law notwithstanding the glaring differences between the two systems of law.

. . .

The Sharia Court of Appeal is essentially an appellate court serving as an intermediate court between the "inferior courts" (Area Courts, Sharia Courts) and the Court of Appeal. The approach of Islamic law to judicial review is different from that of the common law. In Islamic law, a judge can review his own judgment. The doctrine of *res judicata* does not apply. There is a controversy in the Muslim world as to whether or not Islamic law allows appellate review. Some deny the validity of appellate review while others uphold it. The better view is perhaps that Islamic law permits appellate review except in some matters, such as those issues decided based on personal reasoning (*ijtihad*). The powers of the Sharia Court of Appeal with respect to appeals before it are not expressly defined along the lines envisaged by Islamic law. This has, however, not caused any controversy, possibly because judicial review by the Emir or Sultan was accepted in pre-colonial era in northern Nigeria. Another controversy in Islamic law relates to courts consisting of more than one judge. According to Ruxton, "A bench of judges is unthinkable to Muhammadan mind." Under the Constitution, the Sharia Court of Appeal is "duly constituted" by "at least three [q]adis." This again has not generated any controversy.

The arrangement as regards the Sharia Court of Appeal and Islamic law generally does not satisfy the yearning of Muslims. They complain about the narrow jurisdiction of the Sharia Court of Appeal; the High Court's jurisdiction in Islamic law matters; the dominant role of legal practitioners in the administration of Islamic law at the Court of Appeal and the Supreme Court levels; the indifference to Islamic legal education and Arabic by the government; and the non-establishment of a Sharia Court of Appeal in the southern states. Muslims complain that they are subjected to the common law whether they like it or not, although the common law is a product of a Christian culture. To them, Islamic law is also a matter of their constitutional right to practice their religion.

. . .

The controversies surrounding the court are due in the main to religious rivalry in a multi-religious environment and competition between legal orders in a pluralistic legal system. The official organs of Christianity and practitioners of common law are generally opposed to the very existence of the Sharia Court of Appeal as a court recognized by the Constitution and to any expansion of its jurisdiction in particular. The Christian objections are founded on the need to contain Islam. The objectors see any concession to Islam as another step in the perceived Islamization of the country. The reasons behind the objections of legal practitioners to the court are multifarious, but also mundane. Having been raised intellectually to believe in the perfection of the common law system, they cannot contemplate or tolerate the existence of a rival law within the Nigerian legal system, a law which they are totally ignorant of. Above all, they fear for both their livelihood and prestige. The loud criticism of some aspects of Islamic law has obscured the fact that Muslims, too, have their opinion of the common law. Muslims believe that Islamic law has decisive advantages over the common law. To them, the common law is not only arbitrary, expensive, slow, and unduly technical, but also its method of administering justice is more or less like a forensic game which has no business with justice. These criticisms of the common law are not limited to Muslims. Since their introduction into Nigeria, English-style courts have neither been popular nor won the confidence of the peoples of Nigeria. Even today, many culturally conscious intellectuals and even some of the country's most distinguished judges admit to some of these faults.

Ann Black, *Survival or Extinction? Animistic Dispute Resolution in the Sultanate of Brunei*, 13 Willamette J. Int'l L. & Disp. Resol. 1, 8–11 (2005)

The Iban in Brunei Darussalam, along with other animist peoples of Borneo, are heirs to a long tradition of consensual dispute resolution. Animism thrives in an environment where the dense tropical jungle, intricate river systems, and difficult terrain of the interior gave rise to small scattered segmentary groups. In the spirit world, the natural order and the supernatural are believed to interest all human endeavors. . . . At first it may seem incongruous that people who were known as the "headhunters of Borneo" would also adopt a consensual and spiritually based process for settling disputes and employ an essentially egalitarian social structure. However, in all probability, this occurred as a protective reaction against the external violence that permeated Borneo's interior. The longhouse became the vital institutional ingredient in Iban life as it provided a means of defense and protection for its residents. Separate dwellings would have made families vulnerable. One structure was easier to defend because the longhouse was built off the ground on high stilts, making enemy access difficult since the ladders could be drawn up when ended. Longhouses no longer fulfill this protective function, but they have survived as the pivotal social institution into the 21st century.

The longhouse, the application of *adat* and augury, the mediating role played by the headman, and the principles that govern the process of dispute resolution within and outside the longhouse can be identified as the distinctive features of Iban dispute resolution. Each will be discussed in turn.

A. The Longhouse

Iban dispute resolution typically takes place in the longhouse. The longhouse establishes a delineated community and minimization of conflict between members of the house is a priority. A longhouse does not operate strictly in a communal form, but more as a collection of independently owned and inhabited family apartments (*biliks*), joined laterally, and connected with a joint gallery (*ruai*) and open-air veranda (*tanju*).

. . .

[A]fter one's family, an Iban's identity and loyalty are to the longhouse. This is strengthened by kinship and friendship ties. It has been described as an open society "where the most intimate details of family life can be open for public discussion . . . [an Iban] lives in an atmosphere of reciprocity, freedom and egalitarianism. The longhouse binds the individual to his community and his culture." The longhouse is a sovereign unit, acting dually as a collective ritual entity and as a forum for settling disputes between members. Both functions are administered by the longhouse headman and elders, and by an augur.

B. *Adat* and Augury

For the animist Iban two agents regulate their world: *adat* and augury. Each impacts upon the individual and his or her relationships with others, with the longhouse community and with the gods and spirits. Both *adat* and augury govern the processes for dispute resolution. Augury defines the ritual magic-religious requirements for each member and *bilik* family, as well as for the longhouse as a ritual entity. *Adat* is an all-encompassing customary system of beliefs, rules, principles, and practices that guide all behavior, including relations with other humans as well as the natural and supernatural world.... "To the Iban the term *adat* covers all the various customary norms, jural rules, ritual interdictions and injunctions that guide an individual's conduct, and the sanctions and forms of redress by which these norms and rules are upheld."

Adat is the means by which good relations are maintained within an Iban community and can be applied to virtually all spheres of human life, social, economic, religious, and political. It regulates interpersonal relationships by setting out reciprocal responsibilities, rights and duties; by providing sanctions to be imposed for breach of *adat*; and by establishing the moral standards to be valued and attained, such as courage, kindness, and generosity. An Iban can describe a person as having either good or bad *adat*. Good *adat* indicates that he or she possesses admirable personal qualities, as well as adhering to the rules, practices, and beliefs.

A large proportion of *adat* is believed to have been revealed by the gods and spirits, and so a breach of *adat* may require the observance of a ritual. This is to prevent supernatural retaliation for the lack of harmony within the longhouse. Augury further enhances the connection between *adat* and the dictates of the spiritual world. Augury is a form of divination, providing the means by which the will of the gods can be revealed to an Iban through the behaviour of birds, animals, and reptiles. The gods can issue warnings, provide favor and guidance, and foretell future occurrences to those who can interpret the omens and signs. The augur of the longhouse is responsible for correctly interpreting the omens and for securing the ritual status of the longhouse. Of greatest importance are seven augural birds that act as messengers for the most important of the Iban gods, Singalong Burong. Harm is not caused by the omens of evil but by failing to heed the warnings and willfully disregarding the prognostications of the gods. As the Iban explain: "These omen birds, they announce to us those things which are hurtful and those which are not; but if we do not understand their language, if we do not heed them, then we shall suffer." Augury complements *adat*, in that any serious breach of *adat* may necessitate supernatural sanctions and ritual redress to preserve the collective well-being of the longhouse community. In addition, a violation of *adat* that causes injury to the person or property of another is seen as an attack on the spiritual personality or the soul of the victim, which in turn requires spiritual redress, in addition to any other form of redress. It is the responsibility of the headman and the elders, including the augur, to see that correct redress is applied so that the social harmony between individuals and the spiritual health of that community can be restored.

NOTES AND QUESTIONS

1. Is the legal pluralism in Nigeria similar to or different from that in the United States and Canada? Are Nigerian attitudes toward the common law culturally conditioned? For a skeptical view of institutionalized Islam in Nigeria, see Eliza Griswold, *God's Country*, ATLANTIC, March 2008, at 40, 52 ("the implementation of sharia, which is currently on the books in twelve of Nigeria's thirty-six states, has had very little impact. The harsh criminal punishments . . . have proven, for the most part, impossible to implement.").
2. Aside from the questions raised earlier about the role of religious law and tribunals in the public sphere, of what use or relevance are essentially anthropological accounts of religious practices that function as legal institutions in essentially closed societies? Do practices such as those of Brunei's Iban people serve a positive or a negative function in the larger society of a country? Does a reliance on animism, fundamental as it is in Iban society in performing certain functions of legal authority among a subgroup, actually threaten secular authority in countries with an established religion (Islam, in the case of Brunei)?
3. Do Iban practices offer any insights useful in dispute resolution? In international dispute resolution? Leaving augury and *adats* aside, consider the possibility of providing a facility within the UN Secretariat – a kind of longhouse, so to speak – in which religious leaders could maintain offices (bases of diplomatic operations) to sort out and discuss their differences, assess their overall roles in the global order, and perhaps even formulate joint proposals for greater international cooperation. Ann Black offers the following observations in her article:

   > Despite the ascendancy of secularism on the world stage, religion continues in many parts of the world to inform national priorities. It impacts international relations between nations and the intra-national relationships between ethnic and religious groups within nations. Religion has always been an important factor in shaping the social reality of people, and this extends to laying down the approved means for dispute resolution. The nexus between religion and dispute resolution can be overlooked in a Western context, where a secular world view and the separation of church and state distances dispute resolution from the religious priorities and values of the Judeo-Christian tradition. The contemporary aim of Western dispute resolution is to be value-neutral and to utilize an impartial intervener, for whom religious knowledge is irrelevant, even inappropriate, in fulfilling the role – whether as judge, arbitrator or mediator. However, in many parts of the world, religion is not relegated to the private sphere, but directly informs state practice including the means by

> which conflict is de-escalated and disputes are resolved. Religious knowledge and credentials become essential to the process.

Ann Black, *Survival or Extinction? Animistic Dispute Resolution in the Sultanate of Brunei*, 13 Willamette J. Int'l L. & Disp. Resol. 1–2 (2005).

In contrast, should international institutions, in the interest of secular impartiality, observe a separation of church and state?

E. Freedom of Religion

1. National Laws

Gonzalez v. O Centro Espírita Beneficiente União do Vegetal, 546 U.S. 418 (2006)

Chief Justice Roberts delivered the opinion of the Court.

A religious sect with origins in the Amazon Rainforest receives communion by drinking a sacramental tea, brewed from plants unique to the region, that contains a hallucinogen regulated under the Controlled Substances Act by the Federal Government. The Government concedes that this practice is a sincere exercise of religion, but nonetheless sought to prohibit the small American branch of the sect from engaging in the practice, on the ground that the Controlled Substances Act bars all use of the hallucinogen. The sect sued to block enforcement against it of the ban on the sacramental tea, and moved for a preliminary injunction.

It relied on the Religious Freedom Restoration Act of 1993, which prohibits the Federal Government from substantially burdening a person's exercise of religion, unless the Government "demonstrates that application of the burden to the person" represents the least restrictive means of advancing a compelling interest. 42 U.S.C. §2000bb-1(b). The District Court granted the preliminary injunction, and the Court of Appeals affirmed. We granted the Government's petition for certiorari. Before this Court, the Government's central submission is that it has a compelling interest in the *uniform* application of the Controlled Substances Act, such that no exception to the ban on use of the hallucinogen can be made to accommodate the sect's sincere religious practice. We conclude that the Government has not carried the burden expressly placed on it by Congress in the Religions Freedom Restoration Act, and affirm the grant of the preliminary injunction.

In *Employment Div., Dept. of Human Resources of Ore.* v. *Smith*, 494 U.S. 872 (1990), this Court held that the Free Exercise Clause of the First Amendment does not prohibit governments from burdening religious practices through generally applicable laws. In *Smith*, we rejected a challenge to an Oregon statute that denied unemployment benefits to drug users, including Native Americans engaged in the sacramental use of peyote.* *Id.*, at 890. In so doing, we rejected the interpretation of the Free Exercise Clause announced in *Sherbert* v. *Verner*, 374 U.S. 398 (1963), and, in accord with earlier cases, see *Smith*, 494 U.S., at 879–880, 884–885, held that the Constitution does not require judges to engage in a case-by-case assessment of the religious burdens imposed by facially constitutional laws. *Id.*, at 883–890.

Congress responded by enacting the Religious Freedom Restoration Act of 1993 (RFRA), 107 Stat. 1488, as amended, 42 U.S.C. §2000bb *et seq.*, which adopts a statutory rule comparable to the constitutional rule rejected in *Smith*. Under RFRA, the Federal Government may not, as a statutory matter, substantially burden a person's exercise of religion, "even if the burden results from a rule of general applicability." §2000bb-1(a). The only exception recognized by the statute requires the Government to satisfy the compelling interest test – to "demonstrate[e] that application of the burden to the person – (1) is in furtherance of a compelling governmental interest; and (2) is the least restrictive means of furthering that compelling governmental interest." §2000bb-1(b). A person whose religious practices are burdened in violation of RFRA "may assert that violations as a claim or defense in a judicial proceeding and obtain appropriate relief." §2000bb-1(c).

The Controlled Substance Act, 84 Stat. 1242, as amended, 21 U.S.C. §801 *et seq.* (2000 ed. and Supp. I), regulates the importation, manufacture, distribution, and use of psychotropic substances. The Act classifies into five schedules based on their potential for abuse, the extent to which they have an accepted medical use, and their safety. See §812(b) (2000 ed.). Substances listed in Schedule I of the Act are subject to the most comprehensive restrictions, including an outright ban on all importation and use, except pursuant to strictly regulated research projects. See §§823, 960(a)(1). The Act authorizes the imposition of a criminal sentence for simple possession of Schedule I substances, see §844(a), and mandates the imposition of a criminal sentence for possession "with intent to manufacture, distribute, or dispense" such substances, see §§841(a), (b).

O Centro Espírita Beneficente União do Vegetal (UDV) is a Christian Spiritist sect based in Brazil, with an American branch of approximately 130 individuals. Central to the UDV's faith is receiving communion through *hoasca* (pronounced "wass-ca"), a sacramental tea made from two plants unique to the Amazon region. One of the plants, *psychotria viridis*, contains dimethyltryptamine (DMT), a hallucinogen whose effects are enhanced by alkaloids from the other plant, *banisteriopsis caapi*. DMT, as well as "any material, compound, mixture, or preparation, which contains any quantity of [DMT]," is listed in Schedule I of the Controlled Substances Act. §812(c), Schedule I(c).

In 1999, United States Customs inspectors intercepted a shipment to the American UDV containing three drums of *hoasca*. A subsequent investigation revealed that the UDV had received 14 prior shipments of *hoasca*. The inspectors seized the intercepted shipment and threatened the UDV with prosecution.

The UDV filed suit against the Attorney General and other federal law enforcement officials, seeking declaratory and injunctive relief. The complaint alleged, *inter alia*, that applying the Controlled Substances Act to the UDV's sacramental use of *hoasca* violates RFRA. Prior to trial, the UDV moved for a preliminary injunction, so that it could continue to practice its faith pending trial on the merits.

At a hearing on the preliminary injunction, the Government conceded that the challenged application of the Controlled Substances Act would substantially burden a sincere exercise of religion by the UDV. See *O Centro Espirita Beneficiente Uniao do Vegetal* v. *Ashcroft*, 282 F. Supp. 2d 1236, 1252 (NM 2002). The Government argued, however, that this burden did not violate RFRA, because applying the Controlled Substances Act in this case was the least restrictive means of advancing three compelling governmental interests: protecting the health and safety of UDV members, preventing the diversion of *hoasca* from the church to recreational users, and complying with the 1971 United Nations Convention on Psychotropic Substances, a treaty signed by the United States and implemented by the Act. Feb. 21, 1971, [1979–1980) 32 U.S.T. 543, T.I.A.S. No. 9725. See 282 F. Supp. 2d, at 1252–1253.

The District Court heard evidence from both parties on the health risks of *hoasca* and the potential for diversion from the church. The Government presented evidence to the effect that use of *hoasca*, or DMT more generally, can cause psychotic reactions, cardiac irregularities, and adverse drug interactions. The UDV countered by citing studies documenting the safety of its sacramental use of *hoasca* and presenting evidence that minimized the likelihood of the health risks raised by the Government. With respect to diversion, the Government pointed to a general rise in the illicit use of hallucinogens, and cited interest in the illegal use of DMT and *hoasca* in particular; the UDV emphasized the thinness of any market for *hoasca*, the relatively small amounts of the substance imported by the church, and the absence of any diversion problem in the past.

The District Court concluded that the evidence on health risks was "in equipoise," and similarly that the evidence on diversion was "virtually balanced." *Id.*, at 1262, 1266. In the face of such an even showing, the court reasoned that the Government had failed to demonstrate a compelling interest justifying what it acknowledged was a substantial burden on the UDV's sincere religious exercise. *Id.*, at 1255. The court also rejected the asserted interest in complying with the 1971 Convention on Psychotropic Substances, holding that the Convention does not apply to *hoasca*. *Id.*, at 1266–1269.

The court entered a preliminary injunction prohibiting the Government from enforcing the Controlled Substances Act with respect to the UDV's importation and use of *hoasca*. . . . The injunction requires the church to import the tea pursuant to federal permits, to restrict control over the tea to persons of church authority, and to warn particularly susceptible UDV members of the dangers of *hoasca*. . . . The injunction also provides that "if [the Government] believe[s] that evidence exists that *hoasca* has negatively affected the health of UDV members," or "that a shipment of *hoasca* contain[s] particularly dangerous levels of DMT, [the Government] may apply to the Court for an expedite[d] determination of whether the evidence warrants suspension or revocation of [the UDV's authority to use *hoasca*]." *Id.*, at 257a, ¶ 29.

The Government appealed the preliminary injunction and a panel of the Court of Appeals for the Tenth Circuit affirmed, *O Centro Espirita Beneficiente Uniao do Vegetal* v. *Ashcroft*, 342 F. 3d 1170 (2003), as did a majority of the Circuit sitting en banc, 389 F. 3d 973 (2004). We granted certiorari. 544 U.S. 973 (2005).

...

Under the Government's view, there is no need to assess the particulars of the UDV's use or weigh the impact of an exemption for that specific use, because the Controlled Substances Act serves a compelling purpose and simply admits of no exceptions.

A

RFRA, and the strict scrutiny test it adopted, contemplate an injury more focused than the Government's categorical approach. RFRA requires the Government to demonstrate that the compelling interest test is satisfied through application of the challenged law "to the person" – the particular claimant whose sincere exercise of religion is being substantially burdened. 42 U.S.C. §2000bb-1(b). RFRA expressly adopted the compelling interest test "as set forth in *Sherbert* v. *Verner*, 374 U.S. 398 (1963) and *Wisconsin* v. *Yoder*, 406 U.S. 205 (1972)." In each of those cases, this Court looked beyond broadly formulated interests justifying the general applicability of government mandates and scrutinized the asserted harm of granting specific exemptions to particular religious claimants. In *Yoder*, for example, we permitted an exemption for Amish children from a compulsory school attendance law. We recognized that the State had a "paramount" interest in education, but held that "despite its admitted validity in the generality of cases, we must searchingly examine the interests that the State seeks to promote . . . and the impediment to those objectives that would flow from recognizing *the claimed Amish exemption*." 406 U.S., at 213, 221 (emphasis added). The Court explained that the State needed "to show with more particularity how its admittedly strong interest . . . would be adversely affected by granting an exception *to the Amish*." *Id.*, at 236 (emphasis added).

In *Sherbert*, the Court upheld a particular claim to a religious exemption from a state law denying unemployment benefits to those who would not work on Saturdays, but explained that it was not announcing a constitutional right to unemployment benefits for "*all* persons whose religious convictions are the cause of their unemployment." 374 U.S., at 410 (emphasis added). The Court distinguished the case "in which an employee's religious convictions serve to make him a nonproductive member of society." *Ibid.*; see also *Smith*, 494 U.S., at 899 (O'Connor, J., concurring in judgment) (strict scrutiny "at least requires a case-by-case determination of the question, sensitive to the facts of each particular claim"). Outside the

Free Exercise area as well, the Court has noted that "[c]ontext matters" in applying the compelling interest test, *Grutter* v. *Bollinger*, 539 U.S. 306, 327 (2003), and has emphasized that "strict scrutiny *does* take 'relevant differences' into account – indeed, that is its fundamental purpose," *Adarand Constructors, Inc. v. Peña*, 515 U.S. 200, 228 (1996).

B

Under the more focused inquiry required by RFRA and the compelling interest test, the Government's mere invocation of the general characteristics of Schedule I substances, as set forth in the Controlled Substances Act, cannot carry the day. It is true, of course, that Schedule I substances as DMT are exceptionally dangerous. See, *e.g.*, *Touby* v. *United States*, 500 U.S. 160, 162 (1991). Nevertheless, there is no indication that Congress, in classifying DMT, considered the harms posed by the particular use at issue here – the circumscribed, sacramental use of *hoasca* by the UDV. The question of the harms from the sacramental use of *hoasca* by the UDV *was* litigated below. Before the District Court found that the Government had not carried its burden of showing a compelling interest in preventing such harms, the court noted that it could not "ignore that the legislative branch of the government elected to place materials containing DMT in Schedule I of the [Act], reflecting findings that substances containing DMT have 'a high potential for abuse,' and 'no currently accepted medical use in treatment in the United States,' and that '[t]here is a lack of accepted safety for use of [DMT] under medical supervision." 282 F. Supp. 2d, at 1254. But Congress'[s] determination that DMT should be listed under Schedule I simply does not provide a categorical answer that relieves the Government of the obligation to shoulder its burden under RFRA.

This conclusion is reinforced by the Controlled Substances Act itself. The Act contains a provision authorizing the Attorney General to "waive the requirement for registration of certain manufacturers, distributors, or dispensers if he finds it consistent with the public health and safety." 21 U.S.C. §822(d). The fact that the Act itself contemplates that exempting certain people from its requirements would be "consistent with the public health and safety" indicates that congressional findings with respect to Schedule I substances should not carry the determinative weight, for RFRA purposes, that the Government would ascribe to them.

And in fact an exception has been made to the Schedule I ban for religious use. For the past 35 years, there has been a regulatory exemption for use of peyote – a Schedule I substance – by the Native American Church. See 21 CFR §1307.31 (2005). In 1994, Congress extended that exemption to all members of every recognized Indian Tribe. See 42 U.S.C. §1995a(b)(1). Everything the Government says about the DMT in *hoasca* – that, as a Schedule I substance, Congress has determined that it "has a high potential for abuse," "has no currently accepted medical use," and has "a lack of accepted safety for use . . . under medical supervision," 21 U.S.C. §812(b)(1) – applies in equal measure to the mescaline in peyote, yet both the Executive and Congress itself have decreed an exemption from the Controlled Substances Act for Native American religious use of peyote. If such use is permitted in the face of the congressional findings in §812(b)(1) for hundreds of thousands of Native Americans practicing their faith, it is difficult to see how those same findings alone can preclude any consideration of a similar exception for the 130 or so American members of the UDV who want to practice theirs. See *Church of Lukumi Babalu Aye, Inc.* v. *Hialeah*, 508 U.S. 520, 547 (1993) ("It is established in our strict scrutiny jurisprudence that 'a law cannot be regarded as protecting an interest 'of the highest order' . . . when it leaves appreciable damage to that supposedly vital interest unprohibited'" (quoting *Florida Star v. B. J. F.*, 491 U.S. 524, 541–542 (1989) (SCALIA, J., concurring in part and concurring in judgment))).

The Government responds that there is a "unique relationship" between the United States and the Tribes . . . see *Morton v. Mancari*, 417 U.S. 535 (1974), but never explains what about that "unique" relationship justifies overriding the same congressional findings on which the Government relies in resisting any exception for the UDV's religious use of *hoasca*. In other words, if any Schedule I substance is in fact always highly dangerous in any amount no matter how used, what about the unique relationship with the Tribes justifies allowing their use of peyote? Nothing about the unique political status of the Tribes makes their members immune from the health risks the Government asserts accompany any use of a Schedule I substance, nor insulates the Schedule I substance the Tribes use in religious exercise from the alleged risk of diversion.

The Government argues that the existence of *congressional* exemption for peyote does not indicate that the Controlled Substances Act is amenable to *judicially crafted* exceptions. RFRA, however, plainly contemplates that courts would recognize exceptions – that is how the law works. See 42 U.S.C. §2000bb-1(c) ("A person whose religious exercise has been burdened in violation of this section may assert that violation as a claim or defense in a judicial proceeding and obtain appropriate relief against a government"). Congress' role in the peyote exemption – and the Executive's, see 21 CFR § 1307.31 (2005) – confirms that the findings in the Controlled Substances Act do not preclude exceptions altogether; RFRA makes clear that it is the obligation of the courts to consider whether exceptions are required under the test set forth by Congress.

C

The well-established peyote exception also fatally undermines the Government's broader contention that the Controlled Substance Act establishes a closed regulatory system that admits of no exceptions under RFRA. The Government argues that the effectiveness of the Controlled Substances Act will be "necessarily . . . undercut" if the Act is not uniformly applied, without regard to burdens on religious exercise. . . . The peyote exception, however, has been in place since the outset of the Controlled Substances Act, and there is no evidence that it has "undercut" the Government's ability to enforce the ban on peyote use by non-Indians.

The Government points to some pre-*Smith* cases relying on a need for uniformity in rejecting claims for religious exemptions under the Free Exercise Clause, . . . but those cases strike us as quite different from the present one. Those cases did not embrace the notion that a general interest in uniformity justified a substantial burden on religious exercise; they instead scrutinized the asserted need and explained why the denied exemptions could not be accommodated. In *United States v. Lee*, 455 U.S. 252 (1982), for example, the Court rejected a claimed exception to the obligation to pay Social Security taxes, noting that "mandatory participation is indispensable to the fiscal vitality of the social security system" and that the "tax system could not function if denominations were allowed to challenge the tax system because tax payments were spent in a manner that violates their religious belief." *Id.*, at 258, 260. See also *Hernandez v. Commissioner*, 490 U.S. 680, 700 (1989) (same). In *Braunfeld v. Brown*, 366 U.S. 599 (1961) (plurality opinion), the Court denied a claimed exception to Sunday closing laws, in part because allowing such exceptions "might well provide [the claimants] with an economic advantage over their competitors who must remain closed on that day." *Id.*, at 608–609. The whole point of a "uniform day of rest for all workers" would have been defeated by exceptions. See *Sherbert*, 374 U.S., at 408 (discussing *Braunfeld*). These cases show that the Government can demonstrate a compelling interest in uniform application of a particular program by offering evidence that granting the requested religious accommodations would seriously compromise its ability to administer the program.

Here the Government's argument for uniformity is different; it rests not so much on the particular statutory program at issue as on slippery-slope concerns that could be invoked in response to any RFRA claim for an exception to a generally applicable law. The Government's argument echoes the classic rejoinder of bureaucrats throughout history: If I make an exception for you, I'll have to make one for everybody, so no exceptions. But RFRA operates by mandating consideration, under the compelling interest test, of exceptions to "rule[s] of general applicability." 42 U.S.C. §2000bb-1(a). Congress determined that the legislated test "is a workable test for striking sensible balances between religious liberty and competing prior governmental interests." §2000bb(a)(5). This determination finds support in our case; in *Sherbert*, for example, we rejected a slippery-slope argument similar to the one offered in this case, dismissing as "no more than a possibility" the State's speculation "that the filing of fraudulent claims by unscrupulous claimants feigning religious objections to Saturday work would drain the unemployment benefits fund." 374 U.S., at 407.

We reaffirmed just last Term the feasibility of case-by-case consideration of religious exemptions to generally applicable rules. In *Cutter v. Wilkinson*, 544 U.S. 709 (2005), we held that the Religious Land Use and Institutionalized Persons Act of 2000, which allows federal and state prisoners to seek religious accommodations pursuant to the same standard as set forth in RFRA, does not violate the Establishment Clause. We had 'no cause to believe" that the compelling interest test "would not be applied in an appropriately balanced way" to specific claims for exemptions as they arose. *Id.*, at 722. Nothing in our opinion suggested that courts were not up to the task.

We do not doubt that there may be instances in which a need for uniformity precludes the recognition of exceptions to generally applicable laws under RFRA. But it would have been surprising to find that this was such a case, given the longstanding exemption from the Controlled Substances Act for religious use of peyote, and the fact that the very reason Congress enacted RFRA was to respond to a decision denying a claimed right to sacramental use of a controlled substance. See 42 U.S.C. §2000bb(a)(4). And in fact the Government has not offered evidence demonstrating that granting the UDV an exemption would cause the kind of administrative harm recognized as a compelling interest in *Lee*, *Hernandez*, and *Braunfeld*. The Government failed to convince the District Court at the preliminary injunction hearing that health or diversion concerns provide a compelling interest in banning the UDV's sacramental use of *hoasca*. It cannot compensate for that failure now with the bold argument that there can be no RFRA exceptions at all to the Controlled Substances Act. . . .

IV

Before the District Court, the Government also asserted an interest in compliance with the 1971 United Nations Convention on Psychotropic Substances, Feb. 21, 1971 [1979–1980] 30 U.S.T. 543, T.I.A.S. No. 9725. The Convention, signed by the United States and implemented by the Controlled Substances Act, calls on signatories to prohibit the use of hallucinogens, including DMT. The Government argues that it has a compelling interest in meeting its international obligations by complying with the Convention.

The District Court rejected this interest because it found that the Convention does not cover *hoasca*. The court relied on the official commentary to the Convention, which notes that "Schedule I [of the Convention] does not list . . . natural hallucinogenic materials," and that "[p]lants as such are not, and – it is submitted – are also not likely to be, listed in Schedule I, but only some products obtained from plants." U.N. Commentary on the Convention on Psychotropic Substances 387, 385 (1976). The court reasoned that *hoasca*, like the plants from which the tea is made, is sufficiently distinct from DMT itself to fall outside the treaty. See 282 F. Supp. 2d, at 1266–1269.

We do not agree. The Convention provides that "a preparation is subject to the same measures of control as the psychotropic substance which it contains," and defines "preparation" as "any solution or mixture, in whatever physical state, containing one or more psychotropic substances." See 32 U.S.T., at 546, Art. 1(f)(i); *id.*, at 551, Art. 3. *Hoasca* is a "solution or mixture" containing DMT; the fact that it is made by the simple process of brewing plants in water, as opposed to some more advanced method, does not change that. To the extent the commentary suggests plants themselves are not covered by the Convention, that is of no moment – the UDV seeks to import and use a tea brewed from plants, not the plants themselves, and the tea plainly qualifies as a "preparation" under the Convention.

The fact that *hoasca* is covered by the Convention, however, does not automatically mean that the Government has demonstrated a compelling interest in applying the Controlled Substances Act, which implements the Convention, to the UDV's sacramental use of the tea. At the present stage, it suffices to observe that the Government did not even *submit* evidence addressing the international consequences of granting an exemption for the UDV. The Government simply submitted to affidavits by State Department officials attesting to the general importance of honoring international obligations and of maintaining the leadership position of the United States in the international war on drugs.... We do not doubt the validity of these interests, any more than we doubt the general interest in promoting public health and safety by enforcing the Controlled Substances Act, but under RFRA invocation of such general interests, standing alone, is not enough.

...

The Government repeatedly invokes Congress' findings and purposes underlying the Controlled Substances Act, but Congress had a reason for enacting RFRA, too. Congress recognized that "laws 'neutral' toward religion may burden religious exercise as surely as laws intended to interfere with religious exercise," and legislated "the compelling interest test" as the means for the courts to "strik[e] sensible balances between religious liberty and competing prior governmental interests." 42 U.S.C. §§222bb(a)(2), (5).

We have no cause to pretend that the task assigned by Congress to the courts under RFRA is an easy one. Indeed, the very sort of difficulties highlighted by the Government here were cited by this Court in deciding that the approach later mandated by Congress under RFRA was not required as a matter of constitutional law under the Free Exercise Clause. See *Smith*, 494 U.S., at 885–890. But Congress has determined that courts should strike sensible balances, pursuant to a compelling interest test that requires the Government to address the particular practice at issue. Applying that test, we conclude that the courts below did not err in determining that the Government failed to demonstrate, at the preliminary injunction stage, a compelling interest in barring the UDV's sacramental use of *hoasca*.

The judgment of the United States Court of Appeals for the Tenth Circuit is affirmed, and the case is remanded for further proceedings consistent with this opinion.

It is so ordered.

NOTES AND QUESTIONS

What, precisely, are the legal constraints in the U.S. legal system on religious practices? What exactly is the standard for determining a compelling regulatory interest sufficient to deny the normal exercise of religious freedom? Consider a decision from before the modern civil rights era. In *Morison v. Rawlinson*, 7 S.E.2d 636 (S.C. 1940), the Supreme Court of South Carolina upheld an injunction against services at an African American church that had been deemed to constitute a public nuisance. The court found that the plaintiff church members engaged in "weird and unearthly outcries" and

> loud shouting, clapping of hands in unison, and stamping of feet. The incessant use of drums, timbrels, trombones, horns, scrubbing boards and wash tubs add to the general clamor. Some of the votaries are moved to testify; others enter an hypnotic trance. The central pillars of the church are padded to protect them from injury during their transports. The tumult can be heard for many city blocks. Meetings are carried on daily from early hours in the evening until the early hours of the morning. Boisterous and disorderly throngs, unable to enter the crowded building, congregate in the adjoining streets. Fights often occur. White residents who live in the vicinity testified that life is made unbearable by the continual din, which deprives them of all peace and tranquility, and makes sleep impossible.

Id. at 638.

Would the result be any different today? Would any other remedy besides a blanket injunction against a religious practice impose less of a burden on the free exercise of religion and thereby pass constitutional muster as a minimally invasive restriction?

Pitman B. Potter, *Governance of China's Periphery: Balancing Local Autonomy and National Unity*, 19 Colum. J. Asian L. 293, 305–07 (2005)

[In China, c]onstitutional provisions on religion distinguish between freedom of belief and controls on behavior. Article 36 provides that citizens enjoy freedom of religious belief, and protects "normal religious activities." Yet this protection does not extend to behavior that disrupts public order, impairs the health of citizens, or interferes with the educational system of the state. In explaining the meaning of constitutional provisions on religious freedom, Peng Zhen noted that, from a political perspective, the common elements of patriotism and adherence to socialism bind those who believe in religion and those who do not. This underscores the imperative of submission to Party/state control as a condition for enjoyment of religious freedom.

Protection of freedom of religious belief is qualified as well by Article 33 of the PRC Constitution, which conditions the exercise of citizens' rights on performance of their duties. As Peng Zhen explained, these included upholding the Four Basic Principles, which impose a duty to uphold the socialist road, the dictatorship of the proletariat, leadership of the Party, and Marxist/Leninist/Mao Zedong Thought. Thus, the freedom granted religious belief remains conditional not only on compliance with law and regulation, but more fundamentally on submission to the policies and edicts of the Party/state.

The State Council's 1997 White Paper on Freedom of Religious Belief in China reiterated the point that "religion should be adapted to the society where it is prevalent" and that religions must "conduct their activities within the sphere prescribed by law and adapt to social and cultural progress." Pursuant to these principles, the government remained committed to punishing those religions and religious believers who "are a serious danger to the normal life and productive activities of the people" or who "severely endanger the society and the public interest." The coercive themes associated with administration of religion were reiterated at the United Front Work Department's national work conference in late December 1999 by Director Wang Zhaoguo: "[W]e must comprehensively and correctly implement the Party's religious policy, strengthen administration of religious affairs according to law, and actively guide religions to adapt to socialist society." These basic constitutional provisions are echoed in a wide array of central and local regulations that control religious activities, practitioners, and places of worship, and have recently been formalized in national regulations on religious administration.

NOTES AND QUESTIONS

Compare the following constitutional provisions with the provisions in the PRC Constitution, as described above, and with each other:

> United States: "Amendment I: Congress shall make no law respecting an establishment of religion, or prohibiting the free exercise thereof. . . .
>
> France: "Article 1: France shall be an indivisible, secular, democratic and social Republic. It shall ensure the equality of all citizens before the law, without distinction of origin, race or religion. It shall respect all beliefs. It shall be organized on a decentralized basis."
>
> Italy: "Article 3: All citizens have equal social dignity and are equal before the law, without distinction of sex, race, language, religion, political opinions, personal and social conditions. . . .
>
> Article 8: There is, equally before the law, freedom of all religious beliefs (*confessioni*). Religious beliefs other than Catholic have the right to organize in accordance with their own statutes, insofar as they are not in conflict with the Italian juridical order. Their relations with the State are regulated by law on the basis of agreements between their respective representatives. . . .
>
> Article 19: All have the right to profess freely their own religious faith in whatever form, individually, or in association, to propagate it and to exercise it in private or public worship, provided that the rites are not contrary to good morals.
>
> Article 20: The ecclesiastical character and the purpose of religion or worship of an association or institution may not be a cause for special legislative limitations, nor for special fiscal impositions in its constitution, juridical capacity and any form of activity."

How do these provisions, including those of China, differ in effect from one another? From your reading of these provisions and general knowledge, can you identify specific cultural or historical explanations for the apparent variety in expressing the common freedom of religion? Do any of the statutes seek to inhibit the performance of religious activity by evangelical preachers who are not educated or otherwise accredited ministers of religion?

2. International Law

Peter G. Danchin, *The Emergence and Structure of Religious Freedom in International Law Reconsidered*, 23 J. L. & Relig. 455, 522–26 (2007–08)

The modern system for the protection of religious freedom has its origins in the series of minorities treaties drafted at the Paris Peace Conference of 1919 following the end of the First World War. These treaties mark a conscious departure from the Westphalian *cuius regio* principle seeking to establish peace and stability through determining the physical boundaries of the State on the basis of religion. The Allies now sought to establish a conceptual apparatus through which attention was switched to exercising both conditionality and multilateral oversight of obligations placed upon States under international law. In this respect, the establishment of the League of Nations represents a double shift: the first from Great Power diplomacy to international action mediated through multilateral organizations; and the second, from nineteenth-century practice, as typified by the Treaty of Berlin in 1878, to the contemporary international system.

While the Covenant of the League of Nations did not address religious freedom, the so-called "minorities treaties" drafted in the New States Committee in relation to the newly constituted and enlarged States in Central and Eastern Europe did explicitly address the question of religious liberties. They continued the tradition of inserting clauses seeking guarantees of certain rights in treaties conferring recognition on new States. The starting point at the League of Nations Conference for the consideration of minority issues was the protection of Jews in Poland and the Polish Treaty thus served as the model for later minorities treaties.... [T]he Polish Treaty immediately exposed a tension which struck at the core of the "national" self-determination principle upon which the post-war settlement was being conducted, and which continues today to be a source of contestation in international law – the difference between a "national" as opposed to an "ethnic, religious or linguistic" minority. On the one hand, Zionists who viewed the Jews to be a "nation" called for the establishment of a Newish National Home and "national rights" in Central and Eastern European states to protect the culture and religious traditions of Jewish life. On the other hand, those who viewed the Jews as nationals and citizens of the states in which they lived sought more limited "minority" protections against tolerance and discrimination on the basis of religion and religious practices.

For their part, the Poles issued general complaints against the policy of imposing minority obligations on a sovereign state regarding the treatment of its citizens. They further suggested that establishing a system which gave special privileges under so-called "Jewish clauses" would only create further animosity and a "new Jewish problem." By emphasizing the elements of Jewish nationalism reflected in the treaty and the precedent it set, the Poles

> raised the spectre of the Allies themselves becoming subject to similar forms of minority obligations, a possibility that they had resisted, and were continuing to resist, at the cost of some considerable embarrassment.

One of the central concerns was whether allowing the Jews to control their own schools, as proposed under Article 10, would encourage Yiddish to be used in primary and secondary education. It was felt that this would foster the creation of a State within a State.... The Allies thus made clear that the Treaty would impose special protection of only a "minority" rather that "national" kind for the Jewish community in Poland....

Once the Polish Treaty was concluded, the Allied Powers immediately entered into four other minorities treaties with Czechoslovakia and the Serb-Croat-Slovene State (September 10, 1919), Romania (December 9, 1919), and Greece (August 10, 1920). The obligations contained in these treaties were then placed under the guarantee of the League of Nations, which itself came into existence with the entry into force of the League Covenant on January 10, 1920. Minority protections on the Polish Treaty model were further included in the Peace Treaties with Austria, Hungary and Bulgaria; and the Treaty of Sèvres with Turkey, signed by the Ottomans on August 10, 1920, also contained provisions for the protection of minorities.

Together, these five treaties with particular States involving minority problems, provisions on minorities in general peace treaties with four countries, and declarations made by several States as a condition for their admission to the League became known as the minorities system [but] it is difficult to defend these instruments as a "system" given the inconsistency of their application. Minority obligations were not uniformly imposed by the victors on the War's losers since the Treaty of Versailles imposed no such obligations on Germany. Nor were Belgium, France or Denmark required to assume minority obligations though they gained territory at Germany's expense. Similarly, nothing was required of Italy, which received areas of the Southern Tyrol and of the Istrian Peninsula....

We might conclude, then, by observing that the rationale and objectives of the minority system were closely based on two premises. First, the system assumes that a nondiscrimination principle by itself was insufficient to ensure that individuals belonging to minorities enjoyed legal equality with other nationals of the State. This constitutes an early recognition of the distinction between formal and substantive equality. A second, and closely related, premise was that in order to achieve substantive equality it is necessary to have group-differentiated rights protecting differences in religion, language and culture. These two notions were later articulated by the Advisory Opinion of the Permanent Court of International Justice in the 1935 *Minority Schools in Albania* case.[6]

The following documents trace the progression of modern international legal instruments to protect religious freedom, from the generalities of the Universal Declaration of Human Rights, which was not intended to be binding but is commonly accepted today as customary law, to the specificity of later instruments. Regional instruments conclude this parade of leading international legal instruments.

Universal Declaration of Human Rights, G.A. Res. 217A, at 71, U.N. GAOR, 3d Sess., 1st plen mtg., U.N. Doc. A/810 (Dec. 12, 1948)

Article 2

Everyone is entitled to all the rights and freedom set forth in this Declaration, without distinction of any kind, such as race, colour, sex, language, religion, political or other opinion, national or social origin, property, birth or other status.

Article 18

Everyone has the right to freedom of thought, conscience and religion; this right includes freedom to change his religion or belief, and freedom, either alone or in community with others and in public or private, to manifest his religion or belief in teaching, practice, worship and observance.

International Covenant on Civil and Political Rights, Dec. 16, 1966, 993 U.N.T.S. 171 [hereinafter ICCPR]

Article 18

(1) Everyone shall have the right to freedom of thought, conscience and religion. This right shall include freedom to have or to adopt a religion or belief of his choice, and freedom, either individually or in community with others and in public or private, to manifest his religion or belief in worship, observation, practice and teaching.

(2) No one shall be subject to coercion which would impair his freedom to have or to adopt a religion or belief of his choice.

(3) Freedom to manifest one's religion or beliefs may be subject only to such limitations as are prescribed by law and are necessary to protect public

[6] *Minority Schools in Albania* 1935 P.C.I.J. (Ser. A) No. 64, at 17 (suggesting that the protection of racial, religious, or linguistic minorities and the ensuring of "true equality" between a majority and a minority requires "suitable means for the preservation of their racial peculiarities, their traditions and their national characteristics").

safety, order, health, or morals or the fundamental rights and freedoms of others.

(4) The States Parties to the present Covenant undertake to have respect for the liberty of parents and, when applicable, legal guardians to ensure the religious and moral education of their children in conformity with their own convictions.

Declaration on the Elimination of All Forms of Intolerance and of Discrimination Based on Religion or Belief, G.A. Res. 36/55, U.N. GAOR, 36th Sess., Supp. No. 51, at 171, U.N. Doc. A/36/51 (Nov. 25, 1981)

[Article 1 is the same as the first three paragraphs in Article 18 in the preceding ICCPR.]

Article 2

1. No one shall be subject to discrimination by any State, institution, group of persons or person on the grounds of religion or other beliefs.

2. For the purposes of the present Declaration, the expression "intolerance of discrimination based on religion or belief" means any distinction, exclusion, restriction or preference based on religion or belief and having as its purpose or as its effect nullification or impairment of the recognition, enjoyment or exercise of human rights and fundamental freedoms on an equal basis.

. . .

Article 6

In accordance with article 1 of the present Declaration, and subject to the provisions of article 1, paragraph 3, the right to freedom of thought, conscience, religion or belief shall include, *inter alia*, the following freedoms:

(a) To worship or assemble in connexion with a religion or belief, and to establish and maintain places for these purposes;
(b) To establish and maintain appropriate charitable or humanitarian institutions;
(c) To make, acquire and use to an adequate extent the necessary articles and materials related to the rites or customs of a religion or belief;
(d) To write, issue and disseminate relevant publications in these areas;
(e) To teach a religion or belief in places suitable for these purposes;
(f) To solicit and receive voluntary financial and other contributions from individuals and institutions;
(g) To train, appoint, elect or designate by succession appropriate leaders called for by the requirements and standards of any religion or belief;
(h) To observe days of rest and to celebrate holidays and ceremonies in accordance with the precepts of one's religion or belief;
(i)To establish and maintain communications with individuals and communities in matters of religion and belief at the national and international levels. . . .

Katarina Tomaševski, *Rights of Women: From Prohibition to Elimination of Discrimination*, INT'L SOC. SCI. J., no. 158, at 84, 87, 93, 94 (1998) (reprinted with permission of the Blackwell Publishing Ltd.)

Societal norms – forged by our global historical heritage – routinely discriminate against women. We tend to subsume them under the heading of *culture* and shy away from addressing their discriminatory contents in the name of respect for *culture.* From the viewpoint of victims of such discriminatory norms, our behaviour may not look as respectful as we would wish it to appear. A young North African woman, who was sold by her family to her husband and thence into prostitution, commented: "Westerners are too quick to believe that our problems are inherent in our culture. What they mean is that they do not want to do anything about it."

...

The term "culture" is today often used in a negative sense, to denote a barrier to universal recognition of human rights. Debates along the lines of universalism *versus* cultural relativism proliferate, and are fueled by the resurgence of religious and ethnic identities and the corresponding demands for collective rights.

The emergence of gender discrimination on the human rights agenda broadened the reach of human rights from vertical relations between individuals and governments, to horizontal relations, namely between individuals, within families and communities, and ultimately within couples. The human rights argumentation is that women should not be left unprotected from abuse, that governments have to take the lead in eradicating abuse even when it occurs within families and is justified by tradition or religion. Rights of individual women take precedence over respect of family autonomy.

...

Freedom of religion is often counterposed to women's equal rights within the family.

NOTES AND QUESTIONS

1. Notice that, although article 18 of the Universal Declaration of Human Rights (1948) explicitly confirms a right "to change" one's religion, article 18 of the later ICCPR (1966) acknowledges only a right "to have or adopt" a particular religion or belief. On the difficult issue of apostasy and in general whether a right to change one's religion exists, see Peter G. Danchin, *Of Prophets and Proselytes: Freedom of Religion and the Conflict of Rights in International Law*, 49 HARV. INT'L L.J. 249, 270 (2008).
2. The UN mechanism for implementing the principal human rights instruments includes a special rapporteur on freedom of religion and belief who is appointed by the Human Rights Committee under the ICCPR. Member states must respond to the rapporteur's reports and requests in a process of accountability to the United

Nations. The effectiveness of these legal instruments relies heavily on national implementation and enforcement. In the United States, the International Religious Freedom Act of 1998, 22 U.S.C. §§ 6401–6474 (2002), established the Commission on International Religious Freedom to review reports on that topic and make recommendations to the president and Congress. The president must apply diplomatic and economic sanctions against states that have been deemed to violate the principle of religious freedom, and allocation of foreign aid must take account of a prospective recipient's record on religious freedom. These sanctions are nonreviewable. The Act also created a special adviser to the National Security Council and the Office on International Religious Freedom, which is lodged in the State Department and chaired by an ambassador-at-large. The Office is charged with detailed monitoring of practices in other countries, collecting data, and preparing an annual report to Congress on religious freedom.

3. In the Tomaševski reading, inequality seems to be reinforced by the concept of cultural integrity. Do the international instruments make any attempt to reconcile cultural traditions with the principle of equality? Does article 2 of the 1981 UN declaration against religious discrimination address this apparent conflict between two fundamental human rights, or does that provision simply reinforce a primacy of cultural norms even if they reinforce inequality of women and others?

3. Regional Law

Organization of American States, American Declaration of the Rights and Duties of Man, O.A.S. Res. XXX, O.A.S. Off. Rec. OEA/Ser.L/V/I.4 Rev. (Mar. 30–May 2, 1948)

Article III

Every person has the right freely to profess a religious faith, and to manifest and practice it both in public and in private.

Organization of American States, American Convention on Human Rights, Nov. 22, 1969, O.A.S.T.S. No. 36, 1144 U.N.T.S. 123

Article 12
Freedom of Conscience and Religion

1. Everyone has the right to freedom of conscience and of religion. This right includes freedom to maintain or to change one's religion or beliefs, and freedom to profess or disseminate one's religion or beliefs, either individually or together with others, in public or in private.
2. No one shall be subject to restrictions that might impair his freedom to maintain or to change his religion or beliefs.
3. Freedom to manifest one's religion and beliefs may be subject only to the limitations prescribed by law that are necessary to protect public safety, order, health, or morals, or the rights or freedoms of others.

4. Parents or guardians, as the case may be, have the right to provide for the religious and moral education of their children or wards that is in accord with their own convictions.

Organization of African Unity [now African Union], African Charter on Human and Peoples' Rights, June 26, 1981, O.A.U. Doc. CAB/LEG/67/3 Rev. 5, 21 I.L.M. 59 (1982)

Article 8

Freedom of conscience, the profession and free practice of religion shall be guaranteed. No one may, subject to law and order, be submitted to measures restricting the exercise of these freedoms.

Council of Europe, European Convention for the Protection of Human Rights and Fundamental Freedoms, Nov. 4, 1950, 213 U.N.T.S. 221

Article 9

(1) Everyone has the right to freedom of thought, conscience and religion; this right includes freedom to change his religion or belief, and freedom, either alone or in community with others and in public or private, to manifest his religion or belief, in worship, teaching, practice and observance.

(2) Freedom to manifest one's religion or beliefs shall be subject only to such limitations as are prescribed by law and are necessary in a democratic society in the interests of public safety, for the protection of public order, health or morals, or for the protection of the rights and freedoms of others.

ŞAHIN v. TURKEY,
2005-XI Eur. Ct. H.R. 175

I. The Circumstances of the Case

The applicant was born in 1973 and has lived in Vienna since 1999, when she left Istanbul to pursue her medical studies at the Faculty of Medicine at Vienna University. She comes from a traditional family of practising Muslims and considers it her religious duty to wear the Islamic headscarf.

A. Circular of 23 February 1998

On 26 August 1997 the applicant, then in her fifth year at the Faculty of Medicine at Bursa University, enrolled at the Cerrahpasa Faculty of Medicine at Istanbul University. She says that she wore the Islamic headscarf during the four years she spent studying medicine at the University of Bursa and continued to do so until February 1998.

On 23 February 1998 the Vice Chancellor of Istanbul University issued a circular, the relevant part of which provides:

> By virtue of the Constitution, the law and regulations, and in accordance with the case-law of the Supreme Administrative Court and the

> European Commission of Human Rights and the resolutions adopted by the university administrative boards, students whose 'heads are covered' (who wear the Islamic headscarf) and students (including overseas students) with beards must not be admitted to lectures, courses or tutorials. Consequently, the name and number of any student with a beard or wearing the Islamic headscarf must not be added to the lists of registered students. However, students who insist on attending tutorials and entering lecture theatres although their names and numbers are not on the lists must be advised of the position and, should they refuse to leave, their names and numbers must be taken and they must be informed that they are not entitled to attend lectures. If they refuse to leave the lecture theatre, the teacher shall record the incident in a report explaining why it was not possible to give the lecture and shall bring the incident to the attention of the university authorities as a matter of urgency so that disciplinary measures can be taken.

On 12 March 1998, in accordance with the aforementioned circular, the applicant was denied access by invigilators to a written examination on oncology because she was wearing the Islamic headscarf. On 20 March 1998 the secretariat of the chair of orthopaedic traumatology refused to allow her to enroll because she was wearing a headscarf. On 16 April 1998 she was refused admission to a neurology lecture and on 10 June 1998 to a written examination on public health, again for the same reason.

. . .

The Turkish Republic was founded on the principle that the State should be secular (*laik*). Before and after the proclamation of the Republic on 29 October 1923, the public and religious spheres were separated through a series of revolutionary reforms: the abolition of the caliphate on 3 March 1923; the repeal of the constitutional provision declaring Islam the religion of the State on 10 April 1928; and, lastly, on 5 February 1937 a constitutional amendment according constitutional status to the principle of secularism (see Article 2 of the Constitution of 1924 and Article 2 of the Constitutions of 1961 and 1982. . . .

The principle of secularism was inspired by developments in Ottoman society in the period between the nineteenth century and the proclamation of the Republic. The idea of creating a modern public society in which equality was guaranteed to all citizens without distinction on grounds of religion, denomination or sex had already been mooted in the Ottoman debates of the nineteenth century. Significant advances in women's rights were made during this period (equality of treatment in education, the introduction of a ban on polygamy in 1914, [and] the transfer of jurisdiction in matrimonial cases to the secular courts that had been established in the nineteenth century).

The defining feature of the Republican ideal was the presence of women in public life and their active participation in society. Consequently, the ideas that women should be freed from religious constraints and that society should be modernised had a common origin. Thus, on 17 February 1926 the Civil Code was adopted, which provided for equality of the sexes in the enjoyment of civic rights, in particular with regard to divorce and succession. Subsequently, through a constitutional amendment of 5 December 1934 (Article 10 of the 1924 Constitution), women obtained equal political rights with men.

The first legislation to regulate dress was the Headgear Act of 28 November 1925 (Law no. 671), which treated dress as a modernity issue. Similarly, a ban was imposed on wearing religious attire other than in places of worship or at religious ceremonies, irrespective of the religion or belief concerned, by the Dress (Regulations) Act of 3 December 1934 (Law no. 2596).

Under the Education Services (Merger) Act of 3 March 1924 (Law no. 430), religious schools were closed and all schools came under the control of the Ministry for Education. The Act is one of the laws with constitutional status that are protected by Article 174 of the Turkish Constitution.

In Turkey wearing the Islamic headscarf to school and university is a recent phenomenon which only really began to emerge in the 1980s. There has been extensive discussion on the issue and it continues to be the subject of lively debate in Turkish society. Those in favour of the headscarf see wearing it as a duty and/or a form of expression linked to religious identity. However, the supporters of secularism, who draw a distinction between the *başörtüsü* (traditional Anatolian headscarf, worn loosely) and the *türban* (tight, knotted headscarf hiding the hair and the throat), see the Islamic headscarf as a symbol of a political Islam. As a result of the accession to power on 28 June 1996 of a coalition government comprising the Islamist *Refah Partisi*, and the centre-right *Doğru Yol Partisi*, the debate has taken on strong political overtones. The ambivalence displayed by the leaders of the *Refah Partisi*, including the then Prime Minister, over their attachment to democratic values, and their advocacy of a plurality of legal systems functioning according to different religious rules for each religious community was perceived in Turkish society as a genuine threat to republican values and civil peace (see *Refah Partisi (the Welfare Party) and Others v. Turkey* [GC], nos. 41340/98, 41342/98, 41343/98 and 41344/98, ECHR 2003-II).

2. The rules on dress in institutions of higher education and the case-law of the Constitutional Court

The first piece of legislation on dress in institutions of higher education was a set of regulations issued by the Cabinet on 22 July 1981 requiring staff working for public organisations and institutions and personnel and female students at State institutions to wear ordinary, sober, modern dress. The regulations also provided that female members of staff and students should not wear veils in educational institutions.

On 20 December 1982 the Higher-Education Authority issued a circular on the wearing of headscarves in institutions of higher education. The

Islamic headscarf was banned in lecture theatres. In a judgment of 13 December 1984, the Supreme Administrative Court held that the regulations were lawful, noting:

> Beyond being a mere innocent practice, wearing the headscarf is in the process of becoming the symbol of a vision that is contrary to the freedoms of women and the fundamental principles of the Republic.

On 10 December 1988 transitional section 16 of the Higher-Education Act (Law no. 2547 – "the Higher-Education Act") entered into force. It provided:

> Modern dress or appearance shall be compulsory in the rooms and corridors of institutions of higher education, preparatory schools, laboratories, clinics and multidisciplinary clinics. A veil or headscarf covering the neck and hair may be worn out of religious conviction.

In a judgment of 7 March 1989 published in the Official Gazette of 5 July 1989, the Constitutional Court held that the aforementioned provision was contrary to Articles 2 (secularism), 10 (equality before the law) and 24 (freedom of religion) of the Constitution. It also found that it could not be reconciled with the principle of sexual equality implicit, *inter alia*, in republican and revolutionary values (see the Constitution – Preamble and Article 174).

In their judgment, the Constitutional Court judges explained, firstly, that secularism had acquired constitutional status by reason of the historical experience of the country and the particularities of Islam compared to other religions; secularism was an essential condition for democracy and acted as a guarantor of freedom of religion and of equality before the law. It also prevented the State from showing a preference for a particular religion or belief; consequently, a secular State could not invoke religious conviction when performing its legislative function. They stated, *inter alia*:

> Secularism is the civil organiser of political, social and cultural life, based on national sovereignty, democracy, freedom and science. Secularism is the principle which offers the individual the possibility to affirm his or her own personality through freedom of thought and which, by the distinction it makes between politics and religious beliefs, renders freedom of conscience and religion effective. In societies based on religion, which function with religious thought and religious rules, political organisation is religious in character. In a secular regime, religion is shielded from a political role. It is not a tool of the authorities and remains in its respectable place, to be determined by the conscience of each and everyone. . . .

Stressing its inviolable nature, the Constitutional Court observed that freedom of religion, conscience and worship, which could not be equated with a right to wear any particular religious attire, guaranteed first and foremost the liberty to decide whether or not to follow a religion. It explained that, once outside the private sphere of individual conscience, freedom to manifest one's religion could be restricted on public-order grounds to defend the principle of secularism.

Everyone was free to choose how to dress, as the social and religious values and traditions of society also had to be respected. However, when a particular dress code was imposed on individuals by reference to a religion, the religion concerned was perceived and presented as a set of values that were incompatible with those of contemporary society. In addition, in Turkey, where the majority of the population were Muslims, presenting the wearing of the Islamic headscarf as a mandatory religious duty would result in discrimination between practising Muslims, non-practising Muslims and non-believers on grounds of dress with anyone who refused to wear the headscarf undoubtedly being regarded as opposed to religion or as irreligious.

The Constitutional Court also said that students had to be permitted to work and pursue their education together in a calm, tolerant and mutually supportive atmosphere without being deflected from that goal by signs of religious affiliation. It found that, irrespective of whether the Islamic headscarf was a precept of Islam, granting legal recognition to a religious symbol of that type in institutions of higher education was not compatible with the principle that State education must be neutral, as it would be liable to generate conflicts between students with differing religious convictions or beliefs.

On 25 October 1990 transitional section 17 of Law no. 2547 entered into force. It provides:

> Choice of dress shall be free in institutions of higher education, provided that it does not contravene the laws in force.

In a judgment of 9 April 1991, which was published in the Official Gazette of 31 July 1991, the Constitutional Court noted that, in the light of the principles it had established in its judgment of 7 March 1989, the aforementioned provision did not allow headscarves to be worn in institutions of higher education on religious grounds and so was consistent with the Constitution. It stated, inter alia:

> . . . the expression "laws in force" refers first and foremost to the Constitution. . . . In institutions of higher education, it is contrary to the principles of secularism and equality for the neck and hair to be covered with a veil or headscarf on grounds of religious conviction. In these circumstances, the freedom of dress which the impugned provision permits in institutions of higher education "does not concern dress of a religious nature or the act of covering one's neck and hair with a veil and headscarf" . . . The freedom afforded by this provision [transitional section 17] is conditional on its not being contrary "to the laws in force." The judgment [of 7 March 1989] of the Constitutional Court establishes that covering one's neck and hair with the headscarf is first and foremost contrary to the Constitution. Consequently, the

> condition set out in the aforementioned section requiring [choice of] dress not to contravene the laws in force removes from the scope of freedom of dress the act of "covering one's neck and hair with the headscarf[.]" . . .

. . .

D. Comparative law

For more than twenty years the place of the Islamic headscarf in State education has been the subject of debate across Europe. In most European countries, the debate has focused mainly on primary and secondary schools. However, in Turkey, Azerbaijan and Albania it has concerned not just the question of individual liberty, but also the political meaning of the Islamic headscarf. These are the only member States to have introduced regulations on wearing the Islamic headscarf in universities.

In France, where secularism is regarded as one of the cornerstones of republican values, legislation was passed on 15 March 2004 regulating, in accordance with the principle of secularism, the wearing of signs or dress manifesting a religious affiliation in State primary and secondary schools. The legislation inserted a new Article L. 141–5–1 in the Education Code which provides: "In State primary and secondary schools, the wearing of signs or dress by which pupils overtly manifest a religious affiliation is prohibited. The school rules shall state that the institution of disciplinary proceedings shall be preceded by dialogue with the pupil."

The Act applies to all State schools and educational institutions, including post-baccalaureate courses (preparatory classes for entrance to the *grandes écoles* and vocational training courses). It does not apply to State universities. In addition, as the circular of 18 May 2004 makes clear, it only concerns " . . . signs . . . , such as the Islamic headscarf, however named, the kippa or a cross that is manifestly oversized, which make the wearer's religious affiliation immediately identifiable."

In Belgium there is no general ban on wearing religious signs at school. In the French Community a decree of 13 March 1994 stipulates that education shall be neutral within the Community. Pupils are in principle allowed to wear religious signs. However, they may do so only if human rights, the reputation of others, national security, public order, and public health and morals are protected and internal rules complied with. Further, teachers must not permit religious or philosophical proselytism under their authority or the organisation of political militancy by or on behalf of pupils. The decree stipulates that restrictions may be imposed by school rules. On 19 May 2004 the French Community issued a decree intended to institute equality of treatment. In the Flemish Community, there is no uniform policy among schools on whether to allow religious or philosophical signs to be worn. Some do, others do not. When pupils are permitted to wear such signs, restrictions may be imposed on grounds of hygiene or safety.

In other countries (Austria, Germany, the Netherlands, Spain, Sweden, Switzerland and the United Kingdom), in some cases following a protracted legal debate, the State education authorities permit Muslim pupils and students to wear the Islamic headscarf.

In Germany, where the debate focused on whether teachers should be allowed to wear the Islamic headscarf, the Constitutional Court stated on 24 September 2003 in a case between a teacher and the *Land* of Baden-Württemberg that the lack of any express statutory prohibition meant that teachers were entitled to wear the headscarf. Consequently, it imposed a duty on the *Länder* to lay down rules on dress if they wished to prohibit the wearing of the Islamic headscarf in State schools.

In Austria there is no special legislation governing the wearing of the headscarf, turban or kippa. In general, it is considered that a ban on wearing the headscarf will only be justified if it poses a health or safety hazard for pupils.

In the United Kingdom a tolerant attitude is shown to pupils who wear religious signs. Difficulties with respect to the Islamic headscarf are rare. The issue has also been debated in the context of the elimination of racial discrimination in schools in order to preserve their multicultural character (see, in particular, *Mandla v. Dowell*, 'The Law Reports' 1983, 548–570). The Commission for Racial Equality, whose opinions have recommendation status only, also considered the issue of the Islamic headscarf in 1988 in the *Altrincham Grammar School* case, which ended in a compromise between a private school and members of the family of two sisters who wished to be allowed to wear the Islamic headscarf at the school. The school agreed to allow them to wear the headscarf provided it was navy blue (the colour of the school uniform), kept fastened at the neck and not decorated.

In the case of *R (On the application of Begum) v. Headteacher and Governors of Denbigh High School* [2004], the High Court had to decide a dispute between the school and a Muslim pupil wishing to wear the jilbab (a full-length gown). The school required pupils to wear a uniform, one of the possible options being the headscarf and a shalwar kameeze (long traditional garments from the Indian subcontinent). In June 2004 the High Court dismissed the pupil's application, holding that there had been no violation of her freedom of religion. However, that judgment was reversed in March 2005 by the Court of Appeal, which accepted that there had been interference with the pupil's freedom of religion, as a minority of Muslims in the United Kingdom considered that a religious duty to wear the jilbab from the age of puberty existed and the pupil was genuinely of that opinion. No justification for the interference had been provided by the school authorities, as the decision-making process was not compatible with freedom of religion.

In Spain, there is no express statutory prohibition on pupils' wearing religious head coverings in State schools. By virtue of two royal Decrees of 26 January 1996, which are applicable in primary and secondary schools unless the competent authority – the autonomous community – has introduced specific measures, the school governors have power to issue school rules which may include provisions on dress. Generally speaking, State schools allow the headscarf to be worn.

In Finland and Sweden the veil can be worn at school. However, a distinction is made between the burka (the term used to describe the full veil covering the whole of the body and the face) and the niqab (a veil covering all the upper body with the exception of the eyes). In Sweden mandatory directives were issued in 2003 by the National Education Agency. These allow schools to prohibit the burka and niqab, provided they do so in a spirit of dialogue on the common values of equality of the sexes and respect for the democratic principle on which the education system is based.

In the Netherlands, where the question of the Islamic headscarf is considered from the standpoint of discrimination rather than of freedom of religion, it is generally tolerated. In 2003 a non-binding directive was issued. Schools may require pupils to wear a uniform provided that the rules are not discriminatory and are included in the school prospectus and that the punishment for transgressions is not disproportionate. A ban on the burka is regarded as justified by the need to be able to identify and communicate with pupils. In addition, the Equal Treatment Commission ruled in 1997 that a ban on wearing the veil during general lessons for safety reasons was not discriminatory.

In a number of other countries (the Czech Republic, Greece, Hungary, Poland or Slovakia), the issue of the Islamic headscarf does not yet appear to have given rise to any detailed legal debate.

. . .

I. Alleged Violation of Article 9 of the Convention

The applicant submitted that the ban on wearing the Islamic headscarf in institutions of higher education constituted an unjustified interference with her right to freedom of religion, in particular, her right to manifest her religion.

> She relied on Article 9 of the Convention, which provides: [Editor's note: see the quotation of this provision in the materials immediately preceding this case]

A. The Chamber judgment

The Chamber found that the Istanbul University regulations restricting the right to wear the Islamic headscarf and the measures taken thereunder had interfered with the applicant's right to manifest her religion. It went on to find that the interference was prescribed by law and pursued one of the legitimate aims set out in the second paragraph of Article 9 of the Convention. It was justified in principle and proportionate to the aims pursued and could therefore be regarded as having been "necessary in a democratic society[.]" . . .

B. The parties' submissions before the Grand Chamber

In her request for a referral to the Grand Chamber dated 27 September 2004 and in her oral submissions at the hearing, the applicant contested the grounds on which the Chamber had concluded that there had been no violation of Article 9 of the Convention.

However, in the observations she submitted to the Grand Chamber on 27 January 2005 she said that she was not seeking legal recognition of a right for all women to wear the Islamic headscarf in all places, *inter alia* in these terms: "Implicit in the section judgment is the notion that the right to wear the headscarf will not always be protected by freedom of religion. [I] do not contest that approach."

The Government asked the Grand Chamber to endorse the Chamber's finding that there had been no violation of Article 9.

C. The Court's assessment

The Court must consider whether the applicant's right under Article 9 was interfered with and, if so, whether the interference was "prescribed by law," pursued a legitimate aim and was "necessary in a democratic society" within the meaning of Article 9 § 2 of the Convention.

. . .

The Court reiterates that as enshrined in Article 9, freedom of thought, conscience and religion is one of the foundations of a "democratic society" within the meaning of the Convention. This freedom is, in its religious dimension, one of the most vital elements that go to make up the identity of believers and their conception of life, but it is also a precious asset for atheists, agnostics, sceptics and the unconcerned. The pluralism indissociable from a democratic society, which has been dearly won over the centuries, depends on it. That freedom entails, *inter alia*, freedom to hold or not to hold religious beliefs and to practise or not to practise a religion (see, among other authorities, *Kokkinakis v. Greece*, 25 May 1993, Series A no. 260-A, p. 17, § 3; and *Buscarini and Others v. San Marino* [GC], no. 24645/94, § 34, ECHR 1999-I).

While religious freedom is primarily a matter of individual conscience, it also implies, *inter alia*, freedom to manifest one's religion, alone and in private, or in community with others, in public and within the circle of those whose faith one shares. Article 9 lists the various forms which manifestation of one's religion or belief may take, namely worship, teaching, practice and observance (see, *mutatis mutandis*, *Cha'are Shalom Ve Tsedek v. France* [GC], no. 27417/95, § 73, ECHR 2000-VII).

Article 9 does not protect every act motivated or inspired by a religion or belief (see, among many other authorities, *Kalaç v. Turkey*, judgment of 1 July 1997, *Reports of Judgments and Decisions* 1997-IV, p. 1209, § 27; *Arrowsmith v. the United Kingdom*, no. 7050/75, Commission decision of 12 October 1978, Decisions and Reports (DR) 19, p. 5; *C. v. the United Kingdom*, no. 10358/83, Commission decision of 15 December 1983, DR 37, p. 142; and *Tepeli and Others v. Turkey* (dec.), no. 31876/96, 11 September 2001).

In democratic societies, in which several religions coexist within one and the same population, it may be necessary to place restrictions on freedom to manifest one's religion or belief in order to reconcile the interests of the various groups and ensure that everyone's beliefs are respected (*Kokkinakis*, cited above, p. 18, § 33). This follows both from paragraph 2 of Article 9 and the State's positive obligation under Article 1 of the Convention to secure to everyone within its jurisdiction the rights and freedoms defined in the Convention.

The Court has frequently emphasised the State's role as the neutral and impartial organiser of the exercise of various religions, faiths and beliefs, and stated that this role is conducive to public order, religious harmony and tolerance in a democratic society. It also considers that the State's duty of neutrality and impartiality is incompatible with any power on the State's part to assess the legitimacy of religious beliefs or the ways in which those beliefs are expressed (see *Manoussakis and Others v. Greece*, judgment of 26 September 1996, *Reports* 1996-IV, p. 1365, § 47; *Hassan and Tchaouch v. Bulgaria* [GC], no. 30985/96, § 78, ECHR 2000-XI; *Refah Partisi and Others*, judgment cited above, § 91) and that it requires the State to ensure mutual tolerance between opposing groups (*United Communist Party of Turkey and Others v. Turkey*, judgment of 30 January 1998, *Reports* 1998-I, § 57). Accordingly, the role of the authorities in such circumstances is not to remove the cause of tension by eliminating pluralism, but to ensure that the competing groups tolerate each other (*Serif v. Greece*, no. 38178/97, § 53, ECHR 1999-IX).

Pluralism, tolerance and broadmindedness are hallmarks of a "democratic society." Although individual interests must on occasion be subordinated to those of a group, democracy does not simply mean that the views of a majority must always prevail: a balance must be achieved which ensures the fair and proper treatment of people from minorities and avoids any abuse of a dominant position (see, *mutatis mutandis*, *Young, James and Webster v. the United Kingdom*, judgment of 13 August 1981, Series A no. 44, p. 25, § 63; and *Chassagnou and Others v. France* [GC], nos. 25088/94, 28331/95 and 28443/95, § 112, ECHR 1999-III). Pluralism and democracy must also be based on dialogue and a spirit of compromise necessarily entailing various concessions on the part of individuals or groups of individuals which are justified in order to maintain and promote the ideals and values of a democratic society (see, *mutatis mutandis*, the *United Communist Party of Turkey and Others*, judgment cited above, pp. 21–22, § 45; and *Refah Partisi and Others*, judgment cited above § 99). Where these "rights and freedoms" are themselves among those guaranteed by the Convention or its Protocols, it must be accepted that the need to protect them may lead States to restrict other rights or freedoms likewise set forth in the Convention. It is precisely this constant search for a balance between the fundamental rights of each individual which constitutes the foundation of a "democratic society" (*Chassagnou and Others*, judgment cited above, § 113).

Where questions concerning the relationship between State and religions are at stake, on which opinion in a democratic society may reasonably differ widely, the role of the national decision-making body must be given special importance (see, *mutatis mutandis*, *Cha'are Shalom Ve Tsedek*, cited above, § 84; and *Wingrove v. the United Kingdom* judgment of 25 November 1996, *Reports* 1996-V, p. 1958, § 58). This will notably be the case when it comes to regulating the wearing of religious symbols in educational institutions, especially (as the comparative-law materials illustrate – see paragraphs 55–65 above) in view of the diversity of the approaches taken by national authorities on the issue. It is not possible to discern throughout Europe a uniform conception of the significance of religion in society (*Otto-Preminger-Institut v. Austria*, judgment of 20 September 1994, Series A no. 295-A, p. 19, § 50) and the meaning or impact of the public expression of a religious belief will differ according to time and context (see, among other authorities, *Dahlab v. Switzerland* (dec.) no. 42393/98, ECHR 2001-V). Rules in this sphere will consequently vary from one country to another according to national traditions and the requirements imposed by the need to protect the rights and freedoms of others and to maintain public order (see, *mutatis mutandis*, *Wingrove*, judgment cited above, p. 1957, § 57). Accordingly, the choice of the extent and form such regulations should take must inevitably be left up to a point to the State concerned, as it will depend on the domestic context concerned (see, *mutatis mutandis*, *Gorzelik*, judgment cited above, § 67; and *Murphy v. Ireland*, no. 44179/98, § 73, ECHR 2003-IX (extracts)).

This margin of appreciation goes hand in hand with a European supervision embracing both the law and the decisions applying it. The Court's task is to determine whether the measures taken at [the] national level were justified in principle and [were] proportionate (*Manoussakis and Others*, judgment cited above, § 44). In delimiting the extent of the margin of appreciation in the present case the Court must have regard to what is at stake, namely the need to protect the rights and freedoms of others, to preserve public order and to secure civil peace and true religious pluralism, which is vital to the survival of a democratic society (see, *mutatis mutandis*, *Kokkinakis*, judgment cited above, § 31; *Manoussakis and Others*, judgment cited above, p. 1364, § 44; and *Casado Coca*, judgment cited above, § 55).

The Court also notes that in the decisions of *Karaduman v. Turkey* (no. 16278/90, Commission decision of 3 May 1993, DR 74, p. 93) and *Dahlab v. Switzerland* (no. 42393/98, ECHR 2001-V) the Convention institutions found that in a democratic society the State was entitled to place restrictions on the wearing of the Islamic headscarf if it was incompatible with the pursued aim of protecting the rights and freedoms of others, public order and public safety. In the *Karaduman* case, measures taken in universities to prevent certain fundamentalist religious movements from exerting pressure on students who did not practise their religion or who belonged to another religion were not considered to constitute interference for the purposes of Article 9 of the Convention. Consequently, it is established that institutions of higher education may regulate the manifestation of the rites and symbols of a religion by imposing restrictions as to the place and manner of such manifestation with the aim of ensuring peaceful co-existence between students of various faiths and thus protecting public order and the beliefs of others (see, among other authorities, *Refah Partisi and Others*, cited above, § 95). In the *Dahlab* case, which concerned the teacher of a class of small children, the Court stressed among other matters the "powerful external symbol" which her wearing a headscarf represented and questioned whether it might have some kind of proselytising effect, seeing that it appeared to be imposed on women by a religious precept that was hard to reconcile with the principle of gender equality. It also noted that wearing the Islamic headscarf could not easily be reconciled with the message of tolerance, respect for others and, above all, equality and non-discrimination that all teachers in a democratic society should convey to their pupils.

(ii) *Application of the foregoing principles to the present case*

The interference in issue caused by the circular of 23 February 1998 imposing restrictions as to place and manner on the rights of students such as Ms. Şahin to wear the Islamic headscarf on university premises was, according to the Turkish courts (see paragraphs 37, 39 and 41 above), based in particular on the two principles of secularism and equality.

In its judgment of 7 March 1989, the Constitutional Court stated that secularism, as the guarantor of democratic values, was the meeting point of liberty and equality. The principle prevented the State from manifesting a preference for a particular religion or belief; it thereby guided the State in its role of impartial arbiter, and necessarily entailed freedom of religion and conscience. It also served to protect the individual not only against arbitrary interference by the State but from external pressure from extremist movements. The Constitutional Court added that freedom to manifest one's religion could be restricted in order to defend those values and principles (see paragraph 39 above).

As the Chamber rightly stated (see paragraph 106 of its judgment), the Court considers this notion of secularism to be consistent with the values underpinning the Convention. It finds that upholding that principle, which is undoubtedly one of the fundamental principles of the Turkish State which are in harmony with the rule of law and respect for human rights, may be considered necessary to protect the democratic system in Turkey. An attitude which fails to respect that principle will not necessarily be accepted as being covered by the freedom to manifest one's religion and will not enjoy the protection of Article 9 of the Convention (see *Refah Partisi and Others*, judgment cited above, § 93).

After examining the parties' arguments, the Grand Chamber sees no good reason to depart from the approach taken by the Chamber (see paragraphs 107–109 of the Chamber judgment) as follows:

> . . . The Court . . . notes the emphasis placed in the Turkish constitutional system on the protection of the rights of women. . . . Gender equality – recognised by the European Court as one of the key principles underlying the Convention and a goal to be achieved by member States of the Council of Europe . . . was also found by the Turkish

> Constitutional Court to be a principle implicit in the values underlying the Constitution. . . .
>
> . . . In addition, like the Constitutional Court . . . , the Court considers that, when examining the question of the Islamic headscarf in the Turkish context, there must be borne in mind the impact which wearing such a symbol, which is presented or perceived as a compulsory religious duty, may have on those who choose not to wear it. As has already been noted (see *Karaduman*, decision cited above; and *Refah Partisi and Others*, cited above, § 95), the issues at stake include the protection of the "rights and freedoms of others" and the "maintenance of public order" in a country in which the majority of the population, while professing a strong attachment to the rights of women and a secular way of life, adhere to the Islamic faith. Imposing limitations on freedom in this sphere may, therefore, be regarded as meeting a pressing social need by seeking to achieve those two legitimate aims, especially since, as the Turkish courts stated . . . , this religious symbol has taken on political significance in Turkey in recent years.
>
> . . . The Court does not lose sight of the fact that there are extremist political movements in Turkey which seek to impose on society as a whole their religious symbols and conception of a society founded on religious precepts. . . . It has previously said that each Contracting State may, in accordance with the Convention provisions, take a stance against such political movements, based on its historical experience (*Refah Partisi and Others*, cited above, § 124). The regulations concerned have to be viewed in that context and constitute a measure intended to achieve the legitimate aims referred to above and thereby to preserve pluralism in the university.

Having regard to the above background, it is the principle of secularism, as elucidated by the Constitutional Court (see paragraph 39 above), which is the paramount consideration underlying the ban on the wearing of religious symbols in universities. In such a context, where the values of pluralism, respect for the rights of others and, in particular, equality before the law of men and women are being taught and applied in practice, it is understandable that the relevant authorities should wish to preserve the secular nature of the institution concerned and so consider it contrary to such values to allow religious attire, including, as in the present case, the Islamic headscarf, to be worn.

. . .

In the light of the foregoing and having regard to the Contracting States' margin of appreciation in this sphere, the Court finds that the interference in issue was justified in principle and proportionate to the aim pursued.

Consequently, there has been no breach of Article 9 of the Convention.

. . .

NOTES AND QUESTIONS

1. In *Şahin*, note the court's emphasis on the rights of other Muslims to be free of the pressures derived from allowing others to wear headscarves in the name of religion. Given the complexity of freedoms at stake, notice also the Court's acceptance of a margin of appreciation within which Turkey and other members of the Council of Europe could tailor national measures consistent with their own cultural and political traditions – in the case of Turkey, a profoundly secular discouragement of religious practices in public. The particular balancing of freedoms in a national society is therefore within its "reserved domain" so long as it observes minimum international standards of human rights.
2. The *Şahin* judgment raises serious questions. How wide is the margin of appreciation or discretion of a state? How far can it be applied when the issue is observance of generally accepted principles of international law incorporated into worldwide and regional instruments using identical wording? Has the Court been consistent with its own case law quoted in the *Şahin* judgment? Did the Court thoroughly substantiate its assertion that the use of the headscarf by Ms. Şahin on the University of Istanbul's premises implied a serious risk of disrupting public order or affecting the rights of others? Would the Court have granted the same margin of discretion to a state with an official religion that decided to ban the use of symbols proclaiming atheism or agnosticism or adherence to a differing faith? Is the Court's approval based on the margin of appreciation principle of an absolute ban at all educational levels, including universities, helpful in the construction of a European pluralist, equalitarian, and tolerant legal system?

   Natan Lerner, *How Wide the Margin of Appreciation: The Turkish Headscarf Case, the Strasbourg Court, and Secularist Tolerance*, 13 Willamette J. Int'l L & Disp. Resol. 65, 80 (2005).
3. In 2008 the Turkish Parliament, on the initiative of the country's prime minister, voted overwhelmingly to amend the Turkish Constitution so as to permit the wearing of headscarves in university classrooms. Sabrina Tavernise, *Move to Lift a Ban on Head Scarves Gains in Turkey*, N.Y. Times, Feb. 10, 2008, at 3; Sabrina Tavernise, *In Turkey, a Step to Allow Head Scarves*, N.Y. Times, Jan. 29, 2008, at A3. Later the same year, however, Turkey's constitutional court annulled the amendments as violations of the Turkish Constitution's guarantee of secularism. The legal battle continues.
4. *Şahin*, decided by the European Court of Human Rights, addressed an issue of religious dress that resonates in many legal systems. As noted in that opinion (para. 59), the German Constitutional Court overturned a Federal Administrative Court's decision that had upheld a State of Baden-Würtemberg ban on teacher headscarves. Case No. 2 BUR 1436/02, Bundesverfassungsgericht [BVerfG] [Constitutional Court] Sept. 24, 2003. See Cindy Skach, *"Teacher Headscarf" Case*, 100 Am. J. Int'l L. 186, 188–96 (2006).
5. For an analysis of the headscarf issue from a feminist viewpoint, denying the existence of a bright-line rule to govern the underlying human rights issues and arguing for a more contextual gender-sensitive approach, see Karima Bennoune,

Secularism and Human Rights: A Contextual Analysis of Headscarves, Religion Expression, and Women's Equality under International Law, 45 COLUM. J. TRANSNAT'L L. 370 (2007).

6. As also noted in the opinion, the headscarf issue prompted the French Assembly to prohibit the wearing of conspicuous religious dress or symbols. The main legal issue in France involves the concept of *laïcité*, or secularism, which has its roots in the French Revolution of the eighteenth century and is enshrined in article 1 of the French Constitution. Despite this constitutional commitment to secularism, however, churches and other religious establishments receive substantial support from the French government. This support ranges from funding religious broadcasts on state television and providing tax breaks for religious organizations to maintaining historical churches and Muslim cemeteries. Moreover, the following commentary suggests that a prohibition directed at students, like the Turkish law that was at issue in *Şahin*, raises more serious questions than the question raised by restrictions on the apparel or religious symbols worn by teachers:

> Inasmuch as public employees carry actions for the State, and therefore represent the State, they may be forced to disregard their personal religious prescriptions pertaining to the expression of faith when discharging their official functions in order to keep their public positions. The scope of such restrictions varies among States according to the balance that they choose to establish between State neutrality and public order, on the one hand, and freedom of religious expression, on the other hand. Thus France, like some American states or Belgium, prohibits teachers from wearing religious garments or symbols on the work place. Similarly, public school pupils may be constrained in their freedom to express their religious beliefs on the school premises when such a manifestation conflicts with the rules of operation of the school. The question that arises is the extent to which the state is entitled to restrict the religious freedom of students on campus. Because public school students, or generally speaking, recipients of a public service do not represent the State but only take advantage of a service provided by the latter, it may be argued that the restrictions which may be imposed on them cannot have the same scope as the ones forced upon civil servants. It follows that unlike public school teachers, public school students should not be subjected to a prohibition on religious garb. The distinction between the individual who acts in the name of the State and one who takes advantage of the State's action and contributes to social pluralism is then essential in the assessment of the validity of restrictions to religious expression. It must be borne in mind that the renounced religious practices can only [be concerned] with expression of the faith and never the faith itself. Otherwise the freedom of religions would be sacrificed and exacting the renunciation would amount to discriminating on the basis of religion.

Dominique Custos, *Secularism in French Public Schools: Back to War? The French Salute of March 15, 2004*, 54 AM. J. COMP. L. 337, 342 (2006).

7. In 2009, the European Court of Human Rights decided two cases under Article 9. In *Kimlya v. Russia*, Case no. 71, Eur. Ct. H.R. (Oct. 1, 2009), the court ruled

that Russia had violated Article 9 by refusing to list the Church of Scientology as a "religious organization" on the basis that two branches of the church had not existed for at least 15 years, as required by Russia's Religion Act. This basis of refusing registration, the court reasoned, was purely formal and functionally unsupportable. Additionally, the law discriminated against newly emerging religious groups that were not part of an established church hierarchy. The court concluded that the consequent interference with the Scientology members' freedom of religion and association had not been "necessary in a democratic society." In *Lautsi v. Italy*, Case no. 819, Eur. Ct. H.R. (Nov. 3, 2009), the court ruled that the display of Christian crosses in public schools violated both Article 2 of Protocol No. 1 (right of education) and Article 9. The court did not accept Italy's argument that a cross was a secular symbol of the Italian state or that it was just one of the many acceptable symbols in a pluralistic state.

4. Comparative Law

The judicial opinion that follows, which refocuses our attention on national law for comparison, underscores the distinctions made by Professor Custos in question 6.

Cooper v. Eugene School District No. 4J, 723 P.2d 298 (Or. 1986)

LINDE, Justice.

When Janet Cooper, a special education teacher in the Eugene public schools, became a Sikh, she donned white clothes and a white turban and wore them while teaching her sixth and eighth grade classes. In a letter to the staff of the school where she taught, she wrote that she would wear the turban and often wear white clothing as part of her religious practice, and that she had explained this and other changes in her life to her students. She continued to wear her white garb after being warned that she faced suspension if she violated a law against wearing religious dress at her work. The law provides, in ORS 342.650:

> "No teacher in any public school shall wear any religious dress while engaged in the performance of duties as a teacher."

[A]nd, in ORS 342.655:

> "Any teacher violating the provisions of ORS 342.650 shall be suspended from employment by the district school board. The board shall report its action to the Superintendent of Public Instruction who shall revoke the teacher's teaching certificate."

Pursuant to these statutes, the school superintendent, acting for the school board, suspended Cooper from teaching and reported this action to the Superintendent of Public Instruction, who, after a hearing, revoked Cooper's teaching certificate. This order was challenged on constitutional grounds in the Court of Appeals, which set aside the revocation of the teaching certificate as an excessive sanction under the court's understanding of federal First Amendment doctrine. *Cooper v. Eugene Sch. Dist. No. 4J*, 76 Or. App. 146, 708 P.2d 1161 (1985). On petitions by the school district and the Superintendent of Public Instruction, we allowed review.

...

[A] law restricting dress specifically for being "religious dress" cannot stand as a regulation of "conduct" rather than "belief" or "worship." If such a law is to be valid, it must be justified by a determination that religious dress necessarily contravenes the wearer's role or function at the time and place beyond any realistic means of accommodation.

The compatibility of religious dress with the role of public school teachers is an old issue under state laws and constitutions. Generally it involved teaching by nuns while wearing the habits of their orders. It is, of course, a different question whether a constitution itself is claimed to forbid the display of the teacher's religious commitment in the public school or whether a ban on religious dress adopted by law or properly delegated rule contravenes the teacher's religious freedom. . . .

...

The courts' tolerance of overt religious symbolism in public schools has differed over time and perhaps with the religious composition of different communities. Looking beyond the specific facts of the cases, however, the decisions generally have been that more than a teacher's religious dress is needed to show a forbidden sectarian influence in the classroom, but that a rule against such religious dress is permissible to avoid the appearance of sectarian influence, favoritism, or official approval in the public school. The policy choice must be made in the first instance by those with lawmaking or delegated authority to make rules for the schools. The courts' role is to see whether the rule stays within that authority and within the constitution and, if necessary, to give the rule a constitutional interpretation.

III. RELIGIOUS NEUTRALITY IN PUBLIC SCHOOLS

Here the policy choice was made by the legislature. There is no reason to believe that when the Legislative Assembly enacted ORS 342.650 in its present form in 1965, it had any aim other than to maintain the religious neutrality of the public schools, to avoid giving children or their parents the impression that the school, through its teacher, approves and shares the religious commitment of one group and perhaps finds that of others less worthy.

...

The main battleground has been the public schools, as the cases under the constitutional proscriptions of "sectarian influence" and later under the First Amendment show. Parents and lawmakers may and do assume that the hours, days, and years spent in school are the time and the place when a young person is most impressionable by the expressed and implicit orthodoxies of the adult community and most sensitive to being perceived as different from the majority of his or her peers; famous constitutional cases have involved this socializing rather than intellectual function of the schools. In excluding teachers whose dress is a constant and inescapable visual reminder of their religious commitment, laws like ORS 342.650 respect and contribute to the child's right to the free exercise and enjoyment of its religious opinions or heritage, untroubled by being out of step with those of the teacher.

. . .

IV. THE PERMISSIBLE REACH OF ORS 342.650

A court's obligation before invalidating a textually overbroad statute is to see whether it can be interpreted so as to save the legislative purpose as far as the constitution permits, leaving only marginal instances of potentially unconstitutional application to case-by-case decision. *State v. Moyle*, 299 Or. 691, 702, 705 P.2d 740 (1985). The Court of Appeals recognized the need to limit the potential reach of ORS 342.650. Compliance with the statute demands some sacrifice of religious self-expression by a teacher. The statute, of course, does not forbid the wearing of religious dress outright, but it does forbid doing so while teaching. The law could be described either as denying a teacher's right to practice her religion or as denying a person demonstratively committed to a religious vocation the opportunity to teach in the public schools. The two descriptions may invite different responses, but the issue should not hinge on semantics.

To forbid a teacher to disclose personal views that are identified as such and not attributed to the school, including religious views, involves issues of free speech as well as religion. A program hermetically sealed to exclude all controversy and potentially offensive ideas can hardly be defended as education for the world beyond the classroom. Teachers as well as students have been held free to express their objection to national policy symbolically by their dress. A distinction between privileged personal expression and forbidden "indoctrination" or "proselytizing" is easier to assert than to apply; one teacher's personal views and acts can carry more unintended persuasion than another's most determined teaching efforts. Yet if Janet Cooper on December 6, 1983, only had told her class that she had changed her name because she became a Sikh and what this meant, the school district could hardly have discharged her in order to protect her pupils against religious proselytizing. To disqualify her from teaching under ORS 342.650 for dressing as a Sikh one must find greater significance in the forbidden religious dress than in the verbal religious self-identification.

The Court of Appeals stated this greater significance as follows:

> We therefore construe the term "religious dress" to mean clothing that is associated with, and symbolic of, religion. To be symbolic, the clothes must communicate the wearer's adherence to a particular religion. We construe "while in the performance of his duties as a teacher" to include only those duties which systematically bring the teacher, as a teacher, into contact with students. (Footnote omitted).

76 Or. App. at 150–51, 708 P.2d 1161. We agree with this interpretation as far as it goes, but more needs to be added. The quoted paragraph correctly recognizes that "religious dress" must be judged from the perspective both of the wearer and of the observer, that it is dress which is worn by reason of its religious importance to the teacher and also conveys to children of the age, background, and sophistication typical of students in the teacher's class a degree of religious commitment beyond the choice to wear common decorations that a person might draw from a religious heritage, such as a necklace with a small cross or Star of David. A teacher does not violate the statute by wearing a garment or a color that unintentionally happens to imply membership in some religious group, nor, for instance, by dressing in clerical garb to assume a role in a classroom historical exercise or a performance of, say, George Bernard Shaw's *Saint Joan*.

The quoted formulation also recognizes that the "performance of his duties as a teacher" does not include everything that a teacher is paid to do and every hour during which he does it. Under the principles already discussed, the phrase must be confined to those circumstances when a teacher's dressing in accordance with the standards of his or her religion is truly incompatible with the school's commitment to maintaining for its students the atmosphere of religious freedom and neutrality that is the objective of ORS 342.650. This means appearing in religious dress while dealing directly with children in a teaching or counseling role.

The additional element not stated in the opinion of the Court of Appeals is the continual or frequent repetition of a teacher's appearance in specifically religious (not merely ethnic) dress. The religious influence on children while in the public school that laws like ORS 342.650, in their concern with the employment of nuns wearing their special garb as public school teachers, legitimately seek to prevent is not the mere knowledge that a teacher is an adherent of a particular religion. Their concern is that the teacher's appearance in religious garb may leave a conscious or unconscious impression among young people and their parents that the school endorses the particular religious commitment of the person whom it has assigned the public role of teacher. This is what makes the otherwise privileged display of a teacher's religious commitment by her dress incompatible with the atmosphere of religious neutrality that ORS 342.650 aims to preserve, or so the school authorities may decide. The statute therefore would not be violated whenever a teacher makes an occasional appearance in religious dress, for instance on her way to or from a seasonal ceremony. It is the same distinction as that between an occasional religious meeting, parade or brief display in a public park or building and the permanent erection of a religious symbol, as in *Lowe v. City of Eugene*, *supra*. Only wearing religious dress as a regular or frequently repeated practice while teaching is grounds for disqualification.

V. CONCLUSION

We conclude that, when correctly interpreted and applied, ORS 342.650 survives challenge under Oregon's guarantees of religious freedom. As interpreted in this opinion, we believe it also does not violate the federal First Amendment.

NOTES AND QUESTIONS

1. In 2010 the Oregon Legislature repealed ORS §§ 342.650 and 342.655, which were at issue in the *Cooper* case.
2. If the culture-sensitive issue in *Cooper* had involved the religious dress of a student, not a teacher, what should be the result? Would the French law of 2004 concerning student dress, as discussed by Professor Custos, survive U.S. constitutional scrutiny? (The French legal system does not provide for judicial review of constitutional issues in a case or controversy.) Consider the following commentary:

> France has followed a principle that forbids all religious and political symbols from the public schools, which includes head scarves. This is an apt place to show the difference between the French and the U.S. approaches to accommodation.
>
> In the United States, there is a value placed on encouraging a free marketplace of religion. Two First Amendment principles work together to let religion operate in a free and open market. The Free Exercise Clause prevents persecution based on religious belief that would rid the market of certain religious elements and the Establishment Clause prevents the government from supporting religion, which would torque the market away from actual demand toward government-managed demand. The result is not only a truly amazing variety of religious faiths, but also a fascinating blend of a public square filled with religious talk and images, juxtaposed with a government that does not itself take positions in that square on religious belief. The celebration of religious diversity that is at the heart of the First Amendment encourages accommodation, and so a flat ban tends to appear undesirable if religious belief can be accommodated consistent with the public good. The problem in the United States is that too often the drive to accommodate religious conduct takes flight from common sense and public security.
>
> The French appear to have the opposite inclination – a presumption against accommodation. As of March 15, 2004, it became illegal in France to wear clothing, insignia, or symbols that "conspicuously manifest a religious [or political] affiliation." The directive applies across the board to all students, though some believe it was prompted by Muslim girls wearing head scarves to school, at a time of large Muslim migration into France and resulting discord.
>
> The motive behind the French law would not have made it unconstitutional in the United States, because the law is neutral and generally applicable. But the culture created by the First Amendment's robust protection of belief and speech would have set the default position at accommodation. That, in turn, would have opened the door to the Islamists to persuade parliament that head scarves could be worn without harm to the public good. For those in the United States who believe that this country has reached the point of factually separating church and state and has eviscerated all traces of religion

> from public places, the French example provides an outstanding context for understanding that strict separation never was and likely never will capture the spirit of the Religion Clauses.

MARCI A. HAMILTON, GOD VS. THE GAVEL: RELIGION AND THE RULE OF LAW 128–29 (2005) (reprinted with permission of Cambridge University Press).

What historical or cultural experiences help explain the divergent legal approaches of France and the United States within their respective legal frameworks?

F. Concluding Observations

MARTIN E. MARTY, THE ONE AND THE MANY: AMERICA'S STRUGGLE FOR THE COMMON GOOD 90–91 (1997) (reprinted with the permission of Harvard University Press)

God's people wondered how they might stay together and worship in Babylon, the land of their exile. There, elders feared, their language would sound muffled, incomprehensible even to themselves. In another generation those exiles might intermarry with the daughters and sons of their captors. They would forget who they were and become bewildered.

. . .

One more question: how seriously should one take the claims of any particular chorus when so many alternative sets of singers advertise themselves as "the Lord's"?

Groups worry, then, that positive involvement with others in a pluralist society may weaken commitment to their own group. This is less likely to be the case in matters of racial and ethnic contact than in religious or ideological involvements, but it is a threat to leaders in all cases. As long as one occupies a tribal place on one side of a mountain and is "pluralistically ignorant," these problems do not arise. One can always hear portrayals of the evils of the other tribe but have no more contact with it than across battlefields during raids and forays. As long as one is in a ghetto and has no intimate involvement with others, it is easy to inspire conflict and prevent intermarriage or reject the entertainment of ideas uncongenial to one's own tribe. Where there is ignorance one can portray monsters at the edges of the moral map. Thus the cartographer Hartman Schedel long ago drew prototypes for those who reject unfamiliar elements in modern pluralist society. In 1493 at the edges of his own map of the world (following the practice of Gaius Julius Solinus [fl. A.D. 250]), he drew fanciful beings and wrote *haec incoluerunt monstra*, "here be monsters."

If ignorance can create imaginary monsters, knowledge and interaction can potentially humanize "the other." Yet this knowledge can also "demonsterize" the other and thus confuse one's own identity and blur the boundaries of one's group. That is why some tribes and subgroups in recent decades have insisted more strenuously than ever before that they must be separate, exclusive, untainted.

The moment we find groups being exclusivist about their place, their blood and soil, their interests, and even their ideas, we find problems for any who have notions of a common humanity or of the common good in a republic. And when, on the other hand, people do recognize the interchangeability of ideas and do encourage the interaction of groups, the leadership of movements bent on control of their own know that ties of loyalty can be weakened. They do not want to take the risk.

NOTE AND QUESTIONS

In the foregoing reading, Professor Marty advocates education in the interchangeability of ideas and encouragement of interaction between groups as antidotes to the fear of the cultural "other" and anxieties about the erosion of one's own culture. What is the role, if any, of faith-based diplomacy in such initiatives? Or is such diplomacy apt to make things worse by unnecessarily exciting passions and latent anxieties about the security of one's beliefs? Does interaction necessarily lead to greater harmony between groups? And what is the future of religion in the endless effort to encourage virtue, purpose, and justification in global relationships? The concluding readings explore these questions.

Brian Cox & Daniel Philpott, *Faith-Based Diplomacy: An Ancient Idea Newly Emergent*, 1 Brandywine Rev. Faith & Int'l Aff., Fall 2003, at 31, 34

"Reconciliation" is now a familiar term in public discourse, a buzzword today in America, and a common phrase elsewhere. Yet it can also arouse deep passions. In the July 2002 opening of the Institute for Reconciliation in Srinagar, Kashmir, one prominent Kashmiri journalist challenged the very idea of reconciliation. In a moment of passionate anger he shouted out, "Does reconciliation mean submitting lamely to a rapist when you are being raped as we are here in Kashmir?"

Reconciliation, though, is neither a recent trend nor a Western importation. The ancient religions express it most deeply, defining it as the restoration of relationship.

. . .

To be sure, differences abound among and within faith traditions about the meaning of reconciliation and about the relative roles of punishment, forgiveness, apology, atonement, and the practice of these concepts in public law. Still, reconciliation is important in each tradition. It pervades Judaism, in which atonement, central to the Torah, infuses halakhah, the Jewish law, wherein punishment, repentance, and restitution are all arrayed towards restoration. Christianity extends the logic of atonement to God's mercy toward sinners on the cross. In Islam, the Qur'an's repeated references to Allah's mercy and injunctions to forgiveness imply a restorative logic, one indeed practiced in Arabic rituals of *sulh*, designed to bring reconciliation between offenders and victims. In Hinduism the conception of dharma, or human obligations, found in the Laws of Manu, appears to stress retributive punishment, but speaks also of repentance and penance through which an offender is restored in his soul and returned to his rightful place in the social order. Reconciliation reached its height in Hinduism through the life and thought of Mahatma Gandhi, though he drew upon other faiths as well. He once exemplified his vision by counseling a Hindu murderer of a Muslim to find an orphan Muslim boy and raise him as Muslim. The Buddhist faith is epitomized by the restoration of the offender's soul and of relationships among the estranged. Both its compendium of ethics, the Vinaya, and the judicial practice of traditional Tibetan culture stress reconciliation as a response to evil.

If restoration of relationship is found in faith traditions, then so, too, the restoration of political orders wounded by war and injustice is a natural principle for faith-based diplomacy.

Raymond Cohen, Diplomacy in the Holy Sepulchre (unpublished manuscript in preparation for his book Saving the Holy Sepulchre: How Rival Christians Came Together to Rescue Their Holiest Shrine (2008))

[This reading assumes that the value of reconciliation, developed in the previous reading, is broadly accepted, but inquires into the efficacy of its implementation in practice. The setting involves six Christian denominations that coexist in Jerusalem's Church of the Holy Sepulchre that is associated with the crucifixion and resurrection of Jesus Christ. Together they share certain common areas but have largely divided up the space territorially.]

For many centuries, then, the Christian communities sharing the Holy Sepulchre have been embroiled in uncounted numbers of quarrels of varying degrees of severity. Sometimes these disputes have spilled over into violence. Many arise from the friction that is inevitable in a crowded, busy place where hundred of monks from different denominations gather to worship throughout the day, every day. Feasts are celebrated, pilgrims visit, services are prepared and conducted, sacramental objects and furnishings moved, rugs laid, pictures rehung, windows and floors cleaned, sewage, water and electricity maintained, damage repaired, doors repainted, novelties introduced. The *Status Quo*, the patchwork of customs governing relations between the communities, cannot foresee all eventualities. Nor is it uncontested. Some disagreements never go away, though they may go underground for decades only to burst out again. It is extraordinary how unvarying and insoluble some of these disputes are.

. . .

Conflict is a feature of the Holy Sepulchre to an extraordinary degree even though it is a holy place of worship dear to millions worldwide and cherished in a very tangible way by all its resident communities. Obduracy, not compromise, is their default mode of disputation. Indeed, the Holy Sepulchre qualifies as a good example of a *conflict system* displaying in concentrated form many characteristic features of conflict and its handling.

For the student of international relations it is suggestive because its conflicts are typically rooted in bedrock beliefs and principled claims, are endlessly protracted, and cannot be resolved in a definitive sense. They can, however, be evaded, postponed or contained. The basilica also clearly has an international dimension, even though its area is no more than that of a cathedral. It is a world heritage site; the resident communities represent international or transnational actors; states and international organisations often intervene in its affairs; it is of considerable interest to the international media; it has featured prominently over the centuries in diplomatic history. It also uncannily resembles a miniature international society: A set of communities coexist in a state of mixed cooperation and conflict, in the absence of a sovereign or hegemon. An outside arbiter sometimes intervenes. The space they inhabit has territories and borders. There are frontier incidents and a tragedy of the commons. Shared and separate narratives, chronicling the histories and struggles of communities down through the ages, shape their identities and claims. Delegates interact, correspond, negotiate and reach agreement according to all the niceties of protocol. There is the occasional resort to violence.

Dissension is intense, frequent and ubiquitous. Almost everyone may be involved in dispute with everyone else at one time or another. The main contemporary conflicts involve Greeks versus Latins; Greeks versus Armenians; Armenians versus Syriani; Copts versus Ethiopians; Copts versus the major communities. But other disputing combinations occur, such as Latins and Greeks versus Armenians; and Latins and Armenians versus Greeks. Disputes also arise between one or more Christian communities and the Moslem religious endowment, the *Waaf*, and also with the government.

. . .

How, then, are disputes actually dealt with in practice in the Holy Sepulchre? As remarked, there is no prevailing ethic of conflict resolution, quite the reverse. The language of Christian reconciliation did make an appearance at the time of Vatican II. Its high point was the historic visit to the Holy Land by Pope Paul VI in January 1964. Whether ecumenical ideas made any permanent impression on the communities in Jerusalem is questionable. Even Roman Catholics speak of the present state of affairs at the Holy Sepulchre as a "cease fire" rather than a permanent arrangement with any kind of legitimacy.

Since there is no mechanism for resolving conflicts, order in the church has been based for the last century and a half on the preservation of the *Status Quo*. The *Status Quo* is capitalized because it is the specific state of affairs in all its complexity *notionally* existing in the Church of the Holy Sepulchre (and all the other Holy Places of Palestine) in 1852. As a concept it has its origins in the Ottoman diplomatic principle of *ala halihi*, meaning maintaining the *status quo* on the ground after a war or "what you have, you hold." What it did not mean, as revisionist communities were subsequently to discover, was a return to the *status quo ante*, the state of affairs existing before the conquest of territory.

For practical purposes the *Status Quo* in the Holy Sepulchre refers to who holds ("possesses") what; and who can do what, when and where. Attempts to discern any hard and fast logic governing the *Status Quo* have been unsuccessful. In general, it tends to conform to certain Ottoman legal assumptions: The right to clean and pay for the repair of property denotes exclusive possession; the right to hang a lamp or picture denotes exclusive possession of a pillar or wall; possession of a roof denotes ownership of the structure underneath; trespassers can be forcibly evicted by the owners. The *Status Quo* is not, incidentally, necessarily set in concrete. Changes involving trade-offs have taken place in the Holy Sepulchre as a result of negotiations involving all the interested parties. Changes have also occurred as a result of unopposed *faits accomplis*.

. . .

So the *Status Quo* is a device for allowing life to go on in a conflict system given the existence of unbridgeable differences. It depends on the presence of an arbiter able to issue administrative rulings and, if necessary, send in the forces of law and order to keep the protagonists apart. Over the years the sovereign's policing function has been essential. The major communities can keep the minor communities in line but have come to depend on the secular authorities to keep the peace between them. To ensure that Holy Saturday 2003 passed off safely the Israeli authorities were obliged to deploy one thousand police in and around the Holy Sepulchre. Curiously, in time of war and transition between regimes in Jerusalem, the communities have usually managed to keep a lid on their disagreements. There is a suspicion that some disputing is staged for the benefit of the authorities. [See also the description of a similar religious fragmentation in the Church of the Nativity in Bethlehem. *10 Must-See Endangered Cultural Treasures*, SMITHSONIAN, March 2009, at 33. – *Eds.*]

John Updike, *The Future of Faith*, NEW YORKER, Nov. 29, 1999, at 83, 91 (© 2007 by John Updike. Used with permission of Alfred A. Knopf, a division of Random House, Inc.)

The future is not just an extension of the past; like a particle being measured, it eludes prediction. Judaism and Christianity are both religions of waiting – waiting in one case for the Messiah, in the other for the Messiah's Second Coming. Christian time is an interim, which has stretched longer than the prophets and early saints expected. Something might happen in faith's future. Science might come up with a surprise – a loophole among the quarks or a reinstatement of the cosmological constant. Or the dynamic of human nature, as Earth's population rolls past six billion, might produce a qualitative change in the frame of faith, of the world's tired, grotesque, irreplaceable faiths. What occurs won't be easily intelligible – the Gospels took most of a century to get written – but the yearning, the insistence that there be, to again quote William James, "something more," will persist. Our concepts of art and virtue, purpose and jurisdiction are so tied up with the supernatural that it is hard to foresee doing altogether without it.

10. Language and Linguistic Expression

A. The Relationship between Language and Cultural Identity

It seems appropriate to conclude this book with a focus on language and linguistic expression. After all, we have seen throughout the book that language is essential to both culture and law, playing a role that transcends its normal and most obvious function simply as a vehicle of communication. Quite likely, it actually structures and thereby influences individual perceptions and actions. According to the famous Sapir-Whorf hypothesis, language filters sensory information so significantly that it shapes our understanding of reality. The effect is a particularly profound example of the role of culture, given the primacy of language.

The manner in which individuals express themselves can both enhance intercultural communication and help foment conflict. Consequently, and even in the absence of conflict, the use of language often raises serious political and legal questions for society and its governance. Intervention by the state may be necessary but also problematic. For example, a decision to officially recognize one or another language or perhaps more than one language may affect the allocation among persons of social services, education, political participation, the judicial process, and regulation of the media. As we will see, linguistic human rights address the resulting domestic and international issues.[1]

This chapter examines national language laws and planning as well as related problems involving multilingualism. The chapter also considers the human rights framework for promoting and protecting the use of particular languages. Before turning to these themes, however, let us examine more deeply the proposition that language in itself shapes cognition, behavior, and cultural identity.

Stephen May, *Language and Culture, in* Language and Minority Rights: Ethnicity, Nationalism and the Politics of Language 132–35 (2008)

It does not take much to demonstrate that language is a communally shared good since language, almost by definition, requires dialogue. What

[1] For examples of language policy debates around the world, *see, e.g.*, Language and National Identity in Africa (Andrew Simpson ed., 2008); Language and National Identity in Asia (Andrew Simpson ed., 2007).

is harder to determine is whether one's own language is a good. Is a particular language significantly related to one's cultural identity or would any language suffice? This is a crucial question since, if the latter is proved, the case for specific language rights – that is, rights relating to the protection and promotion of specific languages – is dealt a perhaps terminal blow. However, even if the former tenet is accepted, one must be able to account for the historical, social and political construction of the language and identity link and its clear variability, both at the inter- and intra-group level. This is not an easy task by any means but the work of the prominent sociolinguist Joshua Fishman provides us with a useful place to start.

Fishman argues that language and ethnocultural identity are crucially linked in three key ways: indexically, symbolically and in a part-whole fashion. First, a language associated with a particular culture "is, at any time during which that linkage is still intact, best able to name the artifacts and to formulate or express the interests, values and world-views of that culture."[2] This is the indexical link between language and culture. Such a link does not assume that a traditionally or historically associated language is a perfect isomorphic match with an attendant culture, nor that other languages might not be able to replace this traditional link in the longer term. However, in the *short* term (that is, at any particular point in time), "no language but the one that has been most historically and intimately associated with a given culture is as well able to express the particular artifacts and concerns of that culture." In other words, the traditionally associated language reflects and conveys its culture more felicitously and succinctly than other languages, *while that language-in-culture link remains generally intact.*

Fishman's position here reflects a weak version of what is known in linguistics as the Sapir-Whorf hypothesis, . . . named after its proponents, Edward Sapir and Benjamin Whorf. . . . Sapir's argument was that one's social and cultural experiences are organised by language and thus each language represents a particular worldview. His pupil Whorf extended this by arguing that thought is not independent of the language used because language carves up experience according to its particular grammatical structure, categories and types. Accordingly, the key implication of the Sapir-Whorf hypothesis is that people who speak different languages are likely to have somewhat different cultural outlooks on the basis that the particular structure of each language results in a culturally specific structuring of reality. Indeed, a strong version of the hypothesis attests that languages are causal vis-à-vis culturally specific behaviours; a view [which has been] widely rejected as linguistically determinist. However, a weak version of the thesis, as here, highlights the influence of language in shaping our customary ways of thinking and can be regarded as both reasonable and unsurprising. If identity is understood here in relation to habitus as "the background against which our tastes and desires and opinions and

[2] J. Fishman, Reversing Language Shift: Theoretical and Empirical Foundations of Assistance to Threatened Languages 20–21 (1991).

aspirations make sense,"[3] then a traditionally associated language would seem to have a significant part to play. . . .

Language and culture are also linked symbolically; that is they come to stand for, or symbolically represent, the particular ethnic and/or national collectivities that speak them. Accordingly, the fortunes of languages are inexorably bound up with those of their speakers. Languages do not rise or fall simply on their own linguistic merits – indeed, it has long been accepted that all languages are potentially equivalent in linguistic terms. Rather, the social and political circumstances of those who speak a particular language will have a significant impact on the subsequent symbolic and communicative status attached to that language. This fact often escapes speakers of dominant national languages, and particularly speakers of English as the current world language, who take the "natural" ascendancy of these languages for granted. In contrast, the current international currency of a language like English has much more to do with the sociopolitical dominance of those nation-states, notably the [United States], for which English is the accepted language of public discourse. Likewise, national languages reflect the greater sociopolitical status of their speakers in relation to minority languages and cultures within the nation-state.

The final aspect – the part-whole link – reflects the partial identity between a particular language and culture. Since so much of any culture is verbally constituted (its songs and prayers, its laws and proverbs, its history, philosophy and teachings), there are parts of every culture that are expressed, implemented and realised via the language with which that culture is most closely associated. Fishman argues that it is within this part-whole relationship that:

> child socialisation patterns come to be associated with a particular language, that cultural styles of interpersonal relations come to be associated with a particular language, that the ethical principles that undergird everyday life come to be associated with a particular language and that even material culture and aesthetic sensibilities come to be conventionally discussed and evaluated via figures of speech that are merely culturally (i.e. locally) rather than universally applicable.[4]

Fishman's analysis highlights the cultural significance of language to identity. This does not imply, however, the reification of the latter or the assumption that such identity can be 'preserved' in some pure, unaltered state. Nor does it link particular languages inexorably with particular identities. Rather, a traditionally associated language is viewed as a significant resource to one's ethnic identity, both at the level of societal integration and social identification. While such a resource may ultimately be discarded, it remains important until such a time as this occurs. . . .

[3] Charles Taylor, *The Politics of Recognition*, *in* MULTICULTURALISM: EXAMINING THE POLITICS OF RECOGNITION 25, 33–34 (Amy Gutmann ed., 1994).

[4] FISHMAN, *supra* note 2, at 124.

Given this, the concern to repudiate language as a significant feature of identity may be overstated. However, be that as it may, Fishman's argument still needs to account for the exceptions it implicitly acknowledges but does not necessarily explain. How do we accommodate those individuals and groups for whom a particular language is clearly not an important feature of their identity? How do we explain language shift, which suggests that these associations, while important, are by no means irreplaceable? And how do we counter the charge that the language and identity link is largely arbitrary – a social and political construction along the well-rehearsed lines of the 'invention of tradition' argument? . . .

NOTES AND QUESTIONS

1. A stock example of the social and environmental relativity of language is that Arctic peoples have a highly refined vocabulary for snow. The relationship of this vocabulary with Arctic society forges a cultural identity over time. From your knowledge of English and perhaps foreign languages, can you think of other specific examples of how language shapes cognition, behavior, and cultural identity in addition to enhancing social and political integration and identity?
2. Alternatively, is language merely a superficial marker of identity – that is, only a form of "symbolic ethnicity"? When individuals shift to speaking a new language, does this have any effect on ethnic identity? Can you cite evidence that language is not a core aspect of cultural identity? Consider the example of Ireland, where in general English has replaced Irish Gaelic as the dominant ethnic and national language: "Despite the fact that Gaelic has been recognized as an official language since the establishment of the Republic of Ireland in 1919, Gaelic has almost given way to English because efforts to protect it by making it a second language that is compulsory in schools neglected to nourish the mother tongue transmission of Gaelic in the home and community." Marianne Ignace & Ron Ignace, *Canadian Aboriginal Languages and the Protection of Cultural Heritage, in* FIRST NATIONS CULTURAL HERITAGE AND LAW: CASE STUDIES, VOICES AND PERSPECTIVES 417, 427 (Catherine Bell & Val Napoleon eds., 2008). Has this linguistic displacement substantially affected Irish culture?
3. To the extent that language does, indeed, reflect divergent worldviews, it can be challenging to facilitate cross-cultural communication. The study of intercultural communication has become increasingly important in the era of globalization. See, e.g., FRED E. JANDT, INTERCULTURAL COMMUNICATION: AN INTRODUCTION (3d ed. 2001); COMMUNICATING ETHNIC AND CULTURAL IDENTITY (Mary Fong & Rueyling Chuang eds., 2004). For an amusing but apparently true account of an anthropologist's frustration and learning experience in discussing *Hamlet* with an elder of the Tiv tribe in West Africa, see Laura Bohannan, *Shakespeare in the Bush*, 75 NAT. HIST. 28 (1966). The elder's distinctive interpretation, apparently based on deep-seated tribal tradition and mores, demonstrated how profoundly culture influences our understanding of things and how easily it may inhibit cross-cultural communication. Whatever the merits of the Sapir-Whorf

hypothesis, the relationship between language and cultural identity seems to be reciprocal.

4. An excellent source of practical commentary on language and its influence in criminal prosecution of foreign defendants and defendants for whom English is a second language is CULTURAL ISSUES IN CRIMINAL DEFENSE (Linda Friedman Ramirez ed., 2d ed. 2007).

B. Responses of the State to Multilingualism

Of all the symbolic manifestations of cultural identity, the right to speak one's native language is arguably the most controversial. Indeed, language differences often fuel ethnic conflicts. Even if linguistic barriers and related misunderstandings do not generate physical conflict, they may be highly contentious. Language laws and state planning in response to multilingualism are likewise controversial.

Some legal systems have established more than one official language, whereas others have established a single official language. Still others do not recognize any official language, or if they do, it is for specific purposes such as eligibility for citizenship, judicial proceedings, or official documentation. In general, insofar as governments are primarily intent on strengthening the state and forging social cohesion, issues of resistance to assimilation and linguistic human rights readily emerge throughout the world.

Dario Castiglione, *The Challenges of Multilingualism*, *in* THE LANGUAGE QUESTION IN EUROPE AND DIVERSE SOCIETIES: POLITICAL, LEGAL, AND SOCIAL PERSPECTIVES 5–11 (Dario Castiglione & Chris Longman eds., 2007)

Whichever side one takes on the origins of languages, as nature or convention, it is apparent that a language is not simply an abstract means of communication between different people, but – like all other such social "institutions" – it binds them together, while offering them a ground for identification and belonging. Besides, as a means of social exchange, it offers opportunities for power politics and social domination. Thus, communication, identity and power are all processes in which language matters.

On the face of it, the first challenge posed by multilingualism is that there is more than one currency in which communication, identity and power relationships can take place in society. This poses obvious problems of efficiency, complicating all three sets of social relationships, thus endangering the unity of the society in question. Economically, transaction costs are greater, particularly if exchanges take place between people who speak different languages. Politically, people may find it more difficult to come to an agreement, since besides all other barriers, they also need to overcome the one posed by the difficulty in communicating and finding a way of understanding each other. Moreover, linguistic differences are, more often than not, part of a broader pattern of cultural differences due to different historical traditions and experiences developing in different parts of the world across time.

. . .

[I]n a bilingual or multilingual environment, there are two sets of linguistic effects, which derive from the particular way in which two or more languages either enter into conflict or communicate. These effects impact on the languages themselves as systems of communication, but also on the community of speakers who predominantly identify with one language or another, and on the individuals whose interests and identity are variously related to language use and intra-group communication. This complex set of relationships is already evident in the context of social and personal bilingualism that may arise from inter-linguistic marriages, or from the close proximity of different linguistic communities. It acquires a more pregnant meaning, however, when bilingualism takes the form of *diglossia*, i.e., in those contexts where the languages available are not used interchangeably across all roles and levels of social discourse, but contextually, according to specific rules and conventions differentiating the use of one language from the other. There are cases in which diglossia may be regarded as merely functional, as when there may be a more or less tacit agreement between members of a community (or family) to speak one language privately (or at home) and another in public (which is often the case with dialects). There are other cases in which diglossia serves to separate the sacred from the profane, thus establishing a linguistic hierarchy and reinforcing a separation of roles, as when, for instance, it was the practice in the Catholic Church to use Latin in religious services (indeed, remnants of this system are still in place). But when diglossia applies to the political sphere, the functional reasons take on a more direct and divisive meaning, establishing a hierarchy of status and power. In such a case, the variety of relationships that diglossia establishes between languages, groups and individuals become more contested and the direct object, not only of personal psychology, but of political struggle. One of the issues raised by multilingualism in politics is whether there is any alternative to political diglossia (i.e., where one language is selected as the language of the political sphere), and whether any other arrangement is stable enough to guarantee effectiveness of communication while ostensibly offering equality of treatment and dignity to all linguistic groups comprising the political community.

Until recently, the subject of multilingualism in political societies was only perfunctorily addressed, for it was often assumed that the legal and political systems of modern nation states required a common language in order to function. The question of the diversity of languages was seen as operating at the margin of the nation state: either as part of the assimilation process of migrant communities, or as part of the accommodation of relatively small, but concentrated, linguistic minorities. On the rare occasions that language emerged as a political issue, it was either as part of a discourse about national character or as a challenge to the supposed unity of the political 'nation,' rather than to its monolingualism. The other political contexts in which multilingualism mattered were, of course, those of direct domination through either imperial or colonial power.

. . .

Now, in different ways, multiculturalism, globalisation and post-colonialism have re-introduced culture, and the attitude one has towards other people's culture, as a political issue. Linguistic diversity is part of this general problem. But the politics of language, as an aspect of the politics of culture, is both simpler and more complex. It is simpler, in so far as it offers a relatively easy test for the identification of issues of cultural identity and for the elaboration of cultural (i.e., linguistic) policies. In this respect, language is a good example of why and in what sense culture matters in politics and law. It is also simpler because language is a paradigmatic example of the relationship between universalism and particularism and of that between the individual and the community. Indeed, language is something that only comes in a particular form and can only exist as the product of social and interpersonal interaction. And yet, language – in the abstract – is one of the fundamental and universal human capacities. Moreover, individuals can grow up as bilingual or can learn another language with relative ease. In certain conditions, they can make a second language their own, using it to their own advantage, and without this causing them any problem in terms of their personality or detracting from their sense of identity.

But the politics of language present some difficulties, for the way in which language conjugates universalism and particularism, individual and collective expression, often complicates issues of identity, while rendering political choices starker, since the more traditional strategies of toleration, indifference, side-to-side cohabitation, and separate flourishing cannot easily apply in the case of language as they might more readily to other aspects of culture or to religion.

Bruno De Witte, *A Legal Perspective, in* Ethnic Groups and Language Rights 303–13 (Sergij Vilfan ed., 1993)

Among linguistic rights, a broad distinction can be made between rights to freedom and rights to equality. Rights to freedom serve to protect the free choice of language use in private conversations, in meetings, in associations, publications or private schools. Such rights, in the traditional view which was unchallenged during the whole period of review, are negative in scope, and impose on the public authorities only a duty of abstention, not a duty to act. They are therefore of little help for members of a minority when they are confronted with judicial or administrative authorities. The freedom to use one's own language in addressing those authorities is ineffective if those authorities have no corresponding duty to understand and act upon that language; and with "negative" rights, no such duty can be imposed upon them. Indeed, in the absence of such a duty, the individual members of the administration or the judiciary could themselves invoke their own linguistic freedom against that of the citizen with whom they deal. In the context of administrative and judicial usage, the primary interest of minorities is the recognition of a form of linguistic equality rather than linguistic freedom.

That the principle of equal treatment implies the recognition by the state of the linguistic peculiarities of non-dominant ethnic groups is not altogether self-evident. Indeed, throughout the nineteenth century, and even now to a very large extent, the main thrust of the principle of equality has been to eliminate all those "arbitrary" distinctions between persons which were the legacy of the ancient regime. Such direct discrimination, denying persons certain rights and benefits on the sole basis of the language which they speak, has been very tenacious during the period under review. Indeed, the advent of authoritarian regimes after the First World War has led to an increase in such discrimination.

Yet in one basic respect linguistic minorities want to be treated differently: they want to able to use, in dealing with the authorities, a language which is different from that of the majority. Equality is therefore an ambiguous concept; it can be invoked for claiming a treatment which is at the same time identical in substance but differentiated in (linguistic) form.

Theoretical arguments for such differential treatment can be found fairly easily. Indeed, the use of a given language in a public relationship affects the substantive value of this relationship for its participants. In the context of public administration, those who have full command of the language will receive a service which is also more valuable in substance to them than to citizens who do not master the language, and this despite the fact that all citizens have contributed by their taxes to the functioning of the public service without distinction as to the language they speak. In other words, the public authorities, by using a single language in a plurilingual situation do not provide an equal treatment to all but operate what could be called a "cultural redistribution" in favour of those persons who speak the official language.

This "pluralistic" view of equality has been widely recognised only in recent times. In the period between 1850 and 1940, by contrast, it may well be argued that egalitarian ideas have had a detrimental impact on the maintenance of linguistic diversity because they justified policies of assimilation. Certainly the dominant view in the period 1850–1940 was that allowing the official use of a minority language was not a "normal" thing but rather a special and almost privileged treatment resulting more from effective political pressure than from considerations of fairness and justice. Yet a very authoritative statement of the pluralistic view of equality was given, towards the end of the period under review, in the advisory opinion of the Permanent Court of International Justice in the *Case of the Albanian Minority Schools.* Albania wanted to suppress all private schools in the country – whatever their language of instruction. The Greek minority in the country considered that, despite appearances, this was a violation of the principle of equality which Albania had an international duty to observe, because all Greek schools were private and the public schools only used the Albanian language. The court agreed with this point of view on the basis of a distinction between two complementary aspects of equality as understood in the context of the minority treaties:

> The first is to ensure that nationals belonging to racial, religious or linguistic minorities shall be placed in every respect on a footing of perfect equality with the other nationals of the state. The second is to ensure for the minority elements suitable means for the preservation of their racial peculiarities, their traditions and their national characteristics.[5]

Reasonable though it may seem in theory, the equal official use of several coexisting languages has seldom been achieved in the period and in the countries under review, and even where it has been realised this was usually after protracted struggles (such as in Belgium and Catalonia). Several reasons may be advanced for this state of affairs. Some of them are pragmatic reasons. The use of several languages can make communication processes more difficult and the delivery of administrative or judicial services less efficient and, above all, more expensive (in particular due to translation or interpretation costs). This consideration carried weight at a time when administrative and judicial activities were perceived more as the exercise of state authority than as the provision of a public service, more a matter of largesse than of right. But the decisive reasons were, no doubt, of an ideological nature. The period 1850–1940 saw the heyday of linguistic nationalism; as the state was defined in national terms, and the nation, in turn, characterised by a common language, the establishment of linguistic uniformity was seen as desirable both by long-established states and by the newly independent states after the First World War.

The legal regime of any given language within a given country, or part of a country, can be roughly classified in one of three categories: the "pure" categories of full equality; total absence of legal status; and, between those two extremes, the variegated category of minority status. Before embarking on an analysis of those categories it must, however, be emphasised that the comparison of legal regimes which will be undertaken here is essentially a static enterprise. A dynamic historical survey is provided elsewhere, but it must be pointed out that a legal comparison can be made not only between the solutions reached in the various countries, or parts of countries, but also between the same areas at different points of time. The major divide in this respect was the end of the First World War. Some groups moved from a status of a "non-dominant ethnic group" to that of a "dominant nation" (the Czechs, Slovaks, Poles, Slovenes, and the Baltic nations), or vice versa (mainly German-speaking groups, in Czechoslovakia, Belgium, Italy, Poland and France, but also the Hungarians in Slovakia). Other groups remained in a minority position throughout but their position

[5] Minority Schools in Albania, Advisory Opinion, 1935 P.C.I.J. (ser. A, B) No. 64, at 17.

became worse under a new nation-state than it was formerly under a multinational empire (this was the case of the Ukrainians in Poland whose language had been recognised as a Landessprache (provincial language) in Austrian Galicia before the war). The evolution of the status of Catalan was equally traumatic but for reasons internal to Spain; the last decade of the period under review saw, first, a dramatic improvement of its position under the Republic followed by a total collapse after the civil war.

For other languages the evolution in either direction was more gradual. Dutch in Belgium saw its position reinforced through a long but continuous process starting in the late nineteenth century and culminating in the series of language laws of the 1930s. The German[-]speaking minority of that country benefited from this momentum and achieved a major recognition of its language, albeit with some delay and some limitations. The position of Romansh in Switzerland slowly improved until its recognition, at the very end of the period under review, as a national language. This constitutional amendment, however, appears more as a symbolic gesture than as a decisive change in the effective language regime. On the other hand, the position of the Sami languages in the Nordic states worsened as a result of policies of assimilation which even led Norway to claim in the League of Nations that it had no minorities. In the case of Finland the change of status from an autonomous territory within the Russian empire to an independent state did not dramatically change the linguistic situation. The equality of status of the Finnish language had already been recognised some years earlier but was now formally entrenched by the constitution. Finally, it may be noted that the last decade of the period, the 1930s, saw a general deterioration of the status of minority languages throughout most of central and eastern Europe (and particularly in Poland and the Baltic states) due to the spread of authoritarian regimes that were generally hostile to minority cultures.

Absence of Legal Status

In many countries minority languages were not given any legal recognition in the administrative or judicial apparatus. The political attitude underlying this absence of status varied, however, from active persecution to benign neglect. The first attitude is legally characterised by the fact that the use of the minority language, whether orally or in writing, is explicitly prohibited, sometimes even under the threat of criminal sanctions (as for example, in South Tyrol during the Fascist period and in Catalonia after the civil war). In other cases, like that of the Samis, the minority language was not explicitly prohibited but "ignored" in the sense that acts, whether private or public, done in that language could not produce legal effects. At the other end of the spectrum a language might be officially ignored but nevertheless be allowed to play a certain role in practice, depending on the goodwill of the public authorities and their single representatives, and without a firm basis in written legal rules. Objective difficulties of communication between the population and a foreign language bureaucracy existed to a large extent in a period in which mass education and mass literacy had not spread everywhere. Those difficulties often could not simply be ignored but required practical accommodations in order to allow the state machinery to function. This was a constant feature, throughout the many political vicissitudes, of language regulation in Alsace. All successive regimes, be they French or German, were quick to impose the principle of official unilingualism but at the same time allowed for some mitigations of the principle. Those mitigations cannot be qualified as minority rights but as precarious privileges which were intended to vanish after some time.

Only apparently different is the case of total absence of language regulation, or of regulation at a purely local level, as was the case in the early decades of Belgian independence and for most of the time in Romansh Graub[ü]nden and Sami Norway. This absence of a general official status for both the "dominant" and the "minority" language might appear to be a form of equal treatment of both languages and could even be presented, in the Belgian case, as an expression of the constitutional principle of linguistic freedom. Yet the reality was quite clear: absence of legal regulation meant that local elites, whenever feasible, almost exclusively used the socially dominant language (that is, French in the case of Belgium). There were many exceptions to this predominance but they were inspired, again, by the need to make sure that the population understood the content of the messages addressed to them.

Status of Equality

A language has reached the status of full equality when it can be used, within a given country, to the same extent as any other language and is therefore, legally speaking, no longer considered as a minority language, but becomes instead one of the country's official languages. When a language reaches this status of official language an immediate logical consequence seems to be the right, for the citizens, to use that language when dealing with the judicial and administrative authorities. Both Article 14 of the Finnish constitution and Article 2 of the Statute of Autonomy for Catalonia, after having declared that Finnish and Swedish, Castilian and Catalan, have an equal official status, explicitly added the right to use any of those languages in dealing with judicial or administrative authorities. This right seems to be implicit in recognising the official status of a language. What would be the purpose of declaring a language to be "official" if this does not guarantee at least a right for the citizens to use that language when they have to deal with "official" authorities?

Yet full equality does not necessarily mean that the two (or more) official languages can be used interchangeably in all circumstances and throughout the country. Their equal status may be, and usually has been, modulated on a territorial basis. An excellent example is provided by Belgium. The equal status which was finally accorded to the Dutch language in the 1930s did not result in a bilingual regime throughout the country but in a regime of territorial unilingualism. Each of the two official languages (Dutch and French) dominate (within the area where it was spoken by a majority of the population) and a truly bilingual regime was established only in the central administration and in the local administration of the capital

Brussels and of those few localities where the minority language group exceeded 20 per cent of the population. For its part, Finland implemented the principle of equal treatment of the Finnish and Swedish languages first through a system (under the law of 1902) in which both languages could be used throughout the country in dealing with all state authorities; later it was done through a much more restrictive system under 1922 legislation which divided the country into bilingual, unilingual Finnish and unilingual Swedish districts.[6] In the unilingual districts members of the local minority henceforth had only the right to use the language themselves, but had no right to receive the services of courts or administrative authorities in that language as well. Even in post-war Czechoslovakia the legal fiction of a single Czechoslovak language, with its two "literary" forms of Czech and Slovak to be used interchangeably, could not be maintained throughout: it was stipulated that as a rule Czech and Slovak would each be used as the official language in its traditional area of diffusion.

A more restricted form of equality that could be obtained by a minority language was equality within a limited territory, which implied a continuing minority status within a country as a whole. This status was partly 'achieved by the so-called Landessprachen (provincial languages) in Austria before 1918; by German in the Memel territory under its internationally recognised autonomy status; and also, but briefly, by the Catalan language under the Second Spanish Republic. While the constitution firmly entrenched the national primacy of Castilian, the 1932 Catalan Statute of Autonomy recognised the co-official status of Catalan within the limits of the old principality of Catalonia. As Catalonia was fairly homogeneous from the linguistic point of view no further territorial specialisation of the two languages was made, both being official throughout the territory of the region, with a marginal advantage given to Castilian.

In all cases where two official languages coexisted at a given level (mainly, for the period and area considered in this volume, in the central administration of Belgium and Finland or in the bilingual districts of those countries, as well as in Catalonia and some of the old Austrian Under) the external activity of the administration and the working of the judiciary were constrained by the right of individual citizens to use the official language of their choice in their relations with the state. Yet in the internal operation of the public administration those two languages might be used either simultaneously or interchangeably. The latter option is the most flexible and the cheapest but it usually tends to favour the use of one of the two languages. That this does not need to be the state language is shown by the example of Catalonia: the possibility of using Castilian or Catalan on an equal basis during the years of the Second Republic generally served to improve the position of Catalan. If, however, a formal precedence is given to one of the two languages in the operation of the services, then there is

[6] Although the legal mechanism is similar to that adopted in Belgium, the actual numerical relation between the two language groups is, of course, much more asymmetrical in Finland, which meant that the biggest part of the country became, in effect, unilingual Finnish territory.

no longer equal treatment of two languages but one official language with a protected status for the other language.

Minority Status

This remaining category covers all the cases in which some official recognition is given to a language without taking the form of completely equal treatment with the dominant language. The number of possible options and combinations within this category is, of course, almost infinite.

The best position, within this category, is that of a language which was not recognised as an official language and therefore was not used in the internal operation of the administration. Nevertheless, it could be used by the citizens in their relations with judicial and administrative authorities, with a corresponding duty for those to respond in the same language. Typically such a right was territorially limited, excluding thereby those members of the minority who happen to live elsewhere in the country. Thus in Czechoslovakia the general right to address the authorities, and receive their services, in a minority language was limited to those areas in which that language was spoken by at least 20 per cent of all inhabitants, which resulted in the exclusion of almost 300 000 minority language speakers throughout the country.

The right to use one's language may be limited to relations with local as opposed to regional or state authorities. Finnish was officially allowed in dealing with the local administration by laws in 1858 and 1863, that is, long before the granting of a general official status to the language. In Catalonia, during much of the period, there was no explicit prohibition against the use of the regional language in local administration, which was often interpreted as tacit permission to use it.

The scope of minority language use may also be limited to relations with the courts as opposed to administrative services. The case of the German minority in Belgium may be mentioned here. This minority was granted the right to use their language in court by law in 1935, while a corresponding right in relation to the administrative authorities was formally granted by law as late as 1963.

There may be a right to use one's language in addressing either the courts or the administration, but without a corresponding duty for the public service to use that same language from its own side, especially when issuing written documents. This situation prevailed under the 1868 Hungarian Nationalities Act; in Estonia; and also in Graub[ü]nden for the Romansh language.

At the level of the courts a distinction was sometimes made between criminal and civil procedures, and language guarantees were granted more easily in the first type of procedure. This distinction was macroscopic in Belgium. Criminal trials in Flanders had been held in Dutch since 1873 while only in 1935 was the same rule imposed for civil proceedings. The reason for the distinction might be that personal oral evidence is usually more important in criminal trials and that the inability to use one's language not only constitutes a cultural discrimination but also often a violation of fundamental rights of defence and fair trial. The latter consideration inspired legislation which restricted the right to use a non-official language to those ignoring the court's language.

A further option was that language rights were formally recognised but costs attached to the exercise of that right had to be borne by their beneficiary, for instance in providing the translation of a document or paying the cost of an interpreter. This strong deterrent was used, among other cases, against the Sami and the Romansh language.

Finally, instead of granting a subjective right to use a language, one might allow pure or limited discretion to the authorities in deciding whether or not to allow for the use of a non-official language in the given circumstances.

Language Use and Access to Public Employment

The decision on which language(s) the courts or the public authorities must use in given circumstances presupposed the existence of corresponding linguistic abilities among the staff of those authorities. In the long run those abilities could be created through appropriate language teaching either in the educational system generally or specifically in the training of future judges and civil servants (when such special training existed). But in the short run the proclamation of an additional official language could create problems of adaptation. One solution was to make the transition costs bear on the citizens, who would receive only imperfectly bilingual services for a certain time. But if it was really desired to guarantee the right to obtain a service in all official languages then the public authority itself would have to be made responsive to that right. Two major mechanisms could be used for that purpose. One was to divide every basic unit of the administrative and judicial apparatus into separate unilingual sub-units serving each of the language groups concerned, without requiring bilingualism from the civil servants or judges individually. The other solution was to impose linguistic proficiency requirements on new candidates for public employment or on candidates for promotion within the service or even on laymen participating in the exercise of public authority (such as members of a jury).

For the internal operation of the service the latter would be the more practical solution, as it avoided difficult problems of organisation. As far as the users were concerned, however, the picture was more ambivalent. At first sight it might seem more attractive to be able to address every single civil servant in one's mother tongue. On the other hand, the level of proficiency required from the civil servants might, in practice, be so low that minorities might prefer a separate but linguistically fluent service. Finally, candidates for recruitment or promotion may themselves resent linguistic requirements as a discriminatory mechanism which excluded persons for reasons which had nothing to do with their intrinsic capacities as judges or administrators. The counterargument, of course, was that linguistic skills were functionally related to work in a bilingual environment to the same extent as more traditional skills.

In some countries both systems of recruitment were used contemporaneously, with differentiations according to the service concerned. In Belgium a bilingual requirement was established for state civil servants under a 1921 law but was dropped in a 1932 law, though it was maintained for the personnel of the local administration in the Brussels area. During the Second Spanish Republic, proficiency in Catalan was apparently required in Catalonia only for some of the new positions to be filled. A similar distinction was made in Finland between higher and lower judges, linguistic proficiency in both official languages being requested only from the latter.

Regulatory Style

Generally speaking, the regulation of official language use became more and more detailed during the period under review, and "blank spots" on the map of linguistic legislation gradually disappeared.

Two factors may have contributed to that evolution. One general factor was the development of the regulatory and welfare state, which made contacts between the citizens and the state ever more frequent and therefore also increased the need to regulate the way in which those administrations had to function, both internally and in their external relations with the population. In a multilingual setting linguistic rules are an important part of this functioning. This also meant that linguistic regulation became more important for the citizens, because they increasingly had need to deal with public services.

The specific factor favouring linguistic regulation was the dominant ideological mood of linguistic nationalism. Establishing linguistic uniformity within a country became, much more than in earlier centuries, a major policy priority in most countries. Legislation on language use became either the expression of such assimilationist policies or an instrument for regulating conflicting interests when the policy of assimilation had failed.

As a result, by the end of the period all the countries considered were regulating to a certain extent the use of languages by the judiciary and the administration. But the variations between countries were considerable not only, as indicated above, in the content of the rules but also in the formal characteristics of the regulation. The fact, for instance, that linguistic assimilation was a major policy priority did not necessarily mean that it was expressed in a solemn legal instrument. In Fascist Italy, for example, German was excluded from the South Tyrolean administration by a simple prefectoral decree, although the policy decision was clearly taken at the highest national level.

Territorial subdivisions, often made for general purposes and not with exclusive reference to the regulation of language use, frequently had important effects on the substance of the rights granted to minorities. Thus the consolidation during the years 1849–53 of the historical Lander boundaries in Austria, and the (very partial) adjustment of their subdivisions according to national lines, did not directly involve language regulation. However, it set the framework within which decisions on language use would be taken for the following 60 years. Territorial subdivisions were particularly important whenever, as in the case of Czechoslovakia or Finland, the attribution of rights was made dependent on the relative importance of a language within a given area.

Another factor which has to be borne constantly in mind when analysing language regulation in this period is the gap that could exist between the law as laid down and the law in reality. Formal rules were often not implemented in practice. In "old" Austria there was a continuous struggle to implement the promise of equal rights contained in the 1867 constitution. A particularly blatant case was that of the 1867 Hungarian Nationalities Law, which appeared on the face of it to make far reaching concessions to the non-Hungarian minorities, but which in fact served to camouflage continuous discrimination, largely because there were no judicial remedies for enforcing the rights which were granted. The same applies to a very large extent to the treatment of minorities in inter-war Poland. The Polish constitution of March 1921 solemnly proclaimed equality of rights for members of minorities, yet the subsequent language laws of 1924 severely restricted the possibility of using minority languages. Even those limited rights were hardly respected in practice and abolished altogether under the dictatorial regime of the 1930s.

This type of gap between promise and reality was not confined to authoritarian political systems. The equal status of the Romansh language, for example, recognised by the cantonal constitution of Graubünden, contrasted with the daily practice of the administrative and judicial institutions, which was rather restrictive. Yet it would seem that the existence of effective judicial remedies in countries like Belgium, Czechoslovakia, Finland or "old" Austria must be considered as a necessary condition for the effective guarantee of the rights of non-dominant groups. Such remedies are not, however, a sufficient condition, for a number of reasons. First of all, rules of constitutional rank were immune from judicial review. Neither could there be, as a rule, judicial interference with national legislation, as opposed to executive action, so that legislation implementing constitutional principles in a restrictive way could not be challenged. In addition, some aspects of day-to-day administrative decision-making tend to escape judicial control; as an example of such practices, one might mention the organisation of language tests for access to the civil service, which have sometimes been used deliberately in order to influence the ethnic composition of the Service. Furthermore, the judiciary, itself often dominated by the majority group, may give an unduly restrictive interpretation of minority rights that is very liberal if taken at face value; some evidence to that effect is available for Czechoslovakia. Finally, minorities may be reluctant, for a variety of reasons, to use available means of redress, even in the absence of open intimidation by the majority population.

Language planning by states, with its implications for language rights, has also been important in Africa. Because of the hundreds of languages spoken in the large state of Nigeria, its distinct model of language planning is particularly instructive.

F. Niyi Akinnaso, *Linguistic Unification and Language Rights*, 12 Applied Linguistics 139–60 (1994)

Since independence, many African States have been involved in extensive language status planning as part of more general programs in State construction. One of the major goals of such planning is the adoption or imposition of one or more indigenous languages as "national" or "official" languages, to supplement or supplant the colonial languages which have continued to perform various "high" language functions. The processes involved in this language politics have been described variously as "language and national development"; "language rationalization"; "status change"; "national language management"; and so on. Whatever the terms used, the current wave of language status planning in Africa and elsewhere is reminiscent of the processes of linguistic unification, the hallmark of nationalism in nineteenth-century Europe, based on the idea that language, nation, and State should be isomorphic.

There is, however, a growing consensus that linguistic unification will not be the norm in Africa, despite some (partial) success stories, such as Tanzania and Somalia. The consensus is based on the complexity of the language situation; problems of the choice, development, and acceptability of indigenous languages to serve official roles; and the political, economic, and practical problems with the implementation of language policies, particularly those that involve status change from a European to an indigenous language. The implication is that European languages may not lose official status in African States.

One of the key problems with status change in postcolonial States is the resistance of the elite to such change, partly because the European language to be replaced is the language of elite professions (law, medicine, engineering, accountancy, etc.) and partly because education in the European language is often viewed as a necessary step to the reproduction of elite culture.[7] European languages provide the symbolic capital upon which the elite's claim to power and legitimacy is based. Language minorities also resist status change, because of the fear that the elevation of dominant languages to national or official status will further enhance the political hegemony of the dominant groups.

. . .

Although the issue of language rights has always been recognized, it was not subjected to systematic analysis until recently. The term has been used in two senses, both of which underlie the present analysis: language-as-right – that is, the rights of individuals and groups to have their languages developed and used for certain purposes and in certain contexts and

[7] Although there are postcolonial countries, such as Sri Lanka, in which the professional elite advocated and secured the replacement of the colonial language by an indigenous language, the colonial language has retained its importance in the language repertoires, particularly as the language of elite professions. Thus, in Sri Lanka, the elite's claim to political legitimacy continues to be sustained in part by English.

right-to-language, that is, the right of access to the State's legitimate or dominant language(s), including the right to learn even a foreign language in the belief that such knowledge might bring certain benefits to the individual or the society. The duties, obligations, and expectations involved in language rights are complex and wide-ranging, including the rights against discrimination on the basis of language and against interference in private language use. Since language is critical to self[-]expression, social identity, and community membership, language rights are important in preserving the value of autonomy and identity, leading to a convergence of individual and communal rights.

Both perspectives of language rights entail complementary processes of empowerment – one seeks to ensure that minority languages are developed and maintained, while the other seeks to ensure that minorities acquire the appropriate symbolic capital that would guarantee access to the labor market. However, the language-as-right perspective has received the most attention, partly because recognition and development of local languages, especially their use in elementary and adult functional literacy programs and the communication media, are considered vital to the preservation and survival of local traditions and can be a catalyst for social mobilization, agricultural production, effective health management, and "modernization" and partly because language rights are viewed as human rights. . . . No wonder, then, that the language-as-right perspective has been endorsed by major world bodies, notably UNESCO, the World Bank, and the United Nations. Language status planning is often, but not always, at the root of both language-as-right and right-to-language problems, both problems being two sides of the same coin. On the one hand, language-as-right problems arise when certain languages are marginalized and deprived of recognition and resources for development, thereby reducing their "exchange value" in the labor market. On the other hand, right-to-language problems arise when certain languages are privileged over others, by being officially recognized, developed, and legitimated by formal institutions, thus constituting them into a form of symbolic capital which must be acquired in order to have access to power and the labor market. Bilingual education programs often provide opportunities for meeting language-as-right demands, by providing initial mother tongue education, and right-to-language demands, by providing (later) instruction in the legitimate or dominant language(s). This dual objective, however, often raises a critical problem – how to provide minorities with access to the dominant languages without denigrating their first languages and without requiring them to assimilate to the dominant languages.

It should be stressed, however, that, although language status planning may exacerbate the demand for language rights, what is being demanded is often more than either language-as-right or right-to-language; in many cases, the demand for language rights only serves as a smokescreen that masks much deeper social, cultural, economic, and political concerns. This is particularly so in linguistically heterogeneous States like Nigeria, where language boundaries typically coincide with other major cleavages, such as ethnic, cultural, religious, economic, political, and demographic differences. Because language is so often used as an excuse, although sometimes also the reason, for protests, language issues have become an integral aspect of Nigeria's overall development planning. Thus, a variety of language policies and linguistic practices emphasize linguistic unification as part of the national program for political integration. At the same time, however, the demands for language rights from state governments and ethnic minorities and actual linguistic practices at the local level have prompted the government to adopt a parallel set of policies emphasizing language rights.

. . .

The cultivation of a "common language" remains an elusive goal in most postcolonial States in Africa, Southeast Asia and the Pacific islands. Even when Nigeria was divided into only three Regions, it had been predicted that "the political survival of Nigeria as a country would be even more seriously threatened than it is if any one of these three languages [Hausa, Igbo, and Yoruba] were promoted by the Government as being the one national language." Whether or not the present integrative policies would erupt in a political crisis depends on the outcome of the government's plans to evolve a single official language.

. . .

The degree to which the integrative policies could be pursued is dictated partly by the degree to which language rights are recognized and accommodated. This explains why Nigeria's language planning model allows for the inclusion of a variety of "rights" policies: each state may select one or more indigenous languages, in addition to English, for conducting the business of its House of Assembly (Constitution, Section 95); the mother tongue or the language of the immediate community shall be used in early primary education (National Policy on Education, Sections 2:11(3) and 3:15(4); Cultural Policy, Section 9.2.2); Nigerian languages shall be used in the mass media (Cultural Policy, Section 8) and in the criminal courts (Constitution, discussed in Brann 1980); and the government shall promote the development and learning of all Nigerian languages (Constitution, Section 19(4); Cultural Policy, Sections 4.3.5 and 9.2.2).

. . .

Recent developments in [Nigerian] local government reforms have increased the symbolic value of local languages and dialects, whose mastery is often the best guarantee for access to political participation, job opportunities, and other social rewards within particular local governments, in addition to their primary function in maintaining everyday social interaction. Campaigns for local elections, contract negotiations, customary court proceedings, ward meetings of political parties, and many other business meetings are often conducted in the appropriate local language or dialect, although records are often kept in English. The use of appropriate local languages and dialects is obligatory, especially in traditional politics and ritual performances, in the second tier of local administration (the kingdoms and the emirates). Even where the traditional rulers are knowledgeable in other languages, the local language is the preferred medium of communication, even with outsiders. The role of language in the much publicized competition for the post of the Sultan of Sokoto is a case in point. One of the reasons given for the rejection of a top contender was his reply in English to a memo written in Hausa, the supposed official language of the emirate. Thus, in a sense, states, local councils, and traditional political units provide a territorial dimension in the exercise of language rights, by bringing into prominence the linguistic resources within each territory. Thus, local languages and dialects function as a means of both inclusion and exclusion.

In addition to satisfying language-as-right needs, the federal government has also been sensitive to the people's right-to-language needs by providing various avenues for exposure to English and the national languages. Although integrative functions are served by teaching the three national languages in the State's schools, by promoting TV lesson programs in these languages, and by using them in network news broadcasts and advertisements, these efforts should also be viewed from a right-to-language perspective.

. . .

The traditional doctrine that the national language should be the crystallizing focus of national identity underlies contemporary conceptions about the relationship between language and the political economy. Although the centrality of language to notions of identity and nationalism dates back to antiquity, the Enlightenment period marked a turning point. The mother-tongue-education ideology aimed at achieving the Enlightenment ideals of educational expansion soon developed into an association among language, nation, and State, which was then exploited for other political purposes, especially during the revolutionary wars when language became the key symbol of nationalism throughout Europe.

Of what relevance is the language-nation ideology to postcolonial States? Why, for example, should Nigeria, which is culturally and linguistically diverse, but embraces "egalitarianism" and "equal opportunities" for its citizenry, pursue a policy that seeks to cultivate a "common language" for the State? Despite the universal appeal of the ideology, different sets of factors underlie language nationalism in Europe and Africa, because of major differences in historical experiences and the goals of nationalism. In Africa, the factors include anticolonial feelings, especially reactions against English linguistic imperialism; the search for a symbol of "authenticity" – that is, one that represents the people and their past; the need to establish "linguistic self-pride"; and the hope that a national language might promote the integration of diverse ethnolinguistic groups into a single national culture. There are hidden agendas as well. In Nigeria, for example, the three major ethnic groups, whose languages are contenders for national status, are interested in perpetuating their hold on power through the legitimation of their languages at national and regional levels. This is particularly so with the Hausa-speaking group which has maintained political hegemony since independence, having produced seven of ten Heads of State, and has continued to use its privileged position to promote the adoption of Hausa as the State's official language.

Given the commitment of many postcolonial States to linguistic unification, the question is not so much of whether it is necessary as of whether it is practicable or achievable. Although absolute linguistic unification appears to be impossible, some form of language rationalization is indeed possible. However, given the sociolinguistic peculiarities of each State and the variations in the nature and degree of the constraints within which options must be examined, it is fair to conclude that there can be no monolithic path to such rationalization. The Nigerian model illustrates one of three major paths that postcolonial States have followed.

The Nigerian model supports the promotion and legitimation of a few languages, usually those spoken by majority ethnic groups, either through overt language policies, requiring their use, for example, in legislation or education, or through covert policies governing linguistic practices in specific situations or domains, such as the mass media. There are at least two such languages in Kenya, three in Nigeria, four in Zaire, five in Benin, six in Senegal, and seven in Zambia. In choosing more than one language as national languages, the underlying expectation is that one of them might eventually emerge as the national language. Such a development actually took place in Sri Lanka, where the choice of Sinhala as the sole official language in 1956 was preceded by the adoption, in 1943, of a two-language-formula, involving Sinhala and Tamil.

At the other extreme, some countries, such as Somalia and India, attempt to hazard the attendant tension by naming one of the indigenous languages as the national and official language. Somalia even took melodramatic measures in 1972 when it suddenly declared Somali the official language with immediate effect and distributed leaflets on the new orthography by dropping them from helicopters. While India's choice of Hindi led to serious protests and remains largely unimplemented, the choice of Somali posed no such problems, because over ninety-five per cent of the Somali population speaks it. Fewer than ten countries in Africa enjoy such a linguistic luxury! The apparent success of the Somali experiment notwithstanding, the 25-year-long "script war" which preceded the declaration must not be overlooked.

Between the two extremes is a third approach, the choice of either a minority language, such as Bahasa Indonesia (previously Malay) in Indonesia, or a trade language, such as Swahili in Tanzania and Tok Pisin in Papua New Guinea. Other trade languages in Africa, such as Sango in the Central African Republic, Kituba in the Congo, and Pidgin English in Nigeria and Cameroon, could not be elevated to this exalted position for sociohistorical and political reasons. For one thing, none of these trade languages ever had the advantage of missionary and colonial support for its development nor the strong support of a respected and trusted Head of State such as Swahili had in Julius Nyerere.

Nigeria's "gradualist" approach is far more popular than the "radical" approach adopted by Somalia; however, both embrace the ideals of linguistic unification, unlike the "status quo" approach, adopted by countries like Cameroon, which emphasizes the nationist role of colonial languages and the need not to rock the boat. What is particularly interesting about the Nigerian model is the adoption of a system of stratified rationalization in which one or more majority languages are accorded some special status at federal, regional, state, and local levels, while the rights of other languages to exist and be developed are also respected.

. . .

Although several minority languages have fallen under the hegemonic pressures of superordinate languages, the increasing emphasis on language rationalization in modern States has been matched by a proportional increase in the activities of language rights and revival movements, leading to the enhanced status of many regional languages, for example, Catalan in Spain, Flemish in Belgium, French in Canada, Kannada in India, and Ibibio in Nigeria. Even in France, where minority languages were suppressed, even brutalized, for over four centuries, provincial languages are now undergoing unprecedented revival and development. Many former French colonies, once subjected to France's assimilationist language policy, have also been developing their local languages for use in literacy education and other aspects of national life. Moreover, in South Africa, where the Bantu Language Act was previously rejected, writers, journalists, and the liberation movements are beginning to see the important role of local languages and the demands for language rights are now on the increase. In Africa as a whole, attention is being drawn to the functions and vitality of local languages, their right to exist, and the need to develop them appropriately.

Although language rationalization has always been resisted by those whose languages or interests are jeopardized, the escalating demands for language rights in the last three decades can best be explained in terms of recent political, economic, and educational developments. First, a pattern of "internal colonialism" developed in which marked inequalities between the groups relegated the peripheral or minority groups to an inferior position, while the core or dominant groups maintained economic and political power. The hostility of the former to the latter groups led to conflicts which were deepened by linguistic differences. Although this Hechterian formulation was based specifically on the British context, the model remains compelling in many other contexts. We have seen in the Nigerian context how various language minorities have reacted against the dominance of the majority ethnic groups, leading to various demands for civil, political, and language rights. Ironically, however, the federal government's attempts to balance sectional inequalities drew attention to certain inequalities, while also creating others, thereby accentuating further demands for redress.

Second, once the question of the best language in which to inaugurate the child into literacy was decided in favor of the child's mother tongue . . . the empowerment of minorities through literacy in their mother tongues became an integral part of literacy campaigns and the recognition and development of various local languages became a major part of educational and national development planning in developing States. Thus, the rights to education and language became intertwined.

Third, human rights organizations, supranational communities, such as the European Community, and major world bodies, such as the United Nations, have endorsed language rights as part of the process of minority empowerment. This broad coalition of support, the (re)emergence of civil society, and the failure of modern States to meet the growing demands of minorities, have all provided good grounds for the formation of language rights and revival movements as part of the negotiations for greater economic and political participation.

Fourth, many countries have been turning inwards to their internal resources, particularly local languages and traditions, in response to the uncontrollable spread of major world languages, particularly English, and various large-scale sociopolitical processes. In Western Europe, for example, the formation of the European Community, which statutorily requires that member States develop their regional and minority languages, has alerted such States to the need to pay proper attention to language rights. Not only are local languages and traditions now being viewed as a positive resource which ought to be preserved, but nurturing local traditions and local power bases is also viewed as a logical way of preserving democracy. Recent local government reforms in Nigeria and attention to local languages and traditions provide an illustration. However, this sensitivity to the revival and development of local languages still leaves a critical question unresolved – how nation-states might best guarantee language rights, while fostering national identity and political integration.

An important step is to recognize that such rights exist and that they must be protected. This implies that the equal treatment of speakers of all languages must be guaranteed through legislation or other statutory means and specific language policies must be enacted that protect language rights. As indicated above, many national governments, supranational communities, and major world bodies have begun to incorporate language rights in their statutes.

Another step is to provide resources for the development of minority languages and incentives for teaching and learning them. In this regard, regional, state, and local governments must supplement federal efforts. The empowerment of local governments is particularly relevant here. Nigeria again provides a model of political, educational, and economic reforms that could foster the development of local languages and traditions. In politics, Nigerian local governments now function, like Swiss communes, as the first point at which those who wish to succeed in politics must begin their careers; every politician aspiring to office at any level must begin his/her accreditation and nomination here. For the first time, too, local governments are now directly responsible for primary education and have been granted increased federal allocations which can now reach the local governments with minimum intervention by their state governments. Furthermore, local governments are now encouraged to initiate their own development projects and many have set aside some specific day(s) each year for 'homecoming' and fund raising. Although much still remains to be done, these grassroots orientations are already having some impact on local traditions, languages, and even dialects, and such impact is likely to increase in the future.

The federal government should provide access to the dominant languages, although regional and local governments should be involved in the implementation. However, such languages should not be imposed or even used as catalysts for national integration, especially where they coincide with other major cleavages as in Nigeria. Instead, national integration should be sought in social, educational, and political programs and shared symbols, as in Switzerland. The Somali experience shows too well that a successful policy on linguistic unification is no guarantee for national integration. Even in Europe, where language nationalism first developed into a political ideology, the multilingual nature of the individual States and the recent formation of the European Community demonstrate the futility of using languages [as] the most important catalyst of social community.

NOTES AND QUESTIONS

1. What principles governed the landmark decision of the Permanent Court of International Justice in the *Case of the Albanian Minority Schools* (summarized in the fifth paragraph of the De Witte reading)? To what extent are these principles relevant to disputes in the twenty-first century?
2. In your view, what model of state language planning shows the greatest potential for resolving linguistic conflicts? Do federal systems have an advantage in reconciling competing linguistic interests within a polity?
3. As we more specifically see in the next section of this chapter, "[t]he matter of language rights is especially critical in countries like Belgium with more than one significant language group. Rather than deal with this issue through ordinary legislation or by invoking more general guarantees of equality, privacy, education and so forth, some of these countries have enacted rather specific constitutional rules on the right to use the minority language in defined situations." Mark Janis & Richard Kay, European Human Rights Law 407 (3d ed. 2008). Focusing on Canada, the authors observe as follows:

   > Since confederation, the Canadian Constitution has provided that either English or French may be used in legislative or judicial proceedings in the federal government and in the province of Quebec. A similar provision was enacted for the province of Manitoba when it was created in 1870, and for New Brunswick in 1982. Furthermore, in the Constitution Act 1982, very

specific rules were included governing minority language education rights for qualifying citizens of Canada in any province "where numbers warrant." This provision was relied on by the Supreme Court of Canada to strike down parts of the Quebec Charter of the French Language in 1984, insofar as it denied English language education to certain children. In subsequent cases, that Court has held that linguistic minority communities are entitled to some degree of management and control of the minority language instruction, as well as to a "distinct physical setting" for the instruction. The exact character and extent of these latter rights should be determined on a "sliding scale" relating to the number of students involved so that the larger the minority population the more independent its educational establishment must be. The Court, therefore, has held that the provincial duty to supply minority language education "where numbers warrant" could not be satisfied by providing transportation out of the locality. The Court emphasized that the constitutional rule was intended, in part, to promote the cultural development of minority language communities.

Arsenault-Cameron v. Gov't of Prince Edward Island [2001] 1 S.C.R. 3.

4. See generally COLIN H. WILLIAMS, LINGUISTIC MINORITIES IN DEMOCRATIC CONTEXT (2008) (especially Chapter 4, "Language Policy and Planning Issues in Multicultural Societies"); MAPPING LINGUISTIC DIVERSITY IN MULTICULTURAL SETTINGS (Monica Barni & Guus Extra eds., 2008); MAINTAINING MINORITY LANGUAGES IN TRANSNATIONAL PERSPECTIVES (Anne Pauwels, Joanne Winter, & Joseph Lo Blanco eds., 2007); LANGUAGE RIGHTS AND POLITICAL THEORY (Will Kymlicka & Alan Patten eds., 2008).

C. Linguistic Human Rights

Universal Declaration of Human Rights, G.A. Res 217A, at 71, U.N. GAOR, 3d Sess., 1st plen. mtg., U.N. Doc. A/810 (Dec. 12, 1948)

Article 19

Everyone has the right to freedom of opinion and expression; this right includes freedom to hold opinions without interference and to seek, receive and impart information and ideas through any media and regardless of frontiers.

International Covenant on Civil and Political Rights, Dec. 16, 1966, 993 U.N.T.S. 171

Article 27

In those States in which ethnic, religious or linguistic minorities exist, persons belonging to such minorities shall not be denied the right, in community with the other members of their group, to enjoy their own culture, to profess and practice their own religion, or to use their own language.

Declaration on the Rights of Persons Belonging to National or Ethnic, Religious and Linguistic Minorities, GA Res. 135, UN GAOR, 47th Sess., Supp. 49 at 210, U.N. Doc. A/RES/47/135 (Dec. 18, 1992), ***reprinted in*** **32 I.L.M. 991 (1993)**

Article 1

1. States shall protect the existence and the national or ethnic, cultural, religious and linguistic identity of minorities within their respective territories and shall encourage conditions for the promotion of that identity.

Article 2

1. Persons belonging to national or ethnic, religious and linguistic minorities (hereinafter referred to as persons belonging to minorities) have the right to enjoy their own culture, to profess and practice their own religion, and to use their own language, in private and in public, freely and without interference or any form of discrimination. . . .

Article 4

. . . 2. States shall take measures to create favorable conditions to enable persons belonging to minorities to express their characteristics and to develop their culture, language, religion, traditions and customs, except where specific practices are in violation of national law and contrary to international standards.

3. States should take appropriate measures so that, wherever possible, persons belonging to minorities may have adequate opportunities to learn their mother tongue or to have instruction in their mother tongue.

Council of Europe, European Convention for the Protection of Human Rights and Fundamental Freedoms, Nov. 4, 1950, 213 U.N.T.S. 221

Article 14

Prohibition of discrimination

The enjoyment of the rights and freedoms set forth in this Convention shall be secured without discrimination on any ground such as sex, race, colour, language, religion, political or other opinion, national or social origin, association with a national minority, property, birth or other status.

The jurisprudence of linguistic rights under international law is sparse by contrast to that of other human rights. The European Court of Human Rights (ECHR) has generated the bulk of the limited case law, followed by the United Nations Human Rights Committee. The seminal case that follows, the "Belgian Linguistics Case," led to one of the first major judgments of the ECHR. The judgment is particularly instructive in its discussion of the relationship between linguistic and other rights and in its restrictive interpretation of the scope of linguistic rights within the territories of parties to the *European Convention for the Protection of Human Rights and Fundamental Freedoms.*

Case Relating to Certain Aspects of the Laws on the Use of Languages in Education in Belgium,
6 Eur. Ct. H.R. (ser. A), 1 E.H.R.R. 252 (1968)

[French-speaking parents brought action against the Belgian government, claiming that it had violated their right of family life and the educational and language rights of their children by limiting public school instruction in their areas of the country to the Dutch language. The court generally upheld the Belgian system of linguistic districting but struck down arrangements in certain districts around Brussels as discriminatory violations of Article 14 in conjunction with article 2 of Protocol 1 of the European Convention for the Protection of Human Rights and Fundamental Freedoms. The court's discussion, as follows, of article 2 of Protocol 1 has remained definitive. – *Eds.*]

By the terms of the first sentence of this Article, "no person shall be denied the right to education."

In spite of its negative formulation, this provision uses the term "right" and speaks of a "right to education." Likewise the preamble to the Protocol specifies that the object of the Protocol lies in the collective enforcement of "rights and freedoms." There is therefore no doubt that Article 2 does enshrine a right.

It remains however to determine the content of this right and the scope of the obligation which is thereby placed upon States.

The negative formulation indicates, as is confirmed by the preparatory work . . . that the Contracting Parties do not recognize such a right to education as would require them to establish at their own expense, or to subsidise, education of any particular type or at any particular level. However, it cannot be concluded from this that the State has no positive obligation to ensure respect for such a right as is protected by Article 2 of the Protocol. As a "right" does exist, it is secured, by virtue of Article 1 of the Convention, to everyone within the jurisdiction of a Contracting State.

To determine the scope of the "right to education," within the meaning of the first sentence of Article 2 of the Protocol, the Court must bear in mind the aim of this provision. It notes in this context that all member States of the Council of Europe possessed, at the time of the opening of the protocol to their signature, and still do possess, a general and official education system. There neither was, nor is now, therefore, any question of requiring each State to establish such a system, but merely of guaranteeing to persons subject to the jurisdiction of the Contracting Parties the right, in principle, to avail themselves of the means of instruction existing at a given time.

The Convention lays down no specific obligations concerning the extent of these means and the manner of their organisation or subsidisation. In particular, the first sentence of Article 2 does not specify the language in which education must be conducted in order that the right to education should be respected. It does not contain precise provisions similar to those which appear in Articles 5(2) and 6(3)(a) and (e). However, the right to education would be meaningless if it did not imply, in favour of its beneficiaries, the right to be educated in the national language or in one of the national languages, as the case may be.

The first sentence of Article 2 of the Protocol consequently guarantees, in the first place, a right of access to educational institutions existing at a given time, but such access constitutes only a part of the right to education. For the "right to education" to be effective, it is further necessary that, inter alia, the individual who is the beneficiary should have the possibility of drawing profit from the education received, that is to say, the right to obtain, in conformity with the rules in force in each State, and in one form or another, official recognition of the studies which he had completed. . . .

The right to education guaranteed by the first sentence of Article 2 of the Protocol by its very nature calls for regulation by the State, regulation which may vary in time and place according to the needs and resources of the community and of individuals. It goes without saying that such regulation must never injure the substance of the right to education nor conflict with other rights enshrined in the Convention.

The Court considers that the general aim set for themselves by the Contracting Parties through the medium of the European Convention on Human Rights was to provide effective protection of fundamental human rights, and this, without doubt, not only because of the historical context in which the Convention was concluded, but also of the social and technical developments in our age which offer to States considerable possibilities for regulating the exercise of these rights. The Convention therefore implies a just balance between the protection of the general interest of the community and the respect due to fundamental human rights while attaching particular importance to the latter.

The second sentence of Article 2 of the Protocol does not guarantee a right to education; this is clearly shown by its wording. . . .

This provision does not require of States that they should in the sphere of education of teaching respect parents' linguistic preferences, but only their religious and philosophical convictions. To interpret the terms "religious" and "philosophical" as covering linguistic preferences would amount to a distortion of their ordinary and usual meaning and to read into the Convention something which is not there. Moreover the preparatory work confirms that the object of the second sentence of Article 2 was in no way to secure respect by the State of a right for parents to have education conducted in a language other than that of the country in question; indeed in June 1951 the Committee of Experts which had the task of drafting the Protocol set aside a proposal put forward in this sense. Several members of the Committee believed that it concerned an aspect of the problem of ethnic minorities and that it consequently fell outside the scope of the Convention. The second sentence of Article 2 is therefore irrelevant to the problems raised in the present case.

[The court also interpreted article 8 of the Convention, which provides in part as follows: "Everyone has the right to respect for his private and family life, his home and his correspondence." The parents argued that the Belgian government had violated their family rights, and those of their children, by compelling the children either to reside apart from their parents in order to gain access to French-language instruction or, more commonly, receive their education in a language other than that spoken at home. The court responded as follows:]

It is true that one result of the Acts of 1932 and 1963 has been the disappearance in the Dutch unilingual region of the majority of schools providing education in French. Consequently French-speaking children living in this region can now obtain [their] only education in Dutch, unless their parents have the financial resources to send them to private French-language schools. This clearly has a certain impact upon family life when parents do not have sufficient means to enroll their children in private school. . . .

Harsh though such consequences may be in individual cases, they do not involve any breach of Article 8. This provision in no way guarantees the right to be educated in the language of one's parents by the public authorities or with their aid. Furthermore, in so far as the legislation leads certain parents to separate themselves from their children, such separation is not imposed by this legislation: it results from the choice of the parents who place their children in schools situated outside the Dutch unilingual region with the sole purpose of avoiding their being taught in Dutch, that is to say in one of Belgium's national languages.

NOTES AND QUESTIONS

1. The judgment in the *Belgian Linguistic Cases* resulted in a revision of the Belgian constitution to better ensure linguistic rights in public education as well as in several national institutional reforms.
2. Given the patent threat to the linguistic rights of the children of French-speaking citizens, what did the court mean when it so confidently established ("It goes without saying") that regulation of the right to education "must never . . . conflict with other rights enshrined in the Convention"? Doesn't such a high-sounding statement ring hollow in view of the court's acceptance of substantial qualifications of the children's linguistic rights?
3. Reread the provisions from the Declaration on the Rights of Persons Belonging to National or Ethnic, Religious and Linguistic Minorities that are set forth in the introductory list of authority before the excerpts from the *Belgian Linguistic Cases*. If the Declaration had been in force at the time of that case, would it have changed

the outcome? Do such declarations, by contrast to treaty obligations, have any effect at all?

Fernand de Varennes, *Language and Freedom of Expression in International Law*, 16 Hum. Rts. Q. 163–86 (1993) (reprinted with the permission of the Johns Hopkins University Press)

A. Historical Context

During the drafting of the Universal Declaration of Human Rights some contended that the rights of members of linguistic and other minorities were fully protected by Article 2 and by the provisions on freedom of thought, conscience, and religion, on freedom of the press and of expression, on freedom of assembly, on the right to education, and on the right to participate in the cultural life of the community. Indeed, many seem to take for granted that language is implicitly part of the freedom of expression. Professors McDougal, Lasswell, and Chen have pointed out that:

> The rights . . . to freedom of expression, in particular, are intimately linked to freedom of access to language. Thus Lador-Lederer has observed that "the right of any group to use its own language is anchored in Art. 19 of the Universal Declaration."[8]

Some therefore felt during the drafting of the Universal Declaration that such provisions as Article 19 dealing with the freedom of expression protected the rights of individuals speaking languages different from the majority's language. Whether language is an integral part of this freedom of expression does not appear to have been considered directly in the *travaux préparatoires.*

Nevertheless, legal commentators generally have not addressed this matter, and publications dealing with the freedom of expression are largely silent on this point. However, no one seems to have suggested that language is not a constituent of the freedom of expression.

Traditionally, the freedom of expression was deemed to guarantee effective political and social debate essential for the proper operation of any democratic system. More recently, the freedom of expression has evolved into a more individualistically oriented freedom that permits individuals to freely communicate between themselves in order to impart and receive information. Thus freedom of expression seems to extend well beyond the purely political realm, encompassing matters such as science, literature, theater, the arts, and commercial activities.[9]

. . .

[8] Myres S. McDougal et al., Human Rights and World Public Order 726 (1980); *see also* Antoni Milian-Massana, *Droits linguistiques et droits fondamentaux en Espagne*, 23 Revue Generale de Droit 561, 576 (1992).

[9] Thomas M. Scanlon, *Freedom of Expression and Categories of Expression*, 40 U. Pitt. L. Rev. 519 (1978–79); *Markt Intern and Beerman v. Germany*, 12 Eur. H.R. Rep. 161 (1989).

Despite a definite trend in national jurisdictions associating language and freedom of expression, until recently it was far from clear at the international level how language relates to the freedom of expression.

. . .

Freedom of expression obviously emphasizes the content of the opinions expressed, but there remained some ambiguity at the international level on the position language occupies as the means of expressing these opinions. It is at least likely from the above-mentioned national opinions that language may be a constituent of the freedom of expression insofar as it is a necessary component of the expression of opinions. Indeed, a simple reading of Article 19 would seem to support such an interpretation, since the freedom of expression "shall include . . . the freedom to receive and impart . . . information and ideas of all kinds, . . . either orally or in writing."

. . .

On 31 March 1993, the United Nations Human Rights Committee handed down a decision that clarified, apparently once and for all, its position on the relationship between language and freedom of expression. At issue were provisions of the Quebec Charte de la langue francaise, which, in most situations, made French the exclusive language of outdoor commercial signs. In *Ballantyne, Davidson and Mclntyre v. Canada*, the authors were English-speaking residents of the Province of Quebec who claimed that the prohibition against using any language other than French on outdoor commercial signs or in a firm's name infringed upon their freedom of expression. The government of Quebec argued that the freedom of expression protected by Article 19 of the Covenant did not include commercial publicity, but was limited to matters involving political, cultural, and artistic expression. It also maintained that even if commercial publicity were encompassed in the freedom of expression, this freedom did not include an individual's absolute right to choose the language of commercial signs. Finally, the government argued that even if the freedom of expression included freedom in the choice of language in commercial activities, the prohibition contained in the Charte de la langue francaise was reasonable given the importance of protecting the French language and culture in Quebec.

The Human Rights Committee rejected the government of Quebec's attempts to restrict the authors' freedom of expression. The Committee stated that Article 19(2) of the Covenant applies not only to ideas and subjective opinions that can be transmitted to others, but also to any news or information, to any expression, to any commercial publicity or signs, and to any work of art. In other words, the Committee squarely rejected any attempt at limiting the freedom of expression to a narrow field of activity such as political, cultural, or artistic expression. The Committee also set aside the argument that commercial expression was somehow less worthy of protection under the Covenant, and that in such cases governments should have wider discretion in deciding what restrictions were appropriate or necessary in their country. The government of Quebec also contended that its provisions were necessary and reasonable in order to protect the French language in the province. In response, the Human Rights Committee pointed out that Article 19 of the Covenant only permits restrictions on the freedom of expression that are provided by law and necessary either to respect the reputations of others or to protect national security, public order, health, or morals. Though clearly "provided by law," the language restrictions relating to outdoor commercial signs in Quebec were unnecessary, according to the Committee, because they protected neither the rights of other individuals, nor the public order, health, or morals. Furthermore, even if the restrictions were possibly valid based on Article 19(2)(a) or (b), the government would have to establish that the restriction was justified, which the Quebec government made no attempt to do with respect to the provisions of the Charte de la langue francaise, beyond claiming they were simply reasonable. Though the acknowledgement was not strictly required in order to support its decision, the Committee acknowledged that the government could validly seek to protect the French language in Quebec. It recognized that while a state may choose one or more official languages, it may not simply ban the use of non-official languages, at least outside of governmental services or activities. In essence, the Committee recognized that in an entirely non-governmental realm, any attempt at restricting an individual's language choice clearly violates that individual's freedom of expression.

. . .

A number of national jurisdictions clearly distinguish between public use of language and private use of language when dealing with matters involving language and freedom of expression. Matters relating to the public use of language go beyond what is understood in these jurisdictions as the freedom of expression, because such use involves a government's obligation to provide administrative, judicial, or other governmental services – services that are usually provided in the state-sanctioned official language. The prevalent understanding of a freedom is that of non-intervention of the state in private or nongovernmental affairs.

The example of a trial illustrates the importance of the distinction between public and private use of language. In some [international cases], authors of complaints contended that to prohibit an accused from using her primary language, when she could understand the official language of the courts, violated her freedom of expression. However, a trial is not a private affair: it is a public function carried out by a segment of the state apparatus. In other words, it is a state activity. The private citizen cannot assert that the state has no power to intervene in one's private choice of language of expression, because a trial is not a private forum for a citizen to express her point of view. Rather, it is a public activity conducted under the auspices of the state for the public good.

The private use of a language is conceptually quite different from public use, where a state's intervention is solicited or mandatory, because the former would encompass the freedom to express oneself in any language in all non-official activities, such as between private individuals, in newspapers, in theater, in movies, and particularly during political meetings and conferences....

Put differently, an individual has the freedom to impart information or address his government in any language, but the state does not have a corresponding obligation to receive this information or respond to the individual's exercise of his freedom.

...

Some would point out that Article 27 of the International Covenant on Civil and Political Rights already provides for the use of a minority language between persons of that language group so that one need not include language as a necessary element of the freedom of expression. This argument contains a number of weaknesses. It could be valid in some cases, for example, that of a newspaper, but would be of little assistance in the case of an individual trying to address, in a prohibited language, a group of individuals who are not members of the linguistic minority. Nor is this last example far-fetched. Only a few years ago a Kurdish-speaking citizen of Turkey was promptly arrested for addressing a human rights conference in Kurd. The situation may still constitute an offence in Algeria under Articles 18 and 31 of the Loi du 16 janvier 1991 portant generalisation de l'utilisation de la langue arabe. One can also question the effect of Article 27 on national legislation that forbids licenses, as a general rule of policy, to radio stations whose programs are in a minority vernacular.[10] Finally, Article 27 contains a number of restrictions; for example, it pertains only to "linguistic minorities" existing in a given state. This restriction causes a number of misgivings because some states contend that no such minorities exist in their jurisdictions. Furthermore, even the majority's language may be severely restricted by the state.[11]

It would seem preposterous to assert that an individual, involved in a private activity yet forbidden by the state to use his own language, is not a victim of an infringement upon his freedom of expression. By definition the government is attempting to impose its preference involving the medium of transmission of information and ideas on a private activity. For these

[10] This last point involves a very complex and largely unexplored subject. Licensing restrictions can involve questions relating to the freedom of expression, to the nondiscrimination principle, and to the Article 27 minority clause of the International Covenant on Civil and Political Rights. Only a few, rather unsatisfying, U.S. cases have some relevance to this issue. For a description of these, *see*... REPORT OF THE WAITANGI TRIBUNAL ON CLAIMS CONCERNING THE ALLOCATION OF RADIO FREQUENCIES, Wai 26 & Wai 150, 1990 (New Zealand).

[11] This problem was also raised in the *Quebec Commercial Sign Language* Case. Because English-speaking individuals are a majority in Canada, they could not claim their Article 27 rights were violated because they were not a "linguistic minority." Nevertheless, in one of the federal units of the state, the Province of Quebec, they were a linguistic minority. *See also* Asian-American Business Group v. City of Pomona, 716 F. Supp. 1328 (C.D. Cal. 1987).

reasons it is more consistent with traditional definitions of the freedom of expression, and with the conclusions of national jurisdictions and of the UN Human Rights Committee's 1993 decision on this issue, to include language as an integral and necessary constituent of this freedom.

Before 1993, all of the cases that the Human Rights Committee and the European Commission on Human Rights considered involved individuals called to testify before a tribunal or seeking a service from a state institution and compelled to address that state institution, against his will, in a language other than his primary one. Many may feel, as the writer commenting on the *X v. Ireland* case, that this amounts to a violation of one's freedom of expression. In reality, what these predicaments involve is the state apparatus seeking evidence or information or being probed to provide a service: in other words, they involve a state function.

Clearly they do not involve an individual seeking to express his opinion or point of view in the private domain. If the freedom of expression is mainly concerned with ensuring that the people are free to express themselves in private matters such as culture, politics, arts, and business, necessary for venting the populations' ideas and frustrations in order to maintain a healthy society, it does not follow that the state is obliged in all of its information gathering and official operations to give way to the people's linguistic preferences. The state machinery is still perfectly entitled to operate exclusively in the language of its choice in its activities, and is perfectly within its competence to require individuals to submit to this choice if they are able to do so, because individuals are still free to express themselves in any manner outside of the state's governmental activities.

In some situations another right may limit the state's discretion in matters relating to the imposition of its own language preference on individuals in the public sphere; however, this limitation will emanate from other obligations imposed on a state, and not from the freedom of expression.

As shown in *Ballantyne, Davidson and McIntyre v. Canada*, the argument that language does not really affect the substantive right to freedom of expression, as long as one has an accessible language in which to express one's opinion, would appear fallacious. Though the Human Rights Committee did not elaborate on the issue, it did indicate that the freedom of expression extends to any possible medium of expression. Because the expression of opinions, information, and ideas can be conveyed orally, in writing, or in print, one cannot suppose that the state may limit the speaker's choice of medium, other than through the limits provided by Article 19(3) of the International Covenant on Civil and Political Rights and by Article 10(2) of the European Convention. Article 13(1) of the American Convention on Human Rights is categorical in this regard, in that it guarantees:

> freedom to seek, receive, and impart information and ideas of all kinds . . . either orally, in writing, in print, in the form of art, or through any other medium of one's choice.

Logically, if one can express an opinion or idea through art, a non-verbal medium, one can also express an opinion or idea through another medium, a particular language. To maintain that to permit an individual to express himself in only one language has no effect on his freedom of expression is like saying an artist can paint anything as long as it is an abstract painting, and that such a restriction in no way infringes on the artist's freedom of expression. In both cases, the government reaches into a private area and tries to restrict the way in which one chooses to express one's opinions. Any limit to such freedom of expression must be found in the recognized restrictions permissible under the various provisions of the international treaties.

...

Another possible argument not raised in *Ballantyne, Davidson and McIntyre v. Canada* is that the state does not violate the freedom of expression unless an individual is completely unable to use or comprehend the state sanctioned official language of expression. Once again this approach is seriously flawed; it seeks to create a restriction neither recognized nor even implicit in the rights provided for by Article 10 of the European Convention and by Article 19 of the International Covenant on Civil and Political Rights. It presents a de facto state intervention in a private activity, one of the most sacred and cherished freedoms of a democratic society: the right to freely express one's opinions and ideas without government interference, other than those that are strictly necessary. One can illustrate further the weakness of this last argument: if there is no violation of the freedom of expression when an individual is not permitted to express his ideas in his own language, as long as there is another language that he can use, logically one could also claim there is no need for people to express their point of view by way of newspapers, as long as they can do it another way, such as at public meetings. Clearly, such an interpretation is futile intellectual gymnastics. Nothing in the European Convention nor the International Covenant would support the creation of a new limitation on the freedom of expression by governments not provided for in these instruments.

...

As has been shown, attempting to exclude language from the substantive right of the freedom of expression would be a serious error. The approach adopted by the Human Rights Committee, when examined in light of national decisions and current trends, provides much needed clarification on the relationship between language and the freedom of expression.

...

The freedom of expression properly construed requires the removal of or limitations to state intervention in matters properly belonging to the private domain. Such a freedom does not impose a positive duty on the state to offer its services in everyone's language of choice. As the

[UN] Human Rights Committee concluded in *Ballantyne, Davidson and McIntyre v. Canada*, the freedom of expression is so closely interrelated with language that they can never be separated completely. Thus, in most cases, a state's attempt to prohibit or limit in any way the private use of a language, such as in cinema, art, commerce, conferences, publications, or the media, constitutes an infringement of one of the most basic and cherished fundamental human rights. Yet many states limit to some extent the use of languages within their territory, and challenges to these limitations will increase significantly worldwide. International law must respond in a consistent and coherent manner to ensure the peaceful, orderly settlement of a growing area of tension and conflict.

The content of linguistic human rights thus encompasses not merely the right of non-discrimination but also the obligation of states to take positive steps to protect and even promote the usage of minority tongues. Whether they are narrowly or broadly construed by courts of law, linguistic rights have substantial impacts on educational systems, the media, the arts, the law, medicine, and many other social institutions.

Within the member countries of the Council of Europe a *Framework Convention for the Protection of National Minorities* (FCNM) more or less seeks to advance the affirmative agenda (for states to take positive steps) and otherwise underscores linguistic human rights of minorities that are established in the other principal European and international instruments.

The Rights of Minorities in Europe 3–4 (Mark Weller ed., 2005) (reprinted with permission of Oxford University Press)

Although the [Framework Convention for the Protection of National Minorities (FCNM)] is not the first instrument relevant to the protection of national minorities developed by the Council of Europe, it is the most comprehensive document in the field. Its particular relevance derives from the fact that it is the first legally binding, multilateral treaty to address the protection of national minorities in general. Moreover, in Article 1, it is expressly stated that the protection of national minorities constitutes an "integral part" of the international protection of human rights; thus, the FCNM is to be considered a member of the European family of human rights treaties with consequences attached to its interpretation. . . . Articles 7 and 8 guarantee freedom of assembly, association, expression, thought, conscience, and religion, while Article 9 seeks to facilitate access to and the use of media. Furthermore, Articles 10 and 11 deal with: linguistic rights relating, *inter alia*, to the use of minority languages in private and in public, as well as before administrative authorities; the use of one's own name and the use of minority languages for the display of information of a private nature; and for topographical names. Rights linked with education, such as the right to learn and to be instructed in the minority languages (Articles 12, 13, and 14) . . . also fall under this section. See also Patrick

Thornberry & Maria Amor Martín Estébanez, Minority Rights in Europe 137 (2004).

D. Dying Languages

Jack Hitt, *Say No More*, N.Y. Times, Feb. 29, 2004, at 52, 54, 56, 57–58 ()

Languages die the way many people do – at home, in silence, attended by loved ones straining to make idle conversation.

. . .

Linguists now estimate that half of the more than 6,000 languages currently spoken in the world will become extinct by the end of this century. In reaction, there are numerous efforts to slow the die-off – from graduate students heading into the field to compile dictionaries; to charitable foundations devoted to the cause, like the Endangered Language Fund; to transnational agencies, some with melancholic names appropriate to the task, like the European Bureau for Lesser Used Languages. Chile started a modest program, not long after the ugly debates surrounding Christopher Columbus in 1992, to save Kawesquar (Ka-WES-kar) and Yaghan, the last two native languages of Southern Chile. But how does one salvage an ailing language when the economic advantages of, say, Spanish are all around you? And is it possible to step inside a dying language to learn whether it can be saved and, more rudely, whether it should be?

. . .

In two generations, a healthy language – even one with hundreds of thousands of speakers – can collapse entirely, sometimes without anyone noticing. This process is happening everywhere. In North America, the arrival of Columbus and the Europeans who followed him whittled down the roughly 300 native languages to only about 170 in the 20th century. According to Marianne Mithun, a linguist at the University of California at Santa Barbara, the recent evolution of English as a global language has taken an even greater toll. "Only one of those 170 languages is not officially endangered today," Mithun said. "Greenlandic Eskimo."

Without the revitalization of youth, a language can go from being alive to endangered (declining speakers among the young), then moribund (only elderly speakers left alive), then dead (the last known speaker dies) – all linguistic terms of art. William Sutherland, the author of a study in Nature magazine last spring, compared the die-off to an environmental catastrophe. According to Sutherland, 438 languages are in the condition of Kawesquar, that is, with fewer than 50 speakers, making them "critically endangered" – a category that in the animal world includes 182 birds and 180 mammals. Languages "seem to follow the same patterns" as animals.

. . . "Stability and isolation seem to breed abundance in the number of bird and animal species, and they do the same for languages." Conversely, the instability and homogenization of the global economy [are] creating a juggernaut of monoculture, threatening plants and animals. But, Sutherland makes clear, the one life form even more endangered is human culture.

According to Daniel Nettle and Suzanne Romaine, authors of "Vanishing Voices," the last time human language faced such a crisis of collapse was when we invented farming, around 8000 B.C., during the switch-over from highly mobile hunting and gathering to sedentary agriculture. Then the multitude of idioms developed on the run cohered into language families, like Indo-European. Sino-Tibetan and Elamo-Dravidian. The difference this time is that with each language gone, we may also lose whatever knowledge and history were locked up in its stories and myths, along with the human consciousness embedded in its grammatical structure and vocabulary.

One often hears the apocryphal story about the Inuit and their 40 words for "snow." True or not, it acknowledges the inherent human sense that each language, developed over a certain time and geography, is a revelation of what we call "a sense of place." To let languages die out, en masse, is to permit the phrase "terra incognita" to creep back onto our environmental maps. One organization of linguists, biologists and anthropologists, known as Terralingua, is working to keep languages alive by highlighting what gets lost when they fade away. "I remember when I was doing fieldwork in Mexico," said Luisa Maffi, Terralingua's president. She encountered a man whose native Mayan was already blurred with Mexican Spanish. He had traveled with his 2-year-old daughter to a health clinic because she was sick with serious diarrhea. "He no longer knew the word for *yakan k'ulub wamal*," she said, using the Mayan term for a plant long known to cure the problem. "It was probably growing in his backyard."

A handful of linguists dismiss salvage efforts like Terralingua's as futile exercises. They say languages just die, as spoken Latin did, and then are reborn as French, Spanish and Italian. No big deal. Or more bluntly, all this sentimentality about dying languages is just another symptom of academe's mewling, politically correct minority-mongering. In the magazine Prospect, the writer Kenan Malik summarized this position in an essay titled "Let Them Die." "There is nothing noble or authentic about local ways of life; they are often simply degrading and backbreaking," Malik argued. "What if half the world's languages are on the verge of extinction? Let them die in peace."

Linguists counter that yes, there is a natural process of language death; but the order of magnitude of the current die-off is what should create concern. What's happening with human culture now, they say, should shock people the way the Cuyahoga River catching fire in 1969 radically changed how many thought about the environment.

To general linguists, the dismissive position is just deliberate ignorance. But they also argue that the utilitarian case is too narrow. In peril is not just knowledge but also the importance of diversity and the beauty of grammar. They will tell you that every language has its own unique theology and philosophy buried in its very sinews. For example, because of the Kawesqar's nomadic past, they rarely use the future tense; given the contingency of moving constantly by canoe, it was all but unnecessary. The past tense, however, has fine gradations. You can say, "A bird flew by." And by the use of different tenses, you can mean a few seconds ago, a few days ago, a time so long ago that you were not the original observer of the bird (but you know the observer yourself) and, finally, a mythological past, a tense the Kawesqar use to suggest that the story is so old that it no longer possesses fresh descriptive truth but rather that other truth which emerges from stories that retain their narrative power despite constant repetition.

. . .

Among [l]inguists, the sorrowful story of the "last speaker" is practically a literary genre. The names ring out, like a Homeric catalog. Ned Maddrell, the last speaker of Manx, died in the village of Cregneash on the Isle of Man in 1974. Tevfik Esenc, the last speaker of Ubykh, died in Turkey in 1992. Red Thunder Cloud, the last speaker of Catawba, died in 1996. More are coming. Marie Smith-Jones in Alaska, the last speaker of Eyak, is 83 years old.

. . .

[The author then discusses the last-speaker "hustle."] Remember Red Thunder Cloud, the last Catawba speaker? Actually, he was Cromwell Ashbie Hawkins West, the son of an African-American druggist in Newport, R.I. According to Ives Goddard of the Smithsonian, West was "a great mimic and fast learner." He quickly mastered the language, donned some turquoise jewelry and, until his death in 1996, worked the last-speaker circuit. Usually, he could be found at county fairs, hawking Red Thunder Cloud's Accabonac Princess American Indian Tea – "fresh from the American forest to you."

There's a paradox in those last-speaker stories. After all, what is driving these languages off the cliff but sheer economics? It only makes a kind of poetic sense that in their death throes their speakers would resort to economic ploys. But this is also where the environmental metaphor of endangered languages falls apart. Getting down to a few in number is irreversibly the end of, say, a fern or a tiger. For humans, it's often the beginning of politics.

The very success of English as a global language is prompting a revival of ancestral tongues. Compared to the die-off now in progress, it's a drop in the bucket. Still, many native American languages have reacted against these near-death experiences. The Miami in Oklahoma and Mohawk straddling the Canadian border have full-scale programs for language revival. Native Hawaiian, also written off only a few decades ago, has 18 schools teaching a new generation in the original language of the islands.

Language revival as a means of identity may well be the way of the future. The big fight in linguistics over the past two decades has been about English

First. But first is no longer the question. Now the question is, What will be the *second* language? In America, the drift in high school curriculums has always been toward dominant second language – French, Spanish, German, maybe Chinese if you're a rebel. But what if a second language could be that of your ancestors?

That possibility is already proving to be quite popular with many people. As their initiatives succeed and become more visible, they will drive into the open a question for English-speaking Americans, the owner-operators of the dominant linguistic ecosystem. Do we want to dwell in a society that encourages linguistic revival and cultural diversity, knowing that with it may come a lot of self-righteous minority-pitying? Or, shall we just sit contentedly amid a huge cultural die-off, harrumphing like some drunk uncle at the family reunion angrily spilling his beer and growling, "Let 'em die"? Keep in mind that if the actuarial tables are correct, it means that once the languages start to die off in earnest, there will be a "death of the last speaker" article in the papers, on average, every 12 days.

. . .

[W]hile the grown-ups are having their arguments about what we should and shouldn't do – and after the linguists have compiled their dictionaries and put together their grammars – the future of all these resurrections will depend on teenagers. Will it become cool to speak and live and sing and groove in, say, Mohegan? It depends.

Twenty years ago, the distinct language of Welsh was in intensive care, destined to die. Now 21 percent of the people in Wales speak it regularly. Gaelic in Ireland has failed, by comparison. Maybe 3 percent of the people in Ireland speak Gaelic regularly today. Some argue that Wales needed something extra to distinguish itself from the English up the road, while the Irish live on an island. But other observers, like the author David Crystal, point to the influence of the kids. In his book "Language Death," he cites a small scandal that broke out in 1998. The Welsh band Manic Street Preachers promoted a new album in Cardiff by hanging an enormous banner written in the old tongue. When he saw it, Peter Hughes Griffiths, a professor at Trinity College in Carmathen who teaches the language, condemned the banner for using slang.

"You would have thought the group would have made the effort to make sure the poster was grammatically correct," he fumed to an English newspaper. "Standards are not being kept up." The professor was quickly hooted down by newspapers and by the Welsh Language Board. He had missed the point: kids would propel the language, not him. Kids – with their mistakes, bastardizations, slang, import words and poor syntax – will be the ones who breathe new casual life into old formal syntax. That said, there always remains the other possibility – that the next generation will decide that the native tongue is preposterous, and poof.

NOTES AND QUESTIONS

1. To what extent do you think that national and international laws can meaningfully protect and preserve dying languages? Is it worth the money and effort, given that languages have always appeared and disappeared through history? Does the intangibility of language and its dependence on human society make it more difficult to protect from extinction than, say, an endangered species of flora or fauna?
2. In colonial times, many indigenous languages were transcribed in dictionaries by nonindigenous peoples in an attempt to record what was then considered a "dying" aspect of indigenous culture. Can written records alone serve a purpose or are other strategies needed to preserve languages at risk?
3. Linguists and linguistic anthropologists sometimes disagree on the health of living languages. For example, the article by Jack Hitt indicates that Welsh is faring quite well, given a willingness to entrust its development partly to teenage culture. However, Colin Williams, in his book, LINGUISTICS MINORITIES IN DEMOCRATIC CONTEXT (2008), describes Welsh as a threatened language and refers to a current debate whether the "Welsh-speaking heartland" in the north and west of Wales should be officially designated as such to generate protective language planning. (*Id.* at 256–59).
4. For further reading, see ROBERT H. ROBBINS & EUGENIUS M. UHLENBECK, ENDANGERED LANGUAGES (2001); DAVID CRYSTAL, LANGUAGE DEATH (2000). On the struggle to prevent indigenous languages from dying, see Ben Block, *Languishing Languages*, WORLD WATCH, July/August 2010, at 24. Marianne Ignace & Ron Ignace, *Canadian Aboriginal Languages and the Protection of Cultural Heritage, in* FIRST NATIONS CULTURAL HERITAGE AND LAW: CASE STUDIES, VOICES AND PERSPECTIVES 417 (Catherine Bell & Val Napoleon eds., 2008).

E. Affirmative Measures to Implement Linguistic Rights

Does the duty to warn under general tort law imply an obligation on the part of manufacturers of potentially harmful products to provide warning labels in the principal foreign languages of prospective consumers of those products? In other words, is there a duty to warn in languages other than the official or dominant language in a consumer society?

This was precisely the issue presented in *Ramirez v. Plough*,[12] a case that is thought to have been the first of its kind. It involved a Spanish-speaking mother who, unable to read the English label warning on an aspirin bottle, gave her son this nonprescription medication. He had a severe reaction known as Reye's syndrome, which led to blindness, quadriplegia, and serious intellectual disabilities. With the assistance of the American Civil Liberties Union, the mother sued the drug manufacturer. The trial court dismissed her complaint on a motion for summary judgment. The California Court of Appeal, however, reversed the trial court's dismissal and remanded the case to the trial court,

[12] *Ramirez v. Plough*, 6 Cal.4th 539; 25 Cal. Rptr. 2d 97; 863 P.2d 167 (Dec. 1993).

on the ground that there was a triable issue of fact. Ultimately, the California Supreme Court reversed in an opinion that explained as follows:

> We granted review in this case to determine whether a manufacturer of nonprescription drugs may incur tort liability for distributing its products with warnings in English only. Recognizing the importance of uniformity and predictability in this sensitive area of the law, we conclude that the rule of tort liability should conform to state and federal statutory and administrative law. Because both state and federal law now require warnings in English but not in any other language, we further conclude that a manufacturer may not be held liable in tort for failing to label a nonprescription drug with warnings in a language other than English.

The California Supreme Court wrote further that the imposition of such a requirement on businesses should come from the legislature. A policy rationale for the outcome was that mandating multilingual labels on products would be too burdensome for businesses, which was what the company argued in this case.[13]

NOTES AND QUESTIONS

1. Do you agree with the following conclusion concerning the *Ramirez* case?

> Manufacturers of over-the-counter drugs should not be required to provide warnings in foreign languages, except under certain specific circumstances. These circumstances would be similar to the facts present in the *Ramirez* case. If a manufacturer cultivates demand for its product in the native language of a significant minority group, then that manufacturer may assume the duty to warn in that language. Absent these very specific circumstances, it is unjust to place such a burden upon these manufacturers. English is the common language of the United States. To indiscriminately impose a duty to warn in foreign languages upon every manufacturer of over-the-counter drugs creates an undesirable precedent. Such a duty would negate the incentive for immigrants in this country to learn English and become more productive members of society. In today's intensely competitive global economy, our society cannot afford such a luxury.
>
> ...
>
> [The Supreme Court of California] emphasized the importance of uniformity and predictability in drug products labeling and thereby concluded that the state legislature deliberately chose not to require foreign language labeling because the applicable statute expressly required that the warnings be in English. The court presumed that the FDA maintained a similar view because the agency's requirements do not require multilingual warnings. Thus, the court ultimately held that because both state and federal requirements currently mandate warnings only in English, manufacturers may not be held liable for failure to include bilingual labeling on non-prescription drugs.
>
> ...
>
> [T]here remains the important question of whether liability may result in situations where advertising and marketing to non-English-speaking groups is

[13] Jennifer Warren, *Bilingual Warnings Rejected by Justices*, L.A Times, Dec. 10, 1993, at A3.

undertaken in a foreign language. The court noted that when such advertising fails to adequately warn consumers of potential risks, there may be liability if the advertising is viewed as "materially misleading."

Christopher S. Maciejewski, *The Dilemma over Foreign-Language Labeling of Over-the-Counter Drugs*, 15 J. Legal Med. 129–54 (1994).

2. Some commentators have proposed mandatory substitution of widely understood symbols (similar to highway traffic marking) instead of words whose meaning may not be understood by those who speak other languages. What symbols besides the skull and bones would you suggest? Would such internationally standardized symbols adequately warn everyone around the world about the risks associated with a product?
3. Even if states find it administratively convenient to use only one official language, there are inevitably situations in which it is crucial to provide social services in other languages. When emergencies occur, telephone operators must be able to understand persons facing life-threatening situations, law enforcement officers must be able to inform suspects of their constitutional rights,[14] and so on. Affirmative measures are therefore essential.
4. It is difficult to overstate the importance of well-trained language interpreters. The role of these culture brokers is critically important in many institutional settings, including the courts, hospitals, and the military. See, e.g., Martha Carter-Balske, Leslie Kay & Linda Friedman Ramirez, *Use of Foreign Language Interpreters, in* Cultural Issues in Criminal Defense 35 (Linda Friedman Ramirez ed., 2d ed. 2007); Charles M. Grabau & Llewellyn Joseph Gibbons, *Protecting the Rights of Linguistic Minorities: Challenges to Court Interpretation*, New Eng. L. Rev. 227 (1996) (with a copy of the Model Court Interpreter Act). Despite the key function interpreters play, proper certification is a problem that may warrant greater scrutiny and legislative action.
5. Consider the dilemma of the bilingual juror. In *Hernandez v. New York*, 500 U.S. 352 (1991), prosecutors used four peremptory challenges to remove Spanish-speaking potential jurors from a case involving a Latino criminal defendant. The prosecutor volunteered that he had struck two of the potential jurors because he was unsure whether they would listen only to the interpreter's translation of the testimony; instead, they might also listen to the Spanish-language testimony. Apparently, it was presumed that justice requires that all jurors hear the evidence in precisely the same form, in this context, only the English translation of the testimony. Do such challenges violate the equal protection clause of the Fourteenth Amendment? The Court ruled that there was no equal protection violation in the absence of a sufficient nexus between language and ethnicity insofar as some Latinos do not speak Spanish and some non-Latinos do. Given this ruling, however, are bilingual citizens, ironically because of their bilingual capacity, unfairly limited in their ability to survive challenges to serve as jurors? Should affirmative measures be taken to protect their bilingual rights? See Roger Enriquez & John W. Clark III,

[14] Janet Ainsworth, *You Have the Right to Remain Silent, but Only If You Ask for It Just So; The Role of Linguistic Ideology in American Police Interrogation Law*, 1 Int'l J. Speech, Language, & Law 15 (2008).

The Social Psychology of Peremptory Challenges: An Examination of Latino Jurors, 13 TEX. HISPANIC J. L. & POL. 25 (2007).

F. Restrictions of Linguistic Rights

Individuals and societies often feel threatened by linguistic pluralism. The confusion of other languages is therefore often viewed not simply as a problem but also as an actual danger to society. Recall that in the biblical story of the tower of Babel the existence of many languages was interpreted as a consequence of sinful behavior. In modern times, members of minority groups who continue to speak their first languages may be viewed in more secular terms as a threat to the larger community of a magnitude that requires political or legal response. During time of war or other national emergency, in particular, leaders sometimes attack particular foreign languages because of the symbolic identities of those languages with enemies. In retrospect, the resulting suppression of the enemy's language and advocacy of monolingualism almost always seem xenophobic. For example, the anti-German movement in the United States during the First World War illustrated a chauvinistic obsession with patriotism and a presumption that it was incompatible with speaking German. But bad situations may lead to good decisions. In *Meyer v. Nebraska*, 262 U.S. 390 (1923), a landmark case resulting from Germanophobia, the U.S. Supreme Court recognized a fundamental right to use the language of one's choice. The Court's opinions are summarized in the following essay.

Paul Finkelman, *The War on German Language and Culture, 1917–1925, in* CONFRONTATION AND COOPERATION: GERMANY AND THE UNITED STATES IN THE ERA OF WORLD WAR I, 1900–1924, at 177–96 (Hans-Jurgen Schroder ed., 1993) (reprinted with permission of Berg Publishers, an imprint of A & C Black Publishers)

During and after World War I, German-Americans were the targets of official harassment, political suppression, police brutality, and mob violence. This repression was rooted in the hostility to foreigners that reemerged in the late nineteenth century as nativist organizations, such as the American Protective Association, began agitating for an end to non-Anglo-Saxon immigration. Even before the rise of this new xenophobia, conservative Americans had been appalled by the labor radicalism and socialism espoused by many immigrants.

. . .

The superpatriotism of World War I stimulated the attack on education in foreign languages and, more importantly, the teaching of foreign languages. The end of the war did not end the demand for instruction only in English. Former President Theodore Roosevelt set the tone, declaring[,] "We must have in this country but one flag, the American flag, and for the speech of the people but one language, the English language." He advocated night schools for every adult immigrant "and if after, say, five years he has not learned English, he should be sent back to the land from whence he came." The American Legion, organized in 1919, made forcing immigrants to learn English one of its major goals. The American Bar Association joined the crusade two years later.

. . .

While foreign languages in general were under assault, German was the major target during and after war. During the war the National Security League urged a total ban on teaching both German language and German literature. By the end of the war 16 states had prohibited the teaching of German. "Much of the repressive activity of the state councils [of national defense] came to center on the elimination of the use of the German language." Theodore Roosevelt, a scholar in his own right who also had been president of the American Historical Association, supported a ban on teaching German, while a professor at Johns Hopkins University declared that German was "a barbarous tongue" with no cultural or commercial value.

The large German-American population in the West and Midwest led to an intense effort to suppress the German language. In South Dakota the legislature prohibited all foreign language education before the ninth grade. This law simply legitimized the action of South Dakota's State Council for National Defense, which had already "ordered that all teaching of the German language during the period of the war be discontinued in all the schools and educational institutions of the state." In July 1918 the South Dakota Council prohibited the use of German in telephone conversations. The Washington Council for National Defense was less authoritarian and simply requested that the state Board of Education prohibit German language education. The Board complied with this request. The Governor of Montana likewise prohibited the German language in his state's schools, while in Iowa the Governor banned the use of German in any public place. Shortly after the declaration of war, the Nebraska State Council for National Defense verbally assaulted the Lutheran churches of the state for continuing to worship in German, on the grounds that the language "had been a potent preventative means against the Americanization of the people who came under such influence." In April 1918 the Nebraska legislature condemned, but did not prohibit, the use of foreign languages in the state's private schools. While framed in general terms, this resolution was aimed at Nebraska's German speaking Lutheran schools. Indianapolis, which had taught German in the primary grades for decades, abolished such classes during the war. The resolution that achieved this result also declared that the city's school board "subscribes to the belief that the public schools should teach our boys and girls the principle of one nation, one language, and one flag, and should not assist in perpetuating the language of an alien enemy in our homes and enemy viewpoints in the community." After the war was over, Ohio specifically prohibited the teaching of German in elementary schools, while numerous other states required that all instruction be conducted in English. Indiana, which had once required German in high schools, now flatly prohibited the language in all schools.

Louisiana led the nation in its wartime paranoia of the "enemy language." The state's wartime prohibition on teaching German in any public or private school in the state, at all levels from elementary schools to universities, was the most extreme in the nation until Indiana passed similar legislation in 1919. But beyond this, Louisiana also prohibited the display or use of any "sign, insignia, name, designation, title, phrase, circular, or other form of advertisement or description, written, printed or appearing in the German language or that of any of its allies, or derived from any such language." Furthermore, the law prohibited "the sale or disposal in any manner of books, magazines, and papers printed or appearing in the German language or the language of its allies."

Where states did not act, localities and students did. . . . During World War I, thousands of school districts dropped German from their curriculum, never to return to it. By 1922 less than 1 percent of all American high school students studied German.

. . .

With no one learning German, it took little effort to remove German books from the schools and libraries. Book burnings were common, as schools, libraries, and book stores disposed of their German language texts. The public library in Columbus, Ohio sold its German collection for scrap paper. The Cincinnati library cancelled its German language newspapers and removed all German books from its shelves. If this could occur in Cincinnati, where German-Americans were the largest and "most thoroughly organized" ethnic community in the city, it is not surprising that libraries across the nation took similar actions.

Even after the war, the attack on German culture and language continued. . . .

Meyer v. Nebraska: A Bit of Sanity in a Crazy World

In 1919 Nebraska prohibited instruction in any "private, denominational, parochial or public school," except in English. Furthermore, the law prohibited the teaching of any modern foreign language until "after a pupil shall have attained and successfully passed the eighth grade. . . . " A year later Nebraska added a 27th section to its bill of rights, making English "the official language of the state" and providing that it be the language of instruction in "the common school branches . . . in public, private, denominational, and parochial schools."

In 1920 authorities charged Robert T. Meyer, a teacher in a Lutheran school, with violating this statute by teaching biblical studies in German to 10-year-old children during a special hour and a half recess period that the school had instituted after the adoption of this law.

Although this law proscribed all foreign language education, it was aimed at the state's large German-American population. The law's purpose was clearly described by the Nebraska Supreme Court, which upheld its constitutionality:

> The salutary purpose of the statute is clear. The legislature had seen the baneful effects of permitting foreigners who had taken up residence in

> this country, to rear and educate their children in the language of their native land.
>
> The result of that condition was found to be inimical to our own safety. To allow the children of foreigners . . . to be taught from early childhood the language of the country of their parents, . . . was to educate them so that they must always think in that language, and, as a consequence, naturally inculcate in them the ideas and sentiments foreign to the best interests of this country.

By a seven-to-two vote, an odd coalition of justices on the United States Supreme Court rejected this law. In the minority were the relatively liberal Justice Oliver Wendell Holmes Jr. and the extremely conservative George Sutherland. The majority opinion, written by the extraordinarily conservative James C. McReynolds, was supported by the very liberal Louis D. Brandeis. In his opinion of the court, McReynolds, who was notorious for his bigotry and anti-Semitism, showed a remarkable sensitivity to minorities. He was also able to defend minority rights on grounds that were compatible to economic and social conservatives. McReynolds conceded the inherent value of all Americans speaking the same language. He appeared to agree with the "desire of the [Nebraska] legislature to foster a homogeneous people with American ideals, prepared readily to understand current discussions of civic matters." He also agreed that the "unfortunate experiences of the late war . . . were certainly enough to quicken that aspiration." For McReynolds, the goals of the legislature seemed laudable enough; the question was the constitutionality of the methods.

McReynolds found three problems with the Nebraska law. First, it seemed overly broad. It prohibited the teaching of all modem foreign languages before the eighth grade. But was this reasonable? The Justice noted that the "Mere knowledge of the German language cannot reasonably be regarded as harmful. Heretofore it has been commonly looked upon as helpful and desirable." Therefore, was it reasonable to now proscribe it? McReynolds did not directly confront this question because it was easier to strike down the law.

The Justice found that the Nebraska law unconstitutionally deprived foreign language teachers of their liberty to make a living, which was in violation of the Fourteenth Amendment. In a sense this was simply an application of the substantive due process and freedom of contract doctrines used to strike down protective labor legislation in earlier cases, such as *Lochner v. New York*. However, McReynolds also hinted that the Fourteenth Amendment might protect non-economic substantive rights as well:

> While this court has not attempted to define with exactness the liberty thus guaranteed (by the Fourteenth Amendment) the term has received much consideration, and some of the included things have been definitely stated. Without doubt, it denotes not merely freedom from bodily restraint, but also the right of the individual to contract, to engage in any of the common occupations of life, to acquire

> useful knowledge, to marry, establish a home and bring up children, to worship God according to the dictates of his own conscience, and, generally, to enjoy those privileges long recognized at common law as essential to the orderly pursuit of happiness by free men.

McReynolds further found that "it is the natural duty of the parent to give his children education suitable to their station in life." He thus concluded that the Fourteenth Amendment protected the parents' right to educate their children, subject to the "reasonable" police power of the state. Prohibiting the teaching of a foreign language was, in this context, unreasonable.

The unreasonableness of the statute did not stem solely from the inherent value of learning a foreign language. It also reflected the dangers that could result from the overregulation of education. Quoting from Plato's *Republic* and describing education in ancient Sparta, McReynolds showed how a society might undermine the parent-child relationship in order to ensure the proper education of all children. The ancient Greek models, he conceded, would "submerge the individual and develop ideal citizens," but such a system was also "wholly different from" the "ideas touching the relation between individual and state" in the United States. In essence, McReynolds saw the Nebraska law as leading to a totalitarian state which could undermine basic American liberties. While not explicitly stating the point, the McReynolds decision showed that in fighting against German "tyranny," Americans were creating their own, home-grown, system of tyranny and oppression, which violated the guarantees of the Constitution.

In a companion case, the Supreme Court struck down similar legislation from Ohio. The Court also struck down an Iowa statute that flatly prohibited the teaching of German in any school to children of any age. Even Justices Sutherland and Holmes concurred in finding the Iowa act unconstitutional.

NOTES AND QUESTIONS

1. As we have just seen in the summary of *Meyer v. Nebraska*, the U.S. Supreme Court struck down a Nebraska law that restricted all instruction to the English language and, in a companion case, a similar Ohio law. Although Paul Finkelman in his article interprets these rulings as the "first modern civil liberties victory," few parents took advantage of the right to have their children study other languages at an early age. The effect of the judicial decision would therefore seem to have been rather insignificant, but might there not be an alternative measure of the importance of *Meyer* and other such human rights decisions? How, generally, do we determine the effectiveness of judicial decisions based on linguistic human rights?
2. In *Lau v. Nichols*, 414 U.S. 568 (1974), the U.S. Supreme Court held that teaching Chinese American children in English-only classes denied them equal opportunity in violation of the 1964 Civil Rights Act. More recently, the volatile question

of bilingual education reemerged in a political context when California voters approved Proposition 227, which banned the use of any language other than English for instruction in the state's public schools. Bilingual education has remained a hot issue in the United States and elsewhere. What are your views on the legitimacy and efficacy of bilingual education?

3. Minorities have challenged the validity of business policies that require employees to speak the language of the dominant culture in the workplace. In one controversial case, *Garcia v. Spun Steak Co.*, 998 F.2d 1480 (9th Cir. 1993), the Ninth Circuit Court of Appeals addressed the question of whether such a requirement violated title VII of the 1964 Civil Rights Act. The workers characterized their objection as an interference with their cultural heritage, but the court rejected their argument, holding that English-only policies are not presumed to be discriminatory. Thus, the use of English can be a bona fide occupational qualification. See Rey M. Rodriguez, *The Misplaced Application of English-Only Rules in the Workplace*, 14 Chicano-Latino L. Rev. 73 (1994); Juan Perea, *English-Only Rules and the Right to Speak One's Primary Language in the Workplace*, 23 J. Legal Reform 265 (1990).

G. Accent Discrimination and Linguistic Profiling

1. Accent Discrimination

Persons who have learned a second language after their early childhood will normally speak it with an accent. To the extent that they are therefore stigmatized in a monolingualist society, they may experience discriminatory accent discrimination. Of course, there is no neutral, accent-free way of speaking, despite Amy Carter's famous observation in 1976 after her father, the thoroughly Southern-drawling Jimmy Carter, was elected president. Young Amy conjectured that finally the United States would have a president without an accent. Even deaf people speak with an accent "in the way they use American Sign Language. An experienced observer of deaf culture can identify Black signing, upper-class signing, 'hearie' signing, regional signing, teenage signing, 'heavy' signing, and signing associated with certain residential schools. But because of ethnocentrism, we do not recognize our accents and view our way of speaking as the norm. Furthermore, we expect minorities to modify their speech to conform to Standard English."[15]

Accent discrimination has long been a focus of civil rights litigation in the United States. An abiding question has been how best to analyze and respond to this problem within the existing categories of civil rights laws.

Gerrit B. Smith, Note, *I Want to Speak like Native Speaker: The Case for Lowering the Plaintiff's Proof in Title VII Accent Discrimination Cases*, 66 Ohio St. L.J. 231 (2005)

Sophia Poskocil is a middle-aged woman and a native of Bogota, Colombia. She received her high school and college education in Colombia and,

[15] Mari J. Matsuda, *Voices of America: Accent, Antidiscrimination Law, and a Jurisprudence for a Last Reconstruction*, 100 Yale L.J. 1329, 1329–30 (1991).

though her native tongue is Spanish, she speaks English fluently. From 1989 through 1991, Poskocil attended Hollins College, in Virginia, on a part-time basis. She qualified for a teaching certification from the Virginia Department of Education. Moreover, she successfully worked part-time as an adjunct professor at Hollins College and in 1996 taught at Roanoke College in Virginia. From 1992 to 1998, she diligently pursued employment with the Roanoke County School Division and renewed her application annually. As part of her education program at Hollins College, Poskocil interned as a student-teacher at Northside High School in the Roanoke County School Division. Her supervisor at Northside, Karen Lavinder, praised Poskocil for her teaching skills and wrote strong recommendations on Poskocil's behalf. Despite these strong recommendations, Poskocil was unable to attain a regular part-time or full-time teaching position within Roanoke County.

Over the span of six years, Poskocil applied to a total of nineteen positions with Roanoke County schools, but was denied employment each time. On March 20, 1996, she filed charges with the Equal Employment Opportunity Commission (EEOC) accusing the school division of national origin and age discrimination. During the trial, evidence was introduced that the school district based its decision not to hire Poskocil on student evaluations. Students in Poskocil's Northside High School class complained that Poskocil was difficult to understand because of her foreign accent. In their evaluations, students wrote, among other things, that the "instructor [Sophia Poskocil] barely spoke English, [and] was hard to understand."

Ultimately, the district court granted summary judgment in favor of the school district, stating that the plaintiff failed to demonstrate that the county discriminated against her. What is disturbing about the case is that Poskocil was not applying to teach a high school English class, which might have made the students' complaints more relevant, but rather Poskocil was applying to teach Spanish classes. Moreover, it appears that no one at her trial had a difficult time understanding her. However, her apparently substantial foreign accent and the school district's argument that Poskocil's accent interfered with her communication skills led the Poskocil court to find that Roanoke County relied on a legitimate non-discriminatory reason for not hiring her.

To be sure, there are countless Sophia Poskocils whose stories never make it into the hallowed halls of U.S. courts, let alone into the pages of law review articles. Proving discrimination under the Title VII proof scheme is a difficult task, as evidenced by the discussion of the case above. This Note will take a critical look at the developments in Title VII foreign accent discrimination cases. I will argue that rapid changes in the demographic landscape of the United States, specifically the increased influx of immigrants from non-English speaking countries, make combating accent discrimination more important than ever. Because of the increase of non-native speakers looking to enter the American workforce, the likelihood of incidents of accent discrimination – or at least perceived incidents of accent discrimination – will increase and with it litigation. While skilled and educated immigrants like Poskocil will likely not make up the majority of people coming to this country in the future, they undoubtedly represent a growing number in the workforce. This Note will argue that discriminating against non-native speakers based on their foreign accent has serious repercussions for non-native speakers, as otherwise qualified individuals are encouraged or even forced to take lower paying jobs, because of their perceived communication problems. As a result of the prejudice toward foreign accented speakers, many immigrants face a negative economic impact on themselves and their families.

... [T]he first step in remedying this injustice and making it easier for plaintiffs to win foreign accent discrimination cases is to have courts vigilantly exclude customer preference arguments – such as the student evaluations in Poskocil – that operate as a partial defense to foreign accent discrimination and do nothing more than detract from a sound inquiry of whether the plaintiff's English skills are sufficient to perform his or her job satisfactorily. Moreover, despite the general rejection of customer preference defenses by courts in other areas of Title VII cases, arguments that portray a prejudicial posture toward the foreign accented speaker still permeate many accent discrimination cases.

...

The Civil Rights Act of 1964 prohibits discrimination in employment on the basis of race, color, religion, national origin, or gender. Specifically Title VII of the act states the following:

> a) It shall be an unlawful employment practice for an employer – (1) to fail or refuse to hire or to discharge any individual, or otherwise to discriminate against any individual with respect to his compensation, terms conditions, or privileges of employment, because of such individual's race, color, religion, sex, or national origin....

National origin refers to the country of origin a person or his or her ancestors came from. The act never mentions accent discrimination specifically.

However, the EEOC, the agency given the responsibility of enforcing Title VII, has interpreted "national origin discrimination" to mean "the denial of equal employment opportunity because of an individual's, or his or her ancestor's, place of origin; or because an individual has the physical, cultural or linguistic characteristics of a national origin group." The EEOC has remarked that discrimination on the basis of how a person speaks or his or her accent might constitute national origin discrimination and that it will "closely investigate" charges involving denial of employment opportunities on the basis of a person's foreign accent.

...

While the EEOC believes that the preferences of customers, clients, or co-workers generally do not warrant a Bona Fide Occupational Qualification [BFOQ] exception, customer preference arguments have and continue to be raised in a number of employment cases. For example, in *Diaz v. Pan*

American Airways, the airline had a policy discriminating against male applicants for the position of flight attendant. Pan Am argued in part that its passengers strongly preferred to be served by female flight attendants and that the airplane cabin is a unique environment, creating special psychological needs on the part of the passengers. These psychological needs, the carrier argued, were better provided for through female flight attendants. The Fifth Circuit rejected the airline's arguments and held that Pan Am's policy to hire only female flight attendants was not a BFOQ and was not "reasonably necessary to the normal operation" of Pan Am's business. Moreover, the court went on to say that "we feel that customer preference may be taken into account only when it is based on the company's inability to perform the primary function or service it offers."

One area where customer preferences have been considered to be more persuasive is in the context of privacy-based sex discrimination. Discrimination in this area has been allowed where the position requires actual physical touching or the inspection of another person's naked body. This is especially true for jobs that fall into what are considered to be caregiver or security positions, such as nurses and prison wardens. However, some courts have rejected sex discrimination even in these settings.

In the context of national origin discrimination, the EEOC explicitly states that employers may not rely on customer preferences when making employment decisions. The EEOC goes on to give an example of when an employer's customer preference consideration on the basis of national origin would constitute a violation of Title VII:

Alexi, a Serbian-American college student, applies to work as a cashier at a suburban discount store. Although Alexi speaks fluent English, the manager who conducts the routine interview comments about his name and noticeable accent, observing that XYZ's customers prize its "all-American image." Alexi is not hired. XYZ has subjected Alexi to unlawful national origin discrimination if it based the hiring decision on assumptions that customers would have negative perceptions about Alexi's ethnicity.

The example of national origin discrimination already includes a reference to a person's foreign accent, re-enforcing the idea that a person's foreign accent is intertwined with one's national origin.

The EEOC recently updated its guidance to employers in the area of national origin discrimination, including accent discrimination. This change was precipitated by the increasing number of accent discrimination cases in recent years and the continued influx of non-native English speakers. [C]ustomer or co-worker's preference arguments routinely enter into the opinion of the courts in these contexts. For example, in *Ang v. Proctor & Gamble*, the Sixth Circuit rejected a Chinese-American plaintiff's claim of accent discrimination, despite evidence that Proctor & Gamble (P&G) appeared to have had at least a disparaging attitude toward non-native speakers of English. P&G's "Company Norms" brochure at the time stated "that the inability to speak the 'King's English' may be viewed by those in the majority culture as equating to intelligence (i.e. lack of)," suggesting that accented speakers better get rid off their accent in order to be seen as smart and arguably therefore worthy of advancement. In addition, Ang, who had worked for P&G for fourteen years when he was terminated, was continuously admonished in his evaluations by his superiors about his "continuous . . . need for improved communication skills." Nevertheless, Ang was also found to have had "extraordinary technical talent" despite his allegedly poor communication skills. After a weak analysis of Ang's accent discrimination claim, the Sixth Circuit concluded that Ang did not present sufficient evidence to make out a prima facie case of accent discrimination.

Another case, *Yu v. United States Postal Service*, nicely illustrates how preferences and biases by customers and co-workers are used by the employer as a partial defense to the charges of accent discrimination. Susan L. Yu, a part-time distribution clerk of Taiwanese origin, asked to be put on light-duty after a shoulder injury. The Postal Service argued that there was no suitable work for Yu and denied her request to answer the phones. The reason for this decision was given by Yu's supervisor, who justified the agency's action by stating that "[h]er [Yu's] English is not easily understood, which is absolutely necessary for the performance of this job [answering the phones]." Furthermore, the supervisor noted that "when she had a Hispanic . . . answer the phones, she had complaints from customers who were not able to understand him." As a result of this experience, the supervisor decided not to let Yu answer the phones. [But] the EEOC rejected the agency's customer preference arguments, noting that Yu testified at an administrative hearing where the administrative judge had no problems understanding her. In this case, the EEOC reversed the agency's final decision.

As indicated above, the EEOC has recently introduced new guidelines regarding accent discrimination. While the EEOC admonishes employers to "carefully scrutinize" decisions they make based on an individual's accent, the example that is given by the EEOC about when employment decisions based on accent do not violate Title VII is confusing at best. The following example is given by the EEOC, where the EEOC believes the employee's accent materially interferes with performing the functions of the job, and at least in that context customer preferences apparently are acceptable bases for decision making:

A major aspect of Bill's position as a concierge for XYZ Hotel is assisting guests with directions and travel arrangements. Numerous people have complained that they cannot understand Bill because of his heavy Ghanaian accent. Therefore, XYZ notifies Bill that he is being transferred to a clerical position that does not involve extensive spoken communication. The transfer does not violate Title VII because Bill's accent materially interferes with his ability to perform the functions of the concierge position.

The example seems to be in conflict with the statement that "employers may not rely on coworker, customer, or client discomfort or preference as the basis for a discriminatory action." The conclusion that Bill's accent "materially interferes" with his ability to perform his duties as concierge appears to be wholly based on the preferences of the hotel guests. Curiously, based on the example, Bill was obviously hired by someone who did not think that Bill's accent was too heavy to perform the job of concierge. Again, in a country where more and more individuals do not claim English as their first language, do we really want to allow customers or co-workers to decide – or at least influence – what type of jobs an individual can or cannot do? As I have indicated above, I believe the answer to this question should be no, and therefore I believe all customer preference arguments that speak against the comprehensibility of an accented person's communication skills should be excluded at trial, unless the plaintiff uses them to show bias on part of the defendant and to ultimately prove discriminatory conduct. Instead of lay persons' preferences, the focus should be on the evaluations of linguistic experts in regards to the plaintiff's speech. In addition, I believe this assertion is supported by the findings of linguistic research in the area of listener prejudice.

B. Listener Prejudice toward the Accented Speaker

A number of studies have analyzed how native speakers perceive the speech of non-native speakers. Studies have shown that persons with a foreign accent from certain countries were perceived to be "significantly less successful." For example, a Swedish study demonstrated that when the listener was told the accent they heard was from a Kurd, the speaker was perceived as less successful than when the listener was told that the speaker was German, although the same person was speaking. Linguists have found that native speakers will often attach "cultural meanings to an accent which derive from the stereotypes and prejudices that the listener holds toward the race or ethnic group associated with that accent." Speakers with accents of Western European countries, for example, appear to be less discriminated against than non-native speakers from less developed countries. This notion is supported by a review of a number of court cases that show that a great number of accent discrimination cases involve plaintiffs from third world countries. However, while cases dealing with accented speakers from Europe are not as prevalent, this does not mean that courts should scrutinize these cases any less rigorously than cases involving accents from other regions of the world.

One of the most overt cases concerning employer discrimination against accented speakers is *Caroll v. Elliott Personnel Services.* In this case a secretary for an employment agency, Doritt Caroll, was directed by her manager to screen inquiries over the phone. Callers that did not "'speak right'" were not offered a job and the secretary was asked to keep a record of the callers' speech and accent. Reasons why employers might discriminate against an accented speaker may be because of their own prejudices, but another likely reason may be because they feel pressured by their customers. While customer preference defenses have been rejected in the majority of Title VII cases, they are still allowed in accent cases. . . .

Moreover, hostility by some individuals toward accented speakers will likely mean that employers will continue to include customer preference as a defense if courts allow defendants to do so. Perceived problems on the part of customers with employees who are L2 speakers are widely documented.

Whether it is at the doctor's office or fast-food drive-throughs, native speaking customers are apparently "frustrated" more than ever by having to "communicate with people who aren't from here." However, one should not read too much into these "frustrations." As linguist Rosina Lippi-Green notes, "breakdown of communication is due not so much to accent as it is to negative social evaluation of the accent in question, and a rejection of the communicative burden" on the part of the listener. Moreover, this assertion is supported by other research that shows that "a strong foreign accent does not necessarily reduce the intelligibility or comprehensibility of speech produced by non-native speakers." Based on the discussion above, it appears clear that the accented speaker faces a number of challenges to fully participate in the U.S. labor market. One of the tools to discourage employers to discriminate against non-native speakers is to disallow employer and customer preference defenses.

V. Analysis: Abolishing the Customer Preference Defense in Title VII Accent Cases

This exclusion of the customer preference defense in accent discrimination cases should be seen as part of a greater movement of shifting the burden from having the immigrant make herself understandable to others, to encouraging others to make an effort to understand her. Disallowing defendants to use the customer preference defense would be a first step in tilting the scale in favor of the plaintiff in accent discrimination cases. While the customer preference defense is routinely rejected in other Title VII cases, a review of accent discrimination cases . . . demonstrates that the defense is successfully used by the defendant. By disallowing statements into evidence about what customers apparently prefer or what employers think their customers or clients want, the plaintiff has a better chance of being successful with her claim. In the case of Sophia Poskocil, it was the students who complained to the school district that they had a difficult time understanding her. By rejecting this kind of evidence as inadmissible, the court will be forced to focus more of its time and analysis on whether or not the plaintiff's language skills are in fact unsatisfactory. I am mindful about the fact that in the end the courts might very well come out the same way as they did in both *Poskocil* and *Fragante*, but the concentration of the inquiry will inevitably have to focus on more objective criteria. Perhaps more importantly, the plaintiff, even if she loses her case, will likely not feel the same alienation she feels when the case centers around individuals complaining about her accent. Moreover, the fact that most immigrants will never lose their accent further supports the idea that accent discrimination cases need to be at least as fair in terms of process as cases dealing with race and gender.

While the focus of this Note has been primarily on the linguistic and economic arguments for lowering the burden of proving accent discrimination, as suggested above there are also potential psychological repercussions for those individuals [who] are being discriminated against. The effects of discrimination on the victim may include loss of self-esteem, anger, depression, anxiety, and feelings of abandonment. Moreover, these mental effects on the discriminated person often lead to other problems, including disrupting personal relationships and even physical health problems. As implied by the quote of Young Park at the beginning of this Note, sounding different than the majority of speakers may have a psychological impact on the accented speaker, even if [there] is no perceived or actual discrimination. Facing discrimination – and the limited opportunity to advance in one's job that comes with that discrimination – many immigrants have turned to expensive speech classes to reduce their accent. These classes tend to be expensive and their success in reducing an individual's accent is disputed. The question is why should an immigrant have to spend time and money on reducing his accent? If the accented speaker is taking accent reduction classes to gain greater self[-]confidence with the English language, there will be very little objection to this. However, it is more problematic when these classes are taken solely to progress up the career ladder. Issues of fundamental fairness come into play when people are virtually forced to give up their mother-tongue to conform to employer and customer expectations of what an individual's English should sound like by discrimination against the accented speaker of English. Moreover, there are advantages to maintaining the mother tongue, since it allows individuals to retain some of their distinctive culture and "adapt more gradually to the ways of majority Americans than would be the case if they lost their mother-tongue."

The argument for greater tolerance for accented speakers in the workplace is strengthened by the fact that many organizations increasingly rely on written rather than verbal communication. This increased reliance on written communication can be attributed to technological advancement. The use of e-mails and faxes have become common forms of written communication and in many ways have reduced or replaced the need for verbal communication for a number of employment positions. However, I do not mean to suggest that verbal communication and the need for face-to-face interaction are not important. On the contrary, I strongly believe that human interaction at work is vital and, as discussed below, obviously an important avenue for the native speaker to familiarize herself and get used to accented speech. Moreover, commentators have noted that the lack of face-to-face interaction can seriously undermine an organization's cohesiveness and the mental health of an organization's employees. But, as a result of the greater reliance on written work in the employment setting, a person's writing skills have become more important. As I suggested above, many non-native speakers of English who come to the United States will have stronger writing skills than native English speakers, making numerous immigrants more employable than their American-born counterpart on that basis alone.

One thing employers may want to consider when thinking about how to reduce accent discrimination is offering "cross-cultural awareness training and explicit linguistic instruction" on how to comprehend foreign accented speech. Studies show that exposing native speakers to accented speech improved comprehension on the part of native speakers. Besides increasing comprehensibility, native speakers also become more tolerant of listening to accented speech. Based on these studies, offering employees linguistic instruction and cross-cultural awareness training is a wise investment, especially since the labor market will continue to increase in terms of linguistic diversity.

VI. Conclusion

Over twenty years ago, a linguist asked "[w]hy, in a country of immigrants, many if not most of whom were not able to speak English when they arrived, would the matter of discrimination against people with accents not have become a matter of public concern?" Today that question still rings true, as evidenced by the continued use of the customer preference defense in Title VII accent discrimination cases and the overall lack of protection for non-native speakers of English. This Note has argued for a re-thinking of the way the justice system approaches these cases, based in part on the fact that accent is an immutable trait for many immigrants who learn English later in life. Moreover, the United States is experiencing a high influx of immigrants into its workforce and the importance of that influx on economic expansion must not be underestimated.

By discriminating against individuals just because their way of speech appears different, forcing us to concentrate and strain ourselves a bit to comprehend that speech, the United States only injures itself in the long run – culturally and economically. By approaching non-native speakers of English with greater tolerance and ensuring equal treatment under the law when questions arise as to whether or not they have been discriminated against, immigrants will be able to reach their fullest potential. Furthermore, the population as a whole should celebrate the linguistic diversity that has historically characterized the United States. By disallowing the customer preference defense in Title VII accent discrimination cases, a small step toward these goals will have been realized.

NOTES AND QUESTIONS

1. It is apparent that accent discrimination does not fit easily into the established legal categories of human rights concern.[16] In analyzing alleged discrimination in the workplace, a major question is whether unaccented communication is crucial for job performance and therefore a bona fide occupational qualification. Although unaccented communication might be important for telephone operators or those in the media, it seems less so for security guards. One commentator proposes that courts consider four questions to help them evaluate whether speech is critical for job performance: (a) What level of communication is required for the job? (b) Was the candidate's speech fairly evaluated? (c) Is the candidate intelligible

[16] *See* Matsuda, *supra* note 15, at 1348–57.

to the pool of relevant, nonprejudiced listeners, such that job performance is not unreasonably impeded? and (d) What accommodations are reasonable given the job and any limitations in intelligibility? She defends the use of reasonable accommodation language, noting that "[i]t is borrowed from disability law and addresses the potential anomaly of treating physical speech impediments as more deserving of protection than accents." MATSUDA, *supra* note 15, at 1368.

2. It is noteworthy that there exists a hierarchy of status among accents. In their hiring practices, universities often seem to favor European accents, and undergraduates tend to be less enthusiastic about instructors with other types of accents who are said to be "hard to understand." Do students (and others) who react strongly to accented speech harbor unconscious prejudices?
3. How do cartoons affect children's perceptions of accents? Consider the following observation:

> In entertainment, linguistic stereotypes have long been a stock-in-trade. Dialect was used to draw character in Chaucer, and can be followed in the present time. In broadcast and film entertainment, the use of linguistic stereotypes mirrors the evolution of national fears and obsessions: Japanese and German characters in Disney cartoons during the Second World War, Russian spy characters in children's cartoons in the 1950s and 1960s, Arab characters in the era of hostilities with Iran and Iraq. More general stereotyping is also prevalent in television programming and movies: situation comedies (*Beverly Hillbillies, I Love Lucy, Sanford and Son, All in the Family*) and animated films (*Jungle Book, Dumbo*) provide numerous examples.

Rosina Lippi-Green, *Accent, Standard Language Ideology, and Discriminatory Pretext in the Court*, 23 LANGUAGE IN SOC'Y 163, 192 n.10 (1994).

2. Linguistic Profiling

A particularly egregious extension of accent discrimination is linguistic profiling, particularly when it facilitates racial and other outlawed forms of profiling and when it is practiced or sanctioned by governments.

CLIFFORD v. COMMONWEALTH,
7 S.W.3d 371 (Ky. 1999)

Opinion of the court by Cooper, J.

Following a jury trial in the Campbell Circuit Court, Appellant was convicted of one count of trafficking in a controlled substance in the first-degree. He then entered a guilty plea to being a persistent felony offender [PFO] in the first-degree and waived jury sentencing. He was sentenced to ten years in prison for the trafficking conviction, which was enhanced to twenty years for the [conviction]. He appeals to this Court as a matter of right.

Detective William Birkenhauer of the Northern Kentucky Drug Strike Force had an agreement with Gary Vanover, a police informant, whereby Vanover would assist Birkenhauer in setting up drug "sting" operations. On

May 20, 1996, Birkenhauer and Vanover set up a meeting with Appellant for approximately 3:00 p.m. at Vanover's apartment. Birkenhauer instructed Vanover to tell Appellant that he wanted to purchase a quarter of an ounce of crack cocaine.

Birkenhauer testified that when he arrived at the apartment, Vanover answered the door and a female friend of Vanover was also present. Appellant then emerged from the bedroom. Appellant told Birkenhauer he had only $75.00 worth of cocaine with him, because he did not like to carry more than that on his person, but stated that he could complete the order later that afternoon. Birkenhauer told Appellant he would take the "75" and return later for the rest. Appellant then went back into the bedroom and instructed Vanover to follow him. When Vanover came out of the bedroom, he was carrying a baggie of crack cocaine which he gave to Birkenhauer. Birkenhauer gave Vanover the $75.00 and told him to tell Appellant that he would return later for the rest. Vanover reentered the bedroom, then came back out a few seconds later and accompanied Birkenhauer outside to his vehicle. Birkenhauer returned an hour and a half later, but neither Appellant nor Vanover was present at the apartment.

Vanover testified that the crack cocaine actually belonged to him, that he had made the sale to Birkenhauer, and that Appellant was not involved in the transaction. Appellant did not testify.

Unknown to either Appellant or Vanover, Birkenhauer was "wired" with an audio transmitter, and other police officers were in a nearby apartment with surveillance equipment and a receiver. One of those officers, Darin Smith, was listening to the transaction over the receiver. A tape recording of the transaction was produced, but the trial judge determined that the recording was inaudible and it was neither admitted into evidence nor played to the jury. However, Smith was permitted to testify to what he heard over the receiver as the transaction was occurring.

Smith testified that he saw Birkenhauer enter the apartment. He then heard four different voices, the first of which he recognized as being that of Birkenhauer. He then heard the voice of another male, the voice of a female, and, then later, a fourth voice which "sounded as if it was of a male black." Smith testified that he had been a police officer for thirteen years and had spoken to black males on numerous occasions; and that based on that experience, he believed the last voice which he heard was that of a black male. Appellant is a black male; Vanover is a white male.

. . .

Appellant first argues that Smith's testimony amounted to an impermissible interpretation of an inaudible tape recording. However, Smith did not purport to interpret the tape recording. He testified to what he, himself, heard as the transaction was taking place. *Gordon v. Commonwealth*, Ky., 916 S.W.2d 176, 180 (1995); *see also United States v. Cylkouski*, 556 F.2d 799 (6th Cir. 1977) (parties to telephone conversations could testify with respect to those conversations even though the tapes of the conversations had been suppressed).

Appellant next asserts that Smith should not have been permitted to express his opinion that the fourth voice he heard sounded like that of a black male. A nonexpert witness may express an opinion which is rationally based on the perception of the witness and helpful to a determination of a fact in issue. A corollary to this rule is the concept known as the "collective facts rule," which permits a lay witness to resort to a conclusion or an opinion to describe an observed phenomenon where there exists no other feasible alternative by which to communicate that observation to the trier of fact. Thus, lay witnesses have been permitted to testify to the speed of a moving vehicle; the age of a person and whether that person was intoxicated, the degree of physical suffering endured by another, and the mental and emotional state of another; in *King v. Ohio Valley Fire & Marine Ins. Co.*, 212 Ky. 770, 280 S.W. 127 (1926), a witness was permitted to testify that upon arriving at the scene of a fire, he "smell[ed] gasoline." In response to the argument that the witness should have been permitted to merely describe the odor, not to testify that the odor was that of gasoline, the Court held:

Technically, perhaps, that should have been done, but the average man would have great difficulty in telling just how coal oil or gasoline smells, though acquainted with their odors, and perhaps the best description the witness could give was to say he knew their odors, and he could smell coal oil, or he could smell gasoline.

In each of the above examples, the witness was permitted to describe what he observed by use of inference, conclusion, or opinion. Whether the collective facts rule would permit a witness to express an opinion that an overheard voice was that of a particular nationality or race has never before been addressed in this jurisdiction. However, it is not an issue of first impression.

In *People v. Sanchez*, 129 Misc.2d 91, 492 N.Y.S.2d 683 (N.Y. Sup. Ct. 1985), a lay eyewitness to a fatal shooting was permitted to testify that immediately prior to the shooting, he overheard the victim and the killer arguing in Spanish, and that the killer was speaking with a Dominican, rather than a Puerto Rican, accent. The opinion noted that lay witnesses have been permitted to testify to inferences of identity as to race, language, visibility and sounds. The court made the following observation with respect to the subject of accents and dialects:

Accent is a branch of phonetics, which in turn, is a division of linguistics. While some writers use accent and dialect interchangeably, accent relates to how words are pronounced whereas dialect involves not only accent but particular speech patterns of a group or region. It is clear that lay witnesses can often detect the distinctive accent related to particular ethnic or geographic groups. Thus, a lay witness, depending upon his experience, could distinguish between a Yiddish accent and an Italian accent, or between a Russian and an English accent, or between a Spanish and French accent. In addition, within broad categories, certain more specific accents, characteristic of [a] particular region, may be ascertained. For example, the lay witness may be able to reliably identify the "Brooklyn" accent, as distinguished from the "Boston" accent, or the "Southern" accent from the "Cockney" accent. Human experience has taught us to discern the variations in the mode of speech of different individuals.

More specifically, in *Rhea v. State*, 104 Ark. 162, 147 S.W. 463 (1912), it was held that a witness may recognize and know the difference between voices of persons of different nationalities and races. *See also State v. McDaniel*, 392 S.W.2d 310 (Mo. 1965) (testimony that robbers had African-American accents was admissible to identify the probable race of the perpetrators); *State v. Phillips*, 25 N.C. App. 5, 212 S.E.2d 172 (1975) (testimony that robbers "sounded like black people talking" was admissible, because the witness was merely testifying to the dialect that he heard); *State v. Smith*, 307 S.C. 376, 415 S.E.2d 409 (App. 1992) (testimony of radio dispatcher that caller was a white male, approximately forty years old, with a "very country and rugged, scratchy like voice" was admissible even though the witness was not an expert in voice identification); *State v. Kinard*, 39 Wash. App. 871, 696 P.2d 603 (1985) (testimony that one burglar "sounded black to me" and another sounded like a young white male, was held properly admitted).

No one suggests that it was improper for Officer Smith to identify one of the voices he heard as being that of a female. We perceive no reason why a witness could not likewise identify a voice as being that of a particular race or nationality, so long as the witness is personally familiar with the general characteristics, accents, or speech patterns of the race or nationality in question, *i.e.*, so long as the opinion is "rationally based on the perception of the witness." A proper foundation was laid for Smith's testimony. That foundation was not eradicated by Smith's admission that the voices of some black men are indistinguishable from those of white men and vice versa. His inability to more specifically describe or to demonstrate "how a black man sounds" merely proves the reason for the collective facts rule, *i.e.*, that it would be difficult or impossible for the witness to give such a description or demonstration.

. . .

[The court then discussed issues involving hearsay, sufficiency of the evidence and the principle of lesser included offenses, concluding that none of these limited the proceedings in this case.]

Accordingly, the judgments of conviction and sentences imposed by the Campbell Circuit Court are affirmed.

Johnstone, J., concurring.

I concur in the majority opinion in all respects, but write separately to dispute the dissent's misguided assertion that "the majority takes a tremendous step backwards with its holding today and permits prejudice and inference to convict a man where logic and objectivity would not." That is simply untrue.

The contentious issue confronted by the Court in this case is whether a lay witness may express an opinion as to the race of a person from an overheard voice. Despite any inferences to the contrary, other courts have previously addressed this issue and allowed such lay witness opinion testimony. The majority opinion cites cases in which lay witnesses have been allowed to identify voices as sounding like white, as well as black, persons.

. . .

Sadly, the dissent has spun this evidentiary issue into a needless racial diatribe. It is my opinion that as we approach the next millennium, the majority opinion perpetuates the time-honored deference to the discretion of trial judges in this Commonwealth and allows additional valuable evidence to be considered by the diverse group of jurors that serve so diligently in the Kentucky Court of Justice.

Stumbo, J., dissenting.

With much dismay, I must dissent. The majority opinion is not only fundamentally flawed on several levels, but is also tremendously disheartening. The opinion condones the admission of Officer Smith's testimony that the voice of the fourth speaker he heard on the tape "sounded as if it was of a male black." This testimony not only impermissibly bolstered the testimony of Detective Birkenhauer, whose version of events inculpating Appellant had been called into serious question by the testimony of the Commonwealth's own informant, but also was incredibly prejudicial to Appellant, the sole black man sitting at the defense table. Additionally, the testimony was, by Officer Smith's own admission, entirely irrelevant and probative of absolutely nothing. Thus, it should have been excluded under as being more prejudicial than probative.

I must first object to the basic premise which underlies the majority's rationale in this case – that a person's race can be ascertained simply by the sound and cadence of his voice, his pronunciation of certain words – his accent. An accent may be indicative of many things – how a person's parents speak, the countries, regions or even neighborhoods in which he has lived, the schools he has attended, the languages he speaks, his social class, and even whom he admires. What it most definitely cannot indicate is the color of his skin.

Common sense should tell us this. The quality of a particular voice is sensed by hearing, just as the appearance of a person is sensed by sight. It is simply not possible to perceive appearance using the sense of hearing. One might presume that a particular voice or accent would be indicative of how the speaker might look. However, that presumption would be based solely on preconceived ideas, stereotypes, and assumptions, not on logic or reality.

Race, that is, skin color, must be perceived by sight. To say that a person is capable of ascertaining another's race solely by hearing his voice is tantamount to saying the one can "hear a color" or "smell a sound" or "taste a noise." One can no more determine that a person's skin is pale, cinnamon, or ebony simply by hearing his voice, than one can perceive that an individual will have a British accent, a Portuguese accent, a New York accent or an Appalachian accent simply by gazing at his countenance and the color of his skin. Thus, it was entirely improper to permit Officer Smith to testify that the fourth voice on the videotape "sounded black." This type of testimony would be improper in any context, but it is all the more so because the defendant was the lone black man sitting at the defense table. Although Appellant's voice was unknown to both Smith and the jury, the overwhelming inference was that Appellant was the fourth speaker, and thus guilty as urged by Detective Birkenhauer.

The majority holds Officer Smith's opinion that the voice on the tape sounded like that of a black man is perfectly acceptable as lay opinion which is *rationally based* on Smith's perception, because "Smith testified that he had been a police officer for thirteen years and had spoken to black males on numerous occasions." As discussed above, I fail to see any rationality to the notion that *one can hear a person's skin color.* Let us, for the moment, assume that what Officer Smith was inartfully attempting to say, is that the voice he heard on the tape was spoken in an accent or dialect which he associated with African Americans, for reasons which he could not explain because he was not a linguist. This being so, Smith's observations were still entirely inadmissible absent any showing that Appellant, himself, speaks with this kind of accent. As Smith had never heard Appellant speak and as Appellant chose not to testify at trial, there was no way to connect Appellant to the particular type of accent described by Smith. Instead, the jury was simply left with the impermissible inference that because Smith associated the voice with African Americans, and because Appellant was an African American, Appellant must be the person Smith heard.

Smith himself conceded the illogicality and irrelevance of his own testimony. Upon cross-examination, Smith acknowledged not all black men sound alike, nor do all white men. He also acknowledged that some African American men "sound like whites," and that "some white people sound like blacks." In essence, Smith conceded that Appellant's voice and accent might sound like the accent Smith associated with African Americans, but that it might not. He could say no more, because he had never heard Appellant's voice. Evidence is relevant when it tends to make the existence of a disputed issue more probable or less probable than it would be without the evidence. Here, Smith's testimony that the voice he heard sounded like an "African American accent" in no way tended to increase the probability that Appellant was the speaker, because there was no showing that Appellant, himself, spoke in the manner described. As Smith's testimony was clearly irrelevant, yet undoubtedly extremely prejudicial to Appellant, it should have been excluded.

Finally I must take issue with the primary case the majority cites in an effort to find support for its unfortunate holding. Somehow, the majority has improperly broadened the issue before us to that of whether a lay witness may "express an opinion that an overheard voice was that of a particular nationality or race." In so doing, the majority quotes at length from the case of *People v. Sanchez*, 129 Misc.2d 91, 492 N.Y.S.2d 683 (N.Y. Sup. Ct. 1985), a case which is easily distinguishable from the instant controversy. There, the question was whether the suspect was speaking Spanish in a Dominican or Puerto Rican accent. That case in no way dealt with the issue of accent as it relates to race or skin color, but rather as it relates to nationality. Given that he or she grows up in, it is entirely reasonable to permit identification of a nationality based on a particular kind of accent, so long as the listener is familiar with the accent of that particular nationality. Such is not the case with the color of a person's skin, which has absolutely no impact on the way a person speaks. I find the fact that the majority seems unable to grasp this obvious distinction to be extremely disconcerting.

As we approach the next millennium, the majority takes a tremendous step backwards with its holding today and permits prejudice and inference to convict a man where logic and objectivity would not.

NOTES AND QUESTIONS

1. Do you agree with the majority opinion in *Clifford* that the danger of impermissible prejudice against the appellant was remote? Why or why not?
2. The dissent argues that the question of linguistic profiling is distinct from accent discrimination. The judge distinguishes a precedent by noting, "There, the question was whether the suspect was speaking Spanish in a Dominican or Puerto Rican accent. The case in no way dealt with the issue of accent as it relates to race or skin color, but rather as it relates to nationality." After you compare and contrast these two phenomena, consider what analytic framework should be used for linguistic profiling and how it differs from that normally applicable (at least in theory) in accent discrimination litigation.
3. Do you agree with the dissenting opinion in *Clifford* that, because the appellant did not give evidence and thus the officer had no opportunity to compare the appellant's voice with the one he overheard, the officer's [Smith's] evidence was irrelevant? If the appellant had testified, do you think the officer's evidence then would have been relevant? Does the fact that an accused belongs to a racial group whose accents may have contributed to its discriminatory treatment justify the exclusion of any linguistic profiling that is patently prejudicial?
4. What role, if any, should linguistics experts play in cases such as *Clifford*? Consider the discussion of expert versus lay testimony in Dawn L. Smalls, *Linguistic Profiling and the Law*, 15 STAN. L. & POL'Y REV. 579 (2004). The article also contains a discussion of *Clifford* and of the legal contexts of employment, housing, and criminal prosecution in which linguistic profiling is injurious.
5. Will the increasingly common use of e-mail for communications of all types reduce the likelihood of linguistic profiling in the future?
6. In American culture, "seeing is believing," and eyewitness testimony plays a crucial role in the legal system, where there are strict rules against the "ear witness" and hearsay. Consider the provocative essay by Bernard Hibbits, *Coming to Our Senses:*

Communication and Legal Expression in Performance Cultures, 41 EMORY L.J. 874, 895 (1992). It may be considered culturally inappropriate to rely too heavily on the sound of a voice or aural testimony generally. If so, should aural testimony continue to be disfavored?

7. When attorneys at trial use ethnic slurs, judges normally admonish juries to disregard what they heard. Appeals by defendants asking for a mistrial usually fail because even if the judge's ruling was an error, it is usually treated as harmless error. For a compelling analysis of the impact of racial slurs on juries and an argument for a *per se* rule requiring a mistrial whenever a single slur is uttered, see Sheri Lynn Johnson, *Racial Imagery in Criminal Law*, 67 TULANE L. REV. 1739 (1993).

Index

Page numbers for principal cases are in italic type.